HANI–ENGLISH / ENGLISH–HANI DICTIONARY

HANI–ENGLISH / ENGLISH–HANI DICTIONARY

HAQNIQDOQ–YILYIDOQ DOQLO– SOQDAOQ

哈尼语 – 英语词典

COMPILED BY

PAUL W. LEWIS and BAI BIBO (PIU BO)

Routledge
Taylor & Francis Group
LONDON AND NEW YORK

in association with the

INTERNATIONAL INSTITUTE FOR ASIAN STUDIES
Leiden

First published in 1996 by
Kegan Paul International

This edition first published in 2010 by
Routledge
2 Park Square, Milton Park, Abingdon, Oxfordshire OX14 4RN

Simultaneously published in the USA and Canada
by Routledge
711 Third Avenue, New York, NY 10017

First issued in paperback 2016

Routledge is an imprint of the Taylor and Francis Group, an informa business

British Library Cataloguing in Publication Data
A catalogue record for this book is available from the British Library

ISBN 13: 978-1-138-97579-8 (pbk)
ISBN 13: 978-0-7103-0564-0 (hbk)

Publisher's Note

The publisher has gone to great lengths to ensure the quality of this reprint but points out that some imperfections in the original copies may be apparent. The publisher has made every effort to contact original copyright holders and would welcome correspondence from those they have been unable to trace.

Foreword

The International Institute for Asian Studies is proud to present the reader with the first Hani-English/English-Hani dictionary which has ever been published. The IIAS is honoured to have been given this opportunity to publish such a fine linguistic work in association with Kegan Paul International. We did not hesitate when Paul W. Lewis and Bai Bibo asked us in 1995 if we would like to be the publisher of their dictionary. It took them five years of arduous study and labour to compile this impressive, almost 900-page *Hani-English/English-Hani Dictionary*. It is not only important for researchers in the field of Hani studies but also for the Hani people themselves. The Hani, a minority group, live in China and Vietnam and are closely related to their Akha neighbours in Myanmar, Thailand, and Laos. The Hani and Akha population together consist of 2 million people. Hani-irrigated mountain rice terraces are evidence of their complex social organization which dates back thousands of years. They have retained their own cultural identity notwithstanding close contact with the Han Chinese.

The dictionary was officially presented during the Second International Conference on Hani-Akha Culture in Thailand, May 12-18, 1996, which was organized by Dr. D. Tooker, Fellow of the IIAS and Programme Director of the second IIAS research programme, *Cultural Traditions in Endangered Minorities of South and Southeast Asia*, and Dr. L. Alting von Geusau of the Southeast Asian Mountain People's - Culture, Development - Research, Documentation, and Information Centre (SEAMP-CD-RDI) in Chiang Mai, Thailand. A third co-organizer was Dr. I. Hansson of the Lund University, Sweden. Professor Dai Qingxia, Chairman of the Department of Minority Languages and Literature in Beijing, first instigated the compilation of this dictionary, and it was through his good offices that Paul W. Lewis and Bai Bibo were brought together.

Paul van der Velde
Editor
International Institute for Asian Studies

CO-COMPILERS

Paul W. Lewis served as a missionary with the Lahu and Akha people in Burma and Thailand for over 40 years. His training in linguistics and anthropology (he has a Ph.D. in Cultural Anthropology) equipped him for compiling dictionaries in the Lahu and Akha languages, as well as for writing various ethnographic and linguistic materials.

Bai Bibo (Piu Bo in Hani), the key compiler in the field, has his M.A. in Linguistics from the Postgraduate School of the Chinese Academy of Social Sciences in Beijing. He has served with the Institute of Nationality Studies of Honghe Prefecture, Jianshui County in Yunnan, China. He has had experience in helping to produce Hani books, teaching Hani writing to Hani teachers, and studying the varied cultures and dialects of many Hani dialectical groups in China.

DEDICATION

The compilers of this dictionary wish to

dedicate it to the wonderful Hani people,

who made this work necessary,

and to our wonderful wives,

who helped make it possible!

HANI - AKHA AREA

TABLE OF CONTENTS

Introduction: THE HANI PEOPLE AND LANGUAGE -- 1

Hani-English 37

a -- 39
ao -- 63
b -- 71
c -- 100
d -- 128
e -- 162
ee -- 163
ei -- 167
f -- 171
g -- 176
h -- 197
hh -- 230
(ii)
j -- 251
k -- 267
l -- 284
m -- 317
n -- 357
ng -- 390
o -- 395
p -- 397
q -- 419
s -- 435
ss -- 469
t -- 481
w -- 499
x -- 508
y -- 519
z -- 540

English-Hani - 570

a -- 571
b -- 591
c -- 597
d -- 619
e -- 631
f -- 640
g -- 651
h -- 660
i -- 670
j -- 675
k -- 677
l -- 679
m -- 689
n -- 700
o -- 705
p -- 710
q -- 726
r -- 728
s -- 740
t -- 767
u -- 781
v -- 784
w -- 787
x -- 798
y -- 799
z -- 801

Appendix Index - 802

Appendix 1 -- 803
Appendix 2 -- 805
Appendix 3 -- 823
Appendix 4 -- 825
Appendix 5 -- 826
Appendix 6 -- 827
Appendix 7 -- 828
Appendix 8 -- 830
Appendix 9 -- 831
Appendix 10 -- 834
Appendix 11 -- 835
Appendix 12 -- 836

THE HANI PEOPLE AND LANGUAGE

THE PEOPLE

The Language and Name

There are some 1.3 million people who live in Yunnan Province (in the extreme Southwest of China) who are called "**Hani**". These Hani people speak a language which is a member of the Loloish (or Yi) branch of the Lolo-Burmese subgroup of the Tibeto-Burman family of languages. Included in this branch, along with Hani are: Yi (the largest group, also called Nosu and Nyi Pho), Lisu, Lahu, Naxi, Jino, and Akha - although the latter group should be considered as speaking a major dialect of Hani. The Tibeto-Burman family of languages is part of a larger linguistic stock, Sino-Tibetan, which, as the name suggests, includes the Chinese languages.

There are probably other languages which were originally in this linguistic branch, but have since been so inundated with Chinese loanwords that it is difficult to see the Loloish relationship. The Bai (also called Minchia) may be one of these.

The Hani people of Southwest China have a long history. In the records of the Hani found in Chinese sources, they were often referred to as 'Woni' or 'Honi'. After liberation they were called by the name which most of them call themselves, i.e. Hani. They write it in their script as: '**Haqniq**'. The linguistically closely related Akha living in Burma and Thailand would write it as: '**Haˬ nyiˬ**'.

There does not appear to be any special meaning in the name 'Hani'. The name, however, is very close to the term the Akha people use to designate themselves in their proverbs and ancient ballads. That term is 'Zani' (in Hani written: **Ssaqniq**; in Akha: **Zaˬ nyiˬ**.) The Hani refer to the Akha who live in Xishuangbanna as '**Ssaqniq**' (46:200). There appears to be a definite relationship between the terms '**Hani**' and '**Zani**'.

Considering the closeness of the Hani and Akha languages, it is likely that they were one language some 1,000 to 1,200 years ago. The term 'Akha' was evidently only used by those 'Zani' who moved south across the Mekong (Lancang) River.

In China the term "Aini" is often used to designate the Akha who live in the Xishuangbanna area of southern Yunnan. The term "Aini" may be a Dai term, or some feel it could be from the Akha and Hani term for "younger sibling" (**aqnil**). The Akha are also called 'Yani', probably a corruption of **Za̬ nyi̬**.

There were some 1,254,000 Hani living in China at the time of the 1990 census. This includes roughly 150,000 who call themselves "Akha" who live especially in the Xishuangbanna area, and the Lancang Lahu Autonomous County of Southwestern Yunnan.

The Location of the Hani

The central location of most of the Hani in China is the area between the Yuanjiang and Lancang rivers, bounded roughly in a latitude of 21-26 degrees north, and a longitude of from 99-104 degrees east. The elevation of their villages goes from 800 meters to 2600 meters (Zhang Yajin 1993:10). Many of them are under the jurisdiction of the Honghe Hani-Yi Autonomous Prefecture, which includes Honghe, Yuanyang, Luchun and Jinping counties.

Others (although some of these would call themselves Akha) dwell in Mojiang, Jiangcheng, Pu'er, Lancang and Zhenyuan counties in Simao Prefecture; and in Xishuangbanna's Menghai, Jinghong and Mengla counties. There are also Hani in Jingdong and Jinggu counties. Located in Yuanjiang and Xinping, as well as Yuxi Prefecture, and with a few in Eshan and Jianshui, there are many who call themselves Haoni, Biyue, or Kaduo rather than Hani. They are all lumped together in Government statistics as "Hani", however.

Dr. Nguyen Duy Thieu, of the Institute for Southeast Asian Studies, Hanoi, has informed IIAS that as of 1995 there were 12,489 Hani and 1,261 Akha living in Vietnam, along with 58,000 Akha in Laos. We are most grateful to Dr. Deborah E. Tooker for this information.

The History of the Hani

The Hani do not have a written history. From their legends and from Chinese history we know that long ago they tended to be a migratory people, looking for the best mountains for their slash-and-burn agricultural pursuits. Ancient Chinese chronicles may indicate that the "forefathers of the Hani were nomads on the Qinghai-Gansu-Tibetan highlands" (Li Zixian 1993:2).

About the Third Century B.C. the Hani migrated to the Dadu River valley in Sichuan, and at the beginning of the Christian era they continued their southern migration into Yunnan, where they settled down over the next few centuries in approximately the same areas in which they live today.

About the 6th Century A.D. the ancestors of the Hani began to change from a nomadic dryland farming culture into a terraced field rice culture. Compared to the Yi, Naxi, Lahu and others, "the Hani were one of the better developed groups that first constructed terraced paddy fields on the mountains." (Li Zixian 1993:2)

From linguistic evidence, we estimate that around the year 1000-1200 A.D. the group of Hani who later called themselves "Akha" broke away from the main concentration of Hani in the Red River and Ailao mountain area, and continued their migration to the south. When they had crossed the Mekong (Lancang) River they gradually began to call themselves "Akha", and considered themselves as a different group from the Hani, who they accused of "becoming Chinese".

The Akha call the Hani the ones who "remained behind" ("**jol yavq e**", or, "**ga duv e**"). To this day the Akha continue to consider themselves as relatives to the Hani, but many Akha in China feel a closer linguistic and cultural kinship with other Akha living in Burma, Laos and Thailand than they do with the Hani.

The Hani and Akha genealogies are amazingly similar, and show the close relationship they have with each other, and even with other Lolo groups, especially the Yi. The Hani and Akha cultures are quite similar. However, the Hani remaining in the Red River valley and Ailao mountain area of Yunnan have been heavily influenced by the Chinese, as is shown by the numerous Chinese loan words in their language, and the various Sinitic influences in their house construction, their clothing, etc.

The group that migrated to the south and later called themselves "Akha" have had their language and culture heavily influenced by the Dai (also called Tai, or Shan). However, when one compares Hani and Akha proverbs (Lewis 1993) and Hani and Akha funeral texts (Hansson 1993), it can be seen from their older style language and former cultural traits that the Hani and Akha are basically one ethnic group.

The Culture of the Hani

Most of the Hani live in a subtropical mountainous area with fertile land and plentiful rainfall. For well over a thousand years they have been building and planting beautiful rice terraces up the sides of the Ailao and other mountains in that area. They also plant millet, cotton, buckwheat, peanuts, maize, tea and indigo.

They build their houses of mud bricks, stone and wood -- often on steep mountain sides, using thatch grass as the most common roofing material. The houses tend to be very dark, with the front door and an opening in the wall for smoke to go out being the main sources of light. Fortunately, the Government authorities have made electricity available to a large majority of the Hani villages, so that it is not uncommon to see them lighting their homes with electricity now.

Traditionally they built houses so that the family stayed in the upper floor, and the animals and agricultural tools were kept on the lower floor. Many of them now build their houses more like the Chinese, with a living area for the family on both floors, and the animals kept in separate quarters.

When Hani girls marry they go off to live with their husband's family, and accept his "family altar" (**aqpyuq baoqgeel**). At specified times they return to visit their home, just as the Akha of Burma and Thailand do.

There is one deity which is regarded highly by the Hani, called "Momi" (**Molmil**). He is sometimes referred to as "the one who lives in heaven/sky". He is called upon when asking a blessing upon someone, and is also blamed for certain tragedies. Another deity is "**Aqpyuq Miqyeil**", who may be considered their major protector.

The New Year Festival (**Galtaol taol**) takes place early in October, since that is the first month in the Hani lunar calendar. During the week-long festivities various ceremonies are carried out by each village and each home. Pigs and chickens are killed, and special glutinous rice balls are prepared for that celebration (Ma Yin 1989:258).

Once a year in late February or early March there is a "sacred grove ceremony" (**hhaqma tul**) held in each village, led by the "ritual head" of the village (**milguq**). The elders go to the sacred grove above the village and sacrifice a pig there, putting some of the blood on the three "sacred stones" by the "sacred tree".

Meat from the pig is distributed to each family in the village, both to feast on and to use in making ancestral offerings. Prayers are said to the "Lord of the site" (**Milsaol aqpyuq**), which include thanks for past blessings, and requests for good crops, healthy villagers, and an increase in their domesticated animals for the coming year.

There are many other festivals held in Hani villages, some of which are observed jointly with the "ritual head" in charge, and some of which are observed separately by individual households.

The Hani believe that there are 12 souls which inhabit the body (Li Qibo 1993:1). If one or more of these souls leaves the body illness results. The most common cause of "soul loss" (**sullal bal**) is when one is frightened, although it can also happen when one goes to a beautiful spot and the soul (or souls) wishes to remain there. Soul loss is identified by a "**moqpil**" or "**byulmoq**" (who may be called a "spirit priest"), and then the soul (or souls) must be "called back" (**sullal kul**).

The Hani have a proverb which relates the importance of the three main specialists in the Hani culture:

Zyuq maq jol laol biav.
Pil maq jol neivq beeq.
Qivq maq jol xal bial.

(If there is no ceremonial leader, the country falls apart.
If there is no spirit priest, the spirits create chaos.
If there is no blacksmith, the fields are abandoned.)

The function of the former village head (called "**zyuq**" in the proverb), has pretty much been taken over by the "ritual head" (**milguq**). There are some Hani villages where they still have a man called the "**zyuqma**", but the true ceremonial specialist and "ritual head" of the village now appears to be called the **milguq**.

"**Pil**" stands for the Hani 'spirit priests' (the specialists who deal with spirits). "**Qivq**" refers to the blacksmiths who historically provided the Hani with their agricultural tools.

Cultural Development

The People's Republic of China has developed a very progressive policy with their minority groups, of which the Hani are one. Education and economic development schemes have been pushed among the Hani and other groups, so that there are now many educated Hani serving their people and various Government groups in many ways.

THE LANGUAGE

The Dialects

Chinese linguists divide Hani into three major dialect groups:

1. **Hani-Yani** (HA-YA) There are many dialects in this group, with the Luchun dialect being chosen as "standard Hani" for publishing literature. This is the dialect used in this dictionary, but it must be remembered that there are many branch dialects of Luchun (Dolnia). Most of the speakers of this family of dialects live in the Luchun, Honghe, Yuanyang, Jinping counties of the Honghe Hani and Yi Autonomous Prefecture.

   The Akha dialects (YA stands for Yani which is often used to indicate the Akha who are living in China) are mainly spoken in the Lancang Lahu Autonomous County and Xishuangbanna area of China, as well as in Myanmar (Burma), Laos and Thailand.

2. **Haoni-Baihong** (HAO-BAI) Those speaking these dialects mainly live in Mojiang Hani Autonomous County, Yuangjiang Hani, Yi and Dai Autonomous County, and in the Pu'er Hani and Yi Autonomous county.

3. **Biyue-Kaduo** (BI-KA) There are three major dialects in this group: Biyue, Kaduo, and Ngoniu. Those who speak these dialects live mostly in the Simao region, in: Mojiang, Pu'er, Zhenyuan and Jingdong counties, and in Jiangcheng Hani and Yi Autonomous County.

ORTHOGRAPHY

The Hani people did not have a script until 1957, when the orthography now being used was devised by linguists in the People's Republic of China. The script is based on the Pinyin system, using letters from the Roman alphabet. This Hani orthography has been used in preparing many excellent books, pamphlets and newspapers for the Hani people (see the bibliography).

There have been four very capable men who led in developing this orthography:

Senior Lecturer Mr. Bai Zu'e, a Hani linguist who is known as the 'father' of the Hani orthorgraphy (see his book "Haniq Huvqpeiq Lapeiq Puv", 1989)

Prof. Dai Qingxia, who has been a pioneer in the

study of Tibeto-Burman languages as spoken in the People's Republic of China (see his book, "Research on Tibeto-Burman Linguistics", 1990, in Chinese)

Prof. Li Yongsui (see his "Hani Grammar", 1990, in Chinese)

Prof. Wang Ersong, a Hani linguist (see his book "A Brief Introduction to the Hani Language", compiled with Prof. Li Yongsui, 1986, in Chinese)

HANI PHONOLOGY

1. VOWELS

In Hani, as in Akha, there are both ORAL and LARYNGEALIZED (sometimes called 'creaky' or 'tight') vowels. The ORAL VOWELS are characterized by an expanded pharyngeal cavity, with no restriction of the passage of air.

The LARYNGEALIZED VOWELS are characterized by faucalization and laryngealization, with a glottal stop at the end when the syllable occurs in an utterance final position (as at the end of a clause or sentence).

The following nine vowels occur both in oral and laryngealized forms: (International phonetic symbols, as used by Chinese scholars, are given on the far right for the primary allophones.)

-i	high front unrounded (**bil** = to divide) (when it is initial, it is written: yi)	/i/
-ei	lower-mid front unrounded (**ceil** = ten)	/ɛ/
-yu	upper-mid front rounded (**yul** = old)	/ø/
-ee; -ii	high back unrounded (**meeq** = good; **siil** = gold)	/ɯ/
-e	upper-mid back unrounded (**bev** = shoot)	/ə/
-a	lower-mid unrounded (**ba'la** = moon)	/a/
-u	high back rounded (**qu** = care for) (when it is initial, written: **wu**)	/u/
-o	upper-mid back rounded (**goq** = high)	/o/
-ao	lower-mid back rounded (**naolma** = sun)	/ɔ/

When -i occurs initially, the Hani orthography places a **y-** before it (**'yil'** = to go down). When -u occurs initially, a **w-** is placed before it (**'wuqduq'** = head). In neither case is the **y-** or **w-** pronounced.

There are borrowed words where when **w-** is followed by vowels other than **-u**, the **w-** is pronounced as a **w-**. For example: **'weiftiq'** = a problem; question (Chi).) When the consonant **y-** is followed by the **-u** vowel in Hani, then the syllable must be written: '**yiu**', so as not to confuse it with the **-yu** vowel. When **y-** is followed by the **-yu** vowel it must be written: '**yyu**'.

The -ii vowel only occurs with the following consonants:

ciil = to lead	**ciivq** = genealogy
ziiq = to ride	**ziiv** = to itch
siil = gold	**siivq** = seven
ssiil = admit a mistake	**ssiiv** = to oppress

Since none of these four consonants occur with the **-ee** vowel, and the -ii vowel occurs only with these four consonants, the two vowels are allophones of the same phoneme, and could be written with a single symbol.

VOWEL CHART

	FRONT		BACK	
	Unrounded	Rounded	Unrounded	Rounded
High	**i**		**ee/ii**	**u**
Mid	**ei**	**yu**	**e**	**o**
Low			**a**	**ao**

Traditionally Hani has NO DIPHTHONGS. There are a few Han borrowed words which are pronounced as diphthongs by those who are fluent in Chinese:

-iei	**(fuflieiq)**	**-lia**	**(liafciiq)**
-ua	**(gua'li)**	**-iao**	**(diaof)**
-uei	**(gueif)**	**-ie**	**(lieqsual)**

Note: Akha has four vowels which Hani does not appear to have. These are written in Akha as follows:

- **-e** upper-mid front unrounded -- Although Hani uses this vowel in a few words (such as: **li** = "to go up"), the vowel is written as '-i'.
- **-oi** high front rounded
- **-m** a syllabic "m̩", which occupies the low front unrounded category in the Akha pattern
- **-ah** low back unrounded and nasalized

We would presume that these vowels were in the original Hani-Akha language, and were gradually subsumed into other vowels by the Hani, whereas the Akha retained them. (see Appendix 1, and Lewis 1989: 10-11)

2. CONSONANTS

The following consonants are not altered significantly by the quality of the vowels which follow them. (International phonetic symbols for the primary allophones are given on the extreme right.)

b-	voiced bilabial stop (**ba'la** = moon)	/b/
d-	voiced alveolar stop (**aqda** = father)	/d/
g-	voiced velar stop (**galma** = road)	/g/
s-	voiceless alveolar fricative (**sal** = beg)	/s/
z-	voiced alveolar affricate (**zaq** = to eat)	/dz/
x-	voiceless palatal fricative (**xa** = to plant)	/ç/
j-	voiced palatal affricate (**jaq** = to call) (Followed by a laryngealized vowel there is more palatization: **jav** = have)	/dʑ/
ss-	voiced alveolar fricative (**ssama** = elephant)	/z/
y-	voiced palatal fricative (**yal** = field) (Note: Followed by the **-u** vowel this letter is written **'yiu'**, so as to differentiate it from the **-yu** vowel.)	/j/
m-	voiced bilabial nasal (**aqma** = mother)	/m/
n-	voiced alveolar nasal (**nal** = to hurt)	/n/
ng-	voiced velar nasal (**ngal** = I)	/ŋ/
hh-	voiced velar fricative (**hha** = must)	/ɣ/
l-	voiced alveolar lateral (**lal** = come up)	/l/

The following voiceless consonants are **aspirated** when followed by an oral vowel, **unaspirated** when followed by a laryngealized (tight) vowel.

	ORAL (aspirated)		**LARYNGEALIZED** (unasp.)	
p-	**pal** = borrow	/ph/	**pavq** = leaf	/p/
t-	**taq** = don't	/th/	**tav** = sharp	/t/
k-	**alka** = crab	/kh/	**kav** = crossbow	/k/
q-	**qaq** = tired	/tɕh/	**qavq** = to cook	/tɕ/
c-	**cal** = sing	/tsh/	**alcav** = rope	/ts/
h-	**haq** = bitter	/xh/	**havq** = broken	/x/

(Note: **/xh/** has little or no friction when followed by an oral vowel, but when followed by a laryngealized vowel it becomes a partial velarized stop which has friction, and a final glottal stop, much like "**k'a**‸" in Akha.)

The following consonants can be palatalized. Only the voiceless stop **p-** is influenced by the quality of the vowel (i.e., aspirated when an oral vowel follows, unaspirated when a laryngealized vowel follows):

pi-	**piaq** = have a fever	**piav** = to scratch	/pj/

bi- **biaq** = bee **biav** = a coin /bj/
mi- **miaq** = many **miav** = eye /mj/
ni- **nieil** = to forget **nieivq** = to grab /nj/
Note: '**ni**' by itself is always palatalized:
nil = small **niv** = to move

There are two consonants borrowed from Chinese:

f- **feiljil** = airplane (although many Hani may say: **peiljil**); **feiqzaof** = soap /f/
w- **weifseil** = health; **weiqhuaf** = culture /w/
(Note: When this consonant proceeds **-u** in Hani words, it indicates a zero-initial syllable, so the **w-** is not pronounced, as in **wuqduq**.)

CONSONANT CHART

	Bi-labial	Alveo-lar	Palatal	Velar
Stops (voiceless)	**p**	**t**		**k**
Stops (voiced)	**b**	**d**		**g**
Affricates (voiceless)		**c**	**q**	
Affricates (voiced)		**z**	**j**	
Fricative (voiceless)		**s**	**x**	**h**
Fricatives (voiced)		**ss**	**y**	**hh**
Nasal	**m**	**n**		**ng**
Lateral		**l**		
(Borrowed)	**(w)**	**(f)**		

(Note: The fricatives **y-** and **x-** often fluctuate in Hani words. For example, 'mountain field' is pronounced both as: '**yal**' and '**xal**'.)

3. TONES

The TONES in Hani are indicated by final letters. There are THREE tones on **ORAL** vowels:

High - --l (**bal** = attend a festival)
Mid - -- (**ba** = white)
Low - --q (**baq** = thin)

There are TWO tones on **LARYNGEALIZED** vowels:

Mid	-	**--v**	(**bav** = a mistake)
Low	-	**--vq**	(**bavq** = to bring)

There is a RISING tone on certain **BORROWED** words:

--f (**faqyeif** = a legal court - Chi)

There are some instances in which a special indication needs to be made to distinguish the tone marker and the following vowel. For example, in the word for 'moon' (**ba'la**) an apostrophe placed between the two syllables indicates that the first syllable is on the mid tone, and the **'l-'** is the initial consonant for the following syllable.

There are a few words in which the Hani no longer use the apostrophe. They formerly wrote 'discipline' (Chi) as: **ji'liq**, but now they write it as: **jiliq**, since in Hani it would be impossible to have **'-iq'** by itself. Therefore the apostrophe is not needed.

Graphically the tones can be represented as follows, with laryngealization shown by 'plus' (++) marks.

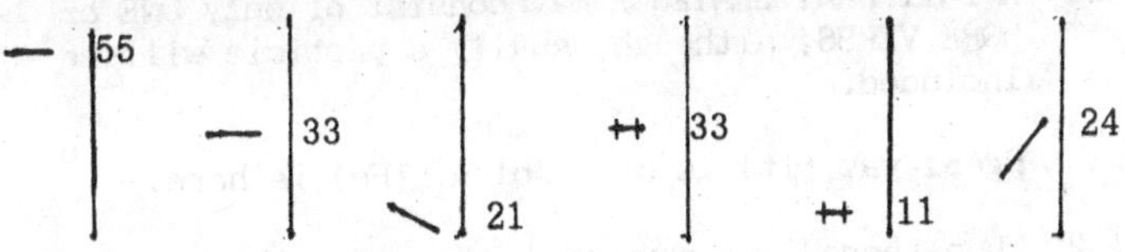

(Note: Many Chinese scholars hear the low tone as going from mid to low, that is: "31". Paul Lewis hears it as a tone that is closer to "21" in utterance intitial positions, and "11", or even "12" in other instances, depending on the tones which precede and follow it.)

TONE CHART

	ORAL		**LARYNGEALIZED**	
High	--l	(**bal**)		
Mid	--	(**ba**)	--v	(**bav**)
Low	--q	(**baq**)	--vq	(**bavq**)

(Note: Certain tonal changes take place in Hani. For example in; **sol pa sol nei sol** = "to smell very sweet", the second syllable is spoken on a high tone, since it is sandwiched between two high tones, but it is written on a mid tone, which is phonemically correct.)

WORD FORMATION

The grammar of Hani is similar to other Tibeto-Burman languages in that all Hani syllables have a CVT pattern: C = consonant, V = vowel, and T = tone. (See Hani Grammar, by Prof. Li Yongsui, 1990.)

Prof. Li Yongsui describes ten parts of speech in detail in his work on the Hani grammar. The three main parts of speech are: VERBS, NOUNS, and PARTICLES. The latter weave their way in and out to give needed direction, clarity of meaning, mood and other peripheral information.

1. THE VERB-PHRASE

All words (and only those) which can follow the negative adverb '**maq**' are in the class of Hani verbs. As in other Tibeto-Burman languages, no tense is indicated in Hani verbs.

1.1 A full Hani **SENTENCE** may consist of only ONE or MORE VERBS, although usually a particle will be included.

Ngeel ya. (It) is so. **Jol a.** (He) is here.

1.2 When there is a noun with the verb, the verb **follows** the noun.

Ngal lal = I come (up). **Nol yil** = You go (down).

1.3 **TWO FULL VERBS** often occur together.

Nal sil al. = Died of being sick.
Nalhaq sal ya. = listen being easy (That is: It sounds nice to me.

1.4 Verbs are often constructed from NOUNS by **REDUPLICATING** the second syllable: **AB B.**

hhosaq = pity, **hhosaq saq** = to pity someone
aoqsseil = rain, **aoqsseil sseil** = rain to rain
lavqduvq = bracelet, **lavqduvq duvq** = to wear a bracelet

1.5 **PRE-HEAD VERB**: The main causative verbs which can come before a main verb are: "**bi**" and "**hha.**

Ssaqguq a bi lal. = Let the young people come.
Ssaqguq hha lal. = The young people must come.

1.6 **POST-HEAD VERBS**, such as: **zaq**, **pal**, **duv**, **lal**, **yil**, **sil**, etc. are full verbs when they occur alone, but when they occur after a main verb, they are subordinate to it, adding some meaning or result to the head verb, or perhaps showing the direction or state of the action.

duv (as full verb) = go/come out
  duv (as post-head verb) = away from the site
    xeiv = to run
      xeiv duv = to run out and away (13:1)

sil (as full verb) = to die
  bev = to shoot
    bev sil = to shoot to death

1.7 **VERB PARTICLES** can never constitute an utterance, but occur after verbs and verb phrases, being subordinate to them.

They are such particles as: **na**, **nia**, **movq**, **qivq**, **qaol**, etc. They indicate the subjective attitude of the actor toward the verb, especially in the area of ability and willingness.

yil (as full verb) = go down
  na (as modal auxiliary) = willing to (vb)
    yil na = to be willing to go down

aol (as full verb) = to do
  nia (as modal auxiliary) = to be able to (vb)
    aol nia = to be able to do (something)

1.8 **ADVERBS** occur before and in close subordination to a main verb or verb-phrase. Nothing else can come in between.

Negative:
  maq = no, not (**maq lal** = not come; **maq zaq deiv siq** = not eat to the full yet)
  taq = don't (**taq lal** = don't come; **taq diq sil** = don't beat it to death)

Positive:
  alciiv = a little (**alciiv kaq** = a little better)
  loyei nei = slowly (**loyei nei eil** = speak slowly)

Comparative:
  hal = all who (**hal jol e colmoq** = all of the old people who are there; **Alheeq hal meeq zeiq e qiq hhaq.** = Alheeq is the best.)

2. THE NOUN-PHRASE

2.1 Hani **NOUNS** consist of one or more syllables:

a. **One-syllable nouns:**
piul = silver (money)
col = person; people

b. **Two-syllable nouns** which can be broken down into their constituent parts:

keelguq = achilles tendon (**keel** = foot/leg, **guq** = tendon/vein)
dama = parents (**da** = father; **ma** = mother)

c. **Disyllabic nouns** which cannot be broken down:

saqlaq = cotton; **albol** = tree; **aqda** = father

2.2 **NOUN REDUPLICATION** is often used in Hani, with various patterns: (and see Appendix 12)

a. the **AB BC pattern:**

haqpeeq = paddy bran
haqpeeq peeqnaoq = soft inner paddy bran

b. the **AB AC pattern:**

milluvq milsaol = guardian lord of the area
daoldiq daolbuvq = a large bird

c. the **AB CB pattern:**

taoqtul laltul = straight up and down
aoqlu millu = earthquake

2.3 **PRONOUNS**

a. **Nominative**
Singular: **ngal** = I; **nol** = you; **aqyoq** = she, he, it
Plural: **ngalya** = we (exclusive); **ngaldu** = we (inclusive); **nolya** = you (plural); **aqya; aqya mavq; aqyo mavq** = they

b. **Objective**
Singular: **ngaq yaol; ngaq a** = to me; **noq yaol; noq a** = to you; **aqyoq yaol; aqyoq a** = to him, to her, to it
Plural: **ngalyaq yaol; ngalyaq a** = to us (exclusvie); **ngalduq yaol; ngalduq a** = to us (inclusive); **nolyaq yaol; nolyaq a** = to you (plural); **aqya yaol; aqya a; aqyo mavq yaol; aqyo mavq a** = to them

c. **Possessive**

Singular: **nga**; **ngaq** e = my; **no**; **noq** e = your; **aqyo**; **aqyoq** e = hers, his, it's

Plural: **ngalya**; **ngaldu**; **ngalyaq** e; **ngalduq** e = our; **nolya**, **nolyaq** e = your; **aqya**, **aqya** e, **aqyo mavq** e = their

2.4 **INTERROGATIVES** Most interrogatives in Hani begin with: **hal---** or **aqsol**

haljivq alnei = why?; **haljivq nei** = with what?
haljivq = what?; **haltaq** = when?; **halgei** = where?,
halmeil leil = how?; **halhe nei** = how big?
Aqsol hev nia ya? Who could know?

In some cases the question asks for a number, or a specific person:

halmiav = how many?; **aqsol** = who?

2.5 **DEMONSTRATIVES** point to the noun they follow:

yul = that, there (**galma yul kaol** = that path)
tyul = that/this (closer to you than me) (**col tyul hhaq** = human that/this person)
xil = this (**aqyol xil mol** = sheep this animal)

2.6 **ADJECTIVES** follow nouns, and are used as a modifier or a predicator. They are distinguished one from the other by their written form:

colmoq = old man (**moq** is a modifier segment)
col **moq** = the man is old (**moq** is a predicator)

a. Some adjectives can be **reduplicated**:

colqoq qoq = to invite a friend to accompany one
alyeiv yeivnil nil = the red flower is red

b. **COMPARATIVE DEGREE** of adjectives is often shown as:

hultav + adjective + **zeiq** = comparative degree
(**Aqda aqma hultav moq zeiq**. = Father is older than mother.)

c. **SUPERLATIVE DEGREE** is shown as:

hal + adjective + **zeiq** = superlative degree
(**Alheeq hal meeq zeiq e qiq hhaq**. = Alheeq is the best person.)
Col e **niuqteil hal goq zeiq e nga**. = (Man's forehead is the highest there is.)

2.7 **NUMERALS** are as follows: (Note: The numeral "3" is pronounced on a high tone when the classifier is on a low tone, but it is pronounced on a low tone when the classifier is on a mid or high tone.)

1 - **qiq**	11 - **ceiltivq**
2 - **niq**	12 - **ceil niq**
3 - **saol (saoq)**	13 - **ceil saol (-saoq)**
4 - **yuvq**	
5 - **ngavq**	20 - **niq ceil**
6 - **kuvq**	21 - **niq ceiltivq**
7 - **siivq**	35 - **saoq ceil ngavq**
8 - **xeivq**	49 - **yuvq ceil hhyuq**
9 - **hhyuq**	90 - **hhyuq ceil**
10 - **ceil**	99 - **hhyuq ceil hhyuq**

100 - **qiq yal**
200 - **niq yal**
1,000 - **qiq taol**
10,000 - **qiq mil**
100,000 - **ceil mil**
1,000,000 - **yal mil**
10,000,000 - **taol mil**
100,000,000 - **milmil; yif** (Chi)
1,000,000,000 - **ceil milmil**
10,000,000,000 - **yal milmil**

2.8 **CLASSIFIERS** occur after nouns, and indicate just how the Hani 'classify' that noun.

a. Classifiers usually occur **following**:

numbers: **moq yuvq kaol** (horses four animals)
the question 'How many': **Col halmiav hhaq** (People how many humans?)
demonstratives: **galma xil kaol** (road this long item)

b. The **most common** classifiers are:

mol = general things and some animals
hhaq = humans
siq = fruit and certain round things
cav = string, cord, rope
kaol = thread & long things; certain animals (cow, donkey, buffalo, etc.)
mavq = a group (animate)
dyul = a group of things

c. Some classifiers simply **use the noun** they classify:

nao = day, **nao kuvq nao** = days six days

d. Some classifiers **repeat** the second part of the noun they classify:

kavmiaq = crossbow arrow, **kavmiaq ceil miaq** = crossbow arrows ten arrows

e. Some nouns can take **more than one** classifier:

yuqlaoq = pot **yuqlaoq qiq siq; yuqlaoq qiq mol; yuqlaoq qiq laoq** = a pot
miqbev = gun **miqbev qiq siq; miqbev qiq mol; miqbev qiq bev** = a gun

3. PARTICLES

3.1 **NOUN PARTICLES** can only follow nouns or another noun particle.

- **yaol** = an indicator of the objective case (**Aqyoq yaol diq sil** = He is beaten to death.)
- **a** = an indicator of the objective case (**Aqyoq a soqhhaq qiq daoq bivq miq.** A copy of the book is given to him.)
- **-gei** = place (**xilgei taq duq** = don't dig here)

ngaoq = if (**xilgei duq ngaoq, hha sil** = if you dig here, you must die)

nei = the actor (**Ngaq nei zaq saq al.** = I am the one who ate it all.)

- **e** = a restrictive indicator (**zaq e aqzal** = food for eating; **dol e wulquvq** = water for drinking)
- **e** = a possessive case indicator (**Piul xildyul ngaq e maq ngeel, noq e.** This money is not mine, it is yours.)

3.2 **INTERJECTIONS** often occur alone, or at the beginning of the sentence:

eiqya !	(ok, yes!)	**aqmiqyil**!	(oh my)
alyol !	(surprise)	**peiq**!	(disgust)
eiq !	(sorry)	**halhal**!	(happy)

3.3 **FINAL PARTICLES** usually follow the verb and come at the end of the sentence. They have various functions which are defined in the dictionary.

zaq = to eat
Zaq joq. Please eat.
Zaq ma laq? Do you want to eat? **Zaq ma.** Yes.
Zaq al laq? Have (you) eaten?
Zaq al. (I) have eaten.
Zaq kal yoq. Let's eat.
Zaq haqhaq. To be eating.
Zaq nadul al. Looks like (he) might have eaten already.
Zaq aqkussal. Perhaps (he) has eaten.
Zaq siq lul. Eat more please.
Zaq teiqteiq. Eat quickly.

WORD DIVISION IN HANI

In the Hani language most syllables have a meaning or a grammatical function. Often the syllables can be written separately, although noun and adjective prefixes must not be separated: **al-** (as in: **albaol; algo; almiuvq**); **aq-** (as in: **aqnil; aqhhavq; aqkeeq**), **yo-** (as in: **yomeeq; yokeel; yoheeq**).

It is often difficult to know just where to divide Hani words, since there are times when the divisions can make a difference in the meaning. For example: **taqzaq** = to deposit (as money in a bank); **taq zaq** = don't eat. **miavgaol** = a hoop; a band; but **miav gaol** means to have 'sharp' eyes (good eyesight).

In the initial stages of writing Hani more syllables were written together than in the last few years. For example, for 'the sky and land to turn black' (as in a bad storm), it was originally written: '**aoqnav milnavmeil**' (30:2), but later it was written: '**aoq nav mil nav meil**' (46:147). For 'the sky and land to be red' it was formerly written: '**aoqnilmilnil**', but now it is written: '**aoq nil mil nil**' (46:155).

In 1992 a group of Hani scholars discussed how words should be divided. Based on their decisions and our own understanding of Hani grammar, as well as our perception of the needs of new literates, we are dividing words as follows;

1. Two syllable nouns and adjectives with the prefixes: **al-, aq-, yo-**, **laqbil; milkaq** must never be divided.

2. Certain four-syllable words should be divided:
   a. Nouns should be divided into two parts:
      aqha hama = hen
      molcyuq cyuqssaq = an orphan
      seifhyuf ziifhhal = social security (Chi)

   b. Those to be divided into individual syllables:
      Verb phrases: **puv lil puv la** = to turn repeatedly
      Adjective or descriptive phrases: **hhyul leiq hhyul sil** = with exceeding joy

3. Certain one syllable words are written separately:
   a. Adjective intensifiers; **pa** (**laolnuv pa nuv nei laol** = very warm water) (Note: when a high tone occurs on both sides of /**pa**/, it is pronounced on a high tone, but written with a middle tone. **navqyol pa yol nei navq** = very deep)
   b. Certain particles: (1) **nei** (**meeq nei** = well

done); (2) **meil** (**yomeeq meil** = goodly; **ju lu ja la meil** = in rags, sloppy)

c. Numerals: **ceil; yal; taol** = 10, 100, 1,000

d. The word for "side"; **pyu** (**ngaq pyu** = my side; **xil pyu** = this side)

4. Three syllable phrases where the first two syllables form a noun, and the last syllable is a verb, the verb is separated from the noun:
   alyeiv yeiv = flowers blossom; **alhhe ziiq** = to ride a swing

USING THE DICTIONARY

ALPHABETIZATION

The standard alphabetization of English is used in this dictionary, with the exception that in the Hani when there is a digraph (two letters) used for writing either a vowel or consonant, they are considered to represent one sound, and are therefore not divided in this dictionary.

Thus all '**a**' vowels, for example, will come before any '**ao**' vowels. When the '**ao**' vowels are completed, then the '**e**' vowels are listed one by one (according to TONE -- see below), followed by the '**ee**' vowels, etc.

1. ALPHABETIZATION OF VOWELS

a	ia	iu
ao	iao (Chi)	o
e	ie	u
ee	iei (Chi)	ua (Chi)
ei	ii	uei (Chi)
i	io	yu

2. ALPHABETIZATION OF CONSONANTS

b	k	s
c	l	ss
d	m	t
f (Chi)	n	w
g	ng	x
h	p	y
hh	q	z
j		

3. ALPHABETIZATION OF TONES

high oral	--l	(as in: **bal**)
mid oral	--	(as in: **ba**)

low oral **--q** (as in: **baq**)
mid laryngealized **--v** (as in: **bav**)
low laryngealized **--vq** (as in: **bavq**)

rising tone (borrowed words) **--f** (as in: **baf**)

4. SPECIAL FEATURES

When there are two identical syllables, but one of them has two hyphens before it (indicating it is a bound form), the syllable without the hyphens is written first: **lav**
-- lav

When a verb is derived from the second segment of a noun, there are two entries:
aoqsseil sseil = the rain to rain
-- sseil, aoqsseil -- the rain to rain
In this way the verb is not lost in the reduplicated pattern.

Also, the pre-head causative verb is shown as:
bi (vb) cause to (vb) (**bi aol** = cause to do)

Post-head verbs are shown as:
(vb) pal again (vb) (**eil pal** = to say again)

In the case of some multi-syllabic terms, we include separate entries for many of the other syllables, in an effort to have a clearer understanding of the morphemic patterns. These are enclosed in equal (=) signs, which show that the actual order is inverted, and that the syllables are joined;

=moq, col= old people
=moq, saqhav hav= old forest
(Note: The expressions are: **colmoq; saqhav havmoq** respectively.)

Sometimes we give a literal translation of the term in parentheses, with single quote marks.

BORROWING

Most of the borrowing in the Hani language comes from Chinese, including words which may have originally been borrowed by the Chinese from English, such as: **salfaq** = sofa; **kalfeil** = coffee.

The Akha of Burma and Thailand, and to a certain extent the Akha (Zani or Yani) of the Xishuangbanna area, have borrowed heavily from Dai (also called Tai, or Shan). The Hani have borrowed very few words from Dai, such as a few names of trees, and some words for certain types of tiles, pots, and knives. If borrowed from Dai the entry is followed with: (Dai)

mamoq mango (Dai)

The words which are clearly borrowed from Chinese are followed with: (Chi)

gueif lao to be strange (Chi)
calgueil to visit (Chi)

There are times when only the first part of the word is from Chinese and the second is Hani. In that case we write:

calkuf laqhyul grannary (A=Chi)
gaolluf galma highway (A=Chi)

If it is the second (or last) segment of the word which is borrowed from Chinese we indicate it as:

soqhhaq laoziiq a written receipt (B=Chi).
moq jalsoq a halter (B=Chi)

Often the borrowed Chinese term can be written in more than one way in Hani, with one more like the Chinese, the other more like what the Hani people say:

tuaq yeiq league member (closer to Chinese)
tyuq yeiq league member (closer to Hani)

When possible, we include both entries (see: **feiljil**; and **peiljil**).

AKHA ENTRIES

Since Prof. Dai Qingxia suggested we include the Akha terms where possible, we have sought to do this, enclosing them in parentheses.

These terms are written in the Akha orthography developed in Burma and Thailand (see Lewis: 1989). When the Hani term can be expressed by more than one word in Akha, or when there is more than one way of saying that word in Akha, we try to use the form which is closest to Hani.

Since the Hani and Akha cultures are fairly different, there are many Akha words which do not correspond 100% to the Hani expression. In a few cases they are quite different, such as '**na ciq**' (as compared to Akha 'ja^ g'a$_{\vee}$'). At the same time, we hope the inclusion of the Akha terms will be helpful for those interested in comparing the two languages.

DIALECTS

There are many dialects of Hani spoken in China. One of us (Bai Bibo, or Piu Bo in Hani) has done a comparative study of the following; Luchun, Qidi, Laza, Jaying, Midie, Ailuo, Guozo, Talaotang, Habi, Yice, Banpo and Doni.

The **Luchun** dialect has been chosen as the major dialect to use in producing literature, but not all Luchun speakers agree on every word -- which is not surprising. This is one reason we often record the place where we have found illustrations of Hani words in Hani literature. The first number in parenthesis is the number of the work (see list: HANI SOURCES). The second number is the page on which that word is found.

The book which is number 50 in our Hani sources is important, in that it represents the efforts of several Hani (including at least one Akha) in developing the best way of writing specialized words. Many words are simply transliterations of Chinese words, but these are important in that they become the "semi-official" way of writing these words, as well as various Hani words, in the Hani language. We do notice a tendency for some of the Hani entries to be rather superficial, however, as there is a scramble on the part of the compilers to find what could be the closest equivalent to the Chinese in Hani -- and it may be quite a ways off!

There are some words which seem to be spoken the same by all Luchun speakers. Usually these are words that are roughly the same as in Akha, such as:

aqda = father; **aqma** = mother; **aqlavq** = arm/hand; **aqkeel** = leg/foot; **miqzaq** = fire; **galma** = road

When there are differences in the way Hani words are written, such as: **nago** and **naogo** (meaning: 'with'), we try to take the most recent Hani literature as our guide in what we use in this dictionary.

Having two Hani words for 'dry mountain field' creates a problem. These are the words '**xal**' and '**yal**'. There are some 20 or so entries under both terms having to do with 'field', such as: "field hut", "weed the field", "go to the field", etc. When possible, we include both of these spellings in the dictionary.

THANKS

We two, Bai Bibo and Paul Lewis are most grateful to various people and organizations who have helped produce this dictionary.

First we wish to thank Prof. Dai Qingxia, chairman of the Department of Minority Languages and Literature in Beijing for his encouragement in getting this project under way, and helping in so many aspects of it. The inclusion of Akha terms in the first section of the dictionary is a result of his suggestion, although it should be realized that the meanings of these Akha terms are not always equivalent to the Hani terms.

A gracious financial grant was made by the Board of International Ministries of the American Baptist Churches/USA, with headquarters in Valley Forge, PA. Apart from that this dictionary never could have been compiled.

We are grateful to Mr. Shi Junchao who introduced Bai Bibo to the project so that he could become a joint compiler of this dictionary. We also wish to thank Prof. Li Zhanxu, Director of the Institute of National Minorities Literature of the Yunnan Academy of Social Sciences, who helped in many ways.

We also thank Mr. Li Qibo, President of the Institute of Nationality Studies, Honghe Prefecture, Yunnan Province. We appreciate the time granted to Bai Bibo to work on this dictionary by Mr. Li and his Institute.

Thanks are also due to Mr. A-Je Kukaewkasem of Chiang Rai, Thailand, for his excellent help in adding many Akha terms to the dictionary. Rob Taylor of SIL also gave excellent suggestions and much encouragement, for which we are most grateful.

Very special thanks is expressed to the INTERNATIONAL INSTITUTE FOR ASIAN STUDIES of Leiden, The Netherlands, who made the printing of this dictionary possible. Our heartfelt thanks go to Director Wim Stokhof and Dr. Deborah Tooker for arranging for this dictionary to be printed as a pre-conference publication for the May 1996 Hani-Akha International Cultural Conference.

For all of those who have labored long and hard to write and produce literature in the Hani language we offer sincerest thanks, and wish to encourage them to continue their excellent work.

Bai Bibo (Piu Bo), Yunnan, PRC
Paul Lewis, USA
February 1996

Ssaoqssaq a Eilgaq e Doq

(to our Hani readers)

Doqlo Soqdaoq xil daoq Haqniqdoq, Aqkaqdoq ssolnei Yilyidoq yaol laqheiq qeil e col qiq mavq a bi ssaoq movq a leil, zaol duv laq e nga.

Haqniq soqmiav miqnieiq aol zaq e col, Haqniq milcaq a soqhhaq meiq zaq e col ssolnei, Haqniq yoliq miqnieiq aol zaq e col qiq mavq, soqdaoq yosiivq xil daoq aqlavq hholqei jav e ngaoq, yoqhhaq soqhhaq aqzeiq zol hev lal nia. Yoqhhaq miqnieiq aqzeiq aol meeq qivq zeiq e maq ceil, aqya yaol liq aqzeiq meil meiq hev nia zeiq, aqya meiqsi Haqniq yoliq liq aqzeiq meil gee loq nia zeiq nga.

Soqdaoq xil daoq hholqei zaoma nei saoq baol kevq nga: wuqduq qiq baol, alkaq qiq baol ssolnei daoqmiq qiq baol.

Qiq. Wuqduq Qiq Baol

Xilgei hholqei aq, eilgaq ssolnei eilloq e doq nga. Xil meevnia qa kevq nga.

1. Haqniqssaq ssolnei Haqniqdoq yoliq wuqzao dyul gee meiq e nga.

Haqniqssaq halmiav nei jol, galhhu halgei jol, ṇiaoq'aol jolduq jolhhal halgei, aol zaq hovq dol miqnieiq halmeil leil, xil mavq saqnei xilgei hholqei gee meiq nga. Haqniqdoq gee e halmeil, Haqniq soqmiav halmeil leil, soqmiav buvq e galquv halmeil leil, xilgei hholqei gee meiq nga.

2. Doqlo Soqdaoq xil daoq halmeil leil ssaoq leil xilgei gee meiq nga.

Haqniqdoq hholqei kevq e Pyulniuldoq yul qa halmeil leil buvq, Dolnia Luqcyul Haqniqdoq maq ngeel meil, Aqkaqdoq ssolnei gee li nia la Haqniqdoq halmeil leil bavq ssaoq laq e leil, xil hholqei gee loq laq e nga.

Doqlo qiq mol naolhao guaqhaof hholqei gee'qa niq mol kevq e yul qa, miqteil qiq mol aq, soqdaoq e gee'qa, naolhao qiq mol aq, doqlo mol lal laq e yul baq e gee'qa nga. Xilgei salhu:
Yiqsav Honghe County (Hani name) (11:130).

Xilgei 11 aq soqdaoq dif 11 daoq e gee qa; 130 aq soqdaoq dif 11 daoq hholqei 130 baq hultav a doqlo "Yiqsav" xil mol jav nga leil nga.

3. Eilpyuqdoq

Doqlo soqdaoq xil mol zaol e Paolu Liuqyisiil ssolnei Piubo nga niq hhaq, soqdaoq xil mol zaol ballal nei hhaqhav tivq haol e col taol hhaq yal hhaq yaol eilpyuq. Xilgei aq col meevnia hhaq e colmiaol buvq dav alnei aqzeiq meil qiq heiq eilpyuq miq wul.

4. Doqlo soqdaoq xil mol zaol e taq, nga niq hhaq zol laq e soqdaoq e colmiaol buvq ssaoq taq.

Yilyi, Pyulniul ssolnei Haqniq soqmiav nei buvq laq e soqdaoq e colmiaol saqnei kevq al. Doqlo yomiaq qiq pav aq, soqdaoq xildyul hultavq nei bavq ssaoq laq e ngeel al.

5. Doqlo soqdaoq xil daoq hholqei buvq kuv laq e soqmiav aqma dyul yaol eilloq. "AK" aq, Aqkaq yaol eil e nga; "CA" aq, Maoq Pov Guq Aqkaq leil eil e nga.

Niq. Alkaq Qiq Baol

Xil qiq baol hholqei niq pav bil pav laq e nga. Huqteil qiq pav aq, Haqniqdoq-Yilyidoq-Aqkaqdoq doqlo nga. Haqniq doqlo dyul soqmiav aqma A... AO... nei Z hev nei, qiq ba qiq ba meil bavq soq taq laq e nga.

Doqlo miaq zeiq e qiq mavq aq, Haqniqdoq, Yilyidoq ssolnei Aqkaqdoq xil saoq qa meil kevq nga. Aqkaqdoq a guaqhaof hholqei bavq dov laq e nga. Xilgei salhu:

alba   older sister (9:1) (a˅ yui˄),
aqda   father; dad; daddy (9:8) (a˯ da).

Doqlo naoq zeiq e qiq mavq aq Aqkaqdoq maq kevq nga.

Naolhao qiq pav hholqei aq, Yilyidoq ssolnei Haqniqdoq, xil niq qa nga. Yilyi doqlo dyul soqmiav aqma A -- Z hev nei, aqyoq e galquv lo'qo bavq soq taq laq e nga. Xilgei salhu: abdomen   wuqma; wuqdeiq
mother   aqma

Saol. Daoqmiq Qiq Baol

Xil baol hholqei aq, eillaoq e soqdoq nga. Paolu ssolnei Piubo nga niq hhaq nyuq e Haqniq soqmiav miqnieiq aol zaq e col qiq mavq Haqniq yoliq niq'eil loq zeiq niq'eil meeq. Xilmeil nei, xilgei Haqniq miqnieiq soqdoq ceil niq qa bavq soq taq laq e nga.

1. Haqniq soqmiav ssolnei Aqkaq soqmiav bavq qeiv.

2. Haqniq dudaq "Beiyaoq Ssolnei Aqssaq". Huqteil pyu aq Haqniq soqmiav. Naolhao pyu aq, Yilyi nei buvq puv laq e nga.

3. Haqniq aqpyuq aqda e ciivq bavq qeiv. Dolnia Luqcyul, Maohei, Mieidieif ssolnei Teifgoq milhaoq e Haqniq aqpyuq aqda ciivq kevq nga.

4. Zaolgoq goqjal hholqei colqa 56 qa colmiaol buvq e galquv.

5. Zaolgoq goqjal sei, sif ssolnei ziifziifqil 31 mol e colmiaol buvq e galquv.

6. Teilsal doqqo qo e galquv.

7. Colqoq alkaq pyuqdoq gul e galquv.

8. "Maq" naogo eil paoq e doqlo loba.

9. Haqniq doq aqma meevnia doq.

10. Haqniq bakaq meevnia mol.

11. Huvq, la, nao

12. Doqlo loyeiv

Ngaq e niq hhaq, Paolu ssolnei Piubo, hhaqhav tivq alnei Doqlo soqdaoq xil mol aol e kuvq huvq huvq biao biao al. Ngaq e niq hhaq, doqlo soqdaoq meeqzav nei, wuqduq daoqmiq leev nei qiq daoq zaol duv alnei, Haqniq soqmiav miqnieiq aol zaq e col qiq mavq a soqhhaq ssaoqmiaoq qiq daoq bivq alnei, xil laqnil Haqniq soqmiav soqhhaq duv e tyul qa meeqduq halmiaq nei bi jav movq ya leil nyuq. Doqlo hal mol lal e, hal jav e saqnei meil, bavq ssaoq movq ya leil nyuq.

Tyulliq, neema nyuq e aqlavq maq aol hev nia. Haqniq doq aqma eil e aqmeil:

"Haqniq soqdoq niq eil niq duv duv;
Joqdei milnil niq duq niq zeq zeq.
Haqniq soqdoq gee saq galcaol maq jav;
Joqdei milnil duq saq daoqdaoq maq jav."

Soqdaoq xil daoq hholqei doqlo maq luvq maq ceil, buvq bav laq e ssolnei eil bav laq e liq, kevq gaoq zeiq ya. Xilmeil nei, halgei maq za, halgei bav nga laq leil nga niq hhaq naogo eilgaq. Aqkal hha zaol duvq pal nia qiq jol jav ngaoq, Doqlo soqdaoq xil daoq aqzeiq qiq teivq zaol meeq dav movq ssa.

Paolu ssolnei Piubo

1996 huvq 2 la

BIBLIOGRAPHY OF BOOKS AND ARTICLES

ENGLISH SOURCES

Bradley, David

1977 Akha and Southern Loloish. Pacific Linguistics A-49:23-65.

1979a Lahu Dialects. Oriental Monograph 23. Australian National University Press, Canberra. 291 pp.

1979b Proto-Loloish. Scandinavian Institute of Asian Studies Monograph Series No. 39. London and Malmo: Curzon Press Ltd.

1994 A Dictionary of the Northern Dialect of Lisu (China and Southeast Asia). Pacific Linguistics Series C-126. The Australian National University.

Deng Qi Yao

1993 The Layout of the Body for the Traditional Funeral Ceremony. First International Conf. on Hani Culture. (28 pg.)

Hansson, Inga-Lill

1982 A Phonological Comparison of Akha and Hani. Linguistics of the Tibeto-Burman Area, 7.1, 63-115.

1984 A Comparison of Akha, Hani, Khatu, and Pijaw. 17th International Conference on Sino-Tibetan Languages and Linguistics, Univ. of Oregon, 7-9 September.

1985 Akha and the Hani Languages of China.

1993 A Preliminary Comparison of Hani and Akha Funeral Texts. First International Conf. on Hani Culture.

Lewis, Paul

1968a Akha Phonology, Anthropological Linguistics 10.2 8-18.

1968b The Role and Function of the Akha Village Priest. Behavior Science Notes 3.4 249-262.

1973 Tone in the Akha Language. Anthropological Linguistics 15.4 183-188.

1986 Lahu - English - Thai Dictionary. Thai Tribal Crafts, Box 3, Chiang Mai, Thailand.

1989 Akha - English - Thai Dictionary. DAPA; 115 M. 2, T. Rimkok, A. Muang, Chiang Rai 57000, Thailand.

1993 A Brief Introduction to Hani Proverbs. First International Conf. on Hani Culture. (6 pgs)

Lewis, Paul and Elaine
1984 Peoples of the Golden Triangle. London: Thames and Hudson.

Li Chonglong
1993 An Introduction to the Hani Regulations Used in their Lives. First International Conf. on Hani Culture. (20 pg.)

Li Kaike
1993 A Brief Discussion of the Social Functions of Hani Folk Dance. First International Conf. on Hani Culture (9 pgs)

Li Qibo
1993 A Study of Soul Recall and Protection in Hani Folklore. First International Conf. on Hani Culture. (13 pg.)

Li Zixian
1993 Water -- the Source of Life and Culture: On Hani Mythology and Terraced Field Rice Culture. First International Conf. on Hani Culture. (11 pgs.)

Liu Jin Wu
1993 The Varied Cultural Characteristics of the Hani Nationality Dance. First International Conf. on Hani Culture (12 pgs.)

Lu Zhaohe
1993 A study of the Cultural Background of the Development of the Hani Population. First International Conf. on Hani Culture. (8 pgs.)

Matisoff, James A.
1973 The Grammar of Lahu. Berkeley: University of California Press.

1988 The Dictionary of Lahu. Berkeley: University of California Press.

Ma Yin (editor)
1989 China's Minority Nationalities. Beijing: Foreign Languages Press.

Tooker, Deborah E.
1995 The Aini zu of the Hani Minority Nationality: Some Comparative Thoughts on Akha in China, Thailand and Myanmar (Burma). in Yearbook of the International Institute of Asian Studies I. 1994. Leiden.

Tsutomu, Inamura
1995 The International Bibliography on Akha-Hani. English, Chinese, Japanese (15, August, 1995)

Wheatley, Julian K.
1982 Comments on the 'Hani' dialects of Loloish. Linguistics of the Tibeto-Burman Area. 7.1, 1-38.

Yang Fang
1993 On Hani Folk Songs. First International Conf. on Hani Culture (19 pgs.)

Yang Jintian
1993 The Male Centeredness of the Hani Culture. First International Conf. on Hani Culture. (3 pgs.)

Zhang Xiaohui and Lu Baohe
1993 Hani Nationality's Customary Law and Its Cultural Value. First International Conf. on Hani Culture. (11 pgs.)

Zhang Yajin
1993 First Probe of Hani Folk Dance Culture. First International Conf. on Hani Culture (12 pgs.)

CHINESE SOURCES

(Many of these come from the International Bibliography on Akha-Hani prepared by Inamura Tsutomu.)

Bai Bibo
1989 Naming System of the Hani
1989 On the Existential Sentences of the Hani Language
1991 The Concept of Zeng and Property in the Hani Language
1991 An Analysis of the Difficult Points when Hani People learn Mandarin

Bai Pozu
1986 The Respectful Manners of Hani for Elders JJ2, pp. 228-229

Bai Zu'e
1988 Migu, Ritual Singer and Pimo

Bai Xueguang
1989 An Analitical Study of the Farewell Song at the Marriage Ritual among the Hani

Bai Yu
1987 On the Historical Poetry of the Hani
1989 Group Imagination of Hani: its Demands and Derivation
1991 An Analysis of Hani Funeral Ceremonies
1992 An Initial Analysis into the Outlook on Life and Death among the Hani

Chen Jianyao
1982 Pima (priest) of the Hani

Dai Qingxia
1990 Research on Tibeto-Burman Linguistics

Duan Kuangle
1991 The Characteristics of the Literary Language of the Hani

Fan Yuanchang
1987 On the Features of Hani Proverbs

Fang Guoyu
1957 An Introduction to Hani History

Gao He
1994 Magic: the Calling the Soul back of the Hani
1994 The Meaning of the Hani Name

Guo Xingang
1983 Premarital Intercourse among the Hani (JJ1, pg. 254)

Han Lai
1988 On the Family Customs of the Hani

Huang Yan
1988 On the Agricultural Activities and the Rituals among the Hani

Jiu Mi
1993 The Ceremonies of the Hani

Li Guowen
1988 Hani Primitive Religion

Li Kechong
1986 The Amatu Ceremony of the Hani: its Activity and History
1989 The Funeral Ceremony of the Hani: Ancestor Worship and the Mopi (priest)

Li Qibo et al
1990 Funeral Songs of the Hani

Li Yuanqin
1991 On the Pluralistic Genealogy: A View of the Patronymic Linkage System of the Hani

Li Yongsui
1986 The Lively Forms of the Adjectives in the Hani Language
1990 Hani Grammar
1992 New Progress made in the Survey of Hani Languages

Li Yongsui and Wang Ersong
1986 A Brief Introduction to the Hani Language

Lilang Bofa
1994 The Village Headman of the Hani

Lu Chaogui
1986 Mopi, Pimo, Nima of the Hani
1991 The Priest and Shaman of the Hani

Mao Youquan
1981 Introduction of Five Hani Folk Customs
1983 On the Hani Folk Songs
1983 Hani Calendar and Festivals
1983 On Pimo (folk priest) of the Hani
1985 New Rice Festival of the Hani
1986 Funeral Ritual of the Hani
1987 The Birth Customs of the Hani
1990 A Classification of Hani Supernatural Beings
1991 Introduction of Hani Culture

Peng Yongsheng
1983 Marriage Customs of the Hani

Shen Xu and Liu Zhi
1988 Hani (Akha, Kaw) in Border Minorities of Southwest China and Southeast Asia.

Shi Junzhao
1987 The Soul of Hani Culture
1987 The Hani Flood Myth; the Source of Fertility

Shi Junzhao et al
1986 The Epic Poetry of Hani

Song Enchang
1986 Wedding Customs of the Hani

Sun Guansheng
1986 On Mopi (priest) of the Hani
1991 The Origin of Hani Legends and History

Tian Zhiyong
1987 On Pima (priest) of the Hani

Wang Ju
1985 Respect for the Elders among the Hani

Wang Qinghua
1991 On the Way of Cultural Transmission among the Hani
1994 Notes on Marriage among the Hani

Wang Zhengfang et al (eds)
1990 The Anthology of Hani Legends and Myths

Xiao Zhuo
1993 Hani Proverbs

Yang Shouchuan
1993 The Cowrie Culture of the Hani

Yang Wanzhi
1990 On the Influences of Buddhism and Christianity on the Hani Tradition
1991 A Historical Study Concerning the Hani Calendar

Yu Dingjian
1988 Hani Marriage Customs

Zhang Nanzhe
1988 A Study of the Traditional Ethics of the Hani

Zhao Guanlu
1983 The Hospitality of the Hani
1984 Several Rituals among the Hani
1987 A Survey of Hani Customs

Zhao Guanlu and Guo Chunli
1989 Shier Nuju: the Creation Myth of the Hani

Zhao Guanlu and Zhou Tianquan
1987 The Epic Poetry of Hani

NUMBERED HANI SOURCES

Following are the sources which have been used in compiling this dictionary. Only the number of the source and the page number are given in the dictionary.

1. Hansson, Inga-Lill (1982) A Phonological Comparison of Akha and Hani. Linguistics of the Tibeto-Burman Area. Vol. 7.1, fall 1982, pp 63-115. (An excellent introduction to the language.)

2. **Haqniq soqhhaq zolkaoq** (1984) The study of the Hani Language for primary students.

3. **Aolzaq Hovqdol e Galquv** (1986) It contains short articles on many subjects.

4. **Ssaqguq caldoq ssolnei bakaq caq** (1986) Songs and riddles for children.

5. Body part words from many of the Tibeto-Burman languages used in China, written for the STEDT project directed by Dr. James A. Matisoff, and given to me by Prof. Dai Qingxia. These are written in IPA. (No date, probably about 1989.)

6. List of Hani, Akha, Haoni and Biyu/Piyaw words sent to me by David Bradley, with the Chinese terms translated by Law̬ Gaw. (It is written in IPA. There is no date.)

7. Hansson, Inga-Lill A Comparison of Akha, Hani, Khatu and Pijaw. (1984)

8. **Haqniq doqdaq** (Hani stories - Book 1) (1988)

9. **Haqniq ssolnei Pyulniul soqhhaq e ciiqhyuf dyufzaof.** Hani to Chinese dictionary. (1984)

10. **Ssaqguq yuvq qa nalgol maq bi duv lal ssolnei nalgol cev e yo'liq** Health book for children. (WHO) (1989).

11. Hani Grammar by Prof. Li Yongsui. (1990) (This includes the story of the dragon and the son-in-law. See Appenedix 2.)

12. A Brief Introduction to the Hani Language. Prof. Li Yongsui (1986) (Mostly in Chinese, but good Hani illustrations are given.)

13. **Haqniq doqdaq** (Hani stories - Book 2) (1990)

14. **Caoqlaolhaoq bialzeil e doqdaq** (Stories by the fireplace) 1990

15. **Seilmif Ziilsiiq (Saosuf miqcuq dama yaol heilmiq.)** Health book for children, part II. (1990)

16. **Yyuweiq (Yyuqnaqsei yuvqhuvq zol e xaoxoq kofbei)** Text book for primary schools (1-4 years). (No date)

17. **Yyuweiq (Kuvqhuvq zol e xaoxoq kofbei)** Text book for Sixth grade. (No date)

18. **Haqniq doqzao zao doq.** Hani proverbs. (1986)

19. **Ngavqhuvq zol e xaoxoq kofbei Sufxoq** (copy 1) Math study book for fifth grade. (No date)

20. **Puvkaq hholqei dieif aol e yo'liq** Electricity in the village (1988)

21. **Deqheq xa zaq e yo'liq** The planting of 'amomum' (1989)

22. **Sufliaof boqmoq hhekaq alnei ceildu xazaq e yo'liq.** The planting of corn (maize) (1989)

23. **Laqpeiv halmeil xazaq alnei miaqnei duv lal nia e galquv** The planting of tea (1989)

24. **Haqniq huvqpeiq lapeiq puv** Hani Songs (1989)

25. **Haqniq aqpyuq colpol pol (Haqniqpaq pol e Halbaq)** Hani ballads (1985)

26. **Leiqfaol e doqdaq** (The Story of Leiqfaol) (1990)

27. **Haqniq Weiqbaof** (27-33 are Hani newspapers) 1988-1991

28. **Haqniq Weiqbaof** August 20, 1989

29. **Haqniq Weiqbaof** Dec. 30, 1988

30. **Haqniq Weiqbaof** Oct. 10, 1988

31. **Haqniq Weiqbaof** May 5, 1989

32. **Haqniq Weiqbaof** Sept. 20, 1988

33. **Haqniq Weiqbaof** Dec. 30, 1988

34. A speech delivered in commemoration of the 70th anniversary of the Chinese Communist Party by Jiang Zemin, in Chinese, on January 1, 1991. Translated into Hani by Yang Yangjiu and Bai Bibo, published 1991.

35. **Haqniq Doqdaq 3** Hani Stories - Book 3 (1991)

36. **Haqniq Doq'aqma** Hani Proverbs (1991)

37. **Haqniq Doq Aqma.** Hani Proverbs (Collected by Bai Zu-e and Bai Bibo)

38. **Haqniq doqdaq 4** Hani Stories - Book 4 (1992)

39. Report on the 14th Conference of the Chinese Communist Party by Jiang Zemin (**Jal Ceiqmiq**) (1992)

40. **Ziilshiqgaol** (1) General Articles (1991)

41. **Pyulniuldoq Haqniqdoq gee** Teaching Chinese with Hani Translations (1992)

42. **Jahhaqhhaqhe naol e yoqmil doqdaq** Poems that sniff the grass (1992)

43. **Yyuqnaq alsiil xazaq yo'liq** The way to plant bananas in Yunnan

44. **Aqqul qul doq** "Sweet Words" -- poetry (1991)

45. **Haqniq Dudaq** 5 Hani Stories - Book 5 (1993)

46. **Haqniq Neeciiv** Hani Festivals (1993)

47. **Maq deivq qiq jivq maq jol** Creation Saga (no date)

48. **Qiq soq bo xa hazal, qiq mil seiq xa hhaqssyuq**

49. **Galmol haolgaoq yaol maq nieil qaol** Unable to forget the Distant Mountains (1994)

50. **Pyulniul - Haqniq Doqlo Yosiivq Ssaoq** The Way to Write Chinese Words in Hani (1994)

51. **Haqniq Soqmiav Meiq Hev Zolkaoq** Textbook for Teaching Hani Writing, Compiled by: Beiq Ju'eq; Zal Peiqziil; Beiq Piubo. 1994

52. **Aqhhavq Halmeil Qu** How to Raise Pigs (1994)

53. **Ceil Cuv Yoliq** Proper way to Plant Rice (1994)

54. **Haqniq Soqmiav Zolkaoq** Textbook for Hani Writing; Compiled by Bai Bibo (1992)

55. Hani cassette (1995) (Segments from Hani Radio Broadcasts)

56. Ethnographic material gathered in December 1994 by Bai Bibo and Paul Lewis from three Hani informants

57. **Beqsiil lHeeq e Haqniqma** (Hani Women in the Reform Period; Ten Outstanding Hani Women in the Market-Directed Economy - Prepared for the Fourth International Women's Conference, 1995)

58. **Haqniq Sanqbovq Zaodmq** (A Book for Studying Hani/Akha) 1995

59. Ethnographic material gathered in November and December 1995 by Bai Bibo and Paul Lewis

ABBREVIATIONS

Ak = Akha
brd = bird
CA = China Akha (as spoken by the Mahᵥ Po^ Akha living in the Xishuangbanna area of China, as well as in Burma and Thailand, the Akha dialect which is probably the Akha dialect which is closest to Hani)
CHA = China Akha, especially related to the way the Akha in China are currently writing their language using the Hani orthography, and refering to their language as 'Hani'
Chi = borrowed from Chinese
(A=Chi) = first segment borrowed from Chinese
(B=Chi) = second segment borrowed from Chinese
Chi-Eng = borrowed from Chinese which in turn borrowed from English (as: **kalfeil** = coffee)
cf. = compare
clf. = classifier
cpt = couplet
Dai = borrowed from the Dai/Tai/Shan
edi = edible (can be eaten)
esp. = especially
fp. = final particle
fp - = a final particle which cannot stand alone)
gram = grammatical term
hs. = a house
lit. = literally
not pf. = not preferred
OB = older brother
op. = opposite of
OS = older sister
pf. = preferred
poet = a poetic way of saying it (as in proverbs), often not used in daily speech
pol = political
(see full) = this means to see the word in its full and normal order
semi-taboo = a word which is usually not used because of its connotations and related meanings
taboo = a word not used in polite society or before elders
TE = a term of endearment (and see Appendix 7)
UL = U Lo Akha, an Akha dialect spoken in Thailand
wm = weights and measures
YB = younger brother
YS = younger sister

HANI - ENGLISH INDEX

a A -- 39

al - 39
a - 48
aq - 49

b B -- 71

ba - 71
bao - 76
be - 79
bee - 80
bei - 82
bi - 84
bia - 87
biao - 90
biei - 91
bio - 92
biu - 92
bo - 93
bu - 94
byu - 97

c C -- 100

ca - 100
cao - 105
ce - 107
cei - 108
ci - 114
cii - 117
co - 118
cu - 123
cua - 125
cyu - 126

d D -- 128

da - 128
dao - 134
de - 139
dee - 140
dei - 140
di - 145
diao - 149
diei - 149
do - 150
du - 156
dua - 160
duei - 160
dyu - 160

e E -- 162

ee Ee - 163

ei Ei - 167

f F - 171

fa - 171
fao - 173
fe - 173
fei - 173
fu - 174

g G - 176

ga - 176
gao - 181
gee - 186
gei - 189
go - 190
gu - 193
gua - 194
gyu - 195

h H - 197

ha - 197
hao - 208
he - 212
hee - 214
hei - 215
ho - 217
hu - 222
hua - 227
huei - 228
hyu - 228

hh Hh - 230

hha - 230
hhao - 238
hhe - 239
hhei - 242
hho - 243
hhu - 247
hhyu - 248

j J - 251

ja - 251
jao - 254
je - 254
jei - 255
ji - 256
jo - 261
ju - 263
jyu - 265

k K - 267

ka - 267
kao - 270
ke - 272
kee - 273
kei - 276
ko - 277
ku - 200
kua - 281
kuei - 282
kyu - 282

l L - 284

la - 284
lao - 284
le - 298
lee - 298
lei - 300
li - 303
lia - 306
lie - 306
liei - 306
liu - 307
lo - 307
lu - 312
luei - 316
lyu - 316

m M - 317

ma - 317
mao - 325
mee - 326
mei - 327
mi - 332
mia - 343
miao - 347
mie - 349

miu - 349
mo - 349
mu - 355
myu - 356

n N - 357

na - 357
nao - 362
ne - 367
nee - 367
nei - 373
ni - 375
nia - 379
niao - 380
nie - 381
niei - 381
niu - 382
no - 384
nu - 386
nyu - 387

ng Ng - 390

nga - 390
ngao - 392
nge - 393
ngee - 393
ngu - 393
ngyu - 394
ngua - 394

o O - 395

p P - 397

pa - 397
pao - 400
pe - 401
pee - 401
pei - 402
pi - 405
pia - 407
pie - 408
piei - 409
pio - 411
piu - 411
po - 412
pu - 413
pyu - 417

q Q - 419

qa - 419
qao - 420
qe - 421
qei - 421
qi - 424
qia - 430
qo - 430
qu - 431
qyu - 434

s S - 435

sa - 435
sao - 444
se - 447
sei - 450
si - 453
sii - 457
so - 459
su - 464
sua - 467
syu - 467

ss Ss - 469

ssa - 469
ssao - 474
ssei - 475
ssi - 477
ssii - 478
sso - 479
ssu - 479
ssua - 480
ssyu - 480

t T - 481

ta - 481
tao - 483
te - 487
tee - 487
tei - 488
ti - 491
tiao - 492
tiei - 492
to - 492
tu - 494
tua - 496
tuei - 497
tyu - 497

w W - 499

wa - 499
wei - 499
wu - 500
wua - 507
wuei - 507

x X - 508

xa - 508
xao - 511
xe - 513
xei - 513
xi - 514
xiao - 517
xii - 517
xo - 517
xu - 517
xyu - 518

y Y - 519

ya - 519
yao - 522
ye - 523
yei - 524
yi - 527
yiu - 529
yo - 530
yu - 536
yyu - 538

z Z - 540

za - 540
zao - 546
ze - 551
zei - 552
zi - 558
zii - 559
zo - 562
zu - 564
zua - 566
zuei - 566
zyu - 567

AL

al interjection, showing surprise, or admiration (Al! **Aqqoq aqda/aqma**! Oh, what a great man/ woman. **Al, zaqqul al**! Oh, how beautiful it is!)

(vb) **al** 1. a final part. indicating completion of action (9:1) (**zaq al** = finished eating), 2. final part. used with negative sentence. (**Maq beq sso al**. Never mind. 41:7)

albal a type of golden bamboo (9:1) (za^ shui˅)
  albal balhhaq the culm sheaths (parchment-like outer membrane) of the golden bamboo (za˅ lo˅)
alba older sister (9:1) (a˅ yui^)
  alba bama the eldest sister (a˅ yui^ yui^ sa˅)
  alba miqhhaol the second eldest sister
  alba miqli the youngest of older sisters
albaq liquor (or) **zilbaq** (46:205) (ji˅ ba˅)
albaol grasshopper; locust (11:26) (nyeh^ bah˅)
  -- albaol leiq, piaqsal -- (see full)
  albaol nieivq to catch a grasshopper as part of a ceremony (see also: **saqsal albaol lao**)
albee a quilt (a˅ bui)
  albee beehov the cover of a quilt
  albee beejal an old quilt (**albee beejal jal** = a quilt to get old) (a˅ bui bui ce˅)
  albee beewul cotton batting or filling used in a quilt
  -- albee, dieifssi -- a theater curtain (A=Chi)
  albee hyulzal woolen blanket (B=Chi); **geivzavq** (Chi)
  albee mieifzii a small quilted covering (B=Chi)
albeil 1. umbilical cord (ca^ beh˅), 2. placenta; afterbirth
  albeil duqduq a place where one's placenta is buried (it is buried behind the door inside the house)
  albeil duqhaoq one's birth place; home village (place where one's placenta is buried)
  albeil duv yi for the placenta to be delivered
  albeil niaov to cut the umbilical cord
albeiv a pod
  albeiv beiv to bear a pod (14:157) (a˅ beh^ beh^-eu)
albiao a trellis for vines
-- albiao, maldei -- trellis for pumpkin vines
albol 1. tree (9:2) (a˅ baw˅), 2. a stalk (used for rice, buckwheat, corn and such)
  albol alhov tree bark (3:1) (a˅ baw˅ ba^ k'o^)
  albol alkaq in the woods; in the forest (46:176)
  albol allavq tree branch (6:169) (a˅ baw˅ u˅ la^)
  albol alqil a root of a tree

albol bolcaoq a grove of trees and bushes (as in the woods); jungle trees (bawˇ tsah˅)
albol boldei an expanse of trees (14:213)
albol bolmoq an old tree (aˇ bawˇ bawˇ maw˅)
albol bolsovq sovq to cut off branches so that a tree grows straight (aˇ bawˇ bawˇ nym˅ nym˅-eu)
albol caqcaoq a wooden wedge (as used in splitting wood)
albol daoqliq a tree stump (or) **daoqliq**
albol daoqpul a tree stump with roots included
albol daoqtao a block of wood used as a stool
albol diqpuq a wooden hammer (put at the village gate to scare away spirits) (38:37) (daˇ kaw˅ di˅ pu˅)
albol gaoqqei dibble stick (aˇ bawˇ gah˅ kaw˅)
albol gubaq zaq for a tall tree to shade something under it (aˇ bawˇ guˇ ba ba da^-eu)
albol haoqmaq a wooden bowl
albol hupievq a pole with a forked top (can be used in building field huts and the like)
albol lavqqivq carpenter (9:1, 41:3) (la˄ saˇ maˇ)
-- albol, milsiil -- a sacred village tree
albol miqbev a wooden gun (put at the village gate to scare away spirits) (38:37) (daˇ kaw˅ mi˅ beu^)
albol moqdev cassava root (daˇ kaw˅ mah˅ coeˇ)
albol naqneil treetop
albol neev'qavq beans from a tree (14:156)
albol saqhav a forest (aˇ bawˇ sah˅ k'a^)
albol soqssaq a sapling (aˇ bawˇ kah˅ za˅)
albol soqtal tal to cut off all the branches and then the top of a tree (as one in a field) (aˇ bawˇ sah˅ cu˅ cu˅-eu)
albol tojeil a wooden knife (put at the village gate to scare away spirits) (38:37)
albol toma a wooden sword (to scare away spirits from a house or a village)
albol tul to cut down a tree (9:2) (aˇ bawˇ tuˇ-eu)
albol ziq resin from a tree (aˇ bawˇ bawˇ dzi˅)

alcav rope; wire; cable (aˇ ca^)
alcav beil bieiq to break free from being tied by a rope (aˇ ca^ behˇ tseh^-eu)
alcav beil ceiv to break free from being tied up (aˇ ca^ behˇ tseh^-eu)
alcav bieiq to untie or loosen a rope or cord (and see: **beil bieiq**) (aˇ ca^ puiˇ-eu)
alcav cavduv fibers twisted into thread or cord
alcav cavkuq a dry rope (aˇ ca^ ca^ ku^)
alcav cavtao pieces of rope (35:67)
-- alcav, kaolbev -- 1. an inked line used in a carpenter's marker (to make straight lines on boards), 2. a rope to lead a buffalo to the left and right when plowing or harrowing
alcav meiqzaq nei hheziivq miq to hit someone or something with a rope's end

alcav xu to make a rope (9:1) (a˅ ca^ yeu˰-eu)

alciiv a little, a bit (a˅ cui^, ui cui^)

alciiv alciiv meil bit by bit, little by little (a˅ cui^ a˅ cui^-eh˅)

alciiv ciivssaq a very little (11:35)

alciiv kaq 1. a little better (13:25) (a˅ cui^ ma˯ ga˅), 2. a little bit far away (ga˅ mah˅ a˅ cui^ ka˯)

alciiv liq maq (vb) not even a little (vb) (**alciiv liq maq guv** = not even a little afraid - 26:45) (a˅ cui^ teh˰-eh˅ k'aw˰ ma˯ (vb))

alciiv meeniav a few (a˅ cui^ na^)

alciivq 1. a joint (as in bamboo etc.) (a˅ tsui˰); 2. a genealogy (**ciivq gee** = to recount one's genealogy) (tsui˰)

alciivq allo structure (50:63)

alcuq kind of small bamboo (9:2, 46:117) (a˅ cu˯)

alcuq cuqdaol a type of wild, small bamboo

alcuq cuqdyuv shoots of a small species of bamboo

alcuq dalgeeq a small bamboo stick (da˅ cui˅)

Aldebo a place name (Chi) (35:24)

Aldil almal Haolteil 'father and mother mountain' (AB=Chi)

aldovq a light; lamp (9:2, 41:42) (tsi˅ k'm˯)

aldovq bia for a lamp to shine (41:42) (tsi˅ k'm˯ bya-eu)

-- aldovq, biaqsaoq -- a beeswax candle

aldovq dexi a lamp wick (B=Chi) (tsi˅ k'm˯ sai˯)

aldovq deilpaol an electric bulb (B=Chi)

aldovq dovq to light a lamp (tsi˅ k'm˯ do˰-eu)

aldovq dovqhovq an oil lamp (tsi˅-eu˯ tsi˅ k'm˯)

aldovq dovqma a big lamp (tsi˅ k'm˯ k'm˯ ma)

aldovq dovqma bia nei a lamp which is burning brightly

aldovq dovqssaq a small lamp (tsi˅ k'm˯ k'm˯ za˯)

aldovq keq dovq dav to light a lamp (tsi˅ k'm˯ keu˯ do˰-eu)

aldu a bud (a˅ cu˯)

aldyul diarrhea of an infant (9:2) (a˅ doe˅)

aldyul dyul infant to have diarrhea (11:42) (a˅ doe˅ doe˅-eu)

aldyuv bamboo shoots (a˅ bye˰)

aldyuv dyuv for bamboo shoots to sprout (9:2) (a˅ bye˰ bye˰-eu)

aldyuv dyuvkuv dried, preserved bamboo shoots (9:2) (a˅ bye˰ ko^)

aldyuv heivq to gather bamboo shoots

aldyuv laolgaol joint in a bamboo shoot (a˅ bye˰ a˅ tsui˰)

algaq dear; dearest (ga˯-eu)

algao thorn (9:2) (a˯ gah)

algao alluq thorn plant fruit

algao alluq luqnav fruit of thorn plant (dark

color)

algo 1. older brother (9:2), 2. fictive older brother, as when meet older man on trail (Chi) (12:126) (a˅ do^)

  algo aqhhaol second eldest brother (A=Chi)

  algo goma eldest brother (A=Chi)

  algo ssaqli the youngest of older brothers (A=Chi)

algoq (TE) dear elder brother

alhaq bitter bamboo shoot (9:2) (a˅ k'a˯)

alhaol wild cat; jungle cat (9:2) (or) **ha'qiq** ('chicken carrier') (a˅ hah˅)

alhaoq peilja clothing

  alhaoq peilniul khaki colored clothing (as for those in the army)

alheiq original; source (50:10)

alhoq zaq to have a rice meal

alhov skin; peel; outer layer of grain (or) **balhov** (ba^ k'o^; sha˯ k'o^)

alhovq empty (9:3) (yaw˯ ngeh˰)

alhuvq 1. age (9:3), 2. a year (a˅ k'o˰)

  alhuvq lal to get on in years; to get old (or) **colmoq moq** (a˅ k'o˰ k'aw^ la˅-eu)

  alhuvq naoq young age (26:45) (a˅ k'o˰ yaw nyi˅)

  alhuvq naoq e ssilxoq a young hero (C=Chi) (26:45)

  alhuvq nil to be young ('age is small') (11:195)

-- **al, hhaq** -- enough; all right

alhhaol laolbao the center (as the center of a page)

alhhaol laolqei the middle part (g'ah˅ ceh)

alhhe a swing (9:2) (eu leu = small, la˰ ceu˯ = village swing)

alhhe haqpaq a frog (which makes a loud noise) (or) **alhhe meiqbieil** (k'a˯ pa˯)

  alhhe hhaqqaol rest house by the village swing

  alhhe hhaqssaol poles for the village swing; **alhhe hhessaol**

  alhhe hhe to swing (la˰ ceu˯ bi˯-eu)

  alhhe hhedaoq a swing board on which people sit or stand when swinging

  alhhe hhepuv ferris wheel type of swing, with 4 persons circling over and around (9:3) (ga˯ la˯ la˯ ceu˯)

  alhhe hhessaol posts used in making the village swing (four of them); **alhhe hhaqssal**

alhhe meiqbieil (see: **alhhe haqpaq**)

  alhhe naqjul the ring to which the swing is tied

  alhhe ziiq to swing in a swing (11:50)

alhhov outer appearance (50:115)

alhhu laldeiq ant (**qiq ba** = a group/line of ants) (27:11) (a˅ ho)

  alhhu laqnil red ants (35:42) (a˅ ho ne˅)

aljeil urine (9:3) (or) **alsyuq** (i˅ shoi)

  aljeil jeil to urinate (9:3) (i˅ shoi shoi-eu)

Aljoqniq name of Trickster in Hani stories (13:11)
alju fluid; liquid (or) **zal'eel**

alka crab (9:3) (aˇ ka)
  alka kahovq the upper body of a crab (aˇ ka aˇ k'aw^)
  alka lavqma pincers of a crab (aˇ ka la^ ma)
alkaq 1. in between, 2. in a given period of time (35:35, 45:54), 3. a line, 4. a frontier (50:88) (aˇ ka⌄)
  alkaq col a witness (tsawˇ ka⌄)
  alkaq galma the middle way ('golden mean') (gaˇ ma g'ahˇ ceh kahˇ)
  alkaq kaq 1. to solve a dispute (or) **alkaq pil** (aˇ ka⌄ piˇ-eu), 2. some space between two things (aˇ ka⌄ ka⌄-eu), 3. to testify; give evidence
  alkaq kaqli central; the core (9:3, 11:32, 34:28)
  alkaq kaqma main division through a Hani village, like a major thoroughfare and also a fire break
  alkaqlaq in the middle; central (11:211, 212)
  alkaq pil to solve a dispute (or) **alkaq kaq** (aˇ ka⌄ piˇ-eu)
  alkaq seiq e to make a line (50:88)
  alkaq zeifweiq the body, or main part of an article (as in a newspaper) (B=Chi)
alkaol thread; fiber (9:3) (sa⌄ kahˇ)
  alkaol hhe to pick out fibers
alku bialhhaq bat (flying mammal) (9:3) (boeˇ ha⌄)
alkuv dry (as dried vegetables) (9:3) (yaw ko^, yaw gui)

allal an interjection (ho!)
  allal oqyil an interjection (ho!, hoy!, oh my)
Allalbeiq Arabic; Arab (54:31)
allavq branch (u⌄ la^)
  -- **allavq, albol** -- a tree branch
  allavq allo 1. branches, 2. groups (46:132)
  -- **allavq, aqtaoq** -- branch of a pine tree
alleil nei for the purpose of (or) **bal nei; ballal nei** (**Haqlaq laqssaq nieiv movq alleil nei, haqlaq jol e milnia hha** li. You must go to where tigers live for the purpose of catching cubs. 11:120)
alleiv a dwarf (lehˇ ti - semi-taboo)
alleiv leiv 1. to be a dwarf (or) **moqleiv leiv** (lehˇ ti - semi-taboo in Ak.), 2. thin and small (or) **alssii ssii**
allo bamboo section (between two joints) (14:163)
allo hhoqpial a plant used as medicine for urinary problems (esp. kidney stones)
alloq hhoqpul wild turnip
allu butterfly (or) **allu zalbaol** (9:3) (aˇ lu)
  allu zalbaol butterfly (or) **allu** (aˇ lu)
Alluv protective village jungle spirits (in a fairy tale) (46:127)

almal to be full; mature (op. of: **alhovq** = empty) (maˇ-eu)
alma miq'aoq 'my humble self' (a female, used in songs and the like)
almil cat (9:3) (aˇ miˇ)
  almil milssaq kitty (29:4) (aˇ miˇ miˇ zaˬ)
  -- **almil, toqla** -- a rabbit
almiyiq ! interjection showing fright (or) **aqmiqyiq** (11:146)
almiq a woman; lady (14:214) (zaˬ miˬ)
almiuvq monkey (9:3) (aˇ myo‸)
  almiuvq baqzuvq a monkey with a wrinkled face (14:178)
  almiuvq miuvqhav daoqnil red-bottomed monkey
  almiuvq miuvqlaol loris (nocturnal, arboreal primate) (myo‸ lahˇ)
  almiuvq miuvqnav gibbon (arboreal ape) (or) **almiuvq miuvqnav lavqhhev** (aˇ myo‸ myo‸ na^; aˇ myo‸ na^)
  almiuvq miuvqniul langur monkey (aˇ myo‸ myo‸ nyoeˇ; aˇ myo‸ nyoeˇ)
  almiuvq miuvqpeel silvered leaf monkey (Presbytis cristatus) (aˇ myo‸ myo‸ puiˇ)
  almiuvq miuvqsiil golden monkey
  almiuvq miuvqssaq 1. a little monkey, 2. a smart child, 3. a very thin child
  almiuvq miuvqtaol a single monkey
  almiuvq miuvqzyuq a 'king' of monkeys (leader of the pack) (aˇ myo‸ sahˬ paˬ)
almol a type of bamboo (maybe: ma saˬ)
almol a fly (9:4, 10:19, 11:26) (aˇ mawˇ; pawˬ teˇ)
  almol kovq a fly to 'bite' (10:19) (aˇ mawˇ kaw‸-eu)

alnal a sore; an ulcer (9:4) (maˇ naˇ naˇ ma)
  alnal nal 1. a running sore (as a skin ulcer), (maˇ k'ehˬ dahˇ-eu); 2. to have a disease; sickness (26:47)
  alnal nalbioq a scar (9:4) (maˇ byaw‸)
  alnal nalbioq bioq sol to have scabs all over one's body
alnav a type of bamboo
alneev a bean,; a soybean (9:4) (aˇ nui^)
(vb) alnei 1. because of (vb) (miˇ neh), 2. and (hawˇ-eu), 3. for the purpose of (11:119)
alnei prematurely sprouted vegetables (**hhoqpavq alnei** = greens that are sprouted)
alniq bamboo strip; bamboo tie (9:4) (aˇ neˬ)
  alniq hoqbav container for rice made of bamboo strips (13:12) (aˇ neˬ hawˬ g'aw^, aˇ neˬ hawˬ ba^)
  alniq lolbiel bamboo rice table made of bamboo strips (hawˬ jeh)
  alniq miaoqgaoq goods made of bamboo strips (14:141)
  alniq niq to make bamboo strips (9:4) (aˇ neˬ neˬ-

eu)
alniq niqhovq the inner part of a bamboo strip (not so useful)
alniq niqmal a strip of bamboo which is useful
alnia father's younger sister (Chi) (9:4, 11:176) (a˯ k'o˯)
alniaq (TE) dear aunty
alniul rafter in roof (9:4) (nymˇ nyoeˇ)
Alniul Han Chinese (or) **Pyulniul** (La˰ bui˯)

alpavq leaf (9:4) (aˇ pa˰)
alpavq hhaqcil leaf lard
-- alpavq, hhoqcyuq -- vegetable leaves
alpavq pavqkuq a dry leaf (or) **alpavq pavqkuv** (pa˰ ko^)
alpavq pavqniul a green leaf (aˇ pa˰ pa˰ nyoeˇ)
alpavq pavqsiil a yellow leaf (aˇ pa˰ pa˰ shuiˇ)
alpeel leprosy (coi˯ doi)
alpia cockroach; **alpia aqma** (aˇ pya; aˇ pya luˇ za) (note: **alpia aqma** is also used for a kind of water weed)
alpia javniuq a water insect that can fly, longer than a cockroach (edi)
alpiaq piaq to have a fever (aˇ pya˯ pya˯-eu)
alpiaq piaqcao cao to have malaria fever
alpieil a type of bamboo (can be very sharp)
alpieil kaol a forest of this type of bamboo
alpieil xaq to be cut deeply by this kind of bamboo
alpuq puq a cluster of something (as grapes; bananas)
-- alpyuv, ceildu -- popped corn
alpyuv pyuv for grain to pop (as rice; corn) (aˇ bo^ bo^-eu; cf. cehˇ bo^)

alqa a clan (aˇ keu; gu˯)
alqil a root (9:4) (du˯ ciˇ)
alqil qilssaq minor root; smaller root (du˯ ciˇ ciˇ za˯)
alqil qiltaoq tap root; main root (du˯ ciˇ ciˇ ma)
alqul albol plantain (simalar to a banana) tree
alqul aldu bud of sweet banana tree
alqul alsiq plantain (like a large banana) (9:4)
alqul alzi young banana plants
alqul qulbol sweet banana tree (or) **alqul albol**
alquv a bud; a sprout (9:4) (aˇ cu˯)
alquv quv a bud to bud; a sprout to sprout; to germinate (11:29) (aˇ cu˯ cu˯-eu)

-- alsavq, milhhuv -- natural gas
Alsaol Haoni (a major branch of the Hani which speaks a different dialect)
alse a type of folk song sung when transplanting rice
alse se to sing the folk song sung when transplanting rice
alsiq fruit (9:5) (aˇ si˯)
alsiq alhov the skin or peel of fruit

alsiq alhhov fruit (cplt.) (aˇ si˯ aˇ lu)

alsiq aqhaoq seil to have smallpox (or) **alzaq zaq**

alsiq siq to produce fruit; bear fruit (9:5, 50:87) (aˇ si˯ si˯-eu)

alsiq siqcaoq fruit orchard; fruit plantation (57:130)

alsiq siqyal fruit orchard (50:68)

alsol 1. alone (**Nol qiq hhaq alsol hoq zaq.** You are eating rice alone.) (13:33), 2. only (**Hhoqcyuq alsol zaq e maq ngeel meil, zilbaq liq alciiv dol.** Not only eat some vegetables, also drink a little liquor. 46:104) (teh˰-ehˇ)

alsuq father's younger brother (Chi) (13:1, 41:7) (a˯ zawˇ)

alsuq Leiqfaol 'uncle' Leiqfaol (term of respect for an older person) (Chi) (26:101)

alsyuq urine (or) **aljeil** (iˇ shoi)

alsyuq syuq to urinate (iˇ shoi shoi-eu)

alsyuq syuqkaoq kaoq to have pain when urinating (usually from kidney stones)

alssi wild taro (or) **alssi moqgaoq**

alssii ssii thin and small (or) **alleiv leiv**

alssyuq seed (9:5) (aˇ yoe˯; aˇ nui^)

alssyuq ssyuq to preserve, as seeds

alssyuq ssyuqssaq baby boy's penis

alssyuq yomeeq good seeds (50:107)

altev lelsel a kind of water insect, oval shaped, can fly (edi)

alteil fame; reputation (or) **colteil dav**

alteivq dav to go up one grade (50:151)

alwuv egg (animal) (9:5) (ya u^)

alwuv ceillaoq an offering of unhusked rice with an egg on top (used in various ceremonies)

alwuv hoqlul fried rice with an egg (ya u^ haw˯ luˇ)

alwuv teil to drop or throw an egg, when trying to find a site for a person's grave (if it breaks, the site is proper for the burial)

alwuv wuv an egg to hatch (11:29) (ya u^ u^-eu; ya u^ ceu˰-eu)

alwuv wuvba the white of an egg (ya u^ pyuˇ)

alwuv wuvdeev an egg soaked in brine (1-2 months)

alwuv wuvhovq egg shell (3:7) (ya u^ k'aw˰)

alwuv wuvnaoq a soft-shelled egg

alwuv wuvnil red eggs (they are dyed with plants during the rice transplanting season in the spring) (46:157) (ya u^ neˇ)

alwuv wuvsiil the yolk of an egg (ya u^ shuiˇ)

alwuv zao to bury an egg in the lower part of the village

alyaovq 1. to express one's feelings, 2. facial expression (50:14)

alyeil a burden (for a person) (**alyeil xao** = to have a heavy burden) (k'a^ beh^)

alyeil eq 1. to be responsible, 2. to carry something (50:54) (k'a^ beh^ pi-eu)

alyeil pi to undertake a 'burden' (responsibility) **ceiqdal** (Chi)

alyeil pial a light burden

alyeil qeivmoq a pack horse

alyeiv flower (9:5) (aˇ yeh^)

alyeiv ba'la pal for a woman to have her menstrual cycle (aˇ yeh^ hehˇ-eu)

alyeiv hualpiq a vase for flowers (B=Chi)

alyeiv ssiiv a floral pattern

alyeiv yeiv a flower to blossom (aˇ yeh^ poˬ-eu)

alyeiv yeivcaoq flowering shrubs (aˇ yeh^ bawˬ)

alyeiv yeivjoq withered flowers (aˇ yeh^ yaw nyoeˬ)

alyeiv yeivnil red flower (aˇ yeh^ yeh^ neˇ)

alyeiv yeivyal a flower garden (50:73)

alyol interjection (11:21); **alyol oq** (38:15); **aqyoq**; **alyal** (11:144) (**Alyol, qavq nal wul yaq**! Oh, it hurts very much! **Alyol! Gol sil la ya**! Oh my, it aches 'to death'. 54:102, 157)

alzaq smallpox (9:5) (or) **alsiq aqhaoq seil** (aˇ siˬ maˇ naˇ naˇ-eu)

alzaq zaq to have smallpox (9:5) (aˇ siˬ maˇ naˇ naˇ-eu) (may also be used for other rashes on the face, especially of children 11:41)

alzaol coffin (9:5) (mawˇ dmˬ)

alzaol a bavq dov to put a corpse in a coffin

alzaol a bavq tao to put in coffin (or) **alzaol hholqei bavq dov**

alzaol bavq yoq for the coffin to be lifted over kneeling children and grandchildren of the dead person before being taken out to be buried

alzaol dev to cut the coffin (a more polite way of saying going to cut the coffin = **colmoq laqhyul qo li**)

alzaol hholqei bavq dov to put corpse in coffin (or) **alzaol bavq dov**

alzaoq a bundle (aˇ dzahˬ)

alzaoq raw; uncooked (or) **yozaoq** (yaw tsah; yaw jmˬ; maˬ aw˰; maˬ ja˰)

Alzeq protective village jungle spirits (in a fairy tale) (46:127)

alzeiq older sister (Chi) (14:233); **alba** (Hani, 41:1)

alzeiv wild banana (9:5) (nga jeh^)

alzeiv albol a wild banana tree (or) **alzeiv zeivbol** (nga jeh^ aˇ bawˇ)

alzeiv aldu the white flower that comes on wild banana trees

alzeiv alsiq a wild banana (nga jeh^ aˇ siˬ)

alzeiv byuqsiq a type of taro (11:127)

alzeiv zeivbol a wild banana tree (or) **alzeiv**

albol

alzil 1. bird (9:5) (aˇ jiˇ), 2. meat (**saq; saqnil** = pf.)

alzil aqpeil wild pear

alzil hhoqqeil a kind of grass

alzil miqbev muzzle-loader type gun (hunt birds)

alzil moqyovq a kind of wild fruit that grows on a vine (not edi.)

alzil zilbeeq a bird nest (9:5, 11:35) (aˇ jiˇ bahˬ)

alzil zilssaq a young bird (aˇ jiˇ zaˬ)

alziq (tree) sap (9:6) (or) **ziq** (aˇ dziˬ)

alziiv an itch (yaw dzui^)

alziiv ziiv for an itch to itch (10:4) (yaw dzui^ dzui^-eu)

A

a on; to; at; in (**Nga qovq laqhyul a zaq li kal.** Let's go eat at my home. 41:7)

(n) **a** topicalizer (or) **aq** (11:128,, 129) (aˬ)

(n) **a** indicates the receiver of something (**Aqyoq a soqhhaq qiq daoq bivq miq.** Give him a copy of the book.) (**Neesoq tullal ngaq a gul.** Call me to get up in the morning. 41:41)

(v) **a** final part. for questions demanding a yes or no answer (**Hhellavq aol e piul biao nei pa hha gaoq a?** Perhaps you have plenty of money for trading?) (see also: **aq**)

adovq dragonfly; **aqbiaoq** (aˬ juˬ ciˇ myah)

a'lo maq qivq quite a lot (11:23)

a'lov nei quietly and slowly (13:23) (aw law^ law^-ehˇ)

AQ

aq ! interjection (11:145) (**Aq, qavq zaqqul wul yaq.** Oh, it is very beautiful! 54:102)

(n) **aq** topicalizer (or) **a** (**xilmol aq** = now as to THIS thing) (-aˬ)

(v) **aq** final part. indicating a question demanding a 'yes' or 'no' answer (**Noq e aqpiq aqbol jol nga siq aq?** Are your grandparents still living? 41:20) (see also: **a**)

(vb) **aq (vb)** to (vb) and (vb) (**ssuq aq ssuq** = to walk and walk - 45:60)

aqbal shadow; shade (35:78) (aˇ baˇ)

-- aqbal, lulhhuv -- (see full)

aqbaq a lover

aqbeq 1. a person who is mute, 2. a person who is foolish (9:8) (cf. Ak.: male: aˬ dzawˬ, female: aˬ byahˬ) (and see: **aqbiaoq**)

aqbeel persimmon (9:7)

aqbeil nasal discharge (naˬ behˇ) (9:8, 46:116)

  aqbeil beilgaol liquid nasal discharge (9:7) (na⌄ behˇ)

  aqbeil beilniul dense or solid nasal discharge

  aqbeil nal'eel liquid nasal discharge (46:116)

  aqbeil nalxiq dry nasal discharge (38:14) (na⌄ behˇ ko^)

  aqbeil nieivq to blow nose; squeeze mucous from nose (9:8) (na⌄ behˇ baw dzeh-eu)

-- aqbei, galhhu -- ancient times

aqbeivq vagina; **aqbovq** (taboo) (a⌄ beh‸; daw⌄ beh‸)

  aqbeivq hav a female to be sexually aroused (taboo)

aqbiaq biaqsaoq wax (46:168)

-- Aqbiaq, Hheivqqivq -- Mr. Trickster in legends

Aqbiavq a clever man's name (and see **Aqbiaq**) (45:1)

aqbiaoq a dragonfly (or) **adovq**

aqbiaoq a foolish person (cf. a⌄ byah⌄)

aqbiaoq biaoq to be weak and limp (or) **keelqaoq lavqaoq qaoq**

aqbieiv bieiv to feel numb; to be numb (9:8) (yaw bui^ bui^-eu)

aqbol 1. grandfather; 2. term of respect for older man (9:8) (a⌄ bawˇ)

  -- aqbol, aoqjiq -- thunder god

  Aqbol laoyiq my lord (B=Chi) (35:25)

  aqbol ssalmol 1. grandpa, 2. old man

  aqbol ssaqmoq 1. grandpa, 2. an old man (35:67) (a⌄ bawˇ tsawˇ maw⌄)

aqbovq vagina (or) **aqbeivq** (taboo) (a⌄ beh‸; daw⌄ beh‸)

aqbul a bath (10:27)

  aqbul ciq 1. to take a bath, 2. to go swimming (1. iˇ cu‸ dzui‸-eu, 2. iˇ di⌄ di⌄-eu)

  aqbul ciq miq to give a bath (10:27)

aqbyul alsiq a kind of sour fruit

aqbyu 1. a hole, 2. the vulva

aqcaq zil to have (contain) philosophy (14:183)

aqcav a kind of poisonous green worm

  aqcav cav a sore to develop on the skin caused by a poisonous green worm

aqcavq a big spoon; a ladle (or) **kuqcavq; yuqcavq; hoqkuq yuqcavq** (ku⌄ tsa‸; ku⌄ tsa‸ tsa‸ mạ)

Aqcaoq ssaq Dai (Tai; Shan) nationality (or) **Biqcaoq; Deicuq** (Chi) (Bi⌄ cm⌄; Mi⌄ cm⌄)

aqcevq a kind of crop

aqciq 1. type of food, 2. soybean condiment (9:8)

  aqciq ciqbieiv a fresh soybean condiment

  aqciq ciqkuv a dried soybean condiment

  aqciq ciqnav black soybean condiment

aqcivq goat (9:6) (ci‸ myeh‸)

  aqcivq civqbu a male goat

  aqcivq civqkuv goat shed (9:6) (ci‸ myeh‸ ku^)

  aqcivq civqma a female goat

  aqcivq civqxiq goat dung (9:6) (ci‸ myeh‸ ca‸; ci‸ myeh‸ ce⌄)

aqciiv nyuq hu to give a thought to something
aqcol people; person
aqcu older brother's wife (9:8, 11:26) (a˯ tsu)
aqcuq (TE) dear elder sister-in-law

aqda father; dad; daddy (9:8) (a˯ da)
-- **aqda, cilja** -- father of one's son-in-law or daughter-in-law
aqda danil step-father (41:2) (a˯ da da nyiˇ)
aqda dassaq young male; young boy
-- **aqda, yosaol** -- (see full)
aqdaq (TE) dearest father (very polite)
aqdaol wing (9:8, 46:117) (a˯ dahˇ)
aqdaol daolhav hard feathers of a bird's wing (a˯ dahˇ dahˇ g'ahˇ)
aqdaol daolhav duv 1. for a hard feather to grow out, 2. for something to become mature
aqdaol daolnaoq soft feathers
aqdaol daolpiaq a whole wing; the full wing
aqdaol daolqiaq the tip edge of a wing
aqdeiqdeiq an interjection (**Aqdeiqdeiq, xilmeil maq gaq lal haoq wul yaq**! Oh, what bad news this is! 54:102)
aqdil really (or) **aqdil meil; ngeeljil meil** (a˯ diˇ)
aqdil meil really (or) **aqdil; ngeeljil meil** (a˯ diˇ)

aq'eil? question ending particle (11:138); **nga aq'eil** (**Miqnieiq mol xilmeil leil maq ngeel nga aq'eil?** Isn't the matter like this?)
Aqgaq a person's name (11:109)
aqgav cold (9:8) (yaw ga^)
aqgav ba'la winter (10:7) (tsah˯ ga^ yam˯)
aqgav gav to feel cold (9:8) (yaw ga^ ga^-eu)
aqgav gavsiq goose flesh (9:8) (yaw ga^ jaˇ teˇ teˇ-eu)
aqgav gavsso to become cold
aqgaoq cevq to divine with thatch grass (three pieces are passed three times up and down the body of the sick person, then checked against his turban length) used to let a soul that has wandered off return to the owner without hindrance
aqgaoq gaoq for a **moqpil** to take a cooked egg and pass it up and down the body of a sick person, then divine from that
aqgeel alsiq a star (9:9) (a˯ guiˇ; a˯ guiˇ si˯)
aqgeel alsiq hama ssaqzeq a constellation that looks like a mother hen and her chicks
aqgeel caqkov the milky way
aqgeelsiq (or) **aqgeel alsiq** star (9:9) (a˯ guiˇ; a˯ guiˇ si˯)
aqgeel siivq massaq the Big Dipper cluster of stars (50:9) ('7 stars, mother and children')
aqgeel sseiv a star to shine (26:101) (a˯ guiˇ

tsehˬ-eu)

aqgeel sseiv sseiv nei sseiv stars to twinkle

aqgee aqnia goqjal other countries (41:208) (aˬ cawˬ miˇ k'ahˬ)

aqgee duv yil to go downstream (14:220) (cf.: iˇ ka-eu)

aqgee gee to count; to enumerate (14:167) (gui-eu)

-- aqgee, naoqmil -- down south

aqgee pyu 1. down; below, 2. west (9:9), south (**naq; naqfal** = Chi) (dzawˬ gui = downslope area of house)

aqgov bedbug (9:9) (aˬ gaw^)

aqgyu kind of nut tree in jungle with flat, bitter nuts (not edi) (11:26) (or) **gyuma albol**

aqha chicken (9:9) (ya ci^) (clf. = **ha; mol**)

aqha buldul upper chicken leg; chicken thigh (13:11) (baw duˇ)

aqha dol duv when a bad-omen chicken occurs

aqha habaoq a chicken which is cooked in the house of a girl before she leaves to marry a boy (the boy provides one, the girl's family provides another)

aqha hadavq cock's spur (ya ci^ da˰; da˰)

aqha hadol a bad-omen chicken

aqha hageel a chicken nest (ya ci^ ya guiˇ)

aqha hahal a young hen (ya k'aˇ)

aqha hakuv chicken house; chicken shed (ya ci^ ya ku^)

aqha hama a hen (9:9) (ya ci^ ya ma)

aqha hama mama a big hen (ya ci^ ya ma ma laˇ-eu)

aqha hamiq yavpyul feather duster made of chicken feathers

aqha hama massaq a small hen (11:36) (ya ci^ ya ma zaˬ)

aqha haniaol chicken feather (46:132) (ya ci^ aˬ dahˇ)

aqha hapyul a rooster (9:9) (ya poeˇ)

aqha hasaq chicken meat (9:9) (ya ci^ shaˬ jiˇ)

aqha haseil chicken louse (ya ci^ ya sehˇ)

aqha hasol a grey hen

aqha hasovq capon (9:9) (ya ci^ ya shaw˰)

aqha hawuv egg; chicken egg (ya u^)

aqha manav a black-skinned chicken

aqha mobiaq comb of chicken (9:9) (naˬ beh)

aqha miavhav chicken basket (or) **hahav** (ya ci^ k'a^ pahˬ)

aqhaoq an interjection (oh!) (35:7)

aqhel! an interjection (**Aqhel, xildyul dyulssaq yaol**! Oh, what a small amount it is.)

aqheq! an interjection (**Aqheq, qavq saoq wul yaq**! Oh, how ugly. 54:102)

aqhuq father's younger sister (9:10) (aˬ k'oˬ)

aqhuq malma father's sister (younger and older

than father) (46:89)

aqhuq ssaqmiq father's sister (she is the one to make a shoulder bag for a **moqpil**)

aqhuq zilhaoq bavq the money which a paternal aunt gives to the groom and bride out of a bowl which has had some liquor poured into it, along with offerings

aqhyuq smoke (9:10) (u˯ k'oe˯)

aqhyuq baoqlo a bamboo water pipe for smoking

aqhyuq daolyeil tobacco smoked in a bamboo water pipe (B=Chi) (ya k'aw˯ baw˯ law; shoi˯ yoi baw˯ law)

aqhyuq hyuq smoke to smoke (billow) (9:10) (u˯ k'oe˯ k'oe˯-eu)

aqhyuq hyuqniul tobacco (ya k'aw˯)

aqhyuq maoqyeil tobacco smoked in a bamboo water pipe (B=Chi) (ya k'aw˯ baw˯ law; shoi˯ yoi baw˯ law)

aqhyuq suv to smoke tobacco (ya k'aw˯ dawˇ-eu)

aqhyuq ziilyeil a cigarette (B=Chi) (clf. = **mol**) (12:126)

aqhhavq a pig (9:9) (a˯ za˰) (a˯ g'a˰ = CA)

aqhhavq gaolzul adult male pig (B=Chi) (a˯ za˰ piˇ)

aqhhavq hhavqcil lard (11:35) (za˰ tsiˇ)

aqhhavq hhavqciil small male pig (a˯ za˰ za˰ byu˯ za˯)

aqhhavq hhavqhal young female pig (a˯ za˰ za˰ ma za˯)

aqhhavq hhavqho old female pig (sow) (a˯ za˰ za˰ ma)

aqhhavq hhavqnav a black pig (46:134) (za˰ na^)

aqhhavq hhavqssaq little pigs (a˯ za˰ za˰ za˯)

aqhhavq meiqzu pig snout (or) **aqhhavq nalmeil**; **aqhhavq nalbaoq** (a˯ za˰ meh˯ boe˯)

aqhhaol second son

aqhhel hhelneev chinaberry

aqhhol 1. official (46:108), 2. 'king' (used of dragon in 11:210, 45:51)

-- **aqhhol, puvlaol** -- village head (or) **puvlaol soqpaq** (and see full)

aqhhovq a needle (9:9) (a˯ g'aw˰)

aqhhovq cov to inject (as medicine) (a˯ g'aw˰ tsaw^-eu)

aqhhovq guvqdaq a thimble (9:9)

aqhhovq guvqnieiq sewing work half finished

aqhhovq hhovqbyu the eye of a needle

aqhhovq sil tao to thread a needle

aqhhuv below; under (9:9, 46:121) (or) **hul'a** (la˰ o^)

aqhhuv aqtav up and down (as a fish in a stream) (13:14)

aqhhuv bi yiuvq to be done in a magical way by a shaman in a trance (nyiˇ pa˯ tseˇ-eu)

aqhhuv daolteil lower back

aqhhuv jol   sit down (41:154) (nuiˇ-eu)

aqhhuv meiqjil   lower lip (meh˯ lu˯ la˰ o^ pyaw˯)

aqhhuv meiqzu   lower lip (meh˯ lu˯ la˰ o^ pyaw˯)

aqhhuv pyu   1. below; lower side (46:125, 132) (la˰ o^ paw), 2. the following (as in: **aqhhuv pyu ssaqguq guqssaq** = the following children)

aqhhuv qiq ciivq   subordinate; at a lower level

aqhhuv qiq lov   1. the country below the world; 2. a bottomless pit, 3. hell

aqhhuv yiuvq   to go into a trance ('sleep below')

aqhhuv yiuvqma   a shaman (nyiˇ pa˯)

aqhhuv yiuvq nia e col   a shaman (nyiˇ pa˯)

aqhhyu   maternal uncle (9:10) (a˯ g'oe)

aqhhyu aqmee seil   game small children play (hold hands and sing Hani songs)

aqhhyu duv   to attend a burial ceremony on behalf of a maternal uncle

aqhhyu hoqbiol lol   to honor maternal uncles who come to attend a burial ceremony by serving them a meal (or) **aqhhyu lol**

aqhhyu lol   (see: **aqhhyu hoqbiol lol**)

aqhhyu paoqciivq bavq   to kneel to the maternal uncles as they come to a funeral

-- aqhhyu, saol ciivq --   (see full)

aqhhyu xaol gav luvq   for the maternal uncle to sleep in the bed of the buried person the first night after burial

aqjaol   a long bar fixed as swing for one or more people, that circles round and round (9:10, 13:39)

aqjaol albaol   a swing pole (lit. a 'swing tree' used in making the long bar used in swinging) (46:184)

aqjaol ziiq   to ride on the long bar fixed as swing (see above) (13:39)

aqjul julkuv   dried loaches (14:159)

Aqjulniq   name of a trickster in legends (38:1) (he appears in legends from Xishuangbanna, telling of a poor man who tricked the wealthy)

aqkal   later; in the future (11:110) (**Aqkal aqyoq heeq lal ngaoq golbaq heeq** lil. If he grows in the future he will have a big body.) (or) **aqkal naolhao; galnee salpeiq** (a˯ kaˇ)

aqkal hhana   sometime in the future

-- aqkal, maq mia --   before long; not long after

aqkal mol   to see (meet) again (41:179) (cf. Eng. "See you later".) (perhaps not used much daily) (a˯ kaˇ mawˇ teh˰-a)

aqkal naolhao daov maq gal nei   in the by and by

aqkeel   foot (9:10) (a˯ kuiˇ)

aqkeel haocavq   leg hair (a˯ kuiˇ ca˰ hm)

aqkeel hhe   1. to lag behind (as in a group where one gets poor marks and pulls the group average down) (26:43), 2. to 'drag one's heels' by not supporting something or someone

aqkeel hhe lal to pull back one's legs (so as not to block another's way) (41:96) (a⌄ kuiˇ caw k'o^-eu)

aqkeel keelhhaq sole of foot (9:10) (a⌄ kuiˇ pya⌄ g'a⌄) (CA)

aqkeel keelnaol foot (apart from sole) (9:10)

aqkeel keelqeiq lame; crippled leg (a⌄ kuiˇ kuiˇ cu⌄) (9:10)

aqkeel nei naoq to stamp with one's foot

aqkeel piaqhhal a foot print (14:148) (a⌄ kuiˇ peh⌄ zaˇ)

aqkeel seiqma pavq to tie the big toes of a dead person together

aqkeel sil leg to be paralyzed (9:10) (a⌄ kuiˇ shiˇ-eu)

aqkeeq dog (9:10) (a⌄ kui⌄)

aqkeeq a suq neiq to give (throw) to dogs (a⌄ kui⌄-ahˇ bi⌄ neh⌄-eu)

aqkeeq daoqmiq hoqsiq qiqsiq nei dav ciivq hhyuq ciivq dav from one grain of rice on the tail of a dog could climb up nine levels (from legend)

aqkeeq jaq suq to ask dogs to 'chase' people home after a funeral (see: **ssaqmiq galkeel leiq huvq**)

aqkeeq keeqhhul male dog (a⌄ kui⌄ kui⌄ huˇ)

aqkeeq keeqma female dog; bitch (a⌄ kui⌄ kui⌄ ma)

aqkeeq keeqmu mad dog (9:10) (a⌄ kui⌄ kui⌄ u⌄)

aqkeeq keeqpaq a male dog (a⌄ kui⌄ kui⌄ huˇ)

aqkeeq keeqsaq dog meat (9:10) (a⌄ kui⌄ sha⌄ jiˇ)

aqkeeq keeqsil dead dog (in 27:12 used as: 'tired as a dead dog') (a⌄ kui⌄ kui⌄ shiˇ)

aqkeeq keeqsiil a yellow (or brown) dog (11:36) (kui⌄ shuiˇ)

aqkeeq keeqsiil siilgov a thin yellow dog (11:36)

aqkeeq keeqwul a male dog (a⌄ kui⌄ kui⌄ huˇ)

aqkeeq miav nei saq a dog's life (lots of trouble)

-- **aqkeeq, saqleiq** -- hunting dog

aqkeiq a question part. which shows that the speaker does not know the answer (11:145) (**Xil hhaq maq ngeel nga siq aqkeiq?** Was it this person or not? 45:60, **Ssaqguq niq hhaq halgei jol siq aq, sil aqkeiq?** Where were the two children - had they died? 45:83)

aqkulssal perhaps (**Zaq aqkulssal.** Perhaps they have eaten.) (fp.- pa⌄)

aqlaqyil interjection of surprise (11:145) (**Aqlaqyil! Qavq hu zaq wul yaq.** Oh my, how very interesting -- as a book, movie.)

aqlavq hand; arm (9:11) (a⌄ la^)

aqlavq bavq cei 1. to raise one's hands (41:62), 2. to give up (as when soldiers raise their hands in surrender) (or) **milhaoq aoq zaq e; aolnieiq pieiq taq** (a⌄ la^ ba^ diˇ-eu)

aqlavq bavq cei nei zaol ceiv to vote by raising the hand (50:92)

aqlavq lavqhhaq palm of hand (9:11) (la^ k'aw^; la^ g'a˅ = CA)

aqlavq hhev to wave the hand (9:11) (or) **aqlavq lavqhhev** (la^ li^ li^-eu; la^ jawˇ jawˇ-eu)

aqlavq hhev nei maq gua to wash one's hands of the business; to refuse to do anything more about the matter (D=Chi) (50:145)

aqlavq lavqbaoq a glove (26:73) (la^ bah˅)

aqlavq lavqhov cupped hands; a cupped hand (la^ k'aw^)

aqlavq lavqhhev a hand gesture

aqlavq lavqluvq a hand with no fingers ('blunt hand')

aqlavq lavqnaol the back of the hand

aqlavq lavqyevq ngaoq to arm wrestle

aqlavq lov 'hands to be free' (that is, to have some free time, spare time) (26:50) (a˅ la^ ngeh^-eu)

aqlavq nei zei nei zei to reach out with the hand

aqlavq pieiq to put aside work; to stop working (26:71) ('throw down hands') (a˅ la^ pyeh˅-eu)

aqlavq tal to burn hand (B=Chi) (a˅ la^ pui^-eu)

aqlavq zei to stretch out one's hand (45:30) (a˅ la^ caw˅ ja-eu)

aqlao lao to wallow in a buffalo wallow (as in a pond or the like) (46:164) (or) **niuqlao lao**

aqlaoq neeyo taq nil don't worry (k'ah˅ ta˅ lahˇ)

aqlaoq yoqssil yoqbo each has a given lifespan (35:53)

aqleil ! interjection of surprise or pity

aqleil air; wind (10:21) (**aqleil liq hha bi tao lal nia** = must let air into home) (ja˅ lehˇ)

aqlil wind (old poetic word)

aqlil an affirmative final particle (11:201) (**Ngal Haqniq soqhhaq zol aqlil.** I study Hani writing. 54:166)

aqli a child (9:11) (za˅) (note: a˅ li = 'boy' in Akha)

aqli mavq children (za˅ gu˅ ba˅ ma^)

aqlivq python; boa (9:11) (li^)

Aqlo baqdiq the area around Luchun (35:84)

Aqlobieil a site in the jungle near **Tavqzaoq** village in Luchun, where 13 villages make yearly offerings to the 'lord of the water divide' (**bieil = bil**) (or) **Aqlo eelbieil**

Aqlobieil lol to make the yearly offering to the 'lord of the water divide' (or) **Aqlo eelbieil lol**

Aqlobieil saqhel pork which is from the site where the offering has been made to the 'lord of the water divide'

Aqlobieil saqyyuq bones from the offering made to the 'lord of the water divide' (later some sew bits of these bones into their clothing to keep them healthy)

Aqlobieil ssaqssyuq children of the Aqlobieil (see above)

Aqlo eelbieil (see: **Aqlobieil**)

-- **aqlo meil, qiq ssil** -- the whole life

aqlul uterus; womb (9:11) (zaˬ jawˇ zaˇ)

aqlyul alsiq citrus fruits

aqlyul lyulma savqbaoq pomelo (big citrus fruit)

aqlyuq penis (taboo); **aqqoq** in some dialects (however this also means 'others') (9:11) (aˬ loeˬ; beu^ leu^)

aqma mother (aˬ ma)

aqma female (-- ma)

aqma 'dear' (an expression of endearment to one's wife, used especially when young)

-- **aqma, ceiljil** -- the spirit of the granary

-- **aqma, cilja** -- mother of one's son-in-law or daughter-in-law

aqma manil step-mother (41:2) (ma nyiˇ)

aqma ssaq 1. mother and children, 2. all living things (45:42)

-- **aqma, ssaqnaoq** -- baby's mother

aqmaq (TE) dearest mother (very polite)

aqmaq deq nei to be numb (cf.: **eqleq deq nei** = numb and staring at something) (14:140) (yaw bui^ bui^-eu = to be numb)

aqmavq deq to stare in surprise (14:140, 26:38) (haw tso^ taˬ-eu)

aqmavq deq nei jol to be stunned; amazed (26:83) (na˰ suiˇ na˰ la˰)

aqmavq mavq to be numb

aqmaol aqda (see: **aqmol aqda**)

aqmeel a 'filler word' in poetry and ceremonies (with no meaning, but it serves to round out the statement)

aqmee wife of father's YB; wife of mother's brother; mother's younger sister (9:12) (aˬ mui)

aqmeil an interjection (**Aqmeil, xildyul pa baol meil**! Oh, how many there are!)

aqmeil 1. like....; it seems; looks alike (9:12, 12:126) (duˇ-eu), 2. for example (50:105)

aqmeil a walnut (9:12, 11:26)

aqmeil duv lal will appear as ... (10:4) (do^ laˇ-eu)

aqmeil meilhav a hard type of walnut (9:12)

aqmeil meilnaoq a soft type of walnut

aqmeil ngeel like (duˇ-eu); same as (10:11) (tiˬ kaw^)

aqmeil zaol do like this (10:13) (heu lo˰-ehˇ jahˇ)

aqmil ! 'oh!' an interjection of surprise

aqmil some time ago (dzeuˇ laˇ-eu)

-- **aqmil, galhhu** -- long, long ago

aqmil qiq jol last time (some time ago)

aqmiqyil! an interjection (**Aqmiqyil! Siil xil miav pa miav meil.** Oh my, there is a lot of gold!); **aqmilyil**

aqmiqyiq (see: **almiqyiq**)

aqmiaovq a boaster; liar; cheater (cf.: ja˯ myaw˄ myaw˄-eu)

aqmiaovq miaovq to boast; to tell a lie (or) **jaqhheivq hheivq** (ja˯ myaw˄ myaw˄-eu)

aqmiaovq miaovq zaq to boast; cheat; lie

aqmol 1. wife's brother, 2. what a sister calls her brother (46:145) (a˯ mahˇ)

aqmol aqda the brothers of a girl, esp. when speaking of her getting married

aqmol bee 1. home of brother (called this from the sister's side), 2. wife's brother's home

aqmol dulma brothers and sisters (mehˇ nmˇ dmˇ ma)

aqmoq 1. horse (mah˯); 2. pubic hair (daw˯ mah˯)

aqmoq moqpiul a white horse (46:188) (mah˯ mah˯ pyuˇ)

aqmu lalmu mu to feel dizzy (u˯ du˯ mo˯ mo˯-ehˇ g'eh-eu)

aqmu lalmu ssovq nei to feel very dizzy

aqmu mu to be dizzy (u˯ du˯ mo˯ mo˯-ehˇ g'eh-eu)

aqnaoq a kind of clay which pregnant women sometimes eat (especially when they lack certain minerals in their diet) (a˯ nah˯)

-- **aqnaoq, milcaq** -- a kind of clay which pregnant women sometimes eat (especially when they lack certain minerals in their diet)

aqnaovq alsiq fruit from this kind of tree (see below)

aqnaovq naovqbol a kind of wild fruit tree

aqneiq birdlime (iˇ ni˯)

-- **aqneiq, tevqlevq** -- parasitic plant

aqnil younger sibling/relative (9:12) (a˯ nyiˇ)

aqnil aqda (TE) dear child's father (used by a young baby's mother when addressing her husband, or on behalf of her child) (or) **ssaqnaoq aqda**

aqnil aqma (TE) dear child's mother (used by a young baby's father when addressing his wife, or on behalf of his child) (or) **ssaqnaoq aqma**

aqnil dalya children's songs (32:3)

aqnil eq to be pregnant (38:35) (a˯ nyiˇ pi-eu; za˯ jeu˯-eu)

aqnil miqli a younger sister (aqnil miqli zaqqul pa qul nei = the younger sister in the family is beautiful) (46:203)

aqnil mul yiuvq to lull a baby to sleep (as with a lullaby)

-- **aqnil, miavssaq** -- pupil of eye

aqnil toqssaq a baby sitter (or) baomu (Chi) (50:7)

aqnil toq zaq to look after a baby

aqnia upstream; upper; up there (9:12) (gaw^ mehˇ;

cf. dzawˬ nya = upper orientation related to a hs. as it is situated on a mountain))

-- aqnia, niamil -- the far north

aqnia pyu 1. upper side, upstream, 2. east (9:12) (gaw^ mehˇ paw)

aqnieivq empty; vacant (9:12) (**aqlavq aqnieivq** = empty hands) (yawˬ ngeh‸)

aqniuq 1. cow, 2. water buffalo (9:12) (1. mawˇ neˇ, 2. aˬ nyoˬ)

aqniuq aqqul cow (buffalo) milk (10:19) (aˬ nyoˬ aˬ coeˇ)

aqniuq laqpil very large type of chili pepper

aqniuq leiq kuv to confine a buffalo in its stable (aˬ nyoˬ ku^ ka‸-eu)

aqniuq niuqnil a cow

aqniuq niuqpeel a buffalo

aqniuq piav zaq to cut open a buffalo and skin it at a funeral

aqnu besides (k'oeˇ ta‸-aˇ); another (9:12) (yawˬ g'aˬ yawˬ; aˬ cawˬ) (cf. Lahu: awˬ nu)

aqnu aqnia other (**aqnu aqnia goqjal** = other countries) (aˬ cawˬ)

aqnu col another person (9:12) (aˬ cawˬ)

aqnu liyal another; others (B=Chi) (11:222)

aqnu mavq others (41:29)

aqnu milhaoq a foreign land; a strange land

aqnyuq a type of tree (or) **heiqnyuq** (45:40)

aqpaq male (-- paˬ)

-- aqpaq, bieivqdaoq -- a man who has no son (taboo)

aqpeil pear (9:12) (siˬ poeˬ tsa‸ aˇ siˬ)

aqpeil albol pear tree

-- aqpeil, alzil -- wild pear

aqpeil peilbol a pear tree (13:14)

aqpeil peilcavq cavq to graft a pear tree

aqpeil peilqul sweet pear

aqpiq grandmother; old lady (9:12) (aˬ piˬ)

aqpiq aqbol grandparents; old people (aˬ piˬ aˬ bawˇ)

aqpiq lol to have the spring festival

aqpiq Molmil 'grandmother God' (4:43, 46:211) (see also: **aqpyuq Molmil**)

aqpiq naqdeiv a talkative person

aqpiq ssaqmoq old woman (11:149) (aˬ piˬ tsawˇ mawˬ)

aqpuv lilpuv puv to rotate; to whirl

aqpuv puv to roll on the ground (26:10) (po^ la^ la^-eu)

aqpyul male animal (limited to certain ones) (9:12) (aˬ poeˇ)

aqpyuq great grandfather (9:12) (aˬ poeˬ)

aqpyuq aqbol ancestors (9:12) (aˬ poeˬ aˬ piˬ)

aqpyuq aqda 1. ancestors (aˬ poeˬ aˬ piˬ); 2. great-great-grandfather (or) **aqpyuq Molmil**

aqpyuq baoqgeel ancestral altar (usually a shelf of

bamboo) (or) **aqpyuq helgeel** (11:203) (a˯ poe˯ paw˰ law˰)

aqpyuq baoqgeel hel to make an ancestral offering (or) **aqpyuq zal hel; zal hel hel**

aqpyuq helgeel ancestral altar (11:203) (or) **aqpyuq baoqgeel** (a˯ poe˯ paw˰ law˰)

-- aqpyuq, joqhyuq -- spirit of the clouds

aqpyuq Hhaolbei Leilseil spring season God

-- aqpyuq, Hhaolduv -- spring ancestor

-- aqpyuq, Hhoqzyuq -- spirit that protects the crops

-- aqpyuq, Milsaol -- Lord of the land (spiritual)

Aqpyuq Miqyeil a supernatural being who is basically a protector for the Hani people, evidently made up of three manifestations: 1. **Byulluvq Aqpyuq Miqyeil** - protects people, 2. **Zeiqluvq Molmil Ssaqli** - last son of **Molmil**, protects animals, 3. **Kalluvq Caqnavq Aqma** - protects crops. (see also: **Molmil; Aqpyuq Molmil**) (46:167) (a˯ poe˯ Mi˯ yehˇ)

Aqpyuq Molmil ancestor god; sky-God (46:210) (see also: Molmil; **Aqpyuq Miqyeil**)

aqpyuq Taoqpaoq a Hani ancestor (46:107)

aqpyuq zal hel make an ancestral offering (or) **zalhel hel; aqpyuq baoqgeel hel**

aqqeil stinkbug (a˯ ciˇ a˯ caˇ)

aqqo daoqmiq servility; slavishness (50:123)

aqqoq others; someone else (9:12) (a˯ caw˯) (Note: This word also means 'penis' in some Hani dialects.)

aqqoq a bi hev miq to let others know; to tell others

aqqoq a bivq miq to give away (a˯ caw˯-ahˇ bi˰ neh˯-eu)

aqqoq e aqzavq one who must take another's orders (or) **aqqoq e jeilma**

aqqoq hav for a man to be sexually aroused (taboo)

aqqoq yaol zaol yoqhhaq yaol kyuq lal to receive back what you do to others (i.e., if you hurt others, you will be hurt in turn)

aqqul 1. sweet, 2. breast, 3. milk (9:13, 11:29) (a˯ coeˇ)

aqqul ceiv to wean (a˯ coeˇ g'eh^ laˇ-eu)

aqqul qulpul the breast (lit. 'the breast root')

aqqul qulpul nal mastitis; breast cancer; breast pain

aqqul qulqeil collostrum (first milk secreted by a new mother)

aqqul qulsiq nipple; teat

aqsal in the future (or) **aqkal; naolhao** (46:76) (a˯ kaˇ)

aqsaoq 1. brother-in-law, 2. older sister's husband (9:13, 11:26), 3. father's younger sister's husband (46:89) (a˯ shah˯)

aqseivq seivq to show off; be proud of oneself (jahˇ g'eh-eu)

aqsol 1. who (a˯ suˇ), 2. single or only one (**qiq hhaq aqsol** = only one person; **qiq mol aqsol** = only one tool)

aqsol hev nia ya? Who could know? (26:2) (A˯ suˇ g'a˯ si˯ nya-eu)

aqsol liq whoever (11:222) (a˯ suˇ g'a˯ k'aw˰)

aqsol liq dal wuqbo everyone has a share of responsibility (50:130)

aqsol mavq whoever (a˯ suˇ g'a˯ ma˯ ka˯)

aqsol movq aqsol sal choose one you want (love) (11:222)

aqsol nei aqsol hev ya? 'who knows by whom?' (13:4)

aqsol sol whoever; 'just who' (11:103) (**Aqsol sol lal?** Just who came?) (a˯ suˇ suˇ g'a˯)

aqssaq son-in-law (9:13, 41:2) (a˯ za˯)

aqssaq kul to 'call' a son-in-law (the groom stays with the girl's family)

aqssaq ssaqsiivq a new son-in-law (a˯ za˯ yaw shui˰)

aqssii ssii to be disgusted; to dislike (byeh-eu)

aqtav above; up (9:13) (la˰ ta^)

aqtav bu dav appeal to a higher court (50:147)

aqtav dav li to raise up (50:147)

aqtav daolteil upper back (la˰ bya^)

aqtav hu e aoq, aqhhuv hu e mil look up it is the sky, look down it is the earth (the meaning; 'the sky and earth are my witnesses, they approve')

aqtav meiqjil upper lip (meh˯ lu˯ la˰ ta^ pyaw˯)

aqtav pyu 1. upper side, up above (9:13) (la˰ ta^ paw), 2. the things above (as written above) (26:104), 3. the Government policy (as being over us) (10:pref)

aqtav qiq daol an upper floor

aqtav soqpaq government (or) **zeiffu qovq** (A=Chi); **goqjal qovq** (A=Chi)

aqtav tul to stand up

aqtaoq pine tree (46:190)

aqtaoq allavq the branch of a pine tree (46:191)

aqteiq 1. single (op. of **aqzao** = double); only, 2. odd (as in odd numbers, not even) (aˇ te˯)

aqxeivq water leech (9:13) (yeh˰ neˇ; yeh˰ nyoeˇ)

aqxu to be less than; not many (9:13) (cf. yaw su˰)

-- **aqyal, taolso** -- myriads ('thousands and hundreds')

aqya they; others (or) **aqya mavq** (27:12) (a˯ yaw˰ ma˰)

aqya bulduq they themselves (yaw˯ haˇ yaw˯ ha; a˯ yaw^ yaw˰)

aqya dyul they (31:3)

aqya mavq they; others (a$_\vee$ yaw$_\wedge$ ma$_\wedge$)

aqya niaq the two of them (a$_\vee$ yaw$_\wedge$ nya$_\wedge$)

aqyaq! an interjection (**Aqyaq! Tyulmeil maq zaol haoq nga lul!** Hey, that must not be done!)

aqyaol particle indicating bewilderment (**Aqyoq lal aqyaol, halgei jol ngaq?** He came, but where is he?)

aqyaoq interjection; exclamation (oh!!) (11:218) (often indicates disgust, anger - 27:12)

aqyeil biul 1. greasy; oily, 2. to be sick of something; fed up with it; 'lazy' to do it (in 11:210, fed up with staying with the dragon) (9:13) (cf. deh-eu; yeh$_\wedge$-eu; and Lahu - bvuh^ ve)

aqyivq a termite (**hhocuv aqyivq** = flying termite) (a$_\vee$ i$_\vee$)

aqyivq 1. oldest daughter, 2. elder sibling (9:13) (1. a$^\vee$ yui$_\wedge$; 2. a$_\vee$ yui$_\wedge$)

aqyivq aqnil 1. older and younger siblings; relatives (11:202), 2. general term for cousin (father's sister's sons); they call each other: **loqbioq** (a$_\vee$ yui$_\wedge$ a$_\vee$ nyi$^\vee$)

aqyivq meilnaol brothers (a$_\vee$ yui$_\wedge$ meh$^\vee$ nm$^\vee$)

aqyivq nilma 'sister' (fictive, what women call each other when they are not related)

aqyol sheep (9:13) (yaw$^\vee$)

aqyol yolbu a ram (male sheep)

aqyol yolhao wool

aqyol yolma a ewe (female sheep)

aqyo his; her's; it's (possessive)

aqyo aqmee 1. younger brother's wife (a$_\vee$ mui), 2. term of endearment men use with women

aqyo bulduq he himself/ she herself (or) **aqyoq bulduq** (yaw$_\vee$ ha$^\vee$ yaw$_\vee$ ha; a$_\vee$ yaw^ yaw$_\wedge$)

aqyo galma yo'liq as a rule (zah$^\vee$ ja^-eu lo$_\wedge$-eh$^\vee$)

aqyo mavq they (9:14) (a$_\vee$ yaw$_\wedge$ ma$_\wedge$)

aqyo niaq the two of them (11:222, 13:31) (a$_\vee$ yaw$_\wedge$ nya$_\wedge$)

aqyo qiq mavq they (10:pref) (a$_\vee$ yaw$_\wedge$ ma$_\wedge$) (& see: **aqyo mavq**)

aqyo qovq his/her family (9:14) (nym$^\vee$ dah$_\vee$ ti$_\vee$ zaw$_\wedge$) (cf.: **qovqbee**)

aqyoq ! interjection of surprise; pain (12:127, 26:60) (or) **aqyoq yoq!** (35:28), **alyol; alyol oq**

aqyoq he; she; it (nominative) (9:14) (a$_\vee$ yaw$_\wedge$)

aqyoq bulduq himself; herself; itself (or) **aqyo bulduq** (yaw$_\vee$ ha$^\vee$ yaw$_\vee$ ha; a$_\vee$ yaw^ yaw$_\wedge$)

aqyoq yaol him; her; it (objective)

aqzal food (9:14) (dza$^\vee$)

aqzal a kind of tree

aqzaq fire (26:14) (mi$_\vee$ dza$_\vee$)

aqzaq keq to set fire (45:33) (mi$_\vee$ dza$_\vee$ keu$_\vee$-eu)

aqzaq miqlaol fire (26:14)

aqzaq miqseil (see: **miqzaq miqseil** = shooting

stars - 35:102)

aqzaq syuq 1. to trouble, 2. to be difficult to deal with

aqzavq to be cheated (bi shuiˇ-eu; bi myaw˰-eu)

aqzavq zavq to cheat someone (myaw˰ dza˯)

aqzao 1. double (op. of single) (nyi˯ mya^), 2. an even number

aqzei zei to stretch out one's body

aqzeiq 1. left over; extra (9:4) (a˯ dzeh˯), 2. more (**Aqzeiq qiq niq zuvq bavq duv yi siq, ngal qiq heiq ceil nial.** Please take out one or two more jackets, I will choose. 41:150), 3. surplus

aqzeiq aol dav to do beyond (or) **yozeiq aol duv**

aqzeiq meil 1. more of; some more (3:2); 2. outstanding

aqzeiq qiq taq once more; one more time (41:62) (ti˯ po^ si˯)

aqzeiq zeiq over; beyond (**jiqgeiq maq ceil nei aqzeiq zeiq al.** passed the exam, and MORE than passed - 26:47)

aqzeiq (vb) **zeiq** more than (vb) (10:32) (**aqzeiq miaq zeiq** = more in number than.....) (dzeh˯-eu; ta˰-ehˇ)

aqzeivq cicada (9:14) (a˯ je˯; a˯ je˯ ca˯)

aqzeivq zeivqsil zeivqsav type of cicada

aqzil song - sometimes a little like a yodel (folk; courting; never sung in house) (9:14)

-- **aqzil, baqsal** -- a love song

aqzil gul to sing (yodel) the above (10:pref) (a˯ ciˇ guˇ-eu = CA)

-- **aqzil, yohhyul** -- a love song

aqziv clitoris (taboo) (or) **beivqniuv; beivqziv** (a˯ dzi˯ meh˯ laˇ)

aqzoq foolish (9:14); fool; idiot (a˯ dzaw˯ - in Akha only used for males)

aqzuq worm; insect; caterpillar (9:14) (a˯ ju˯)

aqzuq yaq to get rid of worms (as in a buffalo) using magical words

Aol

aol 1. to work (9:6) (m˅-eu), 2. to request (13:31), 3. to want (11:187) (**Aqyoq caqdevq aol nga laq?** Does he want salt?) (**Aol maq aol?** Do you want it or not? 11:54) (geu‸ maw‸-eu)
aol alnei beq lal to become rich by means of one's work (50:137)
aolbal taq bi bal to prevent something being done in a superficial way (50:48)
aolbei 1. to start to work; start to do, 2. pioneering work (50:26) (m˅ beh-eu)
aolbei bei to create; to begin; to open up; to start up (50:95)
aolbei heiq a breach; a gap
aolbiq a kind of tree (its flower gives a sweet juice) (34:6); three branches are given to a dead person while telling that person to bathe him or herself
aolbiav to be worn out from working
aolbiei biei to do carelessly (maˬ yah˅ ni m˅-eu)
aolbu wasted work (of no value) (11:115) (m˅ dzeh-eu)
aol cavq to carry on (as a program) (or) **jifceiq** (Chi) (34:2)
=aol, caol'= spindle
aol ceq to succeed
aolcevq cevq to strike a spinning top on the top portion
aol cyuq 1. to build a wall, 2. to fence in an area (45:1) (cf.: ya˅ km˅ m˅-eu)
aol dav 1. to build up; 2. to get ahead
aol daol laq e to follow the path; obey the rules
aoldaoq cov dav to make a tatoo on the skin
aolduq 1. to be useful, 2. place where done; work site (9:6, 50:59) (**Haljivq aolduq jav nga laq?** What is the use of doing it? **Aolduq maq jav.** = It is useless.) (1. ga˅ dah˅, 2. m˅ duˬ)
aolduq aolyal position; front
aolduq dalweif a work unit (B=Chi) (34:96)
aolduq jav obtain employment; take up an occupation (50:92)
aolduq maq bo out of a job; to lose one's position
aolduq maq jav to no avail (or) **qiq daol maq cyuq** ('no value')
aol duvq to mend (gu‸ myahˬ-eu)
-- aol e col, hhellavq -- trader; businessman
aol e hhaq productive forces
aol e za to be applicable; suitable
aol gov laq e nal peiv to have an incurable sickness or disease for many years
aol haol to help do (or) **balhaol** (caw m˅-eu)

aol haol ciq to render a service

aol haol lal to come to the rescue (or) **hhaqhav tivq haol lal** (with all one's might)

aol haol miq to give a lift to (or) **deiq cei miq**

aol hev to realize

aolheiq cuv to start a new job; new work (50:27)

aolheiq qeil enjoyable work (11:196) (m$^{\vee}$ mui$_{\vee}$-eu)

aol huqteil before work starts (26:29) (m$^{\vee}$ dah$_{\vee}$ ma$_{\vee}$ beh k'oe$^{\vee}$)

aolhha to obtain

aolhhaq dav'qeiv level of productive forces (50:151)

aolhhaq juq lose ability to work (as old and weak) (50:146)

-- **aol, hhaqma** -- (see: **hhaqma lol**)

-- **aol, hhuvqdaol** -- to come back

-- **aol, hhyul** -- nutrition; nourishment

aolkal leil qoq an advocate; promoter (50:164)

-- **aol, kaoldaol** -- to fence in

aol koq to start doing (26:89) (m$^{\vee}$ beh-eu)

aolkov a kind of plant which has yellow leaves the Hani sometimes use to color sticky rice yellow (46:156)

aolkov qaqsiil a very large flower (called 'king flower' = **yeivzyuq**)

aol leev to do the work well; properly (m$^{\vee}$ mui$_{\vee}$ nya-eu)

aol leiq to lose (in business) (or) **zaol leiq**

-- **aol lo, aol sil** -- (see full)

aolma a skilled person (50:121)

aol meeq to improve (10:pref.); build up (50:84) (m$^{\vee}$ mui$_{\vee}$-eu)

aolmeiq meiq to set an example; to demonstrate

-- **aol, miq** -- to labor; to work

-- **aol, miqnieiq** -- to labor; to work

aol miaq zaq miaq work more, get more

aol naoq zaq naoq work little, get little (50:147)

aolnaovq willow tree (or) **aolnaovq albol** (9:6, 26:117)

aol nia capable (of doing); energetic (50:120)

aol nia e colssaq a man of business; a person who gets things done

=aol, niaoq'= now

aolnieiq unfinished work; to leave work before it is finished (ma$_{\vee}$ m$^{\vee}$ ji$^{\vee}$-eu$_{\vee}$)

aolnieiq aolpav unfinished work (50:5); half-done work

aolnieiq aolquv function (50:212)

aolnieiq pieiq taq to give up (or) **maq aol zaq; aqlavq bavq cei; milhaoq aoq zaq e**

aol pal sso flexible; adaptable (or) **za; ya; zaol pal**

sso

aolpav rent being half the income

aolpav pav to rent something (paying the owner half of what one gets) (m˅ pa^ pa^-eu)

aolpav pieiq to rent out something, as a field (half of the produce will come back to the owner) (m˅ pa^ pa^-eu)

aol paoq to work cooperatively

=aol, paoq= a spindle

aol pievq to bring about

aolpuq diq to hit a spinning top with a nonspinning top

aolpyuq wages (50:7)

aol pyuq bi bo strive for efficiency (50:84); to be worth one's pay (for work)

aolqeiv qeiv to have competition; to match (or) **diqqeiv qeiv**

aol qivq laqmeil to be in good condition to use; to be useful (57:71)

-- aolquv, aolnieiq -- function

aol saq complete the task; finish doing (m˅ ji˅-eu)

aol sil aol lo 1. to work very hard, but have no results (m˅ seh‸ le‸-eu˯ ti˯ je˯ ma˯ za), 2. to shed one's heart blood (50:125)

aolsiq teiv to play billiards (50:96)

aol soq 1. to manage in good order; to run well (35:52), 2. to solve a dispute; to solve a problem (50:88)

-- aol, soq'aol -- to do morning work

aolsuq suq to neglect one's duty

aol suv skillful at doing something

aol ssiq dav to be going on (26:16)

aolsso to need (26:26 - 'where revolutionary work was needed, there he went')

aoltavq cooperation (50:71)

aoltavq tavq to unite in a project (50:106)

aoltavq tavq e qilniq a joint company or enterprise (B=Chi) (50:71)

aoltavq zaq to work cooperatively (50:71)

aolteiv teiv to hit a spinning top on its side with another top that is spinning (cah˯ ti^-eu)

aol xa to continue

aol xa heil 1. to carry out (a task); 2. to continue (a task) (46:78)

-- aolyal, aolduq -- position; front

aol yoq to surpass (dzeh˯-eu)

aol zaq 1. to work and make a living at it, 2. to manage; to run something (50:91) (m˅ dza˯-eu)

aol zaq haol leev management and administration

(50:91)

aol zaq hovq dol to work for a living (3:cover) (mˇ dzaˬ k'aw‸ dawˇ-eu)

-- aolzaq, hhellavq -- to trade for a living

aolzaq milcaq area under cultivation (50:59)

aolzaqssaq farmers; peasants (11:93) (yaˇ mˇ zaˬ)

aolzaq ssaqyo working people; farming men

-- aolzaq, xal -- to farm; plant fields for a living

-- aolzaq, zal'eel -- to dip meat into a bowl of spicy condiment before eating

aolzei wooden top (for spinning) (cahˬ)

aolzei gaol to spin wooden tops (46:90) (cahˬ biˬ-eu)

aolzei leel to wind up (as to wind up a top to spin it)

aolzei puv for a top to turn (**Huvqlavq aolzei puv maq ceil meil kol.** Years and months went by faster than a turning top. 14:218)

aolzei teiv to play games with wooden tops (cahˬ ti^-eu; cahˬ biˬ-eu)

aolzei zeissaq tev aqmeil 'like a spinning top' (that is, for a person to roam everywhere)

aol zeiq pyuq overtime pay (50:81)

aol zo used to do

Ao

ao interjection (oh!) (11:210)

Aoq

aoq heaven; sky (9:6) (mˬ)

aoq yes (consenting); all right; okay (mˬ; euˬ)

aoq oh! (9:6)

aoq to hold in mouth (9:6) (or) **kovq** (mymˇ-eu)

aoq to sell (9:6) (ahˬ-eu)

aoq aol maq bi hav to keep away drought (50:48)

aoq aoqdaoq horizon ('bottom of the sky' (11:133) (cf. **aoqdaoq aoqzeil**) (mˬ dzeˇ)

aoqbei mil bei huvqlavq the 'golden age' (right after creation all beings lived together in peace)

aoqbia bia sun to rise (9:6) (uˬ bya bya-eu)

aoqbia bia to taq when the sun came up (26:37, 45:61, 50:52) (nahˇ ma do^ laˇ ngeh)

aoq biajul early morning (or) **aoqsoq soq to**

aoqbia to pyu at dawn; when it gets light (uˬ bya laˇ-eu)

aoqboq aqma a tadpole (or) **hoqbioq aqma**

aoqcal sunshine (sun's rays) (46:131, 50:143) (uˬ tsaˇ)

aoqcal calhav hot sunshine (10:6) (uˬ tsaˇ k'a^-eu)

aoqcal calseil laol to get warm in the sun (uˬ tsaˇ

law^ lm^v-eu)

aoqcal calziil twilight

aoqcal cuvq for the sun to shine (nah^v ma tseh_v-eu)

aoqcal tei the sun's rays shine (u_v tsa^v tso^-eu)

aoqcal tei pyu the sunny side

aoq caoq mil caoq 'nets above, snares below' (tight encirclement, as with problems)

aoq ceivq low temperature (50:134)

aoqceivq xa yi for the weather to cool off

aoqcil aol qivq to work all day

aoqcil qivq nei the whole day; all day (38:1, 45:72) (nah lah ni)

aoqcyuq cyuq overcast sky (9:6, 11:205) (m_v zah^v-eu)

aoqdaoq aoqzeil the horizon; as far as one can see ('bottom and side of the sky') (4:32, 14:171) (mya^ haw ti_v haw)

aoqdaoq mildaoq puv la nei everywhere in the world (mi^v k'ah_v k'ah_v lah ni)

aoq daoq mil zeil the ends of the earth; the remotest corners of the eath (m_v dze^v mi^v dze^v)

aoqdeivq mildeivq deivq e the creation of heaven and earth (14:183) (m_v beh mi^v beh beh-eu_v)

aoq duv to make a profit (or) **piul aoq duv** (57:120)

aoq gee mil gee land and sky to be very dry (30:2)

aoq gee zaol gee drought ('sky dried up') (35:28)

aoq he nei as big as the sky (26:45 - hev nei) (m_v hui ni)

aoq hul'a all over the world (or) **milcaq hultav** (mi^v tsa_v k'oe^v ta^ doe ni)

-- **aoq, hhaq** -- 'strength which is sold) (i.e., a wage)

-- **aoq, hhaq'aoq** -- to 'sell strength' (to work for a wage)

aoqhhaq hhel to hire ('buy') labor (50:64)

aoqhhaq quqsiq nei coolish (not hot or cold) (10:7)

aoqhhaq siq yaol 1. a cool place; 2. a thatched house (50:107)

aoqhhaol hav to be dry

aoq hhel galquv knowledge of trading (50:147)

aoq hhel kaqlaq the relationship between supply and demand (50:60)

aoq hhel naqgaq trading information (50:147)

aoq hhel zalsiq xaduq a farm of commodity crops (50:146)

aoqjiq aqbol the thunder god (45:43)

aoqjiq aoqlu 1. thunder, 2. a noise like thunder

aoqjiq aoqmiaovq hha nei thunder and lightening

aoqjiq aoqsseil a storm with thunder and rain (m_v je_v ja_v leh^v k'a^-eu)

aoqsseil baoq ya baoq ya meil sseil yi rain to pour down

aoqjiq coqceiv ceiv strong thunder and lightning

(m˯ je˯ tsaw˯ teh^ teh^-eu)

aoqjiq duq nei thunder to roll (30:2)

aoqjiq jiq to thunder (9:7) (m˯ je˯ je˯-eu)

aoqjiq jiqhav thunder without rain (u˯ yehˇ ma˯ pi m˯ je˯)

aoqjiq jiqteiv teiv to thunder and lightning (m˯ je˯ m˯ teh^ teh^-eu)

aoqkaq milkaq the horizon (50:35)

aoqkul ba'la dry season

aoqkul kul to have a drought (yaw gui gui-eu)

aoqkul kulma kul to have a severe drought

aoq kul mil kul drought (46:114)

aoq kuv mil kuv drought

aoq laol high temperature (50:134)

aoq lavqhhuvq a in the world (34:18) (miˇ k'ah˯ la˰ k'oeˇ)

aoq lavqhhuvq e col all people in the world ('under the sky') (34:12) (miˇ tsa˯ za˯ daw˯ taw^ lu˰)

aoqlaol ba'la summer; hot season (10:7), **sseilzyuq ba'la** (jawˇ la yam˯)

aoqlu millu lu earthquake ('heaven/earthquake') (miˇ lu^ lu^-eu)

aoqma the great heaven; the great sky (34:8)

aoqma siilkav peiqtaoq a golden comb sent down from God (**Aqpyuq Miqyeil**) to help a woman who cannot deliver a baby

aoqmiq a corner ('tail') of the sky (**Haqjil maq saq aoqmiq maq hhao.** If a man is not unhappy he will not roam the earth (i.e. to the corner of the sky) (18:17)

aoqmiaovq miaovq lightning to strike (m˯ myaw˰ myaw˰-eu)

aoq nav mil nav meil sky and land turn black (as in a bad storm) (30:2, 46:147) (m˯ miˇ zahˇ-iˇ-eu)

aoqnao daytime; in the day (12:127, 13:46, 26:82) (nah g'ahˇ)

aoqnao naohhaol at noon (14:188) (nah lo^ ceh laˇ-eu, and cf.: nah g'ahˇ ceh laˇ-eu)

aoq naoq hhel miaq supply falls short of demand; demand exceeds the supply (50:60)

aoqnee daytime

aoqnil red glow of sunset

aoq nil mil nil reddish everywhere (46:155)

aoqniv milniv niv for there to be an earthquake (57:97)

aoq pav half of a day (nah k'oe^)

aoqpeel blue sky

aoqpiul salziq ziqssaq a type of spirit living in the sky that takes souls

aoq puv mil pal 'sky turns, earth changes' (nothing

is permanent, all is changing) (m˯ paˇ miˇ paˇ-eu)

aoq puv mil puv earth-shaking; world-shaking

aoqpuv milpuv puv lots of changes take place ('the sky and earth turn') (11:45)

aoqpuv puvzaq to sell something again

aoqqaol a swan (46:117)

aoq qiq haoq laqhhuv everywhere ('under one sky')

aoqqivq night; dusk (9:7) (u˯ ci˰)

aoqqivq naohhaol meil day and night (u˯ ci˰ nah g'ahˇ)

aoqqivq pyu evening time (11:38) (u˯ ci˰ taw)

aoqqivq qivq late at night (9:7) (u˯ ci˰ ci˰-eu)

aoqqivq qivq lal to be getting dark

aoqqivq qivqto pyu dusk to be approaching (u˯ ci˰ ci˰ le)

aoq qivq yil it's getting dark

aoqsal sal good sky; nice weather (9:7, 26:75) (m˯ mui˯-eu; m˯ yaw law˯)

aoqsal milsal bright, clear day (11:22) (m˯ yaw shawˇ)

aoqsiq siqdaol a cool place (k'awˇ dmˇ)

aoqsoq morning (u˯ shaw˯) clf. **soq** (shaw˯)

aqsoq laqpeiv dol drink morning tea (have breakfast)

aoqsoq navq e col one who gets up early

-- aoqsoq, neesoq -- tomorrow morning

aoq soqpaq lord of heaven

aoqsoq soqlu middle of the morning (35:72)

aoqsoq soqto early morning (or) **aoq biajul**

aoqssaol pillar of the sky

aoqsseil rain (9:7) (u˯ yehˇ)

aoqsseil diq sso to be caught in the rain; for the rain to beat down on one

aoqsseil seq to bring with rain; to come with rain (14:153)

aoqsseil sseil to rain (9:7) (u˯ yehˇ yehˇ-eu)

aoqsseil sseil nao a rainy day (or) **saq e huvqlavq**

aoqsseil sseilma rain to pour down (u˯ yehˇ yehˇ le-eu)

aoqsseil sseilsav sav to drizzle (not a heavy rain, but steady) (11:196) (u˯ yehˇ ma˯ k'a^-a)

aoqsseil sseilseq a type of spirit which is included in the ceremony to drive out the "**ngeeq**" spirit

aoqsseil sseilziivq ziivqma large drops of rain (11:36) (u˯ yehˇ aˇ jui˰ jui˰ ma)

aoq ssol milcaq heaven and earth (8:28, 29, 30) (m˯ hawˇ-eu miˇ)

aoq ssol milcaq haoqbaoq everywhere in the world, in the universe (26:56, 112) (lit. 'in sky and earth' - 46:119)

aoqtav sky; heaven (13:21, 46:130) (m˯ ta^)
aoqtav laolqaol high above the sky (13:40)
aoqtav laolqaol saq suffer an airplane crash (50:98)
aoqtav Molmil god of the sky (38:90)
aoqtaoq miltaoq to become lawless (50:180)
aoqto milzeil in every corner of the world

aoq ya all right; okay (45:32)
-- **aoqyaol, soqhhaq** -- a book store (50:157)

aoq zaq 1. make living by selling (13:38), 2. to sell one's properties (50:13) (ah˯ dza˯-eu)
aoqzaq aol bia night and day; around the clock (50:143) (or) **naocil aollivq**
aoqzaq bia nei overnight (u˯ ci˄ ti˯ miˇ)
-- **aoqzaq, daoqkaoq** -- a prostitute
aoq zaq e daoqma logs for selling; commodity logs (50:146)
aoq zaq e zalsiq food to sell (esp. grains) (50:113)
aoqzeil 'side of the sky' (in the sentence 'the sky has no limit') (11:133) (m˯ dzeˇ)
-- **aoqzeil, aoqjiq** -- a storm
aoqzeil leilto the far edges of the sky (34:7) (m˯ dzeˇ miˇ dzeˇ)
aoqzyuq 'rulers of the sky' (30:2)

BA

bal to attend a festive activity (wedding etc.)
bal (in) **sullal bal** for one's soul to leave the body (thus becoming sick) (suˇ laˇ baˇ-eu)
bal a group; a class (Chi) (26:101)
=bal, aq= a shadow
balbal nei on purpose; for the purpose of (11:25, 114, 26:41)
balceil a bus that travels between towns and cities (not simply within a town) (Chi) (41:156)
balfaq (see: **baffaq** a method; an idea 14:145)
-- bal, Galtaol -- to celebrate the Hani New Year
balhov chaff (outer layer of grain) (or) **alhov**
balhaol to help (A=Chi) (9:15, 10:pref., 11:128, 169) (or) **aolhaol** (caw ba-eu)
balhhaq a shadow (14:173) (baˇ laˇ)
-- balhhaq, albal -- culm sheath (parchment-like outer membrane of golden bamboo)
baljoq nei the whole group (26:114)
ballal for; on behalf of (**no ballal** = for you, on your behalf - 11:200) (g'aˇ duˬ)
ballal nei to some purpose (9:15, 38:7) (see also: **bal nei**)
=bal, lavq= to hinder
ballul (see: **biallul** = catfish) (14:138)
balluvq tob. pipe (both men & women) (46:176) (or) **yahyuq balluvq** (gawˇ luˬ; gawˇ tsui˰)
bal nei for (as, for the people of the border area) (10:pref.); in order to (13:3); for the sake of (see also: **ballal nei**) (see for samples: 11:120)
=bal nei, bal= purposely
balsal to play (not pf.) (niˇ g'a-eu)
-- bal, seilhha -- play with
-- bal, sullal -- for one's soul to leave the body, thus becoming sick
balza group leader; monitor (Chi) (26:42, 50:5)
balzii 1. screwdriver (Chi) (26:29), 2. leading body (Chi) (34:103)

ba clf. for a group (**ssaqguq qiq ba** = a group of children) (11:77, 198, 27:11, 45:45) (aˇ ma˰; baˬ ma˰)
ba light in color; white (yaw ba)
=ba, al= older sister
baba nei very white (11:57) (ba coˬ ni)
=ba, baq= cheek
bacal to be impatient (or) **neema cal; neema teiq; neema maq yeil nia**
badiq an echo (ba so)
badu basket for measuring grain
-- badu, moqceil -- horse-feed bag

bahaol to assist ; help (caw ba)
=ba, heiq= 1. a blackboard; chalkboard, 2. a tree with white nuts
bahuaf a painting (as on a canvas or board) (Chi) (50:5)
=ba, hhoq= white cabbage
bahhul a wind instrument (Chi), called in Hani: **gaoqbil** (9:18)
bahhuq to hold; grasp (Chi) (34:91) (nyeh˰-eu)
bahhuq nei white; cream-colored (46:155) (yaw ba)
bakaq a riddle (4:title, 11:178) (tsa˯ dzo^)
  bakaq caq to guess a riddle (11:178) (tsa˯ dzo^ tsa˯-eu)
ba'la 1. moon, 2. month (ba la)
  ba'la aqzeiq a leap month
  ba'la aoqcal moonlight (14:164) (ba la u˯ tsaˇ)
  ba'la beeljoq a lunar halo
  ba'la ceiqkol early in the lunar month
  ba'la deivq sil aol e to start and end a month (46:83)
  ba'la heeq a long month (31 days)
  -- ba'la, hhulduv -- spring season
  ba'la laceiv end of the lunar month
  ba'la ladav early in lunar month
  ba'la ladaoq del a popular rhyme
  ba'la lahhaol middle of the lunar month
  ba'la la'luv full moon (14:140)
  ba'la neivqkeeq zaq lunar eclipse (50:203) (lit., 'spirit dog eats moon', from a legend) (ba la la kui˯ dza˯-eu)
  ba'la nil a short month (30 days or less)
  ba'la wuqcal seil to play in the moonlight
-- banei, wuqduq -- with white hair

baziq blacksmith (ba ji˯; ba^ ji˯)

baq direction
baq thin (9:16) (yaw ba˯)
baq classifier for 1. the side of a mountain, 2. a page in a book (**soqhhaq qiq baq**)
baqba cheek (9:16) (ba˯ ba)
baqbeiv gill of fish (nga˯ nga^)
-- baqbeiv, ngaqsaq -- gill of fish
-- baqcevq, toma -- a kind of sword
baqcul cul to kiss on the face
-- baqdaq, eelju -- (see full)
baqdel small stool (Chi) (9:16, 10:30, 11:30) (k'aw˯ bo^, nuiˇ gaw˯)
baqdiq diq a slippery and steep mountain
=baq gaq, naq= to hear from
baqgeel facial skin (9:16)
=baq, Haqniq lal= Hani songs
baqhe to get the odor of liquor (11:137) (**zilbaq baqhe naol lal ya** = I get the smell of liquor)
baqhovq a dimple (9:16) (ba˯ ba ba˯ k'aw˰)

=baq, hu= squirrel
=baq, hhu= a door frame
baqhhyul to fall in love with
  baqhhyul aqzil love songs
  baqhhyul hhyul zaq to talk about love matters (46:89)
baqjiq jiq (see: **baqdiq diq** = very slippery and steep) (14:168) (cf.: yaw juˇ)
baqjol jol to be in love
baqka very thin (11:18) (ba˯ lehˇ ni)
baqka kassaq very, very thin (11:58)
baqkyul cheekbone; malar bone (9:16)
=baq, lal= folksong; ballad
=baq, lol= river
baqlu puffed out cheeks (ba˯ ba mˇ pu˯-eu)
baqlu baqlu meil zaq to eat with cheeks puffed out
  baqlu baqlu nei to eat big mouthfuls (with cheeks bulging - 38:2)
  baqlu deiq cheeks puffed out (from eating a lot) (26:85)
  baqlu teiv to eat whole and quickly (as small fruits, nuts)
Baqlufjil Eighth Route Army (Chi)
baqma big river (9:16, 13:47) (lawˇ ba˯)
baqmeeq a lover
=baq, nia= north side of a river
baqpov diq to slap someone in the face with the palm of the hand (ba˯ ba-ahˇ teh^-eu)
baqpuq a protruding face
baqqeil distiller's grains (9:16) (jiˇ ba˯ jiˇ peh^)
-- baqqeil, zilbaq -- distiller's grains
baqsal love matters; a love affair
  baqsal aqzil a love song
  baqsal sal to look for a lover (46:89) (za˯ k'a˯ po^-eu)
  baqsal zol for a young man to learn to talk about love matters
baqseil whiskers (side) (9:16) (ba˯ sheh^)
baqsiq a pimple (nui leh)
baqsov nei very thin (9:16) (ba˯ lehˇ ni)
baqtevq a mark on one's face (maˇ jaw˰)
baqxoq mandible; jaw (genl.) (ba˯ ngeuˇ)
baq zei to throw away (35:73); **bavq zei** (pf.) (bi˯ dzeh-eu)
-- baq, zeiqhhaq -- 1. very little capital (as money and property), 2. weak souls of animals
baqzuvq a wrinkle (46:164) (yaw ju˰)

(vb) bav make a mistake (vb) (**aol bav** = to do something wrong; **eil bav** = to say something wrong; **nyuq bav** = to think something wrong, etc.) (50:20) **coqwuf** (Chi) ((vb) bah˯, (vb) leh˯-eu)
bavdoq wrong sentence (50:15)
=bav, hoq= box; case
-- bav, lav -- 1. to hinder; disturb; 2. make a

mistake
-- **bav lav nei, bil lil** -- uncertain; incoherently
=**bav, laol**= collar
bavlov a bedroom (or) **yiuvq duq; lovkaq**
-- **bav, maq** -- (see full)
-- **bav, nyuq** -- 1. to think wrongly, 2. to misunderstand
=**bav, peilhaoq laol**= a fur collar
-- **bav, qo** -- 1. to lead astray, 2. to incorrectly hand on a message
-- **bav, zaol** -- to make a mistake

bavq 1. to take (9:17), 2. to carry on shoulder (1. yuˇ-eu, 2. ba˰-eu)
bavq al la to bring something up with you (yuˇ da^ la˰-eu)
bavq al li to go up and take something away
bavq al yi to bring down; to take down (yuˇ ka le˰-eu)
-- **bavq, aqhhyu paoqciivq** -- to kneel to the maternal uncles as they come to a funeral
-- **bavq, baolbavq** -- to build terraces in an irrigated field
bavqbuvq freckle (nm˰ si˯ nm˰ shaˇ)
bavqbuvq bavqciv a dirty face (mya^ pyaw˯ yaw jaw˰)
bavqbuvq leiqbuvq for one's face to be covered with dust
bavq cavq 1. to come to help, 2. to connect parts together
bavq caoq to cover over (35:3)
bavq cei 1. to hold up; raise up (9:17, 11:28, 41:62, 45:59, 46:119) (ci˯-eu), 2. to get up (tuˇ laˇ-eu)
-- **bavq cei, aqlavq** -- to raise one's hand
-- **bavqciv, bavqbuvq** -- a dirty face
bavq cuvq 1. to set up (as a ladder), 2. to build a bridge of wood or bamboo
bavqdaq a pad
bavq daol to place a table in preparation for a meal
=**bavq diqkovq, laq**= (see full)
bavqdov to put in (daw^-eu, daw^ ahˇ-eu)
-- **bavq dov, alzaol a** -- to put corpse in coffin
bavqdul a shoulder pole (9:17)
bavq duq to bury someone (du˯ pah˯-eu)
bavq duv to take out (yuˇ do^-eu, ba˰ do^-eu)
bavq gaoq to make a pile of something (35:96) (bymˇ-eu)
bavq goq to raise; heighten; hold up high (50:56)
bavqhav a large basket (or) **havkal**
bavq hel to offer; make an offering (50:52)
bavq heil to send to someone (as money etc.) (26:76)
bavq huvq 1. to take back, 2. to withdraw (as money from a bank)
bavq huvq al la to fetch something
bavq hha to receive
bavq hhuvq to revoke; to withdraw (50:38)

bavq kaq 1. to cure a disease (by drugs), 2. to cover something over (deh˯ ka˯-eu)
bavq kavq to embrace; to cling closely; **bavq quvq** (byaˇ cu˰-eu)
bavq kevq to mix with (9:17) (la^ keu˯-eu)
bavq lal come and take away (11:47) (yuˇ dzeh laˇ-eu)
bavqlavq bavqzaol zaol to be shoulder-to-shoulder (or) **bavqzaol zaol**
bavq laol 1. to make something warm (41:158) (la^ lahˇ-eu), 2. to inspire; hearten (50:63)
bavq laoq to add up; to add onto; put something more in (46:82) (la^ lah˯-eu)
bavq leev to put away; conceal
bavq li to take up; to bring up (ba˰ da^-eu)
bavqlivseq molar tooth; wisdom tooth (9:17) (seu˯ ma ba˰li)
bavqmieiq a plowing rope
bavqmoq miq to take something and face it in a different direction (35:60)
-- **bavq, moqseiq** -- to raise the hoof of a horse for cutting the hoof and shoeing it
bavq pal to exchange (9:17) (paˇ-eu)
bavq pao to open up a cover (ba˰ pah-eu)
bavq paoq 1. to get together; to put together (as people getting together to work on a project - 26:107), 2. to mix; combine (34:27) (ui˯ laˇ-eu)
bavqpia flag (6:185) (paˇ lo˯ paˇ lehˇ)
bavq puv to turn over; to overthrow (34:49) (ba˰ pyawˇ-eu)
bavq pyul to take something over there (ba˰ g'eh-eu)
bavq pyul lal to come and take something away (ba˰ la˯ laˇ-eu)
bavq pyul la to bring something to this side
bavq pyul yil to go to that side (lower) and bring something to this side (higher)
bavq pyul yi to bring something to this side (lower)
bavq pyuq to praise (ja ceu˯-eu, ci˯ poe˯-eu)
bavq qeiv to compare (41:94), to contrast (as color, shape etc.) (yuˇ ceh^ haw-eu)
-- **bavq qeiv, taoqdav** -- to rub from foot to head of a sick person in a spirit driving ceremony
-- **bavq qeiv, taoqtyuq** -- to rub from head to foot on a sick person in a spirit driving ceremony
bavq qu to take care of; to look after (35:52) (cu-eu)
bavq quvq to embrace tightly (or) **bavq kavq** (byaˇ cu˰-eu) (9:17)
bavq sa to send out; send to another place (26:79 = bavq sa) (k'ehˇ g'eh-eu)
bavq seiq to water (as flowers, etc.) (9:17) (iˇ cu˰ sheh˯-eu)
-- **bavqssaq, cyuqssaq** -- poor people
bavq ssaoq to collect together (9:17, 26:75) (la^

ui⌄)
bavq taq to place; to put (9:17) (ta⌄-eu, (vb) ta⌄-eu)
bavq taq huvq to replace
bavqtavq shoulder (6:170) (ba‸ pu)
bavq tao mix in (as soup); put in (10:10)
-- bavq tao, alzaol a -- to put into coffin
=bavq taoq, lavq= to butt heads (as buffaloes)
bavq teiq to hold; get hold of (9:17) (nyeh‸ teh⌄-eu)
bavqteiv a slap (**bavqteiv qiq lavq bi diq** = to give a slap) (46:151) (teh^-eu)
bavqteiv qiq lavq bi diq to give someone a slap (46:151) (ba⌄ ba-ah˅ teh^-eu)
bavqteivq a narrow space on a window or fireplace (14:171)
bavq tul to lift up; to raise up one's head
bavq xa 1. to send down (to lower place, or south) (26:81), 2. to tear down (take apart something, as machinery - 26:33)
bavqyaol 1. palanquin in which to carry officials (11:27), 2. a pack saddle (11:149) (mah⌄ k'a^ da⌄)
bavq yil to go down and bring back up
-- bavq yoq, alzaol -- for the coffin to be lifted over kneeling children and grandchildren before being taken for burial
bavq zavq 1. to do something for a living, 2. to catch and kill something (esp. when one animal kills another -- 35:111)
bavqzaol zaol to be shoulder-to-shoulder (or) **bavqlavq bavqzaol zaol**
bavq zei 1. to throw away (**miqbev bavq zei** = to throw one's gun away), 2. abandon (ba‸ dzeh-eu)
bavq zil zaq to talk and exchange ideas (50:95)
bavq zyuq 1. to choose a ruler (35:49), 2. to support a ruler, 3. to set up (as a company; organization) (50:23), 4. to feed a queen bee

baf to manage (Chi) (26:77)
bafdaofti 1. semi-conductor (Chi) (50:5), 2. radio (old Chi)
baffaq a method; way (Chi) (50:5) (**baffaq maq jav** - there is no method) (9:14)
bafgaolsiiq office (Chi) (9:15, 11:11, 26:51)
Bafpol (place name, district close to Vietnam) (Chi)
bafqeq baseball (Chi) (50:6)
baf ziiqmiqdif baf faoljeif seifhyuf semi-colonial and semi-feudal society (Chi) (50:5)

BAO

baol 1. clf. for a share (9:15) (**Xilmeil nei hhaqhav qiq baol bo e miqnieiq aqzeiq qiq baol aol.** Thus I have shared my strength to do an extra share. 26:68), 2. clf. for a part or share (**Qiq huvq halmiav baol jav?** Into how many parts can a year

be divided? 41:119) (bi˅ pa^-eu)
=baol, al= grasshopper
baolbavq bavq to build terraces in an irrigated field (deh bah˅ = a dike/bund)
baolca a contract for a fixed output (Chi) (41:24)
baolca daofhuf 1. to fix farm output quotas for each household (Chi) (41:24), 2. private production (50:6)
baolcevq cevq to cut away with hoes and then build up mud on the dikes (bunds) of a terrace
=baol, ceil= a rice stack
-- baolciivq, xaldei -- steps between terraces in irrigated rice fields
=baol, dal= bund of earth in a terraced field
baolhhyuq to surround (Chi) (or) **luvqhhao** (**baolhhyuq** ceiqsiif = to surround cities (AB=Chi - 34:6)
-- baol, jeibaol -- a bonfire to burn
-- baol, kavbaol -- to harrow a field into piles
baollaol aol take care of everything concerning a job; take everything on oneself (50:6)
baollaol aolpal take on what ought to be done by others (50:6)
baollaol laq e milyal private fields (50:6)
=baol, luq= a tomb
baolnaoq naoq to stamp (with foot) on dikes of a terraced field (naw˯ teu˅-eu)
baol pav half a share (11:67) (ti˯ pa^)
baoltavq the lap (baw˅ k'ah˅)
baolsov sov to smooth the dikes of terraced fields with a hoe
baoltal tal to cut down an old dike (bund) in an irrigated field and build a new one in its place
baolteiv teiv to pat new mud on the dikes (bunds) of a terraced field with a hoe
baolzii steamed dumpling with pork (Chi) (41:168)

baoguei hhyuyeiq a treasurer (Chi)
baohhyuq (see: **baolhhyuq**)
baojeifzaf public health clinic (Chi) (50:7)
=bao, lao= a swamp; a pond
-- bao, laobao -- to be muddy (yaw pyeh^)
bao'lyu fort; stronghold (Chi) (34:86) (lah˅)
baoma stomach (9:15, 46:166) (baw ma)
baomu a baby sitter (Chi) (50:7) (or) **aqnil toqssaq**
=bao nei, qeil= sourly
-- bao, qiqbao -- unite as one
baose conservative (as in policy) (Chi) (50:7)
baosiiq a diamond (Chi) (50:6)
baowua (see: **baowuei**) (26:118)
baowuei a treasure bowl (Chi)
baoxei to ensure; guarantee (Chi) (or) **baozaf** (Chi) (ka˯ hm˯-eu)
baoya to protect (Chi) (26:119)
baozaq to bet (A=Chi) (da˯-eu)
baozaf to ensure; guarantee (Chi) (34:40) (or) **baoxei**

(Chi) (la^ ma˅-eu)

baozeif 1. to be sure (9:16), 2. pledge (34:38) (Chi) (la˯ ma˯ baw-eu)

baoq to wear (as gloves, socks, etc.) (9:15) (dm-eu)

baoq a wooden container used to measure rice or other grains (k'a^ pu˯)

baoq clf. for: 1. hollow things, such as; bee hive, rice steamer, etc. (bah˯), 2. a measure = about 5 kg (9:15, 11:79)

baoqma = big size, **baoqssaq** = small size

baoq clf. for rain

=**baoq, biaq**= a beehive

-- **baoq, civqbaoq** -- to have a bad temper

baoqdel a bamboo water pipe for smoking tobacco (shoi˯ yoi baw˯ law)

baoq du taoq for a spirit priest (**moqpil**) to beat a bamboo section on a stone to show the dead person he/she is truly dead

=**baoq, eel**= bamboo water container

baoqgeel ancestral altar (tray of bamboo) (a˯ poe˯ paw˄ law˄)

-- **baoqgeel, aqpyuq** -- ancestral altar (shelf of bamboo)

baoqgeel cuv to erect an altar (either ancestral in the home, or for some deity in the jungle)

=**baoq, haoq**= hole in a tree

-- **baoq, haoqbaoq** -- to be hollow (as trees)

-- **baoq, hhobaoq** -- for rice stems to develop

=**baoq, hhovq**= needle case

=**baoq, ja**= fish box of bamboo

=**baoq, juldal dal**= chopstick holder

=**baoq, juq**= 1. waist, 2. weaver's shuttle

=**baoq, kaoq**= throat

baoqkev box; trunk (9:15) (bah˯ keu^, baw˯ keu^ = CA)

baoqkev kevssaq a small box; trunk

-- **baoqkev, saqgeel** -- a leather case

baoqkev xoq lock for a box (9:15)

=**baoq, keel**= women's leggings

=**baoq, laq**= sleeve

=**baoq, lavq**= a glove (la˄ bah˯)

baoqlo a section of bamboo used for various things (or) **boqlo**

-- **baoqlo, aqhyuq** -- bamboo water pipe for smoking

-- **baoqlo, haqbol** -- a bamboo tube in which water flows

baoqlo lokuv a container made of dried bamboo

-- **baoqlo, yahyuq** -- a bamboo water pipe for smoking

baoqma a big wooden measuring box

=**baoq, meiq**= mouth; snout

=**baoq, nal**= 1. the bridge of nose, 2. a pig snout

=**baoq, naov**= stockings

-- **baoq, naovbaoq** -- to wear stockings

baoqssaq a small wooden measuring box

=**baoq, taoq=** a wooden pail
baoqtevq a bamboo container (9:16) (baw⌄ law)

baovlao laoqyev a king in a kingdom (35:86)

=**baovq nei, xao=** heavily

baofceq to get revenge (Chi) (26:15)
baoffaq huf 1. a person who got rich quick, 2. an upstart (Chi) (50:8)
baofgaof a report of the situation (Chi) (57:156)
baofgaof soqdoq to make a report (on literature, crime, etc.) ('A=Chi) (50:8)
baofgaof soqhhaq a written report (A=Chi)
baofkao to register to take an examination (Chi) (50:8)
baofluaf (see: **baoflueil**) (Chi) (34:50)
baoflueif a riot; rebellion (Chi)
baofseif a newspaper office (Chi) (50:8)
baofzii newspaper (Chi) (9:15, 26:44, 41:78, 50:8)

BE

bel diligent; industrious (14:215) (yaw bym; yaw biˇ)
bel to wake up; recover (46:93) (beuˇ laˇ-eu)
-- **bel, keellavq** -- very active; diligent
Belniaq the name of a widow in a fairy tale (46:128)
beltav nei to be clear-headed (46:162)
belzav nei to be diligent (9:20)
=**bel, ziivq=** to shake one's head in order to wake up

beq to scoop out; dip out (9:20) (beu⌄-eu)
beq to be rich (smˇ mui⌄ mui⌄-eu)
=**beq, aq=** a mute person; a foolish person
-- **beq, aqbeq** -- to be foolish (or mute)
beq dav 1. to become rich (smˇ mui⌄ mui⌄ laˇ-eu), 2. to dig up; to pick up (46:97)
-- **beq, loqbeq** -- to become rich; wealthy
-- **beq, maq** -- does not matter; no matter
Beqna Lolbaq Tengtiaojiang River
Beqna Lolma the Tengtiao River, **Beqna Lolma** river (14:144)
Beq Quq'eil Dr. Bethune (Canadian doctor, Chi)
beqsiil skill; ability (Chi) (57:title)
beqtul tul to become rich very quickly (50:113)

bev 1. to play a stringed instrument, 2. to shoot (as a gun or crossbow), 3. to fluff cotton (9:20), 4. to throw (1. di⌄-eu, 2. & 3. beu^-eu, 4. bi⌄-eu)
bev cuv to shoot and stick in (as an arrow)
bevdaoq stock of a gun (mi⌄ beu^ taw^ k'aw^)
bev duv 1. to fire (as a gun), 2. to launch (as a missle) (50:44)
-- **bev, hha** -- to shoot game

=bev, kaol= the line in a carpenter's ink marker
-- bev, laqheq -- to play a three-stringed instrument (or) **laqhev bev**
bev leiq to shoot and miss the target
=bev, miq= gun; rifle
=bev, ngaq= bamboo bow with which to shoot fish
-- bev, pavqcavq -- 1. to shoot at; to aim at, 2. to sentence to death by a firing squad
bevsaol gun barrel
bev sil shoot to death (11:161) (beu^ seh‸-eu)
bev sso to shoot and hit (9:150) (beu^ zaw-eu)
bev tov 1. to execute by shooting (50:135), 2. to shoot to death
bev xa to shoot down (8:18) (beu^ co˯-eu)
bev yoq to throw over something (as over a river)
bevyyuq cotton fluffer (9:20) (sa˯ beu^)
bev zavq to go hunting ('hunt-shoot') (11:218) (sha˯ beh-eu; sha˯ beu^-eu)
bevzao zao an instrumental ensemble

BEE

beel poetic term for 'sun' (or) **beelma**
beel to boil (9:18) (buiˇ-eu; pu‸-eu)
beelduv heiq east (9:18) (do^ k'eh˯ paw)
  beelduv pyu east (6:161, 13:32) (do^ k'eh˯ paw)
-- beel, eelbeel -- for water to boil
beeljoq 1. loops and whorls on fingers (as seen in a person's fingerprints), 2. a halo around the sun or moon
-- beeljoq, ba'la -- lunar halo
-- beeljoq joq, naolma -- for red ring to form around sun (9:117)
beelkaq umbrella (9:18, 11:14) (buiˇ ka˯)
  beelkaq huv to hold up an umbrella (9:18) (buiˇ ka˯ k'o^-eu)
  beelkaq kaqpiul a white umbrella (46:172) (buiˇ ka˯ ka˯ pyuˇ)
  beelkaq piq to shut an umbrella
  beelkaq tuv piei to open an umbrella
beelkeel rays of the sun (or) **naolma beelkeel** (14:199)
beelpaoq a cloth tent (9:18) (sa˯ paˇ seh˯ g'aw^)
beeltav nei diligent (50:137)
beelya pyu west (9:18, 13:32) (ga k'eh˯ paw)

bee a household (13:11) (zaw‸)
=bee, al= quilt (aˇ bui)
beehov a quilt covering (9:18) (bui tuˇ)
  -- beehov, albee -- quilt covering
-- beeja, albee -- old quilt
bee mul to inveigle to come to one's home
beenil a red quilt (46:175) (bui neˇ)
beepavq reed leaves used to wrap glutinous dumplings which are in the shape of a pyramid

beesav measles (15:28), **alsiq aqhaoq seil** (bui sa^)
beesav duv to develop measles (15:28) (bui sa^ sa^-eu)
=bee, sul= the families of others
beeteiq 1. baby-carrying cloth (9:18) (bui teh˯), 2. afterbirth; placenta
beeteiq teiqnav a black carrying cloth for carrying a baby (bui lo˯)
beewul padding or filling for a quilt, jacket
-- beewul, albee -- cotton batting for filling quilts
beewul peilhaoq cotton-padded jacket (26:39)
beexa mosquito net (9:18) (bui ka)
-- bee, yoq -- one's own family
-- bee, yulbee -- to have a wedding party

beeq nest (as for birds); lair (as for wild boars, tigers etc.) (**alzil zilbeeq** = bird nest; **ollol lolbeeq** = snake nest) (bah˯)
beeq 1. to break the law, 2. to be untidy; messy (9:18, 14:171, 50:44)
beeq clf. for a flock of chickens, ducks (11:81); for a litter of pigs
beeqcaoq caoq to ambush (or) **caoqteiq**
beeq (vb) daq (vb) to (vb) something with no purpose (**beeq aol daq aol** = to do something with no purpose; **beeq hu daq hu** = to look with no purpose; **beeq quq daq quq** = to run about wildly, no specific direction) (and see: 46:127, 132)
=beeq, bia= weeds
-- beeq, eelbeeq -- to go swiming
beeq eil daq eil to speak without thinking (ma˯ noe˯ ni ngeh˯-eu)
beeqga nei very untidy (9:18, 45:59), confusion; chaos (50:76)
beeqga pa ga nei very untidy (35:75)
beeqhaq a freckle (nm˯ si˯ nm˯ sha˅)
Beeqhaoq Baihong, a branch of the Hani (46:181)
-- beeq, 10 huvq huvqbeeq -- ten years of civil strife; ten years of internal disorder
=beeq, ja= weeds
-- beeq, joq taoq -- to be foggy
-- beeq, lav -- to disturb; cause disturbance
-- beeq, lavq -- to be deranged
beeq li ga la at sixes and sevens (mixed up); chaotic; disorderly (38:91)
=beeq, miaoq= everything helter-skelter
-- beeq, miaoqbeeq lav -- to make things disorderly
-- beeq, neema -- to be anxious
beeq pieiq daq pieiq meil 1. to herd animals wherever one likes, 2. to put something wherever one likes
=beeq, soq= order; sequence
beeqsu nei to be in disorder
beeq zaq daq zaq zaq to eat simply

-- **beeq, zaol** -- to make trouble

BEI

beil struggle (9:19) (behˇ-eu)
=**beil, al**= umbilical cord
=**beil, aq**= nasal discharge
-- **beil bieiq, alcav** -- to get loose from ropes or chains tied around one
beilcaoq forest; jungle (or) **haoldaol** (bawˇ tsahˬ)
  beilcaoq alsiq wild (uncultivated) fruit
  beilcaoq haqbol wild bamboo (za‸ bawˇ)
  beilcaoq hoqhyuq wild pigeon; turtledove (k'aˬ k'oeˬ)
-- **beil ceiv, alcav** -- to break free from being tied up
-- **beil, civqbaoq** -- 1. to lose one's temper, 2. to have an epileptic seizure
beildul lulcuq rainbow (buˇ deˇ leˇ k'ah; aˇ deˇ leˇ k'ah)
-- **beilgaol, aqbeil** -- liquid nasal discharge
beiljei to open (**miavgeel beiljei** = to open eyes) (26:13) (also: **miavgeel beijei** - 35:35) (mya^ nui^ byeh-eu)
beiljil goiter (or) **beiljil lulpuq** (lawˇ behˇ)
  beiljil lulpuq goiter (or) **beiljil; lulbeil** (lawˇ behˇ)
beiljul a small basket, carried on back (9:19)
beilkuq aqma cuckoo bird; hoopoe bird
  beilkuq hulbu alzil cuckoo bird; hoopoe bird
beil leiq beil sil to struggle (13:14)
beillivq the crop or craw of a bird (behˇ jiˇ)
beillol betel nut (Chi) (9:19) (lu^ pa‸)
  beillol hhyuq to chew betel nut (A=Chi) (11:17) (lu^ pa‸ g'oeˬ-eu)
  beillol hhyuq povq plug of betel after chewing (A=Chi) (11:17)
beillul goiter (5:411) (lawˇ behˇ) (see also: **beiljil**)
=**beil, lul**= goiter
beil movq wants to struggle (13:14) (shaˬ maw‸-eu)
-- **beilniul, aqbeil** -- dense nasal discharge
=**beil, peil**= an apron Hani women wear
-- **beil, sabaoq** -- to lose one's temper
beil sil 1. to be noisy; quarrelsome; **doqlovq** (9:19) (law‸ g'a-eu), 2. to be in one's death throes, 3. to twist and turn violently (as when a pig is tied up) (byehˇ seh‸-eu)
beilsil rattan shoulder bag
beil tul lal to rise suddenly (or) **zei tul lal**
beilyil beillav nei continuously struggling upside down (14:139)

bei a copy (Chi) (11:173)
(vb) **bei** to start; begin (**aol bei** = begin doing)

(9:18) (mˇ beh-eu)
(vb) bei to have (vb) before; to have experienced (9:18, 11:132) ((vb) haw-eu)
beibei to begin; to start (41:74) (beh-eu)
beicaoq wild (not cultivated) (46:117) (see: **beilcaoq** (pf)
=bei, caoq= liver of fowls
beido a tightly woven basket (it is used to carry the stones from the river which are fashioned into the '**milsaol luvcuv**')
bei duv to create something (50:26)
beihhyuf zuyif selfish departmentalism (Chi) (50:10)
beijei to open eyes widely (35:35, 96) (see also: **beiljei**)
beikuq allaq a kind of bird in Hani story (35:115), (or) **bilgu'laq**
beiseiq the natural color (Chi)
beisiif ability; skill (Chi) (9:19, 26:47, 38:35) (or) **beisiiq** (50:10); **beqsiil** (Chi) (nya-eu; bym-eu)
beiyaoq dragon (9:20, 46:119) (bya^ yah˯)
-- bei, yeilbei -- create; establish
beiziiq the essence of something; the nature of something (Chi) (34:91); innate character (50:10)

beiq north (Chi) (6:161) (la‸ ta^ paw)
beiqcal a white vegetable (Chi); Chinese cabbage
-- beiqceil, ssaqbeiq -- the second rice crop
beiqceif a white vegetable (Chi) (9:19)
Beiqcuqdoq language of the Bai people (A=Chi)
Beiqcuqssaq Bai people (A=Chi)
beiqfal north (Chi) (9:19, 26:34) (la‸ ta^ paw)
beiqfaq zafzeil northern expedition (Chi) (34:6)
beiqhoq gaolsiil a department store (Chi) (50:4)
beiqhuafsiil a modern poem (Chi) (50:4)
beiqhuafweiq modern Chinese characters, words (Chi) (50:4)
beiqje wine (Chi) (41:169) (**piqje** = beer) (jiˇ ba˯)
Beiqjil Beijing; Peking (Chi) (9:19, 11:33, 50:94)
Beiq Jilmiq name of a Hani man of the Bai clan (35:53)
Beiqjiq North pole (Chi)
beiqleil Chinese olive (14:145)
beiqleil alsiq fruit from the Chinese olive
beiqqiq a white flag (Chi) (paˇ lo˯ paˇ lehˇ lehˇ pyuˇ)
=beiq, ssaq= rice stubble in the field
beiqssiiqkeiq nalgol whooping cough ('100 days cough') (A=Chi) (10:23) (or) **beiqssiiqkeq** (15:28) (ya ma u˯ tsoe˯ tsoe˯-eu)
beiqyeq asphalt; tar (Chi)
beiq zei to cut away (46:124) (or) **yeiq zei** (deu^ dzeh)

beiv to cut (9:19) (as when clearing field - 11:211)

(tuˇ-eu, myaˬ-eu)
-- **beiv, albeiv** -- for beans to come on the plant
=**beiv, baq**= gill of a fish
beivdaoq the bottom of a basket (14:184)
beivja green bean (9:20) (aˇ beh^)
=**beiv, nee**= green bean
beiv'qeil a kind of sour fruit
-- **beiv, saqbeiv** -- to come down with measles
beivto nei (see: **bieivto nei** = muddy) (14:159)
-- **beiv, xal** -- to cut down trees to make a field

beivq 1.to be blind, 2. vagina (taboo) (9:19) (1. mya^ beh˰ beh˰-eu, 2. aˬ beh˰, awˬ beh˰)
beivq to break; split (peh˰-eu)
=**beivq, aq**= vagina (taboo)
-- **beivq, ceilbao** -- rice to be heading
-- **beivq, coq** -- to break suddenly (as the floor of a house with too many people in it)
-- **beivq, diq** -- hit and break (11:115); break down
beivqhov vulva; labia (taboo) (aˬ beh˰, dawˬ beh˰)
-- **beivq, keelbeivq** -- cracks to develop in skin of foot
beivqlavq to smell bad (beh˰ la˰-eu)
beivqlavq silhe nei filthy with bad smell
=**beivq, miav**= to be blind
-- **beivq, miavbeivq lovq** -- shining brightly enough to blind one
beivqmoq pubic hair (5:1036) (aˬ mahˬ; dawˬ mahˬ)
beivqniuv clitoris (taboo) (or) **beivqziv** (aˬ dziˬ mehˬ laˇ)
beivqqeil something soiled from the vagina (taboo)
beivqsivq menstrual blood (taboo) (aˇ yeh^-eu shiˬ)
beivqsivq duv to menstruate (aˇ yeh^ hehˇ-eu; aˬ shiˬ do^-eu - latter term taboo in Ak.)
beivqziv clitoris (taboo) (or) **beivqniuv** (aˬ dziˬ mehˬ laˇ)

beifmu a bulbous plant of the genus Fritilaria (Chi) (50:9)
beifsil a vest (Chi) (26:61)

BI

bil to divide up; distribute (9:22, 50:50) (biˇ-eu)
bil a type of grass, taller than thatch, that is used to represent a woman pregnant with an illegitimate child
bil clf. for a share (qiq bil = one share) (or) **baol** (41:92)
bil bav lal hhev to be irregular
bilceiv laqbil a flute
bilceiv nei to be horizontal; crossways (as in putting a bag of rice crossways at a person's feet - 11:219)

bil ceiv taq to plan by quota (50:38)
-- **bilduv meil, miavneev** -- protruding eyes
bilduv nei 1. to reveal; show (45:76) (bya˅ haw-eu), 2. to be open; overt; public (50:61), 3. obviously; clearly (50:118)
-- **bil e, miqnieiq** -- to divide up work
=**bil, gal**= a flat road
=**bil, gaoq**= a wind instrument
=**bil, geeq**= flute of brass
bilgu'laq a kind of bird (or) **beikuq allaq**
bil heq 1. to divide; separate (9:22, 38:37), 2. to distinguish (50:138)
bil heq alnei faq dav to punish according to the mistakes (**faq** = Chi) (50:50)
bil hhoq to split; divide; break up (50:50)
bilhhuvq nei to be curved
bilhhuvq laqhhuvq meil to be warped (as wood) (yaw pyaw^)
=**bil, laq**= a type of flute
bil lil bav lav 1. confusion on confusion; 2. incoherently; uncertainly
bil lil biav lav meil brokenly
bil lil hhuvq luvq nei to be bent; not straight (14:168) (yaw ngo˄)
bil lil yovq loq meil leaning to one side (person, pole, building)
billol meil to fall & lean against (9:23)
bilmiq other people (35:19) (old lang.) (a˅ caw˅)
bilmiq ssaqheiq a lover; **ssaqheiq; baqmeeq; milmi ssaqheiq**
=**bil, miav**= tears
bil pav to divide; to separate (50:139) (bi˅ pa^-eu)
bil pav lavqhev a four-stringed plucked musical instrument
bilqei aqma one kind of squirrel
bilqeiq to be askew; aslant (or) **qeiq; yovq**
bilqeiq qeiq to slant
bilqeiq military leadership; military power (Chi) (50:15)
(no.) bil qiq bil one out of (no.) (11:71) (i.e., one out of five, three out of ten, etc.) (**ceil bil qiq bil** = one out of ten)
bilqiqliq ice cream (Chi) (11:17)
bilquq ice hockey (Chi) (50:14)
=**bil, siq**= fragrant tree
bil taq amount divided; shares (50:38)
bilyi object (in a sentence) (Chi)
bilyiq faq military service law (Chi) (50:15)
bilyovq meil crooked (9:23) (or) **hhuvq** (yaw g'o˄)
bil zaq galquv a plan for dividing something (50:50)
-- **bil zaq, xalbaol** -- for a family to divide up their goods and live separately
-- **bil zaq, yovqhhovq** -- divide the family
bilzaf military depot (Chi) (50:15)
bilzuvq meil to be wrinkled; folded (9:23) (yaw ju˄,

kuˬ taw^-i)

bi (vb) to cause to (vb) (**bi dol** = give to drink - 9:20, **soqhhaq bi zol** = had them study - 11:50) (bi dawˇ-eu, bi dzaw-eu, etc.)
bi bucol the defendant; the accused (50:9)
bi caol to be abused (or) **bi yaq** (bi k'ehˬ-eu)
bi dao to clothe someone (bi dm-eu)
bi deivq huvq to bring to life (bi deh^ laˇ-eu)
bi dul a metaphor; analogy; figure of speech
=bi, eel= water spring
bifeil score; points (as the score in a basketball game) (Chi) (41:201)
bigal biscuit (Chi) (41:158)
bi hev to let people know (50:61)
bi hu to show; to demonstrate (or) **zaol hu** (bi haw-eu; bya-eu)
bi hhoq to keep apart (or) **lav hhoq**
bi hhyul to please (13:3)
bi jav to retain (or) **maq bi bial**
bi jeil to drench (or) **jeil duvq**
bi jol pal transferred from place to place (or) **leiq tul** (50:38)
bi'lif proportion (in economic sense) (Chi) (34:38)
bi nyuqgaol to call attention to
bi ngeel maq ngeel to run counter to one's desire; to be the opposite of what one wished
bi qeq to make someone excited (50:55) (or) **neema kev**
biseif to compete in a game or contest (as in basketball) (Chi) (41:203)
bi yaq 1. to be abused (**col nei bi yaq** = abused by people) (13:21) (bi k'ehˬ-eu), 2. to be cursed, 3. to cure a wound by magical means
bi yiuvq to put to sleep (bi yu^-eu)
bi zaq to feed (9:24) (cf.: **qu** = feed/raise, as of animals) (bi dzaˬ-eu; cu-eu)
bi zaq deil to start feeding solid food to an infant
bi zeq to cause to develop (50:44)
bi zeq lal goqjal a developing country (B=Chi) (15:21)

biq to be rich (smˇ muiˬ muiˬ-eu)
biq a pen for writing (Chi) (2:47) (sahˬ duˇ)
biq to spill over (9:23) (yoeˇ dzeh-eu)
Biqcaoqssaq Dai (Tai, Shan) (or) **Aqcaoq; Deicuq** (Chi) (Biˬ cmˬ)
=biq, gal= pen with which to write (B=Chi)
biqjifbei a notebook (Chi) (26:18)
=biq nei, cul= fat; roly-poly
biqniq to graduate (Chi) (**Ngal gaolzaol biqniq naolhao** ..., After I graduated from senior middle school - 41:15) (or) **biqnieiq** (**xaoxoq nei biqnieiq** = a graduate of primary school - 9:24, 26:26)
=biq pa biq nei, cul= chubby; fat & roly-poly
biqseiv nei richly (smˇ muiˬ)

biqsuf laqhyul a villa (A=Chi)
biqssaq meilssaq other people; others (34:6) (a̬ caw̬)
Biqyoqssaq Biyue branch of the Hani (46:208)

bivq 1. to give, 2. to donate (bi̭-eu) (9:24), 3. deliver (50:44)
bivq haol to give something to help someone
-- **bivqhaol, zeiqmiaoq** -- aid financially; subsidize
bivq hev to honor (50:41)
bivq huvq to return something; give back; pay back (or) **heilhuvq** (9:24) (bi̭ k'o̭-eu)
bivq laq to be given (35:27) (bi̭ la̭-eu)
bivq laoq a subsidy; a grant-in-aid (50:16)
bivq laoq piul subsidy money; grant-in-aid (50:16)
-- **bivq, miqbivq** -- to instruct; to give orders
-- **bivq, miaoqbivq** -- 1. to divide the work, 2. to order
bivq neiq to supply; to give to

bifssiqtaoq a condom (Chi) (15:61)

BIA

bial lose; to have lost; be lost (9:20) (or) **gabial** (sm-eu)
bial disappear (12:128, 45:65, 46:77) (byo^-eu)
bialcil layers of lard (tsiˇ)
bialdaoq bialzeil a margin
bialdaoq bialzeil (jol e col) the (people) standing there; the ones surrounding them (28:4, 35:96)
-- **bial, eil** -- negative
bialhhal side of torso (9:20) (byaˇ g'aˇ = side of something)
bialhhal saqyyuq rib (behˇ jeh^) (and see: **bialnaol**)
bial hhuvq to throw oneself on (ga yṷ da^-eu)
biallul catfish (9:20) (nga̬ pa̭ deh̬)
bialnaol rib (9:20) (behˇ jeh^) (and see: **bialhhal saqyyuq**)
=**bial, nil**= to forget (& see below)
=**bial, nieil**= to forget (& see above)
-- **bial, pieiq** -- (see full)
bialsaq a cliff; a very steep place (35:2) (ba̬ g'a)
bialsaq hhaqzeil a cliff edge (4:34) (lo guˇ)
=**bial, xal**= a fallow field
bial yil to die away; to die out (or) **saq yil** (shiˇ byo^-eu)
bial yil nia may disappear (byo^-iˇ nya-eu)
bialzeil beside (9:21, 46:101, 115); to the side; around (46:83) (ba̬ g'a pya̭ = steep side of mountain)
-- **bialzeil, galma** -- side of the road
bialzeil pyu 1. beside (46:175), 2. outside; outsiders (as in 11:206, listen to outsiders)

bia 1. bright; shining, 2. to flash (bya-eu) (9:20)
-- **bia, aldovq** -- for a lamp to shine
-- **bia, aoqbia** -- for the sun to rise
biabeeq weeds (9:20) (ya˅ mo˄)
biabeeq beeqcaoq high grass in jungles (13:31)
bia bia nei very bright (11:57) (bya ceh^ ni)
=**bia, dovq**= illumination; lighting
-- **biajul, aoq** -- early morning
bia lil bia loq meil 1. bright; brilliant; 2. frankly; open and above board (50:65)
-- **bia lil bia loq, neema** -- to be happy; bright-hearted
bia loq bia ceiv for the day to be bright; sunny
bia loq bia jul meil daybreak (u˯ bya bya la˅-eu)
bia'loq loqma meil very, very brightly (zaw˅ bya-eu)
bia'loq nei brightly (11:56) (bya ceh^ ni)
bia'loq pa loq nei brightly (bya ceh^ ni)
=**bia, miq**= a flame; a blaze
bia miv biv mi sparkling (like a star) (50:146)
-- **bia nei, aoqzaq** -- overnight
=**bia, piul**= white

biaq clf. for a piece of pork (jeh˄)
biaq a bee (generic term) (9:21) (bya˯)
biaqbaoq beehive (9:21) (bya˯ bya˯ bah˯)
biaqbyuq young of wasp or bee (edi) (9:21) (bya˯ boe˯)
=**biaq, dei**= 1. dance ground in the village, 2. a flat place
biaqdul ground wasp (9:21) (bya˯ du˅)
biaq'eel honey (3:25) (or) **biaqqul** (bya˯ bya˯ ui˅)
biaqgoq tree wasp (9:21) (must not allow these to build hives in trees near village) (bya˯ gaw˯)
biaqhovq an empty honeycomb (bya˯ k'aw˄)
biaqhheil a kind of bee (must not allow these to build hives in trees near village).
=**biaq, laol**= mane of horse
biaqlov honeycomb (9:21)
=**biaq, mo**= comb of rooster; dragon
=**biaq, moq laol**= mane of horse
biaqqul honey (or) **biaq'eel** (bya˯ ui˅)
biaqsaoq beeswax (9:22) (bya˯ shah˯)
biaqsaoq aldovq candle (6:183, 50:101) (shah˯ leh˯ do˄-eu)
-- **biaqsaoq, aqbiaq** -- wax
biaqsaoq buvqdul a wax writing pen (50:101)
biaqsil honey bee (the kind they raise) (9:22) (bya˯ yaw˯)
biaqyil naqboq yellow weasel; yellow-throated martin (9:22, 11:180) (bya˯ hi˅)
biaqzyuq queen bee
biaqzyuq biaq nei bavq zyuq the queen bee is fed and cared for by bees

biav to fry (9:22) (luᵛ-eu)
biav to collapse (coᵥ pya^ coᵥ sha^-eu)
biav to spread something with hands (yuᵛ bya^-eu)
biav to make (as a cake) (**hhaqlei hhaqbiav biav** = to make buckwheat cakes)
biav to be flat (yaw bya^)
biav clf. for coin; money measure; flat things (as cakes) (see also: **yeiq**) (9:22) (bya^)
-- biav, aol -- to be worn out from working
=biav, caq= a dried brick
-- biav cuqlyul, cuq -- to gossip
-- biav, daobiav -- for there to be bad erosion or a landslide in a field that has been planted
=biav, hoq= a basin
=biav, haoqniaoq niaoq= flat glutinous rice cake
-- biav, hhaqlei hhaqbiav -- to make buckwheat cakes
=biav, lavq= upper arm
biavma yuan (Chinese money) clf. **biav** (26:76)
  biavma qiq biav one yuan (a 'big' yuan, worth 100 cents)
=biav, meel= burned bricks (A=Dai)
=biav, meiq= a big mouth
-- biav, milbiav -- to have a landslide
=biav, nal= a flat nose
biavnav brown sugar (pawᵥ coeᵛ ca₍^₎)
-- biav nei, naqbol -- to listen carefully
=biav, ni= wild grapes
=biav, niaoq= a glutinous rice cake
biav pav half a coin (money measure) (11:67) (bya^ pa^)
biavpiul white sugar
-- biav, poqbiav -- to make jaggery (cane sugar) into cakes
biavsev nei to be flat (bya^ lehᵛ ni)
biavsuq nei to be flat (9:22) (bya^ lehᵛ ni)
biavssaq half a yuan (50 cents)
  biavssaq qiq biav half a yuan (a 'small' yuan, worth 50 cents)
-- biav, wuqbiav -- flattened head
=biav, xiq= dung cakes (**niuqxiq xiqbiav** = buffalo dung cakes)
biav yil scatter out (as cows) (bya^-iᵛ-eu)
-- biav, zaol -- 1. to break something; 2. to damage something
=biav, zaoq= a flat chisel

biavq 1. to lie down (ga yu₍^₎-eu); 2. to fold (9:22) (bya^ dmᵛ-eu)
biavq clf. for a board (bya₍^₎)
biavq biavq cei cei to be colorful
-- biavq, ceilbiavq -- to pile up harvested rice plants
=biavq, coq= magpie
biavqcuv to be nailed down (as floor, wall)

biavqcuv cuv to nail down something, as the floor (11:43)
=biavq, hhal= a plowed up muddy lump of earth
=biavq, nal= a type of nasal disease
-- biavq, pyuq -- medal; decoration (50:192)
=biavq, saq= black and white spots on skin
biavq sov a planed board (9:22) (la‸ saw^)
biavqsov nei to be piebald
biavqsov sov to plane a board (11:43) (la‸ saw^ saw^-eu)
=biavq, teil= plank of wood; board
-- biavq, wuqbiavq -- 1. to drop to the ground; 2. to lie on one's stomach

BIAO

biaol to fly (9:21) (zaw-eu)
biaol pus from an infection (9:21, 11:41) (maˇ byahˇ)
biaol biaol for pus to form (9:21, 11:41) (maˇ byahˇ byahˇ-eu)
biaolfalbil example; model (Chi) (26:100)
=biaol, hu= flying squirrel
-- biaol, huvq -- (see full)
biaol hhao to fly in a circle (4:38) (jawˬ jawˬ-ehˇ zaw-eu)
=biaol, moq= flying horse (in legends)
biaol tao li to fly into (11:47) (zaw ahˇ-eu)
biaoltiq title of a book (Chil) (or) **soqhhaq colmiaol**
biaolyi slogan (Chi) (50:13)
biaolzyuyil standard pronunciation (Chi) (50:14)

biao 1. full; complete (9:21, 10:7), 2. reached (**Ba'la xil siq halmiav nao biao al laq?** How many days have been reached in this month? 41:110) (byah-eu)
biao a watch (Chi) (9:21) (naˬ liˬ)
=biao, dao= wall of terraced field
biaogaoq pa gaoq nei fully (as to fill to the full) (11:171) (tiˬ byah)
-- biao, huvqbiao -- for a year to come around in a full cycle
biaojiq to vote; decide by vote (Chi) (50:14)
biaojiqqeiq the right to vote (Chi) (50:14)
biao nei full (as a table full of food); to have plenty (13:11) (tiˬ byah ni)
biao nei jav to be plentiful (or) **daoqgaoq gaoq nei; miaq nei jav**
biao pa biao nei full; fully (11:58) (tiˬ byah)
biaoxeil to show forth (26:100) (byaˬ haw-eu)
biaoxeif deeds (Chi) (26:100)
biaoyaq to praise, give thanks (Chi) (9:21) (ja ceuˬ-eu, ciˬ poeˬ-eu) (write article of praise - 26:66)

biaoq 1. to shake, 2. to be weak
=biaoq, aq= dragonfly

-- biaoq, aqbiaoq -- to be weak and limp
biaoq, biaoq, biaoq to be moving and shaking
biaoqhhe nei shaking
-- biaoq laoq, biu lu -- to stagger
=biaoq, wuq= baby's soft fontanel on top of head

BIEI

bieil wide (yaw je˅)
bieil clf. for chairs; tables (9:22)
bieil buvq to compile (as written things) (A=Chi) (50:12)
bieildaol a bamboo table full of food
  bieildaol daol to make an offering with a bamboo table full of food (esp. when there is no ancestral altar)
bieildaof write and direct, as a play (Chi) (50:11)
bieil duv to compile; work out; fabricate; invent (A= Chi)
-- bieil, eil -- to make public; to disclose
-- bieilhhao, lolbieil -- a round table
bieiljal frontier; border area (Chi) (9:22, 10:pref.) (mi˅ ka˯)
bieiljiq editor (Chi) (50:12)
  bieiljiq doq editorial (Chi) (50:12)
bieillee a round table
=bieil, lol= a table
bieillo nei very wide (je˅ lo ni)
bieilluq to compile quotations (Chi) (50:12)
bieilmuq to make a catalogue (Chi) (50:12)
bieilpeiq to arrange; lay out (Chi) (50:12)
bieilsei read and edit; be copy editor (Chi) (50:12)
bieilzal food grains other than rice (50:204)

biei 1. to open (as eyes), 2. to open (as blossoms and flowers) (1. byeh-eu, 2. pyeh˅ la˅-eu)
-- biei, aolbiei -- to do carelessly
-- biei, jaqbiei -- to talk animatedly
bieijei to open (as eyes) (pah-eu; byeh-eu)
  -- bieijei, miavneev -- to open one's eyes
bieizal non-staple food (or) **zalbiei**

-- bieiq, alcav -- to untie or loosen a rope, cord
-- bieiq, hhe -- to pull off; to untie
-- bieiq, peel -- untie and let go; unfasten

bieiv 1. to chop; mince (9:23) (byeh^-eu), 2. to be watery; thin (as a thin gruel) (see also: **qavqbieiv bieiv**
-- bieiv, aqbieiv -- to feel numb; to be numb
=bieiv, aqciq ciq= fresh soybeen condiment
-- bieiv, hhaq -- negative; passive
=bieiv, hhaq= to be dejected; lonely; sad
  -- bieiv, hhaqbieiv -- disappointed; lose hope
=bieiv, lao= muddy; marshy

-- **bieiv, laobieiv** -- to be muddy
Bieivma an ancestor's name in Hani genealogy (or) **Bieivma aqbol**
Bieivma aqbol laqdu yoheeq the great ancestor **Bieivma**
=**bieiv, mil**= mud
Bieivnaoq important name in Hani genealogy, younger brother of **Bieivma**
-- **bieiv, niuqxiq xiq** -- watery buffalo/cow dung
-- **bieiv, qavqbieiv** -- cooked to a watery mush; thin gruel (as porridge)
-- **bieiv, saqbieiv** -- to chop up meat
-- **bieiv, xiqbieiv** -- to have diarrhea

bieivqdaoq a no-son person; a bad person (can be used as a curse); **sulbieivq; bieivqdaoq aqpaq** (semi-taboo)
=**bieivq, sul**= a no-son person (see also: **bievqdaoq**)

bieifgeiq to transform (Chi) (34:10)
bieifsuqxal accelerator in car/truck (Chi) (26:33)
bieifzeif dialectical (Chi) (34:71)
  bieifzeiffaq dialectics (Chi) (50:13)
  bieifzeif weiqwuq lueif theory of dialectic materialism (Chi) (50:13)
  bieifzeif weiqwuq zuyif dialectical materialism (Chi) (50:13)
bieifziiq to go bad; to deteriorate (Chi) (50:13)

BIO

biol clf. for a meal (9:23, 11:85) (byaw˅)
=**biol, nal**= scar

bioq 1. tasteless, 2. fade in color or strength (9:23) (byaw˯-eu)
bioq clf. for a torch
-- **bioq, alnal nal bioq** -- to have scars and scabs all over one's body
bioqgav nei tasteless (byaw˯ leh˅ ni)
biaoqgav pa gav nei to be extremely tasteless
=**bioq, hoq**= tadpole
bioqka nei very thin (ba˯ leh˅ ni)

biov 1. short in height (9:23, 11:56), 2. low (46:184) (or) **yobiov** (yaw nym˅, yaw aw)
=**biov, haoqkavq bil**= sponge gourd
biovlov lovssaq very short (11:58)
biovlov nei short (yaw nym˅)
biov yil to become short; low down (14:167) (aw-i˅-eu)

BIU

biul (see: **aqyeil biul**) (9:24)

biuldeiq nei unhappy (14:219) (la˯ k'a˯ ma˯ ceh˅)
biulduvq nei greasily
  biulduvq nei biul to be very greasy; to be nauseated by some food
biulniq nei smoothly (ju˅ k'eu^ ni)
  biulniq nei biul translucent
  biulniq pa niq nei very smoothly

biu lu biaoq laoq to stagger

biuq clf. for bundles (9:24) (dzah˯)

BO

bol clf. for trees (9:24) (baw˅)
=bol, al= tree
=bol, aq= 1. paternal grandfather, 2. old man
Bolbel name of a person born by heaven
-- bolcaoq, albol -- a grove of trees; jungle trees
-- bolcaoq, haqbol -- bamboo forest
=bol, ceil= rice stalk
=bol, haq= bamboo
=bol, hhaq= buckwheat stalk
bolliq glass windows (Chi) (26:89)
bolliq buqssaq a glass jar (A=Chi) (50:15)
  bolliq caqbyu glass window (as in a house) (A=Chi) (14:242)
bollo the lower leg (9:24) (kui˅ du)
-- bolmoq, albol -- an old tree
=bol, naq= the ear
=bol, niaol= banyan tree

bo to be born (9:24) (baw-eu)
bo to have (as to have major item; father, mother, husband, etc.) (baw-eu)
bo 1. to blow (as on a fire, on a wind instrument) (9:24), 2. to fan something (as in threshing, etc.) (9:24) (baw-eu)
=bo aqnil, naoq= younger brothers & sisters
-- bo dovq, miqzaq -- to make a fire; to cook
-- bo, gaoqlaoq -- to have merit/blessing
boheiq cyuq birth control; contraception (50:11)
bo hoq to blow over (baw da^-eu)
bohuvq one's birth year (deh^ le-eu a˅ k'o^)
-- bo, hhaqhav -- to have strength; to be strong
bohhe bellows (as a blacksmith uses) (baw baw-eu)
bo leeq to blow down (baw ka-eu)
bo leiv to blow off (as a cap) (baw dzeh-eu) (11:128)
-- bo, molsavq -- shy; bashful
bonao birthday (9:24, 13:19, 41:111) (baw-eu a˅ nah)
-- bo, neenil maq -- don't forget; without forgetting
Boniaoq name of a person born by earth (34:8)
-- bo, pyuq -- to have prestige; be famous; be popular

-- **bo, savqdol** -- to be shy; bashful; to be ashamed; to have something to be ashamed of
bosev a fan (9:24) (baw seu)
-- **bosev, miqzaq** -- a fan to fan a fire
bo sil a stillborn child; dead when born (baw seh^-eu)
-- **bo, ssil** -- to have a long life
-- **bo tul la, jaqleil** -- for the wind to blow up fiercly
Bozao person's name (11:111)
bo zeq to breed; reproduce (50:46)
bo zei 1. to blow down (as the wind blowing leaves down from trees); 2. blow away (baw dzeh-eu)
bo zivq leil hhev a windstorm

boq 1. to protect; to save (**wuqhol boq e** = to save a person's life - 26:13), 2. to bring luck to people
boq noun part. meaning: questionable; dubious (**maq ngeel boq** = probably that is not so) (ma˅ ngeu˅ pa˅)
boq a treasure (Chi) (33:3)
boq clf. for times of action
boq aqma anything which gives people happiness
boq, boq, boq the sound of knocking (14:234) (po^ po^ po^)
boqheiq jacev black spots (as on face) (9:24)
boqlo a tube (usually bamboo) (and see: **baoqlo**)
-- **boqlo, haqbol** -- bamboo container
-- **boqlo, miqzaq** -- bamboo pipe used to blow on fire
-- **boqlo, yahyuq** -- tobacco water pipe made of bamboo
boq luaf fa zeif to bring order out of chaos; to set things right (Chi) (34:12)
=**boq, naq**= deaf
-- **boq, naqboq** -- to be deaf
boqwuqguei a museum (Chi) (34:65)
boqxoq to exploit (Chi) (9:24, 26:17, 34:10, 50:15)
boqxoq geiljiq an exploiting class (Chi) (50:15)

bovq vagina (taboo) (not pf., see: **beivq**)
=**bovq, hyuq**= smoky
-- **bovq, hyuqbovq** -- to be smoky

BU

bul to float; to flow along (9:25) (bu-eu)
=**bul, aq**= a bath
-- **bul, coq** -- to jump and float (as in a river)
-- **buldeiq nei, neema** -- to be nauseated
buldul thigh (9:25, 46:88) (human = a˅ kui˅ sha˅ pya˅; chicken = baw du˅)
buldul dulma saqyyuq thigh (femur) bone
bulduq oneself (9:25, 11:94) (**Nol bulduq buvq.** You write it yourself.) (yaw˅ ha˅ yaw˅ ha)

-- **bulduq, aqya** -- they themselves
-- **bulduq, aqyo** -- he himself; she herself
-- **bulduq, nol** -- you yourself
-- **bulduq, yoqhhaq** -- oneself
=**bul, eel**= to float in water on stomach
bulhha to float (38:109, 46:201) (bu-eu)
bulhha nei in a floating manner (**bulhhaq nei** in 9:25)
=**bul, luq**= (see full)
bulya nei floating on water (50:137)

bu to wash something clean with water (tsi˯ shawˇ-eu)
bu to accuse (as an official) (27:12, 38:22, 45:51, 46:108)
--**bu, aol** -- to do something which is useless; wasted work of no value
bucaol complement (Chi) (34:38)
=**bu, cei**= to bleach; rinse; clean
=**bu, civq**= male goat
-- **bu dav, aqtav** -- appeal to a higher court
buduq a court; a tribunal (50:45)
buduv bucaoq weeds; grass (or) **jahhaq** (yaˇ mo˄)
bugaq to declare; proclaim (50:190)
=**bu, hul**= cuckoo
bu lal to accuse (as before a magistrate etc.) (13:20)
=**bu, lal**= male buffalo
bu'lavq 1. satin, 2. brocade (9:25)
-- **bu, leiq** -- to wash by rubbing
bu'loq nei cleanly (9:25) (buˇ coe^ ni)
bu'loq nei eilduv honest; frank; confess (cf. Eng. 'come clean')
bu'loq nei mol qivq transparent
=**bu, niuqnil lal**= bull
bu puv 1. to appeal (50:149), 2. to write a rebuttal to an accusation (50:149)
bu puv huvq to countercharge; counterclaim (50:47)
bu puv qeiqlif right of appeal (C=Chi) (50:149)
-- **busiq, lalbu** -- the hump on the neck of an ox
bu soqhhaq to write a complaint (50:217)
buyi a compliment (50:16) (Chi)
-- **bu, yoqbu** -- private prosecution of a case
bu zaq to accuse someone (50:98)
bu zaq qeiqlif the right to accuse someone (B=Chi) (50:98)
bu zaq soqbuvq written accusation (in legal sense) (50:98)

buq to be proud (50:149)
=**buq buqma, haqzeil zeil**= osprey
buqcaoq the cover of a jar (k'aw˯ pym˯)
-- **buq, dalbuq** -- to brag; show off
buqdeil 1. earthworm (bu˯ joe), 2. ascaris (or) **wuqdeiq buqdeil** (buˇ deˇ) (9:25)
-- **buqdeil, wuqdeiq** -- intestinal roundworm

(ascaris)
buqdeil zaol a tangle of ascaris worms
=buq, jaq= proud of riches; a show-off
-- buq, jaqbuq -- to be proud of riches; to show off
buqluq a werewolf; weretiger (the soul of such a person goes out of his or her body and sucks the blood out of people) (or) **buqluq pilsil** (35:85) (piˇ seuˇ)
  buqluq pilsil (see: **buqluq**)
  buqluq puv to drive a werewolf out of a person by magical means
buqma a big jar
=buq, miq= a tail with long hair
buqssaq earthen jar; jug (9:25) (maˇ tsa‸; maˇ tsa‸ oeˬ lahˬ)
  buqssaq naqpavq the collar that goes around a Chinese jar with a lip in it in which water is kept to make it airtight
  -- buqssaq, wulquvq -- large water container
buq zaq to be proud; conceited; arrogant; to boast (Chi) (35:86) (jaˇ g'eh-eu)

=buv, jav= automatically; without thinking; immediately
buv luv biav lav meil biav to get out of repair

buvq to write (9:25) (bo‸-eu)
buvq to rot; decay (9:25) (bu‸-iˇ-eu)
=buvq, bavq= freckle
-- buvq, caldoq -- write words for a song
-- buvq, calteil -- write music for a song
=buvq, col= a clumsy person
buvqcuv handwriting (32:3)
buvqdav to write on (something) (11:47)
  buvqdav miq write it down (as a record) (50:9)
buvqdul 1. writing pen (sahˬ duˇ), 2. writing brush (clf. = **mol**) (26:16, 50:112)
buvqduq handwriting
buvq e soqdaoq a notebook (50:11)
-- buvq, eil -- to libel someone; mock; satirize
=buvq, haqpal pal= patterned cloth
buvqkaoq excercise book (26:41)
buvq lav buvq civ nei variegated
buvqlavq nei to be rotten; corrupt (34:59)
  buvqlavq qeilsuq nei rotten; putrid; decayed (50:52)
  buvqlavq qeilsuq nei neecavq decadent and moribund thought (50:52)
-- buvq, leiq -- to scribble
-- buvq miq, eil -- to say bad things about a person
=buvq, miqca ca= marks on foot from warming at fire
=buvq, nal= pockmark on face
=buvq, naq= ear pus
-- buvq, nyuqbuvq -- to write from memory

=buvq, pal= cotton print cloth
-- buvq, piulbuvq -- to have inflation of money
buvqqo qo depict; portray; delineate (50:115)
-- buvq, soqmiav -- to inscribe; write an inscription
buvqssaq author; writer of a book or article
-- buvqssaq, naqgaq -- newsman; reporter
buvq taq ssaq a record keeper (50:80)
buvq teiq 1. to write down (9:25), 2. to register (bo^ ta˅-eu)
  buvq teiq taq to record something (50:9)
=buvq, zaoq= ribbon
buvqzol soqkaoq to write composition exercises (50:183)

bufceq a step; a measure (of distance) (Chi) (34:56) (or) **bufcef**
bufcef a step; a measure (Chi) (or) **coqsiil** (34:10; 50:17) (or) **bufceq**
bufdyuf army; troop (Chi) (34:80, 50:16) (yeh˅)
bufgaof a notice (as a notice on the wall); a bulletin (Chi) (50:17)
bufji a painted backdrop of scenery for some kind of art troupe or acting group (Chi) (50:17)
bufjiq overall arrangement; layout (Chi) (50:17)
bufmeiq department (Chi) (34:56)
bufpiaof a ration coupon for buying cloth (Chi) (50:17)
bufsuq to dispose; deploy (Chi) (34:115)
bufza a minister in the govt. (Chi) (50:16)
bufziiq to assign (as homework) (Chi) (41:66)

BYU

byuldaoq widower (or) **byuldaoq aqpa** (boe˅ dah˅)
  byuldaoq daoq to become a widower
byuldeivq to be alive; go on living (9:25, 13:21) (yaw deh^)
  byuldeivq deivq to survive; continue to live (46:172)
  byuldeivq huvqlavq the age of humans
  byuldeivq liqhhaol social morality; social ethics (50:148)
  byuldeivq maq deivq qivq cannot live (38:18, 45:59)
  byuldeivq neemeeq humanitarianism (50:141)
byuldyul dyul to be lazy (yaw doe˅ doe˅-eu)
byulkyul clever; genius; talented; difted
  byulkyul aqda a clever man (yaw gah˅)
  byulkyul col a talented person; a person of ability (50:141)
  byulkyul kyul to be clever; to be quick-witted (10:pref., 35:58) (nui gah˅)
  byulkyul kyulma a clever woman
  byulkyul kyulssaq a clever child
  byulkyul kyulteil geeq 'let there be one hundred

schools of thought' (50:4)

Byulluvq Aqpyuq Miqyeil one of three manifestations of God (**Aqpyuq Miqyeil**), who protects people

byulmaoq (see: **byulmoq**)

byulmoq a religious practitioner who is the major go-between for humans and spirits. He does certain ceremonies for the entire village (such as the **Molmil lolzaq** ceremony); also calls souls back and engages in healing ceremonies for families in the village (see more under: **moqpil**) (boeˇ mawˬ; mawˬ piˇ) (11:185)

byulnal a pestilence (45:70)

byulnal duv lal for a type of pestilence or plague which can kill to spread rapidly

byulnal nal to suffer from some pestilence

byulnal sil to die from a pestilence or plague which travels rapidly

byulssaq human; person (old lang., poetic lang) (46:68) (or) **colssaq** (tsawˇ haˬ)

byulssaq meeqduq zaol zyul to infringe upon a citizen's human rights

byulssaq naol human beings (13:47) (tsawˇ haˬ zaˬ)

Byulssaq naol jol lil. Beelma lalma boq, aoqma milma boq. What the Hani call out when there is an earthquake. ('People are here, living under the protection of the sun and moon.')

byulssyuq toqssaq a nurse (Chi pattern) (50:7)

byultaoq anvil (biˇ nahˇ)

byu clf. for a hole (**milbyu qiq byu**) (11:95)

=byu, caq= hole (as in wall)

=byu, daoq= anus

=byu, eel= water hole; water cave

=byu, hoq= a roof

=byu, hho= at the door

-- byu, kovq -- to gnaw a hole; to bite a hole into something

=byu, laol= nape of neck

-- byu, leiq -- to make a hole (in wood, dirt, rock etc.)

byu'lyu gong (9:25) (boe loe)

-- byu'lyu, luqduq -- drum and gong (a pair)

=byu, mil= a cave; a hole

=byu, nal= nostril

=byu, naq= ear canal

byunaoq byusev a tree which has sticky bark they use to seal the sections of a coffin

-- byu, peev -- to be broken from burning

-- byu, suqduq -- a bottomless pit

=byu, xaol= the roof of a house (see: **hoqbyu**)

byuq to butt with horn or snout

byuq dig in earth with snout (9:26) (boeˬ-eu)

byuq baoq a hollow section in a tree (there must not be such in a tree to be used as a coffin)

=byuq, biaq= young wasp/bee
=byuq, ceil= rice worm/insect
byuq daol to dig in the earth with snout to make a way to go (4:42)
byuqduq a bamboo container in which seeds are kept until the next planting (45:53)
=byuq, haq= insects that infest bamboo
byuqkaol silk thread (14:162) (boe˯ sa˯ kahˇ)
-- byuq, laolbyuq -- to carry a baby animal by the nape of the neck
=byuq, nal= scab
byuqnav a cutworm
  -- byuqnav, ceil -- rice weevil
byuqnil a type of taro
byuqnil nil to pick a quarrel; to provoke
byuqpeel a kind of taro (9:26)
byuqpiul a type of white taro
byuq puv to root up and break with the snout (as a pig rooting in weeds or bamboo)
byuqqul byuqbiol aqma turtle (9:26) (boe˯ ciˇ boe˯ yawˇ; boe˯ ku^)
=byuq, seq= (see full)
byuqsil an insect that lives in the earth
byuqsiq taro (generic) (9:26) (bym˯ ma)
byuqsyu bending head (14:144)
byuqssaq worm; insect (9:26) (boe˯ dza˯-eu = insect to bore) (see also: **aqzuq**)
byuq ssil byuq ssav jav flourishing; prosperous (50:46); **byuq ssil byuq ssav meil zeq**
byuq tao li to drop in to visit (14:231)
byuqtaoq taoq to hibernate (9:26) (lo k'ah˯ k'ah˯-eu)
byuqyol a type of wild taro (starchy root)
byuqzeil a kind of plant
byuqzeiv to root with the snout (as a wild pig)
byuqzuq spider (9:26) (a˯ g'o˰ lo˰ ma, bu˯ ju˯ luˇ za)

CA

cal to sing (ca˅-eu)
cal sun to shine (**aoqcal cal** = u˯ tsa˅ tsa˅-eu)
cal to hurry; rush (teh˯-eu)
=cal, aoq= sunshine
caldaof to initiate; propose (Chi) (34:116)
caldoq words in a song (50:57, 71)
=cal, eel= soup
-- cal, eelcal -- watery soup; watery juice
=cal, geeq= bronze/copper pot
calgual to tour; to visit (Chi) (50:19) (see also: **calgueil**)
calgual tuaq a visiting delegation (Chi) (50:19)
calgueil to visit (Chi) (pf.) (or) **calgual** (11:11) (daw˯ deh g'a-eu)
-- calhav, aoqcal -- hot sunshine
=cal, hho= a spinning wheel
caljal to take part in (Chi) (or) **kevq**
caljyul to join the people's army (Chi) (9:26)
calkao reference (as a letter of reference) (Chi) (50:19)
-- cal, kaoqpiul -- to sweat all over
calkuf laqhyul storage bin (rice etc.) (A=Chi) (11:31)
=cal, laq= quickly (vb)
=cal, leil= burning ashes
-- cal, leiq -- urge on; ask to hurry
calmeq to give advice (Chi) (50:19)
calmeqza chief of staff in the army (Chi) (50:19)
calmil nei nervous; tense (50:89)
=cal, nalteiq nal= serious & sudden diseases
=cal, naol= sun's ray
-- cal, neema -- to be impatient
cal nei right away; quickly (or) **laqcal** (11:112)
calpiq a lid (as for a pot) (9:27) (k'aw˯ pym˯)
calqoq qoq antiphonal singing (A=Chi) (50:41)
-- cal, saol -- a metal pot
calteil 1. sound of singing (11:170) (ca˅-eu te˅ sa˅), 2. a song (50:57)
calyif to propose (Chi) (50:22)
calyifyeif the senate (Chi) (50:19)
calzao zao a chorus (50:70)
calzeif to participate in governmental and political affairs (Chi) (34:53)
calzeifda a party that participates in governmental and political affairs (Chi)
-- calziil, aoqcal -- twilight

ca 1. to bake; roast (or) **peev** (pui^), 2. to get warm by a fire (pui^ lah˅-eu)
ca to be missing; short of (9:26)

ca to owe money or something (da^-eu)
ca clf. for a 'thing', a 'type' of something
-- cabuvq, miqca -- (see full)
caca a shovel (Chi)
cabaoq a microwave oven (Chi) (50:96)
=ca cama, mol= very long
ca gee to smoke something until it gets dry (or) **teiv gee** (la^ gui-eu)
-- ca, hhaqhav -- to be a little weak
-- ca, miqca -- to warm one's back by the fire
=ca nei, mol= a long distance
=ca nei, niq= near by
caza a factory director (Chi) (34:42, 50:21)

caq to guess; conjure up (9:27) (sheh^ tsaˬ tsaˬ-eu)
caq to have something break
caq 1. all right; correct, 2. to be "right" with one's neighbors (45:8) (tsaˬ-eu)
caq to check something for contraband (as luggage or goods) (Chi) (tseˇ-eu)
caq a mark
-- caq, bakaq -- to guess a riddle
caqbiav brick (sun-dried) (9:27) (tsaˬ bya^)
  caqbiav caqsiq sun-dried bricks (46:117)
  caqbiav sev to trim a brick (in making) (9:27)
  caqbiav seiv to make bricks (9:27) (tsaˬ bya^ teh^-eu)
  caqbiav seivhuvq a wooden mold for making bricks (9:28)
caqbyu hole (as in wall) (maˇ k'ehˬ); window hole in house (9:28, 10:7, 13:46, 26:37); a window (50:26)
  -- caqbyu, bolliq -- a glass window (A=Chi)
  caqbyu diq cyuq to close the window (10:7) (laˇ g'o^ piˬ tehˬ-eu)
  caqbyu diq pao to open the window (10:7) (laˇ g'o^ pah-eu)
caqcaolzil to do something with direct honesty
caqcaoq a wooden wedge (as for putting into handle to make firm, or used to split log) (9:28) (sehˬ)
caqceiq the great wall of China (Chi) (50:21)
caqciq muddy water used by blacksmith to cool hot metals
caqciivq ginger (9:28) (tsawˬ tsui˰)
caq cuv 1. to be marked (as fields to be dug), 2. to be engaged to someone
  caqcuv cuv to build a mud wall (miˇ tsaˬ ka^ pyawˇ)
  caqcuv laqhyul a building with a mud wall
caqdaoq 1. the edge of a field (yaˇ dzeˇ), 2. plot; circumstances (50:138), 3. purpose (50:119)
  caqdaoq kyuq a serious plot (50:138)
  caqdaoq ya from beginning to end (jiˇ cuˬ ni); the whole matter; to do something completely (50:111), real affairs; concrete affairs (50:93)
caqdevq salt (9:28) (saˬ deu˰)
  caqdevq baoqcavq salt container made of bamboo

(9:28) (sa⌄ deu^ baw⌄ law)

caqdevq caqhaoq a salt bowl (put on table)

caqdevq haq to be too salty

caqdevq hoqbiav salt pounder (9:28) (see also: **caqluv**) (sa⌄ deu^ tah⌄-eu k'aw˅ law⌄)

caqdevq maq haq not to be very salty (or) **caqdevq maq qul**

caqdevq maq qul not to be very salty (or) **caqdevq maq haq**

caqdevq qul to be salty enough

caqdef broad bean (Chi) (and see: **caqdul**)

caqdul broad bean; horse-eyed bean (Chi) (9:28) (and see: **caqdef**)

caqduq a salt well (sa⌄ deu^ lah du⌄)

caq duv to check and find (as a mistake, fault) (A=Chi)

caqgol a song (Chi) (11:169) (cf.: ca˅-eu daw⌄)

caqgol cal to sing a song (A=Chi) (11:169) (or) **caqgol caf** (Chi)

-- caq, gul -- to shout out; call out; disturb someone; to interrupt

=caq, hal= earth; mud

-- caq, haoqquq -- (see full)

caqheq to investigate (A=Chi) (50:21)

caqhu a teapot (Chi) (law˅ baw⌄-eu la^ ceh)

caq hu to give a guess (or) **nyuq hu** (tsa⌄ haw-eu)

caqhhyu member of the standing committee (Chi) (50:21)

Caqjal baqma the Yangtse river (A=Chi) (50:21)

caqjil yaolma the main house (nym˅ ma)

caq jifhuaf long-term plan (Chi) (50:21)

caqkeel 1. the lower part of embankments in an irrigated field (9:28), 2. the lower part of the wall of a building; the foundation

caqkeel keeltov a low wall in an irrigated field which looks like men's leggings in the transplanting season (46:158)

caqkeel sev to clear the weeds off the lower bunds of the terraced rice fields

caqkov ditch around house (9:28) (daw˅ law˅ kaw^)

-- caqkov, aqgeel -- the milky way (star pattern)

caq lal to be possible (or) **za lal**

-- caq, lav -- to disturb someone; cause a disturbance

=caq, lavq= a mark

caqliq flat roof of house

caqloq to check; verify (A=Chi) (50:20)

caqluv pestle for pounding salt (9:28) (see also: **caqdevq hoqbiav**)

(vb) caq maq siq did not know the right way to (vb) (13:7) (**qiq gal jol caq maq siq**)

=caq, meiq= a cracked lip

=caq, mil= earth

caqnavq deep, muddy irrigated fields

caqpaoq under the roof (where they put grass etc.)

caqpeiq mortar for pounding salt and chili (sa⌄ deu^

tah⌄ du⌄)

caqpiq eaves under the roof where it is covered with mud (4:34)

caqqil for a long time (Chi) (34:52) (g'aw myahˇ ni)

caqqiq the horizon (34:6) (miˇ dzeˇ; mya^ haw ti⌄ haw)

-- caqsiq, caqbiav -- sun-dried bricks

caqssaq an illegitimate child; bastard

caqssaq aqda father of an illegitimate child

caqssaq aqma mother of an illegitimate child

caqssaq cavqkeeq ciil ceremony held when an illegitimate baby is born

caq taq 1. a marriage contract (50:76), 2. an engagement; an appointment (50:38)

caqtaoq a mud wall (9:28, 14:231) (miˇ tsa⌄ ka^ pyawˇ)

caqtaoq taoq to erect a mud wall (miˇ tsa⌄ ka^ pyawˇ teh^-eu)

caqto a mud wall (9:28) (miˇ tsa⌄ ka^ pyawˇ)

caqto to to make a mud wall (miˇ tsa⌄ ka^ pyawˇ teh^-eu)

caqtuq an illustration (picture or chart, as in a book) (Chi) (50:20)

caqwuf hhyuyeiqhyuf standing committee (Chi) (50:21)

caqyaq mud; muddy (35:3) (yaw pyeh^ yaw leh^)

caqyaq nil (naoq) to make mud for building (9:29)

caqyaq teil zaq to have a mud fight (14:237)

caqyeq diesel oil (Chi) (26:32) (or) **ceiqyeq**

caqyil laqpeiv tea (A=Chi)

caqzaol to investigate and deal with accordingly (A=Chi) (50:20)

caqzeil the long march (Chi) (34:7, 50:21) (it was 25,000 li, or about 12,500 kilometers)

caqzeif finance (Chi) (34:40) (or) **ceiqzeif**

cav clf. for cords, rope (long) (9:29) (ca^)

=cav, al= rope; wire; cable

-- cav, aqcav -- sore on skin from caterpillar

cavbev a small plow rope

cavdu a cord; strand of strings (cf.: **cavleiq**)

=cav, gal= (see full)

-- cavkuq, alcav -- a dry rope

cavleiq a strand of threads (or) **cavdu**

=cav, miaq= rope for plow

=cav, moq= reins for horse

=cav, nal= nose rope for buffalo/cattle

=cav nei, lavq= to drop down (as tears)

cavni 1. rattan vine (9:29, 27:11, 46:157), 2. a stem to a fruit (4:34) (1. aˇ nyo^)

cavni leelbeil a type of tuberous plant which looks like a large sweet potato and is used for medicine (14:145)

cavni nikuq an old, thin, dry rattan vine

=cav, niuq= rope to tie buffalo/cattle

cavpaoq twine

cavpaoq paoq to make twine
cav'qeiv a portion (50:11)
cavceq ceq sil to commit suicide by hanging
-- cavtao, alcav -- pieces of rope
cavtev qiq tev to pull suddenly and hard (45:76)
cavtevq criterion; yardstick

cavq 1. to connect; join (9:29), 2. to graft (as trees)
cavq to be dirty; dusty (41:148) (cf.: yaw ca^; yaw pahv) (or) **suq**
cavq clf. for spoon (9:29) (tsa^)
=cavq, aqkeel hao= leg hair
-- cavq, aqpeil peilcavq -- to graft a pear tree
=cavq, colmiaol miaol= one's nickname
cavq dav to extend something
=cavq, doq= bad word; dirty word; rumor
-- cavq, doq -- to wait and meet; wait and greet
-- cavq, doqgaq -- to pass on a message
cavq dyu to spread abroad (as a broadcast) (50:26)
=cavq, eel= 1. wash water, 2. a kind of snake that lives in the water
-- cavq, eil -- to mock; slander
-- cavqgaq, sseil sal -- weather forecast
-- cavq, geel -- to weld
=cavq, hao= body and facial hair (not head hair)
=cavq, hu= a rat
-- cavq, kavq -- to be tied together with a rope
-- cavq, laqguq -- to work diligently; willing to work hard
cavq lav heq to separate bad from good (in ceremonies)
=cavq, lavq= an assistant; helper; aid
-- cavq, lavqcavq -- (see full)
=cavq, mal= a bottle
-- cavq, miaoq -- 1. to stick on, 2. to do different jobs
=cavq meil, naoq= following closely
cavqmoq the horse which is led to the grave of a rich person
cavqmoq ciil to lead a horse to the grave of a rich person
=cavq, nal= bad diseases; bad sicknesses
-- cavq, neema -- evil hearted
-- cavq, neema nee -- bad-hearted
cavqni nei dirty; ugly
-- cavq, nieivq -- to connect
-- cavq, pavq -- to carry on; to take over from
=cavq, pavq= (see full)
-- cavq, pieiq -- to breed (animals)
=cavq, pioq= ugly face (appearance)
cavqqeiv maq za out of proportion; out of ratio (50:11)
-- cavq qiq mol, miqnieiq nieiq -- a bad job
-- cavq, seq -- to come to meet someone

cavqsiil siil to read one's mind (35:15); to test one's mind (nui ma tseˇ haw-eu)

cavqsiil siil hu to try reading a person's mind (13:44); to sound out; to feel out

-- cavq, wuq -- to do something bad on purpose

-- cavq, yevq -- to be twisted on (as nuts on bolts)

=cavq, yo= to be bad; evil

=cavq, yuq= a spoon

-- cavq zaq, miqyo -- to commit adultery

-- cavq, zaol -- 1. to pollute; contaminate, 2. to fix; repair

-- cavq, zeq -- 1. a run of good luck, 2. to extend good luck to 'old people'

cafgol cal to sing songs (A=Chi) (26:59) (cf.: sahˬ bo‸ caˇ-eu)

cafpieif a music record; record disk (Chi) (50:22)

CAO

caol to abuse (9:27) (k'ehˬ-eu)

caol to be dense; thick (as plants) (9:27, 11:55) (yaw tsahˇ)

caol clf. for land; field; etc.

caol'aol spindle (for thread) (or) **paoq'aol** (ya ahˇ)

caolcaq a sports ground; a ballground; a playing field (Chi) (26:45) (niˇ g'a duˬ)

caoldaofli super-conductor (electric) (Chi) (50:22)

caolfeil nei to be full; ample (Chi) (34:67)

=caol, gal= crossroad; fork in path

caolheiq a gate or smaller opening to smaller ditches leading off an irrigation canal

caolheiq dav to repair the irrigation ditch diversion where it comes out of the river or stream

=caol hhe, hhoq= thin out seedlings

caolhheq to complete the task and do extra (Chi)

caoljiq dafgoq super-power country (Chi) (50:22)

caollaq meil to be dense; crowded (as a dense forest) (yaw tsahˇ)

=caol, mei= a foot-operated rice pounder

caolpieivq braided hair (6:170) (ca^ pyeh‸)

caolpieivq pieivq to braid hair (11:160) (ca^ pyeh‸ pyeh‸-eu)

caolseilbol ultrasonic wave; supersonic wave (electric) (Chi) (50:22)

caolseil bol to have an extra child (A=Chi)

=caol taoq, mei= to pound rice (& see full)

caolteev a stream that is dammed (tsahˇ tui^)

caolteev teev to dam up a stream (tsahˇ tui^ tui^-eu)

caolziv nei to be dense; crowded (as many plants in a small area) (yaw tsahˇ)

caolziv zivma meil very, very dense (11:59) (zawˇ

tsahˇ-eu)

caolzofga the operating lever of an engine; an engine's control rod (Chi) (**caolzofga hhe niv** = 'pull an engine into motion', i.e. to start it)

-- **cao, alpiaq piaqcao** -- to have malaria

caomeiq strawberry (Chi)

-- **cao, piaqcao** -- to get fever; have malaria

-- **cao, savqcao** -- to pant; breathe rapidly

caoq 1. to cover something (such as snow covering the ground - 26:45, a bowl covering cowrie shells - 46:114) (and see: **caoq laol**) (piˇ tehˇ-eu; mo^ kaˇ-eu), 2. to wear certain items of clothing, 3. to contain (as a wooden container with pig food in it - 33:3)

caoq to be present inside (**Alsiq hholqei alneev caoq.** There is a seed present inside the fruit.) (11:49) (la^ k'oeˇ ahˇ-eu)

caoq winter season (41:116) (or) **caoqgav** (tsahˇ ga^)

caoq a frightening place where spirits live

caoq liver (9:27) (shaˇ tsahˇ)

caoq (w.m.) the width of the palm of the hand (11:78)

caoq clf. for 1. clumps, as: grass, weeds, bamboo (9:27) (**jahhaq qiq caoq** = a clump of grass), 2. a patch (as of ginger - 13:48); 3. a cluster (as of trees), 4. a section (as of a flower or melon), 5. a set of the same things (as houses) (11:205)

=caoq, albol bol= woods; forest

caoq aoqcal the sun's rays (35:19) (nahˇ ma aˇ kuiˇ)

-- **caoq, bavq** -- to cover

-- **caoq, beeqcaoq** -- to ambush

=caoq, beil= forest; jungle

caoqbei liver of birds and all fowls (5:474)

caoqbiaq a clip for bullets to insert in gun

=caoq, caq= a wooden wedge

caoqcaf an ensemble of two or more singers (Chi) (50:24)

caoq dav the beginning of winter season (50:105)

-- **caoq, deiq** -- push down

caoqduv winter (tsahˇ ga^)

caoqgav winter season (46:81) (tsahˇ ga^)

caoqgav aqzil winter songs

caoqgav ba'la winter season (9:27) (tsahˇ ga^ yamˇ)

caoqgaoq a type of large tree (not used for building)

=caoq, haq= a clump of bamboo

=caoq, hov= cymbals

-- **caoq, hha** -- hidden trouble; hidden danger

caoqhhaq govhhaq hhaq part of death ceremonies which takes back the soul of the dead person from the spirits

=caoq, hhavq= pig liver

=caoq, jabeeq beeq= cluster of weeds

caoqjif esteem; respect; revere (Chi) (50:24)

caoq kuv to cover something in (tsahˇ ka˯-eu; mo˄ ka˯-eu)
caoq laol to cover something up (9:27) (and see: **caoq**) (deh˯ ka˯-eu)
caoqlaolhaoq fireplace (9:27, 14:178, 38:15) (or) **caoqleiq** (tsaw˯ g'o˄; tsaw˯ ha˯)
caoqleiq a fireplace (14:161) (or) **caoqlaolhaoq**
caoqleiq since (Chi) (13:12)
=caoq lolgov, miq= (see full)
-- caoq, meelhov -- to tile a roof
=caoq, meiq= covering for mouth/snout
-- caoq, miq -- (see full)
-- caoq, miqcaoq -- an offering to prevent a house from burning (and see full)
-- caoq, molkol -- to take a picture (B=Chi)
-- caoq, moqcaoq -- to lie on one's stomach
-- caoq, navq -- to be stuck
caoq naolma aoqcal sun's rays
caoqnaoq naoq to stamp on the ground with one's feet (26:5) (tsaw˯ naw˯-eu)
=caoq, ngaq= bamboo fish net
-- caoqpeel, wuqcaoq -- grey or blue cap
caoqsaol owner of land, worshipped (6:185) (miˇ sahˇ)
  Caoqsaol albiaol the one who inhabits the sacred grove; a sacred personage that can be addressed
  caoqsaol milsaol a place where spirits (both evil and protective) live
  caoqsaol milsaol lol to make an offering in the middle of the village to the 'lord of the area' where spirits (both evil and protective) live
caoq teiq 1. to ambush (or) **beeqcaoq caoq**, 2. to overlap (**meelhov caoq teiq** = for tiles to overlap), 3. to absorb; assimilate (or) **cuv** (50:149)
-- caoq, wuqcaoq -- to wear a hat; a cap
Caoqxeilcuq Korean people (Chi)
Caoqxeil yaol haol (see: Meigaoq yaol diq - 50:96)

caofjeq to bring up; to train (Chi) (34:109)

CE

celsyujil a water pump (Chi) (50:25)
celtil a drawer (Chi)

ceq hatred (Chi) (bye-eu; muiˇ-eu)
(n) ceq 1. to hang, as a cloth, or a shoulder bag (**palnil ceq** = to hang red cloth) (12:125), 2. to wrap around (**kaoqbaoq yaol ceq** = to wrap around the neck - 14:218)
=ceq dav, kavq= (see full)
=ceq, hal= a sneeze (or) **heilceq** (pf)
=ceq, heil= a sneeze (or) **halceq**
-- ceq, heilceq -- to sneeze
-- ceq, kavq -- to tie up; to hang up (and see full)

-- **ceq, luqyil jil** -- to take a radio along (A=Chi)
-- **ceq, paltaol** -- to carry a shoulder bag
-- **ceq, piav** -- to climb on
-- **ceq, pieiq** -- to hang up
=**ceq, yo**= private property
-- **ceq, zalguv** -- to make a scarecrow

cev 1. to pick (as fruit); pluck (as leaf) (9:32), 2. to separate; wean (or) **hhoq; hhei**
=**cev, boqheiq ja**= black spots (as on face)
cevcev nei very quick (11:57) (yaw kaw$^{\vee}$)
cev ceiv to pinch (18:4) (tsui$_{\wedge}$-eu)
=**cev, naoq**= a type of small bird
=**cev, nee**= a gourd ladle; or a bamboo ladle with which to dip up water or put it in containers
cev nei quickly (**Cev nei ssuq, aoqsseil sseil al.** Walk quickly, it's raining.) (11:111) (kaw$^{\vee}$ kaw$^{\vee}$-eh$^{\vee}$)
cev puv to turn over (as paper, cake, etc.) (tah$_{\vee}$ po^ po^-eu)
-- **cev, puvlav** -- to be quick
-- **cev, saqkaol** -- (see full)
cev ssaoq 1. to gather; collect (50:18), 2. to 'pluck' and put together (as vegetables) (50:18)

cevq to chop (as firewood); to split; cut with an axe (9:32) (or) **dev** (ceu$_{\wedge}$-eu)
cevq to pick (tseu^-eu, etc.)
-- **cevq, aqgaoq** -- to divine with thatch grass (and see full)
cevq'aqma kingfisher (brd)
-- **cevq, aolcevq** -- (see full)
-- **cevq, baolcevq** -- to cut away old mud on the dikes (bunds) of terraced fields (du$_{\vee}$ dzeh-eu)
-- **cevqbu, miqkoq** -- big firewood (which must be cut with an ax)
=**cevq, ceiq**= a digging tool (like a pick)
cevq pav to split (with knife or axe) (or) **dev pav**
cevqpovq albol big-nut chestnut tree
cevqseil albol mid-sized nut chestnut tree
cevqsiq a wart
cevqsiq chestnut (9:32) (tsui$_{\wedge}$ si$_{\vee}$)
cevqsiq albol a small-nut chestnut tree

CEI

ceil unhusked rice; paddy (9:29) (ceh$^{\vee}$)
ceil 1. to select; choose (9:29) (tse$^{\vee}$-eu), 2. to investigate; to check (50:20)
ceil ten (9:29) (tse$^{\vee}$)
ceil to sterilize a female pig
ceil clf. for truck, lorry (Chi) (11:81)
ceil (vb) to (vb) look for (**piaqhhal ceil yil** = went looking for foot prints) (13:20) (po^-eu)
ceil'aqma wild rice stem (9:29)

ceilbaol rice stack (9:29) (ceh$^{\vee}$ bym$^{\vee}$)
-- ceilbaol, hhoyyuq -- stack of rice straw
ceilbao beivq rice in bloom (ceh$^{\vee}$ bym$_{\vee}$ bym$_{\vee}$ la$^{\vee}$-eu)
ceilbiavq biavq to pile up harvested rice plants
ceilbol rice stalk (9:29) (ceh$^{\vee}$ ceh$^{\vee}$ baw$_{\vee}$)
ceilbo a machine for winnowing grain
ceilbyuq rice worm/insect (9:29)
ceil byuqnav a rice weevil
ceilcaoq a cluster of rice stems in a field (14:188)
ceil ceilkol early ripening rice (46:205)
ceil ceilnuv powdered rice grains (cf.: ceh$^{\vee}$ meu)
ceil ceiv 1. to judge (50:127), 2. come to a conclusion (50:127)
ceil dalleil bags in which to carry rice
=ceil, daol= mountain rice
ceildaoq jav to have a result (as for an examination); to have a verdict (as in a a court case) (50:150)
=ceil, dei= irrigated rice field
-- ceil, diq -- to choose out from
ceil diq 1. to thresh ('beat') rice; 2. a general term for rice harvest (ceh$^{\vee}$ di$_{\vee}$-eu)
ceil diq aqzil song of autumn
ceil diq ba'la harvest season; autumn (26:110)
ceil diq baoqbeivq busy season in the autumn
ceil diq jilqiq rice threshing machine (26:26)
ceildu corn, maize (9:30) (a$^{\vee}$ du)
ceildu alpyuv popped corn (a$^{\vee}$ du a$^{\vee}$ pa$_{\vee}$ pa$_{\vee}$-eu)
ceildu ceilpiul corn & (grain) crops (12:127)
ceildu du for corn to ear out; ears begin to form
ceildu duhovq corn cob (a$^{\vee}$ du a$^{\vee}$ kah$_{\vee}$)
ceildu duniaoq glutinous corn (9:30) (a$^{\vee}$ du du nyaw$_{\vee}$)
ceildu dussei hard (field) corn
ceildu duyal corn field (9:30) (a$^{\vee}$ du du ya$^{\vee}$)
ceildu heivq to pick corn; harvest corn (9:30) (a$^{\vee}$ du k'eh$_{\wedge}$-eu)
ceildu meiqmoq corn tassels; corn silk (a$^{\vee}$ du meh$_{\vee}$ mah$_{\vee}$)
ceildu meiqnil red corn tassels
ceildu seqkal corn with few 'teeth' (grains)
ceildu sov to shell an ear of corn (a$^{\vee}$ du pya^-eu)
ceil duv to select out; look for and find; to pick up (13:20) (tse$^{\vee}$ do^-eu)
ceilgeeq broken rice (ceh$^{\vee}$ gui$_{\vee}$)
Ceilgu milhaoq a township in Honghe County (46:173)
=ceil, hal= sand
-- ceil, habaol diq -- to divine with a chicken thigh
ceilhav roughly pounded rice
ceil heq to distinguish (50:13)
ceil heq ceiv bring to trial; to try by trial (50:150)
=ceil, hoq= partially cooked rice
ceilhovq empty rice husk (9:30, 11:188) (ceh$^{\vee}$ k'aw$_{\wedge}$)

-- **ceilhuvq, quvqlaol** -- a thermometer

ceilhhaol a two-stringed musical instrument (or, cil'aol = not pf.)

ceilhhaol hhe to play the above instrument

ceiljeil workshop (Chi) (26:27)

ceiljeil zusseif director of workshop (Chi) (26:27)

ceiljil 1. rice granary (9:30), 2. grain bin, 3. storeroom (cehˇ jiˇ)

ceiljil aqma the spirit of the granary (46:79)

ceiljil aqma lol to make an offering to the spirit of the granary (46:79)

ceiljil jilsiivq a new rice granary (cehˇ jiˇ jiˇ shui^)

Ceiljil Lavqqivq Aqda Jil Byu'lyul master craftsman Jil Byu'lyul (a person's name) (35:40)

ceiljil naqbiaq a round wooden protection put around the posts of a rice granary to keep mice and rats from climbing up (35:41)

ceil jiv jilciq a motorized rice mill (B=Chi)

ceilkaol head hair (9:30) (tsehˇ kahˇ)

ceilkaol kaolpiul white head hair (9:30) (uˬ duˬ uˬ pyuˇ)

ceilkev hoqpiul fine rice; well-pounded rice (the last stage) (9:30) (cehˇ pyuˇ)

ceilkev kev to pound rice lightly (the first pounding)

ceilkol early rice (9:30) (or) **ceil ceilkol**

ceil kov ngavq siil many ways or customs (46:205)

ceilkul fried rice

ceil kuvq sixteen (9:30) (tseˇ ko^)

ceilla galtaol ten-month New Year

ceilla galtaol aqpyuq hel ten-month New Year ancestral offering

Ceilla siq October

ceillaoq a by-election (50:16)

ceille late rice (9:30)

ceillevq very small kind of bamboo

ceil leiq lavqqivq skill to drive a car (A=Chi) (50:82)

ceil loq 1. to interrogate (50:150), 2. to make things clear (50:127), 3. to select; to distinguish (50:127)

ceillyul powdered rice

ceil mil one hundred thousand (tiˬ seh)

ceil milmil one billion

ceil miaol a type of rice

ceil miao rice ripens (cehˇ myah laˇ-eu)

=ceil, moq= horse feed (unhusked rice)

ceilnaq naq a place to keep the harvested rice temporarily until there is a chance to sun it and put it in the granary

ceilnav purple glutinous rice (9:31) (hawˬ nyawˬ na^)

ceilnaol rice ear (9:30, 11:151, 46:206) (cehˇ nmˇ)

ceilnaoq re-pounded rice

ceilneev the rice grain (or) **ceilsiq** (9:31) (ceh^{v} si$_{v}$)

ceil niq twelve

ceil niq puvlaol the second cry of a newborn, which is for the whole village

ceil niq puvlaol dama older villagers; village elders

ceil niq se twelve o'clock (41:30) (B=Chi)

-- ceil ngavq nao, Xeivqla siq -- August 15th, the time of the autumn festival

ceilpiaof train or bus ticket (Chi) (26:90, 50:22) (this could be: **hoceil piaof**)

ceilpiul rice (pounded and winnowed, uncooked) (9:31) (ceh^{v} pyu^{v})

ceilpiul ciq to wash husked rice (before cooking) (9:31) (ceh^{v} pyu^{v} tsi$_{v}$-eu)

ceilpiul pyuqtul a container for rice

ceilpyuv popped rice

ceil qa yal qa many kinds; hundreds of kinds (lit. 'tens of kinds, hundreds of kinds') (46:217) (tse^{v} je$_{v}$ ya^{v} je$_{v}$)

ceilqavq glue (11:28) (gaw$_{v}$; i^{v} ni$_{v}$)

ceilsiq rice grain (or) **ceilneev** (9:31) (ceh^{v} si$_{v}$)

ceilsiivq ceil'yul mil for old rice to last until the new rice crop comes in

ceilsiivq hoq new rice (9:31) (haw$_{v}$ shui$_{\wedge}$)

ceilsiivq hoqtaoq teil to pound new rice

ceilsiivq hoq zaq to eat the new rice festival (haw$_{v}$ shui$_{\wedge}$ dza$_{v}$-eu)

ceilsiivq kalnaol new rice ears

ceil soq to adjust; to regulate (46:76)

ceilssyuq rice seeds (ceh^{v} si$_{v}$ yoe$_{v}$)

ceil taoq to pound rice (9:31) (ceh^{v} tah$_{v}$-eu)

ceiltivq eleven (9:31) (tse^{v} ti$_{\wedge}$)

Ceiltivqla siq November (11:69)

ceiltov badu 1. a measuring basket for grain, 2. a small basket used to take the threshed rice out of the threshing 'boat' (**diqloq**)

ceilxal the class one travels on a train (as first, second, etc.) (Chi) (26:93)

ceil xa to plant rice (46:211) (ceh^{v} ka ka-eu)

ceilyav buqdeiq a board for spreading and collecting rice

=ceil, yeq= a postman's car (Chi)

ceil yeiq to harvest (reap) rice (ceh^{v} yeh$_{v}$-eu)

ceilyeiv rice to head ('flower') (ceh^{v} a^{v} yeh$^{\wedge}$)

ceilyeiv puq nei rice flowers to blossom

-- ceil, zalceil -- to eat selectively

ceilzaf a station (for buses, trains) (Chi) (50:22)

ceilzil zaq consideration; deliberation

cei to take pity on someone (or) **neema cei miq** (g'aw$_{v}$ sha$_{v}$ ga$_{v}$-eu)

cei to stand up (9:29) (yaw‸-eu)
-- **cei, bavq** -- to raise; hold up
ceibu to bleach; rinse; clean (9:29) (tsiˬ shawˇ-eu)
-- **cei cei, biavq biavq** -- colorful; blazing with color
ceicei nei to be very sad (nui ma caw^-eu)
-- **cei, coq** -- to jump up
cei'fa gather news (as reporters) (Chi) (50:18)
-- **cei, hhe** -- to raise up (as sword)
=**cei, moq**= horse cart
=**cei nei, lu**= to puff out
=**cei, niuq**= cart for buffalo/oxen
-- **cei, piav** -- to climb up on
-- **cei qaq, hol** -- to take pity on someone
cei'qeiq biqhef to learn from past mistakes so as to avoid future ones (Chi) (34:109)
=**cei, yaq**= (see full)

ceiq mattock; hoe (9:31) (tsehˬ ma)
ceiq to plow (9:31) (tsehˬ-eu)
ceiq a city (Chi) (34:56) (or) **ceiqssif** (meuˬ)
ceiq to multiply (in math) (Chi) (see also: **ceiqfaq**)
ceiq clf. for hoe, plow (11:95)
Ceiq a surname (26:24)
ceiqbaol to contract (Chi) (34:42)
ceiqca property (Chi) (34:86) (myawˬ)
ceiqcevq a pick (digging tool) (9:31)
-- **ceiq, ceiqyeif** -- to have a test (Chi)
ceiqdal to accept (as in accepting responsibility) (Chi) (or) daqhaol
-- **ceiq, daoltavq niuqceiq** -- to plow mountain fields (non-irrigated)
ceiq duq to dig with a hoe; mattock
-- **ceiq, eeldaoq niuqceiq** -- to plow irrigated fields
ceiqfaq multiplication (math) (Chi)
  ceiqfaq kejiq repeating the multiplication tables by means of a pithy formula (Chi)
ceiqgaol success (**ceiqgaol jav** = to have success, 26:45, 34:4) (Chi)
ceiqgo results (Chi) (34:71)
ceiqhaof times (Chi) (math term, as in 'ten times eight')
-- **ceiq, hoqceiq** -- to eat little by little, making a little food last a long time (as one egg for four meals)
ceiqhuaq talent (Chi) (34:68)
ceiqhuaf to plan (Chi) (50:20)
ceiqhhuvq a hoe (tsehˬ ma)
  ceiqhhuvq hhuvqssaq a small hoe or shovel as used to pick up dung (26:37)
  ceiqhhuvq miavhhuvq hoes and machetes (tools to use in the field)
ceiqjil finance and economics (Chi) (50:18)
ceiqjiq achievement (as grades; evaluation marks as given in school) (Chi) (26:42, 50:23)

-- **ceiq, kavceiq** -- to harrow a field deeply
ceiq kov furrows (in a field)
-- **ceiqkov, niuqceiq** -- a plowed furrow
-- **ceiqla soq, zeiq duv** -- to pay various taxes
ceiqla zalpeil exorbitant taxes and levies (50:97)
-- **ceiqla, zeiqduv** -- to pay heavy taxes
=**ceiq, lavq**= adze
ceiqliq an old hoe (tseh˯ ma yaw oeˇ)
ceiqliq a foundation (Chi) (26:76, 34:1)
ceiqliaol material (Chi) (50:18)
ceiqma a big hoe (tseh˯ ma)
Ceiqmiq Dazaolyal President and Party Secretary (Chi) (see: **Jal Zeqmiq**)
ceiqmuf commercial trade (Chi) (50:18)
ceiqmuf bufmeiq department of commercial trade (Chi) (50:18)
ceiqnaq the opening in the hoe for a handle to fit
=**ceiq nei, nil**= red
ceiqnioq 1. policy (50:20) 2. tactics (Chi) (34:24)
=**ceiq, niuq**= plow (for buffalo/oxen)
Ceiqpiul a personal name (9:31)
ceiq puv to plow a terraced field (turning the mud over) (9:31, 11:18)
ceiqqeiq financial rights (Chi) (50:18)
ceiqsal shirt (Chi) (26:72) (or) **ceiqyil** (Chi) (pehˇ k'ah˯)
Ceiqsal boy's name (11:147)
ceiqsiif town; city (Chi) (26:27, 50:23) (or) **ceiq; ceiqzeif laol** = walled city)
Ceiqsiif Sseiqmiq gaolseif People's Commune in the city (Chi) (26:76)
ceiqso outhouse; water closet; toilet (Chi) (10:16, 50:20) (gaˇ nyiˇ iˇ ku^)
ceiqsuq suq to plow a field shallowly
=**ceiq, ssaq**= a fetus
-- **ceiq, ssaqbeiq** -- (see full)
ceiqssaq lavqdev a small hoe (la^ ngeu˯)
ceiqxif order; procedure (Chi) (34:56)
ceiqyeq diesel oil (or) **caqyeq** (Chi)
=**ceiq, yeil**= luck
ceiqyeif ceiq to have a test (A=Chi) (41:63)
ceiqyyuq a mattock or hoe handle (tseh˯ ma tseh˯ yoe˯) (9:31)
ceiqzal delicious food
-- **ceiqzaq, davceiq** -- to be a step-father
ceiqzeif a town (Chi) (50:23)
ceiqzeif public finance (Chi) (50:18) (or) **caqzeif**
ceiqzeif ciiqziif financial deficits (Chi) (50:18)

ceiv 1. to break (as thread); 2. to interrupt (9:32) (tseh^-eu)
ceiv to compare (ceh^-eu)
-- **ceiv, alcav beil** -- to break free from being tied up
-- **ceiv, aqqul** -- to wean

-- ceiv, aoqjiq coqceiv -- thunder and lightning
-- ceiv, cev -- to pinch
-- ceiv, eil -- to promise; decide
=ceiv, doq= a partial sentence
-- ceiv, eil -- to decide; promise; conclusion; set a regulation
-- ceiv, gee -- an agreement on something
=ceiv, heiq= sambar deer
-- ceiv, heivq -- twist and break
-- ceiv, hhaqbieiv -- to be discouraged
-- ceiv, kuvq -- to estimate (A=Chi)
ceivkyul deer horn (9:32) (u˯ coe˅)
-- ceiv lal, savq -- 1. to stop breathing, 2. to die
=ceiv, la= last ten days of month
-- ceiv, lav -- 1. to break a line; a string, 2. to pluck a stringed instrument
-- ceiv, luvq -- to block the way
-- ceiv, miqdavq -- a young man to visit his girlfriend (taboo)
ceivnav wild goat (11:218)
-- ceiv, neema -- a broken heart; to be discouraged
-- ceiv, neema nyuq -- to persevere
=ceiv nei, bil= horizontal
ceiv nei puv a violent change; change very quickly (50:93)
-- ceivnil, heiqceiv -- a red deer
-- ceiv, nyuq -- to decide
-- ceiv, sil -- to die (finally expire)
-- ceiv xa, nee -- dare to do something; decide to do something
-- ceiv, ya -- to be broken off

ceivq to bark (as dog) (9:32) (tseh˄-eu)
ceivq cool (9:32) (yaw tseh˄)
-- ceivq, coldavq -- for a girl to visit her lover (taboo)
=ceivq, eel= cold water; unboiled water
-- ceivq, heivq -- to twist and break
-- ceivq, laqbavq -- to wrestle
-- ceivq, lav -- to tease
ceivqqaol freezing cold (tseh˄ ga˅ neh-a˯)
ceivqqaol pa qaol nei extremely cold (11:58) (tseh˄ dui dui-eu)

CI

cil tin
cil oil; lard (tsi˅)
cil 1. hot (to touch) (yaw cui˅), 2. to be peppery (9:32) (yaw pi˅)
cil 1. to be clean (of water) (yaw shaw˅), 2. to be silent (ci˯ cu˅ ni)
cil'aol stringed instrument with two strings (9:32) (**ceilhhaol** = pf.)
cilbaoq oil jar; lard jar

cilciq relatives (Chi) (9:33, 11:153, 41:2); **ciciq** (a˯ yui˰ a˯ nyiˇ)

=cil, haq= a bamboo slat

cilhaoq a bowl for oil (in Ak. = a lamp: tsiˇ k'm˯)

=cil, heil= castor oil plant

=cil, hhavq= pig lard

=cil, hhoq= rape plant

cilja a term that husband's and wife's parents call each other (41:2)

  cilja aqda father of one's son-in-law or daughter-in-law

  cilja aqma mother of one's son-in-law or daughter-in-law

=cil, ja= wagtail (brd)

cilkuq dregs of fat (pork rinds) (**hhavqcil cilkuq** = pork fat)

-- cil, laqpil -- 1. to be spicy (with chili pepper), 2. to be stingy

=cil, lavq= sweat on hands

cil lil cuvq luvq nei twittering; gabbling (45:45)

-- cillil, peiqtaoq -- a kind of fruit that looks like a comb

=cil, meiq= cupped lip

-- cil, miavcil -- eyes to become red from pink eye (conjunctivitus)

cilmol mom; mother (Chi) (a˯ ma)

Cilnieiqtueiq Youth League (Chi)

-- cil, nyuq duvq nyuq -- to think deeply and plan carefully

cilpuq a cupping jar for curing diseases (they use a fire in the cup)

  cilpuq zei to cure a disease with a cupping jar

=cil qivq nei, aoq= the whole day

-- cil, soq -- to pay a debt

cilsuq nei to be painful (naˇ seh˰-eu)

ci to pick up something with thumb and two fingers (toe˯ diˇ-eu)

ci clf. for amount of something that can be picked up between thumb and two fingers

ciciq relatives (see: **cilciq**)

-- ci, haolci -- for mold or fungus to develop

cija to ask for a leave of absence (Chi) (9:32)

  cija e tiaoqzii a note asking for leave (from work, school, etc.) (Chi)

ciq to wash (9:33) (tsi˯-eu)

ciq wet; damp (as from rain) (yaw a˯)

ciq muddy water used by a blacksmith to temper hot metals

-- ciq, aol haol -- to render a service

Ciqcaoq Qin dynasty (221-206 BC) (46:83)

ciqdeivq nei very wet; damp

ciqhaq dew (9:33, 14:216) (ceu˯)

ciqhaq ciqpeil a type of medicine they get in the

jungle (bitter and sour)
  ciqhaq puvtav nei to be wet with dew (14:169) (ceuˬ aˬ-eu)
-- **ciq, huq** -- to wash first; to wash before doing something else
ciqhhaol a type of mushroom (or) **haollul** (aˇ hmˇ)
ciqkuaf the situation (Chi)
ciqlavq nei to be damp (aˬ ciˬ ni)
ciqleiq to paint (and see: **ciqleiq leiq**) (leh‸-eu)
-- **ciq, leiq** -- to wash by rubbing
ciqleiq leiq to put medicine on a wound (ja^ g'aˬ leh‸-eu)
-- **ciqma, naciq** -- pharmacist
-- **ciq miq, aqbul** -- to give a bath
=**ciq, miaoq**= to dye cloth indigo
=**ciq, na**= medicine
=**ciq, ngaq**= a vine used to poison fish
ciq pieiq to temper metal by dipping in water (as a blacksmith does) (la^ mi^-eu)
-- **ciq, qiv** -- to brush with water
ciq sol to wash clean (10:16, 11:21) (tsiˬ shawˇ-eu)
ciqwufyeiq odd-job man (Chi) (26:111)
ciq xa to wash away (16:179) (tsiˬ shawˇ-eu)
=**ciq, zaq**= color
ciqzaof the masses; ordinary people (Chi)

civ to graze (28:4) (ga^ dzaˬ-eu)
civciv nei the sound of birds, insects, animals (14:217) (mahˇ-eu teˇ saˇ)
-- **civ, hahao** -- to dress (pluck) a chicken
-- **civ, laqpil** -- to be a miser
=**civ nei, gaol**= clean water
civtaoq taoqma qiq taoq to strike a death blow
civteiq to endure; to last
civzaol nei 1. frequently; very often (9:33, 10:2, 11:110 has samples, 38:33), 2. always (10:10), 3. daily (11:118) (tiˬ k'ehˬ maˬ taˬ ni, aˬ myah lu‸) (or) **ciivzaol nei**
  civzaol nei qiq gao always together

=**civq, aq**= goat
civqbaoq 1. a bad temper (46:104), 2. to be cruel (50:19)
  civqbaoq baoq to have a bad temper (nui ma maˬ muiˬ)
  civqbaoq beil 1. to lose one's temper (46:104) (nui ma pehˇ laˇ-eu), 2. to have an epileptic seizure
  civqbaoq beil sil to have an epileptic seizure (mawˇ bawˬ coˬ-eu)
civqbo one of the spirits which can enter a person ("ngeeq")
civqbu male goat (9:33) (ci‸ myeh‸ ci‸ buˬ)
  civqbuq a long haired goat; certain types of sheep
civqhao goat hair (9:33) (ci‸ myeh‸ ca‸ hm)
civq lav peiv 1. to make someone angry (45:52), 2. to

offend (nui ma la^ pehˇ-eu)
=civq, miaoq= a busy season
civq niq peiv while angry (57:87)
civq peiv to be angry (46:103) (or) **neema peil** (nui ma pehˇ-eu)
civq peiv sil very angry; indignant (13:21) (nui ma pehˇ seh˰-eu)
civq peiv sil peiv lo to be extremely angry (45:53)
civqsaq goat meat (9:33) (ci˰ myeh˰ sha˯ jiˇ)

cifzuq celebration (Chi) (26:76)

CII

ciil to lead (tsahˇ-eu (anim.) sheu˯-eu (peop.)) (9:32, 46:144)
-- **ciil, caqssaq cavq keeq** -- ceremony held when an illegitimate child is born
=ciil, dal= stick; switch
=ciil, hhavq= boar; male pig
-- **ciil, keeqciil** -- (see full)
ciil teiq 1. to lead animals (as horses) (12:126), 2. to hold someone's hand, arm (26:46) (tsahˇ-eu; tsahˇ teh˯-eu)
ciil tul to take up; lift up (26:11) (if a child falls down, you: **ciiltul**) (ci˯ da^-eu)
ciil zul to take someone to a seat (14:193)

cii to breathe heavily
cii clf. for a folksong (35:84)
-- **cii, leelcii** -- to bother others
=cii meil, savqhhol savq= to breathe with difficulty
-- **cii, savq** -- to have breathing difficulty; to suffer from asthma
-- **cii, savqcii** -- to pant; to breathe with difficulty; to suffer from asthma

ciiq a word (Chi) (41:94) (daw˯)
ciiq (w.m.) about one-third of a meter, clf. for a measure of cloth (Chi) (11:77, 41:126)
ciiqdeif recording tape (Chi) (50:27)
ciiqdiei a dictionary (Chi)
ciiqjesif the last (Chi)
ciiqkyul to suffer losses; to get the worst of something (Chi) (14:146)
ciiqteq magnetic core (Chi) (50:27)
ciiqyeil 1. same clan, 2. close friends (46:86) (tsui˰ yehˇ)
ciiqziif deficit (Chi) (50:24)

ciiv nei a moment (9:32) (ti˯ k'eh˯)
ciiv nei qiq heiq after a moment; after a little bit; in a very short time (35:17) (ui cui^ ti˯

k'ehˬ)

ciiv **nei qiq heiq ngeel taoqngaoq** after a moment (35:52) (tiˬ k'ehˬ naˇ)

ciiv **nei za** to be just right

ciiv **teiq** to bear with someone (oˇ tehˬ-eu)

ciiv**zaol nei** often (14:159) (or) **civzaol nei** (14:206) (maˬ myahˇ kaˬ-ehˇ)

ciivq to choke (iˇ cu˰ dawˇ nga˰-eu)

ciivq to pinch (9:32, 46:134) (tseu^-eu)

ciivq genealogy (9:32) (tsui˰) (**ciivq gee** = to recount a genealogy)

ciivq clf. for a joint (as of bamboo, fingers, etc.) (tsui˰)

=ciivq, **al**= 1. for a joint between sections, 2. a genealogy

-- ciivq, **aqhhu qiq** -- a lower level; subordinate

ciivq**coq coq** a genealogy in which there is one or more breaks (i.e., 'jump over') (tsui˰ tsawˬ)

=ciivq, **daol**= one's back (lower)

ciivq**daoq daoq** a genealogy in which there are no male descendants to keep it going

ciivq **daov peiv** very angry (13:3)

ciivq **gee** to recount a genealogy (46:136) (tsui˰ gui-eu)

=ciivq, **haq**= bamboo joint

=ciivq, **kaoq**= larynx

=ciivq, **lavq**= elbow

=ciivq, **laol**= neck (animals; people)

ciivq**naoq** spinal cord (5:555) (dahˇ teˇ)

=ciivq, **nyul**= joint of a finger

=ciivq, **paoqhhuvq paoq**= the hollow behind the knee

-- ciivq, **saqciivq** -- to pinch (in joking or quarreling)

=ciivq, **saqyyuq paoq**= the kneecap

=ciivq, **tavq**= an older generation

=ciivq, **xaldei baol**= steps between terraces in irrigated fields

CO

col people; person; human (9:33) (tsawˇ haˬ)

col clf. for people (or) **hhaq (Col xil col.** 11:95)

col a mistake; an error (Chi) (yaw bahˬ)

-- col, **alkaq** -- (see full)

col **aoq zaq** to abduct and sell a person (50:64)

-- col**ba, gee pil** -- a mediating group; organization

col**buvq** a clumsy person (yaw dza)

col**cavq** a bad person (yaw doeˇ; yaw ca˰)

col**cavq pievq** to become a bad person (yaw doeˇ pyeu˰ laˇ-eu)

col**ceivq colzaq** evil elements from the old society (50:19)

col**ciivq** a generation (tiˬ ziˇ; tiˬ tsui˰)

col**cuv colcavq** a funny person; a foolish person; a

dumb person (28:4)

colcuv colcavq cavq act in collusion with each other (50:101)

coldavq young man (taboo) (9:33) (a˯ li za˯ da˰)

coldavq ceivq for a young woman to go visit a young man (taboo)

col del a person who wanders (or) **col ya col del**

coldel del for a person to wander; roam

coldol a bad person (tsawˇ dawˇ = a taboo term in Akha)

coldyul a loafer; a lazy person (or) **colga**

colga a loafer; a lazy person (or) **coldyul**

colgaq a beloved elder

colgaq aqbol Maoq Zuxiq beloved elder grandfather/ Chairman Mao (C=Chi) (26:101)

colgaq aqyivq meilnaol beloved brothers and sisters (46:217) (ga˯-eu a˯ yui˰ mehˇ nmˇ)

colgaq neegaq gaq e loved (friends) dear (ga˯ caw˯) (relatives) (**Colgaq neegaq gaq e aqyivq meilnaol** = beloved friends; beloved relatives - 26:87)

colgov thin/weak person (yaw jeh)

colgov gov a thin person (11:18) (yaw jeh)

colhav adult; young adult (9:33) (tsawˇ k'a^)

colhav aqda da for a boy to become a young adult

colhav aqma ma for a girl to become a young adult

colhaol an arbiter; an envoy (or) **colkaq** (tsawˇ ka˯)

colhe 1. personality; character (50:141), 2. common feelings of people (50:142)

colhhaq 1. manpower (in terms of how many people can work for what length of time) (11:115, 50:102) (aˇ g'a˯), 2. salary (45:3)

colhhaq aol (zaq) to work for others for a living doing odd jobs

-- col, hhaqhaoq -- a porter

colhhaq hhaqpav 'half manpower' (as a boy would be half the manpower of a man) (50:5)

colhhovq family (9:33) (nymˇ dah˯ ti˯ zaw˰) (cf. Lahu clf. for household: g'o˰)

colhhyul aqda paqssaq beloved elders (46:217)

col hhyul e neivq maq hhyul 'what makes people happy does not make spirits happy'

coljol life; a person's life (10:22)

Coljol bi sal, colssil bi bo. May you have good health and live a long life. (a blessing) (a polite ending to a letter or a blessing when leaving someone)

Coljol bi sal, gaoqlaoq bi bo. May you have good health and good luck. (a blessing)

coljol bi sal movq alnei zilbaq dol to drink to someone's health

coljol bi sal, ssil bi bo may you be healthy and have a long life (a blessing) (41:160) (jawˇ mui˯ jawˇ saˇ do^-awˇ ziˇ baw lu˰-uˇ)

-- col jol, niq lov -- (see full)

coljol sal miq to wish good health to someone

(10:pref.) (guiˬ lahˬ bi‸-eu)

Coljol sal yaq? How are you? (**Sal ya.** = Well. **Maq sal ya.** = Not well. **Daov maq sal ya.** = Not very well.) (Jawˇ saˇ do^ miˇ-a loˇ.)

coljol salzav nei in good health; healthy (jawˇ saˇ do^-eu)

col ju nei a slender and tall person

colkaq 1. a go-between; arbiter; envoy (or) **colhaol**, 2. a witness (9:34) (tsawˇ kaˬ), 3. a go-between who arranges for a wedding

colkaq gee to be a go-between; witness

colkaq kaqceiv a ruling (50:18)

colkaq kaqduq notarization office (50:62)

colkaqssaq a judge

colkyul a clever, smart person (9:34, 13:11) (tsawˇ gahˇ)

colleiv a short person (tsawˇ aw; cf.: lehˇ ti)

col loq ceil col ten people (elaborate) (35:85) (tseˇ g'aˬ)

col loq col meil a mob of people (14:150)

colma an able person (**colssaq colma** = small, able person) (32:3)

col maq bi miaq lal population control (50:98)

col mavq people (tsawˇ haˬ)

colmeeq good people; great people (34:3) (tsawˇ muiˬ)

col miaq doq miaq 'many people - many words' (Hani proverb) (tsawˇ myaˬ dawˬ myaˬ)

col miaq zeiq overpopulated (50:22)

col miav human eye (as when speaking of something that cannot be seen by the 'naked eye') (10:23)

colmiaol name (9:34) (tsawˇ myahˇ)

colmiaol buvq to sign one's name

colmiaol gul to call roll (or) **dieimiq** (Chi) (tsawˇ myahˇ kuˇ-eu)

colmiaol leiqbial remove someone's name from the rolls (50:25)

colmiaol miaol to name someone (9:34) (tsawˇ myahˇ myahˇ-eu)

colmiaol miaolcavq one's nickname (35:40)

colmiaol miaoltaoq one's real name (35:40) (tsawˇ myahˇ myahˇ maˇ)

colmoq old man; old person; elder (tsawˇ mawˬ)

colmoq laqhyul qo li to go cut a coffin for an elder ('to search for a home for the elder' = a very polite way of speaking of death) (or) **alzaol dev** (not so polite)

colmoq moq to get old; to get on in years

colmoqssaq elderly; old people (tsawˇ mawˬ zaˬ) (9:34)

colmu a person who is mad; insane (tsawˇ uˬ)

colmu mu for a person to go mad; go insane (9:115) (tsawˇ uˬ uˬ-iˇ-eu)

colnal a sick person (9:34) (tsawˇ naˇ)

colnav a colored person; a black person

colpeel poor people (27:11) (or) **cyuqssaq** (shaˬ-

eu zah˯-eu tsaw˅ ha˯)

colpol pol to immigrate (14:182, 46:76, 135) (paw˅-eu)

colpuv 1. "people" village (13:2) (pu), 2. a rebel (one who turns against his country) (50:127)

colpuv paoq the same village (14:173) (ti˯ pu)

colpuv puv 1. to rebel; revolt (50:8), 2. one who betrays (50:127)

colpyuq bo to have prestige (or) **colteil dav**

colqa clan (family) name; surname (9:34) (tsaw˅ jeu˯ tsaw˅ ca)

colqa colssaq 1. nationality (46:77); 2. minority nationalities (46:218)

colqi middle-aged (or) **colqi meil** (9:34, 13:2) (tsaw˅ k'a^)

col qiq hhaq one person (3:2) (tsaw˅ ha˯ ti˯ g'a˯)

col qiq ba a crowd of people

col qiq hhaq aqmeil dul nei as one person

col qiq mavq one group of people (3:2) (tsaw˅ ha˯ ti˯ ma˄)

col qoq col alkaq among friends (57:135)

colqoq gaq zav hhyul qaol nei qoq to get on with people; to be a good friend (caw˯ caw˯-eu)

colqoq miavhhaq bo to give honor to (yaw zeu baw-eu)

colqoq pievq huvq to be reconciled

colsaq colga refugees (50:120)

col seivq zyul crime of murdering a human (50:146)

colsil corpse; dead body (9:34) (tsaw˅ shi˅)

colssaq humans; people (tsaw˅ ha˯) (13:53)

colssil one's life span (26:55) (zi˅)

colssil bo e 1. to still be alive (35:110) (deh˄ lu˄-eu), 2. to have a long life span (zi˅ baw-eu)

colssil ssilssaq a short life (26:100) (zi˅ ma˯ baw)

colssyuq colqa ethnic family (46:133, speaking of choosing two young men from a 'good family')

col taol col yal hundreds and thousands of people (57:70)

colteil reputation; fame (50:118, 150)

colteil dav to have prestige (or) **colpyuq bo**

colteiq ssaqnil a person whose child is young

colteiq ssaqnil aqda a man whose child is young (za˯ nah˯ a˯ da)

colteiq ssaqnil aqma a woman whose child is young (za˯ nah˯ a˯ ma)

col xildyul these people (tsaw˅ ha˯ heu deu˯)

col ya col del flee hither and thither (50:109) (and see: col del)

col yaol yaq to call someone bad names

colyaovq the appearance of a person (11:31) (mya^ pyaw˯ na˅ meh˅)

colzaq aqquv strong and handsome; vigorous and graceful (50:84)

colzoq a dumb, foolish person (or) **ssaqzoq**

colzuv native people (50:79)

colzuvssaq a native; local people (50:10)
colzyul criminal (50:2)
colzyul neema zaol pal to change one's mind (50:55)
colzyul zyul for people to gather together (14:241) (tsaw$^{\vee}$ ha$_{\vee}$ dzoe$^{\vee}$-eu)

coma a village announcer
coma to be heavy (only used of people)
coma jol for people (esp. children) to be fat

coq 1. to jump (9:34) (tsaw$_{\vee}$-eu), 2. to stretch out one's hand
coq clf. for a jump (11:85)
coq beivq 1. breaks suddenly (as a floor with too many people on it, or fruit) (9:34, 45:41), 2. to blow up; explode (or) **coq pav**
coqbeivq coqseil chapping, as the skin (or) **havyov nei**
-- **coqbiq, wulquvq** -- a water course made of wood or bamboo
coq biav to break (la^ pa^-eu)
coqbiavq magpie (9:35) (law caw^) (or) **covqbiavq**
coq bul to jump and float (as when jumping into a river) (35:78) (tsaw$_{\vee}$ bu-eu)
coq cei to jump up (41:199) (tsaw$_{\vee}$ di$^{\vee}$)
coq ceiv to break (as a thread) (tsaw$_{\vee}$ pa^)
coqceiv a waterfall (or) **wulquvq coqceiv** (tsaw$_{\vee}$; tsaw$_{\vee}$ ga)
-- **coqceiv, wulquvq** -- a waterfall
-- **coq, ciivqcoq** -- a genealogy in which there are one or more breaks (lit. 'jump over')
-- **coq, neema** -- heart to beat
coqhha jumping (in 26:27 it tells of fire in a refinery 'jumping' like a dragon)
-- **coq, hhyulcoq** -- to dance for joy; to jump up and down for joy
-- **coq, kavcoq** -- to harrow a field here and there
-- **coq, keelcoq** -- jumping
=**coq, koq**= the sound of jumping fish
coqleiq kovq to pass on a disease to another (10:23) (na$^{\vee}$ gaw$^{\vee}$ nyaw$_{\vee}$ le$^{\vee}$-eu)
-- **coq, loqzoq** -- to dance (10:pref.)
coq pav 1. to explode; to blow up (50:8) (tsaw$_{\vee}$ pa^-eu), 2. to break
=**coq, piaq**= chipmunk (small jumping squirrel)
coq puvq to jump into (35:78) (tsaw$_{\vee}$ pu$_{\wedge}$-eu)
coq pyul to jump over (11:127) (tsaw$_{\vee}$ dzeu$^{\vee}$-eu)
coqseil seilba an art troupe (50:93)
coqseil seilmiaol the name of a dance (performed by an art troupe) (50:93)
coqseil seilyaol 1. theater for dancing and singing groups, 2. cinema (50:93)
-- **coq, seiqkaq** -- (see full)
coqsiil a step; a measure (or) **bufcef** (Chi) (34:10)
coq tao li to jump into (26:;24) (tsaw$_{\vee}$ u$^{\vee}$-eu)

coqwuf a mistake (Chi) (34:6); **bav** (bah⌄)
Coqzyuqma the first founder of a Hani village (a female in a Hani legend) (46:112)

cov to pierce into; stick into; stab (9:35, 46:94) (tsaw^-eu)
-- cov, aqhhovq -- to inject with a needle
cov cuv to stick in (46:153)
cov dav to prick (or) **peiv dav**
-- cov, hhovqma -- to give an injection with a needle
-- cov, naciq -- to inject medicine
cov tao to insert
-- cov, xaolyeil -- to give an injection of medicine to bring down swelling and inflamation (A=Chi)

covqbeivq a crack
covqbiavq a magpie (or) **coqbiavq**
covqbiavq aqma a magpie (35:74) (or) **covqbiavq**
covq covq nei the sound of water (14:168) (iˇ cu^ yoeˇ-eu teˇ saˇ)
=covq, ha= a hen which grows rapidly
covqleiq kovq to pass on a disease (or) **coqleiq kovq** (naˇ gawˇ nyaw⌄ leˇ-eu)
covqleivq a skin rash (maˇ toe^ toe^-eu)
  covqleivq dav for a skin rash to appear
  covqleivq kovq to have a skin rash
  covqleivq nieivq to pull the skin in order to cure a disease (thus making deep red spots) (sha^ g'eu-eu)
  covqleivq qiv to rub the skin with a coin or button in order to cure a disease (thus making deep red spots)
covq pal 1. to exchange money, 2. to make change (**Piul covq pal zaq kal**. Let's change money.) (paˇ-eu)
-- covq pieiq lal, ssil -- to cause someone to have a short life
-- covq, ssil -- to have a short life

cofhhuf a mistake (Chi) (yaw bah⌄)
cofsiil a measure (Chi) (34:40)
cofzeiq a setback; a reverse (Chi) (34:85)

CU

cul fat; plump (9:35) (yaw tsuˇ)
cul to kiss (5:395) (meh⌄ cuˇ cuˇ-eu)
-- cul, baqcul -- to kiss on the face
culbiq nei fat; roly-poly (38:20) (tsuˇ dah⌄ ni)
culbiq pa biq nei very fat (as roly-poly children) (11:61) (tsuˇ dah⌄ ni)
-- cul, deiq -- (see full)
=cul, hhavq= pork fat
culjiq primary; first class (Chi) (50:25)
  culjiq geilduaf primitive stage; primary stage

(Chi) (34:35; 50:25)
-- cul, meiqjil deiq -- pouting lips
culxao elementary school (grades 1-3) (Chi)
culzaol junior middle school (Chi) (14:200, 50:25)
culzaol zol to study in a junior middle school (A=Chi)

=cu, aq= older brother's wife
cu'faq to punish; penalize (Chi) (50:25)
cu'li to solve a problem; bring about a settlement (Chi) (34:15, 50:26) (la^ shaw-eu)

cuq a hot spring (cu$_\vee$)
cuq to suck (liquid) (cu$_\wedge$)
cuq to divide (as numbers) (Chi)
cuq the sound of cicadas
cuqba to publish (Chi) (34:65, 50:25)
cuqbaseif a publishing house (Chi) (14:183, 50:25)
=cuq, beildul lul= rainbow
cuq biav cuq lyul to gossip; tell bad things; libel; stir up trouble (11:205) (ja doe$^\vee$-eu)
cuqcal an errand (Chi) (26:94)
-- cuq dav li, lolcuq -- to go upstream (along the river)
-- cuqdaol, alcuq -- a type of small wild bamboo
cuqdoq a bad word (11:208) (daw$_\vee$ doe$^\vee$)
cuqduq a hot spring; a mineral spring (cu$_\vee$; i$^\vee$ lah$^\vee$ cu$_\vee$)
-- cuqdyuv, alcuq -- shoots of a species of small bamboo
cuqfaq division in math (Chi)
cuqfaq kejiq method of repeating division tables in a rhyme (Chi)
cuqjif to promote (as a program) (Chi) (34:55)
cuq luq heif to eliminate six kinds of calamity (Chi) (34:65)
cuq puv to sow dissension; foment discord
cuqsaol aqma the master or owner of the place
cuqteq those in the village who collect money for the various village offerings (Chi)
cuqxuqso a bank (for money) (Chi) (26:76) (pyu$^\vee$ ta$_\vee$ du$_\vee$)
cuqzulceil a taxi ('rent a car') (Chi) (50:25)

cuv 1. to squeeze (grab) with the fingers (or) **piav**; 2. to grasp in talons (as an eagle) (tsu^)
cuv autumn (41:116) (or) **cuvduv**
cuv to build (as house) (9:35) (tso^-eu)
cuv bei to start setting up; the beginning of construction (50:26)
-- cuv, biavqcuv -- to nail to the floor
-- cuv, caqcuv -- to build a mud wall
-- cuv, cov -- to stick in
cuv dav to build up (3:4) (tso^ da^-eu)
cuv dav the beginning of autumn (50:105)

-- cuv, eeldaoq hhocuv -- to transplant rice in terraced fields
Cuvhaoq Haoqdil Emperor Zu Hao (a Hani emperor) (35:48)
=cuv, hoq= 1. fistful of rice, 2. rice dumpling
=cuv, hul= (see full)
-- cuv, hu -- to stare at
=cuv, hho= rice seedling
-- cuv, hhocuv -- transplant rice seedlings
-- cuv, lavqcaq -- to make a mark
-- cuv, lima -- to transplant rice seedlings
=cuv, luv= (see full)
cuv nei 1. properly; rightly (11:216), 2. exactly (**Ngal yeiqnaohuvq cuv nei niq ceil siivq huvq biao al.** This year I am exactly 27 years old. 41:106), 3. at the right time; accurate
-- cuv, puv -- an established village (46:118)
-- cuv, puvcuv -- to establish a village
-- cuv, puvcuv hhaqcuv -- to establish a village and a village sacred grove
=cuv, syuq= to stick into (as ground)
cuv teiq to clamp onto; hold tight (11:197) (nyeh‸ tehˬ-eu; ka‸ tehˬ-eu)
=cuv, yovq= (see full)
Cuvzal miqnieiq aol emperor Zu Hao reigns
=cuv, za= a kneaded dumpling
-- cuv, zacuv -- to make a dumpling
cuv zaq to marry (45:7, 45:7) (or) **cuv zavq** (pf.) (11:203) (sheuˬ dahˬ dzaˬ-eu; mˇ dzaˬ-iˇ-eu)
cuv zavq to marry (11:203); **cuv zaq** (45:7) (not pf.)
cuv zavq lavq e to be married (11:222) (oeˇ mˇ baˇ-eu)
-- cuv zavq, yovqhhovq -- to set up a family (through marriage)
-- cuv, zaolmol -- (see full)

cuvq 1. to build a bridge (tso‸-eu) (see: **laolzaol cuvq**), 2. to squeeze with the hand (cf., nyeh‸ cu‸-eu = to squeeze a dog's mouth shut), 3. to have (as an ear, a handle on a hoe, etc.) (tso‸-eu), 4. to install & fix up (9:35)
cuvq to shine (as the sun) (9:35) (nui tsaˇ tso‸-eu)
-- cuvq, aoqcal -- for the sun to shine
-- cuvq, bavq -- 1. to set up a ladder, 2. to build a bridge of wood & bamboo
-- cuvq, eil -- to accuse falsely
-- cuvq, guvq -- to sew up; sew back on (as a button)
-- cuvq, laolzaol -- to build a bridge
cuvq teiq insist on; persist in (50:82)
-- cuvq, zaol -- to put together
cuvqzyuq ba'la autumn season

CUA

cuaqdal a sheet for a bed (Chi) (41:40)

cuaqtao tradition (Chi) (34:109) (zah˅)

cuafcaoq jilseiq creative spirit (Chi) (34:22), (or) **cuafcaof jilseiq** (50:53)
cuafcaofxif creativity (Chi) (34:102, 50:27)
cuafzoq to compose (as a song, poem, etc) (Chi) (50:27)

CYU

cyulmiq hhyuyeiqhyuf villager's committee (Chi)
cyulniuq to boast; brag (Chi) (ja˅ eh˅-eu)
cyulza village director (Chi); village leader (**cyulza bi gee** = had him become village director) (11:181, 41:3) (dzoe˯ ma)

=cyu nei, laol= very hot
=cyu pa cyu nei, laol= very warmly

cyuq to be poor (9:35) (or) **cyuqssaq; colpeel**, etc. (cf.: coe˯, in: mi˯ coe˯ mi˯ ma)
cyuq to cough (9:35) (tsoe˯-eu)
cyuq to hinder (tsoe˯-eu)
-- cyuq, aol -- 1. to build a wall, 2. to fence in an area
-- cyuq, aoqcyuq -- an overcast sky
-- cyuq, caqbyu diq -- to close a window
=cyuq cyuq, aoq= overcast sky
=cyuq cyuqssaq, mol= an orphan
-- cyuq, dal -- to block; to stop
-- cyuq, deiq -- to block; hinder
-- cyuq, diq -- to close (as a window)
-- cyuq, galtuv tuv -- to set up a village gate to keep evil spirits from entering
cyuqgov hhe tul to help the poor people (50:52)
=cyuq, hhoq= vegetables (g'aw˯ nyoe˅)
-- cyuq, joqhyuq -- to be foggy
-- cyuq, kalwuq -- to take the first ear of corn harvested and hang it on the rack over the fireplace
=cyuq, laq= pants; trousers
-- cyuq, laol -- to prevent; stop
-- cyuq, leiq -- to stop; block; obstruct; thwart
-- cyuq lo, cyuq sil -- 1. very poor, 2. to cough very much
-- cyuq, luvq -- to block the way
=cyuq, ma= a poor woman
=cyuq, miq= a widow
-- cyuq, miqcyuq -- to be widowed
-- cyuq, nalcyuq -- nose to be congested
cyuqnal to have a cold (9:35) (tseh˄ tah na˅-eu)
cyuqnal kovq to catch a cold (15:41, 50:55) (tseh˄ tah nyaw˯-eu)
-- cyuq, pavqcyuq -- to cover with a cover (as a basket of bamboo)

cyuqpeiq cyuqnal diseases (10:pref.) (na$^{\vee}$ gaw$^{\vee}$)

cyuqpyuq cyuqnal nal to have a serious respiratory disease (as: TB, flu)

cyuq sil cyuq lo 1. to be very poor (zaw$^{\vee}$ sha$_{\vee}$-eu); 2. to cough a lot (tsoe$_{\vee}$ ga$^{\vee}$ neh-a$_{\vee}$)

-- cyuq, silbyu nalbyu pavqcyuq -- to stuff cotton in nostrils, mouth and ears of a person who has died

cyuqssaq poor people (9:35) (or) **cyuqssaq bavqssaq** (i$^{\vee}$ sha$_{\vee}$ sha$_{\vee}$-eu; sha$_{\vee}$-eu za$_{\vee}$)

cyuqssaq Molmil haol God bless ('helps') the poor

cyuqssaq sulhhaq the poor and the rich

-- cyuqssaq, ssaqcyuq -- poor people

-- cyuq, teev -- to stop; to dam up

-- cyuq, teiv -- to stop something

cyuq zaq to have ability (13:1) (jah$^{\vee}$ nya-eu)

-- cyuq, zaoqcyuq -- to cough

cyuf unit of length (roughly an inch - 50:29), one-third of a decimeter (Chi)

DA

dal 1. to rely on (**dalja yaol hha dal** = must rely on the people - 26:114, 45:25), 2. to lean on (9:36) (k'aw˯ daˇ-eu)
dal clf. for type of Chinese weight, about 100 kg (Chi) (9:36, 11:79)
dalbaol 1. dike (bund) of earth in irrigated field (9:36, 14:237) (deh bahˇ), 2. a dam (for water)
dalbiav biavssaq a small board
dalbuq a show off; an arrogant person (38:109)
dalbuq buq to show off; brag; be arrogant; conceited; boast (Chi) (26:107, 50:52) (k'ah˯ sehˇ jahˇ g'eh)
dalceil a bicycle (Chi) (14:229, 46:175) (seh^ beˇ; lo ti˯)
  dalceil ziiq to ride a bicycle (A=Chi) (46:175) (seh^ beˇ dzi˯-eu; lo ti˯ dzi˯-eu)
dalciil a stick; switch (9:36) (daˇ cuiˇ)
dalciiq single word; words (Chi) (9:36) (daw˯)
dal cyuq to stop something; to block something (la^ tsoe˯-eu)
dalda what one would call 1. father's younger brother (a˯ zawˇ), 2. father's older sister's husband (9:36, 12:126, 46:89) (a˯ k'o˯)
=dal, dil= ding dong (sound of bell)
daldul a stick or pole which is used for something
  -- **daldul, ngaqhhovq** -- fishing pole
  -- **daldul, loq he** -- oar (for rowing)
dalgeeq bamboo pole for drying things (9:36)
  -- **dalgeeq, alcuq** -- a small bamboo stick
dalgoq to delay (Chi) (9:36, 50:32) (la^ mya˰-eu)
dalgul gul a tall and slender figure (or) **gul nei**
=dal, haq= asparagus; Chinese alpine rush; or grass
-- **dal, haol** -- to rely on
dalhel a stake (9:36, 46:117) (daˇ ta˰)
dalhhyuf a work unit (in the Communist system) (Chi) (50:32)
dalja all (Chi) (9:36, 11:129) (daw˯ taw^)
  dalja dalduq all people (Chi)
  dalja meeqduq overall situation (50:30) (A=Chi)
  dalja neekyul collective wisdom (50:79) (A=Chi)
  dalja nei hev zaq known by all people (A=Chi)
  dalja saq nei all (11:129) (A=Chi)
  dalja xul all agree (50:61) (A=Chi)
=dal, jul= chopsticks
=dal, lavq= 1. an arm rest; 2. a hand rail; 3. reliable
-- **dal, leq** -- to lean
dalleil gunny bag (as for carrying rice) clf. = leil (9:36) (pehˇ zeuˇ)

dalleil leilma a big bag (pehˇ zeuˇ zeuˇ ma)
-- **dal, lol** -- to lean on; depend on
dallul a wide road (Chi) (gaˇ ma yaw huiˬ)
dalma ancestors; parents (when spoken in ritual texts it is usually **dalma**, in daily conversation; **dama**)
-- **dalma, haqdal** -- a type of fern
dalma hhaol liq ancestor's traditions (older term, cf. Akha: zahˇ)
dalmiq dalkeil clearly; obviously (Chi)
dalmiaq 1. a door bolt (9:37), 2. wooden lock
=**dal, miav**= (see full)
dalniaov double layered (9:37) (nyiˬ law^)
dalniaov niaovssaq tweezers (small)
dalpav a board (daˇ pa^)
-- **dalpav, milsov** -- (see full)
-- **dalpav, naolgul** -- a pedal for a loom
dalpial a whip (daˇ cuiˇ)
-- **dal, pieiq** -- to rely on; to trust
dalqei a sharp stick (daˇ ceh)
-- **dalqei, saol** -- a sharp iron bar or rod
dalqei sev to whittle a stick to a point (daˇ ceh ceh-eu)
dalqeiq diaper-type cloth for baby (9:37)
dalqeiq leev wrap up a newborn baby in a cloth
dalqeiv qeiv to measure (50:20)
dalqeiv qeiv alnei aol do what one is capable of; act according to one's capacity (50:107)
-- **dalqul, meiq luq** -- to pout out lips when disagree or disgruntled
dalsil a stick for stringing fish together (for drying, keeping from animals, etc.)
dalsseiv a bamboo stick (ma saˬ daˇ cuiˇ)
dal sso to depend upon (or) **qeq sso e** (g'oe-eu)
-- **daltevq, yojil yoliq** -- criterion of truth
dalteiq a single chopstick (4:39) (tsiˇ daˇ tiˬ teˬ)
dal teiq to hold tightly (14:155) (nyeh‸ tehˬ-eu)
dalteiq teiq to hold onto (46:117) (nyeh‸ tehˬ taˬ)
-- **dalteiq teiq, eqjil** -- to make thatch grass shingles for roofing
dalteivq yaq xa to demote a grade
daltuv a support; a holder (cf. with Ak.: daˇ to^)
daltuv tuv to support; to prop up (tu^ tehˬ-eu)
dalya a very long trumpet-like instrument
dalya bo to play the above instrument
dalya meel to play the above instrument
dalya a ballad; folk song; nursery rhyme
-- **dalya, aqnil** -- children's songs (32:3)
=**dal, zaq**= a bomb (or) **zaqdaf** (Chi)

da a political party (as the Communist party) (Chi)
-- **da** male suffix (**haqjil aqda** = human males)
da a hhoq to quit a political party (A=Chi) (50:172)
=**da, aq**= father
=**da, dal**= (see full)

da e seilhoq the party's committee (A=Chi) (50:32)
da'faol work method of the party (Chi) (50:32)
da'feif party membership fees (Chi) (50:32)
dagal party program (Chi) (50:33)
dagyul party's regulations (Chi) (50:33)
dahojil steel/flint lighter (Chi) (or) **miqdiq**
dahhaf files; records (Chi) (50:33)
da hholqei inner party (Chi) (50:33)
dahhyu party committee (Chi) (9:36, 50:33) (or) **dahhyu hyuf**
dahhyu bafgaolsiiq party committee office (Chi) (26:76)
dahhyu fuf suljif party vice (deputy) secretary (Chi) (50:33)
dahhyu hyuf the party committee (Chi)
dahhyu suljif party secretary (Chi) (50:33)
daji party discipline (Chi) (34:99)
dajiq party membership (Chi) (50:33)
dakof party's class (Chi) (50:33)
da'liq alhuvq number of years in the party (thus determining one's standing in the party) (A=Chi) (50:33)
dama parents (9:37) (sometimes with sense of ancestors - 3:1) (a˯ ma a˯ da)
dama colmoq elders; older people (tsawˇ maw˯ tsawˇ k'a^)
dama colzil respected villagers (see also: **puvlaol dama**)
dama soqdoq poetry (old word) (or) **soqdoq**
dama ssaoqnieiq 1. family heirloom, 2. inheritance from parents (50:26)
damoq father's older brothers and spouses (6:175, 41:1) (a˯ ui˯)
danil stepfather (or) **aqda danil** (a˯ da da nyiˇ) (see also: **davceiq**)
-- **danil, aqda** -- stepfather
dapeif political parties and groups (Chi) (50:33)
da'qiq the party banner (Chi) (50:33)
da quqca a big playing field (soccer; basketball, etc) (Chi)
daxaof party indoctrination school (Chi) (50:33)
dayeiq a party member (Chi) (9:40, 41:3, 50:33)
dayeiq gee dav to join the party (A=Chi) (50:144)
dayeiq wuqcaoq hhe expel from the party (A=Chi) (50:95)
dazal party charter; constitution (Chi) (9:41, 34:103, 50:33)
Dazaolyal Party Central Committee (Chi) (34:28, 50:33)
Daziilbuf a party branch (Chi) (26:21; 50:33)
daziifjil a typewriter (Chi) (50:30)
daziifjil diq to type on a typewriter (A=Chi)
dazu leading party group (Chi) (50:33)
dazuziiq the party organization (Chi) (50:33)

daq 1. to fill with padding or batting (9:39), 2. to substitute
daq to set or place something (**hhadaoq daq** = to set a trap - 14:139)
=daq, aqhhovq guvq= thimble
-- daq (vb), beeq (vb) -- **beeq aol daq aol** = to do something to no purpose, **beeq zaq daq zaq** = to eat simply, **beeq eil daq eil** = to speak thoughtlessly
daq biao fetch full load (water) (11:162)
daqbioq weak wine
=daq, dao= shirt
=daq, diq= threshing stick (used to beat the crop)
=daq, doq= proverb; old saying
=daq, du= a story
daqhaol 1. to catch hold of (9:40) (nyeh‸ tehˬ-eu), 2. to accept (as in accepting responsibility) (or) **ceiqdal** (Chi)
daqhoq to cooperate (Chi) (9:40)
=daq, hoq= a mattress
daqhhal clods of mud that have been plowed up (miˇ tsaˬ miˇ k'oˇ)
daqhhaq 1. ground (8:2, 16, 46:162), 2. an island in a stream
daqhhaq e milsaol owner (spirit) of the ground (miˇ sahˇ; miˇ sahˇ cuˬ sahˇ)
daqhhaq hhaqma the mainland (50:31) (or) **dafluq** (Chi)
daqhhaq hhaol dusk to fall (9:40)
  daqhhaq wuv to be in the shadow (naˇ shmˇ shmˇ-eu)
daqhhoq long grass (good for animals) (28:4, 46:89)
  daqhhoq hhoqdei lawns (46:176)
  daqhhoq loldei a wide lawn
=daq, hhoq= vegetable leaves
daqhhuq ground
daqjeil a bandit; armed robber (or) **diqsseiq** (Chi) (9:40) (tahˇ joe)
=daq, jol= a cushion
daqjul a soldier (Chi) (and see: **daqjyul**)
daqjyul a soldier (Chi) (**daqjyul gee** = to become a soldier) (26:41) (see also: **dafjyul; daqjul; mavqssaq**) (yehˇ; lu suiˇ)
daqlei dalleiq meil something to fall down easily
=daq meil, leiq= wasted
-- daqnieiq, pavqcavq -- a bad person to be executed by a firing squad (can also be used as a curse)
=daq, qaoq= outer cloth for a coat
daqtav in the world (miˇ tsaˬ k'oeˇ ta^)
  daqtav colssaq yokyul alkaq xovq tul to stand among the advanced nations (50:105)
  daqtav jol e living in the world (not under it) (14:236) (miˇ tsaˬ k'oeˇ ta^ jawˇ-eu)
daqyao guest (9:40) (daˬ yah)
  daqyao a bi zaq bi dol to entertain ('give food and drink to guests')
  daqyao gee to be a guest (daˬ yah geu‸-eu)

daqyao kul to invite a guest to come (da˯ yah kuˇ)

daqyao xavqduq guest house (da˯ yah ya˰ du˯)

daqyoq cicada (a˯ je˯; a˯ je˯ ca˯)

Daqzaoq the Dazhai village in Luchun. The dialect spoken in this village was chosen as the one on which the Hani orthography is based (or) **Oltol Tavqzaoq; Holtol Tavqzaoq** (means 'upper village') (41:73)

daqzii courage (Chi) (9:40)

daqzii heeq very brave (A=Chi) ('big courage') (26:48, 46:95) (nui ma k'a˯-eu)

dav to climb up; go up (9:40) (da^-eu)

-- **dav, alteivq** -- to go up one grade

-- **dav, aol** -- to build up

-- **dav, beq** -- to dig up; to pick up

-- **dav, caol heiq** -- to repair the irrigation ditch diversion where water comes out of the river

davceiq step-father (a˯ da da nyiˇ) (see also: **danil**)

davceiq ceiqzaq to be a step-father

-- **davceiv, galdav** -- (see full)

davciivq a flight of steps; a stair

-- **dav, cov** -- to prick

-- **dav, eq** -- to feel disgruntled, sometimes nauseated

=**dav, gal**= path going up

-- **dav, goq** -- to raise up

-- **dav, hu** -- to like; favor

-- **dav, hha** -- to add

=**dav, hhaq**= (see full)

-- **dav, hhuv** -- to pick up

=**dav, ju**= a vine to grow

=**dav, la**= first 10 days of month, early in month

-- **dav, lavqpeiv** -- for a callus to form

-- **dav, maq ya maq** -- not too high, not too low (as, middle class)

-- **dav, meel seiq** -- to apply glaze (A=Dai)

-- **dav miq, seiv** -- to pour out a liquid

=**dav, nee**= pit of the stomach

=**dav, neema gal**= (see full)

-- **dav, niul** -- to turn green (as plants coming up)

-- **dav, ngaoq** -- to pour on

-- **dav, piqkeel** -- to develop a gall bladder disease

dav puv go upward from the river (50:121)

-- **dav, pyuq** -- to spring up (and see full)

-- **dav'qeiv, aolhhaq** -- level of productive forces

davsavq a slight incline

davssaq a plate (9:40) (k'm˯ ma˯)

davtevq something engraved; something with a notch in it

davtevq tevq 1. to engrave something, 2. to make a notch (as in wood)

-- **dav, teil** -- 1. to raise the stakes, 2. to throw something up higher

dav teiq teiq to grow up quickly (46:158) (hui˯ laˇ-

eu yaw kaw˅)
davtivq the first day of a month
davtuv a slight upslope (ga˅ da^)
-- dav, xaoldav -- (see full)
davxov 1. ladder (46:130) (daw˯ dzm), 2. a staircase
dav zaq to mortgage; pawn (50:36)
dav zaq duq a pawn shop (50:33)
-- dav, zaol -- to add (mathematical)
-- dav, ziiq -- to mount and ride (as a horse)
-- dav, zolteivq -- go to a higher grade in school

=davq, aqha ha= cock's spur
=davq, col= young man (taboo)
-- davq, coldavq -- young man in his youth (taboo)
=davq, ha= spur of a rooster
=davq, ma= stepmother
=davq, miq= maiden (taboo)
davqtav wuqdu upper world (i.e., on the earth (11:221) (mi˅ ta^)
davqwuv scrotum
davqwuv wuvsiq testicle (leh˯ u^)

dafbeiqziiq protein (Chi) (11:49, 50:32)
dafbiao (see: **deifbiao**) (Chi) (**sseiqmiq dafbiao** = people's representative - 26:101)
daf difzu a wealthy landlord (Chi) (34:7)
dafdyuf production brigade (Chi) (50:30)
dafgaolsef the 'big' commune period in China (Chi)
dafgaol wuqsiil to be selfless; unselfish (Chi) (34:116, 50:30)
daf geiqmif great revolution (Chi) (50:30)
dafgoq salweiq zuyif great-nation chauvinism (Chi) (50:30)
dafgofzii a tall man (Chi) (26:82)
dafhuaq naciq yellow medicine made from jungle plants (A=Chi) (50:30)
dafhyuf a general meeting; a big conference; a big meeting (Chi) (26:106, 50:30)
dafjyul great army (Chi) (26:14) (see also: **daqjyul**)
Dafli Dali (city northwest of Kunming) (Chi) (50:31)
Dafli galzii the Dali market (Chi) (50:31)
Dafli haqluv marble from Dali (A=Chi) (50:31)
daflitaq a big hall, as for meetings (Chi) (50:31)
dafluq the mainland (Chi) (34:112)
dafmeiq barley (Chi)
dafmiqcuq zuyif big-nationality chauvinism (Chi) (50:31)
dafpaoq a canon (to shoot) (Chi) (26:27) (kaw maw)
dafseilca sum of the products; total production (Chi)
dafsii ambassador (Chi) (50:31)
dafsiigua embassy (Chi) (50:31)
dafxi capital letters (Chi) (9:36) (bo˄ ma)
dafxoq university (Chi) (11:145, 31:3)
dafxoqseil 1. university student (31:3, 50:31), 2. university graduate (57:154)

dafyaofjif big leap forward (Chi) (50:31)
dafyif a righteous cause (Chi) (34:113)
daf ziilca geiljiq important, influential bourgeoise (Chi) (34:7)
dafziifbaof a big character; a capital letter (Chi)

DAO

daol 1. to be; exist (as of a road) (9:37) (dahˇ-eu), 2. to lead to; to lead the way to (45:1)
daol one line (9:37) (kaw^; tiˬ kaw^)
daol to fold (**hhaoldaol daol** = to fold a fold) (bya^ dmˇ-eu)
daol clf. for times (9:37, 46:89) (po^)
daol clf. for big flat items (quilt, mat, buffalo or cow hide, etc.) (11:74)
=daol, aq= wing
-- daol, bieildaol -- to place various foods on a bamboo table to make an ancestral offering (esp. used in homes where no ancestral altar)
daolbo hyulzeiq domestic animals that fly (50:81)
daolbuv fin of a fish (30:2) (yehˇ ma)
daolbyuq cei cei for a bird to raise its wings to fly
daolceil mountain rice (9:37) (dahˇ ta^ cehˇ)
daolciivq one's back; lower back (9:37) (daˇ tsui˄)
  daolciivq waist (jo˄)
  daolciivq saqyuq the backbone; spine (pf.)
    daolciivq saqyoq (daˇ tsui˄ shaˬ yoeˬ)
daol cyuq lolhav to be very poor (57:89)
-- daol dav, helhaoq -- (see full)
daoldav koqyal a field on a mountain (dahˇ ta^ yaˇ)
-- daol daol meil, hhuvq hhuvq -- to come and go
daoldiq diq for a bird to spread its wings (4:39) (g'awˇ pyeh nehˬ-eu)
=daol, eel= wave of water
daolfaol east wind (Chi) (or) **naolheiq jaqleil** (50:39)
=daol, gul= a wooden plow board
=daol, ha= chicken wing
-- daol, haqbol -- a thicket of bamboo
=daol, haqluv luv= rocky area
daolhav a terraced mountain field in which there is water only during rains (9:38, 46:161)
-- daolhav, aqdaol -- a hard feather
daolhav hav ceil a dry mountain rice field which is terraced (cehˇ yaˇ)
  daolhav nuv to transplant dry terraced fields in the rainy season (no irrigation as such)
=daol, haol= mountain
=daol, hhaol= a fold
-- daol, hhaoldaol -- to fold
daolhhaoq the back to be bent
daolhhuvq hunchback (& see: **daollu**)
=daol, kaol= a fence
daolkyul a field at an angle (V shaped)

daollaq musk deer
-- **daol, lav** -- to dredge up
daollu a hunchback (& see: **daolhhuvq**)
daolma 1. backbone, 2. mainstay (50:63)
daolma makov a general plan; overall plan (50:220)
-- **daol maq cyuq, qiq** -- to be worthless; can do nothing
=**daol, millaol laol**= burned place in the woods
=**daol, miaq**= pineapple
-- **daol, naqbol maq** -- to not want to listen to advice
-- **daolnaoq, aqdaol** -- a soft feather
-- **daol, neema** -- candid; straightforward
=**daol, ngaq**= fin of a fish
daolpiaq wings (chickens; birds) (57:69)
daolpiei piei to spread wings (as birds) (m˅ pyeh-eu)
Daolsal a village which left from Daoltyuq village in Yuanyang County (46:123)
=**daol, ssaol**= (see full)
daoltavq hill related (as field, people, etc.) (dah˅ ta^)
daoltavq koqyal a field on a mountain (or) **haoltavq koqyal** (dah˅ ta^ dah˅ ya˅)
daoltavq niuqceiq ceiq to plow the mountain fields (non-irrigated)
daoltavq ngaqlol a kind of nonpoisonous snake ('hill eel')
daolteil back (as on an animal or fish) (46:196)
-- **daolteil, aqhhuv** -- the lower back
-- **daolteil, aqtav** -- the upper back
Daoltyuq an old village in Yuanyang County (46:123)
daolyal hill field; mountain field (9:38, 11:48) (dah˅ ya˅; dah˅ ta^ ya˅)
daolyal kav to harrow (mtn.) field

dao put on; wear (clothes) (9:37) (dm-eu)
dao to be equal to (35:19) (ti˯ kaw^)
daobiav biav for there to be bad erosion or a major landslide in a field that has been planted
daobiao wall of terraced fields (2:48)
Dao Cyuqssyuf hero in People's Liberation Army (26:104)
daodaq a shirt (9:37) (peh˅ k'ah˯)
dao dav put on (as clothes) (26:102) (dm da^-eu)
dao e maq hhyuq no clothes to wear (dm-eu meh˯ tsoe˯ ma˯ ja^)
=**dao haoqseil, mil**= fame
-- **dao, hhe** -- to pull & cover
dao'lul something to wear (**dao'lul maq hha** = nothing to wear - 4:39) (dm-eu meh˯ tsoe˯)
-- **daonei, yeil** -- to be calm; patient
dao zeiv worn out clothing (**naov zeiv** = worn out shoes)

daoq to be tired (g'a˯ doe˅)

daoq to be present (only of liquids) (9:38) (dahˬ-eu)
daoq to be blunt; dull (9:38) (yaw dmˬ) (**tojeil daoq a** = the knife is dull)
daoq clf. for book, paper (46:215) (or) **kaoq** (paˇ dmˬ)
=daoq, bieivq= (see full)
=daoq, byul= a widower
-- daoq, byuldaoq -- to become a widower
daoqbyu anus (5:912) (dawˬ byoe)
daoqbyu sivq duv dysentary (or) **daoqnil nal**
=daoq, caq= 1. edge of a field, 2. a case from beginning to end
daoqcavq wooden floor (on which there are mats) (daˇ kawˬ kawˬ taˬ-eu)
daoqcavq bo to have a filter tip (cigarette) (57:109)
-- daoq, ciivqdaoq -- a genealogy in which there are no male descendants to continue the line
daoqdaoq lower part; bottom (9:38) (dawˬ dahˬ)
daoqdaoq e galkov basic policy (34:115)
daoqdaoq hu duv check out reason behind some matter
daoqdaoq maq bo no end of .... (**soqhhaq ziilsiiq zol saq e daoqdaoq maq bo** = no end of studying books that give knowledge, 26:55) (jiˇ-eu maˬ baw)
daoqdaoq pyu the lower; bottom section (dawˬ dahˬ paw)
daoqdaoq qiq cii basic level; grass-roots unit; primary level (50:78)
daoqdaoq qiq cii dalhhyuf grass-roots unit; lowest unit (C=Chi) (50:78)
daoqdaoq ya to have a conclusion (50:87)
-- daoq, eil -- to persuade
=daoq galzeil, gal= side of the road
daoqgaoq dust (9:38) (k'aˬ lehˇ)
daoq gaoq plenty of liquids present (dahˬ gahˬ-eu)
=daoq, gaoq= foot of the mountain
daoqgaoq gaoqbeeq (see: **gaoqbeeq**)
daoqgaoq gaoq nei to be plentiful (or) **biao nei jav; miaq nei jav**
daoqgu dilgu coq jump up and down with joy (29:4) (tsawˬ tsawˬ-ehˇ laˬ k'aˬ cehˇ-eu)
daoqgu nei coq heart to beat fast (12:127) (or) **neema daoqgu nei coq** (nui ma tsawˬ kawˇ-eu)
=daoq, hha= type of snare
daoqjyu geiq nei slippery (45:63) (or) **daoqju geiq nei**
daoqjyu jyu to crawl on muddy ground (or) **daoqju ju** (miˇ tsaˬ yaw pyeh^-ahˇ joe-eu)
daoqkaoq 1. buttocks of humans (9:38), 2. haunches of animals (dawˬ dahˬ; dawˬ kmˬ)
daoqkaoq aoq zaq to prostitute ('sell one's bottom')
daoqkaoq aoq zaq col a prostitute
daoqkaoq saqpiaq buttocks (dawˬ dahˬ, dawˬ kmˬ)
=daoq, keel= heel of foot
daoqkee a tail rope for ponies (tie to pack saddle)

(9:38)

daoqkee alsiq bamboo rollers on a horsetail rope

=daoq, keeq= a chain for a dog

=daoq, laq= 1. a floor beam, 2. bottom of trouser

daoqlaol the hip (as of an animal) (35:35)

daoqlei nei to feel weak; be very tired; to be blunt (50:129)

daoqliq 1. the stem (of a plant) (9:38) (aˇ bawˬ), 2. the stump of a tree (or) **albol daoqliq**

-- daoqliq, albol -- a tree stump

=daoq, lol= 1. end of a river, 2. end of a dammed stream

daoqlul anus (dawˬ boe)

daoqlul ya duv a prolapsped rectum (some of the intestine comes out through the anus)

daoqluv dilluv meil coq jump up and down (29:4) (tsawˬ tsawˬ-ehˇ teu^-eu)

daoqlyul lyulpuv turned upside down

daoqlyul lyulpuv puv to turn a somersault (koˬ moˬ koˬ toˇ toˇ-eu)

daoqma log (wood) (9:38, 11:159) (dmˬ ma)

daoqma laqhyul a wooden house (11:37, 26:69) (daˇ kawˬ nymˇ)

daoqma naqbol fungus; fungi (arboreal fungus) (9:38, 14:145)

daoqmeil the buttock (4:40, esp. used here after one has had a bowel movement)

=daoq, meiq= chin

-- daoq, meiqbaoq nei eil -- to use 'blunt' words to win an argument

daoqmeiv a seesaw (4:37)

daoqmeiv dilmeiv meiv zaq to play on a seesaw

-- daoqmeiv, jacil -- a kind of wagtail bird

daoqmeiv meiv 1. to go up and down on a seesaw, 2. for a wagtail bird to go up and down like a seesaw

daoqmiq tail (9:39) (dawˬ miˬ)

daoqmiq jiqwei conclusion of an article (as in a magazine or newspaper) (B=Chi)

daoqmiq pyu the tail part; tail section

daoqnaol saqyyuq pelvis (or) **saqpiaq saqyyuq**

=daoq, naov= sole of the shoe

daoqnil nal suffer dysentery (or) **daoqbyu sivq duv** (uˬ ma^ uˬ neˇ neˇ-eu)

=daoq, peil= a cloth women wear around their hips

daoqpei 1. near, 2. in front of, 3. before (1. dawˬ peh, 2-3. mehˬ shi)

daoqpei niqca nei to be close by (not far) (or) **niqcanei**

daoqpeiq root; base; foundation (9:39, 50:78) (dawˬ pehˬ)

daoqpul a tree stump with roots

-- daoqpul, albol -- a tree stump with roots included

daoqpul hhe puv to uproot something

daoqpul pul nei hhe puv to pull up by the roots

(13:48) (duˬ ciˇ g'awˇ-eu)

daoqqil root (9:39) (duˬ ciˇ)

daoqqil qilsal a small root (9:39) (duˬ ciˇ ciˇ zaˬ)

daoqqil qiltaoq a tap root; main root (9:39) (duˬ ciˇ ciˇ ma)

daoqsiq hip (5:581) (shaˬ pyaˬ k'ehˆ)

daoqsiq saqyyuq hipbone (shaˬ pyaˬ mya^)

=daoq, sol= an account book

=daoq, soq= books

daoqsov sov xa to slide down (or) **daoqteil teil xa**

=daoq, ssaoq= plow rope

daoqtao wood (9:39) (**qiq tao** = clf.) (daˇ kawˬ)

=daoq, taoq= bottom of pool in river

daoqtev a jolt; a bump (cf.: **gu lu gaoq laoq**

daoqtev daoqtev bumping and jolting along (57:79)

daoqtev teev to jolt; to bump

daoqteil a bench (or) **naolteil**

daoqteil teil 1. to be slippery (26:99), 2. to tumble down (dawˬ teˇ teˇ-eu - to slip and fall on one's buttocks)

daoqteil teil hal to spill a liquid (46:102) (yoeˇ dzeh-eu)

daoqteil teil xa to slide down (or) **daoqsov sov xa**

daoq'yul aqma a cuckoo (brd)

daoqzul zul to sit on heels; to squat down (dawˬ dzuˇ dzuˇ-eu) (9:39)

daov (vb) very (vb) (**laqpil dyul daov cil** = the chili peppers are very spicy - 11:105) (9:39) (... gaˇ neh-aˬ; ... dui dui-eu; zaw-ehˇ ...)

daov cavq to be base; contemptible (50:9)

daov duvq very strong poison (50:93)

daov dyul 1. very bad, 2. very lazy (doeˇ gaˇ neh-aˬ; doeˇ dui dui-eu; zaw-ehˇ doeˇ-eu)

daov gaol e neenyuq miqnieiq high civilizational spirit (50:56)

daov gaol e zeiqsal miqnieiq high civilizational material (50:56)

daov heeq very big; great (34:22) (zawˇ huiˬ-eu)

daov mol a very long time (50:21)

daov pyuq glorious (34:22)

daov qeil to be very happy (38:20)

daov teiq pressing; urgent (50:89)

daov xao very heavy (50:46)

daov zaq e wonderful; beautiful (50:89)

daov zeifqoq totally correct (B=Chi) (34:22) (tsaˬ dui dui-eu)

daovq fat and strong (or) **hhaqhav bo** (9:39, 38:110)

daovqsiq nei very strong (**daovqsiq nei daovq e aqniuq** = a strong buffalo of great strength - 11:150) (g'aˬ zawˇ k'a^)

daofciiq a verb (Chi)

daofdeiq morals (Chi) (34:58)
daofdeiq gaolsaf noble; lofty ideals; morals (Chi) (26:55)
daofhuf individual household (Chi) (41:24) (zaw^)
daofliq motives (Chi) (34:75)
daofluaf (see: **daoflueif**) (Chi) (34:50)
daoflueif turmoil; disturbance (Chi)
daofteif trends (Chi) (50:39)
Daoftiqhuq name of a lake (Chi) (26:2)
daofwuqxoq zoology (Chi) (50:39)
daofyeiq to mobilize (Chi)

DE

del to collect together (Chi) (la^ uiv-eu)
-- del, coldel -- a person who roams; who wanders
del del meil to collect money for village offerings
del hha 1. to play a game, 2. to roam around (46:129) (or) **qao hha**
=del, mol= a big clay basin

=de, eel= (see full)
-- de le, di li -- 1. the sound of bells (on cows, horses), 2. a clicking noise
-- dexi, aldovq -- lamp wick (B=Chi)

-- deq, eqleq -- (see full)
deqheq a type of edi. berries (amomum, **caoguo**)
deqheq heqsavq smell of berries (9:42)
=deq lal, nee= to be satisfied
-- deq, needeq -- to calculate; to consider
deqzeil struggle (Chi) (26:16) (see also: **defzeil**) (teu^-eu; byehY-eu)

dev to cut; hack (9:42) (deu^-eu)
dev clf. for a piece (as a piece of silver) (13:5)
dev clf. for a cut; a hack (11:85)
dev ceiv to cut down (deu^ tseh^-eu)
devdaq a cutting block for wood (yehv bo^)
-- dev hu, soqyeiq -- (see full)
=dev, juq= the hip
=dev, laq= a small ax
=dev, moq= Chinese yam
devmoq moq to go through the motion of chopping (as cutting down a tree) without actually striking it
dev pav to split (with knife or axe) (or) **cevq pav**
devpovq chips of wood; bamboo (9:43)
-- dev, sevdev -- (see full)
dev sil to cut to death; hack to death (14:210) (deu^ seh^-eu)
dev soq to prune (50:190)
dev tov cut to death (as snake) (11:220) (deu^ seh^)
dev xa to cut down; cut off (11:217, 221) (deu^ ka)

=devq, caq= salt

-- **devq, gevqdevq** --   to tickle

defhaof   a comma (Chi) (50:39)
defzeil   1. to struggle against (**daov saq e defzeil** = a difficult struggle) (26:44, 117), 2. to criticize (Chi) (or) **zafdef** (Chi), 3. to fight (50:39) (see also: **deqzeil**)

DEE

=**dee, leel**=   necklace

deeqhaoq   plate of a small steelyard (in a scale for weighing)
=**deeq, leel**=   a small balance

deev   to soak (9:41) (dui^-eu)

DEI

deil   (a rooster) to crow (9:41) (ya poeˇ doeˇ-eu)
deil   a lamp (Chi) (41:42) **teiqdeil** = desk lamp (Chi)
deil   to have space or room for something or someone; the capacity to contain (46:92, 118) (deˇ-eu)
(vb) **deil**   proper time to (vb) (as old enough to go to school) (11:134)
=**deil, buq**=   ascaris worm
-- **deil, duldeil** --   to fasten a belt
-- **deil, keellavq ciq** --   (see full)
deillu   a basket used to catch fish
deilluv   a strong rooster
deilnil   red loach (type of fish) (9:41)
=**deil, ngaq**=   fish (general term) (nga˯ deˇ)
-- **deilpaol, aldovq** --   an electric light bulb
deilqeiv qeiv   to compete in crowing (doeˇ ceh^ ceh^)
-- **deil, saqdeil** --   (see full)
deilssaol   to prepare; get ready (as food for a meal, soldiers ready for battle) (9:41, 13:11, 26:57, 46:187) (leh˯ hm˯-eu)
deilteil   the sound of crowing (doeˇ-eu teˇ saˇ)
=**deil, teiq**=   a desk lamp (Chi)
-- **deil, yiuvq** --   the time to sleep
-- **deil, zaqdeil** --   to be ripe enough to be eaten
deilziiq   a belt used to support one's waist when lifting heavy items
  deilziiq ziiq   to wear a belt to support one's waist when lifting heavy items

dei   1. level; flat (9:41) (deh saˇ), 2. equal (50:61)
dei   clf. for a piece of land (**milhaoq qiq dei** = one piece of land)
=**dei, albol bol**=   an expanse of trees
deibaq   (see: **deibiaq**) (46:92)
deibiaq   1. the dance ground for the village, 2. a

flat place (as a plain) (18:30, 46:89) (or) **deibaq** (1. deh k'ah$_{\vee}$, 2. deh sa$^{\vee}$)
deiceil rice from an irrigated field (deh ma ceh$^{\vee}$)
Deicuq Dai (Tai) nationality (Chi) (or) **aqcaoq ssaq; Biqcaoq ssaq** (Bi$_{\vee}$ cm$_{\vee}$)
-- **deicuv cuv, puv cuv** -- to establish a village and fields
deidei etc.; and so on (Chi) (34:109) (dui dui)
deigaol merit citation (as in the army) (Chi) (**niq deigaol** = merit citation Class II - 26:101)
-- **deigeel, maldei** -- trellis for a pumpkin vine
-- **dei, haqbol** -- a thicket of bamboo
deihaoq open country; open fields
deihaoq hu to tour (50:110)
deihaoq tavq neighbors (50:129)
deihaof to be equal (in mathematical equations) (Chi)
deihhal dav to harvest rice in the field where the special nine plants from the ancestral altar have been planted
deihhaol a lawn (9:41)
deijiq degrees (as the temperature) (Chi) (50:34)
deijiq ziifduf heirarchy; social estate system (Chi) (50:34)
deikaq outside of house (11:33) (po^ ka)
=**dei, lol**= river valley
=**dei, mal**= pumpkin
deima irrigated field (9:41) (deh ma)
deima loqma a big irrigated field (57:78)
deima loqsal a good field (38:37) (deh ma yaw mui$_{\vee}$)
deimamoq a kind of weed in irrigated fields (deh ma ya$^{\vee}$ mo$_{\wedge}$)
deimamuvq a kind of weed in irrigated fields
deima salseq an orchid (yeh^ sah$_{\vee}$ shui$^{\vee}$)
deima yalqaol hut in a terraced field (ya$^{\vee}$ cm$^{\vee}$)
deimeeq loqhaoq a fertile (good) field (9:41) (**loqhaoq** = clf.) (or) **deimeeq loqma; deimeeq loqsal**
deinei reciprocity; equity (50:41)
dei nei to be flat (9:41) (deh sa$^{\vee}$)
dei pa dei nei very flat (11:57) (deh ga yaw sa$^{\vee}$)
deisal even; flat (50:131) (deh sa$^{\vee}$)
-- **deisal, hhavqtavq** -- a mountain slope and plain
deissaol to prepare; get ready (50:218) (leh$_{\vee}$ hm$_{\vee}$)
deissaol taq to be ready; to be prepared (la^ dah)
deixal fields and gardens; countryside (50:166) (deh ya$^{\vee}$)
=**dei, zoq**= the village playground

deiq 1. scold, 2. push, 3. sting (as bee), 4. empty (4:40 - see also: **zaq leiq** = to consume something until the container is empty (deh$_{\vee}$-eu) (9:41), 5. to dye (or) **xa**
-- **deiq biav alnei nalhaq, naqbol** -- to give an ear; to listen attentively

deiq ca to go close to (14:192) (iˇ peh-eu)
deiq caoq to push down; to cover (9:41) (dehˬ k'aw‸)
deiq cei 1. to push up, 2. to praise, 3. to lift up (1. dehˬ da^; 2. ja ceuˬ; 3. ba‸ da^)
deiq cei miq to give a lift to (or) **aolhaol miq**
deiq ceiq to have both ability and political integrity (Chi) (34:107)
=deiq ceiq, loq= to plow a field a second time
deiq cul to pout; to make a face (with the mouth) (9:42) (aˇ byehˇ byehˇ-eu)
-- deiqcul, meiqjil -- pouting lips
deiq cuv 1. to plant (by sticking in) (dehˬ tso^-eu), 2. to stick on (dehˬ myahˬ-eu)
deiq cyuq 1. to block; hinder (9:42) (la^ tsoeˬ-eu), 2. to cover (**meiqbaoq a deiq cyuq alnei** = covered his mouth - 27:11) (dehˬ ka-eu)
deiq dav to back up (or) **deiq tul** (dehˬ da^)
=deiq deiqju, pavq= flower of a prickly plant
deiq dov to stuff in
deiq dov laq e miaoqgaoq a padded article
deiq duv to select out; to choose out (46:131) (tseˇ do^-eu)
deiq gul to stretch out (35:77) (g'eu cawˬ-eu)
deiqhaol give special help to someone (as to a disabled service man)
deiq hoq spread; lay (45:41) (dehˬ k'awˬ)
-- deiq, huvq ssol la -- (see full)
-- deiq hhovq, zyulmiaoq -- to hide criminal evidence
deiq kaq to cover over (9:42, 50:96) (dehˬ kaˬ-eu)
deiq kavq to struggle against (dawˬ ceh ceh-eu)
deiq leivq to use as an excuse (50:88) (or) **zaol leivq**
deiq loq zaq to argue; to reason things out (50:159)
-- deiq, meiqdeiq -- to quarrel
deiq miaoq to stick on (9:42) (dehˬ myahˬ-eu)
deiq muv to sulk
deiq muvq to bend down; hang down (as head) (46:138) (tahˬ mo‸-eu)
-- deiq, needeiq -- to quarrel in hearts
=deiq nei, biul= to be unhappy
deiq neiq 1. to hand over, as a ticket (26:91) (a nehˬ- eu), 2. to shift responsibility to others (50:171)
deiq niq push; lean against (14:44) (dehˬ-eu)
deiqniv nei suddenly (10:2) (**deiqniv nei nyuq lal** = suddenly wake up) (ja pyuˬ ni)
deiq niul to open one's eyes widely (14:148) (mya^ nui^ g'awˬ loe ni byeh-eu)
deiq piq to close (as window) (or) **diq cyuq** (dehˬ piˬ-eu)
deiq puv 1. to turn over (**albol deiq puv** = a tree turns over - 14:195), 2. to push over (14:195) (ba‸ po^-eu)
deiq pyul to push away (dehˬ pa^-eu; dehˬ dzeh-eu)
deiq qul (see: **deiq cul** -- to pout)

deiq siq to sharpen (a knife; machete) (57:84)
deiq ssil 1. to make a face (with eyes) (9:42), 2. to stare (haw tso^ ta⌄-eu), 3. to glower
deiqssil alnei violently (or) **hhaqhav tivq nei**
-- **deiq ssil, miav** -- to stare angrily
-- **deiqssil, neema** -- crazy
deiq tao to stick into (38:16) (deh⌄ ahˇ-eu)
deiq teiq 1. to prevent (10:27), 2. to press down (deh⌄ teh⌄-eu)
deiq tul 1. to start (as to start pushing a cart, getting it moving - 26:64), 2. to help something develop quickly (50:28), 3. to back up (or) **deiq dav** (deh⌄ da^-eu), 4. to stand up (gaw⌄ yaw‸ yaw‸-eu; tuˇ laˇ-eu)
-- **deiq tul, naqbol** -- to raise its ears (as a cat or dog)
deiq xa to push down (deh⌄ k'aw‸-eu; deh⌄ ka-eu)
deiq yoq to push away (9:42) (deh⌄ dzeh-eu)
deiq zaq quarrel (9:42) (deh⌄ dza⌄ ceh dza⌄-eu)
deiq zei 1. to push away (deh⌄ dzeh-eu), 2. to stretch out
deiq zuvq to frown (mya^ pyaw⌄ mˇ byeh⌄-eu)
deiqzyul to offend (Chi) (46:195) (la^ pehˇ-eu)

deiv satisfied; eaten one's fill (9:42) (deh^-eu)
deivdeiv nei fully (ti⌄ deh^; ti⌄ byah)
-- **deiv, dol** -- to drink to the full
-- **deiv, doqdeiv** -- to be talkative
deivhhuvq nei deivq full of vitality
deiv nei to the full (9:42) (deh^ dui dui-eu)
deiv pa deiv nei very full (as of food) (11:57)
-- **deiv, zaq** -- to eat to the full
-- **deiv zaq, wuqdeiq leiq** -- to seek for food; to work for a living

deivq 1. to be alive; to live, 2. to be born (deh‸-eu)
deivq to be bright (yaw bya)
-- **deivq, byuldeivq** -- to survive
=**deivq, byul**= to be alive; to go on living
deivqdeivq nei talkative (daw⌄ ja ja coeˇ-eu)
deivqhol hav life-force; vitality (50:151)
deivq huvq lal to regain consciousness
deivq hhoq sil hhoq hhoq a dead person is instructed to forget the ones he loved in life and separate from them
deivq hhuvq deivq lal xeiv nei very fresh and lively
deivq hhuvq nei freshly
deivq kevq alnei se instinct (50:10)
-- **deivq lal, deivq hhuvq** -- lively; vivid; vigorous
-- **deivq le, seq le** -- to marry at a mature age and give a late birth
deivq meeq good things to happen which are predestined from birth ('good birth')
-- **deivq, meiqzu** -- to be talkative

deivq mol sil lal kul following the burial, the souls of the whole family are called back to the home
deivqmol ssaqmiq molseq one of the spirits which can enter a person ("**ngeeq**")
deivqmol ssaqmiq molzao one of the spirits which can enter a person ("**ngeeq**")
deivq muv to be dispirited; depressed (nui g'a˯ ju˯)
deivqnao birthday (deh^ le-eu˯ a˅ nah)
-- **deivq, neema** -- 1. to be careful; to work hard, 2. clever; smart; sharp; intelligent
=**deivq nei, niul**= very green and fresh
=**deivq nei, xao**= to be very, very heavy
deivqniv hov nei in a great panic (45:73)
deivq sil tavq life and death together (50:151)
deivq syuq 1. difficult labor; 2. a hard life (deh^-eu yaw sha˯)
-- **deivq, ssaq** -- 1. to give birth, 2. to get interest from invested money
deivq ssol sil col na maq dovq cannot tell when people will live or die (set phrase)
deivq ssol sil lal e miqnieiq a matter of life and death
deivq zyul bad things to happen which are predestined from birth ('bad birth')

=**deivq, yeil**= inherent; innate
=**deivq, yo**= alive
-- **deivq, yodeivq** -- to be alive
-- **deivq, yodeivq ssil** -- to sing about life

deifbiao a representative; delegate (as in congress) (Chi) (9:41, 34:6, 41:4,5, 40:31, 50:31) (or) **dafbiao** (26:101) (cf.: tsaw˅ ka˯)
  deifbiao hefxei sseiq a candidate
  deifbiaotuaq a delegation (Chi) (50:31) representative delegate
deifciiq a pronoun (Chi)
deifkua for the government to lend money (Chi) (14:211) (cf.: pyu˅ bi nga˯-eu)
deifniq unemployed (waiting for work) (Chi) (50:31)
deiftiq to substitute (Chi) (34:23)
Deif Xaopiq Deng Xiaoping (Chinese leader) (Chi) (34:12)
deifyif salary; income (Chi) (50:31)

DI

dil to weigh something in the hand (sa^ haw-eu)
=**dil, aq**= really
dildal 'ding dong' (sound of pony bells) (12:125)
dildev a cattle bell (ja˅ cu˅)
dil dil dil dal ding-a-ling (sound of bells) (12:126)
-- **dil, tyuqdil davdil** -- to seek in every way
dilziiq metal nails (buy in town) (Chi) (shm˅ seh˯)

di to retreat (9:43) (g'aw˅ di^-eu = to retract, as snake or earthworm)

di li de le 1. a clicking noise, 2. the sound of bells (on cows, horses)

-- **di, naoldi** -- to back down; to retreat; to give ground; to move back, to withdraw (as from a battle) (and see full)

-- **di, naolhhuvq** -- to retreat

Di'qal weiqhuaf dogee following the Diqia culture (an ancient nation in China) (Chi) (46:84)

diq to beat; strike (9:43) (di˯-eu) (or) **tuv** (as when knocking on door or table with one's knuckles (deh k'o^-eu)

diq to beat down on, as rain (9:43) (di˯-eu)

diq to pat; clap (9:43) (di˯-eu; teh^-eu)

diq clf. for a hit, a strike (11:85) (la˰)

-- **diq, aolpuq** -- (see full)

-- **diq, baqpov** -- to slap someone in the face with the palm of one's hand

diq beivq hit and break (11:115) (or) **diq pav** (di˯ pya^-eu; di˯ pa^-eu)

diq bial to cancel

diq biov to pat; to persuade (ja jah-eu)

diq ceil to choose out from (10:pref.) (tse˅ do^-eu)

diqciq yeast; distiller's yeast (deh˯ tse˯)

diqciq dalpiaq a type of fern

diq cuv to nail something; to fix something (with nails)

diq cyuq 1. to close (as window) (10:7) (pi˯ teh˯-eu), 2. to seal off; blockade (**faolso** = Chi), 3. to fight (50:35)

-- **diq cyuq, caqbyu** -- to close a window

-- **diq, daziifjil** -- to type on a typewriter (A=Chi)

diqdaq threshing stick for beating grain (or) **diqdul** (9:43) (di˯ ma)

-- **diq, daoldiq** -- for a bird to spread its wings

-- **diq, doqlovq** -- to have a chat

diqdul threshing stick for beating grain (or) **diqdaq** (di˯ ma)

diq duvq to be beaten heavily; sufficiently (di˯ lo˰-eu)

diqdyuf feilzii 1. a hostile element (Chi) (50:34), 2. an opposition member (50:34)

diqdyuf geifxeif a hostile border line (Chi) (50:34)

-- **diq e hhaqhav, geel** -- combat capacity

-- **diq, eeldiq** -- to swim

-- **diq, geel** -- to fight a war

diq gyuq yoqqif percussion instrument (C=Chi) (50:30)

diq hal to turn over and liquid runs out

-- **diq, habaol** -- to divine with a chicken thigh

-- **diq, hav** -- exert force; violence

diq ho 1. to knock (di˯ k'o^-eu), 2. to strike and make a loud noise so as to drive spirits away;

tuv ho
diqhhal a bamboo mat tied to either side of the threshing 'boat' to keep the rice going into the 'boat' (9:43)
diq hhaq to win (9:43) (& see: **diq hhaol**) (**g'aˬ** leˇ-eu)
diqhhavq a fence (kmˇ cehˇ; **yaˇ** kmˇ)
-- **diq, hhavqkuv a** -- to attack a jail
diq hhaol to win; overcome (as in a battle) (& see: **diq hhaq**) (g'aˬ leˇ-eu)
diqhhao a big bamboo container in which crops are put
diq hhao to fence in; to circle a site with poles (46:115, 130) (yaˇ kmˇ mˇ lahˇ-eu)
diqhho maoqdyuf contradictions between ourselves and the enemy (Chi) (50:34)
diqhhoq a pea (9:44, 11:74) (la‸ buiˬ **sahˬ** duˇ)
diq hhoq to strike and separate (diˬ pa^-eu)

diq ju to beat black and blue (cf.: diˬ neˇ diˬ law-eu)
diqka factory-made synthetic cloth (not cotton) (Chi) (9:44, 11:17)
diq kaq a cover; a cap (uˬ k'o^)
diq kaq to cover (9:44) (dehˬ kaˬ-eu)
-- **diq kaq, piqkaq** -- to cover something
diq kavq 1. to strike each other, 2. to fence (cf.: diˬ k'a^-eu; diˬ kaˬ-eu)
-- **diq, kaoldaol** -- to fence in
diq kyuq to beat severely (or) **diqduvq** (diˬ k'a^ le‸-eu)
=diq, laq= jew's-harp (musical mouth instrument)
-- **diq, laqqeq** -- to play basketball (A=Chi)
-- **diq, lavqhov** -- to applaud
diq laol to lock up; to put in prison for some time (50:92) (kawˬ-ahˇ daw^-eu)
diq leeq to beat down; knock down (9:44) (diˬ coˬ-eu)
diq leev to thresh rice and get it into paddy bins (diˬ lui^-eu)
diqloq a wooden container (shaped like a boat) into which they thresh rice (11:27)
-- **diq, lusul** -- to think of an idea; method
diq mei to wipe out (kill all) (9:44) (cf.: meh-eu)
=diq, miq= 1. flint etc. for making fire, 2. modern lighter
diq miaoq bavq to be armed; to hold a weapon (as a gun) (50:24)
diqmoq moq to go through the motion of striking something without actually hitting it
-- **diq, moqseiq** -- to shoe a horse
diq mu hit and make woozy, dizzy (13:24)
diq nal to hit and hurt (9:44) (diˬ naˇ-eu)
diq nuv saq naldul dul sil ya it seems that all (hope) has been struck to pieces (14:141)
diq pav to break down (or) **diq beivq** (diˬ pa^-eu)
diqpaol homemade canon for making a loud noise (Chi)

diq pao to open (as window) (10:7) (pah-eu)
diq paoq to put together; to summarize
diq peel 1. to separate two fighting people or animals, 2. to help someone out of a predicament (50:88)
diqpuq hammer (9:44) (di˯ pu˯)
-- **diqpuq, albol** -- a wooden hammer (put at the village gate to scare away spirits)
diqpuq lavqniaov a set of tools for a blacksmith (clf. = **zuvq**) (11:77) (ba^ ji˯-eu˯ keu ka)
-- **diqpuq, maqzavq** -- hammer for shoeing horses
-- **diqpuq, meiyeil** -- (see full)
diq puv to attack (50:30)
diq puv diq leeq to overthrow (34:16)
diq puv huvq to retaliate (50:30); to fight against (50:47); to counter-attack
diq qaq 1. to be tired of being beaten, 2. to be tired of beating (di˯ doeˇ-eu)
diq qaq diq ga 1. to be very badly beaten, 2. to beat hard (di˯ k'a^-eu)
diqqeiv qeivzaq to have a contest; a game (as a basketball game) (41:191) (or) **aolqeiv qeiv** (jahˇ ceh ceh-eu)
diqqoqliaq dacron (Chi)
diq qov to beat to breaking (di˯ pa^-eu)
diqqul a bell (9:44) (jaˇ cuˇ)
-- **diq, saqhav** -- to cut down a forest
diq seivq strike to death (or) **diq tov; diq sil** (di˯ seh˄-eu)
diq sil 1. to put out a fire (26:69), 2. to kill by beating (1. di˯ siˇ-eu, 2. di˯ seh˄-eu) (la^ mi^-eu)
-- **diq, silpuq** -- to play basketball
diqsiil wilderness (virgin forest with few trees & bushes)
diqsiif to be hostile; antagonistic (Chi) (50:34)
diqsseiq enemy; armed bandit (Chi) (26:15) (or) **daqjeil** (9:40)
diqsseiq diq to get revenge against an enemy (26:15)
diq tao to break into (or) **teiq dov** (tah˯ ahˇ-eu)
diq teiq to control (as to control the basketball) (41:202)
diqteiv diqteiv meil patting gently
diq tov to beat to death; strike to death; **diq sil; diq seivq** (9:44) (di˯ seh˄-eu)
diq tov jil nei to give a death blow
diq tov zaq those killed in war or conflict (they take the 'upper path' according to death ceremonies)
diq tovq to hit something other than what aiming at (yaw˯ je˯ yaw˯-ahˇ di˯ zaw-eu)
-- **diq, wusuq** -- to perform Chinese martial arts (A=Chi)
-- **diq, yaqmoq** -- to kill a buffalo for a dead person

(or) **yaqmoq seivq**

diq **zaq** to beat one another, to fight (11:20) (**diqsseiq naogo diqzaq** = to fight with the enemy 26:104) (diˬ dzaˬ-eu)

diq **zaq** eil **zaq** to have conflict

diq **zaq koqzaq** col 'smash-and-grabber' (50:30)

diq **zaq koq zaq** li to invade and take over (as a territory) (50:137)

diq **zoq** to dress up; to put on make-up

diq **zov** 1. to beat someone all over, 2. to strike something softly

diqzu a landlord (Chi) (35:1) (yaw sahˇ)

div muddy, turbid water (9:44) (iˇ neˇ neˇ-eu)

=div, eel= muddy water

-- div, eeldiv -- water to become muddy

dif'eq **piul bivq** pay money by quota (A=Chi) (50:38)

diffal **faqgyul** the local regulations (Chi) (50:35)

difgoq **zuyiq** imperialism (Chi) (26:1, 16) (or) **difgoq zuyif** (34:8) (**Mei difgoq zuyif** = American imperialism - 34:8)

difhhyu prefecture committee (Chi) (50:36)

difhhyuf the position of a person (Chi) (50:36)

difli geography (Chi) (50:35)

difli **huaqji** geographical conditions (Chi) (50:35)

diflixoq geography (Chi) (50:35)

diflueiq a land mine (Chi) (50:35)

difqil district; region (46:111) (Chi) (miˇ k'ahˬ)

difquq earth (Chi) (or) **milcaq** (Ha) (miˇ tsaˬ)

Dif **Sal Ciif Siifgeif Dafzaf** the Third World War (Chi) (50:35)

Dif **sal siifjeif** Third world countries (Chi); **Dif sal siifgeif** (Chi) (50:35)

difsuljil a stapler (Chi) (50:39)

difsseiq terrestrial heat (Chi) (50:35)

diftuq a map (Chi) (50:36)

difweif position (Chi) (34:38) (yaw duˬ)

difxeif a ground wire (Chi) (50:36)

difyi attributive (gram) (Chi) (50:39)

difyiq the first one (Chi) (or) **huqteil teil** (50:35)

difyiqxeif front line (Chi) (50:35)

difzel fuflieiq prefectural women's affairs (Chi) (10:pref.)

difzu landlord (Chi) (26:1) (yaw sahˇ)

difzu geiljiq landlord class (Chi) (50:36)

DIAO

diaolbao a guard house; blockhouse (military) (Chi) (26:47, 50:38)

diaolkeq to carve (Chi)

diaof to get (goods); to transport (goods) (Chi) (**Kyulmiq a miaoqgaoq diaof li movq.** I want to transport goods from Kunming. 41:15)

diaofcaq to investigate (Chi) (9:43, 10:32, 34:40, 50:38) (tseˇ haw-eu)

diaofcaq baofgaof investigative report (Chi) (50:38)

diaofcaqhyuf research meeting (Chi) (50:38)

diaofcaq yeiljef study and research work (Chi) (50:38

diaofdaof to transfer one's job (Chi)

DIEI

dieilfuq to overturn (Chi) (34:33)

diei'faf a type; model (Chi) (or) **moqfaf** (Chi)

dieimiq to call the roll (Chi) (or) **colmiaol gul**

-- diei, qiq -- iodine deficiency (Chi)

dieizaol o'clock (Chi) (4 **dieizaol** = 4 o'clock) (26:33) (la^)

dieif electricity (Chi) (50:36)

dieifbaof telegraph (Chi) (50:36)

dieifbilxal refrigerator (Chi) (50:36)

dieifbol electric waves (Chi) (50:36)

dieif bosev electric fan (A=Chi) (50:37)

dieif caqhul electric teapot (Chi) (50:37)

dieifcafjil an electric phonograph; gramophone (Chi) (50:36)

dieifceil electric trolley car (Chi) (or) **dieif qiqceil** (Chi) (50:37)

dieifciiq a battery (Chi) (50:37)

dieifcyulfaol electric hair drier (Chi) (50:37)

dieifdeil an electric lamp (Chi) (9:43, 50:37)

dieifdeil hhe sil to turn off ('pull to death') the lamp (A=Chi)

dieifhuafhyuf a meeting by telephone; telephone conference (Chi) (50:37)

dieifqifhuaf to be electrified (as a village to be able to use electricity) (Chi)

dieifhuaf a telephone (Chi) (50:37) (or) **dieifhual** (9:43)

dieifluq an electric stove (Chi) (50:37)

dieifnao computer (Chi) (50:37)

dieif nei zuq sil to be electrocuted; killed by an electric shock (as from a broken wire) (A,C=Chi)

dieif saolcal electric pot (A=Chi) (50:37)

dieifsiif television (Chi) (34:65); movie, film (46:172) (and see: **dieifssi**)

dieifsiifjil TV set (Chi) (9:43, 50:37) (tiˇ viˇ; dehˇ suiˇ = CA)

dieifsiif luqxaf television and video (Chi)

dieifsiifjif a TV program (Chi) (50:37)

dieifsiifteiq a TV station

dieifssi movie (Chi) (11:31) (and see: **dieifsiif**) (biˇ mya^)

dieifssi albee movie screen (curtain) (Chi) (11:31) (bi˯ mya˰ mya˰-eu sa˯ paˇ)
dieifssi hu to watch a movie (or TV program) (A=Chi) (bi˯ mya˰ bya˯ gaˇ haw-eu)
dieifssi mu'luq a film (A=Chi)
dieifssi pieiq to show a movie (or TV program) (A=Chi) (bi˯ mya˰ bya˯-eu)
dieiftaoq flashlight; battery torch (Chi) (9:43, 11:30, 50:37) (nahˇ ma nahˇ do˰; daˇ miˇ; paˇ ta)
dieiftil electric lift (elevator) (Chi) (50:37)
dieifyi film; movie (Chi) (34:65)
dieifyidyuf movie projectionist (Chi) (50:37)
dieifyi fafyifjil movie maker (Chi) (50:37)
dieifyi pieiq to show a movie (A=Chi) (41:207)
dieifyifde an electric iron (Chi) (50:37)
dieif yuqlaoq electric rice cooker (A=Chi) (50:37)
dieifzii electronics (Chi) (46:76)
dieifzii jifsuf electronic techniques (Chi) (50:37)
dieifzii jifsuafjil electric computer (Chi) (50:37)

DO

dol 1. to drink (9:44) (dawˇ-eu), 2. to be straight (yaw dawˇ)
dol bad omen (see below for examples) (dawˇ)
aqha dol duv for a bad-omen hen to occur (must cut off the head on the threshold of the house, if body flies into house eat the hen inside, if it flies out of the house eat it outside) The head is stuck up on a stick and left outside of the village pointing away from the village
hhavqdol duv for a bad-omen pig to occur
keeqdol duv for a bad-omen dog to occur
moqdol duv for a bad-omen horse to occur
niuqdol duv for a bad-omen buffalo or cow to occur
=dol, col= bad-omen people
dol deiv to drink to the full (dawˇ deh^-eu)
-- dol, doqheiq -- (see full)
dolduq a place to drink (dawˇ du˯)
dol duv 1. for a bad omen to occur, 2. for trouble from a bad omen to break out (**ha dol duv** = for a hen to reveal a bad omen) (cf. **yocavq duv**) (dawˇ tah˯ pu˯-eu)
dol eq tao al la for a bad omen to be brought into a village (such as by a barking deer running in) (when spoken rapidly it becomes: **dol eq taol la**)
dolgee below; beneath; down (op.: **dolnia**)
=dol, ha= bad-omen hen (see full)
=dol, hhavq= bad-omen pig (see full)
=dol meil, qiq= straight to one point; mark
dol miaq to drink a lot (cf.: **dol yevq** = to drink to intoxication) (g'aw˯ mya ni dawˇ-eu)
=dol, moq= bad-omen horse (see full)
dol mu to get drunk (or) **dol yevq** (dawˇ yeh˰-eu)
Dolniq a group of Hani who live in Yuanyang and

Jinping counties
dolnia above; upstream (op.: **dolgee**)
Dolnia Luchun (thought by the Hani to be the historical center of the Hani/Akha people) (or) **Dolnia Luqcyul; Luqcyulxeif** (Chi) (11:126)
Dolnia doq the Luchun dialect of Hani (46:84)
=dol, niuq= bad-omen cow/buffalo
dolssiq nei 1. straight, 2. to align (9:44, 46:113, 130) (or) **doqheiq dol** (dawˇ coe ni)
dolssiq nei dol upright
dolssiq nei ssol dei nei straight and level
dolteil the back (naˇ k'ah)
dol yevq to drink to intoxication (dawˇ yeh^-eu)
=dol, zeiq= bad-omen animals (see full)

do to castrate (the term is only used for buffalos, cattle and horses) (9:44) (mawˇ neˇ dawˇ-eu)
do to be neat
dogee a lower place (11:32) (or) **dolgee**
=do, miav= a type of machete used for cutting wood (A=Dai)
-- do, moqdo -- to castrate a horse
=do nei, lee= neatly
=do nei, soq= to be tidy
donia upriver; an upper place (11:32) (or) **dolnia**
dosol dolsol to be fragrant (57:90)

doq word; sentence (9:45) (daw˯)
doq to wait for (9:45, 13:23) (daw˯-eu)
doq'aqma story; proverb
doqbiav bad word; dirty word (9:45) (or) **doqcavq; doqdyul**
doqbiav pieiq to cook up a story and spread it around; to start a bad rumor
doqcavq bad word; dirty words; rumor (or) **doqbiav; doqdyul** (daw˯ doeˇ)
doq cavq wait and meet (9:45) (daw˯ tsa˯-eu)
doq cavq lal come to greet (11:221, 46:133) (or) **doq cavq li** = go to greet
doqceiv partial ('broken') sentence; half of a sentence
doqciivq a set phrase; an idiom; a word (note: often in Ak. this is used for 'meaning of a word')
doqdal special words spoken in ceremonies
doqdaq myth (6:185) a story (9:45) (see also: **dudaq** (daw˯ da˯)
doqdaq daq 1. to tell a story, 2. to speak of another
doqdaq helbiav a souvenir badge (50:81)
doqdaq luvcuv a monument; a memorial stone (50:81)
doqdaq yaolma monument hall (50:91)
doqdeiv deiv to be talkative (or) **doq miaq**
doqdeiv hha to visit (46:109) (daw˯ deh g'a-eu)
doqdeiv hhazaoq zaoq to meet together and talk (46:86)

doq doqma important words (11:36) (daw˯ daw˯ ma)

doqdyul 1. bad words; dirty words (or) **doqbiav, doqcavq**, 2. derogatory term (50:12) (daw˯ yaw doeˇ)

doq eil to make a speech (50:44)

-- doq, eilloq -- 1. to annotate; explain with notes, 2. a preface

doq eil maq zaol divergence; difference; not do what one says one will do (50:50)

doq eil nalhaq to obey (or) **eildoq nalhaq** (ehˇ daw˯ naˇ ha˯-eu)

doq eil naciq ciq for one's words to have an effect

-- doq, galdoq -- to wait for on the way

doqgaq 1. news (9:45, 11:28) (daw˯ ga˯), 2. information (or) **qiqbaof** (Chi), 3. intelligence (50:138)

doqgaq cavq to pass on a message; order

doqgaq zol to pass on a message (35:78)

doq gee caqcaol zil to come to the point (in a discussion)

doq gee geel maq hhuvq blame not the speaker (50:193)

doq gee maq jil dishonest talk (dawˇ coe ma˯ ngeh˯-eu)

doq gee'qoq to talk in private (with a friend)

doq gee zaq to speak in a polite way (50:201)

doqhav maq eil doqnaoq eil avoid the important and dwell on the trivial; keep silent about major charges while admitting minor ones (50:11)

doqhaol haol 1. to appeal to; to call on, 2. to help someone to speak (50:72)

doqheiq dol 1. to live well; for things to be going along well (45:8) (jawˇ mui˯-eu), 2. to align (or) **dolssiq nei**

doqheiq doq introduction to a paper (50:34)

doqheiq lo'lavq a language branch (50:201)

doqheiq loquv a language family

doqheiq lozao language group; language branch

doqheiq teev offensive and defensive alliance; an agreement between partners in crime not to give each other away; a pact to shield each other (50:60)

doqhyuq a secret word (50:2)

-- doq, hheivq -- cheating words

doqhhuvq duv a conflict to break out

doqhhyul sweet words (as to lover) (11:203) (daw˯ mui˯)

doqjil surely (35:19) (diˇ ma˯-ehˇ)

doqkol kolzao a poetic drama (50:152)

doqkol soqdaoq a book of poems; a collection of poems

-- doqkol, yeilgaq -- an epic

doq lavq a clause (gram.) (50:50)

doqlavq doqlo a duplicated word (50:24)

doqlavq lavqpaoq a compound sentence (50:54)

doqlaoq doqlo a couplet ('duplicate word') (such as: **aol zaq hovq dol**) (50:24)

doqlo a word (50:27)

doqlo cuv galquv word building (gram) (50:63)
doqlo doqlaoq "duplicate words" (as; **qul qul bieiv bieiv**)
-- doq lo, doq sil -- to wait and wait for a long time
doqlo loba a phrase (50:28)
doqlo locavq a conjunction (gram) (50:106)
doqlo loceil a grammatical term for the character, as "ngeel" (50:127)
doqlo locuv a set phrase (50:64)
doqlo lodav prefix and suffix of a word (50:28)
doqlo loduv a sentence-making derivative (gram) (50:126)
doqlo loheeq enlarge the meaning of a word
doqlo loheiq etymology (50:28)
doqlo lohovq a functional word (opposite of a theoretical or notional word, see: **doqlo lomal**)
doqlo lo'lyul a segment of a word (50:28)
doqlo lomal a theoretical or notional word (conveying an idea and having full lexical meaning, the opposite of a functional word - see: **doqlo lohovq**) (50:28)
doqlo lonil to narrow the meaning of the word (50:28)
doqlo lopal change the meaning of a word
doqlo lopaoq a synonym (50:168)
doqlo lopuv antonym (words of opposite meaning) (50:47)
doqlo loqa a part of speech (50:27)
doqlo lo'qil a root word (50:27)
doqlo lo'qo word order (50:28)
doqlo lo'quv morphology
doqlo losal elements of a sentence (50:93)
doqlo losiivq a new word (50:151)
doqlo losol a single morpheme word
doqlo loyeiv elaborate expressions (& appendix 12)
doqlo lozao 1. a compound word (50:71); 2. a dictionary (see also: **doqlo soqdaoq; doqlo soqkaoq**)
doqlo soqdaoq a dictionary; **doqlo soqkaoq**
doqlo yodoq 1. basic words; 2. daily words (50:78)
doqlo yo'liq the meaning of a word (50:28)
doq loq doq ngeel true speech (words) (57:76)
doqlovq 1. to be quarrelsome; noisy (or) **beilsil**, 2. to have a chat; 3. to have a noisy conversation
  doqlovq diq to have a chat (41:55, 46:87,109) (daw͜ ngeh͜ caw͜-eu)
  doqlovq lovq to chat; converse in a noisy way
doqma slogans (50:98) (or) **kehaof** (Chi)
doqmeeq good words (daw͜ mui͜) (or) **doq meeq**
  doqmeeq cavq to tell good news (50:8)
  doqmeeq doqlo a commendatory term (50:6)
doqmiaq to be talkative (or) **doqdeiv deiv**
doqmiaol title; subject; topic (50:164)
-- doq, moqdoq -- to use a horse now and pay the owner for it later

doqnaq naqdoq a two-part allegorical saying (50:187)
doqnaoq kind words ('soft words')
doq nei by word of mouth (or) **meiqbaoq wuqduq nei**
doq palpuv col a translator (50:46)
doq pav 'half' of a sentence (an incomplete sentence)
doqpuv 'upside down words' (say 'bad' for 'good', 'light' for 'dark', etc.) (daw˯ po^)
doqqeiv qeiv parallelism (50:126)
doqqo alzil parakeet (Psittacula spp)
doqqoq puq to interview; to have a dialogue (50:41)
doqqul sweet words (daw˯ yaw coeˇ)
  doqqul sov to flatter; to praise excessively (50:126)
=doq, sal= good words
doqsaq tavq to get along; find each other congenial (50:185)
doqsav sav to whisper (9:45) (daw˯ sa^ sa^-eu)
doq sil doq lo to wait and wait for a long time (46:96) (g'aw˯ myahˇ ni daw˯-eu)
doqsii a speech; a word (14:141) (daw˯)
  doqsii doqdeiv to talk freely
  doqsii eil to make a speech
  doqsii eil ceiv to come to terms
  doq sii nei meiqzaoq zaoq when a buffalo is being killed at a funeral, water is poured down its throat to keep it from calling out
  doqsii yeillul gee to speak (daw˯ ngeh˯-eu)
doq taq an appointment; engagement
  doq taq eil ceiv to make an appointment (nah paˇ paˇ-eu)
  doqtaq taq to make an appointment; engagement
-- doqtevq, puvlaol -- village regulations
doqteil a sound; a voice (6:185, 38:1) (teˇ saˇ) clf. = **teil** (**doqteil qiq teil** = one sound) (13:31)
  doqteil teilma a very loud sound (26:10) (teˇ saˇ yaw k'a^)
  doqteil teilpaoq homonym; homophone (50:168)
  doqteil teilsal a pleasant sound (38:91) (naˇ ha˯ mui˯-eu teˇ saˇ)
  doqteil teilsav a soft, whispery sound (26:86) (teˇ saˇ yaw nah˯)
  doqteil teilssaq a small sound; a soft sound
doqxu xudoq elliptical sentences (50:151)
doqza za to compare languages (in 31:3 it is speaking of bilingualism)
doq zaq 1. to wait for; 2. to hope; expect (50:127, 133)
doqzaq laq to reply; to answer (46:90) (ehˇ k'o˰ neh˯-eu)
doqzaq maq laq no answer; no reply (35:43) (ma˯ ehˇ k'o˰-eu)
doqzaol antithesis (50:41)
doqzil a meeting (50:76)
doqzil duv to meet to discuss

doqzil duvduq a meeting room (50:76)
doqzil duvheiq pao to have an opening speech at a conference or meeting (50:95)
doqzil gee to discuss (46:138) (ja uˇ-eu)
doqzil zil 1. to discuss (9:45, 11:190, 26:35), 2. to have a meeting (50:95) (or) **keilhyuf keil** (Chi) (daw˯ baw˯-eu; baw˯ dza˯-eu; daw˯ ja ja uˇ-eu)
doqzil zilduq a meeting place (dzoeˇ du˯)
doqzil zilzaq to discuss together (11:38, 26:103) (baw˯ dza˯-eu)
doqzol zol to have an intelligent conversation; to learn something from a conversation
doqzu a summary (50:81)

dov 1. to put in; to season (as food), 2. to get into (daw^-eu)
-- dov, bavq -- to put in
dovheiq an entrance
dov lal yal easy come easy go (or) **duv yil yal**
dov li enter (up) (uˇ leˇ-eu)
dovlov meil quietly; slightly (9:45) (aw law^ law^-ehˇ; aˇ za za-ehˇ)
dovlov nei kovq to nibble on something
=dov nei, leev= 1. satisfactory, 2. thoroughly
-- dov, pieiq -- put into (as salt and chili into soup)
-- dov, ya -- to drop into
dov yil enter (down) (uˇ-iˇ-eu)

dovq to make a fire; light a fire (9:45) (do˄-eu)
dovq to perch (as a bird) (9:46) (daw˄-eu)
dovq to put on (as clothes); to wear (as a flower, a bandage) (9:46) (dm-eu; geu˄-eu)
dovq for a disease to spread (**nalgol dovq lal** = the disease spreads) (nyaw˯)
=dovq, al= a light; a lamp
-- dovq, aldovq -- to light a lamp
=dovq, a= dragonfly
-- dovqbei, lavqnieivq -- to start a project (put hands on and begin)
dovq bia illumination; lighting (50:208)
-- dovq, eq -- to infect with a disease
dovqhovq a lamp (tsiˇ k'm˯)
-- dovqhovq, aldovq -- an oil lamp
-- dovq, hhe -- to turn on (as a light)
dovqkovq a lamp to be burning
=dovq, neivq= 'will-o'-the-wisp'; phosphorescent light
dovq xa heil to spread out, as a disease (15:62) (nyaw˯ leˇ-eu)

dofciiq (see: **daofciiq**) (Chi) (50:39)

dul 1. similar (9:46) (duˇ-eu), 2. true to life (**qiq dul qiq hevq** = lifelike; true to life) (50:10)
=dul, bavq= shoulder pole
=dul, biaq= ground wasp
=dul, bul= thigh
=dul, buvq= a pen
=dul, caq= broad bean
=dul, dal= a pole that can be used for something
duldeil deil to fasten a belt (46:160) (jo‸ pa‸ pa‸)
=dul, diq= a threshing stick
duldul the cry of doves (46:118) (duˇ-eu)
dul lal to be similar; to look alike (8:12) (duˇ laˇ)
dulma sister (dmˇ ma)
-- **dulma, aqmol** -- siblings (brothers & sisters)
Dulma Jeiseq the name of **Molmil**'s daughter; also called: **Dulma Jeiseq aoqtav miltav colkyul**
dulma ssaqmiq lovely little sister (dmˇ ma yaw mui˯)
-- **dul, maq nyuq maq** -- not to worry
dulmav mav an omen; sign (50:201)
=dul meil, nal= likely
-- **dul, naldul** -- appears to be the same; same as; seems to be...

=du, ceil= corn; maize
-- **du, ceildu** -- for corn ears to begin coming on with grains of corn
dudaq a story (13:38, 30:1) (daw˯ maw˯ daw˯ oeˇ)
dudaq gee zaq to tell a story
dudaq maq ngeel maq gee 'if it were not real there would be no story' (i.e., I would not say it if it were not so)
=du, keel= calf of leg; lower leg
=du, kyul= horn (as buffalo/ox)
=du, lavq= forearm
du lu de le 1. strings of beads, 2. bearing fruit
=du, miq= burning rope from which tobacco can be lit
=du nei, laol= warmly
duniaoq sticky corn; glutinous corn (aˇ du nyaw˯)
=du, ngal= we all (inclusive we)
dupyuv popcorn (aˇ du aˇ pa˯)
du'qu to fill in with earth; pile up earth around (as corn plants) (du˯ dzm-eu)
=du, saol= crowbar
dussei hard corn (du g'ahˇ)
duyal corn field (46:211) (aˇ du du yaˇ)
duyyuq corn cob (9:47) (aˇ du aˇ kah˯)

duq dig (9:46) (du˯-eu)
duq clf. for 1. pools of water (9:46), 2. sound of drum, thunder etc.
(vb) **duq** place to (vb) (**jolduq** = place to live; **aolduq** = place to do, etc.) ((vb) du˯)

duq, duq, duq the sound of knocking at the door; thunder; striking a drum (and see appendix 6)
-- duq, albeil duq -- the place where one's placenta and umbilical cord are buried (one's birthplace)
=duq, aol= 1. to be useful, 2. a place where something is done
-- duq, bavq -- to bury
duq beivq duv puv to dig thoroughly (57:99)
=duq, bul= oneself
-- duqbyu, jaqleil -- a wind hole spoken of in their mythology (& see full)
=duq, byuq= a bamboo container in which seeds are kept until the next planting
duqceiq duq to gamble (Chi) (35:34) (da˯-eu)
duqceiq zeifqeiq autocratic authorities (Chi) (50:40)
-- duq, wuqduq -- leading role; the lead (as in a film); headed by; ring leader (50:215)
-- duq col, wuqduq -- ring leader (50:156)
=duq, cuq= a hot spring
duq cuv to plant (14:173) (ka-eu)
duqcuaf an early model; the first made (as first made model of radio, etc.) (Chi) (50:40)
-- duqduq, albeil -- one's birthplace (i.e., where one's placenta was buried)
-- duq, duqceiq -- to gamble
duq duv to dig dirt and build up a road (gaˇ ma du˯-eu)
duqhaoq a low place in the road/path
duqhovq a hole in the ground (9:46) (du˯ k'ah˯)
duqhovq hovq to dig a hole in the ground, or for there to be a hole in the ground (9:46, 11:44) (du˯ k'ah˯ k'ah˯-eu)
duq hhaq to win at gambling (35:35) (pa˯ da˯ g'a˯-eu)
duq hhuvq to bury (or) **bavqduq** (du˯ pah˯-eu)
=duq, jol= a place where one lives
duqkaoq a cloth patch (9:46) (pehˇ tsahˇ do^-eu)
=duq, keeq= compost; manure pit
Duqlaoq ssaqqa Dulong nationality (A=Chi) (50:40)
duqliq independent (Chi) (34:14)
duqlu a bump (as on a road)
=duq, lu= a pool of water
=duq, luq= a drum
=duq, meeq= goodness
duq nal duq sil hurt and killed by digging (46:195) (du˯ naˇ du˯ seh^)
=duq, naq= a resting place
-- duq nei, aoqjiq -- thunder to roll
=duq, ngaq= a fish pond
-- duq, ngaqduq -- to dig a fishpond (11:18)
duq pal to dig again (paˇ du˯-eu)
duq pao to dig a hole; to dig an opening (33:3) (du˯ k'ah˯ du˯-eu)
=duq, piul= silver buried in ground
-- duq, piulduq -- to bury silver in the ground
duq puv to dig up (9:46) (du˯ po^-eu; du˯ paˇ-eu = to

dig up a body)
duq qu . to dig and pile up (as piling dirt around corn plants) (du⌄ dzo-eu)
duq sal to dig and build with a hoe
=duq, savq= kitchen
duqsul reading (Chi) (26:52) (gui-eu)
duq sul to lose at gambling (35:35) (pa⌄ da⌄ smˇ-iˇ)
-- **duq, syu li** -- place to hide
duq teiq to prevent (**eelpuv duq teiq** = to prevent flooding - 26:57) (k'm⌄-eu)
-- **duq, wuqduq** -- to be the 'head'; leader; have a leading role (as in a film)
=duq, xa= planting methods; planting space
=duq, xavq= sleeping place; camping place
=duq, xiq= a toilet
=duq, yiuvq= a place to sleep
=duq, zaq= a place to eat
duq zei abandoned (or) **bavq zei**
duqziiqzyul dereliction of duty (Chi) (50:40)

duv 1. come/go out of (do^ laˇ-eu; do^-iˇ-eu), 2. to leak (liquid) (dza^-eu) (4:47), 3. to pay for, 4. to take place (**miqnieiq qiq mol duv** = something took place, something happened)
duv al la comes out (as in: **nyuq duv al la; eil duv al la**)
-- **duv, bavq** -- to take (carry) out
-- **duv bei, zaol** -- formerly created
-- **duv, caq** -- (see full)
-- **duv, ceil** -- to select out; to choose out
-- **duv, daoqlul ya** -- a prolapsed rectum
-- **duv, deiq** -- to select out; to choose out
-- **duv, doqzil** -- to meet to discuss
-- **duv, eil** -- to speak out; make clear; confess (and see full)
-- **duv, eilloq** -- to make clear; state clearly
-- **duv, galkeel** -- (see full)
-- **duv, gee** -- to speak out
-- **duv, hal** -- 1. a dispute to develop, 2. to spread a rumor
duvheiq an exit
=duv heiq, beel= east
-- **duv, hu** -- to see; to know; to see through
-- **duv, hhe** -- to draw out; to stick out
-- **duv, hhobaoq hhoduv** -- for rice ears to begin to form
-- **duv, hhuv** -- to go out
-- **duv, jaq** -- to call something out
-- **duv, kov** -- to draw out
-- **duv, kuq** -- to fill and soak
duv lal come out of; appear (9:47, 11:40) (do^ laˇ-eu) (**maq nyuq duv al la** = can't think through)
duv lal to arise (or) **tul lal** (tuˇ laˇ)
duv la comes out (as in: **nyuq duv la; eil duv la,** etc.) (8:6,8,17)

-- **duv laq e, ya** -- to lag behind
-- **duv, leiq** -- to drive out; expel; discharge
-- **duv, mieiv** -- to spit out
-- **duv, naqguv** -- to extort a confession by torture
=**duv nei, bil**= to reveal; to show
-- **duv, nyuq** -- to think out; think through
-- **duv, pieiq** -- (see full)
-- **duv, qeiq** -- to get an idea
duv saq maq hhaol emerge in an endless stream (50:20)
-- **duv, sil** -- to stick out (as from a hole)
-- **duv, sivq** -- to bleed
-- **duv, sulnil** -- to become rusted
-- **duv, wulquvq** -- to flow out
-- **duv, xalsol** -- go to work in the fields
-- **duv, xeiv** -- to run away
-- **duv, yalsol** -- go work in the field
-- **duv yil, aqgee** -- to go downstream
duv yil dov lal to go in and out (or) **yil lal suv nei**
duv yiv to come out (do^-iˇ-eu)
duv yoq to walk through; walk over (cah tseh^-eu)
-- **duv, zaol** -- 1. to show by one's countenance or appearance, 2. to create
-- **duv, zeiq** -- (see full)
-- **duv, zyulzeiq** -- to pay a fine

duvq 1. to mend, patch (9:47) (do‸-eu), 2. to replant in empty places (see: **hhaoldaol duvq**)
duvq poison (do‸)
-- **duvq, diq** -- beat heavily
-- **duvq, hhaoldaol** -- to plant in empty spaces
-- **duvq, jeil** -- to drench
=**duvq, lavq**= a bracelet
-- **duvq, lavqduvq** -- to wear a bracelet
=**duvq, miaq**= poisoned arrows
duvq nei all over; thoroughly (46:212) (jiˇ cuˬ ni)
=**duvq nei, biul**= very greasy
-- **duvq, ovq**-- ripe enough to eat
duvq sil to poison to death (or) **neiq sil** (do‸ neh daw^ seh‸-eu)
-- **duvq, yaqduvq** -- to denounce; condemn
-- **duvq, zaol** -- to mend; repair

DUA

duapieil xaosoq short stories (Chi) (50:40)

Duaf Kuafloq a Hani woman editor (57:156)
duaflieif (see: **dueiflieif**) (Chi) (26:102, 117)
duafloq dafyif the meaning of a paragraph (50:41)

DUEI

dueil a ton (Chi) (50:41)

dueifhaof a dot which acts as a slight pause mark

used to set off items in a series in the Chinese writing system (as "、") (Chi) (50:42)

dueiflieif to temper; train oneself; toughen oneself (as in the great revolutionary movement) (Chi) (**duaflieif** - 26:102)

DYU

dyul lazy; bad (9:47) (doe$^{\vee}$-eu)
dyul those; a group of things; some (inanimate -- **mavq** would be used for animate) (9:47) (deu$_{\vee}$)
dyul a ton (w.m.) (Chi) (41:127)
=**dyul, al**= infant's runny bowel movement
  -- **dyul, aldyul** -- to have diarrhea (usually used of infants)
dyul buq qi 'I am sorry' (Chi)
=**dyul, byul**= lazy
  -- **dyul, byuldyul** -- to be lazy
  =**dyul, doq**= bad, offensive words
  dyulduq a shortcoming; a weak point (26:35, 50:140) (yaw te$_{\vee}$)
  dyulkuq nei lazily (13:33) (yaw doe$^{\vee}$)
-- **dyul, meeq** -- right and wrong
  -- **dyul, yiuvqmav mavdyul** -- to have a bad dream
=**dyul, yoq**= a clumsy manner
dyulzeil same height; as tall as ...

(vb) **dyu** all around (**nalhaq dyu e** = asked all around) (11:200)
-- **dyu, cavq** -- to spread abroad (as a broadcast)
dyu nei everywhere (9:47) (or) **saq nei aol saq al** (yaw$_{\vee}$ ga$^{\vee}$ na lu$_{\wedge}$)
  dyu nei eilgaq to give public notice (50:167)
  dyu nei nalhaq ask all around
  dyu nei zol extensive reading; extensive study (50:47)

dyuq tin (9:47) (bah$_{\vee}$ keu^)
=**dyuq, saol**= a peacock; peafowl

dyuv 1. a bamboo shoot to develop, 2. a clf. for bamboo shoots (9:47) (a$^{\vee}$ bye$_{\wedge}$)
=**dyuv, al**= bamboo shoots
=**dyuv, haq**= a bamboo shoot
-- **dyuv, haqdyuv** -- bamboo shoot to sprout; to come out
-- **dyuvkuv, aldyuv** -- dried, preserved bamboo shoots
=**dyuv, niaol**= short

dyuf buq qi to make excuses (Chi) (or) **yeiqliaf** (Chi)
dyufke ciiq rhymed dialogue (50:41)
dyufwaf keilfaf open to outsiders (Chi) (50:41)
dyufwu army unit (Chi) (26:58) (yeh$^{\vee}$ a$^{\vee}$ ma$_{\wedge}$)
  dyufyeiq team or brigade member (as in the army or party) (Chi) (9:47, 50:41)

dyufza production leader; team leader; brigade team leader (Chi) (9:47, 11:51, 50:41)

dyufziiq confrontation (Chi) (or) **dyufziif** (50:41)

E

el interjection, "Oh" 1. can be used in respectful way (**El, aqbol soqpaq** = Oh elder ruler), 2. can be used to show disgust (**El! Xil qa col yaol haqhhyu maq aol zaq qivq al.** Hey, this person is not reliable!)
Elzel Europe (Chi)

(n) e gen. particle (**ngaq** e = my) (-eu˯)
(vb) e liq even though, although (**ngal piul jav e liq,** = even though I have money...) (11:121) (k'aw˰)
e **ngaoq** if (9:50) (naˇ)

eq to carry on back (or) **pi** (9:50) (eu˯-eu; pi-eu)
eq to be pregnant (**ssaq eq**) (9:50) (a˯ nyiˇ pi-eu)
eq clf. for a load a person can carry (11:83)
-- **eq, aqnil** -- to be pregnant
eq dav to feel disgusted; sometimes nauseated (nui ma bymˇ-eu)
eq dovq to infect with a disease (9:50)
eq haol help someone carry a load
eqjil cogon; thatch grass (9:50) (u˯ jiˇ)
eqjil dalteiq teiq to make thatch grass shingles for roofing (46:117)
eqjil laqhyul a house with a thatch roof (11:148) (u˯ jiˇ nymˇ m˯)
eqjil yaolma a big house with a thatch roof
-- **eq, kalduv** -- to carry new rice back home on one's back
eqleq deq 1. to be dull; to stare blankly, 2. to be stunned; frightened, 3. to be sluggish (**Eqleq taq deq. Ssuq.** Don't be sluggish. Go!) (38:34) (yaw dm˯)
eqleq deqgaq nei to be empty-minded (nui ma yaw˯ ngeh˰)
eqleq ssil deq for listeners to be deeply attracted to Hani folk songs
-- **eq, ssaq** -- 1. to be pregnant, 2. to carry a child on one's back
-- **eq, ssaq diq** -- to become pregnant; with child (in a way contrary to Hani customs)
-- **eq, ssaq lav** -- to become pregnant (in a way contrary to Hani customs)
eq tao bring into water (46:133)
Eqtaoqtuaq Children's League (Chi) (26:12)
Eqtaoq tuaqyeiq member of Children's League (Chi) (26:12)
eq teiq to carry along on one's back (14:216) (eu˯-eu)

EE

eel to laugh; to smile (9:48) (uiˇ-eu)
eelbaoq a water container (of bamboo) (9:48, 46:134) (iˇ bah˯; uiˇ bah˯ = CA)
eelbeq beq to swim frog style (11:110)
eelbeel beel for water to boil (4:33) (iˇ cu˄ ca˄ buiˇ-eu)
eelbil a watershed (where streams divide into different systems) (or) **eelbieil**
-- **eelbil, Aqlo** -- a place near Dazhai village where a yearly offering is made by Dazhai village and 12 other villages to the 'great water divide' (or) **Aqlobieil**
Eelbil a village name
eelbi a water spring (9:48, 11:166) (lawˇ k'aw˄)
=eel, biaq'= honey
eelbul to float or swim on the water (on one's stomach) (iˇ cu˄-ahˇ bu-eu)
eelbul nia to be able to swim (on stomach) (iˇ cu˄ di˯ nya)
eelbyu water hole; water cave (9:48) (iˇ cu˄ lawˇ k'aw˄)
eelcal watery soup (9:48, 10:10, 41:170) (dzaˇ uiˇ)
eelcal cal to make very watery soup or juice (46:202) (dzaˇ uiˇ)
-- **eelcal, hoqqavq** -- water from boiled rice
-- **eelcal, hhoqcyuq** -- soup (with greens or vegetables)
-- **eelcal, kaoqpiul** -- covered with sweat; perspiration
-- **eelcal, neeguq** -- soybean juice
-- **eelcal, zeiqkeeq** -- compost liquid
eelcavq wash-water (water in which things have been washed, sometimes fed to pigs) (9:48) (la^ buˇ-eu iˇ cu˄)
eelcavq a type of water snake (9:48) (lawˇ ba˯ aˇ lawˇ)
eelceiv bamboo water sucker
eelceivq 'cold' water (unboiled water in 10:16) (iˇ cu˄ yaw tseh˄)
eelceivq haoqniaoq glutinous rice grown in mountainous irrigated fields (yaˇ haw˯ nyaw˯)
eeldaol wave of water (9:48) (iˇ lu^) (cf. Lahu: g'ui˯ dawˇ)
eeldaol bi water to form a wave (iˇ lu^ dzeh-eu; iˇ k'awˇ)
eeldaol hhev a wave of water (26:22) (iˇ lu^ dzeh-eu)
eeldaol yaoq nei waves to come (30:2) (iˇ lu^ dzeh-eu)
eeldaoq water in fields all year round (irrigated)

(op. is: **daolhav** = fields that have water only during the rains) (deh ma; **deh** yaˇ)

eeldaoq daoqceil rice from fields with water in the year round (deh **ma** cehˇ)

eeldaoq daoqyal fields with water year around

eeldaoq hhocuv cuv to transplant rice in terraced, irrigated fields

eeldaoq niuqceiq ceiq to plow a terraced, irrigated rice field (deh ma tsehˬ-eu)

eelde 1. bamboo water container with branches forming a handle, 2. a bamboo container that uses water to make a sound to frighten birds and animals away from ripening crops (iˇ bahˬ)

eeldeiq a water insect (uiˇ dehˬ)

eeldiq diq to swim free style (or) **aqbul ciq**

eeldiv muddy water (9:48) (iˇ neˇ)

eeldiv div water to become muddy (iˇ **ne**ˇ neˇ-eu)

eeldiv eelgaol ceil to see the matter through (whether muddy or clear water)

eel doq a joke; a funny story (28:4) (ehˇ niˇ g'a-eu; ja byawˬ-eu gaˇ kawˆ)

eelduq a pool of water; a well of water (lah; lah duˬ)

eel eel meil eil· while laughing said...

eelgal an irrigation ditch (9:49, 46:211) (uiˇ k'**eh**ˬ)

eelgaol clean; clear water (9:49) (iˇ shawˇ; iˇ gahˇ)

eelgaol **gaol** to be clean water

eelgaol niq nei clean; clear water (iˇ shawˇ; iˇ gahˇ)

eelhal nevcev a bamboo water dipper with a handle, used in ceremonies

eelhaq hholqei deivq, eelqul hholqei heeq lal 'I once lived in bitter water, I have grown up into sweet water' (comparing life before and after liberation) (26:77)

eelheiq the opening of a smaller ditch off the main irrigation ditch (9:49) (uiˇ k'**eh**ˬ)

eelheiq soq a ritual offering made at the opening of the main ditch in an irrigated field by individual families (egg, chicken, liquor & rice) (46:114)

eelhhal hhal dirty surface water (12:128) (iˇ jaw‸)

eelhhaol niq pav middle of the water (13:47)

eelhhev a whirlpool (iˇ cu‸ iˇ zeuˆ)

eelhhuvq sil to drown (a 'bad death')

eelhhuvq ssolnei galpeil a spirit which lives in the water, and can enter people (as those who drown)

eeljo a system to prevent flooding

eelju slobber (as of an infant); drool (9:49) (iˇ ju ju-eu)

Eelju name of a village (2:49)

eelju baqdaq a bib to catch the slobber of a baby

eelju eelzav meil wet all over from rain (yaw aˬ yaw ciˬ)

eelkol a 'flying snake' (travels very rapidly)

eel lal maq bi bal lal let the soul of the water never leave
eellavq (see: **hhellavq**) (14:172)
Eellaol name of a village (2:49)
eellaol hot water; boiled water (9:49, 11:28) (iˇ lahˇ; uiˇ lahˇ)
  eel laol hholqei a quq dov to get into hot water (iˇ buiˇ-ahˇ iˇ ahˇ-eu)
  eellaol laol water to be heated (11:61) (iˇ lahˇ lahˇ-eu)
  eellaol laolnuv warm water (9:49, 10:27) (**nuv** = soft, cf. Lahu: nuˉ-ehˍ ve) (iˇ lahˇ)
eellaovq hysterical laughter (uiˇ seh˰-eu)
eelloq water trough (wood or bamboo) (9:49); aqueduct (50:92) (k'awˇ law˯)
-- **eelloq, haqbol** -- a bamboo tube in which water runs
eelluv a water fountain
  eelluv luv for a spring to have water flowing; a fountain of water to be running (57:70)
eelma a loud laugh (uiˇ k'a^)
eelmav mav to smile or giggle in one's dream (9:49) (uiˇ ma^ ma^-eu)
eel **meil** up river; the water source (or) **lolheiq; lolmei** (gaw^ mehˇ)
eelmei mei to drown (ga nui˰ seh˰-eu; ga pu˰ seh˰-eu)
eelmiq down river; the lower part of the river (gaw^ bi)
eelnaq pieiq to make a joke; provoke laughter (or) **lav eel** (ceh˰ leh˰ ka˯-eu)
  eelnaq pieiq e piqhov a distorting mirror (50:69)
eelnav bi tuvq 'may you be bitten by a black viper' (a curse)
-- **eelnav, ollol** -- a black viper
eelnaoq naoq to walk in deep water
-- **eelnaoq, wulquvq** -- (see full)
eelnil nil 1. water becomes 'red' (muddy) (30:2, 46:95) (uiˇ neˇ neˇ-eu), 2. to flood
eelniq nei smilingly (14:242) (uiˇ uiˇ-ehˇ)
eelniul green snake (poisonous)
eelpeel a snake that goes very fast on the ground or in the grass
Eelpuv the name of a village (near the Vietnam border)
eelpuv a flood (see also: **eeltaoq**) (iˇ jeu˯ jeu˯-eu; iˇ cu˰ dah˯ byah laˇ-eu)
  eelpuv leiq to flood (iˇ cu˰ dah˯ da^-eu)
  eelpuv puv to flood (26:57) (iˇ cu˰ dah˯ da^-eu)
eelqal saliva; spittle (9:49) (du˯ k'a˯)
  eelqal qalma saliva; spittle (du˯ k'a˯ dzaˇ peh^)
eel **qaq** to be tired of laughing (14:226) (uiˇ doeˇ-eu)
eelquv a water ditch to divert water into fields
  eelquvq water (45:28, 46:114) (or) **wulquvq** (iˇ cu˰; uˇ cu˰ = CA)
  eelquvq eelsol 'pure water' from the village water

source (used in offerings and ceremonies)
eelquvq gaol clear water; clean water
eelquvq xu for water to run; to flow (50:158) (iˇ cu˰ yoeˇ-eu)
=eel, savq'= steam; vapor (50:158)
eelsaol river otter (9:49) (uiˇ shmˇ; iˇ shmˇ)
eelseq lev to smile (11:203) (uiˇ cawˬ-eu)
eelseq lev nei smilingly (12:126) (uiˇ cawˬ ni)
eelseq maq leev without smiling (45:27) (maˬ uiˇ cawˬ ni)
eel seqniq to smile (5:394) (uiˇ cawˬ-eu)
eelsil still, 'dead' water (50:91)
eelsiq water flecks
eelsol 1. clean water, 2. "holy" water (46:134) (iˇ shawˇ; iˇ gahˇ)
eelsol aqma lord of the water
eelsyu syu tao come down into the water (13:47)
eelssaq small insects etc. in the water family (38:90)
eelssaol large water leech (aˬ yeh˰)
eeltaoq pail; bucket (for water) (B=Chi) (9:49, 11:31) (iˇ cu˰ buˇ naˬ)
eeltaoq taoq to flood (26:22) (see also: **eelpuv**) (iˇ cu˰ dahˬ bym-eu)
-- **eeltaoq, xiq** -- a bucket for dung
eeltev tev to burp or belch (from drinking water) (aˇ eu˰ eu˰-eu)
eeltevq dev to cut the channels in the wooden outlet for irrigation water
eeltevq tevq to make wooden openings to divide the water from the main irrigation ditch
eel teil 1. sound of water (**eel teil gaq** = to hear the sound of running water) (26:23), 2. the sound of laughter (uiˇ-eu teˇ saˇ)
eelxeiv dirty water (iˇ jaw˰)
eelxovq xovq to swim in deep water as if walking or standing in it; to dog paddle
eelxul duv a joke to be told (28:4)
eelxul lav to make a joke (ceh˰ leh˰ ka-eu)
eelxul taolxavq to make jokes (esp. regarding embarrassing matters)
eelxu flowing water (iˇ cu˰ yoeˇ-eu)
eelyiuvq yiuvq to swim on one's back
eel zaq 1. to laugh at someone (uiˇ dzaˬ-eu), 2. pretty water
eelziq juice (46:180)
eelziv spring water
eelziiv to develop an itch from being in dirty water
eelziivq a rain storm (uˬ yehˇ jaˬ lehˇ)

EI

eil to **say**; to **speak** (9:49) (ehˇ-eu)
eil 1. interjection 'oh' (11:143), 2. final part. to denote closeness to the listener (or) **eil eiq; ei eiq**
eil **bav** to say something wrong (ehˇ bah˯-eu; ehˇ leh˯-eu)
eil **bial** negative (50:51)
eil **bieil** to make public; to disclose
eil **buvq** 1. to libel someone; speak badly of or to someone or something (similar to: **eildyul**) (11:28), 2. to mock; satirize (or) **eilcavq; eilkyuq** (ja doeˇ-eu), 3. to belittle (57:134)
eil **buvq miq** to say bad things about or to someone (ja doeˇ-eu)
eil **buvq zaol buvq** to insult; humiliate (50:182)
eil **caq** to stop speaking (ehˇ g'a˯-eu)
eil **cavq** 1. to mock someone, 2. to slander (50:49) (ehˇ doeˇ-eu)
eil **ceiv** 1. to decide, 2. to promise (9:49); pledge; guarantee (50:7), 3. to set a regulation (or) **gyuldif** (Chi) (50:66), 4. to have a conclusion (50:93) (ehˇ tseh^-eu)
eil **ceiv taq e doq** to give a promise
eilceivq diqceivq ceivq cold war (50:104)
eil **cuvq** to accuse falsely; to frame a case against someone (33:3); trump up (50:121)
eildaq luvq to be laughed at by others (bi uiˇ-eu)
eil **daoq** to persuade; convince (57:103)
eildoq nal haq 1. to obey, 2. to accept or adopt a plan or idea (or) **doq'eil nalhaq** (ehˇ daw˯ naˇ ha˯-eu)
eil **duv** 1. to refute (or) **eil loq**, 2. make clear; justify oneself, 3. confess; admit, 4. inform against someone (50:83), 5. to speak out (50:14)
-- **eil duv, bu'loq nei** -- honest; frank; confess
eil **duv la** 1. to speak out (8:17, 11:47) (ehˇ do^-eu) (or) **eilgaq**, 2. to point out (through words)
-- **eilduv, loqnei** -- make clear to all; proclaim publicly
eil **duv qeiqlif** right of accusation (B=Chi) (50:83)
eil **e loq** to speak clearly; distinctly (11:163) (ehˇ law^-eu; law^ ka ni ngeh˯-eu)
eil **eiq** a particle that denotes closeness to the listener and showing sympathetic concern (45:9) (or) **ei eiq; eil**
eilgaq 1. to tell, 2. to announce; spread the news (50:61), 3. to bid farewell to someone (9:50), 4. make a report (or) **naqgaq xa** (50:8) (ehˇ ga˯-eu)
-- **eilgaq, dyu nei** -- give a public notice; spread the news all around

-- **eilgaq, huq** -- to announce in advance

eil **gav miq** to dampen someone's enthusiasm ('speak cooling words') (50:131) (cf. Eng. 'to pour cold water on an idea')

eil **gaol meiq gaol** to advise; to persuade; to educate (50:159) **meiq gaol**

eil **haol** 1. to express support for; to verbally support (50:150), 2. speak in defense of; defend (50:13)

eil **haol liqsiil** a defense lawyer (B=Chi) (50:13)

eilhaoq eilceiv advertise; publicise (50:190)

eil **heeq miaq** to exaggerate (50:99)

eilheiq the topic being talked about (ngeh⌄ lu˄-eu gaˇ kaw^)

eilheiq artemisia; wormwood (at harvest time tie some of this wood to the stems of rice in three places) (or) **eilheiq hoqloq**

eilheiq qeil to say happily (la⌄ k'a⌄ ti⌄ cehˇ ehˇ-eu)

eilheiq za to talk properly (tsa⌄ tsa⌄ ni ngeh⌄-eu)

eil **huvq** to answer (ehˇ k'o˄-eu)

eil **hhaq** the right to speak (50:44)

eil **hhaol** to win over someone; persuade them with words

eil **hhoq zaq** to say goodbye; farewell (41:171) (g'aw⌄ ma lehˇ ehˇ-eu)

Eilkeiqsiil (Frederich) Engels (Eng-Chi)

eil kov eil kov meil eil to speak very quickly

eil **kyuq** 1. to satarize; mock, 2. to hurt someone by what one says (or) **eilnal** (ehˇ coe⌄-eu)

eil lal yaq lal to accuse someone (35:28)

eilla wild yam (large, yellow)

eilla moqdev Chinese yam

eil laol **miq** to 'warm someone's heart' (say kind, encouraging things) (50:131)

-- eil laol, **neema** -- to console; to comfort

eil **laoq** to say more; to add to what was said (ehˇ lah⌄-eu)

eil **laoq doq** a postscript

eilleiv puv to repeat again (50:54)

eil **leivq** to lie; dishonest talk

eil lo **maq mi meil** as soon as stopped speaking (13:44) (ehˇ g'a⌄ neh⌄-ehˇ)

eil **loq** 1. to state; declare; announce (26:57, 50:150), 2. to vindicate; assert one's sincerity (50:14), 3. to explain (12:127) (ja neh⌄-eu), 4. to speak clearly (or) **eil e loq**, 5. to refute (or) **eil duv**

eilloq doq 1. to annotate; explain with notes, 2. a preface (50:216)

eilloq duv to make clear; state clearly (50:214)

-- eil **loq, eil xa** -- to explain and publicise

eillul to say (35:97) (ehˇ-eu)

eil **nal** to satirize; to mock (or) **eilhyuq** (yeh⌄ baw⌄-ehˇ ehˇ-eu)

-- eil **nalhaq, doq** -- to obey what was said
eil **naq maq pieiq** to keep on talking (14:229) (ngehˬ dui dui-eu)
eil**neiq** bamboo strip (or) **alniq** (pf) (18:1) (aˇ neˬ)
eil **neiq** to tell someone
eil**nil miaq** to understate; underestimate (50:99)
eil**niaoq** glutinous yam
eil**nieiq** eil**nieiq nei** while speaking (14:186)
  eil **nieiq** eil **pav** unfinished conversation; unfinished speech (maˬ ngehˬ g'aˬ-eu)
  eil **nieiq meil** while talking (46:98) (ngehˬ lu˰ ngeh)
eil **nyuq** 1. to remind, 2. to hint (ehˇ noeˬ-eu)
  eil **nyuq** eil **ta** 1. to remind, 2. to hint (ehˇ mawˇ nehˬ-eu)
eil **pal siq** to say again (paˇ ehˇ-eu)
eil **peel** to dispute; refute (50:13)
eil **puv** 1. to reply; answer (6:194, 11:161), 2. to talk back (ehˇ k'o˰-eu)
eil **pyuq** 1. to praise (9:50, 11:174, 26:35, 50:14), 2. to encourage (50:63) (ja ceuˬ-eu; ciˬ poeˬ-eu; ehˇ poeˬ-eu)
  eil **pyuq miq** to praise someone (ciˬ huiˬ)
  eil **pyuq zaq** to flatter someone
eil **qoq** to argue with someone (ceh dzaˬ-eu)
eil **sa** 1. to reflect, 2. to report (50:47)
eil**sa lal** to come tell (30:2) (ehˇ nehˬ-eu; ja nehˬ-eu)
eil**saq saq e** to conclude a statement; say the final word (ehˇ saˬ saˬ-eu)
eil **saoq** to say bad things to another; ugly words
eil **soq** 1. to provide an explanation; try to defend oneself (50:13), 2. to speak clearly (50:87)
eil **suv** skillful at speaking (**aol suv** = skillful at doing)
eil **taq** 1. to have promised; 2. to have been decided by discussion (ehˇ taˬ-eu)
eil**teil havma** a good debater (50:13)
  eil**teil heil** to argue; debate (50:13)
  eil**teil heil doqzil** a debate (50:13)
eil **tovq** to speak similar things (as the same name, similar titles of books, etc.)
eil**xa** eil**loq** to explain and publicise (50:190)
eil**yavq xa** to order (50:118)
eil **yevq** to distort; misrepresent ('speak twist') (50:173)
eil **za** to talk and agree
eil **zaq** 1. to say bad things behind the back of another; to gossip (ja bu ja doeˇ-eu), 2. to quarrel

ei, eif ! interjection (see 11:143 for samples)
ei eiq a fin. particle denoting closeness with the listener; often used in a coaxing way (**Aqbiavq ei eiq** - 38:15, **Ngaldu col ei eiq** = We people -

35:19); **eil eiq**

ei eiq an interjection of compassion (**Ei eiq! Hhosaq qavq saq wul yaq**! Oh my, what a poor thing it is.)

eiq ! interjection (may have the feeling of being sorry or apologizing at times) (see 11:142-3 for examples)

-eiq 1. a particle showing sorrow (35:18), 2. a particle showing agreement

eiqdaq nei (see: **leiqdaq nei**) (14:175)

eiqhheiq cherry tree (9:50) (g'eh$_{\vee}$ a$^{\vee}$ baw$^{\vee}$)

eiqlaq 1. final particle used at end of commands, with the idea of 'Isn't that so? Okay?' (9:50, 26:35) (often as a directive) (**Nol lal eiqlaq.** You come, ok?) (2:49), 2. please ... (**taq eil eiqlaq** = please don't say ... - 38:23) (cf. Akha = eh$^{\vee}$ law$_{\vee}$)

eiqmil lalnao the other day (26:84) (yaw$_{\vee}$ nah yaw$_{\vee}$)

eiqmilnao a few days ago; the other day (mi$^{\vee}$ nah hu$_{\vee}$ nah) (9:50, 26:44); day before (13:54)

eiqsi just a moment ago; short time ago (9:50, 11:109) (u$_{\vee}$ soe)

eiqsi aqmil some time ago

eiqsi sihav moment ago; a few moments ago (9:50, 41:174) (or) **eiqsi siha** (26:39, 45:63) (u$_{\vee}$ soe)

eiqxaq laqleiq to grin cheekily (46:148) (ui$^{\vee}$ k'eu$_{\wedge}$ k'eu$_{\wedge}$-eu)

eiqya yes; okay; all right (9:50, 11:21, 142) (eu$_{\vee}$, e$_{\vee}$-a$_{\wedge}$) (**aqyoq eiqya nei qiq doq eil** = he replied with an 'ok'.- 26:47)

-- **eif, xilqil** -- Tuesday (Chi)

FA

falfaq way of doing something; a method (Chi) (34:25)
falhhaf a plan; project; scheme (Chi) (9:51, 50:48)
falqiq tomato (Chi) (or) **haoqgo haolgo alsiq; xilhaoqsiif** (Chi)
falseil to have a new and better life; to turn over a new leaf (Chi); to overturn (with the idea of having a better life) (26:15)
falsiif 1. method (Chi), 2. style (or) **weiqti** (Chi)
falyiq to translate; interpret (Chi) (13:40) (yu˅ do^-eu)
falzeil a policy (Chi) (9:51, 50:48)

fadaof reactionary (Chi) (50:47)
fadaofpeif reactionary person (Chi) (**Goqmiqda fadaofpeif** = the reactionary KMT - 34:8) (Chi)
fadaof taoziif reactionary rule (Chi) (50:47)
fa dif to fight against imperialism (Chi) (34:6)
fa dif fa faoljieif to fight against imperialism and feudalism (Chi)
fa dieilfuq to fight against an anti-revolutionary spirit (Chi) (34:33)
fadueif to oppose (Chi) (50:47)
fadyuf to oppose; fight against (Chi) (34:29)
fageiqmif anti-revolutionary; reactionary (34:6, 50, 50:47) (Chi)
fageiqmif col an anti-revolutionary guide (A= Chi) (50:47)
fageiqmif zyul an anti-revolutionary criminal (A=Chi) (50:47)
fa hoqpiq yeibieif anti-peaceful revolution (Chi) (34:34)
faweif to visit; a visit (Chi)
faweiftuaq a visiting delegation (Chi) (50:48)
fayif to reflect (Chi) (34:63)
faziiq gaolniq textile industry (Chi) (50:48)
fazoqyaof counteraction (Chi) (34:71)

faq magic (Chi) (or) **moqsuq** (Chi)
faq to distribute; give out; divide up (Chi)
faq to fine money (Chi) (or) **geelzeiq hhuvq** (gui˅ o^ ti^-eu)
faqbuf waterproof cloth (Chi) (26:95)
faqbuf let people know the news; spread the news (Chi) (50:44)
faqdif deifli col a legal representative (AB=Chi) (50:45)
faqdieifca electric power station (Chi) (50:44)
faqdieifjil generator; dynamo (Chi) (50:44)
faqfeif tuqqaq work energetically for development (Chi) (26:75)

Faqgoq France (Chi)
Faqgoqcol French people (Chi)
faqgyul laws and regulations (Chi) (50:45)
faqhyul 1. to produce (26:119), 2. to bring into play (34:16) (Chi)
faqji law and discipline (Chi) (34:99)
faqkuei to impose a fine for doing something wrong (Chi) (gui˅ o˄ ti˄-eu)
faqliq law; decree; statute (Chi) (50:45) (or) **faqlif**
faqliq ceiqxif legal procedure (Chi) (50:45)
faqliq e miqnieiq a legal case (A=Chi)
faqliq eil ceiv legal provisions (A=Chi) (50:45)
faqliq faqgyul laws and regulations (Chi) (34:38)
faqliq maq za miqnieiq 1. illegal act; unlawful practice; against regulations, 2. unhealthy tendency (A=Chi) (50:16,17)
faqliq meiqsi aqsol liq qiq qa all people are equal before the law (A=Chi) (50:45)
faqliq nei caq heq investigate in legal order (A=Chi) (50:45)
faqliq nei meiq gaol to educate in the legal system (A=Chi) (50:45)
faqliq nei ssiv teiq legal sanction (Chi) (50:12)
faqliq sesuq lawful procedure (Chi) (50:45)
faqliq wu'qif legal weapon (Chi) (50:45)
faqliq xaofliq legal effect (Chi) (50:45)
faqliq za lawful (A=Chi) (50:71)
faqliq za e piul lawful money (A=Chi) (50:71)
faqliq za e qeiqlif lawful rights (A,C=Chi) (50:71)
faqliq za e zeiq lawful property (A=Chi) (50:71)
faqlif law; decree; statute (Chi) (50:45) (and see under: **faqliq**)
faqpiaof a receipt (Chi) (50:44)
faqquq to serve a ball in a game or sport (as in ping pong, tennis) (Chi)
faqsiifliq vaseline (Chi-Eng) (11:17)
faqti soqmiav complicated words (A=Chi) (50:46)
faqxeif to find; discover (Chi)
faqxilsiil fascist (Chi-Eng) (50:45)
faqyaq to carry on; continue on (as a task) (Chi) (34:2)
faqyaoq calsseif thriving and prosperous (Chi) (34:18)
faqyeiq to make a speech (Chi) (daw˅ ngeh˅-eu)
faqyeif a law court; court of justice (Chi) (9:51, 50:45)
faqyil pronunciation (Chi)
Faqyi French langauge (Chi)
faqza to develop (Chi) (9:51, 34:17)
faqzaof nei heavy; strenuous (Chi) (34:90)
faqziif legal system (Chi) (34:48, 50:45)

faf to let go (Chi) (Hani = **pieiq**)
fafjaf a school term break; school vacation (Chi)

(41:13)
fafpiaof 1. meal tickets (Chi) (41:175), 2. ration coupons for rice (Chi) (50:47)
fafxafjil video camcorder (Chi) (50:49)

FAO

faolbol a disturbance (Chi) (34:50) (la^ **bah**ˬ-eu)
faolgaol hhyujiq a person's great contribution (Chi) (50:51)
faolgeiq style (Chi) (50:51)
faolhhol meiq a briquette of fuel (made in the shape of a honey comb) (A=Chi) (50:51)
faoljeif feudalism (Chi) (50:51
faoljeif difzu a feudalist landlord (Chi) (34:16)
faoljeif seifhyuf feudal society (Chi) (34:3; 50:51)
faoljeif zuyif feudalism (Chi) (50:51)
faolji scenery (Chi)
faolmaof style and features (Chi) (50:51)
faolqif general mood; atmosphere (Chi) (50:51)
faolsaf prevailing custom (Chi) (50:51)
faolso to blockade; seal off (Chi) (34:10) (or) **diq cyuq**

FE

fedif to deny; negate (Chi) (34:48)

feqdaof gaolzii a floating salary (Chi) (50:52)

FEI

feil points (as in an exam) (Chi) (**qiq yal niq ceil feil** = 120 points - 14:241)
feil centimeter (or) **gaolfeil; liqmi** (Chi) (41:127)
feil one-tenth of a 'mu' (length for measuring land) (Chi) (41:129)
feil buvq col a score keeper (in sports) (A=Chi) (50:80)
feilhaof semicolon (Chi)
feiljil airplane (Chi) (50:49) (or) **peiljil** (3:2, 6:183, 9:51, 26:27) (heu biˇ)
feiljil nei hhe air transport (A=Chi) (50:98)
feilliq to separate (Chi) (34:55)
Feilliqbil the country of the Philippines (Chi)
Feilliqbilcol a Filipino (a person of the Philippines) (Chi)
feilmi decimeter (one-tenth of a meter) (Chi) (41:124)
feilmu denominator (the lower number in a fraction) (Chi)
feilsuf a fraction (Chi)
feilxiq to analyse (Chi) (34:25)
feilzaol a minute (Chi) (10:26, 41:29) (**ceil feilzaol bi jol** = have him stay for 10 minutes)

feilzii a numerator in a fraction (the one written above the line) (Chi)

feibiq chalk (Chi) (50:50) (they use in making designs on coffins, which are rubbed off before burial)

feiq to fertilize (Chi) (11:8)
feiqyeil nal to have pneumonia (A=Chi) (15:43)
feiqzaof soap (Chi) (or) **yaqqiv**

feifdef to strive; to struggle; to fight (Chi) (34:2, 24)

FU

fudaof to give guidance in study (Chi)
  fudaofyeiq an assistant; an instructor (Chi)
fuyil a consonant (Chi)
  fuyil ziifmu a consonant letter (in the alphabet) (Chi)

fuqcaoq to obey (Chi) (34:69) (ehˇ daw˯ naˇ ha˯ geu‸-eu)
fuqgaof 1. announce someone's death, 2. give someone's obituary (Chi)
fuqhaof a symbol (as a letter is a symbol) (Chi) (41:76)
  fuqhaof yomiaol the names of punctuation marks, such as; period, comma; semicolon; etc. (A=Chi)
fuqjaof Buddhism (Chi) (50:51)
fuqjif a complex sentence (Chi)
fuqwuf service (Chi) (34:42)
fuqxiq to review a lesson (Chi) (9:51)
fuqyeiq to demobilize (as an army at the end of a war) (Chi)
fuqyifmu a diphthong (Chi) (9:51)
fuqzaq complicated (Chi) (34:74) (yaw bah˯ yaw lahˇ)

fuf- vice-; deputy- (Chi)
fuf balza vice-monitor (as in school) (Chi) (50:53)
fuf bufza vice-minister (in govt.) (Chi) (50:53)
fuf calmeqza vice-advisor in the army (Chi) (50:53)
fuf capi byproducts (not the main ones) (Chi) (50:53)
fufcaza vice-director of a factory (Chi) (50:53)
fufciiq an adverb (Chi) (50:53)
fufdal a burden (Chi) (26:55) (k'a^ beh^)
fufgaol women's association worker (Chi)
fuf guza vice-director of a department (Chi) (50:53)
fuf hhyuyeiqza vice-council president (Chi) (50:53)
fufjalxiq additional punishment (Chi) (50:54)
fuf jaofdaofyeiq vice-political instructor (Chi) (50:53)
fuf jiqza vice-director of a bureau (Chi) (50:53)
fuf kolza vice-director of an office (Chi) (50:53)

fuf liza vice-brigade commander (Chi) (50:53)
fuflieiq women's association (Chi) (50:54)
fuf lieiqza deputy commander (Chi) (26:99); vice company commander (50:53)
fuf miqsulza vice-secretary of an association (Chi) (50:53)
fufnaoq a rich peasant (Chi) (50:52)
fufniq a second job; a second occupation; side occupation (Chi) (9:51, 50:54)
fuf peiqza vice-platoon leader (Chi) (50:53)
fufqaq prosperous and strong (Chi) (34:31)
fuf qilza vice-director of a township (Chi) (50:53)
fuf seiza vice-governor of a province (Chi) (50:53)
fuf seifza vice-team leader (Chi) (50:53)
fuf siillif vice-commander (Chi) (50:53)
fuf siilza vice-division commander (Chi) (50:53)
fuf suljif deputy party secretary (Chi) (50:53)
fuf tuaqza vice-regimental commander (Chi) (50:53)
fuf xalza vice-township leader (Chi) (50:53)
fuf xaofza vice-principal of a school (Chi) (50:54)
fuf xeifza county deputy president (Chi)
fuf yiqza vice-battalion commander (Chi) (50:54)
fuf zao'li vice-premier (Chi)
fufzeiq to have responsibility (Chi)
fuf zeiqziif responsibility system (Chi) (34:42)
fuf ziihyul vice-commander (Chi) (50:54)
fuf zusseif vice-director (Chi) (50:54)
fuf zuxiq vice-president; vice-chairman (Chi) (50:54)

GA

gal to matter (**maq gal** = it does not matter, or, it is not bad) (9:52) (ma˯ gaˇ)
gal a place (9:52) (--gaˇ, as in: heu gaˇ = here)
gal to last
gal clf. for 1. a long ditch; canal (**lolgal**), 2. a place
=gal aol, ssuq= to walk back and forth
-- galbaol, lolgal -- (see full)
galbil a flat road (9:52) (gaˇ ma gaˇ saˇ)
-- galbil, galma -- a flat road or path
galbiq a writing pen (Chi) (11:165) (sah˯ duˇ)
galcav the thread or rope that is tied around the village or village gate at certain times (38:37)
galcaol 1. a crossroad (two paths intersect), 2. a fork in a path (9:52) (gaˇ tsmˇ)
galceiq steel material (Chi)
galceiv half way (on the trail, road) (ti˯ tseh^; ti˯ pa^)
galdav road or path going up (9:52) (gaˇ da^ da^-eu)
galdav davceiv to go half way up the slope (ti˯ tseh^ le da^-eu)
-- galdav, neema -- to be eager for a better life
galdaoq galzeil roadside; side of road (9:52, 13:48) (gaˇ dzeˇ; cf. gaˇ daw˯ gaˇ sha sha-iˇ-eu)
galdoq doq to wait for (someone) on the way (46:105) (gaˇ ma-ahˇ daw˯-eu)
=gal, eel= a ditch
galhal travelling expenses (9:52, 46:157) (gaˇ lo poe˯)
galhaol on the way (35:67) (gaˇ ma-ahˇ)
galhaol luvcuv minister of minerals (A=Chi) (50:104)
galheeq heeq long-distance; far away (10:13, 46:172) (gaˇ mahˇ ka˯-eu)
galheeq hhel aoq long-distance buying and selling (50:21)
galheeq nei from a distance (**galheeq nei hu ngaoq** = if you look from a distance - 14:204)
galheeq pyu a long distance (35:98) (g'aw˯ mahˇ ni ka˯-eu)
galheeq sa nei a long ways; distant (9:52, 26:42, 46:203) (pf.) (or) **galheeq sav nei** (gaˇ mahˇ ka˯-eu)
galheiq 1. the lower side of a village, 2. the place outside of the village where they eat the meat of 'bad-omen' animals (must eat it all there, cannot take any back to the village) (pu dzeˇ pu taw), 3. the gate of the village (46:132)
galhhao galma a winding road; a tortuous road (50:139)
galhhao hhao 1. to make a detour around something

(9:52), 2. to go around something (as a village) (or) **galhhev hhev** (gaˇ jaw jaw-eu)

galhhev hhev 1. to make a detour around something, 2. to go around something (as a village) (or) **galhhao hhao** (gaˇ jaw jaw-eu)

galhhu long ago; formerly; before (9:52) (gaˇ hu; aˇ hu; aˇ hu ba)

galhhu aqbei ancient times (long ago in the beginning) (9:52, 13:3) (gaˇ hu; aˇ hu)

galhhu aqmil in the past; long ago (aˇ hu aˇ nah)

galhhu doqlo historical word (50:106)

galhhu jolduq jolhhal historical position (50:106)

galhhu miqnieiq history (50:106); **liqsii** (Chi)

galhhu soqdaoq historical documents; historical books (50:106)

galhhu wul galhhu long, long ago (46:200) (gaˇ hu ba)

galhhuvq a crooked road or path (9:52) (gaˇ g'o‸)

galhhuvq e haolteil galma a crooked mountain path

galhhuvq gallavq a small winding path (12:125)

galhhyuf one's position (Chi) (50:56)

galjil iron bars put over windows to keep thieves out (Chi) (57:79)

galjil syuniq iron bars used to reinforce cement structures (Chi) (57:126)

galjo a straight path (a short-cut) **qiq kaol** (clf.) (gaˇ ma gaˇ dawˇ)

galju zav nei to slobber (iˇ ju ju-eu)

galkeel to bring comfort to a grieving family

galkeel duv to go for a relative's memorial service

galkov 1. a line (including a political line) (9:52, 50:110) (aˇ kaw^), 2. regular, 3. pattern; design, 4. order; procedure (50:13), 5. a ditch (or) **lolgal; logal galkov** (dawˇ lawˇ kaw^)

galkov kov 1. to be striped (as a tiger) (bya‸ yaw˯ ni), 2. to dig a ditch in a line (gaˇ kaw^ kaw^-eu)

galkov lo'qo nei by rule

galkov wuqzao the reason for the case (legal) (50:2)

gallavq a path that branches off another path

galli program; guiding principle (Chi) (34:115, 50:56)

gal lieif to refine metal (Chi) (26:34)

=gal, lol= a ditch; a water course

gallavq a byroad (or) **galquv**

galluvq a guarded road

galma 1. road; path (gaˇ ma), 2. truth; rule

galma bialzeil the side of the road (12:126) (gaˇ ma gaˇ dzeˇ)

galma dallul a wide road; path; highway (B=Chi) (9:53) (gaˇ ma yaw jeˇ)

galma daol 1. for there to be a road, path (9:37) (gaˇ ma dahˇ-eu), 2. for there to be a course or direction

galma galbil a flat road or path (11:35) (gaˇ ma yaw saˇ)

galma galsiivq a new path; road (gaˇ ma gaˇ shui^)

galma galssaq a path (14:166)

galma galzeil the side of the road or path (11:36) (gaˇ ma gaˇ dzeˇ)

-- **galma, hoceil** -- railway line (A=Chi)

galma luqxeif 1. a line on a road, 2. a political line (B=Chi) (34:27)

galma meiq 1. to give directions, 2. part of the burial ceremonies in which the priest repeats the genealogy of the dead person and tells the soul to take the middle path so as to get to the land of the ancestors

galma qiq kaol qiq li meil all along the path (35:50)

galma ssuq bav to go astray; go on the wrong path (gaˇ ma bah˯-eu)

galma yoq to cross a road/path

galmeiq caqcuv a road marker (50:110)

galmol kaq to be remote (or) **galmol mol**

galmol mol far away (or) **galmol kaq** (gaˇ mahˇ ka˯-eu)

galmol neenyuq long-range strategy (50:207)

galmol ssuq to take a long trip

galnee salpeiq in the future (9:53) (or) **aqkal; aqkal naolhao** (a˯ kaˇ)

galniq nearby (26:66) (**Ngal nolya galniq a jol** = I live near you) (daw˯ peh) (cf. Lahu: aw˯ paˇ neˇ)

galniq niq to draw near (9:53) (daw˯ peh peh-eu)

galniul moss on road (9:53)

gal pav half way (as on a journey) (11:67) (gaˇ pa^; gaˇ k'eh^; gaˇ pehˇ ti˯ k'oe^)

galquv 1. a path (often with deep weeds on the side), 2. the proper way (3:title, 46:204), 3. a byroad (or) **gallavq**, 4. a 'notch' (saddleback) in a mountain (or) **galquv quvssaq**, 5. one's features (50:135)

-- **galquv, bil zaq** -- a plan for dividing something

galquv halhhu traditional ways; customs; old rites (see in 46:79)

galquv niq quv two paths to go on (34:8) (gaˇ ma nyi˯ kahˇ)

galquv suv nei directly into the future (50:65)

galquv taol directional (50:38)

galquv yeil nei bia broad prospects; wide prospects (50:66)

-- **galquv, zaoma** -- general rules; general principles

galsaol members of an irrigation cooperative which distributes irrigation water

galseq e col a leader

galseq seq to lead; guide someone (on path) (11:42) (gaˇ ma sheu˯-eu)

galssaq a path (small)
galtal tal to meet on the way (ga˅ ma-ah˅ tah˯ pu˯-eu)
Galtaol the Hani New Year (ga˅ tah˅)
Galtaol bal to go to celebrate the Hani New Year (or) **Galtaol taol; Galtaol pal** (ga˅ tah˅ pa˅-eu)
galtiq steel (Chi)
galtiq caqceiq a steel wall (Chi) (34:79)
Galtiq gaolsiil name of a steel mill (Chi) (26:26)
galtuv galheiq nei tuv a ceremony to renew the village gate so that evil spirits will not enter the village
galtuv tuv offering to village gate to prevent evil spirits from entering (law˅ kah˯ law˅-eu)
galtuv tuv cyuq set up the village gate so that evil spirits cannot enter (46:132) (law˅ kah˯ du˯-eu)
galtyuq 1. road/path going down, 2. a downhill slope (ga˅ toe˯) (9:53)
galtyuq nei a downslope (38:109) (za˰ ta˰ ta˰-eu)
-- **galtyuq, wuqduq** -- dejected; with head hanging; discouraged

galyaof outline; sketch (Chi) (34:74)
galzeil roadside (45:57) (ga˅ dze˅)
galzii market (Chi) (9:53), **leiv** (leh^)
galzii deikaq in the street (A=Chi) (or) **leivkaq deikaq** (45:60)
galzii hhellavq aol to trade in the market (A=Chi) (50:79)
galzii laolhaol market square (A=Chi) (35:50)
galzii nao market day (A=Chi) (14:143)
galzii qiq nao market day (A=Chi) (26:81)
galzii zuvq go to the market (A=Chi) (11:158) (leh^ dzu˰-eu)

ga bial to be lost (or) **bial**
gadaof to feel emotion; to be moved or touched by something (as someone's brave deed) (Chi) (26:113)
ga dov Haqniq the 'lag-behind' Hani (what the Hani are called in relation to the Akha, who moved south of the Lancang or Mekong River) (or) **ya duv Haqniq**
Gahhaof Hongkong & Macao (Chi) (50:56)
-- **ga la, beeq li** -- disorder; chaotic
=**ga nei, beeq**= very untidy
=**ga, ssaq**= a bad, naughty child
-- **gassaq, ssaqga** -- a bad, naughty child
gatafjif exclamatory sentence (gram) (Chi) (50:55)
gatafhaof exclamation mark (punctuation) (Chi) (50:56)
gaxif to give thanks (Chi) (**noq yaol hha gaxif siq** = we must thank you still) (13:14, 34:21)
gaxifsif a letter of thanks (Chi) (26:68)
ga yi to get down (or) **ya yi** (i˅ ka-eu)

gazaol move and inspire (Chi) (50:56)

gaq to hear (ga˯-eu) (9:55)
gaq long for (g'aw˯ sha˯ ga˯-eu)
gaq 1. to love (9:55) (ga˯-eu), 2. to be beautiful (yaw ja˯)
=gaq, bu= to declare; proclaim
gaqbuf cadre in the Communist party (Chi) (11:52) (see also: **gafbuf**)
=gaq, doq= news
gaqduvq gaqciiv meil 1. deeply in love (ga˯-eu), 2. to be very beautiful (yaw ja˯)
=gaq, eil= to tell; to announce
=gaq, hu= pretty (nice to look at)
gaq lal 1. to hear the answer, 2. to miss someone
gaqli gaqzav nei to be very kind; loving
gaq na to love
=gaq, naq= to hear about
=gaq, nee= to love
=gaq nei, niuq= tamed (both animals & children)
gaqniq niq Hani dance with drums and gongs (46:137)
gaqsaq cei to take care of someone (50:64)
gaq sil 1. to miss someone (noe˯ ga˯-eu), 2. to be in love (cf. Lahu: 'nyi ma ha_ ve suh la yo˯')
gaq sil gaq lo to love deeply
=gaq, yeil= a legend; a story
gaq zaq 1. to love one another (**daov gaq zaq** = to love each other very much) (ti˯ g'a˯ tiˇ g'a˯ ga˯-eu), 2. to be in harmony, 3. to overhear someone (9:55)
gaq zaq hhyul zaq 1. to love each other (26:103) (ga˯ dza˯-eu), 2. to love and take care of each other, 3. to have a close friendship (50:200)
gaqzav beautiful (46:128) (yaw ja˯)
gaq zav hhyul qaol nei 1. to love each other dearly (46:91), 2. to be beautiful, 3. have goodwill, 4. to be hospitable
gaq zav hhyul qaol nei lav qoq miq to give a warm welcome; to give a warm reception (lmˇ bo˯ ni ha geu˰-eu)
gaqzav nei lovely (35:72)
gaqzav pa zav nei beautiful (**gaqzav pa zav nei daov maq gaq** = not very beautiful) (11:60, 45:88)

gav to feel cold (9:55) (ga^-eu)
=gav, aq= cold
=gav ba'la, caoq= winter
=gav, hoq= cold rice
-- gav, laolgav -- for fields to 'cool off' after burning
-- gav, neema -- to be sad; upset
-- gavsiq, aqgav -- gooseflesh
gavsiv nei very cold (9:55) (ga^ seh˰-eu)
gavsiv pa siv nei very, very cold
-- gavsso, aqgav -- to get cold

-- **gav ya, saq ya** -- hardship and cold
gavyov nei disappointed
-- **gav zeiq, saq zeiq** -- poverty; suffering; hunger; hardship
gavzuq zuq to be chilly (or) **saqzuq zuq**

gafbuf cadre in the Communist party (Chi) (9:51, 34:56, 41:3) (see also: **gaqbuf**)

GAO

gaol clean water (2:50, 50:137) (gah$^{\vee}$; yaw gah$^{\vee}$)
gaol well behaved (cf. yaw gah$^{\vee}$ = smart) (9:53)
gaol ahead; to be in the lead (meh$_{\vee}$ hu)
gaol straight (11:55) (daw$^{\vee}$ coe ni)
-- **gaol, aolzei** -- to play with toy wooden tops
gaolca a factory (Chi) (9:54, 26:3, 50:59)
Gaol Caoqyoq a person's name (14:209)
=gaol, ceiq= success (34:4)
gaolceiq engineering project (Chi) (34:66, 50:59)
  gaolceiqbil a soldier engineer (builds bridges, train tracks, highways etc.) (Chi) (26:89)
  gaolceiqsiil an engineer (Chi) (41:4), engineering (50:59)
gaolciv nei clean water (9:54) (i$^{\vee}$ cu$_{\wedge}$ yaw shaw$^{\vee}$)
  gaolciv nei gaol very clear water (11:22) (gah$^{\vee}$-eu i$^{\vee}$ cu$_{\wedge}$)
  gaolciv pa civ nei very clean water (46:114)
gaolciiq a meter (Chi) (41:125)
gaoldaof justice (Chi) (50:61)
gaoldei yeifxaol higher educational schools (Chi) (50:56)
gaoldiq public enemy (Chi) (50:61)
gaoldif a building or work site (Chi) (26:62) (ga$^{\vee}$ m$^{\vee}$ du$_{\vee}$)
gaolduf a high degree of (Chi) (34:71)
-- gaol, eelgaol -- water to be clear
gaolfeil centimeters (Chi) (11:77, 41:127) (or) **feil; liqmi**
gaolfeil work points in the Communist system (Chi) (50:59) (or) **gaolpeil**
gaolfeil hhaqpyuq the value of work points (A=Chi) (50:59)
gaolfeil piq evaluate work and allot workpoints (Chi) (50:131) (& see: **gaolfeil pieiq**)
gaolfeil pieiq to divide up work points (A=Chi) (& see: **gaolfeil piq**)
-- **gaol, gaoqgaol** -- (see full)
gaolgaof qiqceil a public bus (Chi) (50:61)
gaolgual to tackle key problems (Chi) (50:60)
gaolguei (see: **gaoltaq**)
gaolgyuf piziiq noble; high quality (Chi) (26:100)
gaolhyuf labor union (Chi) (9:54, 50:59)
gaolhhalbuf ministry of security (Chi) (50:60)
gaolhhalcuf security department in the prefecture

(Chi) (50:60)
gaolhhal jilgual an administrative unit in the bureau of security (Chi) (50:60)
gaolhhaljiq security bureau (Chi) (50:60)
gaolhhaljyuq Public Security Bureau (Chi)
gaolhhal mavqssaq security troops (A=Chi) (50:60)
gaolhhal peilhaoq police uniform; security person's uniform
gaolhhaq siifqif to maintain high spirits (Chi) (34:80)
gaolhhaltil provincial security department (Chi) (50:60)
gaoljil a kilogram (Chi) (41:127)
gaoljiq 1. high quality, 2. contribution (Chi) (34:28)
gaoljiq gaolceiqsiil senior engineer (Chi)
gaoljiq sseiqmiq faqyeif higher people's court (Chi) (50:56)
gaolkao high university exam (Chi) (14:241)
gaolkao sufxoq high university exam in mathematics
Gaolkeel dialect of Akha called **Aqkel** (A˯ keuˇ) by the Akha, but called this by the people themselves
gaolkof lessons (as for school children) (Chi) (50:60)
=**gaol, lavq**= a finger ring
-- **gaol, lavqma lavqgaol** -- to wear a ring on the thumb
-- **gaol, lavqnyul lavqgaol** -- to wear a ring on the finger
gaolleiq nieivq gaol to spin a chestnut (put a stick in and twist it)
gaolli kilometer (Chi) (26:89, 50:61)
gaolliq calendar (Chi) (50:61)
gaolliaq grain tax (Chi) (9:54)
gaollu galma highway (A=Chi) (pf) (or) **gaolluf galma**
gaolluq a blast furnace (Chi) (50:56)
gaolluf galma (see: **gaollu galma**
-- **gaol, meiq** -- admonish; advise (50:192)
gaolmiq citizenship (Chi) (50:61)
=**gaol, miav**= a hoop; a band
-- **gaol, miav** -- eyes to be sharp; have good vision
gaol naoq lieiqmaoq alliance of workers and peasants (Chi) (50:59)
=**gaol, nee**= bright; clever
gaolniq industry (Chi) (9:54, 26:100)
gaolniq capi industrial products (Chi) (50:59)
gaolniqhuaf industrialized (Chi) (50:59)
gaolniq tixif industrial system (Chi) (50:59)
gaolniq xeifdeifhuaf industrial modernization (Chi) (50:59)
gaolniq nei clean (as water) (14:227) (gahˇ; shawˇ)
=**gaol, nyuq**= to be alert; to pay attention; to think clearly
-- **gaol, nyuqgaol** -- being alert; paying attention

gaolpeil work points in the Communist system (Chi) (gaolfeil = pf.)

gaolquv pure (50:27)

gaolquv nei pure; clean and honest (50:27)

gaolsal gua'li faqgyul regulations of industrial and commercial management (Chi) (50:59)

gaolsal huf family of industry and commerce (Chi) (50:59)

gaolsaljiq department of industry and commerce (Chi)

gaolsalniq industrialism and commercialism (Chi) (34:10)

gaolsaf lofty; noble (as ideals) (Chi) (26:55)

gaolseil pav half a liter (A=Chi)

gaolseif 1. a public hall (26:38), 2. a commune; brigade (Chi) (26:37, 50:61)

gaolseifhuaf communalism (Chi) (50:61)

gaolseif paof anti-aircraft gun (Chi) (50:56)

gaolsiil 1. a company (50:61), 2. a shop, 3. a department store (Chi)

gaolsiif 1. a formula, 2. a public job (Chi) (34:109)

gaolsuf public prosecution (Chi) (50:61)

gaol sufduf high speed (Chi) (or) **sufduf kol** (A=Chi) (50:57)

gaolsuf hhafjeif the public prosecution of a case (Chi) (50:62)

gaolsseiq a worker (Chi) (26:5, 41:3, 50:59) (mˇ zaˬ)

gaolsseiq geiljiq working class (Chi) (50:59) (mˇ dzaˬ zaˬ)

gaolsseiq ssaqnaol ordinary workers (A=Chi) (26:26) (gaˇ mˇ dzaˬ zaˬ)

gaolsseiq yifdaof worker's movement (Chi) (50:59)

gaolssiq nei straight (9:54) (dawˇ coe ni)

gaolssiq pa ssiq nei to be very straight (dawˇ coe ni)

gaoltaq a public hall (or) **gaolguei** (Chi)

gaol taq teiq siq wait a moment (don't be in a hurry) (dawˬ tawˬ; taˬ tehˬ)

gaolwuf public affairs (Chi)

gaolwuf xif public affairs letter (Chi)

gaolxaol hoqzoq seif supply and marketing cooperative (Chi) (50:60)

gaolxaolseif supply and marketing cooperative (Chi)

gaolxao 1. senior premier (Chi) (50:57), 2. upper elementary school (grades 4-6) (26:111)

gaolxil meritorious service (Chi) (50:60)

gaolxoqyeif institute of technology (Chi)

=gaol, yaq= toothpaste (Chi)

gaolyaqgol high pressure steamer (Chi) (50:57)

-- gaol, yavq -- to subject someone to discipline

gaolyeziif public ownership (Chi) (34:16, 50:62)

gaolyeiq 1. the Christian era; A.D.; century (Chi) (46:84), 2. a park (two words in Chinese - 50:62)

gaolyiqliaq crop taxes for government (Chi) (12:128)

gaolyif to provide (Chi) (50:60)

gaolyif miaoqgaoq handicraft articles (A=Chi) (50:60)

(or) **gaolyifpi** (Chi)

gaolyifpi (see: **gaolyif miaoqgaoq**)

gaolyoq 1. a pledge; treaty; pact (Chi) (50:62), 2. an appointment

gaolzaol senior middle school (high school) (Chi) (41:15, 50:57, 71)

gaolzeif bonds (Chi) (50:62)

gaolziil wages; salary (Chi) (34:40, 50:60)

gaolziil hha zaq to have a salary (A=Chi)

gaol ziibiaol high target (Chi) (50:57)

gaolzoq work; a job (Chi) (9:54, 26:26, 41:50, 87, 50:60) (**gaolzoq aol** = to work at an office) (or) **golzoq** (not pf.)

gaolzoq aol zaq to work in an office

gaolzoqdyuf a work team (Chi) (9:54, 50:60)

gaolzoq taolxif one's work address (Chi) (50:60)

gaolzoq za working team (Chi) (50:60)

gaolzua revolves (Chi) (50:62) (& see below)

gaolzuei revolves (Chi) (46:83) (& see above)

gao together (9:53) (ti˯ kaw^ lo˰-eh˅)

=gao, al= a thorn

gaoguf to consolidate; strengthen (Chi) (34:17) (g'a˯ bi˰-eu)

gaoma (see: **yaovma** = cicada)

=gao, ngaq= fish bones ('thorns')

=gao, qiq= together

gaoyeziif public ownership system (Chi) (34:37)

=gao, zaoq= together

gaoq spear (9:54) (gah˯) (see also: **gaoqdul**; **gaoqpyul**)

gaoq before; ahead (**Nol gaoq ssuq**. You go ahead.) (meh˯ hu)

gaoq clf. for piles (as piles of firewood - 11:77); mountains (**haolgaoq** - 11:95) (9:54); stacks

(vb) **gaoq** to have much; be rich (**jav gaoq** = to have plenty; ja^ gah˯)

-- gaoq, bavq -- to make a pile of something

gaoqbeeq weeds; dust; rubbish (14:162) (or) **gaoqbeeq** dalssei (cf.: ya˅ mo˰)

gaoqbil a wind instrument (**bawul** = Chi) (9:18)

gaoqdaoq the foot of the mountain (13:11) (gaw˯ jaw˯ daw˯ dah˯)

gaoqdaoq laoq, gaoqdaoq laoq the sound of a rice pounder going "kathump, kathump" (46:86)

gaoqdul spear handle (50:113)

gaoqduq the saddleback of a mountain (or) **gaoqheiq**

gaoqgaol gaol a fine rash on baby's body (10:23)

=gaoq, haol= a mountain ridge

gaoqheiq saddleback of a mountain (or) **gaoqduq**

gaoqhhaol a mountain side; middle part of the mountain (not too high or too low) (38:37) (gaw˯ jaw˯ gaw˯ dze˅)

Gaoqja a Hani clan (Gao = Chi)

-- **gaoq, keelgaoq** -- to cross one's legs

gaoqlaoq blessing; merit; luck (**gaoqlaoq meeq** = good blessing; **gaoqlaoq heeq** = big blessing) (guiˬ lahˬ)

gaoqlaoq bi meeq lal to bring about good luck; blessings

gaoqlaoq bo to have blessing; merit; luck

gaoqlaoq heeq lal for luck/blessings to increase (guiˬ lahˬ huiˬ-eu)

-- **gaoq laoq, gu lu** -- to be bumpy

gaoqlaoq maq bo to be unlucky (or) **siqhel maq meeq**

gaoqlaoq meeq to have good fortune

gaoqlaoq sal 1. for a newly married couple to go from elder to elder with liquor and water seeking their blessings; 2. for relatives to push with their hands on the abdomen of a sacrificial buffalo killed at a funeral, in the hopes of getting some dung to come out which they carry in the corner of their jackets and take (three times) to certain locations in the home, for 'good luck'

=**gaoq, luv**= a stone heap; a stone pile

-- **gaoq, maq** -- no matter who or what (46:204)

gaoqmeiv meiv to teeter-totter

=**gaoq, mil**= mountainous places

-- **gaoqmiq, haolgaoq** -- the 'tail' of the mountain

-- **gaoq, miaq** -- many; excessive

=**gaoq, miaoq**= things; goods

=**gaoq, nee**= kind of bean

-- **gaoq nei, daoqgaoq** -- to be plentiful

=**gaoq pa gaoq nei, biao**= fully; thoroughly

gaoqpyul head of spear (50:113)

gaoqqa a digging tool with a metal head (gahˬ cehˇ)

gaoq qu to stack up

-- **gaoqssaq, milgaoq** -- a small mountain

gaoqwuq 1. temporary, 2. ahead (as in 'You go ahead') (9:54) (mehˬ hu)

-- **gaoqwuq, haolgaoq** -- the top of a mountain

gaoqzaol upstairs (as in the attic) (27:11) (gui ma)

-- **gaoq, zyulgaoq** -- gathered together

gaofbiqhyuf a farewell meeting (Chi) (41:174)

Gaofcada Communist party (Chi) (9:53, 11:25, 50:62) (or) **Da**

Gaofca dayeiq Communist party member (Chi) (9:53)

gaofca'faol communist drive (Chi) (50:62)

gaofca zuyif communism (Chi) (9:53, 26:56, 50:62)

gaofca zuyif seifhyuf communist society (Chi) (50:62)

gaofca zuyif yifdaof communist movement (Chi) (50:62)

gaofhoqgoq a republic (Chi) (50:62)

Gaofqiltuaq Youth league (Chi) (50:63) (or) **Gaofqiltueiq**

Gaofqil tuaqyeiq Youth league member (Chi) (9:53)

(or) **Gaofqil tueiqyeiq**
gaoftaoq faqyaoq to be prosperous together (Chi)
gaoftaoq galli common program (Chi) (50:62)
gaofxeif 1. devoted to (26:56), 2. contribution (34:28) (Chi)

GE

geldel geldel the sound of the bamboo instrument they make to scare birds away (14:189)

geqmifjal (see: **geiqmifjal**) (Chi) (34:92)

gevq a pheasant (brd) (9:56, 46:117) (geu^)
gevq spotted appearance (cf.: ma˅ byaw^)
gevqdevq devq to tickle (9:56) (kaw˅ doe^ doe^-eu)
=gevq, moq= a black and white horse
gevqpiul a silver pheasant (14:241) (geu^)

GEE

geel war (6:190) (gui˅)
geel to melt; to dissolve (9:55) (gui˅-eu)
geel to shine; to brighten (46:146) (bya-eu)
=geel, aq= a star
=geel, aqpyuq baoq= ancestral shelf of bamboo (& see below)
=geel, aqpyuq hel= ancestral altar (& see above)
geel aol laolcoq a fighting bastion (50:207)
=geel, baq= facial skin
geel cavq to weld ('melt join')
geel diq to fight a war (battle) (9:55, 11:32) (gui˅ deu^-eu)
  geel diq deilssaol to prepare for war (50:9)
  geel diq e hhaqhav combat capacity
  geel diq mavqssaq soldiers; fighting forces
  geeldiq yiqqeiq fighting tactics (50:207)
  geel diq zaq duq a battle ground (gui˅ deu^ deu^ k'ah˅)
=geel, ha= chicken nest
=geel, hhavq= pig skin
geelhhuvq to make things bad (50:47)
  geelhhuvq duvduq a criminal site (place) (50:47)
  geelhhuvq maq hha duv an attempted crime (50:47)
  geelhhuvq yoba a criminal clique (group) (50:47)
=geel, miav= eyelid
-- geel, miavgeel -- to dazzle with light
-- geel, neema -- very sad in one's heart ('heart melting')
geelniq nei brightening (9:55) (bya-eu)
  geelniq pa niq nei very brightly (bya ceh^ ni)
geelnieiv nei geel to glare; to be bright
geelqaq leqhev a water-proofed bamboo rain hat
geelsal a disaster (35:80); dangerous; unexpected (37:72)

geelsal duv e a disaster to take place (46:124)
geelsiq silver ornaments that look like stars which Hani women wear in their hair
-- **geelsiq, ngavq kyul** -- a five-pointed star
geelsseivq nei shining (26:100)
-- **geel, taoq** -- uncovered porch by the house
-- **geeltevq, miavgeel** -- double-fold eyelid
geelzeiq hhuvq to fine in punishment

gee dry (trans.) (9:55) (gui-eu)
gee to do; to assume responsibility (soqpaq gee = to be a lord; ruler) (geu^- eu)
gee to be; become (**daqyao gee** = to be a guest) (9:55, 45:6) (geu^ laˇ-eu, pyeu^ laˇ-eu)
gee 1. to make (a speech); to speak; talk (9:55, 13:6, 41:12) (**doqsii taq gee** = don't speak this word), 2. to count (9:55) (gui-eu)
gee clf. for fires (as different places where fires are burning -- **miqzaq qiq gee** = one fire)
-- **gee, aqgee** -- to count numbers
geebaq the south side of a river (lawˇ gaw^)
=**gee, ca**= to dry with smoke
gee caq 1. to be engaged, 2. the way to count
-- **gee caq, miqssaq** -- to betroth to be married; to arrange a marriage
gee ceiv to reach an agreement on something (50:187)
gee dav to become (50:32)
geedoq bei editor's preface (50:2)
geeda tavq part-time; part-time job; concurrent post (50:82)
-- **gee, daqyao** -- to be a guest
gee dav 1. to count from lower to higher numbers (gui da^-eu), 2. to become something higher (as an officer, higher office, etc.), 3. let it be (as we decided, for example)
gee dav (with neg.) to be careless (see 10:pref.) (ma˯ yahˇ)
-- **gee, doqzil** -- to discuss
gee duv to speak out (50:44)
geeheiq pyu west, or down (as in downriver, downhill)
gee hu try counting it (gui haw-eu)
-- **gee, kaoqbaoq** -- to be thirsty ('throat dry')
geekoq deibil a flat path between mountain fields
gee li nia la approximately; more or less; about (11:70) (ehˇ ga˯)
gee loq to explain (32:3, 50:88)
-- **gee, lovq** dried by the sun
-- **geema, miqzaq** -- fire burning in home
gee meiq to conduct propaganda (50:190)
gee nao term of office; tenure of office (50:143)
geenieiq pieiq 1. to resign from one's position (50:4), 2. to leave the army & return home (50:54)
geepil one of three types of spirit priest (not the highest, which is: **nialpil**)
gee pil to mediate; make peace (50:166)

gee pil colba a mediating group; organization (50:166)

-- **gee, piav** -- to turn upside down to dry

geepuv niapuv neighboring villages (35:84) (lit. 'below and above villages')

=**gee pyu, aq**= down below; west

gee'qa number; amount; to count (**gee'qa maq hev** = do not know numerals)

gee'qev nei very dry (11:63) (gui co^{v} ni)

gee'qev nei daov maq gee not very dry (11:60)

geesav nei dry (9:56) (gui co^{v} ni)

-- **gee, savq** -- to evaporate

gee soq to coordinate; to harmonize (50:187)

-- **gee, soqpaq** -- to be a lord; ruler

=**gee ssaq, zoq**= people who live downstream

gee taq soqkaoq a written agreement (50:187)

-- **gee, teiv** -- to smoke dry by hanging over a fire

gee xa to count down (i.e., from higher to lower number) (gui ka-eu)

gee xul miq to persuade

gee yil nia lal to go everywhere; to every corner (50:120)

geeza 1. to discuss; to consult (9:56, 26:58) (baw$_{v}$ dza$_{v}$-eu), 2. a short commentary; a brief comment (50:40)

geeza doqssaq a short commentary; a brief comment (50:40)

-- **geeza, geezil** -- to consult; talk things over; discuss

geeza zaq to discuss; to consult (or) **geezil geeza**

gee zaq 1. to make happen, 2. to talk and laugh at, 3. to tell (as a story) (13:38) (**dudaq gee zaq** = to tell a story)

-- **gee zaq, dudaq** -- to tell a story

geezil geezaq to talk with each other; to discuss in a friendly way (50:76, 163, 187) (daw$_{v}$ ja ja-eu)

gee zyul to discuss (26:107)

geeq copper; brass; bronze (metals used for pots) (9:56) (gui$_{v}$ ba)

geeq scabies (a skin disease) (9:55) (ma^{v} gui$_{v}$ dzui^-eu)

geeqbaoq a person who has scabies

geeqbil a metal flute or trumpet (usually of copper or bronze) (11:93) (to blow = **bo; meel**)

geeqbil laqbil bo to blow a flute

geeqcal a copper or bronze pot (9:56) (gui$_{v}$ shm^{v})

=**geeq, ceil**= broken rice

=**geeq, dal**= bamboo pole for drying things

geeqdiq geeqcal a copper or bronze pot (or) **geeqcal**

geeq eel geeq nei very happily; actively (26:16) (la$_{v}$ k'a$_{v}$ ti$_{v}$ ceh^{v})

geeqgeeq nei 1. to be active, 2. to be noisy (law$_{\wedge}$ g'a-eu)

geeqhha a copper pot (gui$_{v}$ ba)

=geeq, hhaq= buckwheat husk
geeq jeivq saol jeivq saoq hhev seiq to make three circles in the ground with a metal tool to keep spirits from attacking
geeqkaol a wire (26:73); an electric wire (cf.: mi⌄ dza⌄ aˇ ca^)
geeqkaol albol (ssaolma) a pole for electric wires
=geeq, laol= scabies on the neck
-- geeq, leiqgeeq -- to make someone or something go along very quickly
geeq nal to get scabies (maˇ gui⌄ dzui^-eu)
geeqnav bronze
geeqnil copper (9:56) (gui⌄)
=geeq, ngaq= fish scales
geeqpiul 'white' copper (9:56) (gui⌄ pyuˇ)
geeqsiil 'golden' copper (gui⌄ shuiˇ)
geeqsev albol lacquer tree (9:56)
geeqsev tav something to be lacquered
geeqsiil 'yellow' copper (9:56) (gui⌄ shuiˇ)
geeqsiil meilbiav a brass coin (or) **geeqsiil taoqhaoq** (B=Chi)
geeqsiil taoqhaoq (see: **geeqsiil meilbiav**)
-- geeq, ssuqgeeq -- to go quickly

GEI

geilduaf a period of time (Chi) (34:25, 50:86)
geiljiq a class of people; a social class (as poor, rich, etc.) (Chi) (9:56, 50:86) (**boqxoq geiljiq** = class of exploiters - 34:10)
geiljiq defzeil class struggle (Chi) (26:17, 50:96)
geiljiq diqsseiq class enemies (Chi) (50:86)
geiljiq galquv class ways of doing (A=Chi) (50:86)
geiljiq gaqiq class feeling (Chi) (50:86)
geiljiq gualdiei class viewpoints (Chi) (50:86)
geiljiq hhaqhav class power (A=Chi) (50:86)
geiljiq joqwuf class consciousness (Chi) (50:86)
geiljiq maoqdueif class contradiction (Chi) (50:86)
geiljiq seifhyuf class society (Chi) (50:86)
geiljiqxif 1. classism; 2. class character; class nature (Chi) (50:86)
geiljiq zuziiq class organization (Chi) (50:87)

geicaof to transform; remold something (Chi) (34:10), to create a new world (or) **geigeiq**
gei'faf to liberate; to free (Chi) (26:12) (pyeh⌄-eu)
Gei'fafjyul People's Liberation Army (Chi) (9:56, 50:87)
gei'faf zafzeil liberation war (Chi) (50:87)
geigeiq to reform; to remove (an obstacle) (Chi) (9:56, 34:10, 42, 50:55) (or) **geicaof**
=gei, hal= where?
geijiq to solve (Chi) (**weiftiq xilmol geijiq** = to solve the problem this way - 32:3) (34:26)
geisaf to improve (Chi) (34:46) (la^ mui⌄-eu)

geiqdalhaol cauliflower (Chi)
geiqleiq a reed pipe wind instrument
geiqleiq nei very slowly (50:74)
geiqmif revolution (Chi) (9:56, 26:13, 50:57)
geiqmif aol to take part in revolutionary activities (A=Chi)
geiqmif boqwuqgua revolutionary museum (Chi) (50:57)
geiqmif col revolutionary person (A=Chi) (50:58)
geiqmifhuaf to revolutionize (Chi) (34:107)
geiqmifjal a revolutionist (Chi) (34:28)
geiqmif liqsiif bee col the family of a revolutionary martyr (AB=Chi) (50:57)
geiqmif qiqzaol revolutionary people (Chi) (50:58)
geiqmif taoyiq zafxeif revolutionary united front (Chi) (50:58)
geiqmif yifziif revolutionary thought (Chi) (50:58)
geiqmif zafsiif a revolutionary soldier (Chi) (26:44)
geiqmif zilseiq revolutionary spirit (Chi) (26:61)
geiqyil fuqhaof apostrophe (punctuation mark) (Chi)

geivzavq 1. a fur blanket; a carpet (for floor or bed) (Chi) (11:30), 2. a woolen blanket (or) **albee hyulzal** (B=Chi)

geivq, geivq, geivq the sound of cracking; the sound of creaking (as a creaking door - 45:64) (and see appendix 6)

geifciiq preposition (Chi) (50:88)
geifpieif calcium (Chi)

GO

gol ache; severe pain (especially of teeth and eyes aching) (9:57) (gaw$^{\vee}$-eu)
golbaq stature; body size (Chi) (9:57, 11:111) (cf.: g'aw$^{\vee}$ maw$^{\vee}$; maw$^{\vee}$ do)
golbaq heeq a big body; big stature (A=Chi) (maw$^{\vee}$ do yaw hui$_{\vee}$)
golbaq maq heeq body not big (tall) (A=Chi) (26:37) (maw$^{\vee}$ do ma$_{\vee}$ hui$_{\vee}$)
golbaq nil small; short person (A=Chi) (26:42) (yaw aw)
golcaq a ladle for cooking and for dipping up food (Chi) (ni ceu^)
golful ability (Chi) (or) **beisiif** (26:48) (nya-eu)
=gol, hhavq= adult pig
goljif opera (Chi) (50:57, 71)
=gol, nal= a disease
golpu the music of a song (Chi) (50:57)
golquq a song (Chi) (50:57)
Golsa milcaq a place name (14:209)

-- **gol, seq** -- tooth to ache

golwujif singing and dancing (Chi) (50:57)

golwutuaq art troupe (Chi) (50:57)

gol zeiq to ache more (14:165) (gaw$^{\vee}$ dzeh$_{\vee}$-eu)

=**go, nao**= with

goq high; tall (9:57) (yaw go$^{\vee}$)

-- **goq, bavq** -- to raise; heighten; hold up high

goqbeeq (see: **gaoqbeeq**) (14:170)

=**goq, biaq**= tree wasp

goqciq the condition of the country (Chi)

goqcuq all kinds of nationalities (Chi) (34:107)

goq dav to raise up (38:94)

goqdul capital of a country (Chi) (50:66)

goqfaq 1. defense (26:43, 105, 50:66), 2. national defense (34:79) (Chi), 3. a national law (50:66)

goqfaqbuf ministry of defense (Chi) (50:66)

goqfaq gaolniq defense industries (Chi) (50:67)

goqfaq xeifdeif huaf defense modernization (Chi) (50:67)

goqgol the national anthem (Chi) (50:67)

goq goqdeil goq the sound of hens clucking

goqgyul hhovq cocka-doodle-doo (sound of a rooster crowing) (38:92); **goqgyul lil'o; goqgyul lilhhul** (kaw$_{\wedge}$ toe$^{\vee}$ loe$^{\vee}$ coe$^{\wedge}$ oe$_{\vee}$)

-- **goq, hal miavnei** -- how high?

goqhyul a national emblem (Chi) (50:67)

goqjal a nation; a country (Chi) (9:57, 50:67)

-- **goqjal, aqgee aqnia** -- other countries (C=Chi)

goqjal aoqzaq saolhyuq to be a traitor to your country (A=Chi) ('sell one's country as a thief') (50:112)

goqjal jilgual national departments (Chi) (50:67)

goqjal laqhyul laqnil domestic and international (A=Chi) (50:67)

goqjal qovq government (A=Chi) (or) **aqtav soqpaq; zeiffu qovq** (A=Chi)

goqjal saqhav national forest (A=Chi) (50:67)

goqjal soyeziif national system (Chi) (50:67)

goqjal yoqhhovq haolleev to preserve home and country (A=Chi) (50:7)

goqjal zeiqma national property (A=Chi) (50:67)

goqjal ziilbei zuyif national capitalism (Chi) (50:67)

goqjal zuxiq national president (Chi) (50:67)

Goqjef the name of a city (the capital for Honghe prefecture) (Chi) (11:176) (or) **Gejiu**

goqji hhyufseil jeiyiq gyuldif border sanitation and quarantine regulations (Chi) (50:67)

goqjif international (Chi) (as in WHO) (34:15)

Goqjif Gol International song (Chi) (50:67)

goqjif jiljif zeifziif ciifxif international political economic order (Chi) (34:29)

goqjif seifhyuf international community (Chi)

(34:76)

Goqjif Weifseil Zuziq World Health Organization (Chi) (10:13)

goqjif zafnioq geiqjiq international strategic pattern (Chi) (34:29)

goqkufjeif a treasury bill (Chi) (50:67)

goqliq national power (Chi) (34:18)

Goqmiqda Kuomintang (old Nationalist regime) (Chi) (50:67)

goqmiq jiljif national economy (Chi) (50:67)

goqmiq selssuq national income (Chi) (50:67)

goqpuv bamboo mat for drying crops (9:57) (gaw˯ pu)

goqqiq the national flag (Chi) (miˇ k'ah˯-eu˯ paˇ lo˯ paˇ lehˇ)

goqqifjiq National day (Chi)

goqqifjiq neeciiv national holiday (AB=Chi) (50:67)

goqsa nei very high (9:57, 11:18) (yaw goˇ)

goqsa sama nei goq high to the extreme (11:59) (aˇ dzeh˯-ehˇ goˇ-eu)

goqwufyeif state council (Chi) (9:57, 50:67)

goqyiq country-owned; nationalized (Chi) (34:42)

goqyiq daf zaol xiq big and mid-sized country-owned enterprises (Chi) (34:42)

goqyiq jiljif national economics (Chi) (50:67)

goqyiq naoqca national farm (Chi) (50:67)

-- **goq, zaol** -- to put high up

gov a thin, emaciated, weak person or animal; in poor health (as when thin from lots of illness) 9:57) (**yogov govssaq** = a thin, weak person) (yaw jeh; jeh ngawˇ ni)

=**gov alsiq, ni**= wild grapes

=**gov, aq**= bedbug

-- **gov, colgov** -- a very thin, weak person

=**gov, lol**= valley with water

=**gov, moq**= a thin horse

=**gov nei, xeivq**= very thin

gov sil to die of thinness and weakness (as animals) (12:127) (jeh seh˄-eu)

-- **govtov, seivmoq** -- stilts

=**gov, xal**= 1. a field that is not fertilized, 2. an irrigated field without a good crop

govxeivq nei very thin person

govxeivq pa xeivq nei extremely thin person (aˇ dzeh˯-ehˇ jeh-eu)

-- **gov, yogov** -- to be weak and limp

=**gov, zeiq**= weak domesticated animals

-- **govq, zalgovq** -- to mix up vegetables (& see full)

gofduf transition; interim (Chi) (34:112, 50:68)

gofduf siiqqil transition period (Chi) (50:68)

gofhheif to have a perfect mastery of something (Chi) (34:80)

gofsseiq zuyif 1. selfish (think of oneself, not of others) (Chi) (26:10), 2. individualism (Chi) (50:58)
gofti private (as privately owned) (Chi) (34:10)
  gofti jiljif an individual economy (Chi) (34:39)

GU

gul 1. to name (myahˇ-eu; kuˇ-eu), 2. to call out (guˇ-eu) (9:57)
gul clf. for calling out (11:85)
-- **gul, aqzil** -- to sing a ballad or courting song in the mountains
gulcaq to interrupt; disturb someone (13:3) (la^ bahˬ-eu)
gul cil to shout loudly and get a sore throat (14:189)
-- **gul, dalgul** -- a tall and slender figure
guldaoq a wooden plow
-- **gul, deiq** -- to stretch out
gul huvq to call back (guˇ k'o˰-euˬ; guˇ cawˬ-eu)
gul jiq gul jiq to shout loudly (13:46)
  guljiq jiqma a loud shout (46:104)
=**gul, naol**= a weaving loom
gul nei tall and slender (or) **dalgul gul**
gul nyuq to call forth (guˇ g'eh-eu)
-- **gul, saqgul** -- to blow a buffalo horn when they get large game
gul ssaoq to call together (13:3) (kuˇ uiˬ-eu)
gul teev call to stop (46:98) (guˇ naˬ-eu)
gulteil a sound of calling; shouting (13:39, 26:70) (guˇ-eu teˇ saˇ)
gul zyul to call people together (14:145) (guˇ uiˬ-eu)

gu'liq economic elements (Chi) (34:37)
gu'lif to encourage (Chi) (26:44) (g'aˬ bi˰-eu)
gu lu gaoq laoq 1. to be bumpy; **daoqteev teev**; 2. to pile up in a disorderly way
=**gu nei, nil**= naked
=**gu nei, qeil**= sour taste
gupeiq playing cards made of bone (Chi)
=**gu saqgeel, laol**= skin at nape of neck (as a cat)
guwu to encourage; inspire (Chi) (26:66, 77)

guq to need; to require (2:50, 26:79, 41:97) (loˬ-eu)
guqciv Chinese chives; leeks (9:58)
guqgaf a major person; dynamic leader; specialist (Chi) (34:86)
Guqhal old name for Kunming (Chi) (35:96) Now called **Kyulmiq**
=**guq, haq**= fine bamboo strips
=**guq hhe kuv, lavq**= a cramp in the hand
=**guq, keel**= Achilles tendon

guq lal to be in need (46:108)
=guq, laq= the pulse
guqmal bean curds
=guq, mil= a Hani ritual head, who leads the village in annual offerings
=guq, naol= bamboo or rattan stool
=guq, nee= bean curd
guqpovq soy bean dregs (9:58)
guqpuv woven bamboo mat for drying crops (gaw⌄ pu; ka˅ te˅)
guqqil type of chives similar to kohlrabi (9:58)
=guq, qil= a rattan tie (string)
guqsav a wild yam (small, white, edible)
guqsuq geeqbil meel e siilful one who plays a bronze flute (siilful = player = Chi) (14:156)
guq sso to be necessary; to be needed (lo⌄ la˅-eu)
-- guq zaq, neivqhaq -- for an evil spirit to take one
-- guq zaq, yocavq -- to have bad luck

guv 1. to be afraid (9:58) (gu^-eu), 2. to scare (or) **guv sso**
guvciiq to exploit; to take advantage (Chi) (**guvciiq zaq** e = to exploit someone)
=guv, naq= to frighten someone
=guv neivqyav, neivq= a drug used to set broken bones
guvniq pieiq to frighten someone; cause them to be in awe
guv xa so frightened one falls to the ground (46:147)
guvzuq zuq in a state of great fear ('shivering with fear')

guvq to sew (9:58) (gu^-eu)
guvq the sound of drinking water ('gulp')
guvqciv a type of vegetable
guvq cuvq to sew up; to sew back on (as a button); to fix by sewing (41:31) (gu^ tm˅; gu^ tso^-eu)
guvqduq sewing work (as clothing etc.) (41:149) (gu^-eu)
guvqkaol silk thread (9:58) (boe⌄ kah˅)
guvqkaol aqma silkworm (9:58) (boe⌄ a˅ maw˅)
guvqkov a pattern of sewing
guvqnieiq something being sewn; sewing in process (as pants, shirt, etc.)
guvq taol to patch; mend (9:58, 26:84) (gu^ tm˅-eu)

gufnaoq a farmhand (Chi)

GUA

gual, gual, gual the sound of a gong (46:174)
gualdiei a viewpoint (Chi) (34:25) (or) **gueildiei**
gualjeif 1. the crux (Chi) (34:84), 2. a critical moment (or) **gualke**
gualke crucial moment; critical moment (Chi) (26:44)

(see also: **gualjeif**)
gualliaoq bureaucracy (Chi) (34:16)
  gualliaoq ziilbei zuyif bureaucrat (Chi) (34:8)
gualxif a relationship (Chi) (34:17)
gualyoq glorious (as a glorious day) (Chi) (26:102)

guabo to broadcast (as a radio) (Chi) (34:65) (maw$^{\vee}$ kaw$^{\vee}$-ah$^{\vee}$ ngeh$_{\vee}$-eu)
  guabozaf broadcasting station (Chi) (26:60) (maw$^{\vee}$ kaw$^{\vee}$ do^ du$_{\vee}$)
gua'faf extensive; wide-ranging (Chi) (34:107) (g'aw$_{\vee}$ mah$^{\vee}$ ni)
guagaof advertisement (Chi) (50:65)
gua'li to manage (Chi) (9:57) (or) **guei'li**

guaqhaof brackets; parentheses (punctuation) (Chi) (50:100)

guafceiq to carry out (as a program) (Chi) (34:74)

GUEI

gueildiei view point (Chi) (or) **gualdiei**
gueilliaoq zuyif bureaucracy (Chi)
gueilxil to show concern (Chi) (or) **neema nyuq**

guei'li to manage (Chi) (or) **gua'li**

gueif lao to be strange (Chi)
gueifteq canned goods (Chi) (**malcavq bavq dov laq e zal**)

GYU

gyul to cry; weep (or) **ngyul** (ngoe$^{\vee}$-eu)
gyuldif to stipulate; set a regulation (Chi) (34:103, 41:52, 50:66)
gyulfaf to standardize (Chi) (50:66)
gyulhuaf to make a plan (Chi) (50:66)
gyulji rule; custom (Chi) (50:66)
gyulliq regulation (Chi) (34:11)
gyulmoq scale; scope (Chi) (50:66)
gyulmoq halheeq nei broad in scale (A=Chi) (50:66)
gyulzal rules (Chi) (50:66)
  gyulzal zifduf system of rules; regulations (Chi) (50:66)
gyulzeiq 1. a rule (as in grammar) (Chi) (41:78), 2. a principle (as a principle to follow) (Chi) (50:66)

gyu to thatch a roof (nym$^{\vee}$ m$_{\vee}$ m$_{\vee}$-eu)
gyu kaq to thatch over (nym$^{\vee}$ m$_{\vee}$ shaw$_{\vee}$-eu)
gyuma a nut tree with flat, bitter nuts (8:1) (large tree, but the wood is not used in building)
gyu nieiq gyu pav a roof half thatched

gyuyoq a lazy person (yaw doeᵛ)
gyuzii a bandit (esp. armed robbers) (**Ssiiqbei gyuzii** = the Japanese bandits - 26:2) (cf.: tahᵛ joe)

gyuq 1. roar (as tiger); rumble (joeᵥ-eu), 2. bell rings, 3. cry out (8:1-4), 4. bark of a barking deer (**qilssaq gyuq**)
-- **gyuq, hhe** -- to ring a bell
gyuqma singing birds (14:188)
-- **gyuq, nilzeiq ssaq** -- for a wild animal to cry out
-- **gyuq, salsil** -- for the soul of someone who has died a bad death to cry out, esp. when it is rainy or cold on dark evenings
gyuq teil a sound (14:153) (teᵛ saᵛ)
=**gyuq, wuv**= (see full)

gyufteiq a carton; cardboard box (Chi) (50:66)

HA

hal 1. superlative degree; highest degree (**Aqli hal kyul zeiq e nga.** The youngest boy is cleverest. 11:106. **Alheeq hal meeq zeiq e qiq hhaq** = Alheeq is the best.), 2. comprehensive (**Col e niuqteil hal goq zeiq e nga.** Man's forehead is the highest.) (k'aᵛ)

hal (vb) every (vb); each (vb); **hal zaol movq** = everything you want to do) (k'aᵛ ...)

hal to pour or splash a liquid (k'aᵛ-eu) (9:59)

hal to spit (du˯ k'a˯ k'a-eu) (9:59)

hal (n) (note: this combination is a little like 'wh---' in English (where? what? who? why? etc.) (see: 11:99, 45:7)

hal (clf., clf.) which ... (**hal mol mol?** = which 'one and one?')

hal 1. a bad quarrel; a verbal fight; a dispute (**Yeiqnaohuvq puvkaq a hal maq duv lal qaol al.** This year no disputes have broken out in the village.), 2. a rumor (and see: **hal duv**)

hal aol qaol e aol to do one's best (50:58)

hal aol sso hal bil to receive according to one's need (50:2)

hal aol hal bil to pay wages according to one's labor (50:2)

hal aol hal hha to receive wages according to one's labor (50:2)

halbeiv a kind of small basket (14:142)

halbol bolcaoq bamboo forest (ma sa˯ yaᵛ)

halcaq earth; mud (9:59, 26:59, 46:165) (sha˯ jeh^)

halcaq puqhul big lump or clod of mud (26:59, 46:165) (miᵛ tsa˯ k'oᵛ)

halceq a sneeze (or) **heilceq** (haᵛ ceu˯) (9:59)

halceq ceq to sneeze (or) **heilceq ceq** (haᵛ ceu˯ ceu˯-eu)

halceil sand (9:59, 11:49) (k'aᵛ shui˰)

halceil ceildei a sandy beach (14:147) (or) **halceil loldei**

halceil leildei 1. a sandy strand (as by a river bank), 2. sandy silt on a field or path

halceil loldei a sandy beach (or) **halceil ceildei**

halceil milcaq sandy earth (k'aᵛ shui˰)

Haldei milcaq Hade, a place in Luchun (57:154)

hal duv 1. for a bad dispute or quarrel to develop, 2. for a rumor to spread

hal dyul many; so many (11:210) (g'aw˯ mya ni)

Hal'eibil milcaq Harbin, a city in northern China (57:86)

=hal, gal= travel expenses

hal gaq hal aol to appoint people by favoritism (50:143)

halgei where? (9:59) (a˯ gaˇ)
  halgei gei (just) where and where? (**Aqyoq halgei gei** li? Just where did he go? 11:103)
  halgei ... halgei wherever.... wherever (26:102) (**Da halgei a li nei eil ngaoq, ngal halgei a xeiv al li.** Wherever the party tells me to go, there I will go/run.) (see also: 26:70) (a˯ geu gaˇ k'aw˰)
  halgei halhao everywhere (35:92, 38:14, 45:65, 46:172) (yaw˯ gaˇ na lu˰)
hal he nei heeq how big? (aˇ hui ni)
  hal kaol galquv all the ways; methods (50:58)
  hal hhovq liq every household; whatever household (**hal hhovq liq nao meeq qiq nao ceil** = every household chose an auspicious day).
  halgei jol nga aq? where do you live? (8:36) (a˯ gaˇ jawˇ le)
  halgei li go everywhere
  halgei liq wherever
  halgei maq gee dav nei everywhere; no exceptions (10:20) (goes on to say, 'don't defecate and urinate') (see also 26:3)
  halgei yil halgei hyuq wherever he goes he steals (13:21) (k'aˇ iˇ gaˇ k'oe˯-eu)
  halgei yil ma laq? where are you going? (8:27) (a˯ gaˇ iˇ te)
  halgei yil wul aq? where are you going? (8:27) (a˯ gaˇ iˇ te)
hal goq zeiq the highest (as a place or position that is the highest) (goˇ dzeh˯ dzeh˯-eu)
halhal! **interjection (Halhal! Meeq al!** Ha, it is wonderful!)
=hal, ha= a hen which tries to lay eggs
halhe nei how big? (aˇ hui ni) (**halhe nei heeq?**)
halhev milnia everywhere (yaw˯ gaˇ na lu˰)
halheeq nei very big (9:60) (g'aw˯ loe ni)
  halheeq pa heeq nei extremely big (aˇ dzeh˯-ehˇ hui˯-eu)
-- hal, hoqleivq -- to pour out food to spirits (and see full)
hal huvq which year? (a˯ geu k'o˰)
  hal huvq liq every year; whatever year (12:127) (yaw˯ k'o˰ na lu˰)
=hal, hhavq= female pig (a˯ za˰ ma)
halhhov 1. rice container made from strips of bamboo; also used for carrying meat during religious ceremonies (haw˯ g'aw^), 2. lines on a finger which look like rice containers made of bamboo (they show up in one's fingerprint; the more you have the richer you are)
hal jav e 1. all you have (nawˇ k'aˇ uˇ-eu), 2. the amount (k'aˇ ja^-eu)
  hal jav e col the richest (sahˇ dzeh˯-eu)
  hal jav e zaq saq to eat up all one has (k'aˇ ja^-eu dza˯ jiˇ-eu)
hal jav hal zaq zaq to eat what one has (35:2) (k'aˇ

ja^-eu dza⌄ jiˇ-eu)

haljivq what? (**Xil mol haljivq nga laq?** What is this thing? - 9:60, 10:1) (a⌄ je⌄)

haljivq alnei why? (11:101, 13:20, 30) (a⌄ je⌄ g'eh-eu)

haljivq alnei aol Why did he do these things? (A⌄ je⌄ g'eh-eu heu deu⌄ jahˇ-eu⌄ nga.)

haljivq alnei ngeel nil? Why? What is the reason? (26:80) (a⌄ je⌄ g'eh)

haljivq beeq ya never mind (ti⌄ je⌄-i⌄ ma⌄ ngeuˇ) (**Alciiv nal e haljivq beeq ya.** Never mind this small pain/suffering. 26:47)

haljivq e lulsuq diq alnei liq by whatever means (a⌄ je⌄ ya jiˇ law k'aw^)

haljivq jivq whatever (13:46, 35:75) (a⌄ je⌄ law k'aw^)

haljivq liq 1. whatever (11:103), 2. anything

haljivq loq 'what was that?' (as when you do not understand what someone says to you), 'pardon me, what did you say?' (a⌄ je⌄ lehˇ)

haljivq (vb) movq what do you want to (vb)? (**Nol haljivq aol movq ya leil aol.** Do whatever you want to do. 11:104) (a⌄ je⌄ geu^ maw^ nya) (8:27)

haljivq nei with what? (to do something with an object, as a pen, chopstick, knife) (a⌄ je⌄ neh)

haljivq neivqhaq hhellavq 'what devil of business...' (said in anger)

haljul (see: **havjul**)

halkal (see: **havkal**)

hal kol qivq nei as soon as; as quickly as

hallal small lion in ancient legends; a mythical small animal

hal leiq leiq to chase or hunt for a long time (11:217)

hallyul dust (9:60, 13:13) (k'a⌄ lehˇ)

hallyul meevnei to raise a cloud of dust (46:148) (k'a⌄ lehˇ la^ po⌄-eu)

hallyul puq ya for dust to accumulate (**hallyul daov puq ya** = much dust has accumulated) (k'a⌄ lehˇ ui⌄ leˇ ta⌄-eu)

halmeel meeq nga just so-so (not good, not bad)

halmeeq hal aol appoint people by their merits (50:143)

halmeeq maq gal not bad; not so bad (41:212)

halmeevq almost; virtually (11:114) (mya⌄ mya⌄)

halmeil (vb) how (vb)? (**Soqmiav mol halmeil buvq?** How do you write this character? - 11:102, 178) (a⌄ jo^-ehˇ)

halmeil deivq ya how can we live? (13:21)

halmeil (vb) halmeil (vb) however you (vb) (**Halmeil buvq movq halmeil buvq.** Write however you want to write. 11:103) (a⌄ jo^ lo^-ehˇ k'aw^)

halmeil leil 1. how? what? (**Halmeil leil meeq?** What/which is good? 11:102. **Nol halmeil leil nga**

laq? How about you?) (9:60) (a˯ jo^-ehˇ), 2. what kind of ...? (**Aqyoq halmeil leil e col nga laq?** What kind of person is he? 11:102) (a˯ jo^-ehˇ g'eh-eu tsawˇ ha˯ la)

halmeil leil kul what is (it) called? (a˯ je˯ lehˇ kuˇ te)

halmeil liq certain; must; surely (9:60, 13:11) (a˯ jo^-ehˇ k'aw˰) (cf. Lahu: hk'a˯ hk'e ka˰)

halmeil nei why...? (**Algo halmeil nei maq lal?** Why hasn't the older brother come? 11:102) (a˯ je˯ miˇ neh)

halmeil (vb) ngaoq halmeil (vb) whatever (vb) I will (vb) (**halmeil eil ngaoq halmeil nalhaq** = whatever the leaders say I will do - 26:103) (a˯ je˯ ma˯ ka˯)

halmeil ngeel what happened? (13:14) (a˯ je˯ g'eh-a˯)

halmeil ngeel aqkeiq? how did this happen? (26:40)

halmeil ngeel e liq no matter what; at any cost (a˯ jo^ lo˰-ehˇ k'aw˰)

halmeil ssol nei why? (**Nol halmeil ssol nei Dafjyul gee li ya?** Why did you join the army? - 26:15) (a˯ je˯ miˇ neh; a˯ je˯ g'eh-eu)

halmeil wul leil how about...? (14:207)

halmeil ya laq? what do you (vb) (as think?) (a˯ jo^-ehˇ (vb))

hal miaq e at the most (k'aˇ mya˯-eu)

halmiaq nei many; much (**Alsiq halmiaq nei siq.** It bore much fruit. **Col halmiaq nei jol.** = There are many people. **Wulquvq halmiaq nei daoq.** There is plenty of water. 9:60, 11:41) (g'aw˯ mya ni)

halmiaq nei meeq zeiq how much better it is (26:74) (aˇ na^ ni mui˯ dzeh˯-eu)

halmiav (clf) how many (clf)? how much (clf)? (**Ssaqguq halmiav hhaq jol?** How many children are there?) (9:60, 11:99, 103) (aˇ mya^ g'a˯)

halmiav miav just how many times? (11:103) (aˇ mya^ po^)

halmiav nei how many? (aˇ mya^ ni)

halmiav nei goq how high?

halmiav nei mol how far? (as a road) (aˇ mah ni mahˇ-eu)

halmiav nei tul how thick?

hal molzeiq the longest (farthest away)

halmo nei how long is it? (asking about length of an object) (aˇ mah ni mahˇ-a)

hal nao liq every day ('whatever day') (11:200, 26:2) (a˯ geu nah ma˯ ka˯)

hal naoq zeiq e at least (or) **hal maq miaq e liq**

halnil slander (ehˇ doeˇ-eu)

halnil nil to slander (or) **halnil pieiq** (yeh˯ baw˯-ehˇ ehˇ-eu)

halnil nilcuvq to slander someone; make slanderous remarks (ehˇ doeˇ-eu)

halnil pieiq (see: **halnil nil**)
hal niq hhaq which two people (11:99) (aˬ geu nyiˬ g'aˬ)
hal nyuq duv qivq e lulsul by all means
hal nyuq hal eil speak without inhibition; speak out freely (50:22)
halnyuq nyuq, haldul dul to think alike (11:222)
-- hal, ngaoq -- to pour out; to throw out
hal ngeel every; any; all
hal ngeel aqmeil maq gee zaq na not many people are willing to do the job
hal ngeel meil to be as one pleases (46:131) (k'aˇ mawˆ-eu loˆ-ehˇ
halngeel aqmeil everywhere want to (vb) (**halngeel aqmeil alciivq maq gee haoq** = not proper to repeat one's genealogy everywhere one pleases)
hal pov to yawn (aˇ haˬ heuˇ-eu)
hal puq nei whenever meet up with (12:128) (aˬ myah mawˇ law k'awˆ)
-- halpyul, neivqssaq -- a beetle
hal pyu which direction? (13:19) (aˬ geu paw)
hal pyu baq which side? (9:60) (aˬ geu paw)
hal pyu liq sso every aspect (as to discuss every aspect, or 'every direction' of something (50:115)
hal pyu pyul go to which side? (aˬ geu paw iˇ-eu)
hal qa which kind? (aˬ geu jeˬ)
hal qa aol heiq all the jobs (50:58)
hal qa hal qa many kinds ('which kind of which kind' - 30:1) (g'awˬ mya jeˬ)
hal qiq hhaq which person? (11:99)
halsiil what type of ... (**Halsiil miqnieq aol zaq?** = What kind of work do you do?) (Aˬ jeˬ gaˇ mˇ te.)
halsol coriander (9:60); **halsol solssaq** (yaˇ sawˇ)
halsol solma celery (9:60)
hal soq liq every morning (13:19) (yawˬ shawˬ na luˆ)
hal ssaq which one (of the small things, as little pigs) (**Hal ssaq aol movq laq?** Which little one do you want to buy? 41:134)
hal taq when? (**Nol hal taq hhuvq lal?** When will you come back? (26:23) (aˬ myah) (cf. Lahu: hk'aˬ htaˆ)
hal taq (vb) hal taq (vb) whenever (vb); at that time (**Nol hal taq meivq ngaoq, hal taq zaq.** Eat whenever you are hungry. 11:104) (aˬ myah maˬ kaˬ)
hal taq liq always (aˬ myah luˆ) (10:pref.) (cf. Lahu: hk'aˬ htaˇ kaˆ)
hal taq luldu when? what time? (**ssaq hal taq luldu bo** = what time to have a baby - 15:5) (aˬ myah)
haltyuq halnil talk nonsense and hurt others; to slander; to libel
hal yavq 1. each night, 2. which night (9:60) (aˬ geu miˇ maˬ kaˬ)
hal za e most suitable (15:3)

hal za hal'aol aol to do whatever is needed (50:108)
hal zaol movq at will; do what one wants to

ha hen
=ha, aq= chicken
habaol chicken thigh (used for divining) (46:116) (ya yoe⌄)
habaol baoldaq daq to divine with a chicken thigh
habaol diq to divine with chicken thigh (or) **habaol diq ceil; habaol hu** (ya yoe⌄ ka haw-eu)
habaol hu (see: **habaol diq**)
hacavq peev the custom of killing a chicken and roasting it outside the door (46:209)
haciv the chicken plucking ancestral offering (part of **Kuqzaq zaq** offering)
haciv civ the tradition of plucking chicken feathers (while chicken is alive)
hacovq hen which grows rapidly and lays eggs quickly after a brood of chickens has grown up
hadavq spur of a rooster (9:59) (ya ci^ da‸)
hadaol chicken wing (ya ci^ a⌄ dahˇ) (9:59)
hadol bad-omen hen (in sense that a bad omen is connected to it)
hadul chicken thigh (baw duˇ)
haduq chicken head
haduq dev to cut off a chicken's head
hageel chicken nest (ya ci^ ya guiˇ) (9:59)
-- **hageel, aqha** -- hen nest
hahal hen which tries to lay eggs; a young hen
-- **hahal, aqha** -- young hen
hahav a chicken basket (for live chickens) (9:59, 11:25) (ya ci^ k'a^ pah⌄)
hahao chicken feather (small, soft) (9:59) (ya ci^ ca‸ hm)
hahao civ to pluck a chicken; dress a chicken
ha huvq chicken year (9:59) (za ti⌄ k'o‸)
hakeel chicken foot (46:115)
hakuv chicken house; chicken shed (ya ci^ ya ku^) (9:59)
hama hen (9:60) (ya ci^ ya ma)
hama lolnil red-necked snake (must never allow it to coil over the door of one's house)
hanal 1. chicken disease (ya ci^ naˇ gawˇ), 2. a sick chicken
ha nao chicken day (9:60) (za ti⌄ nah)
hanil nilbu to lodge a false complaint against someone (50:180)
haniq jungle fowl; jungle chicken (9:61) (ya nyi⌄)
haniq niq to be timid; shy (naˇ k'ahˇ nah⌄-eu)
haniq niqma jungle hen (ya nyi⌄ ya ma)
haniq niqpyul jungle rooster (ya nyi⌄ ya poeˇ)
haniaol chicken feather (large; stiff) (9:60) (ya ci^ a⌄ dahˇ)
-- **haniaol, aqha** -- a chicken feather
hapyul rooster; cock (9:63, 41:137) (ya poeˇ)

hapyul pyulbiavq biavqma a large spotted cock (11:36)

ha'qiq wildcat (9:64) (or) **alhaol** (aˇ hahˇ)

haseil chicken louse (ya ci^ ya shehˇ)

hasovq capon (9:66) (ya ci^ ya shaw˄)

hasovq sovq to castrate a cock (11:160) (ya ci^ ya shaw˄ shaw˄-eu)

hawuv chicken egg (9:66), **hawuv qiq siq** (ya u^)

hawuv wuv eggs to hatch (ya ci^ ya za˅ ceu˄-eu)

hawuv xa a hen to lay an egg (ya u^ ka-eu)

haxiq wuqseil a type of bush (in the great tree legend, at first the Hani and others could not cut down the tree, but by rubbing the leaves of this bush on a wooden machete they could cut the tree down)

hazal chicken food (ya ci^ dzaˇ) (9:66)

ha zeq chicken hour (B=Chi)

haq 1. bitter (yaw k'a˅), 2. very salty (sa˅ deu˄ yaw ta^) (9:63) (cf. Lahu: a¯ leh^ hk'aˇ ve)

haq bad odor of one who has passed wind (taboo) (or) **haqbuvq** (taboo)

haq clf. for one time (9:63) (po^, la˄, etc.)

haq'al Yeah! (as when one replies to someone calling from a long distance. A little like "I am here.") (13:43) (a˅ je˅ lehˇ)

haqbaoq dry bamboo

haqbaoq a derisive term about a person (one who often passes gas/wind)

=haq, beeq= freckle

haq beivqlavq to smell the bad odor of one who has passed gas/wind

haqbol bamboo (9:63) (ma sa˅; za˄ bawˇ)

haqbol baoqlo bamboo tube for water to run in (or) **haqbol eelloq**

-- haqbol, beilcaoq -- wild bamboo

haqbol bolcaoq a bamboo forest (14:213) (ma sa˅ yaˇ; za˄ bawˇ yaˇ)

haqbol bolssaq type of small bamboo (13:38)

haqbol boqlo bamboo container (za˄ bawˇ k'aw˅ tsui˄ = bamboo section)

haqbol daol thicket of bamboo (or) **haqbol dei; haqbol haqcaoq**

haqbol daoqciivq bamboo (14:178) (ma sa˅; za˄ bawˇ)

haqbol dei thicket of bamboo (or) **haqbol haqcaoq**

haqbol eelloq a bamboo tube for water to run in; **haqbol baoqlo**

haqbol haqcaoq thicket of bamboo (or) **haqbol daol; haqbol dei**

haqbol haqdyuv bamboo shoots

haqbol kaoldaol a bamboo fence (or) **haqbol laolkaol; kaoldaol**

haqbyuq insects that infest bamboo (9:63) (aˇ boe˅ aˇ mawˇ)

-- haq, caqdevq -- to be too salty

haqcaoq bamboo cluster (9:63) (za‸ bawˇ bawˬ)
-- haqcaoq, haqbol -- a thicket of bamboo
haqcil bamboo slat (za‸ dzaw^)
haqcil zeiv to make bamboo slats (za‸ dzaw^ diˬ-eu)
=haq, ciq= dew
haqciivq bamboo joint (tsui‸)
haqciivq daoqdel a bamboo bowl
Haqdal the temporary name given to every girl at birth, so that the spirits will not name her and take her away (see: **neivqhaq miaol zaq lal**) (or) **Haqdal aqma**
haqdal 1. asparagus, 2. Chinese alpine rush or grass (9:63, 12:126)
haqdal dalma a type of fern (46:117)
haqdal dalpiaq bracken fern (daˇ pya^; daˇ leh^)
haqdyuv a bamboo shoot (9:63) (aˇ bye‸)
haqdyuv dyuv a bamboo shoot to come out (9:63, 11:41) (aˇ bye‸ bye‸-eu)
haqguq fine bamboo strips (**haqmuv**) (aˇ neˬ)
haqguq alzil a parrot
haqguq sseilnaovq shoes made of fine bamboo strips (ma saˬ sehˬ naw^)
haqhaq bitter bamboo (aˇ k'aˬ)
haqhaq 'ha ha' (the sound of laughing) (11:21)
(vb) haqhaq continuous (vb) (**zaq haqhaq** = eating) (... lu‸)
haqhov bamboo tiles
=haq, hu= ferret badger
haqhhal seil to dance & play games (9:64, 46:91, 111, 137) (niˇ g'a-eu)
haqhhal seilduq a stage for presenting drama, music, etc.
=haq, hhaq= bitter buckwheat
haqhheq charcoal (k'aˬ g'euˬ)
haqhheq liqtaf for charcoal to be burning (B=Chi) (k'aˬ g'euˬ pahˬ-eu)
Haqhholssaq Yi; Lolo (or) **Laqhholssaq** (11:30, 41:4)
=haq, hhoq= bitter vegetables
haqjal naqboq sparrow; munia (brd) (6:166) (or) **haqzal naqboq** (k'aˬ jaˇ)
-- haq, ja -- bitter grass/herbs
haqjaf winter holidays (Chi) (50:69)
haqjil 1. a husband, 2. a man (k'aˬ dzeˇ zaˬ)
haqjil aqda human males (11:198) (female; **haqmiq ssaqnaol**) (-paˬ, yo..., li)
haqjil aqda dassaq a young boy (13:43) (aˬ li zaˬ)
haqjil aqda yolqoq the best man at a wedding
haqjilssaq 1. a husband, 2. a man (11:30) (k'aˬ dzeˇ zaˬ)
haqju ju to snow (9:64)
haqju xa huvqhhaq hav a timely snow promises a good harvest (50:144)
haqkaol aviation (Chi) (50:70)
haqlaq tiger (clf. **mol**; **laq**) (11:34) (k'aˬ laˬ)

haqlaq huvq tiger year (k'a˯ la˯ ti˯ k'o˰) (9:64)
haqlaq nao tiger day (11:32) (k'a˯ la˯ ti˯ nah)
haqlaq zeq tiger hour (k'a˯ la˯ ti˯ la˰)
haqleil fine ashes and dust (9:64) (k'a˯ lehˇ)
-- **haqleil, zeiqkeeq** -- dried compost; dust from manure
haqlo bamboo joints (2:50) (za˰ bawˇ aˇ tsui˰)
haqluq culm sheath (parchment-like sheath at the bottom of bamboo joints) (9:64) (za˰ lo˯)
haqluv a stone (9:64) (k'a˯ lo)
haqluv cil petroleum (or) **haqluv cilmal** (36:18)
haqluv hhaqsaol a rock (k'a˯ lo)
haqluv hhaqzeil a boulder (9:64); rock cliff (12:125) (lo guˇ)
haqluv luvbaoq a rock cave (14:130) (k'a˯ lo boe)
haqluv luvbiav a flat stone (46:130) (k'a˯ lo bya˯)
haqluv luvdaol rocky area (9:64) (k'a˯ lo lo yaˇ)
haqluv luvgaoq a stone pile (9:64) (k'a˯ lo bymˇ)
haqluv luvjeivq small stones (13:5) (k'a˯ lo za˯)
haqluv luvma a huge stone (9:64) (k'a˯ lo lo ma)
haqluv qiq teil e galma a stone's throw away
haqmiq wife (za˯ mi˯; mi˯ za˯)
haqmiq haqjil wife and husband (mi˯ za˯ yo za˯; a˯ nya˰ dzeˇ za˯; mi˯ sawˇ yo za˯)
haqmiq ssaqnaol a woman; women (9:64, 10:24, 11:30, 46:112, 171) (za˯ mi˯ za˯)
haqmuv fine bamboo strips (use to make shoes)
=haq, nal= 1. to ask; question; interrogate, 2. to listen, 3. to obey
haqnav soot (9:64) (k'eh˯ na^)
haqnav aqma a crow (brd) (9:65, 46:118) (aw˰-a˰)
haqnil frost (or) **haqnieil** (9:65) (ngehˇ)
haqnil nildev piece of ice
haqnil nilngaoq ice (9:65)
haqnil nilngaoq ngaoq ice to form (9:65)
haqnil ya for frost to form (33:3) (ngehˇ ga-eu)
Haqniq Hani (people) (9:65) (Haˇ ni˯ tsawˇ ha˯)
Haqniq aqciq Hani soybean condiment
Haqniq ba'la Hani calendar (50:122)
Haqniqcuq the Hani people (B=Chi) (Haˇ ni˯ tsawˇ ha˯)
Haqniqdoq Hani language (9:65) (Haˇ ni˯ daw˯)
Haqniq e Goqzoqssaq the Guozhuo branch of the Hani nation (35:43)
Haqniq haoqdil Hani emperor (35:53)
Haqniq lalbaq Hani songs (11:37) (Haˇ ni˯ caˇ daw˯)
Haqniq liqhhaol Hani culture; Hani customs (Haˇ ni˯ zahˇ)
Haqniq loqzoq a Hani dance
Haqniq niqhhal a Hani dance
Haqniq pyuq e aqhhyu the Hani people honor their maternal uncles
Haqniq soqbuvq galkov Hani orthography (Haˇ ni˯ sah˯ bo˰)
Haqniq soqhhaq 1. Hani books, 2. Hani orthography

or script (Haˇ niˬ sahˬ bo˰)

Haqniq soqmiav Hani orthography; script

Haqniqssaq Hani people (Haˇ niˬ zaˬ)

Haqniq yo'liq Hani way; custom (**Haqniq galma**)

Haqniq yoqcol Hani friend; fellow Hani

=haq, neivq= bad type of spirit

haqnil (see: **halnieil**)

=haq, niul= blue sky

haqpal cloth (9:65) (saˬ paˇ)

haqpal palbuvq patterned cloth (9:65)

haqpal palhav hand-woven fine cloth (woven by Hani)

haqpal palkal gauze (or) **salbuf** (Chi)

haqpal palpiul a white cloth (paˇ pyuˇ)

haqpal palsiil yellow cloth (saˬ paˇ paˇ shuiˇ)

haqpal seivqnaov cloth shoes (put on a corpse before burial) (or) **haqpal seiqnaov**

haqpal xa to dye cloth (saˬ paˇ na^-eu; saˬ paˇ ka-eu)

haqpal xaduq a place to dye cloth (saˬ paˇ na^ duˬ)

haqpaq frog (k'aˬ paˬ)

-- haqpaq, alhhe -- loud sounding type of frog

haqpaq qiq coq e galma a frog's hop (away)

haqpav large bamboo strips (46:130)

haqpavq bamboo leaves (9:65) (za˰ bawˇ aˇ pa˰)

haqpeeq inner husks from rice (paddy) (9:65) (k'aˬ puiˬ)

haqpeeq peeqcil the softest type of rice bran

haqpeeq peeqhav outer husks from rice (paddy) (9:65) (k'aˬ puiˬ puiˬ k'a^)

haqpeeq peeqnaoq soft rice bran

haqpeeq peeqnil brown powder from rice bran (k'aˬ puiˬ puiˬ nm^)

haq pieiq to pass wind/gas; have flatulence (5:117) (uˬ k'aˬ pyehˬ-eu) (taboo)

haqpyul a bamboo raft

haqpyulloq bamboo raft (9:65) (poeˇ = raft)

haqqul sweet bamboo (9:65) (aˇ bye˰ coeˇ)

haqqul haqdyuv sweet bamboo shoots

haqsav bamboo (za˰ bawˇ; ma saˬ)

haqseil garlic (9:66, 41:138) (sehˇ puˇ)

-- haqseil, milcaq -- wild garlic

haqsiil golden bamboo (za˰ shuiˇ)

haqsiil dalqei golden bamboo 'nails' (slivers of golden bamboo which are used as nails in a coffin so as not to have metal in it)

haqssiiq leopard; panther (k'aˬ zuiˬ)

haqssiiq haqlaq leopards and tigers (k'aˬ zuiˬ k'aˬ laˬ)

haqssiiq hhadaoq a tiger trap made of wood and vines

haqssiiq nei bi kovq 'may you be killed by a leopard' (a curse)

haqssiiq ssiiqbuvq silver leopard

haqssiiq ssiiqcil leopard; panther (k'aˬ zuiˬ)

haqtaqbaoq not to be satisfied (57:103); **neema maq**

lal **meil** (pf.)
haqteivq nei very bitter (12:126) (k'a˯ ga˅ neh-a˯)
haqteivq pa teivq nei very, very bitter (k'a˯ jaw˰ ni)
haqtieil feiljil a space shuttle (Chi) (50:70)
=haq, wul= intestines
haqyeil dhole (a type of wild dog) (k'a˯ yeh˅)
=haq, yeiqnao nao= just today
haqyiq here, please! (as when you stretch out your hand and ask someone to give you something) (13:31)
-- haq, yiuvqnyuq maq -- don't oversleep; without oversleeping
haqzal sparrow (9:66, 11:30) (ja˅ tseu^)
haqzal naqboq sparrow-like bird (or) **haqjal naqboq**
haqzeil hawk; eagle (k'a˯ dze˅)
haqzeil davxov a ladder (daw˯ dzm)
-- haqzeil, soqhhaq -- kite
haqzeil zeilbuq buqma osprey (k'a˯ dze˅ bu)
haqzeil zeilpia small kind of eagle (k'a˯ dze˅ pyaw^)
haqzeil zeilpiul a white eagle (4:38) (k'a˯ dze˅ pyu˅)

hav to be hard (k'a^-eu)
hav one who flirts; engages in coquetry (both male and female) (taboo) (see also: **aqbeivq hav; aqqoq hav** -- all taboo)
hav clf. for basket (**bavqhav**) (11:80)
-- hav, aqbeivq -- for a female to be sexually stimulated (lubricated) (taboo)
=hav, aqdaol daol= hard feathers of bird wings
=hav, aqmeil meil= hard type of peanut
-- hav, aqqoq -- for a male to have a sexual erection (taboo)
=hav, aoqcal cal= hot sunshine
-- hav, aoqhhaol -- dry
=hav, col= adult person
=hav, daol= dry field
-- hav, deivqhol -- life-force; vitality
hav diq force; violence (50:8)
=hav, ha= chicken basket
=hav, haqpeeq peeq= outer husks from rice (paddy)
=hav, haoq= ancient bowl; antique bowl
-- hav, haoqhav -- to be coarse
=hav, hoqceil ceil= partially cooked rice (hard)
=hav, hhaq= strength
havjul a kind of small basket (or) **haljul**
havkal a large basket (or) **bavqhav**
=hav, kaoq= trachea; windpipe
=hav, luv= a basket filled with stones used to prevent flooding
=hav, meil= hard walnut
-- havma, miaoq'aol -- strong; powerful man
=hav, miav= basket for carrying firewood
-- havmoq, saqhav -- old forest

=hav, neessil nee= extremely angry
hav niv a system of deep breathing exercises (50:134)
=hav, niaoq'aol niaol= just a moment ago
=hav, pial= one kind of thatch grass
-- havpuq, juldal -- chopstick basket
=hav, yal= new fields
=hav, yo= a cruel person
havyov nei chapping (as skin) (or) **coqbeivq coqseil**
=hav, yuq= a basket on which to put a hot pan
=hav, zil= a bird cage

havq broken (9:66) (k'eh‸-eu)
=havq, meiq= (see full)
=havq, nal= broken nose
=havq, seq= a broken tooth

hafweif to defend; guard; protect (Chi) (34:79) (lo‸-eu)
Haf'yi the Chinese language (Chi - Yunnan dialect)
Haf'yyu the Chinese language (Chi) (La‸ bui˯ daw˯)
Haf'yyu pilyil the Chinese language in Roman script (pin yin) (Chi) (32:3)

HAO

haol 1. to set a trap (for game) (k'mˇ-eu; tahˇ-eu), 2. to protect; to save a life (50:92); defend (26:56, 46:153) (see also: **baoweif** = Chi), 3. to serve (Chi) (26:106)
(vb) haol to help (vb) (**aol haol** = to help to do)
=haol, al= wild cat; jungle cat
-- haol, aol -- to help to do
haolbev bev to accompany on a plucked musical instrument (50:5)
haolcal to accompany (as when singing) (50:5)
haolcil a kind of small, white mushroom that grows in rotten wood (baw guˇ aˇ hmˇ)
haolcil qivlevq to hurt one's skin by rubbing
haolci mold (fungus growth) (9:61) (hmˇ tsi)
haolci ci for mold to develop (hmˇ tsi tsi-eu) (9:61, 11:41) (**haolciv civ** - 14:205 - not pf.)
haolcoq partner (as in dancing) (50:5)
haolcul a kind of tree (mix juice from this with buckwheat flour or with fresh pork when eating)
haol dal to rely on (g'oe-eu)
=haol, daq= catch hold of
haoldaol mountain (8:11, 9:61) (gaw˯ jaw˯; dahˇ ta^)
-- haoldaol, beilcao -- forest in mountains
haoldaol daolkuv cold mountain places (50:56)
haoldaol laqliv col mountain people (14:232)
haoldaol laolma forest (9:61) (bawˇ tsah˯)
haoldaol milcaq mountainous area (10:11)
haoldaol saqhav forest in mountain (13:38) (aˇ bawˇ sah˯ k'a^)
=haol, deiq= give special care (as to disabled

servicemen)

-- **haol, eil** -- speak in defense of; plead for; express support

haolgaoq a mountain ridge (8:11, 37, 9:61) (clf. - **gaoq; pyu** - 46:99) (gaw˯ jaw˯ dahˇ teˇ)

haolgaoq daoqdaoq foot of a mountain (gaw˯ jaw˯ daw˯ dah˯)

haolgaoq gaoqmiq 'tail' of a mountain

haolgaoq gaoqssaq hill; little mountain (11:35) (dahˇ ta^ gaw˯ jaw˯)

haolgaoq gaoqwuq the top of a mountain (gaw˯ jaw˯ u˯ du)

haolgaoq maq guv, laoma maq guv not afraid of mountains or oceans (26:112)

haolgaoq wuqduq a mountain ridge

haolhhyuq to guarantee; pledge (includes: **eil ceiv**) (50:7)

haol jil to protect all (45:53)

-- **haollaol, milhaoq** -- to defend public order

haol leev to save; protect; preserve (13:43, 46:92, 50:7) (what **Aqpyuq Miqyeil** does to Hani people)

-- **haol leev, aol zaq** -- management and administration

haol leev col a guardian (50:82)

haol leev mavqssaq a bodyguard (50:177)

haollul a kind of germ (2:50) (cf.: aˇ boe˯ aˇ mawˇ)

haollul straw mushroom (9:61)

haollul laqhyul a building in Yuanyang County for Hani people (mushroom shaped) (14:144)

haollul yaolma mushroom-like buildings (14:204)

haollu hail (frozen rain) (or) **haollu alsiq** (or) **hollu** (not pf.) (huˇ lo = taboo term in Akha) (9:61)

haollu alsiq (see: **haollu**)

haol luvq to defend; guard; protect (50:70)

haolma rattan (or) **cavni; qilguq** (aˇ nyo^)

haolma haolniq a rattan tie

haolma zaqngeeq rattan walking stick; cane

haol miq to help; protect (another) (46:121)

haol na to protect (as the ancestors protect us - 35:96)

haolneiq type of mushroom (9:61)

haolnil red mushroom (aˇ hmˇ neˇ) (9:61)

haolnil buvqciv Asian golden cat; Temmick's cat (Felis temnincki) (seu pa˯)

haolniq strips of rattan (aˇ nyo^ aˇ ne˯)

haolpuq gourd (9:62) (iˇ pu˯)

-- **haolpuq, miqzal** -- gourd used for carrying gun powder

haolpuq neecev a ladle made from a gourd

haolquv a mushroom coming up (young, small) (46:118)

=**haol, saq**= at the right moment

=**haol sil, naol**= to be satisfied

haolssiil post of a building (45:30) (k'awˇ zeuˇ)

haol taq laol insurance (50:7) ('don't worry')

haoltavq mountain; related to mountain (or) **haoltavq haolteil** (dahˇ ta^)

haoltavq haolteil mountain; related to mountain (45:45, 46:77, 50:146) (or) **haoltavq** (dahˇ ta^)

haoltavq koqyal mountain field (9:62) (dahˇ ta^ dahˇ yaˇ)

haolteil mountain slope (9:62, 12:125) (clf. = **teil** - 45:83) (ba˯ g'a)

-- **haolteil, milma** -- mountains

haolteil teilma high mountain (9:62) (gaw˯ jaw˯ goˇ)

haolteil teilma wuqduq high in the mountains; tops of mountains

haolteil teilssaq a small hill (45:58) (gaw˯ duˇ)

haoltov a bamboo noise maker (to scare away birds) (14:189)

=**haol, yaq**= bugle (Chi)

=**haol, yo**= public property

-- haol, zaol -- to help another

haolzeil side of the fireplace

hao feather (ca‸ hm)

hao 1. to be stuck onto something (ngeu˯ leˇ-eu), 2. to smear

haocavq body hair; facial hair (fine, soft) (ca‸ hm) (9:61)

-- **haocavq, aqkeel** -- leg hair

haocavq hhe to pull body hair

=**hao, civq**= goat hair

=**hao, ha**= chicken feathers (soft)

haohaf a good person (Chi) (**ssilxoq haohaf duv** = a hero appears - 26:61) (tsawˇ ha˯ yaw mui˯)

=**hao, hhavq**= pig bristle

hao laol to give consideration to (or) **hu leev** (50:208)

-- **hao'li, naolhao** -- the very last

hao'lyu horse bells (mah˯ jaˇ cuˇ)

=**hao, miav**= eyebrow; eyelash

-- **hao, nalmeil** -- nose hair

=**hao, naol**= afterwards

haonuv feather; fur (ca‸ hm)

haopiul white fur; white feather

=**hao pyu, naol**= behind; back side

haoq clf. for 1. bowl, bowl of rice, 2. Chinese money (jiao) (9:62) ten cents

haoq to be proper; suitable (... k'm˯)

haoq may; can (**eil haoq, maq eil haoq** = can you say that or not? - i.e., is it proper?) (...k'm)

haoq'aol a bear (9:62, 35:17) (k'a˯ hmˇ)

haoq'aol for women to do work with cotton

haoqbaoq hole (as in a tree) (8:20, 9:62) (**aoq ssol milcaq haoqbaoq hul'a deivq e colssaq** .. = the people who lived under the 'hole' in the sky and earth, i.e., all on earth 45:88) (maˇ byoe)

haoqbaoq baoq to be hollow (as in a tree)
-- haoqbaoq, milcaq -- all over the world
haoqbuf lifjiq nothing for oneself; thinks only of others (Chi) (26:10)
-- haoq, caoqlaol -- a fireplace
haoqceivq non-glutinous rice (haw˯ ceh˰)
haoqdaoq laol to defend border area (or) **haoqtaoq laol** (50:12)
haoqdaoq laol mavqssaq border troops (**haoqtaoq laol mavqssaq**) (50:12)
=haoq, dei= open country; open field
haoqdil emperor (Chi) (35:48) (see also: **haovqdil**)
haoqdil bavq zyuq to select an emporer (35:52)
haoqgav gav to be sad in one's heart (50:3)
haoqgoq tomato (or) **haoqgo haolgo alsiq; falqiq** (Chi); **xilhaoqsiif** (Chi) (maˇ k'eu ehˇ)
haoqgual tiaoqjiq macroscopic adjustment (as in economics or politics) (Chi) (34:38)
haoqgual tiaoqkaof macroscopic adjustment and control (Chi) (34:46)
haoqhav ancient bowl (9:62) (k'm˯ ma˯ yaw oeˇ)
haoqhav hav to be coarse
haoqhaol laolseiv purple (4:42)
Haoqhoq Honghe river (Red River); Honghe town (Chi) (9:62, 10:pref, 46:170)
Haoqhoq lolqol Honghe (Red River) delta (A=Chi)
Haoqhoqxeif Honghe (Red River) county (Chi) (9:62, 30:1)
Haoqhoqzel Honghe Prefecture (Chi) (9:62)
Haoqhoqzel miqcuq nieiljeso Honghe Prefecture Institute of Nationality Studies
=haoq, hhaq= valley
haoqhhaolpiul panda
haoqhhyu neesal confidence; faith (50:188)
Haoqjyul the Red army (Chi) (34:7, 50:72)
haoqkavq muddled; confused; not able to think clearly (33:3)
haoqkavq bilbiov sponge gourd (9:62)
=haoq, laq= seat of trousers
=haoq, lavqhhuv= armpit
haoq laol to worry (k'ah˯ lahˇ-eu)
Haoqlizil Young Pioneer ('Red scarf') (Chi) (26:111)
haoqma a big bowl (esp. for soup) (k'm˯ ma˯ ma˯ ma)
haoqmaq a small bowl (9:63, 11:34, 13:33) clf. **haoq** (k'm˯ ma˯)
-- haoqmaq, albol -- a wooden bowl
haoqmaq aqnieivq nieivq to empty one's glass (or) **dol saq**
haoqmaq ciq a wash bowl (13:33) (k'm˯ ma˯ tsi˯-eu; k'm˯ ma˯ jo^-eu)
haoqmaq havdov a bowl-shaped basket
haoqmaq moldel a big porcelain bowl; a pottery bowl; a jar (9:63)
=haoq, mil= country; place; region
haoqmi millimeter (Chi) (41:125)

=haoq, naq=   ear canal
-- **haoq, naqhaoq** --   to be noisy and disturb others
=haoq, nao=   (see full)
=haoq nei, nav=   blackish; darkish
Haoqniq   the Haoni branch of the Hani (or) **Alsaol**
haoqniaoq   glutinous rice (haw˯ nyaw˯)
  haoqniaoq niaoqbiav   glutinous rice cake (46:109) (haw˯ tah˯)
  haoqniaoq niaoqnav   purple glutinous (sticky) rice
  haoqniaoq niaoqnil   red glutinous (sticky) rice (46:179) (haw˯ nyaw˯ neˇ)
  haoqniaoq niaoqsiil   yellow-colored glutinous (sticky) rice (46:157) (haw˯ nyaw˯ haw˯ shuiˇ shuiˇ-eu)
-- **haoq, nyuq liq maq nyuq** --   not proper to think
haoq piul   a white porcelain bowl
haoqqiq   red flag (Chi) (34:7)
haoqquq caq   a game of guessing fingers at the table (while drinking) (A=Chi)
=haoq, savjil sav=   (see full)
haoqseil   1. fame; reputation, 2. to honor or glorify someone (50:65) (k'ah˯ sehˇ)
  haoqseil puv huvq   to rehabilitate a person's reputation
-- **haoq, seil** --   play according to the rules
haoqsuv nei   darkness (50:2)
haoqsuvq suvq   to be unhappy; worried (noe˯ suˇ noe˯ li-eu)
haoqssaq laqma   quail (hah˯ za˯ la˯ ma; k'ah˯ za˯ la˯ ma)
haoqtaoq teil   to pound sticky rice to make cakes (haw˯ tah˯ tah˯-eu)

haovqdil   emporer (Chi) (11:30) (and see: **haoqdil**)
haovq zaq nia   to be good at boasting; cheating (35:48) (myaw˰ nya-eu)
-- **haoq, zaol** --   complimentary

haofneiq naoq   low consumption capacity (A=Chi) (50:70)
haofzaol   to call on someone to do something (Chi) (50:70)
haofzaof   to announce (as a meeting to be held) (Chi) (26:38) (tsa˰ ga˯-eu)
  haofzaof xassif   to answer the call (as the call of the party to do something) (Chi) (26:39)

HE

hel   to pray to ancestral god; to offer to
-- **hel, aqpyuq zal** --   to make an ancestral offering
-- **hel, ceil la galtaol aqpyuq** --   to celebrate the New Year ancestral offering
=hel, dal=   a stake
heldoq   words of worship; praise (35:42) (spoken

while making an offering); words of blessing (50:80)
heldoq soqbuvq funeral oration (50:80)
helgeel ancestral tablets (or) **baoqgeel**
-- **helgeel, aqpyuq** -- ancestral altar
hel haol daol to preprare a small bamboo table with food offerings on it to be used in religious ceremonies
helhaoq a religious offering or sacrifice (46:110) (lawˇ-eu)
helhaoq aol to make a religious offering or sacrifice (46:110)
helhaoq daol dav to make a religious offering or sacrifice (food, eggs, chickens, pigs, etc. 46:111)
-- **hel, heiqhel** -- (see full)
helliq a pole to mark a field (11:204) (yaˇ bya˰)
helliq diq (see: **helliq tavq**)
helliq tavq to put up a pole (to mark a field) (yaˇ bya˰ bya˰-eu)
-- **hel miq, heiqhel** -- 1. to give one joy, 2. to pronounce a blessing
helsiq cowrie shell (46:113) (they put one on each leg and head of a buffalo killed as part of the funeral ceremony) (huˇ si˯)
heltev tev to hiccup (iˇ tui^ tui^-eu)
helyal other (a˯ caw˯)
-- **hel, zalhel** -- offer food to the ancestors

he to smell (beh˰ la˰-eu)
he used in extensive noun phrases (**xil he nei** = this big; **yul he nei** = that big, etc.)
he to row; paddle (9:66) (heu-eu)
he to stir (as food) (heu-eu)
he to dredge up
he perhaps (**Xilmeil ngeelleil he**. Maybe like this.) (9:66) (pa˯)
=**he, baq**= odor of liquor (**zilbaq baqhe naol lal ya** = I get the odor of liquor)
he dav 1. to skim off, 2. to vomit out
-- **he, jalngeel** -- to dredge up from the water the insects called: **jalngeel**
hekal a sieve-like basket for catching fish
-- **he, kaoqhe** -- to snore
=**he, miq**= the smell of fire
he nei since; as; now that (k'oeˇ naˇ)
=**he nei heeq, hal**= how big?
=**he nei, neiq**= very big; large
=**he nei, sil**= the smell of urine
he'qivq a tingling sensation
he qivq to catch sight of; to see something (mawˇ-eu)
he zei to skim and throw away

-- **heq, bil** -- to divide; separate
heqjiv burning charcoal (35:111) (k'a˯ g'eu˯ pah˯-eu)

hev to understand (9:67) (si˯-eu) (also found in Akha proverbs, written as: k'eu^)
hev to arrive; reach (keu^-eu) (or) **hev nei**
-- **hev, aol** -- to realize
hevcav a string on a three-stringed musical instrument
-- **hev, heil** -- take to; get to (50:160)
-- **hev, huvqsiivq** -- to start the New Year
-- **hev, hhaolduv** -- the start of spring season
hev lal to take turns (**nol sso al** = it's your turn)
=**hev, laq**= stringed musical instrument
=**hev, leq**= Chinese style hat
hev nei to arrive at (or) **hev**
=**hev nei, za**= proper
hev nia able to understand (50:143)
-- **hev, nyuq** -- 1. to get the meaning; to understand, 2. to be conscious; aware
-- **hev, qiq savq** -- a long time (and see full)
hev zaq to overhear (26:95) (k'oe˯ ga˯)
hev zaq to hold a festival (46:174)
-- **hev zaq, huvq** -- to 'eat' (celebrate) the New Year

hevq to dig out from hole (as ear) with small thing (as finger) (9:67) (k'eu˰-eu)
=**hevq, naq**= an ear spoon
=**hevq nei, jil**= really; truly; sincerely
=**hevq nei, nul**= plump (as a child; a pig)
=**hevq nei, zil**= tightly
-- **hevq, ngaqlol** -- to dig out eels
-- **hevq, ngaqngal** -- to cure tonsilitis with salt
-- **hevq, seqkaq** -- to pick teeth

hefbifjyul reserve army (Chi) (50:72)
hefbu to be a candidate (Chi) (50:72)
hefgo the consequence (Chi) (34:96)

HEE

heeltev tev to belch; burp (9:66) (aˇ eu˰ eu˰-eu)

heeq big; large (9:66) (hui˯)
-- **heeq, galheeq** -- long distance; far away
heeq heeq nil nil big and small, young and old (34:3) (yaw hui˯ yaw za˯)
heeq lal 1. to get big (4:39); 2. to increase (hui˯ laˇ-eu)
heeq lal mol lal to grow up, big and tall (said of infants) (15:17) (hui˯ laˇ mahˇ laˇ-eu)
heeq luvq for people to mature
heeqma molma the great; the mighty (50:176)
-- **heeq, miqqil** -- very famous; great fame (A=Chi)
-- **heeq miaq, eil** -- to exaggerate
=**heeq nei, gal**= from a distance
heeq nil size (50:66)

heeq nil maq dei not the same size (ti⌄ kaw^ hui ma⌄ ngeuˇ)

-- **heeq, pieiq** -- to enlarge; to increase

-- **heeq, qu** -- (see full)

Heeqsal a boy's name (54:114)

heeqsa nei to be far away (g'aw⌄ mahˇ ni ka⌄-eu)

=**heeq pyu, gal**= a long distance

Heeqsal a boy's name (54:114)

=**heeq, ssaq**= first (oldest) son

heeqssaq meiqma wives of brother

heeqzaq a bully (50:133)

-- **heeq, zaqhaoq** -- (see full)

heeqzaq laqmeil to be proud of oneself

HEI

heil to take away (9:66) (k'ehˇ-eu)

heil to send (person) (or) **miaoqheil heil** (k'ehˇ-eu)

heil to pick up (g'o^-eu)

(vb) heil idea of transition in space and time (**bavq heil** = to take away, **biaol duv heil** = to fly out 13:46, 45:6, 52) (... g'eh-eu)

heil aoq order to sell (50:126)

heilceq 'ahchoo' (the sound of sneezing) (11:21) (or) **halceq** (aˇ ceu⌄-i⌄)

heilceq ceq to sneeze (or) **halceq ceq** (haˇ ceu⌄ ceu⌄-eu)

heilcil castor oil plant (9:67)

heil dav bring up to (as money, etc.) (26:77) (yuˇ da^ la^-eu)

heilduq hatred (A=Chi) (bye-eu)

heilduq jav for there to be hatred (A=Chi)

heil hev to take to; get to (50:160)

heil huvq to give back (or) **bivq huvq** (bi^ k'o^-eu)

=**heil, hhaq**= a servant

-- **heil, miaoqheil** -- 1. to send on an errand (or) **moqheil heil**, 2. to order someone to do something

-- **heilneiq col, soqhhaq** -- postman; mailman

heil niv to mobilize; to arouse (50:39)

heil paoq to put together (9:67) (ti⌄ gaˇ yuˇ ui⌄-eu; la^ ui⌄-eu)

heil qav to draw down (**wulquvq hholqei ya neevq heil qav taq** = he was pulled down into the water - 26:24) (g'eu ahˇ-eu)

-- **heil, xa** -- to fall into (& see **ya heil**)

-- **heil, ya** -- to fall into (& see **xa heil**)

heil zaq to order someone to do something; to command someone (26:7) (k'ehˇ-eu)

heigual 1. customs office (Chi) (50:69), 2. customs department regulations (Chi) (50:69)

heijyul navy (Chi) (69)

heimieiq nadul dul spongy-like (A=Chi) (or) **ovqdei nei; naoqzov nei**

heiseil sea slug (Chi)

heiq an exclamation; an interjection (especially showing disgust) (**Heiq! Ngaq e laqma heiq!** No way, here is my 'thumb' (**laqma ngaoq pyul** = to reach out one's thumb in a gesture of disgust) (**Heiq! Solmil aqbol nol!** Hey, you old fortune teller! (54:175)

heiq clf. for a word, or a mouthful of food or drink (9:67, 11:21)

heiq 'here' (as when handing something to someone) (9:67) (hehˬ)

heiqba a blackboard; a chalk board (used in school) (Chi) (41:64, 50:71) (bo˄-eu teˇ bya˄)

heiqba a type of tree

heiqba albol a nut tree with oval nuts

-- heiq, aolbei -- a breach; gap

heiqcaoq a bird trap made of bamboo strips (lawˬ)

heiqceiv sambar deer (9:67) (k'aˬ tseh^)

heiqceiv ceivnav wild goat; serow

heiqceiv ceivnil a red deer

heiqciq a type of chestnut tree (identified as 'chinquapin' in China) used for making poles (46:117); also used to make a post to which a sacrificial buffalo is tied (zhuili in Chi)

heiq dieifzaf a nuclear power station (Chi) (50:70)

=heiq, doq= subject matter; theme

-- heiqdoq, hoheiq -- preface; foreword

=heiq, eel= (see full)

=heiq, eil= wormwood

heiq'eil aqkeeq dhole; wolf; a wild dog (k'aˬ yehˇ)

heiq'eil daoqmiq the tail of a wild dog

=heiq, gal= 1. downside of village, 2. place outside the village where bad-omen animals are eaten

heiq hav to be disrespectful; impolite; use harsh words (**heiq hav nei eil e maq ngeel** = I do not say this disrespectuflly)

heiqhel hel to pray; to say some ritual words (35:60) (and see below)

heiqhel heldoq an offering prayer; words to accompany an offering (**lavqnieiq dovq e heiqhel heldoq** = words of prayer to be spoken at the beginning of a project (46:86-87, seven lines of four syllables each)

heiqhel hel miq 1. to give one joy (46:113:131) (laˬ k'aˬ la^ cehˇ-eu), 2. to pronounce a blessing

heiq heiq 'ha ha' (sound of laughter) (13:12, 45:32)

=heiq, hho= gate

heiq hhuvq to bend something to make it crooked (ngawˬ ngo˄-eu)

=heiq jacev, boq= black spots (as on face)

=heiq, laq= top of trousers

=heiq, laqbaoq baoq= cuff of sleeve; opening of sleeve

=heiq, laol= collar

=heiq, lol= river source
=heiq, miaoq= business; vocational work
heiqmoq twin (pf) (or) **ssaqzao; heiqmiaoq** (not pf) (9:148, 10:2, 35:72) (tsaw$^{\vee}$ caw$^{\wedge}$ = taboo word in Akha)
=heiq, moq= wooden shoes
=heiq, nal= a scar
heiqnyuq albol a birch-like tree with big leaves (9:67) (These are often planted near the 'hhaqma' tree. The Hani send this leaf, which signifies 'missing' the other person, along with a soy bean, which signifies 'with my whole heart' -- a play on words for 'soybean' and 'heart'.)
=heiq qeil, aol= enjoyable work
-- heiq, savqheiq -- to sigh
heiqsoq seqtevq a pair of 'divining sticks' (made of a plant cut in two, with one side round and one flat side, thrown by spirit priests to divine various things about spirits and souls)
  heiqsoq seqtevq pieiq to throw a pair of 'divining sticks'
heiqsov albol a thorn tree used in religious activities (they use this tree in making the wooden standard carried in front of the coffin for burial)
  heiqsov albol haqzeil a wooden standard carried on the right shoulder of the man who proceeds the coffin, with figures carved into it (from the top) a hawk, the sun, the moon, and some combs (he carries a white umbrella with his left hand)
=heiq, ssaq= a lover
-- heiqssaq, hhoheiq -- back (or side) door
heiqsso lolnil a red clam
heiqtuvq a type of tree (9:67)
heiq wu'qif a nuclear weapon (Chi) (50:70)

=heiq, yeil= marriage affairs
=heiq, yeiq= a mark left from sawing or cutting
-- heiq, yojil meeq -- actual effect; substantial results
-- heiq, yoqhhaq meeq -- private interests

heivq to break; cut; collect (includes cutting and collecting firewood) (9:67) (k'eh$_{\wedge}$-eu)
heivq ceiv to twist and break, as firewood (9:67, 11:18) (k'eh$_{\wedge}$ tseh^-eu)

HI

hiq ! interjection (esp. used when looking down on the person to whom it is said) (11:147)

HO

hol 1. to make a mistake (**eil hol** = to say something wrong) (35:53) (bah˯-eu), 2. to make someone angry

hol cei to take pity on (50:64) (**ssaqcyuq yaol hol hha cei miq nga** = we must take pity on the poor; **hol maq cei na** = not willing to pity someone) (g'aw˯ sha˯ ga˯-eu)

  hol cei **qaq** to take pity on someone (35:73) (g'aw˯ sha˯ ga˯-eu)

hollol to be greedy (eat fast & all you can)

-- **hollol, moq** -- pony bells; horse bells

hollu hail (frozen rain) (or) **hollu alsiq; zeiqkeeq alsiq; haollu** (pf.) (huˇ lo = a taboo word in Ak.)

hol**moq** a religious ceremony (46:161)

  hol**moq aol** to hold a religious ceremony (46:91)

=hol, oq= life of people (or) **wuqhol**

Holtol **Tavqzaoq** the village of Dazhai on the outskirts of Luchun town, the dialect spoken here was chosen as the dialect to be used in writing Hani (or) Oltol **Tavqzaoq**

holtol **tolbuvq** a kind of thorny plant

hoceil a train (Chi) (50:77); **hocei** (not pf.)

  hoceil **galma** train track (A=Chi) (or) **hocei galma**

  hoceil **piaof** train ticket

  hoceil**zaf** railway station (Chi) (50:77)

hocei a train (Chi) (26:34); **hoceil** (pf.)

  hocei **galma** train tracks (or) **hoceil galma**

-- **ho, diq** -- to knock (see full)

Hogal a person's name (11:157)

hoheiq **heiqdoq** a preface; a foreword (50:190)

=ho, **hhavq**= a female pig

-- **ho, hhoq tuv** -- to knock again

hojeif a rocket (Chi) (50:77)

ho'lo horse bell (11:17) (mah˯ jaˇ cuˇ)

hosiiqtuaq the staff in a messhall which prepares food for large numbers of people (Chi) (50:77)

hotyu ham (Chi) (14:235)

=ho, zeiv= to clamor

hoq cooked rice (9:74) (haw˯)

hoq to match; to pair off; to be all right

hoq 1. to spread out something (as mat) (9:74), 2. to pave a road (11:154) (k'aw˯-eu), 3. to live happily together (**colmavq hoq nia** = to live happily with the group - 38:34), 4. to cast; throw (bi˯-eu)

(vb) **hoq** to be correct; right; proper suitable; equal (Chi) (9:75, 10:17, 34:42) (**Xilmeil zaol e hoq maq hoq**? Is this the correct way to do it or not? 11:189) (tsa˯)

hoqbav box; case (9:75) (bah˯ keu^)

  hoqbav piqhov mirror (9:75) (pyaw˯ haw)

hoqbiav basin (9:75) (sehˇ byehˇ)

  -- **hoqbiav, miavciq** -- a wash basin

hoqbiol leiq zaq to roam around looking for meals, as a beggar (po^ dza˯-eu)

hoqbiol lol 1. to invite and give a meal to someone (35:18) (da˯ yah kuˇ-eu), 2. to feast the villagers as a part of the wedding ceremony
-- hoqbiol lol, aqhhyu -- to honor maternal uncles who come to attend a burial ceremony by serving them a meal (or) **aqhhyu lol**
hoqbioq tadpole (9:75) (a˯ byah˯)
hoqbioq aqma a tadpole (or) **aoqboq aqma** (a˯ byah˯ ma)
-- hoq, bo -- to blow over
hoqbyu roof beam (roof of house in 14:216) (nymˇ nyoeˇ)
-- hoqbyu, laqhyul -- a roof beam in a house
-- hoqbyu, yaol -- roof beam in a house
hoqceil partially cooked rice (9:75) (ja˄ zaw zaw-eu)
hoqceil ceilhav partially cooked rice (hard)
hoqceil ceilhav luqduq to partially cook rice so it is 'hard as a drum'
hoqceil hoqtuv a container of partially cooked rice (at the time a household member dies, they flatten the rice in this container so as to see in the morning how much the deceased member has taken)
hoqceiq ceiq to eat slowly and sparingly, savoring the food (as when food is good or there is not much of it) (haw˯ tseh˯ tseh˯-eu)
hoqceivq non-glutinous rice (haw˯ ceh˄)
hoqcuv 1. a fistful of cooked rice (haw˯ tsu^), 2. a hot rice dumpling (46:90)
hoqcuv hoqzoqsef the commune period in China, also called the 'big kitchen' period (B=Chi)
hoqdaq 1. mattress; mat (11:27) (paˇ si˯), 2. pad; cushion (9:75); 3. a sheet of cloth
-- hoq, deiq -- spread; lay
hoqgav cold rice (lunch, as when in field) (9:75) (haw˯ ga^)
hoqgav baoqtevq cold rice carrying container
hoqgeiq qualified (Chi) (34:80)
hoqhaoq diq hal to lose one's job for some failure (lit. 'to throw away one's rice bowl')
hoqhul a rice lump
hoqhual alyeiv lotus flower (A=Chi) (50:71)
hoqhyuq dove; pigeon (9:75) (k'a˯ gu˯, k'a˯ k'oe˯)
-- hoqhyuq, beilcaoq -- a wild pigeon
hoqhhyu aol to be reliable; trustworthy (54:157)
hoqhhyuq chewed up rice (as when feeding a baby)
hoqhhyuq hhyuq for humans to chew up food and then feed it to an infant; for birds to bring food to the mouths of their infants
hoqkuq spoon or ladle for dipping up rice (11:165), **hoqkuq yuqcavq; aqcavq** (haw˯ ku˯ luˇ ma˯)
hoqkyul a pyramid-shaped dumpling made of glutinous rice eaten during the Dragon Boat Festival
-- hoqkyul kyul zaq, ngavq la ngavq nao -- (see full)

hoqlaol one kind of bowl

hoqleivq hal 1. to ritually pour out a little cooked rice with soup, and then throw the bowl away, in order to prevent sickness, 2. to put out a bowl containing small portions from each of the ancestral offerings for the 'bad ancestors'

hoqleivq leivq to mix soup with rice to eat (haw˯ yoe yoe-eu)

-- **hoq li, maq** -- not to live peacefully

-- **hoqloq, hhavqzal** -- a pig trough

hoqlul fried rice (9:75) (haw˯ luˇ)

-- **hoqlul, alwuv** -- fried rice with egg

hoqma havdov a basket in the shape of a bowl (9:75)

hoqmaq bowl (10:30) (**haoqmaq** - pf.) (k'm˯ ma˯)

hoqmiao fully cooked rice (9:75) (sa˰ laˇ-eu˯ haw˯)

hoqneev rice grain (cooked) (9:75) (haw˯ aˇ nui^)

hoq nil red rice

hoqniaoq (see: **haoqniaoq**)

Hoqniaoq Alpal a person's name (38:35)

hoqniaoq niaoq biav flat glutinous (sticky) rice cake (or) **haoqniaoq niaoq biav** (haw˯ tah˯)

hoqniaoq niaoqbiav taoq to pound the glutinous (sticky) rice cakes (haw˯ tah˯ tah˯-eu)

hoqniaoq niaoqcuv glutinous rice dumpling (oe)

hoqniaoq niaoqnav purple glutinous rice (9:63)

hoqniaoq pavqtov eq rice offering given to relatives at a festival

hoqniaoq zabiav (see: **hoqniaoq niaoqbiav**)

hoq pavqtov tov to wrap up cooked rice (in a leaf) (haw˯ cu cu-eu)

hoqpiq rice steamer cover (9:76) (haw˯ pym˯)

hoqpiq peace (Chi) (**hoqpiq miqzu** = peaceful democracy - 34:8)

hoqpiq gaofcu peaceful coexistence (Chi) (34:83)

hoqpiq gofduf peaceful transition (Chi) (50:71)

-- **hoqpiq, siifgeif** -- world peace (Chi)

hoqpiq yeibieif peaceful evolution from socialism back to capitalism (Chi) (34:33)

hoqpiul uncooked husked rice (haw˯ pyuˇ)

hoq qavq to cook rice (food; meal) (haw˯ mˇ-eu)

hoqqavq eelcal the liquid present with boiled rice

hoqqavq qavqbieiv boiled rice porridge; rice gruel (haw˯ ca˰)

-- **hoq qiq gal, maq** -- where there are mistakes

hoqqiqse the flag carrier (as in the army) (Chi) (26:100) (or) **haoqqise** (paˇ lo˯ paˇ lehˇ ba˰-eu g'a˯)

hoqsav nei to spread out (50:50)

hoqsavq steamed rice (or) **savq laq e hoq**

hoqsavqduq cooking place ('rice steaming place') (9:76) (haw˯ sa˰ du˯)

hoqsavqyaol a kitchen ('rice cooking building')

hoqseiv nei 1. comfortable; pleasant (14:182) (yaw saˇ), 2. scattered around different places

(50:108)

hoqsiivq new rice (the first which is harvested) (9:76, 11:28, 46:205) (haw⌄ shui^)

hoqsiivq kalnaol pavq to tie heads of rice as a part of the harvest ceremony

hoqsiivq zaq to eat the new rice festival (10th of the annual ancestral offerings) (haw⌄ shui^ dza⌄)

=hoq, sol= (see full)

=hoq, soq= breakfast ('morning rice')

hoqssa a beggar (9:76, 13:2) (haw⌄ shaᵛ dza⌄-eu tsawᵛ ha⌄)

hoqssa sal la to beg for food (45:51) (haw⌄ shaᵛ shaᵛ-eu)

hoqssa sal zaq to beg for food (haw⌄ shaᵛ dza⌄-eu)

hoqtav the upstairs floor; the upstairs room (**hoqtav dav** li = to go upstairs)

hoqtavq 1. the mat above fireplace (to dry things), 2. the attic area in the house (9:76 - but in 45:64 it is: **hoqtav**) (haw⌄ ta^)

hoqtavq saqkuv dalsil a stick with which to hang meat up above the fireplace to dry

hoqtavq yav to sweep the floor (must not do it after the sun has gone down) (9:76) (k'aw⌄ ta^ ya^-eu)

hoqtaoq seqtevq a contract (A=Chi)

hoqtevq a lunch box

hoqtuv a wooden basin; a wooden water container (33:3)

-- **hoqtuv, hhavqzal** -- a pig trough

hoqyav yavpyul a small broom used to; 1. collect cooked rice into a container, 2. sweep cooked rice, 3. used in ceremonies for the ritual head to brush himself, thus 'cleansing' himself

hoqyiftiq collegiate bench of judges (Chi) (50:71)

hoqyol spoiled rice (haw⌄ yaw bu^)

hoqzal susi zaq to cook food at the time of the funeral to feed the family and guests who come

hoq zaq to eat a meal (rice) (haw⌄ dza⌄-eu)

hoq zaq qiq bial, eel dol qiq heiq a polite way of saying 'to have a meal' (including the drink) (12:126)

hoqzaol susi to cook (and prepare) rice (haw⌄ mᵛ-eu)

hoq zaol zaq to cook and eat rice (13:33) (haw⌄ mᵛ dza⌄-eu)

hoqzii a box (Chi) (bah⌄ keu^)

hoqzoq cooperation; association (Chi) (34:48)

hoqzoqseif a cooperative (Chi)

hoqzyuq dama elders and ancestors

=hov, al= skin; peel; outer layer (as of grain)

=hov, aqlavq lavq= cupped hand

=hov, bee= quilt covering

=hov, beivq= vulva (taboo)

hovcaoq cymbals (9:76) (cehᵛ lehᵛ)

=hov, keel= arch of foot

=hov, lavq= cupped hand
=hov, meel= roof tile
=hov, miav miav= eyelid
hov zavq equal to (**maq hov zavq** = not equal; not an equivalent amount) (ti˯ kaw^)

hovq shriveled and hollow (as grains) (ko^-iˇ-eu)
hovq 1. to fetch water, 2. to catch water in cupped hands (9:76) (k'aw˰-eu; iˇ cu˰ k'aw˰-eu)
hovq clf. for a pit; hole
=hovq, alniq niq= the inner part of a bamboo strip (not very useful)
=hovq, alwuv wuv= egg shell
hovqbiav a basin (41:33)
=hovq, baq= dimple
=hovq, ceil= empty rice husk
hovq cuv to set up a family
-- hovq dol, aol zaq -- to labor (lit., 'do work, fetch water')
hovqdoq daqxa maq nyuq work hard and not be upset by criticism (50:143)
=hovq, dovq= a lamp
-- hovq, duqhovq -- to dig a hole in the ground
hovqdyu a vulture (brd) (je˯ shiˇ k'a˯ dzeˇ)
=hovq, lol= water source, a well; village sacred water source
hovq lol soq to carry out a ceremonial offering to the village water source with a male duck, a cock and a hen, on the first tiger day in lunar Jan.
-- hovqma, puvlaol -- fellow villagers
hovqma ssaqmeeq all of the villagers (45:76, 46:93)
=hovq, meiv= wooden receptical for unhusked rice as a part of the rice pounder
=hovq, nee= chest (of body)
=hovq, neema nee= the sternum; pit of chest (sunken in part)
hovq sal happy family (11:207)
hovqteiq a single family living by itself
hovqtuv wooden pail (11:199)
=hovq, zii= bullet shell; shell case
hovqzyuq ancestors (or) **hovqzyuq dama** (11:202)
hovqzyuq dama ancestors (or) **hovqzyuq** (11:202) (a˯ poe˯ a˯ pi˯)

hofceil a truck (Chi) (50:77)
hofmiei'qeiq right of exemption (Chi) (50:77)

HU

hul clf. for piece of salt, clod of earth (**milcaq qiq hul**), etc. (11:75)
hul the sound of someone calling from far off (27:11) (or) **kul** (kuˇ-eu)
hul'a 1. underneath; below (as in space), 2. below (as in a number) (9:76, 10:pref) (**wulquvq hul'a** =

under water - 13:47) (la‸ o^)

hulbu cuckoo; hoopoe (brd) (9:76, 11:25, 46:155) (si si bo‸)

hulbuq the sound of a cuckoo bird (46:155)

hulcuv three stones used to hold up pots when cooking (9:77, 11:202)

huljil husband (9:76, 28:4); **haqjil** (18:24) (k'a⌄ dze˅ za⌄)

-- huljil, miqssaq -- wife and husband

huljil pyu nei ni lal to be related by marriage (on the male side)

=hul, keeq= a lump of manure

hulle nei spherical

=hul, puq= a lump of dirt; a clod of dirt

hultav 1. up above; on (**peilhaoq hultav milbieiv suq nga** = there is mud on the clothing) (k'oe˅ ta^; la‸ ta^), 2. over; more than (**Aqda aqma hultav moq zeiq.** Father is older than mother.) (na^ ma⌄ tse˅)

-- hultav, miqteil -- more than in the past

hultav pyu on the upper side (13:49) (k'oe˅ ta^ paw)

hu 1. to look; behold (haw), 2. to see (maw˅), 3. to read (gui-eu)

hu- indicates an animal in the rodent family

(vb) hu to try (vb) (**aol hu** = to try doing)

hubaq squirrel (9:76) (ho ca‸ ho ba⌄) (Hani shamans go to where they live while in a trance)

hubaq baqnil red-cheeked ground squirrel

hubiaol flying squirrel (ho byaw)

hucavq to be hostile (34:113) (ma⌄ gaw‸ le˅-eu)

hucavq a mouse; a rat (ho ca‸)

hucavq hubyu a mouse or rat hole (ho ca‸ byoe)

hucavq hubyu aqmeil navhaoq pa haoq nei dark as a rat's burrow

hu ceil to examine; to test (50:95)

hu ceiv in charge of (50:54)

hu cuv to stare at (or) **hu cuv** (26:51) (haw tso^-eu)

hu dav 1. to believe (14:190) (jah-eu), 2. to like; to favor (14:239) (maw‸ le˅-eu)

hu duv to see; to see and recognize; to see through (13:6; 41:88) (si⌄ la˅ maw˅ la˅-eu)

-- hu duv, daoqdaoq -- to check out the reason behind the matter ('get to the bottom of it')

hu duv zaq lal to discover ("see through") (maw˅ la˅-eu)

hu gaq pretty (nice to look at) (11:119) (haw mui⌄-eu)

-- hu, gee -- to try counting (and see full)

huhaq ferret badger (Helictic orientalis) (kui⌄ si^)

(vb) hu hu to try (vb) (**aolhu hu** = to try doing) **salhu** ((vb) haw-eu)

hu huvq rat year (ho ti⌄ k'o‸)

-- hu, hyuq -- to steal a look; a glance

hujil (see: **huljil, haqjil**) (41:2)

hu'laol squirrel
hu laovq to stare at something or someone (45:75) (haw tso^ ta᷇-eu)
hu leev 1. to take care of (45:64); 2. to show concern; give consideration (or) **hu meeq; hao laol**
hu loq to see clearly (13:14)
hu meeq to show concern (or) **hu leev**
-- **hu, miav** -- open one's eyes
hu mol to see ('look-see') (haw mawˇ-eu)
hu mol e col a witness ('one who saw')
-- **hu, mollu** -- to watch a movie
-- **hu, naol** -- to look behind
-- **hu, naolhu** -- to smell out (as a dog)
hu nao rat day (13:19) (ho ti᷇ nah)
hu nil to look down on (**taq hu nil** = don't look down on) (35:30, 46:88, 50:133) (haw te᷇-eu)
Hunil Hunav red stone and black stone (or) **luvnil luvnav**) (46:76)
-- **hu, nyuqhu** -- try to think over
-- **hu, nyuq** -- to think about; consider
hu pal review (**zolpuv** = to review what studied) (haw po^-eu; paˇ haw-eu)
hupiq bamboo gopher (9:77) (ho pi᷇)
hupieivq 1. a forked stick; 2. a pole in a field hut
hupiul porcupine (9:77) (ho puˇ)
hu puv pal to check again (50:54)
hu sal pretty; look nice (9:77) **hu zaq** (haw mui᷇-eu) (cf. Lahu: nyi sha ve)
-- **hu, silpyuq** -- pay one's respects to the remains of someone
-- **hu, sov** -- to try to find out
hussaq all kinds of rodents and rats
hu taq look after; keep watch (9:77) (haw ta᷇-eu)
hu taq zaq e col a watchman (13:13) (lo‸-awˇ haw-eu)
hu teiq to supervise and urge (50:40); superintend; control (50:82); **hu cuv** (haw tso‸-eu)
hu zaq beautiful (or) **hu sal** (haw mui᷇; yaw ja᷇)
hu zaq 1. interesting (**Milqivq e dieifssi tuvqqil hu zaq**. Last night's movie was very interesting.), 2. to come and meet (50:87); **mol**
-- **hu, zaq** -- to taste ('try eating')
hu zaq lov free to look; to watch (as TV, movie)
-- **hu, zaol** -- 1. to demonstrate ('try doing'); 2. to punish
-- **hu, zaolhu** -- to attempt doing something; to explore
hu zeq rat hour (ho ti᷇ la‸)
=hu, zei= (see full)
huzil to take a risk; a chance (13:6)
huzyuq raja rat (Rattus surifer)

huq, huq the sound of blowing wind (26:31)
=huq, aq= father's younger sister
huq aq miqteil the very first (11:203) (aˇ dah᷇ beh-eu)

huq bi gee col an agent (50:31)
huqbu aqma (see: **huqbu miavlavq**)
huqbu miavlavq owl (9:77) (or) **huqbu aqma** (35:78) (haw˯ bu ma)
-- **huqbyu daoqma, yaol** -- a ridgepole in a house
huq caqheq to try a case in advance
huqceiq sister-in-law (a˯ tsu)
huq ciq first time to wash (46:178)
huqcuv naolcavq nei one after another (35:52) (ti˯ hm˯ meh˯ nah ti˯ hm˯; ti˯ je˯ saˇ-iˇ ti˯ je˯)
huq eilgaq to announce in advance (50:201)
huqhyufza **deputy director of the Old Folks Association in the village (Chi)**
huqnao day before yesterday (9:77) (hu˯ nah)
huqnaohu the day before the day before yesterday, i.e. three days ago (hu˯ nah hu)
-- **huqnao, milnao** -- a few days ago
huqnaohuvq year before last (9:77) (hu˯ nui k'o˰)
huqqivq night before last (9:77) (hu˯ ci˰)
huqsal sal to receive a heritage (as from ancestors) (11:202) (je˯ biˇ za-eu)
huq sol hu a budget (50:201)
huqsoq morning before last (9:77)
huqteil 1. ahead of (space, time); in front of; before (2:51), 2. to (vb) ahead, to (vb) first (9:77) (je˯ hu)
huqteil bi teil to have priority; preponderance (50:199)
huqteil kaqceiv the first trial; the preliminary judgment (50:201)
huqteil pyuq doq a preface (50:135)
huqteil qiq hhaq taq teil, naolhao qiq hhaq taq naoq no one go early, no one come late (i.e., all go and come together, a set phrase) (45:22)
huqteil teil 1. to go ahead so as to lead someone (hu˯ teˇ sheu˯ g'eh-eu), 2. the first one (50:35) (or) **difyiq** (Chi) (meh˯ hu˯ hu˯-eu)
huqteil teilli the very first; the earliest (9:77)
huqteil tyul taq at the very first (29:4)
huqxal each other (Chi) (ti˯ g'a˯ tiˇ g'a˯)
huqzu zaq to cooperate as a group
huqzuzu a cooperative group (Chi)

huv to wear; put on (9:77) (k'o^-eu; dm-eu; geu˰-eu)
-- **huv, beelkaq** -- to hold up an umbrella
-- **huv, wuqhuv** -- for a female to wear a turban

huvq to return; come back (9:78) (g'o˰-eu)
huvq 1. year, 2. age (k'o˰, aˇ k'o˰)
huvq clf. for a dish (**hhaoqcyuq qiq huvq**) (k'm˯)
huvq to divorce (man to send wife away) (50:104) (or) **huvqzavq** (mi˯ za˯ k'o˰-eu)
(vb) huvq, (vb) puv repeat (vb) (**eilhuvq, eilpuv** = say again)

=**huvq, al**= age; year

-- **huvq, bavq** -- to take back; to withdraw (as money from the bank)

-- **huvq, bivq** -- to give back; return something; pay back

huvq biaol full years (**huvq biaol ngavq ceil huvq** = a full fifty years; cf. **huvq miaol ngavq ceil huvq** = close to fifty years, but not quite)

huvq biao the cycle of one year (tiˬ k'o˄ aˇ jawˬ)

huvq biao biao for a full year to come around

-- **huvq, bu puv** -- countercharge; counterclaim

-- **huvq, colqoq pievq** -- to be reconciled

huvq deivq the first one (speaking of living things; see also: **hhaol deivq; naoq deivq**)

-- **huvq, ha** -- chicken year

-- **huvq, haqlaq** -- tiger year

-- **huvq, haoqseil puv** -- to rehabilitate a person's reputation

huvq hev la hev hev zaq to celebrate a holiday; to have a seasonal festival (46:80)

huvq hev zaq celebrate ('eat') the New Year (9:78) (gaˇ tahˇ paˇ-eu) (cf. Lahu: hk'aw˄ suh¯ caˇ ve)

-- **huvq, hu** -- rat year

-- **huvq, hha** -- to give back

-- **huvq, hhaq bi bo** -- to be refreshed

-- **huvq, hhavq** -- pig year

-- **huvq, hhel** -- to buy back; redeem former belonging

-- **huvq, hhoq paoq** -- to have a reunion

huvqjoq the whole year (k'o˄ lah ni)

-- **huvq, keeq** -- dog year

huvqlavq 1. an epoch; a period of time; years and months (26:86, 46:75, 50:121), 2. a situation in space and time (50:189)

huvqlavq hultav the history (34:12)

huvqlavq lavqsiivq a new time; a new epoch (50:188)

huvqlavq liqsii history (B=Chi) (34:23)

huvqlavq yosiivq the beginning of a new era; a new epoch; new time (age) (34:9)

-- **huvq, laoq** -- dragon year

huvq li to go back; return (41:41) (g'o˄ leˇ-eu)

huvq lo milhhu the years past (9:78) (dzeuˇ laˇ-euˬ aˇ k'o˄)

=**huvq, milnao**= last year

-- **huvq, miq** -- for a man to divorce his wife (send her back)

=**huvq, miq**= a divorced woman

huvqmiq the end of the year (46:81)

huvq miaol close to; almost (x) number of years (**huvq miaol ngavq ceil huvq** = close to fifty years, but not full; cf. **huvq biaol ngavq ceil huvq** = a full fifty years)

-- **huvq, miuvq** -- monkey year

=**huvq, mol**= a big bowl

-- **huvq, moq** -- horse year

=**huvq, neelya**= next year (and see: **nyulyahuvq**)

-- **huvq, niuq** -- buffalo year
=**huvq, nyulya**= next year (& see: **neelyahuvq**)
-- **huvq, nyuq hu** -- to think over again; reconsider
-- **huvq, pal** -- to redeem the original item back
=**huvq, palpuv**= to exchange back again
huvq pav half a year (41:120) (k'o^ pa^)
Huvqpei Lapei Puv from an old Hani poem referring to the passing of years and months (46:82)
huvqpeiq beginning of year (first few months) (9:78, 46:81)
-- **huvq, peiq** -- to compensate
huvqpeiq lapeiq the beginning of a year
huvqpeiq lapeiq puv to begin a New Year
-- **huvq, puv** -- 1. to turn back, 2. to restore
-- **huvq, sallal** -- year after next
-- **huvq, seil** -- snake year
huvqsiivq New Year (9:78, 46:81) (k'o^ shui^)
huvqsiivq hev to begin the New Year (k'o^ shui^ do^ le-eu)
huvqsiivq hev zaq to spend the New Year holiday (festival) (gaˇ tahˇ paˇ-eu)
-- **huvq, soq** -- to get revenge
huvq ssol là the year and month of birth (used when calculating such things as the proper girl for one's son to marry)
huvq ssol la deiq to check the year and month of birth of a boy and girl to see if they will make a good match (or) **huvq ssol la ceil**
huvq ssol miltiv meil all year round (k'o^ lah ni)
-- **huvq, toqla** -- rabbit year
-- **huvq, wuqduq taoq** -- to apologise and beg another's pardon
=**huvq, xeiv**= to leave earlier than one should
-- **huvq, xo** -- to divorce one's husband
-- **huvq, yoqhhaq xeiv** -- to voluntarily leave one's job
huvq'yul old year (k'o^ oeˇ)
Huvq'yul siq December (last month of the year) (41:107)
huvq za hhaq bo in the prime of life (50:121)
huvqzaq divorce (general term -- see also: **miq huvq; miq seil**)
huvqzavq to divorce (or) **huvq** (miˇ zaˇ k'o^-eu)
-- **huvq, zaol** -- to get revenge
=**huvq, zaoq**= rounded chisel
=**huvq, zol**= school age

huflif mutually beneficial (Chi) (34:82)

HUA

-- **hualpiq, alyeiv** -- a vase for flowers (B=Chi)
hualqeil alyeiv flower wreath (A=Chi) (50:73)
hualyiq welcome (Chi) (34:113) (or) **hueilyiq**

huaqdaqniq gabardine (Chi) (50:73)
huaqji circumstances (Chi) (34:81)
Huaq Jifgual a hero during the Korean war (Chi) (26:41)
huaqqaoq overseas Chinese (Chi) (50:74)
huaqqeiq finger-guessing game (Chi) (or) **lavqnyul lavqma caq zaq**

huafbaof pictorial (Chi) (50:74)
huafbiq paint brush (Chi) (50:74)
huafceiq picture book (Chi) (10:pref) (aˇ baˇ sahˬ bo˰)
huafdeil mu'luq a slide show (A=Chi) (50:74)
huaffeiq chemical fertilizer (Chi)
huaffeiq zeiqkeeq chemical fertilizers (A=Chi) (50:74)
huafgaolca a chemical factory (Chi) (26:27)
huafgaolca ximeiq ceiljeil a chemical manufacturing plant for processing coal (Chi) (26:27)
huafsiiq haqluv a fossil (A=Chi) (50:74)
huafxoq chemicals (Chi) (50:74)
huafyeif 1. to have a medical examination (Chi) (10:33) (goˬ haw-eu), 2. to perform a chemical examination; labratory test (Chi) (50:74)

HUEI

hueilyiq welcome (Chi) (or) **hualyiq**

hueif feilzii bad people (Chi) (tsawˇ haˬ yaw doeˇ)

HYU

hyul inside; domestic (opposite of: **nil** = outside, wild) (laˬ k'oeˇ; la˰ k'oeˇ)
hyul to be extremely comfortable (aˇ dzehˬ-ehˇ saˇ-eu)
Hyuqcuq Hui nationality (Muslim) (41:4)
=hyul, laq= home; house
hyul neivq good spirits, live in house or village
hyulyeilfaq marriage law (Chi) (50:76)
hyulyil ziifduf marriage system (Chi) (50:76)
hyulyil ziifzu freedom to decide on marriage affairs by oneself (Chi) (50:76)
-- hyulzal, albee -- a woolen blanket
hyulzao relatives on the father's side
hyulzao aqbol paternal grandfather
hyulzao aqpyuq paternal ancestors
hyulzao baoqgeel ancestral altar to paternal ancestors
hyulzeiq domesticated animals (9:78, 13:22, 50:81) (jeˬ zaˬ = all animals)
hyulzeiq taoq bribe; bribery (50:47)

hyuq to steal (9:78) (k'oeˬ-eu)

hyuq (vb) to secretly (vb) (**hyuq suv** = to smoke secretly) (k'oeˬ ..., ... k'oeˬ)
=hyuq, aq= smoke
hyuq aoq buy and resell secretly (50:47)
-- hyuqbaq, juqhyuq -- for a haze to be present
hyuq bev shoot from ambush ('steal-shoot') (50:2)
hyuqbovq bovq to be smokey (uˬ k'oeˬ k'oeˬ-eu) (9:78)
hyuqgyulxeif tropic (Chi) (50:75)
=hyuq, hoq= dove; pigeon
hyuq hu to steal a glance; a look (11:200) (k'oeˬ haw-eu)
-- hyuq hhel, hyuq aoq -- to smuggle goods
hyuq hheivq to hide something (13:33)
-- hyuq hheivq meil aol, hyuq leivq -- to do something in a secretive, lying way
hyuq hhyul zaq to feel happy in one's heart
=hyuq, joq= fog; cloud
hyuq kavqtovq to abduct (esp. when abducting a person, such as a girl) (or) **hyuq su zaq**
hyuqleivq hyuqhheivq meil aol to do something in a secretive, lying way
hyuq meil hyuq jav laq e to become rich by stealing from others (57:89)
hyuqniul tobacco (9:78) (ya k'awˬ)
hyuqniul suv to smoke tobacco (9:78) (ya k'awˬ dawˇ-eu)
hyuq nyuq to suspect; to doubt (maˬ jah coeˇ-eu)
hyuqpavq tobacco leaf (9:78) (ya k'awˬ aˇ pa˰)
hyuq seivq to kill secretly (50:2)
hyuq su 1. to spy (50:2), 2. keep watch over someone or something (50:82)
hyuq sussaq one who spies on others (50:83)
hyuq su zaq to abduct (esp. a person, as a girl) (or) **hyuq kavqtovq**
hyuq suv to smoke secretly
hyuq xavq to steal into and stay (14:188)
hyuq xeiv to escape
hyuq xeiv dov al la to trespass
hyuq zaq to steal (k'oeˬ dzaˬ-eu)
hyuq zaq meil stealthily (11:167)
hyuq zaq zo to be a habitual thief (50:65)

hyuvq hheivq to hide something (la^ za˰-eu)

hyufyeiq committee members (Chi) (50:76)
hyufyif a meeting (Chi) (41:14) (bawˬ dzaˬ-eu)

HHA

hhal to winnow (9:68) (za˅-eu; g'a˅-eu = CA)
hhalbiavq a muddy lump of earth from a plowed up field (9:68) (clf. **biavq**)
=hhal, diq= threshing mat
hhaldif tuaqjiq stability and unity (Chi) (34:48) (zi‸-eu)
hhaldif tueiqjiq stability and unity (Chi)
=hhal, eel= dirty water on surface
Hhalgal the name of a steel plant (Chi) (26:27)
=hhal jav, zaq= to have food to eat
hhallaovq laovq to get together (46:202) (ui˯ la˅-eu)
=hhal, li= (see full)
hhallul a toy (**seil e hhallul** = toys to play with - 14:242)
-- hhallul seilhha, ssaqguq -- children to play games
hhalma winnowing tray (9:68) (za˅ ma; g'a˅ ma = CA)
Hhal Niqmiq a hero (26:104)
-- hhalniul, neivqzaq -- (see full)
=hhal, nyuq= faith; belief (50:188)
hhalpeiq an arrangement (50:1) (Chi)
hhalqeiq hhyuyeiqhyuf security committee (Chi) (50:1)
Hhalsal the name of a mountain (Chi) (26:26)
=hhal seil, haq= to dance and play games
hhalseil seil to play a game (46:92, 202) (and see: **hhaseil seil** - 31:3)
hhalsuf albol a eucalyptus tree (A=Chi) (11:31)
-- hhal, ssaqguq yiuvq -- a cradle
-- hhal, yiuvq -- a cradle

hha to get; obtain (9:67) (za-eu; g'a-eu = CA) (cf. Lahu: g'a).
hha 1. to play (see also: **hhalseil**), 2. to visit (daw˯ deh g'a-eu)
hha (vb) must (vb) (ya ...; g'a ... = CA) (3:2) (cf. Lahu: g'a)
hha (vb) due to (**Aqyoq xilgei 5 se hha kev lal.** He is due to arrive here at 5 o'clock.)
hhaba nei daily (45:41) (a˯ yaw‸ nah yaw‸; yaw˯ nah na lu‸)
-- hha, bavq -- to receive
hha bavq hha to have received (as a letter) (57:108)
hha bev to shoot game (35:15)
=hha, bul= to float on water
hha caoq hidden trouble; hidden danger (50:198)
hhacoq coq to jump with joy (57:77)
hha dav must add (as price, quantity, etc.) (daw^ lah˯-eu)
hhadaoq type of snare (with wood or stone)
-- hhadaoq, haqssiiq -- a tiger trap made of wood and vines

-- **hha, del** -- to wander; roam
-- **hha, doqdeiv** -- to pay a visit
hha gaq to hear; to get wind of (or) **naqba gaq lal** (na⌄ ga⌄-eu)
hha, hha, hha the sight of something floating (as a boat); flying; moving about; **hha meil hha alnei** (bu-eu)
hha hha nei going up & down (as fish in pail or a flag blowing in the wind) (11:201)
=**hha, jollal**= daily
hha'la nei by chance (50:125)
-- **hha, lav** -- to make a joke
hha'loq nei open; spacious (50:97)
hha meil hha alnei the sight of something floating on water (as a boat); **hha hha hha nei**
hhana some (**qiq hhaq hhana** = some of the people) (ti⌄ pa^ na deu⌄)
-- **hhana, qiq jol** -- sometimes
-- **hhana, qiq mavq** -- some of them
=**hha, nee**= chest of body
-- **hhaniul, neivqzaq** -- a kind of ogre
-- **hha, qao** -- to wander; roam
hha qeiq may pick up (14:145)
hhaseil seil to dance a dance (31:3) (and see: **hhalseil seil**) (ga˅ nyeh nyeh-eu)
-- **hhazaoq zaoq, doqdeiv** -- to meet together and talk
hhazei fish net (9:70), **ngaqzei** (za; g'a = CA)

hhaq to win (g'a⌄-eu)
hhaq clf. for people (9:68) (g'a⌄)
hhaq strength (9:68) (g'a⌄)
hhaq okay; all right (9:68) (cf.: g'a⌄-a˅ = 'enough')
hhaq buckwheat (and see: **hhaqlei**) (g'a⌄)
(vb) **hhaq** able to (vb) (45:92) (nya-eu)
(vb) **hhaq** ending with the negative, indicating certainty (**maq hha nieil hhaq** = must certainly not forget - 54:110)
hhaq al all right; enough (g'a⌄-a˅)
=**hhaq, aqkeel keel**= sole of foot
=**hhaq, aqlavq lavq**= palm of hand
-- **hhaq, aol e** -- productive forces
hhaq'aoq aoq to 'sell strength' (work for wages) (g'a⌄ ah⌄-eu; g'a⌄ mah˅ mah˅-eu)
hhaqbil the rafter that goes between houseposts on the long side of the house, forming the floor joists for the second floor
hhaq bi bo to give strength (46:103) (g'a⌄ bi^-eu)
hhaq bi bo huvq to refresh
hhaq bi bo lal to give strength to
hhaq bi dav to gather one's breath (as after a strenuous exertion)
hhaq bi jaoq yil to cause to become weak; to weaken
hhaqbiaq a rock bee
Hhaqbiaq a Hani village named from 'rock bees' that live nearby

hhaqbiav a fried buckwheat cake
hhaqbiav biav to fry buckwheat cakes (14:150)
hhaqbieiv to be dejected; discouraged (45:58, 84, 46:172) (g'a˯ byeh^)
hhaqbieiv bieiv to be dejected; discouraged (g'a˯ byeh^ byeh^-eu)
hhaqbieiv ceiv to be dejected; discouraged; melancholy (50:25) (g'a˯ byeh^-eu)
hhaqbol a buckwheat plant (g'a˯ baw˅)
-- **hhaqcaoq, hhaqma** -- the sacred grove area of the village
-- **hhaqcaoq, jahhaq** -- a cluster of weeds; grass
hhaqcil oil (45:65) (see: **hhavqcil**) (tsi˅)
hhaqcil aldovq oil lamp
-- **hhaqcil, alpavq** -- leaf lard
hhaqcil leiqju to lubricate
=**hhaq, col**= manpower
-- **hhaqcuv cuv, puvcuv** -- to establish a village and the sacred village jungle around it
=**hhaq, daq**= 1. ground, 2. island
hhaqdav crossbeams used in joining the house posts on the ends of the house, and forming the floor joists for the second floor (6:177)
hhaq dav for strength to increase (g'a˯ ah˅ la˅-eu)
hhaq daoq for strength to decrease; to lose strength
-- **hhaqdaoq, milma** -- a mountain pass
-- **hhaqdei, jahhaq** -- expanse of grass or weeds
hhaqdeivq roughly made buckwheat cake
-- **hhaq, diq** -- to win; to defeat someone
-- **hhaq, duq** -- to win at gambling
hhaq duv maq naoq al use all strength without letting up (10:pref)
hhaqdyul dyuljo nei very lazily (35:108) (g'a˯ doe˅ doe˅-eu)
hhaqgal cei to think or do beyond one's ability
hhaqgal mol taq nei for a long time (10:15) (g'aw˯ myah˅ ni)
hhaqgeeq soft buckwheat bran
hhaq hal jav e bavq duv alnei to give all of one's strength; all of one's mind
hhaqhaq bitter buckwheat (or) **hhaqpeel**
hhaqhav 1. strength (g'a˯ k'a^), 2. one's power and rights (50:139)
hhaqhav bo to have strength (26:107, 41:198) (g'a˯ k'a^ baw-eu)
hhaqhav ca to be a little weak (41:199) (g'a˯ ju˯-eu)
hhaqhav hal jav e bavq duv to expend all of one's energy; to do one's best
hhaqhav havma healthy; strong (12:128) (g'a˯ k'a^-eu)
hhaqhav havma tivq extreme effort
hhaqhav lalduq motive force; motive power (50:39)
hhaqhav laol limited power (50:139)
hhaqhav maq heeq not strong (26:42) (g'a˯ ma˯ k'a^)

hhaqhav nil to have small strength (26:42) (g'a˯ aˇ cui^ teh˰)
hhaqhav pyu those in power; those with authority (50:32)
hhaqhav tivq with great effort (50:123) (cf. Lahu: g'aˇ hte˰)
hhaqhav tivq haol lal to come to the rescue (or) **aolhaol lal** (cf.: ka k'o˰ laˇ-eu)
hhaqhav tivq nei 1. with all one's strength; with all one's energy (11:218) (cf. Lahu: g'aˇ hte˰), 2. violently (or) **deiqssil alnei**
hhaqhav yobo man to have unusual strength (46:145)
hhaqhaoq valley (9:69) (g'a˯ law˯; lawˇ k'm˯)
hhaqhaoq col a porter (or) **hhaqhaoq eq zaq**
hhaqhaoq eq zaq to be a porter (by trade)
Hhaqheeq name of a man who is good at weaving bamboo goods (14:143)
hhaqheil a servant; one who obeys orders
hhaqheil heil to order someone to do something
hhaqhovq buckwheat husk
=hhaq, ja= grass; weeds
hhaq jaoq yil to become weak
hhaqjeil xaldei terraced irrigated fields (or) **xaldei hhaqjeil**
-- hhaqjeil, xaldei -- terraced irrigated fields
hhaq jol dav recuperate; convalesce (50:108)
hhaqjo jo to exchange manpower by having another work for you (g'a˯ nga˯ nga˯-eu)
hhaqjo soq 1. to return manpower borrowed earlier (46:100), 2. to get revenge
-- hhaqju, hhaqleiq -- a joke
hhaqkaq (see: **alkaq**)
hhaqkaq a valley (14:177) (g'a˯ law˯)
=hhaq, keel= sole of foot
hhaqkeeq a hunting dog (sha˯ teh-eu a˯ kui˯)
hhaqkuv a diq to attack a jail (50:60) (Note: usually 'jail' is spelled: **hhavqkuv**)
hhaqkuv a diq laol to put in jail (or) **hhaqkuv a nieivq tao**
hhaqkuv laqnil nei ziiqxiq let out of jail on probation (C=Chi) (50:82) (Note: usually 'jail' is spelled: **hhavqkuv**)
hhaqkuv nei xeiv duv to escape from prison; to break out of prison (50:202)
hhaqkyuq kyuq to be tired (46:100) (g'a˯ doeˇ doeˇ-eu)
hhaq lal to feel for something which is not visible to the eye (as in a bag, basket, darkness)
=hhaq, lavq= palm of hand
hhaqlei buckwheat (9:69, 11:28) (g'a˯)
hhaqlei hhaqbiav buckwheat cakes
hhaqlei hhaqdeivq buckwheat cakes
hhaqlei hhaqgeeq buckwheat flour with soft bran (used for pig food)

hhaqlei hhaqhaq bitter buckwheat
hhaqlei hhaqhhyuq hhyuq to make an offering of buckwheat
hhaqlei hhaqlyul buckwheat flour
hhaqlei hhaqneev buckwheat seeds, grains
hhaqlei hhaqniuv the best flour from buckwheat
hhaqlei hhaqnyul buckwheat cakes (made like fingers)
hhaqlei hhaqpeel gray, bitter buckwheat
hhaqlei hhaqpiaol buckwheat food
hhaqlei hhaqqul sweet buckwheat
hhaqlei hhaqsiq grains of buckwheat
hhaqlei hhaqteil buckwheat cakes (9:69, 11:35)
hhaqlei hhaqteil maq zaq nia 1. does not eat buckwheat cakes, 2. is not able to make jokes
hhaqlei hhaqyal a buckwheat field (35:16)
hhaqlei hhaqyal beiv to cut a field for planting buckwheat

hhaqleiq a joke
hhaqleiq hhaqju a joke
hhaqleiq leiq to make a joke (ja uiˇ-eu)
hhaqleiq maq ya to dislike a joke
hhaqleiq pieiq to make a joke
hhaqleiq qiq pav meil half jokingly (35:51)
hhaqleiq seil to make a joke

hhaq lil okay; all right; that's fine (35:27, 38:2, 41:137) (g'a˯-aˇ)

Hhaqlol a branch of the Hani (46:111)

Hhaqlol haolgaoq Ailao mountains (where the Hani currently live (A=Chi) (46:76)

-- hhaq lo, hhaq sil -- wealthy

hhaq luv cuvhhal the sacred stones which are in the sacred grove area of the village (see also: **kal luv cuvhhal; saol luv cuvhhal**)
hhaqlyul buckwheat flour (9:69) (g'a˯ loeˇ)

hhaqma the village sacred grove above the village where an annual offering is made (it is also called the 'brother' to the water source = **lolhovq**)
hhaqma albol the sacred village tree in the sacred grove (or) **hhaqmabol; hhaqma hhaqbol**
hhaqma aqbol 1. sometimes used for the ritual head (**milguq**) who presides in the village sacred tree ceremony (46:133), 2. a respectful term for the village 'protector' who resides in or near the sacred grove
hhaqma aol (see: **hhaqma lol**)

hhaqma bi meil to rest and build up one's strength; to rehabilitate (50:189)

hhaqma eelseil centipede (46:100) (la˄ ma uiˇ shehˇ)
hhaqma hhaqbol the village sacred tree (46:154) (miˇ sahˇ lawˇ-eu aˇ bawˇ)
hhaqma hhaqcaoq the sacred jungle area above the village given over to the 'lord of the land'

(46:111)

hhaqma hhaqhhyuq hhyuq to have a religious holiday for the sacred grove ceremony

hhaqma lol to make annual offering in the village sacred grove above the village led by the 'ritual head' (**milguq**) (or) **hhaqma tul zaq; hhaqma aol; hhaqma lol zaq**

hhaqma luvcuv the three stones in the sacred grove

hhaqma saqhel sacrificial pork given in the ceremony to the sacred village tree (46:136)

hhaqma tul annual offering made in the sacred grove, including a pig being killed for the whole village

hhaqma tul zaq (see: **hhaqma lol**) (46:111)

hhaqma zildol kul a feast the ritual head gives to the elders the day after the sacred grove ceremony

hhaq maq dyul meil aol make a sustained effort; make an unremitting effort (50:17)

hhaq maq hhaq? is it okay or not? (11:45) (g'a$_{\vee}$ nga la$_{\vee}$)

hhaqmeil valley (46:170) (g'a$_{\vee}$ law$_{\vee}$)

hhaqmeil col people of the mountains (dah$^{\vee}$ ta$^{\wedge}$ tsaw$^{\vee}$ ha$_{\vee}$)

-- hhaq, miavhhaq -- to have poor eyesight

hhaqnaq naq 1. to rest (9:69) (g'a$_{\vee}$ na$_{\vee}$ na$_{\vee}$-eu), 2. to have a holiday (50:49)

=hhaq, naolcal= solar energy

=hhaq nei, naq= surprisingly

hhaqnyul steamed finger-like buckwheat cakes

(vb) **hhaq nga** 1. ending with the negative (**Hal gee movq e ma gee hhaq nga.** It is not proper to recite a genealogy any time you may want.) (Note: **ma gee = maq hha gee**), 2. question ending (**Xilmeil aol e hhaq ngaq**? Can it be done in this way? Answer: **Hhaq nga.** Yes, okay.)

hhaqpal pal to exchange manpower with someone else (g'a$_{\vee}$ nga$_{\vee}$ nga$_{\vee}$-eu)

hhaqpav half the manpower (g'a$_{\vee}$ pa$^{\wedge}$)

hhaqpeel (see: **hhaqhaq**)

hhaqpiaol tiny dumplings (as big as a grain) made from buckwheat powder

hhaqpiaol piaol zaq to make tiny dumplings from buckwheat powder

Hhaqpu a person's name (35:30)

hhaqpuq a rock (14:168) (k'a$_{\vee}$ lo; lo gu$^{\vee}$)

hhaqpuq diq to storm a fortification (50:60)

hhaqpuq hhaqbaol rock and cliff (lo gu$^{\vee}$)

hhaqpyuq price; expenses; pay (9:69) (a$^{\vee}$ poe$_{\vee}$)

hhaqpyuq dei nei pal zaq exchange of equal value (50:34)

hhaqpyuq yal a cheap price (a$^{\vee}$ poe$_{\vee}$ yaw ya$^{\vee}$)

=hhaq, qao= one who has enough strength to walk

hhaqqul sweet buckwheat (9:69)

=hhaq quqsiq nei, aoq= cool (as the weather)

=hhaqsav nei, naq= very surprisingly

hhaqsaol a rock (k'a˅ lo)
hhaq sil hhaq lo to be very wealthy (sm˅ mui˅)
hhaqsiq buckwheat grain
hhaqsiil naciq a type of powder used to make buckwheat cakes yellow
=hhaq sol meil, yoq= personally
=hhaq, sul= 1. others (a˅ caw˅); 2. rich person
=hhaq, ssiiv= pressure
hhaqtav miqteil teil aim high and achieve more (50:106)
hhaqteil pounded buckwheat cake
-- **hhaqteil maq zaq, hhaqlei** -- (see full)
hhaq tivq to work hard, with all one's strength (cf. Lahu: g'a˅ hte˄)
=hhaq tul, zeiq= to have much capital, property
=hhaq, wuv= a thin eggshell
hhaqxaq a ravine
-- **hhaq, xavq** -- to have sexual intercourse (46:132)
hhaqxovq xovq a part of the burial ceremony whereby the officiating priest gets strength to carry on (repeated several times throughout)
hhaqyal buckwheat field (9:69)
-- **hhaqyal, hhaqlei** -- a buckwheat field
hhaqzeq cavq a ritual ceremony presided over by the 'ritual head' (**milguq**) to carry on and strengthen the sacred grove of the village
hhaqzeil cliff (of rock) (11:217, 33:3)
-- **hhaqzeil, bialsaq** -- cliff edge
=hhaq, zeiq= one's capital; property

=hhav, moq= frame for pack saddle
=hhav, ziiq= riding saddle

hhavq 1. to weave (9:69) (za˄-eu; g'a˄-eu = CA), 2. to knit (or) **ziivq**
hhavq a pig (a˅ za˄; a˅ g'a˄ = CA)
=hhavq, aq= pig
hhavq baqxoq a pig jaw (hung up in the swing rest house)
hhavqcaoq pig liver (9:69, 46:88) (za˄ tsah˅)
hhavqcil pork-lard (9:69) (za˄ tsi˅)
hhavqcil buqssaq a lard jar (9:70)
hhavqcil cilbuvq naol to be rancid (or) **zalhe naol**
hhavqcil cilkuq pork fat
hhavqciil male pig (za˄ pi˅; za˄ pa˅)
hhavqcul a fat pig (9:70) (za˄ tsu˅)
hhavqdol a 'bad-omen' pig (with one or two in litter, or nurses only on one side) (za˄ caw^)
hhavqdol diq to kill and eat the above type of 'bad-omen' pig (za˄ caw^ seh˄ dza˅-eu)
hhavqdol diq duq a place where a 'bad-omen' pig is killed and eaten (za˄ caw^ seh˄ dza˅ du˅)
hhavqdol duv for a 'bad-omen' pig to occur
-- **hhavqduq, hhavqkeel** -- pig feet and head
hhavqgeel pig skin (9:70) (a˅ za˄ ba^ k'o^)

hhavqgol adult pig
hhavqhal female pig, never had litter (za˄ ma)
hhavqhao pig bristle (9:70) (za˄ ca˄ hm)
hhavqhao haopiul white bristle of pigs (46:134)
hhavqhao moltavq pig bristles
hhavqhao tal xa to singe and scrape off pig's bristles
hhavqho female pig (a sow), **hhavqma** (a˅ za˄ ma)
hhavq huvq pig year (9:70) (za˄ ti˅ k'o˄)
=hhavq, hyuq= graft and embezzlement
-- hhavq, kaoldaol -- to fence in
hhavqkeel hhavqduq pig feet and head (when speaking of an offering) (46:126)
hhavqkuv pig shed; pig sty (9:70) **cuv** = to build (za˄ ku^)
hhavqkuv prison; jail (**hhavqkuv nieivq laol** = to put in jail) (ku^; tsawˇ ha˅ ku^)
hhavqkuv a diq to attack a jail
hhavq lal kul to call back the soul of a pig
hhavqma female pig; a sow, **hhavqho** (a˅ za˄ ma; a˅ g'a˄ ma = CA) (9:70)
hhavqnal swine fever (9:70)
-- hhavqnav, aqhhavq -- a black pig
hhavq nao pig day (za˄ ti˅ nah)
=hhavq, pal= a woven belt
hhavqpaq boar (a˅ za˄ pa˅; a˅ g'a˄ pa˅ = CA) (9:70)
hhavq pav half a pig (i.e., they own a share of a pig) (11:67)
hhavqsaq pork (9:70) (a˅ za˄ sha˅ jiˇ)
hhavqseiq a pig hoof (46:88) (a˅ za˄ kuiˇ sah˅)
hhavqssyuq a pig species
hhavqtavq a mountain slope (4:40) (gaw˅ jaw˅ ba˅ g'a; za˄ ta˄)
hhavqtavq deisal a mountain slope and plain
hhavqtavq deisal kaq where a mountain slope and a plain meet
hhavqtavq tavq zaq to raise pigs jointly
hhavqteiq wild boar (9:70) (za˄ te˅; g'a˄ te˅ = CA)
hhavqtovq a pig yoke (put on the neck of pigs to keep them from going through fences into gardens) (za˄ kaw˅ kaw˅-eu)
hhavqwul wulzii pig intestines
hhavqwul wulzoq sausage (a˅ za˄ uˇ dzaw˅)
hhavqxiq pig dung (12:126) (a˅ za˄ ca˄)
hhavqzal pig food (9:70) (za˄ dzaˇ; g'a˄ dzaˇ = CA)
hhavqzal hoqloq pig trough (or) **hhavqzal hoqtuv** (9:70) (za˄ dzaˇ k'awˇ law˅)
hhavqzal hoqtuv pig trough (or) **hhavqzal hoqloq** (za˄ dzaˇ k'awˇ law˅)
hhavqzaq zyul corrupting crimes (50:162)
hhavq zeq pig hour (B=Chi)

hhafjeif a court case (Chi) (50:2)
hhaflaoq feilpeif to divide goods in accordance with one's labor (Chi) (**halmiav aol, halmiav hha** =

you receive as much as you do - 34:38) (or) **hhaflaoq feilpeiq** (34:16)
hhafsiiq laqhyul a dark room (A=Chi)

HHAO

hhaol 1. stiff; hard (9:68, 11:55) (g'ah$^{\vee}$-eu), 2. to be smart (8:11) (g'ah$^{\vee}$-eu; yaw g'ah$^{\vee}$), 3. to win (9:68) (g'a$_{\vee}$-eu)
hhaol springtime (41:116) (or) **hhaolduv**
Hhaolbei Leilseil spring season god (or) **aqpyuq Hhaolbei Leilseil**
=hhaol, ceil= stringed musical instrument
=hhaol, ciq= mushroom
Hhaoldal name of a village in Jinping county (35:44)
hhaoldaol a fold (bya^-eu)
hhaoldaol daol to fold a fold (bya^ dm$^{\vee}$-eu)
hhaoldaol duvq to replant in open spaces (as when there are empty places in a rice field) (ka dzaw$_{\wedge}$-eu)
hhaoldao soq a ceremony held when abnormal human births occur, to drive away evil spirits
=hhaol, dei= a lawn
hhaol deivq the middle one (speaking of living things, see also: **huvq deivq; naoq deivq**)
hhaoldoq old words (words of wisdom from the ancestors) (18:1) (daw$_{\vee}$ oe$^{\vee}$)
hhaolduv springtime (46:81)
hhaolduv aqpyuq spring ancestor (see 46:156 for a poem about how when spring ancestor is born, there is total change in the 'new world'.)
hhaolduv ba'la springtime (9:68, 26:110)
hhaolduv hev to start the spring season (50:105)
=hhaol, gaoq= middle part of mountains (not too high or too low)
=hhaol hhaoldao, nao= daytime
hhaoljov nei very hard (not soft) (9:68, 11:58) (g'ah$^{\vee}$ caw$_{\vee}$ ni)
=hhaol, la= middle of month (second ten days)
-- hhaol liq hhaol, tav liq tav-- sharp and hard (set phrase)
hhaol luvq e for plants, fruits etc. to mature
-- hhaol, maq diq -- not to win; to lose (as in a battle)
=hhaol, miq= second or middle daughter
=hhaol, nao= daytime
=hhaol, nee= daytime
=hhaol niq pav, eel= middle of the water (i$^{\vee}$ cu$_{\wedge}$ ti$_{\vee}$ k'eh^)
hhaol pil a type of spirit priest (does not perform death ceremonies, should not even be present)
=hhaol, ssaq= second oldest son
=hhaol, sseil= rainy season
-- hhaol, teil -- mid-tone; mid-level tone (or) **teil yei**

=hhaol, yaq= pickaxe (Chi)
hhaolzal ancestor's food (18:1) (a˅ poe˅ a˅ pi˅-eu˅ dzaˇ)
hhaol zeiq to win (41:200) (g'a˅ leˇ-eu)

-- hhao, diq -- to fence in; to wall around
-- hhao, galhhao -- 1. to make a detour around, 2. to go around
hhao'lao nei roundish; a circle; circle around (**hhao'lao nei jol taq** = people circled around - 26:66) (lah jo^ ni)
=hhao, lolbieil bieil= a round table
-- hhao, luvq -- to surround
hhao nei surrounding (35:33)
-- hhao, diq -- to fence around; wall in

hhaoq to bend (la^ ngo˄-eu; la^ g'o˄-eu)
hhaoq pillow (also 'to pillow' in 9:68) (u˅ g'm˅)
-- hhao, biaol -- to fly in a circle
hhaoq, hhaoq, hhaoq the sound of a gurgling stream
-- hhaoq lov, wuqhhaoq -- a pillow cover
-- hhaoq, ngaoq -- to bend something
=hhaoq, saol= a metal hoop
-- hhaoq, wuqhhaoq -- to pillow one's head
-- hhaoq, yiuvqhhaoq -- to pillow one's head (when lying down)
hhaoq zaq to try to do something (jahˇ haw-eu)
hhaoqzao bed (9:68, 38:14, 41:32) (ja ci˅)
hhaoqzao hoq to put blankets etc. on a bed (yu˄ zaˇ k'aw˅-eu)
hhaoqzao hultav on the bed (13:33) (ja ci˅ k'oeˇ ta^)
hhaoqzao naqpeiq the portion of the bed where the pillow lies (41:32) (ja ci˅ yu˄ g'm˅ paw)
hhaoqzao zao to make a bedstead; make a new bed (ja ci˅ ci˅-eu)

HHE

hhel buy (9:71) (zeuˇ-eu; g'euˇ-eu = CA)
Hhelbo a person's name
Hhelhovq a supernatural addressed by the ritual head in certain ceremonies, along with **Meqyyul**
hhel huvq to redeem back; buy back one's former belongings (zeuˇ k'o˄-eu; g'euˇ k'o˄-eu = CA)
hhel hhel meil aoq buy often to resell
hhelhhuv pao to give birth to first offspring (deh˄ beh beh le-eu)
hhellavq aol to trade (9:71) (je˅ ga˄ ga˄-eu)
hhellavq aol e col a trader; businessman (je˅ ga˄ ga˄ za˅)
hhellavq aolssaq a trader; a business man (41:4) (je˅ ga˄ ga˄ za˅)
hhellavq aol zaq make a living by trading (13:38, 39) (je˅ ga˄ ga˄ dza˅-eu)

hhellavq lavq caoq in the tide of business (57:70)
hhellavq lavqssaq small business; minor trading ventures (41:15)
hhellavq miqnieiq trading affairs (50:147)
hhellavq pievq a commodity for trade (50:146)
hhellavq zeiqsal trading economics; commodity economy (50:146)

Hhellaoq son of the Hani ancestor **Taoqpaoq** (46:207)
hhellaoq royal; kingly dragon (11:201) (or) **beiyaoq** (bya^ yah˯ sah˯ pa˯)
hhellaoq qovq royal dragon's family
hhellaoq soqpaq dragon king (or) **hhellaoq soqpaq** (38:90), **beiyaoq** (bya^ yah˯ sah˯ pa˯)

hhel luvq to buy enough goods (41:141) (zeuˇ lo˰-eu)
-- hhel, miqhhel -- to buy a daughter
=hhel nei, zil= tasty; good to eat
hhel pyul heil for others to have bought something 'over there'
hhel pyul la for one to buy something 'over there'
=hhel, ssaq= a son who was purchased
hhel ssaoq 1. make purchases for an organization (50:18), 2. to buy and collect
hhel zaq e hhaqhav purchasing power (50:63)
Hhelzel Europe (Chi) (125)

hhe 1. to pull up, 2. to tear (apart) (9:71), 3. to drag (g'eu-eu), 4. to transport goods (as by truck)
hhe to influence; to effect (10:pref., 5)
hhe to play a stringed instrument (beu^-eu; di˯-eu)
=hhe, al= a swing
-- hhe, alhhe -- to swing a swing
-- hhe, alkaol -- to pick out fibers
-- hhe biav, laolkeel -- to break a wall
hhe bieiq to pull off; to untie something (29:4) (g'eu do^-eu)
hhe caq to pull and cover (or) **hhe dao** (g'eu pi˯-eu)
-- hhe, ceilhhaol -- to play a two-stringed musical instrument
hhe cei to raise up (as a sword) (11:221) (ba˰ diˇ-eu)
hhe dav hhe xa appoint and remove (50:143)
-- hhe dav, kavtev -- to cock a crossbow
hhe dao to pull and cover (g'eu pi˯-eu)
hhedaoq the board in a swing (that one sits on)
hhe dovq to turn on (as a light) (29:4) (pah-eu)
hhe duv to draw out; to pull out (g'eu do^-eu)
hhe'fei starch made from lotus root (edi) (Chi) (50:125)
hhe gyuq to ring (a bell) (12:126)
hhe hhao to circle; to mark around (46:113)
hhe hhoq 1. to tear apart (9:71) (g'eu dzeh-eu), 2. to get off (or) **pieiq duv; xeiv leev; ssavq**
-- hhe, hhoqcaol -- to thin out seedlings
hhe hhuvq to bend by pulling (9:71) (g'eu ngo˰-eu)
hhe jiq hhe jiq meil hhe to pull very quickly

(45:76)

hhe jyuq to stretch out (**aqkeel maq hhe jyuq qivq** = could not stretch his legs out) (or) **hhe joq** (not pf.) (g'eu caw˯-eu)

-- **hhe, keellavq** -- influence the arms and legs (i.e. certain diseases affect a growing child)

hhe kuv 1. to pull in (**laolbyu hhe kuv** = to pull head in, so as not to get cold - 26:37) (caw˯ ahˇ; g'eu ahˇ), 2. to retract (**aqlavq aqkeel hhe kuv** = for arms and legs to retract - 26:24) (or) **lav laovq; se'leev**, 3. to curl up (as a dog's tail), 4. to shrink (shu˰-iˇ-eu)

-- **hhekuv, keelguq** -- to have a cramp in a leg

-- **hhekuv, lavqguq** -- to have a cramp in a hand (so cannot stretch it out)

-- **hhekuv, saqguq** -- to have muscle spasms; convulsions

-- **hhe lul dav, neema** -- to pull crazily

hhe pao 1. to open (pull open) (9:71) (g'eu pah-eu), 2. to unfold

hhe piei to open (as mouth) (13:12) (mˇ nga-eu)

hhe piq to pull closed (as a door or a cover) (g'eu pi˯-eu; g'eu pym˯-eu)

hhe puv to pull up (g'eu da^-eu)

hhe qov to pull in order to break (g'eu pya^ g'eu sha^; g'eu k'eh˰-eu)

hhe sa to remove; to relieve someone of his office (50:87)

-- **hhe sil, dieifdeil** -- to turn off a light (A=Chi)

hhe siivq to pull; to tighten (as a knot) (g'eu teuˇ-eu)

hhe sul jol for there to be someone to transport goods (57:122)

hhe ssaoq to bring together (g'eu ui˯-eu)

hhe ssil to grin (uiˇ ce˰ ce˰-eu; uiˇ seu^ seu^-eu)

hhe teiq 1. to hold fast, 2. to pull steadily, 3. to detain; hold in custody (9:71) (g'eu teh˯-eu)

hhe to 1. to lead; 2. to pull something straight (as a rope), 3. to take charge of; uphold; stand for (50:215)

hhe tul 1. to help someone stand up; pull up (57:135), 2. to support (50:52)

hhe xa to cancel; to rescind (50:22)

hhexovq a zipper (Chi) (50:101)

hhe xu 1. to decrease (as money); to reduce (as to reduce people's burden - 26:55, 50:89), 2. to deduct (50:98) (cf.: shu˰-eu)

-- **hhe xu, mavqssaq** -- cut down on military personnel

hhe yoq to pull away

hhe yovq to be pulled so that something is bent (as when rickets bends children's bones) (10:5)

hhe zaq to draw up; pull up (for a living) (**ngaqdeil hhe zaq** = to fish for a living, **miqkoq hhe zaq** = to sell firewood for a living - 45:70)

hhe zei 1. pull and discard (as weeds) (9:71) (g'eu

dzeh-eu), 2. to report something as worthless; to reject; scrap (50:8)

-- **hhe zei, zei nei** -- to pull to a longer length

hhe zeiv torn; pulled to pieces (as a shirt from fighting a fire) (**laqcyuq hhe zeiv** = pants torn - 27:12) (g'eu dzeh-eu; g'eu **pyeh**˅-eu)

hhe ziivq to whip (as a horse) (or) **ziivq** (9:71, 13:33) (jui˄-eu)

-- **hhe ziivq miq, alcav meiqzaq nei** -- to whip someone or something with a rope's end

=hheq, haq= charcoal

hhev 1. to wave one's hand; to gesture (9:71, 46:213) (la˄ li li-eu; la˄ jaw˅ jaw˅-eu), 2. to sway

-- **hhev, aqlavq** -- to wave (with hand) (9:11)

-- **hhev, galhhev** -- 1. to make a detour around something, 2.to go around something (as a village)

=hhev, laq= a whirlpool

-- **hhev, wulquvq taoqhhev** -- a whirlpool

=hhev, zilbaq zil= a funnel used in distilling liquor

HHEE

hheelhuvq Molmil Oh God (used in rituals)

HHEI

hhei 1. to separate (or) **hhoq; cev** (g'eh^-i˅-eu), 2. to wean (8:21) (a˅ coe˅ g'eh^-eu)

hhei to hold a meeting (Chi) (**Keilhyuf hhei zaq yil.**= They are holding a meeting.) (or) **keilhyuf kei**

hhei to be wrong (**Haljivq hhei ya aq**? What's wrong with you?) (leh˅-eu) (Note: This may be closer to the Ak.: g'eh-eu, which indicates a state of being, or a transition of a state of being.)

hhei (vb) to go; to do (**Nol laojal a taqqil hhei li wul aq**? Are you going to see your relatives? (41:14)

-- **hhei, saqbal** -- to go to work in an office (Chi)

=hheiq, eiq= cherry tree

Hheiqjiq Egypt (46:82)

hheiqzeif cancer (Chi) (50:1)

hheivq 1. to deceive (or) **moqleevq leevq**, 2. to cheat (someone) (46:198) (see also: **hheivqleivq**) (myaw˄-eu)

hheivq doq cheating words (35:27) (myaw˄-eu daw˅)

-- **hheivq, hyuq** -- to hide something

hheivqhhaf a false case (B=Chi)

=hheivq, jaq= hypocrisy; a lie

-- **hheivq, jaqhheivq** -- to tell a lie (**javqhheivq hheivq**)

hheivqjo soq to get revenge for someone lying to one

hheivq leivq to cheat (someone) (or) **hheivq**

hheivq meil hheivq jav laq e to become rich by lying and cheating

hheivqmiaovq miaovq to practice fraud (50:123)

Hheivqqivq Aqbiaq name of a hero in Hani stories who plays tricks on rich people

-- **hheivq, silhheivq** -- to be in a coma

hheivqsov pieiq to extort; blackmail (50:136)

hheivqsov pieiq sso to be cheated (35:78) (bi myaw^-eu; bi shuiˇ-eu)

hheivq zaq to cheat (take advantage of by cheating) (13:12); defraud; swindle (myaw^ dzaˇ shuiˇ dzaˇ-eu)

hheivq zaq zo to deceive others habitually (50:65)

-- **hheivq, zaol** -- pretend to do something

-- **hheivqzaol zaol** -- to forge; falsify

hheifgoq to be patriotic; love one's country (Chi) (34:17)

hheifgoq sseiqsiif a patriot (Chi) (34:21)

hheifgoq zuyif patriotism (Chi) (34:19); love for the motherland (50:1)

Hheifniq Akha who live in Xishuangbanna (Chi) (or) Aini (Chi) (13:11)

hheifziil bif AIDS (Chi) (50:1) (& see below)

hheifziil bieif nalgol AIDS (Chi) (15:60) (& see above) (cf.: Eˇ-shiˇ naˇ gawˇ)

HHO

hhol to breathe (sa^ g'awˇ-eu)

hhol clf. for the smoking of a water pipe (**Yahyuq qiq hhol alkaq** = between two smokes of tobacco, or in a very short time) (35:35)

hholcal hho to work at a spinning wheel (14:178)

Hholhhel a twin boy's name in a Hani story (the other twin is: **Moqxuv**) (35:72)

hholkov regulations (or) **galkov; galquv** (46:82) (note: this is in the name of a book of 12 regulations)

hholmol body (9:72) (g'awˇ mawˇ)

hholmol ciq to bathe someone (iˇ cu^ bi dzui^-eu)

hholmol qiq mol meil miqsiq miqzal eq alnei to be armed to the teeth; the whole body to be armed

hholmol qiv to rub a cooked egg up and down a sick person's body and then divine with that egg

hhol puv hhol pal to breathe in and out (sa^ g'awˇ da^-eu; sa^ g'awˇ ka-eu)

-- **hhol pal, hhol puv** -- to breathe in and out

hholqei middle; inside; in the midst (9:72, 10:pref, 13:33) (**qiq taol hhaq hholqei** = in one thousand people) (g'ahˇ ceh)

-- **hholqei, xildyul** -- among these things
=**hhol, yoq**= one's body

hho to spin (9:71) (g'aw$^{\vee}$-eu)
hhobaoq hhoduv duv for heads of rice to begin to form (46:196)
hhobyu at the door (45:25) (la$^{\vee}$ g'o^-ah$^{\vee}$)
hhocal spinning wheel (9:71)
hhocovq early ripening rice
hhocuv rice seedling
hhocuv aqma the spirit of transplanted rice (14:237)
hhocuv aqyivq flying termite (a$_{\vee}$ i$_{\vee}$)
hhocuv aqzil folk song sung when transplanting rice seedlings
hhocuv cuv to transplant rice seedlings (9:72, 11:42) (g'aw$^{\vee}$ ka-eu)
  hhocuv cuv dovq yil a ceremony performed by women at the time they transplant rice into the terraced fields
  hhocuv sullal kul a ceremony done in home after transplanting rice, to call back the souls of family members
-- **hhoduv duv, hhobaoq** -- rice to be budding
hhoheiq gate (9:72) (g'o^ k'eh$_{\vee}$)
  hho heiq duv pal to hold a wedding ceremony and party again for a young woman because she cannot conceive
  hhoheiq heiqssaq the back (or side) door
-- **hhohho meil, meivq** -- long period of famine
hhokeeq rice seedling (9:72, 46:165)
  hhokeeq keeqssaq young rice seedlings (46:159)
  hhokeeq keeqssei old rice seedlings
hhomu emperor
  hhomu haovqdil emperor (B=Chi)
=**hho, nee**= bosom
hhopiul husked ('white') rice (ceh$^{\vee}$ pyu$^{\vee}$)
-- **hho, puvqhho** -- to boil halfway
hho'quv rice bud (9:73)
-- **hho, saqlaq** -- to spin cotton
hhosaq saq pity someone (9:73) (g'aw$_{\vee}$ sha$_{\vee}$ ga$_{\vee}$-eu)
hhoseiq seiq to sow seed (9:73) (si$_{\vee}$ yoe$_{\vee}$ seh$_{\vee}$-eu; a$^{\vee}$ nui^ seh$_{\vee}$-eu)
hhossaq ssaq to till land (50:50)
hhossyuq rice seeds (si$_{\vee}$ yoe$_{\vee}$)
hhoteev threshold of a door (or) **hhuteev**
hhoyyuq rice straw (9:73) (see also in 8:8) (g'o^ yoe$_{\vee}$)
  hhoyyuq ceilbaol rice straw piles
hhozil dol to drink wine after the rice seedlings have been transplanted

hhoq 1. to be lax, 2. to wear (as clothes); be covered (45:59, although '**hhyuq**' is pf.)
hhoq to separate; leave (9:72), **hhei; cev** (g'aw$_{\vee}$-eu)
hhoq again (g'o$_{\wedge}$ ...)

hhoq, hhoq, hhoq the sound of a bulldozer (26:30) (or) **hhaoq, hhaoq, hhaoq**

hhoq (vb) to (vb) again (**hhoq lal** = to come again = g'o^ laˇ-eu)

hhoqba white cabbage (11:118)

hhoqbaf a cruel man; despot; local tyrant (Chi) (26:16, 50:43) (tsawˇ haˬ yaw doeˇ)

hhoqbaf difzu a cruel landlord (Chi) (26:17)

-- **hhoq, bil** -- to split; divide; break up

-- **hhoqbol, loqhhoq** -- a large palm tree

(vb) **hhoq bo** must (vb) (**aol hhoq bo** = must do it; **deivq hhoq bo, sil hhoq maq bo** = must be alive, must not be dead)

hhoqcaol hhe to thin out vegetable seedlings (9:72)

hhoqcil the rape plant (9:72)

hhoqcil alneev rape seeds

-- **hhoqcil geel, neema** -- very sad in one's heart

hhoqcil xalyo rape seed oil

hhoqcyuq a dish (9:72) (k'mˬ maˬ)

hhoqcyuq vegetables (41:130) (or) **hhoqpavq; hhoqniul** (g'awˬ pa^ g'awˬ nyoeˇ)

hhoqcyuq alnei a sprout or vine of a vegetable

hhoqcyuq alpavq vegetable leaves (g'awˬ nyoeˇ pa^)

hhoqcyuq eelcal vegetable soup (10:10) (dzaˇ uiˇ)

hhoqcyuq hhoqdaq leaves of vegetables (g'awˬ nyoeˇ pa^)

hhoqcyuq hhoqdul the stem sections of vegetable leaves

hhoqcyuq hhoqkuv kuv to dry vegetables for future use

hhoqcyuq hhoqtuv a bundle of vegetables (g'awˬ nyoeˇ tiˬ dzahˬ)

hhoqdaq vegetable leaves (g'awˬ pa^)

-- **hhoqdei, daqhhoq** -- lawn-like area (46:176)

=**hhoq, diq**= a pea

Hhoqgoq Russians (Chi) (34:5) (or) **Sullieiq**

hhoqhaq a type of bitter vegetable

-- **hhoq, hhe** -- 1. to pull apart; tear apart, 2. to get off

hhoq, hhoq the sound of a big engine (as a bulldozer) (26:30)

-- **hhoq, hhoqloq nei** -- to separate

hhoqkuv dried vegetables or greens (9:72) (g'awˬ pa^ ko^)

hhoqleiq again (38:2)

-- **hhoq, leiq** -- to drive apart; to separate

hhoqleiqsiq still; again (45:53)

hhoqleivq again and again (9:72) (or) **hhoqleivq meil** (tiˬ po^ saˇ-iˇ tiˬ po^)

hhoqleivq meil again and again (or) **hhoqleivq**

hhoqleivqsiq again (13:4)

hhoq li to depart (up) (**hhoq yil** = to depart down)

hhoqli hhoqquv to collapse; disintegrate

hhoqloq nei hhoq to separate (46:152)

hhoqma albol oil palm tree

hhoqma alpavq oil palm tree leaves

Hhoqma milcaq a place named Hhoqma (14:153)

hhoqna not very (vb) (9:72) (teu na^ na^-ehˇ maˬ ..)

hhoqna maq (vb) not (vb) very much (as: not love very much, **Ngal hu e hhoqna maq huzaq ya.** I am not too much interested in watching that movie.) (teu na^ na^-ehˇ maˬ myaˬ)

hhoqna maq meeq not so good (9:72) (teu na^ na^-ehˇ maˬ muiˬ) (9:72)

=hhoq, naolma du= sunflower

hhoqnil three-colored **amaranth** plant

hhoqniul a green vegetable (or) **hhoqcyuq; hhoqpavq** (g'awˬ nyoeˇ)

hhoqniul zalniul green vegetables (cplt)

hhoq nyuq 1. to think of something again (45:32), 2. to consider; think over (46:82)

hhoqpavq vegetable (9:72) (or) **hhoqcyuq; hhoqniul** (g'awˬ pa˰; g'awˬ pa˰ g'awˬ nyoeˇ)

hhoqpavq peivqcal cabbage (B=Chi) (g'awˬ pa˰ nga du)

hhoqpaoq 1. vegetable seedlings before being transplanted, 2. a seedbed for vegetables

hhoq paoq huvq reunion (g'o˰ k'o˰ laˇ-eu)

hhoqpul Chinese radish; turnip (9:72, 11:78) (g'awˬ buˇ)

-- hhoqpul, alloq -- wild turnip

hhoqqeil pickled Chinese cabbage; any sour greens (9:73, 11:28) (g'awˬ pa˰ g'awˬ cehˇ)

-- hhoqqeil, alzil -- a kind of **grass**

-- hhoqqeil, ngaqsaq -- salted sour fish

hhoqqeil qeil to pickle Chinese cabbage (9:73) (g'awˬ pa˰ cehˇ cehˇ-eu)

-- hhoqquv, hhoqli -- collapse; disintegrate

hhoqsaq nei pitiful (26:57) (g'awˬ shaˬ gaˬ-eu)

hhoqsiq kidney (9:73) (g'awˬ siˬ)

hhoqsol pepper corn (black and white pepper) (9:73)

Hhoqssaq a village name where the Dolniq, a branch of the Hani, live in Yuanyang county

hhoq sseil xa yi to rain down again (46:79) (uˬ yehˇ paˇ yehˇ le-eu)

hhoqssyuq vegetable seed (9:73) (g'awˬ yoeˬ)

hhoqtaoq bitter wild vegetable (14:183)

hhoq tuv ho to knock (at door) again (13:46)

-- hhoq, xeiv -- to run away; to get away

-- hhoq, xoqxaof -- to leave school (A=Chi)

hhoqyal vegetable field (9:73, 11:18)

-- hhoqyal, sseilhhoq -- vegetable fields planted in the rainy season

hhoq ya to set down again (14:160)

hhoq yil to depart (down) (**hhoq li** = to depart up)

Hhoqyi Russian language

hhoqyolceil fennel; **hhoqyyulceil**

hhoq yoq to avoid (something or someone) (50:11)

hhoqyyulceil fennel; **hhoqyolceil**

hhoqyyuq vegetable seed (g'awˬ yoeˬ) (9:73)

hhoqzeiq heel of the foot (a˯ kuiˇ kuiˇ nui˄)
hhoqzi vegetable seedling
Hhoqzyuq aqpyuq an assistant to God, who rides a white horse down to take part in the spring festival (food for the horse is also provided, see: **moq ceil moq zal**) (46:182)
Hhoqzyuq aqpyuq Molmil ssaq li last son of **Molmil** who rides a horse down to attend the Kuqzaq zaq festival (also called: **Hhoqzyuq aqpyuq kuqleivq zaq**)

hhov scales (of fish, snakes, also used of scaly human skin or dandruff as in: **saqhhov**) (g'aw)
hhov brittle (9:73) (yaw zaw^)
hhovceiv nei brittle; easy to break (yaw zaw^)
=hhov, nal= a scab
=hhov, ngaq= fish scale
=hhov, ollol lol= snake skin
=hhov, saq= scaly human skin; dandruff

hhovq clf. for a family (9:73, 11:77) (zaw˄) (cf. Lahu: g'o˄)
=hhovq, aq= a needle
hhovqbaoq a needle case (9:68) (a˯ g'aw˄ bah˯ keu^)
-- hhovqbyu, aqhhovq -- the eye of a needle
=hhovq, col= a family
=hhovq daldul, ngaq= fishing pole
hhovqma a needle for injections (9:73) (a˯ g'aw˄) (cf. Lahu: g'o˄)
hhovqma cov to give an injection (ja^ g'a˯ tsaw^-eu) (9:73)
=hhovq, miq= (see full)
=hhovq, ngaq= fish hook
=hhovq, sseil= needle used to sew palm bark cape
hhovqteiq aol zaq individual family business (50:40)
-- hhovq, xeiv -- to run and hide; hide oneself

HHU

hhul to be active
hhulduv ba'la spring season
hhulla nei to be astute
-- hhul, lav -- to stir something up
hhulqil nei to be very active

hhubaq a doorframe (or) **hhubaq hhussaol**
hhubaq hhussaol a doorframe (or) **hhubaq**
hhubaoq meel to blow a rice stem flute (46:208)
hhu dav to pick up
=hhu, gal= long ago; formerly
hhu lu hhe le meil to hang over something
hhuteev threshold (of a door) (or) **hhoteev**

hhuq hhuq hhuq leil the sound of barking dogs
hhuq meil hhuq alnei the sound of a running machine

=hhuv, aq= under
hhuv pick up something (9:74) (g'o^-eu)
hhuv dav to pick up (g'o^ da^-eu; ba˄ da^-eu)
hhuv duv to go out (do^-iˇ-eu)
=hhuv haoq, lavq= armpit
hhuv leev to tidy up; pick things up (9:74) (g'o^ lui^-eu; la^ lui^-eu)
=hhuv, lul= a door
hhuv pao to open a door (50:95) (laˇ g'o^ pah-eu)
hhuvteev the threshold at the door of a house (certain things must not be done there, as washing one's feet, combing one's hair, etc., whereas certain things must be done there, as cutting off the head of a chicken)

hhuvq 1. to be bent; curved; crooked (g'o˄), 2. to ferment
hhuvq to return (6:196) (g'o˄-eu)
=hhuvq, ceiq= a hoe
=hhuvq, daol= a hunchback
hhuvqdaol aol to come back (g'o˄ laˇ-eu)
-- hhuvq, duq -- to bury
=hhuvq, gal= crooked path
-- hhuvq, heiq -- to bend something
-- hhuvq, hhe -- to bend by pulling
hhuvq hhuvq daol daol meil to go and come (iˇ iˇ laˇ laˇ)
-- hhuvq, heiq -- to bend something so it is crooked
hhuvq huvq lal to return back (from lower place) (g'o˄ laˇ-eu)
hhuvq huvq yiv to return back (from higher place) (g'o˄ le-eu)
hhuvq lal come back from lower place or west (9:74) (g'o˄ laˇ-eu)
=hhuvq, lavq= inner elbow; crook of elbow
-- hhuvq, leiq -- covered with water
hhuvq li to go back from lower place or west (9:74) (g'o˄ leˇ-eu)
=hhuvq, mil= below the ground
=hhuvq, miav= a hooked machete for field work
-- hhuvq puv, naol -- to turn back
hhuvqqeil to ferment
=hhuvq, qeil= watercress
hhuvqseq lower teeth
hhuvq sil to cover over
hhuvq siivq to press on
-- hhuvq, yalsol -- return home from fields
-- hhuvq, yav -- to bury something by sweeping something over it
hhuvq yil to go back from upper or east (9:74) (g'o˄-iˇ-eu)
hhuvq yil wuq mal allowed to return home (45:22)
hhuvq yiv come back from upper, or east (g'o˄ le-eu)

-- **hhuvq, zaol** -- to bury something
=hhuvq, zaol= lower part of the village

HHYU

hhyul to be pleased; delighted; enjoy (9:74)
hhyul to like; love; be friendly with (11:39) (g'oeˇ-eu)
hhyul clf. for number of pipes of tobacco smoked (11:152)
hhyul aol to nourish (as one's own body) (9:74)
hhyul aol to be abundant and nourishing (as mother's milk) (10:8)
hhyulcoq coq to dance for joy; jump up and down for joy
-- **hhyul, doq** -- sweet words
hhyul lal to love (46:107) (ga˯-eu; g'oeˇ-eu ga˯-eu)
hhyul leiq hhyul sil meil with exceeding joy (45:89, 46:177) (la˯ k'a˯ cehˇ seh˰-eu)
hhyul lul hhyul sav very happily (46:91); pleasantly
hhyul maq luvq e nalgol malnutrition ('lack of physical nourishment' disease) (10:15)
hhyulmeil sil for a woman to die in childbirth with the baby still in her womb (za˯ k'a^ k'a^ seh˰-eu)
=hhyul, nee= happily
hhyul nei warm-heartedly (50:141)
hhyulniq nei happy (12:126) (and see below)
hhyulniei nei happily; to be excited by good news (la˯ k'a˯ cehˇ ta^ ni) (9:74, 35:63) (& see above)
hhyulpuq puq to have a party together (50:105)
-- **hhyulqaol nei, gaqzav** -- 1. deeply in love, 2. very beautiful
hhyulqoq friend; close friend (13:43, 44); loving friend (38:94) (caw˯; tsui˰ yehˇ)
-- **hhyul sav, hhyul lul** -- very happily
hhyul sil very happy (exceedingly) (14:188) (la˯ k'a˯ cehˇ seh˰-eu)
  hhyul sil hhyul lo delighted; extremely happy (35:96)
  hhyul sil maq ngeel meil to like it very much (45:7)
=hhyul, zal= healthy food; nutritious food
-- **hhyul zaq, baqhhyul** -- to talk about matters of love (46:208)
-- **hhyul zaq, gaq zaq** -- 1. to love one another, 2. to love and take care of each other, 3. to have a close friendship
hhyulzav nei actively; happily (46:188) (la˯ k'a˯ cehˇ ta^ ni)
hhyul zeiq pyuq zeiq happier and nobler (46:123)
hhyulzuq zuq 1. to be excited (26:76), 2. to be shrivelled up

=hhyu, aq= maternal uncle
hhyudaf great (Chi) (34:63) (hui˯-eu)

hhyutoq to entrust (Chi)
hhyuyeiq a committee member (Chi)
  hhyuyeiqhyuf a committee (Chi)

hhyuq nine (9:74) (g'oe$_{\vee}$)
hhyuq to chew (9:74) (g'o$_{\vee}$-eu; g'oe$_{\vee}$-eu)
hhyuq to be covered (every part and corner); to wear clothes (pf. over '**hhoq**') (dm-eu)
Hhyuqba deidaq the name of an area ('nine flat places') (35:97)
=hhyuq, hoq= chewed up rice (as for infant)
-- hhyuq, hoqhhyuq -- to chew up food and feed it to an infant (human; bird)
hhyuq hu hu ceil hu hu to think and think many times; to consider carefully ('think nine, ten times') (57:185)
-- hhyuq, hhaqlei hhaqhhyuq -- to offer buckwheat
Hhyuqla siq September (11:69)
hhyuq luvq ceil luvq meil sufficient; quite enough (lo$_{\wedge}$-eu; g'a$_{\vee}$-eu)
hhyuq nei everywhere (yaw$_{\vee}$ ga$^{\vee}$ na lu$_{\wedge}$)
hhyuq nuv to chew to bits
hhyuqpovq the residue that is left after one chews something such as sugar cane, turnip, betel
hhyuq qa hhyuq lol zuvq to flourish; be bustling; busy (50:46)
hhyuqxei geelsal to be dangerous (A=Chi) (34:86)
hhyuqyaol an apron (Chi) (or) **laqlaol**
hhyuqzyul to surround (A=Chi) (57:129)

hhyufseil public health (Chi)
hhyufxil a satellite (Chi)

JA

jal old; broken (cf.: cehˇ; as in: nymˇ nymˇ cehˇ) (note: **albee beeja** = old quilt or blanket)
Jalbil Allaq the name of a "**Molmil**" (god) also called: **Zilbiei Alloq** = creator of the earth (**Mil zaol qivq ssol Zilbiei Alloq** = the earth was created by **Zilbiei Alloq**) (cf.: Jaˇ biˇ oeˬ lahˬ)
jalcev laqpil aqma a kind of edible water insect (14:139)
Jalceiq Jiangcheng (46:111)
  Jalceiq xeif Jiangcheng county (46:137)
jalcil aqma a wagtail bird (when it walks and cries its tail moves up and down, which looks like a seesaw) (4:37) (or) **jacil** (jaˇ tsiˇ)
jalgaolca a factory for processing (as for tea, sugar cane, etc.) (Chi) (26:69, 50:81)
jalhaof plus (in mathematical sense) (Chi)
jaljul type of bird (eats rice, looks like sparrow) (9:79) (cf.: jaˇ tseu^)
  jaljul lalhhaq swallow (brd) (26:60) (or) **zilkuv lalssaq**
jaljyul an army general (Chi) (50:84)
jaljyul aqma a sparrow-like bird (14:138)
jalkal a basket for catching fish (14:138)
jalniul green weeds; vegetables (**g'awˬ nyoeˇ**)
jalngeel a water larva which becomes a **dragon** fly (a smaller variety than jalzeiq) (14:138) (edi)
  jalngeel he to dredge up the above mentioned water insects (14:138)
jalqaq to enhance; strengthen (Chi) (34:29, 50:81)
jalsoq a rope used to tie loads on pack saddles (Chi) (14:214)
jaltiq a family (Chi) (15:7, 34:42)
jalxul xul to whistle; **jalxyul xyul** (jahˬ cehˇ cehˇ-eu)
Jal Zeqmiq PRC President and Party Secretary Jiang Zemin
jalzeiq a water larva which becomes a **dragon** fly (a longer and larger variety than **jalngeel**) (edi)
jalzii lolbieil a wooden table (from which they eat) (cf.: hawˬ jeh) (9:79)

ja to expand; stretch out; grow tall (2:51) (ja-eu)
=ja, albee bee= old quilt
jabaoq fish container made of **bamboo** (9:79, 45:89)
jabeeq weeds (9:79) (ja^ guˬ ja^ ga^)
  jabeeq beeqcaoq a big area of weeds (9:79)
=ja, beiv= green bean
jabu nei simply (50:115)
-- jacev, boqheiq -- black spots (as on one's face)
jacil a wagtail (46:165) This bird searches for

insects in mud, with its tail bobbing up and down without stopping. Hani compare women bobbing up and down transplanting rice with this bird. (or) **jalcil** (ja^{v} tsi^{v})

jacil daoqneiv a kind of wagtail (brd)

jadei a pasture (or) **zeiqssaq zeiqdei**

jahaq bitter herbs/grass

jahhaq grass; weeds (cf. Akha: ja^ g'a$_{v}$ = medicine)

jahhaq hhaqcaoq a large area of weeds; grass

jahhaq hhaqdei an expanse of grass or weeds (46:176)

jahhaq hhaqhe smell of grass; weeds (9:79)

jahhaq janiul 1. herbs, 2. grass (including the kind they feed to their animals) (33:3)

-- **jahhaq, keeqmiq** -- a type of grass that looks like dog tails

-- **jahhaq, naciq** -- a medicinal plant

jajoq nei oval shape

jajul loqniuv a snail (9:79) (a$_{v}$ nyo^)

jaju nei long and smooth (57:91)

jakaol a kind of grass used to weave mats (hu^{v} seu a^{v} baw$_{v}$)

ja'la long (**luduq ja'la ja'la nei** = a long pond) (46:155)

-- **ja'la meil, ju lu** -- to be shabby

ja'la nei slender; thin and long (9:79) (for humans: **ju nei**)

ja'lif 1. encourage and reward; award (Chi) (14:241) (or) **jalif** (50:84), 2. bonus (50:84)

-- **jameiq nei, jawuq** -- shabbily dressed; in rags

=**ja, neebeiv beiv**= cowpea plant

janiul weeds that can be used for animal food (33:3) (see also: **jahhaq janiul**) (mah$_{v}$ dza^{v})

-- **janiul, jahhaq** -- 1. herbs, 2. grasses

japi a prize (Chi)

jassaq plants (45:61)

-- **jassaq, soqssaq** -- (see full)

jasiil lecturer (Chi) (50:84)

jawuq jameiq nei shabbily dressed; in rags (45:57)

jaziiq lolbieil a wooden table

jazuaf certificate of merit (Chi) (50:84)

jaq to call (as to call an animal) (36:3) (ja$_{v}$-eu)

jaqbiei biei to talk actively (cf.: daw$_{v}$ ja yaw mya$_{v}$)

jaqbuq pride of wealth

jaqbuq buq to be proud of one's wealth; to show off (50:14)

jaqbuq seil to show off (as in a play, dance, etc. as in speech, or having many goods) (cf.: ja byaw$_{v}$-eu)

jaq duv to call someone or something to come out (46:156)

jaqhhal rib; side (or) **bialhhal** (pf) (14:138) (beh^{v} jeh^)

jaqhheivq hypocrisy (or) **javqheivq**

jaqhheivq aqbol a hypocritical old man
jaqhheivq hheivq to tell a lie (or) **aqmiaovq miaovq** (jaˬ myaw‸ myaw‸-eu)
jaqjiq jiq to hop on one foot
jaqleil wind (9:80) (jaˬ lehˇ)
jaqleil bo the wind to blow (jaˬ lehˇ baw-eu)
jaqleil bo tul la the wind to blow fiercely (30:2)
jaqleil duqbyu a 'wind hole' (spoken of in legends) (jaˬ lehˇ lehˇ boe)
jaqleil leilhha a whirlwind (and see: **jaqleil leilhhev**) (jaˬ lehˇ lehˇ zeu^)
jaqleil leilhhev whirlwind (or) **jaqleil leilhha** (jaˬ lehˇ lehˇ zeu^ zeu^-eu; jaˬ lehˇ lehˇ g'eu^ g'eu^-eu = CA) (11:35)
jaqleil leilma strong wind (9:80) (jaˬ lehˇ lehˇ ma)
jaqleil leilma mama a typhoon; very strong wind
jaqleil leilsev a cool wind (9:80) (jaˬ lehˇ yaw tseh‸)
jaqmal right (hand) side (9:80) (aˇ maˇ; la‸ maˇ)
jaqqal left (hand) side (9:80) (aˇ caˇ; la‸ caˇ)
jaqqal pyu left side (26:99) (la‸ caˇ paw)

jav 1. to have (inanimate), 2. for there to be (9:80) (ja^-eu)
javbuv 1. automatically; without thinking (35:85), 2. immediately
javbuv meil 1. generally (35:85), 2. an estimation
jav gav e aqzeiq remnants; vestiges (50:19)
=jav meil, nee= simply
-- jav, miavhhaq -- to be polite
javsev a mat of straw (9:80) (cf.: huˇ seu = a reed mat)
-- jav, siiqjeil -- to have time (A=Chi)

javq to be well cooked (ja‸-eu)
javqhheivq hheivq to tell a lie (or) **jaqhheivq hheivq; moqleevq leevq**
javqleel nei sleepily (yu‸ yoeˇ-eu)
javqleel nei yiuvq to sleep soundly (9:80)
javqleel nei yiuvq sil to be fast asleep (yu‸ k'a^-eu)
javq nei thoroughly (11:213) (dawˬ taw^ lu‸)
-- javq, qavq -- to cook until done
=javq, zal= digestion
-- javq, zaljavq -- to digest food

jaftiaoq a note asking for leave (Chi) (41:62)
jafsiisiiq driver's housing (as on a truck; tractor) (Chi) (26:32)
jafsiizof driver's seat (Chi) (26:98)
jafziiq gueilnieif viewpoint of value (an economic term) (Chi) (34:88)
jafziiq gyulliq law of value (an economic term) (Chi) (34:46)

JAO

=jaol, aq= (see full)
jaolheiq rubber shoes (Chi) (26:72)
jaolheiq seiqnaov rubber shoes (A=Chi) (50:85)
jaoljei camera film (Chi) (50:85)
jaoltaf refined charcoal (Chi) (26:28)
jaolxayoq symphony (Chi) (50:85)

jaoq 1. to be weak, 2. to wilt; fade; wither (as flowers) (9:79, 11:39) (nyoe⌄-iˇ ko^-iˇ-eu; shawˇ-iˇ-eu)
jaoqdaol a confirmative part. always following 'ngeel' (see: 45:11)
-- jaoq yil, hhaq -- to become weak

jaofdaof zusseif director of the teaching staff (Chi) (50:85)
jaofdyuf to proof read (something printed) (Chi)
jaofgei peiqgao to correct the press (Chi)
jaoqsef professor (Chi) (50:85)
jaofsiil a teacher (Chi) (50:85) (or) **laosiil**
jaofsiiq a classroom (Chi) (41:74) (or) **jaofsiif** (50:95) (or) **soqhhaq zolyaol**
jaofsiif lesson to be studied (as in school) (Chi) (41:74)
jaofsyuf lesson; moral (as a lesson to be learned, the moral of the story) (Chi) (34:71); lesson to be studied in school (or) **jaofsiif** (41:74)
jaoftiaoq doctrinairism (Chi) (34:24)
jaoftiaoq zuyif dogmatism; doctinairism; to go by the book (Chi) (50:85)
jaofwuf teaching affairs (Chi) (50:85)
jaofxoq dafgal teaching program (Chi) (50:85)
jaofxoq hhalpeiq teaching schedule (A=Chi) (50:85)
jaofxoq nyufyaoq contents of teaching (Chi) (86)
jaofxoq tixif teacher's system (Chi) (50:86)
jaofxoq yaolqeq teacher requirements (Chi) (50:86)
jaofyeq to educate (Chi) (50:86)
jaofyeq falzeil educational policy (Chi) (50:86)
Jaofyeqjiq Educational Bureau (Chi) (50:96)
jaofyeilzu teaching and research staff (Chi) (50:86)
jaofyiuq education (Chi) (41:14)

JE

jelpul government (Chi) (or) **zeiffu soqpaq qovq** ('family of rulers')

jejil high proof alchohol (50:91) (Chi)

jefjif supported by the government (Chi) (12:127)
jefsefhyuf the old society (Chi) (26:10)

jeil to be wet (as when clothes get wet) (9:80) (yaw a⌄)
=jeil, al= urine
-- jeil, aljeil -- to urinate (iˇ shoi shoi-eu)
jeilbiuvq pa biuvq nei totally wet; wet all over (9:80) (a⌄ ci⌄ ni)
jeilciiq zeilli to hold firmly to the truth (Chi) (34:22) (zi^ dah ni nyeh^ teh⌄-eu)
=jeil, daq= bandit; armed thief
jeilduq to supervise (Chi) (34:51)
jeil duvq to drench (or) **bi jeil**
jeilhhyuhyuf supervisory commission (Chi) (50:82)
jeiljyuq to be firm; resolute (Chi) (34:98)
jeilkaoq kaoq to feel the urge to urinate
jeilku feifdef to work hard while living simply (Chi) (26:75)
jeilma a woman servant
jeilnaq xeizu difficulties; obstacles (Chi) (34:85)
jeilpal a change of clothing (jehˇ paˇ = UL Ak.)
jeilpal pal to change one's clothes
jeilqaq strong; stronger (Chi) (26:111)
jeilquv pieiq lal to be punished by **Aqpyuq Miqyeil** for committing adultery
jeilso nei to be wet; damp (35:9) **(yaw a⌄)**
jeilso pa so nei wet all over (14:153) (yaw⌄ gaˇ na lu^ a⌄ ci⌄ ni)
=jeil, xaldei hhaq= terraced irrigated field
jeilyi siif double function in a sentence (Chi) (50:82)

jeibaol baol for a bonfire to burn (11:212)
jei caq to examine; inspect; check (as a doctor checks a sick person - 26,90; someone to examine train tickets) (Chi) (50:83) (go⌄ haw tseˇ haw-eu) (& see below)
jeicaq act as procurator (Chi) (50:83) (the Chinese characters for this and the above word are different)
jeicaq hhyuyeiq hyuf committee for procuratorial work (Chi) (50:83)
jeicaqyeif procurator (Chi) (50:83)
Jeidee a person's name (13:43)
Jei'faqjil diqsseiq diq the PLA fight against the enemy (A=Chi) (54:112)
jeihaof minus (as in math) (Chi)
jeihuaf soqmiav simplified characters (A=Chi) (50:83)
Jeike Jack (Eng-Chi)
jeiliq biographical notes (Chi) (50:83) (note: could also be spelled: **jei'liq**)
=jei, miavneev biei= to open one's eyes
jeipu numbered musical notation (Chi) (50:83)
Jeiseq (see: **Dulma Jeiseq aoqtav miltav colkyul**)

jeitao self-criticism (Chi)
jeiyeif biaolzyu the criterion for inspecting, examining (A=Chi) (50:83)

jeiq to be lax
jeiqhhev dovhhev meil when one carries a heavy load, and it almost touches the ground (in this case a bear - 35:17)
=jeiq, laq= musical gourd pipe
jeiqzao compost (rotting leaves, weeds, etc.)

jeiv 1. to scrape something off (9:80) (jeh^-eu), 2. to pull something out (13:6)

jeivq clf. for pieces (meat, bread, mud, etc.) (jeh‸)
=jeivq, haqluv luv= small stones
=jeivq, mil= mud dug out by a rat/mouse
=jeivq, nil= (see full)
-- jeivq, ya -- to crumble

jeifdif col 1. a judge, 2. an inspector (as one who inspects the quality of a product) (A=Chi)
jeifdyuf a naval force; a fleet (Chi) (50:84)
jeifgeiqhaof a dash or point (punctuation) (Chi) (50:83)
jeifgoq to establish the New China (Chi) (34:106)
jeifjiq xeiji indirect election (Chi) (50:84)
jeifseiq to build (Chi) (**gaolniq jeifseiq aol meeq movq** = want to build industries well - 26:40)
-- jeifseiq, seifhyuf zuyif -- to revolutionize to socialism (Chi)
Jeifsyu Jianshui, a county in the south of Yunnan Province (Chi) (41:11)
jeifti naval ships and boats (Chi) (50:84)
jeifxeif boundry line (Chi) (34:76)
jeifyif qeiqliq the right to make suggestions (Chi) (50:84)

JI

jil to finish something (**zaq e maq saq, dol e maq jil** = no problem with food, and drink is not finished yet)
jil all (9:81) (**leil kul jil** = all are called this - 13:40) (jiˇ cu˯ ni)
jil 1. real (9:81) (yaw maˇ; yaw du˯), 2. exact; accurate (**Ssil e lalbaq dyul buvqteiq e daov meeq, daov jil nga.** The ballads we sing are very good, very accurate - 41:91; **Doq maq jil taq gee** - Don't speak words which are not accurate. 18:10) 3. genuine (or) **yojil jil**, 4. honest
jil clf. for a 'catty' (a Chinese measure) (Chi) (about 1.3 pounds, or 500 grams - 2 jil = 1 kg.) (11:31, 41:128)
=jil aqda, haq= human males

=jil, beil= goiter
jilbei galli basic program (Chi) (50:78)
jilbei goqceiq national policy (Chi) (50:78)
jilbei goqqiq the basic condition of the whole nation (or) **jilbei goqciq** (Chi) (34:35)
jilbei lufxeif basic policy line (Chi) (50:78)
jilbei yeiqli basic principles (Chi)
jilbei yeiqzeiq yuvq mol the four principles (Marxism, Leninism, Mao Zedong thought, etc.) (A=Chi)
jilbil jeizeif better troops (or staff) and simpler administration (Chi) (50:89)
Jil Byu'lyul a person's name (35:40)
=jil, ceil= rice granary
jilceiq a grass roots unit; the basic level (Chi) (34:56)
jilceiq sseiqmiq faqyeif basic level people's court (Chi) (50:78)
jilceiq zeifqeiq zuziiq organizations of political power at the grass-roots level (Chi) (50:78)
jilceiq zuziiq primary organization; organizations at the basic level (Chi) (34:85, 50:78)
jilcu foundation (Chi) (**weiqhuaf jilcu** = cultural foundation - 34:12) (daw⌄ peh⌄)
=jil, doq= surely
=jil, eq= cogon grass; thatch grass
jilgaf miqbil primary militia (Chi) (50:78)
jilgef organization; organizational structure (Chi) (34:56, 50:79)
jilgef hhe xu simplify the administrative structure (A=Chi) (50:89)
jil geivq geivq chirp, chirp; creak, creak (as of a door), **qil qeiv qeiv**
jilgeifhuaf mechanized (Chi) (50:79)
jilgual office (41:50); institution; organization (50:79) (or) **jilgueil; jilgef; jilguaf**
jilgualqal miqbev a machine gun (A=Chi) (50:79)
jilgueil office; organization (or) **jilgual**
jilgueil a government work unit (Chi)
jilgueil gafbuf a government worker (Chi)
-- jil, haol -- to protect all
jilhevq nei really; truly; honestly; frankly (13:45, 26:42, 45:26, 46:148) (ma˅ ma˅)
=jil, hul= husband
jilhyuf an opportunity (Chi)
jilhyuf zuyif opportunism (Chi) (50:79)
jil jil yiq yiq cautious and conscientious (Chi) (34:86)
jil jil zal zal nei the sound of sparrows chirping (14:138) (or) **jiv jiv zav zav** (35:74)
jiljif economy; economics (Chi) (9:81, 34:3, 50:90)
jiljif gyulliq economic law (Chi)
jiljif meeqdaq effective result of economics (Chi) (50:90)
jiljif meeqduq economic effective interest (A=Chi)

jiljif teiqqil economic zone (Chi) (50:90)

jiljif wuqliq liq economic crisis (A=Chi) (50:90)

jiljif zeiqhuvq huvq to return what one has unlawfully taken (A=Chi) (50:90)

jiljif zeiqkoq koq economic war (A=Chi) (50:90)

jiljif zeiqkuv kuv economic recession (A=Chi) (50:90)

jilli a manager (Chi) (41:4, 50:90)

jil li jil hevq nei honest (45:93) (dawˇ coe ni)

jilloqbuf a club of people (Chi) (50:93)

jilma a kilogram (**jilssaq** = half a kilogram) (57:150)

-- **jilma, savjil** -- a large scale for weighing

=**jil meil, ngeel**= really

-- **jilmeil, ngeeljil** -- seek truth from facts; to be practical and realistic

=**jil, meiq**= lips

jilmiq hhyuyeiq hyuf neighborhood committee (Chi) (50:92)

jilpav 1/4 of kg., 250 grams (A=Chi) (14:237)

Jilpiq the name of a county (35:44, 74)

Jilpiq Hhaoldal a place in Jinping County (35:43)

Jilpol Kachin; Jingpaw (tribal group, both in Burma and China) (Kaˇ tsawˇ haˬ)

jilqal machine gun (Chi) (or) **miqbev jilqal** (miˬ beu^ gaw ja)

jilqif a machine (Chi) (9:81, 11:155, 26:26, 50:79)

-- **jilqif, ceil diq** -- a rice threshing machine

jilqif col a robot (A=Chi) (50:79)

Jilsaljal the Jinshajiang River (35:96)

jilseiq ceiqfuf 'mental property' (such as copyrights on books, cassettes, etc.) (Chi) (34:27)

jilseiq siiqziiq the substance; essence (Chi) (34:24)

jilseiq weiqmiq spiritual civilization (Chi) (50:90)

jilssaq half a kilogram (**jilma** = a kilogram)

jiltieiqfeif to subsidize; help out with funds (Chi) (26:91)

jilxel ceiljeil repair workshop (Chi) (26:33)

jilxil daofpeiq soul stirring (Chi) (34:97)

jilyaoq finance; banking (Chi) (34:40)

jilyaoq guali faqgyul regulations of financial management (Chi) (50:88)

jilyeif experience (Chi) (34:23, 50:90)

jilyeif zuyif empiricism (Chi) (50:90)

-- **jil, yojil** -- to be genuine; true

jibaof alarm; warning (could be a sign) (Chi) (50:91)

jicaq police (Chi) (50:91)

Jigalsal haolgaoq Jinganshan mountain (A=Chi) (50:91)

jihhyufbal a guard squad (Chi) (50:91)

jihhyufyeiq body guard (Chi) (50:91)

jijaoq nei tamely (50:1)

jiliq 1. discipline (Chi) (34:59), 2. strict rules, 3. principle (as one follows) (50:81) (or) **ji'liq**

(and see: **jiqliq**)

jiliq jeicaq hhyuyeiqhyuf commission for inspecting discipline (Chi) (50:81)

jiseiq landscape picture (Chi) (50:91)

jitiq to be on guard against (Chi) (34:113)

jixiq hold a meeting; hold a conference (Chi) (50:93)

jiq to sift; strain through a sieve (je˯-eu)

-- jiq, aoqjiq -- to thunder

jiqcaol a very fine sieve

jiqgeiq to pass (Chi) (as to pass a course, a class, or in the army to pass a course in throwing hand grenades) (26:42, 50:80)

-- jiqhav, aoqjiq -- thunder without rain

jiqhoq to combine with (Chi) (34:5, 24)

jiqhuaf jiljif a planned economy (Chi) (34:38)

-- jiq, jaqjiq -- to hop on one foot

jiqjiq to be active (Chi) (9:81)

jiqjiq feilzil active person (Chi) (50:78)

jiqjiqxif enthusiasm (Chi) (34:16) (nui ma keu^-eu)

(vb) jiq (vb) jiq meil (vb) to (vb) very quickly (**aol jiq aol jiq meil aol** = to work very quickly, **buvq jiq buvq jiq meil buvq** = to write very quickly) (kawˇ kawˇ-ehˇ mˇ-eu)

jiqkal a sieve with large holes (9:81)

jiqliq to discipline (Chi) (**buqdyuf e jiqliq** = army discipline - 26:103) (and see: **ji'liq**)

jiqliq a solar period (twenty-four in a year) (Chi) (41:118) (or) **jiqqif**

-- jiq, loqjiq -- to stammer

jiqmieif aspect; phase (Chi) (34:48)

jiqmuq items in a performance (Chi) (50:87)

jiq nei like thunder - the sound of snoring (13:33)

jiqnieif to commemorate (Chi) (26:55)

Jiqnieif Beq Qeq'eil Memoirs of Dr. Bethune, a doctor from Canada who helped the Chinese, written by Mao Zedong (Chi) (26:55)

jiqpuceil a Jeep (Chi-Eng) (50:80)

jiqqi to derive (Chi) (34:68) (or) **jiqqiq**

jiqsiif situation (Chi) (50:92)

jiqsuq to finish; to end (Chi) (34:113) (mˇ g'a˯; mˇ lui^; mˇ jiˇ)

jiqti a unit; a collective unit of some sort (Chi) (26:107)

jiqtihuaf collective (Chi) (50:79)

jiqti lidaof collective leadership (Chi) (50:79)

jiqti hoqzoq sef collective co-op period (1966-1976)

jiqti soyeziif collective ownership system (Chi) (50:79)

jiqti zuyif collectivism (Chi) (34:59, 50:79)

jiqwei an ending (as of a letter one writes) (Chi)

jiqxeifxif limited; strict (Chi) (50:92)

jiqxyuf to assemble for training (Chi) (50:80)

jiqyeq sesuq sterilization operation (both male and

female) for family planning (Chi) (50:94) (and see: **jiqzaq**

jiqyif conclusion of meeting; conference (Chi) (50:93)

jiqyoq 1. to save something, as a burning building, 2. to save money (as 10 cents a day) (26:75), 3. to be thrifty (Chi)

jiqyoq neiqse a 'model saver' (Chi) (as to keep from using too much gasoline or other goods) (26:100)

jiqzaq contraception by sterilization (for men and women) (Chi) (50:88) (& see: **jiqyeq sesuq**)

jiqzaol to concentrate; put together (Chi) (34:80)

jiqso lufxeif galma ultra left line (political sense; left-leaning (AB=Chi) (50:80)

jiv to grind (leh˯-eu)

=**jiv jivngaoq, miq**= (see full)

jiv jiv zav zav the noise of chirping birds (35:74) (or) **jil jil zal zal** (14:138)

jivluv a stone mill; a grinding stone (9:81, 11:35, 46:143) (lo leh˯)

jivluv jivniuv central wooden peg in a stone mill

jivluv jivseq gears ('teeth') in a stone mill (11:35)

=**jiv, miq**= burning coals

jiv nuv to mill grain (ceh˅ leh˯ leh˯-eu)

jivseq gears ('teeth') in a mill or grinding stone

-- **jiv, seqjiv** -- to grind one's teeth in a dream

jivtuv a peeler for turnips, potatoes (9:81)

jivyov one kind of taro (9:81)

-- **jiv, zaljiv** -- animals to ruminate; to chew the cud

jivq clf. for a kind of (9:81)

=**jivq jivq, hal**= whatever

=**jivq nei, hal**= (see full)

-- **jivq, qiq** -- (see full)

=**jivq, xil**= this; these

-- **jivqyal aol, neema** -- 1. to think hard, 2. to consider seriously

jifbei soqkaoq a book written for a play; drama (A=Chi) (50:93)

jifbuf to improve; progress (Chi) (34:12, 20) (mui˯ la˅-eu)

jifca theater (Chi) (50:93)

jifdeif modern times (Chi)

jifdeifsii modern history (Chi) (34:59)

jifhaof period; full stop (punctuation mark) (Chi)

jifhuaf a plan (Chi) (9:80)

jifhuaf gua'li planned management (Chi) (34:46)

jifhuaf jiljif a planned economy (Chi) (50:80)

jifliaf dalhhyuf units of measure (Chi) (41:124)

jifsuq skill (Chi) (26:33)

jifsuq geiqmif technical revolution (Chi) (50:80)
jifsuq geiqxil technical reform (Chi) (50:80)
jifsuq liq maq bav their skills are not bad (A=Chi) (41:198)
jifsuq zol to learn a skill (A=Chi) (26:28)
jifti concrete (as a concrete idea) (Chi) (34:46)
jiftihuaf details of a plan (Chi) (or) **juftihuaf** (34:74)
jifzeil to compete (Chi) (34:76)

JIEI

Jiei'faqjil diqsseiq diq the People's Liberation Army's fight against the enemy (A=Chi) (54:112)

JO

jol 1. to be at; be; exist (animate), 2. stay (1-2. jawˇ-eu), 3. to sit (9:82) (nuiˇ-eu)
jol clf. for times
-- jol, aqhhuv -- sit down
-- jol, baqjol -- to be in love
=jol, col= life; a person's life
jol cuv to settle down; to live somewhere permanently (57:145)
jol cyuq for an animate object (as a cow) to block the way (**galma liq jol cyuq saq al** = the path was blocked - 26:90) (jawˇ tsoe˯-eu)
joldaq a cushion (nuiˇ da˯)
jolduq address; place where one lives (jawˇ du˯)
jolduq jolhhal a place to live and stay (38:109, 46:77) (jawˇ du˯ jawˇ zaˇ)
jolduq ssal miq to give place to
jolduq ssivq to gain a footing; to have a firm foundation (jawˇ du˯ zi˰-eu)
jol haol to help just by being there
jolhhal 1. a seat (9:82) (nuiˇ du˯), 2. a place to live (jawˇ du˯)
jolhhal maq bo not to be settled; to have no permanent place to live; to be nomadic (jawˇ du˯ ma˯ baw)
jolhhal maq ssaoq scattered here and there (50:92)
jolhhal sal to have a good place to live ('sit') (jawˇ zaˇ yaw mui˯)
jolhhal xa to settle down in some place (as the army or a work team) (50:2)
jollalhha daily (9:82) (yaw˯ nah na lu˰)
jollalhha e miqnieiq the usual thing
jolmiaoq to sit closely
jolnaq naq to have a holiday (46:141) (jawˇ nah taw˯)
jolnao holiday (9:82) (jawˇ nah)
jol pal to change one's residence; to move (or) **jolduq pal** (jawˇ paˇ-eu; pawˇ-eu)
jol qav to have stayed (45:58) (jawˇ-eu˯)
jolqil 1. a state of mind (11:93), 2. a standpoint

(50:105)
jolqil ssivq to take a firm stand (50:105)
jolqil xa 1. to live happily (jawˇ mui˯-eu), 2. to gain a footing
jolsal healthy; comfortable (9:82) (jawˇ saˇ-eu)
jolsal duv free from inhibitions; carefree (50:22)
jolsaq uncomfortable (11:28) (jawˇ sha˯-eu)
jolsyuq to be hard up; life is hard (9:82) (jawˇ su‸-eu)
jol taq to occupy; to be present (jawˇ ta˯-eu)
jol xa to sit down (41:61) (nuiˇ-eu)
=jol, yeil= a cycle (as of days)
jol zo e used to living (**aqgav gav e milcaq a maq jol zo e liq** ... = even though he was not used to living in a cold climate - 26:34)
jolzyul to come together; to gather (9:82) (ui˯ laˇ-eu)

=jo, hhaq= to exchange manpower
-- **jo, laoljo** -- to make a fire lane in the village
(vb) **jo soq** to get revenge for (vb) (**diqjo soq** = to get revenge for a beating; **hheivqjo soq** = to get revenge for being lied to)

joq 1. to separate (la^ pa^-eu), 2. to have a man's hair cut
joq particle for polite imperative to second person -- (**hoq zaq joq** = please eat) (9:82) (jaw˯)
joq tropical (and see: **joq joq**)
joq (vb) as soon as (vb) (**miav joq biei** = as soon as he opened his eyes - 13:14), (**joq duv yil** = as soon as he went out - 13:19), (**Aoqbia joq bia ngaoq**.. As soon as the sun rose... 11:113)
joqceil lowland rice (deh yaˇ cehˇ)
joqgal galma path in a tropical area
joqhav niabeiv a small basket to hold fish (14:138)
joq hu the first glance (13:11) (haw beh beh-eu)
joqhyuq fog; cloud (9:82) (ju˯ k'oe˯)
joqhyuq aqpyuq the spirit of the clouds (38:91)
joqhyuq cyuq to be foggy (14:209) (ju˯ k'oe˯ tm˯-eu)
joqhyuq hyuqpiul a white cloud (46:171) (ju˯ k'oe˯ k'oe˯ pyuˇ)
joqhyuq lavqmeev taoq nei very thick and dark fog (ju˯ k'oe˯ zahˇ-eu)
joqhyuq qiq kaoq hholqei naolma naolkeel qiq kao kev 'in every cloud there is a ray of sunshine'
joq joq to be a tropical area (warm weather) (op. is: **haoldaol daol** = mountain area)
joq (vb) joq (vb) immediately (10:27) (**joq deivq duv joq eelceivq nei aqbul ciq miq** = immediately at birth give a bath in cold water) (ja pyu˯ ni)
joq mol as soon as he saw (13:11)
=joq, mol= whole body; whole; entirely
-- **joq, naolma beeljoq** -- for red rings to form

around the sun
joq nei at once; immediately (9:82) (ja pyu⌄ ni)
joqnil one of the Hani ancestral offerings
Joqnil siq February (or) **Zyuqnil siq**
joqqaq baqleil a type of olive with small and round fruit (9:82) (cf.: **julleiv**)
=joq, qiq (n, n)= (**qiq yaol yaoljoq** = the whole house, **qiq yavq yavqjoq** = the whole night, etc.)
=joq, soq= annual rings in trees
-- joq, soqjoq -- to peel back bark from trees
joq ssuq to go immediately (13:14)
joq tao the moment he/she/it entered; as soon as he/she/it entered (13:29)
joq taoq fog; thick clouds (ju⌄ k'oe⌄)
joqtaoq beeq to be foggy (14:235)
joqtaoq taoq fog; thick clouds to develop (9:82) (ju⌄ k'oe⌄ tm⌄-eu)
joqto alqul a banana (nga beh^)
joqto haqhhal partridge (brd) (9:82) (nga cehˇ)
joqto haoldaol a tropical mountain (14:188)
joqto miuvqsiil small yellow monkey (lives in warm places) (aˇ myo⌃ shuiˇ)
joq tul as soon as one gets up; as soon as one wakes up (4:38)
-- joq, wuqjoq -- (see full)
joqwuf conscience (Chi) (26:103)
joq yil joq lal to go and come quickly (13:53)
joqyoq to balance out equally (with or without scales)
joqyoq alsiil to divide equally (without scales) (ti⌄ kaw^ mya^ biˇ pa^-eu)
-- joq, yuqjoq -- a vine fence
joqzaq spring festival (46:81)
joqzaq hhoheiq duv ceremony at the end of the spring festival when the villagers all eat together at long tables outside their homes
Joqzaq siq January (lunar) (lit. the month in which the spring festival is held) (46:128) (or) **Zyuqzaq siq**
joqzaq zaq to hold the spring festival (46:78)
joqzyul ringworm (9:83) (k'a⌄ tseh^ tseh^ nyaw⌄ naˇ-eu)

=jov nei, hhaol= very hard (not soft)

jovq nice to look at (haw mui⌄-eu)

JU

jul 1. bald (as a head) (u⌄ de⌄ de⌄-eu), 2. clean (juˇ tsui⌄ ni; juˇ ga⌃ ni = CA)
=jul, beil= basket (smallish)
juldal chopsticks (9:83) (yu daˇ, ju daˇ)
juldal dalbaoq chopstick holder made of bamboo (9:83) (ju daˇ bah⌄)

juldal dalbeiv a holder for a pair of chopsticks

juldal havpuq a woven basket in which to keep chopsticks

=jul, jal= a type of bird (similar to sparrows, eats rice in the fields)

jul jul yaq yaq very smooth (very smooth (juˇ tsui ni)

=jul, keel= fetters for the legs

=jul, lavq= handcuffs

julleiv a type of olive with big and oval fruit (cf.: **joqqaq baqleil**)

julluq nei 1. smooth (juˇ k'eu ni), 2. bald (**wuqduq julluq nei** = the head is bald) (9:83) (uˬ deˬ deˬ-eu; aˬ caˇ caˇ-eu)

julluq pa luq very soft and smooth (14:150)

-- jul, miavjul -- to look intently with a squinty expression, partially closed eyes (13:31)

=jul, naq= earring

julniul jewelry (esp. glass & beads) (or) **julsiq** (juˇ ma)

julniul alsiq a glass or bead ornament (juˇ ma)

=jul, ngaq= a loach (type of small fish)

=jul, saol= handcuffs; fetters

julsiq bead (glass) (or) **julniul** (juˇ ma; juˇ ma juˇ siˬ)

=jul, wuq= bald head

ju to flow (liquids) (yoeˇ-eu)

ju to be smooth (**biavq mol ju nei** = the board is smooth) (yaw juˇ)

ju dav a vine to grow (**alcav judav** = a climing vine) (14:218)

-- ju, diq -- to beat black and blue

ju duv yi to ooze out (or) **milbieiv ju duv yi**

=ju, eel= drool; slobber (as infant) (iˇ ju ju-eu)

ju ju geiq geiq extremely smooth

=ju, haq= snow

-- ju, haqju -- to snow (9:64) (no word in Ak.)

-- ju, hhaqcil leiq -- to lubricate

ju ju ja la meil to be shabby

=ju ju meil, yo= a lot of

-- jukov, miavbil -- tear stains

=ju, loq= long irrigated fields

ju lu ja la meil to be shabby (cf. **peil jal laq jal dao** = to dress in a shabby fashion)

-- juma, moqnil -- sweet potato (mawˬ coeˇ)

ju nei 1. bald; smooth (or) **julluqnei** (yaw juˇ), 2. shiny (as when one has tears in one's eyes) (45:73), 3. slender (as thin humans)

ju nei diq zoq dav to get up

=ju, pavqdeiq deiq= flower of a prickly plant

=ju, sal= vermicelli made from bean starch

-- ju, wuqju -- to crawl on one's stomach

ju xa to drip out; drip down (9:83) (dza^ ka-eu)

juq loose (ya˅ k'eu ni)
juq to throw (as a javelin)
-- **juq, aolhhaq** -- to lose one's strength
juqbaoq 1. the waist (jo‸), 2. a weaver's shuttle (za‸ joe˅)
juqbieiq nei to be loose (9:83) (ya˅ k'eu ni)
juqdev the waist; the hip (35:3, 45:89, 46:152)
juqdev miavjeil a dagger or knife carried at the waist (46:152) (cf.: ji˅ ba^)
juqhyuq a mist
juqhyuq hyuqbaq for a haze to be present
Juqlu Aqsei creator of the heavens
-- **juq, neema** -- to cool off from anger
juqtao za wide adaptability (50:155)
juqzaoq belt (9:83) (jo‸ pa‸; jo‸ tsi˅)
juqzaoq pavq hhal the small of one's back ('where the belt is tied')

=**juv, lul**= bird snare
juv luv juv luv meil a rattling sound given off when something is shaken (as a dried walnut shell) (14:148)
=**juv, wuv**= (see full)

juftihuaf details of a plan (Chi) (34:74) (or) **jiftihuaf**

JYU

jyul, jyul, jyul 1. the sound of ducklings (14:138); 2. the sound of insects
jyulbif jifseif armament race (Chi) (50:94)
jyuldyuf army (Chi) (9:83)
jyulfaq a warlord (Chi) (34:4)
jyulfeilqil military sub-command; military subarea (Chi) (50:94) (it is under the: **jyulqil**)
jyulgoq zuyif militarism (Chi) (50:94)
jyulhhyu army committee (Chi) (50:94)
jyulhhyu zuxiq chairman of the army committee (Chi) (50:94)
jyuljeif loq a battle ship (A=Chi) (50˅94)
-- **jyul, miavjyul** -- to narrow one's eyes
jyulqil military region; military area command (the highest rank of the armed forces) (Chi)
jyulsiif military affairs; matters related to the army (Chi) (26:89, 104, 34:80)
jyulsiif xyuflieif army training (Chi) (26:42)
jyulsiif zafxeif military frontier line (Chi) (50:94)
jyulsiif ziihyulyeiq military commander (Chi) (50:94)
jyulyiq mavqssaq jolduq army camp; barracks (A=Chi) (50:94)
jyulza army commander (Chi) (50:94)
jyulzeif dafxoq military academy (university) (Chi)

(50:94)

-- jyu, daoqjyu -- to crawl on muddy ground
jyu duv to slide away (on something slippery) (14:139) (tah⌄ juˇ g'eh-eu)

jyuq oval (11:55)
jyuqceiq to make policy or strategy decisions (Chi) (34:56)
jyuqdif to decide; to resolve (Chi) (34:80) (noe⌄ tseh^-eu)
jyuqdyu absolute (Chi) (34:80)
-- jyuq, hhe -- to stretch out
-- jyuq, keeljyuq -- to rub one's feet
jyuqlei nei stillness (26:6) (a⌄ ciˇ cu ni)
jyuqsa nei elliptical (9:83)
jyuqza a director (Chi) (14:209)

KA

kal scarce; sparse (9:84, 11:55) (yaw kaˇ)
kal crops (cf.: Kaˇ yehˇ = the spirit that watches over the rice crop)
kal clf. for times; crops
(vb) kal let's (vb) (9:83) (**Ngaldu xilmeil aol kal.** Let's do it this way.) (... kaˇ-euˇ)
=kal, aq= later; in the future
kalbyu nei from the holes in a basket used to catch fish (14:139)
kal cuv kal mal for planted crops to grow and mature well (14:195)
kaldol bad-omen in the crops
kaldol maq bi duv lal let no bad-omen occur in the crops
kalduv eq to carry new rice home (46:209)
kalfaf open to the outside (Chi) (34:12) (or) **keilfaf** (pf.)
kalfeil coffee (Chi-Eng) (ka˯ pi˯)
Kalgyu Lahu (or) **Kalgyussaq; Lalhuq** (Meu˯ seu˯ za˯)
kalhhuv pao to begin planting crops ('open the door') (ka daw˄-eu; ka dah˯ beh-eu)
=kal, jiq= a sieve
-- kal, lavqkal -- hands to be very cold
kal luv cuvhhal a sacred stone at the bottom of the village which is to help protect village crops (see also: **saol luv cuvhhal; hhaq luv cuvhhal**)
Kalluvq Caqnavq Aqma the divine protector of crops (one of three manifestations of: **Aqpyuq Miqyeil**)
kalma a main crop (9:84); major crops (50:30)
=kal, miav= eye glasses
=kal, miaoq= crops
kalnal nal lal e to have crop diseases (46:167)
kalnaol an ear (or head) of grain (usually rice) (9:84)
kalqil roots of plants (35:116) (du˯ ciˇ)
kalqul the fragrance of a crop
kalquv for crops to bud
=kal, saol= iron fence; railing
kalseil nei thinly scattered (9:84) (yaw kaˇ)
kalsiq crops
kalssaq 1. spring crops (46:167), 2. seedlings
kaltov pavq tie grass to the stems of ripened rice hoping there will be more next year
kalwuq cyuq to take the first ear of corn harvested and hang it up on the rack over the fireplace
kalyei crops (cf.: Kaˇ yehˇ = the spirit that watches over the rice crop)
kalyei bavqleev to harvest crops; **kalyei** se leev
kalyei se leev to harvest a crop; **kalyei bavq leev**
kalyei se'leev tovq the time to harvest a crop

kalyeiv crops in flower
  kalyeiv yeiv for crops to flower (kaˇ yeh^ yeh^ laˇ-eu)
kalzal pavq to tie a few ears of rice to the mat (**diqhhal**) tied to the threshing 'boat'
kalzuv to agitate a basket used for fishing (14:139)

=ka, al= crab
=ka, baq= very thin
ka faq zeif a written permit (as a permit to cut down trees) (Chi)
-- kahovq, alka -- the upper body of a crab
-- kassaq, baqka -- to be very, very thin

kaq to be a period of time (kaˬ)
kaq to separate (2:52, 9:85) (kaˬ-eu)
kaq negation; no; not (2:52) (**Tyulmeil leil aol e maq kaq.** It is not good to do it like this. 11:98)
kaq all right; better (9:85, 11:109) (& see above) (maˬ gaˇ)
kaq to recover (after sickness); healed (9:85, 13:14) (maˬ gaˇ laˇ-eu)
kaq 1. different (46:111) (beu gaˇ-eu), 2. distance (50:20)
kaq clf. for umbrella (**beelkaq qiq kaq** - 11:114)
=kaq, al= in between
-- kaq, alciiv -- a little better (slightly recovered)
-- kaq, alkaq -- 1. to solve a dispute, 2. to testify; give evidence; bear witness
=kaq, ba= a riddle
=kaq, bavq= 1. to cover, 2. to cure a disease by drugs
=kaq, beel= umbrella
kaq caq kaq caq the sound of rubbing (14:185) (Chi)
kaqceiv to be judged (50:83)
  -- kaqceiv, huqteil -- first judgment; first trial (50:201)
=kaq, col= a go-between; a witness
=kaq, dei= outside the house
-- kaq, deiq -- to cover over
-- kaq, diq -- a cap; a cover
Kaqdol the Kaduo branch of the Hani (46:79)
-- kaqdoq, colkaq -- statement of a witness
-- kaq e, galmol -- to be remote; far away
-- kaq, gyu -- to thatch over
=kaq kaqssaq, puv= a small village
kaq lal to get better (as from sickness); on way to recovery (maˬ gaˇ laˇ-eu)
-- kaq lal, nalgol -- for a sickness to get better
kaqla beforehand (11:110)
  kaqla mahuvq the years gone by (9:85)
  kaqla manao 1. the other day (38:18) (aˬ yaw˰ nah yaw˰), 2. daily (yawˬ nah na lu˰)
kaqla na maq dul special; peculiar; exceptional

(50:164)
kaqla na maq dul zeifceiq a policy which is different from the former one (E=Chi) (50:164)
kaqlaq 1. among; inside of (14:138) (la˄ k'oeˇ), 2. relationship (50:64)
-- kaqlaq, aoq hhel -- the relation between supply and demand
=kaq, laol= the village ceremonial gate of the Akha
=kaq, meil= medium hard walnut
=kaq, mil= border line
=kaq, miaq= wild arrowhead plant (grows in water)
-- kaq, nal -- recover from sickness
=kaq, pal= cloth woven with an open weave; coarsely woven cloth
kaq saq al to recover fully (ta˅ tseh^ leˇ-eu)
=kaq, seq= the space between two teeth
=kaq, seiq= space between two toes
-- kaqsiivq, puvkaq -- new village
kaq sol fully recovered (13:54) (ta˅ tseh^ leˇ-eu˅)
=kaqssaq, col= a judge
=kaq, xal= field boundary
-- kaq, zaol -- to heal a person; to cure

kav a crossbow (ka^)
kav a harrow (nyo˅ ka^)
kav a comb (paw˅ tsahˇ)
kav to comb (6:192, 9:85) (ka^-eu)
kav to harrow (9:86) (ka^-eu)
=kav alcav, meiq= silver chain
kavbaol baol to harrow a field leaving piles in it
kavceiq ceiq to harrow a field deeply (cf.: **kavsuq suq**)
kavcoq coq to harrow a field here and there (where it is needed)
kavdei to harrow a field to make it level (jeh^ ka^ ka^-eu)
=kav, laq= a harrow
kavlev hhe dav to cock a crossbow (ka^ ngo˄-eu)
kavloq the groove in a crossbow where the arrow fits
kavmiaq a crossbow arrow (9:86) (ka^ mya˅)
kavmiaq miaqbaoq a quiver for arrows (ka^ mya˅ bah˅)
kavniuq a buffalo for harrowing
=kav, niuq= a harrow (for buffalo or cow)
kavngeeq 1. a wooden hook for hanging things, 2. a hooked metal weeder (or) **saol kavngeeq** (cf.: la˄ ngeu˅)
kavpi cord of a crossbow (8:18) (ka^ pi)
kavpuv the main shaft of a crossbow
kavse se to harrow fields flat (ka^ di-eu)
kavseq the 'teeth' in a harrow (jeh^ ka^ seu˅)
kavsuq suq to harrow a field shallowly (cf.: **kavceiq ceiq**)
kavtev crossbow (9:86) (ka^)
kavtev hhe dav to cock a crossbow (ka^ ngo˄-eu)

(vb) **kavq** to be going on; continuous action (35:41) (**diq kavq** = fighting, **dev kavq** = cutting) (lu‸-eu)

-- kavq, bavq -- 1. to embrace, 2. to mix with

kavq cavq to be tied together with a rope (35:68) (ka‸ cuˬ-eu)

kavqceq 1. to hang on (14:166, 46:199), 2. to tie on (45:89); 3. to hang up (45:30) (ciˬ ceuˬ-eu)

kavqceq dav 1. to tie high up (as in tree) (13:13) (pa‸ taw‸-eu), 2. to fine someone for doing wrong (guiˇ o‸ ti‸-eu)

kavq'e from the time of; before that time (**Ngal miqteil kavq'e eil al.** I said it from the first - 11:111) (mehˬ hu)

-- kavq, kovq -- 1. to bite down hard, 2. to bite each other

kavq leev to tie up (ka‸ cu‸-eu; pa‸ taw‸-eu; ka‸ lah-eu)

kavq nei dense (as leaves) (46:130) (yaw tsahˇ)

=kavq, nei= since; from that time

-- kavq nei, tyultaq -- from that time; since that time; from the beginning

kavq paoq to tie together (46:190) (pa‸ dzoeˇ-eu)

kavq puv to tie with a rope (14:201) (ka‸ cu‸-eu)

kavq siivq to tie something tightly (11:162) (ka‸ cu‸-eu; pa‸ teuˇ-eu)

kavq ssivq to fix something (general repair) (or) **zaol ssivq**

kavq tovq 1. to tie; fasten (13:13) (ka‸ taw‸-eu; pa‸ taw‸-eu; tmˬ cu‸-eu), 2. to be tight (9:86)

-- kavqtovq, hyuq -- to abduct (esp. a person)

-- kavqtovq, lavqdu alcav -- to tie a string around the wrist of a person who has had his/her soul called back.

kavq zaoq a bundle (9:86) (aˇ dzahˬ)

kavqzaoq zaoq to make ('bundle') a bundle (aˇ dzahˬ dzahˬ-eu)

kafseso a temporary lock-up for prisoners awaiting trial (Chi) (50:95)

kafzeil fight natural calamities; prevent disasters (Chi) (50:96)

KAO

kaol clf. long things (thread, road, canal, long ditch, etc.) (11:152) (kahˇ)

kaol clf. for certain animals such as: donkey, buffalo, cow (11:18) (cf.: mawˇ = for all animals)

=kaol, al= thread; fiber

kaolbev; kaolbev alcav 1. an inked line in a carpenter's marker (to mark straight lines on boards) (46:117), 2. a rope used to lead a buffalo to go left or right when plowing or harrowing

=kaol, byuq= silk thread

=kaol, ceil= hair of the head
kaolceiqjif empty-city strategum in war (allow the enemy into the city, then ambush them) (Chi) (50:97)
kaoldal to rely on (A=Chi) (cf.: k'aw, daʸ-eu = to lean against)
kaoldaol a bamboo fence (9:84) (or) **laolkaol; haqbol kaoldaol; haqbol laolkaol** (kmʸ cehʸ)
kaoldaol aol to fence in (or) **kaoldaol hhavq; kaoldaol diq**
kaoldaol diq (see: **kaoldaol aol**)
kaoldaol hhavq (see: **kaoldaol aol**)
=kaol, guvq= silk thread
kaolhel pole for climbing beans (46:96)
kaoljyul air force (Chi) (50:97)
=kaol, laol= a fence or wall
kaollee a spool of thread (9:84)
kaolpav half of buffalo, cow, horse (11:67)
kaolpiul cav xu the white string used to tie the umbilical cord
kaolqif air (Chi) (Hani = **aqleil**) (10:26) (ja, lehʸ)
kaolsiq bi siq a knot of thread (14:178) (ca^ tm,)
kaolsiivq kaolnil cev ceiv for a new bride to break a red thread tied to two stakes over a ditch or stream before crossing (a part of marriage ceremony)
kaolto a wall (9:84) (cf.: taw pa^-eu = to wall off something)

kao an examination (as in school) (Chi) (41:897)
kao to blow one's nose (9:84) (na, behʸ baw dzeh-eu)
kao clf. for a hair, straw (kahʸ)
kao dav to pass an examination (50:96)
kaoheiq to test; to have an examination (50:96)
=kao, saq= a line of muscle in meat
kaosiif kao to have an examination (A=Chi) (50:96) (sah, bo^ naʸ ha,-eu)
kaoyeif a test (Chi) (34:89)

kaoq clf. for book, cloth, iron, piece of paper, page in a book (**soqhhaq qiq kaoq** = a page in a book), etc.
-- kaoq, alsyuq syuqkaoq -- to feel pain when urinating
kaoqbaoq throat (6:170, 9:85) (kaw, byah,; ku, byah,)
kaoqbaoq gee to be thirsty ('throat is dry') (ku, byah, gui-eu)
kaoqciivq larynx; adam's apple (9:85) (kaw, tsui^)
=kaoq, daoq= buttocks
=kaoq, duq= cloth patch
kaoqhav 1. trachea; windpipe (9:85) (sa^ g'awʸ byoe), 2. to be coarse
kaoqhav hav to become coarse (or) **kaoqhav laqngaoq**
kaoqhe he to snore (9:85, 11:219, 13:33) (ku, byah,

mah$^{\vee}$-eu)
-- kaoq, jeilkaoq -- to feel the urge to urinate
kaoqlaol neck (outside) (6:170) (kaw$_{\vee}$ lah$^{\vee}$)
kaoqnao nao to choke (9:85) (daw$^{\vee}$ nga$_{\wedge}$-eu)
kaoqnao ziivq nei difficult to swallow (12:126) (myo$_{\wedge}$ ah$^{\vee}$-eu yaw sha$_{\vee}$)
=kaoq, nee= misunderstanding; estrangement
kaoqpiul perspiration; sweat (6:172, 9:85) (or) **koqpiul** (35:58) (ku$_{\vee}$ pyu$^{\vee}$; kaw$_{\vee}$ pyu$^{\vee}$)
kaoqpiul cal to sweat all over (ku$_{\vee}$ pyu$^{\vee}$ do^-eu; kaw$_{\vee}$ pyu$^{\vee}$ do^-eu)
kaoqpiul piulsiq prickly heat rash (9:85)
kaoqpiul yobyu a pore in the skin (5:822) (ku$_{\vee}$ pyu$^{\vee}$ yoe$^{\vee}$ byoe)
kaoqpuq piei nei one's throat to swell with anger
-- kaoq, saqkaoq -- to be a dangerous activity (such as children playing with knives, guns etc.)
kaoqsav sav for the voice to be hoarse (ku$_{\vee}$ byah$_{\vee}$ su$_{\wedge}$-eu)
=kaoq, saol= an iron pan
=kaoq, zol= a text book

KE

kedif to confirm; approve (Chi) (34:28)
kegal a cup; mug (Chi) (26:74)
kehaof slogans (Chi) (or) **doqma**

keq to open something (especially when cutting it open, as: **keq peivq** = to cut open) (note: this is sometimes written as: **keeq**)
keq to make a fire; set a fire; **keq peev** (mi$_{\vee}$ dza$_{\vee}$ keu$_{\vee}$-eu)
keq a gram (a metric measure of mass and weight as used in measuring medicine) (Chi) (10:13)
keq to carve (Chi) (50:38)
-- keq, aqzaq -- to set fire to
keq beivq to cut something open (or) **keq peivq**
keq bil to cut and divide (50:74)
-- keq byu, yobyu -- to cut open a hole
-- keq dovq, aldovq -- to light a lamp
keq pav to cut open (9:87) (or) **keq peivq**
-- keq pav saq, keq beivq -- to cut open every part
keq peev to set on fire (or) **keq** (mi$_{\vee}$ dza$_{\vee}$ keu$_{\vee}$ pui^-eu)
-- keq peev, millaol -- to set a jungle fire
keq peivq 1. to cut something or someone open (peh$_{\wedge}$-eu; yeh$_{\vee}$ pah-eu), 2. to perform a medical operation (**wuqdeiq keq peivq** = to operate on the abdomen) (or) **keq beivq** (peh$_{\wedge}$-eu)
keq peivq keq pav saq to cut open every part
keq peivq to cut open (or) **keq pav**
-- keq pieiq, miqzaq -- to set fire to
keqssaq a knife for dissecting animals

kev to pound rice slightly (not sufficient)
=kev, baoq= box; trunk
-- kev, ceilkev -- to pound rice slightly (the 'first' pounding)
=kev nei, nil= tiny; very small
kev nei nyuq loq suddenly see the light; suddenly realize what has happened (50:75)
-- kev, wuqkev -- to knock on someone's head with the knuckles (a taboo action)

kevq to mix (9:87) (la^ keu⌄-eu)
kevq 1. to be IN something, as in a pocket (11:39, 35:5) in a dish of something (**Hhoqcyuq hholqei saqnil kevq**. There is meat in the vegetable dish. - 11:49), 2. to be present in the sense of being alive (**sil** e **taq wuqduq bavq e qiq hhaq maq kevq** = when I die there will be no living male to bury me - 30:2) (45:8, 46:99), 3. to take part in (50:19) (or) **caljal** (Chi)
kevq e col a party to a lawsuit; a litigant (50:32)
=kevq, lav= to mix
-- kevq, lul -- to fry into; to mix and fry
kevq meil with; together with (**aqyoq kevq meil yil** = to go with him)
-- kevq, nuvq -- to mix with one's hands
-- kevq, pav -- to be involved; to take part in
-- kevq, piav -- to mix

KEE

keel tasty; delicious (9:86) (yaw kuiˇ)
=keel, aq= foot; leg
keelbaoq women's leggings (9:86) (kuiˇ bah⌄)
=keel, beel= the rays of the sun
keelbeivq for the skin of the foot to have cracks in it
keelbeivq beivq for the skin of the foot to have cracks develop in it
=keel, caq= the foundation of an irrigated field or a building
keelciivq leg joints (26:47) (kuiˇ tsui^)
keelcoq coq jumping (14:165) (tsaw⌄-eu)
keeldaoq heel of foot (kuiˇ nui^)
keeldu calf of leg; lower leg (below knee) (9:86) (kuiˇ du du beh^)
keeldu duma big, strong legs (12:128, 46:203)
keelgaoq gaoq to cross one's legs (children must not do this in the presence of elders)
keelguq achilles tendon (sha⌄ gu⌄ = tendon)
keelguq hhekuv to have a cramp in the leg
keelhov arch of foot
keelhhaq sole of foot (9:86) (a⌄ kuiˇ peh⌄ za⌄)
keeljul shackles (fetters) for the legs
keeljul lavqjul shackles for feet and hands

keeljyuq jyuq to rub one's feet (14:165)
-- keel keel, lavq lavq -- hands and feet
keel kuv bent leg; crooked leg (11:218) (kuiˇ ku^)
keel kuv lavq kuv for legs and arms to be bent; crooked
keel kuv zoq to stretch out a bent leg (11:218) (aˬ kuiˇ g'eu caw)
=keel, laq= bottom of trousers
keellavq arms and legs (lit. leg & arm) (9:86) (kuiˇ la^)
keellavq bel to be diligent; active (45:6) (or)
keellavq belzav nei to work diligently (or)
keellavq ciq deil to wash hands and legs and rest (46:165) (cf.: aˬ kuiˇ aˬ la^ dzui^-awˇ neh naˬ-eu)
keellavq hhe 1. something to affect arms and legs (as a disease) (10:15); 2. to disturb; 3. to block someone from doing something
keellavq kavq zaoq bound hand and foot (kuiˇ cu^ la^ cu^ cu^-eu)
keellavq kol quick; agile; fast (with feet and arms)
keellavq leil to exercise arms and legs (B=Chi) (11:193)
keellavq maq hhe not to lag behind ('not to drag one's arms and legs') (41:96)
keellavq nia to be able physically to perform a task (50:108) (kuiˇ la^ nya-eu)
keellavq saq 1. to take trouble for another, 2. one way of saying 'thank you' (for taking trouble for me)
keellavq saqhaol to serve other people (50:52)
keellavq saqhaol miqnieiq a job to serve other people (50:52)
keellavq saqhaol ssaq a servant (50:52)
keellavq seiq 1. to wash the hands and feet (what the maternal uncles do when people return from burial), 2. to wash a sacrificial animal (leg, body, head -- three places)
keellavq sol well-behaved ('pure feet and hands')
keellavq zol to learn to exercise legs & arms (29:4)
=keel, laol= the outside wall of a building
keellol bavqyovq to walk or stand as if drunk; at an angle; to stagger (yaw^ yaw^-ehˇ cah-eu)
keelluvq a foot that has no toes or heel (as from an accident)
keelmil delicious; tasty (11:20, 157) (yaw kuiˇ)
keelmil aol to taste delicious (9:86) (yaw kuiˇ)
keelmiqdaoq at the foot end of the bed (as when one sleeps) (11:218) (aˬ kuiˇ mehˬ dzaˬ)
keelmiav ankle (5:625) (shiˇ mya^ puˇ; kuiˇ mya^ puˇ)
=keel, miav= vision; sight
=keel, moq= hind leg of horse

keelnaol top of foot; instep of foot
keelnaoq dalpav pedal for loom (9:86)
keelnaoq haqluv a stone put at the feet of a dead elder (taken out before the burial by those on the maternal side of the family and thrown away)
keel nei ssuq e to travel by foot
keel niv to point with the foot (46:130) (a˯ kuiˇ neh toe˯ meh˯-eu)
keel niv lavq niv excited (jumping around) (13:32)
keelpul ankle (shiˇ mya^ puˇ; kuiˇ mya^ puˇ)
=keel, qal= the left foot
keelqaoq lavqqaoq qaoq 1. for arms and legs to be weak and limp (as from paralysis); **aqbiaoq biaoq**; 2. for arms and legs to be paralyzed, 3. to be awkward with one's arms and legs
keelqeiq a cripple; lame person (9:86) (kuiˇ caw^)
  keelqeiq lavqqeiq arms and legs to be crippled (la˰ cu˯ kuiˇ cu˯)
keelsaoq toenail (kuiˇ sah˯)
keel sil lavq sil arms and legs to be numb; paralyzed (kuiˇ shiˇ la˰ shiˇ shiˇ-eu)
keelsuv a cupboard; a wardrobe closet (Chi) (35:5)
keeltov men's leggings (9:87) (kuiˇ taw^)
  -- keeltov, caqkeel -- (see full)
  keeltov tov to put on men's leggings (11:28) (kuiˇ taw^ taw^-eu)
keeltuvq a step (14:165) (kuiˇ to˰)
  keeltuvq qiq to step; to walk; to start out (as on a journey by foot - 35:84) (kuiˇ to˰ ci˯-eu)
  keeltuvq qiq dov to be in step
  keeltuvq ssiivq with steady steps; firm steps
  keeltuvq tuvqma qiq to take a stride
  keeltuvq xao the sound of loud footsteps
keelxa duqhovq a footprint (a˯ kuiˇ peh˯ zaˇ)
keelyyuq bones of the leg (a˯ kuiˇ sha˯ yoe˯)
-- keel, zaq -- delicious to eat
keelzav nei to be delicious (9:87) (yaw kuiˇ)
keelzaoq lavqzaoq kavq zaoq to tie feet and hands together (humans; animals) (35:17) (kuiˇ cu˰ la˰ cu˰ cu˰-eu)

=kee, daoq= a rope that goes around the tail of ponies to hold a pack saddle

keeq to be fertile
keeq dog (or) **aqkeeq** (a˯ kui˯)
keeq clf. for dogs (Ak. for all animals: mawˇ)
(keeq) to cut open (46:116) (note: this is usually pronounced and written as: **keq** as in: **wuqdeiq keq** = to cut open the stomach in an operation; **neeguq keq** = to cut open a lump of beancurd) (yeh˯ pah-eu)
=keeq, aq= dog
keeqbuq long hair (fur) of a dog
keeqbuvq to scribble

keeqbyuq laqsyuq dung beetle (nyo˯ ce˯ boi˯ soi^)
keeqciil ciil to lead a dog around the village (A part of the Hani culture, done when bad things happen, such as a girl becoming pregnant before being married.)
keeqdav to mark on something (maˇ byaw˰ byaw˰-eu)
keeqdaoq a chain for a dog
keeqdol diq duq a place where 'bad-omen' dogs are killed and eaten
keeqdol duv for a 'bad-omen' dog to occur
keeqduq 1. a compost or manure pit (9:87), 2. a dog's head
keeqhul a lump of manure (ca˰ ti˯ dzm)
keeq huvq dog year (9:87) (kui˯ ti˯ k'o˰)
=keeq, hho= rice seedling
keeqkovq a fierce dog (a˯ kui˯ yaw k'a˯)
keeqlyul solid manure
keeqma female dog (9:87) (a˯ kui˯ kui˯ ma)
keeqma daughter-in-law (or) **ssaqmiq keeqma** (6:176) (kui˯ ma)
-- **keeqma, ssaqmiq** -- daughter-in-law
keeqmiq jahhaq a type of grass that looks like dogs tails (46:117)
keeqmiq moqzal type of weeds; grass (9:87) ('horse food')
keeqmu a mad dog; a rabid dog (a˯ kui˯ kui˯ u˯)
keeqmu mu a dog to become mad; become rabid
keeqnaq a mole cricket (46:164)
keeq nao dog day (kui˯ ti˯ nah)
-- **keeqnaoq, hhokeeq** -- young & fresh rice seedlings
keeqnuv pieces of manure
keeqpaq male dog (9:87) (a˯ kui˯ kui˯ huˇ)
keeq pav half of a dog (as when two people own one dog, each owns a half) (kui˯ pa^)
Keeqsal boy's name (11:101)
keeqsaq dog meat (9:87) (a˯ kui˯ sha˯ jiˇ)
keeqseil flea (9:87) (kui˯ shehˇ)
keeqsivq dog's blood (46:116) (a˯ kui˯ shi˯)
keeqssaq a young dog; a puppy (kui˯ za˯)
-- **keeqssaq, hhokeeq** -- young rice seedlings
-- **keeqssei, hhokeeq** -- old rice seedlings
keeqtuv galtuv tuv e to stretch out a dog skin outside the village gate, with the head pointing away from the village (38:37) (or) **galtuv tuv e** (kui˯ k'o^ taw-eu; a˯ kui˯ ba^ k'o^ taw-eu)
keeqxiq dog dung (a˯ kui˯ ce˯; a˯ kui˯ ca˰)
keeq zeq dog hour

KEI

keil to drive a car (Chi) (ngaw˯-eu; teh-eu)
keil to attend; to hold (as a meeting) (Chi) (**Ngal zel a miqcuq jaofyiuq hyufyif keil li movq.** I'm going to attend a meeting on nationality education at the prefecture seat. 41:14)

keilfaf open to the outside (Chi) (pf) (or) **kalfaf** (34:12)
keilhyuf keil to hold a meeting (Chi) (4:52) (or) **doqzil zil**
keilsaq a vegetable garden (46:96) (and see below) (yaˇ kmˇ)
keilsavq a vegetable garden (9:87, 35:85) (or) **kul'a** (and see above)
keilteq wuqduq introduction to an article (as in a newspaper) (A=Chi)
keiltiq open a court session; call the court to order (Chi) (50:95)
keilza to launch (Chi) (34:65)

kei to do something (see: **keilhyuf kei**)

keiq a gram (w.m.) (Chi) (41:127)
keiqpav half a gram (A=Chi)
Keiqpu a person's name (35:28)

keivq, keivq the sound of laughter (14:175)

keifmaof a general picture (Chi) (50:55)
keifnieif a concept (Chi) (50:55) (or) **yomiaol**

KO

kol a generation (**aqda qiq kol** = the father's generation) (ziˇ)
kol 1. fast; quick (9:88), 2. fast maturing (when spoken of crops) (yaw kawˇ)
kol clf. for a non-irrigated field
kol (vb) naoq (vb) as you like (11:209)
=kol caovq, mol= to take a picture
=kol, ceil= early maturing rice (fast growing)
kol e hoceil express train (B=Chi)
-- kol, keellavq -- to be agile
kol e soqhhaq express delivery (kawˇ sha ha-eu)
=kol, eel= a very fast type of snake
Kolhhyulteq Kuwait (Chi)
koljif science and technology (Chi) (34:19)
-- kol, keellavq -- to be quick; fast (legs and arms)
kolkol laqcal quickly (yaw kawˇ)
kollal to become fast; quick (kawˇ laˇ-eu)
-- kol, lavq -- 1. quick in doing things, 2. to do magic with one's hands
kol liq kol, meeq liq meeq, leiqdaq liq maq daq achieve greater, faster, better and more economical results (50:42)
=kol, loq= terrace in a field
=kol, mol= a picture; a statue
--kol, neepuv nee'lav -- quick brain; quick reactions (45:12)
-- kol, neivqkol -- speedy; quick like a spirit
kolpu soqkaoq textbook of scientific knowledge

(A=Chi) (50:97)

kolxoq science (Chi) (9:88, 10:pref, 41:80)

kolxoq galquv tav according to the scientific method (A=Chi) (50:97)

kolxoq hhyufxil scientific satellite (Chi)

kolxoq jifsuq science and technology (Chi) (34:19, 50:97) (or) **kolxoq lavqqivq** (A=Chi)

kolxoq lavqqivq (see: **kolxoq jifsuq**)

kolxoq xaldei aol work irrigated fields in a scientific way (A=Chi) (50:97)

-- **kolyaol, molkol** -- temple (house of statues)

-- **kolzao, doqkol** -- a poetic drama (50:152)

koq to grab; to snatch (lu do^-eu; byehˇ cu˯-eu)

koq clf. for group of mountain fields (11:153)

(vb) koq 1. again (vb) (i.e., to take up one's work again) (**aol koq** = to return to what one was doing - 26:61); 2. to go on with what one was doing, 3. shows continuous action (**zaq koq al** = he was eating it all - 38:2)

koqcoq the sound of fish jumping (11:201)

koqdaf zeifseilca expanded production (Chi) (50:100)

koq hha capture; wrest (50:42)

koqjoq (see: **xaoqjoq** = a whole bamboo) (14:142)

koq jul joq luq a great calamity; catastrophe (50:70)

koqlyuq to rape; to seduce (50:82, 135) (yeh˯ baw˯-ehˇ daw^ laˇ-eu)

koqma lalma a large area of terraced fields (14:138)

=koq, miq= firewood

koq pil to grab back (nyeh˰ k'o˰-eu)

koqpial a small stick; a small dry branch (4:32) (gaw˯ yoe˯)

koqpieiv ssaqnaol a person sent from God (**Molmil**) when it is time for a person to die

koqpiul sweat (35:58) (kaw˯ pyuˇ)

koqpiul ju nei duv to be covered ('shiny') with sweat (35:58) (kaw˯ pyuˇ ju ni)

-- **koq, quq** -- to touch on

koqsuv eilneiq bamboo strips (18:1)

koqtavq wuqpiul a white-headed bird

koqteil pull back & forth trying to gain control (13:31)

koqteil qei nei very active; lively (11:167)

koq teiq to occupy (as an army occupies a country) (50:135)

-- **koqyal, daoltavq** -- field on a mountain

-- **koqyal, haoltavq** -- mountain field

koqyil to enlarge (as enlarge the army) (Chi) (50:100)

koqyiljil 1. a megaphone, 2. a loud speaker (Chi) (50:100)

koq zaq 1. to grab and take; 2. to take away by force (as bandits) (13:31) (have: 'to occupy' in 9:88) (ceh geu˰-eu; ka^ geu˰-eu; lu geu˰-eu)

koq zaq zyul a crime of forcibly robbing

kov a line (2:52) (a˅ kaw^)
kov to draw out (9:88)
kov to stir (kaw^-eu)
=kov, caq= a ditch around a house
kovdul a stick for mixing something (as dye) (kaw^ du˅)
kov duv to draw out; to stick out (g'eu do^-eu; kaw^ do^-eu)
=kov, gal= (see full)
-- kov, galkov -- 1. to be striped (as a tiger), 2. to dig a ditch in a straight line
=kov, lavq= lines on the palm of the hand
=kov, lolgal gal= ditch
=kov, miav= line of vision; line of sight
=kov, miavbil ju= line of tear stains
kov puv to stir up
-- kov, qiq -- (see full) (**eil qiq kov** = to say directly; **maq eil qiq kov** = no use to speak)
kov puv to stir up (kaw^ keu˯-eu)
=kov, sol= items of an account; accounts
-- kovtov, seivmoq -- stilts

kovq 1. to bite (9:88) (kaw˄-eu), 2. to carry something in the mouth (as a dog, see also: **aoq**)
kovq to have (stomach) ache (9:88) (u˯ ma^ kaw˄-eu)
kovq clf. for a bite (11:85)
-- kovq, almol -- flies to 'bite' (10:19)
kovq byu to gnaw a hole; to bite into making a hole (46:201) (kaw˄ byoe)
-- kovq, coqleiq -- to pass on a disease to another
-- kovq, cyuqnal -- to catch a cold
kovq daol laq e a tooth mark from a bite (as a dog bite) (11:174)
=kovq, dovq= lamp to be burning
kovq kavq to bite down hard (9:88); to bite each other
=kovq, keeq= a cruel dog
-- kovq, luqbul -- to have trouble urinating because of kidney stones
=kovq, meiq= a bit for a horse
-- kovq, miqqusal -- to have a stroke; some acute disease (cannot speak)
kovq nuv to bite to pieces (13:21) (kaw˄ nm^-eu)
-- kovq, seqkovq -- 1. to grind one's teeth, 2. to bite with teeth
kovq siivq to bite down tightly (14:149) (kaw˄ tso^ g'eh-eu)
kovqsovq a cracking sound (29:4)
kovq teiq to clamp down (as with teeth) (kaw˄ teh˯-eu)
-- kovq teiq, seqpeiq -- to clamp down with teeth
kovqtovq the sound of a bowl breaking

kof a lesson (Chi) (9:87)
kofweiq a text (Chi)

KU

kul to call on; to call out (9:88) (ku$^{\vee}$-eu)
kul to scorch; burn (as when ironing or cooking) (9:88) (ku$^{\vee}$-eu)
kul'a a vegetable garden not far from the village (or) **keilsavq**
-- **kul, aqssaq** -- to 'call' a son-in-law (and see full)
-- **kul, daqyao** -- to invite guests to one's home
kuldoq ask for permission, blessing (50:138)
-- **kul, hhavq lal** -- to call back the soul of a pig
kulkaoq written invitation (50:138)
kul lal yiq yiq what the person calling back a soul says at the beginning and end of the ceremony ('yiq' is a continuous sound)
kul lul kal lal nei scarcely (14:153) (ma$_{\vee}$ mya$_{\vee}$)
kul miq to call (to someone) (35:19) (ku$^{\vee}$-eu)
kul nyuq to 'call awake' (awaken by calling) (13:34) (ku$^{\vee}$ noe$_{\vee}$-eu)
-- **kul, peev** -- to be charred by fire (and see full)
-- **kul, qavq** -- 1. overcooked (burnt) rice, 2. the rice which sticks to the pot
kul qoq to call each other (45:46) (ku$^{\vee}$ caw$_{\vee}$-eu)
kul tul to encourage (34:2) (cf.: g'a$_{\vee}$ bi$_{\wedge}$-eu)
kul yil kal let (me) go to call ... (45:10) (ku$^{\vee}$ la$^{\vee}$-i$^{\vee}$-eu)
-- **kul, zaolkul** -- a final feast at the home of the dead elder after a funeral
kul zil to call a meeting (ku$^{\vee}$ dzoe$^{\vee}$-eu)
kul zyul to call and gather together (ku$^{\vee}$ ym$_{\vee}$-eu; ku$^{\vee}$ ui$_{\vee}$-eu)

kugaf aol to work hard (A=Chi) (m$^{\vee}$ k'a^-eu)
Ku'lu puvkaq the name of a village (14:195)

kuq to fill (as with rice) (9:88)
kuq dip out (**hoq kuq dav la** = to dip up rice) (ku$_{\vee}$-eu)
kuq dry (as of leaves) **alpavq pavqkuq** = dry leaves (or) **kuv** (yaw ko^)
=**kuq, alcav cav**= a dry rope
kuq bil zaq to scoop up one's share (as of meat)
kuqcavq a spoon (or) **aqcavq; yuqcavq** (ku$_{\vee}$ tsa$_{\wedge}$)
=**kuq, cil**= pork rind; cracklings
kuq duv to fill and soak (ku$_{\vee}$ dui^-eu)
=**kuq, hoq**= spoon for dipping up rice
kuqleiv zaq an annual ancestral offering
=**kuq nei, dyul**= lazily
kuqteiv nei dry and shrivelled (ku$_{\vee}$-i$^{\vee}$-eu)
kuqzaq huvq'yul yul nao the eve of the Hani June festival (35:57)

kuq zaq to take by force
=kuq zaq, Yeil= to celebrate the June festival (or) **sseilkuq zaq**
Kuqzaq zaq annual ancestral offering; swing festival (13:39, 46:178); **Yeilkuq zaq; Sseilkuq zaq**
=kuq, zil= (see full)

kuv to shut in (**aqniuq leiq kuv** = to shut a buffalo in a stable)
kuv for a muscle or tendon to contract (**saqguq hhe kuv** = for a muscle to contract)
kuv to dry up (9:89) (ko^-eu)
=kuv, al= dry
=kuv, aldyuv dyuv= dried bambo shoots
=kuv, aqciq ciq= a dried soybean condiment
=kuv, aqcivq civq= goat shed
=kuv, aqha ha= chicken shed
=kuv, ha= chicken shed
=kuv, hhavq= 1. pig shed (a˅ za˄ ku^), 2. prison; jail (an old term)
=kuv, hhoq= dried vegetables or greens
-- kuv, hhoqcyuq hhoqkuv -- to dry vegetables
-- kuv, keel kuv lavq -- legs and arms to be bent
-- kuv, leiq -- to curl on its own
=kuv, lovq= to stretch out to dry
-- kuv, meiqbaoq -- dry lips
-- kuv meivq luv meil, meivq -- starvation
=kuv, moq= horse stable
-- kuv, moqkuv -- to put up a horse stable
-- kuv nei, teiq -- 1. to be crowded, 2. to be narrow
-- kuv, nieivq -- to arrest and put in jail
=kuv, niuq= stable for buffalo/cattle
=kuv, niuqsaq saq= beef jerky
=kuv, pavq= old, dried leaves
=kuv, saq= dried meat
kuvsav nei very dry (as leaves) (ko^ ka^ ni; gui co˅ ni)
  kuvsav pa sav nei extremely dry (as leaves) (ko^ ka^ ni; gui co˅ ni)

kuvq six (9:89) (ko˄)
kuvq ceil sixty
kuvq ceiv to estimate (A=Chi) (11:31)
Kuvqla siq June

KUA

Kuaqsseiq Ssiiqjif the name of a book, Kuangren Riji ('A Maniac's Diary') (57:156)

kuaf a mine (for minerals) (Chi) (26:106)
  kuaf beq to dig a mine (A=Chi) (50:19)
  kuafca an underground mine (gold, silver) (Chi) (50:99)
  kuafniq miqnieiq mining enterprise (A=Chi) (50:99)

kuafsal a mine (for minerals) (Chi) (26:39)
kuafsiiq haqluv mineral stone (from a mine) (A=Chi) (50:99)

KUEI

Kueilmiq Kunming (Chi) (9:88) (**Kyulmiq** = pf.)
kueifjif an accountant; accountancy (Chi) (9:88)

KYU

kyul antler; horn (u˯ coeˇ)
kyul a corner (46:114) (la˰ coeˇ)
kyul to be clever (9:89)
=**kyul, byul**= clever; genius; talented; gifted
-- **kyul, byulkyul** -- to be quick-witted; to be clever
=**kyul, ceiv**= deer antler
=**kyul, col**= clever; smart person
kyulcuv an instrument made of horn for medicinal use
kyuldu horn (as of buffalo) (9:89) (u˯ coeˇ)
kyul lal be clever; good at things (10:pref.) (gahˇ-eu)
=**kyul, laq**= nook; corner (and see below)
=**kyul, lavq**= corner (as of a room) (and see above)
kyulli qeiqleiq nei faltering (14:154)
Kyulmiq Kunming (11:33, 35:96) (see also: **Kueilmiq**) (note: the old name is: **Guqhaq**)
=**kyul, nee**= wisdom; intelligence
=**kyul, niuq**= horn of buffalo/cow
-- **kyul, wuqkyul** -- square-headed
=**kyul, xaldei daol**= (see full)

kyuq to lose (9:89) (coe˯ laˇ-eu)
kyuq 1. to be hurt (coe˯ laˇ-eu), 2. to be tired (9:89)
kyuq to be bad; excessive (**daov kyuq ngaoq**...= if there is severe diarhea - 10:11, 32) (coe˯-eu)
-- **kyuq, eil** -- 1. to satirize; mock, 2. to hurt someone by a spoken word
=**kyuq, hhaq**= tired
-- **kyuq, hhaqkyuq** -- to be tired
-- **kyuq, kyuq sil kyuq lo** -- to experience all kinds of hardships and difficulties
kyuq lal e miqnieiq to do something to cause harm; cause injury (46:131) (coe˯-eu ci^-eu)
kyuqlaq meil 1. to be badly hurt, 2. to be very tired, 3. to have a serious disease
-- **kyuq, lav** -- to harm; to hurt
kyuq leiq kyuq sil very tired; exhausted (13:5, 45:90, 46:85) (g'a˯ doeˇ doeˇ-eu)
kyuqlyu qeiqleiq nei faltering (14:165)
kyuq maq guv qaq maq nyuq nei without fear of hardship and difficulties (38:7) (yaw sha˯ yaw k'a^-ehˇ ma˯ gu^ ni)

kyuqqiv nei harmfully (**Col yaol kyuqqiv nei taq** eil. Don't speak to people in a way that will harm them.) (coe⌄ le˅-eu)
kyuqsei nei to be tired (50:129) (g'a⌄ doe˅ doe˅-eu)
kyuq sil 'dead' tired (g'a⌄ doe˅ doe˅ seh^-eu)
kyuq sil kyuq leiq nei to be very tired (26:2)
kyuq sil kyuq lo kyuq e experienced to all kinds of hardships and difficulties (46:163)
kyuq sil kyuq lo meil very tiresome
kyuq ya to be tired (46:172)
-- kyuq, zeil -- to be tired of working hard (A=Chi)

kyufnaq a problem; a difficulty (Chi) **kyufnaq jav e** = to have problems; difficulties - 26:42) (34:116)

LA

lal to come (up) (9:89) (la˅-eu)
lal to satisfy (**neema lal** = to be satisfied) (deh^-eu)
lal clf. for soul
(vb) **lal** denotes the direction (upward) or increase in amount or size (hui˯ la˅-eu)
=lal, bal= for; on behalf of
lalbaq 1. a loud speaker (Chi) (26:60), 2. a trumpet
lalbaq a folksong; ballad (9:89) (or) **halbaq** (not pf.) (sha˯ zi^)
-- **lalbaq, Haqniq** -- Hani songs; ballads
lalbaq ssil to sing a folksong; ballad; a drinking song, sung by old men in the house (9:89, 10:pref.) (sha˯ zi^ zi^-eu)
lalbaq ssilma a singer of folk songs (11:122)
lalbaq ssilqeiv qeiv to compete in singing folk songs (35:84) (ca˅ ceh ceh-eu)
lalbeil lalya to cry sadly (38:16) (g'aw˯ sha˯-eh˅ ngoe˅-eu)
lalbiaol alyeiv kapok tree blossoms (46:144)
lalbiaol biaolbol the kapok tree (46:144)
lalbu male buffalo (9:90) (a˯ nyo˯ la˄ hi˅)
lalbu busiq the hump on the neck of an ox
-- **laldeiq, alhhu** -- ants
-- **lal, dul** -- to be similar
lalduq a reason to come (**lalduq jav** = there is a reason to come)
-- **lal, duv** -- come out of; appear
lalga lazy; degenerate
lalhav lazy (Chi)
lal hev to arrive (from lower place) (50:7)
lalheiq resources (50:101)
Lalhuq Lahu (people) (Meu˯ seu˯ za˯)
Lalhuqcuq the Lahu people (B=Chi) (or) **Lalhuqssaq** (Meu˯ seu˯ za˯)
Lalhuqdoq Lahu language (10:pref.) (Meu˯ seu˯ daw˯)
Lalhuqssaq the Lahu people (or) **Lalhuqcuq** (Meu˯ seu˯ za˯)
-- **lalhhaq, jaljul** -- a swallow (brd)
-- **lal, hhuvq** -- come back from lower place
lalhhuvq lolqol along a bend in a river (14:189)
-- **lal, kaq** -- getting better
-- **lal, kol** -- become fast; quick
lalkyul 1. the century plant; 2. a cactus
lal lal meil aol comes often (repeatedly) to do the work
lal le to come late (from lower place) (41:62, 50:23) (nah˯-i˅-eu)
lalma tongue (9:90) (meh˯ la˅)
lalma ja nei with one's tongue hanging out in

surprise (57:103)
lalma kovq teiq to bite the tongue (mehˬ laˇ-ahˇ kaw‸-eu)
lalma lalqei the tip of the tongue (or) **lalqei** (mehˬ laˇ mehˬ dzaˬ)
lalma lalssaq the soft palate (or) **lalssaq**
lal maq lal lal to come no matter what
lalmievq savq nei to moisten one's lips with one's tongue (14:181)
-- lal, needeq -- to be satisfied
-- lal, neema -- to be satisfied
lalngavq uvula (5:374) (mehˬ laˇ laˇ zahˇ)
lalngavq ngavq to stammer
=lal, peil= (see full)
lalpieiv pieiv be sure to come; must come (it is settled) (paˬ maˬ laˇ-eu)
lalqei tongue tip (or) **lalma lalqei** (9:90) (mehˬ laˇ mehˬ dzaˬ)
=lal, sal= (see full)
Lalsa Yuanjiang county (in Yuxi Prefecture); **Yeiqyaqxeif** (14:241, 45:70) (also see: **Lalsav**)
Lalsa baqma Yuanjiang river; **Yueiqjalxeif** (Chi) (also see: **Lalsav baqma**)
Lalsav Yuanjiang county (in Yuxi Prefecture) (11:33) (also see: **Lalsa**)
Lalsav baqma Yuanjiang river; **Yueiqjalxeif** (Chi) (also see: **Lalsa baqma**)
Lalsav milcaq Yuanjiang County
lalsav ngaqsaq carp (fish)
Lalsav zeiqssaq Yuanjiang county animals (this is repeated in rituals in that area)
lalsaol saol to eat greedily (dzaˬ naw^ naw^-eu)
lalsaoq to disobey; to be disobedient (14:22) (or) **lavsaoq** (pf.) (ehˇ dawˬ maˬ naˇ haˬ)
lalsoq to disobey; be disobedient (ehˇ dawˬ maˬ naˇ haˬ)
lal sul to disturb someone (26:54) **lav sul** (pf)
lalsul lal to wake up (26:51) **lavsul lal** (pf)
lalssaq soft palate (or) **lalma lalssaq**
-- lal, toq -- to answer; respond
laltov immediately; right away (46:139)
-- laltov nei, qiqhaq -- immediately
-- lalya, lalbeil -- to cry sadly
-- lal, yil -- coming and going
lalzii a mule (9:90, 50:111) (mahˬ sha^ lawˬ)
lalzii aqda male donkey (9:90) (mahˬ liˇ dzeu)
lalzii ziipiul white mule (mahˬ sha^ lawˬ lawˬ pyuˇ)
Lalzul Lazhu, a township in Muojiang county (46:208)

(vb) la an auxiliary verb showing movement (9:89) (... laˇ)
la clf. for month (**qiq la, niq la; qiq siq, niq siq**)
=la, ba'= 1. the moon, 2. a month (ba la)
-- laceiv, ba'la -- the end of the lunar month

laceiv pyu the last ten days of a month
ladav early in the month (9:89)
-- **ladav, ba'la** -- early in the lunar month
ladav pyu the first ten days of a month
-- **la, duv** -- come out (& see full)
laheeq a 'large' month (30 or 31 days)
-- **lahhaol, ba'la** -- middle of the lunar month
lahhaol pyu the second ten days of a month
=**la, ja'**= long
=**la, kaq**= beforehand
la'luv full moon (ba la la lo^)
=**la manao, kaq**= the other day
lamiq the end of a month ('tail')
-- **lamiq, ba'la** -- **late in the lunar month**
=**la nei, pia'**= a careless person
lanil a 'small' month (less than 30 days)
lasiq a month (9:94) (ba la ti$_\vee$ si$_\vee$)

laq to answer (or) **laq miq** (11:214) (eh$^\vee$ k'o$_\wedge$-eu)
(vb) **laq** already (as in 'to learn already') (ji$^\vee$-eu)
laq to borrow something which must be returned (nga$_\vee$-eu)
laq (fp) 1. final particle in questions demanding a yes or no answer, especially with '**nga laq**'. (**Coljol sal nga laq**? Are you healthy? 41:5), 2. final part. with some questions asking 'what?' (**Alzeiq ssol nei aqnil dulma haljivq aol zaq nga laq**? What do your older and younger sisters do? 41:22)
laqbavq ceivq to wrestle (46:89) (or) **lavqbavq yevq** (daw$_\wedge$ ceh ceh-eu)
laqbavq diqkovq for two or more parties to fight over something (13:31)
laqbaoq 1. sleeve, 2. gloves (la$_\wedge$ bah$_\vee$)
laqbaoq baoqheiq cuff of sleeve (9:92, 11:35)
Laqbeq Chinese (or) **Piulniul** (La$_\wedge$ bui$_\vee$)
Laqbeqssaq Chinese people (35:97) (La$_\wedge$ bui$_\vee$ za$_\vee$)
Laqbeqssaq pievq to become 'Chinese' (assimilate)
laqbil a flute (46:175)
Laqbyu milcaq a place name in Luchun Hani area
Laqbyussaq a group of Hani people who live in **Laqbyu** area
Laqcal lolbaq the Lancang (Mekong) River (A=Chi)
laqcal to be quick (35:4) (or) **cal nei** (cf. Lahu: la$_\wedge$ ha$^-$)
-- **laqcal, kolkol** -- quickly
laqcal meil quickly (26:28) (kaw$^\vee$ kaw$^\vee$-eh$^\vee$)
laqcal xeiv hhovq 1. urgent (emergency) to prevent danger, 2. run quickly to a safe place (50:89)
laqcaq 1. baby pants, 2. in a hurry
laqceiq an adze (46:117) (**lavqceiq** = pf.)
laqcyuq pants; trousers (9:92) (la$_\wedge$ di)
laqcyuq laqkeel the cuff of pants (11:36)
laqdaoq 1. the floor beam (k'aw$^\vee$ daw$_\vee$), 2. the bottom of trousers

laqdev a hatchet; a small axe (9:92) (deu^ ha˯)
laqdiq jew's-harp (9:92) (jaˇ oe˯)
laqdul a stalk (of vegetables)
laqdu ciil to lead someone by the hand; to carefully teach someone how to do something (57:152)
laqdu qiq du one arm (26:5) (a˯ la˰ ti˯ la˰)
-- laqdu, xoqbo -- wild taro
laqduq duq to dig a field by hand
=laq, eiq= (see full)
laqga bilnil embroidered cloth (14:192, 35:98)
laqgaol a finger ring (38:4) (la˰ beh˯)
laqgee nei under; after (as 'one person after another'); from (**Aqpyuq Solmil laqgee nei Zyuqtaoqpaoq hev nei** = from ancestor **Aqpyuq Solmil** to ancestor **Zyuqtaoqpaoq**) (35:60, 46:84)
laqguq pulse (9:92) **laqguq tyuq hu** = to take the pulse (shi˯ ca^-ahˇ toe˯ haw-eu)
laqguq cavq willing to work diligently; work hard
=laq, haq= a tiger
Laqhaq milcaq a place name in Luchun Hani area
Laqhaq Laqmil a group of Hani who live in the **Laqhaq** area
laqhaq qeil to show interest in (see: **laqheiq qeil**)
laqhaoq the trouser seat (9:93)
laqhaoq maq cuvq a slit in the crotch of pants (as in a baby's pants)
laqhev a three-stringed musical instrument (9:93, 10:pref, 46:175) (deuˇ-m˯)
laqhev bev to play the above instrument (10:pref) (deuˇ-m˯ di˯-eu)
laqheiq the top of the trousers (9:93)
laqheiq lav qeil dav to become more interested in (34:11)
laqheiq qeil 1. to be happy (26:35) (la˯ k'a˯ cehˇ-eu), 2. to be interested in (50:103)
laqheiq qeiltevq nei to be interested (33:3)
laqheiq qeiltov nei happily; joyfully (26:82) (la˯ k'a˯ ti˯ cehˇ)
laqhual alyeiv orchid flower (A=Chi) (yeh^ sah˯ shuiˇ)
laqhyul house (9:93, 19:pref) (nymˇ; iˇ kahˇ) (cf.: la˰ k'oeˇ = inside)
laqhyul a hhuvq li to return home (up) (iˇ kahˇ g'o˰ le-eu)
laqhyul col family member ('people of the house') (26:76)
laqhyul cuv zaq gaolsseiq to work as a house builder (**gaolsseiq** = Chi) (14:242) (nymˇ tso^-eu g'a˯)
laqhyul hoqbyu 1. the roof beams in a house (9:93) (nymˇ m˯ k'a˯ boe˯), 2. the roof of a building (26:70) (nymˇ m˯)
laqhyul hyulma a large house (11:77) (nymˇ ma)
laqhyul jolduq the house address (26:81) (nymˇ jawˇ du˯)

laqhyul miaoqgaoq tools in the home (50:81)
laqhyul qiqkuaf family affairs (B=Chi) (41:20)
laqhyul yaolgoq multistoried building
laqhyul yaolma 1. a large building; the main building, 2. a large family (26:102) (zaw˰ yaw hui˯)
laqhyul zaol'al a foundation for a house (9:93)
laqhhel handle of a stone mill
laqhhev whirlpool (iˇ cu˰ iˇ zeu^)
Laqhholssaq Yi; Lolo (or) **Haqhholssaq**
laqhhuvhaoq arm pit (la˰ o˰ la˰ tah)
-- **laqjal dao, peiljal** -- to dress shabbily
-- **laqjanei, miaveel** -- tears running down
-- **laqjaq, piaqyiq** -- lizard
laqjeiq musical gourd pipe (la˰ je˯)
laqju nei shining (26:10) (bya-eu)
laqkav 1. a harrow (or) **kav** (9:93) (nyo˯ ka^), 2. a rake
laqkavbieil a decorative border; a flowery design on cloth
laqkeel the lower part of trousers (9:93)
laqkyul nook; corner (as in a room) (50:85) (la˰ coeˇ)
laqlavsov almost (11:146) (aˇ cui^ ma˯ ngeuˇ naˇ)
laqlaol a fathom in length (from fingertip to fingertip with arms outstretched) (9:93) (aˇ lmˇ)
laqlaol 1. Akha skirt; woman's skirt (9:93, 11:131) (clf. = xo) (pi di), 2. an apron (or) **hhyuqyaol** (Chi)
-- **laqleel, qiq puq** -- unite; rally
laqleiq the money given to the couple by the guests at a wedding party
-- **laqleiq, eiqxaq** -- grinning cheekily
laqleiq pieiq for an elder to bless a newly married couple as they come around with drinks
laqlil 1. underpants (9:93), 2. short trousers (46:175) (la˰ di deu; la˰ di daw˯ ka˰)
laqma (see: **lavqma**)
-- **laqma, qeivkeel** -- frame for a pack saddle
-- **laqma, saolhyuq** -- the head of a gang of thieves
laqmeil the same (14:203); so; such (46:172) (ti˯ kaw^; lo˰-ehˇ)
Laqmil a branch of the Hani people
laqnaq 1. handle (as for a cup) (la˰ na˯), 2. evidence
laqnaq teil to take an oath (cf.: saˇ jaˇ bi˰-eu)
laqnaq teil zaq for a tiger or snake to strike someone
laqnil outside (of house) (46:126) (la˰ nyiˇ)
-- **laqnil, alhhu** -- red ants
laqnil duv to leave home
laqnil goqjal a duv yil to go abroad (B=Chi); **dalja nei hev zaq e**
laqnil piqkaq the outer cover
laqnil pyu outside of house; outside direction

(9:93) (la‸ nyiˇ paw)

laqpeiv tea (9:93)(lawˇ bawˬ) (cf. the term for tea in Burmese)

-- **laqpeiv dol, aoqsoq** -- drink morning tea (have breakfast)

laqpeiv peivbol tea plant (9:94) (lawˇ bawˬ aˇ bawˇ)

laqpil chili pepper (9:94) (la‸ piˇ; saˬ piˇ)

laqpil aqbol male miser (tsawˇ tsiˇ aˬ da)

laqpil aqpiq female miser (tsawˇ tsiˇ aˬ ma)

laqpil cil 1. to be hot with chili peppers (saˬ piˇ piˇ-eu), 2. to be a miser (26:75) (or) **laqpil civ** (tsawˇ tsiˇ tsiˇ-eu)

laqpil civ to be a miser (or) **laqpil cil** (tsawˇ tsiˇ tsiˇ-eu)

laqpil davssaq a dish for chili peppers (9:94) (saˬ piˇ k'mˬ maˬ)

laqpil piltev a type of small, very hot chili pepper (9:94) (saˬ piˇ piˇ zaˬ)

laqpil pilzaoq green, fresh chili peppers (14:140)

laqpiq a sewing basket (9:94)

laqpiq piqdel a small sewing basket

laqpul the paw (as of a cat) (29:4) (or) **lavqsaoq** (la‸ sahˬ) (note: in Akha la‸ puˇ = hand; back of hand)

laqpuq puq a cluster of flowers to open up

laqqeq basketball (Chi) (41:190, 50:101)

laqqeq diq to play basketball (A=Chi) (41:52)

laqqiq a dust pan (9:94)

laqquq a basketball (Chi) (9:94)

laqsaoq 1. the claw (as of a cat), 2. a fingernail (or) **lavqsaoq** (11:51) (la‸ sahˬ)

-- **laqsiivq, peilsiivq** -- new clothes (for women and men)

laqsov almost (11:113, 126)

laqsov a plane (a tool for planing wood) (9:94) (la‸ saw^)

laqsovq a bullock (9:94)

laqyil male buffalo (9:94, 46:117) (aˬ nyoˬ la‸ hiˇ)

laqzaoq a belt for trousers (46:176) (jo‸ pa‸)

laqziiq a belt (14:145) (jo‸ pa‸)

laqzu a handle (14:189) (cf.: la‸ naˬ)

laqzu crucial (50:64)

lav 1. to wag the tail (9:94) (**dawˬ miˬ jui‸-eu**), 2. to stir with a stick (heu-eu)

lav bav to make a mistake (la^ bahˬ-eu; la^ lehˬ-eu)

lav beeq to disturb; to cause a disturbance; to confuse; to make disorderly; to cause trouble; to interfere (9:95, 11:28, 50:34,39, 55) (la^ bahˬ)

lav beeq e col to be a troublemaker

lav biav to damage by breaking something (la^ pya^-eu)

lav biov to shorten (or) **lav niaol**

lav caq to disturb someone; cause a disturbance

lav ceiv 1. to break (as a string) (la^ tseh^-eu), 2. to pluck a stringed instrument
lav ceivq to tease (ceh˰ leh˰ kaˬ-eu)
lav daol 1. to dredge, 2. mediate between two parties (persons or groups)
lav eel to provoke laughter (or) **eel naq pieiq**
-- **lav, eelxul** -- to make a joke
lav heeq to enlarge something (50:100)
lav hha to make a joke (9:95) (la^ uiˇ-eu; ehˇ niˇ g'a-eu) (9:95)
lav hhoq to keep apart (or) **bi hhoq** (bi g'oˬ-eu)
lav hhul 1. to cause people to be stirred up, 2. to stir something up
lav kevq to mix (9:95) (la^ keuˬ-eu)
lav kyuq 1. to harm; to hurt someone (50:137) (la˰ coeˬ-eu), 2. to cause a setback; reverse (50:29)
lav laovq to draw in (or) **hhe kuv; se leev** (g'eu ahˇ-eu)
lav nal 1. to bruise; 2. discourage (50:29)
=**lav nei, puv**= to turn upside down
lav niaol to shorten (or) **lav biov** (la^ nymˇ-eu)
=**lav, ngav**= broken
-- **lav pieiv, miqbev** -- to fire a gun accidentally
lav pav to separate
lav puv to turn upside down; to turn over (la^ po^-eu)
lav qoq to answer to (35:85) (ehˇ k'o˰ nehˬ-eu)
lav sa to clear up (**joqhyuq lav sa** = the fog clears, lifts - 26:12) (cf.: yaw lawˬ)
lavsaoq 1. to be fierce (46:127, 137), 2. to be naughty (as a child, a cat) (29:4, 46:176), 3. to be disobedient (14:222) (or) **lalsoq**
=**lavsov, laq**= almost
lav sul to disturb someone; to be awakened by something (as a loud noise) (la^ bahˬ-eu; la^ tuˇ-eu)
lav sul lal to waken someone by disturbing them (la^ bahˬ-eu)
lav su to use a stick to get things together (9:97) (la^ dzoeˇ-eu)
lav ssil to throw down the gauntlet; challenge to battle
lav ssivq consolidate; strengthen (50:62)
lav sso 1. to touch (50:26), 2. to impair; to be harmful to (50:48)
lav tao to put into (9:97) (daw^ ahˇ-eu)
lav yeil laq e alzil a bird startled by the mere twang of a bow-string; a badly frightened person (50:89)
lav zaq to decorate; make up and dress up

lavq 1. a hand (aˬ la˰), 2. a branch of a tree (la˰ mya^; uˬ la˰), 3. a branch of a clan
lavq clf. for times (la˰)
lavq clf. for branches of a tree, hands (la˰)

=**lavq, al=** a branch
lavq a haxiq piav e maq miaoq said of a very clumsy person ('even chicken droppings won't stick to his fingers')
=**lavq, aq=** hand; arm
=**lavq aol, hhel=** to trade (buy & sell)
lavqbal to hinder; disturb (la^ bah˯-eu)
lavqbavq qiq pul taoq koq to wrestle in a wrestling match (14:149) (daw˄ ceh ceh-eu)
lavqbavq taoq to butt heads (as 2 animals) (tah˯-eu)
lavqbavq yevq to wrestle (or) **laqbavq ceivq** (daw˄ ceh ceh-eu)
lavqbaoq glove (6:178) (la˄ bah˯)
lavq beeq to be deranged
lavqbiav upper arm (la˄ bya^)
lavqbiav saqyyuq shoulder blade; scapula (la˄ caw^)
=**lavq, bu'=** satin; brocade
lavqcaq a mark (la^ kaw^)
lavqcaq cuv to make a mark (la^ kaw^ kaw^-eu)
lavqcav nei to drop down (as tears) (**aqbeil miaveel lavqcav nei** - 38:90) (yoeˇ ka-eu; yoeˇ le-eu)
lavqcavq an assistant; helper; aid
lavqcavq aol to give a helping hand ('join hands and do it')
lavqcavq cavq 1. to shake hands (la˄ tsa˄ tsa˄-eu), 2. hand in hand; to unify (or) **tuaqjiq** (Chi), 3. a successor to (**gaofcazuyif lavqcavq cavq** = successor to Communism, i.e. the youth - 26:101) 4. arm in arm (la˄ tsa˄ tsa˄-eu)
lavqceiq an adze (a tool for working with wood) (or) **laqceiq** = not. pf.
lavqcil sweat of hands (9:95) (a˯ la˄ kaw˯ pyuˇ)
lavqciivq elbow; arm joints (26:47) (la˄ tsui˄)
lavqciivq saqyyuq elbow bone (5:6141) (la˄ tsui˄ sha˯ yoe˯)
lavq coq duv to stretch out one's hand (a˯ la˄ caw˯ ja-eu)
lavqdal 1. to be reliable (46:179) (nui ma ta˯ nya-eu); 2. arm rest; hand rail (46:169)
lavqdaq pot holders (la˄ da˯); padding
-- **lavqdev, ceiqssaq** -- a small type of hoe
-- **lavqdev, saolzaol** -- a hatchet; a small axe (see also: **laqdev**)
lavqdu forearm (9:95) (la˄ du)
lavqdu alcàv a string tied around wrist of a person who has had his or her soul called back (la˄ tui^ pa˄-eu)
lavqdu alcav kavqtovq to tie a string around the wrist of a person who has had his or her soul called back (la˄ tui^ pa˄-eu)
-- **lavqdu alcav kavqtovq, ngavq la ngavq nao** -- (see full)
lavqdu dubeiv biceps and muscles of the forearm

(la‸ du du beh^)

lavqdu duma big, strong arms (46:203)

lavqduvq a bracelet (9:95, 46:98) (la‸ du‸)

lavqduvq duvq to wear a bracelet (9:95) (la‸ du‸ du‸-eu)

=**lavq, galhhuvq gal**= a small winding path

lavqguq a muscle (**lavqguq daov deivq** = strong muscle, but really means 'to work hard') (sha˯ jiˇ)

lavqguq deiq duv to go all out (50:63)

lavqguq hhe kuv a cramp in hand (tendon cramps so cannot stretch it out) (9:95) (gu˯ ti ti-eu)

lavqhev three-stringed musical instrument (or) **laqhev**

-- **lavqhev, bilpav** -- four-stringed plucked musical instrument

lavqhov cupped hand (9:95, 46:98) (la‸ k'aw^)

lavqhov diq to clap; applaud ('beat cupped hands') (la‸ k'aw^ teh^-eu)

=**lavq, huvq**= 1. an epoch of time, 2. a situation in space and time

lavqhhaq the palm of the hand (9:95) (la‸ za˯; la‸ g'a˯ = CA) (9:95)

-- **lavqhhev, aqlavq** -- a hand gesture

lavqhhuvhaoq the armpit (la‸ g'o‸ la‸ tah)

lavqhhuvhaoq haocavq underarm hair

lavqhhuvq the inner elbow; the crook of the elbow (46:193)

lavqhhuvq lavqliv 1. in the mountains (14:147) (gaw˯ jaw˯-ahˇ), 2. in remote ('corner') places (50:130)

lavqjul handcuffs (**saoljul** = any metal fetters)

-- **lavqjul, keeljul** -- shackles for the feet and hands

lavqkal kal hand stiff from cold

lavqkaq space between fingers (la‸ noeˇ yaw ka˯)

lavq kol 1. to be fast doing something with hands (yaw kawˇ), 2. to do magic with one's hands

lavqkov lines on palm of hand (9:95) (la‸ kaw^)

lavq lavq keel keel hands and feet (46:160) (a˯ la‸ a˯ kuiˇ)

lavqlaol an armspan (arms stretched out wide) (or) **laqlaol** (aˇ lmˇ)

lavqleiq a gift (50:104) (la‸ saw˯)

lavqliv deep inside (as of a room) (cf.: la‸ k'oeˇ)

lavqlo upper arm (9:96) (la‸ du)

-- **lavqluvq, aqlavq** -- 'blunt' hand (i.e., no fingers)

=**lavq, mal**= right hand

lavqma thumb (9:96) (la‸ ma)

lavqma cavpavq pavq to tie the thumbs of a corpse together with white thread

lavqma lavqgaol a silver thumb ring (used for ornamentation, and also sometimes put into a liquid which is given to a woman to drink who is having a difficult time delivering her baby)

lavqma lavqgaol gaol to wear a ring on one's thumb (la‸ ma la‸ behˬ behˬ-eu)
lavqma ngaoq pyul to hold out one's thumb in a gesture of disgust at someone (cf. **Heiq! Ngaq e lavqma heiq!**)
lavqma xa eel dol to drink water that has a silver thumb ring in it (should help the baby to be born, since the mother is embarrassed to do this)

lavqma needav dav to be nauseous (9:96)

lavqmeevq a servant (35:51) (cf.: zaˬ k'a^)

=lavq meil, beivq= to smell bad

lavqmiav 1. a young branch of a tree (la‸ mya^ mya^ zaˬ), 2. a knothole in a tree (la‸ mya^)

=lavq, moq= foreleg of a horse

lavqnaol the back of the hand (9:96)
-- lavqnaol, aqlavq -- the back of the hand

lavqnia technique (50:80)

lavqniaov tongs (as a blacksmith uses) (9:96) (ci^ nyaw^)

lavqnieiq dovq to begin to work (or) **lavqnieivq dovqbei** (9:96) (mᵛ beh beh-eu; mᵛ dahˬ beh-eu)

lavqnuvq nuvq to knead (nyeh‸-eu)
lavq nuvq lavq xeiv 1. to knead thoroughly, 2. to work hard (mᵛ k'a^-eu)

lavqnyul finger (9:96) (la‸ noeᵛ)
lavqnyul lavqgaol gaol to wear a ring on one's finger (la‸ behˬ behˬ-eu)
lavqnyul lavqma caq zaq to play a finger-guessing game (or) **huaqqeiq** (Chi)
lavqnyul tyuq to sign something; to make one's mark (35:35)

=lavq pa lavq nei, sil= strong smell of urine

lavqpeiv a callus (la‸ peh^)
lavqpeiv dav to form a callus (la‸ peh^ do^ laᵛ-eu)

lavq piav lavq wuvq to have quick and busy hands (57:119)

lavqpiav piav to scratch (57:69)

lavqpul a fist (or) **lavqpiul** (not pf.); **lavqtuv**

lavq pul lavq nieivq 1. unarmed; bare-handed (50:24), 2. empty hands (50:24)

lavqpul lavqciivq the wrist (la‸ lahᵛ; la‸ puᵛ la‸ tsui‸)
lavqpul pulssaq a small fist (14:166)

lavqqaq the little finger (9:96) (caᵛ caˬ)

-- lavqqaoq, keelqaoq -- weak arms and legs

lavqqaoq qaoq paralysis of arms (la‸ shiᵛ shiᵛ-eu)

lavqqeiq a crippled arm (9:96) (la‸ caw^ caw^-eu; la‸ cuˬ)
-- lavqqeiq, keelqeiq -- crippled arms and legs

lavqqiq lines on a finger which 'look like a dustpan' (the more you have the poorer you are) (cf.: **halhhov**)

lavqqivq to be skillfull with one's hands (as a blacksmith, carpenter) (9:96, 50:80) (cf.: la‸ ci‸ = a blacksmith, a term used in ceremonial language)

lavqqivq aqbol older male master craftsman

-- **lavqqivq, neemeeq** -- to be kind-hearted and expert

lavqqivq qivqzol apprentice to master craftsman; learning some handicraft, esp. being a blacksmith

lavqqivq ssaq 1. a skilled person (esp. a blacksmith), 2. a technician (50:80)

lavqqoq a companion (**lavqqoq hhoq** e = for friends to separate - 11:207)

lavq qov a broken arm

=lavq, sal= smell of seafood

lavqsaoq fingernail (9:96) (la‸ sahˬ)

lavqseiv wuqtov a black turban (worn by men)

lavqsiv handkerchief; hand towel (la‸ si^ paˇ jeh)

-- **lavqsiivq, huvqlavq** -- new time (50:188)

lavqsol almost; nearly (46:102)

lavqsov lavqsov nei crawling along on one's hands and knees (26:24)

lavqteiq 1. one-handed (to have only one arm or hand) (9:96) (tiˬ la‸ teh‸-ehˇ), 2. to have a broken arm (14:227) (aˬ la‸ k'eh‸-eu)

lavqtov the shoulder joint in an animal (la‸ puˇ)

lavqtul the length from thumb to mid-finger (11:78) (clf. **tul**) (tiˬ toˇ)

lavqtuv a fist (9:97) (la‸ tu^)

lavqtuv qiq tuv one handful (a measure)

lavqtuv sivq e col a stingy person (tsawˇ tsiˇ)

lavqtuv tuv to make a fist (9:97, 46:94) (la‸ tu^ tu^-eu)

lavqtuv tuvluvq luvq to make a fist (la‸ tu^ tu^-eu)

lavqxa aqhhal a handprint

lavqzaq soq fulfill; carry out (50:110)

Lafcal Lancang County (57:97f)

laffeif to waste (as time); to spend idly (Chi) (41:55) (zmˬ caw^-eu)

Laftiq a township in Honghe county (Chi) (46:173)

LAO

laol a walled town

laol clf. for length, roughly a fathom (the arms held out, from fingertip to fingertip) (11:78) (aˇ lmˇ)

laol to be warm; hot (9:90) (lahˇ-eu; yaw lmˇ)

laol to warm up (as at a fire) (9:90) (lahˇ laˇ-eu)

-- **laol, aoqcal calseil** -- to get warm in the sun

laolbav collar (9:90) (lawˇ baˬ)

-- **laolbav, peilhaoq** -- a fur collar

laolbiaq the mane of a horse (9:90) (mahˬ lahˇ boe; mˬ lahˇ boe)

=laolbiaq, moq= the mane of a horse

laolbyu 1. the nape of the neck (9:91) (kawˬ lahˇ lahˇ dzahˇ), 2. the neck (26:37) (kawˬ lahˇ)

laolbyuq byuq 1. to carry a baby animal by the nape of the neck (as a mother cat does), 2. to carry a load which rests on one's neck, 3. to carry a child on one's shoulders with the legs over the shoulders

-- **laolbyuq byuq, moqqul** -- to carry a baby animal by the nape of the neck

-- **laol, caoq** -- to be covered

laolceq ceq sil to kill by hanging (26:10) (pa^ g'eu seh^-eu)

laolciivq the neck (animals; people) (12:125) (kawˇ lahˇ)

-- **laolcoq, geel aol** -- fighting bastion

laolcyu nei to be very hot (11:58) (or) **laolxavq**

laolcyu pa cyu nei very warmly (as to welcome a person very warmly) (45:90) (yaw cuiˇ yaw lahˇ)

laol cyuq to prevent; obstruct; stop (animate objects) (46:139, 50:48) (or) **jol cyuq** (la^ tsoeˇ-eu)

=**laol dama, puv**= respected villagers

laol dav to warm up

-- **laoldaol, millaol** -- land which has been burned

=**laol, daoq**= the hip of an animal

laoldu nei warmly (46:147) (yaw lmˇ lmˇ-ehˇ)

=**laol, eel**= hot water; boiled water

-- **laol, eellaol** -- for water to get hot

laolgav gav for fields to 'cool off' after burning (they want to plant while they are still 'warm')

-- **laolgaol, aldyuv** -- a joint in a bamboo shoot

laolgeeq scabies on the neck

laolgu saqgeel skin at the nape of the neck (here of a cat 11:197)

=**laol, haol**= 1. give preferential treatment; favored treatment, 2. safeguard; defend; uphold

-- **laolhaol, galzii** -- (see full)

-- **laol, hao** -- give consideration to (or) **hu leev**

-- **laol, haoq** -- to worry ('chest hot')

=**laolhaoq, caoq**= a fireplace

laolheiq the collar ('opening') of shirt/jacket (9:91)

=**laol, hoq**= a kind of bowl

=**laol hovqma, puv**= all of the villagers

laoljo jo to make a fire lane in a village (50:48)

laoljoq the neck (as of a sacrificial pig)

laolkaq a village gate (term from the Akha) (46:122) (lawˇ kahˇ)

laolkaol a fence; wall; bamboo fence (or) **kaoldaol; haqbol kaoldaol; haqbol laolkaol** (kmˇ cehˇ)

=**laol, kaoq**= neck

laolkeel the outside wall of a building (9:91)

laolkeel hhe biav to break down a wall (45:1)

=**laol, laq**= a fathom in length

laollaq meil warmly (yaw lmˇ lmˇ-ehˇ)

=**laol, mil**= a prairie fire (i.e., not in the jungle)

=**laol, miq**= a flame

-- **laolnav, saqhav** -- dense forest
-- **laol, neema eil** -- to console
-- **laol, nieivq** -- to confine someone or something (as to put someone into jail)
laolnuv warm (as water) (9:91) (yaw lahˇ; iˇ lahˇ)
laolnuv nuvma very warm; hot (11:59) (zawˇ lahˇ-eu)
-- **laol, nyuq** -- show consideration; give every care
laolngaol a particle showing purpose (i.e., to make me (vb) (**bi saq movq a leilnei laolngaol** = for the purpose of making me suffer - 11:215)
laolngaoq even though; but (even though the room is large, it is not so bright - 11:126, 140) (**Salbiaoq saoqceil huvq biao alnei laolngaoq, miqssaq maq seq.** Salbiaoq did not even take a wife until he was 30 years old. 11:123) (or) **naolngaoq** (see also: **aqteiq**)
laolngaoq -- maq (neg) except for (**Xilgei ngal qiq hhaq laolngaoq maq jol.** Except for me no one else is here. 11:123) (maˬ ngeuˇ naˇ)
laolpav half a fathom (11:78) (lmˇ pa^)
-- **laol, peilbeil** -- to fold clothes
laolqaol deep inside the woods (bawˇ tsahˬ)
-- **laolqaol, aoqtav** -- the firmament; the vault of heaven
laol qeiq to become warm (38:90) (lmˇ laˇ-eu; lahˇ laˇ-eu)
laolquvq to seal off; close (50:51)
laolsavq to warm up (as the sun); to steam up (14:199) (la^ lahˇ-eu)
laolsil dirty water (9:91) (iˇ jaw˰)
-- **laolsil, neema** -- the heart to be warmed up; to be encouraged
laoltav boiled water; warm water (iˇ cu˰ iˇ buiˇ; iˇ lahˇ)
laoltaoq valley (9:91) (lawˇ k'mˬ; g'aˬ lahˇ)
-- **laol, wuqcal** -- to warm up in the sun
laolxav gracious; warmly (26:14, 50:141) (or) **laolcyu nei** (yaw lmˇ lmˇ-ehˇ)
-- **laol, xoq** -- to shut into; to lock up (or) **xovq laol**
-- **laol, xovq** -- to shut into; close something up (or) **xoq laol**
=**laol za, quvq**= the proper climate
laolzaol a bridge (9:91) (lawˇ dzmˇ)
laolzaol cuvq to put in a bridge (lawˇ dzmˇ tso˰-eu)
-- **laolzaol, saol** -- a metal bridge
-- **laolzaol, saolcav** -- an iron chain bridge
laolzaol zaolteiq a single wooden bridge (aˇ bawˇ lawˇ dzmˇ)

lao to soak in water (as a buffalo does) (**aqniuq niuq lao lao** = the buffalo soaks in the pond) (lah yaˬ-ahˇ lah-eu)
lao the sea; ocean (or) **laoma; lao'laoma** (lah; iˬ

ma la^ sha^)

lao a particle used in certain couplets to show a large quantity. (**Aqtav siq lao siq taol siq yal, siq lao jaljul meiqtuv.** Above thousands of seeds, they look like the beaks of sparrow-like birds.)

-- lao, aqlao -- to wallow in a wallow

laobao a lake; swamp; pond (6:160, 50:73) (lah ma)

laobao bao to be muddy (yaw pyeh^)

-- laobao, sulqeil -- a marsh

laobiao siblings; cousins; relatives (Chi) (13:39) (a˯ yui˰ a˯ nyiˇ; mehˇ nmˇ)

laobieiv muddy; marshy (6:160) (yaw pyeh^)

laobieiv bieiv to be muddy; marshy (9:90) (yaw pyeh^ yaw leh^)

laoduaf monopolize (Chi) (50:110)

Lao Hholnil 'Old Shorty' (a bad name given to the Hani by some Han Chinese, from which the term 'Woni' was no doubt derived -- a name the Hani do not like) (Chi) (57:93)

laojal home town (Chi) (41:14)

lao'laoma the sea; ocean; big lake (9:90, 50:69) (i˯ ma la^ sha^; lah lah ma)

-- lao, nee'lao -- a religious day; a ceremonial day

=lao nei, hhao'= roundish; circular

laopuvsiq an island (50:34)

laosal the third brother/sister (Chi)

-- lao, saqlao -- (see full)

laosil a dirty pond (lah siˇ; lah jaw˰)

lao sil lao hhyuq to spend a ceremonial holiday

laosiil a teacher (Chi) (9:92, 11:212, 41:4, 50:103) (sah˯ bo˰ meh˯-eu g'a˯; sa˯ la˯; kuˇ)

laosiil meeq 'good morning, teacher' (A=Chi) (41:60) (based on Chinese greeting)

Lao Waq 'Old' Wang (Chi) (11:94)

Lao Zal 'Old' Zal (surname) (Chi) (26:71) (written: Laozal)

Lao Zul elder Zhu (14:182)

laoq to increase (9:91) (lah˯-eu)

(vb) **laoq** to add to (**eil laoq** = add more words; **bavq laoq** = put something more in, etc.)

laoqbaq boss; a very rich person (Chi)

Laoqbel a mythical mountain from which **Laoqsel** calls forth the spring (46:156)

laoqdaof labor (Chi) (34:40)

Laoqdaofjiq Labor day (Chi) (26:112)

laoqdaofliaf amount of work one can do (Chi) (50:102)

laoqdaof seilcaliq labor productivity (Chi) (50:102)

=laoq, gaoq= blessing; merit, etc.

laoqgei jail (Chi) (**laoqgei nieivq tao** = put into jail)

laoqgei jilgual administrator of criminal reform (Chi) (50:102)

laoqgei miqnieiq aol 1. reform through labor, 2. punish with hard labor (50:102)
laoqha button quail (9:91) (hah˯ za˯ la˯ ma)
laoqha aqma button quail hen
laoq huvq dragon year (9:91, 11:32) (lah˯ ti˯ k'o˰ = rabbit year in Ak.)
=laoq, hhel= kingly dragon
laoq lal to increase (of animals, humans, money, etc.) (or) **zeq lal**
laoqliaq 1. grains given as tax (Chi) (35:30), 2. taxes (35:30)
laoqlyul millet (9:91) (shaˇ do^)
laoqmeil as; like (duˇ-eu; lo˰-ehˇ)
laoq nao dragon day (9:91) (lah˯ ti˯ nah = rabbit day in Ak.)
Laoqsel a mythical woman who calls out spring (46:156)
Laoqsseil the water protector (46:114)
laoqteq a water tap (Chi) (**wulquvq laoqteq** = a water tap)
laoqteq yevq cyuq to turn off a water tap (A=Chi)
laoq zeq dragon hour (B=Chi)
-- **laoqziiq, soqhhaq** -- written receipt for something purchased (B=Chi)

laovq to be in a stupor (9:92) (cf.: law˰ g'a-eu)
=laovq, eel= hysterical laughter
-- **laovq, hu** -- to stare
-- **laovq, hhallaovq** -- to get together
laovq lal to be attractive
laovq laovq bia bia to have an unclear mind
laovq li to be stupefied
-- **laovq, mu'laovq** -- (see full)
-- **laovq, zaq** -- to attract

LE

=lelsel, altev= (see full)

le to be late (as in: **ceille** = late maturing rice) (9:97, 46:185)
=le, ceil= late maturing rice
lecei nei round (26:85) (yaw lah)
-- **le, lal** -- to come late (arrive late)

leq to fall (ga ka-eu)
leqdal to lean (k'aw˯ daˇ-eu)
leqhev Chinese style hat (9:98) (law˯ heu)
leqhev hevja an old Chinese rain hat
leqsiil the man in charge of cutting the tree for making the swing pole (46:188)

=lev, meiq= thick lips
=lev nei, eelseq= smilingly
=lev nei, peil= (see full)

-- lev, seq -- 1. to show one's teeth, 2. to smile

levq to peel (9:98); to skin (14:171) (leu‸-eu)
=levq la levq meil, qiq= without sorrow
-- levq, moqlevq -- to tell a lie (see: **moqlevq levq zavq**)
-- levq, taoq -- to bump and hurt

LEE

leel for a snake to be coiled up; wrapped around something
leel to roll (also see: **lee; lei**) (leh-eu; yo^-eu)
-- leel, aolzei -- to wind up (as to wind up a toy to spin it)
leelcii cii to bother others (la^ bah⌄-eu)
leeldee necklace (9:97) (law˅ dah)
leeldee saqyyuq collar bone; clavicle
leeldeeq a small balance for weighing light objects
=leel nei, javq= sleepily
=leel nei, ovq= ripe enough
=leel nei, qaq= very tiresome
=leel nei, xeiv= muddy
leeltovq to roll and tie; to twist and tie (yo^-aw˅ neh ka‸ cu‸-eu)

lee to roll (see also: **leel; leeq; lei**) (leh-eu)
lee a roll (as thread, string) (2:53) (leh-eu)
lee whirlwind (9:97) (ja⌄ leh˅ leh˅ zeu^ zeu^-eu)
leecei nei round; in a circle (14:139) (yaw zah; lah jo^ ni)
leedo nei neatly (9:97) (la^ lui^-eu)
=lee, kaol= a roll of thread
=lee, zaoq= (see full)

leeq 1. to fall down (9:97, 46:152), 2. to slip and fall (or) **taoqsil** (co⌄-eu)
(vb) leeq (vb) down (**diq leeq** = to beat down; knock down - 26:17) (di⌄ co⌄-eu)
-- leeq, bo -- to blow down
-- leeq, diq -- to beat down; knock down
-- leeq, diq puv diq -- to overthrow
leeq puvq to fall into liquid (or) **yapuvq** (lah pu‸-eu; ga pu‸-eu)
-- leeq, qil -- to fall down (as from suffering)
leeq taq to lay up (as money in a bank) (or) **toq taq**
leeq tao to fall into (14:165) (ga ah˅-eu)
=leeq, taoq= 1. to fall down (ga ka-eu), 2. to strike down
-- leeq, ya -- to fall down

leev 1. to be protected (57:69), 2. to roll up one's sleeves (9:97) (la‸ lui^ lui^-eu)
-- leev, bavq -- 1. to carry & fix up, 2. to collect, 3. to put away; conceal

leev dav to roll up (14:185) (leh da^-eu)
leevdov nei thoroughly; satisfactorily
-- **leev, haol** -- to save; protect; guard
-- **leev, hu'** -- 1. to take care of, 2. to show concern; give consideration (or) **hao'laol**
-- **leev, hhuv** -- to tidy up
-- **leev, kalyei se'** -- to harvest a crop
-- **leev, kavq** -- to tie up
-- **leev, leiq** -- 1. to drive cattle together, 2. to harvest crops
-- **leev, luvq** -- to keep watch, as over animals
-- **leev nei, wuqduq daoqmiq** -- thorough; everywhere; all affairs ('from head to tails')
leev quvq to cover thoroughly (la^ pym‸-eu)
=**leev, taq**= to preserve; to deposit (as money)
leev teiq 1. to get hold of, 2. to tie down (14:191) (pa‸ taw‸-eu)
-- **leev, toq** -- to take good care of
-- **leev, xeiv** -- to get loose; to run away
-- **leev, yav** -- to sweep clean
-- **leev, zaol** -- to make tidy
-- **leev, zeiqma sol** -- to figure out one's wealth

-- **leevq, moqleevq** -- to deceive; to lie

LEI

leil to drill; to train; to exercise (Chi) (dzaw-eu)
leil to winnow chaff from grain (zaˇ-eu; g'aˇ-eu = CA)
leil clf. for bag of (rice) (from **dalleil**) (11:217) (zeuˇ)
leil .. that (as he said that....) a particle for quotation, usually used within the sentence (**Aqsol liq aqyoq yaol soqhhaq meiq lal leil eil.** Everyone asks him to teach them. 11:129) (..lehˇ)
=**leil, aq**= wind; air (or) **jaqleil** (jaˬ lehˇ)
=**leil, aq**= an interjection showing surprise and pity
leilcal glowing ashes (lehˇ tsaˇ)
=**leil, dal**= a bag in which field produce is carried
=**leil, haq**= fine ashes and dust
leilhhev whirlwind (or) **jaqleil leilhhev** (jaˬ lehˇ lehˇ zeu^ zeu^-eu)
-- **leil hhev, bo ziivq**-- a windstorm
=**leil, jaq**= wind; air
-- **leil, keellavq** -- to exercise arms and legs (B= Chi)
leillel haolgaoq the highest mountain in the area (57:74)
leil lomaq 'like what I just said'
=**leil, luv**= lime (white powder)
-- **leilma mama, jaqleil** -- a typhoon
leilmeev white flying ash (lehˇ tsaˇ; lelhˇ meu‸)

=**leil nei, daoq**= to be very tired; to be weak; to be blunt
-- **leil nei, loqleil pal** -- very clearly
=**leil nei, loq**= clearly
=**leil nei, zoq**= straight way
leiltaoq buqssaq a vat or pot for dyeing (9:97) (meh˯ tah˯ oe˯ lah˯)
-- **leil to, aoqzeil** -- the far edge of the sky
leilzol to exercise (A=Chi)

lei to make a roll (as of thread) (leh-eu)
=**lei, hhaq**= buckwheat
=**lei nei, zyuq**= to be fat; plump
leitaoq xa to dye cloth (meh˯ tah˯ ka-eu; sa˯ paˇ na^-eu; sa˯ paˇ ka-eu)
-- **lei, za'lei** -- to make rice dumplings

leiq 1. to deviate, 2. to twist (thread) (yeu˰-eu), 3. to hunt (**saqleiq; saqqil leiq** = to hunt, as small deer) (9:97) (sha˯ teh-eu), 4. to seek; to look for (35:73) (po^-eu), 5. to drive out (2:53) (teh do^-eu)
leiq to paint (na˯ siˇ leh˰-eu) (**leiqnil** = to paint red; **leiqnav** = to paint black; **leiqbuvq** = to paint black and white)
leiq great-grandchild (oe˯ leh˯)
(vb) **leiq** 1. to (vb) a mistake (**zaol leiq** = to make a mistake); 2. miss something (**bev leiq** = to shoot and miss the target)
leiq bial to cancel; rub out; delete (50:186)
leiq bu to wash something by rubbing (clothes, rice, etc.) (leh˯ tsi˯-eu; nyeh˰ buˇ-eu)
leiq buvq to scribble (9:98); to rub on black (as to blacken a face - 35:77, 46:193) (leh˰-eu)
-- **leiq buvq, bavq buvq** -- a face covered with dust
leiq byu to make a hole (wood, dirt, rock, etc.) (11:161) (maˇ byoe byoe-eu)
-- **leiq byu, yobyu** -- to make a hole
leiq cal to urge on; to ask to hurry, to do quickly (9:98) (la^ kawˇ-eu; la^ teh˯-eu)
leiqcavq to keep in touch (Chi) (50:106)
leiq ciq to wash something by rubbing (9:98) (leh˯ tsi˯-eu)
leiq cyuq to stop; block (13:46) (leh˯ tsoe˯-eu); to catch and stop (35:7)
leiqdaq daq to waste something (50:102)
leiqdaq meil 1. wasted (**leiqdaq meil taq bi jav** = don't let it be wasted), 2. in vain (9:98)
leiqdaq meil bi jav to waste
leiqdaq nei wasted; no value (26:47,48); unnecessary; not needed (26:74)
-- **leiq deiv, wuqdeiq** -- to earn a living
leiq duv 1. expel; discharge (50:95), 2. to drive out (leh˯ do^-eu), 3. to eject (or) **pyuq duv** (esp. for spitting out)

leiq e leiq, suq e suq no matter what ('win or lose') (as in: 'no matter what I will do it') (57:94) (B=Chi)
-- leiq, eelpuv -- to flood
leiqgaoq broom grass (ya^ pyawˇ aˇ do^)
leiqgaoq alpul broom grass roots
leiqgaoq alyeiv blossoms of broom grass (14:146) (ya^ pyawˇ aˇ do^ do^ laˇ-eu)
leiqgeeq geeq to make someone or something go quickly (drive someone or something along quickly) (9:98)
Leiqhoqgoq the United Nations (57:71) **Lieiqhoqgoq**
leiqhoq leiqceiv to scatter
=leiq, hhaq= a joke
-- leiq, hhaqleiq -- to make a joke
leiq hhoq to separate; drive apart (46:76) (la^ g'awˬ-eu)
=leiq, hhoq= again
leiqhhuvq covered with water
-- leiq hhyul sil meil, hhyul -- with exceeding joy
-- leiq ju, hhaqcil -- to lubricate
leiqkev kevma 1. to chase each other, 2. to follow quickly (14:168) (teh-eu)
=leiq kovq, covq= pass on a disease
leiq kuv to curl on its own
-- leiq kuv, aqniuq -- to confine a buffalo in its stable
-- leiq kyuq sil, kyuq -- very tired
leiq leev 1. to drive cattle together, 2. to harvest crops (teh uiˬ-eu; la^ uiˬ-eu)
-- leiq, miavleiq -- 1. to look but not see; turn a blind eye to (50:154), 2. to rub one's eyes (as when one awakens)
leiq mil chase and catch up with (9:98, 11:112, 46:77) (teh miˇ-eu)
-- leiq, miavleiq -- 1. to rub one's eyes, 2. to look but not see (turn a blind eye to something)
leiq nyuq to awaken someone (or) **leiqtul** (la^ noeˬ-eu)
leiqpe a food made from rice water and bean curd (lehˬ peuˇ)
-- leiq, piaqsal albaol -- (see full)
leiq pieiq to drive cattle to the mountains
leiq pieiv to grind into pieces (as a truck running over something or someone)
leiq puv 1. to cast about for, 2. to overthrow; overturn
leiq qiq ciivq e ssaq a great-great-grandchild
-- leiq, qo -- to follow; chase; go after
leiq sa to drive away (teh dzeh-eu)
-- leiq, saqleiq -- to go hunting (following after the game)
leiqsiq leiqsav a kind of nut (with fuzz on it)
leiq suq to spread on (14:217) (la^ k'awˬ-eu)
leiq suv xa laq e to erode
leiqssaq an awl (to make small holes) (9:98) (shmˇ

toe$_{\vee}$)

leiq ssaoq to drive something/one together (9:98) (teh ui$_{\vee}$-eu)

-- **leiq ssaoq, piul** -- to raise funds

leiq teev to stop (38:92) (la^ na$_{\vee}$-eu)

leiq tul 1. to awaken someone (or) **leiqnyuq** (la^ noe$_{\vee}$-eu), 2. transferred from place to place (50:38) (or) **bi jolpal**

-- **leiq tul, ssaqlaol** -- to arouse the masses to action; mobilize the masses

-- **leiqzaq, hoqbiol** -- to roam around looking for meals (as a beggar) (po^ dza$_{\vee}$-eu)

=**leiq zaq, moq**= to trade by using a caravan of horses to carry goods

-- **leiq, zaol** -- 1. to make a mistake, 2. to lose in business

leiq zei to drive away (11:205, 46:148) (teh dzeh-eu)

-- **leiq zei, neivq** -- to drive away evil spirits

-- **leiq, zyulleiq** -- to investigate a case

leiv market (**leiv zuvq** = to go to the market) (leh^)

leiv take off; undress (leh^-eu)

leiv clf. for a time, once (**qiq leiv aol** = to do once) (9:98) as for times of plowing (11:85)

-- **leiv, alleiv** -- to be a dwarf

=**leiv leiv nei, yeiv**= not firm; shakey

-- **leiv, mu lu meiv** -- (see full)

leiv puv to repeat (50:24)

-- **leivssaq nei, teivleiv** -- very, very shallow

leiv zuvq to go to the market (leh^ dzu$_{\wedge}$-eu)

leiv zuvq nao market day

leivq to soak (9:98) (dui^-eu)

leivq for a baby to cry for no reason (a$^{\vee}$ byeh$^{\vee}$ byeh$^{\vee}$-eu)

=**leivq, covq**= a skin rash

-- **leivq, hheivq** -- to cheat

=**leivq, hhoq**= again and again

=**leivq meil, hhoq**= again and again

-- **leivq nei, meiqpov** -- to eat with a full mouth

-- **leivq nei zaq, meiqpov** -- to eat heartily

leivq zavq a naughty, mischievous baby or young child

-- **leivq, zaol** -- a pretense of doing (11:218)

-- **leivq, zaolleivq** -- to pretend to do

LI

lil wind (or) **leil** (pf.) (ja$_{\vee}$ leh$^{\vee}$)

lil affirmative ending of the first person (**Ngal Haqniqssaq ngeel lil.** I am a Hani.) **aqlil** (see 11:133 for more samples)

-- **lil'aq** final particle used in direct questions (**Nol Laosiil gee zaq movq lil'aq?** Do you want to make a living as a teacher? **Nol Haqniqssaq ngeel lil'aq?** 54:168) (for more samples see: 11:138)

(note: **Aqyoq Haqniqssaq ngeel nga laq?** Is he/she a Hani?)

-- lil **bav lav nei, bil** -- uncertain; incoherently

-- lil, **hhaq** -- okay

=lil, **laq**= 1. underpants, 2. short trousers

=lil, **miq**= 1. burning firewood, 2. a short tail

lilpuv opposite (as the opposite direction); upside down

lil **puv lav puv** to rise in rebellion; to revolt (tah˯ po^-eu)

lilpuv meil upside down (13:20, 35:43,74, 46:185); (tah˯ po^ siˇ liˇ-ehˇ)

lilpuv nei in contrast; upside down; the opposite; contrary (35:4, 45:29, 52) (tah˯ po^-ohˇ)

lilpuv puv 1. to turn upside down (tah˯ po^ po^-eu), 2. to be confused, 3. to violate; run counter to (50:178)

-- **lilpuv puv, aqpuv** -- to rotate; to whirl

lilpuv puv ssaq a confused person

lil **puv ssuq puv** to go the wrong direction (50:9)

lil **puv zaol puv** to overturn; subvert (50:36)

li to go (up) (9:98, 11:40) (le-eu = spoken more like an Ak.: 'le')

li half a kilometer (Chi = li) (26:95)

=li, **aq**= child

lidaof 1. to lead (Chi) (26:101), 2. a leader; official (Chi) (26:49) (same as Hani: **aqhhol**)

-- li, **dov** -- to enter (upwards)

ligua a hotel (Chi) (50:110)

lihhal 1. a certain job that time, manpower and materials should be spent on, 2. the price for something

-- li, **hhuvq** -- to go back from a lower place

li'**lueif** theory (Chi) (50:104)

li'**lueifjal** a theorist (Chi) (34:28, 50:105)

li'**lueif jilcu** basic theory (Chi) (50:104)

li'**lueif lieiqxif siiqjif** good & realistic theory (Chi) (50:105)

=li, **miq**= youngest daughter in the family

-- li, **nee'li** -- to think; consider

li'**lueif** theory (Chi)

lima cuv transplanting rice (local dialect) (46:157)

-- li, **neema maq** -- dissatisfied

-- li, **saq** -- epilogue; end

-- li, **savqli** -- difficult to breathe (and see full)

litaq a meeting hall (Chi) (50:104)

lixa an ideal; a hoped for goal (Chi) (26:110, 34:19)

lixa mol 1. to realize or see one's goal; 2. to achieve one's ideal (A=Chi)

lixef a leader (Chi) (50:109)

Lixeiljal name of a river in Luchun county (14:220)

liyal another one (Chi) (usually it is: **aqnu liyal**)

-- **liyal, aqnu** -- another (**liyal** = Chi)

liyiuq a realm (Chi) (34:98)
liza brigade commander (Chi) (50:110)

liq also; too (9:99) (jiˇ; g'eh; k'aw‸) (cf. Lahu Shi: liˇ)
liq one-tenth of a '**feil**' (for measuring land) (Chi) (41:129)
liq a bell (41:29) (**Yiuvqsul tul e liq gyuq al laq**? Has the bell for rising rung yet? (jaˇ cuˇ)
liq zero (Chi)
(vb) **liq** to be worn down (**bo liq** = for a winnowing fan to be worn down; **dev liq** = for a knife to be worn down; **duq liq** = for a hoe to be worn down)
liqcaq standpoint; side (Chi) (**aqsol pyu liqcaq** = whose side are you on?) (34:25)
liqceilyeiq workers on a train (as conductors, those who take tickets, etc.) (Chi) (26:89)
=**liq, daoq**= a stem
liqfaqqeiq legislative power (Chi) (50:105)
liqhaolgei lotus (Chi) (9:99) (lah bo ma)
=**liq, hel**= a pole to mark a field
liqhoqqif a part in a machine (Chi) (26:30)
liqhhaf put on the record; place a case on file for investigation and prosecution (Chi) (50:105)
liqhhaol a calendar (**Haqniq e liqhhaol** = a Hani calendar 46:81, 106)
liqhhaol eil ceiv col the person who decides the policy (50:93)
liqjeif parts (as of a car, machine, etc.) (Chi) (26:33, 73)
liqliaf strength (Chi) (in Hani: **hhaqhav**) (34:15) (g'aˬ)
liqmi centimeter (or) **feil; gaolfeil** (Chi) (41:127)
=**liq nei, to'**= to be tight
liqniq forestry department (Chi) (or) **albol miqnieiq** (50:108)
Liqniq Lenin (Chi) (50:108)
Liqniq Qeiqjiq the complete works of Lenin (Chi) (34:92)
Liqniq zuyif Lenninism (34:5, 50:108)
Liqngal the old name of Jianshui County (or) **Liqngalful** (Chi)
(vb) **liq (vb) saq** something else has been done as well (**qiq nao nei ceil diq saq e maq ceil, eq liq eq leev saq al**. In one day (they) not only threshed all of the rice, but (they) even carried it all home as well. 45:12)
=**liq, seq**= a broken off tooth
liqsef aoq retail; sell retail (A=Chi) (50:108)
liqsiil a lawyer (Chi) (50:111)
liqsii history (Chi) (34:21)
liqsii weiqwuq zuyif historical materialism (Chi) (50:106)
liqsiiq zeiffu provisional government; interim government (Chi) (50:108)

liqsiif luqbaol baolcaoq the grave of a revolutionary martyr (A=Chi) (50:108)
Liqsul the Lisu (people) (Li˯ saw˯)
Liqsulcuq the Lisu people (B=Chi) (or) **Liqsulssaq** (Li˯ saw˯ za˯)
Liqsuldoq the Lisu language (Li˯ saw˯ daw˯) (10:pref.)
Liqsulssaq the Lisu people (or) **Liqsulcuq** (B=Chi) (li˯ saw˯ za˯)
liq ssol hhaol custom; tradition (50:51) (cf.: zahˇ)
liqwaf exception; another one (Chi) (50:106) (or) **aqnu**
liqxul to retire (one who joined his work force before Oct. 1st 1949 and retires from the position because of old age) (Chi) (34:106)
liqzii a small particle, as an atom or neutron (Chi)

=liv, lavq= deep inside (as deep inside a room)
=liv, loq= the craw of a chicken
=liv, lovq= a chicken coop
=liv, ngaqngal laq= the soft palate
=livseq, bavq= a molar tooth; wisdom tooth

=livq, beil= the craw of a bird

lifjif example sentences (Chi) (50:105)

LIA

lia one-tenth of a catty, 50 grams (Chi) (41:129) (or) **mieiv**

liaqguaso grain distribution station and store (Chi) (50:107)
liaqpiaof food coupon; grain ration coupon (Chi) (41:175, 50:107)
liaqsiiq jalgaolca a food processing plant (Chi) (50:107)
liaqsiiqjiq bureau of food and crops (Chi) (50:107)
liaq yil liaq lal meil liaq to measure repeatedly (again and again) (14:150) (**liaq** = Chi)

liafciiq a classifier (grammatical) (Chi) (50:107)

LIE

lieqda caqkaf be placed on probation (Chi) (50:109)
Lieq Saofqiq Liu Shaoqi (former govt. chairman of the Communist Party) (or) **Liuq Saofqiq** (Chi) (34:20, 50:109)
lieqsual acid (or) **lieqsual naciq** (A=Chi) (26:84)
lieqtaol circulation (as in economic use) (Chi) (34:38, 50:109)

LIEI

lieiqbuf a company (as in the army); a command headquarters (Chi) (26:44, 57)
lieiqca associated production (Chi) (34:42)
lieiqciiq conjunction (grammatical) (Chi)
lieiqdyuf an army unit; a company (Chi) (26:51, 54, 50:106) (yeh˅ ma˰)
  lieiqdyuf seza a company commander ('head') (Chi) (26:109)
lieiqfaq united defense work (Chi) (50:106)
  lieiqfaqdyuf united defense team (Chi) (50:106)
Lieiqhoq goq United Nations (Chi) (50:106) (or) **Leiqhoqgoq**
lieiqxalcao albol a certain type of plant which has economic value when grown (A=Chi) (14:210)
lieiqza 1. a captain in the army (Chi) (9:99), 2. a company commander (50:107)
lieiqziifhaof hyphen (punctuation mark) (Chi)

lieifgal to process steel (Chi) (26:28)
  lieifgalluq a steel refinery (A=Chi) (26:27)
lieifmaoq alliance (Chi) (50:106)
lieifxiq to exercise (Chi) (2:53)

LIU

Liuq Liu (surname) (2:53), family name (9:99)
liuqpeif schools of thought (Chi) (34:61)
Liuq Saofqiq Liu Shaoqi (or) **Lieq Saofqiq** (34:20)

LO

lol 1. to offer (as in an offering, or offer someone a meal - 13:2) (law˅-eu), 2. to fall over; to topple (law˅-eu)
lol clf. for a river (9:99)
-- **lol, aqhhyu** -- to honor maternal uncles who come to attend a burial ceremony by serving them a meal (or) **aqhhyu hoqbiol lol**
-- **lol, Aqlobieil** -- to offer to **Aqlobieil** in the 'great water divide' ceremony
lolbaq river (9:99) (clf. **lol** - 11:34) (law˅ ba˯)
  lolbaq baqma a large river (or) **lolbaq lolma, lolma** (law˅ ba˯ law˅ ma; law˅ ba˯ ba˯ ma)
  lolbaq baqssaq a small river (or) **lolbaq lolssaq** (law˅ ba˯ ba˯ za˯)
  lolbaq haqluv a river stone (used in making sacred places) (see: **milsaol luvcuv**)
  lolbaq lolma a large river (46:76) (or) **lolbaq baqma, lolma** (law˅ ba˯ law˅ ma)
  lolbaq lolssaq a small river (or) **lolbaq baqssaq** (law˅ ba˯ law˅ za˯)
  lolbaq taoq a deep pool in a river (11:218) (law˅ ba˯-eu˯ tm˯)

lolbaq yoq to cross a stream (lawˇ baˬ tseh^-eu; lawˇ baˬ yoˬ-eu)

-- **lolbeeq, ollol** -- a snake nest

=**lol, beil**= betel nut

Lolbiq the Luomei branch of the Hani, who live 'down river' (or) **Lolmiq**

lolbieil a table (9:99, 46:134) (hawˬ jeh)

lolbieil bieilhhao a round table (hawˬ jeh)

lolbieil bieilzeil the edge of a table (11:35)

-- **lolbieil, jalzii** -- a wooden table (used for eating)

-- **lolbieil, soqzol** -- a desk

lolbieil wuqduq at the dinner table (35:19)

lolcuq cuq dav li to go upstream along a river (gaw^ mehˇ paw da^ leˇ-eu)

lol dal to lean on; depend on (9:99, 45:46, 50:195) (k'awˬ daˇ-eu)

loldaoq 1. the end of a river, 2. the end of a dammed stream

loldei an irrigated rice field by a river (clf. **dei**) (11:34) (cf.: **lolxaq**) (deh ma; deh yaˇ)

loldei deiyal an irrigated rice field by a river (deh ma; dah yaˇ)

lolgal a ditch, a water course (or) **eelgal** (uiˇ k'ehˬ) (9:99)

lolgal galbaol a dam in a ditch (uiˇ k'ehˬ yaw pyaw˰)

lolgal galkov a ditch; a water course (uiˇ k'ehˬ)

lolgal galloq inside a ditch (uiˇ k'ehˬ la˰ k'oeˇ)

lolgal leiqssaq the man in charge of the irrigation system (see also: **galsaol**)

lolgal taol to dig a ditch (11:158) (uiˇ k'ehˬ duˬ-eu; uiˇ k'ehˬ caˬ-eu; uiˇ k'ehˬ yuˇ-eu)

lolgov a valley with water; a gully (or) **lolxaq** (9:99, 10:20, 11:20, 46:179) (g'aˬ lawˬ)

lolgov govzeil the bank of a valley (14:169) (gaw^ dzeˇ)

lolha diq to beat an offering chicken to death on the stone put at the feet of a dead elder

lolheiq a river source (or) **lolmeil** (9:99)

=**lol, hol**= to be greedy (eat fast etc.)

-- **lol, hoqbiol** -- 1. to invite someone to a meal, 2. to feast the villagers as a part of the wedding ceremony

lolhovq village water source; village well (26:46, 38:37, 46:114, 134) (lawˇ k'aw˰)

lolhovq soq an offering made to the village water source (46:133) (lawˇ k'aw˰ lawˇ-eu)

lolhho a lymph node

lolhho ya for a lymph node to swell

lolhhuvq lolliv a river bend (lawˇ g'o˰)

lolkaq a ditch; a trench (**zafhaoq lolkaq** = a trench used in warfare - A=Chi) (26:48)

lollavq a brook ('branch of a river')

lolma a big river (or) **lolbaq baqma; lolbaq lolma**

(lawˇ baˬ lawˇ ma)

lolmeil a river source (or) **lolheiq; eelmeil**

Lolmeil the Luomei branch of the Hani who live 'upriver' (46:79)

=lol meil, bil= fall and lean against

-- lol, milsaol -- offering to the lord of the land

lolmiq the end of a river; mouth of a river

Lolmiq (see: **Lolbiq**)

=lol, ngaq= an eel (ngaˬ uiˇ ngaˬ lawˇ)

=lol, ol= a snake (aˇ lawˇ)

lolpav pieiq to dam a stream for fishing (11:198) (g'aˬ lahˇ piˬ-eu; ngaˬ lahˇ tsahˇ-eu)

-- lol, peiv -- to stumble

-- lolqaol, aoqtav -- high above the sky

lolqo nei along (13:40)

lolssaq a small river (or) **lolbaq baqssaq; lolssaq** (lawˇ baˬ baˬ zaˬ)

-- lolwuv, ollol -- a snake egg

lolxaq a gully (or) **lolgov**

-- lol zaq, hhaqma -- to make an offering in the sacred grove of the village

lolzeil a river bank; riverside (9:100, 13:30) (lawˇ dzeˇ; gaw^ dzeˇ)

lolzyul where two rivers meet (gaw^ tsmˇ)

lo (fp) a final part. showing affirmation (**Lal lo.** He/she has already come.)

lo a particle or 'filler word' which has no meaning of its own, but rounds out the statement, used in poems, proverbs and couplets (**Da lo xalceiq ceil la laqnil taq bi yoq yil** -- see proverb D4).

lo clf. for a section of wood, bamboo, etc. (9:99) (law)

=lo, bol= the lower leg

locavq a kind of grass

-- loduv, doqlo -- sentence making

=lo, haq= bamboo joints

=lo, ho'= horse bell

=lo, lavq= upper arm

-- lo'lavq, doqheiq -- language branch

-- lomaq (part.) indicating a positive, declarative statement (**Ngal loq lomaq.** Of course I know.)

(vb) lo mi to have time to (vb) (**eil lo mi** = have time to say - 26:67) (aˇ yamˬ ja^-eu)

lonia to the east, or upper side (as of a mountain)

-- lopaoq, doqlo -- a synonym

lo qil lo cavq many joints (as in bamboo)

lo'qo 1. along with (as to go along with) (9:100, 46:155) (nehˬ-ehˇ), 2. according to; following (as a policy) (50:2), 3. a method (**kolxoq lo'qo** = the scientific method - A=Chi) (10:pref.)

-- lo'qo, doqlo -- word order (gram)

lo'qo nei following along (as when looking for where a noise is coming from) (12:125, 41:106) (caw teh g'eh-eu)

-- **loquv, doqheiq** -- language family
-- **losiivq, doqlo** -- new words
loyei nei slowly (9:101) (aw law^ law^-ehˇ)
loyei loyei nei slowly (or) **loyei lolyei nei** (38:94) (aw law^ law^-ehˇ) (cf. Lahu: a yeh¯ a yeh¯)
loyei pa yei nei very slowly (mya‸ dehˬ ni)
-- **lozao, doqheiq** -- language group; language branch

loq 1. to rinse a container with water (as a cup, pot, etc.), 2. to brush one's teeth (la^ jo^-eu)
loq a boat (9:100) (clf. **loq** - 11:34) (lawˬ)
loq 1. to understand (much like siq) (9:100, 46:131), 2. see clearly (as in: **maq hu loq** = not to see clearly) (lawˬ-eu)
loq clf. for irrigated field (9:100, 11:81)
loq a final part. used in questions: 1. demanding a 'yes' or 'no' response ("**Laqhhev loq**?" "A whirlpool? - 46:95) (loˇ), and 2. in some questions demanding an explanation (**haljivq loq** = what was that?)
(n) **loq** a noun particle (**col loq yomeeq** = what a good man - 13:40) (45:58)
loqbeq to be rich (27:11) (smˇ muiˬ)
loqbeq beq to become rich (26:119) (smˇ muiˬ muiˬ-eu)
-- **loqbeq, sulhhaq** -- rich; wealthy
loqbeq za'loq hev nei when one becomes a little wealthy (13:2)
loqbeq zeifceiq a policy to help people become rich (B=Chi) (50:52)
loqbioq what cousins (father's sister's sons) call each other (note: **aqyivq aqnil** = general term)
-- **loq, ceil** -- (see full)
loqdeiq ceiq to plough a field a second time (9:100) (tsehˬ po^-eu)
=**loq, diq**= a wooden container used for threshing rice
=**loq, eel**= water trough
Loq'eil a township in Honghe county (46:184)
-- **loq, eil e** -- to speak clearly; distinctly
-- **loq, eil** -- to refute
-- **loq, gee** -- to explain
-- **loqgov, xaldei** -- a barren irrigated field
loqgual zuyif (see: **loqgueil zuyif**) (34:116)
loqgueil zuyif optimism (Chi) (or) **loqgualzuyif**
-- **loq, haljivq** -- 'what was that?'
loqhaoq sal e good; fertile terraced irrigated fields in the valley
loq he to row a boat (lawˬ heu-eu)
loq he daldul oar or pole for propelling boat or raft (9:100) (or) **loq he dalpav** (lawˬ heu-eu daˇ la^)
loq he dalpav oar or pole for propelling boat or raft (or) **loq he daldul**

loqhef to regress; to go backward (as a country to go backward in development) (Chi) (34:33)
loqheiq a spillway in an irrigated rice field
loq hultav dav to go aboard (as boat, airplane) (**feiljil hultav dav** = board an airplane)
-- **loq, hu** -- to see clearly
-- **loq hu e, yyuq** -- to determine something by consulting bones
=**loq, hhavqzal hoq**= pig trough
loqhhoq a kind of palm tree (the leaves can be used as dishes)
  loqhhoq hhoqbol a large palm tree
  loqhhoq hhoqqeil a sour dish made from leaves of the '**loqhhoq**' palm tree
loqjiq logical (Chi)
loqjiq jiq to stammer; stutter (9:100) (laˇ nga‸ nga‸-eu)
loqju long and narrow irrigated fields
loqkol a terrace in a field (11:204)
  -- **loqkol, xaldei** -- a new irrigated field
loqleil nei clearly (9:100, 46:83) (law˯ ka ni g'eh-eu)
  loqleil pa leil nei very clearly
  loqleil sav nei clearly (as to hear a sound clearly) (11:209)
loqliv the crop or craw of a chicken (behˇ jiˇ)
loqma a large irrigated field (46:160) (clf. **loq** - 11:34) (deh ma)
-- **loq, meiqloq** -- to rinse one's mouth, or brush one's teeth
=**loq, moq**= feeding trough for horses
-- **loq, nalhaq** -- to inquire; to ask
loq naqduq a port for ships (50:112)
=**loq nei, bia'**= brightly
=**loq nei, bu'**= cleanly
loqnei eilduv to make clear to all; proclaim publicly (50:208)
=**loq, niuqtaoq**= donkey
loqniuv a spiral shell (9:100) (a˯ nyo^ lo^)
-- **loq, nyuq** -- 1. to think and understand, 2. to understand each other
loqpeiq a compass (Chi)
Loqpu puvkaq the name of a village
=**loq, puv**= exonerate; rehabilitate
loqsal good terraced fields (46:178)
-- **loqsal, deima** -- a good terraced field
loqsiil a screw (Chi) (26:73)
  loqsiildil a screw and nut (Chi) (26:119)
  loqsiilmaof a screw and nut (Chi)
loqsiiq practicable; workable (Chi) (34:71)
loqyav a lily (9:100) (ja˯ pa‸)
Loqyeq a township in Honghe county (46:184)
=**loq, zal**= a food container
-- **loq zaq, deiq** -- to argue; to reason things out
loqzii mule (Chi) (or) **lalzii** (34:3)

loqzoq to dance (9:100, 46:137) (In Ak., for males to dance: la^ je˅ tsaw˅-eu; for females: gaˇ nyeh nyeh-eu)

loqzoq coq to dance (10:pref., 46:91) (the 'jump' dance with the gourd musical pipe) (la^ je˅ tsaw˅-eu)

lov to be free (to have time) (9:100) (**Haltaq lov ya leil, halmeil liq qiq taq lal.** Come whenever you have time. 11:104) (**siiqjeil jav** = to have time A=Chi) (ngeh^-eu; aˇ yam˅ ja^-eu)
lov clf. for a layer as in a honey comb, piece of paper, a room (12:126) (law^)
=**lov, bav**= a bedroom
=**lov, biaq**= honey comb
-- **lov, hu zaq** -- (see full)
lovkaq a room (or) **bavlov** (ku^ law^)
lovkaq to laq e a screened room (or) **salcual** (Chi)
=**lov lovssaq, biov**= very short
lov maq lov to have time or not (26:24) (aˇ yam˅ ja^-eu ma˅ ja^-eu)

lovq to be noisy (law^ g'a-eu; law^ g'a so^ g'a-eu)
lovq to chat; have a brief conversation (ngeh˅ caw˅-eu)
lovq to dry in the sun (6:197, 9:101, 46:203) (**peilhaoq lovq e miqkoq** = a pole for a clothesline - 26:99)
lovq, lovq, lovq the sound of talking (law^ g'a-eu)
-- **lovq beivq, miavbeivq** -- to shine blindingly bright
-- **lovq, doqlovq** -- 1. to chat; to have conversation 2. to be noisy
lovq gee to be dried by sun (9:101, 11:162) (law^ gui-eu)
lovq kuv to stretch out to dry (law^ gui-eu)
lovqliv a chicken coop (ya ci^ ya ku^) (9:101)
-- **lovq, puvlovq** -- a very active village

LU

lul to fry (6:191) (luˇ-eu)
(vb) **lul** something for (vb) (45:29) (**zaq lul** = food for eating; **dao lul** = something for wearing; **gee lul** = something to talk about)
lul (fp) affirmative final part. (**Ngeel nga lul** = That's so.)
=**lul, aq**= uterus; womb
=**lul, bial**= catfish
lulbeil a goiter (or) **beiljil lulpuq** (lawˇ behˇ)
-- **lulcuq, beildul** -- rainbow
-- **lul, dao** -- something to wear (**dao lul maq hha** = nothing to wear)
luldu when; a moment (**xil taq luldu** = at that moment - 26:43) (.. ngeh; k'oeˇ ngeh)

=lul, haol= 1. a kind of germ, 2. a kind of mushroom
=lul, hoq= fried rice
lulhhuv a door
lulhhuv aqbal the area behind the front door in a house (this is where the females of the family dump three loads each of the dung from the sacrificial buffalo - see also: **gaoqlaoq sal**)
(vb) lul hha post part. of a verb, to have (vb) (**zaq lul hha** = have some food to eat; **dol lul hha** = have some liquid to drink) (**Aqyo niq hhaq qiq gal yil lul maq hha** = The two of them had no place to go. 45:64)
-- lul hha, zaq -- to have food to eat
=lul, hhal= a toy
lulhhuv a door (9:101) (laˇ g'o^)
lulhhuv pao miq 1. to open a door; 2. to answer the door (as when someone comes) (laˇ g'o^ pah-eu)
luljuv a bird snare (9:101) (law˯)
lul kevq to fry into; to mix and fry (46:103) (luˇ keu˯-eu)
lulleil lime (used to make designs on coffins made of dark wood)
lulluv alsiq a stone
-- lulpuq, beiljil -- goiter
lulsiq acne (nui leh)
lulsul 1. to be sure (9:101) (maˇ maˇ ni; pa˯ ma˯ baw-eu), 2. a method, a way (as a suitable way of doing things) (Chi) (13:47, 45:10, 82, 46:91, 50:48) (or) **yiqqeiq** (Hani), 3. ability (50:121)
lulsul jav to have an idea; a method; plan; way (A=Chi) (45:10) (noe˯ ta˯-eu ja^-eu)
lulsul sul to plan; to wish (Chi) (14:176, 45:89, 46:201)
lulwuq dav a blister (from heat) (lahˇ o˯-eu)
lulzuq zuq to develop a sore on one's heel, under the skin, with pus in it

lu 1. protruding, 2. a tumor (**puq lal lu lal** = for a tumor to be growing)
=lu, al= butterfly
-- lu, aoqlu millu -- earthquake
lucei nei to puff out (14:218)
=lu, deil= a basket used to catch fish
luduq pool of water; pond (9:101) (**luduq ja'la ja'la nei** = a long pond) (lah)
luduq duqma a large lake (26:117) (lah lah ma)
=lu, haol= hail
lujeivq nei protruding (as eyes) (26:6)
-- lu, millu -- an earthquake to take place
Lu Miqcel a name (2:53)
=lu, naohhaol hhaol= noon
=lu nei, mal= to be full; mature (as seeds)
lutaoq maggots (9:102) (lu^ tah˯)
lutaoq zaol for maggots to be present
-- lutevq, millu -- the degree of an earthquake

=lu, **teil**= forehead

luzeivq nei (see: **lujeiv nei** = protruding, as of the eyes - 14:144)

luq, luq, luq the sound of a crackling fire

luqbaol a tomb; a grave (6:177, 9:101) (lm̬ bymˇ) (some dialects: **huqbiaol**)

luqbul 1. a flint stone (mi̬ lo), 2. kidney stones (lm̬ bymˇ km̬-eu; lo boe̬)

luqbul bulcov naciq medicine for kidney stones, very bitter, made from roots of the **allo hhoqpial** plant

luqbul kovq to have trouble urinating from kidney stones

Luqcyul Luchun (name of the town after which the dialect is named which has been chosen by the PRC to be the printed Hani dialect. Called **Dolnia** by the Hani. Thought to be the great historical center of the Hani/Akha people) (Chi)

Luqcyulxeif Luchun county (or) **Dolnia; Dolnia Luqcyul**

luqduq a drum (6:185, 9:102, 26:68, 46:111) (tah̬)

luqduq byulyu drum and gong (treated as a pair, if one is beaten the other one is beaten as well)

luqduq naolhao haqhhal seil to dance according to one's own drummer

=luq, **haq**= culm sheath (parchment-like bamboo sheath at base of bamboo stalks)

Luqluqcyul Six-six village (it means it was begun in 1966 - 14:173)

luqluqfei an insecticide (666 BHC - benzene hexachloride) (Chi) (11:25)

luqjyul army (Chi) (50:110)

=luq, **meiq**= lip

=luq, **mol**= (see full)

=luq nei, **jul**= to be bald; to be smooth

luqssao the antler of young stag in velvet (Chi)

luqssiljil a tape recorder (57:145)

=luq, **xa'**= a container for sticks of incense (Chi)

luqxafjil video camera; camcorder (Chi) (50:110)

-- **luqxeif, galma** -- a line on the road (B=Chi)

luqyiljil 1. a radio (46:175), 2. a cassette recorder (Chi) (50:110)

luqyil jil ceq to take a radio along (A=Chi)

-- **luq, zii'luq** -- cheat and rob (grab)

luv clf. for a column of smoke (**aqhyuq qiq luv** = a column of smoke - 26:69)

-- **luvbiav, haqluv** -- a flat stone (46:130)

=luv, **caq**= a pestle for grinding salt

luvcuv 1. stone markers (as those set along roads marking the kilometers), 2. special stones set up at the '**hhaqma albol**' (sacred village tree), in the center of the village, and below the village (46:131)

-- **luvcuv, doqdaq** -- a monument; a memorial stone
-- **luvcuv, milkaq** -- stone boundry markers
-- **luvcuv, saqsaol** -- rocks outside the village where offerings are made to the 'owner' of game animals (**saqsaol**)

Luvgaq the younger son of **Belniaq** in Hani myth (46:128)

luvgaoq a stone heap

=luv, **haq**= a stone

luvhav a big basket filled with stones put into rivers to prevent flooding

-- **luvjeivq, haqluv** -- small stones

=luv, **jiv**= a mill stone

=luv, **la'**= full moon

luvleil lime (white powder) (11:81) (lu boe˯)

-- **luv meiv leiv, mul** -- to be shaky; not firm

=luv, **moqkuv moq**= very old

luvnil luvpiul red and white stone (46:117)

luvniuq lol to make an offering to the 'stone bull' which is about 3 km. from Tavqzaoq village, where a cow or buffalo is offered yearly for the health of villagers in 13 nearby villages **luvniuq tul**

luvniuq tul (see: **luvniuq lol**)

=luv, **ngaq**= basket used to catch fish

=luv, **siq**= a whetstone

luvssaq luvma small and large stones (14:232)

luvssaq luvma dal small rocks depend on big rocks (a Hani saying - 14:183)

=luv, **teiv**= jumping up and down

luvq to guard; protect; herd (9:102) (lo˄-eu)

luvq to be enough; sufficient (9:102, 45:75) (**zaqluvq** = to eat enough) (lo˄-eu)

luvq to be blunt (yaw dm˯)

=**luvq, bal**= tobacco pipe (men & women)

luvq ceiv 1. to ambush (35:76) (k'oe˯ lo˄-eu), 2. to wait in hiding (za˄ ta˯-eu), 3. to block the way (35:76)

luvq col jol duq a sentry post

luvq cyuq to block the way (13:31) (la^ tsoe˯-eu)

-- **luvq, haol** -- to defend; guard; protect

-- **luvq, heeq** -- for people to mature

-- **luvq, hhaol** -- for plants, fruits etc. to mature

=**luvq, gal**= a guarded road

luvqheiq custom house; frontier (50:12)

luvq hhao to surround (jaw˯ lahˇ-eu)

-- **luvq, lavqtuv tuvluvq** -- to make a fist

luvq leev to keep watch (as for animals) (50:82)

luvq leev faqgyul supervising regulations (B=Chi) (50:82)

=**luvq, meiq**= thin lips

=**luvq milsaol, mil**= lord of the land

-- **luvq, moldaol** -- to keep vigil over a corpse while it is in the house, esp. so that no animal will jump over it

-- **luvq, peev** -- to burn and shrivel up
luvqqao qao to be on duty (50:212)
=**luvq, seiq**= feet with short toes
luvqsul one who inherits property (45:24)
luvqssaq a herdsman; a person who guards, protects livestock (as cows etc.) (9:102) (lo‸-eu g'a˯; bo-eu g'a˯; bo sa^-eu g'a˯)
-- **luvq, saqluvq** -- to lie in wait for game
luvq taq to guard; protect (9:102) (lo‸ ta˯-eu)
luvq teiq 1. enforce martial law (50:88), 2. to defend; protect (50:7)
luvqyaol border guard house (50:12)
luvq zaq 1. to herd animals as an occupation (**oq'a luvq zaq** = to herd ducks) (13:2) (bo-eu), 2. to stand around near where others are eating, hoping to get fed
-- **luvq, zaol** -- to enrich

LUEI

lueiqdaq radar (Chi) (50:103)
Lueiqfaol a model worker who died many years ago (Chi) (50:103)
lueiqgua detonator (Chi) (50:103)

LYU

lyul to crash to pieces (9:102) (coe˯ nm^-eu)
=**lyul, ceil**= powdered rice
-- **lyul, cuq biav cuq** -- to gossip
=**lyul, hal**= dust
=**lyul, hhaq**= buckwheat flour
=**lyul, laoq**= millet
=**lyul, mil**= dust
lyulmi nei broken bits; fragments (9:102) (yaw pa^)
-- **lyul puv, daoq lyul** -- to turn a somersault
=**lyul, saol**= iron filings; fragments of iron
-- **lyul, taoq** -- to pound to pieces
lyulyeiv a kind of flower
=**lyul, zal**= flour

lyu aluminum (Chi)
=**lyu, byu'**= a gong
-- **lyu, hao** -- bells used on horses
lyu'qeq softball (Chi) (50:103)

lyuq a man to have sexual intercouse with a woman (taboo) (a˯ loe˯ loe˯-eu)
=**lyuq, aq**= a penis
lyuqcavq cavq to commit gang rape (50:111)
lyuq zaq for a man to have sexual intercourse with a woman (taboo)

Lyuf Sseiqmiq Miqzu Zualzeif On People's Democracy and Dictatorship (a book by Chairman Mao - 26:55)

MA

mal right hand (aˇ maˇ; la‸ maˇ)
mal fertile
mal full ear (as with grains); mature; plump (9:102) (see also: **mallu nei**) (maˇ-eu)
mal final part. in questions, calling for the assent of the one being asked (**Maq ngeel mal**? = Isn't that true? - 32:3)
=mal, alniq niq= a strip of bamboo (useful)
malbal a caravan of pack horses carrying goods (Chi) (12:125)
malcavq a glass bottle (9:103) (maˇ tsa‸; mehˇ tsa‸)
  malcavq alsiq pomegranate
  malcavq bavq dov laq e zal canned goods (or) **gueifteq** (Chi) (bahˬ keu^ dzaˇ)
  malcavq piqzii bottle (B=Chi) (10:19) (maˇ tsa‸)
-- malcavq, yaqhuq -- glass bottle (A=Chi)
maldei pumpkin (Dai) (9:103) (maˇ deh)
  maldei albiao pumpkin vine (A=Dai)
  maldei alneev pumpkin seed (A=Dai) (9:103) (maˇ deh aˇ nui^)
  maldei deigeel a trellis for pumpkin vines to climb (A=Dai)
=mal, jaq= right (hand)
mallavq right hand (9:103) (la‸ maˇ)
mallu nei to be full; mature (as seeds); plump (maˇ-eu)
malma an aunt (9:103, 41:7) (father's OB's wife; father's older sister). (cf. Burm. for 'older sister') (aˬ k'oˬ)
malmul a sterile female horse, cow, buffalo (11:25)
malnaoq a part. used in clause endings to indicate an interrogative mode, somewhat speculating (9:103) (**Ssuq qaq malnaoq**? Are you tired from walking perhaps? **Meivq kyuq malnaoq**? Are you tired from hunger perhaps? 41:158)
-- mal naoq, maq kaq -- maybe impossible
malnee eelcul saqhhyu maq baq not to be afraid (gu^ k'aˇ maˬ za)
malneev a seed of fruit (or) **malniuv** (aˇ nui^)
malniul big hen (34:3) (ya ci^ ya ma)
malniuv 1. fruit seeds (as a pit in a cherry) (or) **malneev** (aˇ nui^), 2. core; kernel; center (46:123)
mal pyu the right side (9:103) (la‸ maˇ paw)
malsal alsiq a kind of fruit (A=Dai)
-- malyeiv, taoqdi -- a kind of flower
malyov alsiq a kind of fruit (A=Dai)

ma to want to (11:130) (this may be a contraction of: **movq a**)

ma a contraction of '**maq hha**' (used in proverbs, as in: **ma dol** = **maq hha dol** = must not drink)

ma clf. for BIG things (**havqluv luvma qiq ma** = one huge stone 11:83) (or) **siq** (cf. Lahu)

ma a final part., used sometimes in statements in the future tense (**Laqhyul hoqbyu ya xa ma al!** = The roof will fall down. - 26:70)

-- **ma** a suffix denoting big, or female

=ma, aq= 1. a mother, 2. a female

=ma, aqha ha= hen

=ma, baq= a big river

=ma, bao= stomach

maceil a horse cart (Chi) (50:112) (& see: **macei**)

macei a horse cart (Chi) (9:103) (la^ law˯)

=ma, ceiq= big hoe

macyuq a poor woman (cf.: mi˯ coe˯ mi˯ ma = widow)

=ma, da= 1. parents ('father/mother'), 2. ancestors (or in poetry: **dalma**)

madaq a motor (Chi) (50:112)

madavq step-mother; **manil** (a˯ ma ma nyi˅)

=ma, daoq= a log

madeil aldovq a lantern (A=Chi)

=ma, dei= an irrigated field

=ma, dul= a sister

=ma, gal= a road; path

=ma, ha= a hen

=ma, haoq= a large bowl (as for soup)

maheiq ssaqseq a single mother with children (as divorced; widowed)

=ma, hhal= a winnowing tray

=ma, hhavq= a female pig

=ma, hhovq= a needle for injections

=ma, kal= the main crop

=ma, keeq= 1. a daughter-in-law, 2. a female dog

Makeiqsiil Karl Marx (Chi) (26:50, 50:112)

Makeiqsiil zuyif Marxism (50:112)

Makeiqsiil Liqniq zuyif Maoq Zeqdaolsiilxa Marxism, Leninism, Mao Zedong Thought (Chi) (or) **Maoq Ceiqdaol Siilxa**

-- **makov, daolma** -- general plan; overall plan

=ma, lal= tongue

=ma, lavq= thumb

=ma, lao'lao= sea; ocean; big lake

Ma'liq zuyif Marxism and Leninism (Chi) (9:103) (not pf.)

=ma, loq= a large irrigated field

=ma, mal= father's older sister

-- **mama, aqha hama** -- a big hen

=ma, meiq= YB's wife

=ma, mil= a female cat

=ma, miq= a wife

=ma, miqli li= the next to last daughter

=ma, miaoq= heavy work; an important job

mamoq 1. first mother (op. of: **madavq; manil**), 2. a polite term for an aunt or an older woman (**Qeiq**

mamoq = Aunty Qian)
=ma, moq= a female horse
mamoq alsiq mango fruit (A=Dai) (or) **malmoq alsiq** (gui˅ g'o^; ma˅ mo)
=ma, muq= a vaulting horse (Chi)
=ma, naol= the sun (nah˅ ma)
-- manao, kaqla -- (see full)
=ma, nee= 1. heart (both the seat of emotions and the physical heart), 2. mind (in certain contexts)
=ma nei, zao= generally; for the most part (Chi)
manil stepmother (aˬ ma ma nyi˅)
=ma, nyul= middle finger (or) **nyultaoq**
Ma Pel a person's name (11:129)
=ma, qeil= wild buckwheat
=ma, qil= wife's younger sister
masev a woman who has daughters but no son (a type of curse word)
massaq mother and son (ma zaˬ = mother & children) (9:104)
=ma, sul= barnyard grass
=ma, ssaq= sister's daughters
-- massaq, paqssaq -- those related to one by blood
=ma, yul= (see full)

maq (fp) a final particle used in questions, esp. used for the future (**Nol li maq**? Will you go? **Halmeil li movq maq**?. How do you want to go?)
maq (vb) not; no (vb); negative (**maq bivq** = not give, **maq gaq** = do not hear) (9:103) (maˬ ...)
-- maq aol, aol wuqbo -- to neglect one's duty
maq aol col maq hha zaq no work, no pay (50:16)
maq aol hha zaq to make money without working (50:16)
maq aol maq qivq yiqqeiq coersive measures; compulsory means (50:135)
maq aol maq zaq (if you do) not work, (you will) not eat (maˬ m˅ na˅ maˬ ya dzaˬ)
maq aol soq nia could not put in order (38:91) (maˬ m˅ shawˬ nya)
maq bav not bad; so-so (**Qiqkuaf maq bav nga**. The situation is not bad. 41:20) (maˬ doe˅)
maq beq does not matter; no matter (46:129) (tiˬ jeˬ-iˬ maˬ ngeu˅)
maq beq sso it doesn't matter (13:5, 26:35) (tiˬ jeˬ-iˬ maˬ ngeu˅)
maq beeq orderly; arranged properly
-- maq beibei, yeilbei -- without precedent in history; unprecedented
maq beiv maq laol not smart; foolish (maˬ gah˅; yaw la^-iˬ)
maq bi bial to retain (or) **bi jav**
maq bi hev e meiqzaq security regulations (50:7)
maq bivq maq qivq meil se force to pay money or taxes (50:135)
maq bivq maq taq qivq must be given (38:16) (maˬ bi^

maˬ g'eh nya)

maq bial saq to become thinner; for muscles to decrease in size (jeh-iˇ nya)

maq biav maq lyul establish oneself in an unassailable position; remain invincible (50:105)

maq bo aqma a barren woman (can have no children)

-- maq bo, aolduq -- out of a job; to lose one's position

maq bo dama a barren couple (they can have no children)

maq bo maq jav not possess; not have ('not rich')

-- maq bo, meeqduq -- invalid

maq buq maq cal to be humble; not proud (50:16)

maq buq zaq to be modest

maq cev kaq qivq e cannot be cured of sickness (50:16) (maˬ taˬ leˇ coeˇ nya)

maq ceil not only; moreover (maˬ tseˇ, na^ maˬ tseˇ) (9:103, 11:118) (**Aqyoq Haqniqdoq gee nia maq ceil, Pyulniuldoq liq gee nia siq.** Not only can he read Hani, he can also read Han Chinese as well. 11:118)

maq ceiv meil without stopping; continuously (41:108, 200) (maˬ naˬ ni)

maq cul maq xeivq not too fat; not too thin (maˬ tsuˇ maˬ jeh)

maq deil li nia not possible to contain; not enough room (maˬ deˇ leˇ nya)

maq diq hhaol to lose (as in a battle); cannot win (38:33) (smˇ-iˇ-eu; maˬ g'aˬ leˇ coeˇ)

maq diq maq nal (if there is) no beating, (there will be) no pain (maˬ diˬ naˇ maˬ naˇ-aˇ)

-- maq dul, kaqla na -- special; peculiar; exceptional

maq dul maq mav meil 1. not to take care of (maˬ la^ sa^-eu); 2. not to give serious thought to

-- maq dul, maq nyuq -- not to worry; not to think

maq duv maq tao (if) nothing is going out, nothing will come in (maˬ iˇ do^ naˇ, maˬ uˇ laˇ nya)

maq eil maq loq (if you do) not tell, (it will) not be clear (maˬ ehˇ nehˬ naˇ, maˬ law^)

maq eil saq qaol al! more than tongue can tell (cannot tell all of it) (26:86) (maˬ ehˇ jiˇ coeˇ nya)

maq eil sso need not say that (26:25) (ehˇ k'aˇ maˬ za)

maq gal never mind (if I am a fool for the sake of my country, **maq gal nga** - 26:109, 46:129) (cf.: ehˬ ngeuˇ-iˬ)

maq gaq maq cavq not too pretty; not too ugly

maq gaq maq hhyul not loving; not warm-hearted (maˬ gaˬ maˬ g'oeˇ)

maq gaoq no matter who; no matter what (46:204)

maq goq maq biov not too high; not too short (maˬ goˇ maˬ aw)

maq guv maq niv firm and indomitable; persistent and

dauntless; fearless (50:82)
=maq, haoq= a bowl (for rice)
maq hev qaol mysterious; not to be known (50:149) (ma˯ si˯ coeˇ)
maq hev qivq e miqnieiq a 'sealed book'; a matter that cannot be known by others
maq heeq maq nil a suitable size (not too big, not too small) (ma˯ hui˯ ma˯ nyiˇ)
maq hoq li not to live peacefully (38:33) (jawˇ-eu ma˯ saˇ)
maq hoq qiq gal where there are mistakes (46:217) (la^ bah˯-eu ja^ gaˇ)
maq hovq maq dol (if you do) not fetch water, (you will) not drink
maq hu dav movq to 'give a cold shoulder'
maq hu loq not see clearly (13:15) (ma˯ haw law˯)
maq hha (vb) **hhaq** must certainly not (vb) (**maq hha nieil hhaq** = must certainly not forget - 54:110)
maq (vb) hhaq must never (vb) (**Ssaqmiq keeqma yiuvqpaq yaol maq taoq qiv hhaq.** Daughter-in-law must never touch the father-in-law.)
maq hhol dav qaol cannot breathe (as when taxes are very heavy) (35:30) (cf.: sa^ ma˯ g'awˇ coeˇ nya)
maq hhoq qivq qiq baol cannot separate (50:16)
maq hhuvq 1. not enough to divide (ma˯ biˇ lo^-eu), 2. don't have (34:4), 3. do not come back
maq hhyul maq gaq not love; not interested
maq hhyul meil reluctantly
maqja mahjong game (Chi)
maqja diq zaq to play mahjong (A=Chi)
maq jav don't have; there is none (inanimate) (ma˯ ja^)
maq jeidal great; wonderful ('not simple') (B=Chi)
maq jil not real; fake (**maq jil Haqniq** = fake Hani - 31:3) (maˇ maˇ ma˯ ngeuˇ-a)
maq jil e colssaq 'a wolf in sheep's clothing'
maq jiqgeiq to fail, as an examination (B=Chi) (or) **siiqbeif** (Chi)
maq jol teiq qaol to be very busy; not time to rest
maq kaq it is not okay; that won't do (disagreement with a previous statement) (26:15) (ma˯ geu^ nya; ma˯ g'eh nya)
maq kaq mal naoq maybe impossible (41:98) (ma˯ g'eh nya pa˯)
maq keel not to taste good (or) **zaq syuq** (ma˯ kuiˇ-eu)
maq lal 1. not present (50:140), 2. not come (from lower to higher place)
-- maq lal, neema nyuq e taoqdav -- things to go contrary to one's wishes
maq laqbal to get clear of something
maq leiq mil nia not able to catch up; to get behind (ma˯ teh miˇ nya)
maq li maq loq not aware of (ma˯ si˯ nya)
maq loq 1. not clear (13:22), 2. not to know (38:94)

(maˬ lawˬ)

-- **maq loq, maq li** -- not aware of

maq luv to be incomplete in number (maˬ lui^)

maq luvq 1. vacancy; short of the quota; lack of something, 2. a defect; a drawback, 3. run out of something; insufficient (50:140) (maˬ lo‸)

maq (vb) maq taq qivq feel compelled to do something (**maq buvq maq taq qive** = Just had to write it)

maq meeq e a defect; not good

maq meeq byuqssaq bad insects (50:69)

maq meeq galquv harmful trends (50:16)

maq meeq maq dyul not good, not bad

maq meiq maq gaol (if there is) no teaching, (there will be) no wisdom (maˬ mehˬ naˇ maˬ gahˇ laˇ)

maq meiq maq kyul (if there is) no teaching, (there will be) no cleverness (maˬ mehˬ naˇ maˬ gahˇ laˇ)

maq mi not catch up with (**laqhyul miqnieiq aol lo maq mi** = no time to catch up with household chores)

maq mia aqkal before long (maˬ myahˇ)

maq miaq 1. few ('not many') (maˬ myaˬ), 2. rare

maq miaol tovq haoq it is not proper to name a child by the same name as someone else in one's ancestry

maq mol kaq nei not long afterwards (13:54; 35:90)

maq mol maq niaol not too long; not too short (maˬ mahˇ maˬ nymˇ)

maq mol sal not want to see; not want to meet (that is, to be ashamed to see someone) (35:18) (maˬ mawˇ maw‸-eu)

maqnaaq or; if not (9:103, 26:76) (maˬ ngeuˇ naˇ)

maqnasiq or; if not (57:155)

maq naq meil 1. all the while (or) **maq pieiq meil** (k'oeˇ ngeh), 2. continue doing something (50:107)

maq naq meil diq kavq to fight without stopping (50:47)

maq naq meil miqteil pyu ssuq to go forward without stopping (maˬ naˬ leˇ ni iˇ-eu)

maq naq nei without stopping; constantly; continuously (26:103) (maˬ naˬ ni)

-- **maq naol, yohe** -- tasteless; unpalatable

maq neiq haoq wulnaq what a pity (46:80)

maq neivq haoq wul yaq what a pity! (46:80); **maq neivq haoq wulnaq** (g'awˬ shaˬ gaˬ laˇ paˬ-eu)

maq niv 1. lazy (yaw doeˇ), 2. not move (maˬ lu^)

maq niv maq guv calm and unhurried (50:28)

maq niv zeiqma fixed assets (50:64); immovable property (as real estate) (50:16)

maq nyuq gaol 1. absent-minded (maˬ noeˬ gahˇ nya-eu), 2. to lower one's guard (50:38)

maq nyuq maq dul not to worry; not to give serious thought to it (k'ahˬ maˬ lahˇ; cf.: maˬ noeˬ maˬ duˇ-eu gaˇ = to be unexpected; not to be prepared)

maq nyuq maq gaq meil by chance (maˬ noeˬ maˬ saˇ du-ehˇ)

maq nyuq maq gaq meil eil duv to speak without thinking (ma˯ noe˯ ni ngeh˯-eh)

maq nyuq maq gaq nei carelessly (26:90); unexpectedly (41:177) (ma˯ noe˯ ma˯ duˇ-eu gaˇ)

maq nyuq puv nia to be stubborn; not change mind

maq nyuq taq nia cannot remember (41:94) (ma˯ noe˯ ta˯ nya-eu)

maq ngeel not so (ma˯ ngeuˇ) (3:2)

maq ngeel a maq leil is it so? (ngeuˇ meh la˯)

maq ngeel aq Isn't that right? (28:4) (ma˯ ngeuˇ-a la˯)

-- maq ngeel, bi ngeel -- to run counter to one's desire; to be the opposite of what one wished

maq ngeel jol maq Isn't that so? (13:34) (ma˯ ngeuˇ-a la˯)

maq ngeel loq otherwise; only (46:90) (teh˰-ehˇ)

maq ngeel maq daq if not so, then no story (i.e., if it were not true I would not be telling you)

maq ngeel maq kaq it must be .. (14:211) (ma˯ ngeuˇ-ehˇ ma˯ g'eh-aˇ)

maq ngeel maq zav meil to have bad behavior (57:121)

maq ngeel ngaoq 1. if not (10:12), 2. or; otherwise (50:51) (ma˯ ngeuˇ naˇ)

maq ngeel siq just a moment (ma˯ ngeuˇ-a si˯)

maq paoq different; not alike (50:40) (ma˯ duˇ)

maq paoq galquv different forms (50:16)

maq pieiq meil all the while (or) **maq naq meil** (cf.: ma˯ na˯ ni)

maq puq bei siq never met yet (35:84) (this is spoken of a man who had never met a person who could win against him in a singing competition) (ma˯ mawˇ haw-a˯)

maq puv maq lav not move; not shake (ma˯ luˆ)

-- maq puv nia, neema -- a rigid way of thinking; stubborn; won't change one's mind

maq pyuq good for nothing (ti˯ je˯-i˯ ma˯ mui˯)

-- maq qaol, nyuq puv -- to regret

maq qeq qivq not to believe (41:97) (ma˯ jah-eu)

maq qil sso not to worry (11:202) (k'ah˯ ma˯ lahˇ)

maq qivq meil hhyul ya extremely happy (46:216) (la˯ k'a˯ cehˇ seh˰-eu)

maq qoq meil ... negative set phrase (**Maq aol movq maq qoq meil maq aol sso.** If you don't want to do it you don't have to. **Nol maq lal movq maq qoq meil maq lal sso.** If you don't want to come you don't have to. **Maq zaq movq maq qoq meil maq zaq sso.** If you don't want to eat you don't have to.)

maq qul maq bioq not sweet; not tasteless -- in between (ma˯ coeˇ ma˯ byaw˯)

maq qu ya qaol to be wild

maq (vb) sal ashamed to (vb) (25:18) (**maq eil sal** = ashamed to speak)

maq sal maq yevq awkward; embarrassed (50:55)

Maqsal puvkaq Masa village ('Unhappy village')

(12:125, 127)
-- **maq sal, yoq jol** -- paralysis; palsy
maq se al not to take along (41:141) (ma˯ seu˯-a̤)
maq sil maq deivq meil being in an extreme situation (not really dead, not really alive) (57:102)
maqsiil neevma a kind of green bean
maq sol maq cavq meil very dirty; not clean (yaw jaw˰) ('without cleanness') (9:104, 10:pref.)
-- **maq ssil, miav qiq ssil** -- dark as a pocket
-- **maq tavq, neegaq** -- merciless; ruthless
maqtel steamed bread (Chi) (41:167)
maq teiq maq cal meil 1. not in a hurry; without hurrying (9:104, 11:219, 13:32, 27:12) (ma˯ teh˯), 2. not nervous (50:104)
maq teiq maq yeil not too narrow; not too wide (ma˯ su˰ ma˯ jeˇ)
maq teiq maq yei not too busy; not too free (ma˯ teh˯ ma˯ yeh˰)
maq teiq sso don't hurry (41::76) (ta˯ teh˯)
maq toq 1. not equal to .... (11:146), 2. not to reply to
maq tul maq taq qivq must get up (26:37) (ma˯ tuˇ-ehˇ ma˯ geu˰ nya)
maq ya maq dav not upper; not lower; not rich; not poor (middle class) (ma˯ goˇ ma˯ aw˯)
maq yevq lal to be careless; not to be careful
maq yevq nei casually
maq yevq nei zaolzyul unpremeditated crime (50:68)
maq yil maq lal not go; not come (ma˯ iˇ ma˯ laˇ)
maq yiuvq maq mi to be too busy to sleep; to work day and night) (ma˯ yu˰ ma˯ na˯)
maq yiuvqsil unable to sleep (ma˯ yu˰ k'a^ nya)
maq za zaol za a flexible regulation; a regulation which can adapt to the circumstances (50:13)
maq zaq haoq zeiq ill-gotten wealth (50:17)
maq zaq maq dol not eat; not drink (ma˯ dza˯ ma˯ dawˇ)
maq zaq saq qaol, maq dao saq qaol have plenty to̤ eat and wear (live a good life) (57:138)
maqzavq horseshoe (Chi) (9:104) (mah˯ kuiˇ)
maqzavq diq to shoe a horse (A=Chi)
maqzavq diqpuq hammer for shoeing horses (A=Chi) (9:104) (mah˯ kuiˇ di˯ di˯ pu˯)
maq zaol haoq forbidden (taboo) (50:89)
maq zol maq hev not to learn; not to understand (ma˯ dzaw ma˯ nya)
maq zyulssaq an innocent person; not a bad person

-- **mav, dulmav** -- omen; sign
-- **mav, eelmav** -- to smile in a dream
-- **mav mav, nyuq nyuq** -- illusion; dreamlike; absent minded
-- **mav, yiuvqmav** -- to dream
-- **mav, zeivqmav** -- to talk while dreaming

mavq a little bit (a˅ cui^)
mavq clf. for the plural of people, animals (animate) (9:104) (-- ma˄, as in: a˅ yaw˄ ma˄)
-- **mavq, aqli** -- children
-- **mavq, aqmavq** -- to be stunned; numb
-- **mavq, col** -- people
=**mavq nei, zoq**= numb; insensitive
mavqssaq soldier (or) **miqbev bavq ssaq** (yeh˅) (cf. Lahu: ma˄ ya˅)
mavqssaq aol e for military use (50:94)
mavqssaq bi miaq enlarge the army (& see: koqyil = Chi) (50:100)
-- **mavqssaq, geeldiq** -- soldiers; fighting forces
mavqssaq geelniv niv army military activities (50:94)
mavqssaq gee zaq to be in military service (50:52)
-- **mavqssaq, haol leev** -- a bodyguard
mavqssaq hhe xu disarmament (50:18)
mavqssaq miqnieiq military affairs (50:94)
mavqssaq neeciiv army festival (50:84)
mavqssaq puv soldiers to mutiny (50:14)
mavqssaq ssaqqa arm of service (as army, airforce, etc.) (50:15)
mavqssaq ssolnei ssaqlaol the army and the people (50:94)
mavqssaq zaqhal grain for the army (50:94)
=**mavq, ssaq**= wife's sister's husband
-- **mavq, ssaqguq** -- children
-- **mavq, ssaqmiq ssaq** -- women
-- **mavq, xil** -- these things

MAO

Maoq Ceiqdaol Mao Zedong (Chi) (34:7, 19, 50:113), **Maoq Zuxiq** (26:54) (Mao tse tung)
Maoq Ceiqdaol siilxa Thoughts of Mao Zedong (Chi) (26:106, 50:113)
Maoq Ceiqdaol Xeijiq the collected works of Mao Zedong (Chi) (26:52, 50:113)
maoqdueif contradiction (Chi) (50:113) (& see: **maoqdyuf**)
maoqdyuf contradiction (Chi) (34:11, 33) (& see: **maoqdueif**)
maoqniq velvet (Chi) (11:31)
maoqniq peilhaoq velvet jacket (A=Chi) (11:31)
Maoqziif milcaq Mengzi county
Maoqziifssaq people who live in Mengzi county
Maoqxei collected works of Mao (Chi) (50:113)
maoqxieif 1. yarn; 2. knitting wool (Chi)
maoqxieif peilhaoq woven sweater (A=Chi) (11:155) (or) **maoqyil peilhaoq** (A=Chi)
maoqxeif saqkaol yarn (A=Chi) (50:112)
Maoq Zuxiq Chairman Mao (Chi) (26:54, 50:113) (see: **Maoq Ceiqdaol**)
Maoq Zuxiq yi'liq Quotations from Chairman Mao (Chi) (50:113)

maofhaof colon (punctuation mark) (Chi) (50:113) (semicolon = **feilhaof**)
maofxei zuyif adventurism (Chi) (34:6)
maofyif trade (Chi) (34:82) (je˯ ga˄-eu)

MEE

meel a glaze (Dai) (**meel seiq dav** = to put a glaze on)
meel 1. singing of birds; crowing of a rooster, 2. to blow a flute (9:104) (baw-eu)
meelbiav bricks which are baked (A=Dai) (mi˅ bya^)
meelgyuq a musical wind instrument (50:65)
meelhaq meil too much (41:189) (a˅ dzeh˯-eh˅)
meelheiq meil too much (11:210) (**Meelheiq meil taq eil.** Don't say too much.) (cf.: a˅ dzeh˯)
meelhov roof tiles (A=Dai) (9:104) (mi˅ k'aw^)
meelhov caoq to tile a roof (A=Dai)
meelhov yaolma a tiled main building (A=Dai)
=meel, qivq= the evening star
meel seiq dav to glaze pottery (A=Dai)
=meel, soq= the morning star
meelteil 1. singing of birds, 2. crowing of a rooster (35:115) (**alzil meelteil** = a bird to sing or crow)
meelyeiv black-headed thrush

=mee, aq= wife of father's YB; wife of mother's brother; mother's YS
Mee'laol a place in Yuanyang County (14:184)
meenia 1. several (10:pref), 2. a few (9:104) (**meenia feilzaol biao al** = a few minutes ago - 41:29) (a˅ cui^ g'aw˯ mya)
meenia (clf) many (clf) (**meenia mol; meenia hhaq; meenia taq**, etc.) (45:52, 46:76) (g'aw˯ mya˯)
meenia ceil huvq for many years ('several tens of years') (13:14) (g'aw˯ mya k'o˄)
meenia gal nei several units (10:pref.)
meenia kaol many ways; many 'roads' (for doing something) (50:42)
meenia nao naolhao several days later (13:20) (a˅ cui^ g'aw˯ mya nah g'eh-aw˅)
meeniav a few (or) **alciiv** (a˅ cui^)

meeq good; well (9:105) (yaw mui˯)
-- meeq, aol -- to improve; build up
-- meeq, deivq -- for good things to happen, predestined from birth
=meeq, doq= good words
meeqduq 1. goodness (9:105, 46:78) (**meeqduq jav** = to have goodness), 2. benefit (**meeqduq bi jav lal e** = for the benefit of...)
meeqduq dei nei jav a balance of good (50:130)
meeqduq maq bo invalid; of no value
-- meeqduq, miaoq'aol e -- 1. effectiveness for a

given period of time, 2. current events; current affairs

meeqduq qiq jivq maq jav good for nothing; of no value (or) **pyuqduq maq jav** (muiˬ duˬ tiˬ jeˬ-iˬ maˬ ja^)

meeq dyul right and wrong; good and bad

meeq dyul ceil loq distinguish (50:50)

meeq dyul eil to criticize (as to whether good or bad); comment; appraise (50:131)

meeq dyul gee to evaluate whether good or bad (50:131)

-- **meeq dyul, neema** -- ideology and moral character

meeq dyul zaol loq to appraise (50:84)

meeq e maq hhyul qiq hhaq maq kevq; dyul e aol movq e qiq hhaq maq jol everyone likes good things; no one likes bad things (set phrase)

-- **meeq, hu** -- to show concern

-- **meeq, laosiil** -- 'good morning teacher' (A=Chi)

meeq li meeq quv constantly improve something; keep improving one's skill (50:90)

-- **meeq li, meeq saq** -- perfect; consumate

meeq loq meeq ya it seems reasonable, but...(50:115)

meeq meeq nei very well (11:57) (yaw muiˬ-ehˇ)

-- **meeq, mil** -- good land; fertile land

-- **meeq, miaoq** -- a deed; an achievement

=**meeq, nao**= propitious day ('good day')

-- **meeq, neema nee** -- kind; good-hearted

meeq nei suitable; proper (10:20) (**meeq nei hha eilmiq** = must tell them what is proper) (muiˬ-eu)

meeq saq al all right

meeq saq meeq li perfect; consumate (50:174; 57:95)

-- **meeq, siqhel** -- to have good luck

-- **meeq, soq** -- a good tree

=**meeqssaq, sul**= rich people (or) **saolmeeqssaq**

meeq ssol dyul good and bad deeds (50:60)

-- **meeq, taoqxoq** -- 'good morning, students'

=**meeq, xal**= fertile field

-- **meeq, yonao** -- good day; propitious day

meeqzav nei well; carefully; properly (**meeqzav nei aol** = do it well) (9:105, 10:20) (yaw muiˬ-ehˇ)

meeqzav pa zav nei very well; very carefully (35:75) (yaw muiˬ muiˬ-ehˇ)

-- **meeq, zaol** -- 1. to improve; make better, 2. to rectify; reoganize

meeq zeiq better (11:99) (muiˬ dzehˬ-eu)

-- **meeq zeiq, sultavq** -- superiority; advantage

=**meev, leil**= flying white ashes

meev nei a cloud of dust (46:153) (k'aˬ lehˇ zaw-eu)

-- **meev nei, hallyul** -- to raise a cloud of dust

=**meevq, hal**= almost; virtually

=**meevq, pavq**= a bubble

meil a particle with different meanings (**Hoq qiq heiq qiq heiq meil hha zaq.** Must eat bit by bit.) (see other samples in 11:131)
meil strong (9:105) (yaw k'a^)
meil (n) full of (n) (**Miavpyuq qiq pyuq meil kaoqpiul** - His whole face was perspiration. 11:82) (ti⌄ byah)
(n) meil all (as in: it rained all day and night - 11:131) (**colpuv qiq puv qiq puv meil** = group after group, all of the villagers = 13:2) (2:54) (daw⌄ taw^)
meil obese; fat (yaw tsu˅)
(vbA) (vbA) meil (vbB) a verbal pattern indicating doing something repeatedly (**yil yil meil ngyul** - to go repeatedly and cry; **lal lal meil aol** = come repeatedly to work; **hhel hhel meil aoq puv** = buy often to sell again; **eel eel meil eil** = to keep laughing while saying)
=meil, aq= 1. a nut (a˅ nui^), 2. like; seems (etc)
-- meilbiav, geeqsiil -- a brass coin
=meil, daoq= the buttocks
meildaoq yoq 'follow me not ceremony' where they make three piles of wild ginger and thorns, then step over them on their way home from burial etc. so that spirits will not follow them
=meil, eel= upriver (toward the source)
meilhav a hard type of walnut
=meil, hhaq= a valley
-- meil, hhaqma bi -- rest and build up strength; to rehabilitate
meilkaq a medium hard type of walnut
-- meil, kevq -- together; with (& see full)
meil lal to (grow) well; be healthy (as crops) (11:39)
=meil, laq= the same; equal
=meil leil kul, hal= what is it called?
=meil leil, yul= that way
=meil, lol= river source
=meil, nal= the nose
meilnaol siblings etc. (meh˅ nm˅)
-- meilnaol, colgaq aqyivq -- dear brothers and sisters
-- meilnaol, paqssaq -- directly related members of one's family, esp. male; what all relatives are called
meilnaoq a soft type of walnut
-- meilnaoq, aqmeil -- a soft type of nut
meilnei all (8:1) (or) **meinei** (daw⌄ taw^; meh˅)
-- meil, niq'eil -- more and more
meilniuv 1. axis, 2. axle
meilquv a type of wild ginger (13:48)
meilquv alpavq leaves of wild ginger (used to make 9 piles to keep spirits from bothering them)
meilquv ssolnei algao wild ginger and thorns used

in the 'follow-me not-ceremony' after burial so spirits will not follow (& see; **meildaoq yoq**)
meilseivq a type of wild ginger
meilsil a tall type of wild ginger
meiltaoq nei healthily; strongly (9:105, 26:13) (jawˇ saˇ do^ do^-ehˇ)
meilyeiv lilac flower

Mei the United States of America (or) **Meigoq** (**Mei difgoqzuyif** = American imperialism - 34:8)
meicaol a foot-operated rice pounder (9:105) (tahˬ tsmˇ)
  meicaol meiv to hold down the rice pounder so that the pounding end is in the air (tahˬ tsmˇ tahˬ diˇ-eu)
  meicaol taoq to pound rice in a foot-operated pounder (cehˇ tahˬ-eu)
  -- **meicaol, wulquvq** -- a water-run rice pounder
=mei, diq= to wipe out (as to wipe out flies or such)
meiduq the head part of the rice pounder (tahˬ tsmˇ uˬ duˬ)
-- **mei, eelmei** -- to drown
meigaol art designing; art designer (50:114)
Meigoq the United States of America (or) **Mei**
  Meigoq yaol diq the Korean ('American') war (A=Chi) (or) **Caoqxeil yaol haol** = war of 'helping Korea' (50:96)
meihovq rice pounder mortar (for unhusked rice) (9:105) (tahˬ tsmˇ siˬ)
meinei all (**meinei silsaq** = all died) (or) **meilei** (dawˬ taw^)
meiniuv the main post of the paddy pounder
meipievq a support for a rice pounder
meisuqjal an artist (Chi) (50:114)
meituv a support for a rice pounder
meixoq aesthetics (50:114) (Chi)
meiyeil the pestle of a rice pounder (9:106)
  meiyeil diqpuq an old pestle from a rice pounder which is now used as a club or hammer
mei yil to die down (as the number of insects) (meh-iˇ-eu)
-- **mei, zaol** -- to make something vanish; to wipe out; kill off

meiq to teach (9:105) (mehˬ-eu)
meiq coal (6:161) (miˇ tsaˬ k'aˬ g'euˬ)
meiq carbon (Chi) (6:184) (sahˬ)
-- **meiq, aolmeiq** -- to set an example; to demonstrate
meiq'aoq aoq teiq to keep in mouth (9:105) (mymˇ-eu)
meiqbaq 1. a bamboo flute (held vertically), 2. a jew's-harp; 3. a horn (metal; wooden; bamboo)
meiqbaoq mouth; snout (9:105) (clf.: **siq** - 11:74, **baoq** - 46:143) (mehˬ boeˬ)
  meiqbaoq kuv dry lips
  meiqbaoq nei eil oral (spoken as op. to written)

meiqbaoq nei eil daoq 'blunt' words used to win an argument

meiqbaoq nei ya duv for words to escape one's lips

meiqbaoq wuqduq nei by word of mouth (or) **doq nei** (mehˬ boeˬ-euˬ dawˬ neh)

-- **meiq, beeqmeiq** -- to issue confused orders; give arbitrary and impractical directions

meiqbivq to ask someone to do something (9:105)

meiqbivq bivq to fix up; arrange (50:17)

meiqbivq dama ancestors who gave us orders; advice (50:64)

meiqbiav a big mouth

-- **meiqbieil, alhhe** -- a type of frog

meiqcaq cracked lips (mehˬ luˬ tsawˬ pa^-eu)

meiqcaoq 1. a gauze mask worn over nose and mouth (as of doctors - 50:98), 2. a covering for mouth or snout (as horses) (9:105) (mehˬ tsahˬ)

meiqcil curled lips; cupped lip (or) **meiqhavq** (mehˬ luˬ mˇ cu‸-eu)

meiqdaoq chin (mehˬ tahˬ)

meiqde carpenter's ink marker (Chi)

meiqdeiq deiq to quarrel (35:19) (iˬ dehˬ iˬ ceh)

-- **meiqduq, soqhhaq** -- a teaching place (as a school)

meiqduvq duvq talkative (50:102) (mehˬ boeˬ yaw ta^)

-- **meiq, galma** -- (see full)

meiq gaol to admonish; advise ('teach wisdom') (9:106) (mehˬ gahˇ-eu)

-- **meiq gaol, eil gaol** -- to admonish; persuade

-- **meiq, gee** -- conduct propaganda

meiqhavq 1. cracked (as lips, cup, etc.) (or) **meiqcaq**, 2. a breach; gap (50:140) (tsawˬ pa^)

meiq haol to guide someone; teach them (50:52)

meiq haol ssaq the instructor; the guide (50:52)

meiq hev caqdaoq the purpose of teaching (50:86)

meiqheiq the opening of a container (14:142, 46:143) (k'awˬ pymˬ pah-eu)

meiqhuv yobaq doq eil havma women with thin lips are talkative women (45:29) (mehˬ luˬ baˬ lehˇ ni g'eh-eu aˬ buˇ-aˬ ngehˬ myaˬ)

Meiqjal Muojiang county (46:181)

meiq jaoltaf coke (used in refining metals) (Chi) (26:28)

meiqjil lips (5:39) (mehˬ luˬ)

-- **meiqjil, aqhhuv** -- lower lip

-- **meiqjil, aqtav** -- upper lip

meiqjil deiqcul lips in a pout (13:31) (mehˬ luˬ mˇ byehˬ-eu)

meiqkavq alcav a silver chain (worn by girls) (pyuˇ lahˇ daw)

meiqkaoq a text book (50:85)

meiqkaoq deilssaol to prepare a lesson from a textbook (50:9)

meiqkovq a bit for a horse (9:106, 11:29) (mehˬ kaw‸; mahˬ kaw‸)

meiqlev thick lips (mehˬ luˬ yaw tuˇ)

meiqloq loq to rinse one's mouth or brush one's teeth) (9:106) (k'a˯ meh jo^-eu; meh˯ jo^ jo^-eu)

meiqluq lip (9:106) (meh˯ lu˯)

meiq luq dalqul to pout out one's lips when disgruntled or disagree

meiqluvq thin lips (meh˯ lu˯ yaw ba˯)

meiqma younger brother's wife (9:106) (a˯ tsu)

meiq miq qu miq to teach and care for

meiqmoq 1. chin whiskers (6:170) (meh˯ mah˯), 2. beard (9:106), 3. moustache (meh˯ ci^)

meiqmoq hhe to pull someone's facial hairs

meiqmoq taq to raise a beard (facial hair) (should only do it after one has grandchildren)

meiqpav 1. cracked lips (or) **meiqhavq** (meh˯ lu˯ tsaw˯ pa^-eu), 2. harelip (meh˯ pyeh˯)

meiqpov one's mouth to be full of food

meiqpov leivq nei to eat with a full mouth (k'a˯ meh ti˯ byah dza˯-eu)

meiqpov leivq nei zaq to eat heartily

meiqpyul a plowshare (9:106)

meiqqei talkative people ('sharp' lips) (meh˯ boe˯ yaw ta^)

meiqqif coal gas (B=Chi) (26:34)

meiqqif yuqduq a gas stove (A=Chi) (50:113)

meiq qul nee haq honey-mouthed and dagger-hearted ('bitter-hearted') (people who talk in a sweet way but are bad in their hearts) (50:98)

meiqsi in front of; before (9:106) (or) **meiqsii** (meh˯ shi)

meiqsi pyu in front of (41:189) (meh˯ shi paw)

meiq sol sol, nee sol sol to calculate using one's mouth and heart

meiqsyu ink (Chi) (6:184, 11:31) (sah˯ uiˇ)

meiqtao to introduce (50:88)

meiqtuv the beak of a bird; the bill of a bird (meh˯ to^)

-- meiq, tyuq -- to guide by pointing out the way

meiqyovq crooked lips (meh˯ lu˯ yaw byeh˯; meh˯ yaw˰)

meiqzaq a bridge head; the end of a bridge (26:14) (lawˇ dzmˇ meh˯ dza˯)

meiqzaq a principle (as an idea) (Chi) (34:43)

meiqzaq a mistake (yaw bah˯)

meiq zaq to teach for a living

meiqzaq daltevq teaching plan (50:85)

meiqzaq duv lal for a mistake to happen (26:120)

meiqzaq laol çyuq take preventive measures (50:48)

meiqzaq lulsul teaching method (50:85)

meiqzaq lulsul sul teaching activities (50:86)

meiqzaq qo taq to place a condition on (50:27)

meiqzeil the corner of the mouth (9:106) (k'a˯ meh meh˯ dzeˇ)

meiqzii wheat (Chi) (9:106)

Meiqziif milcaq (see: **Maoqziif milcaq**)

meiqzu mouth; snout (35:42, 46:151) (meh˯ boe˯)

-- meiqzu, aqhhavq -- pig snout

-- **meiqzu, aqhhuv** -- lower lip

meiqzu deivq to be talkative (45:7)

meiqzu nalzu meil all to talk at once

meiqzu piei to open one's mouth (46:151) (k'a˯ meh m˅ nga-eu)

meiqzu tav a 'sharp mouth' (talkative person) (meh˯ boe˯ yaw ta^)

meiv 1. to be held down (as a rice pounder is held down so that the unpounded rice can be stirred) (tah˯ ka-eu), 2. to be teetering (not firm)

-- **meiv, daoqmeiv** -- 1. to go up and down on a seesaw, 2. for a wagtail bird to go up and down

-- **meiv, gaoqmeiv** -- to teeter-totter

meivhovq the wooden recepticle to hold grain when pounding it

-- **meiv leiv, mu lu** -- to be teetering (not firm)

-- **meiv, meicaol** -- (see full)

meiv pao to lift up and open (4:37) (g'eu pah-eu)

=meiv, yoq= (see full)

meivq 1. to be hungry, 2. to be thirsty (9:106) (meh˄-eu)

meivqhho hho meil a long famine (g'aw˯ myah˅ ni meh˄-eu shu˄-eu)

meivq kuv meivq luv meil starvation (meh˄-eu shu˄-eu)

meivq sil 'hungry to death' (46:198) (meh˄ seh˄-eu) (cf. Lahu; meu˄ ve suh la yo˯)

meivq sil meivq lo starving with hunger

MI

mil, mil, mil the sound a cat makes (29:4) (or) **mil'aol, mil'aol, mil'aol** (mi˅, mi˅, mi˅)

mil ten thousand (9:109) (ti˯ mui˅)

mil to reach; catch up with (9:109) (mi˅-eu)

mil a place; land (or) **yoyal** (50:35)

=mil, al= cat

=mil, aq= an interjection of surprise (esp. when there are too many or too much)

=mil, aq= some time ago

mil'aol, mil'aol, mil'aol sound of cat meowing (29:4) (or) **mil, mil, mil**

=mil aol, keel= to taste something

milbil area; space (as of land) (50:115)

milbia bright earth; shining ground (34:6)

milbiav a landslide (9:109) (mi˅ bya^)

milbiav biav to have a landslide (mi˅ bya^ bya^-eu)

milbieiv mud; muddy (11:82) (sha˯ jeh^)

milbieiv ju duv yi to come out (or) **ju duv yi**

milbyu cave; hole (as where a rat lives) (9:109, 13:19, 46:129) (mi˅ byoe)

milcaq earth (9:109) (mi˅ tsa˯)

milcaq alsiq peanut (6:168, 9:110) (a˅ nui^ pah˯; la˄ bui˯ nui^ pah˯)

milcaq aqnaoq a kind of clay eaten by some women (esp. at time of pregnancy) (miˇ tsaˬ aˬ nahˬ)

milcaq caqmeeq a good place; a good piece of land (33:3) (miˇ tsaˬ miˇ muiˬ)

milcaq haqseil wild garlic

milcaq haolteil an area (14:140)

milcaq haoqbaoq all over the world (38:91) (miˇ k'ahˬ doe ni)

milcaq (vb) hev up to that point (of land) (**milcaq diq hev** = fought to that point - 26:2) (k'oeˇ gaˇ keu^ ni)

milcaq hultav all over the world (or) **aoq hul'a**

milcaq hucavq a mole (animal) (ho pya^ la‸ sehˇ)

milcaq hhoqpul wild turnip

milcaq milbieiv muddy (26:59)

milcaq milquvq wild places

milcaq puvsiq a hill; **puvsiq**

-- milcaoq, aoqcaoq -- surrounded by problems ('nets above and snares below'

mildaol ssivq nei topple the mountains and overturn the seas (50:126)

mildao haoqseil fame (k'ahˬ sehˇ; tsawˇ myahˇ do^-eu)

mil'eel bi ssivq preserve land and water (50:6)

milgaoq mountains; mountainous places (46:76, 168)

milgaoq gaoqdaoq the base of a mountain; the foot of a mountain (46:98) (gawˬ jawˬ dawˬ dahˬ)

milgaoq gaoqssaq a small mountain (45:76) (gawˬ jawˬ jawˬ zaˬ)

milgaoq wuqduq a peak

milguq the village ritual head, who is in charge of major annual ceremonies and the ceremonial places related to the village (35:57, 46:128) (this is the current name for those who were called '**zyuq**' or '**zyuqma**' in the past. **Milguq maq jol ngaoq, caoqsaol milsaol tiq zaq maq jol**. If there were no ritual head, there would be none to hold ceremonies to the great Lords of the area.)

Milguq qovq a branch of the **Siqnaoq** (Bai) Hani clan, called this since many members have been village ritual heads

milguq geessyuq gee'qa from the line of ritual heads (so destined to be a **milguq**)

milguq lavqcavq the helpers to the village ritual head

milguq maq jol ngaoq, caoqsaol milsaol tiq zaq maq jol if there is not a ritual head, the lords of the area would not help us

milhaoq country; place; region; (9:110) (miˇ k'ahˬ)

-- milhaoq, aqnu -- a foreign land; strange land

milhaoq aoq zaq to give up ('to sell one's country') (or) **aqlavq bavqcei; aolnieiq pieiq taq**

milhaoq beeq turbulence; upheaval; unrest

-- milhaoq, Ceilgu -- a township in Honghe county

milhaoq e miq aol local productive activity (46:85)

milhaoq haollaol to defend public order (50:176)

milhaoq haol leev to take care of the country (50:7)
milhaoq haoqsal sal rich and beautiful country
milhaoq leeldov nei complete territory (50:109)
milhaoq milsal a good place; a good region (46:118)
milhaoq milsol a holy place (**sol** = pure) (50:150)
milhaoq sal peace in the land (country at ease) (meu˯ saˇ-eu)
milhaoq sal e taq when there is peace in the land (meu˯ saˇ laˇ ngeh)
-- **mil hel, Molmil** -- make an offering to God
milhhaq naoq to have a good relationship (14:183)
-- **milhhu, huvqlo** -- the years past
milhhuvq below the earth
milhhuvq alsavq natural gas
milhhuvq zaol nei ssyuqbeil ceiv an explanation of earthquakes (the earth is located on a huge fish, which turns from time to time)
miljeivq mud dug out of a hole by a rodent (miˇ jeh˄)
milka lalhuvq the other day (14:194) (miˇ nah hu˯ nah)
milka lalnao a few days ago (12:127)
milkaq border line (between countries, fields, etc.) (9:110, 50:12) (miˇ ka˯)
milkaq leiq duv to deport; expel (50:139)
milkaq luvcuv stone boundary marker (50:88)
milkaq tavq to border on
-- **mil kuv, aoq kuv** -- weather is dry
mil lal soul of the land (14:153)
millaol a 'prairie' fire (an uncontrolled fire that burns outside of a jungle area) (9:110)
millaol keqpeev to set a 'prairie' fire (yaˇ sa˯ keu˯-eu)
millaol laoldaol a place which is burned by a 'prairie' fire (9:110, 46:117)
millaol peev for a 'prairie' fire to burn (yaˇ sa˯ pui^-eu)
-- **mil, leiq** -- to chase and catch up with
millu an earthquake
millu deiq kaq to prevent earthquakes (50:96)
millu lu an earthquake to take place (miˇ lu^ lu^-eu)
milluvq milsaol lord of land ('land god') (13:43, 35:61) (or) **milluvq milsaol aqma; milsaol aqma** (miˇ sahˇ cu˯ sahˇ = lord of land and water)
millyul dust turned to mud (sha˯ jeh^)
milma a female cat (aˇ miˇ ma)
milma haolteil mountain ranges (14:236, 46:166)
milma hhaqdaoq a mountain pass (11:220, 14:149) (cf.: g'a˯ lahˇ = saddleback mountain)
milma hhyuq gaoq zyul e gaoq zyul place where nine mountains meet (one of the places a shaman goes to in a trance)
mil meeq good land; fertile land (46:116) (miˇ mui˯)
milmil one hundred million (or) **yif** (Chi)
milmi ssaqheiq a female lover; a girlfriend (11:208)

-- **mil, miav hu qiq** -- a field of vision
Milmiaol a place name
=**mil, Mol**= God (and see full)
milmu mu to lose one's direction in the forest; to lose one's way (mi˅ bah˯ bah˯-eu)
milnao yesterday (6:163, 9:110) (mi˅ nah)
=**milnao, eiq**= a few days ago
milnao huqnao a few days ago (mi˅ nah hu˯ nah)
milnaohuvq last year (9:110) (mi˅ nui k'o˰)
milneiq clay used for making porcelain
milnil red mud; red dirt (14:173) (mi˅ ne˅)
milnia a place; a point (9:110) (**col daov miaq e milnia** = a place where there are many people - 10:31, 11:120, 45:44, 46:167); a location (ga˅)
milpuq soft earth
milqivq last night (9:110) (mi˅ ci˰)
milqo laqhhoq alsiq a kind of vine
-- **milquvq, milcaq** -- wild places
-- **milsal, milhaoq** -- a good place; a good region
milsaol lord of the land (mi˅ sah˅)
milsaol aqma owner or master of a sacred place in the village (or) **milluvq milsaol aqma**
Milsaol aqpyuq the Lord of the land (spirit) (38:93) (mi˅ sah˅)
milsaol aol ceremony to the Lord of the land (46:165) (mi˅ sah˅ law˅-eu)
-- **milsaol, daqhhaq e** -- spirit owner of the ground
milsaol hha lol zaq to make an offering to the lord of the land (46:78) (mi˅ sah˅ law˅-eu)
milsaol lol to make an offering to the lord of the land (mi˅ sah˅ law˅-eu)
milsaol luvcuv one or three stones set up in the middle of the village in honor of the 'lord of the area', set up by the **milguq**, who uses unblemished river stones (**lolbaq haqluv**)
milseiv rice noodles (Chi)
milsiil albol the sacred village tree
milsiil aqma goddess (lord) of the land (14:174)
=**mil sol, sol**= to tell one's fortune
milsoq yesterday morning (9:110) (mi˅ nah shaw˯; mi˅ shaw˯, which in Akha also means 'this morning' when speaking in the afternoon)
milsov dalpav a board with which to flatten mud walls
milsuv a mud slide on a mountain (46:169)
milsuv suv a mud slide on a mountain to occur
milssaq a kitten (a˅ mi˅ za˯)
milssaol 'post of the earth' (used in proverbs - 18:19, (cf. English: "foundations of the earth")
milsseil sseidev a type of spirit
-- **miltaoq, aoqtaoq** -- become lawless
milteil sal to be famous (14:196) (tsaw˅ myah˅ ja^-eu; tsaw˅ myah˅ do^-eu)
=**mil, toqla al**= a rabbit

milwuvq below the earth (30:2) (mi$^{\vee}$ o^)
milxeiv 1. muddy waters (i$^{\vee}$ ne$^{\vee}$), 2. dirt
milyol a kind of bee
milzal 1. cat food (29:4) (a$^{\vee}$ mi$^{\vee}$ dza$^{\vee}$), 2. a male cat (a$^{\vee}$ mi$^{\vee}$ mi$^{\vee}$ hu$^{\vee}$)
milzeil border area (50:12) (mi$^{\vee}$ ka$_{\vee}$)
-- **mil zeil, aoq daoq** -- the ends of the earth; the remotest corners of the earth
milzeil cuqzeil border areas (10:11; 14:169)
milzul barren earth (cannot grow much on it)
milzul zul earth to become barren (cannot grow much of anything on it)
milzyuq lords of the land (**aoqzyuq qiq mavq gee, milzyuq qiq mavq gee** - some were lords of the sky, some were lords of the land - 30:2)

mi to be free (i.e., to have time)
mi a meter (Chi) (3:1)
=mi nei, lyul= fragments of something
=mi ssaqheiq, mil= a lover; a girlfriend

(vb) **miq** showing action away from subject; action to 3rd person (9:110) (... neh$_{\vee}$) (**eilmiq** = eh$^{\vee}$ neh$_{\vee}$-eu)
(vb) **miq** a part. of being in a certain state (**Ngaq e aqma nal miq taoqngaoq**... Because my mother was sick ...41:62)
=miq, al= woman; lady
miq aol to labor; to work (46:156)
miq aol moqfaf a model worker (B=Chi) (50:102)
miq aol neema mood of labor (50:102)
miq aolssaq workers; working people (26:2) (ga$^{\vee}$ m$^{\vee}$ za$_{\vee}$)
miq aol zei a strong worker (50:102)
miqbao xobaoq ballaol aol an arranged marriage (50:6)
miqbev gun; rifle (mi$_{\vee}$ beu^) (clf. **qiq siq; qiq mol; qiq bev**)
-- **miqbev, albol** -- a wooden gun (put outside the village gate to scare away spirits)
-- **miqbev, miqzal** -- a shotgun
miqbev bavqssaq soldiers; armed forces (or) **mavqssaq** (yeh$^{\vee}$)
miqbev bevdaoq the butt of a gun (mi$_{\vee}$ beu^ beu^ daw$_{\vee}$ da$_{\vee}$)
miqbev dafpaof canon (B=Chi) (50:31)
miqbev lav pieiv to fire a gun accidentally
miqbev lavqzil a sharpshooter; expert marksman (50:149)
miqbev qifqal air rifle; pneumatic gun (to shoot birds and small animals) (B=Chi) (50:134)
=miq, bil= others (old language)
miqbil village militia; local defense in village (Chi) (50:116)
miqbil peiqza militia platoon leader (Chi) (50:116)
miqbivq bivq to instruct; give orders (46:155) (meh$_{\vee}$

neh$_\vee$-eu)

miqbia blaze; flame (9:111, 11:28) (mi$_\vee$ dza$_\vee$ mi$_\vee$ lm$^\vee$) (and see: **miqlaol**)

miqbiaol 'flying girl' (in story) (or) **miqbiaol dulma** (11:203)

miqbuq a tail with long hair (46:155)

miqca ca to warm one's back by the fire (9:111) (mi$_\vee$ dza$_\vee$ lm$^\vee$-eu)

miqca cabuvq marks on the feet caused from warming them at a fire

miqca nei e col close relatives (**miqca nei e col maq aol zaq haoq** = it is not proper to marry close relatives)

miqcaoq caoq to make an offering to prevent a fire in the village (wrap up a piece of charcoal in a wild banana leaf and bury it in a nearby valley) (mi$_\vee$ dza$_\vee$ law$^\vee$-eu)

miqcaoq lolgov a valley in which to make an offering so as to prevent a fire in the village (see also: **miqcaoq caoq**)

miqciiq a noun (gram) (Chi) (50:118)

miqcuq ethnic group; clan; tribal group; nationality (Chi) (9:111, 13:11, 41:4) (tsaw$^\vee$ jeu$_\vee$)

Miqcuq Cuqbaseif Nationalities Publishing House (Chi)

miqcuq gafbuf minority nationality cadre (Chi) (50:117)

miqcuq gaolzoqdyuf a nationality working team (Chi) (50:117)

miqcuq gei'faf to liberate nationalities (Chi) (50:117)

miqcuq gualxif relationship of nationalities (Chi) (50:117)

miqcuq meiqzaq problems of nationalities (A=Chi) (50:117)

miqcuq qilyeq ziifziif nationalities autonomous region (Chi) (50:117)

miqcuq teiqdiei nationalities characteristics (Chi) (50:117)

miqcuq weiqhuaf nationalities culture (Chi) (50:117)

Miqcuq Xoqyeif Nationalities College (in Kunming) (Chi) (9:111)

miqcuq yaqpeiq oppresion of the nationalities (Chi) (50:117)

miqcuq zeifceiq policy of nationalities (Chi) (50:117)

miqcuq ziifziif milcaq autonomous areas of nationalities (AB=Chi) (50:117)

miqcyuq a widow (9:111) (or) **miqcyuq aqma** (mi$_\vee$ tsoe$_\vee$ mi$_\vee$ ma)

miqcyuq aqma a widow (45:81) (mi$_\vee$ coe$_\vee$ mi$_\vee$ ma)

miqcyuq cyuq to be widowed

miqcyuq cyuqssaq bastard ('child of a widow', which means there is no father) (13:3) (taboo) (de$^\vee$ za$_\vee$;

g'o^ ba⌄ la⌃ nyi˅-eu⌄ za⌄)

miqdavq a young (eligible) maiden (taboo) (9:111) (mi⌄ da⌃ = taboo in Ak.)

miqdavq ceivq young man to go looking for a girl (taboo)

=miq, daoq= a tail

=miqdaoq, keel= at the foot end

miqdiq 1. flint, iron and tinder for making fire, 2. modern type of lighter

miqdol duv for a girl to bring a bad-omen on a village by becoming pregnant out of wedlock

miqdol xoldol duv to commit adultery, and thus be a bad-omen for the village

miqdovq yozal material for burning in a furnace (50:141)

miqdu a rope kept burning as a light for tobacco smokers

=miq, eel= down river

miqfaq civil law (Chi) (or) **ssaqlaol e yo'liq**

miqfaol public mood; public atmosphere (Chi) (50:116)

Miqgaq a girl's name (11:131)

miqgaol a worker (Chi) (50:116)

miqhe the smell of burning (pui^-eu beh⌃ la⌃-eu)

miqhoqif a fire extinguisher (Chi) (50:116)

miq huvq for a man to divorce his wife (send her home) (see also: **miq seil**) (mi⌄ za⌄ k'o⌃-eu)

miqhuvq a divorced woman (mi⌄ k'o⌃)

miq huvq xo huvq for a husband and wife to divorce

miq huvq ssaq huvq to divorce one's wife & children

miqhhaol second (middle) daughter (9:111, 13:3)

-- miqhhaol, alba -- second eldest sister

miqhhaol hhaolma the girl in the middle when there are several (11:69)

miqhhaol hhaolssaq a little girl in the middle when there are several (11:69)

miqhhel a daughter that has been purchased

miqhhel hhel to buy a daughter (a⌄ bu˅ zeu˅-eu)

miqhhovq women (old language) (38:16)

Miqhhyu Nationality Affairs Commission (a contraction) (Chi) (54:158)

miqji local police (Chi) (50:116)

miqjidyuf a team of local police (Chi) (50:116)

miqjiv burning coals; charcoal (9:111, 11:28) (mi⌄ ji^)

miqjiv hoqpav a bamboo container for carrying burning coals (so as to start a fire elsewhere)

miqjiv jivngaoq to cure a foot ache by putting out burning charcoal with water and then stepping on the coals which are still hot

miqkoq firewood (9:111) (mi⌄ dza⌄)

miqkoq cevqbu large firewood cut with an ax

miqkoq dalhel (see: **dalhel**) (14:150)

miqkoq daoqdev heavy firewood; large

miqkoq daoqpuq firewood which is big around but short

miqkoq heivq to cut firewood (11:92) (mi˯ dza˯ k'eh˰-eu; mi˯ dza˯ ceu˰-eu)
miqkoq miqjeivq a piece of firewood
miqkoq miqlo long pieces of firewood (as long as can be carried)
miqkoq miqpial firewood and twigs (11:35) (mi˯ dza˯ kaw˯ pyaˇ)
miqkoq xaoqbul straight firewood
miqkyul a clever female (**yokyul** = a clever man) (30:1) (mi˯ gahˇ)
=miq, la= the end of the month
miqlaol 1. a flame (9:112), 2. firelight (and see: **miqbia**) (mi˯ dza˯ mi˯ lmˇ)
Miqleiv 'Miss Shorty'
miqlil burning firewood (9:112) (mi˯ geuˇ)
miqlil a short tail (daw˯ mi˯ mi˯ nymˇ)
miqli youngest daughter in the family (11:69, 41:2, 46:145)
-- **miqli, alba** -- the youngest elder sister
-- **miqli, aqnil** -- younger sister
miqli lima next to last daughter (11:69)
miqli lissaq the youngest daughter (11:69) (a˯ buˇ a˯ nyiˇ nyiˇ sa˯ g'a˯)
=miq, lol= the mouth (outlet) of a river
miqlo a long piece of firewood (it is as long as can be carried) (or) **miqkoq miqlo**
-- **miqlo, miqkoq** -- a long piece of firewood
miqma wife (11:204) (za˯ mi˯ za˯) (cf. **Lahu**: aw˯ miˇ ma)
=miq, moq= a horse's tail
miqmoq yomoq unmarried women and men (14:205)
Miqnav the name of a girl (2:54) (Mi˯ na^)
miq nei peev laq e neivqhaq type of spirit from those who have burned to death
Miqnieilso Nationality Research Institute (a contraction) (Cbi) (54:158)
miqnieiq livelihood; work; job (gaˇ)
miqnieiq aol to work at a job (11:154) (gaˇ mˇ-eu)
miqnieiq aolqeiv qeiv a labor contest; competition (50:102)
miqnieiq bil to divide up the work
-- **miqnieiq, kyuq lal e** -- to cause injury; harm
miqnieiq meiqzaq affairs (50:138)
-- **miqnieiq, miaoq aol e** -- 1. effectiveness for a given period of time; 2. current events; current affairs
miqnieiq nieiqcavq qiq mol a bad job (gaˇ ma˯ mui˯-eu)
miqnieiq nieiqma a great task; a big job (26:59, 104, 41:80) (gaˇ yaw hui˯)
miqnieiq nieiqssaq a small task; a little job (26:114) (gaˇ yaw nyiˇ)
miqnieiq nieiq teiq duv lal an urgent matter to come up (54:109)
miqnieiq qiq mol one type of livelihood (8:27,28)

miqnieiq saqbaol tov to do one's share (50:50)
miqnieiq xilmeil ngeel e ngaoq if this is the case (heu lo‸-ehˇ ngeuˇ-eu law nmˇ-aˬ)
-- miqnieiq, yeilbei -- ancient affairs (creation etc.)
miqnieiq yojil the actual situation (50:152)
miqnieiq yoma the main task; the most important job (26:119)
miqpal pal zaq to have a mixed marriage
miqpavq xopavq pavq to tie a thread around groom's right wrist, and another thread around bride's left wrist as part of the wedding ceremony
-- miqpial, miqkoq -- firewood & twigs
miqqil fame (Chi) (14:241) (tsawˇ myahˇ ja^-ou; k'ahˬ sehˇ ja^-eu)
miqqil heeq to have great fame; to be very famous (14:241) (A=Chi) (tsawˇ myahˇ yaw huiˬ)
miqqiv a match (for lighting a fire) (11:15, 50:77) (miˬ ci^)
miqqoq a bridesmaid, who is a 'friend' of the bride during the travel to the groom's village, the wedding feast and all the related ceremonies (miˬ cawˬ)
miqqusal acute disease, such as a stroke (as when one cannot speak)
miqqusal kovq to have an acute disease, as a stroke
miqqusal nieivq to seek to bring a person out of a stroke by pinching, pulling and hitting the person
miqsaq ngyul 1. to cry and mourn for an elder; 2. to wail for the dead (tsawˇ ngoeˇ ngoeˇ-eu); 3. to sing a sad song
miqsavq 1. soot (9:112), 2. lampblack (k'ehˬ na^)
-- miq, saoq -- to disgust someone
miqseil spark from fire (9:112) (miˬ dzaˬ miˬ dzui‸)
miqseil a woman who is dissatisfied with her marriage
miqseil seil for a woman to be disatisfied with her husband and therefore she leaves him and goes home) (see also: **miqhuvq**)
miqseilma a woman who is dissatisfied with her marriage
miqseif gujiq historical site (as building, area, etc.) (Chi) (50:118)
miqsiq a clever woman (**miqsiq wuqduq zaolmol maq quv** = clever women do not have special marks on their heads)
miqsiq a bullet (9:112, 11:25) (miˬ siˬ)
miqsiq aoqsseil sseil meil ziivq a hail of bullets ('bullets coming like rain') (50:135)
miqsiil a village teacher (not a govt. teacher but pd. by the villagers) (Chi) (50:116)
miqsiivq a bride (miˬ shui‸)
miqsiivq ssaqsiivq a newlywed couple
miqsiivq ssaqsiivq bivq zaq to have a wedding party
miqsiivq ssaqsiivq seq to hold a wedding party (46:105)

miqsiif hhafjeif a civil case (Chi) (50:116)
Miqsol a female name (2:54) (cf.: Mi˯ Saw)
miqsolssaq one's wife (50:128) (za˯ mi˯ za˯)
miqsolssaq gee to arrange a marriage, from the man's point of view (& see: **miqsulssaq**)
miqsul 1. a copy clerk, 2. a secretary to the director (Chi) (50:115)
miqsulkol secretarial department (Chi) (50:115)
miqsulssaq gee to arrange a marriage, from the man's point of view (& see: **miqsolssaq gee**)
miqsulza secretary (Chi) (50:115)
miqsuq suq 1. to pour out water on burning charcoal to drive spirit away at the door of the home when a wild animal is shot and brought back home (the one who shot the game steps over the doused fire), 2. to pour water on a burning fire to prevent evil spirits from entering into a home
miqssaq wife (9:112) (mi˯ za˯)
miqssaq gee caq to betroth to be married; arrange a marriage (or) **miqssaq gee ceiv**
miqssaq gee ceiv (see: **miqssaq gee caq**)
miqssaq huljil wife and husband (mi˯ za˯ yo za˯)
miqssaq maq bo lal na a man who has never married
miqssaq pyu nei niq lal to be related by marriage on the woman's side
miqssaq seq to marry (said of a male) (mi˯ za˯ sheu˯-eu) (and cf. **sulmil yil** for the girl)
miqssiq milssiq firefly (9:112) (a˯ mui ja˯ nyi˯; ja˯ nyi˯ ma)
miqteil first; before; prior to; long ago (46:111) (**Zaqduq dolduq miqteil hultav meeq zeiq nga.** We have more food and drink than we had before. 41:24) (or) **huqteil teilli** (yaw beh; je˯ hu; meh˯ hu)
miqteil a ssuq to go ahead (or) **miqteil a aol dav**
miqteil hultav more than in the past (45:70) (aˇ hu na^ ma˯ tseˇ)
miqteil naolhao nadul nei as usual (yaw jawˇ yaw˯ lo˰-ehˇ)
miqteil nei eil taq to give notice; to tell ahead of time (meh˯ hu ehˇ ta˯-eu)
miqteil pyu in front of (je˯ hu; je˯ hu paw) (11:32)
miqteil teilli first ...(**miqteil teilli qiq hhaq** = the first person 11:67) (yaw beh)
miqteil teilli qiq hhaq the very first person (yaw beh ti˯ g'a˯)
miqteiq a single daughter (9:112) (ti˯ mi˯ teh˰)
-- miqteiq, ssaqmiq -- a single daughter
-- miqteiv, zovqlavq -- (see full)
miqtiq iron (Chi) (shmˇ)
-- miq, toq -- to answer; reply
miqxil a film star; a singing star (Chi) (50:118)
miqxif siilxa superstitious idea (Chi)
-- miq, yaq -- to put a curse on someone

Miqyeil God (46:160, 167) created the world, people, and provided patterns of behavior for people (will punish if people wrong those) (or) **Aqpyuq Miqyeil** (Mi⌄ yeh˅; a⌄ poe⌄ Mi⌄ yeh˅)

-- **Miqyeil, Byulluvq Aqpyuq** -- one of three manifestations of God, the one who protects people

Miqyeil yeilbei customs and traditions handed down from **Aqpyuq Miqyeil** (God) (46:160, 167)

miqyo children (daughters and sons) (30:2) (mi⌄ yo)

miqyo cavq zaq to commit adultery (yu‸ k'oe⌄-eu)

miqzal gun powder (9:112) (mi⌄ dza˅)

miqzal miqbev a shotgun (shot = **savziiq** - Chi)

miqzal teil to pound up gun powder (11:120) (mi⌄ dza˅ tah⌄-eu)

miqzal haolpuq a gourd used to carry gun powder

miqzaq fire (mi⌄ dza⌄)

miqzaq bo dovq 1. to start a fire (mi⌄ dza⌄ baw do‸-eu), 2. to cook something

miqzaq bosev a fan to fan the flames (mi⌄ dza⌄ baw seu^)

miqzaq boqlo a bamboo pipe for blowing fire (9:112) (mi⌄ dza⌄ baw⌄ law)

miqzaq diq sil to put out a fire; extinguish a fire (by beating it out usually) (26:69) (mi⌄ dza⌄ deh mi^-eu)

miqzaq dovq a fire to be ablaze (mi⌄ dza⌄ do‸-eu)

miqzaq geema the major fire burning in a fireplace (no one must step over it)

miqzaq havpuq 1. a brazier in which to make a fire to keep warm, 2. a basket for carrying fire (mi⌄ dza⌄ k'a^ pu⌄)

miqzaq heqjiv (see: **miqzaq miqjiv** = a burning piece of charcoal) (14:139) (mi⌄ dza⌄ mi⌄ ji^)

miqzaq keqpieiq to set fire to (35:108) (mi⌄ dza⌄ keu⌄ do‸-eu)

miqzaq laol to warm up at a fire (mi⌄ dza⌄ lm˅-eu)

miqzaq luqzii a stove (B=Chi) (shm˅ kui˅)

miqzaq miqlaol a flaming fire (26:69) (mi⌄ dza⌄ mi⌄ lm˅)

miqzaq miqlil burning firewood (14:181) (mi⌄ dza⌄ mi⌄ li^)

miqzaq miqseil shooting stars (14:147) (or) **aqzaq miqseil** (a⌄ gui˅ sm˅ mi˅-i˅-eu; pyu˅ a⌄ ma ga-i˅-eu)

miqzaq niq gee alkaq a to be 'between two fires' (cf. Eng.: between a rock and a hard place)

miqzaq sil for a fire to go out (mi⌄ dza⌄ mi^-eu)

miqzaq sseiv something to be ablaze with burning lights

miqzaq yozaq beautiful women; handsome men (30:1)

=miq, zaol= the lower part of a village

miqzeil beside a fireplace (14:142)

miqzeiq bride price (considered the 'cost of mother's milk')

miqzu the fleshy tail piece of a chicken (not

including the feathers) (mi˯ dzo)
miqzu democracy (Chi) (34:8, 31, 50:117) (**hoqpiq miqzu** = peaceful democracy)
miqzu dapeif democratic parties (Chi) (34:20)
miqzu geigeiq democratic reform (Chi) (50:117)
miqzu geiqmif democratic revolution (Chi) (50:117)
miqzu jiqzaol democracy and centralism (Chi) (50:117)
miqzu jiqzaolziif democratic centralism (Chi) (50:117)
miqzu qeiqlif democratic right (Chi) (50:117)
miqzu xeiji democratic vote (Chi) (50:117)

miv to close (eyes) (mya^ nui^ mi^-eu)
-- **miv, miavmiv** -- to wink one's eye
-- **miv, taoq** -- to lower one's head so as to work hard
miflif zuyif commandism (Chi) (50:118)
mifyif destiny; fate (Chi) (34:107)

MIA

mia late (**tul e za nei mia** = got up a little late) (11:106) (mya-iˇ-eu)

miaq many; much (9:107) (yaw mya˯)
miaq clf. for arrows (9:107) (mya˯)
miaq baol the basis; the main purpose
miaq buvq to reforest an area
miaqcav a big rope for a plough (9:107)
=miaq, dal= door bolt
miaqdaol pineapple (9:107, 11:32) (ka teh^)
miaqduvq a poisoned arrow (do˰ leh˰-eu˯ ka^ mya˯)
miaq gaoq many; excessive (mya˯ gah˯)
miaqgaoq pa gaoq nei very many (11:58) (mya˯ gaˇ neh-a˯)
miaqkaq wild arrowhead plant (9:107)
=miaq, kav= an arrow (for a crossbow) (ka^ mya˯)
miaq lal pa lal changeable (46:91)
miaq laq meil many (9:107)
miaqlo miallo aqma 1. an ogre or savage mythical wild person living in the jungle) (9:107) (mah˯ lah˯ mahˇ lahˇ a˯ ma); 2. chimpanzee (the Hani have never seen either of these, so they have one word for both which comes from their legend)
miaq nei 1. many (9:107) (mya˯ ni), 2. too much (10:20) (mya˯ dzeh˯-eu)
=miaq nei, hal= many
miaq nei jav to be plentiful (or) **daoqgaoq gaoq nei; biao nei jav** (g'aw˯ mya ni ja^-eu)
miaq nei qiq puq a great many (zawˇ mya˯-eu)
miaq pa miaq nei very many (11:57) (zawˇ mya˯-eu)
miaqzeiq more; too many; most (mya˯ dzeh˯-eu) (10:22)

miav large quantity (or) **yomiaq**

miav eye (9:107) (mya^)
miav clf. for eyes (mya^); times (mya^)
(no.) **miav** times the number (**niq miav** = double, **saoq miav** = triple, etc.) (11:72) (nyi˯ mya^; sm˯ mya^)
miavbeivq to be blind (9:108) (mya^ beh˄ beh˄-eu)
miavbeivq lovq beivq shining blindingly bright (38:90)
miavbil a tear in one's eye (9:108) (mya^ biˇ)
miavbil duv for tears to run down (mya^ biˇ do^-eu)
miav bilhovq nei sunken eyes (10:12)
miavbil jukov tear stains (mya^ biˇ yoeˇ kaw^)
miavbil ziiq teiq tears to stop running down (mya^ biˇ yoeˇ g'a˯-eu)
miav biei to open one's eyes (13:14) (mya^ nui^ byeh-eu)
miavbiul grey eyes
miavcil cil pink eye (conjunctivitis) (30:2)
miav ciq to wash the face (13:29) (mya^ du˄ pu˄-eu)
miavciq hoqbiav a wash basin (9:108, 41:33) (sehˇ byehˇ)
=**miav, col**= human eye (& see full)
miavcyuq short-sighted (35:17) (mya^ nymˇ)
miavdal silver or gold paper used in women's ornamentation
miav deiq nil angrily
miav deiq ssil to stare angrily (eyes wide open)
miav deivq sharp eyes (alert, keep eyes wide open) (26:29) (mya^ ta^)
miavdo a machete used for cutting wood (A=Dai) (9:108, 35:101, 46:146) (mi cehˇ)
-- **miavdoq, soqmiav** -- standard speech; literary language
miaveel laqja nei tears running (45:42) (mya^ biˇ yoeˇ-eu)
miavgaol a hoop; a band (9:108) (daˇ k'ahˇ)
miav gaol eyes to be sharp; able to see clearly
miavgeel eyelid (or) **miavhov** (5:341) (mya^ nui^ mya^ k'o^)
miavgeel geel to dazzle with light (9:108, 46:98) (mya^ guiˇ guiˇ-eu)
miavgeel geeltevq a double-folded eyelid
miavhav an open-weave basket for carrying firewood (9:108) (k'a^ kaˇ)
-- **miavhav, aqha** -- a chicken coop woven of bamboo
miavhao eyebrow; eyelash (9:108, 26:71) ('hair of the eye') (mya^ nui^ mya^ k'ahˇ)
miavhaoq nillo nei eyes reddened (35:15) (mya^ neˇ)
miavheiq heiqha come clearly into view; leap up vividly before the eyes; in front of your eyes (50:106)
-- **miavhov, miav** -- the eyelid
miav hu to open one's eyes (11:120) (mya^ nui^ byeh-eu)
miav hu ceiv naolngaoq nee nyuq maq ceiv 'the lotus

root snaps, but its fibers stay joined' (although apparently severed, it is actually still connected) (50:125) Although out of sight, still to remember another in one's heart.

miav hu qiq mil the field of vision

miav hu qiq miv a glance

miavhhaq hhaq to have dim eyesight (mya^ nui^ mya^ muˇ muˇ-eu)

miavhhaq jav to be polite (50:104)

miavhhuvq 1. a hooked machete for cutting weeds (A=Dai) (13:45) (mi cehˇ mi ngo‸); 2. machetes used in farming (or) **ceiqhhuv miavhhuv**) (B=Dai) (yaˇ mya˯-eu mi cehˇ)

-- miavjeil, juqdev -- a dagger; knife carried at the waist

miav joq biei as soon as opened eyes .... (13:14)

miavjul to have squinting eyes

miavjul jul for one's eyes to be almost closed (13:31) (pf.) (& see below)

miavjyul jyul for one's eyes to be almost closed (35:27) (& see above)

miavkal eye-glasses; spectacles (9:108) (pyaw˯ ka˯; mya^ taw^)

miavkal dovq to wear eye-glasses (9:108) (pyaw˯ ka˯ ka˯-eu; mya^ taw^ taw^-eu)

=miav, keel= ankle

miavkov one's line of vision; line of sight (50:154)

miav laq seiq to have dim eyesight (46:149) (mya^ g'a˯ g'a˯-eu; mya^ ma˯ shaw-eu)

=miav, lavq= knothole in a tree

miavleiq leiq 1. to rub one's eyes (as when waking up) (mya^ nui^ je˯-eu), 2. to look but not see; to turn a blind eye to something

miavmiv miv to wink the eye (9:108) (mya^ teh^ teh^-eu)

miavmiv qiq miv in the wink of an eye (45:51, 46:147) (mya^ teh^ teh^-eu)

miav miavhov the eyelid (11:36) (mya^ nui^ mya^ k'o^)

miav mol qiq qeiv as far as one can see; the horizon (50:121)

miav mul miav lav seiq 1. to feel dizzy (46:149), 2. to have dim eyesight

miavmul mul to be dizzy (9:108, 46:149) (mya^ nui^ mya^ muˇ muˇ-eu; u˯ du˯ mo˯ mo˯-ehˇ g'eh-eu)

miavmuq lower eyelid (la‸ o^ pa^-eu˯ mya^ k'o^)

miavnal nal to be jealous (or) **miavnil nil**

miavneev the eye; eyeball (9:109) (mya^ nui^)

miavneev bilduv meil to have protruding eyes

miavneev deiq duv to stare at someone or something; to open wide one's eyes (57:102)

miavneev neevnav pupil of eye (mya^ nui^ mya^ na^)

miavneev ngyul duv jil to cry one's eyes out (mya^ nui^ ngoeˇ do^-eu)

miavneev puvluv nei eyeballs turned up (or around) (14:243)

miav nei same; equal (9:109) (or) **qiq kov** (mya^ ni; ti$_\vee$ kaw^)
=miav nei, hal= how many (clf)
miavnil 1. to have red eye, 2. to envy someone; to be greedy (9:109, 35:29) (mya^ na^ na^-eu)
miavnil nil to be jealous (or) **miavnal nal**
miavniul niul to glower at someone; to squint at them in anger (11:43)
miavpiul white of eye (9:109) (mya^ nui^ mya^ pyu$^\vee$)
miavpiul bia nei to make eyes very big in anger, showing the whites of the eyes (12:126)
miavpyuq 1. face (9:109) (mya^ pyaw$_\vee$); 2. one's appearance (50:115)
-- **miavpyuq aoq zaq, yoqhhaq** -- to embarrass oneself ('to sell face')
miavpyuq baqba the whole face (50:115)
miavpyuq ciqduq a place to wash one's face (41:32) (mya^ du$_\wedge$ pu$_\wedge$ du$_\vee$)
miavpyuq heeq nil ceil to discriminate ('to choose between big and little faces') (mya^ pyaw$_\vee$ hui$_\vee$ nyi$^\vee$ tse$^\vee$-eu)
miavpyuq hhe zei to have a long, unhappy face (26:80) (mya^ pyaw$_\vee$ g'aw$_\vee$ mah$^\vee$ ni)
miavpyuq maq hev do not know each other (41:156) (mya^ pyaw$_\vee$ ma$_\vee$ maw$^\vee$ haw)
miavpyuq maq movq meil (vb) seriously; strongly ('without face') (26:30)
miavpyuq mol to meet someone, as a friend (41:5, 50:76)
miavpyuq zaol nal to destroy (ruin) one's face (reputation) (50:76)
=miav, qal= left eye
miav'qeil nal 1. to have an eye disease (mya^ nui^ na$^\vee$-eu), 2. to have a sty in the eye
miav'qei eyes to be crossed
miav'qeiq the corner of one's eye
miav'qeiq qeiq to look out of the corner of one's eye (as when one does not believe the other person) (35:34)
miav'qil nal 1. to have eye disease, 2. to envy someone (38:35) (mya^ na^ na^-eu)
-- **miav, qiq** -- one time
miav qiq ssil maq ssil dark as a pocket
miav'quvq for one's eyes to be somewhat closed all the time (some people are like this) (35:17)
miavsiv a towel (9:109, 46:176) (mya^ si^ pa$^\vee$ jeh)
miavssaq aqnil pupil of the eye (or) **miavssil** (mya^ nui^ mya^ na^)
miav ssil nei to stare (haw tso^-eu)
miavxil xil to aim by looking through one eye
miavxiq mucous in the eyes (35:15) (mya^ ce$_\vee$)
miav yilhovq nei sunken eyes (10:12)
miavzeil corner of the eye
miavzeiv an injured eye (mya^ nui^ na$^\vee$-eu)

(vb) miavq miavq as if they were (vb) (**silmiavq miavq** = as if they were dead - 10:12)
-- miavq, silmiavq -- as if they were dead (see above)

MIAO

miaolcaq cuv to register (50:8)
=miaol, col= a name
-- miaol, colmiaol -- to name someone
=miaol, doq= title; subject; topic
-- miaol, huvq -- (see full)
miaol pal to change the name (as of a child that cries all the time, or is sickly)
miaoltaq 1. original meaning, 2. literal sense (50:10)
miaoltaoq one's true name (children must not call their parents by this name while the parents are alive)

miao 1. cooked fully done, 2. ripe (or) **ovq** (yaw ja˄)
miao second (of time) (Chi)
miao kuv miao sav crops to be thoroughly ripe (myah laˇ-eu)
=miao, hoq= fully-cooked rice

miaoq indigo (or) **miaoqciq** (6:191) (myah˅)
miaoq to stick on (9:107) (myah˅-eu)
miaoq to lean close to (daw˅ peh k'aw˅ daˇ-eu)
miaoq to touch something (**daqhhaq a miaoq** = to touch the ground - 38:109)
miaoq aol to do work (see also: **miaoq'aol yaol**) (myaw˅ mˇ-eu)
miaoq aol baq a 'weak' (poor) worker (50:102)
miaoq aol dav li haq e goqjal the developing countries (final word = Chi) (50:44)
miaoq aolduq jav to have a job (50:102)
miaoq aol e miqnieiq 1. effectiveness for a given period of time, 2. current events; current affairs (50:153)
miaoq aol havma a strong man; a powerful man (9:107) (cf.: g'a˅ k'a^-eu)
miaoq aol xul to be diligent; to work hard (10:pref)
miaoq aol yaol an office (50:5)
miaoq aoqduq a place to sell goods (50:113) (myaw˅ ah˅ du˅)
miaoq bav aol to be perverse
miaoqbaol wuqduq duqssaq a small-group leader (hired by contract)
miaoqbeeq everything helter-skelter; all mixed up (35:74)
miaoqbeeq lav beeq to make things disorderly
miaoqbeeq miaoqga disturbance (50:51)

miaoqbivq bivq 1. to divide the work, 2. to order (or) **miaoqheil heil** (myaw⌄ bi^-eu)
miaoq cavq 1. to stick on, 2. to do different jobs (**miaoq cavq aol** = to do many things) (9:107)
miaoqciq to dye cloth indigo (11:25) (meh⌄ tah⌄ dze˅-eu)
miaoqciq zeil to ferment indigo in preparation for dyeing (4:39)
miaoqcivq a busy season (yaw teh⌄ yam⌄)
Miaoqcuq Miao (Meo; Hmong) people (Chi) (Ceh⌄ myaw^)
miaoq cyuq to seal up; close down (50:20)
-- **miaoq, deiq** -- to stick on
miaoqgaoq things; goods; products (9:107, 11:34, 34:18, 45:88, 50:77) (clf. **bavq** = the amount that one person can carry) (myaw⌄ gah⌄)
miaoqgaoq gaoqssaq aoq zaq to peddle and sell merchandise
miaoqgaoq hhe zaq to transport goods for a living (26:49) (myaw⌄ taw⌄ dza⌄-eu)
miaoqgaoq taq to leave something (myaw⌄ gah⌄ ta⌄ ya^-eu⌄)
miaoqgaoq zalgaoq goods and materials (50:182)
miaoqhav a heavy, difficult job (or) **miaoqma**
miaoqhav aol zalhav zaq to work hard and eat simply
miaoqheil heil 1. to send (a person) (or) **heil** (k'eh˅-eu), 2. to order (or) **miaoqbivq bivq**
miaoq heiq business; vocational work (50:195)
-- **miaoqheiq, zaoma** -- a major project
miaoqhhaq naq an annual ancestral offering when the land, agricultural tools and domestic animals are to rest (or) **moqhhaq naq** (done on 'horse' day = **moq**)
=**miaoq, jol**= to sit closely
miaoqkal crops (13:19, 20)
miaoqkal naciq 1. chemical fertilizer, 2. insecticide ('crop medicine') (50:122)
miaoqkavq to seal
miaoqma heavy work; an important job (11:48) (ga˅ yaw kah; ga˅ yaw sha⌄)
miaoqma teiq very busy (50:46) (myaw⌄ m˅ teh⌄-eu)
miaoq meiq laosiil a tutor; one who trains to do some special work (B=Chi); **moq meiq laosiil** - not pf.)
=**miaoq, moq**= to make funeral arrangements
miaoqnaq pieiq to go on strike (50:4)
miaoq nei to sleep soundly
miaoqsiivq aol bei to start a new task (50:95)
miaoq teiq busy season (50:122) (ga˅ m˅ teh⌄-eu)
Miaoqziissaq Miao (Meo; Hmong) nationality; **Myuqzii** (57:99) (Ceh⌄ myaw^)

miaovq to burn (mi⌄ dza⌄ myaw^-eu)
-- **miaovq, aqmiaovq** -- to tell a lie
-- **miaovq, aoqmiaovq** -- lightning to flash
-- **miaovq zaq, aqmiaovq** -- to boast; cheat; lie (and see full)

MIE

mievq to lick (9:109) (myeu‸-eu)
mievq to vanish (meh-eu; byo^-eu)
mievq tao 1. to swallow (13:24) (myo‸ ahˇ-eu), 2. to merge (as two businesses) (or) **zaqleev; lav paoq**, 3. to embezzle; misappropriate (50:137)
-- **mievq tao, molmievq** -- to gorge oneself with food
mievq xoq to get stuck (myahˬ-eu)

MIEI

Mieitieiv Burma (Myanmar) (or) **Mieitieif** (Chi) (Mam)

mieiv clf. for weight (one-tenth of a catty) (Chi) (9:109) (or) **jil** (41:129)
mieiv duv to spit out (4:41)

mieivqzao carrying rope (men use)

mieifbaol bread (Chi) (26:93) (kaˬ muˇ)
mieiftiaoq noodles (Chi) (41:167)

MIU

=miuvq, al= monkey
miuvqhav daoqnil rhesus monkey (Macaca mulatta) (aˇ myo‸ neˇ)
miuvq huvq monkey year (9:113) (myo‸ tiˬ k'o‸)
miuvqlaol a slow loris (small primate) (myo‸ lahˇ)
miuvq nav a gibbon (and see below) (aˇ myo‸ na^)
miuvqnav lavqhhev gibbon (small type of ape) (aˇ myo‸ myo‸ na^)
miuvq nao monkey day (myo‸ tiˬ nah)
miuvq zeq monkey hour (in the hours of the day) (B=Chi)

MO

mol long (9:113) (yaw mahˇ)
mol to see; catch sight of (9:113) (or) **humol** (mawˇ-eu)
mol brothers (shortened form of **aqmol**, as used in proverbs)
mol clf. for the body; for things (stool, chair, table, pot, knife, finger ring, etc.), and sometimes certain types of animals (11:76) (In Ak. the clf. for general things is: hmˬ. The clf. mawˇ is used primarily for animals, and sometimes animal-like vehicles such as planes, cars, and bad spirits.)
molbaol taq to be engaged to be married (or) **aqssaq**

dav (50:39)

molca cama very long (11:59) (g'aw, mah ah-eu)

molca nei 1. a long distance (9:113) (cf: mah ga neh-a,) (g'aw, mah ka,-eu), 2. long (of things), 3. a long time (50:21)

molca nei gyulhuaf a long-term plan (B=Chi) (50:21)

molca pa ca nei a very long distance (11:132)

molciq lavqjuv aol to take off the clothes of the corpse and wash the body in preparation for burial

molcyuq cyuqssaq an orphan (13:1, 41:2, 45:50) (mu coe a, nm)

moldaol luvq to keep vigil over a corpse while it is in the home, esp. so that no animal will jump over it

moldel a big clay basin (9:113) (mi tsa, seh byeh)

-- **moldel, haoqmaq** -- porcelain bowl for rice

Moldu molqeil an old village name

-- **mol, galmol** -- to be far away; remote

=**mol, hu**= look and see

molhuvq a big bowl (9:113, 13:12) (k'm, ma, ma, ma)

=**mol, hhol**= body

moljoq the whole body (g'aw maw maw lah)

molkol 1. picture (film), 2. clay statue

molkol caoq to take a picture; photo (B=Chi) (50:126, 149) (maw kaw taw,-eu; maw, taw, taw,-eu)

molkol huaf a painting; a portrait (B=Chi) (50:74)

molkol kolyaol a Chinese style temple ('house of statues')

molkol zaol to sculpture; make a statue (50:38)

mol lal to see (14:153) (maw la-eu)

molluq the whole thing (mah lah ni)

molluq a film; movie (Chi) (50:37); **mu'luq; dieifyi** (Chi) (bi, mya, bya,-eu)

molluq hu to go see a movie (or) **mu'luq hu** (bi, mya, bya, ga haw-eu)

molluq soqdaoq the book from which a movie is made (A=Chi) (50:37)

-- **molma, heeqma** -- great; mighty

Molmil a divine being made up of one's ancestors above the level of father, grandfather and great-grandfather. He protects us and our ancestors (9:113)

-- **Molmil, aqpiq** -- grandmother God

-- **Molmil, aqpyuq** -- grandfather God; ancestor God

-- **Molmil, aoqtav** -- god of the sky

Molmil **dama** father/mother god (13:40)

Molmil **eilyi** my God! (an expression of surprise)

Molmil **hev** God knows (**qiq hhaq maq hev, Molmil hev** = no one knows, God knows)

-- **Molmil haol, cyuqssaq** -- God helps the poor

Molmil lolzaq a type of ceremony to protect the whole village or a single family, held after New Year on 'sheep day'.

Molmil milhaol a divine being related to father,

grandfather and great-grandfather (anyone above this 'becomes' **Molmil**)

Molmil milhe God's blessing (46:189)

Molmil ssaqmiq 1. a fairy, 2. the daughter of God (45:41)

molmievq mievq tao to gorge oneself with food

-- mol, neema -- to be greedy

molniaol distance (**galma molniaol hu laq** = to look at the distance of the path - 14:242)

molpeev peev to burn the whole body (maw˅ do do lah ni pui^-eu)

mol saq mol daoq extremely sad

molsavq bo shy; bashful (50:115) (sha^ daw˅-eu)

molsyuq not easy to see

-- moltavq, hhavqhao -- pig bristles

molzaq to be seen; to discover (14:165, 50:44)

molzeiq longer (41:149) (mah˅ dzeh˯-eu)

mobiaq cockscomb of rooster; dragon (38:92) (na˯ beh)

Mo'lal milcaq Mengla, an area in Jinping Country (57:99)

=mo nei, zeiq= lazily

mozuv a phoenix coronet

moq a horse (9:113, 11:95) (clf. **moq, zaol**) (mah˯)

moq to be old (of humans) (9:113) (maw˯)

-- moq a suffix denoting old (... maw˯)

(vb) **moq** will (vb) (**aqyoq wuqhol bial lal moq wul yaq** - he thinks he will lose his life)

=moq, albol bol= old tree

=moq alsiq, ma= mango (A=Dai)

=moq, aq= pubic hair (male)

=moq, aqpiq ssaq= old woman

Moqbeiv a lady's name (14:192)

moqbil a bad habit (Chi) (50:19)

moqbiaol a flying horse

=moq, byul= a spirit priest

moqcav reins for a horse (9:114)

moqcaoq for a 'divining stick' to land flat on the bottom, round on the top when thrown to the ground (see also: **silteil**)

moqcaoq caoq to lie on one's stomach (9:113) (or) **wuqbiavq biavq**

moqceil horse feed (9:114) (mah˯ dza˅)

moqceil badu horse feed-bag

moqceil moqzal the food that is offered to the horse which **Hhoqzyuq aqpyuq** rides down from the sky

moqcei horse cart (B=Chi) (mah˯ la^ law˯)

=moq, col= old person

-- moq, colmoq -- to get old; get on in years

=moq, da= father's OBs and their spouses

moqdev Chinese yam, planted or wild (9:114, 13:4, 46:108)

-- moq, devmoq -- to go through the motion of

chopping

-- moq, diqmoq -- to go through the motion of hitting

moqdol a 'bad-omen' horse (in the sense that a bad-omen is connected with it)

moqdol diqduq the place where a bad-omen horse is killed

moqdol duv for a bad-omen horse to occur

moqdo a castrated horse

moqdo do to castrate a horse

moqdoq doq to use a horse now and pay the owner later

moqdyuv water weeds

moqfaf exemplary; a model (as model village, citizen, etc.) (Chi) (9:114, 26:100, 41:4) (or) **diei'faf** (Chi)

Moqfaf Goqqil tuaqyeiq Model Youth League Member (26:101) (or) **Moqfaf Gaofqil tuaqyeiq**

moqgevq a black and white horse (46:196)

moqgov a thin horse

moqhaoyeiv a flowery design to put on a horse's head (9:114)

moqheiq wooden shoes; bamboo shoes (clf. **zaol**) (11:76)

=moq, heiq= twin sons (plus 2 other ways of saying)

=moq, hol= a religious ceremony

moq hollol pony bells; horse bells (14:125) (mah˯ ja˅ cu˅)

moq huvq horse year (9:114) (mah˯ ti˯ k'o˰)

moqhhaq naq a festival held after spring cultivation when farm tools and farm animals are to rest; on horse day **miaoqhhaq naq; niaqhhaq naq** = the latter is from the Yeche dialect in Honghe

moqhhav a frame for pack saddle (B=Chi) (9:114) (mah˯ k'a^ da˯)

moqhhav qeivkeel frame and pack saddle set (mah˯ k'a^ da˯)

moqhhav qiq zuvq a harness set for horses

moq jalsoq horse halter (B=Chi)

moqkeel the back leg of a horse

moqkuv a stable for horses (9:114) (mah˯ mah˯ ku^)

moqkuv kuv to stable a horse (mah˯ ku^ ka˰-eu)

moq kuv moq luv very old people or animals

Moqlal sseilzeq a man's name (14:170)

moqlavq the front leg of a horse

moqlaolbiaq a horse's mane

moqlevq levq zavq to lie to someone so as to cheat them (or) **hheivq; javqhheivq hheivq**

moqleiq yil to go trading (with horses)

moqleiq zaq to trade by using horses

moqleiv leiv to be a dwarf (or) **alleiv leiv** (leh˅ ti = semi-taboo for Akha)

moq li a person has died (a polite way of saying it)

moq li e peilhaoq yoja 1. a shroud for a dead person, 2. new clothes for an older person's burial

moqloq a feeding trough for horses (or) **moqzal hoqloq** (mah˯ dza˅ k'aw˅ law˯)
moqma a mare (female horse) (mah˯ ma)
=moq, ma= first mother
=moq, meiq= chin whiskers
moq meiq laosiil a tutor; teacher; teaches to do some special work (B=Chi) (50:34) (see: **miaoq meiq laosiil**)
moqmiq a horse tail (46:157) (mah˯ daw˯ mi˯)
-- moq miq, tyuq -- to point out to someone
moq miaoq to make funeral arrangements (50:213)
moq moqgov a thin horse (11:36) (mah˯ yaw jeh)
  moq moqkuv a horse stable (11:36) (mah˯ mah˯ ku^)
=moq, naol= a stool
moq nao horse day (mah˯ ti˯ nah)
moq nei stretching out hand and pointing
moqnil sweet potato (9:114, 11:37) (mah˯; mah˯ coe˅) (and see: **moqqul**)
  moqnil cavni a tendril of sweet potato plant (9:114)
  moqnil juma sweet potato (mah˯ coe˅ ne˅)
moqnieiq woolen cloth (Chi)
moqniuq horses and cattle
  moqniuq taoldei maq sal not to have many horses and cattle
=moq, niuq= old buffalo/cow
=moq, ngaq= an old fish; a mature fish
moqpaq a male horse (mah˯ pa˯)
moqpaq laqsal a praying mantis (insect) (9:114) (mah˯ pa˯ tsa˅ tseh˯ etc.)
moqpil a spirit priest, one who is chosen by the spirits to be a go-between for them and humans. He has important functions in various ceremonies, especially those dealing with soul calling, driving out spirts, healing and funeral rites (or) **pilma** (35:75, 46:144); **byulmoq; pil** (pi˅ ma)
  moqpil galma meiq for a spirit priest to 'teach the way' to the soul of a dead person (boe˅ maw˯ ga˅ ma meh˯-eu)
  moqpil pilma spirit priest (35:75) (pi˅ ma)
  moqpil se lal to 'become' a spirit priest
  moqpil soq for a spirit priest to lead in a special ceremony (see: **hhaoldao soq**)
  moqpil tul for a spirit priest to repeat spirit incantations (cf.: neh˰ to˅ to˅-eu)
moqpiul a white horse (46:196) (mah˯ pyu˅)
moqpuv puv for a horse to roll on its back in the dust (9:114) (cf.: mah˯ po^ po^-eu)
moqqao qao to crawl (9:115) (joe-eu; ci˅ joe joe-eu = on stomach)
  moqqeiv a horse load of goods (13:31) (a rough measure) (cf. **niuqqeiv** = a pack-oxen load) (mah˯ ti˯ taw˯; mah˯ ti˯ da˯)
moqqil husbands of younger sisters (brothers-in-law) (oe˅ k'a˯)

moq qiq huvq horse year (mahˬ tiˬ k'o˰)
moq qiq nao horse day (mahˬ tiˬ nah)
moq qiq zeq horse hour (C=Chi)
moqqul sweet potato (6:168) (and see: **moqnil**) (mahˬ coeˇ; mawˬ coeˇ)
moqqul laolbyuq byuq to carry an animal by the nape of the neck (as cats do)
=moq, saqhav hav= old forest
moqseq front tooth; incisor tooth (lit., 'horse tooth') (juiˇ)
moqseil insects that bother horses (mahˬ shehˇ)
moqseiq horse hoof (9:115) (mahˬ kuiˇ sehˬ)
  moqseiq bavq to raise a horse's hoof for cutting and shoeing
  moqseiq diq to shoe a horse; put a horseshoe on
  -- **moqseiq, piuldev** -- a type of silver bullion which looks like the hoof of a horse
  moqseiq yeiq to cut a horse hoof so as to shoe the horse (mahˬ sehˬ yehˬ-eu)
moqsiq arrowhead plant (9:115)
  moqsiq siqnav black arrowhead plant (9:115)
-- **moqsiq, sivqluv** -- a sharpening stone (older term = **siqluv**)
=moq, soq= an old tree; old people
moqsuq magic (Chi) (or) **faq** (Chi)
moqssa biaq a kind of bee (cf.: byaˬ)
moqssaq a colt; a young horse (mahˬ zaˬ)
Moqssaq the name of a person (38:35)
=moq, ssaq= old people
moqtaol taol to live alone; singly
moqtoqceil motorcycle (Chi-Eng) (50:118)
-- **moq, tyuq** -- to point to something
moqxiq horse dung (mahˬ ceˬ; mahˬ ca˰)
moqxiq diqhhoq a type of small bean
Moqxuv a twin boy's name in Hani story (the other twin is: **Hholhhel**) (35:72)
moqyal fields for dead people (land marked off for the dead to work) (46:160)
=moq, yaq= a sacrifice (as a buffalo) as part of the burial ceremony
Moq'yul one ancestor of the Hani people (**Moq'yulzyuq; Zyuqtaoqpaoq** etc.) (11:218)
Moqyyul a supernatural addressed along with Hhelhovq in certain ceremonies
Moqzal a person's name (35:24)
moqzal horse food (mahˬ dzaˇ)
  moqzal hoqloq horse's feeding trough (or) **moqloq; hoqloq** (mahˬ dzaˇ k'awˇ lawˬ)
  moqzal yeiq to cut horse food (mahˬ dzaˇ yehˬ-eu)
moqzavq horseshoe (B=Chi) (11:31) (or) **mavqzavq** (Chi)
moqzaol a bridge over a river (57:141)
Moqzeq a person's name
moq zeq horse hour (in the time system) (B=Chi)
Moqzeq haolgaoq a mountain in Honghe (46:172)
moqzei nei 1. unexpectedly (35:15) (maˬ noeˬ gaˇ), 2.

languidly (35:15)
=moq, ziiq= a riding horse
moq ziiq to ride a horse (13:4) (mah⌄ dzi⌄-eu)
moq ziiq seivseiv a horse-riding game

(vb) movq to want (vb) (9:115, 41:155) (... maw^-eu)
(vb) movq will be; about to be (**Ngal gaolzoq aol e niq huvq biao lal movq al.** I have been working for almost two years - i.e., it 'wants' to be two years - 41:50)
movq ssa to hope to; to expect to (**hhaq bi bo lal movq ssa** = to hope to strengthen - 46:103) (noe⌄ tm⌄-eu)

mofdyufhueiq name of a type of weed (Chi) (14:159)

MU

mul to coax; entice; lure; cajol (muˇ-eu)
-- **mul, bee** -- to inveigle to come to one's home
mulhuvq a large bowl (clf., **huvq**) (11:33) (k'm⌄ ma⌄ ma⌄ ma)
mul luv meiv leiv to pile up in a disorderly fashion so it will fall over easily; shaky; not firm
=mul, mal= sterile female horse, buffalo, cow
-- **mul, miavmul** -- to be dizzy
=mul miav laq seiq nei, miav= to be dizzy and have poor eyesight
-- **mul yiuvq, aqnil** -- to lull a child to sleep
mul zaq to coax; entice; lure (muˇ-eu)
mul zaq duv to get out of something by lying; or by luring someone

mu 1. to be insane; mad (**colmu mu** = a mad person), 2. for one's head to be dizzy (9:115) (cf: **mul; mu**) (1. tsawˇ u⌄, 2. u⌄ du⌄ mo⌄ mo⌄-ehˇ g'eh-eu)
mu unit of land measurement (0.0667 hectares) (Chi)
=mu, aqkeeq keeq= a mad dog
-- **mu, aqmu** -- to be dizzy
-- **mu, aqmu lalmu** -- to feel dizzy
=mu, col= a mad, insane person
-- **mu, colmu** -- a person to go mad; insane
-- **mu, diq** -- to hit & make woozy
-- **mu, dol** -- to get drunk ('drink crazy')
-- **mu, keeqmu** -- dog to go mad; rabid
mu'laovq laovq to be mad and feel faint
mu lu meiv leiv to be teetering; not firm (yaw^ yaw^-ehˇ)
mu'luq 1. a movie, 2. a performance (Chi) (13:11) (or) **mollu**
-- **mu, milmu** -- 1. to lose one's way, 2. to lose one's direction in forest
-- **mu, samu** -- to go mad, crazy
-- **mu, yiuvqmu** -- to sleepwalk

muqbiaol aim (Chi) (34:17)
muqdiq aim; purpose (Chi) (34:1)
muqluq contents (as of a book) (Chi) (50:119)
muqma a vaulting horse (Chi)
=muq, miav= lower eyelid
Muqtavq a dialect of Hani spoken by those living on Naliang mountain in Jinghong county, Xishuangbanna Aut. Prefecture
muqxal a type of tree (Chi) (50:119)
Muqyeiqzii a salt pit in the vicinity of **Oltol Tavqzaoq** (Dazhai) village (35:67)

muv disorderly (yaw bah$_\vee$ yaw lah$^\vee$)
muv to shrink (shu$_\wedge$-i$^\vee$-eu)
=muv, haq= fine bamboo strips
muv luv meiv leiv piled up so as to fall easily
muvyav nei very disorderly (ti$_\vee$ paw$_\wedge$-i$_\vee$ ma$_\vee$ shaw)

muvq to droop (as rice ears) (46:161) (**Ceil wuqduq ya muvq** = The rice ears droop -- as when very ripe.)
muvq to bow the head (9:115) (u$_\vee$ du$_\vee$ m$^\vee$ mo$_\wedge$-eu)
muvq to weed (9:115) (mo$_\wedge$-eu; ya$^\vee$ mo$_\wedge$ mo$_\wedge$-eu)
-- **muvq, deiq** -- to bend down; hang down (as head)
muvq nei to nod (one's head) (tah$_\vee$-eu)
muvqquq to close or shut one's mouth (35:92) (or) **muvqquvq** (m$^\vee$ cu$_\wedge$-eu)
muvqquvq to close or shut one's mouth (or) **muvqquq** (k'a$_\vee$ meh m$^\vee$ cu$_\wedge$-eu)
-- **muvq, taoq** -- to bend down
-- **muvq, wuqduq taoq** -- to bow the head down
-- **muvq, xalmuvq** -- to weed a field (and see below - **yalmuvq**)
-- **muvq, yalmuvq** -- to weed a field (and see above **xalmuvq**)
muvq zil to aim (as a crossbow) (11:216) (maw$_\vee$-eu)

MYU

Myuqzii Miao (Hmong) group of people (57:99); **Miaoqzii**

NA

nal to be ill; sick; hurt; in pain; ache (9:116) (or) **gol** (naᵛ-eu)
(vb) **nal** to be wounded (**diq nal** = wounded by a blow; **bev nal** = wounded by a bullet, etc.)
=nal, al= sore; ulcer
-- **nal, alnal** -- 1. for a sore to develop, 2. a running sore, 3. a skin ulcer
nalbaoq the nose (8:30, 9:116) (naᵛ mehᵛ)
-- **nalbaoq, aqhhavq** -- pig snout (or) **nalbyuq**
nalbaoq peelsuq nei gloomy; dejected (50:75)
nalbiav 1. the nostril (naᵛ mehᵛ naᵛ byoe), 2. a flat nose (naᵛ mehᵛ yaw bya˯)
nalbiavq a nose disease
nalbiol a scar (maᵛ byaw˄) (see also: **nalheiq**)
nalbuvq a pockmark on one's face (as from smallpox) (11:28)
-- **nal, byulnal** -- to suffer from some pestilence
nalbyu the nostril (naᵛ mehᵛ naᵛ byoe)
nalbyu daol 1. to breathe well (the nose is open) (naᵛ mehᵛ pah-eu), 2. to be bright
nalbyuhao nasal hair (or) **nalmeilhao**
nalbyu maq daol 1. for one's nose to be stuffed up (naᵛ mehᵛ tsoe˯-eu), 2. to think only of oneself
nalbyuq pig snout (or) **nalbaoq** (meh˯ boe˯)
nalbyuq scab (maᵛ naᵛ g'aw)
-- **nalcal, piaqyiq aqma** -- type of civet (a cat-like mammal) with white nose
nalcav a nose rope for cattle & buffalo (9:116) (naᵛ ca^)
nalcavq bad diseases; bad sicknesses (46:132)
=nal, col= a sick person
=nal, cyuq= to have a cold
nalcyuq cyuq for one's nose to be stuffy (9:116) (naᵛ mehᵛ tsoe˯-eu)
=nal, diq= to inflict pain by hitting (di˯ naᵛ-eu)
naldul dul 1. it appears to be, seems to be (12:126, 41:95) (duᵛ-eu; duᵛ leᵛ-eu), 2. to reveal something (as in one's bearing or attitude, as to show how tired one is - 26:95)
-- **naldul dul, qiq qa** -- (see full)
naldul meil to be likely (9:116, 41:95, 46:82)
-- **nal'eel, aqbeil** -- nasal discharge (na˯ behᵛ)
-- **nal, geeq** -- to have scabies
nalgol disease (9:116) (naᵛ gawᵛ)
nalgol bi sol to 'clean' (get rid of) diseases
nalgol faq to get a disease (B=Chi) (26:24) (naᵛ gawᵛ la^ nyaw˯-eu)
nalgol hu li go to see a doctor
nalgol kaq lal for sickness to get better (naᵛ-eu ma˯ gaᵛ laᵛ-eu˯)

nalgol nalniei to be weak; sick; feeble (9:116)

nalgol peiv huvq lal to have a relapse of a former illness

nalgol peil lal to become sick again (paˇ naˇ po^) laˇ-eu)

nalgol pieiq to cause a disease or some other serious problem in some person by means of black magic (or) **neivqhaq pieiq**

-- **nalgol, qaqgol** -- diseases

nalgul a high nose

nalhaq 1. to ask; question; interrogate (9:116; 50:192) (naˇ haˬ-eu), 2. to listen (9:116), 3. to obey (naˇ haˬ geu‸-eu)

nalhaq laovq saq to be attracted to someone's speech; to be astonished at what they say (57:85)

nalhaq sal e nice sound; sounds nice (8:19) (naˇ haˬ muiˬ-eu) (cf. Lahu: na sha ve)

nalhaq tiq question and answer drills (B=Chi)

nalhavq a broken nose

nalheiq a scar (9:116) (see also: **nalbiol**) (clf.: heiq) (maˇ byaw‸)

=nal, hhavq= swine fever

nalhhov a scab (maˇ naˇ maˇ g'aw)

-- **nal, kalnal** -- crops to have diseases

nalkaq to recover from sickness (naˇ-eu taˬ leˇ-eu)

nal kyuq to be very ill (26:3) (naˇ seh‸ taˬ-eu)

nal leil he'qivq to have a tingling sensation

nallao the same (11:202) (lo‸-ehˇ)

nalmeil nose (9:116) (naˇ mehˇ)

nalmeilhao (or) **nalbyuhao** nasal hair (naˇ mehˇ bahˬ ca‸ hm)

=nal, mil= a cat disease (aˇ miˇ naˇ gawˇ)

-- **nal, miavnal** -- to be jealous (mya^ na^ na^-eu)

-- **nal, miav'qil** -- 1. eye disease, 2. to envy someone

-- **nal, neema** -- 1. to envy another, 2. for the heart to be ill, 3. to feel sorry (as for a person with a broken arm)

nalnil red nose (46:139) (naˇ mehˇ yaw neˇ)

=nal, niaoq= (see full)

=nal, niuq= buffalo/cattle plague

nalniuv a kernel (as a kernel if corn etc.) (50:70)

-- **nal, povq** -- lung disease

nalpuv to have a relapse in a sickness (14:154) (naˇ po^-eu)

nal sil e to die of sickness (12:127) (naˇ seh‸-eu)

nalsyuv syuv for something to irritate the nose, such as the odor of burning chili (naˇ mehˇ su‸-eu)

nal sso al ngaoq if (they) get the disease (10:1) (**sso** has meaning of 'getting') (naˇ gawˇ nyawˬ leˇ-eu)

-- **nal, taoq** -- to be hurt; disabled (as by an accident)

nalteiq nalcal serious and sudden diseases (15:7)

-- **nal, wuqpeel** -- to have a disease of the scalp
-- **nal, wuqpieil** -- to have an enlarged spleen
-- **nalxiq, aqbeil** -- nasal mucous (the dry type)
-- **nalyov nei, neema** -- sadly
nalyyuq the bridge of the nose
nalzu the tip of the nose (na$^{\vee}$ meh$^{\vee}$ meh$_{\vee}$ dza$_{\vee}$)
-- **nal zu meil, meiqzu** -- for all to talk at once

(vb) **na** willing to (vb) (**maq nalhaq na** = not willing to listen) (**yil na** = willing to go down) (45:58) (cf.: maw$_{\wedge}$-eu)
(vb) **na** permit to (vb); to allow to (vb) (**maq bi bazaq na** = not permit him to go with the group - 11:198) (bi (vb))
-- **naaq, maq** -- or; if not (ma$_{\vee}$ ngeu$^{\vee}$ na$^{\vee}$)
naciq medicine (9:115) (ja^ g'a$_{\vee}$) (cf. Lahu: na^ tsuh$^{\vee}$)
naciq aqbol male doctor (6:174) (sa$_{\vee}$ la$_{\vee}$ g'o$_{\vee}$, maw$_{\vee}$-aw$^{\vee}$)
naciq aqpiq woman doctor (sa$_{\vee}$ la$_{\vee}$ g'o$_{\vee}$ ma)
naciq bivq to give medicine (ja^ g'a$_{\vee}$ bi dza$_{\vee}$-eu)
naciq ciqyaol a hospital
naciq cov to inject medicine (ja^ g'a$_{\vee}$ tsaw^-eu)
naciq dol to drink medicine
-- **naciq, hhaqsiil** -- alum powder
naciq jahhaq a medicinal plant (herb; grass)
naciq maq ciq 1. not effective medicine, 2. nothing to it (doq'eil naciq maq ciq = his words are not effective; have no value) (57:133)
-- **naciq, neesal** -- a sedative; tranquilizer
naciq sal li go to see a doctor
naciq sov to rub on medicine (as ointment)
naciq zaol paoq to compound medicine (50:128)
nadul dul to be alike; look alike (57:91)
=na, gaq= to love (ga$_{\vee}$-eu)
=na, hhoq= not very (vb)

naq (fp) affirmative ending particle (**Xilmeil ngeel wul naq.** Okay, it's like this. **Zeif maq yiuvq e ngaoq neesoq maq tul lal qaol wul naq.** Again, if we don't sleep now we won't be able to get up tomorrow. 41:38)
naq stop; rest (9:118) (na$_{\vee}$-eu)
naq south (Chi) (6:161) (la$_{\wedge}$ o^ paw)
naqba gaq lal to hear about; to get wind of (or) **hha gaq** (na$_{\vee}$ ga$_{\vee}$-eu)
-- **naqbiaq, ceiljil** -- (see full)
naqbol ear (9:118) (na$_{\vee}$ baw$^{\vee}$)
naqbol biav nei listening carefully
-- **naqbol, daoqma** -- a type of mushroom
naqbol deiq biav alnei nallhaq to listen with one's full attention ('lift up your ears and listen') (cf.: na$_{\vee}$ baw$^{\vee}$ nyi$_{\vee}$ pyaw$_{\vee}$ lu$_{\wedge}$)
naqbol deiqtul to raise its ears (as a cat or dog)
naqbol diqhal not to listen or obey (as to be

disobedient to parents, teachers)

naqbol maq daol dislike to receive advice from others ('no hole in the ear') (ehˇ daw˯ ma˯ naˇ ha˯)

naqbol naqbyu the ear canal (na˯ bawˇ na˯ byoe)

naqbol naqhaoq (see: **naqhaoq**)

naqbol naqpavq for part of the ear to be missing (na˯ yeh˯ yeh˯-eu)

naqbol tao to pierce ears (when about four or five do this to the girls, fear if don't do then after death the spirits will make big holes with huge tools) (na˯ bawˇ na˯ tahˇ tahˇ-eu)

naqboq deaf (9:118, 11:28) (na˯ baw˯)

naqboq boq to be deaf (na˯ baw˯ baw˯-eu)

=naqboq, haqzal= a sparrow-like bird

-- naqboq, pilma -- large type of chili pepper

naqbuv south (Chi) (14:169)

naqbuvq pus in the ear

naqbyu ear canal (na˯ bawˇ na˯ byoe) (and see: **naqhaoq**)

-- naq, ceilnaq -- (see full)

-- naqdoq, doqnaq -- a two-part allegorical saying

naqduq a resting place (46:168) (na˯ du˯)

naqfal south (Chi) (26:34) (cf.: la˰ o^ paw)

naqgaq news; something one hears about (na˯ ga˯)

naqgaq buvqssaq a newspaper reporter (50:80)

naqgaq buvqssaq doqzil cavq a press conference (50:80)

nawgaq gaqniaol short news (50:83)

naqgaq xa to report the news (50:8)

naqguv 1. to frighten someone, or be frightened by someone (9:119, 13:20) (la^ gu^-eu), 2. to bully someone

naqguv duv **to extort a confession by torture (50:189)**

naqhaoq ear canal (na˯ bawˇ na˯ byoe) (and see: **naqbyu**)

naqhaoq haoq to be noisy; disturb others with noise (law˰ g'a so^ g'a-eu)

naqhevq an ear spoon (to take out ear wax)

-- naq, hhaqnaq -- to take a rest (stop doing)

naqhhaq nei 1. surprisingly (13:12), 2. frighteningly (33:3)

naqhhaq sav nei to be overwhelmed by an unexpected favor (35:43); to be very surprised; unexpectedly (or) **naqhhaq sav nei** (35:43)

naqhhaoq 1. a loop (as in a vine swing), 2. a link

Naqjil Nanking (Chi)

Naqjiq South Pole (Chi)

-- naq, jolnaq -- to have a holiday; festival day

naqjul earring (9:119) (na˯ sawˇ, na˯ za)

-- naqjul, alhhe -- (see full)

naqkyul bright mind (50:108)

=naq, laq= handle (as for a cup)

-- naq, moqhhaq -- (see full)

naqneil top of a tree (34:4) (a˅ baw˅ u˯ du˯)
-- **naqneil, albol** -- top of a tree
naqnei astonishing; amazing (50:89)
-- **naq, niaqhhaq** -- (see full)
naq pa naqnei surprised; amazed (50:89)
naqpavq the ear (outer) (9:119) (na˯ pa˄)
-- **naqpavq, naqbol** -- for part of ear to be missing
naqpeiq 1. the temple of the head (9:119), 2. the upper part of a bed where the pillow is (**hhaoqzao naqpeiq** - 41:32)
naqseil ssuv terrified; have great fear (45:64)
naqsiq the earlobe (or) **naqwuv** (na˯ pa˄)
naqtaoq to be hard of hearing (na˯ tah˯)
naqteil xa to warn; caution; admonish (50:91)
naqtul to be stubborn; to be pigheaded; willfull ('thick ear')
naqwuv earlobe (or) **naqsiq** (na˯ pa˄)
Naqxil the Naxi (people) (10:pref.)
Naqxildoq the Naxi language (10: pref.)
naqxiq earwax

nav black (9:119) (yaw na^)
Nav a shortened form for Navssaq (when speaking of the Han Chinese in some proverbs)
=nav, ceil= purple glutinous rice
=nav, ceiv= wild goat
=nav, haq= soot
navhaoqnei blackish; darkish; darkness (9:119, 11:56, 50:76) (na^ gaw ni; na^ k'a˄ ni)
navhaoq haoqma very dark (11:59) (na^ gaw ni)
navhaoqnei nav very dark (11:59) (na^ gaw ni)
navhaoq pa haoqnei very black; dark as a pocket (11:56, 45:42) (na^ caw˄ ni; zah˅ tsui ni)
=nav, hoqniaoq niaoq= purple glutinous rice
=nav meil, xil= this much
=nav, miuvq= gibbon
navnav nei very black (11:57) (yaw na^ na^)
=nav, niaoq= glutinous purple rice
=nav, ollol eel= a black viper
nav'qovq nei jet black (11:57)
nav'qovq pa qovq nei very black (11:59) (na^ caw˄ ni)
navso nei blackish (9:120)
navssul pa ssul nei a crowded, dark area (here a path) (35:50)
=nav, teiq= paint
=nav, yal= new fields (ya˅ na^)

navq to be deep (9:119) (na˄-eu)
navq early (9:119, 46:185) (yaw na˄)
navqcaoq to be stuck (or) **yanevq**
navqguv to frighten someone (54:175)
navq nei 1. earlyish (yaw na˄) (9:119), 2. deepish (9:119) (na˄ sui˅ ni)

navq navq nei 1. earlyish, 2. deepish
navq pa navq nei 1. very early, 2. very deep
=navq, yal= deep terraced fields
navqyol nei very deeply (9:119, 11:63) (na‸ geu ni)
-- navq zo, seq navq yil -- to marry too young
navqyol pa yol nei to be very, very deep (as the sea)

NAO

naol to sniff (in order to smell something)
naol sisters (in proverbs, see also: **nilnaol**; **meilnaol**)
naol clf. for rice heads (**ceilnaol niq naol** = two ears of rice)
=naol, aqkeel keel= (see full)
=naol, aqlavq lavq= the back of the hand
naolba the background (as in a photo) (50:9)
=naol, bial= rib
=naol, byulssaq= human beings
naolcal sun's rays (9:116) (nahˇ tsaˇ)
naolcal hhaq solar energy (50:162)
naolcal yuqduq solar energy stove (50:162)
=naol, ceil= a head of rice
naolciivq a late generation
-- naol dav, ssaqnaol -- to become a youth (46:173)
naoldi di 1. to retreat; withdraw (as from a battle), 2. go back; back down, 3. can also be used for a car going in reverse - 26:98) (46:124) (ji^ g'o‸ le-eu) (cf. g'awˇ di^-eu = to retract)
naoldi di huvq to draw back (g'awˇ di^ k'o‸-eu)
naoldi maq tyul firm and unshakable (50:82) (C=Chi)
naoldiq the part of the plow to which the rope is fastened
naolgul a loom for weaving (saˬ nmˇ)
naolgul dalpav pedal of a loom
naolguq stool (of bamboo or rattan) (9:117, 46:134) (nuiˇ gawˬ; nuiˇ bo^)
naolhaol sil relieved; satisfied (nui k'ahˇ shiˇ-eu)
naolhao afterwards; later (9:117, 41:66) (naˇ k'ah; k'oeˇ naˇ)
naolhao aqnao meeqduq long-term interests (50:21)
naolhao hao'li at last; the very last; in the end (**naolhao hao'li qiq hhaq** = the very last person) (10:25, 13:2, 26:61, 46:169) (aˇ saˬ saˬ-eu)
naolhao hao'li tyul taq at last (mehˬ nah nah saˬ)
naolhao maq hhaq no end of trouble for the future (50:72)
naolhao naoq later ones; to be late (11:128) (mehˬ nahˬ nahˬ-eu)
naolhao nyuq saq fear of trouble back home; disturbance in the rear (50:72)
naolhao pyu behind; the back side (10:4); the last part (41:62) (mehˬ nah)
naolhaol pyu leiq to pursue; to follow after (mehˬ nah caw teh-eu)

naolhao qiq hhaq the next person
naolhao qiq mol the next one (general clf.)
naolhao qiq soq (nao) the next morning (day) (ni shaw˯ ti˯ shaw˯) (8:1, 12, 21)
naolhao xeiv to run after (meh˯ nah ceh^-eu)
naolhao ya duv qavq to drop to the rear

naol hu to look behind (naˇ k'ah haw-eu)

naol hu to try to smell (9:117) (beh˰ la˰-eu)
naolhu hu to smell out (as dog, cat) (13:20)

-- naol hu, siq hu -- to look back and forth

naolhhaol in the daytime; afternoon (46:90)
naolhhaol hhaollu at noon (34:8) (nah lo^ ceh laˇ-eu; nah g'ahˇ)

naolhhuvq to be behind (26:63) (meh˯ nah˯ ga-eu)
naolhhuvq di to retreat
naolhhuvq puv to turn back (38:111) (nahˇ g'o˰ g'o˰-eu)
naolhhuvq zei puv turn head around to look back, behind (9:117, 26:63) (nahˇ g'o˰ g'o˰ haw-eu; meh˯ nah paw haw k'o˰ g'eh-eu)

=naol, kal= head of grain

naolkeel a sun's ray (14:182) (nahˇ ma a˯ kuiˇ)
-- naolkeel, naolma -- the rays of the sun

=naol, keel= top of the foot

=naol, lavq= back of the hand

Naollol Aqcaoq the Hani name for the Luo clan (Chi), which has historical relations to the Dai (as seen in the second part of their clan name)

naolma sun (9:117) (nahˇ ma)
naolma ba'la maq mol extreme hardship ('cannot see the sun and moon') (50:2)
naolma beeljoq a solar halo (50:143)
naolma beeljoq joq for a red halo to form around the sun (9:117)
naolma duhhoq sunflower (nahˇ ma nahˇ g'm; tah˯ pah˯ yeh^ ma)
naolma naolkeel the rays of the sun (14:236) (nahˇ ma nahˇ kuiˇ; nahˇ ma a˯ kuiˇ a˯ la˰)
naolma neivqkeeq zaq an eclipse of the sun (nahˇ ma kui˯ dza˯-eu) (9:117)
naolma qeiq the sun is setting (14:140) (nahˇ ma ga uˇ-eu)
naolma wuqcal sun's rays (nahˇ ma u˯ tsaˇ)
naolma xavq li qavq the sun sets and rests (cf.: nahˇ ma ga k'eh˯-eu)
naolma ya for the sun to set (nahˇ ma ga uˇ-eu)
naolma ya pyu the west (26:69) (nahˇ ma ga k'eh˯ paw)
naolma yaseil aqmeil the sun is setting beyond the western hills (50:143)
naolma ya sil miv nei tyul taq at the time when the sun goes down (nahˇ ma ga ahˇ-eu aˇ yam˯)

=naol, meil= 1. siblings (born of same parents), 2. fellow countrymen

naolmoq a stool; a chair; a seat (29:4, 50:5) (nuiˇ

gaw⌄)

naolnieil a loom (or) **naolgul** (11:210) (sa⌄ nmˇ guˇ)

naolngaoq only (9:117, 10:3) (**niq massaq naolngaoq** = only mother and son - 13:53) (**qiq zal naolngaoq maq bivq qivq** = I can give you only one ticket - 41:209) (teh^; teh^-ehˇ)

naol puv alhuvq for a new year to 'turn over' (for the new year to arrive) (50:75)

=naol saqyyuq, daoq= pelvis

naolteev 1. the back of one's head, 2. a basic, foundation (9:117) (or) **daoqpeiq** (daw⌄ peh⌄)

naolteil stool; bench (46:201) (or) **daoqteil** (nuiˇ gaw⌄; nuiˇ bo^)

naoltovq tovq to tie from the back (as to tie someone's hands behind them) (naˇ k'ah pa^ taw^-eu)

naolzao stool (9:117) (nuiˇ gaw⌄; nuiˇ bo^; k'aw⌄ bo^)

naol zei meil zei to throw back (13:48)

nao to choke (dawˇ nga^-eu)

nao day (nah)

nao clf. for a day (nah)

=nao, bo= birthday

nao buvq soqkaoq a diary book (50:143)

naocil aollivq night and day; around the clock (50:143) (or) **aoqzaq aol bia**

naogo with (13:1) (neh⌄-ehˇ)

-- **nao, ha** -- chicken day

-- **nao, haqlaq** -- tiger day

naohav a 'hard' or 'strong' day (such as: **haqlaq; toqla; hu; niuq; yol**), days on which spirit priests will perform spirit incantations (**neivq tul**)

-- **naohav, yeiqnao** -- just today

naohaoq if (**Xilmeil ngeel naohaoq** = if it is like this) (ngeuˇ naˇ)

-- **nao, hu** -- rat day

=nao, huq= day before yesterday

naohhaol daytime (9:116) (nah g'ahˇ) (and see: **naolhhaol**)

naohhaol hhaoldao daytime

naohhaol hhaollu noon; middle of the day (26:42) (nah lo^ ceh laˇ-eu)

=nao, jol= holiday

=nao, kaqla ma= daily

=nao, kaoq= (see full)

-- **nao, keeq** -- dog day

-- **nao, laoq** -- dragon day

nao'lao lao to observe a religious holiday; **nee'lao lao**

naomeeq an auspicious day; a propitious day; a lucky day (nah mui⌄)

=nao, mil= yesterday

-- **nao, miuvq** -- monkey day

-- nao, moq -- horse day

-- nao, niuq -- buffalo/cow day

nao pal la pal change with each passing day (50:143)

nao pav half a day (**Nao pav ssuq e galma jav nga siq.** It is still half a day's walk from here. 41:159) (nah pa^)

nao'qivq tomorrow evening (9:118) (ni shawˬ uˬ ci‸)

-- nao, sallal -- the day-after-the-day-after tomorrow

=nao, seil= snake day

naosoq tomorrow (or) **neesoq** (ni shawˬ; nui shawˬ)

=nao, toqla= rabbit day

naotyul a calendar (50:143)

naoziil brain (Chi) (iˇ nm‸; uˇ nm‸)

naoq 1. small amount; rare (**zaq e liq naoq** - 10:15, 46:129), 2. soft; fresh (9:118) (nahˬ)

naoq 1. part. of imperative (something like 'de' in Ak., a bit of politeness in it, but still imperative) (**nol salhu naoq** = you look, please - 11:135, 202) (similar to: **joq**), 2. part. for topicalizer (**Aqjulniq naoq = Aqjulniq aq**) (38:6) (**Ngaq e aqda naoq, saoldiq bajiq nga.** As for my FATHER, he is a blacksmith. 41:21) 3. a part. of mood (**Haqniq soqmiav naoq pilyil soqhhaq nga.** The Hani script is in pinyin letters. 41:75)

naoq press down with foot; stamp down (9:118) (nawˬ-eu)

naoq clf. for a kick or stomp of the foot

=naoq, aq= the kind of clay pregnant women sometimes eat (**milcaq aqnaoq**)

=naoq, aqdaol daol= a soft feather

-- naoq, aqkeel nei -- to stamp with one's foot

-- naoq, baolnaoq -- to stamp on dikes (bunds) of terraces when making new ones

naoqbao sabaol the last place a shaman visits when looking for a wandering soul, inhabited by people who died a 'bad death'

naoqbao xabao spirits from those who have died from guns

Naoqbeq a person's name (11:126)

naoqbo aqnil younger brother & sister (aˬ nyiˇ)

naoqca farm land (Chi) (50:122)

naoqcaq a farm (collective) (Chi) (26:26)

naoqcavq meil following closely (9:118) (dawˬ peh cah teh-eu)

naoqcev a tit (small kind of bird) (4:39)

naoqcev aqma a tit (small kind of bird) (4:39) (or) **kalyil aqma**

naoqcyul 1. the countryside (Chi) (34:6, 42), 2. a village (or) **puvkaq**

naoq deivq the last one (speaking of living things; see also: **huvq deivq; hhaol deivq**)

naoq duv to stamp out a path; road (with feet) (34:14) (nawˬ dahˇ-eu)

-- naoq, eelnaoq -- to walk in deep water (trudge)

naoqhaq agricultural bank (Chi) (50:122)

naoqhaq laqdul a kind of weed that looks like a bolt is coming out on top (a type of tea is made of the blossoms)

Naoqhyuf Peasant Association; farmer's association (Chi) (26:12, 50:122)

Naoqhyuf zuxiq chairman of the Peasant Association (26:13)

=naoq, hhokeeq keeq= young & fresh rice seedlings

naoqjilca agricultural processing factory (Chi) (50:122)

naoqjol sapievq ssaqmiq a type of spirit

naoqkoq to stamp on (with foot) (14:47)

naoq lal to become fewer; to be less; to reduce in number (26:36)

naoq leiq to stamp on the wrong place

naoqliq a lunar calendar (Chi)

Naoqliqjiq Farming-forestry Bureau (Chi) (41:197)

=naoq, mal= speculate; maybe

Naoqma aqmeil a place where the Hani people originally lived 'way up north' (35:96) (or) **Naoqma hhaqmeil**

=naoq, meil= soft type of walnut

naoqmil aqgee down south (la˄ o^ paw; cf.: dzaw˅ gui = downslope of house)

-- naoq, milhhaq -- to have a good relationship

naoqniq agriculture (Chi) (26:26, 50:122)

naoqniq gaolsseiq agricultural productive workers (Chi) (50:122)

naoqniq hoqzoqhuaf agricultural cooperative (Chi) (50:122)

naoqniq jilbei jeifseiq basic foundation for agriculture (Chi) (50:122)

naoqniq pyu agricultural sector (A=Chi) (26:100)

naoqniq qilhuaf agricultural areas (Chi) (50:122)

naoqniq syul agricultural taxes (Chi) (50:122)

naoqniq 8 miav xeiffaq the Eight-Point Words for agriculture: soil improvement, rational application of fertilizer, water conservancy, improved strains, rational close planting, plant protection, field management, and improvement of farm implements (AB=Chi) (50:122)

naoqniq zafxeif agricultural front line (Chi) (50:122)

naoqniq zaolxoq middle school for agricultural training (Chi) (50:123)

naoqniq zaoca ziiq total value of agricultural output (Chi) (50:123)

naoq nuv to stamp into pieces (38:23) (naw˅ nm^-eu)

naoq pieiv to trample on

naoqseil sesame seeds (9:118) (nm˄ si˅)

naoqsiq purple perilla (a type of round sesame, that is used when pounding glutinous rice to make rice cakes)

naoqssaq younger generation; descendents (46:161)
naoq ssaq miaq ssaq yaol paoq li the minority is subordinate to the majority and must follow (from a Chinese saying) (50:147)
-- naoq, ssaq -- to give birth
naoqteev maq hha not to have enough food to eat
naoqxo nei softly; tenderly (9:118) (yaw nah˯; nah˯ yu ni) (see also: **naoqxu nei**)
naoqxu soft (14:206) (yaw nah˯; nah˯ yu ni)
naoqxu nei softly; tenderly (35:29) (see also: **naoqxo nei**) (yaw nah˯; nah˯ yu ni)
=naoq, zaol= (see full)
naoqzeiq less (cui^ dzeh˯-eu)
naoqzov nei 1. freshly, as vegetables etc. (9:118) (nah˯ yu ni), 2. softly (11:18, 56), 3. spongy (or) **ovqdei; heimieiq nadul dul** (A=Chi)
naoqzov nei naoq 1. fresh and soft (11:59, 46:165), 2. weak and soft (as bones)
naovbaoq stockings (9:118) (naw^ bah˯)
naovbaoq baoq to wear stockings (naw^ bah˯ bah˯-eu)
naovdaoq sole of shoe (9:118)
naovpeiv peiv to wear shoes with one's feet just part way in

=naovq, ciivq= the spinal cord
=naovq, sseil= palm bark shoes

NE

-- necev, haolpuq -- gourd ladle

NEE

neelyahuvq next year (or) **nyulyahuvq** (na˯ ya˄ k'o˄)

-- neebaq, neenaoq -- timid ('soft hearted')
neebeiv green bean (9:120) (aˇ beh^; aˇ nui^)
neebeiv beivja cowpea (9:120) (nui^ coeˇ aˇ beh^)
neecev a ladle for fetching water (nyi cui^)
nee ceiv a determination; to determine (to do something) (50:93) (noe˯ tseh^-eu)
nee ceiv xa 1. dare to do something (jahˇ peu˯-eu), 2. decide to do something (35:73)
neeciiv festivals; festival days (26:112, 46:title)
neeciiv nee'la festival time (57:89)
needav the pit of the stomach (9:120)
-- needav dav, lavqma -- to be nauseous
needeq deq 1. to calculate, 2. to consider (9:120, 46:94, 50:171) (sawˇ dzm-eu; shaˇ noe˯ shaˇ sawˇ-eu)
needeq lal to be satisfied (deh^-eu; nui k'ahˇ shiˇ-eu)
needeq ssao lal have one's wish fulfilled; achieve one's wishes (50:144)

needeiq deiq to quarrel in hearts (35:19) (nui ma la$_{\wedge}$ k'oe$^{\vee}$ pyeh$^{\vee}$-eu)

needeiq maq deiq for the heart not to become angry (35:19) (nui ma ma$_{\vee}$ peh$^{\vee}$)

neegaq to love (11:28) (ga$_{\vee}$-eu)

neegaq maq tavq merciless; ruthless

neegaol bright; clever (yaw gah$^{\vee}$)

neegaoq kind of bean (9:120) (nui^ gah$_{\vee}$)

neeguq bean curd (9:120) (a$_{\vee}$ ci$_{\vee}$)

neeguq eelcal soybean milk (9:120, 10:33)

neeguq eeldeev salted bean curd

neeguq guqbuvq fermented bean curd (9:120)

neeguq guqpovq the residue from beans after making soybean milk

neehaol sil 1. to be satisfied (38:34) (nui k'ah$^{\vee}$ shi$^{\vee}$-eu), 2. to vent one's hatred (50:87) (see also: **naolhaol sil**)

neehaol silzav nei to be very satisfied (nui k'ah$^{\vee}$ shi$^{\vee}$ dui dui-eu)

neehovq chest (of body) (46:151) (k'ah$_{\vee}$)

neehha chest (of body) (8:30, 9:120) (k'ah$_{\vee}$)

-- **neehha, peilhaoq** -- (see full)

neehha saqyyuq breastbone; sternum

neehhaol daytime (6:164) (nah g'ah$^{\vee}$ nah ga^)

neehhaol hhaollu noon (nah lo^ ceh la$^{\vee}$-eu)

neehho bosom (k'ah$_{\vee}$)

-- **neehhuvq, neepeel** -- unfeeling; callous; grim; cold-hearted

neehhyul happily (9:120) (la$_{\vee}$ k'a$_{\vee}$ ceh$^{\vee}$ ta^ ni)

neejav meil 1. easily (33:3), 2. simply (9:120) (yaw aw$_{\vee}$ aw$_{\vee}$-eh$^{\vee}$)

neekaoq a misunderstanding; an estrangement

neekaoq jav to have a misunderstanding; estrangement (46:131)

neekaoq soq to give vent to personal spite; to get revenge

neekyul widsom; intelligence (50:213)

-- **nee'lav kol, neepuv** -- quick brain; quick reaction

nee'lao lao observe a religious day; a ceremonial day **nao'lao lao** (9:120, 46:132) (nah lah lah-eu)

nee'laoq daytime (18:26 - proverb) (or) **nao'laoq** (nah g'ah$^{\vee}$ nah ga^)

nee'li li to think; consider (noe$_{\vee}$-eu; sha$^{\vee}$ noe$_{\vee}$-eu)

neema 1. the heart (both the seat of emotions and the physical heart) (9:121), 2. the mind (in certain contexts (nui ma)

neema alyeiv yeiv very happy ('flowers bloom in one's heart') (13:16) (la$_{\vee}$ k'a$_{\vee}$ ceh$^{\vee}$ dui dui-eu)

neema bavq duv to be determined in one's heart; to set one's heart on doing (26:29; 57:141)

neema bel alert; sharp-witted (50:79)

neema beeq to be worried; anxious (9:121) (nui ma bym$_{\vee}$-eu; k'ah$_{\vee}$ lah$^{\vee}$-eu)

neema bia lil bia loq to be bright-hearted; happy

(50:65)
neema bia'loq nei hearts are happy (13:16)
neema buldeiq nei to be nauseated
neema cal to be impatient (or) **neema teiq; neema maq yeil nia; bacal**
neema cavq evil-hearted
neema cavqsiil siil 1. to test one's mind (35:59), 2. to test someone to see if they will be a good worker (50:96)
neema cei to show one's sympathy ('reach out with one's heart') (57:106)
neema ceiv a broken heart; discouraged; sad (50:3) (or) **neema qil; neema nee'qil qil ceiv** (nui ma caw^ seh^-eu)
neema coq heart to beat (nui ma ciˇ tahˇ tahˇ-eu; nui ma tsawˇ-eu) (10:25)
neema daol candid; straightforward ('straight heart') (50:163)
neema daoqdaoq maq bo never to feel satisfied ('no bottom to one's heart') (57:95)
neema deiq ssil to be crazy (46:103) (tsawˇ uˇ uˇ-eu)
neema deivq 1. to be careful about something (yahˇ-eu), 2. to work hard on something, 3. clever; smart; sharp; intelligent (50:79)
neema eil laol to console (9:121) ('speak warmth to the heart')
neema galdav 1. to be greedy; to want more (13:53), (mehˇ juiˇ juiˇ-eu), 2. to be eager for a better life
neema gav to be very sad; unhappy ('cold in heart') (13:1) (nui ma caw^-eu)
neema gav sil la to be sad in the extreme (13:1) ('cold heart to death') (nui ma caw^ seh^-eu)
neema gavyov nei coldly; sadly; to be disheartened; to be in low spirits (46:94)
neema geel very sad in one's heart ('heart is melting')
neema hhe lul dav to pull crazily (45:76)
neema hholqei luqduq diq aqmeil guv as frightened as if a drum was beating in his heart (26:23)
neema hhoqcil geel to be very sad (or) **neema ceiv** (nui ma caw^ seh^ taˇ-eu)
neema javduq ssivq to feel easy; comfortable in one's heart; at peace (nui ma yaw saˇ)
neema jil to be honest (27:12) (yaw sui yaw dawˇ)
neema jivqyal aol to consider seriously (35:86) (cf.: shaˇ noeˇ k'a^ le^-eu)
neema juq to cool off from anger (nui pehˇ shu^-iˇ-eu)
neema kev to make someone excited (50:55) (or) **bi qeq**
neema kev nei heartfelt; deep; profound
neema kyuq to be unhappy (11:218); to feel regret

(50:3)

neema lal to be satisfied (41:151) (nui k'ahˇ shiˇ-eu)

neema laqhyul in one's heart (12:126) (nui ma la‸ k'oeˇ)

neema laol to be interested in something; to be happy about something ('heart to be warm') (26:34)

neema laolcyu nei (vb) warmheartedly (as in: warmheartedly said.... - 26:40) (nui ma yaw lmˇ)

neema laolsil for the heart to warm up; to be encouraged (14:218) (nui ma lmˇ laˇ-eu)

neema luq to feel satisfied; feel one has enough (57:78)

neema maq cal patiently (not feel hurried) (35:62) (nui ma maˬ tsaˇ)

neema maq lal not satisfactory (38:34) (nui k'ahˇ maˬ shiˇ)

neema maq lal leil eil to complain

neema maq laovq meil to be clear-minded (50:133)

neema maq li dissatisfied (9:121) (nui k'ahˇ maˬ shiˇ)

neema maq luvq dissatisfied (14:161)

neema maq puv nia to be stubborn; won't change one's mind; a rigid way of thinking (or) **maq nyuq puv nia**

neema maq qil sso not to worry (26:42) (k'ahˬ maˬ lahˇ)

neema maq sal unhappy (9:121) (nui ma maˬ saˇ-eu)

neema maq sal maq hev to be unhappy; uncomfortable in one's heart (26:31) (nui ma maˬ saˇ-eu)

neema maq xeivq to be generous (nui k'ahˇ maˬ huiˬ)

neema maq xeivq haoq one must not be greedy (27:12) (nui k'ahˇ maˬ huiˬ k'mˬ)

neema maq yeil nia to be impatient (or) **neema cal; neema teiq; bacal** (nui ma maˬ jeˇ; nui ma maˬ mahˇ)

neema meeqdyul ideology and moral character (50:159)

neema meeq e col amiable person; good-hearted person (nui ma yaw muiˬ)

neema mol to be greedy ('long heart') (35:1, 45:75) (yaw lo‸ maˬ baw; nui k'ahˇ yaw huiˬ)

neema nal 1. to be 'heart-sick', 2. to envy someone, 3. to feel sorry (as for a person with a broken arm) (14:227) (cf.: nui ma naˇ-eu)

neema nalyov nei sadly (38:4) (nui ma cawˆ-eu)

neema nav'qovq nei evil people ('black-hearted') (26:5) (tsawˇ haˬ yaw doeˇ)

neema navq to be greedy; stingy; miserly ('deep heart') (57:131)

neema nee cavq a bad-hearted person (nui ma maˬ muiˬ; nui ma yaw g'o‸)

neema neehovq the indentation in the chest (just below the sternum or breastbone) (46:152)

neema nee meeq a kind person ('good-hearted')

(nui ma yaw mui⌄)

neema neesiq the heart (as an organ in the body) (nui ma si⌄)

neema neexeivq selfishness (50:219)

neema nee yul the former mind-set ('old heart') (nui ma yaw oeˇ)

neema neezaq lofty character and morals (50:24)

neema nyuq to show concern (or) **gueilxil** (Chi)

neema nyuq ceiv perseverance (50:72)

neema nyuq e taoqdav maq lal things go contrary to one's wishes

neema nyuq pal to change one's mind (nui ma noe⌄ paˇ-eu)

neema nyuq puv to change one's mind (57:115)

neema nyuq savq to have a bad conscience

neema pal change 'heart' (mind); correct one's emotions (13:21) (nui ma paˇ-eu)

neema peil to be angry (or) **civqpeiv** (nui ma pehˇ-eu)

neema pieiq to stop a job; take rest ('to release one's heart') (26:54)

neema piul to be frank; friendly ('white heart') (35:15) (nui ma yaw mui⌄)

neema puv to change one's mind (26:112) (nui ma po^-eu)

neema puv zaq to retreat; to turn away (26:44)

neema qil to break one's heart (or) **neema nee'qil qil ceiv; neema ceiv** (nui ma caw^-eu)

neema qilkuq nei to be worried (26:80) (nui ma bym⌄-eu; k'ah⌄ lahˇ-eu)

neema qil sil worried to death (14:221) (nui ma lahˇ seh‸-eu; k'ah⌄ lahˇ seh‸-eu)

neema qiq gao unity; solidarity (34:17) (nui ma ta‸-eu)

neema qiq siq meil (vb) to (vb) be of one heart with others (in unity) (26:39) (nui ma ti⌄ si⌄ teh‸-ehˇ)

neema qiq siq qiq li meil to apply one's self (or) **yoqhhaq hholmol kevq nei bivq**

neema qiq siq tavq with all one's heart; with one's whole heart (nui ma jiˇ ni)

neema salduq ssivq one's heart to be comfortable; to be satisfied (45:8) (nui ma leh^ ni)

neema salqiq peiv to be angry (38:7) (or) **neema salcivq peiv** (nui ma pehˇ seh‸-eu)

neema salza nei geeza peace talks (50:71)

neema ssil to be angry (45:24) (nui ma pehˇ-eu)

neema ssilpuq nei angrily (45:53)

neema tavq to have one heart; one mind (50:133)

neema tavq e yolqoq a bosom friend; close friend

neema teiq 1. in a hurry; impatient (or) **neema maq yeil nia; bacal; neema cal** (26:30), 2. to be worried (26:43) (nui ma teh⌄-eu; nui ma lahˇ-eu)

neema xao to be heavy-hearted (nui ma kah-eu)

neema xeivq to be a miser; to be stingy (33:3)

(or) **neexeivq** (yaw yui yui-eu; tsaw$^{\vee}$ tsi$^{\vee}$ tsi$^{\vee}$-eu)

neema ya laq to be kindly (57:94)

neema yeil to be patient; even tempered ('wide-hearted') (nui ma yaw je$^{\vee}$)

neema yeildao nei patiently (26:107); kind-hearted (13:21) (nui ma je$^{\vee}$ ni)

neema yomeeq to be good-hearted; good-natured (nui ma yaw mui$_{\vee}$)

neema yo'qul good-hearted ('heart is sweet') (13:40) (nui ma yaw mui$_{\vee}$)

neema yoxeivq xeivq to be miserly

neema za satisfied (9:121) (nui k'ah$^{\vee}$ shi$^{\vee}$-eu)

neema zaq good-hearted (50:188)

neema zuv nei deep feeling; deep love (50:149)

neemeeq lavqqivq to be kind-hearted and expert (50:200)

neemeeq neezaq virtue; moral excellence (50:114)

neenaoq neebaq timid ('soft-hearted') (50:144)

neenil 1. chicken spleen, 2. a type of green bean

neenil maq bo don't forget (without forgetting) (18:1) (ma$_{\vee}$ ngeh$^{\vee}$ ni)

neenil miaqcav a tough vine used for ploughing, and in making the village swing

nee nieil hawuv bi zaq an egg fed to a new mother to help her 'forget' the hardship of birth

neenyuq 1. what one thinks (45:92), 2. what one hopes, 3. one's opinion (nui noe$_{\vee}$)

neenyuq aolzaq mental work (50:120)

-- **neenyuq, galmol** -- long-range strategy

neenyuq meil willingly (**neenyuq meil yiv** = to go willingly) (13:2)

neenyuq nyuq za to think properly; thoughtfully

neenyuq hhaq tul inspire enthusiasm; encourage the spirit (50:209)

neenyuq wuqduq ideology

neepeel neehhuvq unfeeling; callous; grim; cold-hearted (50:104)

nee puv to reflect; to react (41:95)

nee puv nee la kol quick reaction; quick brain (45:21; 57:97, 120)

nee'qeil to be willing to do something

nee'qil the sternum

-- **neesal, haoqhhyu** -- confidence; faith

neesal hha optimistic (50:103)

neesal hha doqgaq an announcement (50:1)

=**nee salpeiq, gal**= in the future

neesaq saq to be sad in one's heart (26:4) (noe$_{\vee}$ sha$_{\vee}$-eu)

neesiq soy bean (9:121) (or) **neevsiq** (nui^ pya^)

neesiq the heart (as an organ in the body) (nui ma si$_{\vee}$)

neesoq tomorrow (or) **naosoq** (nui shaw$_{\vee}$; ni shaw$_{\vee}$)

neesoq aoqsoq tomorrow morning (ni shaw$_{\vee}$ u$_{\vee}$ shaw$_{\vee}$)

neesoq salpeiq in a few days (lit., 'tomorrow and

day-after-tomorrow') (45:10) (ni shawˬ saˇ pehˬ)
neesoq salsoq the day after tomorrow
neesuv to be disgruntled (nui ma yaw su˰; byeh laˇ-eu)
neesuvq suvq to be disgusted (9:121) (nui ma yaw su˰)
neessil angry (11:39, 13:20, 50:8) (nui ma pehˇ-eu)
neessil neehavq angrily; extremely angry (13:15, 27:12); indignation; wrath (50:50) (nui ma pehˇ seh˰-eu)
neetavq neezyul to be of one heart and mind (50:168) (nui ma ta˰-eu)
neetaoq taoq obstinate; stubborn (50:174)
neexeivq selfish; stingy (tsawˇ tsiˇ)
-- **neexeivq, neema** -- selfishness
neexeivq xeivq to be selfish; miserly; **neema yoxeivq xeivq** (tsawˇ tsiˇ tsiˇ-eu)
neexul agreeable (50:103) (nui ma tsaˬ-eu)
neeyul bavq teiq to keep the old ideas (conservative) (50:7)
-- **nee zyul, nee tavq** -- to be of one heart and mind

neev clf. for beans, grains (9:121, 11:74) (nui^; siˬ)
=neev, al= a bean; soybean
neevbyuq worm that eats beans (nui^ boeˬ)
neevceil a type of small bean
=neev, ceil= a rice grain
neevguq eelcal (see: **neeguq eelcal**)
=neev, hoq= a cooked rice grain
=neev, miav= the eyeball
neevnav a type of black bean (nui^ na^)
neevnil climbing green beans (46:96)
neev'quv bean sprouts (2:55) (nui^ pya^ nui^ ji)
neevseiv a type of green bean (nui^ nyoeˇ)
neevsiq 1. a seed; kernel; bean (nui^ siˬ), 2. soy bean (nui^ pya^)
neevsiq aqciq fermented soy bean (aˬ ciˬ)

neevq to drown (9:121) (nui˰ seh˰-eu)
neevq sil to die of drowning (nui˰ seh˰-eu)
-- **neevq, sulmil maq** -- a woman who has never married
-- **neevq, ya** -- to drown

NEI

nei with (9:122) (neh, as in: aˬ yaw˰ neh iˇ-eu = he went with him)
nei from (**Naoqbeq milnao Dolnia nei lal** = Yesterday **Naoqbeq** came from **Dolnia** = 11:126) (gaˇ neh)
nei a particle which indicates the actor involved in the action (**Ngaq nei zaq saq al**. I have eaten it all up.)
nei a particle which indicates what is used (**dalciilnei diq** = beat with a stick - 11:127)

nei a particle which follows adjectives and adverbs (**meeqnei aol** = to work well)
-- **nei, hhyuq** -- everywhere
nei kavq since...; from that time (41:159) (or) **neikavq'e** (11:202) (k'oeˇ naˇ)
nei lal laq e originated from (45:6)
-- **nei, mei** -- all
-- **nei, miaq** -- 1. many (g'awˬ mya ni), 2. too much
-- **nei, miav** -- same; equal
-- **nei, navq** -- 1. earlyish, 2. deepish
-- **nei, suv** -- (see in full)

neiq 1. pliable but strong, 2. durable (or) **neiqgu nei** (yaw nehˬ)
neiq to give someone something to eat (bi dzaˬ-eu)
-- neiq, bivq -- to supply
-- **neiq, deiq** -- (see full)
-- **neiq, eil** -- (see full)
neiqhe nei very big; large (g'awˬ loe ni)
neiqliq ability (26:119) (nya-eu)
neiqliaf energy (Chi) (50:121)
=**neiq, mil**= porcelain clay
=**neiq, poq**= malt sugar
neiq sil to kill by poison (34:58) (or) **duvq sil** (do˄ daw^ seh˄-eu)
neiqyeiq energy (such as workers, etc.) (50:121) (Chi)

neiv shaking (as a bamboo bridge) (zu^-eu)

neivq a spirit (or) **neivqhaq** (neh˄)
neivq beeq to be bothered by spirits (neh˄ guˬ-eu)
neivqdovq 'will-o'the-wisp'; phosphorescent light; ignis fatuus ('spirit lamp') (sha^-aˇ shiˇ-euˬ miˬ dzaˬ)
neivqguv neivqyav a medicine used to set broken bones
neivqhaq a spirit; a bad spirit (or) **neivq** (9:122, 45:64) (neh˄ k'aˬ; neh˄ dzeu^)
neivqhaq guq zaq to be taken by a spirit; possessed by a spirit (see: **ngeeq**)
neivqhaq he nei to be bold as a devil (spirit)
neivqhaq miaqdaol wild pineapple (9:122) (yaˇ seh˄ ka^ teh^)
neivqhaq miaol zaq lal for spirits to name a baby and take it away
neivqhaq mo'luq black magic; black art
neivqhaq neivqdovq will-o'-the-wisp (ignus fatuus) (or) **neivqdovq**
neivqhaq oqngyul egret (9:122) (uiˇ dzoeˬ yaw pyuˇ)
neivqhaq oq'a wild duck (9:122) (yaˇ saˬ gawˬ guˇ)
neivqhaq pieiq to perform black magic (or) **neivqhaq pieiq dov; nalgol pieiq**
neivqhaq tul to repeat spirit incantations (neh˄ toˇ toˇ-eu)

neivqhaq tul duv to drive away evil spirits by repeating spirit incantations (or) **neivqhaq tul zei**
neivqhaq tul zei to drive away evil spirits by repeating spirit incantations (neh˄ to˅ to˅ dzeh-eu)
neivqhaq zaol 1. to perform black magic (ja˯ neh˄ neh˄-eu), 2. to play tricks; make mischief (50:34), 3. to do a bad or evil thing (sometimes secretly) (35:6)
neivqhaq zeilngyul a swan
neivqkeeq the 'spirit dog' in the eclipse story
-- neivqkeeq zaq, naolma -- the eclipse of the sun
neivqkol kol to be speedy ('quick as a spirit') (50:150)
neivq leiq to drive out spirits from houses and the village
neivq leiq galtuv tuv the ceremony of driving out the spirits from houses and the village, ending at the village gate at the east or upper side of the village
neivq leiq zei to drive away evil spirits (or) neivq tul zei (neh˄ to˅ dzeh-eu; neh˄ teh dzeh-eu)
neivqniuq gaur (large, wild, bovine animal, sometimes called a 'wild buffalo') (neh˄ nyo˯)
neivqniuq kyulteiq rhinoceros
neivqssaq aolkov a kind of wild flower
neivqssaq halpyul a beetle (neh˄ ya ci^; neh˄ ku˯ coi)
neivqssaq wuqcaoq the cloth which is a gift to the spirits, sent with the coffin to the grave, but not buried (lit., 'spirit cap')
neivq zaol nia to be able to perform black magic
neivqzaq hhalniul a kind of ogre (46:93); evil monster; some type of ghost (or) **neivqzaq lalniul**

NI

nil to forget (or) **nieil** (26:59) (ngeh˅-eu)
nil little; small (9:124) (yaw nyi˅)
nil 1. red, 2. to make red (9:124) (yaw ne˅)
nil the outside; wild (op. of: **hyul** = inside; domesticated) (cf.: la˄ nyi˅ - as in: nyi˅ neh˄ = outside spirits as opposed to: k'oe˅ neh˄ = inside, or household spirits)
-- nil final part. used in questions (Chi) (**Halmeil duv lal nil**? - 10:23)
-- nil particle showing something not necessary (Chi) (**xilmeil maq zaol sso nil** = it is not necessary to do this)
-- nil, alhuvq -- to be young ('years small')
=nil, aq= younger relative
=nil, alwuv wuv= (see full)

=nil, **aqda da=** stepfather
=nil, **bee=** a red quilt
nilbial to forget (12:126, 26:116, 46:163) (ngehˇ-eu)
-- **nilbu, hanil** -- to lodge a false accusation against someone
-- nil, **byuqnil** -- to pick a quarrel; provoke (50:192)
-- nil, **caqyaq** -- to make mud for building
nilceiq nei reddish (neˇ tseu^ ni)
=nil, **da=** stepfather
nil dol duv yi a ceremony designed to prevent problems from the bad omen of a wild animal (such as a barking deer) coming into the village
-- nil, **eelnil** -- 1. water becomes muddy, 2. to flood
=nil, **geeq=** copper ('red' variety)
Nilgo a village in Yuanjiang County (Chi) (46:92)
nilgov alsiq wild grapes (14:219) (aˬ gaˬ)
nilgu nei naked (neˇ myaw^ ni)
-- nil, **halnil** -- to slander; instigate; incite (and see full)
=nil, **haq=** frost
=nil, **haqpeeq peeq=** bran from rice
-- nil, **hu** -- to look down on someone
=nil, **hhoq=** three-colored amaranth
niljeivq 1. a small building, 2. a building attached to the side of the main house (**xaolssaq**) (the main house is called: **xaolma**)
nilkev kevssaq nei from childhood (11:59) (zaˬ-ahˇ ngeh neh)
nilkev kevssaq nei maq nil not very small (11:60) (teu na^-ehˇ maˬ nyiˇ)
nilkev nei tiny; very small (9:124) (yaw zaˬ; yaw nyiˇ)
nilkev pa kev nei to be very tiny (yaw zaˬ; yaw nyiˇ)
=nil, **laq=** outside of the house
-- **nillo nei, miavhaoq** -- eyes reddened
nillul nei carelessly
nilma sister-in-law; how the older sister addresses her younger sisters and brother's wife; what the brothers and their wives call the wife of husband's younger brothers (nyiˇ ma)
=nil, **ma=** a stepmother
nilma gul for a shaman to go into a trance (or) **aqhhuv yiuvq** (pf.) (nyiˇ paˬ shiˇ-eu)
=nil, **miav=** (see full)
-- nil, **miavnil** -- (see full)
=nil, **moq=** a sweet potato
=nil, **nal=** a red nose (46:139)
=nil, **nee=** 1. chicken spleen, 2. a type of green bean
nil neivq good spirits; live in house or village
nil nil huq huq brilliant; splendid (50:75)
=nil, **niuq=** cow ('red buffalo')
nilpaq shaman (an Asian type of medium) (and see: **nilma**) **aqhhuv yiuvq** (pf.) (nyiˇ paˬ)

=nil, pavq= a red leaf (46:179)
=nil, peeq= soft bran
=nil, peiv= black tea
nilpuq ceiq nei reddish (neˇ tseu^ ni)
Nilpuvlaol a place in Luchun
nil qav to forget something (13:12) (ngehˇ ta˯-eu)
=nil, qil= small red field rat
nilqul nei very red (as when red-faced = **miavpyuq nilqul nei**) (11:18, 13:30, 46:174) (neˇ kah ni; neˇ tseu^ ni)
nilqul pa qul nei very red
nilqul qulssaq nei nil red to the reddest (11:59) (neˇ dui dui-eu)
-- nil, seqnil -- to stain one's teeth red
nilso nei reddish (neˇ tseu^ ni)
=nil, sul= rust to form
niltel nei scarlet
niltel nei nil vermillion
nil teiq catch and hold on (as rope, braid) (11:201) (nyeh˰ teh˯-eu)
niltuvq nei red (as of a healthy face) (**miavpyuq niltuvq nei** = a red, healthy face)
=nil, wuq= bald head
nilyahuvq next year (or) **neelyahuvq** (na˯ ya˰ k'o˰)
=nil, yo= small
nil zaq to forget (14:182)
nilzaq pieiv part of what the priest does in the funeral ceremony
nilzav nei very thin (9:125) (yaw jeh = thin humans; ba˯ lehˇ ni = thin objects)
nilzao relatives on mother's side; maternal relatives
nilzao aqbol maternal grandfather
nilzao aqpiq maternal grandmother
nilzao aqpyuq maternal ancestors
nilzao baoqgeel ancestral altar to the wife's ancestors
nilzao dama ancestors on the wife's side
nilzao maq nil, hyulzao maq heeq maternal relatives are not smaller and paternal relatives are not bigger (i.e., all of one's relatives are of the same closeness and importance)
nilzao qovq a family of maternal relatives
nilzeiq wild animals (or) **nilzeiqssaq; nivzeiq** (13:22) (yaˇ sa˯ je˯ za˯; and cf.: je˯ za˯ = all animals)
nilzeiq mavq various animals
nilzeiq saqgeel a wild animal skin (je˯ za˯ ba^ k'o^)
nilzeiqssaq wild animals (46:127) (or) **nilzeiq** (yaˇ sa˯ je˯ za˯)
nilzeiq ssaq gyuq for wild animals to cry out
nilzu lean pork (no fat) (41:140) (sha˯ neˇ)

nibiav wild grapes (46:157) (or) **puqtaol** (Chi) (a˯ ga˰)

nibuvq a type of vine (it has a bad odor)
=ni, cav= rattan
nigov alsiq wild grapes
nihav cavni a kind of wide vine used to tie up a sacrificial buffalo to a post before killing it at a funeral (cf.: ciˇ ni)
-- ni lal e, huljil pyu nei -- to be related by marriage on the male side
nima laolhhyul a type of vine with red juice (used to tie a dog when a father of an illegitimate child leads it around the village)

niq to be close; not far (**niq** li = go up closer - 26:103) (daw˯ peh) (cf. Lahu: aw˯ paˇ neˇ)
niq while (**galma niq ssuq aqmeil alsiq zaq** = to eat fruit while one is walking) (... ngeh)
niq two (9:125) (nyi˯)
Niq a shortened form for **Haqniq** (found in proverbs)
=niq, al= bamboo tie (strip)
niq bolssaq both grandfather and grandson (14:186)
niqca nei near by; close by (9:125, 35:84) (or) **daoqpei** (daw˯ peh) (cf. Lahu: aw˯ paˇ neˇ)
-- niqcanei, daoqpei -- to be very close; nearby
niq ceil twenty
  niq ceiltivq twenty-one
-- niq, deiq -- to push; lean against
niq eel eil to say smilingly (26:64)
  niq eel meil smilingly
  niq eel niq xeiv xeiv to run smilingly (26:67) (uiˇ uiˇ-ehˇ ceh^-eu)
niq'eil meil more and more (10:15) (ngeh˯-ehˇ (vb) naˇ, ngeh˯-ehˇ..)
  niq'eil maq eil sso one needn't speak about it (12:26)
  niq'eil nyuq niq'eil neema maq sal the more he thought the more unhappy he was (26:43) (ngeh˯-ehˇ noe˯ naˇ ngeh˯-ehˇ nui ma caw^-eu)
-- niq, galniq -- nearby
-- niq, gaqniq -- a Hani dance with drums and gongs
=niq, ha= jungle fowl
-- niq, haniq -- to be timid
=niq, Haq= Hani (Haˇ ni˯)
niq haoq ten cents (two five cent pieces)
niq hu niq bial bial the more one looks the less one can see (13:33)
  niq hu niq loq loq the more one looks the clearer it becomes (26:14) (ngeh˯-ehˇ haw naˇ ngeh˯-ehˇ mawˇ laˇ-eu)
niq hhaq seq bigamy (50:24) (nyi˯ g'a˯ sheu˯-eu)
niqjil a kilogram (kiˇ loˇ)
niq jil ssaq a couple (husband and wife) (35:73) (nyi˯ dzeˇ za˯)
Niqla February ('month two')
niq li to go closer; to draw near (35:26) (or) **niq lal** (peh laˇ-eu) (cf. Lahu: neˇ la ve)

niq lov two layers (nyi˯ law^)
niq lov col jol children living with their step-father or step-mother
niq lov peilhaoq clothes made of two layers (nyi˯ law^ pehˇ k'ah˯)
niq massaq mother and son (33:3) (nyi˯ ma za˯)
niq miav puv redouble (50:46)
niq moqssaq a couple (nyi˯ dzeˇ za˯)
=niq nei, eel= smilingly
=niq nei, geel= brightening
=niq nei, hhyul= happy
niq (vb) **niq** (vb) the more (vb) the more (vb) (**niq duq niq zeq zeq** = the more you dig the more there is)
niq (vbA) niq (vbA) meil (vbB) while doing one thing also doing something else (**niq ngyul niq ngyul meil eil** = while crying she said.. - 46:146)
niq paqssaq father and son (nyi˯ da za˯)
niq pyu both sides (4:39) (nyi˯ paw lu˄)
niq pyu col a double-dealer; double-faced person (50:107)
niq pyu dei two sides are balanced (equal) (50:130)
niq pyu lavq cavq aol reciprocal (or) **niq pyu meeqduq jav**
niq pyu meeqduq jav reciprocal (or) **niq pyu lavq cavq aol**
niq saoq ceil (clf.) 20 or 30 (clf) (**niq saoq ceil hhaq** = twenty or thirty people) (57:84)
niq ssuq niq seiq seiq sowing seeds while walking (from a proverb)
niq ssuq niq ssuq (vb) while walking, doing something else (as singing) (46:176)
niq taq twice; two times
niqwuf main subject (as the subject of a study) (Chi) (26:50)
niqyiq laosiil part-time teacher; spare-time teacher (26:101)
niq zol niq zol the more one studies (**Niq zol niq zol miqzaq miqlaol aqmeil neema laolcyu nei.** The more he studied the more his heart became warm like a flame. 26:45) (ngeh˯ dzaw naˇ ngeh˯-ehˇ ..)

niv moving; action (9:126, 50:77) (ji^-eu)
niv meil niv alnei for something to be shaking; quivering
niv, niv, niv for something to be shaking; quivering
-- niv, heil -- to mobilize; arouse
-- niv, keel -- to point with the foot
-- niv, maq -- to be lazy (not move)
-- niv nei, deiq -- suddenly
niv niv nei moving all the time (yaw˯ jawˇ na lu˄ lu^-eu)
-- niv, ngaoq -- to move something
niv qivq can be moved (46:151) (ji^ nya-eu)
-- niv, sov -- to push and move

-- **niv, taoq** -- to hit and move something
-- **niv, yoqniv** -- take the initiative
nivzeiq animals (Chi) (or) **nilzeiq** (13:19, 20)

NIA

(vb) **nial** part. showing a willingness to (vb); of one's own volition (**ngal meiq miq nial** = I will teach) (9:123, samples in 11:136) (...nyaˇ)
nialpil a spirit priest considered the highest of three types (he is the one who performs funeral ceremonies) (see also: **hhaol pil; gee pil**)

(vb) **nia** able to (vb); can (vb); capable of (vb) (or) **qivq; hhaq; qaol** (9:123, 11:40) (nya-eu)
=nia, al= father's younger sister
=nia, aq= upstream; upper
niabaq north side of a river (gaw^ mehˇ)
=nia, Dol= Luchun (town after which the main Hani dialect is named)
niagaoq up above (33:3) (la‸ ta^)
niaheiq pyu east or upriver (see also: **geeheiq pyu**)
Nia maq nia? Are (you) able or not? (11:46)
=nia, mee= several
=nia, mil= a place; a point
niamil aqnia the far north (38:33)
=nia ssaq, zoq= people who live upstream

niaq a contraction of: **niq hhaq** (2 persons) (aˬ nya‸)
-- **niaq, aqyo** -- the two of them
niaqhhaq naq a Hani festival held after the spring cultivation to rest the farming tools and animals (Yilcessaq dialect) **moqhhaq naq** = Luchun dialect (46:170)
-- **niaq, no** -- you two
Niaqziil one of three ancestors in Hani history, later they became three large clans (46:182)

NIAO

niaol short in length (9:123, 45:42) (yaw nymˇ)
niaolbol banyan tree (9:124) (nyehˇ dzahˇ aˇ bawˇ)
niaoldyuv to be short (yaw nymˇ)
niaoldyuv pa dyuv nei very short (11:58) (zawˇ nymˇ-eu)
=niaol, ha= large, hard chicken feather
-- **niaolhav, niaoq'aol** -- just a moment ago
niaolju 1. a kind of tree, 2. a kind of flower
=niaol, mol= distance
niaolsav a kind of tree
niaolseiv a shuttlecock
Niaolsoq aqpyuq cyulzao Alpeel an important ancestor in the Niaol **soqssaq** clan (Li clan)
Niaol soqssaq the Hani name for the Li clan (Chi)

niaoq 1. to spread, as a contagious disease (nyaw˯), 2. to be sticky (or) **niaoqkavq nei**
niaoq'aol now (9:123) (nym˯-m˅)
niaoq'aol hev nei by now; by this time
niaoq'aol niaolhav just a moment ago (11:109)
niaoq'aol qivq this evening; tonight (9:124) (nym˅ ci˰)
niaoq'aol soq this morning (9:124) (nym˅ shaw˯)
niaoqbiav glutinous rice cakes (14:239) (haw˯ tah˯)
=niaoq, hoq= glutinous rice
niaoqnal a contagious disease, especially a venereal disease such as syphilis (ga˯ la˯ na˅-eu)
niaoqnal nal to suffer from a contagious disease, especially a venereal disease such as syphilis
niaoqnav purple rice (9:124) (haw˯ nyaw˯ na^)
-- **niaoqnil, haoqniaoq** -- red glutinous rice
-- **niaoqsiil, haoqniaoq** -- glutinous rice colored yellow
niaoqsol sweet purple rice (9:124, 11:28) (haw˯ nyaw˯ na^)

niaov 1. to use chopsticks in eating (tsi da˅ neh dza˯-eu), 2. to use scissors in cutting (9:124) (teh˯ da˅ teh˯-eu)
niaov clf. for the amount of food that chopsticks can pick up at one time
-- **niaov, albeil** -- to cut the umbilical cord
niaov ceiv to cut apart (as cloth)
=niaov, dal= double layered
=niaov, lavq= tongs (to use around fire)
-- **niaovssaq, dalniaov** -- tweezers
niaov teiq 1. to pick something up with tongs, chopsticks or the like (35:61) (tsi da˰-eu), 2. to pluck off (35:61)

NIE

Nieqkao Niukong, a place in Luchun County

niev niev nei to be painful (but hard to locate the exact spot)

nievq thoroughly (as to be soaked thoroughly) (50:150)

NIEI

nieil forget (or) **nil** (6:196) (ngeh˅-eu)
nieilbial to forget (or) **nil** (11:39) (ngeh˅-eu)
nieil qav to leave behind unintentionally; to forget something (ngeh˅ ya˰-eu)
=nieil, haq= frost (also: **haqnil**)
nieiljef to study (Chi) (34:40) (dzaw-eu)
=nieil, naol= a loom for weaving
nieil qav to leave something behind; to forget

something (ngehˇ ya˰-eu)

=nieil, **saq**= meat (pork) which has congealed in its juice

-- **nieil, saqnieil** -- for meat (porkl) to become congealed in its juice

nieil **zaq** to forget (11:112) (ngehˇ-eu)

=niei, **nalgol nal**= to be weak; feeble

=niei **nei, hhyul**= happily

-- niei niei **nei, wuqduq** -- shaking one's head up and down in affirmation

-- **niei, wuqduq** -- to salute

nieizii a stone roller (Chi)

nieiq to remain (46:94) (jawˇ ta˯-eu; ja^ ta˯-eu)

nieiq **aol** nieiq **kyuq** further intensified; further aggravated (50:13) (**ngeh˯**-ehˇ jahˇ ngeh˯-ehˇ coe˯)

=nieiq **dovq, lavq**= to begin to work

nieiq'eil **(vb)** nieiq'eil more and more; the more the (vb) (ngeh˯-ehˇ (vb) naˇ, ngeh˯-ehˇ (vb)

nieiq'eil **navq** e nieiq'eil **meeq** the sooner the better (ngeh˯-ehˇ na˰ naˇ, ngeh˯-ehˇ mui˯)

nieiq'eil **ngaoq** nieiq'eil **(vb)** more and more (**nieiq'eil ngaoq nieiq'eil miaq lal** - become more and more - 11:23) (ngeh˯-ehˇ naˇ ngeh˯-ehˇ mya˯ laˇ-eu)

nieiq**hev nei** knowing it ahead of time (35:91)

nieiqjiq grade (Chi) (6 nieiqjiq = sixth grade - 26:20)

-- **nieiqma, miqnieiq** -- a great task; a big job (or) **daolma**

-- nieiq **meil, eil** -- while talking

=nieiq, **miq**= livelihood; work; matter

nieiq **nyuq** to think clearly; to think well (14:235) (yaw mui˯-ehˇ shaˇ noe˯-eu)

(vb) nieiq **pieiq** to stop (vb) (**ngyul** nieiq **pieiq** = to stop crying - 11:209) (vb - pyeh˯-eu)

nieiq**qilhuaf** to make younger (Chi) (34:107)

=nieiq, **zol**= to study a course

nieivq to catch; grab hold of; grasp (9:124) (nyeh˰-eu)

nieivq to massage; squeeze (nyeh˰-eu)

=nieivq, **aq**= empty; vacant

-- nieivq, **albaol** -- to catch a grasshopper as a part of a ceremony

-- nieivq, **aqbeil** -- to blow nose; squeeze off mucous from nose

nieivq **cavq** 1. to contact; 2. to connect; establish relationships (46:76)

nieivq **kuv** to arrest and put in jail (50:21)

nieivq **laol** 1. to close up something or someone (9:124), 2. to detain; take into custody (50:78, 82)

-- nieivq **laol, hhavqkuv** -- to put in jail

nieivq puv to wind up (as to wind up a toy)
nieivq sil 1. to squeeze to death (nyeh˰ seh˰-eu), 2. to put out a light
nieivq teiq to catch and hold (9:124) (nyeh˰ teh˯-eu)
nieivq tul to erect ('take hold of - stand up')
nieivq zao to reconstruct; put together (46:76)
nieivq zovq anaesthesia (50:112)
  nieivq zovq naciq anaesthetic (50:112)

NIU

niul to glare at
niul 1. green (9:125); 2. jade (green stone, in riddle 4:40) (yaw nyoeˇ)
=niul, al= a roof rafter
niulbiaq albol banyan tree (**niaolbol** = pf.) (57:78)
niulbol 'jade' tree (in riddle 4:40)
niul dav to turn green (as new plants) (35:117) (nyoeˇ laˇ-eu)
niuldeivq nei very green and fresh (9:125, 11:58, 33:3, 45:83, 46:130) (nyoeˇ ya˯ ni; nyoeˇ jaw˰ ni)
Niuldoq Han (Chinese) language (shortened from: **Pyulniuldoq**) (9:125, 10:1, 32:3) (La˰ bui˯ daw˯)
=niul, gal= moss on a path
niulhaq blue sky (m˯ puiˇ)
=niul, hyuq= tobacco
=niul, hhoq= green vegetables
niul lu nav laq black and green spots (as in a forest of trees)
-- niul, miavniul -- to make an angry face at someone
=niul, neivqzei hhal= a ghost
niul niul nei very green/fresh (11:57) (nyoeˇ jaw˰ ni)
=niul, ollol eel= a green viper
=niul, paq= a green frog
=niul, pavq= green leaves
=niul, peil= green clothing
niulsiq a pearl (50:118)
niulsiq haqluv jade (stone)
niulsivq nei green; fresh (57:79)
niul taoq taoq extremely green (57:74)
=niul, xaol= rafter (for the roof)
niulzaovq nei very fresh (as vegetables)

niuq water buffalo (sometimes for cow) (a˯ nyo˯ = buffalo, mawˇ neˇ = cow)
niuq to wither (nyoe˯-iˇ-eu)
niuq clf. for cattle, buffalo (or) **kaol** (mawˇ)
niuqbaoq a disease of the skin, sometimes used for leprosy (see: **alpeel**)
  niuqbaoq nal to have a disease of the skin, sometimes leprosy (see: **alpeel nal**)
niuqcav a rope to tie buffalo/cow (4:40, 9:125) (nyo˯ ca^)

niuqcei an oxen cart (**moqcei** = horse cart) (nyo˯ la^ law˯)
niuqceiq a plow (for buffalo) (9:125, 11:28) (nyo˯ tseh˯)
niuqceiq ceiqkov a plowed furrow
niuqdiq niuqma dalciil a stick (from a small bush) they use to beat buffalo when herding them (cf.: daˇ mya^)
niuqdol a bad-omen cow/buffalo (nyo˯ caw^)
niuqgaq nei tamed (both of animals and children that are not active) (9:125) (yaw yah)
niuqgeel a buffalo skin (14:173, 46:174) (a˯ nyo˯ ba^ k'o^)
niuq huvq buffalo year (9:125) (nyo˯ ti˯ k'o˰)
niuqjuq niuljul a cricket (9:125) (nyoi˯ oi˯)
niuqkav a harrow (9:125) (nyo˯ ka^)
=niuq, kav= a buffalo that can harrow a field
niuqkav kavseq the 'teeth' of a harrow (nyo˯ ka^ la˰ g'ah˯-eu˯ seu˯)
niuqkav laqma big 'teeth' in a harrow
niuqkuv buffalo/cow stable (9:124) (nyo˯ ku^)
niuqkyul horn (buffalo/cow) (9:126) (u˯ coeˇ)
niuqkyul alqul a big banana (like horn)
niuqlao duqhovq buffalo wallow (9:126) (a˯ nyo˯ nyo˯ lah)
niuqlao laoduq buffalo wallow; **niuqlao duqhovq**)
niuqmoq an old buffalo (nyo˯ maw˯)
niuqmoq daoqpei ceilhhaol hhe 'to play one's guitar to an old buffalo' (it means you have chosen the wrong audience)
niuqnal cattle plague (9:126) (a˯ nyo˯ naˇ gawˇ)
niuq nao cow/ buffalo day (nyo˯ ti˯ nah)
=niuq, neivq= gaur
niuqnil cow ('red buffalo') (9:126) (mawˇ neˇ)
niuqnil lalbu bull (male cow) (mawˇ neˇ mawˇ gaw)
niuqpav half of buffalo, cow (sometimes they own this much) (11:67) (nyo˯ pa^)
niuqpeel water buffalo (9:126) (a˯ nyo˯)
niuqpeel ssolnei niuqnil zuvq to offer a buffalo and a cow for a dead person (or) **peel nil zuvq**
niuqqul milk (cow or buffalo) (10:16) (mawˇ neˇ a˯ coeˇ; a˯ nyo˯ a˯ coeˇ)
niuqsaq beef (buffalo/cow) (9:126) (mawˇ neˇ sha˯ jiˇ; a˯ nyo˯ sha˯ jiˇ)
niuqsaq saqkuv dried beef; jerky (9:126) (a˯ nyo˯ sha˯ ko^)
niuqsaol a plowshare (nyo˯ tseh˯)
niuqseil a buffalo (cow) louse (45:50)
niuqtavq a partner in a group that owns a buffalo
niuqtaoqloq a donkey (mah˯ tah˯ la^)
niuqteil forehead (9:126) (naˇ k'awˇ)
niuqxiq buffalo/cattle dung (9:126, 12:126) (a˯ nyo˯ ce˯/ca˰; mawˇ neˇ ce˯/ca˰)
niuqxiq haollul a type of mushroom
niuqxiq xiqbieiv watery buffalo/cattle dung

niuqxiq xiqkuv dried buffalo/cattle dung

niuqzal buffalo/cattle feed (9:126) (a$_{\vee}$ nyo$_{\vee}$ dza$^{\vee}$; maw$^{\vee}$ ne$^{\vee}$ dza$^{\vee}$)

niuq zeq cow/ buffalo hour (B=Chi)

niuqzyuq a big cricket (cf.: nyoi$_{\vee}$ oi$_{\vee}$)

=niuv, beivq= the clitoris

=niuv, loq= a spiral shell

=niuv, mal= a seed in fruit; core; kernel; center; quality; nature (see: 50:189)

=niuv, sseil= (see full)

=niuv, yeiv= the stamen (in a flower)

NO

nol you (nominative, sing.) (9:126) (naw$^{\vee}$)

nol bulduq you yourself (naw$^{\vee}$ yaw$_{\vee}$ ha$^{\vee}$ yaw$_{\vee}$ ha)

nol da miqssaq "you are a bad omen" (you are illegitimate -- said to a woman)

nol halmeil zaol movq a maq? what can you do? (with the idea of 'wanting to do' implicit) (26:8) (Naw$^{\vee}$ a$_{\vee}$ je$_{\vee}$ jah$^{\vee}$ nya te; naw$^{\vee}$ a$_{\vee}$ je$_{\vee}$ jah$^{\vee}$ maw$_{\wedge}$ nya)

nol ma huljil "you are a bad omen" (you are illegitimate -- said to a man)

nol meeq ngal meeq 1. a greeting based on a Chinese formula; 2. help each other for mutual benefits (50:73)

nol ngaq yaol hu, ngal noq yaol hu to look at each other (wondering who it was) (26:84) (ti$_{\vee}$ g'a$_{\vee}$ ti$^{\vee}$ g'a$_{\vee}$ haw-eu)

nol qiq doq ngal qiq doq eil each spoke up; each gave his opinion (lit., 'you said a word, I said a word') (45:2) (naw$^{\vee}$ ti$_{\vee}$ daw$_{\vee}$ nga$^{\vee}$ ti$_{\vee}$ daw$_{\vee}$-eh$^{\vee}$ ngeh$_{\vee}$-eu)

nolya you (plural) (9:127) (naw ma$_{\wedge}$)

no your (possessive) (**no beewul peilhaoq** = your quilted jacket - 26:39) (naw$_{\vee}$-eu$_{\vee}$)

no alba (TE) dear older sister (used by older generation to younger generaion on behalf of his or her child, showing that the listener is older than his or her child)

no algo (TE) dear older brother (used by older generaion to younger generation on behalf of his or her child, showing that the listener is older than her or his child)

no alnia (TE) dear aunty (used by a male who is speaking to a younger female on behalf of his child)

no alsuq (TE) dear uncle (used by the same generation)

no alsuq laosiil (TE) dear uncle teacher (used by same generation, where listener is male, the speaker is older than listener, the speaker has a child, and is showing great politeness (or) **no dalda laosiil**

no aqbol (TE) dear grandfather (used by the same generation)

no aqcu (TE) dear sister-in-law (patterns the same as: **no algo,** but used in speaking to a female)

no aqhhyu (TE) dear maternal uncle (used by the same generation)

no aqmee (TE) dear aunty (used by the same generation)

no aqmee laosiil (TE) dear aunty teacher (used by a person of the same generation where the speaker is older than the listener, the speaker has a child, the listener is female, and showing great politeness)

no aqnil (TE) dear younger brother (used by a person of an older generation on behalf of his or her child, showing that the listener is younger than his or her child)

no aqpiq (TE) dear grandmother (used in the same generation in a very polite way)

no aqpyuq (TE) dear great-grandfather; great-grandmother (used in the same generation, but on behalf of the great-grandchild)

no aqsaoq (TE) dear uncle (used by the same generation)

no dalda laosiil (see: **no alsuq laosiil**)

no damoq (TE) dear uncle (the speaker must be a father or mother, and the speaker and listener must be of the same generation)

no malma (TE) dear aunty (used by the same generation)

no niaq the two of you (13:31) (naw nya$_{\wedge}$)

no qovq your family (9:126) (naw zaw$_{\wedge}$)

  no qovq bee your house (naw$_{\vee}$-eu$_{\vee}$ zaw$_{\wedge}$; naw$_{\vee}$-eu$_{\vee}$ nym$^{\vee}$)

noq a 'to you' (objective) (as in: he gave the book to you. But if it is to 'hit' you: **noq yaol**) (cf. Lahu: naw$_{\vee}$ ha$_{\wedge}$) (11:19) (naw$_{\vee}$-ah$^{\vee}$)

noq e your (naw$_{\vee}$-eu$_{\vee}$)

  noq e alsuq (TE) dear brother (my dear child's uncle) (35:16)

  noq e damoq (TE) dear older brother (term of high respect to an older man - 27:11)

noqmil aqgee (see: **naoqmil aqgee**) (14:161)

Noqsol Aqheil the name of a Hani king (35:97)

noq yaol 'to you' (objective)

NU

nul to be plump; fat (as a young pig) (yaw tsu$^{\vee}$)

  nulhevq nei to be plump; fat (as a young pig) (9:127) (yaw tsu$^{\vee}$)

=nu, aq= besides; another
nuda a word said in anger; a strong swear word (27:11)
=nu mavq, aq= others

nuqlif seifhyuf slave system (Chi) (50:123)
nuqlifziif slave system (Chi) (57:156)

nuv to break into pieces (di˯ nm^-eu)
-- nuv, daolhav -- to transplant rice in non-irrigated terraced fields during rainy season
=nuv, eellaol laol= warm water
=nuv, hao= feather; fur
=nuv, keeq= a lump of manure
-- nuv, kovq -- to bite to pieces
=nuv, laol= warm water
-- nuv, naoq -- to stamp into pieces
nuvyav nei pieces (yaw nm^)
-- nuv, teil -- to pound to pieces
-- nuv, yeiq -- to cut up into pieces
-- nuv, zeilnuv -- (see full)

nuvq kevq to mix with one's hands (beu˯ keu˯-eu)
-- nuvq, lavqnuvq -- to knead
nuvq pieiv to squeeze to pieces (nyeh˰ nm^-eu; deh˯ pyeh^-eu)
nuvqyav nei to be smashed into little pieces (57:69)

NYU

nyul clf. for a finger (**lavqnyul qiq nyul**) (11:95) (noeˇ)
nyulciivq joint of a finger; knuckle (noeˇ tsui˰)
=nyul, hhaq= steamed buckwheat cake
=nyul, lavq= finger
nyulma the middle finger (or) **nyultaoq** (noeˇ ka˯)
nyulqaq the small finger (or) **lavqqaq** (caˇ ca˯)
nyultaoq the middle finger (or) **nyulma** (noeˇ ka˯)
nyultul (wm) length from thumb to outstretched index finger (clf. **tul**) (11:78) (toˇ; ti˯ tsi)
nyulyahuvq next year (6:162, 35:27); **neelyahuvq** (na˯ ya˰ k'o˰)
nyulzeil the ring finger (11:128) (noeˇ doe˯)

nyuq 1. to think (noe˯-eu), 2. to wake up (noe˯ laˇ-eu) (9:127)
nyuq bav 1. to think wrongly, 2. to misunderstand (46:119) (noe˯ leh˯-eu; noe˯ bah˯-eu)
nyuqbeel to realize; consciousness (50:93) (nui ma-ahˇ noe˯-eu)
nyuqbia to think good ('bright') things (cf.: noe˯ bya-eu)
nyuqbuvq buvq to write from memory (50:118)
nyuqcaq maq siq to waver; to wonder whether one is right or wrong

nyuq ceiv to decide (noe˯ tseh^-eu)

nyuq ceiv nyuq loq to decide and be sure (34:4)

nyuq duv to think out; to think through (or) **nyuq duv la** (noe˯ do^-eu)

nyuq duvq nyuq cil think deeply and plan carefully (50:149)

-- **nyuq, eil** -- to remind

nyuqgaol have a clear mind; be careful; be alert; attentive (9:127, 46::187); be on guard against; have a clear mind (50:91) (13:47, 26:24) (noe˯ gahˇ-eu)

nyuqgaol gaol to think clearly; to be careful; to be alert; to pay careful attention; be on one's guard against; keep a clear, bright mind (50:91)

nyuqgaol leil eilgaq miq to give warning; to tell someone to be careful (noe˯ gahˇ lehˇ ehˇ neh˯-eu)

nyuq hev 1. to understand the meaning; to recognize (50:91) (g'o^ shaw-eu); 2.vigilent; alert (50:91), 3. to be conscious; aware

nyuq hoq to take care of (14:187)

nyuq hu to think about; to consider (45:94, 50:96) (shaˇ noe˯-eu, cf. Lahu: dawˇ nyi ve)

nyuq hu hu to try to think through

nyuq hu huvq to think over again (paˇ shaˇ noe˯ haw-eu)

-- **nyuq, hyuq** -- to suspect; doubt

nyuq hhal have faith; have a belief (50:188)

nyuqhhal maq hha uncertain; indistinct (50:116)

-- **nyuq, kul** -- call to wake up

nyuq laol to show consideration; give every care (50:165)

-- **nyuq, leiq** -- to awaken someone

nyoq liq maq nyuq haoq it is not proper to think

-- **nyuq lo, nyuq sil** -- (see full)

nyuq loq to think and understand (26:75, 50:104) (g'o^ shaw-eu)

-- **nyuq loq, nyuq ceiv** -- to decide and be sure

=**nyuq meil, nee**= on purpose

=**nyuq, nee**= 1. what one thinks, 2. what one hopes, 3. one's opinion

-- **nyuq, neema** -- to show concern

=**nyuq, nieiq**= to think clearly

nyuq nyuq mav mav 1. illusion; dreamlike (50:114), 2. in a trance, 3. absent minded (50:75) (written in the latter as: **nyuqnyuq mavmav**)

nyuq puv 1. to change one's mind; to repent (noe˯ po^-eu), 2. to bring back to one's mind (or) **nyuq duv**, 3. introspection; self-questioning (50:47)

nyuq puv dav repent and mend one's ways (50:75)

nyuq puv maq qaol to regret

nyuq sal to make oneself comfortable (noe˯ saˇ-eu)

nyuq saq 1. to think through everything (or) **nyuq saq nyuq li**, 2. to be sad; unhappy (noe˯ sha˯-eu) (13:4), 3. to worry (26:51)

nyuq savq to feel embarrassed (sha˰ dawˇ-eu)

-- **nyuq savq, neema --** a bad conscience

nyuq sil nyuq lo 1. to desire very much; 2. to have an ambition (26:105), 3. to miss someone very much (noe⌄ keu^ seh^-eu)

nyuq syuq to worry about (14:179) (noe⌄ zah⌄-eu)

=nyuq, ssaqguq guq= an impossible dream ('a child's thoughts')

-- nyuq, ssaqguq guqnyuq -- have a fantastic idea

nyuq teiq 1. to remember (9:127, 10:28, 46:97), 2. to memorize (noe⌄ ta⌄-eu)

nyuq tovq reason; rational (50:105)

nyuqtovq hev rational knowledge (50:105)

nyuq za 1. to think properly; clearly (9:127) (noe⌄ shaw-eu), 2. to show understanding and sympathy for; make allowances for (50:165)

nyuq za alnei ssaoq to spend according to the plan (50:80)

nyuq zil nyuq za to analyze (50:50)

nyuq zoq 1. to forgive (lit. 'to think straight', a polite way of asking for forgiveness in an honest way - 41:177), 2. to overcome (as some trouble; sadness) (50:97)

nyuvqyav nei nyuq hu to think carefully and in detail (57:99)

nyufgoq cabinet (Chi) (50:120)

nyufzeif internal affairs; domestic affairs (Chi) (50:120)

NGA

ngal I (nominative singular) (9:122) (ngaˇ)
ngaldu we all (inclusive) (9:122) (aˇ dui ma‸; aˇ dui; aˬ dui)
ngaldu algo eil eiq (TE) dear older brother (said in a sympathetic way)
ngaldu aqbol eil eiq (TE) dear grandfather (said in a sympathetic way)
ngaldu aqnil eil eiq (TE) dear younger brother (said in a sympathetic way)
ngaldu aqpiq eil eiq (TE) dear grandmother (said in a sympathetic way)
ngaldu aqhuq eil eiq (TE) dear aunty (said in a sympathetic way)
ngaldu aqhuq malma eil eiq (TE) dear aunty (said in a sympathetic way)
ngaldu niaq we two (inclusive) (11:207) (aˇ nya‸)
ngal noq yaol I to you (8:27) (ngaˇ nawˬ-ahˇ)
=ngal, ngaq= tonsils
ngal ssuq movq al "I'll be going" (lit. 'I want to go'); a polite term a younger person says when about to leave (41:160)
ngalya we (exclusive) (9:122) (nga ma‸)

nga my (possessive sing.) (**Ngal nga milhaoq yaol gaq.** I love my country.)
nga to open (as the mouth) (5:3715) (nga-eu)
-- nga final part.(10:12) (**Maq ngeel ngaoq sil lal nga.** = If you don't (take to hospital) they may die).
-- nga aq? a final interrogative particle; **-- aq?**
nga eil? final question particle (46:138) (or) **ngaq eil?**
nga laq? a final particle showing that the statement is a question, demanding a yes or no answer (see 11:137) (**Ngal gaq e nol Haqniq soqhhaq zol bei leil ngeel nga laq**"? I heard that you have studied Hani writing, is that true? 41:72) (or) **nga aq**
nga nei an opening (nga-eu)
nga qovq my family (9:123) (ngaˬ-euˬ pyaˬ)
nga yil final particle. 'it is said' (11:216, 13:55) (jeˇ)

-- ngaq? final interrogative particle (**Aqyoq haljivq aol ngaq?** What is he doing?); **-- aq?**
ngaq to borrow; lend (in which the same thing is given back to the owner, as a hoe) (9:122) (ngaˬ-eu)
ngaq to step over (9:122) (k'ah dzeuˇ-eu)
ngaq -- fish -- (see: **ngaqsaq**)
ngaqbev a bamboo bow with which to shoot fish (ngaˬ

beu^)
ngaqbuvq a black and white fish (nga˯ beu˰)
ngaq buvq for fish to spoil (nga˯ bu˰)
ngaqcaoq a bamboo fish net ('fish cap') (11:28)
ngaqciq vine used to poison fish (9:122) (cf.: **ciq** and: **naciq**)
ngaqdav a medium-sized carp (nga˯ da^)
ngaqdaol the fin of a fish (or) **yiqciif** (Chi) - this is more specifically shark fin (yeh˅ ma)
ngaqdeil fish (general) (9:122) (nga˯ sha˯)
ngaqduq a fish pond (11:18) (clf.: **duq**) (nga˯ sha˯ lah)
ngaqduq duq to dig a fish pond (11:18) (nga˯ sha˯ lah du˯-eu)
ngaq e my (**ngaq e miqbev** = my gun) (or) **nga** (**nga qovq** = my family) (nga˯-eu˯)
ngaq e Molmil aq oh, my God (26:38) (exclamation)
ngaq e ssaq e nga it is my son's (tractor) (41:160) (heu-a˯ nga˯ li-eu˯)
ngaq eil? a question part. (46:138) (or) **nga eil?**
ngaqgao a fish bone ('thorn') (nga˯ sha˯ a˯ gah; nga˯ gah)
ngaqgeeq scale of fish (nga˯ sha˯ nga˯ g'aw^) (and see below)
ngaqhhov scale of fish (9:123, 11:27) (nga˯ sha˯ nga˯ g'aw^) (and see above)
ngaqhhovq fish hook (9:123, 11:16) (nga˯ jui˰)
ngaqhhovq daldul a pole for fishing (nga˯ jui˰ kaw˯ du˅)
ngaqhhovq pieiq puvq to throw a fish hook into the water (to go fishing) (45:72) (nga˯ jui˰ ka-eu)
ngaqjul loach (a type of small fish, often living in their rice terraces) (9:123, 11:129)
ngaqlaoq a kind of fish
ngaqlol eel (9:123, 11:151) (nga˯ ui˅ law˅)
ngaqlol hevq to dig for eels (11:188)
ngaqlol heeq lol byu heeq easy come, easy go
ngaqlol ngaqjul eels and loaches (14:148)
ngaqluv a basket used to catch fish
ngaqmoq an old, mature fish (38:90) (nga˯ maw˯; nga˯ sha˯ sha˯ maw˯)
ngaqngal 1. tonsils (11:25), 2. perhaps also palate (in mouth)
ngaqngal hevq to cure tonsilitis using salt (11:25)
ngaqngal laqliv the soft palate
ngaqpuq a fish container (14:147) (nga˯ pu˯)
ngaqpyuq rent (50:25)
ngaqsaq fish (nga˯ sha˯)
ngaqsaq albaol shrimp (9:123) (nyeh bah˅ coe˅ k'o˰)
ngaqsaq baqbeiv fish gill (9:123) (nga˯ nga^)
ngaqsaq haqdal a type of water fern
ngaqsaq hhoqqeil sour salted fish (nga˯ sha˯ ceh˅)
ngaqsaq leiqssaq a fisherman
ngaqssa dam across stream so as to catch fish (nga˯ sha˯ lah)

ngaq yaol 'to me' (objective)
ngaq yoq to step over; to get over (9:123) (k'ah dzeuᵛ-eu)
ngaqzaoq raw, fresh fish (14:140) (ngaᵥ shaᵥ yaw jmᵥ)
ngaqzei fish net (or) **hhazei** (za)
ngaqzei zeicyuq ragged fish net (3:1)

ngavlav to be broken (tseh^-iᵛ-eu; pa^-iᵛ-eu)

ngavq to get stuck (ngeuᵥ-eu; tsmᵥ leᵛ-eu)
ngavq five (9:123) (ngaᵥ)
ngavq baol qiq pav five and a half shares (11:67)
ngavq ceil fifty
ngavq ceil keiq fifty grams (C=Chi)
ngavq kyul geelsiq a five-pointed star (50:181)
=ngavq, lal= uvula
ngavq la ngavq nao the fifth day of the fifth lunar month a festival is held (and see the following three entries for what is done)
ngavq la ngavq nao hoqkyul kyul zaq to make pyramid-shaped dumplings of glutinous rice on the fifth day of the fifth lunar month (a Hani custom)
ngavq la ngavq nao lavqdu alcav kavqtovq to tie colored cotton threads on the forearm to show the difference between humans and evil spirits
ngavq la ngavq nao zalgovq zaq to have various vegetables cooked together on the fifth day of the fifth lunar month (a Hani custom)
Ngavqla siq May
ngavq pyu meeq 'five-goods' (a Chinese concept) (50:181)
ngavq pyu meeq e yovq a family of the 'five goods'

NGAO

=ngaol, laol= (see full)

ngaoq if (3:1, 2, 8:28) (**aoq sal e ngaoq** = if it is good weather - 11:21) (see also 11:122 for samples) (naᵛ)
ngaoq freezing weather
ngaoq to turn over a big object (9:122, 46:131) (ngawᵥ-eu)
-- ngaoq, aqlavq lavqyevq -- to arm wrestle
ngaoq dav to pour on (35:91) (sheh^ da^-eu)
ngaoqdul a lever
ngaoqhal to pour out (14:188, 35:16) (ngawᵥ k'aᵛ-eu)
-- ngaoq, haqnil nil -- for ice to form
ngaoqhhaoq to bend something (ngawᵥ-eu)
=ngaoq, laol= even though; but
=ngaoq, naol= only
ngaoq niv to move something (fairly large) (11:142) (ngawᵥ lu^-eu)
-- ngaoqqul, wuqduq -- to raise one's head up
ngaoqseiq to pour on (35:89)

=ngaoq, taoq= because
ngaoq ya to be very cold

NGE

-- ngeq, geeldiq diqngeq -- armed provocation

NGEE

ngeel yes; to be so (or) **ngeel ssa** (9:123) (ngeuˇ)
ngeel al yes indeed (or) **ngual** (in rapid speech), sometimes becoming **'wal'**
-- ngeel, hal -- every; any; all
ngeel jaoqdaol yes indeed (note: **jaoqdaol** = a confirmative part. which always follows **'ngeel'**)
ngeeljil jilmeil to seek truth from facts; to be practical and realistic
ngeeljil meil really (cf. **aqdil; aqdil meil**) (9:123, 13:20)
ngeel laq ssa inferring something to be the case (13:6)
ngeel lo maq of course! (50:32)
ngeel maq ngeel is that right or not? (26:54)
-- ngeel meil, hal -- to be as one pleases
ngeelmoq maq syuq maybe yes; probably so (46:121) (ngeuˇ paˬ)
ngeel naolhaoq 1. as to (noun); concerning (noun) (ngeuˇ naˇ), 2. after which
ngeel nga 'that is true' (an ending used for emphasis (see: 11:51) (ngeuˇ nga)
ngeel nga laq is that so? (**maq ngeel nga** = it isn't so) (ngeuˇ nga laˬ)
ngeel ssa yes; to be so (or) **ngeel**
ngeel wul naq positive ending (sometimes contracted to: **ngul naq; ngul naoq** - 11:22)
ngeel zeiq wul yaq maybe that is true (33:3) (ngeuˇ-eu paˬ)
ngeel zeiq ya perhaps it is so (35:18) (ngeuˇ paˬ)
ngeel zeiq ya leil nyuq to think it must be true (35:18)

ngeeq a type of spirit which can enter people (when that happens they say: **neivqhaq guqzaq lal**)
=ngeeq, kav= a short, hooked hoe
=ngeeq, savjil sav= (see full)
=ngeeq, yav= a hoe made of wood

NGU

ngulnaq (final part.) it is really so; it is really like that (contraction of: **ngeel wul naq**) (57:71)
ngulnaoq yes indeed (a contraction of: **ngeel wul naoq**) (45:7)

NGUA

ngual yes indeed (a contraction of **ngeel wul al**, said in rapid speech)

NGYU

ngyul to cry; weep (ngoe˅-eu)
-- **ngyul lo, ngyul sil** -- to sob and cry
ngyulma female goose
ngyulzal male goose; gander
-- **ngyul, miqsaq** -- to wail for dead elder
ngyulngavq ngavq to sob (to cry with catches in the throat) (26:9)
=**ngyul, oq**= goose
ngyulsavq nei to sob
ngyul sil ngyul lo to cry very hard (cry one's heart out) (26:4, 38:18) (ngoe˅ seh˄-eu)
ngyul teil the sound of crying (26:4) (ngoe˅-eu te˅ sa˅)
-- **ngyul, yiuvqngyul** -- 1. to feel sleepy (9:166, 11:43), 2. to doze off; nod off

NGUA

ngual yes indeed (**said in rapid speech, from: ngeel** al; in rapid speech sounds like; **wal**)

o O o O o O

OL

ol! an interjection (**Ol, meeq al!** Oh, it is good!)
olhoq Molmil interjection; 'oh, my God'
ollol a snake (9:127) (aˇ lawˇ)
  ollol beivdev a poisonous, short, flat-headed snake that moves slowly
  ollol eelkol a 'flying' snake (it goes very fast)
  ollol eelkol kolma king cobra (aˇ lawˇ uiˇ na^; uiˇ k'aˬ uiˇ puiˇ)
  ollol eelnav a black viper (aˇ lawˇ uiˇ na^)
  ollol eelniul a green viper (aˇ lawˇ nyoeˇ)
  ollol lolbeeq a snake nest
  ollol lolhhov a snake skin (aˇ lawˇ lawˇ g'aw)
  ollol lolhhov pal a snake to shed its skin (aˇ lawˇ lawˇ g'aw g'aw-eu)
  ollol lolwuv a snake egg
  ollol saqgeel a snake skin (that is, as taken off by people and not merely shed by a snake) (aˇ lawˇ ba^ k'o^)
  ollol sovq'eel a spotted snake (steals chicken eggs)
Oltol Tavqzaoq old name of Dazhai village in Dolnia (Luchun) county (Hani writing is based on the dialect of this village) (35:67)
Oltyuqlyu a Hani ancestor (son of **Sulmil**) (46:107) (Oˇ toeˬ loe)

O

o'lov meil nei slowly; softly; politely (aw law^-ehˇ)
o'lov o'lov meil slowly and carefully (aw law^ aw law^-ehˇ)
  o'lov nei maq ngeel not a small amount (it means there is a lot) (aˇ cui^ teh‸ maˬ ngeuˇ-a)

OQ

oq ! exclamation (11:21, 141) (**Oq, xilmeil nga laq!** Oh my, it is like this!) (oˇ)
oq'a duck (9:127) (gawˬ guˇ)
  =oq'a, neivqhaq= a wild duck
  oq'a oqpeev roast duck (14:235)
oqhal a young female duck
oqhol life (as to be concerned for life of another, or concerned for your own life) (or) **wuqhol**
  oqhol maq movq to fear nothing; determined to do something even though you die trying ('not want life') (or) **wuqhol maq movq**
oqma 1. a duck, 2. a big duck, 3. a female duck (9:127) (gawˬ guˇ)

oqngyul goose (9:128) (jeh^ k'a$_{\vee}$)

-- **oqngyul, neivqhaq** -- egret

oqssaq a duckling

oqwuv a duck egg (9:128) (gaw$_{\vee}$ gu$^{\vee}$ u^)

oqzal a male duck (9:128) (gaw$_{\vee}$ gu$^{\vee}$ a$_{\vee}$ poe$^{\vee}$)

ovq ripe; done (both fruit, and cooking) (9:128) (aw$_{\wedge}$ la$^{\vee}$-eu)

ovqdei nei to be spongy (or) **naoqzov nei; heimieiq nadul dul** (A=Chi)

ovq duvq ripe enough to eat

ovq duvq ovq ciq over-ripe

ovqleel nei to be ripe enough (aw$_{\wedge}$ lo$_{\wedge}$ la$^{\vee}$-eu)

ovqleel pa leel nei ovq al 1. for fruit to be ripe and becoming over-ripe (aw$_{\wedge}$ lo$_{\wedge}$ la$^{\vee}$-eu), 2. to be tired and overly tired

PA

pal to change; exchange (as exchanging food coupons for money - 41:175) (9:128); substitute (50:31) (paˇ-eu)
pal to borrow/ loan (not return the same) (9:128) (paˇ-eu)
(vb) **pal** (vb) again (eil **pal** = say again) (in Akha it means to repeat something, but to make a change in what is said) (ehˇ paˇ-eu)
-- **pal, bavq** -- to exchange
palbuvq cotton print cloth
-- **pal, covq** -- (see full)
paldiq meicaol a symbolic wooden rice pounder outside the village and facing away from it, propped up in a threatening position (at least threatening to spirits)
paldoq a borrowed word (50:88)
-- **pal, Galtaol** -- to celebrate the Hani New Year
=**pal, haq**= cloth
palhav handwoven cloth (9:128) (sa˯ paˇ)
-- **pal, hu** -- to review
pal huvq to redeem the original one back with goods (paˇ k'o˄-eu)
pal hhaq to allow to change or exchange (46:144) (in negative: **maq hha pal hhaq** = not allowed to change)
palhhavq a woven belt (14:214) (jo˄ pa˄)
palhhavq naolgul a loom (sa˯ nmˇ guˇ)
palhhovq a woven belt (jo˄ pa˄)
-- **pal, jeilpal** -- to change one's clothes
paljil the sound of walking in mud, rain (26:95)
-- **palkal, haqpal** -- gauze cloth
palkaq a cloth with an open (coarse) weave (cf. Lahu: hpa hka˄-eh_)
palnav black cloth (9:128) (paˇ na^)
palnil red cloth (paˇ neˇ)
palnil ceq 1. to hang a red cloth (12:125) (paˇ neˇ ceu˯-eu), 2. to be praised
palngaq borrow or lend money (50:88)
palpeel grey cloth (9:128)
palpievq to exchange (paˇ-eu)
palpiul white cloth (9:128, 46:175) (paˇ pyuˇ)
palpiul leqhev a white umbrella carried in the left hand of the man who carries the wooden standard in front of the coffin on the way to burial
palpiul wuqtov tov to wear a white turban (done by relatives of the person being buried)
-- **pal, puv** -- change; transform
pal puv huvq to exchange back again (paˇ k'o˄-eu)
palsev nei (see: **pialsev nei** = to be light)
palsiil yellow cloth (paˇ shuiˇ)

-- pal, soqmiav zaol zuvq -- reform of a writing system
paltaol 1. shoulder bag, 2. satchel or overnight bag to carry things in (9:128) (pehˇ tahˇ)
paltaol ceq to carry a shoulder bag (pehˇ tahˇ ceu˯-eu)
paltaol hucavq a kangaroo
paltaol hucavq cavqma a bandicoot rat (or) **leillov hucavq cavqma**
-- paltaol, saqgeel -- a leather bag
-- paltaol, soqhhaq -- a school bag
paltaol taolssaq a small bag (26:51) (pehˇ tahˇ tahˇ za˯)
-- pal, yil -- for a woman to marry again
pal zaq to exchange (paˇ-eu)
-- pal, zaol -- 1. to mend something (paˇ tsahˇ do˄-eu), 2. to adjust; regulate; revise

pa 1. a part. meaning may; might (**pa ngeel aq** = it might be, **pa jav aq** - perhaps I have - 41:157), 2. perhaps not (in neg.) (**maq jol pa ngeel aq** = perhaps he is not here) (pa˯))
-- pa -- a particle used in adjectives and adverbs to make the statement much more intense (**nilqul pa qul nei** = very red, **navq pa navq nei yil** = to go very early) (note: as stated in the introduction, when '**pa**' occurs sandwiched between two high tones, it is spoken on a high tone, otherwise it is spoken on a mid tone. The written form is always on a mid tone.)
pa guv lima frightened (13:48) (gu^-eu)
pa guv nei awful
-- pa leel nei, qaq leel -- extremely tired

paq clf. for frogs, toads (mawˇ)
-- paq male suffix for certain words (**yuqpaq** = grandson) (see also: **da; pyul; zal**)
=paq, aq= male
paqbiav aqma a toad
paqbieiv aqma a toad (9:129) (k'a˯ pa˯ bui^)
paqduv laqsiq a type of frog that lives in forest ponds
=paq, haq= a frog
=paq, hhavq= a boar
=paq, keeq= a male dog
=paq, moq= a male horse
Paqmoq ssaqmoq Old People's Association (in village)
=paq, nil= a shaman (an Asian type of medium)
paqniul a type of green frog (k'a˯ pa˯ pa˯ nyoeˇ)
paqpuv lavqsil a shrew (a small rodent) (ho ca˄ biˇ ceh)
paqqa patrilineal (46:86, 131)
paqqa ciiqyeil patrilineal kinship (46:86)
paqqei a type of field frog
paqsal a type of field frog

paqsev a woman who has sons but no daughters (a type of curse)
paqssaq father and son (9:129, 11:27) (da za˯)
-- **paqssaq, colhhyul aqda** -- dearest elders
paqssaq massaq 1. those related by blood, 2. what all closely related family and friends are called
paqssaq meilnaol what all relatives are called; directly related members of one's family
=**paq, sseil**= a type of green frog

pav to break; to separate (**puvkaq pav yil** = the village broke up) (pa^-iˇ-eu)
pav half (ti˯ pa^) (9:129)
-- **pav, coq** -- to break
-- **pav, doq** -- half of a sentence
-- **pav, gal** -- halfway (as on a journey)
-- **pav, gyu nieiq gyu** -- a roof only half thatched
=**pav, haq**= large bamboo strips
=**pav, hhaq**= half the manpower
-- **pav, keq** -- to cut open; **keq peivq**
pav kevq to be involved; take part (50:88)
-- **pav, keeq** -- half a dog (as when two people own one dog, each owns one-half)
-- **pav, nao** -- half a day
=**pav pieiq, lol**= to dam a stream for fishing
=**pav, sa**= a sharp length of bamboo fashioned so that it can cut grass
-- **pav, teiv** -- to kick and break open
-- **pav, xal** -- to rent a field to someone who will pay back one-half of what is made on it
=**pav, ziq**= hemp thread

pavq to wear (esp. things tied, as a belt) (9:129) (pa˄-eu; dm-eu)
pavq clf. for a leaf (9:129) (pa˄)
pavqbil a 'leaf organ' (a leaf that can be used for making music) (9:129)
pavqbil meel to blow a 'leaf organ'
pavqbul canvas (50:46)
pavq cavq to carry on; to take over from
pavqcavq 1. a target (aˇ pyaˇ), 2. a bad person to be executed by a firing squad (a curse)
pavqcavq bev to shoot at a target (aˇ pyaˇ beu^-eu)
pavqcavq daqnieiq for a bad person to be executed by a firing squad (often used as a curse)
-- **pavqcavq, salsil** -- bad death caused by being executed
pavqcyuq a cover, as for bamboo basket (**pavqcyuq cyuq** = to cover a basket) (pym˯ teh˯-eu)
pavqdeiq a nettle (a prickly plant that stings if touched) (9:129) (pa˄ deh˯)
pavqdeiq deiqcal a type of nettle
pavqdeiq deiqhav a type of nettle
pavqdeiq deiqju the flower of a type of nettle
pavqdeiq deiqzal a type of nettle

=pavq, haq= bamboo leaves
-- **pavq, hoqsiivq kalnaol** -- to tie ears of rice as part of the rice harvest
pavqhovq 1. a type of big leaf (used when they want a drink in the jungle) (9:130), 2. a cup made from a big leaf
=pavq, hyuq= a tobacco leaf
=pavq, hhoq= vegetables
-- **pavq, kaltov** -- (see full)
-- **pavq, kalzal** -- (see full)
pavqkuq aqxeivq a land leech (yeh^ ne^v; yeh^ sa^)
pavqkuv dried, old leaves (pa^ ko^)
-- **pavq, lavqma cavpavq** -- to tie the thumbs of a corpse together with a white thread
pavqmeevq a bubble (boe^v loe^v)
-- **pavq, miq pavq xo pavq** -- to tie a thread around the groom's right wrist and the bride's left wrist as part of the wedding ceremony
=pavq, naq= outer ear
pavqnaoq soft leaves (9:130) (pa^ nah_v)
pavqnil a red leaf (179) (pa^ ne^v)
pavqniul green leaves (pa^ nyoe^v)
pavqpiq piqdei a grass which can be used as pig's food (46:117) (za^ dza^v)
pavqsiil a yellow leaf (46:157) (pa^ shui^v)
pavqsiivq new, fresh leaves (pa^ shui^)
pavqtov a packet made with a leaf (50:6) (pa^ toe^)
  pavqtov tov to wrap up in a leaf (pa^ toe^ toe^-eu)
pavq tovq to tie (pa^ taw^-eu)

pafcu to be sentenced (Chi) (50:127)
  pafcu xiqfaq sentence to corporal punishment (Chi) (50:127)
pafgoq feilzii one who betrays the motherland (Chi) (50:127)
pafjiq court decision; judgment (Chi) (50:127)
paf pal to change the original sentence (A=Chi) (50:55)

PAO

pao to open (9:129) (pah-eu)
-- **pao, bavq** -- to open up a cover
-- **pao, hhelhhuv** -- to give birth to the first child
-- **pao, hhe** -- 1. to open; pull open, 2. to unfold
-- **pao, kalhhuv** -- to begin ('open door') planting crops
-- **pao, meiv** -- (see full)
pao'quq a ball; a basketball (Chi) (or) **laqquq** (cf.: baw dui^v)
=pao, saol= 1. metal pot for steaming rice, 2. a steam boiler
-- **pao, yoheiq** -- prologue; prelude
-- **pao, zovq** -- to unlock

paoq to sow seedlings (pah˯-eu)
paoq to come together (cf. Lahu: hpawn˯ da˰ ve)
paoq identical; the same (**qiq qa paoq**) (ti˯ kaw^; du˅ du˅ deh˰ deh˰) (9:129)
paoq'aol a spindle (or) **caol'aol** (ya ah˅)
=paoq, beel= a cloth tent
=paoq, caq= (see full)
-- paoq, cavpaoq -- to make twine
paoqciivq a knee (9:129) (paw˯ tsui˰)
-- paoqciivq bavq, aqhhyu -- to kneel to the maternal uncles as they come to a funeral
  paoqciivq paoqhhuvq the hollow behind the knee
  paoqciivq saqyyuq the kneecap (paw˯ tsui˰ a˅ beu^)
  paoqciivq tuv to kneel down (9:129, 46:134) (paw˯ tsui˰ paw˯ dm˯ dm˯-eu)
  paoqciivq tuv xa to get down on one's knees (paw˯ tsui˰ paw˯ dm˯ dm˯-eu)
-- paoq, heil -- put together
=paoq, hhoq= a seedbed for vegetable seedlings
-- paoq, kavq -- to tie together
paoqkeeq a yoke worn on shoulders (for carrying loads) (9:129) (paw˯ kui˯)
  paoqkeeq laqcav a rope (tumpline) for a wooden yoke (9:129) (paw˯ kui˯ kui˯ ca^)
paoqleiq a tire (for car etc.) clf.: **leiq** (11:33, 26:99) (a˅ beu^)
-- paoq, piav -- to mix up
-- paoq, seiqpaoq -- to plant rice seeds into a seedbed
paoqtaoq the sound of something falling into water ("splash") (11:218)
paoqzaq to cooperate (35:26)

paovtaov a tax collector (Chi)

PE

peq to eat a meal by scooping food into one's mouth from the bowl (as children do) (beu˯-eu)
peq rotten (as wood) (9:131) (yaw peu˯)
(vb) peq dare to (vb) (9:131, 11:40) (... peu˯-eu)
peqdaq to decay; rot (9:131) (peu˯-eu)

PEE

peel blue; grey (2:56) (yaw pui˅)
peel to release; untie (13:15, 35:4) (pui˅-eu)
peel bieiq to untie; unfasten; untie and let go (9:130, 13:15) (pui˅-eu; pyeh˯-eu)
=peel, byuq= kind of taro
=peel, col= poor people
-- peel, diq -- help someone out of a predicament
-- peel, eil -- to dispute; refute
peel juq to relax; to untie (50:49)
peel nil zuvq a ceremony of offering a buffalo and

cow for a dead person (or) **niuqpeel ssolnei niuqnil zuvq**

=peel, niuq= water buffalo
peel pa peel nei very grey (11:58)
=peel, sal= a gourd (wax gourd)
peelsev nei greyish
=peel, sul= thatch grass; cogon grass
peelsuq nei very grey (9:130, 46:165); sky blue
=peel, wuq= (see full)

=peeq, haq= inner bran when rice is husked
peeqhav outer (hard) rice husks (9:130) (ceh˅ k'aw‸)
peeqkaq medium-soft rice bran (k'a˯ pui˯)
peeqnaoq very soft rice bran
peeqnil soft rice bran (reddish)
peeqnuv soft rice bran

peev to burn (9:130) (pui^-eu)
peev to roast (or) **ca** (ba-eu)
peev byu to be broken from burning (as a pot) (14:235)
-- **peev, keq** -- to set on fire
peev kul to be over-roasted; burned; charred (pui^ ku˅-eu)
peev laq e to be burned
peev luvq to burn and shrivel up (pui^ ku˯-eu)
-- **peev, millaol** -- for a fire to burn in the jungle
-- **peev, molpeev** -- to burn the whole body
peev saq to burn away (pui^ byo^-eu; keu˯ dzeh-eu; pui^ dzeh-eu)
peev sil to burn to death (pui^ seh‸-eu)

PEI

peil an astringent taste (it makes one's lips puckery, as tea, pears) (9:130, 11:55) (yaw peh˅)
=peil, aq= pear
peilbeil an apron women wear
  peilbeil laol to fold clothes (meh˯ tsoe˯ bya^-eu)
peil biavq guvq to make an outfit of black and white cloth for an elder to keep his or her lifespan tree (**ssilzaol**) from falling down
  peil biavq zaq hal sal asking for longer life and more food (esp. after 66 years of age, considered the normal age span)
peildaoq a cloth Hani women wear around their hips
peilhaoq clothing (shirt, jacket) (9:130) (peh˅ k'ah˯)
  peilhaoq daodaq a shirt (peh˅ k'ah˯)
  peilhaoq peilja old clothes (9:130) (peh˅ k'ah˯ peh˅ ceh˅)
  peilhaoq laolbav a fur collar
  peilhaoq neehha upper front part of clothes
  peilhaoq peillov a pocket (in clothes) (or) **peillov** (11:35) (paw˯ beh^)

peilhaoq peilmol a long coat for women or old men (peh˅ k'ah˯ peh˅ mah˅)

peiljal laqjal 1. old clothing; old pants (35:76), 2. shabby clothing (**peiljal laqjal dao**) (see also: **ju lu ja la meil**) (meh˯ tsoe˯ yaw oe˅), 3. clothing in general (one dialect)

peiljil airplane (or) **feiljil** (Chi) (heu bi˅)

peilju laqjal old, ripped clothes; trousers (or) **peilja laqja; peilju peilja** (peh˅ ju peh˅ ja)

peillal a narrow vest-like cloth Hani men wear, with buttons on it; **peilhaoq peillal** (lit., 'tongue of clothing')

peillev nei an astringent taste (it makes the lips puckery) (or) **peiltuv nei** (yaw peh˅)

peillil a short coat for women; a woman's vest (no sleeves)

peillov a pocket in clothes (or) **peilhaoq peillov** (9:130) (paw˯ beh˄)

peillov a beq to put a hand in a pocket to search for something (35:93) (paw˯ beh˄-ah˅ beu˯-eu)

peillov hucavq cavqma bandicoot rat (Bandicotta spp)

-- peil, neema -- to be angry

peilniul green clothing (4:39) (pa˅ nyoe˅)

peil peil tuv tuv astringent taste; puckery; **peiltuv**

peilpi button 'hole' (actually a loop of cloth through which the button is fastened) (9:130)

peilpiul white clothing (4:35) (cf.: pa˅ pyu˅)

peilsiq button (9:130, 11:27) (peh˅ si˯)

peilsiivq new clothes (9:130, 46:160) (cf.: pa˅ shui˰)

peilsiivq laqsiivq new clothes (for women and men) (46:160)

peiltuv an astringent taste (makes lips puckery); **peil peil tuv tuv**

peiltuv nei an astringent taste (or) **peillev nei** (yaw peh˅)

peiq an exclamation (**Peiq! Aqssii qavq ssii wul yaq.** Oh, how dirty and disgusting!)

peiq playing cards (Chi) (**peiq diq zaq** = to play cards, an older term, the newer is: **puqkeiq diq zaq**)

peiq to pay for (Chi)

peiq clf. for a basin (Chi) (9:131)

peiqcaq jiljif syusiiq compensate for economic loss (Chi) (50:128)

peiqcaol fine-tooth comb (9:131) (paw˯ tsah˅)

=peiq cyuqnal, cyuq= diseases

=peiq, daoq= a base; foundation (daw˯ peh˯)

peiqfalpiq to mix medicine (Chi) (15:37)

peiq huvq to compensate (A=Chi)

=peiq, huvq= beginning of the year

peiqji flower arangement in a jar or vase (Chi) (50:130)

=peiq, naq= 1. temple of the head (on both sides of the head), 2. a place on a bed near where the pillows are kept

peiqqeq volleyball (Chi) (50:126)

peiq tao (see: **pieiq tao** = to put into - 14:147)

peiqtaoq cillil a kind of fruit (it looks like a comb)

peiqtaoq peiqcaol combs made of wood and carried on the wooden banner before the coffin (see: **heiq sov albol haqzeil**)

peiqya to educate; train; develop; cultivate; nurture; foster (Chi) (26:106, 34:59)

peiqyif typesetting and printing (Chi) (50:126)

peiqza a platoon leader (Chi) (50:126)

peiqziif composing; typesetting (Chi)

peiv 1. to pick out a splinter (9:131) (peh^ do^-eu), 2. to hold with a stick (**alcav peiv** = to hold a rope with a stick) (14:214)

peiv 1. to have a sickness or disease that continues (**aol gov laq e nal peiv** = a continuous sickness), 2. to have a relapse of a sickness; a sickness to recur

peiv clf. for a drop of dew (35:73)

-- **peiv, aol gov laq e nal** -- to have an incurable sickness or disease for many years

-- **peiv, civq** -- to be angry

-- **peiv, civq lav** -- 1. to make someone angry, 2. to offend someone

peiv dav to prick (or) **cov dav**

peiv lal for a sickness to recur

-- **peiv lal, nalgol** -- to become sick again

=peiv, laq= tea

=peiv, lavq= a callous

peiv leeq to trip and fall down (26:24) (dawˬ teˇ teˇ-eu)

peiv lol to stumble (9:131) (sahˬ ti‸ ti‸-eu)

peivnaovq nei to be dense; thick (as porridge) (11:150) (yaw tuˇ)

-- **peiv, naovpeiv** -- to wear shoes just half on

-- **peiv, neema salqiq** -- to be very angry

peivnil black tea

-- **peiv, salqiq** -- to be very angry

peiv sil peiv lo to be very angry

peivq to vomit (peh‸-eu) (9:131); **yuqpeivq peivq**

peivq 1. to pick out thorns or pus (see also: **peiv**), 2. to let water go out (**Xaldei wulquvq peivq.** To let water out of irrigated fields.), 3. to cut open; to operate

-- **peivq, keq** -- to cut someone or something open

-- **peivq, yuqpeivq** -- to vomit

peif to send (Chi) (**feiljil peif** = to send a plane - 26:78) (k'ehˇ g'eh-eu)

peifbiq a group; school; faction (as in politics) (Chi) (34:103)
peifcuq jilgual agency (Chi) (50:126)
peifcuqso local police station (Chi) (50:125)
peifdieifsiiq power distribution station (Chi) (50:128)
peiftaof to form a complete set (Chi) (34:74)

PI

pil a 'spirit priest'; one who is the go-between for humans and spirits in the Hani culture (just '**pil**' is used when naming the three great ones: **zyuq, pil, qivq**); **pilma; moqpil** (piˇ ma)
-- pil, alkaq -- to solve a dispute (aˇ ka˯ piˇ-eu)
pilduv to spell out (A=Chi) (32:3)
pilfaq wholesale (Chi) (50:129)
=pil, gee= (see full)
-- pil, gee -- to mediate; make peace
-- pil, koq -- to grab back
=pil, laq= chili pepper
pilma a 'spirit priest'; one who is the go-between for humans and spirits in the Hani culture; **moqpil; pil; byulmoq** (see more under: **moqpil**) (piˇ ma)
pilma naqboq a type of large chili (sa˯ piˇ piˇ ma)
=pil, moq= (see full)
pilpaf to criticize someone severely (Chi) (50:129)
pil pil pal pal the sound of crackling fire (Note: the stops may be unaspirated, depending on the speaker) (11:21)
pilpiq to criticize (Chi) (26:31, 50:129)
  pilpiq qeiqliq the right to criticize (Chi) (50:129)
pilse never in any case (or) **pieilse**
  pilse taq (vb) no matter what (you) must not (vb) (9:132) (a˯ jo^-ehˇ k'aw˄ ta˯ (vb))
pilsil a type of thatch
-- pilsil, buqluq -- (see: **buqluq**)
  pilsil luljuv aqma a small light-colored bird, nests in roof (said to use fur from tiger, dragon and other wild animals to make its nest)
Piltavq a boy's name (11:106)
-- pil, taoq -- to separate
piltev a type of small chili
pilxi to spell (Chi) (41:78)
Pilyil Pinyin system of writing Chinese in English (Romanized) letters (Chi) (9:132, 32:3, 50:130)
pil zaq to settle; solve (**alkaq pil zaq** = to settle a dispute) (piˇ-eu)
Pilzeq a boy's name (11:176)
pilzyu to permit someone to do something (Chi) (or) **xul** (50:129)

pi 1. carry on back (or) **eq** (pi-eu; eu˯-eu), 2. to be pregnant (pi-eu), 3. to take on responsibility

pideq quality (Chi) (or) **pideiq** (50:130)
=pi, kav= cord of a crossbow
-- pi, ssaq -- 1. to carry child on one's back, 2. to be pregnant
pi teiq nia able to carry on duties; able to lead others; **pi to nia**
pi to nia able to carry on duties; able to lead others; **pi teiq nia**

piq to close; shut; cover (9:132) (pi˅-eu)
piq to be slow (Chi) (11:55)
piq clf. for a bottle (Chi) (**piqzii qiq piq** - 26:116)
=piq, aq= grandmother; old lady
piqbaol leather bag (Chi)
-- piq, beelkaq -- to close an umbrella
piqbi to compare; to appraise by comparing (Chi)
=piq, cal= a cover (as for a pot)
=piq, caq= (see full)
piqciq a tape measure (Chi) (14:150)
piqdaof a TV channel (Chi) (50:130)
piqdei equal (Chi) (50:130)
-- piqdei, pavqpiq -- a grass which can be used as a pig food
-- piq, deiq -- to close (as window)
piqgo alsiq apple (A=Chi) (50:131)
piqheiq leather shoes (Chi)
Piqhoq a township in Luchun county
=piq, hoq= 1. rice steamer cover, 2. peace (Chi)
piqhov a mirror (12:125, 26:41, 46:79) (pyaw˅ haw)
=piqhov, hoqbav= a mirror
=piq, hu= a bamboo gopher
-- piq, hhe -- to pull closed (door; cover)
piqjaf to appraise (Chi) (34:28)
piqje beer (Chi) (41:169) (note: **beiqje** = wine)
piqje zilbaq beer (A=Chi) (50:129)
piqjil zuyif egalitarianism (Chi) (34:38, 50:131)
piqkaq a lid
piqkaq diq kaq to cover something with a lid (as food, to keep off flies) (10:19) (deh˅ ka˅-eu; pi˅ ka˅-eu)
-- piqkaq, laqnil -- an outer covering
piqkeel gall bladder; gall; bile (pya˅ kuiˇ; pi˅ kuiˇ = CA)
piqkeel dav to develop a disease of the gall bladder
piqlaq kohlrabi (a vegetable) (Chi)
=piq, laq= a small basket in which women carry their sewing
piqnaoq a poor peasant (Chi) (26:3)
piqnieiq a normal year; a non-leap year (Chi) (41:115)
piqqeq a ball (Chi) (or) **siilpuq**
piqqeiq 1. crippled; lame (kuiˇ caw^ caw^-eu), 2. to become limp (38:90)

piqqeiq meilssuq to limp (5:682) (kuiˇ dzaˇ dzaˇ-eu)
piqqil temper; temperament (or) **piqqif** (Chi) (**aqniuq piqqif** = a buffalo's temper - 26:58)
piqquq basketball (Chi)
piqssaq grandmother and grandchildren (45:12)
piqzii bottle (Chi) (or) **malcavq piqzii** clf.= **piq** (10:19, 26:116) (maˇ tsa˰)
-- piq, zovq -- to lock (9:174)

PIA

pial light in weight (9:131) (pyaˇ-eu)
pialhav a kind of thatch grass
pialku nei very light in weight (11:58)
pialseiv seivssaq nei very, very light in weight (11:59) (or) **pialsev nei; palsev nei**

pia 1. to have no root, 2. a light-hearted, shallow person
=pia, bavq= a flag
=pia, haqzeil zeil= small kind of eagle
pia'la nei a careless person

piaq to have a fever (9:131) (pyaˬ-eu)
-- piaq, alpiaq -- to have a fever
=piaq, aqdaol daol= the whole wing (as of a bird)
piaqcao malaria; high fever (9:131, 50:124) (miˇ hiˬ)
piaqcao cao to suffer from malaria; have a high fever (10:24) (miˇ hiˬ pyaˬ-eu)
piaqcoq Asiatic chipmunk (Eutamias sibericus) (ho ca˰ pyaˬ tsawˬ)
piaqgol nalgol dav huvq a ceremony held when many people and or animals die in a year
piaqhhal footprint (9:131) (pehˬ zaˇ; pehˬ g'aˇ = CA)
piaqkaq crotch (5:59) (same as groin in Ak) (pyaˬ kaˬ)
piaqsal albaol leiq a festival to kill grasshoppers and insects, after the rice comes up (46:79)
=piaq, xaol= eaves of a house
piaqyiq a masked (gem-faced) civet cat (a small mammal) (pyaˬ iˬ)
piaqyiq aqma nalcal 1. a masked civet cat with a white nose (a small mammal), 2. a natural instinct not easy to change (cf. Eng.: 'cannot change a leopard's spots')
piaqyiq laqjaq a monitor lizard (k'aˬ lehˇ buˇ jehˇ)
piaqyiq yiqpeel a larger type of civet cat (a small mammal) (pyaˬ iˬ puiˇ)

piav to pull down (as a house); to remove (as something built) (**laqhyul piav** = to tear down a house) (pya^-eu)
piav to do something with fingers, as to scratch,

seize something (scratching an itch, a chicken scratching in the ground, etc.) (cf. **cuv**) (pya^-eu)
piav to pick cotton (pya^-eu)
piav ceq to climb up on (as a cat on a person - 29:4)
piav gee to turn upside down to dry (g'eu pya^ gui-eu)
piav kevq to mix up (la^ keu˯-eu)
-- piav pao, qiq piav -- to scratch open
piav paoq to mix up (9:132) (la^ keu˯-eu)
piav puv to search; to check on things (as what is in a case or bag); to research (go˯ haw-eu)
piav qivq can be touched (46:151)
=piav, seiq= to meet danger
piav soq piav leev to manage; to run well (50:65)
piavsov to be slow in action (yaw mya˰)
piav ssaoq to put things together
piav tao 1. to climb into (as a window) (13:45) (pya^ ahˇ-eu); 2. to scramble and put into
piavteiq a spring trap for birds and small animals (pya^ teh˯ tahˇ-eu) (**saol piavteiq** = metal traps)
piav teiq 1. to grab and hold onto (9:132, 13:24) (nyeh˰ teh˯-eu), 2. to hold against something (as the wall) (38:18)
-- piav, teiq sil teiq -- running around in circles; in a frantic rush; in a muddle
piav tul to wake up (14:149) (noe˯ laˇ-eu)
piav xa to scrape off (as moss from the roof) (14:217) (pya^ dzeh-eu)
-- piav zaq, aqniuq -- to cut open a buffalo and skin it at a funeral
piav ziil 1. to scratch something flat (11:215); 2. to make something clean

PIAO

piaol clf. for points given for work in the Communist system (Chi); a minute (Chi)
=piaol, hhaq= food made of buckwheat
-- piaol zaq, hhaqpiaol -- to make tiny dumplings from buckwheat flour

piaof ticket (as for a train) (Chi) (26:90)
piaof luvq taq to scrutinize balloting (A=Chi) (50:82)
piaof luvq taq col one who scrutinizes balloting (A=Chi) (50:82)
piaof tyuq huvq to return a ticket (A=Chi) (41:176)

PIE

pievq to become; change to (9:132) (**Laqbeqssaq pievq** = to become Chinese) (pyeu˰-eu)
pievq to grow up; increase (hui˯ laˇ-eu)

=**pievq, hu=** a pole in a field hut; a forked stick with a crotch in it
-- **pievq, hhellavq** -- commodity (for buying and selling)
=**pievq, seq=** (see full)
-- **pievq, zaol** -- to succeed

PIEI

pieil to cheat (Chi) (myaw^-eu shuiˇ-eu)
pieilheeq swollen spleen (shiˇ pyehˇ huiˇ-eu)
pieilse taq (vb) must not (vb) (under any circumstances) (11:220, 221) (or) **pilse**
=**pieil taoq, wuq=** (see full)

piei to open; spread (including birds spreading their wings) (mˇ pyeh-eu)
-- **piei, daolpiei** -- to spread wings (as bird)
-- **piei, hhe** -- 1. to open (as mouth), 2. to force open (as someone's mouth), 3. to spread out
-- **piei, meiqzu** -- to open one's mouth
piei nei to open (**meiqbaoq piei nei** = to open mouth - 26:49, 46:168); to be wide (35:57)
-- **piei nei, kaoqpuq** -- throat swells with anger
-- **piei, tuv** -- to open an umbrella or the like

pieiq 1. release; let go (9:132); 2. to show, as a movie; a TV program (41:191) (pyehˇ-eu)
-- **pieiq, aolpav** -- to rent out, as a field (half of produce comes back to the owner)
pieiq beeq pieiq ga overflow; spread unchecked (50:47)
pieiq bial to give up something (as land) (45:52) (**xaldei liq pieiq bial saq** = he gave up that field as well) (byehˇ-eu)
pieiqbial bial to release on parole (50:81)
pieiq biaol to release a bird (let it fly away)
pieiq cavq to breed (as animals)
pieiq ceq to hang up (14:168, 45:25) (g'eu ceuˇ-eu)
-- **pieiq, ciq** -- to temper metal by dipping in water
pieiq dal to rely on; to trust (g'oe-eu)
-- **pieiq, dieifyi** -- to show a movie (A=Chi)
-- **pieiq, doqbiav** -- cook up a story and spread it around; start a rumor
pieiq dov to put in (as seasoning in food) (11:117)
-- **pieiq dov, wuqdeiq hholqei haqluv** -- to put stones in another's stomach by means of black magic
pieiq duv 1. to give forth; 2. to get off; 3. to let go (or) **hhe hhoq; xeiv leev; ssavq**
-- **pieiq, eel naq** -- to provoke laughter
-- **pieiq, eil naq maq** -- to keep on talking
-- **pieiq, gaolfeil** -- distribute work points
-- **pieiq, guvniq** -- to awe; frighten
-- **pieiq, halnil** -- to slander

-- **pieiq, haq** -- to break wind; pass gas, flatulence (taboo)
pieiq heeq to enlarge; to increase in size
-- **pieiq, hhaqleiq** -- to make a joke
pieiqjuq to loosen; relax (9:132)
-- **pieiq lal, jeilquv** -- to be punished for committing adultery
-- **pieiq lal, ssilcovq** -- to cause a person to have a short life
-- **pieiq lal, yeilquvq** -- for **Aqpyuq Miqyeil** to punish someone
-- **pieiq, laqleiq** -- for an elder to bless a newly married couple as they come around with drinks
-- **pieiq, leiq** -- to drive cattle to the mountains
-- pieiq, lolpav -- to dam a stream for fishing
-- **pieiq, nalgol** -- to cause disease by black magic
-- **pieiq, neivqhaq** -- to perform black magic
-- **pieiq puvq, ngaqhhovq** -- to throw in a fish hook (when fishing)
pieiq suvq to drain (or) **peivq suvq; wulquvq pieiq suvq**
pieiq taq 1. to stop, 2. to put down (pyeh˯ ta˯-eu) (9:132)
pieiq xa to let go; let down; transfer to a lower level (as doing manual work in the countryside) (50:184) (pyeh˯ g'eh-eu) (cf. **xa** with Lahu: hk'a, as in: yawˇ hta˄ piˇ hk'a.) (13:15)
pieiq xu to relax; to mitigate (50:74)
pieiq yeil 1. relax restrictions (50:49), 2. to enlarge (50:100)
pieiq zeil to filter (dze do^-eu)
pieiq zei abandon; give up (50:49)

pieiv to peel (9:132) (leu˄-eu; pyeh^-eu)
pieiv to cut up (as cloth) (9:132) (teh˯-eu) (pyeh˄-eu = to cut tubular things, including the umbilical cord)
pieiv ceq 1. to put up or hang up (as on wall) (9:132, 46:132), 2. to grab (as a vine 'grabbing' one's feet - 27:11) (nyeh˄ teh˯-eu)
pieiv ceiv to cut apart (as cloth)
-- **pieiv, lalpieiv** -- sure to come
-- **pieiv, leiv** -- to grind into pieces
-- **pieiv, naoq** -- to trample to pieces
-- **pieiv, nuvq** -- to squeeze to pieces
-- **pieiv, qaoqdaq** -- to cut cloth for an outler layer of a coat
-- **pieiv, ssiivq** -- suppress; repress; put down (50:209)
pieivto a limited time
-- **pieiv, zul** -- to sit down with low spirits

pieivq to braid (pyeh˄-eu)
=**pieivq, caol**= braided hair
-- **pieivq, caol pieivq** -- to braid the hair (as

into a pigtail)

PIO

pioq face; appearance (or) **pyuq** (**mya**^ pyaw˅; pyaw˅ na˅)
pioqcavq an ugly face; ugly appearance (pyaw˅ na˅ yaw doeˇ)
pioqkaq haqpal a piece of cloth given (along with a chicken and egg) by relatives to be carried out to the burial site with the coffin (used to wipe away the paintings on the coffin)
pioqzaq a beautiful face; beautiful appearance (pyaw˅ na˅ yaw mui˅)

PIU

piul silver; money (9:132) (pyuˇ)
piul white (9:132) (yaw pyuˇ)
-- piul, aqmoq moq -- a white horse
piulbia white (14:205) (yaw pyuˇ; yaw ba)
piul buvq devalued money; money which has depreciated in value (50:12)
piulbyuvq byuvq to have inflation; for money to lose value (50:167)
piulcav a silver chain (9:132, 11:27) (yeh˅ saw˅)
=piul, ceil= husked rice
piuldev a silver lump (9:133, 33:3) (pyuˇ k'oˇ; pyuˇ kaw˅)
piuldev moqseiq a silver lump in the shape of a horse's hoof
piulduq silver buried in ground (pyuˇ du˅)
piulduq duq to bury silver in the ground
=piul, gevq= a silver pheasant (brd)
=piul, geeq= a white metal ('white copper')
=piul, hao= white bristles (as on a pig)
=piul, haoq= a white porcelain bowl
=piul, hoq= white (husked) rice
=piul, hu= a porcupine
=piul, kaoq= perspiration; sweat
piul leiq ssaoq to raise funds; collect money (50:80)
=piul, miav= the white of the eye
=piul, moq= a white horse
Piulniul Chinese (or) **Pyulniul; Alniul; Navssaq; Laqbeq** (La^ bui˅)
piul sal zaq 1. to earn money, 2. to beg for money (pyuˇ shaˇ dza˅-eu)
piul se joq! 'here is the money' (41:151
piul sessaoq zaq e col a money collector; treasurer (11:134)
piulseiq nei whitish (9:133) (pyuˇ pya ni)
piulseiq pa seiq nei glistening white (11:57)
piulsiil silver and gold (11:82) (pyuˇ shuiˇ)
piulsiil duq gold and silver buried in ground (50:6)

piul siil gua'li faqgyul regulations to manage silver and gold (B=Chi) (50:88)
piulsol pure silver (pyu˅)
piul sol an old type of Chinese silver coin (clf. = **biav**), worth about 40 yuan in 1995
piul ssaq deivq zeq lal to draw interest on money
piulssaq se hha a realistic tax rate (50:153)
piul ssaoq duv to spend money freely (or) **zeiq ssaoq duv** (**zeiq** = an old word for one's property, including animals)
piul taq yaol a bank for money ('money placing building')
piultavq tavq to save ('stack') silver/money (pyu˅ ta‸ ta‸-eu)
piultaoq bone marrow (sha˯ yoe˯ i˅ nm‸)
piul towtaq miaoqgaoq hha to deposit money and get in kind (50:153)
=piul, wuq= white-headed person
=piul, zal= niter

PO

pol to migrate (paw˅-eu)

poqbiav sugar; candy (9:133, 10:13) brown sugar from semi-refined sugar cane (**qiq biav**) (paw˯ coe˅ ca‸ a˅ si˯)
poqbiav biav to form cane sugar into flat cakes
poqbiav biavnav brown sugar; cakes of cane sugar (jaggery) (11:157) (paw˯ coe˅ ca‸)
poqbiav biavpiul white cane sugar
poqneiq malt sugar
poqpil laqpeiv a frgrant type of grass from which they can get an expensive type of oil, and also make tea (57:130)
poqqul sugar cane (9:133), **pyuqqul** (paw˯ coe˅)
poqsalfaol tetanus (Chi) (**poqsalfaol duv** = to develop tetanus - 15:28)
Poqsyu Jiq a water festival for the Dai people (in the book: **Poqxyu Jiq** - 14:237) (Chi)

-- pov, hal -- to yawn (**hal pov tyul taq** = when he yawns)

povq lungs (9:133, 11:16) (sha˯ paw‸)
povq 1. to get soft (**Hhoqpul povq al**. Turnips get soft.), 2. to be empty; used up (**beillol hhyuq povq** = a quid of betel after being chewed)
-- povq, beillol hhyuq -- a quid of betel after chewing it
=povq, guq= dregs left over after making soybean milk
povq nal 1. lung disease (10:pref.); 2. pneumonia (sha˯ paw‸ na˅-eu)
povqnal duv lal 1. for lung disease to develop;

2. to come down with pneumonia (10:22)
povqsav nei to be softened

pofhueif to destroy (Chi) (34:10) (la^ caw^-eu)
pofhueifsif to damage; to harm (Chi) (50:131)
pofzeiqhaof a dash (punctuation mark) (Chi)

PU

pul clf. for a set (**niuqceiq qiq pul** = set of things for plowing) (11:76)
pul clf. for a song (11:161) (bymˇ, and cf. Lahu: pu^)
pul ! sound made when complaining about a bad odor
=pul, hhoq= Chinese radish; turnip
=pul, keel= ankle (or) **keelmiav**
=pul lavqciivq, lavq= wrist
-- **pul luq meil, puq lu** -- to fall and roll
pulqu nei (see: **puv'qu nei** = a pile; a hill - 14:167)
pulsiq a hill (35:97, 46:168) (or) **puv siq** (gaw˯ duˇ)

Pu'e Pu'er county (46:181)
pujiq to permeate (Chi) (or) **seiftef** (Chi)
pujiq jaofyeq universal education (Chi) (50:132)
pupieif gyulliq universal law (Chi) (34:23)
pupieif zeilli general idea (Chi) (50:132)
Putaolhuaf Mandarin (Chi) (50:132)

puq 1. to swell (9:133) (pu˯-eu), 2. a tumor (or) lu
puq clf. for a bunch of fruit, for a hive of bees, strings of things (beads, keys), a cluster (bamboo; grass; trees)
puq, puq, puq 1. the sound of many birds flying, 2. fog or steam to be floating along
=puq, baq= a protruding face
=puq ceiq nei, nil= reddish
puqcil pa cil nei puq swollen up very much (11:59) (pu˯ laˇ dui dui-eu)
=puq, diq= hammer
puqduv daoqmiq a fox (9:133)
=puq, haol a gourd
puqhul a lump of earth; a clod (46:177) (miˇ tsa˯ ti˯ bymˇ)
puqkeiq playing cards (a newer term than: **peiq**) (Chi) (14:195)
puqkeiq diq to play cards (A=Chi)
puq lal to meet; to come across someone by luck (45:61) (or) **taoqpuq; taoqzyul** (pu˯ laˇ-eu; tah˯ pu˯-eu)
puq lal lu lal for a tumor to be growing
puqleiq nei softly (57:80)
puq lu pul luq meil to fall and roll
=puq, mil= soft earth
puq nei sparkling suddenly (35:102)

puqnil tiny baby or tiny animal (35:73) (za˯ nah˯)
=puq piei nei, kaoq= (see full)
-- **puq, qaq** -- to meet accidentally
-- **puq, qao** -- to meet on purpose
-- **puq, qo** -- to meet
=puq, quq= to meet without engagement
puqsuf simple (as a simple life) (Chi) (26:74)
puqtaol wild grape (Chi) (or) **nibiav alsiq**
=puq, wuq= to have a big belly (u˯ ma^ pu˯-eu)
-- **puq, wuqdeiq** -- to have a swollen stomach
puqzii a shop (Chi) (26:2)

puv 1. to roll, 2. to betray, 3. to cross; get over (45:63) (po^-eu)
puv 1. to turn over (9:133) (po^-eu), 2. to turn around (**Huvqlavq qiq huvq qiq huvq meil puv al.** The village turned around over the years and months.) (po^ la˅-eu)
(vb) **puv** to repeat (vb) (**nal puv** = to get sick again 13:53, **eil puv** = to say again) (... po^-eu, as in: m˅ po^-eu; eh˅ po^-eu, etc.)
puv clf. for a village (pu)
-- **puv, aqpuv lilpuv** -- to rotate; to whirl
-- **puv, aolzei** -- for a top to turn
-- **puv, bavq** -- to turn over; to overthrow
-- **puv, buqluq** -- to prevent a werewolf doing anything by cursing it
-- **puv, cev** -- to turn over (as a page, a cake, etc.)
-- **puv, ceiq** -- (see full)
-- **puv, ceivnei** -- a violent change
=puv, col= a village (or) **puvkaq**
puv cuv an established village (38:33, 46:118) (pu tso^)
  puvcuv cuv to establish a village (46:112) (pu tso^ tso^-eu)
  puvcuv deicuv cuv to establish a village and fields (46:112)
  puvcuv hhaqcuv cuv to establish a village and a sacred grove for a village
puvcyuq a poor village (57:71)
puvdav to add to (A=Chi) (11:31) (daw^ lah˯-eu)
puv dav roll up onto something (po^ da^-eu)
puvdav davqaol the place in a village to hold discussions (must not build a house there)
-- **puv, deiq** -- to turn over; to push over
-- **puv diq leeq, diq** -- to overthrow
Puvdo a village that split off of Salpuv (46:123)
=puv, doq= upside down words (and see full)
-- **puv, eil** -- to reply; answer
=puv, goq= bamboo mat for drying crops
puvhaoq deihaoq haoq to establish a village and a living place (46:112)
puv huvq 1. to restore (as an old tradition or political practice) (50:54), 2. to turn back
puv huvq lal to be recovered (50:75)

puvhhaol a village site (46:115) (pu dzahˇ zaˇ)
puvhhaol qo mol to find a site for the middle of the village (46:114)
-- **puv, hhe** -- to pull up
-- **puv hhol pal, hhol** -- to breathe in and out
puvkaq village (9:133) (clf. = puv) (pu)
puvkaq bialzeil edge of a village (13:48), **zaolzeil** (pu dzeˇ)
puvkaq kaqsiivq a new village (or) **puvsiivq** (pu shui^)
puvkaq kaqssaq a small village (35:72) (pu **yaw** zaˇ)
puvkaq puvma 1. an old village (pu oeˇ), 2. a big village (46:122) (pu ma)
puvkaq puvzeil the side of the village (9:133, 35:17) (pu dzeˇ)
puvkaq zaolzeil the side of the village
-- **puv, kavq** -- to tie with a rope
-- **puv, kov** -- to stir up
puv lal uprising; revolt; insurrection (50:134)
-- **puv, lav** -- to turn upside down; turn over
puvlav cev to be quick (13:47) (yaw kawˇ)
puvlav cev nei quickly (yaw kawˇ kawˇ-ehˇ) (11:205)
puvlav nei to turn upside down (po^ la^ la^-eu)
puvlav teiv nei quickly; **puvlav cevnei**
puvlav teiv nei cev puv turn over quickly
puvlaol related to the village (35:14)
puvlaol aqhhol the village head (or) **puvlaol soqpaq** (35:34) (pu dzoeˇ ma)
puvlaol dama 1. respected villagers (see: **dama colziil**), 2. all villagers (26:10; 41:3) (tiˇ pu siˇ)
puvlaol doqtevq village regulations (50:185)
puvlaol hovqma all of the villagers (a term of endearment, as when addressing them) (35:43); elders; fellow villagers (46:93, 131)
puvlaol hovqma ssaqmeeq dearest fellow villagers ('good people' is added) (46:153) (cf. pu cawˇ yaw muiˇ)
puvlaol soqpaq village head; village ruler (historically this would be the **zyuqma**, but currently it tends to be the 'ritual head' -- **milguq** -- in most cases)
-- **puv, leiq** -- overthrow; overturn
-- **puv, leiv** -- to repeat
-- **puv, lilpuv** -- 1. to turn upside down (la^ po^ la^ paˇ-eu), 2. to be confused (see: **lilpuv puvssaq**), 3. to violate; run counter to (50:176)
puv lil puv la 1. to turn over repeatedly, 2. to do something repeatedly (35:42) (**puv lil puv la meil aol** = to do something over and over)
-- **puv, lil puv lav** -- rise in rebellion; revolt
puv li puv lal winding (14:191)
puv li puv lav backward and forward
puv li qav e huvqlavq the year which is past (50:90)

puvliq liq lal for a village to disappear (as when all the people in it die)
puvloq to exonerate; to rehabilitate (50:208)
puvlovq lovq a very active village (35:74)
-- **puvluv nei, miavneev** -- for eyeballs to turn up
puvma tul to offer to the village spirit (46:111)
puvma zaolteil one (or three) stone erected in the middle of the village to the 'lord of the area' (**milsaol luvcuv**)
=**puv meil, lil**= upside down
puvmiaol hovqmiaol eil to give the name of the village as part of the funeral ceremony
-- **puv, moqpuv** -- a horse to roll on its back in the dust
-- **puv, nal** -- to have a relapse in sickness
-- **puv, naolhhuvq** -- to turn back
=**puvnaoq, yul**= (see full)
-- **puv, nee** -- to reflect; to react (41:95)
=**puv nei, lil**= in contrast; upside down; opposite; contrary
puvnil a 'glorious' village (14:181)
-- **puv, nieivq** -- to wind up (as to wind up a toy)
-- **puv, nyuq** -- (see full)
puv pal to change; transform (50:217)
-- **puv, piav** -- to do research; search; rummage; check on things (as to what is in a case or bag)
(vb) **puv** (vb) **tav** over and over again (**hu puv hu tav** = looking at the letter again and again - 26:80)
puvqu a pile of something
puvsal sal a very happy, fortunate village (35:74) (pu yaw sa˅)
-- **puv, saq** -- to return to suffering
puvsaq saq an unfortunate, unhappy village (46:118) (pu yaw shaˬ)
-- **puv, saqyoq lilpuv** -- to rebel
puvsiq a hill (gawˬ du˅)
puvsiivq a new village (or) **puvkaq kaqsiivq** (pu shui˄)
puvsiivq puvssaq a small new village (46:123) (pu zaˬ pu shui˄)
-- **puv, xa** -- to plant again
puv yil puv lal turn back and forth (46:90)
-- **puv yil, xeiv** -- to turn back
-- **puv, yoqpuv** -- rotation
-- **puv, zalpuv** -- to ruminate
puv zaq 1. to rebel (or) **saqyoq lilpuv puv**, 2. to betray someone or something (50:9)
puvzeil pyu outside of the village (14:214) (pu dze˅)
puvzei zei to be strong (57:70)
-- **puv, zol** -- to review; to re-read
-- **puv, zyul** -- to repeat one's mistakes; to revert to bad ways; to be a habitual criminal
-- **puv, zyulpuv** -- habitual criminal

puvq 1. to boil, 2. to cook (9:133) (pu˄-eu)

puvq to enter into water (liquid) (pu^-eu)
-- puvq, coq -- to jump into
puvqhho hho to boil (or simmer) something so it is half done; to parboil
-- puvq, leeq -- to fall into liquid
-- puvq, ya -- to fall into water
-- puvq, zei -- to fall into liquid

PYU

pyul to move away (as to another village) (**pyul li qavq** = they have moved away) (11:99) (pawˇ-eu)
pyul to pass someone (as when walking); to cross a road (11:165) (tseh^-eu)
pyul male suffix for certain animals (**hapyul** = a rooster) (see also: **paq; da; zal**)
pyul clf. for a broom
(vb) pyul (vb) toward (**hu pyul** = looked toward; **xeiv pyul** = ran toward - 26:48)
=pyul, aq= a male animal (not used for all animals)
=pyul, aqha ha= a rooster; cock
-- pyul, bavq -- to take something over there
-- pyul, coq -- to jump over
=pyul, ha= a rooster; cock (ya poeˇ)
-- pyul heil, hhel -- to have bought something over there
pyul lal 1. to come up to this side, 2. to move to (35:97) (pawˇ laˇ-eu)
-- pyul la, bavq -- to bring to this side
-- pyul la, zul -- to move closer
pyul li to go up to that side (pawˇ leˇ-eu)
=pyulloq, haq= a bamboo raft
=pyul, meiq= a plowshare
=pyul, neivqssa hal= a beetle
Pyulniul Han Chinese (or) **Piulniul; Alniul** (41:4) (in Akha proverbs and legends: Pehˇ nyoeˇ. In daily speech: La^ bui˯)
Pyulniuldoq the Chinese language (41:title) (La^ bui˯ daw˯)
Pyulniul huvqsiivq the Chinese spring festival (50:27)
pyul yil to go down to that side (pawˇ ka-iˇ-eu)
pyul yi to come down to this side (pawˇ ka le-eu)

pyu 1. side; direction (50:48), 2. towards (**yulzeil pyu pyul** = face that direction) (9:133) (paw)
-- pyu, aqhhuv -- below
pyu baq the side; the direction (50:48)
--pyu baq, hal -- which side (direction)?
pyu ciq ! interjection of disgust, unbelief (11:146) (almost like the sound of spitting. cf.: poe-eu)
-- pyu, hal -- which direction?
-- pyu, mal -- right side
-- pyu, niq -- both sides
-- pyu, qal -- left side/direction

-- **pyu, yul pyu xil** -- here and there; this side that side (46:170)
-- **pyu, zeil** -- to the side (46:139)

pyuq 1. expensive, 2. to be worthwhile; an object of great value (6:204), 3. to be worthy (14:182) (poeˬ-eu)
pyuq to blow gently (as to blow a feather, blow some water away from something) (poeˬ-eu)
pyuq to spring up (9:134)
pyuq the cost (9:134) (aˇ poeˬ)
pyuq face; appearance (or) **pioq** (mya^ pyawˬ) (cf. Lahu: meh^ hpfuhˇ)
=**pyuq, aq**= great-grandfather
-- **pyuq, bavq** -- to praise
pyuq biavq a medal; decoration (an honor) (50:192)
pyuq bo to be famous; have prestige; be popular (50:175)
pyuq dav springs up (as shavings of wood springing up from a wooden plane) (4:43) (pyeu^ da^-eu)
pyuqdoq a term of endearment; respect
pyuqduq one's reputation (34:15)
pyuqduq maq jav no value; good for nothing (or) **meeqduq qiq jivq maq jav** (gaˇ dahˇ maˬ tsoeˬ)
pyuq duv to spray
-- **pyuq, eil** -- to praise; encourage
pyuq gaq hhyul gaq friendship
pyuqgaq hhyulgaq friendship (14:182) (cawˬ)
=**pyuq, hhaq**= price; expense
pyuq lal to come over
-- **pyuq lo meil, pyuq sil** -- to be very proud; wildly arrogant
-- **pyuq, maq** -- good for nothing
pyuqmil fame (14:182) (tsawˇ myahˇ ja^-eu)
=**pyuq, miav**= face
pyuqqul sugar cane (or) **poqqul** (pf.) (57:116)
-- **pyuq, saol** -- 1. to praise; respect; honor, 2. to celebrate
pyuq seiq 1. to pour out (of mouth) (14:222) (sheh^ do^-eu), 2. sprinkling irrigation (50:129)
pyuq sil pyuq lo meil to be very proud; wildly arrogant (50:99) (jahˇ g'eh-eu)
=**pyuq, sol**= to respect
pyuqtaoq pyuqcaol a coarse comb and a fine-toothed comb
pyuqtul basket of rattan or bamboo which can be closed (9:134) (pawˬ tuˇ; puˬ tuˇ)
-- **pyuq zaq, eil** -- to flatter someone
pyuq zaq laq meil to be arrogant (jahˇ g'eh-eu)
-- **pyuq zeiq, hhyul zeiq** -- happier and nobler
=**pyuq, zol**= tuition fee; tuition

pyuv something to pop (rice; corn) (11:10) (poˬ laˇ-eu)
-- **pyuv, alpyuv** -- for grain to pop (as rice; corn)

QA

qalbeil belly button; navel (9:134) (ca^ tahˬ)
=qal, eel= spittle
=qal, jaq= left (hand)
qalju saliva; slobber (46:104) (iˇ ju; duˬ k'aˬ)
  qalju baqdaq a slobber bib for a baby
  qalju zav nei to slobber (iˇ ju ju-eu)
qalkeel the left foot (14:222) (aˇ caˇ kuiˇ)
qallavq left (hand) (9:134) (la˰ caˇ)
qalluvq a melon that does not grow well
  -- qalluvq, siqhuvq -- a small cucumber that does not grow very well
qalmiav left eye (aˇ caˇ nui^)
qal pyu left side; left direction (aˇ caˇ paw)
  qal pyu baq left side (41:211) (la˰ caˇ paw)
=qal qalma, eel= spittle

qa a kind (of something); a type (of something) (cf. tiˬ jeˬ tiˬ ca)
qa clf. for a kind of, a type of, thing (**qiq qa** = one kind of) (9:134, 11:77) (cf.: tiˬ jeˬ tiˬ ca)
=qa, col= 1. a clan (tsawˇ ca); 2. a surname
=qa, gaoq= a digging tool with a metal head
-- qa, hal -- which kind?
-- qa, xil -- this kind
-- qa yal qa, ceil -- many kinds; hundreds of kinds ('tens, hundreds of kinds')

qaq tired (9:134, 11:217, 41:157) (g'aˬ doeˇ doeˇ-eu)
(vb) qaq being tired of (vb) (**civq peiv qaq** = to be extremely angry) (cf. Lahu = (vb) bawˬ, as in: chehˇ bawˬ, hpeh˰ bawˬ etc.)
qaq one person (a contraction of: **qiq hhaq** - 11:208) (tiˬ g'aˬ)
-- qaq, diq -- (see full)
qaqgol nalgol diseases (38:38) (naˇ gawˇ)
-- qaq, hol cei -- to take pity on someone
qaq lal nal lal to get tired and sick
=qaq, lavq= the little finger
qaqleel nei very tired; very tiresome
  qaqleel pa leel nei extremely tired (g'aˬ doeˇ doeˇ-eu)
qaq liq qaq, laol liq laol not only tired, also hot and exhausted (10:24)
=qaq, nyul= the little finger
qaq qaq meil one person after another (35:60) (tiˬ g'aˬ saˇ-iˇ tiˬ g'aˬ)
qaq qaq yaol balhaol to help each other (50:73)
qaq qaq yaol hu teiq zaq supervise each other (50:73)
qaq qaq yaol maq diq zaq not to beat on each other;

nonaggression (50:73)

qaq qaq yaol maq hu nil respect each other; not look down on each other (50:73)

qaq qaq yaol zol learn from each other (50:73)

qaqqeiq 1. hegemony (34:15), 2. power; might (34:82) (Chi)

-- qaq, saq -- tired of suffering; tired of having a hard life

qaq sil laq e tired "to death" (26:16) (g'a˯ doe˅ doe˅ seh˄-eu)

qaq sil qaq lo to be very tired (45:58) (doe˅ dui dui-eu)

=qaq, siq= plum

qaqtov nei to feel tired (50:129)

(vb) qav (vb) away (**xeiv li qav** = ran off to...) (13:32), (**duq yil qav al** = he has gone to dig 13:4, 45:6, 58, 46:76)

-- qav, jol -- to have stayed

-- qav, nieil -- to leave something behind; to forget something

qavq to boil; cook (9:135) (ca˄-eu)

(vb) qavq a part. showing past time, and when speaking of someone else (**yil qavq** = he has gone) (9:135) (cf.: i˅ g'a˯ meh; i˅ ji˅ meh; i˅ meh˯.)

qavq very

qavqbeeq (see: **biabeeq**) (14:157)

qavqbieiv rice gruel; cooked to mush; porridge (9:135) (ca˄ byeh^)

qavqbieiv bieiv to cook to mush (9:135, 11:44) (ca˄ byeh^ byeh^-eu)

=qavq, ceil= glue

=qavq eelcal, hoq= rice water (i.e., water from boiled rice)

-- qavq, hoq -- a cook

qavq javq to cook done (38:2, 45:60) (la^ ja˄-eu)

qavqkul 1. over-cooked rice; burnt rice (9:135, 11:28), 2. rice which sticks to the pot (haw˯ ko^)

qavqlol the eve of four major offerings; **hhaqma, kuqzaq, luvniuq, Gal taol**

qavq miao cooked done (13:33) (ja˄ le˅-eu)

qavq salhu 1. please look at (11:217), 2. to see immediately; correctly

qavqsaoq to dislike; be repulsed by; to be very displeased (**qavqsaoq wul yaq** = what an ugly thing) (13:20) (byeh˅ la˅ pa˯-eh˅ g'eh-eu)

qavq sil to boil clean; sterilize (as baby's milk bottles) (10:19) (ca˄ shaw˅-eu; ca˄ bui˅-eu)

qavq'yuq qavqlaoq pots and pans (clf.: **zuvq**) (11:77, 46:201) (gui˯ ba oe˯ lah˯)

QAO

(vb) qaol able to (vb); can (vb) (or) **hhaq; nia**

(9:134, 10:25) (... coe˅-eu)
=**qaol, aoqtav laol=** the firmament; the vault of heaven
=**qaol, ceivq=** freezing cold
-- **qaol e aol, hal aol** -- to do one's best
=**qaol, laol=** deep inside the woods

qao 1. to crawl (as a young baby), 2. to roll about without a purpose
qao hha 1. to walk leisurely, 2. to wander (or) **del hha** (cah ni˅ g'a-eu)
qao hha li to go on a journey
qaohhaq to have enough strength to walk (cah coe˅-eu)
-- **qao, luvqqao** -- to be on duty
qao puq to meet without intention (accidentally) (or) **qao puq taoq puq** (tah˯ pu˯ tah˯ dzoe˅-eu)

qaoq paralysis (**keelqaoq lavqqaoq qaoq** = arms and legs are paralyzed) (kui˅ shi˅ la˄ shi˅ shi˅-eu)
qaoqbaol overseas Chinese relatives (Chi) (50:136)
qaoq daq the outer layer for a coat
qaoqdaq pieiv to cut cloth for the outer layer of a coat
qaoq hha to wander; roam
-- **qaoq, keelqaoq lavqqaoq** -- 1. for arms and legs to be weak and limp (as from paralysis), 2. for arms and legs to be paralyzed, 3. to be awkward; clumsy
-- **qaoq, lavqqaoq** -- paralysis of arms and legs
qaoqpeiq to play bridge (Chi) (50:136)
qaoqsuq overseas Chinese relatives (Chi) (50:136)
qaoqteqbao sentry at a bridge (Chi) (50:136)
qaoqwuf overseas affairs (Chi) (50:136)

QE

qeq to believe (12:126, 46:125) (jah-eu)
qeq peilfuq to admire someome (B=Chi) (50:128)
qeq qaq qeq ga superstition; superstitious belief (50:115)
qeq sil to believe in very much (45:93:
qeq sso to depend upon (or) **dal sso**
qeq zaq to believe in (35:91)
qeq zaq na to believe in (14:197) (or) willing to believe

=**qev nei, gee'=** very dry

QEI

qeil sour (9:135) (yaw ceh˅)
qeil 1. to like/love something or someone (9:135, 46:176) (ga˯-eu), 2. to be happy (in certain contexts)
(vb) qeil like to (vb) (**zaq qeil** = like to eat) (11:157) (cf.: maw˄-eu)

-- **qeil, aolheiq** -- enjoyable work
=**qeil, baq**= distiller's grains
qeilbao nei sour (yaw cehˇ)
  qeilbao pa bao nei extremely sour (cehˇ myaw^-eu)
qeilbiq pencil (Chi) (sah˯ bo˄ daˇ duˇ)
-- **qeil, daov** -- to be very happy
-- **qeil, eilheiq** -- to say happily
qeilgu nei to be sour (cehˇ myaw^ ni)
  qeilgu pa gu nei very sour (11:132) (zawˇ cehˇ-eu)
=**qeil, hhoq**= pickled Chinese cabbage; sour greens
-- **qeil, hhoqqeil** -- to pickle Chinese cabbage
qeilhhuvq watercress
Qeilhhuvq loldei a place name in Luchun county
qeilkuv sour dried vegetables (11:27)
-- **qeil, laqhaq** -- 1. to show interest in; 2. to be happy; **laqheiq qeil**
qeilma wild buckwheat
Qeilma lolbaq the Qeima river in Luchun County
=**qeil, ngaqsaq hhoq**= salted sour fish
=**qeil, saq**= sour meat
qeil sil to love very much (45:6) (ga˯ seh˄-eu)
qeiltav nei sharp-pointed (50:82)
qeiltaoq albievq a wild plant (they eat the shoots, which are sour)
-- **qeil, zaq** -- like to eat; prefer to eat
qeilzaoq fresh sour vegetables
qeil zeiq to love more; to love best (46:102) (ga˯ dzeh˯-eu)

=**qei, dal**= a sharp stick
=**qei, hhol**= the middle; inside; in the midst
=**qei, meiq**= 'sharp lips' (& see full)
=**qei, miav**= crossed eyes
=**qei, lal**= the tip of the tongue
=**qei, paq**= a type of field frog
=**qei, saol**= a sharp iron rod
=**qei, saol dal**= a sharp iron rod
-- **qei, taoqteil** -- butting competition (between two animals)
qeituv one's weak points
-- **qei, tyuq** -- to point out (with finger)
qei zaq to argue (13:31) (ceh dza˯-eu)

qeiq 1. to be lame (arm or leg) (9:135, 11:24) (kuiˇ caw^ la˄ caw^), 2. to be unbalanced (**moq qeiv qeiq** = the horse load is unbalanced) (11:24), 3. to be askew; aslant (or) **bilqeiq; yovq**
=**qeiq, aqkeel keel**= lame; crippled legs
-- **qeiq, bilqeiq** -- to slant
=**qeiq, dal**= a type of cloth for a baby (in the general shape of a diaper)
qeiq duv to have an idea (lit. "an idea to come out") (46:99) (noe˯ do^-eu)
Qeiqfuqzual a village name in Yuanyang county (46:130)

qeiqgaol one who works with tools (Chi) (26:33)
qeiqgoq the whole nation (Chi) (26:75) (mi˅ k'ah˯ k'ah˯ lah)
qeiqgoq deifbiao dafhyuf a National representative (Chi) (34:103)
qeiqgoq sseiqmiq deifbiao dafhyuf National People's Congress (Chi) (50:139)
qeiqgoq zao gaolhyuf national workers union (Chi) (50:139)
qeiqhhaf the whole case (Chi) (50:139)
qeiqjyul the whole army (Chi) (34:80)
=qeiq, keel= a crippled leg
=qeiq, lavq= a crippled arm
-- qeiq, laol -- to become warm
qeiqliq influence (Chi) (or) **yixa** (Chi)
qeiqliq jilgual administrative unit (Chi) (50:139)
qeiqmiq soyeziif national ownership system (Chi) (50:139)
-- qeiq, miav -- (see full)
-- qeiq, miavqeiq -- to look out the corner of one's eye
=qeiq, piq= to become limp
qeiq sil to put someone to death (46:146) (la^ seh^-eu)
qeiqtiqxif anemia (Chi) (in Hani = **sivq maq luvq nalgol** = 'blood insufficient disease') (10:33)
-- qeiq, tyuq qeiq dav qeiq to seek in every way
qeiq xa to take off something (as a sword) by luring, cheating (46:100)
=qeiq, yiq= a method
qeiq zaq to cheat (45:26) (myaw^-eu shui˅-eu)
qeiqzii pliers (Chi) (26:29)

qeiv carry on horseback (9:135, 13:6) (mah˯ taw˯-eu)
qeiv to compare; to measure (as how long) (9:135) (ceh^-eu)
qeiv to compete (as to run a race) (6:189, 50:11)
qeiv clf. for a load that a horse can carry (11:83) (ti˯ taw˯)
-- qeiv, aolqeiv -- to have a competition (in working)
-- qeiv, bavq -- to compare
-- qeiv, deilqeiv -- a rooster to compete in crowing
-- qeiv, diqqeiv -- to have a contest; a game (as in basketball)
qeivdul the pole of the frame to which they tie loads for packhorses (35:68)
qeiv hu to compare (50:11)
qeivkeel a frame for the pack saddle
qeivkeel laqma a frame for the pack saddle
=qeiv, moq= a horse load of goods
-- qeivmoq, alyeil -- a pack horse
-- qeiv, qiq qeiv -- one load carried by a horse
-- qeiv, seilqeiv -- to compete in dancing
-- qeiv, xeiv'qeiv -- to race; a running competition

qeivzaqduq sports ground (50:11)

QIL

qil to be firm; durable; to last a long time (as clothing) (9:135, 11:119, 46:118) (ziˆ-eu)
qil to worry (9:136) (noeˬ shaˬ-eu; noeˬ zahˬ-eu) (cf. Lahu: dawˇ hki⁻ ve)
qil to insult someone (Chi)
=qil, al= a root
qildal a receipt (Chi) (50:137)
=qil, daoq= a root
qilgaoljiq bureau of light industry (Chi) (50:137)
qilgaolniq light industry (Chi) (50:137)
qilgaolso a township site (Chi) (50:139)
qilguq a type of rattan (roots edible) (9:136) (or) **cavni; haolma** (ciˇ guˬ)
 qilguq byu'lyu a type of rattan (roots edi.)
 qilguq cavni a rattan string; tie
qilgualqiq lacquer (Chi)
qilhhyu township committee (Chi) (50:139)
 qilhhyu suljif party secretary of the township (Chi) (50:139)
=qil, kal= roots of plants
qil leeq to fall down (as from suffering) (46:97)
qilma wife's younger sister (aˬ nyiˇ)
=qil, miq= fame
=qil, moq= husbands of one's younger sisters
qil nal to be sick from missing and worrying about a loved one for a long time
 qil nal duv to become sick from missing a loved one for a long time
qilnil a small red field rat
qilniq an enterprise (Chi) (34:42, 50:134)
-- qilnieiq, ziilsiiq -- school graduates (A=Chi)
qil qeivq qeivq chirp, chirp; twitter, twitter; the sound of an opening door (45:64), **jil geivq geivq**
qilsaq barking deer meat (9:136) (ciˇ haˬ shaˬ jiˇ)
-- qil, seq -- to have firm teeth
qilseiq side roots (duˬ ciˇ zaˬ)
-- qil sil, neema -- worried to death
qilssaq Muntjac (barking) deer (9:136)
 qilssaq gyuq a barking deer to 'bark'
qiltaoq tap root; main roots
qilyeq ziifziif autonomous region (Chi) (50:139)
qilyiuq region (Chi) (34:55)
qilza governor of region or township (Chi) (50:139)
qilzaol 1. middle of a school term (as compared to the beginning and end of term) (Chi), 2. end of terms (50:133) (note: different characters are used in Chi)
qilzeiffu government of township (Chi) (50:139)
qilzuxiq township chairman (Chi) (50:139)

qi 1. can stand, 2. can offer for something

(vb) qi able to (vb) (46:78) (**maq hhel qi** = not able to buy, cannot afford to buy) (38:24) (coeˇ; nya)

=qi, col= middle-aged

qidaofqif a starter (on a motor, machine, car) (Chi) (50:134)

qitif a substitute regulation or system (Chi) (34:44)

qiq to lift up (9:136) (ci⌄-eu)

qiq one (note: **tivq** is used in 11, 21, 31, etc., the same as Akha) (2:57, 9:136) (ti⌄; ti‸)

qiq ba a group (ti⌄ ma‸)

qiq ba meil zaol zyul a gang of criminals (50:93)

qiq ba naolhao qiq ba zol to learn something class after class (as in a training school) (50:111)

qiqbao bao to unite as one (46:124) (la^ dzoeˇ-eu; la^ ui⌄-eu)

qiqbaof information (Chi) (or) **doqgaq**

qiq beeq ssaq to be of the same clan (or) **qiq hhovq col**

qiq bei a copy (B=Chi) as to write a copy (11:173)

qiq bil (see: **qiq baol** = a share) (14:174)

qiqceil a car; automobile (Chi) (or) **qifceil** (11:30, 26:27) (lo; law⌄ li⌄)

qiqceil bil a trucker; a lorry driver (Chi)

qiqceil galma a highway (A=Chi) (50:61)

qiq cei to lift up (or) **qiq** (ci⌄-eu)

qiq cei nei leiq pieiv to knock down and crush into pieces (as by a truck)

qiq ciivq one generation (ziˇ ti⌄ tsui‸)

qiq daol maq cyuq to have no value; to be of no avail (or) **aol duq maq jav**

Qiqdil a branch of the Hani (46:111)

qiq di qiq di meil one place to another place (35:78) (ti⌄ gaˇ neh ti⌄ gaˇ)

qiqdiei one's shortcoming; weak point (as always being late) (Chi)

qiq diei a lack of iodine (Chi)

qiqdol meil straight to the point; to the mark

-- qiq dol, qiq pieiv -- same age (or almost the same age)

-- qiq doq ssaoq, doqteil -- with one voice

qiq gal one place; a certain place (ti⌄ gaˇ)

qiq gal jol caq maq siq did not know the right place to sit (13:7)

qiqgao together; together with; at the same time (ti⌄ kaw^ lo‸-ehˇ)

qiqgao nieivq cavq end to end

qiqgao pa taoq taoq (in phrase: **paoqciivq meiqdaoq qiqgao pa taoq taoq** = the knees and the chin were almost touching - 14:202)

qiqgao qo'leiq to go hand in hand

qiqgao ssaoq to get together (or) **qiqgao zyul**

qiqgao zyul to get together (or) **qiqgao ssaoq**

qiq gaoq a stack of something

=qiq, ha'= wildcat
qiq haq one time; once (or) **qiq heiq**
qiq haq laltov nei immediately; suddenly (30:2, 35:1, 45:83) (or) **qiq heiq laltov**
qiq haol help carry; help lift up (26:89)
qiq haoq ten cents (when figured in Chinese); five cents (when figured in Hani) (26:74)
qiq heiq 1. a moment (ti˯ k'eh˯...) (3:18), 2. a mouthful
qiq heiq (vb) please (vb) (**zabiav xil dyul qiq heiq bavq laq a!** = please accept these mooncakes - 26:87)
qiq heiq laltov immediately (13:43, 26:24); suddenly (26:39); all at once (or) **tuqssaq meil** (A=Chi)
qiq heiq meil maq soq sso e zeil give credit to
qiq heiq nei at once; immediately (10:23)
qiq heiq nyuq an idea; to think of something once (ti˯ po^ noe˯)
qiq heiq pilzyu aq 'Please give your permision' (as when asking for leave from work or school) (a set phrase) (54:106)
qiq huvq huvqjoq the whole year (41:120, 50:21) (k'o˰ lah ni)
qiq huvq maq leiq every year; without missing a year (46:92) (yaw˯ k'o˰ na lu˰)
qiq huvq qiq taq once a year (ti˯ k'o˰ ti˯ po^)
qiq hhaq kaq qiq hhaq every other person (nyi˯ g'a˯-ahˇ ti˯ g'a˯)
qiq hhaq liq maq nyuq hev bei contrary to all expectations
qiq hhaq liq qiq hhaq yaol one to the other; each to the other (46:124) (ti˯ g'a˯-ahˇ neh ti˯ g'a˯)
qiq hhaq maq hev, Molmil kev no one knows, only God knows (Mi˯ yehˇ ta˰-aˇ ti˯ g'a˯-i˯ ma˯ si˯ nya-a)
qiq hhaq qiq hhaq meil one person after another
qiq hhaq qiq jol jav every person has his/her chances in life ('every dog has his day')
qiq hhovq the whole family (4:41)
qiq hhovq col to be of the same clan (or) **qiq beeq ssaq**
qiq hhovq hhovqjoq the whole family (ti˯ zaw˰ lah ni)
qiqjei jeigoq build up the country through thrift and hard work (Chi) (50:137)
qiq jivq one thing (ti˯ je˯)
qiq jivq aoq lul maq hha nothing to sell (35:49) (ti˯ je˯-i˯ ah˯-eu ma˯ ja^)
qiq jivq e doq maq jav 1. I have nothing to say (ti˯ je˯-i˯ ngeh˯-eu ma˯ ja^), 2. I would like to hear your comments (45:7)
qiq jivq guq to need something (41:160)
qiq jivq liq maq nyuq didn't think anything (38:93) (ti˯ je˯-i˯ ma˯ shaˇ noe˯-eu)
qiq jivq maq (vb) not any (vb) (**qiq jivq liq maq jav** = I have nothing) (ti˯ je˯-i˯ ma˯ ---)

qiq jivq maq aol nia to be clumsy; not able to do anything (ti⌄ je⌄-i⌄ ma⌄ mˇ nya)

qiq jivq maq cyuq 1. no use; valueless (26:113), 2. trivial (gaˇ dahˇ ma⌄ tsoe⌄)

qiq jivq maq jav to have nothing (ti⌄ je⌄-i⌄ ma⌄ ja^)

qiq jivq maq ngeel never mind (ti⌄ je⌄-i⌄ ma⌄ ngeuˇ)

qiq jivq maq zaol qivq nothing can be done (ti⌄ je⌄-i⌄ ma⌄ jahˇ nya)

-- qiq jol, aqmil -- last time (some time back)

qiq jol hhana sometimes (14:225) (ti⌄ po^ na)

qiq jol maq ceil every now and then (ti⌄ k'eh⌄ ma⌄ ta⌄ ni)

qiq jol maq nyuq bei he never thought that ..... (26:27) (ti⌄ jawˇ-i⌄ ma⌄ noe⌄ haw-eu)

-- qiq, keeltuvq -- to take a step

qiq kov same as; equal (or) **miav nei** (ti⌄ kaw^)

qiq kov dei nei ssuq to walk in step

qiq kov miav nei to share equally (9:136) (ti⌄ kaw^ lo^-eh)

qiq kov miav nei heeq equal size (largeness)

qiq kov miav nei yeil equal width

qiqkuaf circumstance; situation; affair (Chi) (34:76)

-- qiqkuaf, laqhyul -- affairs of the home; affairs of the family; situation of the family

Qiqla siq January (or) **Zyuqzaq siq; Joqzaq siq**

=qiq, lavq= (see full)

qiq lavq nei niq tao to chop something in two with one blow (35:58)

qiq laoq zaq eat together (from one pot) (50:23)

qiq levq la levq meil without sorrow

qiq li nei directly into (as an injection of medicine) (13:40) (dawˇ coe ni)

qiq ma bossaq born of one mother (ti⌄ ma za⌄)

qiq mavq some (of the people) (cf.: ti⌄ pa^ na deu⌄)

qiq mavq hhana some of them (10:23) (**aqnu yol qoq qiq mavq hhana** = some of his friends - 26:68, **Qiq mavq hhana Haqniqssaq colmiaol miaol e ..** Some of the Hani people name their names .. 41:111)

qiq mil ten thousand

qiq miq maq seq bei a man who has never married

qiq miav one time (41:132) (ti⌄ po^; ti⌄ la^)

qiq mol kaq qiq mol every other one (nyi⌄ g'a⌄-ahˇ ti⌄ g'a⌄)

qiq mol moljoq nei the whole body (26:32) (g'awˇ mawˇ mawˇ lah)

qiq mol naolhao qiq mol done in its turn (after one another)

qiq naq maq naq yil never stop (continuous) (26:105, 45:60) (ma⌄ na⌄ ni)

qiq nao aqmeil to do something every day (35:89)

qiq nao aoqcil the whole day (ti⌄ nah nah lah)

qiq nao aoqcil qivq nei the whole day (nah lah ni)

qiq nao hultav qiq nao increased one day after

another (45:12) (cf.: tiˬ nah saˇ-iˇ tiˬ nah)

qiq nao laqgal day by day (or) **qiq nao maq leiq** (tiˬ nah saˇ-iˇ tiˬ nah)

qiq nao maq leiq day by day (without exception) (or) **qiq nao laqgal** (11:208, 13:21, 29:4) (yawˬ nah na lu˰)

qiq nao naolhao qiq nao day after day (tiˬ nah saˇ-iˇ tiˬ nah)

qiq niq taq one or two times (once or twice) (tiˬ po^ nyiˬ po^) (10:11)

qiq niv maq niv not to move at all (13:3, 26:52) (maˬ lu^ maˬ la^)

qiq niv maq niv, qiq puv maq puv does not move at all; does not turn over (46:114) (maˬ lu^ maˬ la^)

qiq piav piav pao to scratch open (pya^ pah-eu)

qiq pieiv qiq dol same generation; same age (or almost the same age)

qiq puq laqleel united; rallied together (50:170)

qiq puq laq luq a round sum

qiq puv laolhaol the same village (35:67)

qiq puv qiq laol the whole village (11:205, 46:159) (cf. Lahu: hk'a^ yaˇ lawˬ yaˇ) (tiˬ pu siˬ; pu lah siˬ)

qiq pyu..., qiq pyu... while ..., while ... (**qiq pyu saqnil zaq, qiq pyu zilbaq dol** - while eating meat he drank liquor - 13:11), on the one hand... on the other hand (**qiq pyu ngyul, qiq pyu kul** = on the one hand he cried, on the other hand he called out - 26:5)

qiq pyu ssuq, qiq pyu doq gee on the one hand walking, on the other hand talking (26:24)

qiq pyu zei, qiq pyu eel on the one hand threw (stones), on the other hand laughed (46:177)

qiq pyu zeiqkeeq hhuv, qiq pyu doqsii on the one hand they collected dung, on the other hand they talked with each other (26:39)

qiq qa the same kind; same thing (tiˬ jeˬ-iˬ teh˰)

qiq qa ceil qa many kinds (57:84)

qiq qa col to be of the same nationality (or) **ssaqqa qiq qa**

qiq qa naldul dul to look alike (the same thing; the same kind) (tiˬ jeˬ duˇ leˇ-eu)

qiq qa paoq the same (41:110)

qiq qa qiq qa meil one thing after another (57:115)

qiq qeiv qeiv to carry one load by horse (13:30) (mahˬ tiˬ tawˬ tawˬ-eu)

qiqqiq keikei diligent; conscientious (Chi) (34:86)

qiq quq nei immediately; at once (13:7) (tiˬ po^ teh˰-ehˇ)

qiq savq for a long time (35:5) (g'awˬ myahˇ ni)

qiq savq hev for a long time (13:29) (**Noq yaol maq mol qiq savq hev yaq.** It has been a long time since I saw you last. 41:5) (50:21) (or) **siiqjeil** (Chi) (g'awˬ myahˇ k'aw^ laˇ-eu)

qiq savq (jol) a short time (26:41) (g'awˬ myahˇ

ma˯ k'aw^)

-- qiq savq, xil -- these days; recently

qiq siq siqjoq one whole month (when speaking of **ba'la** - 41:120) (ba la ti˯ si˯ si˯ lah ni)

qiq siil qiq qa one thing (subject) after another (26:50) (ti˯ je˯ saˇ-iˇ ti˯ je˯)

qiqsiiq feasible; realistic (Chi) (34:97)

qiq ssil aqlo hhaq tivq struggle all one's life (50:50)

qiq ssil aqlo meil the whole life (26:120, 45:57), one lifetime (26:45) (ti˯ ziˇ)

qiq ssil miqnieiq lifetime plan (50:4)

qiq taq hhana sometimes; at times (**qiq taq hhana aqda aqma** = sometimes parents... - 10:pref.) (ti˯ po^ na)

qiq taq maq leiq nei without stopping (26:65); again and again (ma˯ na˯ ni)

qiq taq nei niq hhaq deivq 'two born at once' (twins)

qiq tevq qiq tevq nei ceiq tevq to plow one furrow after another (46:164)

qiq teev a deadlock

qiq xa xajoq the whole township (mid. = Chi)

qiq yal ssilmiq pyu end of the century (50:10)

qiq yavq maq leiq each and every night (yaw˯ miˇ na lu˰)

qiq yavq yavqjoq the whole night (ci˰ miˇ lah ni)

qiq yaol yaoljoq the whole house (ti˯ nymˇ nymˇ lah)

qiqyibiao barometer; weather guage (Chi) (50:138)

qiq zaol a couple

qiqzaof yifdaof people's movement (Chi) (50:140)

qiqzaof zuziiq people's non-government organization (Chi) (50:140)

qiq zeil one side

qiq zeil (vbA) qiq zeil (vbB) simultaneously (**qiq zeil ngyul qiq zeil eil** = at the same time crying and talking - 46:145)

qiv to rub off (cf.: deh˯ leh˰-eu)

qiv ciq to brush with water (9:136)

-- qiv, hholmol -- to rub a cooked egg up and down a sick body and then divine with it

=qiv, miq= a match (for lighting a fire)

qivq 1. to be able; skillful; as silversmiths, carpenters and blacksmiths (9:136); 2. used in proverbs for 'blacksmith' (ci˰ ma = old word for blacksmith)

(vb) qivq become (vb) (**duv lal qivq nga** = became..) (pyeu˰ laˇ-eu)

(vb) qivq able to (vb) (**maq mol qivq** = not able to see it - 11:135)

=qivq, aoq= night; dusk

-- qivq, aoqcil -- the whole day; all day

-- qivq, he -- to catch sight of something

qivqhoq evening rice meal (9:136) (**qivqhoq zaq** =

eat the evening meal - supper) (ci^ haw˅)
=qivq, huq= night before last
qivq meel evening star (Venus) (ci^ mui˅)
-- qivq meil hhyul ya, maq -- extremely happy
=qivq, mil= last night
=qivq, nao'= tomorrow evening
-- qivq, niv -- can be moved
=qivq, niaoq'aol= this evening; tonight
qivq pav the middle of the night (11:67) (seh g'ah˅ lah˅ ceh)
-- qivq, piav -- can be touched
qivqsol lolto dusk (or) **aoqqivq; qivqsol lolto pyu** (zah˅ mo˅ zah˅ sheh˅)
-- qivqzol, lavqqivq -- apprentice (in learning some handicraft, esp. being a blacksmith)

qifceil auto; car (Chi) (or) **qiqceil** (9:135, 26:51, 46:77, 50:134) (lo; law˅ li˅)
qifceilbil a person who works with a lorry; truck (26:49)
qifceil galma a highway (Chi)
qiqceil gaolsiil automobile company (Chi) (50:134)
qifdaf meiqsuf gentamicin (a broad-spectrum antibiotic) (Chi) (50:138)
qifdeil kerosene lamp (pump up to light) (Chi) (50:134)
qifdieifcuaq a steam boat (Chi) (or) **qifdieif loq** (A=Chi) (50:134)
qiffeil atmosphere (Chi) (34:61)
qifxafdyuf weather station team (Chi) (50:134)
qiqxafzaf weather station (Chi) (50:134)
qifyeq petrol; oil (50:134)
qifzuq to celebrate (Chi)

QIA

=qiaq, aqdaol daol= the tip edge of a wing (as of a bird)

QO

qo to look for; search for (9:136) (po^-eu; go˅-eu)
qo bav 1. to lead astray; follow a wrong path (sheu˅ bah˅-eu), 2. incorrectly relay a message (46:122)
-- qo, buvqqo -- depict; portray; delineate
qo ceil saq investigation results (50:209)
-- qo heq, qo ceil -- to investigate & examine
qo leiq 1. to follow (13:19, 26:68), 2. to chase after (13:49) (2. cf.: co ko˅ co na˅ teh-eu = driving spirits from the village once a year)
qo leiq zaq to go after (or) **salqo zaq**
=qo, lo'= 1. along with, 2. a method
qo puq to meet (35:111) (cf.: tah˅ pu˅-eu; dzoe˅-eu)
-- qo, salsil galquv -- 'may you die a terrible death' (a curse)

qo yil qo lal pace up and down; hesitate; waver (50:126)

qo zaq 1. to search for (po^-eu); 2. to visit each other

-- **qo, zyulzeiq** -- find out who is to blame (as in an accident)

qoq to invite (kuˇ-eu) (cf. Lahu: hk'o ve)

=**qoq, aq**= others; someone else

-- **qoq, aolkal leil** -- advocate; promoter

qoq'eel seminal fluid (taboo) (aˇ diziˬ).

-- qoq, eil -- to argue with someone

=**qoq, hhyul**= friends

-- **qoq, kul** -- to call each other

qoqlal to invite (kuˇ-eu)

-- **qoq, laq** -- to reply (as by song)

-- **qoq, lav** -- to answer

qoqliq to establish (Chi) (34:10, 17)

-- **qoq meil, maq** -- negative used in set phrases (see full)

=**qoq, miq**= a bridesmaid; a girl companion

qoq sil qoq lo meil to invite with great urgency

=**qoq, ssaq**= (see full)

qoqtevq glans penis (taboo) (beu^ leu^ uˬ duˬ)

-- **qoq, yolqoq** -- to make a friend

=**qoq, zeivq**= to gossip back

qoq zil to call together

-- **qoq, zilbaq dol qoq** -- to drink with friends

=**qoq, zol**= a classmate; schoolmate

=**qoq, zyuq**= (see full)

qov broken (as a stick, a rock) (k'eh‸-eu; pa^-eu; peh‸-eu)

-- **qov, hhe** -- to pull and break

-- qov, lavq -- a broken arm

-- **qov, taoq** -- to be broken (as the roof of a house)

qovq a clan; a family (nymˇ dahˬ; pyaˬ)

-- **qovq, aqyo** -- his/her family

qovqbee family (13:1) (pehˬ zaˬ)

-- **qovq, hhellaoq** -- royal dragon family

=**qovq nei, nav'**= jet black

=**qovq, seq**= Chinese cassia tree

QU

qul sweet (8:28, 9:136) (yaw coeˇ)

=**qul alsiq, al**= plantain (similar to banana)

-- **qul, caqdevq** -- salty enough

=**qul, diq**= a bell

=**qul, doq**= sweet words

=**qul, haq**= sweet bamboo

qulhaq qulhaq nei sweet and bitter (happy and unhappy) (14:216) (yaw coeˇ yaw k'aˬ)

=**qul, hhaq**= sweet buckwheat

qulju nei   sweetly (11:56) (coeˇ o^ ni)
qulju pa ju nei   very sweet (11:63) (zawˇ coeˇ-eu)
qulju pa ju nei maq qul   not very sweet (11:60) (yaw k'a^-ehˇ maˬ coeˇ)
=qul, moq=   sweet potato
=qul, neema yo'=   good-hearted ('sweet-hearted')
=qul nei, nil=   very red (as red-faced)
=qul, niuq=   milk from buffalo/cow
qul qul bieiv bieiv   sweet and mushy; sweet & soft
qul qul nei   very sweet (11:57) (zawˇ coeˇ-eu)
qulsiq   nipple of breast; bottle (10:19) (aˬ coeˇ coeˇ siˬ)
qulsol   a sweet smell (14:226) (yaw sawˇ)
qulsul   a small bell (jaˇ cuˇ zaˬ)
qultuv   a spindle (ya ahˇ)
-- qul, wuqduq ngaoq --   to raise one's head

qu   to raise; care for; feed; support (**ssaqmiq ssaqyo qu** = to support a family) (9:136) (cu-eu; cu huiˬ-eu)
qu   clf. for a pile (bymˇ)
-- qu, bavq --   to take care of; to look after
-- qu, duq --   fill in with earth (as around corn stalks)
-- qu, gaoq --   to stack up
qu heeq   to bring up; to raise to adulthood (cu huiˬ-eu)
qu hu   to visit; to drop in (**taq qu hu lal** = don't come to visit - 13:4) (35:18)
qu meiq   to raise and teach; instruct (50:128)
-- qu miq, meiq miq --   to teach and care for
=qu, puv=   a pile of something
qu'qeiq hu   to spy on someone
qu'qeiq hu e col   a spy; a person who spies on others
qu qu bieiv bieiv   sweet and soft
-- qu, ssaqmeeq --   well-raised; well-educated
qu yal   to raise easily (cu yaˇ-eu)
qu ya   to be tame
qu zaq   to adopt and raise a child
qu zaq miaoq   raise domestic animals; animal husbandry (50:194)
qu zeq   to raise and increase (as animals) (50:128)

quq   a ball (Chi)
quq   to rush up; to run (11:221) (tehˬ-eu; ceh^-eu)
quqceiv pa ceiv nei   extremely still (see: **quvqceiv nei** = calmly; quietly - 14:168) (maˬ lu^ maˬ la^ ni)
quq duv   1. to come out (as a snake out of its hole) (13:53); 2. to stretch one's neck to look (9:136)
quq koq   to touch on (la^ ci^-eu)
quqma   general term for laughing thrush (brd) (coˬ hoˬ)
quqma baqcal   white-crested laughing thrush (brd)

(coˬ haˬ baˬ pyuˇ)

quqma baqnav black-throated laughing thrush (brd) (coˬ hoˬ na^)

quqma quqsiil greater necklaced laughing thrush (brd) (or) **quqsiil** (coˬ hoˬ shuiˇ)

quq muvq to bow one's head (9:136) (uˬ duˬ mˇ mo˰-eu)

quq peev to run into and burn (13:3) (coeˬ pui^-eu)

quq puq to meet accidentally; to meet up with (26:39), (or) **taoq puq** (tahˬ puˬ-eu)

quqseiv daolnil a red-winged thrush (brd)

quq sil to bump to death (coeˬ seh˰-eu)

quqsiq lal to bump into (as a cat to bump into someone's foot) (29:4) (coeˬ tahˬ)

quqsiq nei to be cool; to cool off (9:137, 10:26) (yaw co˰)

quqsiil greater necklaced laughing thrush (brd) (9:137) (or) **quqma quqsiil** (coˬ hoˬ shuiˇ)

quq tao li to enter into (**haoldaol saqhav quq tao li** = to enter into the jungle - 14:209) (uˇ leˇ-eu)

quq tov to bump against something causing death; to fall (as on rocks) and die (coeˬ tahˬ seh˰-eu)

quq tovq bump against (9:137) (tahˬ-eu)

quv 1. to weed with a hoe (9:137) (co^-eu), 2. to bud (aˇ cuˬ cuˬ-eu)

quv clf. for a path in the jungle (35:7)

=quv, al= a bud

-- quv, alquv -- to sprout; to germinate; to bud

-- quv, eel -- a ditch to divert water (as for irrigation)

=quv, gal= 1. the proper way, 2. a mountain pass

=quv, hho'= a rice bud

=quv, kal= for a crop to bud

=quv, meil= a type of wild ginger

-- quv, nee nyuq -- thought; thinking

=quv, neev'= bean sprouts

quv soq to trim or prune branches with a knife

quvq to suck (cu˰-eu)

quvq to be very narrow (yaw su˰)

quvq 1. to be quiet (ciˬ cuˇ ni), 2. to be cool (yaw co˰)

-- quvq, bavq -- to embrace

quvqceiv nei to be quiet; still; tranquil (9:137) (ciˬ cuˇ ni)

quvqceiv pa ceiv nei very quietly (35:74) (ciˬ cuˇ ni g'eh-eu)

=quvq, eel= water; **wulquvq**

quvqlaol ceilhuvq a thermometer (50:177)

quvq laol za a good climate; the proper climate

quvqmiavq a type of jungle fruit (9:137)

=quvq, seiq= bound feet

-- quvq, tov -- to bind up; wrap up

=quvq, wul= water; **eelquvq**

QYU

qyul'aqma woodpecker (9:137) (ciˇ yawˇ)

qyuqzaof the people; the masses (Chi) (34:56, 41:3)

SA

sal to be comfortable; happy; enjoy (or) **hhyul** (saᵛ-eu)
sal to beg; ask for (9:137) (shaᵛ-eu)
sal 1. to be flat (saᵛ leh^ ni), 2. for there to be fine weather
sal 1. to earn money (**zeiq sal** = to earn money for a living), 2. to ask for money (**piul sal zaq**)
sal to look for new land (**xalmil sal** = to seek a field)
(vb) **sal** to be easy; healthy (**jolsal**), etc. (... saᵛ-eu, as in: jawᵛ saᵛ do^-eu)
-- **sal, aoqsal** -- a good sky; nice weather
-- **sal, baqsal** -- to seek a lover
Salbiaoq a person's name (11:123)
Salbo a boy's name (54:113)
Salcaq Shancha (lit. 'Camellia') the magazine sponsored by the Yunnan Acadamy of Social Sciences (Chi) (46:120)
Salcel a girl's name (54:113)
salcivq peiv (see: **salqiq pieiv**)
salcuvq a lightning 'bolt', of metal or stone, which comes from the sky and splits a tree open (**Salcuvq nei diq cov laq e albol miqkoq maq heivq haoq**. It is not proper to gather firewood from a tree struck by a lighting bolt.) (tso‸)
  salcuvq diq for a lightning 'bolt' to strike (50:103)
  salcuvq nei bi diq 'may you be struck by a lightning bolt' (a curse)
Saldee the name of a person (14:194)
=sal, dei= even; flat
saldei nei to be flat (9:137) (saᵛ leh^ ni)
saldieif store; emporium; cooperative store (Chi) (9:138)
saldoq good words (daw⌄ mui⌄)
  saldoq haoqyal a broadcasting station (50:37) (a term used by the Akha in Xishuangbanna)
-- **saldul, salnyuq** -- illusion; fantasy
salfaq sofa (Chi-Eng) (9:138, 50:146)
-- **sal, gaoqlaoq** -- (see full)
=sal, geel= a disaster; dangerous; unexpected
salhaq influenza; flu (Chi) (26:6) (**tseh‸ tah naᵛ-eu**)
salhe naol to smell of fish
salhe nei the smell of seafood (9:138)
salhu 1. to test; try (including to try someone - 35:58); 2. have a look; to watch (9:138)
-- **sal, hu** -- pretty to look at
salhu hu to test; try; have a look (8:2, 6)
salhu li miq to go to visit (as a sick person) (50:4)
-- **salhu, qavq** -- 1. please look at... 2. to see

immediately; correctly
salhuq coral (Chi)
-- **sal, huqsal** -- to receive a heritage
salhha 1. to play a game (or) **seilhha** (pf.) (9:138) (niˇ g'a-eu), 2. to visit (or) **seilhha** (pf.) (dawˬ deh g'a-eu)
Saljei boy's name (Chi)
saljiq soye three systems of ownership: 1. national, 2. collective, 3. individual (Chi) (or) **saol teivq soye** (B=Chi) (50:145)
=**sal, jol**= healthy; comfortable
-- **sal, jolhhal** -- to have a good place to live/ sit
salju vermicelli made from bean starch
salkuv salnaol a plant with a heartshaped leaf (cordate houttuynia) (edi)
salkyul a shell
sal lal to come to beg (shaˇ laˇ-eu)
sal lal 1. to become better (as to have a better life), 2. for weather to clear up (muiˬ dzaˬ laˇ-eu)
sallalhuvq three years from now
sallalnao three days from now (& see: **sallaqnao**) (saˇ pehˬ ngeh nah)
sal la to have begged (and received) (shaˇ za-eu)
sallaqnao three days from now (pf) (& see: **sallalnao**) (pehˬ zaˇ ngeh nah)
sallavq the smell of seafood
sal li to go up to beg; to ask for (shaˇ leˇ-eu)
-- **sal lo, sal ssil** -- (see full)
=**sal, loq**= good terraced rice fields
-- **sal, milhaoq** -- to have peace in the land
-- **sal, milteil** -- to be famous
salmuq albol a spruce tree (A=Chi) (or) **ssaolbol**
salmuqsuf a fir tree (Chi)
-- **sal, nalhaq** -- to sound nice
-- **sal, neema maq** -- unhappy; discontent
salniq bufmeiq trading departments (Chi) (50:147)
salniqjiq bureau of trade (Chi) (50:147)
salnyuq to wonder; contemplate (shaˇ noeˬ-eu)
-- **sal, nyuq** -- to make oneself comfortable
salnyuq saldul illusion; fancy; fantasy (50:74) (cf. shaˇ noeˬ shaˇ sawˇ-eu)
=**sal, paq**= a kind of field frog
salpeel a wax gourd
salpeiqhuvq year after next (9:138) (na^ nui^ k'o^)
salpeiqnao day after tomorrow (**saˇ pehˬ** nah) (6:163, 9:138)
-- **salpeiq, neesoq** -- in a few days; before long
salpi products (Chi) (34:38)
salpi jiljif commodity economy (Chi) (34:87)
Salpuv a village which left Daolsal village (46:123)
-- **sal, puvsal** -- a very happy village
salqiq pseudo ginseng (Chi) (9:138)
salqiq peiv to be very angry; **sacivq peiv** (nui ma

peh˅ seh‸-eu)
-- **salqiq peiv, neema** -- to be angry
salqivqnao four days from now (pehˬ saˬ ngeh nah)
salqo to look for (9:138, 13:24) (or) **leiq puv** (sha˅ caw-eu)
-- **sal, seilhha** -- to amuse
-- **sal, seilsal** -- to enjoy; take pleasure in
salsil to die a bad death, as from lightning, drowning, killed by a wild animal, etc. (46:116, 131) (sha^ shi˅)
salsil galquv qo 'may you die a bad death' (a curse)
salsil gyuq for the soul of one who died a bad death to cry when it is rainy or cold, esp. on dark evenings
-- **sal, ssaq yal** -- happy descendants
salssil forever (11:112, 46:130) (Note: in negative, 'never') (mˬ maˬ maˬ bya^ za˅ zi˅)
salssil maq (vb) never (vb) (maˬ jah˅ haw)
salssil sal lo generation after generation (9:138); for a long time; forever; have a long history (30:1) (tiˬ zi˅ sa˅-i˅ tiˬ zi˅)
salteil a pleasant sound (na˅ haˬ muiˬ-eu te˅ sa˅)
salteil duv a pleasant sound to come forth (14:195)
=sal, teil= (see full)
saltuq cruel and ferocious (50:19)
-- **sal, xalmil** -- to look for a field
sal xavq to ask to stay overnight (13:4) (sha˅ ya‸-eu)
-- **sal, yalmil** -- to look for a field
sal yil to go down to beg; to ask for (sha˅-i˅-eu)
salyo pa yo nei very happily (38:108) (laˬ k'aˬ tiˬ ceh˅)
salzal Chinese hawthorn (plant) (Chi) (14:145)
sal zaq to beg for food (lit. 'beg-eat') (9:138, 13:2) (sha˅ dzaˬ-eu)
salzav nei happily (9:138) (laˬ k'aˬ ceh˅-eu; laˬ k'aˬ ceh˅ ta^ ni)
salzav pa zav nei very happily (35:74) (laˬ k'aˬ ceh˅ seh‸-eu)
Salzaol Qeiqhyuf Third Plenary Session (Chi) (14:195) (very important in Chinese history)
Salzeq a person's name (11:38, 131)
-- **sal, zeiq** -- to earn money
salzol zaq to go after (or) **qo'leiq zaq**
Salzul the name of a person (38:6)
Salzyu piqqeiq the name of the old man in the legend who learned how to cut down the giant tree

sabaoqbeil to lose one's temper (or) **civq peiv; civqbaoq beil** (nui ma peh˅-eu)
sacivq peiv to be angry (and see: **salqiq peiv**) (nui ma peh˅-eu)
-- **sa, leiq** -- to drive away
samu a mad person; crazy person (9:138) (tsaw˅ uˬ)

samu mu to go mad; crazy (tsawˇ uˬ uˬ iˇ-eu)
sa nei far away (g'awˬ mahˇ kaˬ-eu)
=sa nei, goq= very high (yaw goˇ)
=sa nei, jyuq= eliptical
Saniqssaq the Sani people (a branch of the Yi)
sapav a sharp length of bamboo fashioned so it can cut grass
-- sa, ssaqmiq seq -- to take one's daughter to a boy to marry
saweiq prose (Chi) (50:145)
sazual to purchase one by one (Chi) (50:145)
sazyuq a bad person
  sazyuq aqhhol a scolding word for a bad man (35:18) (or) **sazyuq ssaqhav; sazyuq koqkaq**
  sazyuq koqkaq a scolding word for a bad man (35:18) (or) **sazyuq aqhhol; sazyuq ssaqhav**
  sazyuq ssaqhav a scolding word for a bad man (or) **sazyu aqhhol; sazyuq koqkaq**

saq to be suffering; to be poor; hard up; state of misery (shaˬ-eu)
saq to pity (or) **hhosaq saq** (g'awˬ shaˬ gaˬ-eu)
saq muscle; **meat** (9:140) (shaˬ; shaˬ jiˇ)
(vb) saq to finish (vb), to complete (vb) (**aol saq** = finished doing - 9:140) (**pal saq** = all has changed - 12:126) (jiˇ-eu; g'aˬ-eu)
saq al to encounter hardship; to suffer from something (as cold and hunger) (shaˬ-eu)
(vb) saq al (vb) completely (**ngal hoq zaq saq al** = I have eaten it all up) (cf. **ngal hoq zaq al**. I have eaten)
=saq, aqkeeq keeq= dog meat
-- saq, aoqtav laolqaol -- to suffer an airplane crash
saqbal hhei go to work in an office (Chi) (41:51)
saqbaol 1. a share; a part; a portion (9:140, 11:135, 46:191) (as a share of the inheritance - 13:4) (shaˬ bymˇ); 2. a task (50:143)
  saqbaol dei 1. share equally, 2. average (50:131)
-- saq, bial -- a cliff; a steep place
saqbeiv beiv for measles to break out with a rash (bui sa^ sa^-eu)
saqbiavq dark and white spots on one's skin
saqbieiv bieiv to chop up meat (shaˬ byeh^ byeh^)
saqcaoq a bush (**algao saqcaoq** = a thorn bush) (11:208) (baw du^)
saqcil leiq nei to sweat all over (9:140) (kawˬ pyuˇ do^-eu)
=saq, civq= goat meat
saqciq a boil (pus-filled swelling of the skin) (6:172) (shaˬ ciˬ)
saqciivq ciivq to pinch (in joking, or when quarreling)
saqcul the fat of meat (9:140) (shaˬ tsuˇ)
Saqdeq a person's name (11:183)

saqdeil deil pieces of meat hung to dry (sha˯ ko^)
saqduq a dead-fall trap (or) **saqduqbyu**
saqduq duqbyu a bottomless pit
saqduq duqbyu ya dov to be trapped (or) **hhadaoq nei diq teiq**
saqduq gavduq suffering hardships; difficulties (sha˯-eu zah˯-eu)
saq e gav e hardships; difficulties; poverty (26:87) (sha˯ dui sha˯ duiˇ-eu)
-- **saq, eilsaq** -- to conclude a statement; say the final word
saqgeel animal skin; leather (9:140) (ba^ k'o^; **sha˯** k'o^; sha˯ jiˇ ba^ k'o^) (cf. Lahu: sha_ gui˯)
saqgeel baoqkev a leather case (ba^ k'o^ bah˯ keu^)
saqgeel gaolca hide factory (B=Chi) (50:129)
-- **saqgeel, nilzeiq** -- a wild animal skin
-- **saqgeel, ollol** -- a snake skin (when skinned by people)
saqgeel paltaol a leather bag (sha˯ k'o^ pehˇ zeuˇ)
saqgeel seiqnaov leather shoes (ba^ k'o^ seh˯ naw^), **saqgeel seivqnaov**
saqgul gul 1. to blow a buffalo horn when get large game, 2. to flush out animals by making lots of noise (27:11)
saqguq tendon; nerve; ligament; pulse (of a vein) (9:140, 46:152) (sha˯ gu˯)
saqguq hhe kuv to have a convulsion; muscle spasms
saqguq pieiv to cut up meat (as when cut up buffalo meat during funeral ceremonies)
saqhav forest (pf. over: **baolcaoq**) (8:11, 9:140) (aˇ bawˇ sah˯ k'a^; bawˇ tsah˯)
-- **saqhav, albol** -- a forest
saqhav diq to cut down a forest; to clear a forest of trees (not currently permitted) (cf.: yaˇ mya˯-eu)
saqhav havmoq an old forest (yaˇ sa˯ oeˇ)
-- **saqhav, haoldaol** -- a forest in the mountains
saqhav laolnav a dense forest
saqhaol at the right moment (aˇ yam˯ tsa˯ ngeh)
saq haol miq to condole; to offer one's condolences (50:38)
saqhaol qil haol to share someone's cares and burdens (50:50)
saqhao haossaq 1. soft feather, 2. body hair (45:45) (ca˰ hm)
saqhel pork which they offer in the ancestral offerings (**aqpyuq lol**)
-- **saqhel, zyuqzaq** -- Spring festival offering meat
saqhe the smell of meat (9:140)
=**saq, hhavq**= pork
saqhhol saqcii nei to be panting; out of breath (26:57) (sa˰ li li-eu)
-- **saq, hhosaq** -- to pity someone; to sympathize with
saqhhov scaly human skin; dandruff
saqjal jal duv force someone to admit something

(50:10)

=saq, jol= uncomfortable

saqkaol cotton thread (9:140) (clf. = **kaol**) (sa˯ kahˇ)

saqkaol cev for a new bride to break a red thread strung between two sticks at the entrance of her husband's house as she enters (she is not to enter his house before this part of the wedding ceremony is completed)

saqkaol kaollee a spool of thread (9:140) (sa˯ kahˇ sa˯ lah)

saqkaol naolnieil a loom set up (with some cloth in it) (11:210)

saqkaol paoq'aol a spindle for spinning cotton thread by hand (ya ahˇ)

saqkao a line of muscle in meat

saqkaoq to be in a dangerous situation

saqkaoq kaoq to be a dangerous activity (as riding a horse too fast, playing with knives)

saqkaoq kaoq sso have gone through all kinds of hardships and difficulties (50:63)

saqkaoq maq guv not fear danger (50:113)

-- saq, keellavq -- to trouble someone (also used in thanking a person for taking trouble)

=saq, keeq= dog meat

=saq, keil= vegetable garden

saqkuv dried meat

saqkuv bi kuv to dry meat (sha˯ ko^ ko^-eu)

saqlaq cotton (9:140) (**sa˯** la˯)

saqlaq albee a cotton quilt

saqlaq bevhuvq bevdul fluffing equipment for preparing cotton to be spun (including the bow)

saqlaq haqpal cotton cloth

saqlaq hho to spin cotton (sa˯ la˯ g'awˇ-eu)

saqlaq laqhho hho to spin cotton thread by hand

saqlaq saqlei a spool of cotton (sa˯ kahˇ lah)

saqlaq saqyeiv cotton flower (sa˯ la˯ aˇ yeh^)

saqlaq xa to plant cotton (46:212) (sa˯ **la˯** ka-eu)

saqlao lao to feed the villagers in a ceremonial way when one has shot big game

saq leil taq a tragedy (50:8)

saqlei a roll of cotton (for spinning) (9:141) (sa˯ lah)

saqlei lei to roll up cotton in prepration for spinning thread (14:166) (sa˯ lah lah-eu)

saq leiq to hunt (9:141, 11:28) (sha˯ teh-eu)

saqleiq aqkeeq a hunting dog (sha˯ teh a˯ kui˯)

saqleiq leiq to go hunting (following after the game)

saqleiq ssaq a hunter

saqleiq zaq to go hunting (general term)

saq li **an epilogue; the end (50:177)**

-- saq lo, saq sil -- (see full)

saqlu lymph nodes (swollen) (5:412) (sha˯ zaw^ ga-eu)

saqluvq luvq to wait for game being driven to one by

others (11:220) (or) **saqluvq luvq teiq** (sha˯ lo˄ lo˄-eu)

saqnav a mole on the skin (9:141) (sha˯ na^)

saqnav nav to have a mole on the skin (46:101) (sha˯ na^ na^-eu)

saq nei all; completely; thoroughly (9:141, 50:22) (Col **dyul saq nei kuvqceil hhaq.** There are 60 people in all. 11:108) (daw˯ taw^; meh teu^)

saq nei aol saq al all over (or) **dyu nei**

saq nei qiq qa all the same

saq nei qiq qa aol the same is required of all people (50:195)

saq nei sil lal everyone dies

saq nei xul to pass through (50:167)

saqnil lean pork (red meat) (9:141, 41:167) (sha˯ neˇ)

saqnil nilsol 'pure' lean pork with no bones (used in offerings) (or) **saqnil nilzuv**

saqnieil meil meat which is congealed in its juice

=saq, niuq= buffalo/cow meat

-- saq, nyuq -- to be sad

=saq, ngaq= fish

=saq ngyul, miq= to weep and mourn for an elder

saqpeeq an old field; not cultivated for a long time (11:24) (yaˇ sa˯; yaˇ peu˯)

-- saq, peev -- to burn away

saqpiaq the thigh; upper leg (9:141) (sha˯ pya˯)

saqpiaq saqyyuq the pelvis (or) **daoqnaol saqyyuq**

saqpiaq alkaq the groin (pya˯ ka˯)

saq puv to return to suffering (11:206) (sha˯ po^-eu)

-- saq, puvsaq -- an unfortunate village

saq qaq tired of suffering and having a hard life (46:140) (sha˯ doeˇ la˄-eu; sha˯ deh^ la˄-eu)

saqqavq cooked meat (14:172) (sha˯ jiˇ yaw ja˄)

saqqeil sour meat (sha˯ cehˇ)

saqqil meat from a barking (Muntjac) deer (ciˇ ha˯ sha˯ jiˇ)

-- saq, qoceil -- investigation results

saq qoq gav qoq a friend through thick and thin (lit. 'a friend in difficulties and cold') (or) **aoqsseil sseil qoq; keeq diq e yolqoq**

saqsal albaol lao a ceremonial day when they search for grasshoppers, wrap some in leaves and wedge them into poles by the fields (**siqmavq pavq hheil aqtov**)

saqsal dei pa dei nei a flat place; a leveled out place (yaw deh; deh saˇ)

saqsaq li e the ending; the last (eil **saqsaq** li e **doq** = the very last word) (aˇ sa˯ sa˯-eu)

saqsaol lol make an offering to the 'owner' of the game (in hopes of getting game in their hunt)

saqsaol luvcuv rocks placed outside the village where they make offerings to the 'owner' of game animals (**saqsaol**)

saqse se a prayer offered to big animals when they

shoot them ('I did not want to kill you, but you made a mistake...')

saq sil saq lo miserable; suffering; having a hard life (46:144, 197) (sha˯ seh˰-eu)

saqsiq a blemish of the skin (5:821) (maˇ byaw˰ byaw˰-eu)

saqsiivq fresh meat (sha˯ jiˇ yaw jm˯)

saqteil wooden cutting block (for meat, vegs.) (9:141) (k'aw˯ bo^)

saq ya gav ya hardship and cold (14:183)

saq yil to die away; to die out (or) **bial yil**

saqyoq bone; **saqyyuq** (sha˯ yoe˯)

saqyoq lilpuv puv to rebel ('the bone grew in the wrong way') (or) **puvzaq**

saqyyuq bone (9:141, 46:152); **saqyoq** (sha˯ yoe˯)

-- **saqyyuq, Aqlobieil** -- (see full)

saqyyuq loqkol skeleton (5:841) (sha˯ yoe˯ yaw ngaw ngaw-ehˇ)

-- **saqyyuq, paoqciivq** -- the kneecap

saqyyuq piultaoq bone marrow (or) **saqyyuq yyuqnaoq** (9:141) (sha˯ yoe˯ iˇ nm˰)

saqyyuq qiq xaoq sol nei as lean as a rake; just skin and bones (sha˯ yoe˯ teh˰-ehˇ jeh k'awˇ ni)

saqyyuq yyuqnaoq cartilage (or) **saqyyuq piultaoq**

saqzaq haqlaq a pig-eating tiger (35:85) (sha˯ dza˯-eu k'a˯ la˯)

saqzav gav zav nei in poverty (**saqzav gav zav nei jol** = to live in poverty - 26:2) (sha˯ dui sha˯ duiˇ-eu; sha˯-eu zah˯-eu)

saqzaoq fresh meat (sha˯ jiˇ yaw jm˯)

saqzaoq zaoq saqbieiv bieiv to make a special dish with fresh meat

saq zeiq gav zeiq poverty; suffering; hardship; hunger (45:71) (sha˯-eu zah˯-eu)

-- **saq, zilbaq dol** -- to drink up (bottoms up)

saqziv ziv not a good relationship (quarreling, fighting, etc.)

-- **saq, zol** -- to graduate

saqzuq zuq 1. to be chilly; to shiver; 2. shudder (9:141, 11:43) (yaw dzu˯ dzu˯-eu)

sav to file (**saolsav nei sav** = to file with a file) (50:29)

sav coarse; rough (2:57) (yaw sa^; sa^-eu)

sav to weigh (9:141) (sa^-eu)

sav clf. for a certain weight (used in weighing meat) (11:78) (sa^-eu)

-- **sav, aoqsseil sseilsav** -- to drizzle

-- **sav, doqsav** -- to whisper

=sav, haq= bamboo

savjil a scale for weighing (9:141)

savjil jilma a large scale

savjil savhaoq the pan used in the scale for weighing

savjil savyyuq the beam of the scale (see below)

savjil savmiav a scale for weighing (10:2, 13:38)
savjil savsiq the sliding weight of the scale (see above)
-- sav, kaoqsav -- to be hoarse
savmiav ngavq keiq weight of five grams (C=Chi)
savmiav ssol dalqeiv weights and measures
=sav nei, kuv= to be very dry
-- sav nei, naqhhaq -- unexpectedly
=sav nei, povq= to be softened
savngeeq a hook on a scale for weighing things (9:141) (cf.: la‸ ngeuˬ)
=sav, saol= a metal file
-- sav, teilsav -- to whisper
savtuv nei coarse; rough (2:58) (yaw sa^)
savtuv pa tuv nei roughly (13:44) (yaw sa^)
savyov nei to be rough (9:142) (yaw sa^)
savziiq shot (used in a shotgun) (Chi)

savq a breath (clf.: savq) (11:34) (sa‸)
savq steam (or) **savqhyuq** (9:142) (sa‸ k'oeˬ)
savq gas (9:142) (sa‸)
savq to cook by steaming (9:142) (sa‸-eu)
savq a period of time (**Aqyoq maq lal e qiq savq hev al.** He hasn't come here for a long time.)
savqbaoq wooden steamer (for rice) (hawˬ sa‸ bahˬ) (9:142)
savqcao cao to pant (11:43) (sa‸ huiˬ huiˬ-ehˇ g'eh-eu)
savq ceiv lal 1. to stop breathing (10:26), 2. to die (26:99) (sa‸ tseh^ leˇ-eu)
savq ceiv movq nei at death's door (or) **sil movq ca nei**
savq cii to have breathing difficulty; to suffer from asthma
savqcii cii to wheeze; breathe with difficulty, as from asthma (cf.: sa‸ g'awˇ dah-eu)
savqdaol bo (see: **savqdol bo**)
savq diq dov to fill the air
savqdol to be ashamed; shy (pf); **molsavq bo** (sha‸ dawˇ-eu)
savqdol bo something to be ashamed of; to be shy about; to be shy; bashful (50:115)
savqdol sil laq embarrassed to death (13:3) (sha‸ dawˇ seh‸-eu)
savqduq a kitchen
savq'eel steam; vapor
savq gee to evaporate (50:210)
-- savq hev, qiq -- (see full)
savqheiq heiq to sigh (26:93) (uiˇ huiˬ ka-eu)
savqhyuq steam (or) **savq** (9:142) (sa‸ k'oeˬ)
savq hhol to breathe (9:142) (sa‸ g'awˇ-eu)
savqhhol savqcii meil to breathe with difficulty (cf.: sa‸ g'awˇ dah-eu)
=savq, laol= to steam up; warm up (as the sun)
savqli li to pant; difficult to breathe; short of

breath (9:142, 10:25) (cf.: sa^ li li-eu)

savqmei mei to be bored

=savq, miq= soot

-- savq, neema nyuq -- to have a bad conscience

=savq nei, ngyul= to sob

savqpiq ziiq teiq to take a deep breath (35:102) (sa^ g'awˇ mahˇ ni g'awˇ-eu)

savqpuq an air balloon (50:134)

-- savq, qiq -- for a long time

=savq, xil qiq= these days; recently

-- savq, zilbaq -- to distill liquor

safbal to go to work (Chi) (26:29) (gaˇ mˇ-iˇ-eu)

safbal saf saq to resign; to leave one's work (Chi) (26:29)

safcaol morning exercise (Chi) (26:84)

safcaol coq to perform morning exercise (A=Chi) (50:147)

safcaol saf to perform morning exercise (Chi) (26:84)

safceiq jeifzuq 1. realm of the superstructure (Chi) (34:34, 50:147), 2. upper strata; upper levels (50:147)

Safhei Shanghai (Chi) (57:86)

safjiq higher organization (an organization over yours) (Chi) (41:88)

safkof saf to have a lesson (as in school) (Chi) (41:60)

saf saq to leave work (Chi) (26:29)

-- saf, safkof -- to have a lesson (as in school) (Chi)

SAO

saol to shut in (ka^ tehˬ-eu)

saol iron (metal) (9:139) (shmˇ)

saol three (Note: '**saol**' is used when the classifier is on a low tone, '**saoq**' is used when the classifier is on a mid or high tone.) (smˇ; smˬ)

saolbaoq a metal pipe (Chi) (57:89)

saolbeel iron chain (9:139) (shmˇ ca^)

saolcal iron pot; metal pot (B=Dai) (9:139, 13:33) (or) **saol cal** (38:2)

saolcav laolzaol an iron chain bridge (50:167)

=saol, caoq= spirit owner of the land (they make offerings to)

saol ciivq aqhhyu three generations of maternal 'uncles' (mother's brothers are first generation; their sons are the second, and grandsons the third)

saol dalqei a sharp metal rod (38:111); **saolqei** (shmˇ ceh)

saol diq baziq blacksmith (9:139) (shmˇ diˬ-eu ba jiˬ)

saol diqpuq a metal hammer

saoldu a crowbar
saoldyuq a peafowl; peacock (9:139, 14:237) (shmˇ doe⌄)
=saol, eel= an otter
saol geel to melt steel (26:26) (shmˇ baw guiˇ-eu)
saol geelbaoq a refining pot
saolhaovqliq a double plow (Chi)
saolhyuq a thief (9:139, 13:30) (smˇ k'oe⌄)
saolhyuq laqma the leader of a gang of thieves (tahˇ joe la^ ma)
saolhyuq saolhheivq cheaters; liars
saolhhaol midnight (or) **sulhhaol** (9:139, 26:51) (u⌄ ci^ sehˇ g'ahˇ)
saolhhaoq a metal hoop or band
saoljul handcuffs; fetters (la^ kaw^)
saolkal an iron railing; an iron fence
saol kavngeeq a hooked metal hoe (used for weeding) (cf.: la^ ngeu⌄)
saolkaoq an iron pan
saolkeel a trivet (for cooking); an iron tripod (9:139) (shmˇ kuiˇ)
-- saol, lalsaol -- to be greedy (to eat)
saol laqdul a steel rod (26:27) (shmˇ kah⌄)
saol lavqkav iron harrow
saol laolzaol a metal bridge
saol luv cuvhhal the sacred stone (stones) in the middle of the village which are for the 'Lord of the land' (see also: **hhaq luv cuvhhal; kal luv cuvhhal**)
saollyul small pieces of iron; iron filings (cf.: shmˇ ce⌄)
saolmeeqssaq rich people (smˇ mui⌄)
=saol, mil= lord of the land (spiritual 'owner' of an area)
=saol, milluvq mil= lord of the land (and see above)
saolmiaoq a magnet (50:27)
saol paqssaq three members of a family (parents with a child) (45:70) (smˇ peh⌄ za⌄)
saolpao 1, a metal pot for steaming rice (9:139), 2. a steam boiler (50:210)
saol piavteiq metal traps (for large animals)
saolpuq urinary bladder (5:97) (iˇ shoi baw duiˇ)
saolpuq a bubble (30:2) (boeˇ loeˇ)
saolpuq teivq nei bubbles to form (30:2) (boeˇ loeˇ loeˇ-eu)
saol pyuq 1. to praise (50:57), 2. to celebrate (50:138)
saol pyuq miq 1. to praise; respect; honor (46:129) (ci⌄ poe⌄-eu), 2. to celebrate (50:138)
saolqei a sharp iron rod; **saol dalqei** (shmˇ ceh)
saolsav a metal file for filing down wood (kaˇ shiˇ - the Ak. is from Dai)
saol saoldev a piece of iron (used in making their tools) (11:36)
saolseiv cast iron

=saol, soq= the inner part of a tree; the tree core
saolsul a saw (9:139, 11:32) (yeh⌄ ma)
saolsul sulpovq sawdust
saolsyuv dalpav 1. a metal spade (26:59), 2. a metal plow blade (as on a bulldozer) (26:34)
saol teivq soye (see: **saljiq soye**) (50:145)
saoltyuq an awl (made of iron) (9:139) (shmˇ toe⌄)
saolwuqcaoq a metal helmet ('metal cap')
saolxiq iron filings (shmˇ ce⌄)
saolyeiqyil an oral vowel (as opposed to a laryngealized vowel) (Chi) (2:57)
saolzaol an axe for cutting wood, with sharp and blunt sides (9:139, 43:143, 46:153) (deu^ ha⌄)
saolzaol lavqdev a hatchet; a small axe (deu^ ha⌄)
saolzaol zaolpuq the blunt side of a big axe (used to kill the bull at the stone bull ceremony)

sao huaq to eliminate pornographic material (Chi) (34:65)
saomaq to eliminate illiteracy (Chi)
saomaqba a literacy class (Chi) (57)150)
saosuq a minority (Chi) (10:14) (or) **saosuf miqcuq** a minority nationality (Chi) (10:14)
saosuq miqcuq ssaqlaol minority nationality people (AB=Chi)

saoq jungle fowl (ya nyi⌄)
saoq to dislike; to be disgusted with (9:139, 13:25); to hate (38:6) (bye-eu)
saoq three ('**saoq**' is used when the classifier is on a mid or high tone, '**saol**' is used when the classifier is on a low tone) (sm⌄; smˇ)
=saoq, aq= brother-in-law; older sister's husband
-- saoq, biaq -- beeswax
saoq ceil thirty (9:140) (sm⌄ tseˇ)
saoq feil qeq (qiq mol bi zeitao naq) a three-point basket (in basketball) B=Chi) (41:202)
=saoq, keel= a toenail
Saoqla siq March
saoqla xeivqnao ssaqmiq neeciiv March 8th Women's Festival (50:145)
=saoq, laq= 1. a claw (as of a cat), 2. a fingernail
=saoq, lav= to be fierce
saoq miq to disgust someone (45:50)
saoq nao saol yavq three days, three nights (46:90) (sm⌄ nah sm⌄ miˇ)
-- saoq, qavq -- to be very displeased
=saoq, seiq= a toenail; talon; claw
saoq sil to hate; to be very disgusted (13:39) (noe⌄ byoe-eu; bye seh^-eu)
saoq sil laq to be ugly (11:171)
saoq yuvq lasiq March and April ('months three-four') (12:126)
saoq zaq look upon with hatred (35:108)
saoqzeiv nei disgusting (bye laˇ pa⌄-ehˇ g'eh-eu;

byeh laˇ)

saofxeil dyufyeiq young pioneers (Chi) (50:148)

SE

sel to receive (as a letter) (Chi)
-- sel to develop (this is also sometimes used in girl's names = Miqsel)
selgefdieif a purchasing station (Chi) (14:146)
selssuq incomes (esp. monetary) (Chi) (34:44)
selyiljil a radio set (Chi)
sel yi to have led someone to a place (arrived)
sel zaq to collect (A=Chi) (14:146)

se to collect; to get the price (Chi) (9:142, 41:141)
se to move an object (as clothes) (9:144) (sheu-eu)
se to become (as: **moqpil se** = to become a spirit priest) (seu-eu)
se clf. for wooden container to measure rice (9:142) (holds roughly 12 kg.)
se clf. for an hour (**siqse qiq se ssuq** = to walk for an hour - 11:85) (na˯ li˯ ti˯ la˰; na˯ li˯ ti˯ moˇ) (2:58)
se to sing folk songs (cf.: **alse se**) (caˇ-eu)
-- se, alse -- to sing folk songs (especially when transplanting rice)
sebiao wristwatch (Chi) (or) **siqse lavqduvq**
sebuvq buvq e col the village 'artist' (makes decorations for funerals, including the wooden standard carried in front of the coffin)
secuafxif jilseiq creative initiative; pioneering spirit (Chi) (34:16)
seduq stature of one's body (45:6)
seduaf means; method (Chi) (34:45); **sedueif**
sedueif means; method (Chi); **seduaf**
segaolniq handicraft (Chi) (34:10)
se hha piul income; money that one gets (50:156)
-- se hha, piulssaq -- a realistic tax rate
sekevq true qualities; natural color
se leev 1. to get; collect (9:143, 11:221), 2. to be cleaned up (26:7), 3. to draw in (or) **lav laovq; hhe kuv**
-- se leev, kalyei -- to harvest a crop
se'lieqdaf a hand grenade (Chi) (26:42)
se'loq nei neat and clean (shawˇ jeh^ ni)
se'qeiv to compare two things (50:11)
-- se, saqse -- (see full)
sesuf zaol to operate on someone (A=Chi) (50:39)
se ssaoq to collect together (la^ ui˯-eu)
setyulceil a handcart (Chi) (26:63)
seza head (as head of a company) (Chi) (26:109) (in Hani: **wuqduq**)

seq to lead (by hand); guide; take along (9:144) (sheuˬ-eu)
seq to marry a woman (9:144) (sheuˬ-eu)
seq a tooth (9:143) (seuˬ)
seqbiaq tooth (poetic)
seqbyuq a tooth 'worm' (they believe this is what causes cavities in a tooth) (seuˬ boeˬ)
seqcavq bad teeth
seq cavq to come to meet someone (35:57)
seqdaoq gums (or) **seqpeiq** (seuˬ seuˬ dahˬ)
seq deil yil deil alhuvq lawful age to marry (50:45)
-- **seq, galseq** -- to lead along a path; to guide
seqgaoq overlapping teeth (9:144) (seuˬ ka˰)
seq gol for a tooth to ache (seuˬ gawˇ-eu)
seqhavq 1. a broken tooth, 2. a person with a broken tooth (seuˬ ga)
seq hev to have led someone to a place (arrived)
seqjiv jiv to grind one's teeth (as in a dream) (seuˬ teu˰-eu)
seqkaq the space between the teeth (4:41) (seuˬ kaˬ)
seqkaq hevq to pick one's teeth (seuˬ kaˬ kaw^ dzeh-eu)
seqkaq teiq to have something (as food) between two teeth (4:42) (seuˬ kaˬ tehˬ-eu)
seqkovq kovq 1. to bite down with one's teeth (14:149), 2. to grind one's teeth (here in anger) (38:6) (seuˬ kaw˰ kaw˰-eu)
seq le deivq le to marry at a mature age and give a late birth
seq lev 1. to show one's teeth (4:36), 2. to smile
=**seq lev nei, eel**= smilingly
seqliq a broken off tooth (seuˬ k'eh˰; seuˬ pa^)
seqma an incisor (5:3181)
-- **seq, miqsiivq ssaqsiivq** -- to hold a wedding party
-- **seq, miqssaq** -- for a man to take a wife; to marry (from the male perspective)
=**seq, moq**= a front tooth; incisor tooth ('horse tooth')
seq navq yil navq zo to marry too young (50:205)
seqnaoq a baby tooth (seuˬ nahˬ)
seqnil an insect that forms lac
seqnil a tooth stained red (seuˬ neˇ)
seqnil nil to stain one's teeth permanently red (seuˬ neˇ neˇ-eu)
seqnil pieiq to raise the insects that create lac (the Hani get good money for the lac produced)
seq pal for a child to get permanent teeth (seuˬ paˇ-eu)
seqpeiq gums (of teeth) (or) **seqdaoq** (seuˬ seuˬ dahˬ)
seqpeiq siil tov to have a tooth plated with gold (seuˬ shuiˇ yaw-eu)
seqpievq two overlapping teeth
seqqil the root of a tooth (seuˬ dahˬ)

seq qil to have firm teeth (seu˅ yaw zi˄)
seqqovq Chinese cassia tree
seq sa to see someone off (9:144, 11:39)
-- seq sa, ssaqmiq -- (see full)
-- seq, sullal -- to lead souls
seq ssaoq to collect (9:144) (la^ ui˅-eu)
seqtevq a mark (as in stone); a notch (as in wood) (9:144) (ca^ teu˄ teu˄-eu)
seqtevq tevq to engrave; to carve (46:79) (seu˅ teu˄ teu˄-eu)
seq to to guide; lead; take along (46:132, 50:109) (or) **ziidaof** (Chi) (sheu˅ g'eh-eu)
seq to jilgual leading administration (B=Chi) (109)
seq to wuqzao main body of leadership (Chi) (50:109)
-- seq to, zaoqgao -- unified leadership
seqtov tov to plate a tooth with a metal (as gold or silver)
=seq, wuq= (see full)
seqxiq tartar on teeth (seu˅ seu˅ ce˅)
seqyil animal doctor; veterinarian (Chi) (41:23)
seq yil to go to lead someone someplace
seq yi to have been to a place to lead someone back down
seqzaol the two upper front teeth (9:144) (or) **seqma**
seqziil canine tooth (in humans); fang; **ziilqei** (seu˅ juiˇ)

sev 1. to shave (jeh^-eu), 2. to have a haircut (or) **wuqduq sev** (u˅ du˅ teh˅-eu) (cf.: seu^-eu = to scrape), 3. to love (35:85)
sev a gentle breeze (cf.: seu^ seu^-ehˇ = the sound of wind blowing)
=sev, bo= a fan
-- sev, caqkeel -- to clear off weeds from the lower bunds of terraced fields
-- sev, dalqei -- to whittle to a point
sevdev dev the custom of when the coffin has been cut and is returned to the village, a house member (pf. the oldest son), holding a knife in his left hand, circles the coffin three times holding a fire and an egg in his right hand. He then throws the egg and fire on the ground near the coffin, and makes three cuts in the coffin with the knife.
=sev, geeq= lacquer tree
=sev, jaqleil leil= a cool wind
sevle nei (not) even a little (13:11) (**sevle nei maq qeq** = did not believe even a little, or, did not believe it at all)
sevlev a little (35:75, 46:99) (aˇ cui^)
=sev nei, biav= to be flat
sev nei maq cyuq to know nothing (41:86) (ti˅ je˅-i˅ ma˅ si˅ nya)
=sev nei, peel= greyish
sevpil albol a kind of tree

-- **sev, wuqduq** -- to have a hair cut
-- **sev, xaldei daobiao** -- to weed a terrace wall in an irrigated rice field with a hoe

sefhyuf zuyif socialism (Chi) (9:142) (or) **seifhyuf zuyif** (pf.)

SEI

seil louse (9:142) (shehˇ mawˇ)
seil a liter (Chi)
seil to play (as cards) (14:195)
-- **seil, alsiq aqhaoq** -- to have smallpox
-- **seil, aqhhyu aqmee** -- (see full)
-- **seil, ba'la wuqcal** -- to play in the moonlight
=**seil, baq**= whiskers
seilbaoq onion (9:142) (sehˇ bawˬ)
  seilbaoq baoqma a large onion (sehˇ bawˬ bawˬ ma)
seilbei bei doq an announcement (as in a program) (50:8)
  seilbei eilgaq col an announcer (as in a program) (50:8)
seilbeiv silver dangles (like tiny trumpets) worn on the front of a woman's headdress or in her hair
  seilbeiv pavq for a woman to wear silver dangles in hair or in front of her headdress
seilca production (Chi) (26:54) (mˇ za-eu)
  seilcadyuf a production team (Chi) (9:142, 26:39)
  seilca'liq productive forces (Chi) (34:33)
  seilcazei a production worker (Chi) (26:100)
  seilca ziilliaof means of production (Chi) (34:16)
seilciiq new words (Chi) (41:66) (dawˬ yaw shui‸)
seildaof hoqboq lively; vigorous (Chi) (34:48)
seildiaof tones (as in a tonal language) (Chi) (9:143) (teˇ g'ahˇ teˇ nahˬ)
  seildiaof fuqhaof tone marks (phonetics) (Chi)
seilduq a playground (50:103)
seilfaq one's appearance (Chi)
seilfeifzeif identity card (Chi) (50:149)
=**seil, ha**= chicken louse
=**seil, haq**= garlic
-- **seil, haqhhal** -- to dance; play games
seil haoq to play according to the rules (46:90)
seilhoq life (as to give one's life for one's country) (Chi) (26:73, 34:74)
  seilhoq pyu daily life (A=Chi) (26:108)
seil huvq snake year (9:143) (shehˇ tiˬ k'o‸)
-- **seil, hhalseil** -- to play a game (but see also: **seilhha**)
seilhha to play; to play a game (niˇ g'a-eu) (9:143) (see also: **hhalseil seil**)
seilhha to visit (or) **salhha** (11:210) (dawˬ deh g'a-eu)
  seilhha sal to amuse
-- **seil, hhaqleiq** -- to make a joke

-- **seil, jaqbuq** -- to show off one's wealth; display one's wealth
=**seil kav, xal**= (see full)
=**seil, keeq**= a flea ('dog louse')
seillaoq sorghum (9:143) (shaˇ lah˯)
=**seilma, miq**= woman dissatisfied with her marriage (often will go home)
=**seil, miq**= a spark from a fire
seilmif life (Chi) (15 title)
seilmif ziilsiiq basic knowledge about life (Chi)
=**seil, moq**= horse louse (insects that bother horses)
seilmu initial (as an initial consonant - phonetics) (Chi) (41:76)
seil nao snake day (cf.: shehˇ nah ti˯ nah)
=**seil, naoq**= sesame
=**seil nei, kal**= thinly scattered
seilpavq garlic leaf (9:143) (sehˇ puˇ pa˰)
seilqeiv qeiv to compete in dancing
seilqi to submit an application (Chi) (50:149)
seilqi soqhhaq application paper (A=Chi) (50:149)
-- **seilqi soqkaoq, ssuqda** -- application to join the party (AB=Chi)
seilqoq a musical troupe (dancers, singers, but not the star performers) (50:128)
seil sal a pleasant place to play (14:220)
seilsal sal to enjoy; take pleasure in (50:174)
seilse a teacher (Chi) (sa˯ la˯)
=**seil, wuq**= 1. head lice, 2. grey-headed
-- **seil, wuqseil** -- to become grey-headed
seilwuv louse eggs (shehˇ mawˇ ya u^; ya shehˇ ya u^)
seilxoq to study further (Chi) (41:87) (dzaw da^-eu)
-- **seil, zeiseil** -- to be extravagent

sei province (Chi) (10:22) (**ngaldu sei** = our province; **Yyuqnaq Sei** = province of Yunnan 50:227)
seicaq to check something or someone (as the papers) (Chi) (50:150)
seipafza presiding judge (Chi) (50:150)
seiza provincial governor (Chi) (41:3)

seiq a poisonous plant
seiq the hoof of an animal (9:143) (kuiˇ seh˯)
seiq a bamboo stick on which to roll cotton in preparation for spinning it (9:143)
seiq 1. to water (as plants) (seh˯-eu), 2. to spread or sow (as seeds, manure) (9:143) (seh˯-eu)
-- **seiq, bavq** -- to water (as vegetables)
seiq dalpav a wooden paddle used in a loom (pulls back the thread to make the cloth firm)
seiq dav to pour on (3:4) (sheh˯ da^-eu)
seiq dov pal to resow (as where seeds washed out)
-- **seiq, geeq jeivq saol jeivq saoqhhev** -- to make three circles on the ground with a metal tool to keep spirits from attacking
seiqhoqziiq a young man (Chi) (14:154) (a˯ li za˯

gu⌄)

=seiq, hhavq= pig hoof

-- seiq, hhoseiq -- to sow seeds

seiqkaq the space between two toes (kuiˇ noeˇ ka⌄)

seiqkaq coq 1. to visit friends which are scattered (do not all live in the same area), 2. to visit selectively (i.e., go visit some but not all)

-- seiq, keellavq -- to wash hands and feet (see full)

seiqluvq feet with short toes

seiqma the big toe (kuiˇ noeˇ ma)

-- seiq, miav laq -- to have dim eyesight (46:149)

=seiq, moq= a horse hoof

seiqnaov shoes; sandals (or) **seivqnaov** (9:143) (seh⌄ naw^)

seiqnaov naovbaoq socks; stockings (41:151) (note: **seiqnaov; naovbaq** = shoes and socks) (naw^ bah⌄)

seiqnyul toes (kuiˇ noeˇ)

-- seiq, ngaoq -- to pour on

seiqpaoq a seedbed for rice (11:43)

seiqpaoq lav to make a seedbed for rice seedlings

seiqpaoq paoq to sow seeds in seedbed

seiqpiav to encounter danger

-- seiq, pyuq -- to pour out (of mouth)

=seiq, qil= side roots

seiqquvq bound feet (as Chinese women used to do)

seiqsaoq 1. the claw of an animal (la^ sah⌄), 2. the talon of a bird (aˇ jiˇ-eu⌄ la^ sah⌄), 3. a toenail (kuiˇ sah⌄)

=seiq seiq, hho= to sow seeds

seiqsiil an installation; facility (including equipment) (Chi) (50:148)

seiq tao to spread something into (45:53)

seiqtivq tivq to tumble; to trip (sah⌄ ti^ ti^-eu)

seiqtivq tivqlevq to tumble and be injured

seiqxal musk; musk ox (Chi)

seiv 1. to pour; to pour out (9:143, 11:8) (or) **seiv seiq** (35:61), 2. to pour into a mold for casting (as iron), 3. to form mud in a mold to make bricks

-- seiv, caqbiav -- to make bricks

seiv dav miq to pour out a liquid (46:149) (sheh^ do^-eu)

seiv duv to pour out (as water) (sheh^ k'aˇ-eu)

seivhuvq a mold for making bricks (11:27)

seivmoq kovtov stilts (children walk on them) (46:126) (mah⌄ naw⌄ naw⌄-eu)

seivseiq to pour out (35:61) (sheh^ do^-eu)

=seiv seiv, moq ziiq= horse-riding games

seiv tao to pour into (11:47) (sheh^ uˇ-eu)

-- seiv, zilbaq -- (see full)

seivq to kill (9:143) (seh^-eu)

(vb) seivq to kill by (vb) (**diq seivq** = to kill by hitting) (... seh^-eu, di⌄ seh^-eu)

-- **seivq, aqseivq** -- to display oneself in a proud way; to strut
-- **seivq, diq** -- to strike to death
seivqnaov shoes; sandals (or) **seiqnaov** (both Hani words are used) (seh⌄ naw^)
-- **seivqnaov, saqgeel** -- leather shoes
-- **seivq, yaqmoq** -- to kill a buffalo for a dead person

seifdyuf qilniq an enterprise managed by a production team (Chi) (50:148)
seifhyuf society (Chi) (34:33)
seifhyuf baoxei society insurance (Chi) (50:148)
seifhyuf ciifxif social orders (Chi) (50:148)
seifhyuf gualxif social relationships (Chi) (50:148)
seifhyuf hoqdaof social activities (Chi) (50:148)
seifhyufhuaf socialize (Chi) (50:148)
seifhyuf jefjif social relief (Chi) (50:148)
seifhyuf yillyuf public opinion (Chi) (50:148)
seifhyuf yifsiiq social ideology (Chi) (34:71)
seifhyuf ziifhhal social security (Chi) (50:148)
seifhyuf zuyif socialism (Chi) (26:20)
seifhyuf zuyif e davbei bei the primary stage of socialism (A=Chi) (34:35)
seifhyuf zuyif jeifseiq to bring about socialism through revolution (Chi) (26:29)
seifhyuf zuyyif yaol poqhueif to harm socialism (Chi) (50:131)
seiflif to be victorious (Chi) (26:44, 34:22)
seiflyuf 1. editorial (Chi) (50:148), 2. important news item in newspaper given by the govt. (Chi) (50:148)
seiftef to permeate (Chi) (34:33)
seifyeiq commune members (Chi) (26:38, 50:148)

SI

sil 1. to die (9:145), 2. to go out (as fire; light), 3. to the extreme of something (see: **neehaol sil; gaq sil**, etc.), 4. to kill (**dovq sil** = to kill by poison) (shiˇ-eu)
sil to put a stick or a bamboo tie through a fish or piece of meat (to carry it) (siˇ-eu)
sil final part. indicating 'again; still', the same as: **siq**
sil clf. for the above
sil for the (foot) to be tired or painful (9:145)
-- **sil, aqkeel** -- a paralyzed leg
-- **sil, bev** -- to shoot to death
-- **sil, beil** -- 1. to be noisy; quarrelsome; 2. to be in one's death throes, 3. to twist and turn violently (as when a pig is tied up)
=**sil, biaq**= honey bee (the kind they raise)
-- **sil, bo** -- stillborn baby

-- **sil, byulnal** -- to die of some type of 'plague' or epidemic which travels quickly

silbyu nalbyu pavqcyuq cyuq to stuff cotton in nostrils, mouth and ears of a person who has just died (it is removed before the burial)

Silcaqzeil the New Long March (Chi) (14:228)

Silcaqzeil **Tuqjiqse** Pioneers on the New Long March (Chi) (14:228)

sil ceiv to die; expire (not just to be in a coma) (13:39) (shiˇ tseh^-eu)

-- **sil, civqbaoq beil** -- to have an epileptic convulsion

-- **sil, civq peiv** -- to be very angry

=sil, col= a corpse; a dead body

-- **sil, dev** -- to cut to death

-- **sil, diq** -- 1. to kill by beating; striking dead, 2. to put out a fire (by beating)

-- **sil, duq nal duq** -- to hurt and kill by digging

sil duv to stick out (as out of a hole, or between slats) (13:44)

-- **sil, eelhhuvq** -- to drown (a 'bad death')

-- **sil, gaq** -- to miss someone very much

silhe nei the smell of urine

silhheivq hheivq to be in a coma (or) **yiuvqmu mu**

-- **sil, hhuvq** -- to cover over

-- **sil, hhyulmeil** -- for a woman to die in childbirth with the baby still in her

sil lal maq nyuq without fear of death (i.e., did not worry about whether he died or not) (13:48) (shiˇ gaˇ ma˯ gu^ ni)

sil lal saq lal maq guv not to fear death or difficulties (shiˇ gaˇ ma˯ gu^ ni)

(vb) sil laq (ya) (vb) to the ultimate (**qeq sil laq ya** = believe it 'to death') (12:128) (...seh˄)

(cf. Lahu: yon_ ve suh la yo˯)

sillavq pa lavq nei a strong smell of urine

=sil lavqsil, keel= arms and legs to be paralyzed

=sil, laol= dirty water

=sil, lao= a dirty pond

sil laoq huvq a prayer before the buffalo is killed during funeral rites

-- **sil li, civqbaoq beil** -- to have an epileptic seizure

-- **sil, miqzaq diq** -- to put out a fire by beating

silmiavq miavq to act as if they were dead

-- **sil, naolhaol** -- relieved; satisfied (see also: **neehaol sil**)

-- **sil, neehaol** -- to be reliable; satisfied (or) **naolhaol sil**

-- **sil, nieivq** -- 1. to squeeze to death, 2. to turn out a light

-- **sil nyuq lo, nyuq** -- to miss someone very much

-- **sil, peev** -- to burn to death

=sil, pil= a type of thatch

silpuq diq to play basketball (46:186)

silpyuq hu to pay one's respects to the remains of someone
-- **sil pyuq** lo **meil, pyuq** -- to be very proud
-- **sil, qavq** -- to boil clean; sterilize
-- **sil, qeq** -- believe in very much
-- **sil, qeiq** -- to put someone to death (la^ seh‸-eu)
Silqil luq Saturday (Chi) (14:220) (**Silqil luq qiq nao** = 'the day of Saturday')
-- **sil, quq** -- to bump to death
silquvq miavhav a special 'wedding basket' prepared for the bride-to-be by her family to take with her to the wedding
silsav albol a tree which is important in ceremonies (Pyrensria cf. camelliiflora) (siˇ sa^ aˇ bawˇ)
-- **sil, saoq** -- to hate
sil **taol la** to stick into (4:44) (soe˯ ahˇ-eu)
sil **tao** to drown (as a mouse in a pond) (12:126) (ga pu‸-eu)
sil **tao** to pass through (as thread through a needle) (soe˯ ahˇ-eu)
-- **sil tao, aqhhovq** -- to thread a needle
silteil when a 'divining stick' lands with the flat side up it is called this (see also: **moqcaoq**)
silteil nei lying on one's back (26:32)
silteil teil to lie on one's back (k'aw˯ daˇ-eu)
sil **tovq** a death penalty; death sentence
sil **tovq hev** death penalty time arrives
sil **tovq zyul** a capital offence; a capital crime (50:160)
=**sil, zaol**= to kill; cause to die

=**si, eiq**= a moment ago
=**si, meiq**= in front of; before

siq 1. to sharpen a knife (9:145) (si˯-eu), 2. to bear fruit (si˯-eu)
siq clf. for months (9:145) (si˯)
siq clf. for round things as fruit; small stones etc. (si˯)
siq 1. too, 2. again, 3. still (9:145) (si˯)
(vb) **siq** still; yet (46:214) (... si˯)
=**siq, al**= fruit
=**siq, baq**= pimple
siqbiav wild grape (or) **siqbiav nibiav** (a˯ ga‸)
=**siq, byuq**= taro
=**siq, ceil**= a grain of rice
-- **siqdaol, aoqsiq** -- a cool place
siqguq a kind of fig (ficus) tree (si˯ gu˯)
siqhaq a bitter fruit (edi) (9:145)
=**siq, hel**= a cowrie shell
siqhel maq meeq unlucky (or) **gaoqlaoq maq bo** (gui˯ lah˯ ma˯ hui˯)
siqhel meeq to have good luck (35:61) (gui˯ lah˯ hui˯-eu)
siqhu naolhu to look back and forth (45:6)

siqhuvq a cucumber (9:145) (si˯ k'o˯)
siqhuvq qalluvq a small cucumber that does not grow very well
siqhhaoq a peach (9:145, 11:116) (si˯ ym˯)
siqhhaoq albol a peach tree (si˯ ym˯ a˅ baw˅)
siqhhaoq alsiq a peach (fruit) (si˯ ym˯ a˅ si˯)
siqhhaoq hhaoqyeiv peach blossom (9:145) (si˯ ym˯ a˅ yeh^)
Siqhhel lolbaq the name of a river (14:231)
=siq, hhoq= a kidney
=siq, jul= a glass bead
=siq, la= a month
=siq, lul= acne
siqluv a whetstone for sharpening tools (or) **sivqluv moqsiq** = old, poetic term) (mi ceh˅ si˯ lo)
siqlyul an orange (11:34) (si˯ loe˅)
siqlyul malcavq alsiq pomegranate ('citrus bottle fruit') (a˅ ka ka u^ a˅ si˯ = 'crab's eggs fruit')
siqmavq pavq hheil aqtov a ceremony of catching some grasshoppers, wrapping them in leaves of the **siqma** tree and wedging them in slits of poles stuck in the ground by the fields
siq meeq good fruit (4:40) (a˅ si˯ yaw mui˯)
=siq, miq= a bullet
=siq, moq= arrowhead plant
=siq, naq= the earlobe
Siqnaoq a large, old Hani clan (Bai = Chi), one of the branches is called: **Milguq qovq**
=siq nei, daovq= strength (strong)
siqpuv a fig (si˯ gu˯)
=siq, puv= a hill
siqpyuq a kind of sour fruit (46:176)
siqqàq plum (ka^ ca˯)
siqse 1. time; hour (Chi) (9:146, 46:110), 2. a clock
siqse lavqduvq a wrist watch (A=Chi) (or) **sebiao** (Chi) (na˯ li˯)
siqse za nei timely; at the right moment (a˅ yam˯ tsa˯ ngeh)
siqsov red bayberry (9:146)
siqtaq canteen; dining hall (Chi)
=siq, zyuq= (see full)

siv to wipe (si^-eu)
=siv, lavq= a handkerchief; hand towel
=siv, miav= a face towel
=siv nei, gav= to be very cold
sivssaq a kind of migratory bird

sivq blood (or) **sivqnilpuq nei** (9:146, 11:163) (shi˯)
=sivq, beivq= menstrual blood (taboo)
sivq duv to bleed (shi˯ do^-eu; shi˯ yoe˅-eu)
sivqduv moqsiq a sharpening stone (old, poetic term) (14:199), **siqluv** = modern term (mi ceh˅ si˯ lo)
sivqguq a vein; artery (5:871) (shi˯ shi˯ ca^)

sivq maq luvq nalgol anemia (10:32,33) (shi˯ ma˯ lo^-eu naˇ gawˇ)
sivqnilpuq nei blood (or) **sivq**

siffuq happiness (Chi) (26:112) (la˯ k'a˯ cehˇ-eu)
sifyaofsef credit cooperative (Chi) (9:144)

SII

siil 1. gold; 2. yellow (9:144) (shuiˇ)
=siil, **almiuvq miuvq**= golden monkey
=siil, **aqkeeq keeq**= yellow dog
siilbia nei yellowish (14:164) (shuiˇ teu ni)
-- siil, **cavqsiil** -- (see full)
siilcaoq trend of thought; ideological trend (Chi) (34:88)
-- siil, **ceil kov ngavq** -- many ways or customs
siilceiq work; daily affairs; matter (Chi) (Hani = **miqnieq**)
Siildafliq 80 haof tyutujil Stalin No. 80 bulldozer (Chi) (26:32)
Siildafliq 80 haof tyutujil eilloq e soqhhaq instruction manual for the Stalin No. 80 bulldozer (Chi)
siildev a gold lump (35:90) (shuiˇ k'oˇ)
Siildiq a person in a Hani myth (46:125)
siilfaqjiq judicial bureau (department) (Chi) (50:159)
siilful master workman (has apprentices under him) (Chi) (26:34); master (skilled in something) (14:155, 26:28, 50:152)
Siilgaoq Hhavqnav a place in Luchun County (35:84)
=siil, **geeq**= brass ('yellow copper')
=siil, **haq**= golden bamboo
=siil, **haqpal pal**= yellow cloth
siiljil a driver (as of a car, bulldozer, etc.) (Chi) (26:27)
siilla nei thin and pale (or) **govniv nei**
siillif commander (Chi)
Siilmaoq Simao district (10:pref, 46:111)
-- siil, **neema cavqsiil** -- to test one's mind
siilniq nei yellowish (14:139) (shuiˇ nyeh^ ni)
siilnieiv nei yellowish (11:60) (or) **siilniei nei** (35:110, 45:83) (shuiˇ nyeh^ ni)
=siil, **pal**= yellow cloth
=siil, **pavq**= a yellow leaf
siilpuq a ball (or) **piqqeq** (Chi) (baw duiˇ)
=siil siil, **cavq**= (see full)
siilsseiq personal; private (Chi)
siilxa thought; ideology (Chi) (26:111) (**Maoq Ceiqdaol siilxa** = Mao's thought - 26:106)
siilxa gei'faf open-minded; liberated ideology (34:12)
siil xa to 'plant' gold (in a story) (35:24) (shuiˇ ka-eu)

siilyeziif system of private ownership (Chi) (34:38)
siilyeiv golden flowers (4:43) (shuiˇ aˇ yeh^)
siilyeiv yeiv golden flowers to blossom (4:40) (shuiˇ aˇ yeh^ yeh^ laˇ-eu)
=siil, zal= sulphur
siilza to put to good use (Chi) (34:68)
siilzev yellowish (shuiˇ nyeh^ ni)
siilzev zilbaq yellow liquor (14:207)
siilzevq characteristics (Chi) (14:203)

siijiq a diplomatic envoy (Chi)
siisiil an epic (as to write a long epic) (34:5)

siiqbeif to fail, as in an exam (Chi) (26:45) (or) **maq jiqgeiq** (B=Chi)
siiqdaf cuajaf a brave man for that time (**cuajaf** = a brave person) (Chi) (26:45) (cf.: tsawˇ haˬ yaw k'aˬ)
siiqjeil 1. time (Chi) (**siiqjeil taq bi yoq** = don't be late) (13:22, 41:97) (**hhaqnaq naq e siiqjeil** = free time; resting time - 26:43), 2. a long time (or) **qiq savq hev** (cf.: aˇ yamˬ)
siiqjeil hev the time has arrived (or is up) (Chi) (13:23) (aˇ yamˬ keu^ laˇ-eu)
siiqjeil jav to have time (A=Chi)
siiqjei to practice (Chi) (34:68)
siiqjei'lyuf a practical theory (Chi) (50:152)
siiqliq actual strength (Chi) (34:18) (g'aˬ)
siiqmiqwa a white fibrous substance (asbestos?) they dig out of the ground, use to make tile (Chi)
Siiqqil a spirit sent by **Molmil** to protect the crop (rides a black and white horse - 46:196)
siiqse qiq se one hour (Chi) (26:63) (naˬ liˬ tiˬ la˰)
siiqsiif currently; at the present time (Chi) (26:50) (nymˬ-mˇ)
siiqsiif quqsiif to seek truth from reality; to be practical; realistic (Chi) (34:75)
siiqsiif zeifceiq current policy (Chi)
siiqsov gyuq to cry loudly; to make loud noises (such as running water) (50:128)
siiqtaq canteen (as in a factory); dining room (Chi) (41:53)
siiqtaq bal the common dining hall in the 'big commune' (Chi)
siiqxeif to realize (Chi) (34:64) (noeˬ siˬ-eu)
Siiq yiq geif salzaol qeiqhyuf the Third Plenary Session of the Eleventh Central Committee of the Communist Party of China (Chi) (34:12)

siivq seven (9:144) (shi˰)
siivq new (yaw shui˰)
siivq to be tight; firm (**Nol hhoyyuq dyul zaza nei zaoq siivq.** You must tie these straws a little tightly) (11:108, 38:109, 46:94) (yaw zi˰)

siivq ceil seventy (shi^ tse^v)

siivqdao nei very tight (35:102) (zi^ dah ni; deu^v keu^ ni)
siivqheiq nei tightly (9:146, 10:26) (**siivqheiq nei taq tov'quvq miq** = don't wrap the child tightly) (yaw deu^v)
=siivq, hoq= new rice
=siivq hoq, ceil= new rice (cooked)
=siivq, huvq= New Year
-- siivq, hhe -- to pull a knot tight
-- siivq, kavq -- to tie tightly
Siivqla siq July
=siivq, pavq= new (fresh) leaves
=siivq, saq= fresh meat
-- siivq, soqmiav miav -- new wood
siivqxa nei fresh (9:145) (yaw jm^v)

siif city; municipality (Chi) (**Beiqjil Siif** = City of Beijing) (50:226)
siifca tiaoqjiq market adjustment (as in the economy) (Chi) (34:38)
Siifcyul milcaq Sichuan Province (A=Chi)
siifgeif hoqpiq world peace (Chi) (34:15) (mi^v k'ah^v yaw sa^v)
siifjeif the world (Chi) (34:23)
siifjeifgual world outlook (Chi) (34:60)
siifwuf affairs (Chi) (34:56)
siifwufza daily affairs officer (Chi) (26:85)
siif xaf jilbei yeiqzeiq four basic principles (Chi) (34:29)
siifyiq'eif April 12th (Chi) (34:6)

SO

sol fragrant aroma; smell good (9:146) (saw-eu)
sol 1. clean, 2. pure (in Hani sense) (9:146) (**aqpyuq sol alqaq** = the ancestors are 'pure', i.e. no abnormal births or bad deaths) (yaw shaw^v)
sol to calculate (9:146) (saw^v-eu; saw^v haw-eu)
sol only (13:4) (cf.: teh^)
=sol, al= (see full)
=sol, aq= who? (and see full)
sol ceiv a final calculation (50:93)
-- sol, ciq -- to wash clean
sol daoq an account book (50:208)
=sol, hal= coriander
solhoq to calculate correctly (sha^v saw^v tsa^v-eu)
solhoq zaq to judge impartially; equally (50:70)
-- sol hu, huq -- a budget
solhhaol (see: **sulhhaol** = midnight)
=sol, hhoq= peppercorn (as spice)
-- sol, kaq -- fully recovered
-- sol, keellavq -- to be well-behaved
solkov items of an account; accounts

=sol, lavq= almost; nearly

sollavq nei a good smell; fragrant (14:140) (saw k'eu‸ ni)

  sollavq pa lavq nei a very good smell (14:139) (saw k'eu‸ ni)

=sol lolto, qivq= dusk

sol meil alone; single-handed (2:58) (teh‸-ehˇ)

solmil sol to tell one's fortune (ja maw maw-eu)

=sol, niaoq= sweet purple glutinous rice

sol pa sol nei sol very clear (11:60) (shawˇ jeh^ ni)

solpeiq Chinese abacus (Chi) (11:30)

  solpeiq sol to calculate with an abacus (Chi)

Solpiaol a person's name (11:157)

-- sol, piul -- an old type of silver coin

=sol, piul= pure silver

solpyuq to respect (46:88) (ciˬ poeˬ-eu)

=sol, qul= a sweet smell

solsol meil one by one (singly) (9:146) (tiˬ g'aˬ saˇ-iˇ tiˬ g'aˬ)

solssaoq to add up (daw^ lahˬ-eu)

=sol, xal= to go work in the fields

solxeiv nei to smell good; good aroma (11:58, 46:155) (saw k'eu‸ ni)

  solxeiv pa xeiv nei to be very fragrant (46:104)

  solxeiv pa xeiv nei sol intensely fragrant (11:59)

solxu nei to smell good (14:206) (saw k'eu‸ ni)

solyeil nei very clean (among other things used of the stones in the **milsaol luvcuv** which must be river stones with no blemish) (9:146, 10:21, 26:112) (shawˇ jeh^ ni)

  solyeil pa yeil nei very clean; pure (11:58) (shawˇ jeh^ ni)

solzal accounts (Chi) (9:146); to calculate (26:75) (sawˇ-eu)

  solzal aol to keep accounts (financial) (Chi) (or) **solzal sol** (11:20)

  solzal maq lal for things not to work out as one calculated they would (57:127)

solza to verify; check (50:70)

=so nei, jeil= to be wet; damp

=so nei, nav= blackish

soq a type of tree (good for furniture)

soq to redeem; return (yuˇ k'o‸-eu; sheuˬ k'o‸-eu; zeuˇ k'o‸-eu)

soq to be tidy (yaw shaw)

soq a little dry (as: **ciqhaq soq** = the dew has dried up) (yaw gui)

soq clf. for morning (8:1) (tiˬ shawˬ)

(vb) soq to (vb) in order (**aol soq** = to do in order; to put in order - 38:91)

soq'aol aol to do morning work (13:1) (shawˬ mˇ-eu)

=soq, aoq= morning

soqbeeq order; sequence

-- **soq, ceil** -- to adjust; to regulate
soq ceivq 1. to separate; 2. to divide the good from the bad
soq cil to pay a debt (14:211) (dzi˅ dzo^ tsoe˯-eu)
soqdaoq 1. a book (46:82) (sah˯ bo˰ pa˅ dm˯), 2. a historical document (or) **galhhu soqdaoq** (50:178)
-- **soqdaoq, doqkol** -- a book of poems; collection of poems
-- **soqdaoq, galhhu** -- historical documents
=**soq, dev**= to prune
soqdo nei neatly; tidily (9:146) (yaw tsi˯ yaw lui^)
  soqdo pa do nei neatly (yaw tsi˯ yaw lui^)
soqdoq 1. old words (46:82, 183) (daw˯ oe˅), 2. poetry (or) **dama soqdoq**
-- **soq, eelheiq** -- (see full)
-- soq, eil -- to explain; defend oneself
-- **soq, gee** -- to coordinate; to harmonize
-- **soq, guv** -- to trim or prune branches with a knife
soq heeq a large tree (35:86) (a˅ baw˅ ma)
soqhoq breakfast ('morning rice') (shaw˯ haw˯)
-- **soq, hovq lol** -- to make an annual offering to the village water source to purify it
=**soq, huq**= (see full)
soq huvq revenge (50:7)
soqhhaq paper; book; letter (9:146) (seu˯ g'a˯)
  soqhhaq aoqyaol a book store)50:157)
  soqhhaq biaogeiq 1. table (as in a book or paper) (B=Chi), 2. a paper form to be filled in (50:14)
  soqhhaq baofzii paper; writing paper (or) **soqhhaq gaozii** (not pf.) (B=Chi)
  -- **soqhhaq, bu** -- a written complaint (50:217)
  soqhhaq buvqkaoq an exercise book for writing school lessons (26:19) (bo˰ dm˯)
  soqhhaq colmiaol title of a book (or) **biaoltiq** (Chi)
  soqhhaq gaozii (see: **soqhhaq baofzii**) (26:66)
  -- **soqhhaq, Haqniq** -- Hani books
  soqhhaq haqzeil a kite ('paper hawk') (50:51)
  soqhhaq heilneiq col a postman; mailman
  -- **soq, hhaqjo** -- (see full)
  soqhhaq haqzeil a kite (to fly for fun)
  soqhhaq laoqziiq a written receipt for something purchased (B= Chi)
  soqhhaq meiqduq a place where teaching is done
  soqhhaq miqteiv a firecracker (9:146, 50:8) (ma˯ teh˰)
  soqhhaq paltaol school bag; book bag (41:72) (sah˯ bo˰ peh˅ tah˅)
  soqhhaqsif a letter (B=Chi)
  soqhhaq siffaol an envelope (B=Chi)
  soqhhaq taqyaol a library (34:65)
  soqhhaq tiaoqziiq a written receipt for something bought (B=Chi) (11:31)
soqhhaq zol to study; to go to school; to read (11:131) (sah˯ bo˰ dzaw-eu)

soqhhaq zolduq a school (sah˯ bo˰ dzaw nymˇ)
soqhhaq zolpeiq a textbook (26:18) (dzaw-eu sah˯ bo˰)
soqhhaq zolqoq a classmate; school mate (sah˯ bo˰ dzaw caw˯)
soqhhaq zolssaq a student (41:4) (or) **xoqseil** (Chi) (sah˯ bo˰ dzaw-eu g'a˯)
soqhhaq zolyaol school (sah˯ bo˰ dzaw nymˇ; hoˇ heˇ) (6:187)

-- **soq, hhaoldao** -- a ceremony held when abnormal human births occur in the village

=**soq, jal**= a rope used to tie loads on packsaddles

soqjoq an annual ring (in a tree)
soqjoq joq to peel away tree bark

soqkaoq a paper; as a letter (26:94) (sah˯ bo˰; seu˯ g'a˯)
-- **soqkaoq, buvqzol** -- to write composition exercises
-- **soqkaoq, gee taq** -- a written agreement
soqkaoq lo'qo doqjeivq hhuv to do everything according to the textbook (50:9)

=**soq, lal**= to disobey; to be disobedient

-- **soq, lavqzaq** -- to carry out

-- **soq, lolhovq** -- make an offering to the village sacred water source

soqma a big tree

soqmeel morning star (Venus) (shaw˯ muiˇ)

soq meeq a good tree (or) **soq meeq albol** (46:116)

=**soq, mil**= yesterday morning (and see full)

soq miq to return back to (46:127) (g'o˰ laˇ-eu)

soqmiav the alphabet (6:184); characters; words (11:23); script (**Haqniq soqmiav zol** - to study the Hani script - 41:72) (cf.: **soqmiav aqma; soqziil**)
soqmiav aqma the alphabet (main letters)
soqmiav buvq to inscribe; write an inscription (50:164)
soqmiav diqssaq a typist (50:30)
-- **soqmiav, Haqniq** -- Hani orthography; script
soqmiav miavdoq standard speech; literary language (50:179)
soqmiav miavpyul initial letter in a word (as **'b'** in the word: **ba'la**)
soqmiav zaol zuvq pal to reform a writing system (50:179)
soqmiav zolteil the sound of the letters; the pronunciation of the letters (32:3)

soqmoq 1. an old tree (aˇ bawˇ bawˇ oeˇ), 2. an old person (bawˇ maw˯)
soqmoq dalgyu albol 1. old trees, 2. old people

-- **soq, moqpil** -- (see full)

soqnavq pa navq nei early in the morning (u˯ shaw˯ yaw na˰-ehˇ)

=**soq, nao**= tomorrow (or) **neesoq**

=**soq, nee**= tomorrow (or) **naosoq**

-- **soq, neekaoq** -- give vent to personal spite; to

get revenge
=soq, niaoq'aol= this morning
soqpaq an official; a ruler (sah˯ pa˯)
soqpaq bee lord; ruler (although 'king' is: **zyuq**) (sah˯ pa˯)
soqpaq gee to be a lord; ruler (sah˯ pa˯ geu˄-eu)
-- soqpaq, hhellaoq -- the lord dragon
-- soqpaq, puvlaol -- the village head (and see full)
soqpaq qovq government ('family of rulers')
soqpovq pieces of wood (daˇ kaw˯)
soqsaol the inner core of the tree (sah˯ nyo^)
soqsaol hav albol hardwood
soqssaq young trees (aˇ bawˇ za˯)
-- soqssaq, albol -- a sapling
soqssaq jassaq 1. trees and grass, 2. plants in general
soqtal tal to cut away small branches; to prune (bawˇ cu˯ cu˯-eu)
-- soqto, aoqsoq -- early morning
soqyeiq dev hu to make many cuts on three sides of a tree in a field where one wishes to divine whether it is proper to make a field there or not (cf. 'she loves me, she loves me not')
-- soq, yobeeq piav -- bring order out of chaos
-- soq, zaol -- 1. do things smoothly; make things tidy; 2. administer; govern; bring under control (50:213)
-- soq, zeil -- to pay for
soqziil written Chinese characters (clf. **ziil**) (**soqmiav** = Hani) 11:31
soqzol lolbieil a desk (50:157)
soqzyuq 'king' of trees (and see below)
soqzyuq hoqtuv massaol a mythical tree which was cut down in Hani legend, so that the sun and moon could shine and rain could fall (35:86, 46:156)

sov 1. to rub, 2. to stroke, 3. to plane (as wood) (saw^-eu)
-- sov, baolsov -- (see full)
-- sov, biavq sov -- to plane a board
-- sov, ceildu -- to shell corn
=sov dalpav, mil= (see full)
-- sov, doqqul -- to flatter excessively
sov hu 1. to try to find out (46:101) (po^ haw-eu), 2. to feel with one's hand (saw^ haw-eu)
=sov, laq= 1. a plane for planing wood, 2. almost
=sov, laqlav= almost
=sov nei, baq= very thin
sov niv to push and move (deh˯ ji^-eu; ngaw˯ ji^-eu)
-- sov pieiq sso, hheivq -- to be cheated
sovpovq wood shavings (9:147, 11:149)
-- sov xa, daoqsov -- to slide down

sovq to castrate (shaw˄-eu)

=sovq, aqha ha= a castrated cock (capon)
sovq'eel a kind of nonpoisonous snake (loves to steal hen's eggs) (or) **ollol sovq'eel**
=sovq, ha= a castrated cock (capon)
-- sovq, hasovq -- to castrate a cock
=sovq, laq= a bullock (cf.: mawˇ neˇ dawˇ-eu)

SU

sul others (aˬ cawˬ, and cf.: aˬ suˇ) (cf. Lahu: shu)
sul lose (in a game) (Chi) (smˇ-iˇ-eu; maˬ g'aˬ leˇ-eu)
sul to stay overnight (ya˰-eu)
sul aqma water rail (a small black brd.)
sulbee the families of others
sulbieivq a no-son person; a bad person (can be used as a curse) (see: **bievqdaoq**) (shmˇ byeh˰) (semi-taboo)
sulcol others; guests (9:150) (aˬ cawˬ) (cf. Lahu: shu)
suldieif a book store (Chi) (9:150) (sahˬ bo˰ ahˬ duˬ)
-- sul, duq -- to lose at gambling (Chi)
sulhhaq 1. rich people (smˇ muiˬ); 2. others (aˬ cawˬ)
sulhhaq a bivq miq to give possession to (aˬ cawˬ-ahˇ bi˰ nehˬ-eu)
sulhhaq aqda a rich man (smˇ muiˬ aˬ da)
-- sulhhaq, cyuqssaq -- rich and poor
sulhhaq hhaq to be rich (smˇ muiˬ muiˬ-eu)
sulhhaq loqbeq to be rich (13:3) (smˇ muiˬ muiˬ-eu)
sulhhaq loqbeq qiq hhovq a rich family (13:3) (smˇ muiˬ muiˬ-eu aˇ zaw˰)
sulhhaq neema other people's heart (**sulhhaq neema maq jil e col** = other people who are not honest in their heart - 54:76)
sulhhaq soqhhaq other people's books (46:120) (aˬ cawˬ-euˬ sahˬ bo˰)
sulhhaol midnight (45:64) (or) **solhhaol** (sehˇ g'ahˇ)
sulhhaol aqmeil navhaoq pa haoq nei black as midnight
sulhhaol qiq pav deep into the night (11:218) (uˬ ci˰ sehˇ g'ahˇ ceh laˇ-eu)
suljaf a shelf (as for books) (Chi)
suljiq recording secretary (as for a committee) (Chi) (26:21) (or) **suljif** (41:3); **miqsul**
sul jol e mavq there are people (**sul** = **sulhhaq** = other people) (14:140) (cf.: tsawˇ haˬ baˬ ma˰)
sulkeeq aqma corn crake (a type of bird with grey feathers)
sullal soul (the Hani state that each person has 12 souls) (9:150) (sa˰ laˇ; suˇ laˇ)
sullal bal for one's soul (or souls) to leave the body, resulting in illness (laˇ baˇ baˇ-eu)
sullal guv bial soul (or souls) to be frightened

away (26:2) (suˇ laˇ baˇ-iˇ-eu)

sullal kul to call back one or more souls (laˇ kuˇ kuˇ-eu)

sullal kul huvq a part of the funeral ceremony where the soul (or souls) of the dead person is called back (suˇ laˇ kuˇ k'o˰-eu)

sullal seq to lead souls (46:191) (sa˰ laˇ sheuˬ-eu)

sullaq duckweed

-- sul, lav -- to be awakened (as by a loud noise)

Sullieiq Russians (Chi) (or) **Hhoqyi; Hhoqgoq**

=sul, lul= a suitable way of doing things

sullul seilleil jingle jangle (sound of silver ornaments)

-- sul, luvq -- a man who inherits property

sulma barnyard grass (when young it looks very similar to rice seedlings) (shmˇ ma)

sulmeeq a rich family (smˇ muiˬ)

sulmeeq miqli aqnil a young lady from a rich class (smˇ muiˬ zaˬ miˬ)

sulmeeqssaq rich people (or) **saolmeeqssaq**

sulmil maq neevq a woman who has never married

Sulmil'ol Hani ancestor (father of **Oltyuqlyu**) (46:108) (Smˇ miˇ oˇ)

sulmil yil a woman goes to get married (9:151, 45:12) (smˇ miˇ iˇ-eu) (cf. **miqssaq seq** = for a man to get married)

sulnil rust (9:151) (shmˇ kaw)

sulnil deima irrigated fields where the crop is diseased by rust

sulnil duv for rust to form; for something to become rusty (or) **sulnil tuvq** (shmˇ kaw kaw-eu)

sulnil tuvq for rust to form; for something to become rusty (or) **sulnil duv** (shmˇ kaw kaw-eu)

sulpeel thatch grass; cogon grass (or) **eqjil** (uˬ jiˇ)

-- sulpovq, saolsul -- sawdust

sulpuq a basketball

sulqeil laobao a marsh (lah yaˬ)

sulqeil yaldei marshy fields (lah yaˬ)

=sul, qul= a small bell

sulsaof piqdeif a conveyer belt (in a factory) (Chi) (26:34)

sultavq meeqzeiq superiority; best of all (50:199)

sultavq ssaqmeeq a good person in the world (tsawˇ haˬ yaw muiˬ)

sultavq zeiq superiority; preponderance (50:199)

=sul tul, yiuvq= to wake up from sleep and get up

=sul, yiuvq= to wake up

su to mix (keuˬ-eu)

-- su, lav -- to use something (as a stick) to rake things together

susi to adorn oneself (9:151, 46:151)

-- su zaq, hyuq -- to abduct (esp. a person)

suq to throw away (or) **suqzei**
suq 1. sticking on, 2. to be marked (as with ink) (**peilhaoq hultav milbieiv suq nga** = there is some mud on the clothing)
suq to be dirty; dusty (41:148); (or) **cavq**
=suq, al= father's younger brother (Chi)
-- suq, aolsuq -- to neglect one's duty
-- suq, ceiqsuq -- (see full)
suqduqbyu a bottomless pit
-- suq, kavsuq -- to harrow a field shallowly
suq lal to become dirty; muddy (as on body) (14:238)
-- suq, leiq -- to spread on
suqlu hhaqlaq 1. dusk; twilight; getting dark (11:17) (u˅ ci˄ taw˅), 2. confused; perplexed; dazed; not clearly seen (50:114)
suqlu hhaqlaq meil unclear; dim; vague (9:150)
-- suq, miqsuq -- (see full)
=suq nei, biav= to be flat
suqsuq nei the sound of wind blowing (26:85) (seu^ seu^-eh˅)
=suq, taoq= a torch of pitchpine sticks
suqxaf any of the 12 animals representing the year in which a person is born (Chi) (41:107)
suq zei to throw away (or) **suq** (bi˅ dzeh-eu)

suv to be skillful (9:150) (nya-eu; bi˅-eu)
suv to smoke (as opium; tobacco) (9:151) (daw˅-eu; shu^-eu)
suv to study well
(vb) **suv** to be used to (vb) (**jol suv** = to be used to living)
-- suv, aqhyuq -- to smoke tobacco
-- suv, aol -- skillful at doing
-- suv, eil -- skillful at speaking
-- suv, hyuqniul -- to smoke tobacco
=suv, mil= a mudslide on a mountain
suv nei 1. skillfully, 2. directly to (daw˅ coe ni)
=suv nei, yo= 1. smoothly, 2. happily
suv ngavq to choke (9:151) (i˅ cu˄ daw˅ nga˄-eu)
-- suv, ssil -- good at singing folksongs
-- suv, taoqsuv -- to tie a loose knot
-- suv, xiqsuv -- diarrhea

suvq for the voice to be hoarse (9:151) (ku˅ byah˅ su˄-eu)
suvq 1. for a swelling to subside (shu˄-eu) (9:151), 2. to reduce in volume (as water supply in fields) (shu˄-eu)
-- suvq, haoqsuvq -- to be unhappy; worried
-- suvq, neesuvq -- to be disgusted
-- suvq, wulquvq -- for water to recede; for there to be less water
-- suvq, wulquvq pieiq -- to drain off water

sufciiq numeral (Chi)
sufduf kol high speed (A=Chi) (or) **gaol sufduf** (Chi) (50:57)
sufliaof peilhaoq a rain coat (A=Chi) (26:60)
sufxoq mathematics (Chi) (14:241)
-- **sufxoq, gaolkao** -- a high university exam in mathematics
sufxoqtiq mathematic exercises (Chi) (50:157)
sufxoqxif Department of Mathematics (Chi) (54:106)
sufziiq quality (Chi)

SUA

sual acid (or) **sueil** (Chi) (10:12)

SUEI

sueil acid (or) **sual** (Chi)

SYU

syul a tax (kaw⌄)
syul a sworl of hair or fur on humans and animals (can tell if the person or animal is good or bad by looking at these.) (**syul maq meeq** = the sworls are not good)
Syul Zaolsal Dr. Sun Yatsen (34:4)

syubiq buqdul a fountain pen (A=Chi) (11:31)
syuciiq a well of water (Chi) (12:128) (lah du⌄)
syudieifzaf a water power station (Chi) (41:22)
syugua (see: **syuguei**)
syuguei water pipe (for water distribution) (Chi) (12:128) (or) **syugua** (iˇ cu^ baw⌄ law)
syu li duq a place to hide (13:3) (ceh^ za^ du⌄)
syu'lueiq a type of water bomb (Chi) (50:158)
syuniq cement (Chi) (11:31)
Syuwuq jyuq a tax office (Chi) (14:209) (kaw⌄ ta^ du⌄)

syuq 1. to be difficult (9:151, 50:99), 2. to bother others (26:113) (yaw sha⌄)
syuq 1. to turn over something (with a spade), 2. to spade (26:59)
=syuq, al= urine
-- **syuq, alsyuq** -- to urinate
-- **syuq, aqzaq** -- 1. to trouble, 2. to be hard to deal with
syuq cuv to stick into (as into the ground) (45:31, 46:153) (soe⌄ ahˇ-eu; soe⌄ tso^-eu)
-- **syuq, jol** -- to be hard up; poor (life is hard)
syuqkoq to put into
syuq kuv syuq luv to spade hard and repeatedly (as when digging a field) (4:42)
syuq liq ngeel, yal liq ngeel it was both difficult

and easy (14:196) (yaw sha⌄ k'aw^ ngeu˅, yaw ya˅ k'aw^ ngeu˅)

-- **syuq, mol** -- difficult to see

-- **syuq, ngeel moq maq** -- maybe; probably so

-- **syuq, zaq** -- difficult to eat

syuv a root to grow deep into the ground

syuv to look for food; scavenge for food (as a duck in the water, a pig in the jungle) (po^ dza⌄-eu)

-- **syuv, nalsyuv** -- for the nose to be irritated by some odor (as something burned, chili, etc.)

syuv zaq to look for food; scavenge for food (po^ dza⌄-eu)

syuflieif to train (as for sports) (Chi) (26:89

syuf piul tax money (A=Chi) (or) **ssase piul** (A=Chi)

syufsel tax revenue (Chi) (34:40) (kaw⌄ ta^-eu)

syufsuq math; arithmetic (Chi) (26:22)

syufwufjiq excise bureau; Tax Collection Bureau (Chi) (50:158)

SSA

ssal quick; fast (9:147) (yaw kawˇ)
ssal to give away something (land, fruit, etc.) (Chi) (bi‸-eu)

ssa to pick up (9:147) (g'o^-eu)
ssa 1. a particle ending for positive or negative statements (**miqnieiq mol xilmeil maq ngeel ssa** = the matter is not like that, showing the opinion of the speaker), 2. final particle used in imperative 'Let's...' patterns (54:20)
=ssa, hoq= a beggar
ssama elephant (9:147) (ya ma)
  ssama seq elephant tusk (or) **ssama ssaziil** (ya ma juiˇ)
  ssama ssaziil ivory (or) **ssama seq** (ya ma juiˇ)
=ssa, ngaq= a fish dam (used to catch fish)
-- ssa, ngeel -- yes; to be so
ssase piul tax money (A=Chi), **syuf piul** (A=Chi)
ssayyuq an elephant bone (4:39) (ya ma sha˯ yoe˯)
-- ssa, zeiqkeeq -- to collect manure for compost

ssaq son; child (za˯ = child in Ak. 'son' is: za˯ yo)
-- ssaq -- son, -- small, -- nation
ssaq clf. for: 1. chickens, fish, pigs (9:147, 11:73), cats (11:156) (mawˇ), 2. something small, as small stones (**haqluv luvssaq qiq ssaq** - 11:84); small pigs (**aqhhavq yul ssaq** - 41:134)
-- ssaq a suffix denoting little; young
=ssaq, aq= son-ipeh˯)
ssaqbeiq beiqceil a second rice crop
  ssaqbeiq ceiq to plow rice stalks under
ssaq bo 1. to have children (jawˇ-eu), 2. to give birth to a child (za˯ baw-eu)
  ssaqbo aqma mother of an infant (za˯ baw a˯ ma)
  ssaq bo nyuq za birth control (50:80)
ssaqbul aqda father of a baby (za˯ baw a˯ da)
=ssaq, buq= a jar; jug
=ssaq, byul= a human; person (old lang.)
=ssaq, byuq= a worm; insect
ssaqceiq a fetus (za˯ tseh^)
  ssaqceiq beq zei induced abortion (50:141) (za˯ bi dzeh-eu)
ssaq ciq puv laol dama the third cry of an infant; asking the helper to pick it up
=ssaq, col= humans

=ssaq, colmoq= elderly people

ssaqcyuq poor people (9:147) (iˇ shaˬ zaˬ; & cf.: coeˬ-eu)

ssaqcyuq cyuqssaq poor people (iˇ shaˬ shaˬ-eu tsawˇ haˬ)

ssaqcyuq wuqcaoq mol bavq zei 'to take off one's poverty cap' (i.e., to get out of poverty)

=ssaq, dav= a plate

ssaq deivq 1. to give birth (zaˬ ciˬ-eu; zaˬ deh˰-eu), 2. to get interest from money

ssaq diq eq to become pregnant; be with child (in a way not acceptable to the Hani) (or) **ssaq lav eq**

ssaqdov colpeel very poor people (45:12) (iˇ shaˬ zaˬ)

ssaqdul nephew on brother's side (6:176, 9:147, 13:1) (aˬ duˇ)

ssaq e beeteiq afterbirth; placenta (or) **albeil**

ssaq eq 1. to be pregnant (zaˬ pi-eu), 2. to carry child on back (9:50, 10:24) (zaˬ euˬ-eu)

ssaqga a bad, naughty child (zaˬ yaw doeˇ)

ssaqga gassaq a bad, naughty child (zaˬ yaw doeˇ)

ssaqgaq neema the pure heart of a newborn baby (50:24)

ssaqguq youngster; child (9:147, 50:147) (zaˬ guˬ)

ssaqguq guqcal children singing (50:43)

ssaqguq guqnyuq an impossible dream or ideal ('childish thought')

ssaqguq guqnyuq nyuq to have a fantastic idea (50:197)

ssaqguq haqhhal children's performance (50:43)

ssaqguq hhallul seilhha to play games (35:108) (niˇ g'a-eu)

ssaqguq mavq children (zaˬ guˬ deuˬ)

Ssaqguq neeciiv Children's Day festival (Jan. 1) (50:43, 109)

ssaqguq seilduq children's playground (50:43)

ssaqguq soqdoq books for children (50:43)

ssaqguq ssaqnaol younger generation (cf.: zaˬ ziˇ)

ssaqguq tuaq a troop of children (B=Chi) (50:43)

ssaqguq tuaqyeiq Young Pioneers (B=Chi) (50:43)

ssaqguq yiuvqhhal a cradle (or) **yiuvqhhal**

=ssaq, haqjil= a man

ssaqhav one who serves others (9:147)

ssaqheeq first (oldest) son (aˬ yui˰ yui˰ saˬ)

ssaqheil heil to ask one's own son or daughter to do something

ssaqheiq 1. a lover, 2. boy or girl friend (50:41) (zaˬ k'aˬ = semi-taboo in Ak.)

=ssaq, hu= a rat; all kinds of rodents

ssaqhhaol middle son; second oldest son

ssaqhhaol hhaolma middle sons (when there are three or more) (11:69, 41:2)

ssaqhhel a son that was bought/adopted (zeuˇ cu-eu zaˬ)

=ssaq, hhoheiq heiq= the back (or side) door (laˇ

g'o^ na˅ k'ah)

=ssaq, ja= plants (in general) (cf. **yossaq**)

ssaqjeil ordinary people (26:7) (tsaw˅ ha˯ za˯)

ssaqjeil ssaqlaol common people; all the people; ordinary people (50:142); working people (26:1, 45:26, 46:92, 129) (cf.: za˯ lah˅ = followers; students; apprentices)

=ssaq, kal= 1. spring crops, 2. seedlings

=ssaq, keeq= a young dog; a puppy

=ssaq, lal= soft palate

ssaq lav eq to become pregnant; be with child (in a way not acceptable to the Hani) (or) **ssaq diq eq**

ssaqlaol the masses; ordinary people (10:14, 41:3, 50:140) (in Ak. za˯ lah˅ = follower; student)

ssaqlaol alkaq kaq zaq civil mediation (50:116)

ssaqlaol dudaq folk stories (50:116)

saqlaol e yifsuq folk art (B=Chi) (50:116)

ssaqlaol e yo'liq civil law (or) **miq faq** (Chi)

ssaqlaol galkaol policy for the people (50:140)

ssaqlaol koq zaq deiq zaq a civil dispute; a public issue (50:116)

ssaqlaol leiq tul to arouse the masses to action; to mobilize the masses (50:44)

ssaqlaol naogo neema tavq have a heart which is sympathetic to ordinary people (50:114)

ssaqlaol saoqduvq duvq to have earned the hatred of the people (50:116)

ssaqlaol soqdaoq a book of folk stories (50:116)

-- ssaqlaol, ssaqjeil -- common people; ordinary people; working people

ssaqlaol weiqhuaf people's culture (B=Chi) (50:140)

ssaqlaol yaol gaq love the people (50:1)

=ssaq, leiq= an awl

ssaqli youngest son (9:148, 11:69, 41:2, 159) (a˯ li li za˯ g'a˯)

ssaqli lima next to the last son (11:69)

ssaqli lissaq youngest son (11:69)

=ssaq, luvq= a herdsman; a guard

ssaqma sister's daughters (za˯ ma); nieces

ssaqmavq wife's sisters' husbands; husbands of younger sisters

-- ssaqmeeq, puvlaol hovqma -- good fellow-villagers

ssaqmeeq qu well-raised; well-educated (50:199)

=ssaq, mil= a young cat

ssaqmiq woman; daughter; feminine (6:172, 9:148) (za˯ mi˯ a˯ bu˅)

=ssaq, miq= wife

ssaqmiq aqyivq oldest daughter (11:69) (a˯ bu˅ a˯ yui^ yui^ sa˯ g'a˯)

ssaqmiq bivq to give a daughter in marriage (9:148) (a˯ bu˅ bi m˅ dza˯-i˅-eu)

ssaqmiq e qeiqlif woman's rights; woman's authority (B=Chi) (50:54)

ssaqmiq galkeel leiq huvq following all of the

funeral ritual those who have come are 'invited' to return home ('driven home'), asking a dog to chase them (**aqkeeq jaq suq**), the idea being that 'we do not want this type of thing to happen often or soon'

ssaqmiq jolduq aoqzeil milzeil 'the girl's place is far away' ('edge of the world'), giving the ideal marriage, which is for the girl to be from a village very far away from the groom's village

ssaqmiq keeqma daughter-in-law (or) **keeqma** (kuiˬ ma)

=ssaq, miqli li= youngest daughter

ssaqmiq miqgaq a beautiful girl (14:237, 46:148) (aˬ buˇ yaw muiˬ)

ssaqmiq miqqoq friend of the bride (bridesmaid) (50:5)

ssaqmiq miqsiivq seq to fetch a bride (miˬ zaˬ sheuˬ-eu)

ssaqmiq miqssaq a girl; little girl (zaˬ miˬ zaˬ; aˬ buˇ) (8:26, 9:148)

ssaqmiq miqteiq a single daughter

ssaqmiq miqteiq qiq teiq a single daughter (35:1) (zaˬ miˬ tiˬ g'aˬ tehˬ)

ssaqmiq ssaqmavq women (zaˬ miˬ zaˬ deuˬ)

-- ssaqmiq, Molmil -- 1. a fairy; angel, 2. a daughter of God

ssaqmiq seq to bring home a wife ('bring a daughter-in-law home') (zaˬ yo kuiˬ ma laˬ-eu)

ssaqmiq seq sa to take one's daughter to a boy to marry (zaˬ miˬ mˇ dahˬ dzaˬ-iˇ-eu)

ssaqmiq siqtov bavq the daughters of the dead elder furnish a feast for those who went to cut the coffin

ssaqmiqssaq woman (8:26, 9:148) (zaˬ miˬ zaˬ; zaˬ miˬ aˬ buˇ)

ssaqmiq ssaqmavq women

ssaqmiq ssaqnaol young woman (41:3) (zaˬ miˬ zaˬ guˬ)

ssaqmiq ssaqyo daughters and sons (13:3) (zaˬ miˬ zaˬ yo)

ssaqmoq old people (tsawˇ mawˬ)

=ssaq, moq= colt (young horse)

-- ssaqmoq, aqbol -- old man; grandfather

-- ssaqmoq, aqpiq -- old woman; grandmother

Ssaqnaq a person's name (11:111)

ssaqnaol young people (9:148, 41:3, 50:137)

ssaqnaol alhuvq youth; young age (50:137) (zaˬ guˬ)

ssaqnaol naol dav to become a youth (46:173) (zaˬ guˬ guˬ laˇ-eu)

ssaqnaoq baby (10:pref., 41:3) (zaˬ nahˬ)

ssaq naoq 1. to give birth (zaˬ nahˬ ciˬ-eu), 2. to have a young child

ssaqnaoq aqma 1. a baby's mother, 2. a polite term of endearment to or about one's wife (zaˬ nahˬ aˬ ma)

ssaqnaoq naoqmieiv a baby (za˯ nah˯)
ssaqnaoq naoqmieiv mieivssaq a babe in arms (za˯ nah˯ ci˯ lu˄-eu)
ssaqnil 1. a baby (9:148), 2. one whose child is still young
Ssaqniqssaq Yani (Akha) branch of the Hani living in Xishuangbanna (46:200) (Za˯ nyi˯ za˯; A˯ ka˯ za˯)
=ssaq, oq= a duckling
ssaq pi 1. carry child on back; 2. to be pregnant (za˯ pi-eu)
ssaqqa nationality (50:117)
ssaqqa qiq qa to be the same nationality (or) **qiq qa col**
ssaqqa ssaqlaol various nationalities (50:58)
ssaqqoq a friend of the bridegroom (young man)
=ssaq, saolmeeq= rich people
-- ssaqseq, maheiq -- children with stepmother
Ssaqseil a person's name (11:168)
-- ssaqsiivq, aqssaq -- a new son-in-law
=ssaq, soq= young trees
ssaqssyuq progeny; offspring ('seed') (46:108)
ssaqteiq an only son (41:2) (ti˯ li teh˄)
=ssaq, xalduq= a peasant; farmer
ssaq yal sal happy descendants (46:117)
ssaq ya to abort a baby (za˯ dzeh-eu)
=ssaq, yaol= a small building attached to a main building
ssaqyivq 1. the oldest son (9:148, 11:69); 2. oldest daughter (45:7) (a˯ yui˄ yui˄ sa˯ g'a˯)
ssaqyo a man; boy; son (za˯ yo; a˯ li)
=ssaq, yo= living things in general (cf. **jassaq**)
ssaqyo aqyivq eldest son
ssaqyossaq a man (9:148) (za˯ yo)
ssaqyo yo teiq a single son; an only son (46:138) (a˯ li ti˯ li)
ssaq'yul a nephew (sister's son) (9:148) (za˯ oeˇ)
=ssaq, yul= (see full)
ssaq zaq xa an abortion to take place (za˯ dzeh-eu)
ssaqzao twin (little used) **heiqmoq** (pf) (9:148) (tsawˇ caw^ - taboo in Ak.)
ssaq zei a baby that dies shortly after birth
=ssaq, zeiq= a domesticated animal; all kinds of domesticated animals
=ssaq, zil= a bird; all kinds of birds
ssaqzoq dumb; stupid; foolish person (or) **colzoq** (a˯ dzaw˯ = male; a˯ byah˯ = female)
ssaqzoq zoq to be a dumb, stupid person

ssav to quarrel and be noisy (law˄ g'a so^ g'a-eu)
-- ssav lav, ssuv luv -- (see full)
ssavssav nei to be very noisy (law˄ g'a-eu)
ssav, ssav, ssav the sound of quarreling (daw˯ pyehˇ pyehˇ-eu)

ssavq 1. to go down (9:148), 2. to get off; to get

down (or) **pieiq duv; hhehhoq; xeivleev** (za^-eu)
ssavq yil to descend (za^-iˇ-eu)
ssavq yi to go down (27:11, 46:130) (za^ ka-iˇ-eu)
ssavq yiv to come down (za^ le-eu)

SSAO

ssaolbol a spruce tree (or) **salmuq albol** (A=Chi)
ssaoldaol ground floor for penning cattle
ssaoldaoq foundation stones on which house posts are set (9:147)
=ssaol, deil= to prepare (as food); get ready
ssaolma main house post; a pillar (9:147, 29:4, 46:117) (k'awˇ zeuˇ zeuˇ mahˇ)
=ssaol, mil= (see full)

=ssao, luq= (see full)
ssao nei (vb) (vb) well; carefully (**ssao nei nyuq hu** = think carefully; think well) (11:21, 207) (**Nol alniq ssao nei niq.** Cut the bamboo strips carefully. 11:42) (**ssao nei yiuvq** = sleep well - 11:184) (yaw mui˯-ehˇ)
ssao nei aol tavq to work closely together; cooperate (50:114)
ssaossao nei carefully

ssaoq get together
ssaoq spend; use (as money, etc.) (9:147) (zm˯-eu)
-- ssaoq, bavq -- to collect; to gather
-- ssaoq, cev -- 1. to gather; collect, 2. to 'pluck' and put together, as vegetables
ssaoqdaoq a plow rope
ssaoq duv to consume
-- ssaoq, heel -- (see full)
-- ssaoq, hhe -- to bring together
ssaoq lal to come together (50:79)
-- ssaoq, leiq -- to drive animals or people together
ssaoq ma leil e piul flexible money; available money (50:78)
-- ssaoq, piav -- to collect things; put things together
ssaoqsaol 1. an iron tool (9:147) (shmˇ keu ka), 2. metal farming tools (50:122) (**miaoq aol ssaoqsaol** = a tool of production 50:151)
-- ssaoq, seq -- to collect together
-- ssaoq, sol -- to add up
ssaoq sso to go into effect; become effective (50:151)
-- ssaoq, taoq -- to save up
-- ssaoq, yiul -- to divert; misappropriate; embezzle
ssaoq zeiq 1. overspend, 2. go over the budget (50:22)
ssaoq zyul 1. to bring together, 2. to use money illegally (50:80)

sseil rainy season; summer (or) **sseilhhaol** (41:117) (yehˇ g'ahˇ)
sseil to rain (uˬ yehˇ yehˇ-eu)
=sseil, aoq= rain
sseilbol a palm tree (9:149) (deu^ gawˬ; do^ bawˬ)
sseilbol yov to peel palm bark (or) **sseilhov yov**
sseilbyul insects that live in palm bark
sseilcav coir rope (made from fiber of coconut husk) (9:149)
sseildu a palm bud
sseilgeel a palm bark rain cape (9:149, 14:190) (must not wear it backward)
sseilgeel daoqmiq the 'tail' of a palm tree, used as a broom when sweeping the house after a coffin has been taken out
sseilhov palm bark (9:149)
sseilhov bavqpov a palm leafstalk; a palm petiole
sseilhov hovmiq palm bark tail (2:58)
sseilhov yov to peel palm bark (or) **sseilbol yov**
sseilhhaol rainy season; summer (46:81) (uˬ yehˇ yehˇ yamˬ)
sseilhhaol ba'la rainy season (26:22) (yehˇ g'ahˇ yamˬ)
sseilhhaol dav the beginning of summer (50:105)
sseilhhaol lalna during rainy season (uˬ yehˇ yehˇ yamˬ)
sseilhhoq hhoqpavq a green vegetable that grows in the rainy season
sseilhhoq hhoqyal dry mountain fields, where vegetables are planted in the rainy season
sseilhhovq a needle used to sew a palm bark cape
sseilkaol palm 'silk' (9:149)
sseilkaol kaolhav thick palm bark
Sseilkuq zaq to celebrate the June festival; the swing festival (or) **Kuqzaq zaq** (yehˇ kuˬ dzaˬ-eu)
Sseillaoq a man who leads a dog to go around a village site (46:116)
sseilmuv soft palm bark; palm fiber (9:149)
sseilnaovq palm bark sandals
-- **sseilnaovq, haqguq** -- shoe made of bamboo strips
sseilniuv the tip of a palm tree
sseilpaq a type of green frog
sseilpavq a palm leaf (9:149)
sseilpiaq palm leaves
sseilsal cavqgaq a weather forcast (50:165)
sseilsiq palm seed
-- **sseil xa yi, hhoq** -- to rain down again
sseilzyuq ba'la summer; hot season (or) **aoqlaol ba'la** (yehˇ g'ahˇ ba la)

ssei wilted; withered (as vegetables) (**hhoqpavq ssei al** = the green vegetables are old/wilted)

=ssei, hhokeeq keeq= old rice seedlings

sseiq to tear to pieces (as bamboo strips)
Sseiqbei (see: **Ssiiqbei**)
sseiqhuq a thermos bottle (50:141)
sseiqmiq people (Chi) (26:55, 50:141)
sseiqmiq bal nei deivq, sil e ssaqjeil bal nei sil live for the people, die for the people (26:101) (A=Chi)
sseiqmiq deifbiao dafhyuf caqwuf hhyuyeiqhyuf the standing committee of the People's Congress (Chi) (50:142)
sseiqmiq faqyeif people's court (Chi) (50:142)
sseiqmiq gaolseif people's commune (Chi) (26:108, 50:142)
Sseiqmiq Gei'fafjyul People's Liberation Army (Chi) (26:102, 50:142)
sseiqmiq jeicaqyeif people's procurator (Chi) (50:142)
sseiqmiq miqzu people's democracy (Chi) (34:48)
sseiqmiq miqzu zualzeif people's democratic dictatorship (Chi) (50:142)
sseiqmiq peiqseiyeiq people's assessor (Chi) (50:142)
sseiqmiq tuaqti people's organization (Chi) (34:20)
sseiqmiq yilxaoq jifnieif luvcuv monument for the people's heroes (B=Chi) (50:142)
sseiqnaol happy, enjoyable time (Chi) (11:177) (and see below) (byaw˯ gaˇ neh-a˯)
sseiqnaof lively; bustling with excitement (Chi) (26:66) (and see above) (byaw˯ gaˇ neh-a˯)
sseiqqiq warmth; enthusiasm (Chi) (34:19)
sseiqseilgual people's outlook on life (Chi) (34:60, 50:142)
sseiqseil qeiqlif personal rights; individual rights (B=Chi) (50:142)
sseiqsyupiq a thermos (Chi) (41:33)
sseiqxif people's nature (B=Chi) (50:142)
=sseiq, Yoq= the Yao people

sseiv a loud voice (teˇ saˇ yaw k'a^)
sseiv a bright light (bya ceh^ ni)
-- **sseiv, aqgeel** -- stars to shine
-- **sseiv, aqgeel sseiv sseiv nei** -- for stars to twinkle
-- **sseiv, miqzaq** -- something to be ablaze with burning lights
sseiv nei very brightly; glistening (9:149, 46:98) (cf: yaw sheh˰)

sseivqyil 1. a small kind of bird, 2. a small kind of grass

sseifsiiq to know each other (Chi) (ti˯ g'a˯ tiˇ g'a˯ si˯ nya-eu)

sseifsiiqlueif theory of knowledge (Chi) (50:143)
sseifsiiq siifgeif to understand the world (Chi)
sseifsyudaf a hot water bottle (Chi) (26:62)
sseifwuf an urgent task (Chi) (26:81,109)

SSI

ssil to sing folk songs at the table; to sing drinking songs (sha˯ zi^ zi^-eu)
ssil lifespan; generation (9:149) (ziˇ)
ssil clf. for generation; lifespan (9:150) (ziˇ)
ssil bi bo, coljol bi sal 'may you have a long life, may you be healthy' (parting blessing) (41:160) (ziˇ bi baw law)
  ssil bo to have a long life (35:53, 50:21) (ziˇ baw-eu)
  ssil covq to have a short life (35:53) (ziˇ ma˯ baw)
  ssil covq pieiq lal to cause to have a short life
=**ssil, deiq**= (see full)
Ssilgoq England (Chi) (Meu˯ Piˇ la˯ miˇ k'ah˯)
-- **ssil, hhe** -- to grin
-- **ssil, lalbaq** -- to sing a folksong
-- **ssil, lav** -- throw down the gauntlet; challenge to battle
ssilma a singer of folk songs (50:57)
-- **ssilma, lalbaq** -- a singer of folk songs (11:122)
ssil maq bo to have a short life (can be caused by being disrespectful to **Aqpyuq Miqyeil** and the elders)
=**ssil, nee**= to be angry
-- **ssil, neema** -- to be angry
-- **ssil nei, miav** -- to stare at
ssilpav qiq pav half of one's lifespan
-- **ssilpuq nei, neema** -- angrily
ssilqil mil aq gul miaoq the first cry of an infant, asking for a lifespan (or
-- **ssilpuq nei, neema** -- angrily
ssilqil mil aq gul miaoq the first cry of an infant, asking for a lifespan (or
-- **ssilpuq nei, neema** -- angrily
ssilqil mil aq gul miaoq the first cry of an infant, asking for a lifespan (or) **ssilzeq aoq a gulmil**
ssil suv to be good at singing folksongs
ssilxaoq a hero (Chi) (26:104)
  ssilxaoq haohaf pan (or) **ssilqil mil aq gul miaoq**

ssi 1. to hide (za˰-eu), 2. to not grow very well
ssihaof a quotation mark (Chi)
ssikuv nei to be weak (g'a˯ ju˯-eu)

ssiq to be wet (yaw a˯)
ssiq to shake (jui˰-eu)
(vb) **ssiq** to be going on; continuous action (**Duqceiq**

duq ssiq al. Continued gambling. 35:35) (cf.: lu‸-eu)

ssiqhaq a bank (for money) (Chi) (26:74) (pyuˇ ta⌄ du⌄)

ssiqnaol nei to be wet (11:61) (yaw a⌄)

ssiq nei shaky

=ssiq nei, gaol= straight

ssiqniq ziiqzaof a license to conduct business (Chi)

ssiqza a battalion commander (Chi)

-- ssiv, alyeiv -- a floral pattern

ssivdyul to enslave; keep in bondage (50:123)

ssivq firm; stable (46:131) (zi‸-eu)

ssivqdao nei firm; stable (9:150) (zi‸ dah ni)

-- ssivq, kavq -- to fix up (general repair)

-- ssivq, lav -- to consolidate; strengthen

-- ssivq, neema salduq -- heart to be comfortable; to be satisfied

-- ssivq, zaol -- to fix up (general repair)

ssifmu vowels; finals (as opposed to initial consonants) (41:76) (or) **yifmu**

ssifsullieiq transportation unit (as in the army) (Chi) (26:49)

SSII

ssiil 1. to confess; admit a mistake; acknowledge (9:150, 13:4, 50:23), 2. to give in

ssiildoq a statement made by the accused under examination (50:98)

ssiil duv to admit something (50:60)

=ssiil, haol= post of a building; pillar of a building

-- ssiil, yoqzyul yoqssiil -- voluntarily surrender onself; confess one's crimes

-- ssii, alssii -- thin and small

-- ssii, aqsii -- to be disgusted; to dislike

Ssiiqbaof a daily paper (46:120)

Ssiiqbei Japan (Chi) (pf) (or) **Sseiqbei** (Je⌄ bu⌄ miˇ k'ah⌄)

Ssiiqbeicol Japanese people (Je⌄ bu⌄ tsawˇ ha⌄)

Ssiqbei diq e geeldiq Japanese war (A=Chi) (50:96)

Ssiiqbeidoq Japanese language (Je⌄ bu⌄ daw⌄)

Ssiiqbeissaq Japanese people (Je⌄ bu⌄ za⌄)

ssiiqbol the tree of heaven (in their mythology) (9:149)

ssiiqbuvq Chinese toon (a plant they eat) (9:149)

=ssiiq, haq= a panther

ssiiqjif a diary (Chi) (26:79)

ssiiq nei hu tao to attach importance to

ssiiv to oppress (9:149) (k'ehˬ-eu k'a^-eu)
-- **ssiiv, alyeiv** -- a floral pattern
ssiiv teiq to oppress; suppress; hold down (46:132); **zeifyaq** (Chi)

-- **ssiivq, keeltuvq** -- with steady steps; steadily (50:179)
ssiivq nei earnestly; carefully (41:76)
ssiivq pieiv suppress; repress; put down

SSO

ssol and... (hawˇ-eu; ...-awˇ) (8:1) (**silssol** = shiˇ-awˇ)
ssolgov alpeel a small reptile in tropical jungles (a little similar to a crocodile)
-- **ssol la, huvq** -- computing the years and months of birth to determine a good marriage ('my son's **huvq ssol la** is thus and so')
ssolnei and (8:1, 9:150) (...-awˇ neh) (**bavq ssolnei** = to take and ...) (see samples in 11:117)

(vb) **sso** can be (vb) (**Maldei haolgaoq xa sso.** Pumpkins can be planted in mountains. 11:38)
sso to shoot at a target
-- **sso, aoqsseil diq** -- to be caught in the rain; for rain to beat down on one
-- **sso, bev** -- to shoot and hit (9:150)
sso al final part. (a command here) (10:7)
sso al to have gotten (10:1)
-- **sso, dal** -- to depend upon
-- **sso e, qeq** -- to depend upon
-- **sso, guq** -- to be necessary; needed
-- **sso, lav** -- (see full)
-- **sso, maq teiq** -- don't hurry
-- **sso, ssaoq** -- go into effect; become effective
-- **sso, taoq** -- to touch
-- **sso, teil** -- (see full)
ssozaq to be punished
-- **sso, zaol** -- 1. to punish, 2. to persecute

SSU

ssul for a bird to fan out its tail feathers (as a peacock)
ssulqil nei for a bird to fan out its tail feathers (as a peacock)
ssul nei a lot of (g'awˬ mya ni)

ssuq to walk; to go (9:150) (kuiˇ zoˬ cah-eu)
ssuq let's go (13:45, 41:7) (or) **ssuq kal yoq** (dzoˬ-awˬ; iˇ kaˇ-euˇ)
-- **ssuq bav, galma** -- to go astray
ssuqda geifsaof col to introduce a party member to the party (A=Chi) (50:144)

ssuqda seilqi soqkaoq application for joining the Communist party (50:144) (AB=Chi)
ssuqdaol aol to correspond with one another (50:106)
ssuqgal passing by (26:12) (cah tseh^-eu)
ssuqgal aol 1. to walk back and forth (45:40), 2. to be on guard duty (26:38)
-- **ssuq, galmol** -- to take a long trip
ssuqgal taol to have a road for travel (50:85)
ssuqgeeq geeq to go quickly (9:150)
ssuq kal yoq let's go (dzo$_{\vee}$-aw$_{\vee}$; i$^{\vee}$ ka$^{\vee}$-eu$^{\vee}$)
-- **ssuq movq al, ngal** -- 'I'll be going' (lit: 'want to go') a polite term a younger person says when leaving an elder (41:160) (nga$^{\vee}$ g'o$_{\wedge}$-i$^{\vee}$ ma de)
ssuq niv to walk along; move along (11:27)
ssuq pyul la to come to (26:14) (la$^{\vee}$-eu; oe-eu)
ssuq qaq to be tired from walking (cah doe$^{\vee}$-eu)
ssuqteiq teiq to go quickly (9:150) (kaw$^{\vee}$-eh$^{\vee}$ i$^{\vee}$-eu)
ssuq yoq li to go by (cah tseh^-eu)

ssuv to shake (as a tree) (zu^ la$^{\vee}$-eu)
ssuv luv ssav lav meil to be noisy (or) **wul li wual lal** (law$_{\wedge}$ g'a-eu)
-- **ssuv, naqseil** -- terrified; fearful
ssuv xa to shake something down (as fruit from a tree) (45:52) (zu^ ka-eu)

ssuvq to rub (9:150) (saw^-eu)
ssuvq pieiv to trample on (50:143)

SSUA

ssuagaol ointment; paste (Chi) (50:144)
ssuaguqbif rickets (Chi) (10:1) (see: **ssueiguqbif**)
ssuajeif softwear (as for a computer) (Chi) (50:144)

SSUEI

ssueiguqbif nalgol rickets (pf.) (A=Chi) (or) **ssuaguqbif** (lit. 'soft-bone disease')

SSYU

=ssyuq, al= a seed
-- **ssyuq, alssyuq** -- to preserve, as seeds
=ssyuq, col= race
=ssyuq, hhavq= pig species
=ssyuq, hho= rice seeds
ssyuq taq to preserve; to save up; to keep
ssyuq xa yiv to carry on from long ago
=ssyuq, zeiq= species of animal (je$_{\vee}$ za$_{\vee}$-eu$_{\vee}$ jeu$_{\vee}$)

ssyufnieiq leap year (Chi) (41:115)

TA

tal to be burning hot (Chi) (pui^ lahᵛ-eu)
-- **tal, albol soqtal** -- to cut off branches and the top of a tree (in a field)
-- **tal, aqlavq** -- to burn one's hand (B=Chi)
-- **tal, baoltal** -- cut down an old dike (bund) in a terraced field and build a new one
-- **tal, galtal** -- to meet on the way
Talmu Bassaq e Yaolssaq Uncle Tom's Cabin (57:156)
-- **tal, soqtal** -- to cut away small branches; to prune
taltuq nei directly (26:69) (dawᵛ coe ni)
talwul fuhuaf corruption and degeneration (Chi) (34:96)
-- **tal xa, hhavqhao** -- to singe and scrape off a pig's bristles
-- **tal, yiuvqnyuq** -- to wake up

taq clf. for times (once, twice, etc.) (9:153)
taq sour food (such as pickled) (cehᵛ ta^ ni)
taq (vb) don't (vb); negative imperative (9:153) (ta᷾ ...)
(vb) taq time when (vb); ni)
taq (vb) don't (vb); negative imperative (9:153) (ta᷾ ...)
(vb) taq time when (vb); at thq -- to place; put
taq bi hev don't leak something; keep the secret (50:7)
-- **taq, doqtaq** -- to have an appointment; engagement
-- **taq, eil** -- 1. to have promised, 2. to have decided
-- **taq, hal** -- when?
-- **taq, hu** -- to look after; to keep watch
taq hu nil don't look down on someone or something (35:33) (ta᷾ haw te᷾)
-- **taq, jol** -- 1. to occupy, 2. be present
taqkeq an army tank (Chi)
taq leev to preserve; to deposit (as money)
-- **taq, luvq** -- to guard; protect
-- **taq nil, aqlaoq neeyo** -- don't worry
taq ngeel siq just a moment (9:153) (ti᷾ k'eh᷾ jawᵛ taw᷾)
Taqpaoq (see: **Taoqpaoq** = an ancestor of the Hani - 14:183) (Tah᷾ pah᷾)
-- **taq, pieiq** -- to stop; put down
taqqil (go to) visit one's relatives and friends (Chi) (41:14)
=taq, siq= kitchen (Chi)
taqssaoq to save up; accumulate; put together (26:108, 50:78) (and see: **taoqssaoq**) (ta᷾ ui᷾ ta᷾-eu)
taqssaoq laq e what is saved up (as money) (26:76)

(ta⌄ ta⌄-eu)
taq ssaoq don't use (as money) (ta⌄ zm⌄)
-- **taq, ssyuq** -- to preserve; to save up
taq xa to leave (50:87)
-- **taq, ssyuq** -- to keep; preserve
-- **taq, toq** -- to preserve
-- **taq, tyul** -- then; that time
-- **taq, xil** -- this time
-- **taq, yiul** -- to put; take and place
taqzaq to deposit (35:41) (**piul bavq taqzaq** = to take money and deposit it)
taq zaq don't eat
-- **taq, zaol** -- to have done
=**taq, zaol**= palm bark covering for a horse carriage
taq ziv a command to be still and quiet ('don't move') (or) **taq lovq** (ta⌄ lu^)
taq zol yo don't study (41:88) (ta⌄ dzaw)

tav sharp (as a knife) (9:153) (ta^-eu)
=**tav, aq**= above; up
=**tav, aoq**= sky; heaven
tav aoq piul saziq ziqssaq a sky spirit (causes epilepsy)
-- **tav, geeqsev** -- for something to be lacquered
=**tav, hul**= above; over
=**tav, laol**= hot water; boiled water (and see full)
tav liq tav, hhaol liq hhaol sharp and hard (46:200) (cf.: ta^ k'aw‸ ta^, g'ahᵛ k'aw‸ g'ahᵛ)
-- **tav, meiqzu** -- sharp mouth (talkative)
tav pa tav nei very sharp (11:57) (yaw ta^)
tavtaoq nei exactly; precisely (13:20)
tavyol nei very sharp (9:153) (yaw ta^)
tavyol pa yol nei to be very sharp (13:45) (zawᵛ ta^-eu)

tavq to chisel (9:153) (dzah⌄ ta‸ ta‸-eu)
tavq to be related to (**aqyivq aqnil tavq lal** = related to older and younger siblings) (ta‸ leᵛ-eu)
=**tavq, bavq**= shoulder
=**tavq, baol**= the lap
tavqciivq an older generation (35:59)
-- **tavq, deivq sil** -- life and death together
-- **tavq, doqsaq** -- to get along; find each other congenial
=**tavq, hhavq**= a mountain slope
=**tavq, niuq**= (see full)
-- **tavq, piultavq** -- to stack silver/money
tavqseq upper teeth
tavqssaq a chisel (dzah⌄ ta‸)
-- **tavq, yoqsaq** -- to have blood relationship
-- **tavq zaq, hhavqtavq** -- to raise pigs jointly (as in a co-op)
Tavqzaoq Hani name of a village (see: **Oltol Tavqzaoq**)
Tavqzaoq zulbal a local ruler from **Tavqzaoq** village

who ruled in pre-liberation times (**zulbal** may be from the Dai = cao fa)

tafciiq interjection (gram) (Chi)
tafsoq to explore; probe (Chi) (34:61) (po^ maw$^{\vee}$-eu)

TAO

taol thousand (6:206, 9:151) (he$^{\vee}$; pa$^{\vee}$)
taol to speak
taol to make a plow or harrow (9:151) (tah$_{\vee}$-eu; tseh$_{\vee}$-eu; ka^-eu)
=taol, almiuvq miuvq= a single monkey
=taol, Gal= Hani New year
-- taol, Galtaol -- to celebrate the Hani New Year
taolgof to get through (Chi)
-- taol, guvq -- to patch; mend
taollaljil a tractor (Chi) (26:26) (or) **tollaljil**
-- taol la, sil -- to stick into; poke into
-- taol, lolgal -- to dig a ditch
taollul milsavq thousands of something
taol mil ten million (tse$^{\vee}$ lam)
-- taol, moqtaol -- to live alone; singly
taol nao often; always ('one thousand days') (13:4, 39, 50:106) (yaw$_{\vee}$ jaw$^{\vee}$ na lu$_{\wedge}$)
taol nao nei every day ('1000 days') (26:119) (yaw$_{\vee}$ nah na lu$_{\wedge}$)
taol so aqyal myriads ('thousands and hundreds) (38:90) (or) **yogaoq gaoq meil** (tah$^{\vee}$ saw$^{\vee}$ a$^{\vee}$ ya$^{\vee}$)
Taolzeq name of an old man (14:154)

tao to enter (2:59) (u$^{\vee}$-eu)
tao clf. for piece of wood, bamboo
=tao, alcav cav= a piece of rope
-- tao, aqhhovq sil -- to thread a needle
-- tao, bavq -- mix in (as into soup)
-- tao, cov -- to insert
-- tao, deiq -- to stick into
-- tao, diq -- to break into
-- tao, eq -- to bring into water
-- tao, eelsyu syu -- to enter water
tao'feil unity and division (Chi) (34:42)
taojiq statistic (Chi) (15:28)
-- tao, lav -- to put into
-- tao, leeq -- to fall into
tao li 1. to go into a higher place (50:89) (u$^{\vee}$ le$^{\vee}$-eu), 2. to study in detail (50:149)
-- tao li, byuq -- to drop in to visit
-- tao li, quq -- to enter into
tao'lyu to discuss (Chi) (ja saw$^{\vee}$-eu)
-- tao, mievq -- 1. to swallow, 2. to embezzle; misappropriate
-- tao, naqbol -- to pierce the ear
-- tao, piav -- 1. to climb into (as a window), 2. to scramble and put into

-- **tao, sil** -- 1. to die in (as a mouse in a pond), 2. to pass through (as thread through a needle)
-- **tao, ssiiq nei hu** -- attach importance to
-- **tao, xa** -- planted into (as into the ground)
tao yil to go down and into a lower place (uᵛ-iᵛ-eu)
tao yi to come into from a higher place (oe uᵛ-eu)
taoyiq unity (Chi) (34:17)
taoyiq zafxeif a united front (Chi) (34:17)
-- **tao, zaol** -- fastened into
-- **tao, zei** -- to throw into - as a basketball into a hoop
taoziif to rule (Chi) (34:16)

taoq to pound (9:152) (tah˯-eu)
taoq 1. to butt (**lavqbavq taoq** = to butt heads, as animals), 2. to touch or rub against each other (**Ssaqmiq keeqma yiuvqpaq yaol maq taoq qiv hhaq.** The daughter-in-law must never touch the father-in-law.) (tah˯-eu)
-- **taoq** a particle used in questions, with a meaning similar to "Well, what about ..." (**Nol aq taoq?** What about you? - 41:6, **Noq e aqnil ssaqyo taoq?** What about your younger brothers? 41:23)
taoq clf. for a pail; bucket
=**taoq, aq**= a pine tree (46:190)
taoq ba to pound until white
taoqbaoq a wooden pail
taoqbiq tassels
=**taoq buqssaq, leil**= a vat or pot for dyeing cloth
=**taoq, byul**= anvil
=**taoq, byuq**= hibernation
-- **taoq, byuqtaoq** -- to hibernate
Taoqca Tongchang, a place in Jinping County
=**taoq, caq**= a mud wall; a wall
-- **taoq, caqtaoq** -- to build a mud wall
taoq ceiv half a bucket
=**taoq, colmiaol miaol**= one's real name
taoq dav upwards; to make progress (50:89)
taoqdav bavqqeiq to rub from feet to head on a sick person as part of a ceremony to drive out spirits
taoqdav pyu direction from low to high
taoqdaol daolma a big whirlpool (30:2) (iᵛ cu˰ iᵛ zeu^)
taoqdaoq bottom of pool in a river
taoqdel a water pond (lah)
taoqdi malyeiv a kind of flower (46:173)
taoq dov to thrust in
taoq'eqso kindergarten (Chi) (14:242)
=**taoq, eel**= a pail; a bucket
taoqgao harsh and unreasonable cruelness (50:72)
taoqgeel 1. flat roof for drying crops outside of the main building; 2. historically an uncovered porch by the house, but now they usually do not have, so for ceremonies they simply construct a little altar of bamboo (the Akha in Xishuangbanna

continue to have the porches) (35:41) (gui˅ ga)

taoqgeel e ceiljil granary (as the Akha in Thailand build) (ceh˅ ji˅)

taoqgeel laqhyul a typical Akha style building

taoqguq Chinese onion (Allium chinense) (9:152)

taoqhaoq a copper coin (Chi) (9:152); money (11:30)

-- taoq, hoqniaoq niaoqbiav -- to pound sticky rice to make cakes

-- taoq, joqtaoq -- for fog, thick clouds to develop

taoqkeeq pangolin (scale-covered mammal that eats ants) (9:152) (tahˬ kuiˬ)

=taoq, laol= a valley

taoq levq to bump and hurt; to injure one's skin by pounding (tahˬ na˅-eu)

taoq leeq 1. to strike down (26:25); 2. to fall down; fall over (here a bucket) (35:89) (tahˬ ka-eu)

-- taoq, lolbaq -- a deep pool in a river

=taoqloq, niuq= a donkey

=taoq, lu= maggots

taoq lyul to pound to pieces (tahˬ loe˅-eu)

-- taoq, meicaol -- to pound rice

taoq miv to bend one's head to work hard (tahˬ mo˄-aw˅ m˅-eu)

taoq muvq to bend down (**wuqduq taoqmuvq** = to bend the head down, as in submission - 34:15) (tahˬ mo˄-eu)

-- taoq, naqtaoq -- to be hard of hearing

=taoq nei, meil= healthy & strong

taoq nal to be hurt; disabled (as by an accident) (26:87) (tahˬ na˅-eu)

-- taoq, neetaoq -- obstinate; stubborn

taoq niv to hit something and cause it to move (38:109) (tahˬ ji^-eu)

=taoq, nyul= middle finger (or) **nyulma**

taoqngaoq because (and see below) (teu mi˅ neh)

(vb) taoqngaoq while (vb); after (vb); because of (vb) (9:152, 13:2, 41:62) (see 11:122 for samples)

taoqpaol the copper covered end of a musket (Chi)

Taoqpaoq great Hani/Akha ancestor (Tahˬ pahˬ)

Taoqpaoq ssaqzaol ceil a ceremony that is held in a Hani home when twins or what they consider as other abnormal births occur

taoq pil to separate (4:40) (g'awˬ-i˅-eu)

=taoq, piul= bone marrow

taoq puq meet up with by luck; to come across someone (6:194, 9:152) (tahˬ puˬ-eu)

-- taoqpuq, qaoqpuq -- to meet accidentally

taoq puv to knock over (as a tree, a post) (26:99) (tahˬ po^-eu)

taoq pyul to throw towards (14:148) (or) **toq pyul** (a different dialect) (biˬ g'eh-eu)

=taoq pyuqcaol, pyuq= open comb and fine-toothed comb

taoq qov broken (as roof tiles) (14:243) (yaw k'eh˄; yaw peh˄)

Taoqsil the name of a daughter of God (35:57)
taoqsil to have fallen down (9:152, 11:114)
taoq sil e to fall to death (12:127) (tah˅ seh˄-eu)
taoqsiq a knot; a knob (9:152, 46:116) (ca^ tm˅)
taoqsiq siq teiq to have knobs (46:116)
taoqsuq pitch pine (9:152) (or) **tuqsuq** (mi˅ shu˅)
taoqsuq albol a pine tree (6:167, 9:152) (mi˅ shu˅ aˇ bawˇ)
taoqsuq aldovq a pine torch
taoqsuq alneev a pine seed (9:152) (mi˅ shu˅ aˇ nui^)
taoqsuqziq pine resin (9:153)
taoqsuv a loose knot (ma˅ pa˄ teuˇ ni)
taoqsuv suv to tie a loose knot
taoqsyu dehydrated (Chi) (10:12)
taoq ssaoq to save up (9:152) (and see: **taq ssaoq**) (ta˅ ui˅ ta˅-eu)
taoq sso to touch (toe˅-eu)
taoqteil qei to butt each other (in competition) (tah˅ ceh ceh-eu)
taoq teiq to control; press down (used here in sense of keeping the other basketball team on the defensive - 41:202)
taoqtiv lolnavq large river (lawˇ ba˅ ba˅ ma)
taoqtul laltul meil very straight (up and down)
taoqtul meil straight (9:153) (dawˇ coe ni)
taoqtul tul very straight up & down (11:217)
taoqtul tul zol zol for an infant to learn to stand up (45:46)
taoqtul xovq to stand erect
taoqtyuq 'from bad to worse'; from up to down
taoqtyuq bavqqeiv to rub from the head to the feet on a sick person, as part of a ceremony to drive out evil spirits
taoqtyuq pyu the down slope; from high to low (za˄ ta˄ ta˄-eu)
taoqtyuq ssaq a person who has gone from 'bad to worse' (11:25)
-- **taoq, wuqduq** -- 1. to pray (bow head), 2. to bow head and body in a kowtow; to genuflect
-- **taoq, wuqpieil** -- (see full)
taoq xa to break off (**seq qiq seq taoq xa** = a tooth breaks off - 27:11)
-- **taoq, xiqtaoq** -- to be constipated
taoqxoq mavq students (A=Chi) (41:177) (aˇ bo˄ dzaw za˅)
taoqxoq meeq 'good morning students' (formal statement made by the teacher to the class, based on a Chinese expression (A=Chi) (41:61)
taoqyiu tung oil (Chi)
taoq zaq 1. animals fight (as cows, buf., goats) (9:153) (tah˅ dza˅-eu), 2. people fight (14:177)
-- **taoq zaq, wuqduq** -- to beg for mercy; to ask forgiveness
Taoqzeq a human who married God's daughter, (her name

is **Taoqsil**) (35:57)

taoqziif comrade (Chi) (9:153, 11:19, 26:28, 41:3)

taoqziif mavq comrades (Chi) (11:19)

taoq zyul to come together by luck; to meet (or) **taoq puq; puq lal** (tah˯ dzoeˇ-eu)

TE

teq to shoot a basketball (Chi) (41:199)

teqbiq nei especially (34:23) (A=Chi)

teqdiei characteristics; peculiarities (Chi) (or) **teqye; teqzeil**

teqqeiq privilege; prerogative (as a position) (Chi) (34:14)

teqxaq to surrender (as soldiers putting up their hands and surrendering) (Chi) (26:41)

teqye characteristics; peculiarities (Chi) (34:45)

teqzeil characteristics (Chi) (46:83)

tev to jump (as of grasshoppers and fleas) (teu^-eu; tsaw˯-eu)

-- **tev, eeltev** -- to belch (from having drunk water)

=**tev, hel**= a hiccup

-- **tev, heltev** -- to hiccup (iˇ tui^ tui^-eu)

=**tev, kav**= a crossbow (ka^)

=**tev, pil**= a small-sized chili pepper

tevq to gnaw (as on a bone) (teu˄-eu)

tevq 1. to have marks on something (as marks on a ruler), 2. sometimes used for small letters as op. to capital letters

tevq to crack (9:154) (teu˄-eu)

tevq to engrave (or) **davtevq**

=**tevq, baoq**= a bamboo container

=**tevq, cav**= criterion; yardstick

-- **tevq, davtevq** -- to engrave

-- **tevq, eeltevq** -- to make a wooden opening from the main ditch into an irrigated field

tevqlevq parasitic plants

tevqlevq aqneiq parasitic plants (can make glue from them)

=**tevq, miavgeel geel**= double-folded eyelid

-- **tevq, qiq tevq qiq tevq nei ceiq** -- to plow one furrow after another

-- **tevq, seqtevq** -- to carve; engrave

TEE

teev 1. to dam up (as a ditch) (iˇ tsahˇ tui^-eu), 2. to stop

-- **teev, caolteev** -- to dam up (as a stream)

teev cyuq 1. to dam up, 2. to stop (tsahˇ tui^-eu)

-- **teev, daoqteev** -- to bump; to jolt (and see full)

-- **teev, doqheiq** -- a pact to shield each other; an agreement between partners in crime not to give

each other away
-- **teev, gul** -- call to stop
=**teev, hhu**= the threshold (of door)
-- **teev, leiq** -- to stop
=**teev, naol**= 1. basic; foundation, 2. back part of one's head
-- **teev, qiq** -- a deadlock
-- **teev, zaolteev** -- (see full)

TEI

teil to pound sticky rice so as to make cakes (9:153) (haw˯ tah˯ tah˯-eu)
teil to throw (as a rock) (**Haqluv qiq siq bavq alnei, Lazeq yaol teil ma leil zaol.** He picked up a rock and wanted to throw it at Lazeq. - 27:12) (bi˯-eu)
'**teil**' the sound of an arrow leaving a crossbow (11:216) (also spoken as both: **teiv**, and **teil** - with the 't' unaspirated)
teil clf. for mountain or mountain range (12:127)
teilbiavq a board (9:154); a level board (te˅ bya˄)
-- **teil ceiv, laqnaq** -- to swear to the truth of something ('if I'm lying may lightning strike me')
teil dav 1. to put in more (as when gambling, to raise the stakes) (daw^ mya˯-eu), 2. to throw something up higher, 3. to be famous; known; **teilma dav**
=**teil, daol**= the back
-- **teil, daoqteil** -- (see full)
=**teil, doq**= a sound; a voice
teil duv galquv a typical experience (50:36)
teil duv naqgaq typical news (50:36)
teil duv seilhuvq musical instruments; folk music (50:116)
-- **teil, eel** -- the sound of laughter
=**teil, gul**= a sound of calling; shouting
=**teil, haol**= mountain slope
-- **teil, haoqtaoq** -- to pound sticky rice for making cakes
=**teil, huq**= ahead of; in front of
-- **teil, huqteil** -- to lead
-- **teil, huqteil bi** -- to have priority; preponderance
teil hha zaq to play games (**haqluv teil hha zaq** = to play games with stones - 14:234) (k'a˯ lo neh ni˅ g'a-eu)
=**teil, hhaq**= cakes made of pounded buckwheat
teil hhaol a mid-tone; mid-level tone (or) **teil yei**
=**teil, koq**= pull back & forth trying to gain control
-- **teil, laqnaq** -- to take an oath
teillu central part of forehead (na˅ k'aw˅)
teilma dav to have a great reputation
=**teil, miq**= first; before; etc.
-- **teil, miqzal** -- to pound gun powder

=teil, **naol**= stools; benches
=teil, **niuq**= forehead
teil nuv to pound to pieces (tahˬ nm^)
-- **teilpaoq, doqteil** -- homonym; homophone
teilsal 1. a pleasant sound (naˇ haˬ muiˬ-eu), 2. reputation; name (as in 'a good name') (35:43, 46:77) (tsawˇ myahˇ do^-eu)
=teil, **sal**= a nice sound; pleasant sound
teil sal ye nei pleasant sounds (46:87) (teˇ saˇ yaw muiˬ)
teilsav a whisper (46:116) (dawˬ sa^ sa^-eu)
teilsav sav to whisper
-- **teil, silteil** -- to lie on one's back
-- **teilssaq, haolteil** -- a small hill
teil sso 1. to throw and hit, 2. to hit on (**wuqduq a teil sso** = to hit the head -- with stones here - 14:234) (biˬ zaˬ-eu; biˬ tahˬ-eu)
-- **teil xa, daoqteil** -- to slide down
teil yei mid-tone; mid-level tone (or) **teil hhaol**
=teil, **yoq**= the sound of one's own voice
-- **teil, Zalteil** -- to celebrate New Year (or) **galtaol taol; galtaol pal**
-- **teil zaq, caqyaq** -- to have a mud fight

tei to face toward the sun
-- **tei, aoqcal** -- the sun's ray's shine
-- **tei pyu, aoqcal** -- the sunny side

teiq 1. to be in a hurry; to be busy (9:154); 2. to be worried (26:90) (tehˬ-eu)
teiq narrow (9:154) (yaw su‸; & cf.: teˬ-eu)
teiq to be crowded (9:154) (yaw tsahˇ)
teiq to hold; squeeze in between (nyeh‸ tehˬ-eu)
teiq clf. for one of a pair (one shoe, one chopstick, one earring, etc.) (11:75) (tiˬ teˬ)
(vb) **teiq** in a state of (vb) (... tehˬ-eu)
=teiq, **aq**= single; odd number
-- **teiq, bavq** -- to hold on
=teiq, **bee**= 1. a baby-carrying cloth, 2. the placenta; afterbirth
-- **teiq, buvq** -- 1. to write down, 2. to register
teiqcal doqcavq a warning (50:8)
-- **teiq, civ** -- to endure; to last
-- **teiq, ciil** -- to lead animals (as horses)
-- **teiq, cuv** -- clamp onto; hold tight
=teiq, **dal**= a single chopstick
-- **teiq, dal** -- to hold tightly
-- **teiq, dav teiq** -- to grow up quickly
teiqdeil a desk lamp (Chi) (41:42)
-- **teiq, deiq** -- to prevent; to press down
-- **teiq, diq** -- (see full)
teiq dov to break into (or) **diq tao**
-- **teiq, eq** -- to carry along on one's back (euˬ-eu)
-- **teiq, eqjil dalteiq** -- to make thatch grasss shingles for roofing

-- **teiq, hu** -- to keep one's eyes on something or someone

=**teiq, hhavq**= a wild boar

-- **teiq, hhe** -- 1. to hold fast, 2. to pull steadily, 3. detain; hold in custody

teiqhhuf a spy (Chi) (k'oeˬ sho haw-eu g'aˬ)

Teiqhhueil Taiwan (Chi) (Taiˬ waˬ)

-- **teiq, kovq** -- to clamp down with teeth

teiqkuv kuvssaq very, very narrow (11:59) (su˰ ti ni)

  teiqkuv nei 1. to be crowded, 2. very narrow (9:154) (su˰ ti ni)

teiqlaq meil to be busy (9:154) (yaw tehˬ)

=**teiq, lavq**= (see full)

-- **teiq, leev** -- to tie down

teiq li cal lal meil hurriedly; quickly (13:48) (tehˬ law tsaˇ law-ehˇ)

  teiq li teiq cal meil hurriedly (9:154) (tehˬ law tsaˇ law-ehˇ)

-- **teiq, luvq** -- to defend, as a garrison

=**teiq, miq**= single daughter

=**teiq nalcal, nal**= serious & sudden disease

teiqnav paint

-- teiq, **neema** -- to be impatient

-- **teiq, nil** -- catch and hold (as rope, braid)

-- **teiq nia, yoqhhaq** -- to restrain oneself

-- **teiq, niaov** -- 1. to pick up (as with tongs, chopsticks or the like, 2. to pluck off

-- **teiq, nieivq** -- to catch and hold

-- **teiq, nyuq** -- 1. to remember, 2. to memorize

teiq pa teiq nei very narrow (11:57) (su˰ ti ni)

-- **teiq, piav** -- (see full)

teiqqeiq privilege; prerogative (Chi)

-- **teiq, seqkaq** -- to have something (as food) between one's teeth

teiq sil teiq piav quickly; hurriedly (13:13, 32, 26:89, 46:211) (tehˬ tehˬ-ehˇ; kawˇ kawˇ-ehˇ)

-- **teiq, ssiiv** -- to suppress; oppress; hold down

-- **teiq sso, maq** -- don't hurry

-- **teiq, ssuqteiq** -- to go quickly

-- **teiq, taoq** -- (see full)

-- **teiq, taoqsiq siq** -- to have knobs

(vb) **teiq teiq** (vb) quickly (13:32) (**yiuvq teiq teiq** = to go to bed quickly - 26:46) (tehˬ tehˬ-ehˇ)

-- **teiq, tuv** -- 1. to support something with something else, 2. to master; to know well

-- **teiq, wuqdeiq bavq** -- (see full)

-- teiq, yevq -- to clamp down on; twist down on

teiq yil a hurried-up marriage

teiq yil teiq lal nei hurriedly (26:90) (tehˬ tehˬ-eu)

-- teiq, ziivq -- to control oneself

teiv kick with foot (9:154) (beh^-eu) (cf. Lahu: hte^ ve)

teiv shallow (9:154) (ma˅ na˄)
teiv to stamp with foot (9:154) (naw˅-eu)
-- teiv, aolzei -- to play game with wooden tops
-- teiv, aoqjiq jiqteiv -- thunder & lightning
-- teiv, baqlu -- to eat something whole and quickly (as small fruits, nuts)
=teiv, bavq= a slap (**bavqteiv qiq lavq bi diq** = to give a slap
-- teiv, baolteiv -- (see full)
teiv cyuq to stop something (la^ na˅-eu)
teiv gee to smoke dry by hanging over a fire (cf.: **cagee** = to smoke dry by a fire) (teh^ gui-eu)
teiv kuv to dry on the rack above the fireplace (14:140) (teh^ ko^-eu)
teivleiv leivssaq nei very, very shallow (11:59) (ti˅ paw˄-i˅ ma˅ na˄-eu)
teivleiv leivssaq nei maq teiv not very shallow (yaw k'a^-ehˇ ma˅ na˄-eu)
teivluv jumping up and down (46:139) (tsaw˅ diˇ-ehˇ teu^-eu)
=teiv nei, zuvq= of a wrinkled appearance
teiv pav to kick and break open (46:199) (beh^ pa^-eu)
=teiv, yuq= a shallow pot; earthen pot

teivq 'slap' (the sound of a slap) (46:151) (teh^)
teivq clf. for steps in a terrace; stories of a building (9:154) (teh˄; ti^)
teivq, teivq, teivq the sound of rain drops falling (teh^, teh^, teh^)
=teivq nei, haq= very bitter
-- teivq nei, saolpuq -- for bubbles to form

teifduf attitude (Chi) (or) **yoyaovq; neenyuq**
Teifgoq milcaq Thailand (A=Chi)

TI

tihyuf 1. to learn something (Chi) (**ngal tihyuf alciiv jav** - I learned a little 26:40); 2. to have some idea
tixeif to show; display (Chi) (34:61) (cf.: bya˅-eu)
tixif system (Chi) (34:18)
tiyeq sports; physical culture (Chi) (34:19)
tiyyuq spirits (Chi) (26:89) (neh˄)
tiziq xaqpav to dismiss; to get rid of the old system (roughly in the period of 1962-1965, when the former system was abolished and the Hani people were able to rebuild their ancestral altars) (Chi)

tiqcal an advocate (Chi) (34:61)
tiqdaof railway track (Chi) (26:30)
tiqgaol to enhance (Chi)
=tiq, nalhaq= question and answer drills (50:179) (B=Chi)

tiqqeiq ahead of schedule (Chi) (26:100)

tivquq tuv to take money by force or by cheating

tivq one (see: **qiq**)
=tivq, ceil= eleven
-- **tivq, hhaq** -- to work hard with all one's strength
-- **tivq, hhaqhav** -- to work hard; with great effort (and see full)
-- **tivq, seiqtivq** -- to tumble

TIAO

tiaoqgei to mediate (Chi) (2:59)
tiaoqjeif condition (Chi) (34:88)
tiaoqjiq to regulate, adjust (Chi) (34:44)
tiaoqyoq cuv taq to conclude a treaty (A=Chi) (50:35)
tiaoqzei to adjust; re-adjust (as in a machine or the like) (Chi) (26:30)
tiaoqzii 1. a note; a memo (Chi) (9:154), 2. a receipt for something purchased

TIE

tieilzi a courtyard (Chi)

TO

tollaljil tractor (Chi) (9:155) (deh ma tsehˬ-eu lo)
tollaljil se a tractor man (in this case the driver) (Chi) (26:100)

to to stretch tight; to tighten (9:155) (teuˇ-eu)
tobaq knife for cutting vegetables (9:155) (g'awˬ nyoeˇ mi cehˇ)
tobeiv sheath for knife (9:155) (mi cehˇ taw^ k'aw^)
-- **to, caqto** -- to make a mud wall
-- **to, hhe** -- 1. to lead; 2. to pull something straight (as a rope), 3. to take charge of; uphold; stand for
tojeil knife (general term) (9:155, 26:112, 46:193) (mi taw^; mi cehˇ jiˇ ba^)
=to, kaol= an enclosing wall; an enclosure
to'liq nei to be tight (yaw bya)
toma a sword (9:155, 11:220, 46:97, 132) (mi cehˇ taw^ ma)
-- **toma, albol** -- a wooden sword, to scare away spirits from a house or a village
toma baqcevq a type of sword (mi cehˇ taw^ ma)
=to, pieiv= a limited time
tossaq a dagger (9:155) (taw^ ma)
tossaq wuqqei the sharp tip of a dagger (taw^ ma mehˬ dzaˬ)
toyyuq the handle of a knife (mi cehˇ yoeˬ)

toq to take care of children (cu-eu)
toq to answer; to reply (13:43) (or) **toq miq** (cf.: o˯ to˯-eu)
toq to be comparable; equal to
toqdi alyeiv azalea (flower) (46:155) (or) **toqdi malyeiv**
toqdi mayil a type of azalea (flower)
toq'eqsov kindergarten (Chi)
toq heeq la to raise a child to adulthood
toq lal to answer; respond (**aoq a gul e maq toq lal, mil a gul e maq gaqlal** = I call to the heavens, no answer, I cried to the earth, no response - 26:4) (or) **gaq lal** (cf.: o˯ to˯-eu)
toqla rabbit; hare (tah˯ la^ = mule in Ak., lah˯ = hare) (9:155)
toqla almil a rabbit (38:4) (lah˯; tah˯ la^)
toqla aqpeil a type of tree
toqla nao rabbit day (lah˯ ti˯ nah; tah˯ la^ ti˯ nah)
toqla huvq rabbit year (9:155) (tah˯ la^ ti˯ k'o˄ = mule year in Ak., lah˯ ti˯ k'o˄ = rabbit year)
toq leev 1. to take good care of (yaw mui˯-eh˅ la^ sa^-eu), 2. to reserve
toq leev aolssaq a storekeeper (50:7)
toqmaq 'taking off the illiteracy cap' (Chi) (that is, to become literate) (41:79)
toq miq to answer; to reply (or) **toq** (cf.: o˯ to˯-eu)
toqsuq a pine tree (shu˯ li˅; mi˯ shu˯)
toqsuq ziq pine resin
toq taq 1. to preserve (35:75), 2. to get in (as crops) (or) **zalsiq se'leev** (ka˅ yeh˅ la^ lui^-eu), 3. to lay up (as money in a bank) (or) **leeq taq**
toq taq laq e zalsiq stored up grain
-- **toq taq miaoqgaoq hha, piul** -- deposit money and get in kind
toqteil to reply (when someone calls)
-- **toqzaq, aqnil** -- to look after a baby

tov 1. to wrap up (9:155) (pa˄ toe^ toe^-eu), 2. to get a share (as of a pig at a ceremony)
tov clf. for wrapped up packages (11:161) (toe^)
-- **tov, diq** -- to beat to death; strike to death
-- **tov, hoqpavq** -- rice wrapped in a leaf
-- **tov, hoq pavqtov** -- to wrap rice in a leaf
=**tov, keel**= men's leggings
-- **tov, keeltov** -- to wind leggings on (men)
=**tov, lal**= right away; immediately
=**tov, lavq**= joint of the shoulder in an animal
tovma a big package (toe^ ma)
-- **tov, palpiul wuqtov** -- to wear a white turban (as at a funeral)
-- **tov, pavqtov** -- to wrap up in a leaf
tov quvq to bind up; wrap up (9:155, 26:86) (gu˄ taw˄-eu)
=**tov, seq**= a tooth plated with some metal (usually

silver or gold)

-- **tov, seqpeiq siil** -- (see full)

=**tov, seivmoq kov**= stilts

tovssaq a small package (toe^ za⌄)

tov teiq to wrap up (toe^-eu)

-- **tov, wuqtov** -- for a man to wrap a turban around his head

-- **tov, yevq** -- to twist to death (as a chicken's head)

tovq 1. to meet (by chance), 2. to agree; be in accord (46:77)

(vb) **tovq** at the moment of (vb) (13:39, 46:106)

-- **tovq, diq** -- to hit something other than what aiming at

-- **tovq, eil** -- to say similar things; to have similar titles of two books, etc.

tovqhaq a reed (aˇ to^)

=**tovq, hhavq**= a pig yoke (to keep out of gardens)

-- **tovq, kalyei se leev** -- time to harvest the crop

-- **tovq, kavq** -- 1. to tie; fasten, 2. to be tight

=**tovq, kovq**= sound of a bowl breaking

-- **tovq, leel** -- to roll and tie

-- **tovq, naoltovq** -- to tie from the back

-- **tovq, nyuq** -- to reason

-- **tovq, pavq** -- to tie up; to tie down

-- **tovq, sil** -- time for the death penalty; time for the execution

-- **tovq, tul** -- time to arise

-- **tovq, xoq** -- to lock (as a door) (or) **xovq tovq**

-- **tovq, xovq** -- to lock (as a door) (or) **xoq tovq**

=tovq, **yo**= seasonable; right time

TU

tul to cut down a tree (**albol tul**) (tuˇ-eu)

tul stand up (tuˇ laˇ-eu)

tul thick (yaw tuˇ)

tul to measure a hand span (see below) (aˇ toˇ toˇ-eu)

tul clf. for a hand span (thumb to middle finger) (9:155, 11:78) (aˇ toˇ toˇ-eu)

-- **tul, albol** -- to cut down a tree

-- **tul, aqtav** -- to hold something up

-- **tul, beqtul** -- quickly become rich; new wealth

-- **tul, ciil** -- to take up; to lift up

-- **tul, deiq** -- to set up; establish

-- **tul, halmiav nei** -- how thick?

-- **tul, hhaqma** -- (see: **hhaqma lol**)

-- **tul, joq** -- as soon as one gets up; as soon as one wakes up

-- **tul, kul** -- to encourage

tul lal 1. to stand up (9:156) (or) **xovq tul lal** (tuˇ laˇ-eu), 2. to arise (or) **duv lal**

=**tul, lavq**= length from thumb to mid-finger

-- tul, leiq -- 1. to awaken someone, 2. to transfer from place to place
tulluq nei to be thick (12:126) (yaw tuˇ)
-- tul, moqpil -- for a Hani spirit priest to drive spirits away
=tul, naq= stubborn; pigheaded; willful ('thick ear')
-- tul, neenyuq hhaq -- inspire enthusiasm; encourage the spirit
-- tul, nieivq -- to erect
=tul, nyul= length from thumb to outstretched index finger
tul pa tul nei very thick (11:60) (yaw tuˇ)
tul pa tul nei maq tul not very thick (11:60)
-- tul, piav -- to wake up
-- tul, puvma -- to offer to the village spirit
-- tul, taoqtul -- straight up and down
tul tovq time to arise (38:94) (tuˇ laˇ yam˯)
tulxavq nei to be very thick (tuˇ dzaw˯-eu)
-- tul, xovq -- to stand up
tul zaq 1. make offerings, 2. hold religious activities (46:119)
-- tul zaq, hhaqma -- make annual ritual offering in the sacred grove
-- tul zei, neivqhaq -- to drive out evil spirits by means of spirit incantation

tudif geigeiq land reform (Chi) (26:16)
tugei land reform (Chi) (26:15)
tusiil local master; official (from pre-liberation times) (Chi)

tuq 1. to surrender, 2. to last a long time (**Hoq zaq maq tuq** = The rice for eating did not last a long time. 35:40)
tuq a picture (aˇ baˇ)
tuq, tuq, tuq the sound of birds spreading their wings (tu˯, tu˯, tu˯)
tuqdif apprentice (or) **tudif** (Chi)
tuqjiqdyuf a shock brigade (Chi)
Tuqjiqse Pioneers (Chi)
-- Tuqjiqse, Silcaqzeil -- Pioneers of the New Long March (Chi)
tuqjif a way; channel (Chi) (34:46)
tuqsuq pitch pine (or) **taoqsuq**
tuqssaq meil all at once (A=Chi) (or) **qiq heiq laltov meil**

tuv to hold in one's hand (tu^-eu)
tuv 1. to support, 2. to hold onto (cf.: daˇ to^)
tuv 1. to peck or strike (as a bird or snake) (**ollol nei tuv** = for a snake to strike) (9:156, 11:20) (to^-eu), 2. to chop again & again with an axe
tuv to knock on door or table with knuckles (or) **diq** (tu^-eu; k'o^-eu)

tuv clf. for a handful (as grass) (9:156, 11:83) (tu^)
-- **tuv, daltuv** -- to support; to prop up
=**tuv, dav**= a slight upslope
-- **tuv, galtuv** -- an offering to the village gate to prevent evil spirits from entering
tuv ho to knock on a door (laˇ g'o^ k'o^-eu)
=**tuv, jiv**= a turnip and potato-peeler
-- **tuv, keeqtuv galtuv** -- to stretch out a dogskin
-- **tuv, lavqtuv** -- to make a fist
tuv liq to shorten (as a walking stick that is worn down)
=**tuv, mei**= a support for a rice pounder
=**tuv, meiq**= beak of a bird
tuv nei straight to the place (**tuv nei seq hev** = led right to the place)
=**tuv nei, sav**= (see full)
tuvnil measles (bui sa^ sa^-eu)
-- **tuv, paoqciivq** -- to kneel down
=**tuv, peil**= to be astringent
tuv piei to open an umbrella or the like (9:156) (pyeh laˇ-eu = for a flower to open)
-- **tuv piei, beelkaq** -- to open an umbrella
=**tuv, qei**= one's weak points
=**tuv, qul**= a spindle
tuv teiq 1. to support something with something else (tu^ tehˬ-eu), 2. to master; to know well (50:207)
-- **tuv, tivquq** -- to take money by force, or by cheating
-- **tuv tuv, peil peil** -- an astringent taste
-- **tuv xa, paoqciivq** -- to get down on one's knees
-- **tuv, zaqngeeq** -- to hold a walking-stick (gawˬ

tuvq to be stained or dirtied with something (**hholmol hultav yoxeiv tuvq nga** = to have something filthy on one's body) (la^ jawˆ-eu)
tuvq clf. for footsteps (11:152, 46:99)
tuvq (vb) extremely (or) **duvq** (9:47) (aˇ dzehˬ-ehˇ)
=**tuvq, keel**= a step (as in taking a step)
-- **tuvqma qiq, keeltuvq** -- to step a stride
=**tuvq nei, nil**= red (as a healthy face)
tuvqqil meil (vb) (vb) very much (**tuvqqil meil gaq** = to love very much - 29:4, **tuvqqilmeil saoq** = very disgusted - 13:25) (45:74, 46:118) (cf.: g'awˬ mya ni)
tuvqqilnei extremely; very (50:131)
-- **tuvq, sulnil** -- for rust to form
tuvq tuvq tuvq nei the sound of the bubbling from a bamboo water pipe (14:170)
-- **tuvq, yoxeiv** -- (see full)
-- **tuvq, zaol** -- to be very cruel

TUA

tuaqfeif League member dues (Chi) (26:74)

tuaqjiq to unite (Chi) (**dalja yaol hha tuaqjiq nia** = must unite all people - 26:114) (see also: **tueiqjiq**) (la^ ui˯-eu)

tuaqjiqbaof United Paper (name of a local newspaper) (50:171)

tuaqyeiq a League member (Chi) (9:155, 41:3) (see also: **tyuqyeiq; tueiyeiq**)

tuaqzal a Youth League member (Chi) (26:32) (see also: **tueiqzal**)

tuaqzal soqhhaq a membership card for the Youth League (26:32) (A=Chi)

TUEI

Tueiqhhyu Youth League Committee (Chi)

tueiqjiq to unite (pf.) (Chi) (see also: **tuaqjiq**)

tueiqyeiq League member (Chi) (see also: **tuaqyeiq; tyuqyeiq**)

tueiqzal Youth League charter (Chi) (or) **tuaqzal**

TYU

tyul that (often used when speaking of something closer to you than to me) (2:59); that one (9:156) (see also: **tyulmol**) (teu)

tyul e liq but; however (9:156) (ehˇ k'aw˰)

tyulgei there (k'oeˇ gaˇ) (9:156)

tyulliq but; however (ehˇ k'aw˰) (8:2, 10:pref., 11:121) (or) **yulmeil liq**

tyulmeil that way; in that manner (9:156) (teu lo˰-ehˇ)

tyulmeil nei therefore (k'oeˇ miˇ neh; teu miˇ neh)

tyulmeil ngaoq if so; if that is the case (41:74) (k'oeˇ lo˰-ehˇ law naˇ)

tyul mol that one (indefinite) (teu hm˯)

tyul taq then; that time; that moment (k'oeˇ ngeh) (8:16, 9:156, 10:25)

tyultaq kavq nei from that time; since that time; from the beginning (11:219)

tyultujil a bulldozer (Chi) (26:27)

tyuq an exclamatory word when pointing out something to a second person

tyuq said when handing someone something, often with a lengthening sound (**tyuq-yuq-yuq**); **heiq**

tyuq 1. to touch with finger, 2. to press, 3. to point out (9:156, 35:5) (toe˯-eu)

tyuq to be steep down (gaˇ toe˯ toe˯-eu)

tyuq a there (at your place) (teu-a˯)

tyuq beil dav beil beil to struggle up and down (26:111)

tyuq dil dav dil dil 1. to seek in every way, 2. to work very hard ('work up and down')

tyuq duv to expose; bring to light; unmask (50:87)

tyuq duv maq jil report a false case to the authorities (50:83)

=tyuq, gal= road or path going down

-- tyuq huvq, piaof -- to return tickets (as for a refund)

tyuq hhev lal hhev nei hhev to turn round and round (as on a slippery surface) (26:99)

-- tyuq, lavqnyul -- (see full)

tyuq meiq to guide by pointing out the way (toe˅ meh˅-eu)

tyuq moq to point to something (13:2) (toe˅ meh˅-eu)

tyuq moq miq to point out (to someone) (46:95) (toe˅ neh˅-eu)

=tyuq nei, gal= a downslope

=tyuq pyu, taoq= a downslope

tyuq qei to point out (with fingers) (toe˅ meh˅-eu)

tyuq qeiq dav qeiq qeiq to seek in every way

tyuqyeiq a League member (Chi) (11:134) (see also: **tueiqyeiq; tuaqyeiq**)

WA

wal? a final part. in questions (**Halgei li wal?** Where have you been? 41:5)
wal a particle ending which combines: **wul al** (35:84)

Wa Wa people (Ceh˯ ba˄; Keh˯ ba˄)
Wacuq the Wa people (B=Chi) (Ceh˯ ba˄ tsawˇ ha˯)

Waq surname of the Wang clan (Chi)
Waq Ssoqfeil a hero (Chi) (26:112)
Waq Ssoqfeil Jeilyeq Hholqei Jol name of a book which tells of this hero being in jail (A=Chi) (26:112)

Wafli caqceiq the great wall (Chi)
waf siif buq qeq sseiq every problem is solved by oneself (Chi)
waf syuf long life (Chi) (**Maoq Zuxiq waf syuf** = long live Chairman Mao - 26:19) (or) **ssil bo** (ziˇ baw)
wafyeiqhuf a family with a 10,000 yuan income (Chi)

WEI

weil! well!; oh my (interjection) (Chi) (13:43)

weiq hello (Chi)
weiqfaq luafji (see: **weiqfaq lueifji**)
weiqfaq lueifji to violate law & discipline (Chi) (34:88)
weiqhuf to safeguard; defend (Chi) (34:80)
weiqhuaf culture (Chi) (26:104) (**this** includes reading, writing, etc. - 26:50)
weiqhuaf daf geiqmif Cultural Revolution (Chi) (34:11), **weiqhuaf geiqmiq** (14:210)
weiqhuaf ziilsiiq cultural knowledge (Chi) (34:93)
Weiqjaofjiq Cultural and Educational Bureau (Chi) (41:197) (and see below)
Weiqjaofjyuq Cultural and Educational Bureau (Chi) (14:241) (**weiq** = cultural; **jaof** = educational; **jyuq** = bureau) (and see above)
weiqmiq civilization (Chi) (34:31)
weiqseil hygiene; health (or) **weifseil** (Chi) (15:47)
weiqseilsuf vitamin (Chi) (10:1)
weiqti style (Chi) (or) **falsiif** (Chi)
weiqsul recording secretary (Chi)
Weiqwuq'e cuq Uygur nationality (Chi)
weiqwuq zuyif materialism (Chi) (34:71)
Weifxaof nursing school; health school (Chi) (41:23)

weiqxoq literature (Chi)
weiqzal articles (as in newspapers) (Chi) (32:3)

weifgoq milcaq a foreign country (A=Chi)
weifhaof a question mark (Chi)
weifhef to extend cordial greetings (Chi) (34:21)
weifjaol diplomacy; foreign affairs (Chi) (34:82)
weifseil hygiene; health (Chi) (WHO = **Goqjif Weifseil Zuziq** - 10:13) (or) **weiqseil**
  weifseiljiq public health bureau (Chi)
  weifseilyeif township hospital (Chi)
weiftiq a problem; a question (Chi) (32:3, 34:116)
weifweifsif a condolence letter (Chi) (26:78)

WU

wul intestines (or) **wulhaq** (9:156) (baw u˅)
wul affirmative ending in sentences with 'I' or 'we' (see 11:134) (41:11); it sometimes adds some 'zip' to the statement (**Halgei wul**! Well! - 41:16)
(vb) **wul al** final part. indicating 'want to (vb)' (**Aqkeeq mol noq a bivq wul al**. I want to give you a dog. 38:15)
(vb) **wul aq?** final part. showing it is a question (9:157) (**Nol Dolnia a haljivq aol wul aq?** What have you been doing in Luchun? 41:12) (**Nol laojal a taqqil hhei li wul aq?** Are you going to visit your relatives? 41:14)
=wul, aqkeeq keeq= a male dog
(vb) **wulbo** should (vb); must (vb) (11:40, 45) (**maq aol wulbo** = must not do - 11:45) (see also: **wuqbo**) (cf.: ma˯ m˅ k'm˯-eu)
wulhaq intestines (or) **wul** (baw u˅)
wulhyul duvluv ssaqnaol dwarfs; trolls who live underground in Hani legends (said to use duck eggs as rice steamers; chicken eggs as pots); **wulhyuq duvluv aqma ssaqnaol** (both are used)
Wullalguq the name of a mountain along the **Beqna Lolma** River (14:144)
Wullalhoq lolbaq the Wullalhoq River (14:168)
-- wul, lav -- to stir something up
wullavq body and mind (50:149)
wullavq appendix (in body) (baw u˅ u˅ dzeh˯)
wulleil 'would...' (**Aqsol zol huhu wulleil aqlavq bavq cei**. Would those who would like to try raise their hands. 54:11)
wul li wual lal nei to be noisy (14:156), **ssuv luv ssav lav** (Chi) (law˰ g'a so^ g'a-eu)
wul loq final part., showing surprise in asking a question (**Haqniq soqmiav zol li wul loq?** Oh, are you going to study Hani? - 32:3)
wulma large intestine (baw u˅ u˅ ma; baw u˅ yaw hui˯; u˅ dah˯) (9:157)
wulmeil ngaoq if that's the case... (or) **yulmeil**

ngaoq (to^-ehˇ maˇ-iˬ)

wul naq final part. showing it is finished (see: 11:134) (9:157) (probably the same as: **wul yaq; wul al**)

wulquvq water (9:157) (iˇ cu˰; uˇ cu˰ = CA)

wulquvq aqma a water god/goddess (35:78)

wulquvq buqssaq a large water container

wulquvq coqbiq a water course made of bamboo or wood (tsawˬ biˬ)

wulquvq coqciivq a waterfall (50:158) (tsawˬ)

wulquvq duv to flow out

wulquvq eelnaoq slowly running water (iˇ g'aˬ maˬ k'a^-eu)

wulquvq haolpuq water bubbles (iˇ cu˰ boeˇ loeˇ)

Wulquvq Hovqseiq Zaq to hold the Dai water festival (14:240)

wulquvq lolgal a water ditch

wulquvq meicaol water-run rice pounder (iˇ cu˰ tahˬ tsmˇ)

wulquvq necev bamboo water container with long handle

wulquvq nei bul zaq to float away in water

wulquvq nei leiq zei to wash away with water

wulquvq pavqmeevq water bubbles (or) **wulquvq haolpuq** (iˇ cu˰ boeˇ loeˇ)

wulquvq pieiq suvq to drain off water (or) **peivq suvq; pieiq suvq**

wulquvq seiq to sprinkle water (11:20) (iˇ cu˰ shehˬ-eu)

wulquvq suvq for water to recede; to be less water (iˇ cu˰ shu˰-eu)

wulquvq taoqhhev hhev a whirlpool

-- **wulssaq, aqkeeq keeqwul** -- young male dog

wulssaq small intestines (9:157) (baw uˇ uˇ zaˬ)

wul wul the sound of a baby crying (14:165)

wul wul al al nei gyuq the sound of crying (Chi) (14:186)

wul yaq final part. showing it is a positive statement; a particle of confirmation (**Ngeel wul yaq**. That's it. **Zaq wul yaq**. I have already eaten.)

wulziil pig's small intestine (no feces, so small sections can be eaten after boiling and roasting)

wulziil meivq ziil hungry; to have an empty stomach

wulziil zaq to eat boiled and roasted sections of pig's small intestines

wulziil ziil a pig's small intestines

wulzoq sausage (uˇ dzawˬ)

wulzoq zoq to make sausage (aˬ za˰ uˇ dzawˬ dzawˬ)

wu feil five cents (Chi) (41:132)

Wuji bufdyuf Armed Police (Chi) (34:21)

wu joq five jao = fifty cents (Chi) (41:132)

Wusiif Yyuqdaof May the 4th Movement (Chi) (34:5) (an important movement that took place in China in

1919)

wusuq diq to perform Chinese martial arts (A=Chi) (41:190)

wuteiq a platform (as in politics) (Chi) (**goqjif wuteiq** = international platform - 34:15)

wuxaf jilbei yeiqzeiq five principles of peaceful coexistence (Chi) (34:83)

Wuyiq May First (Chi) (26:112)

wuqbiav biav a flattened head (fish; person) (45:42)

wuqbiavq biavq 1. to drop to the ground (ga yu^ g'eh-eu); 2. to lie down on one's stomach

wuqbiaoq a baby's soft fontanelle

(vb) **wuqbo** should (vb) (**hhaqnaq naq wuqbo** = should take a break - 26:33), must (vb) (**aol wuqbo** = must do, **zaq wuqbo** = must eat - 26:66) (**Tyulliq qiq heiq hu wuqbo nga**. However it is worth watching/ ought to watch it. 41:212) (38:2, 46:190) (see also: **wulbo**)

wuqcal sun's rays (9:157) (u˯ tsaˇ)

wuqcal laol to warm in the sun

=wuqcal, naolma= sun's rays (nahˇ ma u˯ tsaˇ)

wuqca proletariat (Chi)

wuqca geiljiq geiqmif proletariat class revolution (Chi)

wuq cavq something bad done on purpose (45:33)

wuqcavq cavq to do something bad on purpose (46:184)

wuqcavq lav 1. adultery; illicit sexual relationship, 2. rape (50:82)

wuqcavq meil to do something bad on purpose (and see: **wuvqcavq...**) (or) **wuqcavq meil aol zyul** (50:64)

wuqcavq xa 1. to do bad things on purpose (13:20); 2. to make a false charge against someone (35:61), 3. to make trouble

wuqcavq xa huvq 1. to make reprisals; 2. make a false charge against (50:8)

wuqcaoq a cap; hat (9:157, 11:128) (u˯ k'o^)

wuqcaoq caoq to wear a cap; hat (9:157) (u˯ k'o^ k'o^-eu)

-- **wuqcaoq mol bavq zei, ssaqcyuq** -- to 'take off one's poverty cap' (i.e., to get out of poverty)

-- **wuqcaoq, saol** -- a metal helmet

wuqcaoq caoqpeel a grey or blue cap (46:126)

=wuq dav, lul= to cause a blister to form (from heat)

wuqdeiq stomach; abdomen; belly (9:157) (or) **wuqma** (u˯ ma^)

wuqdeiq bavq teiq to hold stomach (as after eating a big meal) (26:83) (u˯ ma^ tu^ teh˯-eu)

wuqdeiq buqdeil roundworm; intestinal worm (ascaris) (buˇ deˇ)

wuqdeiq hholqei haqluv pieiq dov to put stones in another person's stomach by means of black magic

wuqdeiq leiq to look for food (14:173)

wuqdeiq leiq deiv zaq to seek for food; to work for a living

wuqdeiq puq 1. to be pregnant (za˅ jeu˅ la˅-eu; a˅ nyi˅ pi-eu), 2. to have a swollen stomach (u˅ ma^ pu˅-eu)

wuqdeiq suv diarrhea (10:pref., 26:57); **wuqdeiq yil** (u˅ ma^ yoe˅-eu; u˅ ma^ ka-eu)

wuqdeiq wuqssaq lower belly (9:157) (u˅ ma^ dah˅)

wuqdeiq yil to have loose bowels; to have diarrhea; **wuqdeiq suv** (u˅ ma^ yoe˅-eu; u˅ ma^ ka-eu)

-- **wuqduq** -- in the space of (time) (**saoq nao wuqduq** = in the space of three days; **hhyuq nao ceil nao wuqduq qiq taq** = once in nine or ten days)

wuqduq head (9:157) (u˅ du˅)

wuqduq ba nei with white hair (46:140) (cf.: u˅ du˅ pyu˅)

wuqduq ceilkaol hair of head (u˅ du˅ tseh˅ kah˅) (5:27)

wuqduq ceilkaol hhe to pull head hairs

wuqduq ceilkaol leiq kuv to have curly head hair

wuqduq ceiv 1. for the head to be split open (as a deep wound when fighting - 26:104), 2. to cut off a head (26:112) (u˅ du˅ yu˅-eu)

wuqduq daoqmiq hev nei ever since ....

wuqduq daoqmiq hev nei hu hev to get to the bottom of something

wuqduq daoqmiq leev nei thorough; everywhere; all affairs ('from head to tail')

wuqduq daoqmiq li nei thoroughly; from head to tail; all along (13:49, 35:3) (cf.: **galma qiq kaol qiq li meil**)

wuqduq duq to be the 'head'; leader; to be the lead (as in a film) (11:42) (u˅ du˅ geu˄-eu; a˅ yui˄ geu˄-eu)

wuqduq duq col a ring leader

wuqduq duqli at the very top (as of a letter)

wuqduq duv to be a leader

wuqduq galtyuq nei dejected; discouraged; head bowed down, bent down (as in grief - 26:80, 35:25) (cf.: u˅ du˅ ga˅ mo˄-eu)

-- **wuqduq, haolgaoq** -- a mountain ridge

-- **wuqduq, haolteil teilma** -- high in mountains; tops of mountains (12:127)

wuqduq hhev hhev nei to shake the head saying "no" (u˅ du˅ jui˄-eu)

wuqduq kav to comb hair (u˅ du˅ ka^-eu)

wuqduq niei niei nei shaking head up and down in agreement (27:11, 35:61) (u˅ du˅ jui˄-eu)

wuqduq ngaoq qul to raise up one's head, as when proud (a dragon in 38:109) (u˅ du˅ ba˄ leu˅-eu)

wuqduq saltaoq to surrender; yield (50:139)

wuqduq sev to give a hair cut (28:4) (u˅ du˅ teh˅-eu)

wuqduq seil head louse (sheh˅ maw˅)

wuqduq taoq 1. to bow the head (as before ancestral

altar) (11:203, 45:65), 2. to pray (u⌄ du⌄ tah⌄-eu), 3. to kowtow (u⌄ du⌄ tah⌄-eu)

wuqduq taoq huvq apologise and beg another's pardon (50:128)

wuqduq taoq muvq to bend the head down (as in capitulation to the enemy - 34:15, 35:25) (u⌄ du⌄ tah⌄ mo^-eu)

wuqduq taoqqoq friend of the groom (best man) (50:5); kowtows with groom at weddings

wuqduq taoq zaq to beg for mercy; to ask for forgiveness

wuqduq wuqhhov dandruff

wuqduq wuqpeel a head disease; favus of the scalp (45:53)

wuqduq wuqtov a male turban (46:158) (u⌄ dzah⌄ dzah⌄-eu)

wuqduq yevq yevq nei to shake one's head (here in wonderment or disagreement) (35:9) (u⌄ du⌄ jui^-eu)

wuqduq zaolhhaol crown of head; pate (u⌄ dzahˇ lahˇ g'ahˇ)

wuqduq zei puv 1. to turn the head (46:139) (u⌄ du⌄ ci⌄ pyaw⌄-eu), 2. to turn around

=wuq, gaoq= 1. temporary, 2. ahead

wuqgeel scalp (head-skin) (9:157, 11:27)

wuqhol life (10:22, 13:32, 34:8) (cf.: yaw deh^; ziˇ)

wuqhol bo to have life; to live (14:228, 46:153)

wuqhol boq to save a life

wuqhol haol col a body guard (50:6)

wuqhol liq maq movq meil ... with disregard for life (13:32)

wuqhol maq movq afraid of nothing; determined to do it (even though it means giving one's life)

wuqhol maq movq meil diq kavq 1. to fight without fear for one's life; 2. to fight to the death (50:93)

wuqhol niq hol two ways to go ('two lives') (34:8)

wuqhol zeiqpyuq a pension for the disabled or family of the deceased (50:52)

wuqhov skull (9:158) (u⌄ du⌄ k'm⌄)

wuqhuv a turban for females (9:158)

wuqhuv huv a female to wear a turban (9:158) (cf.: u⌄ k'o^ k'o^-eu = to wear a cap)

wuqhuv taoqbiq tassels of a woman's turban

wuqhhaoq pillow (or) **yiuvqhhaoq** (6:178, 9:157) (u⌄ g'm⌄)

wuqhhaoq hhaoq to put a pillow under head (9:158) (u⌄ g'm⌄ g'm⌄-eu)

wuqhhaoq hhaoqlov pillow cover

wuqhhov dandruff (i.e. the white that flakes off, see also: **wuqniaoq** = the dark that flakes off) (9:158, 11:119)

-- **wuqhhov, wuqduq** -- dandruff

wuqhhyul a pregnant woman (or) **wuqhhyul aqma**

wuqjoq joq 1. to have a haircut (man) (u⌄ du⌄ teh⌄-

eu), 2. whorl of hair on the back part of head (10:4)

wuqjul bald ('shiny') head (uˬ deˬ)

wuqjul jul to become bald

wuqju ju to crawl on one's stomach (ciˇ joe joe-eu)

-- wuqju meil, wuqleiq -- 1. to crawl on one's stomach, 2. to work hard

wuqkev kev knock at head with knuckles (taboo action for Hani)

wuqkyul horn; antler (45:93) (uˬ coeˇ) (note: the Ak. term is what the Akha women's headdress is called)

wuqkyul kyul head to be squarish (in Ak. uˬ coeˇ coeˇ-eu means for a woman to wear a headdress) (10:4)

wuqkyul wuqquq a horn-like woman's headdress

Wuqliaqsal the Wuliangshan mountains, along the Lancang River where the Hani people now live (46:76)

wuqleev leevzaq to make a living (33:3) (mˇ dzaˬ k'aw‸ dawˇ-eu)

wuqleiq wuqju meil 1. to crawl on one's stomach (mˬ ma^ neh ga^-eu), 2. to work hard

wuqma belly; abdomen (5:57) (or: **wuqdeiq**) (uˬ ma^)

wuqma eel beivq jil nei a good laugh (cf. Eng.: 'a belly laugh')

wuqmieivq woman's carrying rope (tumpline)

wuqnaovq brain (iˇ nm‸) (uˇ nm‸ = CA) (cf. Lahu: u¯ naw‸ neh^)

wuqnaovq cuv to suck brains out (what imperialistic landlords did to the people before liberation - 26:1)

wuqnaovq zeq to be clever, quick-minded

wuqneil a treetop (4:32) (aˇ bawˇ uˬ du)

wuqnil bald ('red') head (uˬ duˬ yaw deˬ)

wuqniaoq dark ('dirty') dandruff (see also: **wuqhhov**)

wuqniuv a tree bud (14:172)

wuqpavq 1. inside section of woman's headdress (**wuqhuv** = the outside section), 2. silver trumpet-shaped ornaments Hani women wear

wuqpavq pavq for women to wear 1. inside section of headdress, 2. silver hair ornaments

wuqpeel the head of a person suffering from a scalp disease (favus of the scalp)

wuqpeel nal a head disease

-- wuqpeel, wuqduq -- to have a head disease; favus of the scalp (45:53)

wuqpieil spleen (9:158) (shiˬ pyehˇ)

wuqpieil nal an enlarged spleen

wuqpieil taoq to cure an enlarged spleen with a hot iron rod

wuqpiul white-headed person (uˬ pyuˇ)

wuqpiul luvma a huge white rock not far from **Aqlo Puvteil** village, where a white pig is sacrificed on the way to the 'great water divide' ceremony

wuqpuq a big belly

wuqpuq ssaqheil aqma a pregnant woman
-- **wuqquq, wuqkyul** -- a horn-like woman's headdress (46:175) (u˯ coe˅)
wuqsev tossaq a small knife for shaving heads
wuqseil grey-headed person (u˯ du˯ pyu˅-eu)
wuqseil head louse (see also: **wuqduq seil**) (u˯ du˯ sheh˅ maw˅)
wuqseil jol for a head louse to be present (sheh˅ maw˅ u˅-eu)
wuqseil seil to become grey-headed (u˯ du˯ u˯ pyu˅ pyu˅-eu)
wuqsei top; tip (9:158) (meh˯ dza˯)
wuqsoq morning (not pf.) (6:164) (u˯ shaw˯)
wuqtov turban worn by males (6:177, 9:158) (u˯ dzah˯)
wuqtov tov a male to wrap on a turban (u˯ dzah˯ dzah˯-eu)
wuqtov tovpiul a white turban (worn only at funerals)
-- **wuqtov, wuqduq** -- a turban worn by males
=**wuq, xal**= the upper part of the field
wuqxavq xavq to choke from smoke
=**wuq, zaol**= the upper part of a village
Wuqziiljiq Goods and materials department
wuqziiq materialism (Chi) (34:12)
wuqziiq weiqhuaf material culture (Chi) (34:33)

wuv to hatch (as birds) (9:158) (ceu˄-eu)
=**wuv, al**= an egg
-- **wuv, alwuv** -- for an egg to hatch
-- **wuvba, alwuv** -- the white of an egg
wuvbuvq a rotten egg (9:159, 11:25) (ya u^ bu˄)
=**wuv, davq**= a testicle
wuvdeev eggs pickled in brine (ya u^ ceh˅)
wuvgyuq to have a hernia ('crying testicle')
=**wuv, ha**= a chicken egg (ya ci^ ya u^)
-- **wuv, hawuv** -- for chicks to hatch
wuvhhaq a thin eggshell (ya u^ k'aw˄ yaw ba˯)
wuvjuv a bad egg (check by shaking it)
=**wuv, naq**= earlobe
wuvnaoq a soft-shelled egg
-- **wuvnaoq, alwuv** -- a soft-shelled egg
wuvnil a brown ('red') egg (ya u^ ne˅)
-- **wuvnil, alwuv** -- (see full)
=**wuv, ollol lol**= a snake egg
=**wuv, oq**= a duck egg
wuvpiul the white of an egg (9:159)
=**wuv, seil**= louse eggs
wuvsiil yolk of egg (9:159) (ya u^ shui˅)
-- **wuvsiil, alwuv** -- the yolk of an egg

wuvq to have (only used of specialized items)
wuvq to soak in water and cover (wuvq deil wul'al = the right time to soak seeds in water -- 54:166)
wuvqhol one's life (**wuqhol** = pf.)

WUA

wuafgoq a foreign country (Chi) (34:40)
wuafgoq col foreign people (A=Chi)

WUEI

wueifgoq a foreign country (Chi)
wueifjiaolbuf the ministry of foreign affairs (Chi)
wueiftiq a problem; a question (Chi) (11:11)

XA

xal field (9:159) (Note: the terms for 'mountain field', **xal** and **yal** are used almost interchangeably, according to the dialect. For other words having to do with 'mountain fields' see: **yal**.) (ya$^{\vee}$)
xal township (which is under county administration) (Chi) (34:56)
xal aoq to do farm work ('make a field')
xal aol jilqif agricultural machinery (B=Chi) (50:122)
xal aolssaq a farmer; a peasant (41:4, 50:122) (ya$^{\vee}$ m$^{\vee}$ za$_{\vee}$)
xal aol ssaoqmiaoq materials for agriculture (50:123)
xal aol zaq to farm ('to make fields') (ya$^{\vee}$ m$^{\vee}$ dza$_{\vee}$-eu)
xal aol zeiqssaq a farm animal used for plowing
xalbaol bil zaq to divide up family property and live separately (45:50)
xal beiv to cut down trees for a field (ya$^{\vee}$ mya$_{\vee}$-eu)
xalbial an old, abandoned field; or one left fallow (9:159, 11:25, 38:35) (ya$^{\vee}$ sa$_{\vee}$; ya$^{\vee}$ peu$_{\vee}$)
  xalbial duq 1. to open up wasteland (50:95), 2. to mark off a part of a field so that a person who has died can cultivate it
Xalceil a general name for boys when they are born (so that spirits will not name them)
xal ceiq xal kav kav 1. to plow and harrow irrigated fields (ya$^{\vee}$ tseh$_{\vee}$ ya$^{\vee}$ ka^ ka^-eu), 2. to engage in farm work (ya$^{\vee}$ m$^{\vee}$ dza$_{\vee}$-eu)
xalceiv a deed for a field
xaldahhyu a township party committee (Chi)
xaldaoq lower section (foot) of a field (9:159, 11:211) (ya$^{\vee}$ dah$_{\vee}$)
xaldei irrigated field (9:159) (or) **yaldei** (deh ma; deh ya$^{\vee}$)
  =xal, dei= fields and gardens; countryside
  xaldei baolciivq the steps between terraced irrigated fields
  xaldei dalbaol terraces in an irrigated field (deh ma deh bah$^{\vee}$) (9:159)
  xaldei dalbaol qiq to build a dam for a terraced field (lah tui^-eu)
  xaldei daolkyul irrigated field in triangular shape
  xaldei daobiao sev to weed the dikes (bunds) of terraces in an irrigated field
  xaldei hhaqjeil terraced irrigated field (or) **hhaqjeil xaldei** (deh ma)
  xaldei loqju a long and straight irrigated field
  xaldei loqkol a new irrigated field (deh ma yaw

shui^)

xaldei loqgov a barren irrigated field

xaldei loqma a very large irrigated field (9:160) (deh ma yaw huiˬ)

xaldei loqteiq a single irrigated field

xaldei xa zaq to plant and cultivate fields (26:3) (deh ma mˇ dzaˬ-eu)

xalduqssaq a farmer; a peasant (yaˇ mˇ zaˬ)

xalgov 1. a field that is not fertilized (9:160), 2. an irrigated field without a good crop

xalhhaoq the upper section of a field (11:211) (yaˇ g'mˬ)

Xaljal lolbaq the name of the Xiang river (A=Chi) (26:4)

xalkaq the boundary of a field (yaˇ kaˬ)

-- **xalkav, xalceiq** -- to plow & harrow a field

xal maq aol zaq col non-agricultural population (i.e., city and town dwellers) (50:49) (yaˇ maˬ mˇ dzaˬ-eu tsawˇ haˬ)

xalmeeq a fertile field (yaˇ yaw muiˬ)

xalmil sal to look for a place to make a field

xalmuvq muvq to weed a field (46:163) (yaˇ mo^ mo^-eu)

xalpav land rent (as for a field where one gives half of the produce to the owner) (50:36)

xalqaol a field hut (9:160) (yaˇ cmˇ)

xalqaol qiq qaol a field hut (8:1-3) (yaˇ cmˇ)

xalseil kav to harrow a field the first time

xalsol duv go to work in the fields (14:166, 35:40) (yaˇ smˇ-iˇ-eu)

xalsol hhuvq lal to return from the field (11:199) (yaˇ smˇ g'o^ laˇ-eu)

xalwuq the upper area of the field (35:3) (yaˇ g'mˬ)

xalwuq nei xaldaoq hev nei from the top to the bottom of the field (35:3) (yaˇ g'mˬ-ahˇ neh yaˇ dahˬ keu^ ni)

-- **xal, xa hu** -- experimental plot for planting seed

xalyeq sesame seed oil (Chi)

xalyeq aqdal an oil lamp (14:181)

-- **xalyeq, hhoqcil** -- rape seed oil (B=Chi)

-- **xal, yyuq** -- to pass on; to hand on (as from the ancestors)

xalza a township leader (below county level) (Chi) (41:3)

xal zaq to mortgage a field

xalzaof perfumed soap (Chi) (41:33)

xalzeil the side of the field (11:216) (yaˇ dzeˇ)

xalzeiffu township, or brigade government (the lowest government unit in China) (Chi) (26:26)

xa here (**xa hev nei** = to arrive here - 11:207, **xa alnei** = from here); **xaq a** (more like 'right here'); **ya** (heu gaˇ)

xa to plant (as vegs.) (9:159, 46:113) (ka-eu)

xa to dye (9:159) (saˬ paˇ ka-eu)

xa to lay eggs (**hawuv xa** = hen to lay an egg) (ya u^ ka-eu)

xa a joss stick

(vb) **xa** particle showing lively transition in space or time (**aol xa** = to continue doing) (cf. in Lahu: ... hk'a)

-- **xa, aol** -- 1. to continue, 2. to carry out; execute

=**xa, bee**= a mosquito net (bui ka)

-- **xa, ceil** -- to plant rice

-- **xa, ciq** -- to wash away

-- **xa, daoqsov sov** -- to slide down

-- **xa, daoqteil teil** -- to slide down

-- **xa, dev** -- to cut down/off

xaduq planting methods; planting space

xa duv miaoqgaoq agricultural products (50:122)

-- **xa, guv** -- so frightened one falls to the ground

-- **xa, hawuv** -- hen to lay an egg

-- **xa, haqpal** -- to dye cloth

xa heil to fall into (ga ka-eu)

-- **xa heil, dovq** -- to spread, as a disease

xa hu xal an experimental plot for planting seeds (50:154)

-- **xa, hhavqhao tal** -- to singe and scrape off a pig's bristles

-- **xa, hhe** -- cancel; write off

-- **xa, jol** -- to sit down

-- **xa, jolqil** -- to live happily

-- **xa, ju** -- to drip down

-- **xa laq e, leiq suv** -- to erode

-- **xa, leitaoq** -- to dye cloth

xa'luq a container for joss sticks (Chi)

-- **xa, naqteil** -- to warn; caution; admonish

-- **xa, nee ceiv** -- dare to do something; decide to do something

-- **xa, piav** -- to scrape off (as moss from the roof)

-- **xa, pieiq** -- transfer to a lower level; transfer to do manual labor in the countryside or factory (and see full)

xa puv to plant again (18:25) (ka po^-eu)

-- **xa, qeiq** -- to take off something by luring; cheating

-- **xa, saqlaq** -- to plant cotton (46:212)

-- **xa, ssaq zaq** -- to have an abortion by taking medicine

-- **xa, ssuv** -- to shake something down (as fruit, leaves from tree)

xa tao to plant 'into' (as into ground) (11:214) (ka uˇ-eu)

-- **xa, taoq** -- to break off

xataoq paulownia trees

xataoq taoq buvq miqjiv jiv hhaol 'decayed paulownia trees still produce hard charcoal' (meaning: 'weak people can still produce wonderful results')

-- xa, wuqcavq -- 1. to make a false charge against someone, 2. to make trouble
-- xa, ya -- to drop down
xa zaq havma a skilled farmer
-- xa, zav -- to drop (as liquid) (or) **ya**
-- xa, zaol -- to destroy; to make something bad
-- xa, zei -- 1. to throw away; 2. to fall down from

xaq to cut open (by something sharp, as a knife, a sharp leaf, etc.) (peh^-eu)
xaq a here; right here (**xaq a yiv** = come here) much like; **xilgei a**
-- xaq, alpieil -- to be cut deeply by the **alpieil** type of bamboo

xav incense; a joss stick (Chi)
xav keq to burn incense (A=Chi)
xav nei grand; solemn (46:110)
xavpiq a sling shot (Chi) (caᵥ oeᵥ)
xavpiq bev to shoot a sling shot (A=Chi) (caᵥ oeᵥ beu^-eu)

xavq 1. stay overnight; spend the night (or) **yavq** (9:160) (ya^-eu); 2. sleep with spouse (46:132) (yu^ ta^-eu)
xavqduq 1. a sleeping place (ya^ k'aᵛ, and cf.: ya^ duᵥ = a roost for a chicken), 2. a camping place
xavq hhaq to have intercourse; make love (46:132) (yu^ ta^-eu; aᵥ loeᵥ loeᵥ-eu)
=xavq nei, tul= very thick
-- xavq, wuqxavq -- (see full)

xafbal to go off to work (Chi) (41:51) (yaᵛ smᵛ-iᵛ-eu)
xafjaol rubber (Chi) (or) **zaqgev** (jaw^ jiᵛ jaw^ g'eu^)
xafjaol albol rubber tree (A=Chi) (or) **zaqgev albol**
xafqiq Chinese chess (Chi) (14:195)
Xaf Xaozeif an ancient Chinese book about the calendar called Xia Xiaozheng (Chi) (46:83)
Xaf Xeflif name of a hero (Chi) (26:70)
xafzeil a token; a symbol (Chi)

XAO

Xaol a surname (Chi)
xaol to respect (esp. old people) (Chi)
xaolbyu the roof of a house (38:92) (nymᵛ mᵥ)
xaolcyuq old, broken house (clf. = **yaol**) (13:4) (see also: **yaolcyuq**) (ymᵛ ymᵛ cehᵛ = CA)
xaoldav dav 1. to celebrate moving into a new house (while alive), 2. to celebrate moving into a new 'house' (i.e. a coffin) in death (nymᵛ da^ da^-eu)
Xaoldifpeiq Brothers brand of a machine for weaving

sweaters (Chi) (57:95)
xaolfaqceil a fire engine (Chi) (26:70)
xaolfaq dyufyeiq firemen; fire fighters (Chi) (26:70)
xaol hoqbyu daoqma a ridgepole in a house (or) **yaol hoqbyu daoqma**
xaolma the main house of the Hani; **yaolma** (**xaolssaq** = small hs.) (nymᵛ ma)
xaolniul a roof rafter in house (or) **alniul** (46:117)
xaolpiaq eaves of a house (45:53)
xaolsueil nitric acid (Chi)
xaolssaq a small house (46:101) (**xaolma** = main house) (nymᵛ za˯)
xaolxiq news (Chi) (daw˯ ga˯)
xaolyeil an inflamation or swelling (Chi) (10:25)
xaolyeil cov an injection of medicine to diminish swelling and inflamation (A=Chi) (10:25)

xao a heavy weight (9:160) (yaw kah)
xaobaovq nei to be very heavy (9:160) (yaw kah)
xaobaovq pa baovq nei to be very, very heavy (13:31) (zawᵛ kah-eu)
xaodeivq nei heavily (or) **xaobaovq nei**
xaodeivq pa deivq nei very heavy (11:58)
Xao.Fal 'little' Fa (a person's name) (Chi) (26:20)
xaogaol a part-time job (Chi) (14:186)
xaohoqzii a young man (Chi) (26:48) (za˯ gu˯)
xaojovq nei to be heavy (26:93) (yaw kah)
xaokal a comfortable life (to be relatively well off) (Chi) (34:18) (deh˰ ziᵛ yaw saᵛ)
-- **xao, keeltuvq** -- the sound of loud footsteps
Xao Leiq 'little' Leiqfal (Chi) (26:28)
Xao Li 'little' Li (Chi)
-- **xao, neema** -- a heavy heart
xaosiiq an hour (Chi) (1 **xaosiiq** = one hour - 26:33) (na˯ li˯ ti˯ la˰)
xao tiqdaof a small railway track (26:31) (Chi)
xaoxi 'small' (lower case) letters (Chi)
xaoxoq a primary school (Chi) (11:176, 41:85)
Xao Yiq 'little' Yiq (Chi) (26:23)
xaozu a group (Chi) (9:160) (aᵛ ma˰ aᵛ muᵛ)

xaoq clf. for long items (sugar cane, stick, bamboo, rafter, needle) (Chi) (9:160, 11:75) (kah˯)
-- **xaoqbul, miqkoq** -- straight firewood
xaoqjoq a whole tree; whole bamboo; whole sugar cane, or whatever is being described
xaoq tovq (see: **xoq tovq** = to lock)
xaoqxil zuafziif lofty aspirations; great ideals (Chi) (34:70) (nui noe˯ yaw hui˯)

xaovq laol to shut into; close something in (35:116) (or) **xovq laol** (pf.) (pi˯ teh˯ ahᵛ-eu)

xaofliq efficiency (Chi) (34:56)

XE

xelli to repair (as a tractor) (Chi) (26:32)
xelzeif cofwuf to correct one's mistakes (Chi) (34:22) (la^ tsa⌄-eu)

XEI

xeilcuaq (see: **xeilcueiq**) (Chi) (41:50)
xeilcueiq propaganda (Chi) (34:67)
xeilcueiqbuf ministry of propaganda (Chi)
xeilfaol moqfaf vanguard and model (Chi) (34:86)
xeiljif advanced (Chi) (26:100) (and see: **xeilzif**) (meh⌄ hu paw da^ le˅-eu; mui⌄ la˅-eu)
xeiljif seilcazei a model worker (Chi) (26:100)
Xeilpaq the name of a person (38:108)
xeilseil mister (Chi) (comes after the name) (**Syul Zaolsal xeilseil** = Mr. Syul Zaolsal)
xeilsiif to swear to follow a policy (Chi)
xeilzif to advance; improve (Chi) (26:106) (and see: **xeiljif**) (mui⌄ la˅-eu)
xeilzif jiqti advanced collective unit (Chi) (26:101)

xei to be fragrant (11:200) (yaw saw)
xeiji to elect; to vote (Chi) (34:51) (cf.: tse˅-eu)

xeiv to run; flee (9:160) (ceh^-eu)
xeiv al la come running over here (ceh^ g'eh la‸)
xeiv al li run up to there (ceh^ da^ la‸)
xeiv al yi run down to there (ceh^ ka le‸)
xeiv bial 1. to run and disappear, 2. to run and hide (13:40) (ceh^ bya^-eu; ceh^ byo^-eu)
xeiv duv to run away (13:1) (ceh^ do^-eu)
-- **xeiv duv, hhavqkuv nei** -- escape from prison; break out of prison
xeiv heil to run away (ceh^ byo^-eu)
-- **xeivhuvq, yoqhhaq** -- to voluntarily leave one's job
-- **xeiv, hyuq** -- to escape
xeiv hha to run about; do exercises (11:130)
xeiv hhoq to get away; to run away
xeiv hhovq to run and hide (9:160), to take refuge; seek asylum (50:11) (ceh^ za‸-eu) (**yoqhha bulduq xeiv hhovq** = to go hide oneself)
xeiv hhovq duq a shelter
-- **xeiv, lavqnuvq lavq** -- 1. to knead thoroughly, 2. to work hard
xeivleel nei muddy (yaw pyeh^ yaw leh^)
xeiv leev 1. to run away (13:24), 2. to get off (or) **ssavq; pieiq; duv; hhe hhoq**, 3. to get loose
=xeiv, mil= muddy
-- **xeiv, naolhao** -- to run after; to chase after
xeivnaovq dirty (as machinery) (9:160, 11:24, 26:32)

(yaw jaw^)
  xeivnaovq nei very dirty (9:161) (jaw^ la^ ni)
  xeivnaovq xeivleel nei very, very dirty (jaw^ dui dui-eu)
xeiv puv yil to turn back (14:235) (ji^ k'o^-eu)
xeiv pyul li to run over to someplace (13:32) (ceh^ g'eh-eu)
xeiv qeiv qeiv 1. to race (9:161), 2. to have a running competition (ceh^ ceh ceh-eu)
xeiv tul la to start it running (in this case a machine) (la^ deh^-eu)
=xeiv tuvq, yo= to get filthy
xeiv yoq to make way; move out of the way (as when horses, or carts or the like are coming) (9:161); dodge; evade (50:75) (gaᵛ ma ji^ dahᵛ-eu)

xeivq eight (9:161, 11:65) (yeh^)
xeivq thin (person) (9:161) (yaw baᵥ)
(vb) **xeivq** to be selfish (**neexeivq xeivq** = to be selfish; miserly)
=xeivq, aq= water leech
xeivqgov nei very thin (yaw jeh)
Xeivqla siq August
  xeivqla siq ceil ngavq nao autumn festival (August 15th)
xeivqmieiv half of a kilogram (an older term) (or) **xeivqmeiv** (14:237)
=xeivq, nee= selfish
-- **xeivq, neexeivq** -- to be selfish; miserly

xeif county (Chi) (**Caqsal Xeif** = Caqsal county - 26:3, 46:111)
  xeifceiq a county site (Chi)
xeifdeifhuaf modernization (Chi) (34:12)
  xeifdeifsii contemporary history (Chi) (34:60)
weifgoq a foreign country (57:126)
xeifhhyuhyuf county committee (Chi) (26:26)
xeifsiiq reality; actuality (Chi) (34:61)
xeifza county magistrate; county president (Chi) (9:160, 11:176)
xeifzeiffu county government headquarters (Chi) (11:187)

XI

xil (n) this (clf.) (8:8, 13, 21) (This must have a classifier or number with it - 9:161) (heu (n))
xil! 'sh!' (asking a person to be quiet) (13:6)
xilbuf western (Chi) (26:87)
xildeiq what one has learned or gained (as from what one reads) (Chi) (26:52)
xildyul these; this much (a large amount)
  xildyul dyulssaq this few (a small amount)
  xildyul hholqei among these
  xildyul palbaol this many (large amount)

xildyul sol 1. all of these; 2. only these

xilfal west (Chi) (34:48)

xilgei here; **xilgei a; xaq a** = a shortened form (heu gaˇ)

xilhaoqsiif tomato (Chi) (or) **haoqgo haolgo alsiq; falqiq** (Chi) (maˇ k'eu cehˇ)

xilhe hessaq this small (11:145)

xilhe nei heeq this big (heu hui ni)

Xilheif geiqmif Revolution of 1911 (Chi) (34:4)

xil hhaq this person (heu g'a˯)

xil hholqei scope; limits (50:47) (heu la˰ k'oeˇ)

xiljivq this; these (heu je˯; heu deu˯)

xil mavq these things (3:1, 10:pref.) (heu myaˆ ni)

xilmeil nei this way; like this (as in: 'do like this') (9:161, 11:20) (heu lo˰-ehˇ)

xilmeil ngaoq if it is like this; if this is the case (heu lo˰-ehˇ g'eh naˇ)

xilmeil ngeel leilhe Maybe like this. (Heu lo˰-ehˇ ngeuˇ nga.)

xilmeil qiq nao the other day (29:4) (hu˯ nah)

xil miqzu zuyif new democracy (Chi) (34:7)

xil miqzu zuyif geiqmif new democracy revolution (Chi) (34:13)

xil miav this much (12:125) (heu myaˆ)

xilmiav nei these (9:161) (heu myaˆ ni)

xilmiav nei biov this low

xilmiav nei goq this high (heu mah ni)

xilmiav qiq bil (all) this much (12:125, 41:92)

xilmiav pa miav heeq e so very large (35:9)

-- xil, miavxil -- to aim at something using one eye

xilmiavq nei this many (heu myaˆ ni)

xilmo nei mol this long (heu myah ni)

xilnav meil this much (heu myaˆ ni)

xil naolhao after this (8:8, 13, 21) (k'oeˇ naˇ) (cf. Lahu: chi hk'aw˰ naw¯)

xil niq nao these two or three days (11:87) (heu myaˆ nah) (cf. Lahu: chi nyiˇ nyi = these several days)

xil qa this kind (heu je˯)

xilqil a week (Chi) (9:161, 41:52) (jawˇ nah ti˯ jaw)

Xilqil eif Tuesday (eif = two) (Chi)

Xilqil kuvq nao Saturday (A=Chi)

Xilqil luq Saturday (Chi) (**luq** = six in Chi)

Xilqil nao Sunday (A=Chi)

Xilqil niq nao Tuesday (A=Chi)

Xilqil ngavq nao Friday (A=Chi)

Xilqil qiq nao Monday (A=Chi)

Xilqil saoq nao Wednesday (A=Chi)

Xilqil teil Sunday (Chi) (26:62) (jawˇ nah ngeh nah)

Xilqil wu Friday (**wu** = five) (Chi) (41:52)

Xilqil yuvq nao Thursday (A=Chi)

xil qiq savq these recent days; recently (41:6, 50:89) (cf.: dzeuˇ laˇ-eu˯ heu myaˆ nah)

xilseil sacrifice (Chi) (34:116)

Xilsual banaq Xishuangbanna (or) Sipsongbanna (Chi) (38:1) a tropical prefecture in the extreme southern part of Yunnan Province -- where most of the Akha in China live (Siˇ sawˇ pa^ na)

xilssil hholqei in this century; this generation (50:10)

xil taq this time (9:161) (heu po^)

xil taq luldu at this very moment (30:2) (hehˬ nymˬ-mˇ)

xilwaf to hope (Chi) (34:114) (noeˬ tmˬ-eu)

xilweiq news (Chi) (34:65)

xilxil halhal laughing and joking (Chi) (14:191)

=xil, yaq= gramaphone; record player (Chi)

xil Zaolgoq New China (Chi) (26:22; 57:156)

xil Zaolgoq jeifseiq to build the new China (Chi) (26:22)

xilzeil pyu this side (9:161) (heu paw)

ximeiq ceiljeil workshop in a coal refinery for washing coal (Chi) (26:27)

xiq feces (human and sometimes animal) (9:162) (ceˬ)

=xiq, aqbeil nal= dry nasal discharge

=xiq, aqcivq civq= goat dung

xiqbiav a dung cake (**niuqxiq xiqbiav** = buffalo dung cake) (46:152)

xiqbieiv bieiv to have diarrhea (uˬ ma^ yoeˇ-eu)

xiqduq a toilet (cf.: gaˇ nyiˇ iˇ ku^)

xiq eeltaoq a bucket for dung/ excrement (35:89)

xiqhualgaol a kind of face cream (Chi) (11:17)

=xiq, hhavq= pig dung

xiqjyul germ; bacteria (Chi) (15:50)

=xiq, keeq= dog dung

xiqmaofsiil hhaoqzao a bed with innerspring mattress (A=Chi)

=xiq, miav= eye discharge; secretion

=xiq, moq= horse dung

=xiq, naq= earwax

=xiq, niuq= dung from buffalo/cow

=xiq, saol= iron filings

xiqsiif form; way (Chi) (34:38)

xiqsuv suv diarrhea (uˬ ma^ yoeˇ-eu)

xiqtaoq taoq to be constipated (uˬ ma^ g'ahˇ-eu)

xiqtiaoq to coordinate (Chi) (34:72)

xiq xiq to defecate (dawˬ ceˬ ceˬ-eu)

xiqyaoqciiq an adjective (gram) (Chi)

xiqyif an agreement (Chi) (34:114)

xiqzeif administration (Chi)

xiqzeif gua'li administration; management (Chi) (34:40)

xifnieif faith; belief; conviction (Chi) (34:89) (jah-eu)

XIAO

xiaopiweiq a short, popular essay (Chi)

XII

xiifziiq nature; character (Chi) (34:25)

XO

xo clf. for clothes (9:162) (kahˇ)
xodol duv a bad-omen relation, when a man marries a close relative, or sleeps with a girl to whom he is not married
xo huvq to divorce one's husband
-- xohuvq, miqhuvq -- for husband and wife to divorce
=xo nei, naoq= softly; tenderly

xoq to lock; **xovq** (pf), **xaovq** (mahˬ taw˰ taw˰-eu)
=xoq, baq= jaw
-- xoq, baoqkev -- a lock for a box
xoqbo laqdu wild taro
xoqhhyuf academic degree (as: Ph.D., M.A., B.A., etc.) (Chi)
xoq laol 1. to pen up (9:162) (lahˇ taˬ-eu), 2. to lock up (**xovq laol; xaovq laol** - 35:116)
xoqseil a student (Chi) (11:23) (sahˬ bo˰ dzaw zaˬ)
xoqsoq theory; doctrine (Chi) (34:52)
xoq tovq 1. to close (9:162) (taw˰ tehˬ-eu), 2. to lock (as a door) (or) **xovq tovq**
xoqxaof a school (Chi) (**Xoqxaof halgei nga laq?** = Where is the school?) (9:162, 11:101, 31:3, 41:13) (sahˬ bo˰ dzaw nymˇ) clf. is: **mol**
xoqxaof hhoq to leave school (A=Chi)
xoqxiq to study; learn (Chi) (26:67) (dzaw-eu)

xov clf. for a pair of trousers (11:87) (kahˇ)

xovq 1. to stand; be standing (9:162, 13:3, 26:52) (yaw˰-eu), 2. to lock; **xovq** (pf); **xaovq**
-- xovq, hhaqxovq -- a part of the burial ceremony
xovq laol to shut into; close something into (pf.) (or) **xaovq laol** (35:116) (piˬ tehˬ ahˇ-eu)
-- xovq, taoqtul -- to stand erect
xovq tovq (see: **xoq tovq**)
xovq tul to stand up (50:134) (tuˇ laˇ-eu)

XU

xul 1. to be willing; 2. to agree with (**nol xul maq xul** - do you agree or not?) (**ngal liq xul al** = I also agree - 38:15) (26:58, 45:7, 46:144) (cf.: nui ma tsaˬ-eu), 3. to relax; to loosen (saˇ suˬ ni)
xul to run water (iˇ cu˰ yoeˇ-eu)

(vb) xul likes to (vb) (**Aqbol naoq e zaq xul**. The old man likes to eat soft things.) (11:64) (maw^-eu)
-- **xul, jalxul** -- to whistle
-- **xul, miaoq aol** -- diligent; work hard
-- **xul, saqnei** -- pass through; adopt
xulsifyi a modifier (gram) (Chi)

xu to flow
xu to make rope (9:162, 45:32) **alcav xu** = to make a rope (aˇ ca^ yeu^-eu)
xu to reduce amount; get less (9:162) (shu^-eu)
-- **xu, alcav** -- to make a rope
=**xu, aq**= less than; not many
-- **xudoq, doqxu** -- elliptical sentence
=**xu, eel**= for water to flow
-- **xu, eelquvq** -- water to run; flow
-- **xu, hhe** -- to reduce; decrease
=**xu, naoq**= to be soft (nahˇ yu ni)
=**xu nei, sol**= to smell good (or) **sol xo nei**

XYU

xyuflieif training (as in the army) (Chi) (26:42)

YA

yal hundred (9:163)(yaˇ)
yal easy (9:163, 10:21) (**zaljavq yal e zal hha bi zaq** = must give food easily digested) (yaw aw˯)
yal 1. cheap; inexpensive (9:163) (yaw yaˇ), 2. simple (50:83)
yal mountain field (but also: **xal**. Look under that entry also for terms related to 'mountain fields'.) (yaˇ)
yalbial fallow field; old field (9:163, 26:63) (or) **yalcyuq** (yaˇ sa˯; yaˇ peu˯)
yalcyuq an old field (or) **yalbial**
=yal, daol= mountain field
yaldei irrigated rice field (or) **xaldei; yaldei yalzeil**
yaldei loqheiq lav pao when a newly married couple goes out to the irrigated field at daybreak after marriage, she 'opens' the ditch with her left foot, showing that the fields are hers as well as his (she says: '**Dulma ssaqmiq qal keel beil puv loqheiq lav**')
-- **yaldei, sulqeil** -- marshy fields
yalgoq mosquito (9:163) (caˇ gaw˯)
yalhav a new field (or) **yalnav** (yaˇ na^)
=yal, hhaq= buckwheat field
=yal, hhoq= vegetable field
yalhhyul a tobacco pipe (14:178, 46:176) (gawˇ lu˯; gawˇ tsui˄; shoi˯ yoi baw˯ law)
yalleel nei to be modest (50:135)
yalleiv nei easily (or) **yalzav nei** (9:163, 10:3,24, 26:69) (yaw aw˯ aw˯-ehˇ)
yal mil a million (lam) (1,000,000)
yal milmil ten billion (10,000,000,000)
yalmil sal to look for a field (9:163)
=yal, moq= fields for dead people (land marked off for the dead to cultivate)
yalmuvq muvq to weed a field (yaˇ mo˄ mo˄-eu)
yalnav a new field (or) **yalhav** (yaˇ na^)
yal navq deep terraced fields
yalpieif zafzeil opium war (Chi) (34:3)
yalqaol field hut (13:44) (yaˇ cmˇ)
-- **yalqaol, deima** -- a hut in a terraced field
-- **yal, qu** -- to raise easily
yalsol duv to go to field to work (9:163) (yaˇ smˇ iˇ-eu)
yalsol hhuvq return from field after work (9:163) (yaˇ smˇ g'o˄ laˇ-eu)
yalzav nei easily (or) **yalleiv nei** (yaw aw˯)
=yal, zaol= 1. building and field, 2. private property
yal zeiq 1. cheaper (41:137) (yaˇ dzeh˯), 2. easier

(aw˯ dzeh˯-eu)

yal zeiq gaoq 1. much cheaper, 2. much easier (41:95)

ya to fall down (9:162) (ga ka-eu)

ya a final part. used only in the first person and expressing some kind of emotion, 1. used in affirmative statements, often intensifying the statement (**jav gaoq ya** = there are plenty), 2. used in negative sentences (**Nol Haqniqdoq gee e daov maq bav ya.** Your spoken Hani is not bad. 41:12), 3. in somewhat polite statements (for examples see: 11:98, 133)

(n) ya to form (**haqnil ya** = for frost to form)

yabiav laq caca nei almost broken; fragile

ya ceiv broken off (**Ngaq e peilhaoq peilsiq ya ceiv al.** A button has come off my jacket. 41:31)

-- ya, daoqdaoq -- to make a conclusion; summary

ya dov to drop into (35:92)

-- ya duv, daoqlul -- a prolapsed rectum

ya duv Haqniq the 'lag behind' Hani (spoken of them in relation to the Akha who went across the Lancang/ Mekong river) (or) **ga dov Haqniq**

ya duv laq e to lag behind (26:2) (meh˯ nah˯ ga ya˄-eu)

=ya, eiq= yes; okay

-- ya, haqnil -- for frost to form

ya heil to fall down (or) **xa heil** (9:159) (ga ka-eu)

=yahuvq, neel= next year (& see below)

=yahuvq, nyul= next year (& see above)

yahyuq tobacco; cigarette (or) **yahyuq hyuqniul** (9:163) (ya k'aw˯)

yahyuq balluvq tobacco pipe (used by either male or female) (gaw˅ lu˯ = used by Akha males; gaw˅ tsui˄ = used by Akha females)

yahyuq baoqdel (see: **yahyuq baoqlo**)

yahyuq baoqlo water tobacco pipe made of bamboo (9:163, 11:148) (or) **yahyuq baoqdel** (shoi˯ yoi baw˯ law)

yahyuq hyuqyei tobacco (14:171) (ya k'aw˯)

yahyuq suv to smoke tobacco (ya k'aw˯ daw˅-eu)

yahyuq ziiyeil a cigarette (B=Chi) (50:213)

-- ya, hhoq -- to set down again

ya jeivq to crumble

-- ya, kyuq -- to be tired

ya leeq to fall down; to drop (9:163, 13:48) (ga ka-eu)

ya'leil final particle of affirmation

-- ya, lolhho -- for a lymph node to swell

-- ya maq dav, maq -- not too high, not too low (in the middle)

-- ya, naolma -- for the sun to set

ya neevq to drown (ga nui˄ seh˄-eu)

Yaniq Akha (living in Xishuangbanna) (or) Aini (A˯ ka˯)

=ya, nol= you (plural)
=ya, ngal= we (exclusive)
-- ya, ngaoq -- to be very cold
ya puvq to fall into water (or) **leeq puvq** (ga pu^-eu)
-- ya, qu -- to be tame
-- ya sil miv, naolma -- (see full)
-- ya, ssaq -- to abort a baby
ya tao to drop down (45:61)
ya xa to drop down (11:216) (ga ka-eu)
ya yi to get down (or) **ga yi** (iˇ ka-eu)
yazeil a remnant; survivor (50:19)
-- ya, zei -- to fall into

yaq 1. to accuse someone (9:164, 14:234), 2. to curse someone (such as: 'may you be struck by lightning; may you be bitten by a black viper', etc.) (ya˯ k'ehˇ ya˯-eu)
-- yaq part. indicating a question (**keel yaq** = is it delicious? **kyuq yaq** = are you tired?) (la˯; loˇ)
yaq a here (**Nol yaq a lal.** = You come here.) (11:143) (heu gaˇ)
-- yaq, aqzuq -- to get rid of worms (as in a buffalo) with magical words
-- yaq, aqzuq bi -- to use magical curse words to cure a disease
-- yaq, bi -- (see full)
yaqcei a musket (old type of gun) (Chi)
Yaqceiq a man's name (younger brother of **Yaqdee**) (35:14)
yaqciiq porcelain (Chi) (26:74)
Yaqdee a man's name (older brother of **Yaqceiq**) (35:14)
yaqduvq duvq to denounce; condemn (50:150)
yaqgaol toothpaste (Chi) (26:73) (seu˯ jo^ ja^ g'a˯)
yaqhaol bugle (Chi)
yaqhuq malcavq glass bottle (maˇ tsa^)
yaqhhaol pickaxe (Chi)
Yaq Keqsal name of a man (14:144)
yaqkul armpit odor (9:164)
Yaq Laosiil Teacher Yang (**Yaq** = surname) (54:106)
yaqliq 1. pressure (Chi) (34:15), 2. solar calendar (Chi) (41:114)
yaqmee Yamen, a government office in feudal China (Chi) (35:48)
yaq miq to put a curse on someone (46:212) (ya˯ k'ehˇ ya˯-eu)
yaqmoq a person who knows how to perform black magic
yaqmoq an offering as part of burial ceremony (ya˯-eu -- as in: a˯ nyo˯ ya˯-eu)
yaqmoq diq to kill a buffalo for a dead person (or) **yaqmoq seivq** (a˯ nyo˯ ya˯-eu)
yaqmoq seivq (see: **yaqmoq diq**)
Yaqniq the Yani (Akha) branch of the Hani (46:79) (note: this is probably a corruption of **Za˯ nyi˯**

which is the old term for the Akha.)
yaqpeiq basin (Chi) (11:23, 30) ('foreigner's basin')
yaqqiv soap (or) **feiqcaovq** (Chi) (saˇ byaˬ; saˬ buˬ)
yaqsaoq toothbrush (Chi); **yaqsuaq**
yaqsuaq a toothbrush (Chi) (41:33); **yaqsaoq**
yaqxil gramaphone; rècord player (Chi)
yaqyiul byuqsiq potato (Chi) (yaˬ yiˇ mawˬ coeˇ) (6:168, 10:3)

yav to sweep (9:164) (ya^-eu)
yavcev a broom of bamboo branches (9:164) (ma saˬ ya^ pyawˇ)
-- **yav, hoqtavq** -- to sweep the floor
yav hhuvq to bury with a broom (by covering with dirt and dust) (ya^ kaˬ-eu)
yav leev to sweep clean (38:23) (ya^ lui^-eu; ya^ shawˇ-eu)
=**yav, loq**= lily
=**yav nei, muv**= disorderly
=**yav, neivqguv neivq**= drug used to set broken bones
yavngeeq a hoe made of wood for scraping grain into piles (38:33) (cf.: la‸ ngeuˬ)
yavpyul a broom (9:164) (ya^ pyawˇ)
yav sol to sweep clean (26:112, 46:85) (ya^ shawˇ-eu)
yav zavq to walk around looking for food (po^ dzaˬ-eu)

yavq 1. to stay overnight (2:60) (ya‸-eu), 2. to force (50:10)
yavq clf. for number of nights staying someplace (9:164) (miˇ)
yavq to press on (Chi)
yavq gaol to subject someone to discipline (50:65)

yafpi a sample (Chi)

YAO

yaol building (8:1, 46:119) (nymˇ; ymˇ = CA)
yaol clf. for building, house (11:86) (nymˇ; ymˇ = CA)
yaol receiver of the action (8:1, 6) (-ahˇ)
=**yaol, bavq**= 1. palanquin, 2. pack saddle
yaolbiav hut (or) **yaolcyuq** (yaˇ cmˇ)
yaolcyuq 1. hut (or) **yaolbiav** (yaˇ cmˇ), 2. old broken house (or) **xaolcyuq** (nymˇ nymˇ cehˇ)
yaol hoqbyu roof of house (nymˇ mˬ)
yaol hoqbyu daoqma ridgepole in a house (or) **xaol hoqbyu daoqma**
(vb) **yaolliq** already (vb) (11:219)
yaolma main building (house) (9:163) (nymˇ ma)
yaolpiaq eaves (9:163)
yaolqeq to request or demand something (as from an official or in an economic sense) (26:46, 34:38)

(Chi)
yaolssaq a small building attached to the main building (9:164) (nymˇ za˯)

yao to avoid direct contact (**Yoqpaq keeqma hha yao nga**. Father and daughter-in-law should avoid direct contact.)
=yao, daq= guest

=yaoq, bei= dragon
-- yaoq nei, eeldaol -- waves to form

yaovma cicada (or) **gaoma** (46:161)

=yaovq, yo= 1. form; appearance; shape (50:189), 2. attitude (as one's attitude toward something or someone)

YE

yeldiei merit (Chi) (34:52)
yelxef excellent; the best (Chi) (26:48, 100)

-- ye nei, teil sal -- pleasant sound
yeqil tuqxiq to set the term of imprisonment (Chi) (50:200)

yeqceil postman's car (Chi) (50:199)
yeqdieifjiq post & telecommunications office (Chi) (50:199) (and see: **yeqjyuq**)
yeqjiqdyuf guerrilla forces; a guerrilla detachment (Chi) (50:199)
yeqjyuq post office (Chi)(26:78) (and see: **yeqdieifjiq**)
yeqpeif the right (pol. speaking); the right wing (Chi) (50:200) (or) **yefpeif**
yeqpiaof a postage stamp (Chi) (50:199)
yeqxiq a parade; march; demonstration (Chi) (50:200)
yeqyif to hesitate (Chi)

yevq to be drunk (9:165, 46:149) (jiˇ ba˯ yeh˄-eu)
yevq to twist; wrench (9:165) (yeu˄-eu)
yevq to be convenient
yevq cavq to be twisted on (as nuts twisted on to bolts) (26:119)
-- yevq, dol -- to drink to intoxication
-- yevq, eil -- to distort; misrepresent
-- yevq, lavqbavq -- to wrestle
=yevq ngaoq, aqlavq lavq= to arm-wrestle
yevq teiq to clamp down on
yevq tov to twist to death (as the neck of a chicken) (38:15) (yeu˄ seh˄-eu)
-- yevq, wuqduq yevq -- to shake one's head (here in wonderment or disagreement)
yevq yevq nei strutting (35:35)

-- **yevq, zilbaq** -- to be drunk

yef right deviation (Chi) (34:91) (political designation)
yefpeif the right wing; a right deviationist (Chi) (political designation) (or) **yeqpeif**
yefqi teqxaq zuyif right deviation capitulation clique (Chi) (34:6) (political designation)

YEI

yeil broad; spacious; wide (9:164) (yaw je˅)
yeil clf. for a load one can carry on back (9:164), for sacks and bags (as of rice) (11:152, 211, 33:3) (yeh˅)
yeil'a salnei tradition (50:26)
yeil'a salnei jiqmuq traditional items (as in a performance) (B=Chi)
yeilbei 1. historical (46:216), 2. to gather history (50:26)
yeilbei bei to create; establish (46:90) (cf.: a˅ dahˬ beh-eu)
yeilbei galma the original way; the old customs; the historical way (46:92)
yeilbei laqnaq conditions of reality (50:97)
yeilbei maq beibei without precedent in history; unprecedented (50:154)
yeilbei miqnieiq ancient affairs (creation etc.) (50:97)
-- **yeilbei, Miqyeil** -- customs and traditions from **Aqpyuq Miqyeil** (God)
yeilbei salbei beginning of the world (50:97)
yeilceiq luck (cf.: guiˬ lahˬ)
=yeil, ciiq= close relatives and friends
yeildao nei to be calm in one's heart; patient (50:131)
-- **yeildaonei; nui ma** -- to be calm in one's heart; patient
yeildeivq inherent; innate (50:166)
yeil deivq saqsal dei ecological balance (50:151)
yeilgaq a story; a legend (13:19, 26:94, 32:3, 50:149) (aˬ poeˬ dawˬ oe˅)
yeilgaq doqkol an epic (50:153)
yeilgaq dudaq legend's story (50:149)
yeilgaq gee to tell a story (13:19)
=yeil, haq= a dhole; a type of wild dog
yeilheiq affairs related to marriage
yeilhhaoq inkstone (Chi)
yeiljol a cycle of time (as of days) (35:116) (cf.: tiˬ yeh˅; tiˬ jaw)
yeilkav nei to be polite (50:135)
Yeilkuq zaq to celebrate the June festival; **Sseilkuq zaq**
yeillaol haoq the place where ancestors are
yeillaol haoq eelbi for a barren woman to have a

spirit priest make an offering for her of one duck (from her brothers) and a hen and rooster (from her husband) at the village water source, in order to become pregnant
Yeillaoq Aqhhol an ancestor of **Hhaqma** (sacred grove)
yeillo loma meil very, very wide (11:59) (zawˇ jeˇ-eu)
  yeillo nei very wide (9:164) (jeˇ lo ni)
  yeillo pa lo nei very wide (11:58) (jeˇ lo ni)
-- **yeillul gee, doqsii** -- to speak
yeilma a big load (33:3) (yehˇ ma)
-- **yeilmeeq, yeilsal** -- good tradition
yeil meil yeil to be patient in one's heart; to have a 'wide heart'
=**yeil, mei**= a pestle of a rice pounder
Yeilmoq Aqma 'mother nature'
yeilquvq pieiq lal for **Aqpyuq Miqyeil** to punish someone
Yeil sal one (or more) supernatural beings (**zyuq Yeil ssol sal nei bivq**) (cf. Miqyeil; and cf. Lahu: G'ui˯ sha)
yeilsal peace; to be at peace (50:1, 71)
yeilsal yeilmeeq good tradition (50:199)
yeilyiq to be addicted to smoking (dawˇ dzaw ta˯-eu)

yei cycle of days or years (**qiq yei** = 13 days or yrs., **niq yei** = 25 days or yrs.) (11:198) (ti˯ yeh)
yei more (**Zaq e bi tuq, dol e bi yei**. 35:43)
yei to save some food (50:87)
yei e **tyul taq** at one's convenience (or) **caq e tyul taq**
yeigeif eyesight (Chi) (26:111)
yeigo a deed of merit (Chi) (11:30)
=**yei, kal**= crops
=**yei nei, lo**= slowly
-- **yei nei, teilsal** -- a sound coming from far away
-- **yei, teil** -- mid-tone; mid-level tone (or) **teil hhaol** (teˇ yeu; teˇ g'ahˇ - note: the latter signifies the high tone in Akha)

yeiq slice; cut; saw (9:164) (yeh˯-eu)
yeiq to burn (9:164) (mi˯ dza˯ do˰-eu) (**miqkoq bavq yeiq** = to add wood to the fire)
yeiq strict; severe (Chi) (34:56)
yeiq money (or) **biav** (6:208) (bya^)
yeiq ceiv to cut down; cut off (9:165, 50:87) (yeh˯ tseh^-eu)
Yeiqdaf Neeciiv New Year's day (A=Chi) (50:201)
Yeiqfaol Yuanfeng (an ancient Chinese kingdom) (Chi) (46:84)
yeiqgeiq strict (Chi) (or) **yeiq; yeiqmiq** (all Chi)
yeiqheiq a mark in wood made from sawing or cutting
yeiqhuvq sickle with saw-like blade (9:165, 11:137) (yeh˯ k'o˰)

Yeiqjalxeif e Yaqgeil xal the YangJie Township in Yuanjiang County (a place where Hani live) (46:91)
yeiqjef to research (Chi) (po^ dzaw-eu)
yeiqjif severe; stern (Chi) (34:89)
yeiqkuq harsh; bitter (Chi) (34:97)
yeiqli principle (Chi) (50:201)
yeiqliaof raw material (Chi) (50:201)
yeiqma sickle (9:165) (yeh˯ ma) (in Ak. this means: a saw)
yeiqmiq strict (Chi) (34:84)
-- **yeiq, moqseiq** -- to trim horse's hoof so as to put on a horseshoe
yeiqnao today (9:165) (i˯ nah) (cf. Burmese)
  yeiqnaohuvq this year (9:165) (tsui˰ nui^ k'o˰)
  yeiqnao naohav just today (41:40)
yeiq nuv to cut up (or) **yeiq ceiv; yeiq zei; zaol kyuq** (yeh˯ tseh^-eu)
  yeiq nuv yeiq ya to cut to pieces (yeh˯ pa^-eu)
yeiq pao to cut open (operate) (50:88) (peh˰-eu)
yeiqseiq color (Chi) (41:148)
yeiqsii seifhyuf primitive society (Chi) (50:201)
yeiqsuaf marshal; supreme commander (Chi) (50:201)
Yeiqyaq Yuanyang, a county in the south of Yunnan Province (Chi) (41:11) (and see below)
  Yeiqyaqxieiq Yuanyang county
yeiqyei opium (Chi) (ya˯ yeh = Bur. Ak., ya piˇ = Thai Ak.)
yeiqyil a vowel (Chi)
yeiqyil ziifmu a letter (vowel) (Chi)
yeiqzaof nei to be serious; grave (Chi) (34:85)
yeiq zei to cut away (or) **beiq zei**
yeiqzeiq principle (Chi) (50:201)
yeiqziidaf atom bomb (Chi) (50:201)
  yeiqziineiq atomic energy (Chi) (50:201)

yeiv to flower (**alyeiv yeiv**) (aˇ yeh^ yeh^-eu)
yeiv clf. for a flower (9:165) (yeh^)
yeiv not firm (ma˯ zi˰)
-- **yeivcaoq, alyeiv** -- flowering shrubs
-- **yeivjoq, alyeiv** -- withered flowers
=yeiv, kal= a crop in bloom (kaˇ yeh^ yeh^ laˇ-eu)
yeivleiv leiv nei not firm; shaky (ma˯ zi˰-eu)
=yeiv, lyul= (see full)
=yeiv, meil= lilac flowers
=yeiv, moq hao= flowery design on horse's head
yeivniuv stamen (in a flower)
yeivpuq yeivluq 'let a thousand flowers blossom' (idea from Chinese) (50:4)
-- **yeiv, siil** -- golden flowers
-- **yeiv, siilyeiv** -- golden flowers blossom
yeivzyuq a big flower ('king flower') (46:155)

yeifxaof college and university (Chi) (50:201)
yeifza 1. president of a college, 2. president of a law court (Chi) (50:201)

yeifzii a courtyard (Chi)

YI

yil to go (down) (pronounced 'il') (9:165, 11:40) (Note: to go up is li, but pronounced like Ak: le) (iˇ-eu)
Yilcessaq the Yeche people (a branch of the Hani) (46:78, 170, 181)
-- yil, dov -- enter down
yilhoq hoq sound of some high-spirited activity (14:156)
-- yilhovq nei, miav -- sunken eyes
-- yil, hhuvq -- go back from higher place
yiljiq syllable (Chi)
Yilkuq a hero sent to the Hani area by **Miqyeil** (46:202)
yilkuq zaq (see: **kuqzaq zaq; sseilkuq zaq**) (46:183) (yehˇ ku˯ dza˯-eu)
yil lal coming and going (iˇ iˇ laˇ laˇ)
yil lal e alzil a migratory bird (or) **yil yil lal lal e alzil**
yil lal maq ceiv in an endless stream (50:111)
yil lal maq loq do not know where he/she is from (50:101)
=yil, laq= a male buffalo
yilleiq yilpiq meil wasteful
yil maq yil yil no matter what, go! (a˯ jo^-ehˇ law k'aw˄ iˇ)
yilmeil nei because of that (9:165) (k'oeˇ miˇ neh)
Yilnaq a Dai (Tai) woman's name (14:228)
yil pal to marry another man (smˇ miˇ iˇ paˇ-eu)
Yilsal milcaq Yisha, a town in Honghe County
yilseil doctor (Chi) (10:5, 26:99) (sa˯ la˯ g'o˯; maw˯-awˇ)
Yilsul Jesus (Chi) (Ye˯suˇ)
-- yil, sulmil -- for a woman to get married
yilsuf a factor; an element (Chi) (34:55)
-- yil, tao -- to go into from a higher to lower place
=yil, teiq= to have a hurry-up marriage
-- yil, wuqdeiq -- to have diarrhea; to have loose bowels
yilxaoq hero (Chi) (41:4)
yilyao to be heroic; brave (Chi) (34:108)
yilyeif jol be in the hospital; be hospitalized (Chi) (50:216) (or) **yilyieif jol**
yil yil lal lal to go and come repeatedly
yil yil lal lal e alzil migratory bird
yil yil meil ngyul went there again and again and cried
Yilyi English (Chi)
Yilyidoq English language (A=Chi)
yilyieif hospital (Chi) (10:5, 26:87) (or) **yilyeif** (14:228, 50:216)

yi'faq grammar (Chi)
yipieif film; movie (Chi) (50:198)
yisiif film and TV programs (Chi) (50:199)
-- yi, tao -- to come in from a higher place
yiweiq language & literature (Chi) (26:21, 50:201) (and see: **yiyeiq**)
yixa affect; influence (Chi) (50:199) (or) **qeiqliq** (Chi)
yiyeiq language (Chi) (and see: **yiweiq**)
yiyeiq xoqjal linguist; philologist (Chi) (50:201)
yiyil a raincoat (Chi) (26:96)

yiqbal in general (Chi); **yiqbal nei**
yiqbal gyulliq universal law (Chi) (34:45)
yiqciif shark fin (Chi) (26:118) (or) **ngaqdaol**
Yiqcuq the Yi people (Chi)
Yiqduvssaq Indians; the people of India (Chi)
Yiqhaq a Dai woman's name (14:222)
yiqjeif comments (**Nol yiqjeif jav maq jav**? Do you have any comments to make about this? - 26:29) (Chi)
yiq keiq a quarter of an hour (Chi)
yiqliaq gaolliaq rice taxes (Chi)
yiqloq hoqdaof recreational activities (Chi) (34:65)
Yiqnaq Vietnam (Chi) (50:202)
=yiq, piaq= civet cat
yiqqeiq idea; method (Chi) (11:179, 46:99), measure; step (29:3) (cf.: nui noe$_{\vee}$)
-- yiqqeiq, geeldiq -- fighting tactics
yiqqeiq maq hev hhaq jil to waste one's strength (labor) for lack of a method
yiqqeiq qeiq duv to develop a method (50:148)
Yiqsa Honghe county (Hani name); **Yiqsav**
Yiqsav Honghe county (Hani name) (11:130); **Yiqsa**
yiqsiil the meaning (Chi) (14:142)
yiqya nutrition (Chi) (34:68)
yiq yuan one yuan (coin) (Chi) (41:131) (note: in Hani this is "big yuan", one of which equals two "little yuan".)
yiqzaq a kind of weed (that is sharp) (14:173)

yiv to come (down) (9:166, 11:40) (oe-eu)
=yiv, hhuvq= come back from higher place

=yivq, aq= termite
yivq sso meilnaol older and younger brothers and sisters (14:145) (a$_{\vee}$ yui$_{\wedge}$ haw$^{\vee}$-eu meh$^{\vee}$ nm$^{\vee}$)
yivq zeiq older than

yif 100 million (Chi) (11:65, 26:75) (**mil mil** = Hani)
yifbif dayeiq probationary Party member (Chi) (50:201)
yifbif qil probationary period (Chi) (50:201)

yif dav to print with colors (Chi)
yifdaof sports (Chi) (50:203)
yifdaofhyuf sports meet; games (Chi) (50:203)
yifhyuf ziifduf parliamentarianism (Chi) (34:48)
yifjeif a view; opinion (Chi) (cf.: nui noe⌄)
yifjeif nalhaq solicit an opinion; ask or seek an opinion (A=Chi) (50:210)
yifmu vowels (Chi) (2:60)
yifsiil meaning (Chi)
yifsiiq xiqteif ideology (Chi) (34:66)
yifsul gaolsiil a transport company (Chi) (50:203)
yifsuqjal an artist (Chi) (50:197)
yifsuaq to print (Chi) (2:60) (sah⌄ bo^ ya⌄-eu)
yifxiq jilziif running mechanism (as in the economy) (Chi) (34:38)
yifyif meaning; significance (Chi) (34:66)
yifzeif to participate in political affairs (Chi) (34:53)
yifziif mental power by which a person can direct thoughts and actions of other people (50:196)

YIU

yiul to take (yuˇ-eu)
yiul jiq excellent rank (Chi)
yiul ssaoq to divert; misappropriate; embezzle (50:124)
yiul taq to put (yuˇ ta⌄-eu)
yiulxiuf outstanding; excellent (Chi) (9:165)

yiuqjiq post office (Chi) (9:165) (or) **yeqdieifjiq**

yiuvq to sleep (9:165) (yu^-eu) (**yiuvq e maq meeq jol e maq sal** = could not sleep or eat well -- as when worried - 38:34)
-- **yiuvq, aqhhuv** -- to go into a trance
-- **yiuvq, bi** -- to put to sleep
yiuvq deil the time to sleep (26:46) (yu^ yam⌄)
yiuvqduq 1. a sleeping place, 2. a bedroom (or) **bavlov** (yu^ du⌄)
yiuvq hhal a cradle (or) **ssaqguq yiuvq hhal**
yiuvqhhaoq a pillow (or) **wuqhhaoq** (yu^ g'm⌄)
yiuvqhhaoq hhaoq to put a pillow under one's head (as when lying down)
-- **yiuvq, javqleel nei** -- to be fast asleep
yiuvqma mother-in-law (9:165); **yoqma** (pf.) (tsawˇ maw⌄; a⌄ maw⌄ = for either mo. or fa.-in-law in Ak.)
yiuvqmav a dream (9:166) (yu^ ma^)
yiuvqmav liq taq mav zaq 'don't even dream of that' (i.e., don't dream of doing that, etc.) (38:8) (yu^ ma^ k'aw^ ta⌄ ma^)
yiuvqmav mav to dream (9:166) (yu^ ma^ ma^-eu)
yiuvqmav mavbeeq bad dreams (14:159)
yiuvqmav mavdyul dyul a bad dream; a nightmare

(11:61) (yu˰ ma^ ma^ doeˇ-eu)

yiuvqmav mavsal sal dream world; dream land (50:15)

yiuvqmav mavtuv tuv to have a bad dream (50:114)

yiuvqmu mu 1. to sleepwalk (9:166, 11:433) (mya^ to^ to^-eu), 2. to be in a coma (or) **silhheivq hheivq**

yiuvqnyuq maq haq don't oversleep; without oversleeping (18:1)

yiuvqnyuq tal to wake up (9:166) (noe˯ laˇ-eu)

yiuvqngyul ngyul 1. to feel sleepy (9:166) (yu˰ yoeˇ-eu), 2. to doze off

yiuvqpaq father-in-law (9:166); **yoqpaq** (pf.) (tsawˇ maw˯; a˯ maw˯ = either fa.- or mo.-in-law in Ak.)

yiuvqsal naciq sleeping medicine (50:1)

yiuvq sil to be sound asleep; fast asleep (9:166, 11:219, 13:33) (yu˰ k'a^-eu)

yiuvqsul to wake up (yu˰ noe˯ noe˯ laˇ-eu)

yiuvqsul tul to wake up from sleep and get up (35:73) (noe˯ laˇ-awˇ tuˇ laˇ-eu)

YO

yol sheep (yawˇ)

=yol, aq= sheep

-- **yolbu, aqyol** -- a ram (male sheep)

-- **yolhao, aqyol** -- wool

yol huvq sheep year (yawˇ ti˯ k'o˰)

yoljil meil truly (14:178)

yollal soul (see also: **sullal**) (clf.= mol) (13:3) (sa˰ laˇ)

-- **yolma, aqyol** -- a ewe (female sheep)

yol nao sheep day (9:167) (yawˇ ti˯ nah)

=yol nei, navq= very deeply

=yol oq, al= an interjection

yolqoq friend (caw˯) (8:1, 9:167) (cf. Lahu: yaˇ chawˇ)

yolqoq gee to make friends with; go along with (caw˯ caw˯-eu)

yolqoq qoq to make friends (13:39) (caw˯ caw˯-eu)

yoltaol yolyal myriads; thousands and hundreds (14:212) (yaˇ tahˇ)

yolyal high mountain field (9:167) (dahˇ yaˇ)

-- **yolyal, yoltaol** -- myriads; thousands and hundreds

yol zeq sheep hour (B=Chi)

yo- prefix of adjectives (**yosol** = clean; **yomeeq** = good, etc.)

yoba yoba meil many of; a lot of (35:48) (g'aw˯ mya ni)

yobeeq piav soq bring order out of chaos (50:15)

yobei the start; the begining (9:166, 50:25) (yaw beh; aˇ dah˯ beh-eu)

-- **yobo, hhaqhav** -- a man with unusual strength

yobuvq 1. clumsy, 2. rotten (yaw bu˰)

yobuvq pievq to go bad (as fruit) (bu˰-iˇ-eu)

yobyu a hole (9:166, 46:201) (yaw boe)
 -- **yobyu, kaoqpiul** -- a sweat gland; pore in the skin
 yobyu keq byu to cut open a hole (yeh˯ pah-eu)
 yobyu leiq byu to make a hole (9:166) (maˇ boe boe-eu)
yocavq to be bad; evil (46:131) (yaw ca˰)
 yocavq duv to be evil; immoral
 yocavq guq zaq to have bad luck (cf.: gui˯ lah˯ ma˯ mui˯)
yoceq private property
-- **yoceil, yomeeq** -- outstanding; excellent
yocul fat (9:166) (yaw tsuˇ)
yodaoq leev the end ('tail') (50:87)
yodev a solid (not a liquid or gas) (50:64)
yodev dev to solidify (50:121)
yodeivq alive (yaw deh˰)
 yodeivq deivq to be alive (in 26:86) (yaw deh˰ deh˰-eu)
 yodeivq ssil deivq to sing about life (46:170)
yoduq a camp (50:209)
yodyul bad (11:26) (yaw doeˇ)
yogaoq gaoq meil a great multitude (a thousand and one) (or) **taol so aqyal** (tsawˇ ha˯ ba˯ ma˰)
yogee to be dry (11:55) (yaw gui)
yogov gov to be limp and weak
yogov govssaq very weak (people, countries, etc.) (34:4) (g'a˯ ju˯-eu)
yohav a cruel person (cf.: yaw k'a^ = strong; difficult) (nui ma yaw doeˇ)
yohaol public property; a collective (50:61, 79)
 yohaol ceil crops which are given as taxes (50:61)
 yohaol meeqduq 1. collective welfare (50:79), 2. in the public interest (50:61)
 yohaol miqnieiq public affairs; public works (50:61)
 yohaol ssaoq piul public welfare fund (50:62)
 yohaol taq ssaoq piul accumulation of a socialist economics collective (50:61)
 yohaol yaol kyuq lal social effects of pollution; environmental pollution (50:61)
 yohaol zeiq public property (50:61)
 yohaol zeiqsal collective economics (50:79)
yohe maq naol tasteless; unpalatable (50:180)
yoheeq big; large (9:166) (yaw hui˯)
yoheiq pao the prologue; prelude ('open the gate')
yohhyul aqzil love songs (ga˯-eu caˇ daw˯)
yojal old (as cloth) (11:26) (in 26:74: **yoja**)
yoja pants; trousers (13:4, 46:193)
yojaq (or) **yozaq** beautiful (3:1) (yaw ja˯) (and see: **zaq; huzaq** etc.)
yojil surely; certainly; true; real (11:203, 50:209) (maˇ maˇ ni ngeuˇ meh)
 yojil galquv realistic methods (50:97)
 yojil jil to be genuine

yojil meeq heiq actual effect; substantial results (50:153)
yojil meil regularize; standardize (50:211)
yojil meil jav existentialism; existing reality (50:97)
-- yojil, miqnieiq -- the actual situation
yojil ngeel al it is certainly true (38:91)
yojil yoliq truth (50:209)
yojil yoliq daltevq criterion of truth (50:209)
yoju ju meil a lot of (g'aw˅ mya ni)
yokyul a clever man (30:1) (**miqkyul** = a clever woman) (yaw gahˇ = clever)
yo'lal 1. fame; reputation; soul; 'face'; 'name' (**yo'lal aoq zaq** = to ruin someone's reputation) (13:21, 46:122, 171), 2. a soul; **sullal**
yoliq 1. rule; custom (9:167) (zahˇ, cf. Lahu = aw˅ liˇ), 2. to be polite (follow the customs) (50:104) (or) **yo'liq**
yoliq liqma fundamental law (50:58)
yoliq lo'qo regulation; policy (based on Chi) (50:2)
yoliq lo'qo aol to follow the policy (based on Chi) (50:2)
yoliq maq za illegal; unlawful (50:49)
yoliq maq za meil laolcyuq to keep something away unlawfully (50:49)
yoliq maq za meil nieivqkuv take into custody illegally (50:49)
-- yoliq, yojil -- truth
yoliq za rational; reasonable; equitable (50:71)
-- yoma, miqnieiq -- most important tasks
=yo mavq, aq= they (a˅ yaw˄ ma˄)
yomeeq good (9:167) (yaw mui˅)
yomeeq ceil e baffaq optimum method for choosing (D=Chi) (50:199)
yomeeq yoceil outstanding; excellent (50:199)
yomeeq yosal good and happy things (50:114)
=yo, miq= daughter and son
yomiaq a large quantity
yomiaq qiq baol most of the group (26:83); for the most part (38:6) (mya˅ mya˅ ti˅ pa^)
yomiaq qiq bil most of; for the most part (10:pref) (mya˅ ni-a˅)
yomiaol 1. name (9:167) (tsawˇ myahˇ), 2. a concept (or) **keifnieif** (Chi)
yomiao cooked (not raw) (9:167, 11:26) (yaw ja˄)
yonao a day (46:108) (aˇ nah)
yonao gee taq to fix a date (50:38)
yonao meeq propitious day; lucky day ('good day') (nah mui˅)
yoneiq not too new; not too old (ma˅ shui˄ ma˅ oeˇ)
yonil 1. small (yaw nyiˇ), 2. red (yaw neˇ)
yoniq doqlo words with a closed meaning (50:89)
yoniq yoqcol close relatives (50:89)
=yo pa yo nei, sal= very happily

yopyuq miaoqgaoq baoqkev a treasure box (26:73)
yopyuq naqgaq news tidbits; filler (50:209)
yo'qa kind; type; variety (50:214)
yosaq maq tavq rough; boorish (50:28)
yosaol 1. owner; householder (9:168), 2. a host (yaw sah˅)
yosaol aqda 1. male head of household, 2. husband (yaw sah˅ a˯ da)
yosaol aqma 1. female head of household; mistress of the house, 2. hostess (9:168) (yaw sah˅ a˯ ma)
yosaol nieivq pal ownership to change hands
yosiivq new; fresh (9:168, 10:6) (yaw shui˄)
yosiivq zaol bring forth new ideas (50:26)
yosiivq zaol duv to invent something new
yosuv nei 1. smoothly (38:37), 2. happily
yossaq living things (45:61)
yossaoq ssaoq to condense (50:121)
yotaol yomil myriads; thousands and tens of thousands (46:76)
yotaol yoyal hundreds of thousands (45:57)
yoteil 1. a sound (9:168, 50:150) (te˅ sa˅), 2. one's reputation (34:28), 3. pronunciation (32:3)
yoteil dav famous (50:216)
yoteil buvq phonetic notation (50:216)
yoteil teilma loudly (26:61) (te˅ sa˅ yaw g'ah˅)
yoteil teilnaoq softly (26:67) (te˅ sa˅ yaw nah˯)
-- **yo teiq, ssaqyo** -- a single son; only son
yotovq seasonable; the right time (46:110) (a˅ yam˯ tsa˯-eu)
yoxeiv 1. dirty, 2. dirt (9:168, 10:27) (yaw jaw˄) (**yoxeiv taq bi leivq** - don't let it get dirty)
yoxeiv tuvq to get filthy (la^ jaw˄)
yoxeivq 1. miserly, 2. to be thin
-- **yoxeivq, neema** -- miserly-hearted
yoyal 1. fields (13:20) (ya˅), 2. place; land (or) **mil** (50:35), 3. easy (yaw aw˯), 4. cheap (yaw ya˅), 5. a hundred; hundreds (4:40)
yoyaovq 1. form; appearance; shape (50:189), 2. attitude (as one's attitude toward something or someone) (or) **neenyuq; teifduf** (Chi) (nui noe˯)
yoyul old (things) (yaw oe˅)
yozaq beautiful (or) **yojaq** (yaw ja˯; yaw mui˯)
yozaoq 1. raw (not cooked) (9:168, 11:26, 35:61) (yaw jm˯), 2. wet (yaw a˯)
yozaoq yomiaol general knowledge (50:21)
yozeiq 1. left over; extra (9:168) (yaw dzeh˯), 2. more than (**ssaqnaoq deivq e ceil nao yozeiq** = when it is more than 10 days after the birth of the baby) (yaw dzeh˯)
yozeiq aol duv to go beyond (or) **aqzeiq aol dav**

yoq 1. to pass (as time) (9:167, 13:6), 2. to cross (**lolbaq yoq** = to cross a river, **eq yoq** = to carry across; **galma yoq** = to cross a road; **lolbaq yoq** = to cross a stream (tseh^-eu), 3. to pass through

yoq to make way

yoq oneself (**yoq gyuq yoq guv** = one cries and frightens oneself -- i.e., as a barking deer being frightened by its own bark)

yoq part. showing imperative (let's) (9:167) (kaˇ-euˇ)

yoq (see: **yoqhhaq** = oneself) (yaw˯ ha)

-- **yoq, alzaol bavq** -- for the coffin to be lifted over kneeling children and grandchildren

=**yoq, aq**= he/she/it

=**yoq, aq**= an interjection

-- **yoq, aol** -- to surpass

yoq aol yoq duv self-reliance; regeneration through one's own efforts (50:219)

-- **yoq aol, yoq miaoq** -- duty; obligation; responsibility

yoq aol yoq saq one suffers from what one does (cf. 'he who plays with fire gets burned') (50:174)

yoq aol yoq zaq self sufficiency (50:219)

-- **yoq, bev** -- to throw something over something else (such as a river)

yoq bee one's own family (yaw˯ ha-eu˯ peh˯ za˯)

yoqbu bu private prosecution of a case (50:219)

yoq ca yoq eil self-criticism (50:219)

yoqcol a close friend or relative (9:167) (cf. Lahu; yaˇ chawˇ)

yoqdaq meil wasted (no benefit) (11:115)

-- **yoq, deiq** -- to push away

-- **yoq dol, yoq hovq** -- support oneself by one's own labor; earn one's own living

yoq dyul a clumsy manner (35:19)

yoqdyuf orchestra; band (Chi) (50:202)

yoq eil yoq puv to take back what one has said (50:9)

yoq eil yoq gaq to him/herself (**yoq eil yoq gaq meil** eil = said to him/herself - 26:66) (a˯ yawˇ yaw˄)

yoq haol yoq leev 1. self-protection, 2. self-government (or) **yoq haoq yaq teiq**

yoqhaoq doq a dialect; a sub-dialect (50:48)

yoqhaoq yo'liq local nationalism (50:35)

yoq haoq yoq del moved out of one's hometown (50:9)

yoqhaoq yoqleev sovereign rights; sovereignty (50:215)

yoq haoq yoq teiq 1. autonomy; self-government, 2. self-protection (or) **yoq haoq yoq leev** (50:219)

yoqhol maq zyuq meil jav to have a great deal of something in life, esp. wealth

yoqhol nei sulhol haol give one's life to rescue someone; sacrifice oneself to save others (50:148)

yoq hovq yoq dol support oneself by one's own labor; earn one's own living (50:219)

yoqhhaq oneself (or) **yoq** (yaw˯ ha)

yoqhhaq aolssaq an individual laborer (50:58)

yoqhhaq aol zaq work on one's own (50:32)
yoqhhaq bulduq oneself (yaw⌄ haˇ yaw⌄ ha)
yoqhhaq bulduq eil heeq to brag; exhalt oneself (yaw⌄ haˇ yaw⌄ ha ja seh-eu)
yoqhhaq bulduq jol sal to enjoy oneself (yaw⌄ haˇ yaw⌄ ha byaw⌄ g'a-eu)
yoqhhaq bulduq nei by one's self (no help)
yoqhhaq bulduq seivq to commit suicide; kill oneself
yoqhhaq e albeil duq duq one's birthplace (i.e., where one's umbilical cord and placenta are buried behind the door inside the house)
yoqhhaq hhazaq hhaduv to assume sole responsibility for an enterprise's profits or losses (50:219)
yoqhhaq hhaqduq oneself (13:2) (yaw⌄ ha)
yoqhhaq hholmol kevq nei bivq to apply one's self
yoqhhaq jolduq sulhhaq a bivq miq to give way to someone (as when get in their way) (gaˇ ma pah neh⌄-eu)
yoqhhaq jol teiq nia to restrain oneself
yoqhhaq meeq heiq private interests (50:159)
yoqhhaq miavpyuq aoq zaq to give oneself away ('to sell face') (yaw⌄ ha mya^ pyaw⌄ ah⌄-eu)
yoqhhaq pyuq a to come over to one's side (45:62)
yoqhhaq sol meil personally
yoqhhaq teiq nia to restrain oneself
yoqhhaq xeiv huvq to voluntarily leave one's job (50:219)
yoqhhaq yaol qiq jivq liq maq nyuq to be totally unconcerned (cf.: ti⌄ paw^-i⌄ ma⌄ noe⌄)
yoqhhaq zeiqsal individual (private) economics (50:58)

-- **yoq, hhe** -- to pull away

yoqhhol one's body (46:202) (yaw⌄ ha-eu⌄ mawˇ do)
yoqhhol qiq hhol one's whole body (14:149) (yaw⌄ ha mawˇ do do lah ni)

-- **yoq, hhoq** -- to avoid something or someone

yoqhhyul one's body (34:7)

yoqjol haol leev naciq aqbol health care doctor (50:7)

yoqjol maq sal paralysis; palsy (50:162)

-- **yoq leev, yoq haol** -- protect oneself

-- **yoq leev, yoq haoq** -- sovereign rights; sovereignty

yoq li to walk past (13:49) (cah dzeuˇ-eu)

yoqma mother-in-law (pf); **yiuvqma** (A=Chi) (11:210) (a⌄ maw⌄)

yoqmeiv 1. a seesaw, 2. a pole used in pressing out oil, 3. a pole used as a lever in moving a large object

yoq miaoq yoq aol duty; obligation; responsibility (50:212)

yoq miaoq yoq leev to maintain independence and keep the initiative in one's own hands (50:40)

yoqniv niv to take the initiative (50:215)
yoqnyuq subjective (50:215)
-- **yoq, ngaq** -- to step over
yoqpaq father-in-law (pf) (A=Chi); **yiuvqpaq** (11:31, 210) (tsaw˅ maw˯)
yoqpu musical score (Chi) (50:203)
yoqpuv puv rotation (50:220)
yoqqif musical instrument (Chi) (50:203)
yoqsaq tavq to have blood relationship
Yoqsseiq the Yao nationality (14:197, 41:4) (Chi) (Ceh˯ yao˯)
yoqteil the sound of one's own voice (yaw˯ ha-eu˯ te˅ sa˅)
-- **yoqteiq, yoqhaoq** -- autonomy; self-government (or) **yoq haoq yoq leev**
-- **yoq, xeiv** -- 1. to make way; move out of the way (and see full); 2. to run away
-- yoqzal, yoqhaoq -- local products
yoqzyul yuqssiil ssiil voluntarily surrender oneself; confess one's crimes (50:169)

yov to peel bark or skin (leu˰-eu)
=yov nei, neema nal= sadly
-- **yov, sseilbol** -- to peel palm bark
-- **yov, sseilhov** -- to peel palm bark

yovq a home
yovq aslant, askew (9:168)
yovq cuv 1. to start a family (settle down and live with the family), 2. to be married (46:118) (nym˅ dah˯ dah˯ dza˯-eu)
-- **yovq, hhe** -- pulled so that it is bent
yovqhhovq a family (clf. **hhovq**) (11:34) (nym˅ dah˯ ti˯ zaw˰)
yovqhhovq bil zaq family to divide (9:168)
yovqhhovq cuv zavq to establish a family (13:2) (nym˅ dah˯ dah˯ dza˯-eu)
yovqhhovq hhovqma a big family
yovqhhovq yovqhol one's own family (38:20) (yaw˯ ha-eu˯ zaw˰; yaw˯ ha-eu˯ peh˯ za˯)
yovq laol family to be happy ('warm')
=yovq meil, bil= crooked
=yovq, meiq= crooked lips

YU

yul that (9:168) (Note: Sometimes '**wul**' is used for this meaning, but '**yul**' is pf.) (k'oe˅)
yul old (6:203) (yaw oe˅)
yul aol to have a wedding
yulbal bal to have a wedding (oe˅ m˅ ba˅-eu)
yulbee bee to have a wedding party (oe˅ m˅ ba˅-eu)
yulgei there (9:168, 41:39); **yuq a = yulgei a** (k'oe˅ ga˅)
yulgei qiq heiq xilgei qiq heiq here and there

(**yulgei qiq heiq xilgei qiq heiq nei nalhaq** = asked here and there - 26:94)

yulhovq zaq go to a wedding

=yul, huvq'= the old year

yulma what the two mothers of a married couple call each other (cf.: **yulssaq**)

yulmeil like that; that way (9:168, 11:20) (k'oeˇ lo^-ehˇ)

yulmeil leil that way (k'oeˇ lo^-ehˇ)

yulmeil liq however (11:198) (ehˇ k'aw^)

yulmeil nei because of that (k'oeˇ miˇ neh)

-- yul, neema nee -- the old mind/heart

yulpuvnaoq those on the bride's side who go to meet the groom's family (cf. **yulzaol**)

yul pyu xil pyu here and there; this side and that side (46:170) (heu paw k'oeˇ paw)

yul qa that kind (9:168) (k'oeˇ jeˇ)

yulssaq what the two fathers of a married couple call each other (cf. **yulma**)

yul taq that time; then (k'oeˇ ngeh; k'oeˇ tiˇ k'ehˇ) (10:24)

yul taq hev e ngaoq by then; by that time (k'oeˇ ngeh)

yul taq kavq nei from that time (or) **yul taq neikavq**

yul taq luldu right then (13:4) (k'oeˇ naˇ)

yulxavq savq for a boy going to fetch his bride to stay a night in her parent's house (if this is done the villagers are to be fed)

yulzaol companions, when going to meet the bride (cf. **yulpuvnaoq**)

yulzaol zaolma a gift which is a guarantee of marriage (can be money, a cloth, etc.)

yulzeil pyu that side; over there (9:168, 38:17) (k'oeˇ paw)

=yul, zeiq'= 1. one's heritage, 2. a pregnant female animal

yulzil dol to drink liquor at a wedding party

yuq grandson; granddaughter (cf. **yuqpaq; yuqma**) (oeˇ paˇ; oeˇ ma)

yuq a there (**yuq a** li = go up there); **yuq a** = **yulgeil**

yuqcavq spoon; ladle (for dipping up rice) (or) **kuqcavq; aqcavq** (oeˇ tsa^; kuˇ tsa^)

-- yuqcavq, hoqkuq -- a ladle for dipping up rice

yuqduq fireplace (9:169, 46:192) (tsawˇ g'o^)

yuqduq aqma the fireplace goddess (must not step over the fire)

yuqduq duqhaoq fireplace (13:3) (miˇ dzaˇ tsawˇ bym)

yuqduq milsaol 'lord of the fireplace' (13:3) (miˇ sahˇ)

-- yuqduq, naolcal -- solar energy stove

yuq eil yuq eil leil the sound of pigs grunting

yuqhav a basket on which to place a pan (when the

pan is hot)

yuqjoq joq a vine fence

yuqlaoq a pot for cooking (10:30) (oe˯ lah˯)

yuqma granddaughter (9:169) (oe˯ ma)

yuqnilduq a hev li to reach death's door

yuqpaq grandson (9:169) (oe˯ pa˯)

yuqpaq yuqma descendants (oe˯ pa˯ oe˯ ma)

yuqpeivq peivq to vomit (10:21) (u˯ peh˰ peh˰-eu)

yuq ssol leiq grandchildren, and great-grandchildren (oe˯ pa˯ oe˯ ma)

yuq ssol ssaq grandchildren; offspring; the next generation (9:169, 10:pref, 30:1, 41:2)

yuqteiv a shallow pot; an earthen pot (9:169) (oe˯ lah˯ teh^-eu = to make it in Akha)

yuvq four (9:169) (oe˯)

Yuvqla siq April

yuvq ngavq taq four or five times (oe˯ nga˯ po^) (10:11)

yuvq liv yuvq kyul four corners (as the four corners of the world, i.e., everywhere) (9:169, 45:83) (oe˯ coeˇ oe˯ baw˯)

yuvq seil maq daol disabled; maimed (50:19) (**seil** = a part of the body, esp. leg, arm, head)

yuvq seil maq daol mavqssaq disabled soldiers (50:19)

yuvq seil maq jav to have a disability (50:19)

YUEI

Yueiqjalxeif Yuanjiang County (Honghe) (Chi) (or) **Lalsav** (Hani term)

YYU

yyuq ! wow! (interjection) (13:5) (a˯ heuˇ)

=yyuq, bev= a cotton fluffer

yyuqbi zabiav a moon cake (26:85) (A=Chi)

=yyuq, ceiq= a handle for a large hoe (mattock)

yyuqdaoq a bone (sha˯ yoe˯)

=yyuq, du= a corn cob

yyuqhe qulbaq nei a sweet fragrance (14:138)

=yyuq, hho= rice straw

yyuq loq hu to determine something by reading bones (34:7)

=yyuq, nal= the bridge of the nose

Yyuqnaq Yunnan (Chi) (9:169, 46:1201, 50:203)

Yyuqnaq sei Yunnan province (Chi)

yyuqnil a red bone

=yyuq, savjil sav= (see full)

=yyuq, ssa= elephant bone (4:39)

yyuq xal to pass on; to hand on (as the ancestors have handed down customs from generation to generation) (41:89) (sha g'eh-eu)

yyufmu a final (in phonological sense, as a 'final consonant') (Chi)

ZA

zal food (9:169) (dzaˇ)
zal chapter; section (Chi) (50:207)
zal clf. for tickets (Chi) (41:193)
=zal, aq= food
zalbi a by-product
zalceil ceil to choose good food to eat ('choose out food') (dzaˇ tseˇ dza˯-eu)
zalceiq solution; way (Chi) (50:207)
zalcii cii to have indigestion
zaldu a rope kept lit for smokers (9:170)
zalduvq poisonous food
zal'eel 1. a spicy sauce in which certain types of food are dipped and eaten (9:169), 2. fluid; liquid, 3. juice (or) **alju**
  zal'eel aol zaq to dip meat into a bowl of spicy sauce (sha˯ jiˇ leh˰ dza˯-eu)
zalfaq presentation of ideas in a piece of writing (Chi) (50:207)
-- zalgaoq, miaoqgaoq -- goods and materials
zalgovq govq to mix up vegetables as a part of a ceremony to keep the village healthy
zalgovq hhoqcyuq zaq a ceremony to keep the whole village healthy by eating various vegetables
-- zalgovq zaq, ngavq la ngavq nao -- (see full)
zalguv a scarecrow (9:170)
  zalguv ceq to make a scarecrow
=zal, ha= chicken food
=zal, haq= sparrow
zalhel a sacrificial offering (46:87, 125) (lawˇ-eu)
  zalhel hel to offer food to the ancestors
zalhel lolbieil a bamboo table on which offerings are placed for various ceremonies
zalhe naol to have a rancid odor (or) **hhavqcil cilbuvq naol**
zalhev nei proper; suitable size (tsa˯-eu)
=zal, hhavq= pig food
zalhhyul healthy food; nutritious (50:194)
zaljavq digestion (10:8) (dzaˇ ji^ ji^-eu)
  zaljavq javq to digest well
zaljiv jiv to chew the cud; to ruminate (dzaˇ ji^ ji^-eu)
zalkavq a kind of plant with very sticky grains (not edible)
zalkeel zalniuv delicious food (45:61) (dzaˇ yaw kuiˇ)
zallaq lark (brd) (8:19) (jaˇ la˯)
Zallaq xal a township in Jianshui county (46:135)
zalloq a food container
zallyul 1. powder, 2. flour (cf.: **yaw loe**ˇ)
zalmaof wuqcaoq a Western style hat (A=Chi) (11:31)

=zal, mil= a male cat
=zal, miq= gun powder
=zal, moq= horse food
zalnaf a disaster (Chi) (34:3)
=zal, niuq= food for buffalo/cow
-- zalniuv, zalkeel -- delicious food
=zal, oq= male duck
=zal, pavqdeiq deiq= a small prickly plant
zalpavq zalcev horse and pig food (**zalpavq zalcev hha cev taq** = must cut food for horses and pigs before some long ceremonies)
zalpiul niter (used in making gun powder)
zalpuv puv to ruminate (dza˅ ji^ ji^-eu) (9:170)
zalqil a miasma; thick vaporous atmosphere (9:170)
zalqil a disaster area (Chi) (26:78)
zalsiq 1. food (9:170, 46:123), 2. grain
zalsiq aqzal crops (couplet)
zalsiq aol dav to increase production of food (grains)
zalsiq diqduq a threshing ground for grains
zalsiq se leev to get in (as crops)
zalsiil sulphur (mi˯ dza˅ dza˅ shui˅)
zalsol 1. things eaten with rice (vegs., chili, salt, etc.) (9:170), 2. spice
zalsol flavorful and aromatic food (13:1)
Zalteil teil celebrate the New Year festival (14:201, 46:182) (or) **Galtaol pal; Galtaol taol** (ga˅ tah˅ pa˅-eu)
zalyiq ngaqdeil octopus (A=Chi) (50:207)
zalyyuq cooking (14:165)
zal zaq to eat a meal (dza˅ dza˯-eu)
zal zaq hhyul aol to take nourishing food to build one's health

za 1. fit; suitable; proper (9:169, 45:9, 46:76, 50:71) (tsa˯-eu), 2. flexible; adaptable (or) **ya; aol pal sso; zaol pal sso**
(vb) **za** proper to (vb); suitable to (vb) (26:31)
-- za, aol e -- to be applicable; suitable
zabiav cake (as moon cakes made at the moon festival) (26:7, 46:86) (clf. = **biav**)
zabiav tal to stir-fry
zacuv a kneaded dumpling
zacuv cuv to make a dumpling (cf.: ja leh leh-eu)
-- za e, hal -- most suitable
-- za, eil -- talk and agree
=za, gee= 1. to consult; to discuss (or) **geeza zaq** = to discuss, 2. a short commentary; a brief comment
zagyuf shopkeeper; manager of a shop (Chi) (50:207)
zahev nei 1. proper; suitable size (tsa˯-eu), 2. a little bit later (30:2), 3. appropriate (or) **zahe nei**
zahhoq to master (Chi) (34:24)
-- za, juqtao -- wide adaptability
zakuq a dumpling spoon

za lal to be possible (or) **caq lal**
za'lagua exhibition center (Chi) (50:206)
za'lei rice dumpling (rice ball used in certain ceremonies, including when there is an earthquake) (9:170) (ja leh)
za'lei lei to make a dumpling (9:170) (ja leh leh-eu)
Za'lei teil New Year in one dialect (see: **Galtaol taol**) (gaˇ tahˇ paˇ-eu)
za'lei zakuq spoon with which to retrieve rice dumplings out of the water
-- **za, neema** -- to be satisfied
za nei 1. a little (n) (or) **zaza nei** (**Aqyoq miavpyuq za nei nav.** His face is a little black.) (11:107) (aˇ cui^), 2. middle-sized (41:199), 3. punctual; on time; on schedule (50:218), 4. for a moment (11:200) (tiˬ k'ehˬ)
za nei qiq savq for a little while; one moment (35:7) (tiˬ k'ehˬ)
-- **za nei, siqse** -- at the right moment; timely
-- **za, nyuq** -- 1. think properly; clearly (noeˬ shaw-eu), 2. show understanding and sympathy for; make allowances for

zaq to eat (9:170) (dzaˬ-eu)
zaq to be beautiful (10:4) (or) **hu sal; hu gaq** (and see: **yojaq**) (yaw jaˬ)
(vb) **zaq** ending used after a main verb, with the meaning: to be in such a state (as fighting, eating, doing) (**soqhhaq zol zaq** = study books; **niuqceiq hhel zaq** = buy a plow; **qei zaq** = argue; fight) (ceh dzaˬ-eu)
=zaq, al= smallpox; cowpox
-- **zaq, alzaq** -- to have smallpox
-- **zaq, aqniuq piav** -- to cut open and skin a buffalo at a funeral
-- **zaq, aol** -- work and make a living
-- **zaq, aoq** -- to make a living by selling; a merchant
zaqceil delicious food
zaqciq color (50:193)
-- **zaq, cuv** -- to marry (in the sense of starting a family), **cuv zavq**
-- **zaq, cyuq** -- to have ability (nya-eu; yaw biˇ)
zaq cyuq zaq peel to eat one out of house and home
zaqdal a bomb (Chi) (ma‸ puˇ puˇ ma)
zaqdal sseiv nei magnificent; gorgeous (50:74)
zaqdal zaol duv to put on make-up; beautify oneself (50:74)
zaq dav dol dav (maq meeq e miqnieiq) to be addicted to something bad to eat or drink
zaqdaol hand hay-cutter (Chi) (9:170)
zaqdeil deil ripe enough to be eaten
zaq deiq to eat something until the container is empty; to consume (4:40) (dzaˬ ngeh‸-eu)

-- **zaq, deiq** -- to quarrel
zaq deiv to eat to the full (dza˯ deh^-eu)
zaq deiv dol deiv eat and drink to the full (dza˯ deh^ dawˇ deh^)
-- **zaq, diq** -- to beat one another; fight
-- **zaq, doq** -- to wait for
zaqduq the place to eat (dza˯ du˯)
zaqduq dolduq the place to eat & drink (14:172, 46:111) (dza˯ du˯ dawˇ du˯)
zaq e dyul haljivq nga laq? what things did you eat? (13:1) (Nawˇ a˯ je˯ dza˯ le?)
zaq e maq hhaol dol e maq saq to have enough to eat and drink, and to spare
zaq e maq qil dol e maq saq not to worry about food and drink (45:43)
-- **zaq, eel** -- to laugh at someone
-- **zaq, eil** -- (see full)
-- **zaq, gaq** -- to overhear
-- **zaq, gaq** -- 1. to love one another, 2. to have harmony
zaqgev rubber (or) **xafjaol** (Chi) (jaw˄ jiˇ jaw˄ geu˄)
-- **zaq, gee** -- (see full)
-- **zaq, geeza** -- to discuss
zaqgyu aqma blackbird (cf.: aw˄-a˄ = crow)
zaqhal food for eating (11:217) (dza˯-eu dzaˇ)
zaqhal hhel kaoq a coupon for buying food (50:63)
zaq haqhaq eating (continuous action) (dza˯ lu˄-eu)
zaqhaoq aqzal edible food (dza˯ nya-eu dzaˇ)
zaqhaoq heeq greedy for food to eat (dza˯ deh^-eu ma˯ baw-eu)
-- **zaq, hev** -- to hold a festival
-- **zaq, heil** -- to order someone to do something
-- **zaq, hoq** -- to eat a meal
zaqhoq hoq to exact a village fine
zaq hu to taste ('try eating') (dza˯ haw-eu)
-- **zaq, hu** -- 1. beautiful 2. to watch (as TV or a movie) (50:155)
-- **zaq, huvqhev** -- to celebrate New year
-- **zaq, hyuq** -- to steal (k'oe˯-eu)
-- **zaq, hyuq su** -- to abduct (esp. a person)
zaq hhal jav to have food to eat (or) **zaq lul hha**
zaq hhal ssa wuqdeiq deiv 'the one who comes last eats fully' (proverb) (can never be too late to have some food)
-- **zaq, hhaqhaoq eq** -- to make a living as a porter
-- **zaq, hhaoq** -- to try to do something
-- **zaq, hheivq** -- to cheat; to take advantage of by cheating; defraud; swindle
zaqhhyul aol healthy, nourishing food (11:119)
zaqjaol hybridization (Chi) (50:204)
zaqjaol ceil hybrid rice (A=Chi) (50:204)
zaqjaol ceildu hybrid corn (maise) (A=Chi) (50:204)
zaq keel to be delicious (9:170) (dza˯ kuiˇ-eu)
-- **zaq, koq** -- to take away by force
-- **zaq laq meil, pyuq** -- to be arrogant

-- **zaq, lav** -- decorate; make up and dress up
zaq laovq to attract (46:177)
zaq leev to merge (as two businesses) (or) **mievq tao; lav paoq**
zaqlul food (30:2) (dzaˇ)
zaqlul hha to have food to eat (or) **zaq hhal jav** (dzaˬ-eu dzaˇ ja^-eu)
-- **zaq, luvq** -- 1. to herd animals as an occupational, 2. to stand around near where others are eating, hoping to get fed
zaq luvq dol luvq sufficient food and drink
-- **zaq, lyuq** -- a male to have intercourse (taboo)
zaqma dolma ma one who eats and drinks a lot; a glutton (50:30)
-- **zaqmeil, hyuq** -- stealthily
-- **zaq, meiq** -- to teach for a living
=**zaq, miq**= fire
-- **zaq, moqleiq** -- trade by using a caravan of horses
-- **zaq, mul** -- to coax; entice
-- **zaq, naolma neivqkeeq** -- eclipse of the sun
-- **zaq, neema** -- good-hearted
-- **zaq, neema puv** -- to turn away; retreat (in heart or mind)
-- **zaq, nieil** -- to forget
zaqnieiq left over food; remaining food (9:170, 11:116) (dzeuˇ laˇ-euˬ dzaˇ)
zaqngeeq a walking stick; a cane (9:170, 46:130) (gawˬ yoeˬ) (cf.: la˰ ngeuˬ)
zaqngeeq tuv to hold a walking stick (gawˬ yoeˬ to^-eu)
-- **zaq, pil** -- to settle; solve (**alkaq pil zaq** = to settle a dispute)
=**zaq, pioq**= beautiful face; beautiful appearance
zaq qeiq like to eat; prefer to eat (41:167) (dzaˬ coeˇ-eu)
-- **zaq, qeiq** -- to cheat
zaq qivq e jahhaq janiul edible herbs
-- **zaq, qo** -- 1. to visit each other, 2. to search for
zaqqul beautiful (9:170, 11:199); pleasing to the eye (50:114) (and see: **zaq; yoja**) (yaw jaˬ)
zaqqul nei very beautiful; good looking (9:170, 11:56, 46:173) (yaw jaˬ; aˇ g'ehˇ muiˬ-eu)
-- **zaq, pal** -- to exchange
zaqqul pa qul nei beautifully (46:173)
-- **zaq, puv** -- 1. to rebel, 2. to betray
-- **zaqqul pa qul nei, aqnil miqli** -- the youngest sister in the family is very beautiful
-- **zaq, qu** -- to adopt and raise a child
zaq salxa, jol sal xa, teil sal xa 1. to eat and live at ease (with no problems), 2. to have a good reputation
-- **zaq, saoq** -- to look on with hatred
zaqsiiq sturdy; solid; down-to-earth (Chi) (34:107)
zaq syuq difficult to eat (9:171)

-- **zaq, syuv** -- to look for food; scavenge for food
-- **zaq, Sseilkuq** -- spring festival; June festival
-- **zaq, sso** -- to be punished
-- **zaq, taoq** -- animals or humans to fight
-- **zaq, tul** -- 1. to make offerings, 2. to hold religious ceremonies (46:119)
-- **zaq, wuqleev leev** -- to make a living
-- **zaq, xaldei xa** -- to cultivate fields
-- **zaq, yeilkuq** -- to celebrate the June festival
zaqzal food (**zaq e aqzal**)
-- **zaq, zal** to eat a meal
zaq zaq yavq yavq 1. to eat; to sleep; eat-sleep (showing the passage of time with nothing unusual happening) (11:22); 2. to eat and sleep idly
zaqziif magazine (Chi) (50:204)
-- **zaq, zyuq** -- to seek to dominate; seek hegemony
-- **zaq, Zyuqzaq** -- June festival; spring festival

zav to drip (dza^-eu)
zav clf. for a drop to drip (9:171) (dza^)
zav dav to drop a liquid on something (as blood on stones in the 'sacred grove' ceremony)
=**zav, gaq**= beautiful (yaw mui$_\vee$ yaw ja$_\vee$)
zavlav nei directly; straight (as a bird which is shot and falls straight down from a tree) (11:216) (daw$^\vee$ coe ni)
=**zav nei, bel**= to be diligent
-- **zav nei, galju** -- to slobber
=**zav nei, gaq**= to be lovely (or) **gaq zav nei**
=**zav nei, gaqli gaq**= to be kind, loving
-- **zav nei, gaqzav pa** -- beautiful
=**zav nei, hhyul**= happily
=**zav nei, keel**= delicious
=**zav nei, meeq**= well; carefully; properly
zav xa to drip (or) **ya**
-- **zav zav, jiv jiv** -- the chirping of birds

-- **zavq, aqzavq** -- to cheat someone
-- **zavq, bavq** -- (see full)
-- **zavq, bev** -- to go hunting
zavqbeeq col one who teaches and incites others to do wrong things (50:85)
-- **zavq, cuv** -- to marry; **cuv zaq**
=**zavq, geiv**= fur blanket
-- **zavq, hov** -- to be equal to
=**zavq, leivq**= a baby or young child that is naughty; mischievous
-- **zavq, yav** -- to walk around looking for food

zaf a unit of length; 3.33 feet (over a yard in length, about a meter) (Chi)
zafceif hhoqqeil hot pickled mustard tuber (A=Chi) (50:206)
Zafcuq Tibetan nationality (Chi)
zafdaf a bomb (Chi) (50:206)

zafdef struggle to get (Chi) (or) **defzeil** (Chi)
zafgol songs of praise (Chi) (50:204)
zafhaoq a trench (for soldiers) (Chi) (26:48)
zafmeisiil a hymn (Chi) (50:204)
zafnioq strategy (Chi) (34:24)
zafnioqjal a strategist (Chi) (34:28)
zafsiiq nei temporary (Chi) (34:85)
zafteiq a platform (Chi) (50:207)
zafye mavq army mates; friends (A=Chi) (26:59)
zafyoq an explosive; dynamite (Chi) (50:206)
zafza head of a station (Chi) (50:207)

ZAO

zaol raw (6:203) (yaw jm˯)
zaol to do; make; prepare (9:171) (jahˇ-eu) (used when asking, 'What are you doing?')
zaol clf. for a pair (9:171, 11:76, 13:19, 46:115) (can be a pair of friends, chopsticks, shoes, chickens - which would be a rooster and hen, etc.) (gu)
zaol 1. clf. for a hive of bees or wasps (11:195), 2. clf. for a bridge (kahˇ)
=zaol, al= a coffin
zaol bav to make a mistake (jahˇ leh˯-eu)
-- zaol, bavqlavq bavqzaol -- shoulder to shoulder
-- zaol, bavqzaol -- shoulder to shoulder
zaol beeq to make trouble
zaol biav 1. to break something (la^ pa^-eu), 2. to damage something (50:131) (la^ caw^-eu)
-- zaol, buqdeil -- a tangle of entertwined ascaris worms
-- zaol buvq, eil buvq -- insult; humiliate
zaol cavq to fix; to repair (50:2)
zaol cavq pollute; contaminate (50:180)
zaolceiq loyal; faithful; staunch (Chi) (50:214)
zaol cuvq to put together (26:119)
zaol dav to add (**Xilmeil ssaqguq a fufdal zaoldav miq pa ngeel aq**? Does this perhaps add a burden to the students? 41:85)
zaoldaoq lower side ('bottom') of village (46:125, 168) (dzahˇ dah˯)
zaoldaoq zaolwuq village surroundings ('bottom and top of village')
zaoldaoq zaolzeil all around the village; all of the environs of the village (must not let certain bees makes their hives in trees in this area)
zaoldul 1. to play the part (as in a play or dance) (50:5), 2. to pretend to be (50:113)
zaol duv 1. to show something in one's countenance or appearance (**neessil aqmeil zaol duv alnei eil... =** he looked like he was angry and said... - 26:67); to pretend (35:2), 2. to create
zaol duv bei formerly created
zaol duvq to mend; to repair (jahˇ mui˯-eu; la^ sa^-

eu)

zaolgao 1. to feel wronged; 2. to put someone to great inconvenience (Chi) (or) **zaol sso** (50:176)

-- zaol gee, aoq gee -- drought

zaol goq to put high up (yuˇ goˇ-eu)

Zaolgoq China (Chi) (9:171, 26:22, 50:214) (**Zaolgoq milcaq** = the country of China - A=Chi) (26:91) (La^ bui˅ miˇ k'ah˅)

Zaolgoq Gaofcada the Chinese Communist Party (Chi) (50:214)

Zaolgoq Ssaqlaol e Gei'faqjyul People's Liberation Army (Chi) (34:21) (or) **Zaolgoq Sseiqmiq Jei'fafjyul** (note: **Gei'fafjyul** = alternate sp.)

Zaolgoq Sseiqmiq Jei'fafjyul People's Liberation Army (Chi) (26:41) (or) **Zaolgoq Ssaqlaol e Gei'faqjyul** (note: **Gei'fafjyul** = alternate sp.)

Zaolgoq teqdiei China style (Chi) (34:24)

zaolgov alpeel a clam (aˇ caˇ caˇ k'aw^)

Zaolha milcaq a place name (35:24)

zaol haol to help (14:146) (caw ba-eu)

zaol haoq complimentary (50:16)

zaolheil puv to chase out bad spirits before entering a new house

zaol hoq comprehensive (Chi) (34:18)

zaolhul to take care of (Chi) (10:21, 26:58) (haw lahˇ-eu)

zaol hu to punish (35:30)

zaol hu 1. to demonstrate (or) **bi hu,** 2. to experiment; test (50:154), 3. to practice

zaolhu hu 1. try doing; attempt doing (13:14) (jahˇ haw-eu), 2. to explore (50:154)

zaol huvq to get revenge (50:8)

zaolhuaq hhaq tul hhaq dav build up China; promote China (A=Chi) (50:209)

Zaolhuaq miqcuq the Chinese nation (34:7) (La^ bui˅ tsawˇ jeu˅)

Zaolhuaq Sseiqmiq Gaofhoqgoq People's Republic of China (PRC) (Chi) (34:8)

zaolhhal a base; foundation; house site (11:204) (or) **daoqpeiq** (daw˅ peh˅)

zaolhhaol a whorl of hair on the top of the head

zaol hheivq to pretend to do something (**nal ya leil zaol hheivq** = pretend to be sick) (13:19) (see also: **zaolleivq leivq**) (cf.: jahˇ g'eh-eu)

-- zaol, hheivqzaol -- to forge; falsify

zaolhhuvq lower part of a village (pu dzahˇ dah˅)

zaol hhuvq to bury something (35:16) (du˅ pah˅-eu)

zaoljaof religion (Chi) (34:55, 50:220) (cf.: zahˇ)

zaoljaof xifnia ziifyeq freedom to believe in religion (Chi) (50:220)

zaol kaq to cure; to heal (10:pref, 35:111, 46:153), to make well (la^ ta˅-eu)

zaolkaq a street; a lane (50:87); the empty places between houses in a village

zaol keeq leiq for a man to lead a dog around an area where a village is to be built (all houses must be built in that circle)

zaol keeq leiq e col the man who leads the dog around the village site

zaol kevq to mix together (50:128)

zaolkul kul a final feast at the home of the dead elder on the day after the burial, when the children call out their parent's name (thus the name for the feast includes 'to call')

=zaol, laol= bridge (law˯ dzmˇ)

Zaollaoq the brother who was stranded in a gourd with his sister during the great flood (her name; **Zaolsol**)

zaol leev to make tidy; put in order (50:210) (la^ lui^-eu)

zaol leiq 1. to make a mistake (11:208) (jahˇ leh˯-eu), 2. to suffer loss; to lose in business; **zaolsu** (B=Chi), 3. to make something worse

zaolleivq leivq to pretend (13:46) (see also: **zaolhheivq**) (leh˯ hm˯-eu; jahˇ g'eh-eu)

zaol lil planned to (**ngaq e huljil hu li movq leil zaol lil** = I planned to go see my husband - 26:90)

zaol loq to improve (as a policy) (12:127) (la^ mui˯-eu)

-- zaol, lutaoq -- to have maggots

zaol luvq to enrich (50:24)

zaol meeq 1. to improve; make better (jahˇ mui˯-eu), 2. to rectify; reorganize (50:210)

zaol meeq zaol zaq to make good and beautiful (50:114)

zaol mei 1. to make vanish, 2. to kill out; wipe out (46:202) (jahˇ meh-eu)

zaolmi zaolluvq aqma the spiritual lord and protector of the house (cf. Akha 'dzahˇ miˇ')

zaolmiq lower section of a village (pu dzahˇ dah˯)

zaolmol a visible symbol; mark (**Miqsiq wuqduq zaolmol maq quv.** = A clever woman has no mark on her head showing her cleverness.)

zaolmol cuv a visible symbol or mark to develop (as a horn on a baby buffalo to begin to grow)

zaolmoq a roof

zaol movq willing to do (jahˇ maw˄-eu)

zaolnaoq middle-class peasant (not rich, not poor) (Chi)

=zaol nei, civq= frequently; often (or) **ciivzaol nei**

-- zaol nia, neivq -- capable of performing black magic

zaol pal 1. to mend (11:161) (jahˇ paˇ-eu), 2. to adjust; regulate; revise (50:166)

zaol pal sso to be flexible; adaptable (or) **za; ya; aol pal sso**

zaol paoq to put many things together (50:128)

zaolpeil lolqoq 1. neighbor (9:171), 2. neighborhood

(50:108)
zaolpeif zuyif sectarianism; factionalism (Chi) (50:220)
zaol pievq to succeed
zaol puv zaq e moqpil a priest who can counteract black magic (such as taking stones out of a person's stomach)
zaolqeljiq moon festival (Chi) (26:85)
zaolqeljiq neeciiv hevzaq to celebrate the moon festival (26:7)
zaolqif paoqpoq full of youthful spirits (Chi) (34:102) (or) **zaolqif paoqpoq**
zaolqo qo to imitate (50:48)
zaol sal to make peace
zaol sil to cause to die; to kill (seh˰-eu)
Zaolsol the sister who was in the gourd with her brother during the great flood (the brother; **Zaollaoq**)
zaol soq 1. to do things smoothly; 2. to make things tidy (or) **aol soq; aol suv** (50:105), 3. to administer; govern; bring under control (50:213)
zaol siivq solidarity; to make firm (34:10) (la^ zi˰-eu)
zaol ssivq to fix (general repair) (50:64) (or) **kavq ssivq**
zaol sso 1. to punish (27:11), 2. to persecute (50:131)
zaoltaq palm bark covering for a horse carriage
zaol taq 1. to lay down; draw up; formulate (Chi) (50:213), 2. to be done; finished doing (jahˇ ta˯-eu)
zaol tao to do something inside (as a room) (12:125)
zaolteev teev for one's skin to crack from the cold
-- **zaolteiq, laolzaol** -- single wooden bridge
zaol tuvq to be very cruel (B=Chi) (50:19)
zaolwuq upper part of a village (pu dzahˇ hu˯)
zaolxa to destroy; to make something bad (la^ caw^-eu)
zaolxoq middle school (Chi) (50:214)
zaolyal 1. building and field, 2. private property
Zaolyal Central committee (Chi)
zaolyil Chinese medicine (Chi) (50:214)
zaol zaq to have sexual intercourse (polite) (or) **lyuq zaq** (not so polite) (yu˰ ta˰-eu; a˯ loe˯ loe˯-eu)
-- **zaol zaq, hoq** -- to cook and eat rice
zaolzeil the side of the village (46:89) (or) **puvkaq bialzeil** (cf.: pu dzeˇ pu taw)
-- **zaolzeil, puvkaq** -- sides of village & houses
zaolziiq aim; purpose (Chi) (34:79)
zaol zol 1. to practice, 2. to learn
zaol zo to develop a habit (9:171)
zaol zyul to commit a crime

zao main body; main part (50:215)

zao to fill in with mud
zao clf. for 1. a cent (Chi) (9:171, 26:74, 41:130), 2. a bed
-- **zao, bevzao** -- an instrumental ensemble
zaocaol morning exercises (Chi) (41:29, 50:204)
zaocaol zof to do morning exercises (Chi) (41:29)
zaodeifli general agent (Chi) (or) **zaozilli** (Chi)
zaodiei breakfast (Chi) (41:175) (shaw˯ haw˯)
zaogal general programs; general principle (Chi) (50:220)
=**zao, hhaoq**= a bed
-- **zao, hhaoqzao** -- to make a bed; to make a bedstead
zaojiq to sum up; summarize (Chi) (34:12, 50:220)
zao'li premier (Chi)
zao'lufxeif the general line; the official line (Chi)
zaoma 1. generally; for the most part (Chi) (26:28), 2. main (as the main one), 3. focal point; stress; emphasis (50:215)
zaoma galquv general rules; general principles (A=Chi) (50:220)
zaoma nei generally; for the most part (Chi) (mya˯ mya˯ ti˯ pa^)
zaoma nei meeq dav basic improvement (A=Chi) (50:58)
zaoma miaoqheiq a major product (A=Chi) (50:215)
zaoma nei nieivqceiv briefly introduced (A=Chi) (50:83)
zaoma xoqxaof key schools (Chi) (50:215)
=**zao, naol**= a stool; a block of wood
zao nei generally; for the most part (Chi) (mya˯ mya˯ ti˯ pa^)
zaosii alsiq jujube (wild) (A=Chi)
zaosuljif general secretary (Chi) (41:3)
zaosso to be cheated (35:60)
zaozilli general agent (Chi) (or) **zaodeifli**

zaoq clf. for a bundle (including: rice, straw) (9:171, 11:82); a unit (50:79) (aˇ dzah˯)
zaoq to bundle something (6:192) (aˇ dzah˯ dzah˯-eu)
zaoq raw; uncooked (or) **yozaoq** (11:55) (yaw jm˯)
zaoqbiav a flat chisel
zaoqbuvq a ribbon
zaoqcyuq cyuq to cough (9:171, 10:1) (u˯ tsoe˯ tsoe˯-eu)
-- **zaoq, doqdeiv hhazaoq** -- to meet together and talk
-- **zaoq, doq sii nei meiqzaoq** -- to pour water down the throat of a sacrificial buffalo to keep it from calling out when killed
zaoqgao together; integrate; unify (50:169) (ti˯ kaw^ lo˰-ehˇ
zaoqgao aol to work together (50:15)
zaoqgao aol meeq to work and make progress together (50:63)
zaoqgao aoq state monopoly for marketing (50:169)
zaoqgao bev to play musical instruments together

(50:133)

zaoqgao cal to sing songs together (50:133)

zaoqgao hhel a state monopoly for purchasing (50:169)

zaoqgao lavssiq to work and fight together (50:63)

zaoqgao seqto unified leadership (50:169)

zaoqgao zaol zyul common crime (50:63)

zaoqgao zol to read/study together (50:133)

zaoq gee a place which is at a lower location

zaoqhuvq a rounded chisel

zaoq huvq resurgence; reversion (50:75)

=zaoq, juq= belt (jo^ pa^)

-- zaoq, kavq -- 1. to bundle; 2. to bite each other

-- zaoq, kavqzaoq -- to bundle a bundle

=zaoq, laq= belt for trousers

=zaoq, laqpil pil= green, fresh chili peppers

zaoqlee a four-angled chisel

zaoqmavq nei to be numb; insensitive

=zaoq, ngaq= raw, fresh fish

zaoqpeiv phlegm; spittle (9:171) (du˅ k'a˅ dza˅ peh^)

=zaoq, qeil= fresh sour vegetable

=zaoq, saq= fresh meat

zaoqssaq a chisel for working with stone (A=Chi) (11:31)

=zaoq, yo= 1. wet, 2. raw (uncooked) (yaw jm˅)

-- zaoq, zilzaoq -- to drink together

=zaovq nei, niul= very fresh (as vegetables)

zaofpieif picture; photo (Chi) (50:208)

zaofxafjil a camera (Chi) (14:191, 50:208)

zaofyaofxif importance (Chi) (34:49)

Zaofyifyeif House of Representatives (Chi) (50:215)

ZE

zel prefecture; district; region (Chi) (41:14, 46:106)

Zel Eilleiq Zhou Enlai (a famous leader in China) (Chi) (34:20)

Zelhhyu the prefecture Party committee (Chi) (57:71)

zelza prefecture governor (Chi) (41:3)

zeq to increase; enlarge (**heeq zeq lal** = to get bigger - 26:56) (9:173, 11:39) (jeu˅-eu)

zeq clf. for time (this is based on the 24 hours in a day, with the name of one of the 12 animals used in naming the years being given to each two-hour segment in the day - 11:221) (Chi)

zeq cavq 1. a run of good luck, 2. to extend good luck to old people

-- zeq, ha -- chicken hour (B=Chi)

-- zeq, haqlaq -- tiger hour (B=Chi)

-- zeq, hu -- rodent hour (B=Chi)

-- zeq, hhavq -- pig hour (B=Chi)

-- zeq, keeq -- dog hour (B=Chi)

zeq lal 1. to develop (13:24), 2. to reproduce; for animals, humans, money etc., 3. to increase (or) **laoq lal** (jeuˬ laˇ-eu)
-- **zeq lal, zeiq taol** -- domestic animals to increase by thousands
-- **zeq, laoq** -- dragon hour (B=Chi)
-- **zeq, miuvq** -- monkey hour (B=Chi)
-- **zeq, moq** -- horse hour (B=Chi)
-- **zeq, niuq** -- buffalo/cow hour (B=Chi)
-- **zeq, seil** -- snake hour (B=Chi)
-- **zeq, toqla** -- rabbit hour (B=Chi)
-- **zeq, wuqnaovq** -- clever; quick-minded
-- **zeq, yol** -- sheep hour (B=Chi)

=zev, siil= yellowish

ZEI

zeil debt (9:172) (dziˇ dzo^)
zeil to strain out; to filter (9:172) (dze-eu)
zeil what remains; the amount left over (dzeuˇ laˇ-eu)
zeil a line (aˇ kaw^)
zeilbil miqnieiq conscription work (A=Chi) (50:210)
=zeil, bial= beside; side (as side of a mountain)
zeil ca to owe (Chi) (dziˇ dzo^ da^-eu)
=zeil cuqzeil, mil= border areas (miˇ kaˬ)
zeil do nei lined up in a straight line (11:216)
zeil duv to seep out
=zeil, haq= hawk; eagle (k'aˬ dzeˇ)
=zeil, haol= side of fireplace
=zeil, hhaq= a rock cliff
zeiljil a swift (brd)
zeilkaol a vacuum (Chi) (34:97)
zeil kyuq to be tired of working hard (A=Chi) (g'aˬ doeˇ doeˇ-eu)
zeilli truth (Chi) (34:25)
zeilliefsyu eelquvq distilled water (A=Chi) (50:210)
=zeil, lol= riverside; river bank
=zeil, meiq= corner of one's mouth
=zeil, miav= corner of one's eye
-- **zeil, miaoqciq** -- to ferment indigo in preparation for dyeing cloth
zeilnuv spend freely; squander (50:75)
zeilnuv nuv 1. to blame someone unreasonably, 2. to spend money unreasonably
=zeil, nyul= ring finger
zeilngyul wild goose (9:172, 11:151) (jeh^ k'aˬ)
-- **zeilngyul, neivqhaq** -- crane
zeilpia small kind of eagle (9:172) (k'aˬ dzeˇ)
-- **zeil, pieiq** -- to filter
zeil pyul li to turn the head (11:162)
zeil pyu direction to the side (46:113, 139) (gaˇ dzeˇ paw)
=zeil pyu, puv= outside the village (pu la‸ nyiˇ paw)

=zeil **pyu, yul=** that side
zeilqi to win; to gain (Chi) (34:81) (g'a˯ le˅-eu)
-- **zeil, qiq** -- one side
zeilqifjil steam engine (Chi) (50:210)
zeil soq to pay for (9:172) (a˅ poe˯ bi˄-eu)
=**zeil, zaol=** the side of the village (pu paw dze˅)
Zeil zeifxiq hhyuyeiq Prefecture Political Consultant Member (Chi)
zeil zuv a debt (to owe money) (A=Chi) (11:31) (dzi˅ dzo^ da^-eu)
zeil zuv maq leiq cal meil loyei nei bi soq to give time to
zeilzuvq eggplant (9:172, 11:25) (ma˅ k'eu)

zei 1. to throw away (byeh˅ dzeh-eu), 2. to stretch out (9:172, 13:44) (**aqlavq zei** = to stretch out the hand)
zei to have strength (g'a˯ k'a^-eu)
-- **zei, aqlavq** -- to stretch out one's hand
-- **zei, aqzei** -- to stretch out one's body
=**zei, aol=** wooden top for spinning (cah˯)
-- **zei, baq** -- to throw away
-- **zei, bavq** -- to throw away; to abandon
-- **zei, bo** -- to blow away
-- **zei, cilpuq** -- (see full)
zei duv to throw (as a hand grenade) (26:42) (bi˯-eu)
zeiduaf (see: **zeidueif**) (34:65)
zeidueif to rectify (Chi) (or) **zeiduaf**
zei'faol reform; adjust; rectify incorrect style of work (Chi) (26:54, 50:210)
=**zei hhalniul, neivq=** an ogre; evil monster
=**zei, hha=** fish net
-- **zei, hhe** -- 1. pull and discard (as a weed) (g'eu dzeh-eu), 2. to eliminate through selection or competition, 3. to report something
zeihu 1. to visit and take care of, 2. to investigate (as a detective)
-- **zei, leiq** -- to drive away; to drive out
zei nei hhe zei to pull to a long length (g'eu ja-eu)
=**zei nei, moq=** unexpectedly
-- **zei, neivqhaq tul** -- to drive away evil spirits by using spirit incantations
-- **zei, neivq leiq** -- to drive away evil spirits
=**zei, ngaq=** fish net
-- **zei puv, wuqduq** -- 1. to turn the head, 2. to turn around
zei puvq to fall into a liquid (11:218) (ga u˅-eu; ga pu˄-eu)
zeiseil seil to be extravagant (50:132)
-- zei, soqbuvq halzei -- to communicate freely
zei tao to throw into (38:16) (bi˯ u˅-eu); to throw a basketball into a hoop (41:200)
zei tul lal to rise suddenly (or) **beil tul lal**
zei xa to throw away (bi˯ dzeh-eu); to fall down from (34:56)

zei ya to fall into (45:61) (ga uᵛ g'eh-eu)

zeiq 1. domestic animals (je⌄ za⌄), 2. money and property (9:172, 50:18)
zeiq to surpass (**zeiq li nia** = able to surpass others)
(vb) **zeiq** more than (**miaq zeiq** = more than = mya⌄ dzeh⌄) (9:172)
(vb) **zeiq** probably (**zaol taq laq e ngeel aq zeiq ya** = he probably did that) (11:200)
(n) **zeiq** more than; older than (**yivq zeiq** = older than) (... dzeh⌄-eu)
zeiq left over; extra (or) **aqzeiq** (dzeᵛ laᵛ-eu)
=**zeiq, aq**= left over; extra (and see full)
zeiqbo aqhhol a rich man (not cruel)
zeiqbo havma a cruel rich man (33:3, 35:75)
zeiqdol bad-omen or abnormal animals (in the sense that there is a 'bad omen' connected with them) (je⌄ caw^)
zeiqdoq doq to get fertilizer in advance and pay for it later
zeiq **duv** to pay a fine for some wrong deeds (guiᵛ o‸ ti‸-eu)
zeiq duv ceiqla bivq to pay heavy taxes
zeiq duv ceiqla soq 1. to pay various taxes (45:76) (kaw⌄ ta‸-eu), 2. to have heavy taxes (or) **syuf** (Chi)
zeiq e **zalsiq** surplus (food) (50:200)
(vb) zeiq **gaoq** much ... (more) (**yal zeiq gaoq** = much easier) (mya⌄-eu; mya⌄ dzeh⌄-eu)
-- **zeiq, gol** -- to ache more
zeiqgov weak; thin domesticated animal
zeiqgov poisonous insects that live in mud
zeiqgov lavqniav aqma a poisonous insect that lives in mud
zeiqgov ziiv for feet to itch from contacting the poisonous insect described above
zeiqgu zeiqga old, weak domesticated animals (28:4)
zeiqheiq source of capital; money (50:18)
zeiqheiq yei nei daol open all sources (50:65)
=**zeiq, hyul**= domesticated animals
zeiq **hyuq neiq** to bribe
zeiqhhaq one's assets; one's capital or property; financial resources; financial capacity (50:18) (myaw⌄ gah⌄)
zeiqhhaq baq little capital and property (poor) (myaw⌄ gah⌄ yaw cui^)
zeiqhhaq tul large capital and property (wealthy)
zeiqhhol money 50:18) (myaw⌄ gah⌄ yaw mya⌄)
zeiq **hhyul** for animals to be pregnant
zeiqkeeq animal manure (9:172, 11:151) (je⌄ za⌄ ce⌄)
zeiqkeeq alsiq hail (or) **hollu** (frozen rain) (huᵛ lo -- taboo term in Ak.)
zeiqkeeq eelcal liquid present in compost

zeiqkeeq haqleil dust and dried matter from manure (9:172) (cf.: k'a˯ leh˅)
zeiqkeeq huaffeiq chemical fertilizer (57:146) (B=Chi)
zeiqkeeq keeqbaol a pile of compost (ca‸ ti˯ bym˅)
zeiqkeeq keeqduq a compost pit; manure pit (or) **keeqduq**
zeiqkeeq keeqqu a manure heap; compost pit
zeiqkeeq laqqiq a scoop for collecting manure and compost (9:172)
zeiqkeeq lav to spread compost with running water from higher in the field
zeiqkeeq luduq a compost pit (9:172)
zeiqkeeq ssa to collect animal manure for composting
zeiq koqzaq zyul the crime of stealing property (50:136)
zeiqkuv a stable for animals (9:172) (je˯ za˯ ku^)
zeiqli philosophic theory; philosophy (Chi) (50:208)
zeiq li e 1. to spend a great deal of money; 2. for something to be expensive
Zeiqluvq Molmil Ssaqli the last son of Molmil, who protects Hani animals
zeiqluvqssaq herder of animals (41:3) (je˯ za˯ bo-eu g'a˯)
zeiqma capital (as money) (9:173, 50:218)
zeiqma bial 1. loss of one's capital (sometimes by theft); 2. have a deficit (50:99)
zeiqma biav to lose one's property (perhaps through corruption) (50:131)
zeiqma sol leev to figure up one's wealth (property etc.) (50:137)
zeiqma xu bial lose money in business; lose one's capital (50:99)
zeiqmeeq qo exploration; prospecting; search for treasure (50:95)
=zeiq, miaq= more; too many; most
zeiqmiaoq bivqhaol aid financially; subsidize (50:219)
zeiqmo nei lazily (38:18)
zeiqnal animal disease (9:173) (je˯ za˯ na˅-eu)
=zeiq, naoq= less (cui^ dzeh˯-eu)
zeiq nei more than (dzeh˯ ni)
zeiqnei nei to be elastic
=zeiq, nil= (see full)
=zeiq, niv= (see full)
-- zeiq, qeil -- to love more; to love best
zeiq qu maq pievq lal not able to raise animals
zeiq qu miqnieiq animal husbandry (50:119)
zeiq qu zeiq zeq to raise animals and have them increase
zeiq sal to earn money (pyu˅ m˅ za-eu)
zeiqsal albol trees which can be sold and produce income (50:90)

zeiqsal galquv the regulation of the economy (50:90)
zeiqsal galquv zaol meeq rectify economic order (50:210)
zeiqsal kalyeiv economic crops (50:90)
zeiqsal kaq peelduq court to solve economic disputes (50:90)
zeiqsal lavqkavq economic dispute (50:90)
zeiqsal meeq e huvqlavq a good time of year for getting money
zeiqsal salpaoq paoq a united financial group (50:90)
zeiqsal yiqqeiq method of determining economic policy (50:90)
zeiqsal zeiqpyuq economic value (50:90)
-- zeiq, sultavq -- superiority; preponderance
zeiqssaq 1. domesticated animals (9:173) (je˅ za˅), 2. the net income (50:27), 3. profit; gain (50:198)
zeiqssaq hao fur (animal) (5:814) (je˅ za˅ ca˄ hm)
zeiqssaq luvqssaq animal herder; shepherd; cowherder (50:119)
=zeiqssaq, nil= wild animals
zeiqssaq pieiqduq pastoral area (50:119)
zeiqssaq zeiqdei a pasture (or) **jadei**
zeiqssaq zeiqkuv cuv to build a stall for animals
zeiqssaoq duv to spend money and goods freely (**zeiq** = an old word for one's property, including animals) (or) **piul ssaoq duv** (cf.: pyu˅ zm˅-eu)
zeiqsseif duty; responsibility (Chi) (50:205)
zeiqsseifziif system of job responsibility (Chi) (34:42, 50:205) (or) **fufzeiqziif**
zeiqssyuq species of animals
zeiq taol zeq lal domestic animals to increase by the thousands (46:117)
zeiq toq toq laq e to deposit
zeiqxoq philosophy (Chi) (50:208)
-- zeiq ya leil nyuq, ngeel -- to think it must be true
-- zeiq ya, ngeel -- perhaps it is
zeiq'yul 1. one's heritage (je˅ bi˅), 2. a pregnant female animal
zeiqzal animal feed (9:173) (je˅ za˅ dza˅)
=zeiq, zyul= a fine (money to pay a fine)
zeiqzyuq the animal leader in an animal group

zeiv to cut into pieces (deu^ nm^-eu)
zeiv broken (9:173) (k'eh˄ tseh^-eu)
=zeiv, al= wild banana
-- zeiv, dao -- worn out clothing
-- zeiv, haqcil -- to split bamboo into slats
zeivho to clamor (45:24)
-- zeiv, hhe -- torn; pulled to pieces
=zeiv, miav= an injured eye
=zeiv nei, saoq= disgusting
zeivnuv zeivyav meil broken into pieces; shattered (la^ pa^-eu)

zeivq 1. to gossip (k'oe$_{\vee}$ sa^ sa^-eu), 2. to have an argument

=zeivq, aq= cicada

zeivq beeq to talk in a wrong way, or a disturbing way (13:20) (ngeh$_{\vee}$ doe$^{\vee}$-eu)

zeivqmav mav to talk in a dream (ngeh$_{\vee}$ ma^ ma^-eu)

zeivqqoq to gossip back (k'oe$_{\vee}$ sa^ k'o$_{\wedge}$-eu; ja k'o$_{\wedge}$-eu)

zeif again (Chi) (**Zeif maq yiuvq e ngaoq neesoq maq tul lal qaol wul naq.** Again, if we don't sleep now, we won't be able to get up tomorrow. 41:38)

zeifbei qilyeiq to radically reform; thoroughly overhaul (Chi) (34:12)

zeifbieif a coup d'etat (Chi) (34:6)

zeifceiq policy (as, the policy of the Communist party) (Chi) (9:172, 11:192, 26:103, 50:211)

zeifceiq galma seq to guide along the way in accordance with the policy (12:127) (A=Chi)

zeifda a political party (Chi) (34:35, 50:211)

zeiffu government (Chi) (9:172, 50:211)

zeiffu qovq government (A=Chi) (or) **aqtav soqpaq; goqjal qovq** (A=Chi)

zeifgaolso township site (Chi) (50:209)

zeifhhyu political commissar (Chi) (50:211)

zeifjeif 1. a bond; a debenture (Chi) (50:206), 2. credentials; papers; certificates (Chi) (50:211)

zeifji political discipline; government regulation (Chi) (34:99, 50:211)

zeifmiq prove; testify; certificate (Chi) (50:211)

zeifqeiq political power (Chi) (34:4)

zeifqeiq col a creditor (A=Chi) (50:206)

zeifqeiq zuziiq political organization; authority (Chi) (50:211)

zeifweiq main body of an article or letter (Chi)

zeifwuf a debt; liability (Chi) (50:206)

zeifxil to vitalize (Chi) (34:21)

zeifxiq Chinese People's Political Consultative Conference (shortened form) (Chi) (50:211)

zeifyaq to suppress (Chi)

zeifyida a party out of political office; a minority party (Chi) (34:53)

zeifza township governor (Chi) (50:209)

zeifziif politics (Chi) (**siiqsiif zeifziif** = current politics - 26:50) (as a subject in school - 41:13)

zeifziifbuf political department (Chi) (50:211)

zeifziif guafsuaf put politics before everything; put politics in charge of everything (Chi) (50:211)

zeifziif heiqxil the political core (Chi) (34:42)

zeifziif qeiqlif bavq zei to deprive someone of their political rights (AB=Chi) (50:15)

zeifziif weiqjil political crisis (Chi) (50:211)

zeifziif xiqsal political consultant (Chi) (34:52)
zeifziif xiqsal hyufyif Chinese People's Political Consultative Conference (Chi) (or) **zeifxiq** (shortened form) (50:211)

ZI

zil watertight
zil a crunchy taste (as nuts)
zil well made (as a plow)
zil to take aim at a target (dziˇ-eu)
zil accurate (**teq daov zil** = very accurate at shooting a basketball - 41:199)
zil clf. for birds
=zil, al= a bird (aˇ jiˇ)
=zil, aq= folk songs (sha˅ zi^ zi^-eu)
zilbaq liquor; wine (9:174) (jiˇ ba˅)
zilbaq baqqeil distiller's grains (jiˇ ba˅ jiˇ cehˇ)
zilbaq buqssaq liquor jar; wine jar (9:174)
zilbaq dolqoq qoq to drink with friends
zilbaq dol saq to drink up (bottoms up)
zilbaq dol yevq to be drunk (jiˇ ba˅ dawˇ yeh˄-eu)
zilbaq savq to distill liquor (11:127) (jiˇ ba˅ sa˄-eu)
zilbaq seiv for young married couples to give liquor to elders while asking for their blessing
zilbaq yevq to be drunk (jiˇ ba˅ yeh˄-eu)
zilbaq zilduvq poisonous wine (35:60) (jiˇ ba˅ dzaˇ do˄)
zilbaq zilhhev a funnel used in distilling liquor
zilbaq zilkeel good-tasting wine (35:60) (jiˇ ba˅ yaw kuiˇ)
zilbaq zilqul liquor or wine made from sticky rice (9:174) (haw˅ nyaw˅ jiˇ ba˅)
zilbaq zilsol 'pure' liquor (used in ceremonies, no one else must have drunk of it, and it must have nothing in it) (jiˇ ba˅ jiˇ shawˇ)
zilbeeq a bird nest (11:126, 45:53) (aˇ jiˇ bah˅)
Zilbiei Alloq the 'god' (**Molmil**) who created the earth (or) **Jalbil Allaq** (45:43) (Ja bi oe˅ lah˅)
zilcov cov youngsters climb up into the attic and through a hole let down small coins and cigarettes wrapped at the end of a pole, to the elders seated at table below, who then wrap up food in banana leaves and send it back up on the same pole to the children waiting above
-- zil, doqzil -- 1. to discuss, 2. to have a meeting
zilhav a bird cage
zilhaoq a winecup (35:53) (jiˇ ba˅ k'm˅ ma˅)
zilhevq nei tightly (zi˄ dah ni)
zilhevq pa hevq nei very tightly (46:118) (zi˄ dah ni)
zilheil old wine; liquor
=zil, hu= to take a chance

zilhhel nei tasty; very good to eat (yaw kuiˇ)
ziljif economic (Chi)
=zil, kul= to call a meeting (kuˇ dzoeˇ-eu)
zilkuq a ladle for dipping up wine
zilkuv lalssaq a swallow (brd) (or) **jaljul lalhhaq** (45:53)
zillovq lovq to drink and talk together (46:105)
-- zil, muvq -- to aim (as a crossbow)
zil nil zil siil red and golden birds (14:188)
-- zil, nyuq duvq nyuq -- careful consideration
Zilpiqxeif (see: **Jilpiqxeif**) (14:169)
zilqiq army chess; military chess (Chi) (14:195)
-- zil, qoq -- to call together
zilseiq spirit of a person (or) **zilsei** (Chi) (**aqyoq e zilseiq hal taq hev** = his spirit is with us always - 26:99) (cf.: sa‸ laˇ)
zilsiivq zilnil a canary (brd)
zilssaq bird (aˇ jiˇ)
ziltieiq a subsidy; an allowance (as a special allowance for soldiers - 26:74) (Chi)
zilxeiq rank (as in the army) (Chi) (or) **deigaol** (Chi)
zilyeif experience (Chi)
zilzaoq zaoq to drink together (46:87) (ti‿ kaw^ lo‸-ehˇ dawˇ-eu)

zi clf. for a young plant, seedling (aˇ ji)
=zi, hhoq= vegetable seedling
ziyeiqssil laryngealized ('tight') vowel (Chi)

ziq 1. hemp (dzi‿), 2. sap from tree (or) **alziq** (aˇ dzi‿)
=ziq, al= sap
-- ziq, albol -- sap or resin from a tree
=ziq, ba= blacksmith
=ziq, eel= juice (46:180)
ziq nei straight (dawˇ coe ni)
ziqpav hemp thread
ziqyiq directly (Chi) (34:66) (dawˇ coe ni)

=ziv, aq= clitoris (taboo)
=ziv, beivq= clitoris (taboo)
=ziv nei, caol= very dense; very thick
-- ziv, taq -- a command to be quiet ('don't move')

zivq 1. season (46:81), 2. a quarter of time (in the sense of a season) (50:81)

ZII

ziil a written character (Chi) (**ziil buvq** = to write a character - (A=Chi) (41:77)
ziil to buzz (or) **zil** (zi)
ziilbeijal a capitalist (Chi) (50:218)
ziilbei zuyif capitalism (Chi) (50:218)

ziilbuf Party Branch (Chi) (50:211)

ziilca geiljiq bourgeoisie; capitalist class (Chi) (34:29, 50:218)

ziilca geiljiq ziifyeqhuaf bourgeoisie liberalism (Chi) (50:218)

ziilciiq to support (Chi) (34:51)

ziilgeiq qualification (Chi) (34:99)

ziilhyul to instruct in some skill (as teaching a person how to drive a car - 26:98) (Chi) (or) **ziihyul**

ziil nei maq gal not so bad

-- ziil, piav -- 1. to scratch something flat, 2. to make clean

ziilqei a fang; canine tooth (or) **seqziil** (seuᵥ juiᵛ)

=ziil, seq= fang; canine tooth

ziilsiiq basic knowledge (Chi) (50:212) (**seilmif ziilsiiq** = basic knowledge about life - 15:title, 26:50)

ziilsiiq feifzii an intellectual; intelligentsia (Chi) (34:20, 50:212) (or) **soqhhaq hev col**

ziilsiiqhuaf to intellectualize (Chi) (34:107)

ziilsiiq qilnieiq school graduates (A=Chi) (50:212)

ziilsiiq xaopi a short play; a short story (50:212)

ziilsul a party branch secretary (Chi) (41:3, 50:211)

ziilyeiq resources; natural resources (Chi) (50:219)

ziilyeiq yil go to support someone in what they are doing (A=Chi)

ziilyoq a poisonous drug from a tuberous plant (but if cooked will not be poisonous, and is used for medicine) (Chi)

ziilziil nei the sound of liquid being drunk ('gurgle, gurgle, gurgle') (14:181)

zii clf. for a market (9:173) (cf. **Lahu: tcuh**)

zii to inflate; pump up (as a ball) (11:11)

ziidaof to guide (Chi) (34:28) (sheuᵥ mehᵥ-eu)

ziidaof falzeil a guiding principle (Chi)

ziidaof siilxa guiding ideology (Chi) (50:213)

ziidaofyeiq a political instructor; a political commander (as in an army unit) (Chi) (26:68, 50:213)

ziihovq a bullet shell; a shell casing

ziihyul (see: **ziilhyul**)

ziihyulbuf a command post; a headquarters (Chi)

ziihyulteiq control tower; command tower (Chi) (50:213)

ziijaol lac-producing insects they raise on trees, use the project in writing and staining teeth red (Chi) (14:228) (cf. **seqnil**)

=zii, lal= mule (and see full)

zii'luq luq cheat and rob (grab) (50:72) (lu geu˄-eu)

ziinaqzeil compass (Chi) (50:213)

ziiwafxieif ultraviolet rays (Chi) (10:6)

ziiq to wear shoes (9:173, 11:20) (naw˅-eu)
ziiq to ride (as a horse) (9:173) (**moq ziiq** = to ride a horse); to go by air; ship; car; etc. (dzi˅-eu)
-- **ziiq, alhhe** -- to swing on a swing (sit on it) (11:50, 46:109)
-- **ziiq, aqjaol** -- to swing on a long pole
ziiqbal duty (Chi) (as to be on duty - 26:28)
ziiqbal zusseif a service director (Chi)
ziiqceil the title of a technical or professional post, such as engineer, professor, lecturer, etc.) (Chi) (50:212) (**xoqhhyuf** = academic degree, such as: Ph.D., M.A., B.A. etc. = Chi)
ziiq dav to mount (as on a horse) (13:32)
ziiqfaq jilgual an administrative unit which makes sure the law is being carried out (Chi) (50:212)
ziiqhhav a riding saddle (dzi˅ g'a)
ziiqliaf quality (as the quality of coal, oil, etc.) (Chi) (26:35)
=**ziiq lolbieil, ja**= a wooden table
ziiqmiqdif a colony (Chi) (34:3, 50:212)
ziiqmiq zuyif colonialism (Chi) (50:212)
ziiqmoq a riding horse (46:160) (dzi˅ mah˅)
-- **ziiq, moq** -- to ride a horse
ziiqneiq function (Chi) (34:49)
ziiqniq occupation; vocation; profession (Chi) (50:212)
ziiqqeiq powers; authority of office (Chi) (34:51, 50:212) (cf.: bao˅)
-- **ziiq teiq, miavbil** -- for tears to stop running
ziiqwuqxoq botany (Chi) (50:212)
ziiqxaqsiif municipality directly under the government (Chi) (50:212)
ziiqzeif da the party in power (Chi) (50:213)

ziiv to itch (9:173) (dzui^-eu)
-- **ziiv, alziiv** -- for an itch to itch

ziivq to whip or beat with a stick (or) **hhe ziivq** (jui˄-eu)
ziivq 1. to compile (2:61); 2. to lay bricks (as in building a wall - 9:174; 226:63) (tso^-eu; gaw˅ da^-eu); 3. to weave (rattan, bamboo) (9:174) (dzeu˄-eu), 4. to knit (or) **hhavq**
ziivqbel for one to shake one's head in order to wake up (u˅ du˅ jui˄-eu)
ziivq e jilqiq machine to weave cloth (B=Chi) (50:12)
=**ziivq, eel**= a rainstorm
-- **ziivq, hhe** -- to beat with a stick or whip (as a horse)
=**ziivq nei, kaoqnao**= to be difficult to swallow
ziivq teiq to control oneself (50:98)
=**ziivq ziivqma, aoqsseil sseil**= large drops of rain

ziif to move mountains; control rivers (Chi) (as an

engineer) (26:100)

ziifbif jefsseiq to cure the illness to save the patient (Chi) (34:109)

ziifdif to come to a conclusion (Chi) (34:5)

ziifduf 1. a system (Chi) (50:213) (**boqxoq ziifduf** = an exploitative system - 34:10), 2. a regulation, a rule (as in the army) (Chi) (26:47)

ziifduf huaf a system (Chi) (34:74)

ziifhyuf wisdom; intelligence (Chi) (34:77) (tsaw˅ gah˅)

ziifhhal public order; public security (Chi)

ziifjif to salute (Chi) (34:21)

ziifjoq nei consciousness (A=Chi) (34:46)

ziifli to administer; to govern (Chi)

ziifliq geilseil self-reliance; independence (Chi) (26:54)

ziiflieqdif plot of land for personal use; private plot (Chi) (50:219)

ziifmu 1. the alphabet (2:61, 41:76), 2. a letter of the alphabet (Chi) (41:77)

ziifmubiao alphabet (Chi)

ziifqaq unremitting (Chi) (34:19)

ziifssaqgeif natural world (Chi) (50:219)

ziifssaq gyulliq natural law (Chi) (50:219)

ziifssaq kolxoq natural science (Chi) (50:219)

ziifssaq ziilyeiq natural resources (Chi) (50:219)

ziifxifxil self-confident (Chi) (34:19)

ziifyeq freedom; liberty (Chi) (26:112, 50:219)

ziifyeqhuaf liberalization (Chi) (34:29, 50:219)

ziifziif autonomous (Chi) (34:55)

ziifziif jilgual autonomous administration (Chi) (50:219)

ziifziif qeiq autonomy (Chi) (50:220)

ziifziifqil an autonomous region (Chi) (50:219) (**Nyufmaoggu Ziifziifqil** = Neimenggu Autonomous Region (50:226)

ziifziifxeif autonomous county (Chi) (50:220)

ziifziifzel an autonomous prefecture (Chi) (50:220)

ziifzu qeiq act on one's own; decide for oneself (Chi) (50:220)

ziifzualxil (see: **ziifzueilxil**) (34:19)

ziifzueilxil self-respect; self-esteem (Chi)

ZO

zol 1. to read; study; learn (45:53) (dzaw-eu; gui-eu) (cf. saw˅-eu). 2. to emulate (50:191)

zolcol lal kaoq letters from readers (as in a newspaper) (50:40)

-- **zol, culzaol** -- to study in a junior middle school (A=Chi)

zol deil old enough to study; old enough to go to school (57:80)

-- zol, **doqgaq** -- to pass on a message

-- **zolduq, soqhhaq** -- a school ('book study place')

zolhuvq school age (50:191)
zolkaoq a textbook (50:97)
=zol, lavqqivq qivq= an apprentice
zolmeiq puv to restudy (50:16)
zolnieiq to study a course (dzaw-eu)
zolnieiq pieiq for school or class to be over (50:49)
zol puv to review; re-read (9:174) (gui po^-eu; dzaw po^-eu)
zol puv bal a make-up class (B=Chi) (50:16)
zol puv hu to review what studied or read (50:54)
zol puv zoldaol daol to review one's lessons (50:177)
zolpyuq tuition fee; tuition (50:191)
zolqoq a classmate; schoolmate (dzaw caw⌄)
-- zolqoq, soqhhaq -- classmate; schoolmate
zol saq to graduate (50:11)
zolseil seil to read out loud (50:102)
zolssaq student; apprentice; trainee; disciple (50:170, 191)
zolteil 1. pronunciation, 2. the sound of reading (9:174)
-- zolteil, soqmiav -- the sound of letters; pronunciation
zolteivq dav to go to a higher grade in school (50:151)
-- zolyaol, soqhhaq -- school
-- zol, zaol -- 1. to practice, 2. to learn (dzaw-eu)

zo to have a habit (dzaw-eu)
zo to have ever (vb) (**gaq zo** = to have loved, **mol zo** = to have seen) (vb haw-eu)
zo left deviation (Chi) (34:91)
-- zo, hyuqzaq -- a habitual thief
-- zo, hheivqzaq -- to be a habitual liar
zo qi left deviation; left-leaning (in political sense) (Chi) (34:6, 50:222)
-- zo, zaol -- to form a habit

zoq to stretch out straight (as a leg) (9:174)
zoq to be foolish; stupid)
=zoq, aq= foolish (a⌄ dzaw⌄ = foolish male in Ak.)
zoqdei a playground in a village (deh k'ah⌄)
zoqdei deima a large playground in a village (deh k'ah⌄)
zoqfaol style; way; style of work (Chi) (50:222)
zoqgee in front of the house (9:174) (dzaw⌄ gui = downslope area of house in Ak.)
zoqgee ssaq people who live downstream (14:232)
zoqgee zoqnia the back and front of a house
zoqjal a writer (Chi) (50:222)
-- zoq, keel kuv -- to stretch out one's legs
zoq lal at the time (A=Chi) (14:142)
zoqleil nei straight way (daw˅ coe ni)
zoqleil pa leil nei very straight (46:113)
zoqleiq kovq to communicate a disease; infect

someone else (10:23) (na$^{\vee}$ gaw$^{\vee}$ nyaw$_{\vee}$-i$^{\vee}$-eu)
=zoq, loq= to dance
zoqmavq nei to be numb; insensitive (14:149)
zoqniq school assignment; homework (Chi) (41:66, 50:222)
zoqnia up (as behind the house) (9:174, 11:219) (**zyuqnia** = poetic language) (dzaw$_{\vee}$ nya = upslope area of the house)
zoqnia ssaq people who live upstream (14:232)
-- zoq, nyuq -- 1. to forgive; 2. to overcome
zoqpi works (as, 'works of art', 'works of literature') (Chi) (34:61)
-- zoq, wulzoq -- to make sausage
zoqyaof function (Chi) (34:42)
zoqzaofhaof mark of emphasis (Chi) (50:218)
zoqzii desk; table (Chi) (26:89)

=zov nei, **naoq=** 1. freshly, 2. softly, 3. spongy

zovq a lock (6:181, 9:174) (mah$_{\vee}$ taw$_{\wedge}$)
zovq clf. for a lock (11:34)
zovqdul a key (to a lock) (mah$_{\vee}$ taw$_{\wedge}$ da$^{\vee}$ du$^{\vee}$)
zovqlavq Chinese prickly ash (it has a cone which is spicy hot, used as a condiment)
zovqlavq miqteiv a play gun made of bamboo (za$_{\wedge}$ baw$^{\vee}$ mi$_{\vee}$ beu$^{\wedge}$)
=zovq, nieivq= anesthesia
zovq pav to change (as money) (50:41)
zovq pao to unlock (mah$_{\vee}$ taw$_{\wedge}$ pah-eu)
zovq piq to lock a lock (mah$_{\vee}$ taw$_{\wedge}$ pi$_{\vee}$-eu) (9:174)

-- **zof, zaocaol** -- to do morning exercises (Chi)

ZU

zul to squat on one's heels (daw$_{\vee}$ dzu$^{\vee}$ dzu$^{\vee}$-eu)
zulbal local rich lord (used esp. before liberation) (35:48)
-- zul, ciil -- to take someone to a seat
Zul Deiq a person named Zhu De who was an important official (zulbal) in Dazhai village (**Oltol Tavqzaoq**) (Chi) (34:20)
-- zul, milzul -- land to be barren (cannot grow much of anything on it)
zul pieiv to sit down with low spirits (45:23)
zul pyul la to move closer (38:15)
Zul Xaohoq Zhu Xiaohe, a famous Hani folksong singer (14:182)

=zu, aqhhavq meiq= pig snout
=zu, aqhhuv meiq= the lower lip
zubieil chief editor (Chi) (50:215)
zugoq motherland; homeland (Chi) (34:29)
zugoq yaol gaq love the motherland (A=Chi) (50:1)
zugual zuyif subjectivism (Chi) (50:215)

zuhoqgyuf a cupboard with sections in it; a cabinet (Chi) (50:221)
=zu, miq= chicken tail (the meaty portion)
=zu, nal= the tip of the nose
=zu nalzu meil, meiq= all to talk at once
zu'qeiq 1. territory (35:15); 2. sovereign rights (Chi) (34:82)
zusseif director (Chi) (50:215)
=zu tav, meiq= a talkative person
zuti main body; principal part (Chi) (34:38)
zutiq theme; subject (Chi)
zuxiq 1. chairman (Chi) (26:13) (**zuxiq Paoq** = chairman Paoq - 26:13), 2. principal penalty (Chi) (50:215)
zuxiqteiq a platform for speakers etc. at meetings (Chi)
zuyaof mainly (Chi) (41:13) (**Zuyaof nei yiweiq meiq.** I mainly teach Chinese. 41:13) (myaˬ myaˬ)
zuyi subject (in gram.) (Chi) (50:216)
zuyif doctrine; doctrinism (Chi) (50:216)
zuzal to advocate; stand for (Chi) (34:76) (tsawˇ kaˬ)
zuza group leader (Chi) (9:175) (aˇ muˇ aˬ yui^)
zuziiq organization (Chi) (WHO = **Goqjiq Weifseil Zusiiq**) (10:13) an organized group (as, Communist party's organization - 26:103, 34:42, 50:221)
zuziiqbuf 1. a committee; 2. organization (Chi) (50:221)
zuziiq yeiqzeiq the discipline of an organization (Chi) (34:102)

zuq to tremble; shiver (5:121)
=zuq, aq= a worm; insect
=zuq, byuq= a spider (aˬ g'o^ lo^ ma)
-- zuq, gavzuq -- to be chilly ('shivering with cold')
-- zuq, guvzuq -- in a state of great fear ('shivering with fear')
zuqhof to congratulate (Chi)
-- zuq, hhyulzuq -- 1. to be shrivelled, 2. to be excited by good news
-- zuq, lulzuq -- (see full)
-- zuq, saqzuq -- to shiver; tremble
zuqyil a method (Chi)

zuv to stir up and down (9:174)
zuv 1. very sharp (yaw ta^), 2. easy to cut deeply
zuv to owe money (pyuˇ da^-eu)
zuv luv zeiv leiv pieces of (35:49)
zuv nei carefully (11:201) (**zuv nei salhu** = watch carefully)
=zuv, zyuq= hereditary system

zuvq 1. nothing overlooked in doing a job; everything complete & perfect (50:174), 2. to have enough

equipment for the task (57:137)
zuvq clf. for a set (as of clothes, tools, pots and pans) (9:174, 11:77) (**diqpuq lavqniaov qiq zuvq** - set of tools for a blacksmith) (ti̬ sheh^)
zuvq to wrinkle (as forehead) (9:175) (yaw jṷ)
zuvq to go to market (**galzii zuvq** = go to market) (9:175, 11:158) (leh^ dzṷ-eu)
=zuvq, baq= a wrinkle
-- zuvq, leiv -- to go to market (leh^ dzṷ-eu)
=zuvq meil, bil= wrinkled; folded
zuvq nei all (as all the flavor) (13:2)
zuvqsaq complete; integrated; intact (50:174)
zuvqteiv nei of a wrinkled appearance (yaw jṷ)
Zuvqyiv Alsal a person's name (in a Hani legend about their moving south - 38:33)

zufceiq register (Chi) (50:216)
zufciiq a particle (gram.) (Chi)
zufse assistant (Chi) (26:98)
zufxoqjil (piul) stipend: grant-in-aid (Chi) (50:216)
zufyil ziifmu the phonetic alphabet (Chi) (50:216)

ZUA

zualjal expert; specialist (Chi) (50:217)
zualmeiq liqsseiq to do for others; to be altruistic (or) **zualmeiq lifsseiq** (Chi) (26:100) (a̬ caw̬ g'aˇ du̬ mˇ-eu)
zualmeiq sseiqceiq people with professional skill (Chi) (50:217)
zualniqhuf professional family (Chi) (50:217)
zualniqhuaf to specialize; professionalize (Chi) (34:107, 50:217) (and see: **zueilniqhuaf**)
zualyeiq dignity; honor (Chi) (34:15) (also used in the expression: 'sanctity of the law') (k'ah̬ sehˇ)
zualzeif dictatorship (Chi) (34:48) (& see: **zualziif**)
zualziif dictatorship (Chi) (50:217)
zualzof to respect (or) **zualzaof** (Chi) (34:15) (see also: **zueilzof; zyulzaof; zyulzif**)

zuaniq for an army man to be transferred to civilian work (Chi) (50:217)
zuazeif for a temporary worker to become a regular worker (Chi) (50:217)

zuafkuaf condition; state of affairs (Chi) (50:217)
zuafyi adverbial modifier (Chi) (50:217)

ZUEI

zueiljal an expert (Chi)
zueilniqhuaf to professionalize (Chi) (or) **zualniqhuaf**
zueilzof to respect (or) **zualzof; zualzaof; zyulzaof;**

zyulzif (yaw zeu baw-eu)

ZYU

zyul to meet together; to assemble; come together (cf.: tah$_\vee$ dzoe$^\vee$-eu; dzoe$^\vee$ tsa$_\wedge$-eu)
zyul a crime; guilt (Chi) (50:221)
zyul to be blamed (45:72)
zyulbev bev sil to sentence to death by shooting (50:127)
-- zyul, colzyul -- for people to gather together
=zyul, deiq= to offend (Chi) (46:195)
-- zyul, deivq -- some bad things predestined from birth (such as a bad death; cf. **deivq meeq**)
zyulduq nyuq hev show repentance; show penitence (50:76)
zyulgaoq gaoq gathered together (34:1)
zyulgol bi bial amnesty; general pardon; to remit (50:31, 148)
-- zyul, gul -- to call (people) together
-- zyul, hhavqzaq -- corrupting crimes (50:162)
zyuljif respect; honor; esteem (Chi) (50:221)
=zyul, jol= to come together
=zyul, joq= ringworm
-- zyul, kul -- to call and gather
zyul lal to meet together (50:79)
zyulleiq leiq to investigate a case (50:218)
zyulleiq leiqtevq term of investigating (50:218)
=zyul, lol= confluence of two rivers
zyulma principal criminal (50:215)
zyul meiqzaq zaol bial destroy the evidence of a crime (50:76)
zyul miaol ceil to judge a criminal (A=Chi)
zyul **miaol eil ceiv** final charge (legal); last accusation (A=Chi) (50:221)
zyulmiaoq deiq hhovq to hide criminal evidence (50:198)
zyul puv to repeat one's mistakes (crimes) (50:24); to revert to bad ways (50:24)
zyulpuv puv repeatedly commit crimes; one who is a habitual criminal (50:110)
-- zyul, siltovq -- capital offence; capital crime
-- zyul, ssaoq -- 1. to bring together, 2. to use money illegally
-- zyul, taoq -- to meet up with
zyultaoq taoqma guilty of the most heinous crimes (A=Chi) (50:221)
Zyulxyul Zhuanxu, name of an ancient king in China (Chi)
-- zyul, zaol -- to commit a crime
zyulzaof to respect; value; esteem (Chi) (26:29) (as in: one must respect the master craftsman) (see also: **zualzof; zyulzif**) (yaw zeu baw-eu)
zyulzeiq a fine; money paid for a punishment (50:44) (gui$^\vee$ o$_\wedge$)

zyulzeiq duv to pay a fine; to pay the money for punishment (50:44) (gui˅ o˄ ti˄-eu)

zyulzeiq hha leiq investigate and affix responsibility for an accident (50:217)

zyulzeiq qo find out who is to blame for an accident (50:218)

zyulzif to hold in high esteem; to respect (as elders, army leaders, etc.) (Chi) (26:103, 120) (see also: **zyulzaof; zualzof**) (ciˬ poeˬ-eu)

zyu'qoq accurate (Chi)

zyuq 1. a term formerly used for the headman of a village (see: **zyuqma**), although now **milguq** is generally used, 2. king, 3. leader (or) **zyuqma; zyuqmoq** (dzoeˬ ma)

zyuq, pil, qivq shortened terms for the 'great three' in a Hani village (**zyuqma, moqpil**, and **qivq** = village leader, spirit priest, blacksmith/ carpenter)

=**zyuq, almiuvq miuvq**= king of the monkeys; leader

-- **zyuq, bavq** -- (see full)

=**zyuq, biaq**= queen bee (byaˬ sahˬ ma)

zyuqdal scissors (6:182, 9:175) (tehˬ da˅)

=**zyuq, hovq**= ancestors (aˬ poeˬ aˬ piˬ)

zyuqlei nei fat and big; plump (35:17) (yaw tsu˅)

zyuqma 1. a term formerly used for the headman of a village or any major officer in the village, 2. a village head (or) **zyuqmoq** (most of his duties now taken over by the **milguq**) (cf. dzoeˬ ma = village founder, village head), 3. commander-in-chief (50:169)

zyuqma aqpiq ruler's wife (or) **zyuqma miqssaq**

zyuqma mama jolhhal the highest organ of state power (50:221)

zyuqma miqssaq ruler's wife (or) **zyuqma aqpiq**

zyuqmoq 1. respectful term for an older ruler (in this case by the wife of an ogre to the ogre (46:104), 2. see: **zyuqma**

Zyuqnil siq February (9:175, 11:68, 41:107) (or) **Joqnil siq**

zyuqnia up (as behind the house) in poetic lang.

zyuqpiaq the rear leg of large animals killed in the jungle, which is given to the **zyuqma**

zyuqqoq village headmen who are friends

zyuqsiq an official symbol of power & position

Zyuqtaoqpaoq a Hani ancestor (son of **Moq'yulzyuq**) (46:108) (Dzoeˬ tahˬ pahˬ, son of: Mawˬ oe˅ dzoeˬ)

zyuq zaq seek hegemony; dominate (50:23)

zyuqzaq January spring festival

zyuqzaq saqhel ritual meat offered during the spring festival

Zyuqzaq siq January (9:175, 11:68, 41:107) (or) **Joqzaq siq**

zyuqzaq zaq to celebrate the spring festival; the

June festival
=zyuq, zeiq= (see full)
zyuqzuv the hereditary system (dzoe˯ dza˯)

zyufgaol lixa highest ideals (Chi) (34:98)

ENGLISH - HANI INDEX

a A -- 571

b B -- 591

c C -- 597

d D -- 619

e E -- 631

f F -- 640

g G -- 651

h H -- 660

i I -- 670

j J -- 675

k K -- 677

l L -- 679

m M -- 689

n N -- 700

o O -- 705

p P -- 710

q Q -- 726

r R -- 728

s S -- 740

t T -- 767

u U -- 781

v V -- 784

w W -- 787

x X -- 798

y Y -- 799

z Z -- 801

a A a A a A

A a soqmiav aqma hholqei huqteil teilli qiq mol

---

abacus **solpeiq** (Chi) (11:30, 50:161)
abandon, to; give up **pieiq zei**
abandoned **duq zei; bavq zei**
abdomen; belly **wuqma; wuqdeiq**
abduct, to **hyuq kavqtovq; hyuq su zaq** (latter used esp. for abducting a person)
  abduct and sell a person **col aoq zaq**
ability, to have **cyuq zaq; neiqliq** (26:119); **golful** (Chi) (26:48); **gaolful; beqsiil** (Chi) (57:1, pf.); **beisiiq** (Chi) (26:47, 50:10)
a bit **alciiv**
ablaze 1. **miqzaq dovq** (as a fire); 2. **miqzaq sseiv** (as something ablaze with burning lights)
able **qivq** (11:40) (see also: **nia**)
  able person, an **colma** (32:3); **nia e col**
  able to (vb) **(vb) qaol; (vb) hhaq; (vb) nia; (vb) qi**
abortion (to take place) **ssaq ya**
  abortion, induced **ssaqceiq beq zei**
about; concerning (see: concerning)
above; upper **hultav; aqtav; aqtav pyu**
absent-minded **maq nyuq gaol; nyuq nyuq mav mav**
absolute **jyuqdyuf** (Chi)
absorb; assimilate **caoq teiq; cuv; suv**
abundant **miaq nei**
abuse, to **caol**
  abuse someone, to **halnil nil**

academic title (as: Ph.D., M.A., B.A., etc.) **xoqhhyuf** (Chi)
accelerator (for machinery) **bieifsuqxal** (Chi) (26:33)
accept **daqhaol; ceiqdal** (Chi) (as in accepting responsibility)
accomplishment **sufya** (Chi) (50:160)
according to **lo'qo**
according to rule **yo'liq galkov lo'qo**
account book **soldaoq** (50:208)
account for, to **eil loq**
account items **solkov** (50:208)
accountant **kuefjif** (Chi)
accounts **solzal**
  account, to keep an **solzal sol**
  account, to make an **solzal aol**
accumulate, to **taqssaoq** (26:108)
accurate, to be **zil; cuvnei; zyu'qoq** (Chi)
accusation, written (in legal sense) **bu zaq soqbuvq**
accuse, to **bu** (27:12); **bu lal bu zaq; yaq; bi yaq** (**col nei bi yaq** - accused by people); **eil lal yaq lal**

accuse, right to **bu zaq qeiqlif** (B=Chi)
accused, the; the defendant **bi bucol**
accuse falsely, to **eil cuvq** (33:3)
ache, to **gol**
ache (as in stomach and head) **kovq**
ache more **gol zeiq**
Achilles tendon **keelguq**
acid **lieqsual; lieqsual naciq** (A=Chi) (26:84)
acknowledge, to **ssiil**
acne **lulsiq**
act; move **niv**
act a part, to **zaol leivq; zaol hheivq**
action 3rd person **(vb) miq** (**eil miq** = said to him)
active **hhulqil nei** (10:pref)
active, to be **jiqjiq** (Chi) **koqteil qei nei; keellavq bel**
actively; happily **geeq eel geeq nei**
active village **puvlovq lovq**
act one's part **yoqhhaq aolnieiq aol**
actuality; reality **xeifsiiq** (Chi)

Adam's apple; larynx **kaoqciivq**
adaptability **juqtao za** (50:155)
add to (as soup to rice) **leivq**
addicted to, to be **zaq dav dol dav (maq meeq e miqnieiq)**
addicted to smoking **yeilyiq** (Chi)
addition (vb) **laoq** (**eil laoq** = add more words; **bavq laoq** = put something more in)
address; place where one lives **jolduq**
add to, to **puv dav** (A=Chi) (11:31); **hha dav; zaol dav** (as to add to a burden)
add up, to **sol ssaoq; bavq laoq**
address (of house) **laqhyul jolduq** (26:81)
adjective **xiqyaoqciiq** (Chi) (50:189)
adjust; reform **zei'faol** (Chi)
adjust; regulate, to **ceil soq; tiaoqjiq; tiaoqzei** (Chi) (26:30)
administer; to govern **ziifli** (Chi)
administration **xiqzeif** (Chi) (50:189)
administration; management **xiqzeif gua'li** (Chi)
administrative law **xiqzeif faqgyul** (Chi) (50:189)
admit a mistake **ssiil**
admonish, to **meiq gaol** (50:192)
admonish, to; caution **naqteil xa**
adopt, to 1. **qu zaq** (as a child); 2. **eildoq nal haq** (as to adopt a plan or idea)
adorn; fix up **susi**
adult **colhav**
adultery **miqyo cavq zaq; taoljeil** (Chi) (50:167)
adultery; illicit sexual relationship **wuqcavq lav**
advance; improve **xeilzif** (Chi) (26:106)
advanced collective unit **xeilzif jiqti** (Chi) (26:101)
advanced nations; stand among **daqtav colssaq yokyul**

alkaq xovq tul
adventurism **maofxei zuyif** (Chi) (34:6)
adverb **fufciiq** (Chi)
advertise; publicise **eilhaoq eilceiv** (50:190)
advice **meiq gaol**
advise, to **meiq gaol; eil gaol meiq gaol**
advocate, an **tiqcal** (Chi)
advocate, to **zuzal** (Chi)
adze **laqceiq; lavqceiq**

aesthetics **meixoq** (Chi)

affairs **siifwuf** (Chi)
affairs; situation **qiqkuaf** (Chi)
affect; influence **yixa** (Chi)
affectionately toward **gaqzav hhyulqaol nei**
afraid, to be **guv**
after (vb) **taoqngaoq; naolhao**
after a little bit **ciiv nei qiq heiq** (13:12)
afterbirth **albeil; beeteiq (ssaq e beeteiq)**
afternoon; daytime **naolhhaol**
after someone (as name a person after someone; to do something after someone) **laqgee nei**
after this **xil naolhao**
afterwards **naolhao**

again **hhoq; hhoqleivq; hhoqleiq; hhoqleiqsiq** (13:4); **zeif** (Chi)
again; still **hhoqleiqsiq; siq**
again; too **siq; sil**
(vb) again **(vb) pal (eil pal** = to say again); **hhoq (vb) (hhoq lal** = come again); **(vb) puv (nal puv** = to get sick again); **(vb) koq (aol koq** = to return to the work one was doing)
again and again **hhoqleivq; hhoqleivq meil; qiq taq maq leiq**
age; year **huvq; alhuvq**
age of a man, the **byuldeivq huvqlavq**
agency **peifcuq jilgual** (Chi)
agenda; order of the day **hha aol miqnieiq** (50:197)
agent, an **huq bi gee col**
agile **keellavq kol**
agree, to **xul (ngal liq xul al** = I also agree)
agreement **xiqyif** (Chi)
agreement, reach an **gee ceiv** (50:187)
agree with, to **xul**
agricultural **naoqniq** (Chi) (**naoqniq pyu** - 26:100)
agricultural front line **naoqniq zafxeif** (Chi) (50:122)
agricultural machinery **xal aol jilqif** (B=Chi)
agricultural materials **xal aol ssaoqmiaoq**
agricultural workers that are productive **naoqniq gaolsseiq** (Chi)

ahead **gaol**

ahead (as in 'go ahead') **gaoqwuq**
ahead of (in time, space) **huqteil**
ahead of schedule **tiqqeiq** (Chi) (26:100)

AIDS **hheifziil bieif** (Chi) (15:60); **hheifziil bif nalgol** (AB=Chi)
Ailao mountains (where the Hani live) **Hhaqlol haolgaoq; Hhaqlol haolteil**
aim, the **muqbiaol** (Chi) (34:17)
aim, the; the purpose **muqdiq** (Chi) (34:1); **zaolziiq** (Chi)
aim, to (as a crossbow) **muvqzil**
aim high and achieve greater things **hhaqtav miqteil teil**
Aini (Akha who live in Xishuangbanna) **Hheifniq** (Chi)
air (as to have fresh air for sick person) **aqleil** (10:21); **kaolqif** (Chi)
airplane **feiljil** (Chi) **peiljil**
  airplane crash **aoqtav laolqaol saq**
air rifle (pneumatic, to shoot birds and small animals) **miqbev qifqal** (B=Chi)

Akha **Yaniq; Yaniq Alka; Ssaqniqssaq; Aqkaq; Aqkaqssaq** (those Akha living in Xishuangbanna)

alarm; warning **jibaof** (Chi)
alert; careful **nyuqgaol; nyuqgaol gaol**
  alert; sharp eyes **miav deivq** (26:29)
  alert; sharp-witted **neema bel**
  alert; vigilent **nyuq hev**
align **dolssiq nei; doqheiq dol**
alive, to be **yodeivq; deivq; byuldeivq; yodeivq deivq; byuldeivq deivq**
all **saq nei; meilnei; jil; dalja; dalja saq nei (A=Chi); zuvq nei**
all (n) **(n) meil (colpuv qiq puv qiq puv meil** - all villages; from one village to another)
all along **wuqduq daoqmiq li nei; galma qiq kaol qiq li meil**
(vb) all around **(vb) dyu (nalhaq dyu** = asked all around)
all at once **tuqssaq meil** (A=Chi); **qiq heiq laltov meil**
all day long **aoqcil qivq nei**
alliance, to form **taoqmaoq jyul** (50:168)
alliance; pact; agreement by partners in crime not to give each other way **doqheiq teev**
all in all **hal jav e**
all means **hal nyuq duv qivq e lulsul**
all of a sudden **qiq heiq laltov meil; tuqssaq meil** (A=Chi)
all over **dyu nei; saq nei aol saq al**
all over the world **aoq hul'a; milcaq hultav**
allowance; subsidy **ziltieiq** (Chi)
all people **ssaqjeil ssaqlaol** (26:1)

all people in the world ('under the sky')
aoq lavqhhuvq e col
all right **meeq saq al**
all right; correct; right **caq**
all right; okay **hhaq; eiqya; kaq**
all the same **saq nei qiq qa**
all the while **maq naq meil; maq pieiq meil**
all together **saq nei (Col dyul saq nei kuvq ceil hhaq jol.** There are 60 people in all. 11:108); **kevq meil** (11:191)
all year round **huvq ssol miltiv meil**
almost (virtually) **halmeevq** (11:114)
almost **ziil nei maq gal; laqsov; laqlavsov**
almost (vb) **laqsov** (see 11:113 for samples)
alone **alsol (Nol qiq hhaq alsol hoq zaq ..** = you alone eat (ate) the rice)
alone; single-handed **sol meil**
along with (as to go along with) **lo'qo**
alphabet **soqmiav aqma** (50:219); **ziifmu; ziifmubiao** (Chi)
already (as in 'to learn already') **(vb) laq al**
already (vb) **(vb) yaolliq**
also; too **liq**
although **(vb) e liq (ngeel e liq** = although it is so)
altruistic **zualmeiq liqsseiq** (Chi) (26:100)
aluminum **lyu** (Chi)
alumnus **xaofye** (Chi) (50:187)
alum powder **hhaqsiil naciq**
always **hal taq; hal taq liq** (10:pref.); **civqzaol nei**

amaranth (three-colored) **hhoqnil**
amazed; astonished **naq nei; naq pa naq nei**
ambassador **dafsii** (Chi)
ambition, to have **nyuq sil nyuq lo**
ambush **caoq teiq; beeqcaoq caoq**
amiable **neema meeq e col**
amnesty; general pardon **zyulgol bi bial** (50:31)
among; inside of **kaqlaq**
amount **saq nei; hal jav e**
ample; full **caolfeil nei** (Chi)

anaesthesia **nieivq zovq**
anaesthetic **nieivq zovq naciq**
analyze, to **nyuq zil nyuq za; feilxiq** (Chi)
anarchism **wuqzeiffu zuyif** (Chi) (50:180)
ancestor **aqpyuq aqbol; hovqzyuq; hovqzyuq dama; aqpyuq aqda; dama** (in poetry: **dalma**)
ancestor God (female) **aqpiq Molmil**
ancestor God (male) **aqpyuq Molmil**
ancestral food **hhaolzal**
ancestral shelf **aqpyuq baoqgeel; aqpyuq helgeel** (11:203)
ancient matters **yeilbei miqnieiq**
ancient times **galhhu aqbei**
and **alnei** (with other meanings too, see 11:119);

ssol; ssol nei (**sil ssol nei** = shiˇ-awˇ neh) (see 11:117 for samples)

anemia **sivq maq luvq nalgol** (10:32, 33); **qeiqtiqxif** (Chi) (10:33)

angel **Molmil ssaqmiq** ('Molmil's daughter')

anger someone, to **civq lav peiv**

angrily **neema ssilpuq nei; miav deiq nil**

angrily stare **miav deiq ssil**

angry, to be **neessil; neema ssil; civq peiv; civq peiv sil; neema peil; salcivq peiv; neema salqiq peiv; needeiq deiq**

angry, extremely **peiv sil peiv lo**

angry, very **civq daov peiv** (13:3); **neessil neehav** (13:15); **neessil neehavq; civq peiv sil; salqiq peiv**

angry expression **miavniul niul** (11:43)

animal **nilzeiq; nivzeiq** (Chi)

animal cry **gyuq; nilzeiq ssaq gyuq** (wild animals); **qilssaq gyuq** (barking deer barks)

animal disease **zeiqnal**

animal, domestic **hyulzeiq; zeiqssaq**

animal feed **zeiqzal**

animal husbandry **zeiq qu miqnieiq**

animal, wild **nilzeiq; nilzeiqssaq**

animal skin, wild **nilzeiq saqgeel**

animals in the twelve-cycle zodiac **suqxaf** (Chi)

animals to fight **taoq zaq**

ankle **keelmiav; keelpul**

announce; tell, to **eilgaq; haofzaof** (as to announce a meeting to be held) (Chi) (26:38)

announce in advance **huq eilgaq** (50:201)

annual ring (in a tree) **soqjoq**

another **aqnu; aqnu liyal** (B=Chi)

another person **aqnu col**

answer; reply **eil puv; eil huvq; laq** (as in: **doqzaq laq** = to answer what someone has said); **toq toq lal; toq miq; lav qoq**

answer the door (open the door) **lulhhuv pao miq**

ant **alhhu; alhhu laldeiq**

ant, red **alhhu laqnil**

antagonistic; hostile **diqsiif** (Chi)

antelope; serow **heiqceiv ceivnav**

antenna **tieilxeif** (Chi) (50:166)

anti-aircraft gun **gaolseif paof** (Chi)

anti-revolutionary, to fight against **fageiqmif** (Chi)

antithesis **doqzaol**

antler of deer; horn of animals **kyul**

antonym **doqlo lopuv**

anus **daoqbyu**

anvil **byultaoq**

anxious **neema beeq**

anything **haljivq liq**

apologize and beg another's pardon **wuqduq taoq huvq**

apostrophe **geiqyil fuqhaof** (Chi)

appeal to; call on **doqhaol haol**
appear; come out **duv lal**
appear; to show **naldul dul** (26:95)
appearance of person **colyaovq** (B=Chi) (11:31)
appearance of person (face) **pyuq; pioq**
appendix (in body) **wullavq**
applaud, to **lavqhov diq**
applicable; suitable **aol e za** (50:155)
apply one's self, to **neema qiq siq qiq li meil; yoqhhaq hholmol kevq nei bivq**
appointment; engagement **doqtaq taq**
appoint people by their merits **halmeeq hal aol**
appraise, to **meeq dyul zaol loq; piqjaf** (Chi)
appraise; comment; criticize (whether good or bad) **meeq dyul eil**
apprentice **lavqqivq qivqzol; tuqdif** (Chi)
apprentice; trainee **zolssaq** (50:191)
appropriate; proper **zahev nei; zahe nei**
approve; confirm **kedif** (Chi)
approximately **gee li nia la** (11:70)
April **Yuvqla siq**
April 12th **siifyiq'eif** (Chi) (34:6)
apron **laqlaol; hhyuqyaol** (Chi)

aqueduct **eelloq**

Arab **Allalbeiq**
arbitrary and impractical directions **beeqmeiq meiq** (50:183)
arch of foot **keelhov**
area; country **milhaoq**
argue, to **qei zaq; deiq loq zaq** (50:159)
arise **duv lal; tul lal**
arithmetic **suafsuq** (Chi) (50:161)
arm; hand **aqlavq**
arm (not hand) **lavqbiav**
arm, crippled **lavqqeiq**
arm, upper **lavqdu; lavqlo; lavqbiav**
armament race **jyulbif** (Chi)
armed bandit **diqsseiq**
armed force (soldiers) **mavqssaq; miqbev bavqssaq**
armed to the teeth **hholmol qiq mol meil miqsiq miqzal eq...**
armed with a weapon **diq miaoq bavq**
arm in arm **lavqcavq cavq**
arm muscles **lavqdu dubeiv**
armpit **lavqhhuvhaoq**
armpit odor **yaqkul**
armrest; hand rail **lavqdal**
arms; weapons **ssaoqsaol; miqbev; wuzual** (Chi) (50:181)
arms and legs **keellavq**
arm's span **lavqlaol**
arm wrestle **aqlavq lavqyevq ngaoq**
army **jyuldyuf** (Chi)

army affairs **jyulsiif** (Chi)
army clothing **alhaoq peilniul**
army commander **jyulza** (Chi)
army mates; friends **zafyemavq** (Chi) (26:59)
army personnel; troop **bufdyuf** (Chi)
army training **jyulsiif xyuflieif** (Chi) (26:42)
army unit **lieiqdyuf; dyufwu** (Chi) (26:54, 58)
army work **jyulsiif** (26:89)
aroma good; smells good **solxeiv nei**
arouse, to; to mobilize **heil niv**
arouse the masses to action; mobilize the masses **ssaqlaol leiq tul**
arrange, to **meiqbivq bivq**
arrange a wedding party; hold a wedding party **yulbee bee**
arrangement, an **hhalpeiq** (Chi)
arrest (and put in jail) **nieivq kuv**
arrive at; reach **hev; hev nei hev**
arrogant, to be **pyuq zaq laq meil; pyuq sil pyuq lo**
arrogant; conceited **dalbuq buq** (26:107); **buq zaq**
arrow (of a crossbow) **kavmiaq**
arrowhead plant, cultivated **moqsiq**
arrowhead plant, wild **miaqkaq**
arrow, poisoned **miaqduvq**
art **yifsuq** (Chi) (50:197)
art designer **meigaol** (Chi)
articles (as in a newspaper) **weiqzal** (Chi) (32:3)
artist **yifsuqjal** (Chi) (50:197)

as; like **laoqmeil**
as a matter of fact **aqdil meil**
as a rule **aqyo galma yo'liq**
as far as **hev nei**
ashamed; shy **savqdol; savqdol bo; savqdol sil laq; molsavq bo**
ashamed to speak **maq eil sal**
ashes **haqleil**
ashes, burning **leilcal**
ashes, flying **leilmeev**
Asian golden cat (Felis temmincki) **haolnil buvqciv**
Asiatic chipmunk (Eutamias sibericus) **piaqcoq**
as if **nadul meil**
ask; listen; obey **nalhaq**
ask all around **dyu nei nalhaq**
ask for **nalhaq**
ask for; beg **sal; sal zaq**
ask for explanation **caq nalhaq** (50:213)
ask for leave of absence **cija** (Chi)
ask to stay overnight **sal xavq** (13:4)
askew; aslant **yovq; qeiq; bilqeiq**
as lean as a rake **saqyyuq qiq xaoq sol nei**
asleep; sound asleep **yiuvq sil**
as one man **col qiq hhaq aqmeil dul nei**
asparagus **haqdal**
asphalt **beiqyeq** (Chi)

aspect; phase **jiqmieif** (Chi)
assemble; come together **zyul**
assign (as homework) **bufziiq** (Chi)
assimilate, to **zaljavq javq** (to digest); **pievq** (**Laqbeqssaq pievq** = to become Chinese); **caoqcaf** (Chi) (also 'to absorb' - 50:149)
assistant **zufse** (Chi) (26:98)
as soon as (vb) **joq (vb)** (**joq mol** = as soon as he saw it, **miav joq biei** = as soon as he opened his eyes - 13:14) (**Aoqbia joq bia ngaoq** = As soon as the sun comes up)
as soon as one gets up **joq tul**
as the case may be **miqnieiq lo'qo**
as this is the case **miqnieiq xilmeil ngeel e ngaoq**
asthma-like panting; wheezing **savqcii cii**
astonishing; amazing **naq nei; naq pa naq nei**
astringent (as tea, pears) **peil** (11:55); **peiltuv; peil peil tuv tuv**
astute **hhulla nei**
as usual **miqteil naolhao nadul nei**
as well as **liq; ssol nei; kaq**

at any cost **halmeil ngeel e liq**
at bottom **daoqdaoq; wuqduq daoqmiq meil saq nei**
at cost **aqyo hhaqpyuq nei**
at death's door **savq ceiv movq nei; sil movq ca nei**
at first **huqteil; huqteil tyul taq** (29:4)
at home **laqhyul a**
at its glory **hal beq hal pyuq zeiq e tyul taq**
at last **naolhao haoli** (10:25); **naolhao haoli taq** (13:2); **naolhao haoli tyul taq**
at least **halnaoq zeiq e; hal maq miaq e liq**
at moment of (vb) **(vb) tovq** (13:39)
atmosphere **qiffeil** (Chi)
atmosphere; general mood **faolqif** (Chi)
at most **hal miaq e**
atom bomb **yeiqziidaf** (Chi) (50:201)
atomic energy **yeiqziineiq** (Chi) (50:201)
at once; immediately **qiq heiq nei** (10:23); **joq nei; qiq quq nei** (13:7)
at one's best **hal meeq e**
at one's command **eildoq nalhaq**
at one's convenience **yei e tyul taq; caq e tyul taq**
at one's earliest convenience **nieiq'eil navq e nieiq'eil meeq** ('the earlier the better')
at one's leisure **aqlavq nieivq e jol**
at peace (the country) **milhaoq sal e taq**
at present **niaoq'aol**
at sixes and sevens **beeq li ga la**
attach importance to **ssiiq nei hu tao**
attack a jail **hhavqkuv a diq**
attempt, to **zaolhu hu**
attend (as a meeting) **keil** (Chi)
at the door **hhoheiq a**
at the right time **cuv nei**

at the same time **qiqgao meil**
at that moment **joq yil joq lal**
attic; or mat hung over fireplace **hoqtavq**
at times **qiq taq hhana**
attitude (as one's attitude toward something or someone) **yoyaovq; neenyuq; teifduf** (Chi)
attitude; manner **teifduf** (Chi) (50:162)
attractive, to be **laovq lal**
at will **hal zaol movq e**

August **Xeivqla siq**
aunt (father's older sister; father's older brother's wife) **malma; aqhuq malma**
aunt (father's younger sister) **alnia** (11:176)
aunt (wife of father's younger brother; wife of mother's brother; mother's younger sister) **aqmee**
auspicious day **naomeeq**
author of an article; writer **buvqssaq**
auto; car **qifceil; qiqcei** (Chi) (3:2, 11:30)
automatically; without thinking **javbuv**
automobile **qifceil; qiqcei** (Chi)
autonomous **yoq haoq yoq teiq; yoq haoq yoq leev** (50:219); **ziifziif** (Chi)
  autonomous administration **ziifziif jilgual** (Chi) (50:219)
  autonomous county **ziifziifxeif** (Chi) (50:220)
  autonomous district **ziifziifqil** (Chi)
  autonomous prefecture **ziifziifzel** (Chi) (50:220)
  autonomous region **ziifziifqil** (Chi) (50:219)
autonomy **ziifziif qeiq** (Chi) (50:220)
autumn **ceildiq ba'la** (26:110); **cuv**
  autumn festival **zaolqeljiq (26:7); Xeivqla siq ceil ngavq nao**
  autumn season **cuvzyuq ba'la**

aviation **haqkaol** (Chi)
avoid direct contact (taboo relation) **yao**

awakened by something (as a loud noise) **lav sul**
awaken someone, to **leiq nyuq; leiq tul**
awaken someone by calling **kul nyuq**
award **ja'lif** (Chi)
awhile **ciiv nei qiq heiq**
awkward **keel qaoq lavq qaoq meil**
  awkward; embarrassed **maq sal maq yevq** (50:55)
awl **leiqssaq**
awl made of iron **saoltyuq**

axe (for cutting wood) **saolzaol**
axe (small); hatchet **laqdev; saolzaol lavqdev**
axis **meilniuv**
axle **meilniuv**

azalea **toqdi alyeiv; toqdi malyeiv**

B b **soqmiav aqma hholqei niq mol e qiq mol**

---

babe in arms **ssaqnaoq naoqmieiv mieivssaq**
baby **ssaqnil; ssaqnaoq; ssaqnaoq naoqmieiv**
baby-carrying black cloth **beeteiq; beeteiq teiqnav**

baby cries (for no reason) **leivq**
baby's mother **ssaqnaoq aqma**
baby wrapper **dalqei**
bachelor (young) **coldavq** (taboo)
back **daolteil**
backbone **daolciivq saqyyuq** (pf); **daolciivq saqyoq**
back, hunched **daolhhuvq**
back, lower **aqhhuv daolteil; daolciivq**
back of hand **lavqnaol; aqlavq lavqnaol**
back, small of **daolciivq**
back; spine **daolciivq saqyyuq**
back, upper **aqtav daolteil**
back door (or side) **hhoheiq; heiqssaq**
back down, to **naoldi di**
back to back **deiq tul; deiq dav**
backward **loqhef** (Chi) (34:33)
backward and forward **puv li puv lav**
bacteria; germ **xifjif** (Chi) (50:183)
bad **yodyul; maq meeq; gyuzii** (as in: **Ssiiqbei gyuqzii** = the bad Japanese) (Chi)
bad, dirty words **doqdyul**
bad conscience **neema nyuq savq**
badger, ferret (Helictic orientalis) **huhaq**
bad habit **moqbil** (Chi)
bad-hearted **neema nee cavq**
bad job, a **miqnieiq nieiq cavq qiq mol**
bad; lazy **dyul; yodyul** (11:26)
bad luck, to have **yocavq guq zaq; gaoqlaoq maq meeq**
bad omen **dol**
  bad-omen buffalo/cow **niuqdol duv**
  bad-omen chicken **aqha dol; aqha hadol**
  bad-omen dog **keeqdol duv**
  bad-omen horse **moqdol duv**
  bad-omen pig **hhavqdol duv**
  bad-omen person **coldol**
bad person **colcavq; sazyuq**
bad smell **beivqlavq**
bad temper **civqbaoq** (**civqbaoq beil** = to get into a bad temper)
  bad temper, to have **civqbaoq baoq**
bad things predestined from birth **deivq zyul**
bad word **doqbiav; cuq doq; doqcavq**
bag (as a rice-bag); gunnysack **dalleil**
bag for school things **soqhhaq paltaol**
bag, shoulder **paltaol**
bag, small **paltaol taolssaq**

Bai language **Beiqcuqdoq** (A=Chi)
Bai people (minority group in China) **Beiqcuqssaq** (A=Chi)
bake, to **ca**
balcony **caqliq**
bald; smooth **julluq nei; ju nei**
bald head **wuqjul; wuqnil**
ball **siilpuq; piqqeq** (Chi)
ballad; folksong **lalbaq** (to sing = **lalbaq ssil**)
ballad; folksong; nursery rhyme **dalya; aqnil dalya**
ballet; dance drama **wujif** (Chi) (50:181)
bamboo **haqbol; haqbol haqdyuv; haqbol daoqciivq; haqsav**
bamboo, bitter **haqhaq**
bamboo bowl **haqciivq daoqdel**
bamboo cluster **haqcaoq**
bamboo container **haqbol boqlo; baoqtevq**
bamboo culm sheath (parchment-like outer membrane at the bottom) **haqluq; albal balhhaq** (for the golden bamboo)
bamboo fence **kaoldaol; laolkaol; haqbol kaoldaol; haqbol laolkaol**
bamboo forest **haqbol bolcaoq; beilcaoq haqbol**
bamboo, golden **haqsiil**
bamboo gopher **hupiq**
bamboo infesting insect **haqbyuq**
bamboo joint **haqciivq; haqlo**
bamboo, jungle **beilcaoq haqbol**
bamboo leaf **haqpavq**
bamboo length **haqbaoq**
bamboo mat for drying crops **goqpuv; goqpov**
bamboo noise maker (to scare birds away) **haoltov**
bamboo pipe for blowing on fire **miqzaq boqlo**
bamboo pole for drying things **dalgeeq**
bamboo raft **haqpyul; haqpyulloq**
bamboo section (between two joints) **allo**
bamboo section in which rice and seeds are preserved **byuqduq** (45:53)
bamboo shoes (made of: **haqmuv**) **haqguq sseilnaovq**
bamboo shoots **haqdyuv; aldyuv; aldyuv dyuv; dyuv; alcuq cuqdyuv**
bamboo shoots, bitter **alhaq**
bamboo shoots, preserved **aldyuv dyuvkuv**
bamboo shoots, sweet **haqqul haqdyuv**
bamboo shoots to sprout **haqdyuv dyuv**
bamboo slats **haqcil** (**haqcil zeiv** = to cut the bamboo and make slats)
bamboo, small variety **haqbol bolssaq; alcuq**
bamboo stick (small) **dalsseiv; alcuq dalgeeq** (B=Chi)
bamboo strip (fine, for making shoes) **haqmuv**
bamboo strip (large) **haqpav**
bamboo strip (small) **alniq** (**eilneiq; koqsuv eilneiq** - not pf.)
bamboo strips, to make **alniq niq**
bamboo (sweet variety) **haqqul**

bamboo table with offerings **zalhel lolbieil**
bamboo ties (as used in building) **alniq**
bamboo trough **haqbol eelloq**
bamboo tube **haqbol baoqlo; haqbol eelloq** (for water)
bamboo types **alcuq; albal; alnav; alpieil; almal,** etc.
bamboo water container **eelbaoq**
bamboo water container with its branches as handles **eelde**
bamboo water container with long handle (for getting water) **wulquvq necev**
bamboo water gun **eelceiv**
bamboo, wild **beilcaoq haqbol**
banana **alqul**
banana (sweet type) **alqul; alqul albol; alqul qulbol; alqul alsiq**
banana tree, wild **alzeiv albol; alzeiv zeivbol**
banana, wild **alzeiv**
band; hoop **miavgaol; saolhhaoq**
bandicoot rat **peillov hucavq cavqma**
bandit (armed) **diqsseiq** (Chi); **daqjeil gyuzii** (in the sense that the Japanese were 'bandits' when they invaded China - 26:2)
bank (for money) **piul taq yaol; ssiqhaq** (26:74); **cuqxuqso** (Chi) (26:76); **yiqhaq** (Chi) (50:198)
bank deposit **yiqhaq cyuq taq piul** (A=Chi) (50:198)
banking; finance **jilyaoq** (Chi)
banyan tree **niaolbol**
bark (of dog) **ceivq**
bark (of tree) **albol alhov**
barking deer **qilssaq**
  barking deer, meat of **qilsaq**
  barking deer barks **qilssaq gyuq**
barley **dafmeiq** (Chi)
barometer **qiqyibiao** (Chi)
barrel of a gun **bevsaol**
barren couple **maq bo dama**
barren land **milzul zul**
barren woman **maq bo aqma**
base; foundation **zaolhhal; daoqpeiq**
base of mountain (see: mountain base)
bashful; shy **savqdol bo; molsavq bo**
basic; foundation **naolteev**
basic improvement **zaoma nei meeq dav**
basin **hovqbiav; hoqbiav; yaqpeiq** (Chi)
  basin of clay **moldel**
  basin (Western style) **yaqpeiq** (Chi) (11:30)
basis; foundation (as a house) **caqkeel**
basis; the main purpose **miaq baol**
basket **miavhav**
  basket (lg. type) **bavqhav; havkal**
  basket (sm. type) **haljul**
  basket (sm. type carried on back) **beiljul**
  basket, type of **halbeiv**
  basket; bowl **hoqmaq havdov**

basket for carrying fire **miqzaq havpuq**
basket for carrying firewood **miavhav**
basket for catching fish **ngaqluv; deillu**
basket for measuring grain **badu**
basket, small (for holding sewing) **laqpiq; laqpiq piqdel**
basket, tightly woven **beido**
basket which has a cover (rattan or bamboo) **pyuqtul**

basketball **laqqeq** (Chi, pf.); **pao'quq; laqquq** (Chi); **siilpuq; silpuq**
basketball, to play **siilpuq diq; silpuq diq; laqqeq diq** (A=Chi)

bastard's father **caqssaq aqda**
bastard's mother **caqssaq aqma**

bat (bird-like mammal) **alku bialhhal**

bath, a **aqbul**

bath, to give (infant) **aqbul ciq miq** (10:27)

bath, to take **aqbul ciq**

bathe someone, to **hholmol ciq**

battle, to fight a **geel diq** (50:207); **diq zaq** (50:207)
battlefield **geel diq zaq duq**

bayberry, red **siqsov**

be; become **gee**

be (as for a liquid to be present) **daoq**

be (as for a path/road to be present) **daol**

be abused **bi caol; bi yaq**

be correct **ngeel**

be; exist (animate) **jol**

be (of same clan) **qiq beeq ssaq; qiq hhovq col**

be (of same nationality) **qiq qa col; ssaqqa qiq qa**

be; to be so **ngeel**

bead (glass) **julsiq**
beads, string of **du lu de le**

beak; bill of bird **meiqtuv**

beam for roof **hoqbyu**
beam in house (main one between posts going the width of the house, and forming joists for the second floor) **hhaqdav**
beam in house (ones going between posts the length of the house, and forming joists for second floor) **hhaqbil**

bean **alneev**

bean, a kind **diqhhoq** (11:74)

bean, broad **caqdul** (Chi)

bean, climbing green **neevnil**

bean condiment **aqciq** (see in Hani-Eng. as well)

bean curd **neeguq**

bean curd (fermented) **neeguq guqbuvq**

bean, green **neebeiv; beivja; neenil**

bean; seed; kernel **neevsiq**

bean sprouts **neev'quv**

bear, a (animal) **haoq'aol**

beard **meiqmoq**

bear fruit, to **siq**
  bear fruit -- string of it **du du de le**
bear with, to **ciiv teiq**
be at, to (implying sitting) **jol**
beat, to **diq**
beat black and blue, to **diq ju**
beat down; knock down **diq leeq**
beat down on (as rain) **diq**
beat flat, to **cevq biav**
beat heavily **diq duvq; diq kyuq**
beat one another; fight **diq zaq**
beat thoroughly **diq duvq**
beat to breaking **diq qov**
beat to death **diq tov; diq sil**
beautiful **zaq; yojaq; hu zaq; hu gaq; husal**
  beautiful; deeply in love **gaqzav hhyulqaol nei**
  beautiful face **pioqzaq**
  beautiful girl **ssaqmiq miqgaq**
  beautiful women and handsome men **miqzaq yozaq**
  beautiful, very **zaqqul nei; gaqzav nei; gaqzav pa zav nei; hu zaq; zaqqul pa qul nei**
because **taoqngaoq**
because of this or that **xilmeil nei; xilmeil taoqngaoq**
become, to **pievq; gee**
become (vb) **qivq** (**duv lal qivq nga** = became something from something else)
become active, to **hhul lal; hhul dav lal**
become something (in special cases) **se** (**moqpil se** = to become a spirit priest)
bed **hhaoqzao** (**hhaoqzao hultav** = on the bed)
bed (with innerspring mattress) **xiqmaofsiil hhaoqzao** (A=Chi) (50:183)
bedbug **aqgov**
bed for seedlings (in garden) **hhoqpaoq**
bedroom **bavlov; yiuvqduq**
bedstead, to make **hhaoqzao zao**

bee (generic) **biaq**
beef **niuqsaq** (from either cow or buffalo)
beef, dried **niuqsaq saqkuv**
beehive **biaqbaoq**
bee, honey (domesticated) **biaqsil**
bee, queen **biaqzyuq**
beer **piqje** (Chi)
beeswax **biaqsaoq**
beetle **neivqssaq halpyul**
before; first (in time) **miqteil**
before; in front of **meiqsi**
before; long ago **galhhu; miqteil**
beforehand **huqteil; kaqla** (11:110)
before long **maq mia aqkal**
before one's eyes **miav hu teiq alnei; meiqsi nei**
beg; ask for **sal**
  beg another's pardon (restricted usage) **maq ngeel**

ya siq
beg for food (for a living) **sal zaq**
beggar **hoqssa**
begin **bei; yobei; (vb) bei (aol bei** = to begin doing); **beibei**
beginning of construction **cuv bei**
beginning of world **yeilbei salbei**
beginning of year **huvqpeiq** (as January...)
begin to work **lavqnieiq dovq**
behind **naolhhuvq**
behind; the back side **naolhao pyu** (10:4)
behind the house **zoqnia**
Beijing **Beiqjil**
belch, to **heeltev tev**
belch, to (from drinking water) **eeltev tev**
belief; faith; conviction **nyuqhhal** (50:188); **xifnieif** (Chi)
believe, to **qeq; hu dav**
believe in, to **qeq zaq; qeq zaq na**
believe in very much **qeq sil**
bell **diqqul**
bell (as in a school) **liq (liq gyuq al** = the bell has rung -- as for class)
bell for horses **ho'lo** (11:17); **hao'lyu**
bell, small **qulsul**
bellows (for a blacksmith) **bohhe**
bell sound (like 'tinkle, tinkle') on cows and horses **di li de le; dil lil del lel**
belly **wuqma; wuqdeiq**
belly button **qalbeil**
belly, lower **wuqdeiq wuqssaq**
below; lower **aqhhuv pyu**
below the earth **milhhuvq**
below; under **hul'a; aqhhuv**
belt **juqzaoq; laqziiq; laqzaoq** (46:176)
belt, to fasten **duldeil deil** (46:160)
belt, to support when lifting **deilziiq (deilziiq ziiq** = to wear such a belt)
belt, woven **palhhavq**
bench; stool **naolteil; daoqteil**
bend, to **ngaoq hhaoq; hhaoq**
bend; to make crooked **heiq hhuvq**
bend by pulling **hhe hhuvq**
bend down, to **taoq muvq (wuqduq taoq muvq** = to bend the head down - 34:15)
bend down; hang down (as the head) **deiq muvq** (46:138)
bend head, to **byuqsyu**
bend one's head **quq muvq**
bend something, to **heiq hhuvq; ngaoq hhaoq**
bend the mind **neema bavq duv**
beneath **hul'a; aqhhuv**
benefit **meeqduq (meeqduq bi jav lal** = for the benefit of)
bent **hhaoq; bil lil hhuvq luvq**

bent arms and legs **keel kuv lavq kuv**
bent (as with rickets) **hhe yovq** (10:5)
bent legs **keel kuv**
berries (amomum) **deqheq**
beside **bialzeil**
besides; another **aqnu**
best; excellent **yelxef** (Chi) (26:48)
best man (at a wedding) **haqjil aqda yolqoq**
be sure **halmeil liq; aqdil meil**
betel, to chew **beillol hhyuq** (A-Chi) (11:17)
betel nut **beillol** (Chi)
betel quid (which they spit out after chewing) **beillol hhyuq povq** (A=Chi) (11:17)
Bethune, Dr. (from Canada) **Beq Quq'eil** (Chi)
betroth, to **miqssaq gee caq; miqssaq gee ceiv**
better **meeq zeiq** (11:99)
better, a little bit **alciiv kaq**
better, to be **kaq; kaq lal; sal lal**
between, in **alkaq**
between two fires, to be **miqzaq niq gee alkaq a (meiqsi naolhao meil saq)**
between you and me **nol ssol ngal alkaq (aqnu qiq hhaq maq bi hev qivq)**
beyond, over **aqzeiq zeiq**

bicycle **dalceil** (Chi)
bicycle, to ride **dalceil ziiq** (A=Chi)
big **heeq; yoheeq**
big, very **halheeq nei; halheeq pa heeq nei; neiqhe nei**
bigamy **niq hhaq seq**
bile **piqkeel**
billiards (game and ball) **teiqqeq** (Chi) (50:162)
billion, one **yal mil**
bill of bird **meiqtuv**
bind up, to **tov quvq**
biographical notes **jeiliq** (Chi)
birch-like tree **heiqnyuq albol** (the Hani send this leaf, which signifies 'missing' the other person, along with a soy bean which signifies 'with my whole heart')
bird **alzil; zilssaq**
bird cage **zilhav**
bird fans out feathers **ssulqil nei**
bird nest, a **zilbeeq; alzil zilbeeq**
bird snare **luljuv**
birds, red and golden **zil nil zil siil**
bird, young **alzil zilssaq**
birds chirping **jiv jiv zav zav**
birds singing **meel**
birth, to give **ssaqdeiv; ssaq bo**
birth control **ssaq bo nyuq za; boheiq cyuq**
birthday **bonao**
biscuit (cookie, etc.) **bigal** (Chi)
bit, a **alciiv**

bit (for horse) **meiqkovq**
bit by bit **alciiv alciiv meil**
bite, to **kovq**
bite down hard **kovq kavq**
bite down tightly **kovq siivq**
bite down with teeth **seqkovq kovq**
bite each other **kavq zaoq**
bite the tongue (lit.) **lalma kovq teiq**
bite the tongue (remain quiet) **doq maq gee**
bite to pieces **kovq nuv**
bitter **haq; siqhaq**
bitter; harsh **yeiqkuq** (Chi)
bitter, very **haqteivq nei**
bitter herbs **jahaq**
bitter to extreme **haqteivq pa teivq nei**
Biyue branch of the Hani **Biqyoqssaq** (46:208)

black **nav**
black; jet black **nav'qovq nei** (11:57)
black, very **nav'qovq nei; nav'qovq pa qovq nei; nav nav nei** (11:57)
black and white horse **moqgevq** (46:196)
black arrowhead plant **moqsiq siqnav**
black art **neivqhaq mo'luq** (& see: black magic)
blackboard **heiqba**
black cloth **palnav**
blackhearted **neema nav'qovq nei** (26:5)
blackish; darkish **navhaoq nei; navhaoq nei nav; navhaoq pa haoq nei**
black-like **navsov nei**
black magic, to do **neivqhaq zaol** (**neivq zaol nia** = to be able to perform black magic)
blackmail; extort **hheivqsov pieiq**
black pig **aqhhavq hhavqnav** (46:134)
blacksmith **baziq; saol diq baziq; qivq** (in flowery language)
black spots (as on face) **boqheiq jacev**
black viper **ollol eelnav**
bladder (urinary) **saolpuq**
blame someone, to **zeilnuv nuv**
blamed, to be **zyul** (45:72)
blanket **geivzavq; albee hyulzal**
blast furnace **gaolluq** (Chi)
blaze; flame **miqbia**
bleach, to (rinse; clean) **ceibu**
bleed, to **sivq duv**
blemish of skin **saqsiq**
blessing **gaoqlaoq**
  blessing, big **gaoqlaoq heeq**
  blessing, give **heiqhel hel miq**
  blessing, good **gaoqlaoq meeq**
  blessing, have (merit) **gaoqlaoq bo**
  blessing, typical **Coljol bi sal, colssil bi bo.** (May you have good health and live a long life.) **Coljol bi sal, gaoqlaoq bi bo.** (May you have good

health and good luck.)
blessing words **heldoq**
blind **miavbeivq; beivq**
blinded by shining light **miavbeivq lovq beivq**
blister (from heat) **lulwuq**
blister (to form) **lulwuq dav**
block, to (animate objects) **jol cyuq** (26:90); **laol cyuq**
block, to (to hinder) **deiq cyuq; leiq cyuq; luvq cyuq; dal cyuq**
block; stop **leiq cyuq**
blockade; seal off **faolso** (Chi) (34:10)
blockhouse (military fortification) **diaolbao** (Chi)
block someone from doing something **keellavq hhe** (and see under Hani)
block way **luvq cyuq; luvq ceiv**
blood **sivq**
blood of dog **keeqsivq**
blood relationship **yoqsaq tavq**
blossom **yeiv**
blossom, to **alyeiv yeiv**
blow, to **bo**
blow a flute **meel; bo**
blow down, to **bo leeq**
blow nose, to **aqbeil nieivq; kao**
blow off (as hat) **bo leiv** (11:128)
blow over, to **bo hoq; bo zei**
blow up, to **coq beivq; coq pav**
blue; grey **peel; peelsuq nei**
blue sky **aoqpeel**
blunt **daoq**
blunt hand (no fingers) **aqlavq lavqluvq**

boa **aqlivq**
boar **hhavqpaq**
boar (wild) **hhavqteiq; hhavqpaq**
board; plank of wood **biavq; teilbiavq**
boast, to **cyulniuq** (Chi)
boast; cheat; lie **haovq; aqmiaovq miaovq zaq**
boaster, a **aqmiaovq**
boat **loq** (clf. = **loq**) (11:34)
body **hholmol; golbaq (golbaq heeq** = big body)
bodyguard **haol leev mavqssaq** (50:177)
body, one's body **yoqhhol** (46:202)
body; substance; object **wuqti** (50:182) (Chi)
body member (as arm, leg, head) **seil (yuvq seil maq daol** = to be maimed; disabled; missing a body part)
body, whole **qiq mol moljoq nei** (26:32); **yoqhhol qiq hhol**
body and mind **wullavq** (50:149)
boil (as water) **beel**
boil, cook **qavq; puvq**
boiled rice (rice gruel) **hoqqavq eelcal** (10:10)
boil, a **saqciiq**
boil clean; sterilize **qavq sil**

boiled water; hot water **eellaol**
boil water, to **eelbeel beel**
boil partially **puvqhho hho**
bolt and nut **loqsiildil** (Chi) (26:119); **loqsiilmaol** (Chi) (26:73)
bolt (in a door) **dalmiaq**
bomb **zaqdal** (Chi) (50:206)
bomb, atom **yeiqziidaf** (Chi) (50:201)
bonds **gaolzeif** (Chi)
bond; debenture **zeifjeif** (Chi) (50:206)
bone **saqyyuq; saqyoq** (not pf.); **yyuqdaoq**
bone, red **yyuqnil**
bone of the leg **keelyyuq**
bonfire, a **jeibaol**
bonfire, to burn **jeibaol baol**
book **soqdaoq; soqhhaq; soqmiav**
book; paper; letter **soqhhaq**
bookstore **soqhhaq aoqyaol** (50:157); **suldieif** (Chi)
boorish; rough **yosaq maq tavq**
border, the **milkaq**
border area **milzeil cuqzeil** (10:11); **bieiljal** (Chi)
border guardhouse **luvqyaol** (50:12)
borderline **milkaq**
border on, to **milkaq tavq**
border sanitation and quarantine regulations **goqji hhyufseil jeiyiq gyuldif** (Chi)
borrow (repay in kind) **pal**
borrow (return what was borrowed) **ngaq**
borrow or lend money **pal ngaq**
bowl, bamboo **haqciivq daoqdel**
bowl, large **mulhuvq**
born, to be **bo**
borrow; lend **ngaq** (repay what borrowed) **pal** (not repay the same)
bosom **neehho**
bosom friend **neema tavq e yolqoq**
botany **ziiqwuqxoq** (Chi) (50:212)
bother others, to **syuq** (26:113); **leelcii; cii**
both of them **aqya niaq**
both sides **niq pyu**
bottle **malcavq; malcavq piqzii** (B=Chi); **piqzii malcavq** (A=Chi)
bottle, glass **yaqhuq malcavq**
bottom; lower part **daoqdaoq**
bottomless pit **saqduq duqbyu; aqhhuv qiq lov**
boulder **haqluv hhaqzeil**
boundary line **jeifxeif** (Chi)
boundary markers **milkaq luvcuv**
bound hand and foot **keellavq kavq zaoq**
bourgeoisie **ziilca geiljiq** (Chi)
bourgeoisie, big **daf ziilca geiljiq** (Chi) (34:7)
bowed down; bent down (as in grief) **wuqduq galtyuq nei** (26:80)
bowel movement (usually runny) **aldyul dyul**
bow head, to **muvq; wuqduq taoq** (as before the

ancestral altar)
bow with which to shoot fish **ngaqbev**
bowl **haoqmaq** (clf. = **haoq** - 11:34)
bowl, ancient **haoqhav**
bowl (basket-shaped) **haoqma havdov**
bowl, big **mulhuvq**
bowl, for washing **haoqmaq ciq**
bowl, large **mulhuvq** (clf. = **huvq**)
bowl, porcelain **haoqpiul**
bowl, rice **haoqmaq**
box **baoqkev**
box; case (as for tobacco) **hoqbav**
box for measuring **baoqssaq**
box, small **baoqkev kevssaq**
boy **ssaqyo**
boy (young) **haqjil aqda dassaq**
boyfriend; girlfriend **ssaqheiq**

bracelet **lavqduvq**
bracelet, to wear **lavqduvq duvq**
bracken fern **haqdal dalpiaq**
brackets (punctuation) **guaqhaof** (Chi)
brag, to; show off **dalbuq buq**
braid **pieivq**
braid hair, to **caolpieivq pieivq**
braided hair **caolpieivq**
brain **wuqnaoq; naoziil** (Chi)
bran, rice (soft, reddish) **peeqnil**
branch (dry); small stick **koqpial**
branch (of a clan) **lavq**
branch (of a language) **doqheiq lo'lavq** (cf. **doqheiq lozao** = language group)
branch (tree) **allavq; albol allavq**
brass **geeq**
brass coin **geeqsiil meilbiav; geeqsiil taoqhaoq** (B=Chi)
brave **daqzii heeq** (A=Chi) (26:48)
brave; heroic **yilyao** (Chi)
brave person, a **cuajaf** (26:45)
brave to (vb) **(vb) peq**
breach; gap **meiqhavq**
bread **mieifbaol** (Chi) (26:93)
bread, steamed **maqtel** (Chi)
bread, steamed with pork **baolzii** (Chi)
break, to **coq pav**
break (as thread) **ceiv; heivq ceiv; coq ceiv; lav ceiv**
break; cut **heivq** (as firewood)
break; interrupt **ceiv**
break down, to **diq beivq; diq pav**
breakfast (drink tea) **aoqsoq laqpeiv dol** (50:204)
breakfast (morning rice) **soqhoq; zaodiei** (Chi)
break into, to **diq tao; teiq dov**
break off, to **taoq xa** (27:11)
break one's heart, to **neema ceiv; neema qil; neema**

nee'qil qil ceiv
break out, to (as a bad omen) **dol duv** (**hadol duv** = if a hen eats an egg, or tries to crow, must be killed because that is a 'bad omen' = **dol**)
break something **zaol biav**
breaks suddenly (as a floor with too many people on it) **coq beivq**
break up; split **beivq**
break wind; flatulate **haq pieiq** (taboo)
break with, to **maq ya lo nia; maq caq lal nia**
breast; udder **aqqul** (11:29); **aqqul qulpul** (lit. 'breast root')
breastbone; sternum **neehha saqyyuq**
breast cancer; breast pain **aqqul qulpul nal**
breath; steam; gas **savq**
breath, a **savq** (clf. **savq**) (11:34)
breathe, to **savq hhol**
breathe in and out **hhol puv hhol pal**
breathe out, to **pyuq**
breathe with difficulty **savqli li savqcii cii; savq hhol savq cii meil**
breed (as animals) **pieiq cavq**
brewery rice; distiller's grains **zilgul**
bribe; bribery **zeiq hyuq neiq; hyulzeiq taoq**
brick, baked **meelbiav**
brick mold **caqbiav seivhuvq**
brick, sun dried **caqbiav**
brick, to make (sun dried) **caqbiav seiv**
brick, to make (to be fired) **meelbiav diq**
brick, to trim (in making) **caqbiav sev**
bride price **miqzeiq**
bridge **laolzaol**
bridge-head (end) **meiqzaq** (26:14)
bridge, metal **saol laolzaol** (50:167)
bridge, wooden (single) **laolzaol zaolteiq**
bridge, to build **bavq cuvq**
brigade; commune **gaolseif** (Chi)
brigade commander **liza** (Chi)
brigade government (lowest unit of govt. in China) **xalseiffu** (Chi) (26:26); **xalzeiffu**
brigade production leader **dyufza** (Chi)
bright; clever **neegaol**
bright day **bia loq bia ceiv; aoqsal milsal** (clear sky)
brightening **geelniq nei**
brighten; shine **geel**
bright-hearted; happy **neema bia lil bia loq**
bright, shining **bia**
bright, very **bia bia nei; bia'loq loqma meil**
brightening **geelniq nei**
brightly **bia'loq nei; bia loq nei** (11:56); **bia'loq pa loq nei**
brightly; frankly **bia lil bia loq meil**
brightly, very **sseiv nei; geelniq pa niq nei**
brilliant; magnificent **bia lil bia loq**

brilliant; splendid **nil nil huq huq**
bring (from another place here) **bavq al la**
bring about, to **aol pievq**
bring back, to (as in memory) **nyuq puv; nyuq duv**
bring something up (as some article) **bavq al la**
bring together, to **hhe ssaoq**
bring to life, to **bi deivq huvq**
bring to mind, to **nyuq duv; nyuq puv**
bring up, to **qu heeq**
bring up to **heil dav** (26:77)
bring up; train **caofjef** (Chi)
briquette of fuel (made in the shape of a honey comb) **faolhhol meiq** (A=Chi)
bristle of pig **hhavqhao; hhavqhao moltavq**
bristle with anger **neessil neehavq**
brittle **hhov; hhovceiv nei**
broadcast (as the radio) **guabo** (Chi)
broadcasting station **guabozaf** (Chi) (26:60); **saldoq haoq yal** (from the Akha name used in Jinghong)
broad; spacious **yeil**
broad in scale **gyulmoq halheeq nei** (A=Chi)
brocade; satin **bu'lavq**
broken **zeiv; havq; ceiv; qov** (as a stick); **ngavlav**
broken (as roof tiles) **taoq qov**
broken arm **lavq qov**
broken bits; fragments **lyulmi nei**
broken from burning **peev byu**
broken heart, a **neema ceiv**
brokenly **bil lil biav lav meil**
broken off **ya ceiv**
broken rice **ceilgeeq**
brook, a **lollavq**
broom **yavpyul; yavcev** (26:70)
broom grass **leiqgaoq alyeiv**
broom of bamboo sticks **yavcev**
brother, eldest **algo goma** (Chi)
brother-in-law (older sister's husband) **aqsaoq**
brothers and sisters (TE) **colgaq aqyivq meilnaol** (46:217)
brother; second eldest brother **algo aqhhaol** (A=Chi)
brother; youngest elder **algo ssaqli** (A=Chi)
brown sugar **poqbiav biavnav**
brush teeth; rinse mouth **meiqloq loq**
brush with water **qiv ciq**
brush-tailed porcupine **hu'laq**

bubble, a **saolpuq** (30:2); **pavqmeevq**
bubbles form **saolpuq teiv nei** (30:2)
bucket; pail **eeltaoq**
bucket for dung **xiq eeltaoq**
buckwheat **hhaq; hhaqlei**
buckwheat, bitter **hhaqhaq; hhaqlei hhaqhaq**
buckwheat, sweet **hhaqqul; hhaqlei hhaqqul**
buckwheat, wild **qeilma**
buckwheat bran (soft) **hhaqgeeq**

buckwheat cake (pounded) **hhaqlei hhaqteil** 11:35); hhaqlei hhaqbiav; **hhaqlei hhaqdeivq**
buckwheat cake (steamed) **hhaqnyul**
buckwheat field **hhaqyal; hhaqlei hhaqyal**
buckwheat 'fingers' (type of food) **hhaqlei hhaqnyul**
buckwheat flour **hhaqlyul; hhaqlei hhaqlyul**
buckwheat flour with soft husks (can be used as pig food) **hhaqlei hhaqgeeq**
buckwheat food (of some kind) **hhaqpiaol**
buckwheat husk **hhaqhovq**
buckwheat plant **hhaqbol**
bud, a **alquv; aldu**
bud on a tree **wuqniuv**
Buddhist temple **molkol kolyaol**
budget **huq sol hu** (50:201)
bud of a bean **neev'quv**
bud to bud, a **alquv quv**
bud to bud (as a crop) **kalquv**
buffalo **niuqpeel**
buffalo, water (or cow) **aqniuq**
buffalo (old) **niuqmoq**
buffalo day **niuq nao**
buffalo dung **niuqxiq; niuqxiq xiq bieiv; niuqxiq xiq kuv**
buffalo horn **niuqkyul**
buffalo hour (as time of day) **niuq zeq** (B=Chi)
buffalo louse **niuqseil**
buffalo, male **niuqpeel lalbu; niuqpeel laqyil**
buffalo meat **niuqsaq**
buffalo rope **niuqcav**
buffalo shed; stable **niuqkuv**
buffalo skin **niuqgeel**
buffalo wallow **niuqlao duqhovq**
buffalo, wild (gaur) **neivqniuq**
buffalo year **niuq huvq**
bugle **yaqhaol** (Chi)
build (as house) **cuvq; jeifseiq** (as in 'want to build industries well') (Chi) (26:40)
building (clf.) **yaol**
building site; work site **gaoldif** (Chi) (26:62)
building, main **yaolma; laqhyul yaolma** (26:102)
building, small (or room) **yaolssaq**
build up, to **cuv dav; ziivq; aol dav**
bull (cattle) **niuqnil lalbu**
bulldozer **tyultujil** (Chi) (26:27)
bullet **miqsiq**
bullet hole **bevheiq**
bullet shell **ziihovq**
bulletin; notice **bufgaof** (Chi)
bullock, a **laqsovq**
bully, a **heeqzaq** (50:133)
bully, to **naqguv**
bump against **quq tovq**
bump and hurt **taoq levq**
bump on a road **duqlu**

bumpy, to be **gu lu gaoq laoq; daoqteev teev**
bund (or dike) between fields **dalbaol**
bundle, a **zaoq; kavqzaoq**
bundle, to **kavqzaoq zaoq**
burden, a **alyeil (pi; eq); fufdal** (Chi) (26:55)
  burden to be light **alyeil pial**
bureaucracy **gualliaoq** (Chi) (34:16)
  bureaucrat **gualliaoq ziilbei zuyif** (Chi) (34:8)
Burma; Burmese **Mieitieif; Mieitieiv** (Chi)
burn, to **peev; yeiq**
burn a bonfire **jeibaol baol**
burn and shrivel up **peev luvq**
burn away, to **peev saq**
burn hand, to **aqlavq tal** (C=Chi)
burn one's whole body, to **molpeev peev**
burning hot **tal** (Chi)
burnt, to be **kul; peev laq e**
burn up, to **haqleil peev pievq saq**
bury, to **bavq duq; duq hhuvq**
  bury silver in the ground **piulduq duq**
  bury with a broom (by covering with dirt) **yav hhuvq**
bus (long distance, between towns) **balceil** (Chi)
bush **saqcaoq (algao saqcaoq** = thorn bush)
bushy-tailed porcupine **hupiul**
business, to do **yiqniq** (Chi) (50:198)
business (small) **hhellavq lavqssaq**
business is business (not in joking) **hhaqleiq maq leiq qivq e miqnieiq**
business license **ssiqniq ziiqzaof; yiqniq ziiqzaof** (Chi) (50:198)
businessman; trader **hhellavq aol e col; hhellavq aolssaq**
bustling with excitement; lively **sseiqnaof** (Chi)
busy, to be **teiq; teiqlaq meil**
busy; bustling; flourishing **hhyuq qa hhyuq lol zuvq**
busy season **miaoqcivq; wafjif** (Chi) (50:175)
but **tyulliq** (10:pref, 11:121); **tyul e liq; yulmeil liq**
but; even though **laolngaoq**
butt, to **taoq**
  butt heads (as animals) **lavqbavq taoq**
  butting contest **taoqteil qei**
butterfly **allu; allu zalbaol**
buttocks **daoqkaoq; daoqkaoq saqpiaq; daoqmeil** (in a riddle where it means the buttocks after a bowel movement)
butt of gun **miqbev bevdaoq**
button **peilsiq**
buttonhole (Hani version) **peilpi**
button quail (type of quail) **laoqha**
buy, to **hhel**
buy and resell secretly **hyuq aoq**
buy back former belonging; redeem **hhel huvq**
buzz, to **ziil; zil**

by accident **maq nyuq maq gaq meil**
by all means **halmeil e liq**
by and by **aqkal naolhao daov maq gal nei**
by any means **halmeil e liq**
by chance **maq nyuq maq gaq meil**
by foot, to travel **keel nei ssuq**
by hand **aqlavq nei**
by heart **neema hholqei nyuq teiq**
by mouth **meiqzu wuqduq nei; doq nei**
by no means **halmeil liq maq ....**
by now **niaoq'aol hev nei**
by one's self **yoqhhaq bulduq nei**
bypath **gallavq; galquv**
byproduct **zalbi; fuf capi** (Chi) (50:53)
byroad **gallavq; galquv**
by rule **galkov lo'qo nei**
by then **yul taq hev e ngaoq**
by usage **aolduq lo'qo**
byway **gallavq; galquv**
by word of mouth **doq nei; meiqbaoq wuqduq nei**

c C c C c C

C c **soqmiav aqma hholqei saoq mol e qiq mol**

---

cabbage **hhoqpavq peivqcal** (B=Chi); **hhoqpavq** (also for greens)
cabbage, white **hhoqba** (11:118)
cabinet **nyufgoq** (Chi)
cactus **lalkyul**
cadre **gafbuf** (Chi)
cajole; lure **mul**
cake (as a moon-festival cake) **zabiav** (26:7)
caladium (see: taro)
calamity; catastrophe **koq jul koq luq**
calcium **geifpieif** (Chi)
calculate, to **sol; solzal** (26:75); **needeq deq**
calculation (final) **sol ceiv**
calendar **gaolliq** (Chi)
  calendar, Hani **liqhhaol** (46:81)
  calendar, lunar **naoqliq** (Chi)
  calendar, solar **yaqliq** (Chi)
calf (buffalo, cow) **niuqssaq**
calf (of the leg) **keeldu**
call, to **kul; gul**
call an animal **jaq**
call and gather, to **kul zyul**
call attention to **bi nyuq gaol**
call back, to **gul huvq**
call each other **kul qoq**
call forth, to **gul nyuq**
call names, to **col yaol yaq**
call on, to **kul**
call on together **gul zyul**
callous; unfeeling; cold-hearted **neepeel neehhuvq**
call out, to **gul; kul; gul caq**
call out something, to **jaq duv** (46:156)
call roll, to **colmiaol gul; dieimiq** (Chi)
call soul back **sullal kul**
call to (someone) **kul miq**
call together **gul ssaoq; kul zyul; qoq zil**
callus **lavqpeiv**
  callus to develop **lavqpeiv dav**
calm and unhurried **maq niv maq guv**
calm in one's heart **yeildao nei; neema yeildao nei**
calmly; quietly **quvqceiv nei; quqceiv nei** (both)
camera **zaofxafjil** (Chi) (50:208)
camp, a **yoduq** (50:209)
camping place; sleeping place **xavqduq**
can (vb) (capable) **(vb) nia**
can (vb) (willing) **(vb) qaol**
cancel, to; to rescind; to write off **hhe xa** (50:216); **diq bial**
candid; straightforward **neema daol** (50:163)
candidate **hefbu** (Chi)

candidate for representative **deifbiao hefxei sseiq** (Chi)
can do (skillful) **qivq**
candle (beeswax) **biaqsaoq aldovq**
cane, sugar **poqqul**
cane; walking stick **zaqngeeq**
cane sugar (not fully refined) **poqbiav**
cane sugar, to make **poqbiav biavnav**
canine tooth **seqziil**
canned goods **malcavq bavq dov laq e zal; gueifteq** (Chi)
cannot remember **maq nyuq taq nia**
cannot win (as in a battle) **maq diq hhaol**
canon (for firing) **dafpaoq** (Chi) (26:27)
can stand **qi**
canteen (as in a factory); dining room **siqtaq** (Chi)
canvas **pavqbul**
caogo (amomum) plant with clusters of red at the base (in the same family as ginger) **deqheq**
cap; hat **wuqcaoq; diqkaq**
capable **nia**
capital (as money; animals) **zeiqma** (50:218)
capital crime; capital offence **sil tovq zyul** (50:160)
capitalism **ziilbei zuyif** (Chi) (26:16, 50:218)
capitalist **ziilbeijal** (Chi) (50:218)
capitalist class **ziilca geiljiq** (Chi) (50:218)
capital letter **dafxi**
capitol (as prefecture; province; region) **sefu** (Chi) (50:156); **sedul** (Chi) (50:156) **seihyuf** (Chi) (50:151)
capon **hasovq; aqha hasovq**
captain in army **lieiqza**
capture; wrest **koq hha**
car; auto **qiqceil** (Chi) (11:30); **qifceil** (Chi) (3:2, 9:135)
carbon **meiq; tafjil** (Chi) (50:163)
carbon ink **tafsuf meiqsyu** (Chi) (50:163)
cards, to play **puqkeiq** (Chi)
care for, to (emphasis on feeding, raising) **qu; bavq qu**
care for, to (emphasis on teaching) **meiq miq qu miq**
careful; alert **nyuq gaol**
careful in work; to work hard **neema deivq**
carefully; earnestly **ssivq nei**
carefully; well **meeqzav nei**
(vb) carefully **ssao nei (vb)** (**alniq ssao nei niq** = cut the bamboo ties carefully - 11:42); **ssaol nei (vb)** (**ssaol nei nyuq hu** = think carefully); **zuv nei** (**zuv nei salhu** = watch carefully); **ssaossao nei**
careless person, a **pia'la nei**
carelessly, to do **aolbiei biei; maq nyuq maq gaq nei**
carpenter **albol lavqqivq** (see also: blacksmith)
carpeting (for floor or bed) **geilzavq** (Chi) (11:30)
carry; take **bavq**

carry along (on back) **eq teiq**
carry and fix up **bavq leev**
carry by nape of the neck (baby; animal) **moqqul laolbyuq byuq**
carrying cloth (for baby) **beeteiq** (it also means: placenta)
carrying pole **bavqdul**
carrying rope (for men) **mieivqzao**
carrying rope; tumpline (for women) **wuqmieivq**
carry off, to **bavq zei**
carry on, to (as a program) **aol cavq; jifceiq** (Chi) (34:2); **faqyaq** (Chi) (34:2)
carry on back **eq; pi**
carry on horse **qeiv** (**qiq qeiv qeiv** = to carry a load on an animal)
carry on neck **laolbyuq byuq**
carry on pole **bavq**
carry on shoulder **bavq**
carry out, to **aol xa heil; guafceiq** (Chi)
carry something in mouth, as dog **kovq; aoq**
carry; transport **miaoqgaoq hhezaq**
carry with hands; lift up **qiq**
cart **maceil; macei** (Chi)
cart, horse **moqcei** (B=Chi)
carton box **gyufteiq** (Chi)
cart, oxen **niuqcei** (B=Chi)
cartilage; soft bone **saqyyuq yyuqnaoq**
carve, to **diaolkeq** (Chi)
carve, to; to engrave **seqtevq tevq; davtevq tevq**
case; box (as for tobacco) **hoqbav**
cash; money **piul** (50:185)
cassava **albol moqdev**
cassia tree, Chinese **seqqovq**
cast about for something, to **leiq puv; salqo**
cast down; discouraged **neema ceiv**
castor tree **heilcil**
castrate, to **sovq** (11:160)
castrate, to (only horse; buffalo or cow) **do**
castrate a cock, to **hasovq sovq** (11:160)
castrate a horse, to **moqdo do**
castrated horse **moqdo**
casually **maq yevq nei**
cat **almil**
catalogue, to make a **bieilmuq** (Chi)
catastrophe **koqjul koqluq**
catch **nieivq**
catch and hold **nieivq teiq; piav teiq**
catch and stop, to **leiq cyuq**
catch hold, to **daq haol**
catch hold of (as rope, vine, braid of hair) **nil teiq** (11:201)
catch sight of, to see (see: to see)
catch up to **mil; leiq mil** (11:112)
caterpillar **aqzuq**
caterpillar-caused sore on skin **aqcav cav**

cat, female **milma**
catfish **biallul**
catfood **milzal** (29:4)
Catholicism **Tieilzujaof** (Chi) (50:166)
cat, kitten **milssaq**
cat, male **milzal**
cattle (and buffalo) **niuq**
cattle plague **niuqnal**
catty (500 grams) **jil**
caught in the rain **aoqsseil diq sso**
cauliflower **geiqdalhaol** (Chi)
causative (because) **alnei**
causative (a pre-verb) **bi (vb)** (**bi dol** = give to drink; **bi aol** = have somebody do, etc.)
cause a disturbance; disturb someone **lav beeq**
caution, to; to warn; admonish **naqteil xa**
cautious and conscientious **jil jil yiq yiq** (Chi)
cave; hole (in dirt) **milbyu**
cave (in stone) **haqluv luvbaoq** (14:130); **haqluv haoqbaoq**

celebrate New Year **huvqhev zaq; Galtaol taol; huvqsiivq hev**
celebrate **qifzuq** (Chi)
celery **halsol solma**
cement **syuniq** (Chi) (11:31)
cent, one **zao** (Chi) (**qiq zao** = one cent - 26:74)
center; core **alkaq kaqli; malniuv**
center (as of a page) **alhhaol laobao**
centimeter **gaolfeil; feil; liqmi** (all Chi) (11:77)
centipede **hhaqma eelseil**
central **alkaq kaqli**
centralize; concentrate **ssaoq zyul**
century **ssillo** (50:154)
century plant **lalkyul**
certain; surely **halmeil liq**
certificate; credentials; papers **zeifjeif** (Chi) (50:211)
certificate of merit **jazuaf** (Chi)

chaff; husks **balhov; alhov**
chain for a dog **keeqdaoq**
chain made of iron **saolbeel**
chain of silver **meiqkav alcav**
chair; stool **baqdel** (Chi) (11:30); **naolmoq** (29:4)
chairman **zuxiq** (Chi) (26:13)
Chairman Mao's quotations **Maoq Zuxiq yi'liq**
challenge to battle **lav ssil** (50:167)
chance, by **hha'la nei**
change, radical **aoq puv mil pal**
change, to (to exchange) **pal**
change; to become **pievq**
changeable **miaq lal pal lal**
change, violent **ceiv nei puv**
change hands, to **yosaol nieivq pal**

change in the extreme (lit., 'sky and earth turn')
aoqpuv milpuv puv (11:45)
change one's mind **neema nyuq pal**
change one's mind; to repent **nyuq puv; neema puv**
change one's quarters, to **jol pal; jolduq pal**
change with each passing day **nao pal la pal**
channel; a way **tuqjif** (Chi)
chaos; confusion **beeqga nei**
chaotic **beeq li ga la**
chapping (as skin) **havyov nei; coqbeivq coqseil; coqbeivq coqseil nga nei** (wide breaks in skin)
chapter; section **zal** (Chi) (50:207)
character; personality **colhe**
characteristics; peculiarities **teiqdiei** (50:164); **teqseq; siilzevq; teqzeil** (all Chi)
charcoal **haqhheq; jaoltaf** (Chi)
charcoal (burning) **miqzaq miqjiv; miqzaq heqjiv; haqhheq liqtaf** (B=Chi)
charred by fire **peev kul**
chase after **qo'leiq**
chase and catch **leiq mil**
chase animals by making loud noise (type of hunting) **saqgul gul**
chase each other, to **leiqkev kevma**
chat, to (also it sometimes includes the idea of boistrous sounds; noisy) **doqlovq lovq; doqlovq diq**
cheap **yal**
cheaper, to be **yal zeiq**
cheap price **hhaqpyuq yal**
cheat, to **hheivq; hheivq zaq; hheivq leivq; aqzavq zavq; qeiq zaq** (45:26)
cheat; boast; lie, to **haovq; aqmiaovq miaovqzaq**
cheat and rob **ziiluq luq**
cheated, to be **hheivqsov pieiq sso; zaosso**
cheating words **hheivq doq**
check; examine **huafyeif** (Chi) (10:33)
check out a reason for a matter **daoqdaoq hu duv** (i.e., to get to the bottom of a matter)
check something (as train tickets); inspect **jeicaq** (Chi)
check; verify **solza** (50:70)
cheek **baqba**
cheekbone; malar bone **baqkyul**
cheek swollen (from having mouth full of food) **baqlu deiq** (26:85)
chemical examination; lab. test **huafyeif** (Chi)
chemical factory **huafgaolca** (Chi) (26:27)
chemical fertilizer **zeiqkeeq huaffeiq** (B=Chi)
cherry tree **eiqhheiq**
chess, Chinese type **xafqiq** (Chi)
chess, military type **zilqiq** (Chi)
chest (body) **neehha; neehovq**
chest (hollow area at sternum) **neema neehovq**
chestnut tree (flat, bitter nut) **aqgyu albol; gyuma**

albol
chestnut tree (large nut) **cevqpovq albol**
chestnut tree (medium nut) **cevqseil albol**
chestnut tree (oval-shaped nut) **heiqba albol**
chestnut tree (smallest nut) **cevqsiq albol**
chew, to **hhyuq**
chick **hassaq**
chicken **ha; aqha** (11:34) (clf. = **mol; ha**)
chicken (castrated; capon) **aqha hasovq**
chicken basket **hahav; aqha miavhav**
chicken coop **aqha hakuv**
chicken day **ha nao**
chicken egg **hawuv**
chicken feather **hahao; aqha haniaol** (46:132)
chicken feather (lg., hard) **haniaol**
chicken food **hazal**
chicken hour **ha zeq**
chicken house **hakuv; aqha hakuv**
chicken leg **aqha buldul** (13:11)
chicken louse **haseil**
chicken meat **aqha hasaq**
chicken mites **aqha haseil**
chicken nest (chicken coop) **hageel**
chicken shed **aqha hakuv**
chicken spleen **neenil**
chicken tail (meat part at the base) **miqzu**
chicken thigh **aqha buldul**
chicken wing **hadaol**
chicken year **ha huvq**
child **ssaqguq; aqli** (esp. of the last child in a family)
child; son **ssaq**
childish; naive **nee hyuq maq hav** (50:200)
child of fortune **sulmeeq sulsal sal ssaq**
children **aqli mavq; ssaqguq mavq; miqyo mavq** = daughters and sons
children and grandchildren **yuq ssol ssaq** (10:pref)
Children's league **Eqtaoqtuaq** (Chi) (26:12)
Children's league, member of **Eqtaoq tuaqyeiq** (Chi) (26:12)
chili pepper **laqpil**
chili pepper (green, fresh) **laqpil pilzaoq**
chili pepper (large) **aqniuq laqpil; pilma naqboq**
chili pepper (small but hot) **laqpil piltev**
chili pepper dish **laqpil davssaq**
chilly; cool **saqzuq zuq; gavzuq zuq**
chimpanzee; ogre; jungle savage (the Hani have not seen so use the same name for all) **miaqlo miallo** (11:17)
chin **meiqdaoq**
China **Zaolgoq** (Chi) (26:22, 50:214)
China (country of) **Zaolgoq milcaq** (A=Chi) (26:91)
chinaberry **aqhhel hhelneev**
Chinese **Pyulniul; Laqbeq; Laqbeqssaq; Navssaq** (or; **Nav** = found in some proverbs)

Chinese alpine rush; asparagus **haqdal**
Chinese cabbage, pickled **hhoqqeil**
Chinese (Han) language **Pyulniuldoq; Haf'yyu** (Chi)
Chinese (Han) language (written in Roman script) **Haf'yyu pilyil** (Chi) (32:3)
Chinese (Han) nation **Pyulniul: Zaolhuaq miqcuq** (Chi)
Chinese onion **taoqguq**
Chinese radish; turnip **hhoqpul**
Chinese style **Zaolgoq teqseiq** (Chi); **Zaolgoq teqdiei** (Chi)
Chinese toon (a plant they eat) **ssiiqbuvq**
Chinese yam **moqdev**
chipmunk (Asiatic) **piaqcoq**
chip out, to **caq (vb)**
chirping of birds **jiv jiv zav zav; qil qeivq qeivq; jil geivq geivq** (latter two also used for creaking door)
chips of wood or bamboo **devpovq**
chisel, to **tavq**
chisel, flat **zaoqbiav** (A=Chi)
chisel for stone **zaoqssaq** (A=Chi) (11:31)
chisel, rounded **zaoqhuvq** (A=Chi)
choke, to (on a liquid) **dol ngavq; kaoqnao nao**
choke, to (on a solid) **suv ngavq**
choose; select **ceil**
choose out of **diq ceil; ceil duv; deiq duv**
chop; mince **bieiv**
chop (as firewood); to split **cevq**
chop (so as to make one side flat) **cevq biav**
chopping board for meat and vegetables **saqteil**
chopping board for wood **devdaq**
chopsticks **juldal; dalteiq** (a single one)
chopstick holder **juldal dalbaoq; juldal havpuq**
chop up meat **saqbieiv bieiv**
chorus **calzao zao**
Christian era (A.D.) **gaolyeiq** (Chi)
chubby (fat & short) **nulhevq nei; culbiq pa biq nei**

cicada **aqzeivq; yaovma** (46:161); **gaoma**
cigarette **yahyuq ziiyeil** (B=Chi) (50:213) **yahyuq** (clf. = **mol**)
circle around, to **hhao'lao nei; hhe hhao**
circular; round **leecei nei**
circulate **lieqtaol** (Chi)
circumstances **huaqji** (Chi)
circumstances; situation **qiqkuaf** (Chi)
city **ceiq; ceiqsiif** (Chi) (10:32, 26:27)
City People's Commune **Ceiqsiif sseiqmiq gaolseif** (Chi) (26:76)
civet cat **piaqyiq; piaqyiq yiqpeel**
civet cat (one type) **biaqyil naqboq**
civet cat (with a white nose) **piaqyiq aqma nalcal**
civil case **miqsiif hhafjeif** (Chi)
civil dispute; a public issue **ssaqlaol koq zaq deiq zaq**

civil law **miq faq** (Chi); **ssaqlaol e yo'liq**
civil mediation **ssaqlaol alkaq kaq zaq**
civilization **weiqmiq** (Chi) (50:178)
clamor, to **zeiv ho**
clamp down, to **kovq teiq; yevq teiq**
  clamp down with teeth **seqpeiq kovq**
clamp onto, hold tight **cuv teiq**
clan, a **alqa**
clan; surname **colqa**
clap; pat **diq**
class (as rich class, poor class, exploited class)
  geiljiq (Chi)
classifier (grammatical) **liafciiq** (Chi)
CLASSIFIERS for
  amount of weight **sav**
  animals (certain) and things **mol; ssaq**
  arrows **miaq**
  bags of rice **leil (dalleil)**
  bamboo **bol; lo**
  bamboo shoots **dyuv**
  basins **peiq**
  baskets **hav (bavqhav)** (11:80)
  beans **neev**
  big things **ma** (11:83)
  bites **kovq** (11:85)
  boards **biavq**
  boats **loq**
  bodies **mol**
  book; paper **kaoq; daoq**
  bowl (as bowl of rice) **haoq**
  buffalo and horse **kaol**
  bundles **zaoq; biuq**
  calling out **gul** (11:85)
  canals; long ditches **gal (lolgal qiq gal)**
  cats (and certain small animals) **ssaq** (11:156)
  cattle (cows, buffalos) **niuq; kaol**
  cent **zao**
  chairs; tables **bieil; mol**
  chickens and pigs **ssaq**
  Chinese money (jiao) **haoq**
  clothes **xo**
  clusters (as trees) **caoq**
  coins **biav**
  containers (wooden) to measure rice **se**
  cords; ropes etc. **cav**
  cows, buffalos, horses, donkeys **kaol** (11:18)
  cuts; hacks **dev** (11:85)
  cutting (as trees) **lavq** (11:211)
  days **nao (qiq nao)**
  dishes (lg.) **huvq**
  donkey **kaol**
  drops (liquid) **zav**
  eyes **miav**
  families **hhovq**
  fields (as rice) **loq** (11:81)

fields (non-irrigated) **kol**
fingers **nyul (lavqnyul qiq nyul** - 11:95)
fish (and other small animals) **ssaq** (11:73)
flat objects **biav**
flocks (chicken, ducks etc.) **beeq** (11:81)
flowers **yeiv**
fruits (and other round things) **siq**
general things (including stools, pots, knives, rings, etc., and some animals) **mol** (11:76)
generations; lifespans **ssil**
grains; beans; pills, etc. **neev**
grass; weeds; bamboo **caoq**
ground-wasp hives **zaol** (11:195)
groups (as of houses) **caoq**
groups (as of mountain fields) **koq** (11:153)
groups (as of people) **ba (qiq ba = 1 group)** (11:77)
hairs; straws, etc. **kao**
handfuls (as of grass) **tuv**
handspans **tul**
hits; strikes **diq; lavq** (11:85)
hives (bee); rice steamers **baoq**
hoes; plows **ceiq** (11:95)
holes (as of rats) **byu (milbyu qiq byu)** (11:95)
hollow things **baoq**
horses; buffalos (certain other animals) **moq; kaol** (11:95)
hours **se (siqse qiq se ssuq = walk for an hour)**
houses **yaol** (11:86)
irrigated fields **loq**
jumps **coq** (11:85)
kicks **naoq** (11:218)
kinds of things **qa** (11:77)
large, flat objects (mat, quilt, hide of a buffalo) **daol** (11:74)
layers of clothing; honey combs **kaol**
leaves **pavq**
lines **daol**
loads (a horse can carry) **qeiv** (11:83)
loads (a human can carry on back) **yeil; eq**
long things (sugar cane, bamboo, rafter, needle) **xaoq** (11:75); **kaol**
lumps (as of salt); clods; etc. **hul**
meals **biol**
money **biav**
month **siq**
mountain ranges **teil**
mountains **gaoq (haolgaoq qiq gaoq** - 11:21)
mouthfuls **heiq (qiq heiq dol)** (11:21)
nights **yavq**
one of a pair **teiq** (1 shoe, 1 chopstick, etc.) (11:75)
pails **taoq**
pairs **zaol** (**juldal qiq zaol**)
paths in the jungle **quv**

pairs of trousers **xov** (11:87)
patches (as of ginger) **caoq**
people **hhaq; col (Col xil col.)**
pieces of silver **dev**
pieces of wood and bamboo **tao; lo**
pigs; chickens (other smaller animals) **ssaq**
piles (as of firewood) **gaoq**
pipes of tobacco smoked **hhyul**
plural numbers (people) **mavq**
ponds; pools of water **duq; mol**
rain **baoq**
rivers **lol; baq**
roads **kaol**
rooms **lov**
ropes; cords **cav**
round objects (esp. small) **siq**
sacks; bags **yeil** (11:211)
sets of things (as for plowing, black-smithing, etc.) **pul (niuqceiq qiq pul** - 11:76)
sets of things (as pots, pans, tools) **zuvq** (11:77)
sides of mountains **baq**
something **jivq (qiq jivq); mol; qa**
songs **pul** (11:161)
spoons **cavq**
steps (as when walking) **tuvq**
steps in terrace **teivq**
sticks (Chi) **xaoq**
stones (small) **siq; ssaq** (11:84)
storeys (in a building) **teivq**
strings of things (beads, etc.) **puq**
suits of clothes **zuvq**
things (types) **qa**
threads **kaol** (11:152)
times **leiv; haq; daol; lavq; miav; taq**
times (related to crops) **kal**
times (based on animals, two hours for each of the 12 annual animals) **zeq** (Chi)
times (once, twice, etc.) **taq**
times of plowing **leiv** (11:85)
trees **bol**
trucks **ceil** (Chi)
umbrellas **kaq (beelkaq)** (11:114)
villages **puv** (11:152)
weights **ceil** (Chi); **mieiv dal** (Chi); **jil** (Chi)
words; mouthfuls of food **heiq**
wrapped packages **tov** (11:161)

class character; class nature **geiljiqzif** (Chi)
class feeling **geiljiq gaqiq** (Chi)
classmate; schoolmate **zolqoq; soqhhaq zolqoq**
classroom **jaofsiif** (Chi); **soqhhaq zolyaol**
class struggle **geiljiq defzeil** (Chi) (26:17)
clause (gram) **doq lavq**
clavicle; collarbone **leeldee saqyyuq**

claw; toenail; talon **seiqsaoq**
claw of cat **laqsaoq** (11:51)
clay (a type sometimes eaten by pregnant women) **aqnaoq; milcaq aqnaoq**
clean **sol; solyeil nei** (26:112)
clean (as water) **gaol nei**
clean, very **sol pa sol nei sol** (11:60); **solyeil pa yeil nei** (11:58); **se leev** (26:7)
clean and honest; pure **gaolquv nei**
clean and neat (as the type of room in which a sick person should stay) **solyeil nei** (10:21)
clean, to; rinse; bleach **ceibu**
clean, very **solyeil pa yeil nei**
cleanly **bu'loq nei; solyeil nei**
clean water; clear water **gaolciv nei; eelgaol**
clear day; bright day **aoq sal mil sal** (11:22)
clear field of trees for planting, to **xal beiv**
clear up (as the weather) **lav sa**
clear water; clean water **gaolciv nei; eelgaol miq nei**
clear water, very **gaolciv pa civ nei**
clearly **loqleil nei; loqleil sav nei** (11:209)
clearly (vb) **(vb) loq (maq hu loq** = not see clearly)
clearly, very **loqleil pa leil nei**
clever; bright **neegaol**
clever; smart; intelligent **neema deivq**
clever, to be **kyul; byulkyul kyul** (10:pref.)
clever child **byulkyul kyulssaq**
clever person **colkyul**
clever person (female) **miqkyul** (30:1); **byulkyul kyulma**
clever person (male) **yokyul** (30:1); **byulkyul aqda**
click, to **di li de le**
cliff, a **bialsaq hhaqzeil; bialsaq saq**
cliff edge **bialsaq hhaqzeil**
cliff of rock **haqluv hhaqzeil**
climate, proper **quvqlaol za**
climb into **piav tao**
climb on, to **piav ceq**
climb up, to **dav**
cling closely to **bavq kavq**
clitoris **beivqniuv** (taboo)
clock **siqse** (Chi)
clod **puqhul**
close; shut **piq; xoq tovq**
close (as eyes) **miv**
close (as window) **deiq piq; diq cyuq** (10:7); **caqbyu diq cyuq**
close and lock **xoq tovq**
close by, to be **daoqpei; niqca nei**
close down; seal up **miaoq cyuq**
close-fisted **lavqtuv sivq e col; laqpil aqbol**
close (not far) **niq; niqca nei; daoqpei niqca nei**
close to something (to move) **zul pyul la; deiq ca**
close up something, to; confine **nieivq laol**
closer, to go **niq; niq li** (26:103)

cloth **haqpal**
cloth, cotton print **palbuvq**
cloth, handwoven **palhav; haqpal palhav**
cloth, patterned **haqpal palbuvq**
cloth, red **palnil**
cloth, synthetic **diqka** (Chi)
cloth, white **haqpal palpiul**
cloth with an open weave **palkaq**
cloth, yellow **haqpal palsiil; palsiil**
clothes, new **peilsiivq laqsiivq** (46:160)
clothes, old and ragged **peilju laqjal; peilja laqja; peilju peilja**
clothes padded with cotton **beewul peilhaoq**
clothe someone, to **bi dao**
clothes, to change **jeilpal pal**
clothing **peilhaoq**
clothing, green **peilniul**
clothing, new **peilsiivq**
clothing, white **peilpiul**
cloud; fog **joqhyuq**
clouds (thick); fog **joqtaoq**
clump, a **caoq** (**albol qiq caoq** = a clump of trees; **jahhaq qiq caoq** = a clump of grass)
clumsy, to be **qiq jivq maq aol nia; yobuvq** (note: this is also the word for 'rotten')
clumsy manner **yoqdyul**
clumsy person **colbuvq**
clumsy, very **lavq a haxiq piav e maq miaoq** (lit., 'even chicken dung does not stick to his hands')
cluster; clump **puq; caoq** (bamboo, grass, trees)

coal **meiq** (Chi)
coal gas **meiqqif** (B=Chi) (26:34)
coals burning **miqjiv**
coarse, to be **kaoqhav hav; kaoqhav laqngaoq**
coat, long **peilhaoq peilmol**
coat, short **peillil**
coax, to; entice **mul zaq**
cobra, king **ollol eelkol kolma**
cobweb **byuqzuq bavhhav**
cock; rooster **hapyul**
cock, spotted **hapyul pyulbiavq**
cock a crossbow, to **kavtev hhe dav** (13:32)
cocka-doodle-doo (sound of rooster crowing) **gaqgyul hhovq; goqgyul lil'o**
cockroach **alpia; alpia aqma** (the latter also means a kind of water weed)
cockscomb **molbiaq; mobiaq**
cockspur **aqha hadavq**
coercive measure; compulsory means **maq aol maq qivq yiqqeiq** (C=Chi)
coffee **kalfeil** (Chi-Eng)
coffin **alzaol**
coffin, to put in **alzaol a bavq dov; alzaol hholqei bavq dov**

cogon grass (thatch) **eqjil**
coin **biav**
coin, copper **taoqhaoq**
coir rope (of coconut husk) **sseilcav**
coke **meiq jaoltaf** (Chi) (26:28)
cold (to be) **ceivq; gav**
cold (to become) **aqgav gav sso**
cold (to feel) **aqgav; aqgav gav** (3:3)
cold, to have a **cyuqnal; cyuqnal kovq** (15:41)
cold, very **gavsiv nei; gavsiv pa siv nei; ceivqqaol; ngaoq ya**
cold rice (as take lunch to field) **hoqgav**
collapse, to **milbiav; biav; milsuv** (46:169)
collapse; disintegrate **hhoq li hhoq quv** (50:173)
collar **laolbav; laolheiq**
collar, fur **peilhaoq laolbav**
collar, opening at **laolheiq**
collarbone; clavicle **leeldee saqyyuq**
collect, to **bavq ssaoq; se; seq ssaoq; bavq leev; sel zaq** (A=Chi)
collect, to get collected **piav ssaoq**
collect; gather **cev ssaoq**
collect; get **se leev; se ssaoq**
collective welfare **yohaol meeqduq**
collectivism **jiqti zuyif** (Chi)
collect manure for compost **zeiqbeiq ssa**
collect money; raise funds **piul leiq ssaoq**
collect together **se leev** (11:221); **bavq ssaoq**
college and university **yeifxaof** (Chi) (50:201); **xoqxaof** (Chi); **dafxoq** (Chi)
collusion, to act in **colcuv colcavq cavq**
colon (punctuation) **maofhaof** (Chi)
colonialism **ziiqmiq zuyif** (Chi) (50:212)
colony, a **ziiqmiqdif** (Chi) (34:3, 50:212)
color **zaqciq** (50:193); **yeiqseiq** (Chi)
colorful **biavq biavq cei cei** (50:181)
colt (young horse) **moqssaq**
coma (to be in) **yiuvqmu mu; silhheivq hheivq**
comb (fine-toothed) **peiqcaol**
comb (for hair) **peiqtaoq; kav; pyuqtaoq**
comb, to **kav (wuqduq kav)**
comb; harrow **kav**
comb of rooster; dragon **aqha mobiaq; molbiaq; mobiaq**
combat capacity **geel diq e hhaqhav**
combine, to **jiqhoq** (Chi) (34:5)
combine; mix **bavq paoq**
come, to **lal** (when it occurs with some other verbs, there may be some tonal changes)
come about, to **duv lal**
come across, to **taoq puq lal**
come and go, to **yil lal**
come back; return **hhuvq lal; hhuvqdaol aol**
come back from lower place or west **hhuvq lal**
come back from upper place or east **hhuvq yiv**
come down, to **yiv**

come down upon, to **duvq nei bi diq; bi hu nil zaq**
come from a higher place **tao yi**
come in, to **dov lal; hev lal**
come in its turn, to **qiq mol naolhao qiq mol meil duv lal**
come in sight, to **mol lal**
come out (as a snake) **quq duv**
come out, to **duv; duv yiv; duv lal; duv al la**
come over, to **pyul lal**
come short, to **lav xu; maq hha**
come short of, to **maq ceq; maq aoq caq**
come to, to **deivq huvq lal**
come to an end, to **naq**
come together, to **jol zyul**
come together by luck **puq lal; taoq puq; taoq zyul**
come to greet **doq cavq lal**
come to life, to **deivq huvq lal**
come to meet **seqcavq**
come to terms, to **doqsii eil ceiv**
come to the ears of **naqbol a gaq lal**
come to the point, to **doq gee caqcaol zil**
come to the rescue **aolhaol lal; hhaqhav tivq haol lal**
come up to, to **duv hev**
comfortable; healthy **jolsal; hoqsei nei; nyuq sal; maq jol saq**
coming and going **yil lal**
coming and going repeatedly **yil yil lal lal**
comma (punctuation) **defhaof** (Chi)
command to be quiet **taq ziv**
commander **siilliif** (Chi) (50:159)
commander, daily affairs **siifwufza** (Chi) (26:85)
commander-in-chief **zyuqma** (50:169)
command headquarters **lieiqbuf** (26:57)
commemorate, to **jiqnieif** (Chi)
comment, to **eil suv** (50:131); **gee zaq** (50:197)
comment; appraise; criticize (whether good or bad) **meeq dyul eil**
comments **yiqjeif** (Chi) (26:29)
commercialism; industrialism **gaolsalniq** (Chi)
commit a crime **zaol zyul**
committee (standing) **caqwuf hhyuyeiqhyuf** (Chi)
committee; organization **zuziiqbuf** (Chi)
committee chairperson **hhyuyeiqza** (Chi) (50:176)
committee member **hhyuyeiq** (Chi) (50:176)
commodity **hhellavq pievq**
commodity economy **hhellavq zeiqsal**
common crime **zaoqgao zaol zyul**
commune; brigade **gaolsef; gaolseif** (both are Chi)
commune members **seifyeiq** (Chi) (26:38)
commune; people's commune **sseiqmiq gaolseif** (Chi)
communicate a disease, to **zoqleiq kovq** (10:23)
communicate freely, to **soqbuvq halzei zei** (50:168)
communism **gaofca zuyif** (Chi) (26:56)
communist drive **gaofca'faol** (Chi)
Communist party **Gaofcada; Da** (Chi)

Communist party, Chinese **Zaolgoq Gaocada** (Chi) (50:213)
Communist party member **Gaofca dayeiq** (Chi)
companion **lavqqoq**
company, a; shop **gaolsiil** (Chi)
company (in the military) **lieiqdyuf** (Chi)
company commander **lieiqdyuf seza** (Chi) (26:109)
comparable; equal to **toq**
compare, to **qeiv; bavq qeiv; zeiv hu; se'qeiv**
compass **ziinaqzeil** (Chi) (50:213)
compensate, to **peiq huvq**
compensate for economic loss, to **peiqcaq jiljif syusiiq**
compete, to **jifzeil** (Chi); **seilqeiv qeiv**
competition; match (as basketball game) **biseif** (Chi)
competition, to have **aolqeiv qeiv**
compile, to **ziivq; bieil duv** (to work out; invent)
complain, to **neema maq lal leil eil**
complaint, written **bu soqhhaq** (50:217)
complement, a **buyi** (Chi)
complement, to **bucaol** (Chi)
complementary **zaol haoq**
complete; full **biao**
completed action **(vb) saq (pal saq** = all changed)
completely **saq nei**
completely (vb) **(vb) saq al (ngal hoq zaq saq al** = I have completely eaten up the rice)
complete the task **aol saq**
complicated **fuqzaq** (Chi)
composing; type setting **peiqziif** (Chi)
composition (as of a painting); setting **bufji** (Chi)
composition (as a student would write) **buvq zol soqkaoq** (50:183)
compost **zeiqkeeq haqleil**
compost, liquid **zeiqkeeq eelcal**
compost pit (animal manure used) **zeiqkeeq luduq; zeiqkeeq keeqduq**
compound word **doqlo lozao** (50:71) (it also can mean: dictionary)
comprehensive **zaolhoq** (Chi)
comprehensive degree **hal**
compulsory means; coersive measures **maq aol maq qivq yiqqeiq** (C=Chi)
comrade **taoqziif** (Chi) (11:19, 26:28, 50:168)
conceited; arrogant **buq zaq** (Chi); **dalbuq buq**
concentrate; centralize **ssaoq zyul**
concentrate; put together **jiqzaol** (Chi)
concern, to show **neema nyuq; gueilxil** (Chi)
concerning; as to **ngeel naolhaoq**
conclude, to **aol saq e; eilsaq saq e**
conclude a treaty, to **tiaoqyoq cuv taq** (A=Chi)
conclusion of an article **daoqmiq jiqwei** (B=Chi)
conclusion, to reach **ziifdif** (Chi) (34:5)
concrete **jifti** (Chi)

condense, to **yossaoq ssaoq**
condition **tiaoqjeif** (Chi)
condition; state of affairs **zuafkuaf** (Chi) (50:217)
condole; to offer one's condolences **saq haol miq**
condolence letter **weifweifsif** (Chi) (26:78)
condom **bifssiqtaoq** (15:61); **bifssiqtaof** (Chi)
conference, a **dafhyuf** (Chi) (26:106)
confess **eil duv** (50:84)
confession by torture, to extort **naqguv duv** (50:189)
confidence; faith **haoqhhyu neesal** (50:188)
confine in, to (as jail, a pen, etc.) **nieivq laol**
confirm; approve **kedif** (Chi)
conflict; contradict **doqhhuvq duv**
conflict, to have **diq zaq eil zaq**
confrontation **dyufziiq** (Chi)
confuse, to **lav beeq**
  confused, to be **lilpuv puv**
  confused; perplexed; dazed **suqlu hhaqlaq**
  confusion; chaos **beeqga nei**
  confusion on confusion **bil lil bav lav**
congratulate, to **zuqhof** (Chi)
conjecture; infer **needeq deq** (50:171)
conjunction (gram) **lieiqciiq** (Chi)
connect, to **nieivq cavq; cavq**
connect parts together **bavq cavq**
conscientious; diligent **qiqqiq keikei**
conscious **nyuq hev** (50:219)
consciousness **joqwul; joqwuf** (Chi) **ziifjoq nei** (Chi)
consent, to give **heiq**
consequence **hefgo** (Chi)
conservative **baose** (Chi)
consider; calculate **needeq deq**
consider; think **nee'li li; hhoq nyuq**
  consider; think about **nyuq hu**
  consider seriously **neema jivqyal aol**
considerate, to be **nyuq laol** (50:165)
  consideration; careful **nyuq duvq nyuq zil**
  consideration; deliberation **ceil zil zaq**
console, to **neema eil laol**
consolidate; strengthen **lav ssivq; gaoguf** (Chi)
consonant (phonological) **fuyil** (Chi)
constantly; without stopping **maq naq nei** (26:103)
constipated, to be **xiqtaoq taoq**
constitution **xeiffaq** (Chi) (50:185)
  constitution for the party **dazal** (Chi)
consult, to **gee za; gee zil gee za** (50:187)
consume, to **zaq deiq** (eat until empty, i.e., a container of something); **ssaoq duv; zaq ssaoq** (50:186)
contact, to make **nieivq cavq**
contain, to **caoq** (33:3)
contain, to (to be in) **kevq**
container, bamboo **baoqtevq; haqbol boqlo**
contemplate; wonder **salnyuq**

contemptible **daov cavq**
contest; match **diq qeiv qeiv zaq**
continue; carry out **aol xa; aol xa heil**
continuous action **(vb) haqhaq** (**zaq haqhaq** = eating); **(vb) koq** (**Zaq koq al** = He was eating it all.); **(vb) ssiq** (this is more like 'still')
continuously **maq ceiv meil**
contraband goods **maq hha aol qaol miaoqgaoq** (50:176)
contraception; birth control **boheiq cyuq**
contract, a **hoqtaoq seqtevq** (A=Chi)
contract, to **ceiqbaol** (Chi)
contradict; conflict **doqhhuvq duv**
contradiction **maoqdyuf** (Chi) (34:11)
contrary; opposite **lilpuv nei**
contrary to all expectations **qiq hhaq liq maq nyuq hev bei**
contrast, to **bavq qeiv (dul maq dul)**
contribution **gaoljiq** (Chi); **gaofxeif** (Chi)
control (as to control the basketball) **diq teiq** (41:202)
control oneself **ziivq teiq**
control; press down **taoq teiq** (41:202)
control; supervise **hu teiq**
control tower; command tower **ziihyulteiq** (A=Chi) (50:213)
convalesce, to **hhaq jol dav**
conversation, to have; to chat **doqlovq lovq**
conveyer belt **sulsaof piqdeif** (Chi)
conviction; faith; belief **xifnieif** (Chi)
convulsion, to have **saqguq hhe kuv**
cook, to **qavq**
cook, to (as a meal) **susi** (**hoqzaol susi** = to cook a meal)
cook, to (as a meal at the time of a funeral) **hoq zal susi zaq**
cook and eat rice **hoq zaol zaq**
cook; boil **qavq; puvq**
cook done, to **qavq javq**
cooked done (not raw) **miao; yomiao; qavq miao**
cooked meat **saqqavq**
cooked to mush; porridge **qavqbieiv; qavqbieiv bieiv**
cooking place (in house) **hoqsavq duq**
cook rice and eat, to **hoq zaol zaq** (cook and eat)
cook rice and prepare a meal, to **hoq zaol susi**
cool, to be **quqsiq nei; ceivq; ceivqqaol**
cool off (from anger) **neema juq**
cool off (weather) **aoq ceivq xa al yi**
cool, or to cool **quqsiq nei** (10:26)
cool, very **ceivqqaol pa qaol nei** (11:58)
coop, chicken **aqha miavhav**
cooperate, to **daqhoq** (Chi) **paoqzaq**
cooperative, credit **xifyaofseif** (Chi) (50:188)
cooperative store **saldieif** (Chi)
coordinate, to **xiqtiaoq** (Chi)
coordinate; harmonize **gee soq** (50:187)

copper **geeq** (Note: this is a fairly general term for metals which are not gold, silver or iron)
copper, 'red' **geeqnil**
copper, 'white' **geeqpiul** (some type of white metal.)
copper, 'yellow' (brass) **geeqsiil**
copper pot **geeqcal**
copulate, to (from man's viewpoint) **lyuq zaq**
copy editor **bieilsei** (Chi)
copy of (as book) **bei** (Chi) (11:173)

coral **salhuq** (Chi)
core; kernel; center **malniuv** (46:123)
coriander **halsol; halsol solssaq**
corn (maize) **ceildu**
corn, glutinous **ceildu duniaoq**
corn, hard variety **ceildu dussei**
corn, hybrid **zaqjaol ceildu** (A=Chi) (50:204)
corn, popped **ceildu alpyuv**
corn, to pick **ceildu heivq**
corn, to take grains off of cob **ceildu sov**
corncob **duyyuq**
corner (as in a room) **laqkyul; lavqliv; kyul**
corner of mouth **meiqzeil**
cornfield **ceildu duyal**
corn tassels **ceildu moqceil; ceildu meiqmoq**
corn with few grains **ceildu seqkal**
corpse; dead body **colsil**
corpse in coffin, to put **alzaol a bavqdov**
correct; right; equal **hoq** (Chi) (**Xilmeil zaol e hoq maq hoq.** Is this the correct way to do it or not?) **caq; daov zeifqoq** (B=Chi)
correction of the press **jaofdyuf; jaofdyuf yeiq** (Chi)
correct the press, to **jaofgei peiqgao** (Chi)
correspond with, to **soqhhaq buvq neiq zaq**
corruption and degeneration **talwul fuhuaf** (Chi)
corrupt; rotten **buvqlavq nei**
corruption; graft **hhavq zaq** (50:162)
cost **pyuq; hoq**
cotton **saqlaq**
cotton cloth **saqlaq haqpal**
cotton fluffer **bevyyuq**
cotton-padded clothes **beewul peilhaoq**
cotton quilt **saqlaq albee**
cotton, to plant **saqlaq xa** (46:212)
cough, to **cyuq; zaoqcyuq cyuq**
cough very much, to **cyuq sil cyuq lo** (or) to be very poor
count, to **gee**
countercharge; counterclaim **bu puv huvq**
counterclaim (see: countercharge)
count from higher to lower numbers **gee xa**
count numbers, to **aqgee gee**

country; area; place **milhaoq**
country; nation **goqjal** (Chi)
countryside **naoqcyul** (34:6) (Chi)
countryside; fields and gardens **deixal** (50:166)
count something (to see how much have) **gee hu**
count upward (as 1 to 100) **gee dav**
county **xeif (Caqsal Xeif** - 26:3)
county, autonomous **ziifziixeif** (Chi)
county committee **xeifweihyuf** (Chi)
xeifhhyuhyuf (26:26)
county deputy president **fuf xeifza**
county government headquarters **xeifzeiffu** (Chi)
county president **xeifza**
coup d'tat **zeifbieif** (Chi) (34:6)
couple (husband and wife) **niq jil ssaq; qiq zaol**
coupon for food **liaqpiaof** (Chi)
courage **daqzii** (Chi)
court (legal); law court **faqyeif** (Chi) **buduq**
courtyard **yeifzii** (Chi)
cousin (father's sister's son) **aqyivq aqnil** (general); **loqbioq** (what they call each other)
cover, a (as for a bamboo basket) **pavqcyuq (pavqcyuq cyuq** = to cover)
cover, a; lid (as for a pot) **calpiq; piqkaq**
cover for rice steamer **hoqpiq**
cover, to **diq kaq; deiq kaq; piq; piqkaq; bavq kaq; deiq cyuq** (27:11 - to cover one's mouth); **hhuvq sil; bavq caoq**
covered, to be **caoq laol; hhyuq; caoq** (as a place to be covered by snow - 26:45)
covered with water **leiq hhuvq**
covering for a mouth (as surgical mask) **meiqcaoq**
covering for a snout (as a muzzle) **meiqcaoq**
cover over, to **bavq caoq; hhuvq sil; bavq kaq** (the latter can also mean to cure a disease with drugs)
cover thoroughly **leev quvq**
cow **niuqnil** (note: buffalo = **niuqpeel**)
cow day **niuq nao**
cow dung **niuqxiq**
cow feed **niuqzal**
cow herder; animal herder **zeiqluvqssaq**
cow hour **niuq zeq** (B=Chi)
cowpea **neebeiv beivja**
cowrie shell **helsiq**
cowshed **niuqkuv**
cow's milk **aqniuq aqqul** (10:19)
cow year **niuq huvq**

crab **alka**
crack, a **covqbeivq**
crack, to **tevq**
cracking sound **kovqsovq** (29:4)
cradle, a **yiuvqhhal; ssaqguq yiuvqhhal**
cramp in hand **lavqguq hhe kuv**
cramp in leg **keelguq hhe kuv**

crash to pieces **lyul**
craw of bird **beillivq**
crawl, to **moqqao qao; lavqsov lavqsov nei** (26:24)
crawl on muddy ground **daoqju ju; daoqjyu jyu**
crazy **neema deiqssil**
crazy person; insane **samu**
creak of door; chirp of birds **qil qeivq qeivq; jil geivq geivq**
cream of the crop (best of the best) **colkyul hholqei colkyul aqda; haqjil hholqei haqjil jilma**
create; establish **yeilbei bei; zaol duv; bei duv**
creative initiative; pioneering spirit **secuafxif jilseiq** (Chi)
creativeness; creativity **cuafcaofxif** (Chi)
creation of heaven and earth **aoqdeivq mildeivq deivq**
creative spirit **cuafcaoq jilseiq** (Chi)
creativity **cuafcaofxif** (Chi)
credentials; certificates; papers **zeifjeif** (Chi) (50:211)
credit cooperative **sifyaofseif** (50:188)
creditor **zeifqeiq col** (A=Chi) (50:206)
cricket, a **niuqjuq niuljul**
crime, to commit **zaol zyul**
crime of forcibly robbing **koqzaq zyul**
crime site **geelhhuvq duvduq**
criminal clique (group) **geelhhuvq yoba**
criminal element **xiqsiif fafzyuf feilzii** (Chi) (50:188)
criminal evidence **zyulmiaoq deiq hhovq**
criminal justice **xiqsiif sufsaof faq** (Chi) (50:189)
crippled, arm **lavq qeiq**
crippled; lame leg **aqkeel keel qeiq; keel qeiq**
crippled leg and arm **keel qeiq lavq qeiq**
crisis, political **zeifziif weiqjil** (Chi) (50:211)
criterion; yardstick **cavtevq** (50:218)
critical moment; crucial moment **gualke** (Chi) (26:44); **gualjeif** (Chi)
criticize, to **pilpiq** (26:31, 50:129); **pilpaf** (50:129) (both Chi)
criticize; appraise; comment (whether good or bad) **meeq dyul eil**
crooked **bilyovq meil; hhuvq (hhuvq e haolteil galma** = a crooked path)
crooked arms and legs **keel kuv lavq kuv**
crooked lips **meiqyovq**
crooked road/path **galhhuvq; hhuvq e haolteil galma**
crop **kalyei; miaoqkal**
crop diseases **kalnal nal** (46:167)
crop, main **kalma** (50:30)
crop of bird **loqliv**
crops **kalyei; kal; miaoqkal**
crops to bud **kalquv**
crop tax for government **gaolyiqliaq** (Chi)
cross, to **yoq**
cross a road **galma yoq**

cross a stream **lolbaq yoq**
crossbeam **hhaqdav**
crossbow **kavtev**
crossbow arrow **kavmiaq**
crossbow cord **kavpi** (8:18)
cross marriage **miqpal pal zaq e**
crossroad **galcaol**
crossways **bilceiv**
crotch (human) **piaqkaq**
crow (bird) **haqnav; haqnav aqma**
crow, to (as a cock) **deil**
crowbar **saoldu**
crowd, a **col qiq ba**
crowded **teiq; teiqkuv nei**
crown of head; pate **wuqduq zaolhhaol**
cruel; ferocious **saltuq; zaoltuvq tuvq**
cruel landlord **hhoqbaf difzu** (26:17)
cruel person **hhoqbaf** (Chi) (26:16); **yohav**
cruel rich man **zeiqbo havma** (33:3)
crumble, to **ya jeivq**
crux; key **gualjeif** (Chi)
cry; weep **ngyul; gyuq**
cry of someone, the **gyuq**
cry one's eyes out **miavneev ngyul duv jil nei**
cry out **gyuq**
cry saldly **lalbeil lalya**
cry very hard; sob **ngyul sil ngyul lo**

cuckoo **hulbu; beilkuq allavq; beilkuq hulbu alzil**
cuckoo, sound of **hulbuq** (46:155)
cucumber **siqhuvq**
cuff of pants **laqcyuq laqkeel** (11:36)
cuff of sleeve **laqbaoq baoqheiq**
culm sheath (on bamboo) **albal balhhaq**
cultivate; educate **peiqya** (Chi) (26:106)
cultivate fields (for a living) **xaldei xa zaq** (26:3)
cultivated area **aol zaq milcaq**
Cultural and educational bureau **Weiqjaofjyuq** (Chi)
cultural bureau **weiqhuafjiq** (Chi) (50:178)
cultural exchange **weiqhuaf jaollieq** (Chi) (50:178)
cultural knowledge **weiqhuaf ziilsiiq** (Chi)
cultural palace **weiqhuafgaol** (Chi) (50:178)
cultural revolution **weiqhuaf daf geiqmif** (34:11);
Weiqhuaf Geiqmiq; weiqhuaf geiqmif (Chi) (50:178)
culture (here used in speaking of reading, writing, etc.) **weiqhuaf** (26:50, 50:178)
cup **haoqma; kegal** (Chi) - 26:74
cupboard, a **keelsuv**
cupped hand **lavqhov; aqlavq lavqhov**
cure, to **zaol kaq** (10:22); **bi yaq**
cure a disease by drugs, to **bavq kaq**
cure pork, to **saqdeil deil**
curl (on its own) **leiq kuv**
curl up (as a dog's tail) **hhe kuv**
curly (hair) **wuqduq ceilkaol leiq kuv**

current **siiqsiif** (Chi) (26:50)
current events; current affairs **miaoq aol e miqnieiq** (50:153)
curse, to **yaq**
curses **pavqcavq daqnieiq** = 'may you be executed by a firing squad' (there are others; 'may you be struck by lightning'; 'may you be struck by a viper', 'may you die a terrible death', etc.)
curved **bilhhuvq nei**
cushion; pad **hoqdaq**
custom; rule **yo'liq**
custom house (on border) **luvqheiq**
customs and traditions (from God) **Miqyeil yeilbei** (46:160, 167)
customs, to have many **ceil kov ngavq siil** (46:205)
cut (to cut or hack, as a plant) **dev; cevq**
cut, to **beiv**
cut, to (as hair) **niaov**
cut, to (as rice) **yeiq**
cut; hack, to **dev**
cut; slice; saw **yeiq**
cut and gather (as firewood) **heivq**
cut away, to **yeiq zei; beiq zei**
cut down; cut off **dev ceiv; yeiq ceiv; dev xa; hhe xu**
cut down a tree **albol tul**
cut firewood **heivq**
cut into pieces **yeiq nuv yeiq ya**
cut off; cut down **yeiq ceiv**
cut off a head **wuqduq ceiv**
'cut one's coat according to the cloth' **haqpal yaol hu alnei peilhaoq pieiv** (a literal translation); **lavq hholqei zeiq yaol salhu alnei ssaoq** (the actual meaning; 'consider the resources you have and carry on accordingly')
cut open, to **keq pav; keq peivq**
cut open a hole **yobyu keq byu**
cut open every part **keq peivq keq pav saq**
cut to death, to **dev sil**
cut to pieces, to **yeiq niuv yeiq ya**
cut up, to **yeiq nuv; yeiq ceiv; yeiq zei; zaol kyuq**
cut up (as cloth) **pieiv**
cut with machete **beiv** (as in clearing field) (11:211)
cut with scissors **niaov qivq** (11:54)
cutworm, a **byuqnav**

cycle of days or years **yei** (**qiq yei** = 13 days or years; **niq yei** = 25 days or years, etc.); **yeiljol**
cymbals **hovcaoq**

D d soqmiav aqma hholqei yuvq mol e qiq mol

dacron **diqqoqliaq** (Chi)
dad; daddy; father **aqda**
dagger 1. **juqdev miavjeil** (46:152 - knife carried at waist); 2. **tossaq**
  dagger tip **tossaq wuqqei**
daily **jollalhha; civzaol nei** (or often) (11:118); **kaqla manao; hhaba nei**
Dai (Tai) nationality **Aqcaoqssaq, Biqcaoqssaq; Deicuq** (Chi)
Dali (lake and town in NW Yunnan) **Dafli** (Chi)
dam; reservoir **syukuf** (Chi) (50:158); **eelquvq laobao** (50:158)
damage, to 1. **kyuq** (eil **kyuq** = to damage by what one says); 2. **lav biav** (to damage by doing something)
damp; wet (as wet ground) **ciq; jeilso nei**
dam; stop up **teev cyuq; caolteev teev**
dam stream for fishing **lolpav pieiq; ngaqssa**
dance, to **loqzoq coq** (10:pref.)
  dance and play games **haqhhal seil; hhaseil seil**
  dance for joy, to **hhyulcoq coq**
  dance ground in village **deibiaq**
  dance to one's own tune (drummer) **luqduq naolhao haqhhal seil**
  dance with drums and gongs (Hani style) **gaqniq niq** (46:137)
dandruff **wuqduq wuqhhov; wuqniaoq** = darkish type
danger, to meet **seiq piav; seiq duv lal**
dangerous **geelsal; hhyuqxei geelsal** (A=Chi)
dangerous situation **saqkaoq; saqkaoq kaoq**
dare to (vb) **(vb) peq**
dare to do something **neeceiv xa**
dark **navhaoq nei**
dark, getting **aoq qivq yil; aoqqivq qivq lal**
dark, very **navhaoq pa haoq nei** (11:56); **navhaoq haoqma** (11:59)
dark as midnight **sulhaol aqmeil navhaoq pa haoq nei**
dark as a pocket **miav qiq ssil maq ssil; navhaoq pa haoq nei**
dark as pitch **hucavq hubyu aqmeil navhaoq pa haoq nei**
darkish; blackish **navhaoq nei**
darkly dark **navhaoq nei nav** (11:59)
darkness **haoqsuv nei**
dark room **hhafsiiq laqhyul** (A=Chi)
dash (punctuation mark) **pofzeiqhaof** (Chi)
daughter **ssaqmiq**
  daughter, middle (if three) **miqhhaol; miqhhaol hhaolma**
  daughter, middle (when more than three) **miqhhaol hhaolssaq** (11:69)
  daughter, next to the last **miqli lima** (11:69)

daughter, oldest **ssaqmiq aqyivq** (11:69)
daughter, single **miqteiq; ssaqmiq miqteiq qiq teiq**
daughter, to buy **miqhhel hhel**
daughter, youngest **miqli** (46:145); **aqli** (11:69)
daughter, youngest of several **miqli lissaq** (11:69)
daughter and son **miqyo** (30:2)
daughter-in-law **keeqma; ssaqmiq keeqma**
dauntless; indomitable; persistent **maq guv maq niv**
dawn, to **aoqbia bia**
day **nao**
day; whole day **qiq nao aoqcil; qiq nao aoqcil qivq nei; aoqcil qivq**
day after day **qiq nao naolhao qiq nao**
day after tomorrow **salpeiqnao; neesoq salsoq**
day after the day after tomorrow **sallaqnao**
day after the day after the day after tomorrow **salqivqnao**
day before **eiqmilnao**
day before yesterday **huqnao**
day by day **qiq nao maq leiq; qiq nao laqgal**
daybreak **bia loq bia jul meil**
days past **kaqla manao**
daytime **naohhaol; naohhaol hhaoldao; neehhaol; aoqnao** (26:82); **nee'laoq; nao'laoq**
dazed; confused; perplexed **suqlu hhaqlaq**
Dazhai village in Luchun, where the Hani dialect was chosen as the one to be written **Oltol Tavqzaoq; Holtol Tavqzaoq**
dazzle, to **miavgeel geel**
dazzling; make one's head swim **miavmul miao laq seiq** (46:149)

dead body; corpse **colsil**
deadlock, a **maq niv qivq e; qiq teev**
deaf **naqboq**
deaf, to be **naqboq boq**
dear **algaq**
dear elders (TE) **colhhyul aqda paqssaq** (46:217)
dear grandmother (term of respect to older woman) **no aqpiq**
dear older brother (term of respect to older man) (27:11) **noq e damoq; ngaldu algo ei eiq**
dear younger brother **ngaldu aqnil ei eiq**
death sentence; death penalty **sil tovq** (50:160)
death's door, to be at **yuqnilduq a hev li**
debate, a **eilteil heil doqzil**
debate, to; discuss **gee zil gee za**
debt **zeil** (Chi) **zeil zuv** (A=Chi) (11:31)
debt; liabilities **zeifwuf** (Chi) (50:206)
decadent & moribund thought **buvqlavq qeilsuq nei neecavq**
decay; rot **peqdaq** (esp. wood); **buvq** (as meat & food)
decayed; rotten; putrid **buvqlavq qeilsuq nei** (50:52)
deceive, to **hheivq; moqleevq leevq**
deceive habitually, to **hheivq zaq zo**

December **Huvq'yul siq**
decide, to **nyuq ceiv**
decide and be sure **nyuq ceiv nyuq loq** (34:4)
decide and resolve **jyuqdif** (Chi)
decided; promised **eil taq; eil ceiv**
decimeter (one tenth of a meter) **feilmi** (Chi)
declare; announce **eil loq**
declare; proclaim **bugaq** (50:190)
decline, to **ssii**
decorate; dress up **lav zaq** (50:190)
decoration; medal **pyuq biavq** (50:192)
decrease; reduce **hhe xu**
deduct, to **hhe xu**
deeds **biaoxeif** (Chi) (26:100)
deed of merit **yeigo** (Chi) (11:30)
deep **navq; navqyol nei; taoq** (as in **lolbaq taoq** = deep river)
deep inside **lavqliv**
deepish **navq nei**
deepish (or 'earlyish') **navq nei**
deep, very **navqyol nei**
deep love; deep feeling neema zuv nei
deer, barking **qilssaq**
deer horn **ceivkyul**
deer, sambar **heiqceiv**
defeat, to **zaol leiq; diq hhaq** (50:207)
defecate, to **xiq xiq**
defect, a **maq meeq e**
defect; drawback; short of quota **maq luvq**
defect, to **qiqdiei** (Chi)
defend; guard; protect **haol luvq; hafweif** (Chi)
defendant; the accused **bi bucol**
defend public order **milhaoq haollaol** (50:176)
defense **haol; baoweif** (Chi) (26:56); **goqfaq** (Chi) (26:43) (the latter is used especially for national defense)
defense lawyer **eil haol liqsiil** (B=Chi)
deficit, financial **ceiqjil; ciiqziif** (Chi)
defraud; swindle **hheivq zaq** (50:206)
degenerate, to **tyufhuaf bieifziiq** (Chi) (50:171)
degenerate; lazy **lalga**
degeneration and corruption **talwul fuhuaf** (Chi)
dehydrated **taoqsyu**
dejected, to be **hhaqbieiv; wuqduq galtyuq; nalbaoq peelsuq nei**
delay, to **dalgoq** (Chi)
delegate; representative **deifbiao** (Chi)
delicious **keel; keelzav nei; zaq keel; keelmil**
delicious food **zalkeel zalniuv**
delighted **hhyul**
demobilize from army **tyufwu** (Chi) (50:171)
democracy **miqzu** (Chi) (34:8)
democracy and centralism **miqzu jiqzaol; miqzu jiqzaolziif** (Chi)
democracy, peaceful **hoqpiq miqzu** (Chi)

democratic centralism **miqzu jiqzaolziif** (Chi)
democratic parties **miqzu dapeif** (Chi) (34:20)
demonstrate, to **bi hu; zaol hu; aolmeiq meiq** (50:154)
demonstration; parade; march **yeqxiq** (Chi) (50:200)
Deng Xiaoping (Chinese leader) **Deif Xaopiq** (34:12)
denounce; condemn **yaqduvq duvq**
dense; thick (as plants) **caol; kavq nei** (46:130)
dense, very **caolziiv nei; caolziiv ziivma meil**
deny, to **fedif** (Chi); **zeivq beeq**
depart, to **hhoq yil** (down); **hhoq li** (up)
depend upon, to **dal sso; qeq sso e**
depict; portray **buvqqo qo**
deploy, to; dispose, to **bufsuq** (Chi)
deport; expel **milkaq leiq duv**
deportment **bufmeiq** (Chi)
deposit, a; a cash pledge **yaqjil** (Chi) (50:193)
deposit, to **zeiq toq taq**
deputy commander **fuf lieiqza** (Chi) (26:99)
deputy party secretary **fuf suljif**

deranged, to be **zaol beeq**
dereliction of duty **duqziiqzyul** (Chi) (50:40)
derive, to **jiqqiq** (Chi)
derogatory term **doqdyul**
descend, to **ssavq yil**
descendants **yuqpaq yuqma**
descendants, happy **ssaq yal sal**
desk (for studying) **soqzol lolbieil** (50:158)
desk; table **zoqzii** (Chi) (26:89)
destiny; fate **mifyif** (Chi)
destroy ('make bad') **zaol xa; pofhueif** (Chi) (34:10)
destroy one's reputation **miavpyuq zaol nal**
destroy the evidence **zyul meiqzaq zaol bial**
details (as of a plan) **juftihuaf** (Chi)
detain, to **hhe teiq**
detain; arrest **nieivq laol**
deteriorate; go bad **bieifziiq** (Chi) (50:13)
determination **neeceiv**
determined in heart/mind **neema bavq duv** (26:29)
detonator **lueiqgua** (Chi)
detour around, to **galhhao hhao**
devalue money, to **piul buvq**
develop, to **faqza** (Chi) **zeq lal**
develop someone; train someone **peiqya** (Chi)
developing country, a **bi zeq lal goqjal** (15:21)
deviate, to **leiq**
deviation to the left (pol) **zo** (Chi)
deviation to the right (pol) **yef** (Chi)
'devil' (bad person) **colcavq**
devil (spirit) **neivq; neivqhaq**
devoted **gaofxeif** (Chi) (26:56)
dew **ciqhaq**
dew, to be wet with **ciqhaq puvtav nei**

dhole (wild dog) **haqyeil**

dialectical **bieifzeif** (Chi)
dialectical materialism **bieifzeif weiqwuq zuyif** (Chi) (50:13); **weiqwuq bieifzeiffaq** (Chi) (50:176)
dialectics **bieifzeiffaq** (Chi) (50:13)
diaper-like cloth for baby **dalqeiq**
diarrhea **wuqdeiq suv** (10:pref., 26:57); **wuqdeiq yil; xiqbieiv bieiv; xiqsuv suv**
diarrhea, infant **aldyul**
diary, a **ssiiqjif** (Chi) (26:79)
dibble stick (for planting crops) **albol gaoqqei**
dictation, to take **nalhaq alnei buvq** (50:167)
dictatorship **zualziif** (Chi) (50:217)
dictionary **doqlo soqdaoq; doqlo soqkaoq** (50:27); **ciiqdiei** (Chi)
die, to (actually and figuratively) **sil**
die; to expire **sil ceiv**
die; to stop breathing **savq ceiv** (26:99)
die a bad death **sal sil**
die away, to **bial yil**
die down, to **mei yil**
die in (as a pond) **sil tao**
die of sickness **nal sil**
die of starvation **gov sil**
die out, to **bial yil; saq yil**
die out (as fire to die out, or electricity to go off) **sil** (= to die)
diesel oil **caqyeq** (26:32); **ceiqyeq** (Chi)
difference; divergence **doq eil maq zaol**
different **maq paoq; kaq**
difficult **syuq**
difficulties; obstacles **jeilnaq xeizu** (Chi)
difficulties; problems; questions **kyufnaq** (**jav e** = to have) (Chi) (26:42); **saq ssol gav**
difficult to eat **zaq syuq**
difficult to see **mol syuq**
dig, to **duq**
dig a ditch **lolgal taol** (11:158)
dig again, to **duq duvq**
dig a hole **duqhovq hovq** (11:44); **duq pao**
digest, to **zaljavq** (10:8)
digging tool (with metal tip) **gaoqqa**
dignity; honor **zualyeiq** (Chi) (34:15)
dig or root with the snout (as a pig) **byuq**
dig out, to **duq duv**
dig out of small hole **hevq**
dig up, to **duq puv**
dig up; pick up **beq dav**
dike (bund) as in a terraced field **dalbaol**
diligent **bel; bel tav nei; belzav nei keellavq bel**
diligent; conscientious **qiqqiq keikei** (Chi)
diligent; work hard **miaoq aol xul** (10:pref.)
dim; vague; unclear (also: dusk; twilight) **suqlu hhaqlaq meil**

dimple **baqhovq**
'ding dong' (sound of bells) **dildal; dildil daldal**
dining hall; canteen **siqtaq** (Chi)
diphthong (gram) **fuqyifmu** (Chi)
dip into **kuq** (11:9)
diplomacy; foreign affairs **hhueifjaol** (Chi) (50:173)
diplomatic envoy **siijiq** (Chi)
dip meat into sauce **zal'eel aol zaq**
dip out; scoop out **beq**
direction; side **pyu; zeil pyu**
directional **galquv taol**
direction from low to high **taoqdav pyu**
directly **zav lav nei** (11:216); **qiq li nei; taltuq nei; ziiqjiq** (Chi)
director **zusseif (Chi) (50:215) jyuqza** (Chi); **soza** (Chi) (50:161)
director of workshop **ceiljeil zusseif** (Chi) (26:27)
dirt **milxeiv**
  dirty **yoxeiv** (10:27)
  dirty (as food) **maq sol maq cavq**
  dirty (as machinery) **xeivnaovq** (26:32)
  dirty; dusty **suq; cavq**
  dirty; muddy **suq lal**
  dirty; ugly **cavqni nei**
  dirty, very **xeivnaovq nei; maq sol maq cavq nei**
  dirty water **laolsil**
disabled; maimed **yuvq seil maq daol; yuvq seil maq jav**
disabled by an accident **taoq nal** (26:87)
disappear **bial**
disappointed; lose hope **hhaqbieiv bieiv**
disarmament **mavqssaq hhe xu** (50:18)
disaster, a **geelsal; zalnaf** (Chi) (34:3)
disaster area **zalqil** (Chi) (26:78)
discharge; expel **leiq duv**
discipline **ji'liq** (Chi); **jiqliq** (26:103)
discipline of an organization **zuziiq yeiqzeiq** (Chi)
discipline someone, to **yavq gaol**
disclose, to; make public **eil bieil** (50:151)
disconsolate; melancholy **hhaqbieiv ceiv**
discouraged, to be **hhaqbieiv ceiv**
discover, to ('see through') **hu duv zaq lal**
discriminate, to **miavpyuq heeq nil ceil**
discuss, to **doqzil zil; doqzil zil zaq** (26:103); **doqzil gee** (46:138); **gee za; gee zil gee za** (50:163); **geeza zaq; gee zyul** (26:107)
discuss together **doqzil zil zaq** (11:38)
disease **nalgol; qaqgol nalgol; cyuqpeiq cyuqnal** (10:pref.)
disease, pass on **covqleiq kovq**
disease of the scalp (favus of the scalp) **wuqduq wuqpeel**
diseases, bad **nalcavq** (46:132)
diseases, serious and sudden **nalteiq nalcal** (15:7)
disgusted with; dislike **saoq; saoqzeiv nei; neesuvq**

suvq; aqssii ssii
disgust someone, to **saoq miq**
dish, a **hhoqcyuq**
disheartened **neema gavyov nei**
dislike; disgusted with **saoq**
disobey; naughty **lavsaoq**
disorder **beeqsu nei; beeq li ga la; muvyav nei**
dispirited, to be **neema qil; wuqduq galtyuq**
display; show **tixeif** (Chi)
displeased, very **qavq saoq**
dispose; deploy **bufsuq** (Chi)
dispute, a **hal duv**
dispute; refute **eil peel**
dispute, to solve **alkaq kaq; alkaq pil**
disregard, to; ignore **maq nyuq; maq hu** (50:180)
dissatisfied **neema maq li; neema maq lal; neema maq luvq**
dissolve, to **geel**
distance **molniaol (galma molniaol hu laq** = look at the distance -- i.e., of the path)
distant (far away) **galheeq sa nei** (26:42)
distill liquor, to **zilbaq savq**
distiller's grains **baqqeil**
distinguish **meeq dyul ceil loq; ceil heq**
distort, to; misrepresent **eil yevq** (50:173)
distribute, to **bil**
district; region **difqil** (Chi)
disturb; hinder **lav sul; lav bav**
disturbance (things) **miaoqbeeq miaoqga**
disturbance; turmoil **lav beeq**
disturb someone; cause a disturbance **lav beeq; lavq caq** (11:28); **lav sul** (26:54); **daofluaf** (Chi); **faolbol** (Chi)
disturb someone; interrupt someone **gul caq**
disyllabic (two syllables) **fuqyifmu** (Chi)
ditch **eelgal; lolgal; lolgal galkov; galkov** (26:59)
ditch around house **caqkov**
ditch, irrigation **lolgal**
ditch opening or watergate **eelheiq**
ditch or trench (for warfare) **lolkaq; zafhaoq lolkaq** (A=Chi) (26:48)
divergence; difference **doq eil maq zaol**
divert; misappropriate; embezzle **yiul ssaoq**
divide, to **bil; bieil heq; bil heq; bil pav**
divide up family property **xalbaol bil zaq**
divide work, to **miaoqbivq bivq**
divine with bones **yyuq loq hu**
divine with chicken thigh **habaol diq**
divine with thatch grass **aqgaoq cevq** (they take three pieces of thatch grass, pass it three times up and down the sick person's body, then check the lengths against a turban to divine the sickness and cure)
division (in math) **coqfaq** (Chi)
division of labor **miqnieiq bil e**

divorce, to **huvq zaq; miqhuvq xohuvq**
divorce one's husband, to **xohuvq**
divorced woman, a **miqhuvq**
dizzy, to be **miavmul mul**
dizzy and poor eyesight **miav mul miav laq seiq nei**
dizzy head **mu; aqmu mu; aqmu lalmu mu**

do, to (assume responsibility) **gee**
do, to (idea of making something, also use this when you want to know what a person is doing) **zaol**
do beyond one's ability **hhaqgal cei**
doctor **naciq aqbol** (see also: doctor, man and: doctor, woman) **yilseil** (Chi)
doctor, go to see **nalgol hu li; naciq sal li**
doctor, man **naciq aqbol**
doctor, woman **naciq aqpiq**
doctrinaire **jaoftiaoq** (Chi) (34:24)
doctrinairism; dogmatism **jaoftiaoq zuyif** (Chi)
doctrine; doctrinism **zuyif** (Chi) (50:216)
doctrine; theory **xoqsoq** (Chi)
documents; papers; instruments **weiqjeif** (Chi) (50:178)
dodge; evade **xeiv yoq**
doesn't matter **maq beq; maq beq sso; maq gal**

dog **aqkeeq**
dog, female **keeqma; aqkeeq keeqma**
dog, ferocious **keeqkovq**
dog, mad **aqkeeq keeqmu**
dog, male **keeqpaq; aqkeeq keeqhhul**
dog blood **keeqsivq**
dog chain **keeqdaoq**
dog day **keeq nao**
dog dung **keeqxiq**
dog for hunting **hhaqkeeq**
dog head **keeqduq**
dog hour **keeq zeq**
dog intestine **keeqwul**
dog meat **keeqsaq; aqkeeq keeqsaq**
dog's life (i.e., having problems) **aqkeeq miav nei saq**
dog to bark **ceivq**
dog, wild (dhole) **haqyeil**
dog with long hair **keeqbuq**
dog year **keeq huvq**
dog, yellow/brown **aqkeeq keeqsiil**
dog, young **keeqssaq**
dogmatism; doctrinairism **jaoftiaoq zuyif** (Chi)
do honor, to **colqoq miavhhaq bo**
Dolniq village (Yuanyang county) **Hhoqssaq**
domestic affairs; internal affairs **nyufzeif** (50:120)
domestic animal **zeiqssaq; hyulzeiq**
dominate; rule **taoziif** (Chi) (50:169)
dominate; seek hegemony **zyuqzaq** (50:23)
donate, to **bivq**

done (as completed) **zaol taq**
done (as cooked food); ripe **ovq; miao**
donkey, male **lalzii aqda; moqlalzii** (13:30)
don't (vb) **taq (vb)**
don't hurry **maq teiq sso**
don't oversleep **yiuvqnyuq maq haq**
don't worry **aqlaoq neeyo taq nil**
do odd job, to **colhhaq aol zaq**
do one good, to **miqnieiq yomeeq aol**
do one's best, to **hhaqhav hal jav e bavq duv; hhaq hal tivq qaol e tivq**
do oneself justice, to **hal aol nia e aol**
door **lulhhuv**
door bolt **dalmiaq**
doorframe **hhubaq; hhubaq hhussaol**
door threshold, a **hhoteev**
do over again, to **aol pal siq (eil pal siq = say over** again)
do something bad on purpose **wuqcavq**
double-dealer **niq pyu col**
double-dealing **aqmiaovq**
double-layered **dalniaov**
double up, to **yomiav bavq dav; hhaoldaol daol dav**
doubt; suspect **hyuq nyuq**
dove; pigeon **hoqhyuq**
doves calling (the sound) **duldul** (46:118)
do well, to **aol meeq**
down (come) **ssavq yiv**
down below; lower side **aqhhuv pyu**
down river **eelmiq**
downside of village **galheiq**
downside, or west **aqgee pyu**
downslope **taoqtyuq pyu; galtyuq nei**
downstream, to go **aqgee duv yil**
downstream people **zoqgeessaq**
doze off, to **yiuvqngyul ngyul**

drag, to **hhe**
dragon **beiyaoq; hhellaoq soqpaq**
dragon day **laoq nao**
drag one's feet (in negative) **keellavq maq hhe maq ceil**
dragonfly **adovq; aqbiaoq**
dragon hour **laoq zeq**
dragon king; Hani ancestor (Taoqpaoq) **Hhellaoq** (46:207)
dragon year **laoq huvq**
drain, to **pieiq suvq; peivq suvq; wulquvq pieiq suvq**
drama; play **xifjif** (Chi) (50:183)
draw attention, to **bi nyuq gaol**
draw back, to **naoldi di huvq**
draw in, to **lav laovq; hhe kuv; se leev**
draw interest, to **piul ssaq deivq zeq lal**
draw near, to **niq li; niq lal**
draw out, to **kov; kov duv; hhe duv**

dream, a **yiuvqmav**
dream, to **yiuvqmav mav**
dreamlike; illusion **nyuq nyuq mav mav** (50:114)
dream; nightmare **yiuvqmav mavdyul dyul** (11:61)
dream world; dreamland **yiuvqmav mavsal sal**
dredge up from the water **jalngeel he; lav daol**
drench, to **jeil duvq; bi jeil**
dress a chicken, to (pull out the feathers) **hahao civ**
dress up **diq zoq**
dried **gee; geesav nei**
dried beef; jerky **niuqsaq saqkuv**
dried in the sun **lovq gee**
dried vegetable **hhoqkuv**
drill; train **xyuflieif** (Chi) (50:192)
drink, to **dol**
drink heavily, to **dol miaq; dol yevq**
drink together **zilzaoq zaoq**
drink to someone **zilbaq dolqoq qoq**
drink to someone's health **coljol bi sal movq alnei zilbaq dol**
drink to the full **dol deiv**
'drink up', to **zilbaq dol saq**
drip out, to **ju xa**
drive apart, to **leiq hhoq**
drive away **leiq zei; leiq sa**
drive away spirits **neivq leiq zei; neivq tul zei**
drive cattle together **leiq leev**
drive cattle to the mountains **leiq pieiq**
drive out, to **leiq duv; leiq zei**
driver (of car, bulldozer) **siiljil** (Chi)
driver's seat **jafsiisiiq** (Chi) (26:32)
drive together, to **leiq ssaoq**
drive together (as cattle) **leiq leev**
drizzle (light rain), to **aoqsseil sseilsav sav**
drop, a **zav**
drop, to **ya; zav xa**
drop down **ya xa; ya tao**
drop down (as tears) **lavqcav nei**
drop; fall down **ya muvq**
drop in, to **qu hu**
drop into, to **ya dov**
drop to the rear **naolhao ya duv qavq**
drought, to have **aoqkul kul; aoq kul mil kul; aoq kuv mil kuv; aoq gee mil gee; aoq gee zaol gee**
drought, to have severe **aoqkul kulma kul**
drought, to keep from having **aoq aol maq bi hav** (50:48)
drown, to **neevq; neevq sil; eelmei mei; eelhhuvq sil; ya neevq**
drum, a **luqduq**
drum people together, to **luqduq nei col diq ssaoq; col gul ssaoq**
drunk **yevq; zilbaq yevq; zilbaq dol yevq**
dry, to (vegetables for future use) **hhoqcyuq hhoqkuv**

kuv
dry, to be **kuv; alkuv; aoqhhaol hav**
dry (a little, as when dew dries up) **ciqhaq soq**
dry (as dry lips) **kuv (meiqbaoq kuv** = dry lips) (10:12)
dry (as vegetable) **alkuv**
dry, very **gee'qev nei** (11:63)
dry, very (as leaves) **kuvsav nei; kuvsav pa sav nei**
drying frame above fireplace **hoqtavq**
dry in sun, to **lovq; lovq gee**
dry meat, to **saqkuv bi kuv**
dry season **aoqkul ba'la**
dry up (as drying fish, fruit) kuv

dubious; questionable noun part. **boq (maq ngeel boq** = probably not so)
duck **oq'a**
duck, big; or female **oqma**
duck egg **oqwuv**
duck, male **oqzal**
duck, roast **oq'a oqpeev**
duck, young female **oqhal**
duckling **oqssaq**
duck, wild **neivqhaq oq'a**
duckweed **sullaq**
due (as in 'due to arrive') **hha (vb) (Aqyoq xilgei 5 se hha hev lal.** He is due to arrive here at 5 o'clock.)
dull (as a knife) **daoq (tojeil daoq al.** The knife is dull.); **eqleq deq**
dumb; foolish person **colzoq; ssaqzoq**
dumb; mute **aqbeq**
dumpling **za'lei**
dumpling (a kneaded variety) **zacuv**
dumpling, to make **za'lei lei; zacuv cuv**
dumpling ladle **za'lei zakuq**
dumpling made of sticky rice **hoqniaoq niaoqcuv; haoqniaoq niaoqcuv**
dung **xiq (niuqxiq** = cattle dung; **hhavqxiq** = pig dung, etc. Also said of human feces.)
dung cakes **xiqbiav** (buffalo dung cakes = **niuqxiq xiqbiav** - 46:152)
dung from buffalo **niuqxiq**
duplicated word **doqlo doqlaoq**
durable, to be **neiq; neiq gu nei**
dusk **aoqqivq; qivqsol lolto**
dusk to be approaching **aoqqivq qivqto pyu** (i.e., getting dark)
dusk to fall **daqhhaq hhaol; suqlu hhaqlaq** (11:17)
dust **hallyul; daoqgaoq**
dust cloud **meev nei**
duster (made of chicken feathers) **aqha hamiq yavpyul**
dustpan **laqqiq; zeiqkeeq laqqiq**
dust to accumulate **hallyul puq ya (hallyul daov puq ya**, or: **hallyul puq gaoq ya** = lots of dust

present)
dust; weeds **gaoqbeeq**
dusty; dirty **suq; cavq**
duty (as to be on duty) **luvqqao qao** (50:212); **ziiqbal** (Chi) (26:28)
duty; obligation; responsibility **yoq miaoq yoq aol** (50:212); **zeiqsseif** (50:205)
duty, to neglect **aolsuq suq** (50:174)

dwarf **alleiv leiv; moqleiv leiv**
dwarfs; trolls (in legends) **wulhyul duvluv ssaqnaol; wulhyuq aqma ssaqnaol**

dye, to **xa; deiq**
dye cloth, to **miaoqciq** (11:25); **haqpal xa; miaoqciq; leitaoq xa**
dyeing pot or vat **leiltaoq buqssaq**
dynamite; explosive **zafyoq** (50:206)
dynamo; generator **faqdieifjil** (Chi) (50:44)
dysentery, to suffer **daoqnil nal; daoqbyu sivq duv**

E e soqmiav aqma hholqei ngavq mol e qiq mol

---

each (vb) **hal (vb)**
each night **qiq yavq maq leiq**
each other **huqxal** (Chi)
eagle; hawk **haqzeil**
  eagle, large **haqzeil zeilbuq buqma**
  eagle, small kind **zeilpia; haqzeil zeilpia**
  eagle, white **haqzeil zeilpiul**
ear **naqbol**
  ear canal **naqbyu; naqhaoq**
  ear of grain **kalnaol**
  ear of rice **ceilnaol**
  ear (outer) **naqpavq**
  earlobe **naqsiq; naqwuv**
earliest; first **huqteil teilli**
early **navq; naolngaoq**
early, very **navq pa navq nei**
'early bird' **aoqsoq navq e col**
early in the month **ladav**
early in the morning **soqnavq pa navq nei**
earlyish **navq nei**
early maturing **kol** (**ceil kol** = early maturing rice)
earn a living **wuqdeiq leiq deiv**
earnestly; carefully **ssiivq nei**
earn money, to **zeiq sal**
earring **naqjul**
ear spoon **naqhevq**
earth **milcaq; difquq** (Chi)
earth; mud **halcaq**
earth, soft **milpuq**
earthen jar **buqssaq**
earthquake **millu lu; aoqlu millu lu** (heaven and earth)
earthquake, degree of **millu lutevq** (50:209)
earth-shaking; world-shaking **aoq puv mil puv**
earthworm **buqdeil**
earwax **naqxiq**
easier **yalzeiq**
easily **yalleiv nei** (10:3, 24, 26:69); **yalzav nei; neejav meil** (33:3)
east **aqnia pyu** (also, upper side) **beelduvheiq; beelduv pyu**
easy **yal**
easy, very **yalleiv nei**
easy come, easy go **dov lal yal; duv yil yal; ngaqlol heeq lol byu heeq**
easy to (vb) **sal**
eat **zaq**
  eat a meal, to **hoq zaq; zal zaq**
  eat and drink to the full **zaq deiv dol deiv**
  eat and sleep idly **zaq zaq yavq yavq**

eat heartily, to **meiqpov leivq nei zaq**
eating place **zaqduq**
eat one out of house and home, to **zaq cyuq zaq peel**
eat one's heart out **neema hhoqcil geel; neema ceiv**
eat selectively, to **zalceil ceil**
eat simply, to **beeq zaq daq zaq zaq**
eat sparingly (make a little last a long time) **hoqceiq ceiq**
eat to the full **zaq deiv**
eat up, to **zaq jul; zaq saq**
eaves of house **yaolpiaq; xaolpiaq** (45:53)

echo **badiq**
eclipse of moon **ba'la neivqkeeq zaq** (50:203)
eclipse of sun **naolma neivqkeeq zaq**
ecological balance **yeil deivq saqsal dei** (50:151)
economic court **zeiq sal kaq peel duq**
economic dispute **zeiqsal lavqkavq**
economic law **jiljif gyulliq** (Chi)
economics **jiljif** (34:3)
economic shrinkage **jiljif zeiqkuv kuv** (A=Chi)
economy **jiljif** (Chi)
economy, national **goqmiq jiljif** (Chi)
economy, planned **jiqhuaf jiljif** (Chi)

edge **bialzeil**
edge of village **puvkaq bialzeil; zaolzeil**
edible food **zaqhaoq aqzal**
editorial **seiflyuf** (Chi)
educate; cultivate **peiqya** (Chi)
educate in the legal system **faqliq nei meiq gaol** (A=Chi)
education **jaofyiuq** (Chi)
education, universal **pujiq jaofyeq** (Chi) (50:132)
educational policy **jaofyeq falzeil** (Chi)
educational system **xoqziif** (Chi) (50:192)

eel **ngaqlol** (clf. = **ssaq**) (11:151)
eel, to dig out of holes **ngaqlol hevq** (11:188)

effect; influence **yixa** (Chi) (50:199)
effective, to be **ssaoq sso** (50:151)
efficiency **xaofliq** (Chi)
efficiency, strive for **aol pyuq bi bo**
effort (with great) **hhaqhav tivq**

egalitarianism **piqjil zuyif** (Chi)
egg **alwuv; aqha hawuv; hawuv** (chicken egg)
egg, brown in color **wuvnil**
egg, duck **oqwuv**
egg, hen to lay an **hawuv xa**
egg, red (colored during certain festivals) **alwuv wuvnil** (46:157)
egg, rotten **wuvbuvq** (11:25)
egg, snake **ollol lolwuv**

egg, soft **wuvnaoq**
egg, white of **wuvpiul; alwuv wuvba**
egg fed to mother to help her 'forget' hardship of birth **nee nieil hawuv bi zaq**
eggplant **zeilzuvq**
eggshell **alwuv wuvhovq**
egg soaked in brine (1-2 mo.) **alwuv wuvdeev**
egg to be laid **hawuv xa**
egg to hatch **wuv**
egg yolk **wuvsiil**
egg yolks (salted) **wuvdeev** (see also: **alwuv wuvdeev**)
egret **neivqhaq oqngyul**
Egypt **Hheiqjiq**

eight **xeivq**
eighth **xeivq mol e qiq mol**
Eighth Route Army **Baqlufjil** (Chi)

eject, to **leiq duv; pyuq duv** (as in 'spit out')

elaborate expression **doqlo loyeiv**
elastic **zeiqnei nei**
elbow **lavqciivq**
elbow bone **lavqciivq saqyyuq**
elbow (inside) **lavqhhuvq**
elder brother **algo** (Chi)
elder brother's **wife** **aqcu**
elderly **dama colmoq; colmoqssaq**
elder sibling **aqyivq**
elder sibling/sister **aqyivq**
eldest daughter **ssaqmiq aqyivq**
eldest son **ssaqyo aqyivq**
elect, to; select **ceil; xeiji** (Chi) (50:190)
election date **xeiji yonao** (A=Chi) (50:191)
electoral district **xeiqil** (Chi) (50:191)
electoral law **xeiji faq** (Chi) (50:191)
electric iron **dieifyifde** (Chi)
electricity **dieif** (Chi)
electric lamp **dieifdeil** (Chi)
electric power station **faqdieifca** (Chi)
electronic **dieifzii** (Chi)
element; factor **yilsuf** (Chi)
elementary (primary) school (grades 1-3) **culxao** (Chi)
elementary (primary) school (grades 4-6) **gaolxao** (Chi) (26:111)
elephant **ssama**
elephant bone **ssayyuq**
eleven **ceiltivq**
ellipsis dots (...) **seinioqhaof** (Chi)
elliptical **jyuqsa nei**
ellipical sentence **doqxu xudoq** (50:151)

embarrassed **savqdol** (13:3); **savqdol bo**
embarrassed; awkward **maq sal maq yevq** (50:55)
embarrassed to death **savqdol sil laq** (13:3)

embassy **dafsiigua** (Chi)
embezzle; misappropriate **mievq tao; yiul ssaoq**
embezzlement; graft **hyuq hhavq** (50:162)
embrace, to **bavq quvq; bavq kavq**
embroidered cloth **laqga bil nil**
emerge in endless stream **duv saq maq hhaol**
emperor **haoqdil** (Chi)
empiricism **jilyeif zuyif** (Chi)
employment; to obtain **aolduq jav**
empty **aqnieivq; nieivq; alhovq** (as in an empty shell or grain); **deiq**
empty hands; unarmed **laq pul lavq nieivq**
empty one's glass **haoqmaq aqnieivq nieivq; dol saq**

encourage, to **gu'lif** (26:44); **guwu** (26:66) (Chi); **kul tul** (34:2)
encourage and reward **jalif** (Chi)
encouraged **neema laol sil**
end, to; to finish **jiqsuq** (Chi)
ending (as of an article) **jiqwei** (Chi)
ENDING PARTICLES: these differ according to the type of sentence; the speaker's viewpoint; the emotion with which the statement is made, etc.
ending particle **nga** (positive, narrative) (see: 11:133)
ending particle **nga yil** ('it is said') (11:216)
ending particle **ngeel; ngeel nga** (showing emphasis) (11:51)
ending particle **ngeel wul naq** (shortened form is: **ngu naq**) (11:222)
ending particle **wul** (affirmative)
ending particle **wul yaq** (slight surprise)
ending particle **ya** (personal statement expressing some emotion) (see: 11:133)
ending particle for questions **aq'eil** (11:138); **nil** (Chi) (11:219); **nga laq** (11:145); **ngaq**
endless stream **yil lal maq ceiv**
end of month **lamiq**
ends of the earth **aoqdaoq milzeil**
end to end **qiq gao nieivqcavq**
endure, to **civteiq**
enemy **diqsseiq** (26:15)
energy **beisiif** (Chi); **neiqyeiq** (Chi)
engaged to marry **gee caq; molbaol taq; aqssaq dav; caq cuv** (the latter can also mean to mark where fields are to be dug)
Engels **Eilkeiqsiil** (Chi-Eng)
engineer, an **gaolceiqsiil** (Chi)
engineer soldier **gaolceiqbil** (Chi)
English (the language) **Yilyidoq** (A=Chi)
engrave, to **tevq; davtevq**
enhance, to **tiqgaol** (Chi)
enhance; strengthen **jalqaq** (Chi)
enjoy, to **hhyul; sal**
enjoy oneself **yoqhhaq bulduq jol sal**

enlarge; increase **zeq** (**heeq zeq lal** = to get bigger - 26:56); **pieiq heeq**
enough **luvq**
enough; all right **hhaq al**
enough food and drink and to spare **zaq e maq hhaol dol e maq saq**
enough to (vb) **(vb) luvq** (**zaq luvq** = enough to eat)
enough, to buy **hhel luvq**
enrich, to **zaol luvq**
enslave, to; keep in bondage **ssiv dyul**
ensure; guarantee **baozaf** (Chi); **baoxei**
enter **tao; dov**
enter (down) **dov yil**
enter (up) **dov li**
enter into, to **quq tao li**
enter into water **puvq; eelsyu syu tao**
enterprise **qilniq** (Chi)
entertain, to **daqyao a bi zaq bi dol**
enthusiasm **jiqjiqxif** (Chi) (34:16)
enthusiasm, to dampen **gav miq**
enthusiasm; warmth **sseiqqiq** (34:19)
entice, to **mul zaq**
entrance, an **dovheiq**
entrust, to **hhyutoq** (Chi)
envelope, an **soqhhaq siffaol** (B=Chi)
environmental pollution; social effects of pollution **yohaol yaol kyuq lal**
envoy (as for a marriage) **colkaq**
envoy (general) **colhaol**
envoy, diplomatic **siijiq** (50:154)
envy, to **neema nal** (note: this can also mean one's heart is sick); **miav'qil nal; miavnil nal** (these last two expressions can also mean to have an eye infection)

epic **yeilgaq doqkol** (50:153)
epic (as to write a long epic) **siisiil** (Chi) (34:5)
epilepsy, to have **civqbaoq beil**
epileptic convulsion **civqbaoq beil sil**
epoch (of time) **huvqlavq**

equal; correct **hoq** (Chi)
equal; same **miav nei; qiqgao dei nei** (50:196)
equal size **qiq kov miav nei heeq**
equal to, to be **dao; hov zavq**
equal width **qiq kov miav nei yeil**
equals (math) **deihaof** (Chi)
equity; reciprocity **deinei**

erect, to **nieivq tul**
erode, to **leiq suv xa laq**
errand **cuqcal** (Chi) (26:94)

escape, to **hyuq xeiv**
escape the lips, to (i.e., to speak without thinking)

meiqbaoq nei ya duv; maq nyuq maq gaq meil eil duv
especially **teqbiq nei** (A=Chi)
essay; article **weiqzal** (Chi) (50:179)
essay; short, popular **xiaopiweiq** (Chi)
essence; nature; innate character **beiziiq** (Chi)
essence; substance **jilseiq siiqziiq** (Chi)
-est (as longest, biggest, etc.) **hal (vb) zeiq** (**hal molzeiq** = the longest)
establish, to **yeilbei bei; qoqliq** (Chi) (34:10)
esteem; respect; revere **caoqjif** (Chi)
estimate, to **kuvq ceiv** (A=Chi) (11:31)
estimating; generally **javbuv meil**
estrangement; misunderstanding **neekaoq**

etc., and so on **deidei** (Chi)
ethnic group **miqcuq** (Chi)
etymology **doqlo loheiq**

eucalyptus **hhalsuf albol** (A=Chi)
Europe **Elzel** (Chi)

evade; dodge **xeiv yoq** (50:75)
evaluate work and allot workpoints **gaolfeil piq** (Chi)
evaporate **savq gee** (50:210)
even; flat **deisal**
evening **aoqqivq; qivqsol lolto; qivqsol lolto pyu**
evening rice meal; supper **qivqhoq**
evening star (Venus) **qivqmeel**
evening time **aoqqivq pyu** (11:38)
even number **aqzao**
even though 1. **laolngaoq** (as in: 'even though the room is large, it is dark); **laolngaoq maq (vb)** (as in: 'even though he takes medicine, he is not better'), 2. although **(vb) e liq (ngal piul jav e liq** = although I had money...)
ever since **wuqduq daoqmiq hev nei**
every; any; all **hal ngeel** (50:46)
every aspect (as to discuss every aspect) **hal pyu liq sso**
'every cloud has a silver lining' **joqhyuq qiq kaoq hholqei naolma naolkeel qiq kao kev** ('in a cloud there is a ray of sunshine')
every day **hal nao liq** (26:2); **qiq nao maq leiq** (not leaving out even one day)
every day ('1000 days') **taol nao nei**
every morning **hal soq liq**
every now and then **qiq jol maq ceil**
every other (one) **qiq mol kaq qiq mol**
every person in village **puvlaol hovqma ssaqmeeq**
everywhere **halgei maq gee dav nei; dyu nei; hhyuq nei; halgei liq; halhao milnia; halgei halhao; halhev milnia**
every year **hal huvq liq; qiq huvq maq leiq**
evidence **laqnaq** ('handle'); **piaqhhal** ('footprint')
evidence; facts **miqnieiq yojil**

evidence, material **lavqzu** (50:182)
evil **yocavq**
evil-hearted **neema cavq**
evil omen **dol (dol duv lal; yocavq duv lal)**
evil spirit **neivq; neivqhaq**

ewe (female sheep) **aqyol yolma**

exact; real **jil** (and see in Hani)
exactly; precisely **cuv nei; tavtaoq nei (tavtaoq nei maq hha mol ya** = I could not see exactly)
exaggerate **eil heeq miaq**
exam; test **kao** (Chi) (41:87)
examination, to have an **kaosiif kao** (Chi)
examination, university entrance exam **gaolkao** (Chi)
examination paper **kaosiif tiq soqhhaq** (A=Chi)
examine a person, medical test **huafyeif** (Chi) (10:33); **jei caq** (26:62)
examine; inspect **jei caq**
example; model **biaolbil** (Chi) (26:100)
exceedingly (vb) **(vb) sil (hhyul sil** = 'happy to death' - 13:16)
excellent **yelxef** (Chi) (26:100)
excellent; outstanding **yomeeq yoceil** (50:199)
excellent rank **yiul jiq**
excessive; many **miaq gaoq**
exchange, to **bavq pal; pal pievq**
exchange; change **pal; pal zaq**
exchange (carry and exchange) **bavq pal**
exchange back again, to **pal puv huvq**
exchange money **covq pal (Piul covq pal zaq kal.** Let's change **money.**)
exchange of equal value **hhaqpyuq dei nei pal zaq**
excited, to be **hhyulzuq zuq** (26:76)
excited; jumping aound **keel niv lavq niv** (13:32)
exclamation; interjection **tafciiq** (Chi) (50:163)
exclamation mark (punctuation) **gatafhaof** (Chi)
excuse, to make **yeiqliaf** (Chi); **dyuf buq qi** (Chi)
excuse, to use as **deiq leivq; zaol leivq**
exemption, right to **hofmiei'qeiq** (Chi)
exercise, to **xeiv hha** (11:130); **keellavq leil** (B=Chi) (11:193); **lieifxiq** (Chi); **leilzol**
exercise, morning **safcaol; safcaol saf** (Chi) (26:84); **zaocaol** (Chi) (50:204)
exercise book **soqhhaq buvqkaoq** (26:19); **buvqkaoq** (26:41)
exclamation of pain, surprise, etc. **aqyoq; aqyaq** (26:60)
exhalt yourself, to **yoqhhaq bulduq eil heeq**
exhausted; tired **kyuq leiq kyuq sil; kyuq sil; kyuq sil kyuq leiq**
exhibit; show; open up before one's eyes **bi duv** (50:206)
exhibition center **za'lagua** (Chi) (50:206)
exist; be (animate) **jol**
exit, an **duv heiq**

exorcise (evil spirit) **neivqhaq tul zei; neivqhaq tul duv; neivqhaq (aqzuq) yaq duv**
expand; stretch out, to **ja**
expanded production **koqdaf zeifseilca** (Chi)
expect, to; to hope for **movq ssa**
expel; discharge **leiq duv**
expel from the country; deport **milkaq leiq duv**
expel from the party **dayeiq wuqcaoq hhe** (A=Chi)
expenses, to pay **hhaqpyuq**
expensive **pyuq**
experience **jilyeif** (Chi)
experienced (vb) **(vb) bei (aol bei** = have done it; have experienced doing it) (11:132)
experiment; test **zaol hu** (50:154)
expert, an **zualjal** (Chi) (50:217)
explain, to **eil loq; geeloq** (32:3)
explain and publicise **eil xa eil loq** (50:190)
explode, to **coq beivq**
exploit, to **boqxoq** (Chi) **guvciiq; guvciiq zaq**
exploration; prospecting **zeiqmeeq qo**
explore, to **zaol hu**
explore; probe **tafsoq** (Chi)
explosive; dynamite **zafyoq** (Chi) (50:206)
expose; bring to light **tyuq duv**
express delivery (mail) **kol e soqhhaq**
express something, to **zaol duv** (26:67)
express support, to **eil haol**
express train **kol e hocei** (B=Chi)
extend something, to **cavq dav**
extensive; wide-ranging **gua'faf** (Chi)
extort; blackmail **hheivqsov pieiq**
extra; left over **yozeiq; aqzeiq**
extravagant **zeiseil seil**
exteme of something (vb) **sil (neehaol sil; gaq sil;** etc)
extremely **tuvq** (vb); **tuvqqilnei** (50:131)

eye **miav; miavneev** (clf. = **miav**)
eyeball **miavneev**
eyebrow; eyelash **miavhao** (lit., 'eye hairs')
eye, corner of (edge of the eye) **miavzeil**
eye, corner of (the eye itself) **miav'qeiq**
eye discharge **miavxiq**
eyeglasses; spectacles **miavkal**
eyeglasses, to wear **miavkal dovq**
eyelash; eyebrow **miavhao**
eyelid **miavgeel; miavhov; miav miavhov** (11:36)
eyelid, double-folded **miavgeel geeltevq**
eyelid, lower **miavmuq**
eye, pupil of **miavneev neevnav**
eyes become red **miavcil cil** (30:2)
eyes crossed **miavqei**
eyes, to open **miavneev bieijei**
eyesight, dim **miav laq seiq**
eyes open **miav hu** (11:120)

eyes protruding **miavneev bilduv meil**
eyesight **yeigeif** (Chi) (26:11)
eyesight poor **miavhhaq hhaq**
eyes sunken **miav bilhovq nei**
eyes wide open **miavjyul jyul**

fabric (not cotton) **diqka** (Chi)
fabricate; fake; trump up **eil cuvq**
face **miavpyuq**
face; appearance **pyuq; pioq**
face covered with dust, to make **bavqbuvq leiq buvq**
face cream (general) **faqsiifliq** (Chi) (11:17)
face cream (one kind) **xiqhualgaol** (Chi) (11:17)
facial hair (fine, soft) **haocavq**
facial skin **baqgeel**
facility; installation **seiqsiil** (Chi)
fact, a **yojil** (50:155)
faction; group; school of thought **peifbiq** (Chi)
factionalism; sectarianism **zaolpeif zuyif** (Chi) (50:220)
factor; element **yilsuf** (Chi)
factory **gaolca** (Chi) **jalgaolca** (26:69)
factory director **caza** (Chi)
facts; evidence **miqnieiq yojil**
fade, to **jaoq**
fade color; lose taste **bioq**
fail (as in an exam) **siiqbeif** (Chi); **maq jiqgeiq** (B=Chi)
failure **siiqbeif** (Chi) (26:45)
fairy; daughter of God **Nolmil ssaqmiq**
faith; belief; conviction **nyuqhhal** (50:188); **xifnieif** (Chi)
faith; confidence **haoqhhyu neesal** (50:188)
fall, to **leeq**
  fall and roll **puq lu pul luq meil**
  fall down; drop **muvq; taoqsil** (11:114); **ya leeq; ya; ya heil; xa heil**
  fall into, to **xa heil; ya heil; zei puvq; leeq tao; zei ya** (45:61)
  fall into water, to **leeqpuvq; yapuvq**
  fall on one's bottom **daoqteil teil** (11:147)
  fall over; topple **lol; taoq leeq**
  fall to death **taoq sil**
fallow field **yalbial; xalbial**
false; not real **maq jil** (31:3 (**maq jil Haqniq** = fake Hani)
false accusation against **hanil nil bu** (50:180)
false accusation crime **hanil nil zyul** (50:180)
false case **hheivqhhaf** (B=Chi)
false charge, to make **wuqcavq xa**
falsify; forge **hheivqzaol zaol** (50:177)
faltering **kyuqlyu qeiqleiq nei; kyulli qeiqleiq nei**
fame **haoqseil; pyuqmil; miqqil** (Chi)
fame; good reputation **teilsal; milteil sal**
fame; reputation **yo'lal** (**yo'lal aoq zaq** = to ruin a reputation); **mildao haoqseil; colteil** (50:118)

family   **colhhovq; qovq** (clf. = **hhovq** - 11:34); **qovqbee; jaltiq** (Chi)
  family affairs   **laqhyul qiqkuaf** (B=Chi)
  family, happy   **hovq sal; yovq laol**
  family member   **laqhyul col**
  family, my   **nga qovq**
  family name   **liuq** (Chi)
  family, one's own   **yovqhhovq yovqhol; yoq bee**
  family, set up   **yovqhhovq cuv zaq**
  family, your   **no qovq**
  family to divide   **yovqhhovq bil zaq**
  family, whole   **qiq hhovq; qiq hhovq hhovqjoq**
famous   **milteil sal; pyuq bo; miqqil heeq** (A=Chi); **yoteil dav** (50:217); **teilma dav**
fan   **bosev**
fan (for fanning a fire)   **miqzaq bosev**
fan, to   **bo**
fang, a   **seqziil; ziilqei**
fantasy; illusion   **salnyuq saldul**
far away   **galmol mol; galheeq heeq** (10:13); **galheeq sav nei**
farewell; saying goodbye   **eil hhoq zaq**
  farewell meeting   **gaofbiqhyuf** (Chi)
farm animal (as for plowing)   **xal aol zeiqssaq**
farm, collective   **naoqcaq** (Chi) (26:26)
farm, to   **xal aol zaq**
farm of commodity crops   **aoq hhel zalsiq xaduq**
farmers; peasants   **aolzaqssaq** (11:93); **xalduqssaq; xal aolssaq**
  farmers (men)   **aolzaq ssaqyo**
  Farming-forestry bureau   **Naoqliqjiq** (Chi)
fart, to (pass gas, flatulate)   **haq pieiq**
fascist   **faqxilsiil** (Chi-Eng)
fast; quick   **kollal; lavqkol**
  fast as a spirit; speedy   **neivqkol kol**
fast asleep, to be   **javqleel nei yiuvq**
fasten; put on   **dovq**
fasten into   **zaol tao**
fasten onto, to   **kavq tovq**
fasten tightly   **kavq tovq; siivq**
fat   **cul; yocul**
  fat (as of meat)   **saqcul**
  fat; obese   **cul; meil**
  fat; plump (as a bird)   **zyuqlei nei**
  fat, very   **culbi pa bi nei** (as of children) (11:61); **culbiq nei**
  fat and strong, to be   **daovq**
fate; destiny   **mifyif** (Chi)
father   **aqda**
father and son   **niq paqssaq**
father-in-law   **yoqpaq** (pf); **yiuvqpaq**
father's ancestors   **hyulzao aqpyuq**
father's older brothers   **damoq**
father's older brother's wife   **malma**
father's older sister   **malma**

father's sister's husband **dalda**
father's younger brother, father's sister's husband **dalda; alsuq** (Chi)
father's younger brother's wife **aqmee**
father's younger sister **alnia; aqhuq**
father's younger sister's husband; brother-in-law; older sister's husband **aqsaoq**
fathom (roughly six feet; the distance between outstretched hands used as a measure) **laqlaol; laol** (clf. = **laol**)
favor, to **hu dav**

fear, to **guv**
fearless; dauntless **maq guv maq niv**
fear of trouble back home **naolhao nyuq saq**
feasible; realistic **qiqsiiq** (Chi)
feather; fur **haonuv**
feather of chickens **hahao** (soft) **haniaol**
feathers, stiff and large **aqdaol daolhav; haniaol** (of chicken)
feathers, soft **aqdaol daolnaoq**
February **Joqnil siq; Zyuqnil siq**
feces **xiq** (runny feces of a baby: **aldyul**)
feeble; weak (as from disease) **nalgol nalniei**
feed, to **bi zaq; qu** (for animal)
  feed (as the queen bee) **bavq zyuq**
feed and care for **qu**
feel something (as the cold) **tihyuf** (Chi)
feel something (with hand) **sov hu**
feelings about something **xildeiq** (Chi) (26:52)
feelings; to express **alyaovq** (50:14)
feet, bound **seiqquvq**
fellow villagers (TE) **puvlaol hovqma** (46:131)
female **aqma; ssaqmiq; haqmiq ssaqnaol** (male: **haqjil aqda**)
female pig **hhavqma**
feminine **ssaqmiq**
fence **kaoldaol; laolkaol**
fence in, to **kaoldaol aol; kaoldaol diq; kaoldaol hhavq; cyuq; aol cyuq**
  fence in; wall in **diq hhao** (46:130)
fence of bamboo **haqbol kaoldaol**
fennel (a plant) **hhoqyolceil; hhoqyyulceil** (both)
ferment, to **hhuvq; hhuvqqeil**
fern, bracken **haqdal dalpiaq; haqdal dalma**
ferocious; cruel **saltuq**
ferret badger **huhaq**
fertile field **deimeeq loqhaoq; deimeeq loqma; loqhaoq sal e**
fertilize, to **feiq** (Chi)
fertilizer (manure) **zeiqkeeq**
festival, to have a **hev zaq** (46:174); **huvq hev la hev hev**
festival day **neeciiv** (26:112)
festival, spring **joqzaq** (46:81)

fetch goods, to **bavq huvq al la**
fetch water **hovq** (**hovqdol e** = fetch water & drink)
fetters; handcuffs **saoljul**
fetus **ssaqceiq**
feudalist landlord **faoljeif difzu** (34:16) (Chi)
feudal society **faoljeif seifhyuf** (Chi) (34:3)
fever, to get **piaqcao cao lal** (10:24) (Note: this can also be used for malaria.)
fever, to have **piaq; alpiaq piaq** (Note: This can also be used for malaria.)
few **meenia; maq miaq** (lit., 'not many')
few days ago **eiqmilnao; milka lalnao; milnao huqnao**
few moments ago **eiqsi sihav**

fiction; novel **xaosoq** (Chi) (50:186)
field (irrigated, on mountainside) **xal; yal; yoyal** (13:20); **yolyal; hhoqyal** (11:18) (Note: '**xal**' and '**yal**' are used almost interchangeably. For example, for 'fallow fields' both **xalbial** and **yalbial** occur. '**yal**' is like the Akha and Burmese words for 'field', and may be the older form.)
field, abandoned **xalbial; yalbial; saqpeeq**
field, big **loqma**
field, fertile **xalmeeq**
field, go look for **xalmil sal; yalmil sal**
field, go work in **yalsol duv; xalsol duv**
field, high mtn. **yolyal; yoyal** (13:20); **daolyal** (11:48); **daoltavq koqyal**
field boundary **xalkaq**
field edge **caqdaoq**
field, good **deimeeq loqhaoq; deimeeq loqma; deimeeq loqsal**
field hut **xalqaol**
field, irrigated **xaldei; yaldei; hhaqjeil xaldei; xaldei hhaqjeil**
field, irrigated (large) **xaldei loqma (yaldei loqma)**
field, look for **yalmil sal; xalmil sal**
field, lower section **xaldaoq**
field lying fallow **xalbial; yalbial**
field, new **yalhav; yalnav**
field, old **yalbial** (26:63); **yalcyuq**
field, return home from **yalsol hhuvq; xalsol hhuvq**
field, side of **xalzeil**
field, unfertilized **xalgov (yalgov)**
field left fallow **yalbial; xalbial** (11:25)
field of buckwheat **hhaqlei hhaqyal**
field of vegetables **keilsavq**
field on mountain **haoltavq koqyal; daoltavq koqyal**
field's lower part **xaldaoq (yaldaoq)**
field's upper part **xalhhaoq**
fierce **lavsaoq**
fifty grams **ngavq ceil keiq** (C=Chi)
fig **siqpuv; siqpuv laqhhaoq**
fight; beat on one another **diq zaq; taoq zaq**
fight against **fadyuf** (Chi) (34:6) (and see: **feifdef**)

fight against imperialism **fa dif** (Chi)
fight a war **geel diq** (11:32)
fighting **diq zaq** (11:20, 26:104)
fight; strive **feifdef** (Chi) (and see: **fa dif**)
fight to the death **wuqhol maq movq meil diq kavq**
file, metal **saolsav**
file, to **saolsav nei sav**
files; records **dahhaf** (Chi)
fill (as rice) **kuq**
fill and soak **kuq duv**
filler; news tidbits **yopyuq naqgaq**
fill in with earth (as around corn plants) **du'qu**
fill the air **savq diq dov**
fill with padding **daq**
film; movie **dieifyi** (Chi); **dieifssi** (Chi), **yipieif** (Chi) (50:198); **dieifssi mu'luq** (A=Chi)
filter **pieiq zeil**
filter out; strain out **zeil**
filthy **yoxeiv; yoxeiv tuvq**
final (phonological, as a final consonant) **yyufmu** (Chi)
final charge (legal); last accusation **zyulmiaol eil ceiv**
final part., command **naoq; joq** (11:135)
final part., declaring one's own feelings **(vb) ya** (**jav gaoq ya** = I have a lot) (when declaring the feelings of others the particle is: **nga**, as in: **jav gaoq nga** = there is a lot)
final part., 'it is said' **nga yil**
final part., narrative **nga** (**puvkaq hholqei zyuq maq jol nga** = in the village there is no headman)
finals (linguistic sense, i.e. vowel) **ssifmu; yifmu** (Chi)
finance **ceiqzeif** (pf.); **caqzeif** (Chi)
finance; banking **jilyaoq** (Chi)
finance and economics **ceiqjil** (Chi)
financial resources; financial capacity **zeiqhhaq**
financial rights **ceiqqeiq** (Chi)
finance, public **ceiqzeif** (Chi)
fine; okay **hhaq lil**
fine, a (for doing something wrong) **zyulzeiq; faq** (Chi); **zeiq duv**
fine day **aoqsal sal** (26:75)
fine someone **zyulzeiq duv; geelzeiq hhuvq**
finger **lavqnyul**
finger, little **lavqqaq; nyulqaq**
finger, middle **nyulma; nyultaoq**
finger-guessing game, to play **huaqqeiq** (Chi); **lavqnyul lavqma caq zaq**
fingernail **lavqsaoq**
finger; ring finger **nyulzeil**
finish; to end **jiqsuq; jil**
finish class; get out of class **zolnieiq naq** (50:184)
finish doing **aol saq**
finished (vb) **(vb) saq** (**aol saq** = finished doing)

fin of fish **ngaqdaol; daolbuv** (30:2)
fire **miqzaq; aqzaq; aqzaq miqlaol** (26:14)
fire, to (as a gun); launch (as a missle) **bev duv**
fire; to light a fire **dovq; miqzaq bo dovq; keq; taoqsuq; miqzaq keq pieiq; aqzaq keq**
fire, to put out **diqsil; miqzaq diqsil**
fire, to set in jungle or open area **millaol keqpeev**
fire a gun **miqbev bev**
fire a gun accidentally **miqbev lav pieiv**
fire burning brightly **miqba**
fire burning jungle, ground **millaol; millaol peev**
firecracker **soqhhaq miqteiv**
fire engine (to fight fires) **xaolfaqceil** (Chi) (26:70)
fire extinguisher **miqhoqif** (Chi)
firefly, a **miqssiq milssiq**
fire for cooking at home **miqzaq geema**
fire goes out **miqzaq sil**
fire lane, to provide **laoljo jo**
firelight **miqlaol**
firemen; fire fighters **xaolfaq dyufyeiq** (Chi) (26:70)
fireplace **caoqlaolhaoq; caoqleiq**
fireplace (as in 'kitchen') **yuqduq; yuqduq duqhaoq**
fireplace, side of **haolzeil**
firewood **miqkoq**
  firewood, big **miqkoq cevqbu**
  firewood, big but short **miqkoq daoqpuq**
  firewood, gather **lavqniaov** (11:25)
  firewood, go cut **miqkoq heivq** (11:92)
  firewood, heavy **miqkoq daoqdev**
  firewood and twigs **miqkoq miqpial** (11:35)
  firewood basket **miavhav**
  firewood burning **miqlil; miqzaq miqlil**
  firewood, straight **miqkoq xaoqbul**
firm **qil; ssiivq; ssiivqdao nei**
firm (as to be tied firmly) **siivq**
firm; resolute **jeiljyuq** (Chi)
firm; solid **zaol siivq** (to make firm)
firmament (vault of heaven) **aoqtav laolqaol** (46:162)
firm and indomitable; persistent and dauntless **maq guv maq niv**
firm and unshakable **naoldi maq tyul** (C=Chi)
first **miqteil; miqteil teilli** (**miqteil teilli qiq hhaq** = the first person - 11:67)
first; earliest **miqteil teilli; huqteil teilli**
(vb) first, (vb) ahead **huqteil (vb)**
first birth (to give) **hhelhhuv pao**
first month of the year **joqzaq siq; jyuqzaq siq; zyuqzaq siq**
fir tree, a **salmuq suf** (Chi)
fish (general term) **ngaqdeil; ngaqsaq** (this indicates the meat of a fish)
fish, mature (old) **ngaqmoq**
fish, raw **ngaqzaoq**
fish, salted and sour **ngaqsaq hhoqqeil**

fish, small type (in rice paddies) **ngaqjul** (11:129)
fish, to (by damming stream) **lolpav pieiq** (11:198)
fish basket of bamboo **jabaoq**
fish bones ('thorns') **ngaqgao**
fisherman **ngaqsaq leiqssaq**
fishery **ngaqsaq qu miqnieiq** (50:200)
fish gill **ngaqsaq baqbeiv**
fish hook **ngaqhhovq** (11:27)
  fish with a hook, to **ngaqhhovq pieiq puvq**
fishing basket (for catching fish) **jalkal**
fish net (of bamboo) **ngaqzeil; hhazei**
    ngaqcaoq (lit. 'fish cap') (11:28)
fish-poison vine **ngaqciq**
fish pole **ngaqhhovq daldul**
fish pond **ngaqduq** (11:18) (clf. = **duq**)
fish pond, to dig **ngaqduq duq** (11:18)
fish scale **ngaqhhov**
fish smell **salhe naol**
fist **lavqpul; lavqtuv**
fist, small **lavqpul pulssaq**
fist, to make **lavqtuv tuv; lavqtuv tuvluvq luvq**
fit; suitable **za**
five **ngavq**
fix, to (as with nails) **diq cuv**
fix, to (general repair) **kavq ssivq; zaol ssivq**
fixed assets **maq niv zeiqma**

flag **bavqpia**
flag carrier (as in the army) **haoqqiqse; hoqqiqse**
flag, national **goqqiq** (Chi)
flame **miqlaol; miqbia** (11:28)
flame; blaze **miqbia**
flaming fire, a **miqzaq miqlaol** (26:69)
flash, to **bia**
flashlight **dieiftaoq** (Chi)
flat (as a dish) **biav; biavsev nei**
flat; even **dei; saldei nei; deisal**
flat, very **dei pa dei nei** (11:57)
flattened head **wuqbiav biav**
flatter, to **eil pyuq zaq**
  flatter; lick someone's boots **doqqul sov**
flattish **dei nei; biavsuq nei**
flatulate; break wind **haq pieiq** (taboo)
flavorful **zalsol**
flea **keeqseil**
flee, to **xeiv**
  flee hither and thither **col ya col del**
fleet; a naval force **jeifdyuf** (Chi)
flexible; adaptable **za; ya; aol pal sso; zaol pal sso**
  flexible money **ssaoq ma leil e piul**
  flexible regulation **maq za zaol za**
flint etc. for making fire, or modern lighter **miqdiq**
float, to **bulhha; bulya nei**
  float along **bulhha nei**
  float away, to **wulquvq nei bul zaq**

flood, to **eelpuv puv** (26:57); **eeltaoq taoq** (26:22); **eelpuv leiq**
floor (as of house) **caqpiq**
floor beam **laqdaoq**
floral pattern, a **alyeiv ssiiv**
flour **zallyul**
flourishing; bustling **hhyuq qa hhyuq lol zuvq**
flourishing; prosperous **byuqssil byuqssav jav**
flow, to **xu**
  flow out, to **wulquvq duv**
  flow swiftly, to **bul**
flower **alyeiv**
  flower, to **yeiv (alyeiv yeiv)**
  flowers, golden **siil yeiv**
flower wreath **hualqeil alyeiv** (A=Chi)
flu (influenza) **salhaq** (Chi) (26:6)
fluffing equipment (for cotton, including the bow) **saqlaq bevhuvq bevdul**
fluff up (cotton), to 'shoot' (cotton) **bev**
fluid; liquid **alju; zal'eel**
fluorescent screen (Chi) **yiqgualpiq** (Chi) (50:198)
flute **laqbil** (46:175); **bilceiv laqbil; meiqbaq** (latter made of bamboo)
flute (made from a rice stem) **hhubaoq meel**
flute (made of copper or bronze) **geeqbil** (11:93)
fly (noun) **almol**
fly, to **biaol**
fly in a circle **biaolhhao**
fly into, to **biaol tao li**
flying horse **moqbiaol**
'flying snake' (it is very fast) **ollol eelkol**
flying squirrel **hubiaol**

fog **joqhyuq**
fog; thick clouds **joqtaoq taoq**
foggy, to be **joqhyuq cyuq; joqtaoq** beeq
fold, a **hhaoldaol**
fold, to **biavq; daol; hhaoldaol daol**
fold clothes, to **peilbeil laol**
folded; wrinkled **bilzuvq meil**
folksong; ballad (the type sung in house) **lalbaq** (note: this is **halbaq** in one dialect)
  folksong; ballad (to sing the above) **lalbaq ssil**
  folksong; ballad; nursery rhyme **dalya**
  folksong; courting (the type sung outside of house) **aqzil**
  folksong; courting (to sing the above) **aqzil gul**
  folksong singer, a famous one **Zul Xaohoq**

follow, to **qo leiq**
following, the (i.e., the one about to be mentioned) **aqhhuv pyu** (10:pref.)
following along **lo'qo nei**
following closely **naoqcavq meil**
'follow-me-not' ceremony **meildaoq yoq**

foment discord; sow dissension **cuqpuv**
fontanel **wuqbiaoq**
food **zal; aqzal; zalsiq aqzal; zaqlul; zaqzal**
  food; rice; meal **hoq**
  food container **zalloq**
  food coupon **liaqpiaof** (Chi)
  food for buffalo **niuqzal**
  food for eating **zaqhal** (11:217)
  food left over **zaqnieiq**
  food which is delicious **zalkeel zalniuv**
fool; idiot **aqzoq; aqbiaoq**
foolish **aqzoq**
foolish; dumb **colcuv colcavq** (28:4)
foot **aqkeel; keeldu**
foot (top of foot) **aqkeel keelnaol; keelnaol**
foot, cracks in skin of **keelbeivq beivq**
foot and hand **keellavq**
foot end (as the foot end of a bed) **keelmiqdaoq**
foot of mountain **gaoqdaoq** (13:11)
footprint **piaqhhal; aqkeel piaqhhal; keelxa duqhovq**
for (as in FOR the people) **bal nei** (10:pref.); **ballal**
for a long time **hhaqgal mol taq nei** (10:15)
force open, to **hhepiei**
forearm **lavqdu**
forehead **niuqteil; teillu**
foreign affairs; diplomacy **weifjaol** (Chi)
  foreign affairs' work **wafjaol miqnieiq** (A=Chi) (50:173)
foreign country **aqnu goqjal** (B=Chi) (50:173) **weifgoq; wuafgoq** (Chi)
foreign exchange **aqnu goqjal piul** (B=Chi) (50:173)
foreign land **aqnu milhaoq** (50:197)
Foreign Minister **wafza** (Chi) (50:174)
foreign trade **wafmuf** (Chi) (50:174)
forest **haoldaol laolma; haoldaol saqhav**
forest, dense **saqhav laolnav**
forest, in mountain **haoldaol saqhav; beilcaoq haoldaol**
forest, jungle **beilcaoq; haoldaol**
forest, old **saqhav havmoq**
forever **salssil** (11:112) (when used in the negative it means: never); **salssil sallo** (30:1)
foreword; preface **yoheiq heiqdoq** (50:190)
forget, to **nieil; nieil bial; nieil zaq; nieil qav** (11:39, 112); **nil** (26:59); **nil qav** (13:12); **nilbial; nilzaq**
forgive, to **nyuq zoq** (lit. 'think straight' - 41:177)
fork in path; crossroad **galcaol**
forked stick **hupievq**
form; appearance; shape **yoyaovq** (50:189)
form; way **xiqsiif** (Chi)
formerly **galhhu**
formula **gaolsiif** (Chi)
formulate; draw up; lay down **zaol taq** (50:213)
forum; symposium **doqzil puq** (50:222)
for purpose of **alleil nei; bal nei; ballal nei**

(11:120)
for someone; on behalf of someone **ballal (no ballal** = for you, on your behalf)
fort; stronghold **bao'lyu** (Chi)
for the most part **yomiaq qiq baol**
fortune, to tell **solmil sol**
forward looking **huqteil pyu hu** (50:185)
fossil **huafsiiq haqluv** (A=Chi)
foundation, a **caqkeel; jilcu** (Chi) (34:12);
foundation; base **daoqpeiq; naolteev**
foundation stone **ssaoldaoq**
four **yuvq**
four corners **yuvq liv yuvq kyul**
four principles **jilbei yeiqzeiq yuvq mol** (A=Chi)
fowl, jungle **haniq**
fox, a **puqduv daoqmiq**

fragile (almost broken) **yabiav laq caca nei**
fragrance of a crop **kalqul**
fragrant aroma **sol; sollavq nei**
fragrant aroma, very **solxeiv nei** (11:58); **solxeiv pa xeiv nei; solxeiv pa xeiv nei sol** (11:59); **sollavq pa lavq nei**
frame a case against; accuse falsely **eilcuvq; nieiq hev meil halnil nil** (50:200)
frame for a pack saddle **moqqeiv; qeivkeel laqma**
frank; friendly **neema piul**
frank; honest **bu'loq nei eil duv** (50:163)
frankly **bia lil bia loq meil**
frankly; honestly **jilhevq nei**
fraud; to practice **hheivqmiaovq miaovq**
freckle **bavqbuvq; beeqhaq**
free, to be (have time) **lov (Hal taq lov ya leil, hal meil liq qiq taq lal.** No matter what, come whenever you are free. 11:104)
freedom; liberty **ziifyeq** (Chi) (26:112, 50:219)
freezing cold **ceivq gaoq**
frequently; always **civzaol nei**
fresh **siivqxa nei**
fresh (as vegs.) **niulzaovq nei; yosiivq nei**
fresh, soft **naoq**
freshly **deivqhhuvq nei; deivqhhuvq deivq lal xeiv nei**
freshly; softly **naoqzov nei; naoqzov nei naoq**
Friday **Xilqil ngavq nao (A=Chi); Xilqil wu** (Chi)
fried rice **hoqlul**
fried rice with an egg **alwuv hoqlul**
friend, a **yolqoq; hhyulqoq**
friend, to make a **yolqoq qoq**
friend (very close, or relative) **yoqcol** (11:112)
friend in need, a **saq qoq gav qoq** ('a friend in the midst of difficulties'); **aoqsseil sseil qoq** ('a friend in the midst of rain'); **keeq diq e yolqoq** ('a friend who helps beat the dog attacking you')
friendly; frank **neema piul**
friendship **pyuq gaq hhyul gaq; gaq zaq hhyul zaq**

(50:200)
frighten someone, to **navqguv; naqguv**
frightened **paguv lima; naqhhaq nei** (33:3); **guvzuq zuq** ('shivering with fear')
frightened so much falls to ground **guv xa** (46:147)
frightening place (where spirits live) **caoq**
frog **haqpaq**
frog, types **paqbieiv aqma; paqniul; sseilpaq; paqsal; alhhe haqpaq; alhhe meiqbieil; paqqei; paqduv laqsiq**
frog that lives in forest pools **paqduv**
from; with **nei**
from head to tail (all) **wuqduq daoqmiq li nei**
from that time **yul kavq nei; yul taq neikavq**
front; before **meiqsi; miqteil pyu; meiqsi pyu**
front of house (outside) **zoqgee**
frontier **bieiljal** (Chi)
front of, in **miqteil pyu**
frost **haqnil; haqnieil**
frost to form **haqnil ya** (33:3)
frown, to **deiq zuvq**
fruit **alsiq; alsiq alhhov**
fruit, good **siq meeq**
fruit, to **alsiq siq**
fry, to **lul; biav**
fry into; mix and fry **lul kevq**

fulfill; carry out **lavqzaq soq**
full; ample **caolfeil nei** (Chi)
full; complete **biao; biao nei**
full; mature (as grains; seeds) **mal; mallu nei**
full; satiated (as of food, drink) **deiv**
full, very **biao pa biao nei** (11:58)
full mouth, to eat with a **meiqpov leivq nei**
full of (n) **meil (n)** (**Miavpyuq qiq pyuq meil kaoqpiul**. One's face covered with perspiration. 11:82)
full of food, very **deiv pa deiv nei** (11:57)
fully **biaogaoq pa gaoq nei** (11:171)
function **aolnieiq aolquv** (50:212); **zoqyaof** (Chi); **ziiqneiq** (Chi)
fundamental law **yoliq liqma**
funeral oration **heldoq soqbuvq**
fungus on trees (arboreal fungus) **daoqma naqbol**
fungus; mold **haolci**
funnel for liquor **zilbaq zilhhev**
fur (animal) **haonuv** (also feather)
fur blanket; fur carpet **geivzavq**
furrows (as in field) **ceiqkov**
furrow (plowed) **hhalbiavq**
further intensified; further aggravated **nieiq aol nieiq kyuq**
future, in the **galnee salpeiq**
future; later **aqkal; aqsal; naolhao**
future, some time in the **aqkal hhana**

G g **soqmiav aqma hholqei siivq mol e qiq mol**

---

gabardine **huaqdaqniq** (Chi)
gain; win **zeilqi** (Chi)
gain a footing, to **jolduq ssivq; jolqil xa**
gain over, to **heel pyul la**
gall **piqkeel**
gallbladder **piqkeel**
  gallbladder disease **piqkeel dav**
gamble, to **duqceiq duq** (A=Chi)
  gambling (to lose at) **duq sul** (Chi)
  gambling (to win at) **duq hhaq** (A=Chi)
game, to play **seilhha; ssaqguq hhallul seilhha**
game children play while singing **aqhhyu aqmee seil**
gang of criminals **qiq ba meil zaol zyul**
gap; breach **meiqhavq; aolbei heiq** (50:169)
garden **yal; kol'al**
  garden, vegetable **keilsaq**
garlic **haqseil**
  garlic, wild **milcaq haqseil**
gas, natural **milhhuvq alsavq**
gas (which can expand) **zii**
gate **hhoheiq**
gather; collect **cev ssaoq**
gathered together **zyulgaoq gaoq** (34:1)
gather one's breath **hhaq bi dav**
gaur **neivqniuq**
gauze **haqpal palkal**; salbuf (Chi)
  gauze mask **meicaoq** (50:98)
gaze, to **hu cuv**

genealogy **ciivq**
  genealogy, to repeat **ciivq gee**
  genealogy which ends (no males to continue)
    ciivqdaoq daoq
  genealogy with breaks ('jumps') **ciivqcoq coq**
general agent **zaozilli; zaodeifli** (Chi)
general knowledge **yozao yomiaol**
generally; for the most part **zao nei; zaoma nei** (26:28); **javbuv meil; yiqbalnei** (A=Chi)
general pardon; amnesty **zyulgol bi bial**
general picture **keifmaof** (Chi)
general secretary **zaosuljif** (Chi)
generation **ssil; kol (aqda qiq kol** = father's generation)
generator; dynamo **faqdieifjil** (Chi)
generous, to be **neema maq xeivq**
genitive **(n) e**
gentamicin (broad-spectrum antibiotic) **qifdaf meiqsuf** (Chi)
genuine, to be **jil; yojil jil**
geographical conditions **difli huaqji** (Chi)

geography **diflixoq** (Chi)
germ; bacteria **xifjif** (Chi) (50:183)
germinate, to **alquv quv**
get; collect **se leev**
get; obtain **hha**
get ahead, to **aol dav; faqza dav** (A=Chi)
get along, to **aol dav**
get among, to **dov li; pievq li**
get at the truth, to **zaol loq**
get away, to **xeiv hhoq**
get back, to **hhuvq huvq lal (yil; yiv; li); hhal huvq**
get behind, to **naolhav ya duv; maq leiq mil nia**
get better, to **nalgol kaq lal**
get by, to **ssuq hev; ssuq yoq**
get by heart, to **nyuq taq** (teiq)
get clear, to **maq laqbal**
get down, to **ya yi; ga yi**
get down on one's knees, to **paoqciivq tuv xa**
get drunk, to **dol yevq; dol mu**
get free, to **alcav beil bieiq**
get hold of, to **bavqteiq**
get home, to **laqhyul a hhuvq li**
get in, to **toq taq; zalsiq se leev**
get in the harvest, to **zalsiq se leev**
get into holes, to **saqduq duqbyu a yadov**
get into hot water, to **eel laol hholqei a quqdov**
get in with **gaq zaq hhyul zaq nia**
get loose, to **xeiv leev**
get off, to **hhehhoq; pieiq duv; xeiv leev; ssavq**
get on, to **ziiq dav; dao dav; aol meeq**
get one's hand in, to **aol suv; aol nia**
get on in years, to **alhuvq lal; colmoq moq**
get on with, to **colqoq gaq zav hhyul qaol nei qoq**
get out of, to **mul zaq duv; hhe duv; xeiv duv**
get out of repair, to **buv luv biav lav meil biav**
get over, to **ngaq yoq; zaol duv**
get ready, to **dei duv; deissaol taq**
get rid of, to **maq aol zaq**
get sight of, to **he qivq**
get the worst of it, to **maq hhaq**
get through, to **aol dav; taol gof** (Chi)
get to, to **hev**
get together (as people getting together for a project) **bavqpaoq** (26:107); **qiq gao ssaoq; qiq gao zyul; hhallaovq laovq** (46:202)
get to the bottom of it **wuqduq daoqmiq hev nei hu hev**
get under, to **diq xa; diq sil**
get up (from sleep) **piav tul** (13:33); **aqtav tul bavq cei; ju nei diqzoq dav**
get up; wake up **yiuvqsul; yiuvqsul tul**
get wind of, to **naqba gaq lal; hha gaq**
get with child, to **ssaq lav eq; ssaq diq eq**

ghost **neivqzei hhalniul (salsil; buqluq; neivqhaq)**

gibbon **almiuvq miuvqnav; miuvqnav; miuvqnav lavqhhev**
gifted; genius; talented **byulkyul** (50:165)
gill (of fish) **baqbeiv; ngaqsaq baqbeiv**
ginger, wild **meilquv**
ginseng-like plant (pseudoginseng) **salqiq**
girl; woman **ssaqmiq; ssaqmiq miqssaq; ssaqmiqssaq**
girl companion (esp. at a wedding) **miqqoq**
girlfriend; boyfriend **ssaqheiq**
girlfriend; female lover **milmi ssaqheiq**
give, to **bivq**
give a call to **hu li; quhu li**
give a daughter in marriage **ssaqmiq bivq**
give a deathblow, to **cuvtaoq taoqma qiq taoq; diq tov jil nei**
give a guess **caq hu; nyuq hu**
give a false impression **maq ngeel meil zaol duv; zaol hheivq e**
give a hand to **aqqoq a lavqzu bi nieivq teiq e**
give a lift, to **deiq cei miq; aolhaol miq**
give all one's strength to **hhaq hal jav e bavq duv alnei**
give an ear to **naqbol deiq biav alnei nalhaq**
give an order; instruct **miqbivq bivq**
give a thought to **aqciiv nyuq hu**
give a warm reception **gaqzav hhyulqaol nei lav qoq**
give away **aqqoq a bivq miq**
give back **hha huvq**
give back, to (return something) **bivq huvq**
give birth, to **ssaq bo**
give consent **heiq**
give credit **qiq heiq meil maq soq sso e zeil**
give directions, to **galma meiq**
give forth, to **pieiq duv; eil duv; eilgaq**
give ground, to **naoldi di**
give in, to **eilgaq; ssiil**
give medicine **naciq bivq**
give notice, to **miqteil nei eil taq; eilgaq**
give one joy **heiqhel hel miq**
give oneself away **yoqhhaq miavpyuq aoq zaq**
give oneself up, to **yoqhhaq bulduq eil duv; maq kaq lal leil nyuq; yoqhhaq bulduq aoq zaq**
give one to understand **eilgaq; bi gaq; bi hev**
give out, to **eil duv; buvq duv; zaol leivq; hhaqhav tivq qaq; aol qaq alnei maq niv nia**
give over, to **aol saq; baq zei; maq hha deivq qivq al leil nyuq**
give place to **jol duq ssal miq; galma taq miq**
give room, to **yoqhhaq jolduq sulhhaq a bivq miq**
give strength, to **hhaq bi bo lal**
give the cold shoulder, to **maq hu dav movq**
give time, to **zeilzuv maq leiq cal meil loyei nei bi soq**
give to the dogs **aqkeeq a suq neiq**
give up, to **maq aol zaq; aqlavq bavqcei; milhaoq**

aoq zaq; aolnieiq pieiq taq
give warning, to **nyuq gaol leil eilgaq miq**
gizzard **caoqbei**

glance, a **miavhu qiq miv**
glans penis **qoqtevq** (taboo)
glare, to (be bright) **geel nieiv nei geel**
glass bottle **malcavq**
glasses, eye **miavkal**
glass windows **bolliq** (Chi) (26:89)
glistening **sseiv nei**
glistening white **piulseiq pa seiq nei** (11:57)
gloomy; dejected **nalbaoq peelsuq nei**
glorious **daov pyuq; gualyoq** (Chi) (26:102)
glove **lavqbaoq; aqlavq lavqbaoq** (26:73)
glue **ceilqavq** (11:28)
glutinous (sticky) rice **haoqniaoq; eelceivq haoqniaoq**
glutinous (sticky) rice, purple **haoqniaoq niaoqnav; ceilnav**
glutinous rice, yellow **hoqniaoq hoqsiil**

gnaw, to **tevq**
gnaw a hole; bite a hole **kovq byu** (46:201)

go, to **yil** (down); **li** (up)
go; walk **ssuq**
go aboard (boat) **loq hultav dav**
go aboard (plane) **feiljil hultav dav**
go abroad, to **laqnil goqjal a duv yil; dalja nei hev zaq**
go after, to **salzol zaq; qo'leiq zaq**
go ahead, to **miqteil a ssuq; miqteil a aol dav**
go and (vb) **(vb) yil; (vb) yi; (vb) li**
go and come **hhuvq hhuvq daol daol meil**
goal; ideal **lixa**
goal - to realize it **lixa mol**
go along with, to **yolqoq gee; galma ssuqqoq**
go around, to **galhhao hhao**
go aside, to **galma aol bav; miqnieiq aol bav**
go astray, to **galma ssuq bav**
goat **aqcivq**
goat, female **aqcivq civqma**
goat, long-haired **civqbuq**
goat, male **civqbu; aqcivq civqbu**
goat, wild **ceivnav**
goat dung **aqcivq civqxiq**
goat hair **civqhao**
goat meat **civqsaq**
goat shed **aqcivq civqkuv**
go back (from lower place, or west) **hhuvq li**
go back (from upper place, or east) **hhuvq yil**
go bad, to **colcavq pievq; yobuvq pievq**
go behind, to **daoqdaoq hu duv**
go between, to **colkaq gee**
go-between; witness **colkaq**

go beyond (in doing) **yozeiq aol duv; aqzeiq aol dav**
go by, to **ssuq yoq li**
God (sky-God) **Molmil** (cf. **Aqpyuq Miqyeil**)
God (mother/father God) **Molmil dama** (13:40)
'God forbid' **maq aol haoq e miqnieiq**
God knows (only God knows) **Qiq hhaq maq hev. Molmil hev.**
god of nature (see: Mother nature)
god of the sky **aoqtav Molmil**
god of water **wulquvq aqma**
God's 'blessing' **Molmil milhe** (46:189)
go down, to **ssavq; yil; ssavq yil**
go far, to **aol daq qi; ssaoq daq qi**
go forward, to **maq naq meil miqteil pyu ssuq**
go hand in hand with **qiqgao qo'leiq**
go in and out **duv yil dov lal; yil lal suv nei**
go into, to **kevq li; dov li; tao li; tao yi**
go into operation, to **aol kovq**
goiter **beiljil; beiljil lulpuq; lulbeil**
gold; yellow **siil**
golden age ('time of creation') **aoq bei mil bei huvqlavq**
golden bamboo **haqsiil**
golden mean ('middle path') **alkaq galma**
golden monkey **almiuvq miuvqsiil**
gold lump **siildev**
go mad, to **samu mu**
gong **byu'lyu**
gong, sound of **gual, gual, gual** (46:174)
good **meeq; yomeeq**
good for nothing, to be **meeqduq qiq jivq maq jav; pyuqduq maq jav; maq pyuq**
good fortune **gaoqlaoq meeq; gaoqlaoq heeq**
good, very **meeq meeq nei** (11:57)
good at, to be **nia; aol nia**
good behavior **yoqyaovq zaq** (50:189)
goodbye; farewell **eil hhoq zaq** (41:171)
good company, to be **gaq qoq hhyulqoq**
good health **coljol salcav nei**
good-hearted **neema yo'qul; neema meeq; neema yomeeq; neema zaq** (50:188)
good land; fertile land **milmeeq**
good laugh, a (belly laugh) **wuqma eel beivq jil nei**
good-looking; beautiful **zaqqul nei**
good luck **siqhel meeq**
good luck, run of **zeq cavq**
good morning, students **taoqxoq meeq** (A=Chi)
good morning, teacher **laosiil meeq** (A=Chi)
good name; fame **teilsal**
good nature **neema yomeeq**
goodness **meeqduq**
good person **haohaf** (Chi) (26:61)
goods and materials **miaoqgaoq zalgaoq** (50:182)
goods; things **miaoqgaoq** (clf. for a load of goods: **bavq**)

good sky; nice weather **aoqsal sal**
good temper **neema yeil**
good things predestined from birth **deivq meeq**
good to eat; delicious **keel**
goodwill **gaqzav hhyulqaol nei**
good words **saldoq; doq meeq**
go on a journey, to **qao hha li**
goose **oqngyul**
goose, female **ngyulma**
goose, male (gander) **ngyulzal**
goose, wild **zeilngyul**
gooseflesh **aqgav gavsiq**
goose-like **zeilngyul**
go out, to **hhuvduv**
go out (as a fire; a light) **sil**
gopher, bamboo **hupiq**
go quickly **ssuqgeeq geeq; ssuqteiq teiq**
gorge, a **lolxaq**
gorge, to (by eating) **molmievq mieivq tao**
gorgeous; magnificent **zaqdal sseiv nei** (50:74)
gossip; libel people **cuq biav cuq lyul**
gossip back, to **zeivqqoq**
go to school; study **soqhhaq zol**
go to support **ziilyeiq yil**
go to work **safbal** (Chi) (26:29); **xafbal** (Chi)
go up, to **dav; li** (Note: the latter is spoken closer to English 'lay', but without the offgide)
gourd; bottle (for water) **haolpuq**
gourd, wax **salpeel**
gourd musical pipe **laqjeiq**
govern, to (administer) **ziifli** (Chi)
government **zeiffu** (Chi) (50:211); **jelpul; jelful** (Chi) **soqpaq qovq** (lit., 'family of rulers'); **zeiffu qovq** (A=Chi)
government, national **goqjal qovq; aqtav soqpaq; zeiffu qovq** (Chi)
government, provisional; interim **liqsiiq zeiffu** (Chi)
government regulation **zeifji** (Chi) (50:211)
government-supported **jefjif**
government worker **jilgueil gafbuf** (Chi)
government work unit **jilgueil** (Chi)
governor of prefecture **zelza** (Chi)
governor of township **zeifza** (Chi) (50:209)
go work in field **yalsol duv; xalsol duv**

grab, to **koq zaq**
grab and take **koq zaq**
grab back, to **koqpil**
grab with fingers, to **cuv; piav**
graceful; fine; exquisite **salzavnei** (50:199)
gracious, to be **laolxav nei** (**lolxav nei e doq** = a gracious word)
grade (as sixth grade) **nieiqjiq** (Chi) (26:20)
grades; marks (as in school) **ceiqjiq** (Chi) (26:42)
graduate, to **biqniq; biqnieiq** (Chi); **zol saq**

('finished studying')
graduates, school **ziilsiiq qilnieiq** (A=Chi) (50:212)
graft (as a tree), to **cavq**
graft; corruption **hhavq zaq** (50:162)
grain, a (of rice) **ceilsiq**
grain (as stored grain) **zalsiq**
grain bin; granary **ceiljil**
grain crops **ceildu ceilpiul**
grain distribution station and store **liaqguaso** (Chi)
grain for the army **mavqssaq zaqhal**
grain ration coupon **liaqpiaof** (Chi)
grain tax **gaolliaq**
gram, a (wm) **keiq** (Chi) (41:127); **keq** (Chi) (10:13)
gramaphone; phonograph **yaqxil** (Chi) electrical: **dieifcafjil** (Chi)
grammar **doq eil galquv** (50:201); **weiqfaq** (Chi) (50:178)
granary; grain bin **ceiljil**
granary spirit **ceiljil aqma**
grand; solemn **xav nei**
grandchildren; offspring **yuq ssol ssaq** (30:1); **yuq ssol leiq**
granddaughter **yuqma**
grandfather (and term of respect for an older man) **aqbol; aqbol ssalmol; aqbol ssaqmoq**
grandmother (and term of respect for an older woman) **aqpiq**
grandmother and grandchildren **piqssaq** (45:12)
grandparents; old people **aqpiq aqbol**
grandson **yuqpaq**
grant-in-aid; subsidy **bivq laoq**
grape **puqtaol** (Chi); **nibiav alsiq**
grape, wild **siqbiavq; siqbiav nibiav; nigov alsiq; nibiav** (46:157)
grasp; hold onto **nieivq; bawuq** (Chi)
grasp in talons **cuv**
grass (including animal feed) **jahhaq janiul** (33:3)
grass, barnyard **sulma**
grass, long type (good for cattle) **daqhhoq** (28:4)
grass, types of **haqdal; alzil hhoqqeil**
grass; weeds **jahhaq**
grasshopper **albaol**
grass in jungle (high) **biabeeq beeqcaoq**
grave, a **luqbaol; huqbiaol**
grave; serious **yeiqzaof nei** (Chi)
grave of a revolutionary martyr **lifsiif luqbaol baolcaoq** (Chi)
gray (see: grey)
graze, to **civ** (28:4)
greasy; oily **aqyeil biul** (also to be sick of something)
great **hhyudaf** (Chi)
great; big **daov heeq**
great effort **hhaqhav havma tivq**
great-grandchild **leiq**

great-grandfather **aqpyuq**
great-grandparents/great-grandfather **aqpyuq aqda; aqpyuq aqbol**
great-great-grandchild **leiq qiq ciivq e ssaq**
great-great-grandfather **aqpyuq aqda; aqpyuq Molmil**
great many, a **miaq nei qiq puq**
great; mighty **heeqma molma** (50:176)
great-nation chauvinism **dafgoq salweiq zuyif** (Chi)
great people **colmeeq** (34:3)
greedy **hollol** (as when eat fast to get more. op. of **hoqceiq ceiq**); **neema galdav; neema mol** (long heart)
greedy to eat (more than others) **lalsaol saol**
green **niul**
green, very **niul niul nei** (11:57)
green and fresh **niuldeivq nei** (11:58)
green clothing (as soldier's) **alhaoq peilniul** (26:12)
green to extreme **niuldeivq nei**
green viper **ollol eelniul; eelniul**
greet someone (as coming to visit) **doqcavq lal** (11:221)
grenade, hand **se'lieqdaf** (Chi) (50:156)
grey; blue **peel**
grey, very **peelsuq nei; peel pa peel nei** (11:58)
grey cloth **palpeel**
grey-headed person **wuqseil**
greyish **peelsev nei**
grey or blue cap **wuqcaoq caoqpeel** (46:126)
grin, to **hhe ssil**
grin cheekily **eiqxaq laqleiq** (46:148)
grind, to **jiv**
grind into pieces (as by a truck) **leiq pieiv**
grindstone, a **jivluv**
grindstone gears **jivseq**
grind teeth, to **seqpeiq** (13:13)
grind teeth (as in a dream) **seqjiv jiv**
ground, the (earth) **daqhhuq; daqhhaq** (the latter also sometimes means 'island')
ground under, to be (as by a truck) **qiqcei nei leiq pieiv**
ground wire, a **difxeif** (Chi)
group **ba (qiq ba)**; **bal** (Chi) (26:101); **xaozu** (Chi) (50:186)
group (animate) **mavq**
group (inanimate) **dyul**
group leader **xao zuza** (Chi) (50:186); **balza** (Chi) (26:42)
group of people **col mavq** (11:26); **col qiq mavq**
grove, a **albol bolcaoq**
grove, sacred **hhaqma; hhaqma hhaqcaoq**
grow up; increase **pievq; heeq lal mol lal** (said esp. of infants getting bigger) (15:17)
grow up quickly **dav teiqteiq**
gruel, rice **hoqqavq qavqbieiv**

guarantee; ensure eil ceiv (50:7); **baozaf** (Chi)
guard; a herdsman **luvqssaq**
guard, to **luvq; luvq taq**
guard; protect; defend **haol leev** (50:177), **haol luvq; hafweif** (Chi)
guarded road **galluvq**
guard house **diaolbao** (Chi) (26:47)
guardian, a **haol leev col**
guard squad **jihhyufbal** (Chi)
guard, to stand **luvq** (50:207)
guerrilla forces; guerrilla detachment **yeqjiqdyuf** (Chi) (50:199)
guess, to **caq**
guest **daqyao**
  guest, to be **daqyao gee**
  guest, to invite **daqyao kul**
  guesthouse **daqyao xavqduq**
guide; lead; take along **seq; seq to; ziidaof** (Chi)
guide; show the way **tyuq meiq**
guiding principle, a **ziidaof falzeil; galli** (Chi) (50:56)
guide of a great cause; tutor **moqmeiq laosiil** (B=Chi)
gully, a **lolxaq; lolgov**
gulp (sound of drinking water) **guvq**
gums of teeth **seqpeiq**
gun, air (pneumatic, for shooting birds) **miqbev qifqal** (B=Chi)
gun, muzzle-loader ('bird') **alzil miqbev**
gun; rifle **miqbev**
gun barrel **bevsaol**
gun butt **bevdaoq**
gunnysack; bag **dalleil**
gunpowder **miqzal**
gunpowder, to pound **miqzal teil** (11:120)
gunpowder container **miqzal haolpuq**
gun stock (wooden part) **bevhov**
gun, wooden (as to put at the village gate to scare away spirits) **albol miqbev**
Guozhuo (branch of the Hani) **Haqniq e Goqzoqssaq**

H h **soqmiav aqma hholqei xeivq mol e qiq mol**

---

habit **zaol zo**
habitual thief **hyuq zaq zo**
hack; cut **dev**
ha ha (sound of laughing) **haqhaq** (11:21); **heiq heiq** (13:12)
hail **haollu; hollu alsiq; zeiqkeeq alsiq**
hair (body and face) **haocavq**
  hair (head) **ceilkaol**
  hair (leg) **aqkeel haocavq**
  hair (nose) **nalbyuhao; nalmeilhao**
  hair (underarm) **lavqhhuvhaoq haocavq**
  hair, soft body hair (or feather) **saqhao haossaq**
  hair; to pull **ceilkaol hhe** (head); **haocavq hhe** (body); **meiqmoq hhe** (beard)
  haircut; shave **sev** (**wuqduq sev** = shave the head; **meiqmoq sev** = shave facial hairs); **wuqjoq joq** (haircut for a man)
  hair, white **ceilkaol kaolpiul**
half **pav** (**qiq pav** = one half)
half a bucket **taoq ceiv**
half a day **nao pav**
half a dog **keeq pav**
half a gram **keiq pav** (A=Chi)
half a liter **gaolseil pav** (A=Chi)
half a year **huvq pav**
half-day **aoq pav; nao pav**
halfway (as on a path or trip) **gal pav; gal ceiv**
halo (as around sun or moon) **beeljoq**
halter for horse **moq jalsoq** (B=Chi)
ham **hotyu** (Chi)
hammer **diqpuq; saol diqpuq**
hammer for shoeing a horse **maqzavq diqpuq**
hammer, wooden (as to put at the village gate to scare away spirits) **albol diqpuq**
Han (Chinese) language **Niuldoq** (10:1)
  Han (Chinese) nation **Pyulniul; Alniul; Laqbeq**
  Han (Chinese) people **Laqbeqssaq; Pyulniulssaq; Navssaq** (or) **Nav** -- latter only used in proverbs)
hand; arm **aqlavq**
hand, back of **aqlavq lavqnaol; lavqnaol**
hand, to **kavqceq**
handball **se'qeq** (Chi) (50:156)
handcart **setyulceil** (26:63) (Chi)
handcuffs; fetters **saoljul; lavqjul; keeljul**
handful **lavqtuv qiq tuv**
hand gesture **aqlavq lavqhhev**
hand grenade **se'lieqdaf** (Chi) (50:156)
handicraft **segaolniq** (Chi) (34:10)
  handicraft industry **segaolniq** (Chi) (50:156)
  handicraft maker, skilled **lavqqivq ssaq** (50:156)

hand-in-hand; to shake hands **lavqcavq cavq**
handkerchief **lavqsiv**
handle (for a cup) **laqnaq**
handle (for a hoe) **ceiqyyuq**
handle (general) **laqzu**
hand on; pass on (as a custom from the ancestors) **yyuq xal**
hand over (as a ticket) **deiq neiq** (26:91)
handprint, a **lavqxa aqhhal**
handrail; arm rest **lavq dal**
hands and feet **lavq lavq keel keel**
handsome men and beautiful women **miqzaq yozaq**
hand-span (measure of length, from thumb to index finger) **nyultul** (clf. = **tul**) (11:78)
hands to be free (that is, spare time) **aqlavq lov** (26:50)
handwoven cloth **palhav**
handwriting **buvqcuv** (32:3); **soqmiav buvq e galquv** (50:157)
hang, to (cloth) **ceq** (**palnil ceq** = to hang up red cloth)
hang down; bend down (as head) **deiq muvq**
hang on, to **pieiv ceq**
hang over a fire **teiv gee**
hang over something **hhu lu hhe le meil**
hang to death, to **laolceq ceq sil** (26:10)
hang up, to **pieiq ceq**
hang up, to; to tie up **kavq ceq**
Hani **Haqniq**
  Hani ancestor (son of **Taoqpaoq**) **Hhellaoq** (also: a dragon king)
  Hani books **Haqniq soqhhaq**
  Hani condiment of fermented soybeans (a specialty) **Haqniq aqciq**
  Hani language **Haqniqdoq**
  Hani orthography, script **Haqniq soqmiav; Haqniq soqhhaq**
  Hani people **Haqniqssaq; Haqniqcuq** (B=Chi); **Niq** (shortened form used in some proverbs)
  Hani songs **Haqniq lalbaq** (11:37)
  Hani way **Haqniq yo'liq; Haqniq galma**
Haoni (branch of the Hani) **Alsaol; Haoqniq**
happier and nobler **hhyul zeiq pyuq zeiq** (46:123)
happily **neehhyul; salzav nei; hhyulniei nei; hhyul leiq hhyul sil meil; hhyulzav nei; hhyul lul hhyul sav; hhyul sil hhyul lo**
happily; actively **geeq eel geeq nei** (26:16)
happily; smoothly **yosuv nei**
happily, very **salzav pa zav nei; salyo pa yo nei**
happily say **eilheiq qeil**
happiness **siffuq** (Chi) (26:112)
happy, to be **laqheiq qeil** (26:35); **laqhaq qeil; hhyulniq nei; hhyulniei nei; laqheiq qeiltov nei** (26:82); **neehhyul**
happy; bright-hearted **neema bia lil bia loq**

happy experience (cf. Thai: 'sanuk') **sseiqnaol** (Chi) (11:177)
happy, extremely **hhyul sil hhyul lo; daov qeil; maq qivq meil hhyul ya** (46:216)
happy feeling **qeil; sal; salzav nei; neema alyeiv yeiv** ('flowers bloom in heart') (13:16); **neema bia loq nei** (13:16); **hhyulniq nei**
happy village **puvsal sal**
hard; stiff **hhaol**
hard, very (op. of soft) **hhaoljov nei** (11:58)
hard life; suffer a lot **saq sil saq lo; deivq syuq** (the latter implies predestined hardship from birth)
hard of hearing **naqtaoq taoq**
hardship and cold **saq ya gav ya**
hardships and difficulties, to suffer **kyuq sil kyuq lo kyuq** (46:163)
hard up, to be (life is hard) **jol syuq**
hardwood **soqsaol hav albol**
hare; rabbit **toqla**
harm, to **lav kyuq**
  harm; cause injury **kyuq lal e miqnieiq**
harmful to one's health **coljol kyuq lal** (50:175)
harmful trends **maq meeq galquv** (50:16)
harmony; love one another **gaq zaq**
harness for horses (the set) **moqhhav qiq zuvq**
harrow, a **niuqkav; laqkav**
  harrow, to **kav niuqkav**
  harrow a field, to **daolyalkav**
  harrow (deeply) **kavceiq ceiq**
  harrow (here and there) **kavcoq coq**
  harrow (into piles) **kavbaol baol**
  harrow (shallowly) **kavsuq suq**
  harrow made of iron, a **saollaqkav**
harsh; bitter **yeiqkuq** (Chi)
harsh and unreasonable cruelness **taoqgao**
harvest a crop **kalyei se leev; kalyei bavq leev;** (26:82); **leiq leev**
harvest rice, to **ceil yeiq**
harvest season **ceil diq ba'la**
  harvest season (busy time) **ceil diq baoqbeivq**
harvest time **huvqlavq; kalyei se leev tovq**
hat; cap **wuqcaoq**
hat (Chinese style) **leqhev**
hat (Western style) **zalmaof wuqcaoq** (A=Chi) (11:31); **zalmaov wuqcaoq** (A=Chi)
hatch, to (as eggs) **wuv**
hatch chicks, to **hawuv wuv; alwuv wuv** (11:29)
hate, to **saoq sil** (13:39); **saoq; saoq zaq**
haunches of animal **bialhhal**
have, to (general) **wuvq**
have, to (inanimate) **jav**
have, to (large, important) **bo**
have, to (liquid) **daoq**
have a try (in examining something) **salhu; huhu**

have time; free **lov** (11:104)
hawk; eagle **haqzeil**
hawthorn, Chinese **salzal** (Chi)
hazy, to be **juqhyuq hyuqbaq**

he/she/it **aqyoq**
head **wuqduq**
head, back of **naolteev**
head, to nod up & down **wuqduq niei niei nei** (27:11)
head (as head of a military unit) **seza** (Chi) (26:109)
head bent down (as in capitulation) **wuqduq taoqmuvq** (34:15)
headdress for women (outside section) **wuqhuv**
headed by; someone as leader **wuqduq duq** (50:176)
head hair **ceilkaol**
head lice **wuqduq seil; wuqseil** (Note: this is the same as for a grey-headed person, cf. **wuqseil seil** = to become grey-headed)
head lice to be present **wuqseil jol; wuqseil zaol**
headman (or any official of village) **zyuq; zyuqma; zyuqmoq** (note: in most Hani villages the 'ritual head', or; **milguq**, now serves also as 'headman')
headmaster; principal (of a school) . **xaofza** (Chi) (50:187)
head of house **yosaol**
head of station **zafza** (Chi) (50:207)
headquarters of government; capitol of prefecture or province or region **sefu** (Chi) (50:156)
headquarters of government official **yaqmee** (Chi)
heal, to **zaol kaq**
healed (from sickness) **kaq**
health **weifseil** (Chi) (10:13)
health school; nursing school **weifxaof** (Chi)
healthy; comfortable **jolsal; coljol salzav nei**
healthy and strong **meiltaoq nei; hhaqhav havma**
healthy food **zalhhyul** (11:119)
hear, to **gaq**
hear about, to **naqba gaq lal**
hearing immpaired **naqtaoq taoq**
hear from, to **naqba gaq**
hear of, to **naqgaq**
heart (mind) **neema**
heart (physical) **neema neesiq**
heart, in the **neema laqhyul**
heartbeat **neema coq** (10:25)
heartfelt; deep; profound **neema kev nei** (50:149)
heart to beat fast **neema daoqgu daoqgu nei coq**
heart, to be sick at **neema nal** (note: or 'to envy')
heaven; great heaven **aoqma**
heaven; paradise **yeillaolhaol** (50:166)
heaven; sky **aoq; aoqtav** (50:165)
heaven and earth **aoq ssol milcaq**
heaven and earth's vault; firmament **aoqtav laolqaol**
heavy **xao**
heavy (only used of people) **coma; coma jol**

heavy; strenuous **faqzaof nei** (Chi)
heavy, very **xaobaovq nei; xaodeivq nei xaodeivq pa deivq nei** (11:58); **xaojovq nei** (26:93)
heavy heart **neema** xao
heavy job **miaoqma** (11:48); **miaoqkav**
heel **keeldaoq**
hegemonism **qaqqeiq** (Chi) (34:15)
he himself/she herself **aqyo bulduq**
height the same; as tall as **dyulzeil**
heighten; raise **bavq goq** (50:164)
heirarchy; social estate system **deijiq ziifduf** (Chi)
heirloom of the family **dama ssaoqnieiq**
help, to **balhaol** (Chi); **zaol haol; haol miq** (46:121)
help carry burden, to **eq haol**
help each other; be good to one another **yoq meeq sul meeq**
helping hand **lavqcavq aol e**
help lift up **qiq haol** (26:89)
help to do, to **aol haol**
helter skelter; all mixed up **miaoqbeeq**
hemp thread **ziqpav**
hen **hama; aqha hama**
hen, big **malniul** (prov.)
hen, young **aqha hahal**
hen day **ha nao**
hen hour **ha zeq** (B=Chi)
henhouse **ha kuv**
hen year **ha huvq**
herbs **jahhaq janiul**
herbs (edible) **zaq qivq e jahhaq janiul**
herd, to (cows, ducks etc.) **luvq**
herd as an occupation **luvq zaq**
herder (of animals) **zeiqluvqssaq**
herdsman; guard **luvqssaq**
here **xilgei; xa** (**xa hev nei** = to arrive here; **xa alnei** = from here); **yaq a** (**Nol yaq a lal.** You come here. 11:143); **xaq'a** (**xaq a yiv** = come over here)
here and there; this side that side **yul pyu xil pyu** (46:170)
hereditary system **zyuqzuv**
heritage **huqsal sal; zeiq'yul**
hernia, to have **wuvgyuq**
hero **ssilxaoq** (26:104) (Chi)
heroic; brave **yilyao** (Chi)
hero in the PLA **Dao Cyuqssyuf** (Chi) (26:104)
herself/himself **aqyoq bulduq**
hesitate, to **yeqyif** (Chi)
hesitate in mind; remain undecided **maq nyuq ceiv nia** (50:200)
hey! (exclamation) **haqyiq**

hibernate, to **byuq taoq**
hiccup, to **heltev tev**

hide (oneself)   **xeiv hhovq (yoqhhaq bulduq xeiv hhovq**
= to hide oneself)
hide criminal evidence   **zyulmiaoq deiq hhovq**
hide something   **hyuqhheivq**
hiding place   **syu li duq** (13:3)
high; tall   **goq**
high, very   **goqsa nei**
higher quality; noble   **gaolgyuf piziiq** (Chi)
highest degree   **hal goq zeiq; goqsav savma nei goq**
(11:59)
high up, to put   **zaol goq**
highway   **gaollu galma** (A=Chi); **gaolluf galma; galma**
dallul (B=Chi) 11:31)
hill, a   **puvsiq; milcaq puvsiq**
hill, small   **haolteil teilssaq**
hillside field   **daolyal**
himself/herself   **aqyoq bulduq**
hinder, to   **cyuq; deiqcyuq**
hinder; disturb, to   **lav bav; lav bal** (Chi)
hinge; crux   **gualjeif** (Chi)
hip   **juqdev; daoqsiq**
hipbone   **daoqsiq saqyyuq**
hip of an animal   **daoqlaol**
hire labor, to   **aoqhhaq hhel** (lit. 'buy strength')
historical   **yeilbei** (46:216)
historical position   **galhhu jolduq jolhhal**
history   **huvqlavq liqsii** (B=Chi); **liqsii** (Chi);
huvqlavq hultav (34:12); **galhhu miqnieiq**
history, contemporary   **xeifdeifsii** (Chi); **jifdeifsii**
(Chi)
hit, to   **diq**
hit (as to hit horse with a whip)   **hhe ziivq** (13:33)
hit and break   **diq beivq** (11:115)
hit and cause to move   **taoq niv**
hit and hurt   **diq nal**

Hmong; Meo   **Miaoqziissaq; Meiqziiqssaq; Maoqziif**

hoarse voice   **suvq; kaoqsav sav**
hoe (general)   **ceiqhhuvq**
hoe, hooked (for weeds)   **kavngeeq**
hoe, large   **ceiqma; ceiqpaoq**
hoe, mattock   **ceiq**
hoe, short variety   **kavngeeq**
hoe, small   **ceiqssaq lavqdev; ceiqhhuvq hhuvqssaq**
(26:37)
hoe handle, a   **ceiqyyuq**
hoe made of wood   **yavngeeq**
hoes and knives (tools for farming)   **ceiqhhuvq**
miavhhuvq
hold, to   **tuv** (Note: Also the clf. for a handful);
bavq teiq; ciil teiq (aqlavq ciil teiq = to hold
hand, arm - 26:46); **dal teiq**
hold; grasp   **bawuq** (Chi)
hold fast   **hhe teiq**

hold in between **teiq**
hold in mouth **aoq**
hold onto **tuv**
hold up; raise up **bavq cei**
hold up; support **davtuv tuv**
hole **yobyu; aqbyu** (also can mean: vulva)
hole; cave **milbyu**
hole, to dig **duqhovq hovq** (11:44)
hole, to make **leiq byu** (11:161); **yobyu leiq byu; yobyu keq byu**
hole in ground (dug) **duqhovq**
hole in ground (natural) **milbyu**
hole in tree **haoqbaoq**
hole in wall **caqbyu**
holiday (ceremonial) **jolnao**
holiday (refrain from work) **jolnaq naq** (46:141); **hhaqnaq naq**
hollow (not full) **haoqbaoq baoq** (as trees); **kuq** (as fruit); **hovq** (as grain crops)
hollow behind the knee **paoqciivq paoqhhuvq**
home **yovq**
home of brother or sister, or of wife's brother **aqmol bee**
home town **laojal** (Chi)
homework **zoqniq** (Chi)
homonym; homophone **doqteil teilpaoq** (50:168)
honest **jil; jil li jil hevq nei; neema jil** (27:12)
honest; confess; frank **bu'loq nei eil duv** (50:163)
honest; truly **jilhevq nei**
honey **biaq'eel; biaqqul**
honey bee (the kind they raise) **biaqsil**
honey comb **biaqlov**
honey comb (empty) **biaqhovq**
Honghe **Yiqsa; Yiqsav**
Honghe county **Haoqhoqxeif; Yiqsav; Yisav**
Honghe delta **Haoqhoq lolqol**
Honghe prefecture **Haoqhoqzel**
Honghe prefecture capital **Goqjel** (11:176)
Honghe Prefecture Institute of Nationality Studies Haoqhoqzel miqcuq nieiljeso (Chi)
Honghe River **Haoqhoq; Lalsabaqma**
Honghe Town **Haoqhoq**
Hong Kong and Macao (Aomen) **Gahhaof** (Chi) (34:21, 50:56)
honor; dignity **zualyeiq** (Chi)
honor, to (to praise; respect) **saol pyuq miq; bivq hev**
honor; respect; esteem **zyuljif** (Chi) (50:221)
hoof (of animal) **seiq**
hoof of horse **moqseiq**
hoof of pig **hhavqseiq**
hook (for fishing) **ngaq hhovq**
hook (for hanging things) **kavngeeq**
hooligan **colbuvq colcavq zyul**
hoop; band **miavgaol**

hoopoe (kind of bird); cuckoo **hulbu; hulbu aqma**
hoop, iron **saolhhaoq**
hop on one foot **jaqjiq jiq**
hope, to **neenyuq; xilwaf** (Chi)
hope, to; to expect **movq ssa**
horizon **aoqdaoq aoqzeil** (26:14); **caqqiq; aoqkaq milkaq** (50:35); **aoqzeil leilto**
horizontal **bilceiv nei**
horn **kyuldu; kyul; wuqkyul**
horn (metal; wooden; bamboo) **meiqbaq**
horn of buffalo/bull **niuqkyul; kyuldu**
horn of deer **ceivkyul**

horse **moq** (note: in some dialects horse is: **aqmoq**, but this means 'male pubic hair' in the Luchun dialect)
horse, castrated **moqdo**
horse, female (mare) **moqma**
horse, male **moqpaq**
horse, pack **alyeil qeivmoq**
horse, thin **moq moqgov** (11:36)
horse, white **moqpiul**
horseback, to carry on **qeiv**
horse bell **ho'lo**
horse bit **meiqkovq** (11:29)
horse cart **moqcei** (B=Chi)
horse day **moq nao; moq qiq nao**
horse dung **moqxiq**
horse-eye bean **caqdul**
horse feed **moqceil; moqzal**
horse feed, to cut **moqzal yeiq**
horse feed bag **moqceil badu**
horse hoof **moqseiq**
horse hour (in telling hours of the day) **moq zeq; moq qiq zeq** (B=Chi)
horse load **moqqeiv** (13:31)
horse-riding games **moq ziiq seiv seiv**
horse to roll on back in dust **moqpuv puv**
horse's 'flower' (tassle on horse's head) **moqhaoyeiv**
horseshoe **maqzavq** (A=Chi)
horse stable **moq moqkuv** (11:36); **moqkuv**
horsetail **moqmiq**
horse train **malbal** (Chi) (train of horses carrying goods)
horse year **moq huvq; moq qiq huvq**
hospital **naciq ciqyaol; yilyeif** (Chi) (50:196)
hospitality **gaqzav hhyulqaol nei**
hospitalized **yilyeif jol** (50:216)
host **yosaol**
hostess **yosaol aqma**
hostile, to be **hucavq; diqsiif** (Chi - 50:34)
hostile border **diqdyuf geifxeif** (Chi)
hostile element **diqdyuf feilzii** (Chi)
hot (to be) **laol**
hot (to touch) ciil

hot; burning hot **tal** (Chi)
hot; peppery **cil**
hot, very **laolcyu nei** (11:58)
hot season; summer **aoqlaol ba'la**
hot spring **cuq; cuqduq**
hot water **eellaol**
hot-water bottle **sseiqsyudaf** (Chi)
hot with chili **laqpil cil**
hour **se; xaosiiq** (Chi)
hour, one **siiqse qiq se** (26:63) (Chi)
hour; time **siqse**
house, **laqhyul** (clf. = **yaol**)
house, clf. **yaol**
house, inside **laqhyul**
house, large **laqhyul hyulma** (11:177)
house, old & in poor shape **xaolcyuq** (13:4) (clf. = **yaol**)
house, outside **laqnil**
house foundation **laqhyul zaol'al**
household **bee** (13:11); **daofhuf** (Chi)
householder, female **yosaol aqma**
householder, male **yosaol**
house made of wood **daoqma laqhyul** (11:37)
House of Representatives **Zaofyifyeif** (Chi) (50:215)
house site **zaolhhaol**
house, small **xaolssaq; yaolssaq**
how? **halmeil leil**
how are you? **Coljol sal yaq?** (**Sal ya.** = Well. **Maq sal ya** = Not well. **Daov maq sal ya.** Not very well.) (Note; the final particle '**ya**' is only used when speaking of oneself.)
how big? **halhenei**
how do you ....? **halmeil** (vb) (**Soqmiav mol halmeil buvq?** How do you write this character? 11:102)
however; but **yulmeil liq; tyulliq** (11:121) (or); **tyul e liq** - 9:156)
how far? **halmo nei**
how high? **halmiav nei goq**
how long? **halmiav nei mol**
how many? **halmiav miav** (11:103); **halmiav nei**
how many (clf.)? **halmiav nei** (clf) (**Ssaqguq halmiav hhaq jol?** = How many children are here? 11:103, **halmiav mol** = how many things/animals)
how many people? **halmiav hhaq**
how much? **halmiav nei**
how thick? **halmiav nei tul**

Hui nationality (Muslim) **Hyuqcuq** (Chi)
human; person **col; byulssaq**
human beings **byulssaqnaol; byulssaq; colssaq**
humanitarianism **byuldeivq neemeeq** (50:141)
humiliate; insult **eil buvq zaol buvq** (50:182)
hump on an ox **lalbu busiq**
hunchback **daolhhuvq**
hundred **yal**

hundreds **yoyal**
hundred million **milmil; yif** (Chi) (26:75)
hundred thousand **ceil mil**
hungry (& thirsty) **meivq**
hungry (with an empty stomach) **wulziil meivq ziil**
hunt, to **leiq; saq leiq**
hunt barking deer **saqqil leiq**
hunting dog **saqleiq aqkeeq; hhaqkeeq**
hurriedly **teiq li teiq cal meil; teiq sil teiq piav meil** (33:3); **teiq yil teiq lal nei** (26:90); **teiq li cal lal meil**
hurry, to be in a **teiq; neema teiq** ('heart in a rush') (26:30)
hurt (as in an accident) **taoq nal**
hurt; sick **nal**
hurt; tired **kyuq**
hurt someone else, to **lav kyuq**
hurt someone with words **eil kyuq**
husband **huljil; haqjil; haqjil aqda**
husband; man **haqjilssaq**
husbands of older sisters **aqsaoq**
husbands of younger sisters **ssaqmavq**
husk, buckwheat **hhaqgeeq**
husk, rice (outer, cannot be eaten) **haqpeeq peeqhav; peeqhav**
hut **yaolcyuq; yaolbiav**
hut in field **yalqaol**
hybridization **zaqjaol** (Chi) (50:204)
hybrid corn (maize) **zaqjaol ceildu** (A=Chi) (50:204)
hybrid rice **zaqjaol ceil** (A=Chi) (50:204)
hygiene **hhyufseil** (Chi) (50:177)
hyphen **lieiqziifhaof** (Chi)
hymn, a **zafmeisiil** (Chi) (50:204)
hypocrisy **jaqhheivq**
hypocrite (old man) **jaqhheivq aqbol**

I i **soqmiav aqma hholqei hhyuq mol e qiq mol**

I **ngal**
ice **haqnil nilngaoq**
ice, piece of **haqnil nildev**
ice cream **bilqiqliq** (Chi) (11:17)
ice hockey **bilquq** (Chi)
ice to form **haqnil nilngaoq ngaoq**
idea **lulsul** (Chi) (**lulsul diq; lulsul jav** = to have an idea); **qiq heiq nyuq**
idea; method **yiqqeiq** (11:179); **baffaq balfaq**
idea to come **qeiq duv**
ideal; hoped for goal **ssaqguq guqnyuq; lixa** (Chi) (26:110) -- to realize it = **lixa mol** (A=Chi)
idealism **weiqxil zuyif** (Chi) (50:176)
ideals, highest **zyufgaol lixa** (Chi)
identical **paoq**
identity card **seilfeifzeif** (Chi) (50:149)
ideology **neenyuq wuqduq; yifsiiq xiqteif** (Chi)
ideology and moral character **neema meeq dyul**
idiot; fool **aqzoq**

if **(vb) ngaoq (nol li ngaoq** = if you go); **(vb) e ngaoq (aoq sal e ngaoq** = if the weather is good 11:21) see examples in: 11:122
if not **maq ngeel ngaoq; maqnaaq**
if so **tyulmeil ngaoq**
if that's the case **yulmeil ngaoq; tyulmeil ngaoq**
if this is the case **wulmeil ngaoq; yulmeil ngaoq**

ill; sick **nal**
illegal; unlawful **yoliq maq za** (50:49)
illegal act; unlawful practice **faqliq maq za miqnieiq** (A=Chi)
illegally take into custody **yoliq maq za meil nieivq kuv**
illegitimate child **caqssaq**
illegitimate child ceremony **caqssaq cavqkeeq ciil**
illegitimate child's father **caqssaq aqda**
illegitimate child's mother **caqssaq aqma**
ill-gotten wealth **maq zaq haoq zeiq** (50:17)
illusion; fantasy **sal nyuq sal dul** (50:74)

immediately; at once **joq nei; qiq heiq nei; joq ssuq; qiq heiq laltov** (26:24); **qiq quq nei** (13:7); **laltov** (46:139); **qiq haq laltov meil** (30:2)
immigrate, to **colpol pol**
immoral, to be **yocavq duv**
immoral person; hooligan **colbuvq colcavq zyul**
impair; be harmful to **lav sso** (50:48)
impatient, to be **neema cal; neema teiq; neema maq yeil nia; ba cal**

imperialism **difgoq zuyif** (Chi) (26:16) (**Mei difgoq zuyif** = American imperialism - 34:8)
imperialism, to fight against **fa dif** (Chi)
imperialism and feudalism, to fight against **fa dif fa faoljieif** (Chi)
imperialists **difgoq zuyif ze** (Chi)
importance **zaoqyaofxif; zaofyaofxif** (Chi)
impossible (probably) **maq kaq mal naoq**
improve, to **aol meeq; zaol meeq; zaol loq** (as a policy); **jifbuf** (Chi) (34:12), **geisaf** (Chi)
improve; advance, to **xeilzif** (Chi)
improve; become more skillful **meeq li meeq quv** (50:40)

in a hurry **laq cal**
in a moment **ciiv nei**
in awhile **ciiv nei qiq heiq**
in between **alkaq**
incense **xav** (Chi)
incense, to burn **xav keq** (A=Chi)
incisor **moqseq** (lit., 'horse tooth'); **seqma; seqzaol**
incite; instigate **halnil nil** (50:167)
incoherent; uncertain **bil lil bav lav nei**
income **se hha piul; selssuq** (Chi)
incomplete in number, to be **maq luv**
increase (animals, humans, money) **zeq lal; laoq lal**
increase; grow up **pievq**
increase production **zeq lal; laoq lal**
independence **ziifliq geilseil** (Chi) (26:54); **duqliq** (Chi) (34:14)
Indian people **Yiqduvssaq** (Chi)
indignant, to be **civq peiv; neema peil**
indignation; wrath **neessil neehav**
indigo **miaoq; miaoqciq**
indigo fermenting for dyeing **miaoqciq zeil**
indistinct; uncertain **nyuqhhal maq hha** (50:116)
induced abortion **ssaqceiq beq zei** (50:141)
industrialism and commercialism **gaolsalniq** (34:10) (Chi)
industry **gaolniq** (Chi)
industrious; diligent **bel**
inexpensive; cheap **yal**
infect someone (with disease) **eq dovq**
inflamation subsides **xaolyeil**
inflate; pump up **zii** (11:11)
inflation (financial) **piulbuvq buvq** (50:167)
influence **yixa** (Chi); **qeiqliq** (Chi)
information **doqgaq; qiqbaof** (Chi)
in front **meiqsi**
in general **yiqbal; yiqbal nei**
inhale, to **suv**
inherent; innate **yeildeivq** (50:166)
inheritor (man) **luvq sul** (45:24)
initial (as in "initial consonant") **seilmu** (Chi)
initiate; propose **caldaof** (Chi)

initiative **zudaofxif** (Chi)
inject, to **aqhhovq cov** (50:216)
injection (to give) **hhovqma cov; xaolyeil cov** (A=Chi) (10:25); **aqhhovq cov**
injection needle **hhovqma**
inject medicine, to **naciq cov**
injure skin (as by pounding with something) **taoq levq**
injustice **bav e hhafzil** (C=Chi), **maq jil maq hoq hhafzii** (E=Chi) (50:201)
ink **meiqsyu** (11:31) (Chi)
innate; inherent **yeildeivq** (50:166)
innate character; essence; nature **beiziiq** (Chi)
in order to... **balnei** (13:3)
inquire, to **nalhaq loq**
insane person; crazy **samu**
inscribe, to **soqmiav buvq** (50:164)
insect **aqzuq; byuqssaq**
insect infesting bamboo **haqbyuq**
insecticide ('666 powder') **luqluqfei** (Chi) (11:25)
insensitive; numb **zaoqmavq nei**
insert, to **cov tao**
inside (as op. to outside) **laqhyul** (note: this also can mean 'house')
inside (as inside body, pot, village etc.) **hholqei** (10:1, 13:33)
inside; middle **hholqei** (& see 'in the midst of')
inside something, to reside **(vb) caoq** (**Alsiq hholqei alneev caoq**. There IS a seed inside the fruit. 11:49)
insist on; persist in **cuvq teiq**
inspect, to **qo hu** (50:154)
inspect; examine; check up **jeicaq** (Chi)
inspector (for quality); judge **jeifdif col** (A=Chi)
inspire, to **bavq laol** (50:63); **guwu** (Chi) (26:77)
installation; facility **seiqsiil** (Chi) (50:148)
instep (of foot) **keelnaol**
in step, to walk **qiq kov dei nei ssuq**
instigate; incite **halnil nil** (50:167)
instinct **deivqkevq alnei se**
institution **siifniq dalhhyuf** (Chi) (50:155)
institution; office **jilgual** (Chi) (50:79)
institution; system **ziifduf** (Chi) (50:213)
instruct; give orders **miqbivq bivq** (46:155)
instruct (as in driving) **ziilhyul** (Chi) (26:98)
instructor **fudaofyeiq** (Chi)
instructor; teacher; mister; sir **seilse** (Chi) (50:184)
insult; humiliate **eil buvq zaol buvq** (50:182)
intellectual **ziilsiiq feilzii** (Chi) j(50:212)
intellectualize, to **ziilsiiqhuaf** (Chi)
intelligence; information **doqgaq**
intelligence; wisdom **ziifhyuf** (Chi)
intercourse, to have sexual **xavq zaq** (46:132); **zaol zaq**
interested **laqheiq qeiltevq nei** (33:3); **neema laol**

(26:34)
interested, become more **laqheiq lav qeil dav** (34:11)
interesting **hu zaq** (**Milqivq e dieifssi tuvqqil hu zaq** = last night's movie was very interesting. (11:107)
interim; transition **gofduf** (Chi) (50:68)
interim government; provisional government **liqsiiq zeiffu** (Chi) (50:108)
interjection (as a part of speech) **tafciiq** (Chi) (50:163); **gataf ciiq** (Chi)
interjections: **heiq!** (11:141); **oq!** (11:141); **eiqya!** (11:142 - meaning of yes, okay); **eiq!** (11:142-3), **eil!** (11:143); **alyol; aqyoq; alyal** (11:144); **eiq** (sorry, apologetic at times - 11:144); **ei; eif** (11:143); **aqlaqyil** (surprise - 11:145); **hiq** (11:147); **pyu eiq** (11:146); **almiyiq; aqmiqyiq** (11:146), **aq** (11:145); **eiqya** (11:21); **alyol!** (11:21); **ao; aqyaoq** (like oh! - 11:210, 218); **aqhaoq; aqdeiqdeiq; aqhel; peiq**; etc.
international **goqjif** (Chi) (34:15) (as in World Health Organization) (10:13)
international community **goqjif seifhyuf** (Chi)
interrogate, to **ceil loq**
interrupt; break **ceiv**
interrupt someone; disturb someone **gulcaq**
intestine **wul; wulhaq**
intestine, large **wulma**
intestine, small **wulssaq** (of pig: **wulziil ziil**)
in the future **aqkal; aqkal naolhao; galnee salpeiq**
in the midst of **hholqei** (& see 'inside, middle')
in the past **galhhu** (long ago); **eiqsi** (short time)
into **dov**
introduction (to a paper) **doqheiq doq**
introspection; self-questioning **nyuq puv**
in vain **leiqdaq meil**
invalid **meeqduq maq bo** (50:180)
invent, to **yosiivq zaol duv**
investigate **qo ceil** (50:209); **qo ceil qo heq; diaofcaq** (Chi)
investigate a case **zyulleiq leiq** (50:218)
investigate and deal with accordingly **caqzaol** (A=Chi)
investigate the legality of a case **faqliq nei caq heq** (A=Chi)
investigative report **diaofcaq baofgaof** (Chi)
investigative results **qo ceil saq**
invite, to **qoq lal**
invited to a meal **hoqbiol lol**
involved, to be **pav kevq**

iodine deficiency **qiq diei** (Chi)

iron **saol**
iron, piece of **saol saoldev** (11:36)
iron chain **saolbeel**

iron fence; railing **saolkal**
iron filings **saolxiq**
iron fragments **saollyul**
iron pan **saolkaoq**
iron pot **saolcal**
iron rod (sharp) **saolqei**
iron tool **ssaoqsaol**
iron tripod (used as cooking stand) **saolkeel**

irregular **bil bav lal hhev**

irrigated field **deima; loldei** (11:34, clf. **dei**)
irrigated field, large **loqma** (clf. - **loq**)
irrigated fields, terraced **xaldei hhaqjeil**

irrigation ditch **lolgal**
irrigation ditch opening into a field **eelheiq**
irrigation ditch, to repair **caolheiq dav**
irrigation system **syu'lif jeifseiq** (Chi) (50:158)

irritate the nose, to **nalsyuv syuv**

Islam **Yilsiillaqjaof** (Chi) (50:196)

island (or) ground **daqhhaq**

itch, an **alziiv**
itch, to **ziiv; alziiv ziiv** (10:4)
itch (from dirty water) **eelziiv**

it doesn't matter **maq beq sso**

items in a performance **jiqmuq**

it seems **aqmeil** (8:18)

itself **aqyoq bulduq**

ivory **ssama ssaziil**

J j soqmiav aqma hholqei ceil mol e qiq mol

Jack **Jeike** (Chi-Eng)
jackal **heiq'eil aqkeeq**
jacket **peilhaoq; dalyil** (Chi) (26:72)
jacket, quilted **beewul peilhaoq** (26:39)
jade (stone) **niulsiq haqluv**
jade green; green **niul**
jade green tree **niul bol**
jaggery (unrefined brown sugar) **poqbiav biavnav** (11:157)
jail; prison; pig shed **hhavqkuv; laoqgei** (Chi)
jail, to put in **hhavqkuv a nieivq laol; hhavqkuv a nieivq tao**
January (lunar) **Joqzaq siq; Zyuqzaq siq** (A=Chi); **qiqla siq**
Japan **Ssiiqbei** (26:1)
jar; jug **buqssaq**
jaw; mandible **baqxoq**

jealous, to be **miavnal nal; miavnil nil**
jerky; dried beef **niuqsaq saqkuv**
Jesus **Yilsul** (Chi)
jew's harp **laqdiq; meiqbaq** (this can also mean: bamboo flute)

Jiangcheng county **Jalceiq xeif** (46:137)
Jiang Zemin (PRC President and Party Secy.) **Jal Zeqmiq**
Jianshui (city in Yunnan) **Liqngal** (Hani name); **Jeifsyu** (Chi)
Jingphaw (Kachin) **Jilpol**
Jinping county village **Hhaoldal**
Jinshajiang river **Jilsaljal**

job, big; important task **miqnieiq nieiqma** (26:59)
job, to lose **hoqhaoq diq hal** ('throw away one's rice bowl')
job; work **miqnieiq (11:32); aolnieiq** (11:27); **gaolzoq** (Chi); **sseifwuf** (Chi) (26:109)
join; connect **cavq**
join people's army **caljyul** (Chi)
joint (as in arm/hand) **lavqciivq** (26:47)
joint (as in bamboo) **alciivq**
joint (as in bamboo shoot) **aldyuv laolgaol**
joint (as in finger) **nyulciivq**
joints, many (as in bamboo) **lo qil lo cavq**
joke, a **eel doq** (28:4); **hhaqleiq**
joke, don't make a **eelxul taq lav**
joke, to **lav hha; eelxul duv** (28:4); **eelxul lav; hhaqleiq seil**
joke, to make a **hhaqleiq pieiq; hhaqleiq leiq**

jokingly ('half-jokingly') **hhaqleiq qiq pav meil**
joss stick **xav**
joss stick, to burn **xav keq**
joss stick container **xa'luq** (Chi)
joy; joyful **hhyul leiq hhyul sil meil**
joyfully; happily **laqheiq qeiltov nei**

judge, a **colkaqssaq; jeifdif col** (A=Chi)
judge (presiding judge) **seipafza** (Chi) (50:150)
Judicial Bureau **Siilfaqjiq** (Chi) (50:159)
jug; jar **buqssaq**
juice **eelziq** (46:180); **zal'eel**
juice; soup **eelcal cal**
jujube (fruit from a wild tree) **zaozii alsiq** (A=Chi)
July **Siivqla siq**
jump, to **coq**
jump and float **coq bul**
jump into, to **coq tao li** (26:24); **coq puvq**
jumping **keelcoq coq**
jump over, to **coq pyul**
jump up, to **coq cei**
jump up and down **teivluv** (46:139)
jump up and down with joy **daoq gu dil gu coq** (29:4); **daoq luv dil luv meil coq** (29:4)
June **Kuvqla siq**
June festival; swing festival **Kuqzaq zaq; Sseilkuq zaq; Yeilkuq zaq**
jungle; forest **beilcaoq; haoldaol**
jungle cat; wild cat **alhaol; ha'qiq** (lit., 'chicken catcher')
jungle fire (to set) **millaol keq peev**
jungle fowl **haniq**
jungle set aside as sacred for the village **hhaqma hhaqcaoq**
just, to be **dei; dei nei**
just a moment **taq ngeel siq**
justice **gaoldaof** (Chi) (50:61)
justice, criminal (law for) **xiqsiif sufsaof faq** (Chi) (50:189)
just now **eiqsi**
just right, to be **ciivnei za**

k K k K k K

K k soqmiav aqma hholqei ceil tivq mol e qiq mol

Kachin (Jingphaw) **Jilpol**
Kaduo (a branch of the Hani) **Kaqdol**
kangaroo **paltaol hucavq**
kapok tree **lalbiaol biaolbol**
kapok tree blossoms **lalbiaol alyeiv**

keep, to **taq**
keep; preserve **ssyuq taq**
keep apart, to **lav hhoq; bi hhoq**
keep eyes on, to **hu teiq; hu cuv**
keep watch; look after **hu taq**
kernel; seed; bean **neevsiq**
key (to lock) **zovqdul**

kick with foot **teiv**
kidney **hhoqsiq**
kill, to **seivq; diq tov; diq sil; diq seivq; zaol sil**
kill by beating **diq sil** (also means: **beat out a fire**)
kill by cutting **dev tov** (as a snake) (11:220); **dev sil**
kill; cause to die **zaolsil**
kill oneself, to **yoqhhaq bulduq seivq**
kill out; wipe out **zaol mei**
kilogram **niqjil** (B=Chi); **gaoljil** (Chi - 41:127)
kilometer **gaolli** (Chi) (26:89)
kind; a type (of thing) **qa** (**qiq qa** = one kind of thing)
kind; good-hearted **neema nee meeq**
kind; loving **gaq li gaq zav nei**
kindergarten **toq'eqso** (Chi)
kind-hearted **neema yeildo nei**
king; official **aqhhol** (used of dragon) (11:210); **zyuq; zyuqma; zyuqmoq**
king cobra **ollol eelkol kolma**
kingfisher (brd) **cevq'aqma**
king in a kingdom **baovlao laoqyevq**
kingly; royal (see: royal)
kinship, patrilineal **paqqa ciiqyeil**
kiss (on the face) **cul; baqcul cul**
kiss (on the mouth) **meiq cavq cavq zavq**
kitchen **savqduq**
kite **soqhhaq haqzeil**
kitty **almil milssaq** (29:4)

knead, to **lavqnuvq nuvq**
knead thoroughly, to **lavq nuvq lavq xeiv** (it also means: to work hard)
knee **paoqciivq**
kneecap **paoqciivq saqyyuq**
knee hollow (back of knee) **paoqciivq paoqhhuvq**

kneel down **paoqciivq tuv**
knife (genl.) **tojeil**
  knife for cutting grass (made of bamboo) **sapav**
  knife for cutting greens & vegetables **tobaq**
  knife for dissecting **keqssaq**
  knife, wooden (at village gate to scare away spirits) **albol tojeil**
knit, to ziivq; **hhavq**
knitted sweater, a **maoqyil peilhaoq** (A=Chi)
knobs, to have **taoqsiq siq teiq**
knock (on door) **diq ho; tuv ho**
knock (on door or table with knuckles) **tuv; diq**
knock at head with knuckles (taboo action) **wuqkev kev**
knock down; beat down **diq leeq** (26:17)
knock over (as a tree, post) **taoq puv** (26:99)
knot, a **taoqsiq**
knot, a loose **taoqsuv** (tie a loose knot = **taoqsuv suv**; to tighten a loose knot = **hhe siivq**)
knot in thread **kaolsiq bi siq**
know; to see (as to see through something) **hu duv**
know, to (understand) **hev**
know by experience **hha hev** (50:165)
know each other, to **miavpyuq hev; sseifsiiq** (Chi)
knowledge, basic **ziilsiiq** (15:title, 26:50, 50:212)
knowledge; learning **xoqweif** (Chi) (50:191)
known by all people **dalja nei hev zaq**
know nothing **sev nei maq cyuq**

kohlrabi **guqqil**
kowtow **wuqduq taoq**

Kunming **Kyulmiq** (11:33 - pf.); **Kueilmiq** (Chi)
  Kunming, old name **Guqhaq**
Kuwait **Kolhhyulteq** (Chi)

L l soq miav aqma hholqei ceilniq mol e qiq mol

labor **laoqdaof** (Chi); **miqnieiq**
labor, to **miqnieiq aol; miq aol** (46:156)
labor, physical **miaoq miaoqhav** (50:165)
Labor day **Laoqdaofjiq** (Chi) (26:112)
labor union **gaolhyuf** (Chi)
lac-making insect **seqnil** (**seqnil pieiq** = to raise such insects)
lacquer **qilgualqiq** (Chi)
lacquer tree **qiq albol**
lacquered, to be **geeqsev tav**
ladder **davxov**
ladle **haolpuq neecev; neecev; kuqcavq**
lag behind, to **ya duv laq e** (26:2)
lag behind (in sense of pulling group down) **aqkeel hhe** (26:43)
'lag behind Hani' **ga dov Haqniq**
Lahu **Lalhuq** (10:pref.); **Lalhuqcuq; Lalhuqssaq; Kalgyu; Kalgyussaq**
Lahu language **Lalhuqdoq** (10:pref.)
lair, a; nest **beeq**
lake, huge (sea) **lao'laoma**
lake, large **luduq duqma** (26:117)
lame, to be **qeiq** (also it means: unbalanced, as a load on a horse)
lame (crippled leg) **aqkeel keelqeiq; keelqeiq**
lamp **aldovq; dovqhovq; dieifdeil** (Chi)
lamp to shine **aldovq bia**
lamp, big **aldovq dovqma**
lamp, oil **xalyiu aqdal; hhaqcil aldovq**
lamp, small **aldovq dovqssaq**
lamp, to be burning **aldovq dovq** (11:29); **dovqkovq; aldovq qo**
lamp, to light **dovqkovq; aldovq dovq**
lampblack **hhaqcil aldovq; miqsavq**
lamp burning brightly **aldovq dovqma bia nei**
lamp chimney **aldovq dovqhovq**
lamp wick **aldovq dexi** (B=Chi)
Lancang (Mekong) River **Laqcaljal lolbaq** (A=Chi)
land; country **milcaq; milhaoq**
land; lord of the land **milluvq milsaol**
land (burned by fire) **millaol laoldaol**
landlord **diqzu** (Chi) (26:1)
landlord, big **daf difzu** (Chi) (34:7)
land mine **diflueiq** (Chi)
land reform **tudif geigeiq** (Chi) (26:16, 50:170); **tugei** (Chi) (26:15)
land reform revolution **tudif geiqmif** (Chi)
land rent (for a field) **xalpav** (50:36)
landslide, to have a **milbiav biav**
language; word **doq**

language and literature **yiweiq** (Chi) (50:201)
language family **doqheiq loquv** (50:201)
languidly **moqzei nei**
langur monkey **almiuvq miuvqniul**
lantern **madeil aldovq** (A=Chi)
lap **baoltavq**
lap up; lick **mievq**
lard (pig) **hhavqcil; aqhhavq hhavqcil** (11:35)
lard jar **hhavqcil buqssaq**
large in size **yoheeq**
large intestine **wulma**
larynx **kaoqciivq**
last; endure **civ teiq**
last, the **ciiqjesif** (Chi)
last (the very last) **naolhao hao'li** (46:169)
last month of the year **huvqyul siq**
last one (clf.) **naolhao haoli (clf)** (**naolhao haoli qiq hhaq** = the last person 11:68)
last night; yesterday evening **milqivq**
last part, the **naolhao pyu**
last time **aqmil qiq jol**
last year **milnaohuvq**
late (as 'late rice') **le**
late (vb) **(vb) le** (**lal le** = to come late)
late (in time) **mia** (**tul e za nei mia** = get up a little late - 11:106)
late maturing **le**
later; in the future **aqkal; naolhao; aqsal** (46:138)
later (ones) **naolhao naoq**
laugh, to **eel**
laugh at someone, to **eel zaq**
laughed at by others **eildaq luvq**
laughing and joking **xilxil halhal** (Chi)
laughter, sound of **eel teil**
laugh until tired **eel qaq**
launch, to (as a program) **keilza** (Chi)
law, universal **pupieif gyulliq** (Chi); **yiqbal gyulliq** (Chi)
law and discipline **faqji** (Chi)
law court **faqyeif** (Chi) (50:45)
lawful age to marry **seqdeil yildeil alhuvq**
lawful procedure **faqliq sesuq** (Chi) (50:45)
lawless, to become **aoqtaoq miltaoq** (50:180)
laws and decrees **faqlif** (Chi)
laws and regulations **faqliq faqgyul** (Chi) (50:45)
lawn, a **deihhaol**
lawyer **liqsiil** (Chi)
  lawyer for defence **eilhaol liqsiil** (B=Chi)
lawsuit document **bu zaq e weiqjeif** (C=Chi) (50:160)
lawsuit; litigation **bu zaq** (50:160)
  lawsuit regulations **bu zaq faqliq** (B=Chi) (50:160)
lay; spread **deiqhoq**
lay bricks, to **meelbiav ziivq; caqbiav ziivq**
layer of something **lov** (**qiq lov** = one layer)
lay up (as money in a bank) **toq taq; leeq taq**

lazily **dyulkuq nei; zeiqmo nei**
lazy; bad **dyul; byuldyul dyul**
lazy; degenerate lalga
lazy; not move **maq niv**
lazy person **byuldyul; colpeel**
'lazy snake' **ollol beivdev**

lead, to **seq to** (to lead by going ahead); **lidaof** (Chi) (26:101)
lead along (as path) **galseq seq** (guide - 11:42)
lead along (by pulling) **hhe to**
lead animal (as horse) **ciil teiq**
lead astray **qo bav** (46:122)
lead by hand; guide; take along (animate) **seq**
leader (to be the head) **wuqduq duq; galseq seq e col**
lead (metal) **qeil** (Chi)
lead souls, to **sollal seq** (46:191)
lead the way, to **daol**
leaf, a **alpavq**
leaf, bamboo **haqpavq**
leaf, dry **alpavq pavqkuv; alpavq pavqkuq**
leaf, fresh **pavqsiivq**
leaf, green **alpavq pavqniul**
leaf, yellow/brown **alpavq pavqsiil**
leaf 'harp' (make music using a leaf) **pavqbil**
leaf lard **alpavq hhaqcil; bialcil**
leaf, red **pavqnil** (46:179)
leafstalk of palm tree **sseilhov bavqpov**
leaf which is soft **pavqnaoq**
leaf whistle **pavqbil**
  leaf whistle, to blow **pavqbil meel**
leaf, yellow **pavqsiil** (46:157)
League member **tueiqyei** (pf.); **tuaqyeiq; tyuq yeiq** (Chi)
  League member fee **tueiqfeif** (pf.); **tuaqfeif** (26:74) (Chi)
leak, to (liquids) **duv**
lean, to **lol dal; leq dal**
lean against **deiq niq**
lean meat (very little fat) **saqnil**
lean on; rely on **dal**
leaning to one side **bil lil yovq loq meil**
learn (from doing) **zaol zol**
learn (from studying) **zol**
learn from (as learn from the people) **xoqxiq** (Chi) (26:67)
leather **saqgeel**
leather bag **saqgeel paltaol**
leather case **saqgeel baoqkev**
leather shoes **saqgeel seivqnaov; saqgeel seiqnaov**
leave behind **taq**
leave; separate **hhoq**
leave home, to **laqnil duv**
leave something behind (forgetting it) **nieil qav**
leaving school **xoqxaof hhoq** (A=Chi)

leech (lives in water) **aqxeivq**
leech (lives on land) **pavqkuq aqxeivq**
leeks **guqciv**
left deviation (pol) **zo'qi** (Chi) (50:222), **zo** (Chi)
left foot **qalkeel**
left hand **qallavq; jaqqal**
left over **aqzeiq; yozeiq**
left side **jaqqal; jaqqal pyu** (26:99); **qal pyu; qal pyu baq**
leg (general term for leg and foot) **aqkeel**
leg (lower part, knee down) **bollo**
leg (thigh of chickens) **buldul**
leg (thigh of humans) **saqpiaq**
legal case, a **faqliq e miqnieiq** (A=Chi)
legal effect **faqliq xaofliq** (Chi)
legal procedure **faqliq ceiqxif** (Chi)
legal provisions **faqliq eilceiv** (A=Chi)
legal representative **faqdif deifli col** (AB=Chi)
legal sanction **faqliq nei ssiv teiq** (A=Chi)
legal system **faqziif** (Chi) (50:45)
legal weapon **faqliq wu'qif** (Chi)
legend; story **dudaq; yeilgaq** (Chi) (32:3)
leggings, men's **keeltov; keeltov tov** (to wind them around the legs - 11:28)
leggings, women's **keelbaoq**
leg hair **aqkeel haocavq**
leg joint **keelciivq** (26:47)
lend, borrow **ngaq; pal**
Lenin, his complete works **Liqniq Qeiqjiq** (Chi)
Leninism **Liqniq zuyif** (34:5) (Chi)
leopard; panther **haqssiiq; haqssiiq ssiiqcil**
leprosy, to have **alpeel nal; niuqbaoq nal** (the latter may signify another type of skin disease)
less **naoqzeiq**
less in number (not many) **aqxu**
lesson **kof** (Chi)
lesson; moral (as 'the moral of the story') **jaofsyuf** (Chi)
lesson, to have **safkof saf** (Chi)
let go; release **pieiq; pieiq duv; faf** (Chi)
let me (vb) **(vb) nial (meiq miq nial** = here, let me teach); **kal (Ngal aol kal.** Let me do it.)
let others know; tell others **aqqoq a bi hev miq**
let's (vb) **(vb) kal; (Ngaldu zol kal.** Let's study.) **(vb) joq**
let's (imperative particle) **ssa (aol zaq movq ssa** = let's do it)
let's go **ssuq kal yoq**
letter (consonant) **fuyil ziifmu** (Chi)
letter (vowel) **yeiqyil ziifmu** (Chi)
letter (written); a note **tiaoqzii** (Chi)
letter of the alphabet **ziifmu** (Chi)
letter; paper; book **soqhhaq**
level; flat **dei**
leveling board, a **teilbiavq; biavq**

lever **ngaoqdul**

liabilities; debts **zeifwuf** (Chi) (50:206)
libel someone, to **eil buvq; cuq biav cuq lyul** (the latter is more 'to gossip')
liberalization **ziifyeqhuaf** (Chi)
liberate, to **gei'faf** (Chi) (26:12)
library **soqhhaq taqyaol; tuqsulgua** (Chi) (50:170)
lick, to **mievq**
lid, a **piqkaq**
lid of Chinese pickling jar (keep water in the collar of it to keep it airtight) **buqssaq naqpavq**
lie, to **aqmiaovq miaovq; jaqhheivq hheivq; moqlevq levq; eil leivq**
lie; cheat; boast **moqlevq levq zavq; aqmiaovq miaovq zaq**
lie down, to **wuqbiavq biavq; biavq**
lie on back **silteil teil**
lie on stomach **moqcaoq caoq**
life **wuqhol** (10:22) (cf. **coljol** = one's life, a person's life - 10:22) (**wuqhol liq maq movq meil** = with disregard for life...); **seilmif** (Chi) (15:title); **seilhoq** (as to give one's life for the country) (Chi) (26:73)
life, daily **seilhoqpyu** (Chi) (26:108)
life, long **ssilbo; waf syuf** (Chi) (26:19)
life, short **ssil covq**
life, to save a **wuqhol boq**
life, whole **qiq ssil aqlo meil** (26:120)
life imprisonment **qiq ssil nieivq kuv** (50:180)
life is hard; to be hard up **jolsyuq; jolsaq**
lifeline; life blood **ssilkov** (50:151)
life span **ssil; colssil** (26:55)
lifetime, one **qiq ssil aqlo** (26:45)
lift, to **deiq cei**
lift up, to **qiq; qiq cei** (also the idea of carrying with hands); **ciiltul** (as to lift up a fallen child - 26:11)
ligament; muscle; vein **saqguq**
ligation (for sterilization) **jiqzaq** (Chi)
light, a **aldovq**
light, white **bia; bawuq nei**
light a fire, to **dovq; keq dovq**
light a lamp **aldovq keq dovq** (11:135)
light burden **alyeil pial**
light in weight **pial**
light in weight, very **pialseiv seivssaq nei; pialkul nei** (11:58,59); **pialsev nei**
lighter, a **miqdiq** (This is also used for flint etc. used in making fires.)
lightning, to flash **aoqmiaovq miaovq**
lightning bolt **salcuvq** (note: probably what they find and consider to be 'lightning bolts' are stone age axe heads and the like, which they find in the ground, and consider to be the items which have

split trees open that have been stuck by lightning)

like ... **aqmeil**

like; same as **aqmeil ngeel** (10:11); **laoqmeil**

like; to be friendly with **hhyul; qeil**

like, to; to favor **hu dav**

like (vb) (as like to do something) **(vb) qeil (zaq qeil** = like to eat - 11:157)

likely **naldul meil**

like that **yulmeil** (11:20) (as in: 'do like that')

like this **xilmeil** (11:20) (as in: 'do like this')

lilac flowers **meilyeiv**

lily **loqyav**

lime (powder) **luvleil** (11:81)

limited time **pieivto**

limits of authority **hhaqhav laol** (50:139)

limp, to **piqqeiq meilssuq**

limp, to become **piqqeiq**

limp and weak, to be **yogov gov**

line, a **galkov**

line (as a line of print in a book) **kov**

line (as in writing) **daol**

line (as on a road; a political line) **galma luqxeif** (B=Chi)

line (clf.) **kov**

lined up **zeil do nei** (11:216)

Lin Shaoqi (see: Liu Shaoqi)

lines of hand **lavqkov**

linguist; philologist **yiyeiq xoqjal** (Chi) (50:201)

link, a **naqhhaoq**

lip **meiqluq; meiqjil**

lip, cracked **meiqcaq**

lip, cupped **meiqcil**

lip, lower **aqhhuv meiqzu**

lip, thick **meiqlev**

lip, thin **meiqluvq**

lip, upper **aqtav meiqjil**

liquor **zilbaq; albaq** (46:205)

liquor (made of sticky rice) **zilbaq zilqul**

listen; ask **nalhaq**

listen carefully **naqbol biav nei**

listen; obey **nalhaq**

Lisu **Liqsul** (Chi); **Liqsulcuq; Liqsulssaq**

Lisu language **Liqsuldoq** (10:pref)

liter **seil** (Chi)

literate, to become **toqmaq** (Chi) (lit., 'take off the cap of illiteracy')

literature **weiqxoq** (Chi) (50:178)

literature and language **yiweiq** (Chi) (50:201)

literature types **ticeiq** (Chi) (50:165)

litter (as of pigs) **beeq (hhavqssaq xil beeq** = this litter of pigs - 11:87)

little, a **alciiv; za nei; zaza nei (Aqyoq miavpyuq za nei nav.** His face is a little black. 11:107)

little; small **nil**

little better **alciiv kaq**
little bit **za nei; naoq** (10:15)
little while, for a **za nei qiq savq**
Liu Shaoqi **Liuq Saofqiq** (Chi)
live, to **deivq**
live happily, to **jolqil xa; jolsal**
livelihood **miqnieiq**
lively; actively (as of children) **koqteil qei nei** (11:167)
lively; bustling with excitement **sseiqnaof** (Chi) (26:66)
lively; vigorous **deivq hhuvq deivq la xeiv nei; deivq hhuvq nei** (50:151); **seildaof hoqboq** (Chi)
liver **caoq**
  liver of fowls (chicken, duck, goose, etc.) **caoqbei**
  liver of pig **hhavqcaoq**
living, to make a **wuqleev leev zaq** (33:3)
living area **jolduq jolhhal**
living things **yodeivq ssaq** (50:151), **yossaq** (45:61)

lizard **piaqyiq laqjaq**
lizard (lives in water) **eelssaol**

loach (type of fish) **ngaqjul**
loafer (lazy person) **coldyul; colga**
load (for a pack-animal) **qeiv** (**moqqeiv qiq qeiv** = one horse load)
load (for a person) **alyeil** (**alyeil xao** = to have a heavy burden)
loan from government **jolqil** (Chi) (11:93)
location, a **milnia**
lock **zovq** (clf. = **zovq** - 11:34)
lock, to (as a door) **xoq tovq**
lock, to (or to be locked) **xoq laol**
lock, to lock it **zovq piq**
lock (made of wood) **dalmiaq; dalxoq**
lock box **baoqkev xoq**
locust; grasshopper **albaol**
lodge, to **xavq**
lofty; noble **gaolsaf** (26:55) (Chi)
log **daoqma** (11:159)
logical **loqyiq** (Chi)
lonely and sad **hhaqbieiv** (46:175)
long **mol; ja'la**
long (of things) **molca nei**
long, long ago **galhhu; galhhu aqbei; galhhu wul galhhu** (46:200)
long, very **molca cama nei** (11:57); **molca pa ca nei** (11:132)
long ago; before **galhhu**
long ago; very **galhhu aqmil**
long distance **molca nei; gal heeqsa nei**
long distance, far away **galheeq heeq** (10:13); **galheeq pyu; galheeq sav nei; galma mol**
longer **mol zeiq**

longest **hal molzeiq** (farthest away)
long for; love **gaq**
long history **sal ssil sal lo**
long life **ssil bo**
long march, the (10,000 li = 5,000 km.) **wafli caqzeil** (Chi) (50:175)
long time **qiq savq hev; mol; caqqil** (Chi)
long-wearing (as clothing) **zil** (11:119)
look; see; read **hu**
look; watch **salhu**
look after; keep watch **hu taq; bavq qu**
look alike **aqmeil** (& see 'look like')
look and see **hu mol**
look at **hu**
look back and forth, to **siq hu naol hu**
look behind **naolhao pyu hu**
look down on **hu nil**
look for, to **salqo; qo**
look for and find **ceil duv**
look for food **wuqdeiq leiq e**
look intently **miavjul jul**
look like **dul** (& see 'look alike')
look nice; pretty **husal; huzaq**
loom (for weaving) **palhhavq naolgul; naolgul; naolnieil**
loom pedal **keelnaoq dalpav**
loose, to be **juq bieiq nei**
loosen, to **bieiq (alcav bieiq** = loosen the cord)
loosen; relax **pieiq juq**
lord; ruler **soqpaq (soqpaq gee** = to be the lord; ruler)
'lord of the fireplace' **yuqduq milsaol** (13:3)
'lord of the land' (local gods) **milsaol; caoqsaol; milzyuq** (in: **aoqzyuq qiq mavq gee; milzyuq qiq mavq gee** - 30:2); **milluvq milsaol; milsiil aqma; milsaol aqpyuq**
'lord of the land', to offer to **milsaol lol** (46:78)
loris; slow loris **almiuvq miuvqlaol**
lose; lost **bial**
lose, to **kyuq**
lose, to (as in a battle) **maq diq hhaol**
lose hope, to **hhaqbieiv bieiv** (50:152)
lose in business **aol leiq; zaol leiq**
lose one's soul **sullal bal**
lose taste; fade in color **bioq**
lose temper, to **civqbaoq beil; saqbaoq beil**
lose the way, to **milmu mu**
lost, to be **ga bial; bial**
lot of, a **yoju ju meil**
lotus **liqhaolgei** (Chi)
loudly **yoteil teilma** (26:61)
loud sound, very **doqteil teilma** (26:10)
loud speaker **lalbaq** (Chi) (26:60)
louse **seil**
louse, buffalo **niuqseil**

louse, chicken **haseil**
louse, cow **niuqseil**
louse, head **wuqseil**
louse eggs **seilwuv**
love; beautiful **gaq zav hhyul qaol nei**
love, to **gaq; gaq zaq** (latter is reciprocal); **hhyul** (11:39); **neegaq** (11:28); **gaq na; hhyul lal**
love, to be in **baqjol jol**
love, to fall in **baqhhyul**
love each other (take care of each other) **gaq zaq; gaq zaq hhyul zaq** (10:pref., 26:103)
love each other dearly **gaq zav hhyul qaol nei**
lovely **gaqzav nei**
love matters (courting; flirting, etc.) **baqsal**
love matters (learn how to court) **baqsal zol; baqhhyul hhyul zaq** (46:208)
love more; love best **qeil zeiq**
love one another **gaq zaq**
love one's country; patriotic **hheifgoq** (Chi)
love or like something **qeil**
lover **milmi ssaqheiq; ssaqheiq; baqmeeq; aqbaq; baq; bavq; bilmi ssaqheiq**
lover, to seek a **baqsal sal**
love songs **baqhhyul aqzil; yohhyul aqzil**
love very much **qeil sil**
loving, very **gaqliq gaqzav nei** (26:104)
loving and kind **gaqliq gaqzav nei**
low **biov; yobiov** (11:56)
lower jaw; mandible **meiqdaoq**
lower leg **keeldu**
lower lip **aqhhuv meiqjil**
lower part; bottom **daoqdaoq**
lower part of village **galheiq**
lower place **dogee** (11:32)
low place in road **duqhaoq**
lower section **aqhhuv**
lower side; down below **aqhhuv pyu**
lower side of village zaoldaoq
loyal; faithful **zaolceiq** (Chi) (50:214)

lubricate, to **hhaqcil leiqju**
Luchun (region of the Hani in China) **Luqcyul; Dolnia** (the Hani term); **Dolnia Luqcyul** (B=Chi) (11:126)
Luchun dialect of Hani **Dolnia doq** (the name of the dialect used in this dictionary)
luck **yeilceiq**
luck, good **siqhel meeq**
lucky day; propitious day **nao meeq**
lump (on body) **saqlu**
lump of earth **puqhul**
lunar eclipse **ba'la neivqkeeq zaq** (50:203)
lunar halo **ba'la beeljoq**
lung **povq**
lung disease (sometimes pneumonia) **povq nal (duv lal)**

(10:22)
Luomei branch of the Hani **Lolmeil**

lying on one's back **silteil nei (26:32)**
lymph node **saqlu**
lymph node (groin) **lulsiq**

M m soqmiav aqma hholqei ceil saoq mol e qiq mol

machete **miavdo** (A=Dai)
  machete for cutting firewood **miavdo** (A=Dai)
  machete for cutting weeds (hooked) **miavhhuvq** (A=Dai)
machine **jilqif** (Chi)
machine gun **jilqal** (Chi); **miqbev jilqal** (B=Chi)
mad; insane **mu; colmu mu; samu mu**
mad dog **aqkeeq keeqmu; keeqmu mu**
mad person, a **samu; colmu**
magazine **zaqziif** (Chi) (50:204)
maggot **lutaoq**
magic **faq** (Chi); **moqsuq** (Chi)
magistrate, county **xieifza** (Chi)
magnet, a **saolmiaoq**
  magnetic core **ciiqteq** (Chi)
magnificent and brilliant; open and above board **bia lil bia loq** (50:65); **zaqdal sseiv nei**
magpie **covqbiavq; covqbiavq aqma**
maiden **miqdavq** (taboo)
mailman; postman **soqhhaq heilneiq col** (50:169)
maimed; disabled **yuvq seil maq daol**
main (as the main one) **zaoma**
  main body; principal part **zuti** (Chi)
  main body of an article; letter **zeifweiq** (Chi)
  mainland **dafluq** (Chi)
  mainstay **guqgaf** (Chi)
  main subject (as a subject of study) **niqwuf** (Chi)
major person; dynamic leader; specialist **guqgaf** (Chi)
make an appointment **doqtaq eilceiv**
make a bed, to **hhaoqzao zao**
make a living, to **aol zaq**
make peace, to **zaol sal**
maize; corn **ceildu**
make; do **zaol**
make, to (as a speech) **gee**
make a face (with eyes) **deiq ssil**
make a face (with mouth) **deiq cul**
make a mark (notch) in wood **seqtevq**
make a plow or harrow **taol**
make to be **gee zaq** (note: can also mean 'to talk and laugh at')
make trouble, to **zaol beeq**
make-up, to put on **zaqdal zaol duv**
make way; move out of the way **xeiv yoq**
malar bone; cheekbone **baqkyul**
malaria **piaqcao cao**
male **haqjil aqda** (female = **haqmiq ssaqnaol**)
male (suffix) -- **paq** (**yuqpaq**); **da** (**haqjil aqda**); **pyul** (**hapyul**); **zal** (**oqzal**)
male animal (for some) **aqpyul**

male dog **aqkeeq keeqhhul**

man **ssaqyo; ssaqyossaq; haqjilssaq** (11:30)
man; husband **haqjilssaq**
manage, to **aol zaq** (50:91), **guei'li; gua'li** (Chi) **baf** (Chi)
manage in good order **aol soq; piav soq piav leev**
management **xiqzeif guei'li; gua'li** (Chi)
management, planned **jifhuaf gua'li** (Chi)
management and administration **aol zaq haol leev** (50:91)
manager, a **zagyuf** (Chi) (50:207); **jilli** (Chi)
mandible; lower jaw **baqxoq**
mane of horse **laolbiaq; laolbial; moq laolbiaq**
manger (for horse) **moqloq; moqzal hoqloq; hoqloq**
mango **mamoq alsiq** (cf. **malmoq alsiq**) (A=Dai)
manpower **colhhaq** (11:115)
mantis, praying **moqpaq laqsal**
manure (as fertilizer) **zeiqkeeq**
manure, lump of **keeqhul**
manure heap **zeiqkeeq keeqqu**
manure pit; compost pit **keeqduq; zeiqkeeq keeqduq**
many **miaq; miaq nei; miaqlaq meil; halmiaq nei**
many (clf) **meenia** (clf) (**meenia hhaq** = many people)
many; excessive **miaq gaoq**
many, very **miaq gaoq pa gaoq nei** (11:58); **miaq pa miaq nei** (11:57)
many kinds **hal qa hal qa** (30:1)
many kinds **ceil qa yal qa** (46:217) (lit. 'tens of kinds, hundreds of kinds')
many of; a lot of **yoba yoba meil**
many people, many words **col miaq doq miaq**
many years **meenia ceil huvq**
Mao's Thoughts **Maoq Ceiqdaol Siilxa** (26:106)
Mao Zedong **Maoq Ceiqdaol** (Chi) (34:7); **Maoq Zuxiq** (26:54) (**Maoqceiqdaol** - 34:6) (Chi)
marble from Dali **Dafli haqluv**
March (the month) **Saoqla siq**
mare (female horse) **moqma**
margin; edge **bialdaoq bialzeil**
mark, a **laqcaq; lavqcaq**
mark (to make a mark on something) **laqcaq cuv** (Note; **caq cuv** can also mean to be engaged to someone)
market **leiv; galzii** (Chi)
market, to go to **leiv zuvq; galzii zuvq**
market day **leiv zuvq nao; leiv nao qiq nao; galzii nao; galzii qiq nao** (26:81)
marks on something (sometimes cracks) **tevq**
marriage contract **caq taq laq e**
marriage (for female) **sulmil yil**
marriage (for male) **miqssaq seq**
marriage, to arrange (from groom's side) **miqssaq gee caq; miqsulssaq gee li**
marriage affairs **yeilheiq**
marrage feast **yulbee bee**

marriage law **hyulyeilfaq** (Chi)
marriage, reached the age for **seq deil yil deil alhuvq**
marriage system **hyulyeil ziifduf** (Chi)
marrow **saqyyuq piultaoq; saqyyuq yyuqnaoq**
marrow, spinal **piultaoq**
marry, to **cuv zaq** (45:7); **cuv zavq; cuv zavq lavq e** (11:222)
 marry a man **sulmil yil**
 marry a woman **seq**
marsh, a **sulqeil laobao**
marshy fields **sulqeil yaldei**
martial arts (Chinese), to perform **wusuq diq** (A=Chi)
Marx, Karl **Makeiqsiil; Ma Keiqsiil** (Chi) (26:50)
Marxism **Makeiqsiil zuyif** (Chi)
 Marxism-Leninism **Maliq zuyif** (Chi)
 Marxism, Leninism, Mao Zedong Thought **Maliq zuyif Maoq Ceiqdaol ssilxa**
mask, surgical **meiqcaoq** (also used for feeding bags for horses, and muzzles for other animals)
massage, to **nieivq**
masses, the (the people) **qyuqzaof** (Chi); **ssaqjeil**
mass media; media **doqgaq xa miaoq** (50:200)
master, a (highly skilled in something, has apprentices under him) **siilful** (Chi) (26:28)
master, to **zahhoq** (Chi) (34:24)
master copy; original manuscript **huq buvq soqkaoq** (50:201)
mat **hoqdaq** (11:27)
match (for making fire) **miqqiv** (11:151)
match; competition (as basketball) **biseif** (Chi)
match; contest **diq qeiv qeiv zaq** (41:191)
match, to **aolqeiv qeiv; diqqeiv qeiv**
material culture **wuqziiq weiqhuaf** (Chi)
materialism **weiqwuqlyuf; weiqwuq zuyif** (Chi) (50:176); **wuqziiq; wuqzii** (Chi)
materials; means **aolmiaoq ssaoqmiaoq** (50:218)
maternal uncle **aqhhyu**
math; arithmetic **syufsuq** (Chi) (26:22); **sufxoq** (Chi)
mathematic department **sufxoqxif** (Chi)
mathematic exercises **sufxotiq** (Chi) (50:157)
mat hung above fireplace; attic **hoqtavq**
mat of bamboo for drying things **goqpov**
mat of straw **javsev**
matter; substance **miaoqgaoq** (50:182)
matter of life and death **deivq ssol sil lal e miqnieiq**
mattock; hoe **ceiq**
mattress; mat **hoqdaq** (11:27)
mature, to be **hhaoldav** (pf.); **aqdaol daolhav**
 mature, to (for people) **heeq luvq**
 mature, to (for plants, fruits, etc.) **hhaol luvq**
 mature; full (as seeds) **mallu nei**
 mature early, to **kol**

mature late, to **le**
May **Ngavqla siq**
may (vb) **(vb) nia; sso (vb)**
maybe **malnaoq; nadul**
maybe yes (probably) **ngeel moq maq syuq** (46:121)
May Day **Wuyiq** (Chi) (26:112)
mayor **siifza** (Chi) (50:154)
May the Fourth movement (1919) **Wusiif Yyuqdaof** (Chi) (34:5)

meal (clf.) **biol**
meal; rice; food **hoq**
meal, to eat **alhoq zaq**
meaning **yifsiil** (Chi) (50:196)
meaning; sense; significance **yifyif** (Chi) (50:196)
means; materials **aolmiaoq ssaoqmiaoq** (50:218)
means; method **sedueif; seduaf** (Chi)
means of production **seilca ziilliaof** (Chi) (34:16)
measles **tuvnil; beesav** (15:28) (**beesav duv** = to develop measles)
measure, a (or a step, as in politics) **bufceq** (Chi); **bufcef; coqsiil** (Chi) (34:10)
measure; units of measure **jifliaf dalhhyuf** (Chi)
measure, to (as how long) **qeiv**
meat **saq; saqnil** (esp. pork); **alzil**
meat, cooked **saqqavq**
meat, dried **saqkuv**
meat, fresh **saqsiivq**
meat, frozen **saqnieil**
meat; muscle **saq**
meat, not dry **saqzaoq**
meat, pickled **saqqeil**
meat, raw **saqzaoq**
mediate, to **gee pil** (50:166); **alkaq pil; tiaoqgei** (Chi)
medical examination **huafyeif** (Chi)
medical expert **yilxoqjal** (Chi) (50:196); **naciq aqbol**
medical team **yilliaoqdyuf** (Chi) (50:196)
medical worker **yilwuf sseiqyeiq** (Chi) (50:196)
medicinal plant **naciq jahhaq**
medicine **naciq**
medicine, Chinese **zaolyil** (Chi) (50:213)
medicine, to give **naciq bivq**
meet, to **qo puq; puq lal**
meet; agree; be in accord **tovq**
meet (as a friend) **miavpyuq mol** (lit., 'see face')
meeting, a **hyufyif** (Chi)
meeting, attend a **hyufyif keil** (Chi)
meeting, to call a **kul zil**
meeting, to have a **doqzil zil; keilhyuf keil** (Chi)
meet by chance **quq puq**
meet on purpose, to **qao puq**
meet on the way, to **galtal tal**
meet someone, to **seq cavq**
meet to discuss **doqzil duv**

meet up with **taoq puq; taoq zyul; quq puq** (26:39)
megaphone **koqyiljil** (Chi)
Mekong (Lancang) River **Laqcaljal lolbaq** (A=Chi)
melon, watermelon **eelquvq maldei** (B=Dai)
melt **geel**
melt steel, to **saol geel e** (26:26)
memo; note **tiaoqzii** (Chi)
memoirs **jiqnieif** (Chi)
memoirs of Dr. Bethune **Jiqnieif Beq Qeq'eil** (26:55) (Chi)
memorize, to **nyuq teiq** (includes memorizing their genealogy)
mend, to **zaol pal** (11:161); **aol duvq; zaol duvq**
mend, to (patch) **guvq taol; duvq**
menstrual blood **ba'la alyeiv** (polite); **beivqsivq** (taboo)
menstrual cycle **alyeiv ba'la pal**
menstruate, to **alyeiv ba'la pal** (polite); **beivqsivq duv** (taboo)
mental property **jilseiq ceiqfuf** (Chi)
mental work **neenyuq aol zaq**
Meo; Miao; Hmong **Miaoqziissaq; Miaoqcuq** (Chi)
merchant **aoq zaq**
merge, to (as two businesses) **mievq tao; zaq leev; lav paoq**
merit **yeldiei** (Chi)
merit; blessing, etc. **gaoqlaoq**
message, a **doqgaq**
message, to give **doqgaq cavq; doqgaq dov; doqgaq cavq dov**
messy, to be **beeq**
metal helmet **saol wuqcaoq**
metalurgical industry **yijil gaolniq** (Chi) (50:195)
metaphor; figure of speech **bi dul**
metaphysics **xiq'eiq safxoq** (Chi) (50:189)
meter **mi** (Chi); **gaolciiq** (Chi)
method **lo'qo** (10:pref) (**kolxoq lo'qo** = scientific method); **baffaq** (Chi) **balfaq** (Chi); **lulsul** (Chi)
method; idea **yiqqeiq** (11:179)
method; means **sedueif** (pf.); **seduaf** (Chi)
methods, all **hal kaol galquv**

Miao (Meo; Hmong) nationality **miaoqcuq** (Chi); **Miaoqziissaq** (A=Chi)
miasma **zalqil**
microscope **xeiweiqjif** (Chi) (50:184)
microwave oven **weiqbolluq** (Chi) (50:175)
middle **alkaqlaq**
middle; inside **hholqei**
middle-aged **colqi meil**
middle daughter **miqhhaol** (13:3)
middle of day **naohhaol hhaolluv** (26:42)
middle of water **eelhhaol niq pav**
middle school **zaolxoq** (Chi) (50:214)

middle size **za nei**
middle son; second son **ssaqhhaol**
midnight **saolhhaol; sulhhaol** (26:51) (**sulhhaol qiq pav** - deep into the night, past midnight)
might; power **qaqqeiq** (Chi)
mighty; great **heeqma molma** (50:176)
migratory birds **yil lal e alzil; yil yil lal lal e alzil**
milestones **luvcuv**
militarism **jyulgoq zuyif** (Chi)
military academy (university) **jyulzeif dafxoq** (Chi)
military affairs **jyulsiif** (Chi) (26:104)
military area command (top rank of armed forces) **jyulqil** (Chi)
military depot **bilzaf** (Chi)
military power **bilqeiq** (Chi)
military service **mavqssaq gee zaq**
military sub-area command (below military area command) **jyulfeilqil** (Chi)
militia **miqbil** (Chi)
milk **aqqul; niuqqul** (10:16 = cow or buff. milk)
Milky Way (constellation) **aqgeel caqkov**
mill, to **jiv nuv**
mill, rice, grain mill **ceil jiv jilqif**
millet **laoqlyul**
millimeter **haoqmi** (Chi)
million **yal mil** (ten million = **taol mil**; one hundred million = **milmil**)
millstone **jivluv**
mince; chop **bieiv**
mind/heart **neema**
mine (in earth) **kuafsal** (26:39); **kuaf** (26:106) (Chi)
mineral spring **cuqduq**
Ministry of Culture **weiqhuafbuf** (Chi) (50:178)
minority **saosuq** (10:14) (Chi)
minority nationality **colqa colssaq** (46:218); **saosuq miqcuq** (10:14) (Chi)
minus (in math sense) **jeihaof** (Chi)
minute, a **feilzaol** (Chi) (10:26, 15:37); **piaol** (Chi)
mirror **hoqbav piqhov; piqhov** (26:41)
mirror which distorts **eelnaq pieiq e piqhov**
misappropriate; embezzle **mievq tao; yiul ssaoq**
mischievous; naughty **lavsaoq** (50:174)
miser **neema xeivq; neema yoxeivq; laqpil civ** (pf.); **laqpil cil**
miserable; suffering a hard life **saq sil saq lo** (46:197)
miserly; selfish **neexeivq xeivq**
misery **saq**
misrepresent; distort **eil yevq**
miss someone or something, to **gaq sil; nyuq sil nyuq lo; gaq lal**
mist **juqhyuq**

mistake   **bav; coqwuf** (Chi) (34:6)
mistake, to   **lav bav**
mistake (to happen)   **meiqzaq duv lal** (26:120)
mistake, to make   **(vb) bav; zaol leiq; zaol bav; hol** (**eil hol** = to make a mistake in speaking) (note: **hol** can also mean to make someone angry)
mistaken idea   **nyuq bav**
mister   **xeilseil** (**Syul Zaolsal xeilseil** = Mr. Syul Zaolsal)
mister; teacher; instructor; sir   **seilse** (Chi) (50:184)
mistress of house   **yosaol aqma**
misunderstanding   **nyuq bav** (46:119)
misunderstanding; estrangement   **neekaoq**
mix, to   **lav kevq; piav kevq**
mix, to; to combine   **bavq paoq**
mix in; put in (as soup)   **bavq tao** (10:10)
mix medicine   **peiqfalpiq** (Chi) (15:37)
mix mud for building   **caqyaq nil**
mix together   **kevq**
mix up, to   **piav paoq; piav kevq**
mix with   **bavq kevq; lav kevq**
mix with one's hands   **nuvq kevq**

mob of people   **col loq col meil**
mobilize; to arouse   **heil niv; ssaqlaol leiq tul** (50:44)
mock, to   **cavq**
mock someone, to   **eil cavq; eil nal; eilhyuq**
model   **moqfaf** (Chi)
model; example   **biaolbil** (Chi)
model worker   **xeiljif seilcazei** (Chi) (26:100)
Model Youth League Member   **Moqfaf Gaoqqil tuaqyeiq** (Chi)
modernization   **xeifdeifhuaf** (Chi) (34:12)
modernize   **xeifdeifhuaf** (Chi) (50:185)
modern times   **jifdeif** (Chi) (34:17)
modest, to be   **maq buq zaq; yalleel nei**
modifier, a   **xulsifyi** (Chi)
molar tooth   **bavqlivseq**
mold (as for making bricks)   **seivhuvq** (11:27)
mold (fungal growth)   **haolci**
mold to develop   **haolci ci**
mole (animal)   **milcaq hucavq**
mole on skin   **saqnav**
moment, a   **luldu** (**xil taq luldu** = at this moment (26:43); **qiq savq**
moment, after a   **ciiv nei qiq heiq ngeel taoqngaoq**
moment, at this very   **xil taq luldu; niaoq'aol niaolhav**
moment, for a   **za nei**
moment ago   **eiqsi; eiqsi sihavq** (11:109 for samples); **eiqsi siha** (26:39)
moment, just this (now)   **niaoq'aol niaolhav; xil taq luldu**

moment; season **yotovq**
Monday **Xilqil qiq nao** (A=Chi)
money **taoqhaoq** (Chi) (11:30)
money; cash **piul** (50:185)
money; silver; white **piul**
money and property **zeiq**
money collector; treasurer **piul se ssaoq zaq e col**
money measure **biav; yeiq** (Chi)
monitor lizard **eelssaol**
monkey **almiuvq**
monkey, golden **almiuvq miuvqsiil**
monkey, red-bottomed **almiuvq miuvqhav daoqnil**
monkey, silver leaf **almiuvq miuvqpeel**
monkey, rhesus **miuvqhav daoqnil**
monkey day **miuvq nao**
monkey hour **miuvq zeq** (B=Chi)
monkey with wrinkled face **almiuvq baqzuvq**
monkey year **miuvq huvq**
monogamy **qiq miq qiq jil galquv** (50:196)
monopolize **laoduaf** (Chi)
month **ba'la; lasiq**
month, a **lasiq**
month, early in **ladav**
month, end of **lamiq**
monument; memorial stone **doqdaq luvcuv**
mood; tone; manner of speaking **doq eil yoteil** (50:200)
moon **ba'la**
moon, full **ba'la la'luv**
moon-cake **yyuqbi zabiav** (26:85) (A=Chi)
moon festival **zaolqeljiq** (Chi) (26:85)
moonlight **ba'la aoqcal**
moral (as moral of the story; lesson of the story) **jaofsyuf** (Chi)
moral character and ideology **neema meeq dyul**
moral excellence; virtue **neemeeq neezaq**
morals **daofdeiq** (Chi) (26:55) (**daofdeiq gaolsaf** = noble; lofty morals and ideals)
more **zeiq aqzeiq**
more and more **nieiq'eil meil** (10:15); **nieiq'eil (vb) nieiq'eil**
more of **aqzeiq meil**
moreover; not only **maq ceil**
more than **zeiq nei; miaq zeiq**
more than (vb) **(vb) zeiq; miaq zeiq** = more than; **yozeiq** (10:7 = as when it is more than 10 days after a baby is born); **hultav (vb) zeiq (Aqda aqma hultav moq zeiq.** Father is older than mother.)
morning **aoqsoq**
morning (early) **aoqsoq soqto; aoq biajul**
morning, one **soq (qiq soq)**
morning, middle of **aoqsoq soqlu**
morning-before-last **huqsoq**
morning exercises **zaocaol** (Chi) (50:204)

morning star **soqmeel**
morning work, to do **soq'aol aol**
morpheme (single morpheme word) (gram) **doqlo losol**
morphology **doqlo lo'quv**
mortar (for grinding salt and chili) **caqpeiq**
mortgage, to; to pawn **dav zaq**
mortgage a field **xal zaq**
mosquito **yalgoq**
mosquito net **beexa**
moss (on ground, road) **galniul**
most **hal**
most, the **hal miaqzeiq** (10:22)
most of **yomiaq qiq bil** (10:pref)
most of the group **yomiaq qiq baol** (26:83)
most suitable **hal za e**
mother **aqma**
mother, first (i.e., birth-mother) **mamoq**
mother, subsequent (i.e., step-mother) **madavq**
mother and child **niq massaq**
mother and children **aqma ssaq**
mother and son **niq massaq**
mother-in-law **yoqma** (Chi) (pf) (11:31); **yiuvqma**
motherland **zugoq** (Chi)
'mother nature' (goddess in charge of nature) **Yeilmoq Aqma**
mother's brother **aqhhyu**
mother's younger sister; wife of father's YB; wife of mother's brother **aqmee**
motion (as to make a); proposal **yifhhaf** (Chi) (50:197); **tiqhhaf** (Chi) (50:164)
motive **daofliq** (Chi)
motive force; motive power **hhaqhav lalduq**
mount (as a horse) **ziiq dav** (13:32)
mountain **haoldaol; milma haolteil** (13:53); **haolgaoq; milgaoq**
mountain, high **haolteil teilma; haolteil teilma wuqduq** (as peaks)
mountain, large **haolteil teilma**
mountain, small **milgaoq gaoqssaq**
mountain, tropical **joqto haoldaol**
mountain base; foot of the mountain **milgaoq gaoq daoq; milma hhaqdaoq**
mountain field **daolyal; daolhav; haoltavq koqyal**
mountain, foot of **gaoqdaoq** (13:11)
mountainous area **haoldaol milcaq** (10:11)
mountain pass **galquv** (note: also means 'proper way'); **milma hhaqdaoq**
mountain people **haoldaol laqliv col**
mountain places **milgaoq** (46:168)
mountain ridge **haolgaoq; haolgaoq wuqduq**
mountain slope **haolteil; hhavqtavq**
mountain slope and plain **hhavqtavq deisal**
mountain 'tail' **haolgaoq gaoqmiq**
mountain top **haolgaoq gaoqwuq**
mourn and cry for an elder **miqsaq ngyul**

mouse **hucavq**
moustache **meiqmoq**
mouth **meiqzu; meiqbaoq** (clf. = **siq**)
mouth, to hold in **meiq'aoq aoqteiq**
mouth, corner of **meiqzeil**
mouth organ (made of gourd and bamboo) **laqjeiq; geiqleiq**
move, to **niv** (**qiq niv maq niv** = do not move at all)
move and inspire (as by a speech or report) **gazaol** (Chi)
move closer to **qul pyul la**
move larger objects (as boulders) **ngaoq niv** (**Taq ngaoq niv.** Don't move it. 11:142)
move smaller objects (as clothes) **se**
moved by something (as brave deeds) **gadaof** (Chi) (26:113)
movement; action **niv**
move out of village **pyul** (**pyul li qavq** = move away - 11:99)
move out of the way; get out of the way **xeivyoq**
move over here **xilgei pyul lal**
movie **dieifssi** (Chi) (11:131); **yipieif** (Chi) (50:198)
movie screen **dieifssi albee** (A=Chi) (11:31)
movie to be shown **dieifyi pieiq** (A=Chi)
moving all the time **nivniv nei**

much easier **yal zeiq gaoq**
mucous (nasal, liquid) **aqbeil**
mucous (nasal, solid) **aqbeil beilniul**
mud **laobieiv; milbieiv** (11:82)
mud; earth **halcaq**
mud, very sticky **milneiq**
muddled (not able to think clearly) **haoqkavq** (33:3)
mud dug out by rat/mouse **miljeivq**
muddy, to be **milbieiv; milcaq milbieiv; laobieiv bieiv; xeivleel nei; laobao bao; bieivto nei; caqyaq; milxeiv**
muddy water; turbid **eeldiv; eeldiv div; milxeiv**
mud fight, a **caqyaq teil zaq**
mud slide, a **milsuv**
mud slide to occur **milsuv suv**
mud wall **caqto**
mud wall, to build **caqcuv cuv; caqto to**
mule **lalzii; loqzii**
mule day (actually 'rabbit' day in Ak.) **toqla**
multiplication tables (repeat with formula) **ceiqfaq kejiq; cuqfaq kejiq** (Chi)
multistoried **laqhyul yaolgoq**
munia bird **haqzal naqboq** (or) sparrow
Muntjac deer (barking deer) **qilssaq**
murder **col seivq zyul**
muscle **saq**
muscle, strong (means: to work hard) **lavqguq** (**lavqguq daov deivq** - 26:35)
museum **boqwuqguei** (Chi)

mush (cooked to mush)   **qavqbieiv**
mushroom   **haollul; ciqhhaol**
  mushroom (types of)   **haolneiq; haolnil**
  mushroom shoot (small; young)   **haolquv**
music   **yilyoq** (Chi) (50:197)
musical instruments   **teil duv seilhuvq**
musical instrument (four strings)   **bilpav lavqhev**
musical instrument (three strings)   **laqhev**
musical instrument, to play above   **laqhev bev**
musician   **yilyoqjal** (Chi) (50:197)
music score   **yoqpu** (Chi) (50:203)
musk   **seiqxal** (Chi)
  musk ox   **seiqxal** (Chi)
musket (old fashioned gun)   **yaqcei** (Chi)
must; certain; surely   **halmeil liq**
must (vb)   **hha (vb); halmeil (vb) liq** (10:19, 22)
must (vb)   **(vb) wuqbo** (aol **wuqbo** = must do) (26:66)
must not (vb)   **pilseq taq (vb); pieilse taq**
    (vb); **maq (vb) wulbo** (must not do that - 11:45)
must; ought   **wuqbo** (46:211)
mute; dumb   **aqbeq**
mutiny (of troops)   **mavqssaq puv**
mutually beneficial   **huflif** (Chi)
muzzle   **bevheiq** (this also means: bullet hole)
muzzle-loader gun   **alzil miqbev**

my   **ngaq e; nga** (as in: **nga qovq** = my house)
my God!   **ol, molmil eilyi; ol, aqpyul molmil eilyi**
myriads   **yoltaol yolyal** ('thousands and hundreds')

nail, to **diq cuv**
nail something, to (as a board) **diq cuv**
nail the floor **biavqcuv cuv** (11:43)
naive; childish **nee hyuq maq hav** (50:200)
naked **nilgu nei**
name **colmiaol; yomiaol**
name, real **colmiaol miaoltaoq**
name someone, to **colmiaol miaol; gul**
Nanking (city in China) **Naqjil**
nape of neck **laolbyu**
  nape of neck (the skin, as in a cat) **laolgu saqgeel**
narrow **teiq**
narrow, very **teiqkuv nei; quvq; teiq pa teiq nei** (11:57); **teiqkuv kuvssaq nei** (11:59)
narrow one's eyes **miavjyul jyul**
nasal discharge (liquid) **aqbeil; aqbeil beilgaol; aqbeil nal'eel**
  nasal discharge (solid) **aqbeil beilniul**
  nasal discharge (thick) **beilniul**
nation; country **goqjal** (Chi)
nation, whole **qeiqgoq** (Chi) (26:75)
national anthem **goqgol** (Chi)
national economy **goqmiq jiljif** (Chi) (34:10)
national emblem **goqhyul** (Chi)
national holiday **goqqifjiq neeciiv** (A=Chi)
national income **goqmiq selssuq** (Chi)
National People's Congress **Qeiqgoq sseiqmiq deifbiao dafhyuf** (Chi) (50:139)
nationalities (all kinds) **goqcuq** (Chi)
Nationalities Publishing House **miqcuq cuqbaseif** (Chi) (10:1)
nationality **colqa colssaq; miqcuq** (Chi)
Nationality Affairs Commission (abbreviated) **Miqhhyu**
Nationality Research Institute (abbreviated) **Miqnieilso**
national power **goqliq** (34:18)
national property **goqjal zeiqma** (A=Chi)
national representative **qeiqgoq sseiqmiq deifbiao** (Chi)
native people **colzuv**
natural color; one's basic attitude **beiseiq** (Chi)
natural color; true qualities **sekevq** (50:10)
natural gas **milhhuvq alsavq** (50:165)
natural law **ziifssaq gyulliq** (Chi) (50:219)
natural resources **ziifssaq ziilyeiq** (Chi) (50:219)
natural science **ziifssaq kolxoq** (Chi) (50:219)
natural world **ziifssaqgeif** (Chi) (50:219)
naughty; mischievous **lavsaoq** (50:174)
naughty child **ssaqga gassaq; lavsaoq** (29:4)
nauseous **lavqma needav dav; neema buldeiq nei**

naval force **jeifdyuf** (Chi)
naval ships and boats **jeifti** (Chi)
navel **qalbeil**
Naxi (Nashi) **Naqxil**
Naxi (Nashi) language **Naqxildoq** (10:pref.)

near **galniq niq; daoqpei**
nearby **galniq niq; niqca nei**
nearly; almost **lavqso**
neatly **leedo nei; soqdo nei**
neatly, very **soqdo pa do nei**
necessary; to need **guq sso**
neck **kaoqlaol; laolbyu** (esp. the nape area)
necklace **leeldee**
neck of horse **laolciivq**
need **guq lal; aolsso** (26:26) (where revolutionary work was needed, there he went)
need; necessary **guq sso**
need; want; require **guq** (26:79, 50:190)
needle **aqhhovq**
needle case, a **hhovqbaoq**
needle for injections **hhovqma**
needle used to sew palm bark **sseilhhovq**
need something, to **qiq jivq guq**
negate; deny **eil bial; fedif** (Chi)
negative **maq** (vb); **maq; maq xul**
negative imperative **taq**
neighbor **zaolpeil lolqoq**
nephew on brother's side **ssaqdul**
nephew on sister's side **ssaq'yul**
nerve; tendon; pulse **saqguq**
nervous; tense **calmil nei**
nest **beeq**
nest of bird **zilbeeq; alzil zilbeeq**
nest of hen **aqha hageel**
nest of snake **ollol lolbeeq**
net (for fishing) **ngaqzei; hhazei**
nettle, a **pavqdeiq** (with many kinds, such as: **pavqdeiq deiqcal; pavqdeiq deiqhav**, etc.)
neutrality **alkaq jol** (50:214)
never **salssil maq (vb)** (when in negative it means 'never' - by itself it means 'forever') (11:112)
never mind **maq gal; qiq jivq maq ngeel; maq beq; maq beq sso; haljivq beq ya** (**Alciiv nal e haljivq beq ya.** Never mind this pain/suffering. 26:47)
new **siivq; yosiivq**
newborn (animal, human) **puqnil**
New China **xil Zaolgoq** (Chi) (26:22)
New China, to build **xil Zaolgoq jeifseiq** (Chi)
new democracy **xil miqzu zuyif** (Chi)
new democracy revolution **xil miqzu zuyif geiqmif** (Chi)
new epoch; new age **huvqlavq yosiivq** (34:1)
New long march **Silcaqzeil** (Chi)
newly-wed couple **miqsiivq ssaqsiivq**

new rice **hoqsiivq**
new rice (to carry it) **kalduv eq** (46:209)
new rice festival **hoqsiivq zaq**
news **doqgaq; xiaolxiq** (Chi); **xilweiq** (Chi)
news agency; news service **naqgaq xaduq** (50:168)
newsman; reporter **naqgaq buvqssaq** (50:188)
newspaper **baofzii** (Chi); **soqhhaq baofzii** (B=Chi) (26:66)
newspaper (daily) **Ssiiqbaof** (46:120) (Chi)
New Year **Galtaol; Zalteil, Za'lei; huvqsiivq**
New Year (lunar; ten-month) **Ceilla Galtaol**
New Year (to celebrate) **Galtaol taol; Galtaol pal; Zalteil teil; Za'lei teil; huvqsiivq zaq; huvq hev zaq**
New Year's day **huvqsiivq nao; Yeiqdaf Neeciiv** (A=Chi) (50:201)
next one (see: '**the next**')
next year **neelyahuvq; nilyahuvq; nyulyahuvq**

nibble on something, to **dovlov nei kovq**
nickname **colmiaol miaolcavq**
niece **ssaqma**
night; dusk **aoqqivq**
night, late at **aoqqivq qivq**
night, middle of **qivq pav** (11:67)
night, the whole **qiq yavq yavq joq**
night-before-last **huqqivq**
nine **hhyuq**
nipple (on bottle) **qulsiq**
nipple (breast) **aqqul qulsiq; qulsiq**
nitre **zalpiul**
Niukong (a place in Luchun county) **Nieqkao** (Chi)

no **maq ngeel**
no; not **maq (vb)**
no hurry; no rush **maq teiq maq cal**
noble; lofty **gaolsaf** (Chi)
noble; higher quality **gaolgyuf piziiq**
noble; lofty ideals **daofdeiq gaolsaf** (Chi)
nod head (gesturing yes) **wuqduq niei niei nei**
noisy **ssuv luv ssav lav meil; wul li wual lal nei** (Chi)
noisy; quarrelsome **beil sil; ssavssav nei**
noisy and disturbing **naqhaoq haoq**
no matter who or what **maq gaoq** (46:204)
nonagression **qaq qaq yaol maq diq zaq** (50:73)
non-agricultural population **xal maq aol zaq col**
noodles **mieiftiaoq** (Chi)
nook; corner **laqkyul**
noon **naohhaol hhaollu; aoqnao naohhaol**
norm; criterion; standard **tevqkov** (50:218)
north **beiq; beiqfal** (Chi)
northern expedition **beiqfaq zafzeil** (Chi) (34:6); **beiqfaq zafzeil**
north, far **niamil aqnia**

nose **nalmeil (nalbaoq)**
nose, flat **nalbiav**
nose, high **nalgul**
nose bridge **nalyyuq**
nose broken **nalhavq**
nose disease (one type) **nalbiavq**
nose hair **nalmeilhao; nalbyuhao**
nose, red **nalnil** (46:139)
nose rope for buffalo/cattle **nalcav**
nose tip **nalzu**
nose to be stuffy **nalcyuq cyuq**
'no-son' person **sulbieivq (semi-taboo)**
nostril **nalbyu**
not; no **maq**
not bad; so-so **maq bav; halmeeq maq gal**
notch in mountain, a **galquv; galquv quvssaq**
notch in wood, a **davtevq**
note; memo **tiaqzii; tiaoqzii** (Chi)
note asking for leave **jafliaoq** (Chi)
notebook, a **biqjifbei** (Chi) (26:18)
not equal to **maq toq** (11:146)
not even a little **sev'le nei (sev'le nei maq qeq na** - did not believe it even a little)
not grow normally; decline **ssii**
nothing **qiq jivq maq (vb) (qiq jivq maq jav** = I have nothing) 10:pref.
notice (as a notice on a wall); bulletin **bufgaof** (Chi)
notice, public **dyu nei eilgaq** (50:167)
notify; inform; give notice **eilgaq** (50:168)
not long after **maq mol kaq nei**
not love, not interested **maq hhyul maq gaq**
not only; moreover **maq ceil**
not salty enough **caqdevq maq qul**
not same size **heeq nil maq dei**
not so bad **ziil nei maq gal**
not so good **hhoqna maq meeq**
not taste good **maq keel; zaq syuq**
not the same **maq paoq** (11:156)
not to be afraid **malnee eelcul saqhhyu maq baq**
not to be so **maq ngeel**
not too salty **caqdevq maq haq**
not to worry **neema maq qil sso** (26:42)
not very (vb) **hhoqna maq (vb) (hhoqna maq meeq** = not very good) (13:1)
nourish, to **hhyul aol**
nourishment; nutriment **zalhhyul** (50:194)
no use; useless **qiq jivq maq cyuq** (26:113)
noun **miqciiq** (Chi)
nourishment; nutrition **hhyul aol**
novel; fiction **xaosoq** (Chi) (50:186)
November **Ceiltivqla siq**
now **niaoq'aol**

numb, to be **aqbieiv bieiv**

numb; insensitive **zoqmavq nei**
numb; paralyzed **keel sil lavq sil**
numbers, to count **aqgee gee**
numeral **gee'qa (gee'qa maq hev** = do not know the numbers); **sufciiq** (Chi)
nursery; child-care center **toq'eiqso** (Chi) (50:172)
nursing school; health school **weifxaof** (Chi)
nurtured and cultivated (as by the Communist party) **peiqya** (Chi) (26:111)
nut **aqmeil** (11:26)
nut (hard type) **aqmeil meilhav**
nut (soft type) **aqmeil meilnaoq**
nutriment; nourishment **zalhhyul** (50:194)
nutrition **yiqya** (Chi)
nutrition; nourishment **hhyul aol**
nutritious food **zalhhyul (zal zaq hhyul aol** = to take nourishing food to build one's strength)

o O o O o O

O o soqmiav aqma hholqei ceil ngavq mol e qiq mol

---

oar (for raft or boat) **loq he dalpav; loq he daldul**
oath, to take **laqnaq teil**

obedient **hal eil hal na** (50:176)
obese (see: fat)
obey, to **fuqcaoq** (Chi)
obey; listen **doq eil nalhaq; eil doq nalhaq**
object, an; a thing **miaoqnieiq** (50:155)
object (gram) **bilyi** (Chi)
obligation; duty **yoq miaoq yoq aol**
obstacles; difficulties **jeilnaq xeizu** (Chi)
obstinate; stubborn **neetaoq taoq** (50:174)
obstruct; thwart **leiq cyuq** (50:221)
obstructed, to be **laol cyuq**
obtain, to **aolhha**

occupation, to obtain **aolduq jav**
occupy, to **jol taq**
occupy by force **koq zaq**
ocean; sea; big lake **lao'laoma**
o'clock **dieizaol** (Chi) (26:33) (4 **dieizaol** = 4 o'clock)
October **Ceilla siq**
octopus **zalyiq ngaqdeil** (A=Chi) (50:207)

odd (as different from even) **aqteiq; laolngaoq** (also: single, only)
odd-job man **ciqwufyeiq** (Chi) (26:111)
odor, bad **beivqlavq**
odor of something **he (Zilbaq baq he naol lal ya.** I get the odor of liquor.)

offend, to **civq lav peiv; deiq zyul** (Chi) (46:195)
offer, to **bavq hel**
offer, to (including to offer a meal to someone) **lol**
offer a meal to someone **hoqbiol lol**
offer condolences **saqhaol miq**
offering **lol** (general); **hel; soq** (religious); **tul** (related to propitiating spirits)
offering, ancestral **aqpyuq zal hel**
offering to 'great water divide' **Aqlobieil lol**
offering to irrigation ditches **eelheiq soq**
offering to 'lord of the land' **milsaol lol**
offering to prevent fire **miqcaoq caoq**
offering to sacred grove **hhaqma lol; hhaqma lol zaq**
offering to village gate (to prevent evil spirits from coming in) **galtuv tuv**
offering to village spirit **puvma tul**
office **bafgaolsiiq; gaolzoq** (Chi); **miaoq aol yaol**
office; institution; organization **jilgueil** (pf.);

jilgual (Chi)
office, to work there **gaolzoq aol**
official; from the past **zulbal** (Chi) (35:48)
official; king **aqhhol** (11:210); **lidaof** (Chi) (26:49); **zulbal** (Chi)
official; local master ('warlord') **tusiil** (Chi)
official; ruler **soqpaq; zyuq**
often **ciivzaol nei** (11:110 - samples); **civzaol nei**
often; always **taol nao nei** (13:4)
often; daily; frequently **civzaol nei** (11:118)

ogre, a kind of **neivqzaq hhalniul**
ogre; wild person; chimpanzee (they have seen none of these so use this term for all) **miaqlo miallo aqma; miallo**

oh! **aoq; el** (**El aqbol soqpaq** = Oh ruler!)

oil (cooking; and used in machinery) **cil**
oil (petroleum) **haqluv cil**
oil lamp **hhaqcil aldovq; yalyeq aqdal**
oil-palm tree **hhoqma albol**
oil-palm tree leaves **hhoqma alpavq**
ointment; paste **ssuagaol** (Chi)

okay; all right; fine **eiqya; hhaq; hhaq lil; aoq ya**

old **yoja** (26:74); **ssei**
old, very **moqkuv moqluv**
old (as cloth) **yojal** (11:26)
old (as goods) **yul; yoyul**
old (as pants) **peiljal laqjal**
old (as people) **moq; colmoqssaq**
old blanket **albee beeja**
older (of people) **yivq zeiq**
older brother **algo** (Chi)
older brother's wife **aqcu**
older sister's husband; brother-in-law **aqsaoq**
oldest daughter **aqyivq**
oldest son **ssaqyivq**
old lady; grandmother **aqpiq**
old man; grandfather **aqbol ssaqmoq; colmoq**
old mind (heart) **neema nee yul**
old people; grandparents **aqpiq aqbol**
old people or animals **moq kuv moq luv**
old person **colmoq**
old society **jefsefhyuf** (Chi) (26:10)
old things **yoyul**
old woman **aqpiq ssaqmoq** (11:149)
old year **huvq'yul**
olive 1. type with small, round fruit **joqqaq baqleil**
2. type with big, oval fruit **julleiv**

omen; sign **dulmav mav** (50:201)
omen (bad) **dol** (**dol duv** - bad omen to appear)

on **hultav** (as in 'there is mud on the clothes')
on behalf of; for **ballal**
once more; one more time **aqzeiq qiq taq**
on duty **ssuqgal aol** (26:38)
one **qiq** (or, **-tivq** - as in: 11, 21, 31 etc.)
one after another **qiq (clf) naolhao qiq (clf)** (**qiq hhaq naolhao qiq hhaq** = one person after another)
one by one; singly **solsol meil**
one-handed (to have only one hand or arm) **lavqteiq**
one heart; one mind **neetavq neezyul** (50:168)
one hundred million **yif** (Chi); **milmil** (Hani) (11:65)
one hundred thousand **ceil mil** (Chi)
one more time; once more **aqzeiq qiq taq**
oneself **yoq; yoqhhaq; yoqhhaq bulduq; bulduq** (**Nol bulduq buvq**. You write it yourself. 11:94); **yoqhhaq hhaqduq; sulhhaq**
onion **seilbaoq**
only **laolngaoq; naolngaoq** (**niq massaq naolngaoq** - only mother and son - 13:53); **sol**
only; otherwise **maq ngeel loq**
only son **ssaqteiq**
on purpose **neenyuq meil; balbal nei** (26:41)
on the one hand (vb) **qiq pyu (vb) qiq pyu (vb)** (**qiq pyu ngyul qiq pyu kul** = on the one hand he cried, on the other he called out - 26:5)

ooze out, to **ju duv yi; milbieiv ju duv yi**

open, to **pao**
open; to pull open **hhe pao; hhe piei** (13:12)
open (as eyes) **biei; miavneev biei nei**
open (as mouth) **nga; meiqzu piei** (46:151)
open (as mouth, by force) **hhe piei; meiqbaoq piei nei** (26:49)
open (as umbrella) **tuv piei**
open (as window) **diq pao** (10:7)
opening of a container **meiqheiq**
open-minded (liberated ideology) **siilxa gei'faf** (Chi) (34:12)
open one's eyes widely **deiq niul; bei nei**
open; overt; public **bilduv nei** (50:61)
open; spacious **hha'loq nei**
open to the outside **keilfaf** (pf.); **kalfaf** (Chi) (34:12)
open up; pioneer work **aolbei bei**
open up; to cut open **peivq**
open up; split **beivq**
open up; spread out **hhe piei** (50:206)
open up a cover **bavq pao**
open up umbrella or the like **tuv piei**
operate (medical) **keq peivq**
operate (to cut open stomach) **wuqdeiq keq peivq**
operation **sesuq** (Chi) (50:156)
operating table **sesuqteiq** (Chi) (50:156)

opinion **neenyuq**
opium **yaqyei** (Chi) (50:193)
opium war **yalpieif zafzeil** (Chi) (34:3)
opportunism **jilhyuf zuyif** (Chi)
opportunity **jilhyuf** (Chi)
oppose; fight against **fadyuf** (Chi)
opposite (as the opposite direction) **lilpuv nei**
opposite; contrary **lilpuv nei**
opposite; upside-down **lilpuv nei**
oppress, to **ssiiv**
oppress; repress **yaqpeiq** (Chi) (50:193)
optic nerve **miavhu seiqjil** (B=Chi) (50:154)
optimism **loqgueil zuyif** (Chi); **loqgual zuyif** (Chi)

or; if not **maqnaaq** (26:76)
oral (as op. to written) **meiqbaoq nei eil**
orange (fruit) **siqlyul** (11:34)
orchestra; band **yoqdyuf** (Chi) (50:203)
orchid **laqhual alyeiv** (A=Chi)
order; procedure **ceiqxif** (Chi)
order, to **miaoqheil heil; miaoqbivq bivq; miqbivq bivq**
ordered someone **heil zaq** (26:7)
orderliness; proper arrangement **tiaoqli** (Chi) (50:166); **maq beeq**
ordinary **naoqmil aqgee** (pf); **noqmil aqgee**
ordinary people; working people **ssaqjeil ssaqlaol**
organization **jilgef** (Chi) (34:56, 50:79) **jilgueil; jilgual; zuziiq** (Chi)
organize; form **zuziiq** (Chi) (31:3, 50:221)
original way; historical way **yeilbei galma**
orphan **molcyuq cyuqssaq**

osprey **haqzeil zeilbuq buqma**

other **aqnu; aqnu aqnia; helyal**
other; guest **sulcol**
other countries **aqnu aqnia goqjal** (34:7)
other day **xilmeil qiq nao** (29:4); **eiqmil nao** (26:44); **eiqmil lalnao** (26:84); **kaqla manao**
other people **aqqoq; biqssaq meilssaq; sulhhaq**
others (old language) **bilmiq**
others; someone else **aqqoq**
others; they **aqya; aqnu mavq**
otherwise; only **maq ngeel loq**
otter **eelsaol**

ought; must **wuqbo**
outer cover **laqnil piqkaq**
outhouse; water closet; toilet **ceiqso** (Chi) (10:16)
outlaw, to; to ban **qitif** (Chi)
outline; general picture **keifmaof** (Chi)
outline; sketch **galyaof** (Chi)
out of proportion; out of ratio **cavqqeiv maq za**
outside **laqnil**

outside; outsiders **bialzeil pyu** (as 'to listen to outsiders')
outside of house **laqnil pyu; deikaq** (11:33)
outstanding **yomeeq yoceil** (50:199); **yiulxiuf** (Chi); **aqzeiq meil** (50:169)

oval **jyuq** (11:55)
over; above **hultav**
over and above **aqzeiq zeiq**
over and over again **(vb) puv (vb) tav (hu puv hu tav** = looked at it over and over again)
overcast sky **aoqcyuq cyuq**
overcome (as in a battle) **diq hhaol** (26:54)
overhaul thoroughly; radically reform **zeifbei qil yeiq** (A=Chi)
overhear someone, to **gaq zaq; hev zaq**
overlap, to **caoq teiq (meelhov caoq teiq** = tiles overlap)
over-ripe **ovq duvq ovq ciq**
overseas Chinese relatives **qaoqsuq** (Chi)
overspend **ssaoqzeiq** (50:22)
over there; that side **yulzeil pyu**
overtime pay **aol zeiq pyuq**
overthrow, to **bavq puv; diq puv diq leeq** (34:16)
overthrow (turn upside down) **falseil** (26:15) (can be with the idea of having a better life)
overturn, to **dieilfuq** (Chi)
overturn; subvert **lilpuv zaol puv**

owe, to **zeil zuv; zeil ca**
owe money or some item **ca**
owl **huqbu miavlavq; huqbu aqma**
owner **yosaol; caoqsaol**
owner of the land (spirit) **daqhhaq e milsaol**

ox **aqniuq; aqniuq niuqnil**

pack animal's load **moqqeiv; niuqqeiv**
packet (made with a leaf) **pavqtov** (**pavqtov tov** = to package something in a leaf)
pack horse **alyeil qeivmoq**
pack saddle **bavqyaol** (11:149)
pack saddle frame **moqqeiv; moqhhav**
pact; treaty **tiaoqyoq** (Chi) (50:166)
pact to protect each other **doqheiq teev**
pad; cushion **hoqdaq; bavqdaq**
padded article **deiq dov laq e miaoqgaoq**
padding or filling (as for a quilt) **beewul**
paddle, to (or row) **he**
paddle of a loom **seiq dalpav**
paddy (unhusked rice) **ceil**
paddy field (irrigated rice field) **yaldei; xaldei**
paddy pounder (used to husk rice) **meicaol**
page, a (**soqhhaq qiq**) **kaoq; baq**
pail; bucket **eeltaoq**
pail, wooden **hovqtuv; taoqbaoq**
pain, to have **nal; gol**
painful; sick **nal**
paint **teiqnav**
pair, a **zaol**
palace, cultural **weiqhuafgaol** (Chi) (50:178)
palanquin (covered litter carried on poles) **bavqyaol** (lit., 'carrying house') (11:27)
palate **ngaqngal**
palate, soft **ngaqngal laqliv**
palm (tree) **sseilbol**
  palm bark **sseilhov; sseilbol**
  palm bark, soft **sseilmuv**
  palm bark, thick **sseilkaol kaolhav**
  palm bark ending **sseilhov hovmiq**
  palm bark rain cape **sseilgeel**
  palm bark insects **sseilbyul**
  palm bud **sseildu**
  palm cord; coir rope **sseilkaol**
  palm fiber **sseilmuv**
  palm leaves **sseilpiaq**
  palm seed **sseilsiq**
  palm tree **sseilbol**
  palm tree, large **loqhhoq hhoqbol**
  palm tree, oil **hhoqma albol**
palm of hand **lavqhhaq; aqlavq lavqhhaq**
palsy; paralysis **yoq jol maq sal** (50:162)
panda **haoqhhaolpiul**
pangolin **taoqkeeq**
panic **guvzuq zuq** ('shivering with fear')
panic, in great **deivqniv hov nei**
pant, to **savqli li; savqcii cii; savqcao cao** (11:43);

saqhhol saqcii nei
panther; leopard **haqssiiq; haqssiiq ssiiqcil**
pants cuff **laqcyuq laqkeel**
pants; trousers **laqcyuq; yoja**
paper; book; letter **soqhhaq**
parade; march; demonstration **yeqxiq** (Chi) (50:200)
paradise; heaven **yeillaolhaol** (50:166)
parakeet **doqqo alzil**
parallelism **doqqeiv qeiv**
paralysis; palsy **yoq jol maq sal** (50:162)
paralysis of arms and legs **lavqqaoq qaoq; keelqaoq lavqqaoq qaoq**
paralyzed; numb **keel sil lavq sil**
paralyzed leg **aqkeel sil**
parasitic plants **tevqlevq**
parchment **miavdal**
pardon (as in 'pardon me, could you say that again?') **haljivq loq**
parenthesis (punctuation mark) **guaqhaof** (Chi)
parents **dama; aqda aqma** (**dalma** = poetic)
parliamentarianism **yifhyuf ziifduf** (Chi)
parrot **haqguq alzil**
part; share **saqbaol; baol**
particle (physics, as atom, neutron) **liqzii** (Chi)
particle (gram) **zufciiq** (Chi)
particle showing a question **wul'aq**
particle showing certainty, a positive statement **wul yaq**
particle showing completed action **wul naq**
particle showing imperative **naoq**
particle showing inclusive imperative (let's) **kal**
particle showing past time **qavq; yil qavq** ('he has gone')
particle showing willingness to volunteer **nial**
particle used at end of commands **eiqlaq**
particle which indicates the one doing the action **nei**
part in a machine **liqhoqqif** (Chi) (26:30); **liqjeif** (Chi) (26:33)
parting blessing **coljol bi sal; ssil bi bo**
parting word ('I'll be going') **ngal ssuq movq al**
partition **bieil**
partridge **joqto haqhhal**
part-time **geeda tavq**
part-time teacher **niqyiq laosiil** (Chi) (26:101)
party (as the Communist party) **da** (Chi)
party branch **Daziilbuf** (Chi) (26:21)
Party Central Committee **Dazaolyal** (Chi)
party charter **dazal** (Chi)
party committee **dahhyu** (Chi) **dahhyu bafgaolsiiq** (Chi) (26:76); **dawei** (Chi)
party committee office **dahhyu bafgaolsiiq**
party constitution **dazal** (Chi)
party member **dayeiq** (Chi)
party membership (length of) **da'liq alhuvq** (A=Chi)

party organization **dazuziiq** (Chi)
party program **dagal** (Chi)
party training school **daxaof** (Chi)
party vice (deputy) secretary **dahhyu fuf suljif** (Chi)
pass, to (as a course, a class) **jiqgeiq** (Chi) (26:42)
pass, to (as in walking past another) **pyul** (11:165)
pass, to (as time) **yoq**
pass gas, to (fart) **haq pieiq** (taboo)
passing by **ssuqgal** (26:12)
pass on; hand on (as a custom handed down from the ancestors) **yyuq xal**
pass on a message **doqgaq zol; doqgaq cavq**
pass on disease **zoqleiq kovq** (10:23); **covqleiq kovq**
pass through (as a river) **yoq**
pass through (as thread through a needle) **sil tao**
past, in the **galhhu eiqmil** (13:29)
paste; ointment **ssuagaol** (Chi)
pasture, a **jadei; zeiqssaq zeiqdei**
pat; clap **diq**
pat; persuade **diq biov**
patch, a **duqkaoq**
patch, to (mend) **guvq taol; duvq**
patch made of cloth **duqkaoq**
path; road **galma**
path; small **galma galssaq**
path between two mountains **geekoq deibil**
path deep with weeds **galquv**
path going down **galtyuq**
path going up **galdav**
path in tropical area **joqgal galma**
patience **yeildo nei; neema yeil** ('wide-hearted')
patiently **neema yeildo nei** (26:107); **neema maq cal**
patrilineal **paqqa** (46:86)
patrilineal kinship **paqqa** (46:131)
patriot **hheifgoq sseiqsiif** (Chi)
patriotic **hheifgoq** (Chi)
patriotism **hheifgoq zuyif** (Chi)
pattern; design **galkov**
pause mark (in Chi) **dueifhaof** (Chi)
pave a road **hoq** (11:154)
pawn, to; to mortgage **dav zaq**
pawn shop **dav zaq duq**
paw of an animal **seiqsaoq; laqpul** (29:4)
pay; expenses **hhaqpyuq**
pay a debt, to **soq cil**
pay back, to **bivq huvq**
pay careful attention **nyuq gaol** (26:24)
pay for, to **zeil soq; duv**
pay tribute; pay taxes **zeiq duv ceiqla bivq**

pea **diqhhoq**
peace **milhaoq sal; hoqpiq** (Chi) (34:8)
peaceful coexistence **hoqpiq gaofcu** (Chi)
peaceful democracy **hoqpiq miqzu** (Chi) (34:8)
peace talks **neema salza nei geeza**

peach **siqhhaoq**
peach blossom **siqhhaoq alyeiv**
peacock (see: peafowl)
peafowl **saoldyuq**
peak, a **milgaoq wuqduq**
peanut **milcaq alsiq**
pear **aqpeil**
pear, sweet **aqpeil peilqul**
pear, wild **alzil aqpeil**
pear tree **aqpeil peilbol** (13:14); **aqpeil albol**
pear tree, to graft **aqpeil peilcavq cavq**
Peasant association **Naoqhyuf** (Chi) (26:12)
peasants; farmers **aolzaqssaq** (11:93); **xal aolssaq; xalduqssaq**
peasants, poor **piqnaoq** (Chi) (26:3)
peck (as a bird); strike (as a snake) **tuv; meiqtuv**
peculiarities; characteristics **teqye** (Chi)
pedal of a loom **naolgul dalpav**
peddle and sell, to **miaoqgaoq gaoqssaq aoq zaq**
peel, a **alhov**
peel, to **levq; pieiv**
peel; strip (bark from tree) **soqjoq joq**
peel; strip (palm bark) **sseilhov yov**
peeler for turnips, potatoes **jivtuv**
peeling, a **alhov**
Peking **Beiqjil**
pelvis **daoqnaol saqyyuq; saqpiaq saqyyuq**
pen (with which to write) **buvqdul** (26:16); **syubiq** (Chi) (50:158), **galbiq** (11:165)
pen, fountain **syubiq buvqdul** (11:31)
penalize; punish **cu'faq** (Chi)
penis **aqlyuq** (taboo) (in another dialect = **aqqoq**, but this means 'others' in the Luchun dialect)
penis (baby boy's) **alssyuq ssyuqssaq**
penny, a **taoqhaoq qiq siq**
pension for the disabled or family of the deceased **wuqhol zeiqpyuq** (50:52)
pen up, to **xoq laol**
people **colssaq; colmavq; col; ssaqlaol** (10:14); **ssaqjeil ssaqlaol** (**saosuf miqcuq ssaqlaol** = minority nationality people); **sseiqmiq** (Chi) (26:55)
people, foreign **wuafgoq col** (A=Chi)
people; humans **byulssaqnaol; sseiqmiq** (26:55)
people, mob of **col loq col meil**
people, old **ssaqmoq; colmoqssaq**
people, ordinary **ssaqjeil** (26:7)
people; person **aqcol**
people; the masses **qyuqzaof** (Chi)
people's commune **sseiqmiq gaolseif** (Chi) (26:108)
people's court **sseiqmiq faqyeif** (Chi)
people's democracy **sseiqmiq miqzu** (Chi)
People's Liberation Army **Gei'fafjyul** (Chi) **Sseiqmiq Gei'fafjyul** (26:102); **Zaolgoq Sseiqmiq Jei'fafjyul** (26:41); **Zaolgoq Ssaqlaol e Gei'faqjyul** (Chi)

people's non-government organization **qiqzaof zuziiq** (Chi)
People's Republic of China (PRC) **Zaolhuaq sseiqmiq gaofhoqgoq** (Chi) (Yyuweiq pg. 78, 34:8)
pepper, black and white **hhoqsol**
peppery hot **cil**
perch, to (as a bird) **dovq**
percussion musical instrument **diq gyuq yoqqif** (C=Chi)
perform; show; put on a play **seil** (50:194)
performance (as of magic, slide show, movie) **mu'luq**
perhaps **he; aqkulssal** (**Zaq aqkulssal.** Perhaps they have eaten.); **maq (vb) pa** (**maq jol pa** = perhaps not present); **pa (vb)** (**pa ngeel aq** = perhaps it is so; **pa jav aq** = perhaps you have)
perhaps it is **ngeel zeiq ya**
period; full stop (punctuation mark) **jifhaof** (Chi)
period of time **kaq**
perish; die out; pass away **zaolmei** (50:186)
permeate, to **seiftef** (Chi); **pujiq** (Chi)
permit (vb) **(vb) na** (**Maq bi ba zaq na** - not permit him to go with the group)
permit; written (as to cut down trees) **ka faq zeif** (Chi)
persecute **zaol sso**
perseverance **neema nyuq ceiv**
persimmon **aqbeel**
persist in; insist on **cuvq teiq**
person **col; aqcol**
person; human **byulssaq**
personal; private **siilsseiq** (Chi)
personality; character **colkaq**
personally **yoqhhaq sol meil**
perspiration; sweat **koqpiul; kaoqpiul**
persuade, to **gee xul miq; eil daoq**
persuade and educate **eil gaol meiq gaol** (50:159)
perverse, to be **miaoq bav aol**

pestilence, a **byulnal**
pestilence, to die of **byulnal sil**
pestilence, to suffer from **byulnal nal**
pestle for salt **caqluv**
petroleum **haqluv cil; haqluv cilmal** (36:18)

pharmacist **naciq ciqma** (50:195)
phase; aspect **jiqmieif** (Chi)
pheasant **gevq**
pheasant, silver **gevqpiul**
phenomenon; appearance **xeifxaf** (Chi) (50:185)
philologist; linguist **yiyeiq xoqjal** (Chi) (50:201)
philosophic theory **zeiqli** (Chi) (50:208)
philosophy **zeiqxoq** (Chi) (50:208)
phlegm; spittle **zaoqpeiv**
phonetic notation **yoteil buvq** (50:216)
phonograph; gramaphone (electric) **dieifcafjil** (Chi)
phosphorescent light; will-o'-the-wisp **neivqdovq**

photo; picture **zaofpieif** (Chi) (50:208)
physical culture; sports **tiyeq** (Chi) (34:19, 50:165)
physics **wuqlixoq** (Chi) (50:182)
physics, laws of **wuqli** (Chi) (50:182)

pick (digging tool) **ceiqcevq**
pick; pluck **cevq**
pickaxe **yaqhhaol** (Chi)
pick corn, to **ceildu heivq**
pick cotton, to **saqlaq piav**
pick fruit, to **cev**
pickled Chinese cabbage; sour greens **hhoqqeil**
pickled greens **hhoqkuv**
pick out, to **ceil duv**
pick out a splinter, to **peiv**
pick teeth **seqkaq hevq**
pick up, to **ssa; hhuv dav**
pick up; dig up **beq dav**
pick up (as with chopsticks); pluck off **niaov teiq**
pick up something, to **hhuv**
picture; statue **molkol**
picture, to take **molkol caovq** (B=Chi)
picture book **huafceiq** (Chi) (10:pref.)
piebald **biavqsov nei**
piece (as meat, bread, mud) **jeivq**
piece (of firewood) **miqkoq miqjeivq**
pieces of **zuv luv zeiv leiv**
pierce into, to **cov**
pig **aqhhavq; hhavq**
pig, adult **hhavqgol**
pig, adult male **hhavqciil; aqhhavq gaolzul** (B=Chi)
pig, baby male **hhavqciil**
pig, female (sow) **hhavqho**
pig, female (sow, never given birth) **hhavqhal; aqhhavq hhavqhal**
pig, small **aqhhavq hhavqssaq**
pig bristle **hhavqhao**
pig considered to be a bad-omen **hhavqdol**
pig day **hhavq nao**
pig dung **hhavqxiq**
pigeon; dove **hoqhyuq**
pigeon, wild **beilcaoq hoqhyuq**
pig fat **hhavqcul**
pig feet and head (used in offerings) **hhavqkeel hhavqduq** (46:126)
pig food **hhavqzal**
pig grunting **yuq eil yuq eil leil**
pig hoof **hhavqseiq**
pig hour **hhavq zeq** (B=Chi)
pig intestine **hhavqwul wulziil**
pig intestine (small) **wulziil ziil**
pig lard **hhavqcil**
pig liver **hhavqcaoq**
pig pen; shed; sty **hhavqkuv** (**cuv** = to build) (it also means 'jail' in some contexts)

pig trough **hhavqzal hoqtuv; hhavqzal hoqloq**
pigs, fat **hhavqcul**
pigs, little **aqhhavq hhavqssaq**
pig skin **hhavqgeel**
pig snout **aqhhavq meiqzu; naqbyuq**
pigtail (hair tied in braids) **caolpievq** (11:160)
pigtail, to braid a **caolpievq pievq** (11:160)
pig trough **hhavqzal hoqloq; hhavqsal hoqtuv**
pig year **hhavq huvq**
pig yoke (to keep pigs out of gardens) **hhavqtovq**
pile, to **gaoq**
pile of dirt **puv'qu; pulqu nei** (not pf)
pile up, to **gaoq dav; qu; bavq gaoq**
pillar, a **ssaolma** (29:4)
pillar (of sky) **aoqssaol**
pillow **wuqhhaoq; yiuvqhhaoq**
pillow, to (one's head) **wuqhhaoq hhaoq; yiuvqhhaoq hhaoq**
pillow cover **wuqhhaoq hhaoq lov**
pimple **baqsiq**
pincers of crab **alka lavqma**
pinch, to **ciivq; cev ceiv**
pinch (in joking, or quarreling) **saqciivq ciivq**
pineapple **miaqdaol**
pineapple, wild **neivqhaq miaqdaol**
pine (tree) **taoqsuq albol; aqtaoq** (46:190)
pine branch **aqtaoq allavq** (46:191)
pine resin **taoqsuq ziq**
pine seed **taoqsuq alneev**
pine torch **taoqsuq**
pinyin system of writing **pilyil** (Chi)
pioneer **tuqjiqse** (Chi)
pioneering spirit; creative initiative **secuafxif** (34:16) (Chi)
pioneering work **aolbei** (50:26)
pipe (for blowing on fire) **miqzaq boqlo**
pipe (for smoking, both men & women) **balluvq** (46:176); **yahyuq balluvq; yalhhyul; yahyuq baoqdel**
pit, bottomless **suqduq byu**
pitcher; bowl **haoqpiul**
pitch pine **taoqsuq**
pitiful **hhosaq nei**
pity; take pity on **hol cei qaq**
pity, what a **maq neivq haoq wul yaq**
pity someone **hhosaq saq; hol cei qaq**

place, a **gal; milnia** (10:31, 11:120); **milcaq haolteil**
place; region; country **milhaoq**
place, to (to put) **bavq taq**
place to (vb) **(vb) duq (jolduq; aolduq; zaqduq** etc.) (i.e., place to live; place to work; place to eat; etc.)
place (point) **milnia**
place (where live) **jolduq**

placenta; afterbirth **albeil; beeteiq; ssaq e beeteiq** (note: **beeteiq** can also mean 'carrying cloth')
placenta burial place (one's home town, since the placenta is buried inside the door of the home) **albeil duqhaoq**
plague; pestilence **byulnal**
plague; pestilence (to die of) **byulnal sil**
plain, a (level area) **deibiaq; deibaq**
plait (hair), to **caolpievq pievq**
plan, a **jifhuaf** (Chi)
plan (for dividing something) **bil zaq galquv**
plan, to (and wish for) **lulsul sul e**
plan; project; scheme **falhhaf** (Chi)
plane; airplane **feiljil** (Chi)
plane a board, to **biavqsov sov** (11:43)
plane, a (for planing wood) **laqsov**
plank; wooden board **biavq; teilbiavq**
planned economy **jifhuaf jiljif** (Chi)
planned to **zaol lil** (26:90)
plant again, to **xa puv**
plant in the ground (sticking in) **deiq cuv**
plant rice, to **ceil xa**
plant, to (as vegetables) **xa; duq cuv**
plant into, to **xa tao**
plants **jassaq**
plate, a (as for eating) **davssaq**
platform, a **zafteiq** (Chi) (50:207)
platform (as a political platform) **wuteiq** (Chi) (34:15)
platform (in an auditorium) **zuxiqteiq** (Chi)
platform (international) **goqjif wuteiq**
platoon leader in militia **miqbil peiqza** (Chi)
play, to **seilhha; salhha; balsal**
play a game, to **seilhha**
play cards **puqkeiq** (Chi); **seil**
play games **haqhhal seil; teil hha zaq**
playground in village **zoqdei**
play in moonlight **ba'la wuqcal seil**
play musical gourd pipe **laqjeiq bo**
play stringed instrument (pluck, strum) **bev**
play three-stringed instrument) **laqhe bev**
play two-stringed instrument) **ceilhhaol hhe**
play tricks; make mischief **neivqhaq zaol** (50:34)
pleasantly **hhyul lul hhyul sav meil**
pleasant sound **salteil; teilsal ye nei**
please (vb) **(vb) eiqlaq (Nol lal eiqlaq** = Please come. **Taq eil eiqlaq** = Please don't say it); **(vb) naoq (Nol sal hu naoq.** You please think.)
pleased, to be **hhyul**
'please give permission' **qiq heiq pilzyu**
pledge **baozeif** (Chi)
pledge; treaty; pact **gaolzeif** (Chi)
plentiful, to be **daoqgaoq gaoq nei; biao nei jav; miaq nei jav**
plenty, to have **biao nei; miaq nei**

pliers **qeiqzii** (Chi) (26:29)
plow, a (use with buffalo, oxen) **niuqceiq**
plow, a (wooden) **guldaol**
plow rope (big) **miaqcav; ssaoqdaoq**
plow rope (small) **cavbev**
plowshare, a **meiqpyul**
plow, to **ceiq**
plow a field a second time **loqdeiq ceiq**
plow again, to **ceiq puv**
plow and harrow a field **xalceiq xalkav**
plowed furrow **niuqceiq ceiqkov**
plowed lumps of mud **hhalbiav**
pluck; pick **cev**
pluck a chicken; dress a chicken **hahao civ**
plum **siqqaq**
plump (as a pig) **nulhevq nei**
plump; fat **cul**
plus (as in math) **jalhaof** (Chi)

pneumonia, lung disease **povq nal** (**duv lal**) (10:22); **beiqssiiqkeiq** (Chi) (10:23); **feiqyeil nal** (A=Chi)

pocket in clothes **peillov; peilhaoq peillov** (11:35)
pockmarks on face (as from small pox) **nalbuvq**
pod, a **albeiv**
poem, a **doqkol** (50:152)
poems, collection of **doqkol soqdaoq** (50:152)
poet, a **doqkol ssaq** (50:152)
poetic drama **doqkol kolzao** (50:152)
poetry (old word) **soqdoq; dama soqdoq**
point; place **milnia**
point, to (or touch with finger) **tyuq; tyuqmoq**
point at something, to **tyuq**
point out (with foot) **keel niv** (46:130)
point out (with hand, finger) **tyuq qei; tyuq moq miq**
point out (with words) **eil duv**
point out (with words and hand) **tyuq duv eil duv** (50:213)
points (as in an exam) **feil** (Chi); **feilsuf** (Chi)
poison **duvq**
poison, to **neiq sil**
poisonous **duvq lal e; duvq kevq e; sual** (Chi)
poisonous food **zalduvq**
poison to death, to **neiq sil; duvq sil**
pole for marking field **helliq** (put into ground: **helliq diq; helliq tavq**)
pole for propelling boat or raft **loqhe daldul**
police, armed **wuji mavqssaq** (A=Chi) (50: 181); **wuji bufdyuf** (Chi)
police station (local) **doqlo loduv**
policy (as the policy of the party) **zeifceiq** (Chi) **falzeil** (Chi)
policy, basic **daoqdaoq e galkov** (A=Chi)
policy, current **ziidaof yeiq** (Chi) (50:213); **siiqsiif zeifceiq**

polite, to be **miavhhaq jav; yeilkav nei**
polite; civilized **weiqmiq limaof** (Chi) (50:178)
polite ending **(vb) naoq** (please go, etc.)
political commander **ziidaofyeiq** (Chi) (26:43)
political crisis **zeifziif weiqjil** (Chi) (50:211)
political instructor **ziidaofyeiq** (26:68)
political party **da; zeifda** (50:211); **dapeif** (Chi) (34:35, 50:33)
political power **zeifqeiq** (Chi)
politics **zeifziif** (Chi) (26:50; 34:4)
politics, current **siiqsiif zeifziif** (Chi) (26:50)
pollute; contaminate **zaol cavq** (50:180)
polo, water **syu'qeq** (Chi) (50:158)
pomegranate **siqlyul malcavq alsiq**
pool of water **luduq**
pond, a **luduq; laobao**
pond, dirty **laosil**
pool of water **luduq; taoqdel**
poor people **cyuq; jol syuq maq ya maq dav meil**
poor; suffering **saq**
poor, very **cyuq sil cyuq lo**
poor and rich people **cyuqssaq sulhhaq**
poor health **gov**
poor people **ssaqcyuq; cyuqssaq; colpeel; ssaqcyuq cyuqssaq; cyuqssaq bavqssaq; ssaqdov colpeel**
poor woman **macyuq**
porcelain **yaqciiq** (Chi) (26:74)
porcelain bowl **haoqpiul; haoqmaq moldel** (lg. type)
porcelain clay **milneiq**
porcelain and pottery **taoqciiq** (Chi) (50:163)
porch on house (uncovered) **taoqgeel**
porcupine **hupiul**
porcupine, brush-tailed **hulaq**
pore **kaoqpiul yobyu; koqpiul yobyu**
pork **hhavqsaq**
pork fat **hhavqcil cilkuq**
pork offered in ancestral offerings **saqhel**
pork, lean (no fat) **nilzu; saqnil**
pornographic book **yiqsul** (Chi) (50:198)
porridge; cooked to mush (a watery gruel) **qavqbieiv bieiv**
porter, to be a **hhaqhaoq col; hhaqhaoq eq zaq**
portion **saqbaol**
portray; depict **buvqqo qo**
position **difweif** (Chi)
possible, to be **za lal; caq lal**
post; pillar **haolssiil**
postage stamp **yeqpiaof** (Chi)
postscript **eil laoq doq**
post for house (large) **ssaolma**
postman's car **yeqceil** (Chi) (50:199)
post office **yieqjyuq** (pf.); **yiuqjyuq; yeqjyuq** (Chi) (26:78)
pot **yuqlaoq** (10:30)
pot, copper **geeqcal**

pot, metal **saolcal** (13:33) (B=Dai)
potato **yaq yiul** (Chi) (50:194), **yaqyiul byuqsiq** (A=Chi) (10:3)
pot for steaming rice **saolpao**
pot holder (padded) **lavqdaq**
pot made of clay **yuqteiv**
pot (copper/bronze) **geeqdiq geeqcal; geeqcal**
pot made of iron **saolcal** (B=Dai)
pot sticker (rice that sticks to pot) **qavqkul** (11:28)
pottery and porcelain **taoqciiq** (Chi) (50:163)
pottery bowl; jar **haoqmaq moldel**
pound, to **taoq**
pound grains **meivhovq**
pound new rice, to **ceilsiivq hoqtaoq teil**
pound rice, to **ceil taoq; meilcaol taoq**
pound rice in pounder **meilcaol taoq** (11:159)
pound rice lightly, to **ceil kev**
pound sticky rice to make into cakes **haoqtaoq teil; hoqniaoq niaoqbiav taoq; teil**
pound to pieces **taoq lyul; teil nuv**
pour, to **seiv; hal; seiq dav**
pour into, to **seiv tao** (11:47); **seiv seiq**
pour on, to **ngaoq seiq; ngaoq dav; seiq dav**
pour out, to (as water) **seiv; seiv duv; seiv dav** (46:149); **ngaoqhal**
pour out food to spirits **hoqleivq hal**
pour water on burning fire to prevent spirits from entering a home **miqsuq suq**
pout, to **deiq cul**
pouting lips **meiqjil deiq cul**
pouting when disagree or disgruntled **meiq luq dalqul; meiqjil deiq cul**
poverty; suffering; hardship **saq zeiq gav zeiq** (45:71)
powder **zallyul**
powdered rice; rice flour (not bran) **ceillyul**
power; might **qaqqeiq** (Chi)
power, those with **hhaqhav pyu**
powerful man; strong man **miaoq aol havma**
power station (hydro) **syudieifzaf** (Chi)

practicable; workable **loqsiiq** (Chi)
practice, to **aolhu** (50:152); **siiqjei** (Chi)
practice; to learn **zaol zol**
praise, to **eil pyuq; biaoyaq** (Chi) **bavq pyuq; saol pyuq**
praise; respect; honor **saol pyuq miq** (46:129)
praise; to thank **eil pyuq; biaoyaq** (Chi) (26:66)
pray (say a 'fortunate' word) **heiqhel hel**
pray (the idea of bowing the head) **wuqduq taoq**
prayer when offering **heiqhel hel doq** (see 46:87 -- there are seven lines, four syllables per line)
praying mantis **moqpaq laqsal**
precisely (see: exactly)
predicate (gram) **hhyufyi** (Chi) (50:177)

preface; foreword **yoheiq heiqdoq** (50:190); **eil loq doq**
prefecture **zel** (Chi)
  prefecture governor **zelza** (Chi)
pregnant, to be **ssaq eq; aqnil eq; aqnil pi; wuqdeiq puq**
  pregnant female animal **zeiq'yul**
prelude; prologue **yoheiq pao** (50:190)
prepare, to **deissaol** (50:201)
prepare; get ready; plan **deilssaol** (50:218)
prepare (as food for meal) **deilssaol** (13:11, 26:57)
prepare a meal **susi** (**hoqzaol susi zaq** = cook a meal to eat)
preponderance; superiority **sultavq zeiq** (50:199)
prerogative; privilege **teqqeiq** (Chi)
present, to be (in something) **kevq** (**Hhoqcyuq hholqei saqnil kevq.** There is meat in the vegetables. 11:49 has more samples.)
preserve, to **taq leev; toq taq**
preserve; to keep **ssyuq taq**
press, to **ssiiv**
press conference **naqgaq buvqssaq doqzil cavq**
press down; prevent **deiq teiq**
press down with foot **naoq**
press on, to **hhuvq siivq**
pressure **ssiivhhaq** (50:193); **yaqliq** (Chi) (34:15)
prestige, to have **colteil dav; colpyuq bo**
pretend to **maq dul zaol dul** (50:177); **zaol hheivq** (**Nal ya leil zaol hheiv** = pretend to be sick); **zaolleivq leivq; zaol duv**
pretty **zaq** (10:4); **zaqqul nei**
pretty; look nice **zaq; hu sal; hu gaq**
prevailing custom **faolsaf** (Chi)
prevent; obstruct; stop **laol cyuq**
prevent, to **deiq teiq** (10:27)
prevent by digging (as to stop a flood) **duq teiq** (26:57)
price; expenses; pay **hhaqpyuq**
prick, to **cov dav; peiv dav**
prickly heat rash **kaoqpiul piulsiq**
priest, a Han **jiqsiil** (Chi)
  priest, spirit (Hani) **moqpil; pilma**
  'priest' of the Hani (ritual head) **milguq**
primary militia **jilgaf miqbil** (Chi)
primary school **xaoxoq** (Chi) (50:186)
prime minister **sexaf** (Chi) (50:156)
prime of life **huvq za hhaq bo**
primitive society **yeiqsii seifhyuf** (Chi) (50:201)
principal; headmaster (of school) **xaofza** (50:187)
principle **meiqzaq** (Chi)
principle part **zuti** (Chi)
print, to **yifsuaq** (Chi)
print (with colors) **yif dav** (A=Chi)
prior to **miqteil**
priority; precedence **huqteil bi teil** (50:199)

prison; jail; pig shed **hhavqkuv; laoqgei** (Chi)
private **gofti** (Chi) (34:10)
private; personal **siilsseiq** (Chi)
private property **yoceq**
private ownership **siilyeziif** (Chi)
privilege; prerogative **teiqqeiq** (Chi) (50:164)
prize, a **japi** (Chi)
probably (vb) **(vb) zeiq (Aqyoq nei zaol taq laq e ngeel aq zeiq ya.** He probably did this.)
probably so; maybe so **ngeel moq maq syuq**
probation, to be placed on **lieqda caqkaf** (Chi)
probationary party member **yifbif dayeiq** (Chi) (50:201)
probationary period **yifbif qil** (Chi) (50:201)
probe; explore **tafcaq** (Chi)
problem **wueiftiq** (Chi) (11:11); **weiftiq** (Chi) (32:3)
problems; difficulties **kyufnaq** (Chi)
procedure; order **ceiqxif** (Chi) (34:56)
process steel, to **lieif; lieifgal** (Chi) (26:28)
processing factory **jalgaolca** (Chi)
proclaim; declare **bugaq** (50:190)
procurator **jeicaqyeif** (Chi)
produce, to **faqhyul** (26:119)
production **seilca** (Chi) (26:54)
production brigade **dafdyuf** (Chi)
production increase **zalsiq aol dav**
production leader; brigade leader **dyufza** (Chi)
production, means of **miaoqguq miaoqgal** (50:151)
production team **seilcadyuf** (Chi) (26:39)
production tools **miaoq aol ssaoqsaol** (50:151)
production worker **seilcazei** (Chi) (26:100)
products **salpi** (Chi)
profession; occupation; vocation **ziiqniq** (Chi) (50:212)
professionalize **zueilniqhuaf** (Chi)
progeny **ssaqssyuq**
program; guiding principle **galli** (Chi) (50:56)
progress **jifbuf** (Chi) (34:20)
project; plan; scheme **falhhaf** (Chi)
prolapsed rectum **daoqlul ya duv**
proletariat **wuqca geiljiq** (Chi) (50:180)
proletariat class revolution **wuqca geiljiq geiqmif** (Chi) (26:56)
proletariat ideology **wuqca geiljiq siilxa** (Chi) (50:180)
prologue; prelude **yoheiq pao** (50:190)
prolong life, to **ssil bi bo**
promise, a **eil ceiv taq e doq**
promise, to **eil ceiv; eil taq**
promote, to **tiqgaf deiq dav** (A=Chi) (50:164); **cuqjif** (Chi)
promoter; advocate **aolkal leil qoq** (50:164) (the idea is from Chi)
pronoun **deifciiq** (Chi)
pronounce a blessing **heiqhel hel miq** (note; this can

also mean to 'give one joy')
pronunciation **zolteil; yoteil** (32:3)
pronunciation; standard **biaolzyuyil** (Chi)
proofread **jaofdyuf** (Chi)
propaganda **xeilcuei** (pf.); **xeilcuaq** (Chi)
propaganda, to conduct **geemeiq** (50:190)
proper; suitable; appropriate **zahev nei**
properly **cuv nei** (11:216); **meeqzav nei** (11:56)
proper time to (vb) **(vb) deil**
proper to (vb) **(vb) za** (26:31); **(vb) hoq** (Chi)
properly; carefully **meeqzav nei**
property **ceiqca**
property and money **zeiq**
proper way **galquv**
propitious day; lucky day **naomeeq; yonao meeq**
proposal; draft resolution; motion **tiqhhaf** (Chi) (50:164)
proposal; motion **yifhhaf** (Chi) (50:197)
propose **calyif** (Chi)
propose; initiate **caldaof** (Chi)
propose; suggest; move **tiqyif** (Chi) (50:165)
prop up, to **daltuv tuv**
prose **saweiq** (Chi)
prosperous (together) **gaoftaoq faqyaoq** (Chi)
prosperous and strong **fufqaq** (Chi)
prosperous and thriving **byuqssil byuqssav meil zeq** (50:46); **faqyaoq calsseif** (Chi) (34:18)
prostitute **daoqkaoq aoq zaq col**
prostitute, to **daoqkaoq aoq zaq**
protect, to **haol leev; haol luvq; baoya** (Chi)
protect (as the ancestors protect us) **haol na**
protect; guard **luvq taq; hafweif** (Chi)
protect; help **haol miq**
protect; save **haol leev; haol luvq**
protect all, to **haol jil**
protect oneself, to **yoq haol yoq leev**
protein **dafbeiqziiq** (Chi) (50:32)
protruding (as eyes) **lujeiv nei; luzeivq nei**
proud, to be very **pyuq sil pyuq lo meil; pyuq zaq laqmeil**
proud of, to be **buq zaq**
proud of oneself **aqseivq seivq**
proud of riches **jaqbuq**
proverb **doq'aqma**
province **sei** (Chi) (10:22) (**ngaldu sei** = our province) (**Huqnaq sei** - 26:3)
provincial governor **seiza** (Chi) (50:152)
provoke, to (pick a quarrel) **byuqnil nil** (50:192)
provoke laughter, to **eel naq pieiq; lav eel**
prune, to **dev soq** (50:190)
prune and top a tree (as in a field) **albol soqtal tal**
prune tree (so it grows straight) **albol bolsovq sovq**
prune tree (to keep from shading other plants) **albol gubaq zaq**

psychology **xillixoq** (Chi) (50:188)
pubic hair **beivqmoq** (women); **aqmoq** (men) (the latter can mean 'horse' in some subdialects)
public affairs (letter) **gaolwuf** (Chi)
public hall **gaoltaq; gaolguei; gaolseif** (Chi) (26:38)
public health bureau **hhyufseil bufza** (Chi) (50:177)
public health clinic **baojeifzaf**
public indignation **neessil neehav**
public issue, a; a civil dispute **ssaqlaol koq zaq deiq zaq**
publicise; advertise **eil haoq eil ceiv** (50:190)
publicise; explain **eil xa eil loq** (50:190)
public mood; public atmosphere **miqfaol** (Chi)
public opinion **seifhyuf yillyuf** (Chi)
public order; public security **ziifhhal** (Chi)
public ownership **gaoyeziif** (Chi) **gaolyeziif** (Chi)
public property **yohaol**
public prosecution **gaolsuf** (Chi)
public welfare fund **yohaol ssaoq piul**
publishing **cuqba** (Chi)
publishing house **cuqbaseif** (Chi)
puckery **peil; peillev nei; peiltuv nei; peil peil tuv tuv**
Pu'er County **Pu'e** (46:181)
puff and blow, to **savq cii**
puff out, to **lucei nei**
pull, to **hhe; hhe teiq**
pull and cover **hhe dao; hhe caq**
pull and discard (as weeds) **hhe zei** (note: **yalmuvq muvq** = to weed a field)
pull away **hhe yoq**
pull back and forth (trying to gain control) **koqteil**
pull closed (as door, cover) **hhe piq**
pull head hair, to **wuqduq ceilkaol hhe**
pull in **hhe kuv**
pull off; untie **hhe bieiq**
pull open, to **hhe pao**
pull out, to **jeiv** (13:6)
pull steadily **hhe teiq**
pull straight **hhe to**
pull tight **hhe siivq**
pull to break **hhe qov**
pull to long length **zei nei hhe zei**
pull to pieces **hhe zeiv** (26:71)
pull up, to **hhe puv**
pulse **laqguq** (**laqguq tyuq hu** = take the pulse)
pulse of a vein **saqguq**
public notice, to give **dyu nei eilgaq** (50:167)
pump (water) **syubol** (Chi) (50:158)
pumpkin **maldei** (Dai)
  pumpkin seed **maldei alneev** (A=Dai)
  pumpkin vine **maldei albiao** (A=Dai)
pump up; inflate **zii** (11:11)
punctual; on time **za nei** (50:218)

punctuation marks (names of) **fuqhaof yomiaol** (A=Chi)
punish, to **zaol sso** (27:11); **zaol hu**
punish; penalize **cu'faq** (Chi)
punished, to be **sso zaq**
punishment; penalty **xiqfaq** (Chi) (50:188)
pupil (in school) **xaoxoqseil** (Chi) (50:186)
pupil of eye **miavneev neevnav; miavssaq aqnil; miavssil**
purchasing power **hhel zaq e hhaqhav** (50:63)
purchasing station **selgefdieif** (Chi)
pure, to be **sol** (**aqpyuq sol alqaq** = 'pure' ancestors, i.e., no abnormal births or bad deaths)
pure; clean; honest **gaolquv nei**
'pure water' (from the village water source) **eelquvq eelsol**
purple **haoqhaol laolseiv**
purple glutinous rice **haoqniaoq niaoqnav**
purpose; aim **muqdiq** (Chi); **zaolziiq** (Chi)
purposely **wuqcavq meil; wuqcavq** (11:215); **balbal nei** (11:114)
pursue, to **naolhao pyu leiq**
pus **biaol**
pus in the ear **naqbuvq**
pus to form **biaol biaol**
push; sting; bite; scold **deiq**
push, to **deiq**
push and move, to **sov niv**
push away, to **deiq yoq**
push down, to **deiq caoq; deiq xa**
push down and cover, to **deiq caoq**
push over, to **deiq puv**
push up; lift up **deiq cei; deiq cei miq**
put; place **bavq taq**
put, to **yiul taq; bavq taq**
put away (conceal) **bavq leev**
put down; stop **pieiq taq**
put down; suppress; repress **ssiivq pieiv**
put in, to **bavq dov; dov** (as in a bag, or salt in food); **lav tao; pieiq dov** (as salt and chili into soup) (11:117); **yiul taq**
put in; mix in **bavq tao**
put in coffin, to **alzaol a bavq tao**
put into, to **lav tao; syuqkoq**
put more **teil dav**
put on; fasten **dov**
put on; wear (as clothes) **dao; dao dav**
put on; wear (as hat) **huv**
putrid; rotten; decayed **buvqlavq qeilsuq nei**
put together **nieivq zao; piav ssaoq**
put to sleep **bi yiuvq**
put together, to **heil paoq; zaol cuvq; bavq paoq**
put together; summarize **diq paoq**
put up (as on a wall) **pieiv ceq**

python **aqlivq**

Qin dynasty (221-206 BC) **Ciqcaoq**

quail **haoqssaq laqma**
quail, button (a type of quail) **laoqha; laoqha aqma**
qualification **ziilgeiq** (Chi)
qualified **hoqgeiq** (Chi)
quality **sufziiq** (Chi) (50:160)
quality (as quality of coal, oil, etc.) **ziiqliaf** (Chi) (26:35)
quality; nature **malniuv** (50:189)
quantity (large) **miav; yomiaq**
quarrel **deiq zaq; meiqdeiq deiq**
quarrel in hearts **needeiq deiq**
quarrelsome; noisy **doqlovq; beil sil**
quarter of an hour **yiq keiq** (Chi)

queen bee **biaqzyuq**
quench, to **ciq pieiq**
question; problem; issue **meiq zaq** (50:179)
question ending **laq; ma laq; wul aq**
question mark **weifhaof** (Chi) (50:179)
questions; difficulties; problems **kyufnaq** (Chi)
question part. **ngaq eil?** (46:138)

quick; fast **kol; ssal; kol lal**
quick, to be **cev nei** (**Cev nei ssuq, aoqsseil sseil al**. Walk quickly. It's raining. 11:111); **keellavq kol** ('fast legs and arms' -- as a person who is fast in his or her work)
quick, very **cev cev nei** (11:57)
quick brain **nee puv nee lav kol** (45:21)
quickly **laqcal meil** (10:12, 26:28); **teiq li cal lal meil**
quickly (vb) **(vb) teiqteiq** (as in: say quickly); **laqcal (vb)** (**Laqcal duv yil teiqteiq** - Go out quickly; **teiq sil teiq piav; (vb) jiq (vb) jiq meil (vb)** (**hhe jiq hhe jiq meil hhe** = to pull very quickly); **teiq li cal lal meil; teiq li teiq cal meil**
quickly; right away **cal nei; laqcal** (11:112)
quick-witted, to be **byulkyul kyul**
quiet, be **taq ziv; taq lovq**
quiet; still **quvq (lal)** (11:185); **quvqceiv nei**
quiet, very **quvqceiv nei**
quietly; calmly **quvqceiv nei; dovlov meil; a'lov nei**
quietly, very **quvqceiv pa ceiv nei**
quilt **albee**
quilt, old **albee beeja**
quilt covering **beehov; albee beehov**
quilt filler **beewul; albee beewul**

quilt, red (colored) **beenil** (46:175)
quiver (for arrows) **kavmiaq miaqbaoq**
quiver; shake **niv meil niv alnei; niv niv niv nei**
quota, to plan by **bil ceiv taq** (50:38)
quotation mark (single and double) **sseihaof; ssihaof** (Chi)

R r soqmiav aqma hholqei ceil xeivq mol e qiq mol

rabbit; hare **toqla; toqla almil**
rabbit day **toqla nao**
rabbit hour **toqla zeq** (B=Chi)
rabbit year **toqla huvq**
rabid dog (mad dog) **keeqmu mu**
race (people) **colssyuq** (50:214)
race, to **xeivqeiv qeiv**
radically reform; thoroughly overhaul **zeifbei qil yeiq** (Chi) (34:12)
radio **selyil jil** (50:156); **luqyil jil** (both Chi) (46:175)
radio, take along **luqyil jil ceq**
radish (Chinese); turnip **hhoqpul**
raft, a **haqpyul**
rafter (for roofing material) **alniul; xaolniul**
railing; iron fence **saolkal**
railway track **hoceil galma** (50:167); **tiqdaof** (Chi) (26:30); **xao tiqdaof** (small track) (Chi) (26:31)
rain **aoqsseil**
rain, to **aoqsseil sseil**
rainbow **beildul lulcuq**
raincape of palm bark **sseilgeel**
raincoat **sufliaof peilhaoq** (A=Chi) (26:60); **yiyil** (Chi) (26:96)
rain hat (Chinese style) **leqhev**
rain hat (old) **leqhev hevja**
rain hat (shellacked version) **geelqavq leqhev** (11:156)
rain heavily **aoqsseil sseilma**
rain large drops, to **aoqsseil sseilziivq ziivqma**
rainy day **aoqsseil sseil nao**
rainy season **sseilhhaol ba'la** (26:22); **sseilhhaol**
raise; care for **qu**
raise animals **qu; qu zaq**
raise easily, to **qu yal** (11:162)
raise funds; collect money **piul leiq ssaoq**
raise head proudly **wuqduq ngaoqcul cul**
raise; heighten **bavq goq** (50:164)
raise one's hand **aqlavq bavq cei**
raise pigs jointly (cooperatively) **hhavqtavq tavq zaq**
raise stakes (as in gambling) **teil dav**
raise up, to **goq dav**
raise up (as a sword) **hhe cei** (11:221)
raise up (hold up) **bavq cei** (11:28)
raise up one's head **wuqduq ngaoq cul**
raise up; hold up **bavq cei** (46:119)
raja rat (Rattus surifer) **huzyuq**
rake, a **laqkav**
ram (male sheep) **aqyol yolbu**
rancid, to be **zalhe naol; hhavqcil cilbuvq naol**

rank (as in the army) **deigaol** (Chi) (26:101); **zilxeiq** (Chi)
rape; seduce **koqlyuq; wuqcavq lav**
rape plant **hhoqcil**
rape seed **xalyeq** (Chi)
rape seed oil **hhoqcil xalyeq** (B=Chi)
rare, to be **naoq; maq miaq**
rash (skin) **covqleivq**
rat **hucavq**
rat, bandicoot **peillov hucavq cavqma; paltaol hucavq cavqma**
rat, field (small, red) **qilnil**
rat day **hu nao**
rat hour **hu zeq** (B=Chi)
rat year **hu huvq**
ration coupon for buying cloth **bufpiaof** (Chi)
rattan **cavni; haolma; qilguq** (**cavni** can also be used for the stem in fruit)
rattan, one type (roots edible) **qilguq**
rattan tie (like a string) **haolma haolniq**
rattan or bamboo basket (can close) **pyuqtul**
rattling sound (as when shake a walnut) **juv luv juv luv meil**
ravine, a **hhaqxaq**
raw; uncooked **yozaoq**
raw meat **saqzaoq** (or, **saqzoq** - not pf.)
rays of the sun **naolma wuqcal; naolma beelkeel**

reach; arrive **hev**
reached (in time) **biao**
reach; to catch up with **mil**
reach with hand, to **aqlavq zei nei zei**
react; reflect **nee puv**
react quickly **nee puv nee lav kol**
reactionary; anti-revolutionary **fa geiqmif** (Chi) (34:6)
reactionary person **fadaofpeif** (Chi) (34:8)
read, to **zol; gee; duqsul** (Chi) (26:52); **soqhhaq gee**
read; see; look **hu**
ready; prepared **deilssaol** (Chi) (26:101)
real; exact (and see in Hani) **jil**
real estate; fixed assets **maq niv zeiqma**
realistic; feasible **qiqsiiq** (Chi)
realistic; seek truth from facts **siiqsiif quqsiif** (Chi)
reality **yojil xeifsiiq** (B=Chi)
realize, to **hha hev** (50:165); **aol hev** (50:153); **siiqxeif** (Chi)
really **ngeeljil meil; aqdil; aqdil meil; meelheiq** (11:210); **jilhevq nei**
realm **liyiuq** (Chi)
reap rice, to **ceil yeiq**
rebel, to **puv zaq; saqyyuq lilpuv puv** ('the bone grows in the wrong way')
rebellion; riot **baoflueil** (pf.); **baofluaf** (Chi)

receipt for something purchased **soqhhaq tiaoqzii** (B=Chi) (11:31)
receive, to **bavq hha**; **sel** (Chi)
receive according to one's need **hal aol sso hal bil**
recently; these days **xil qiq savq**
reciprocal **niq pyu lavq cavq aol; niq pyu meeqduq jav**
recognize, to **hu duv** (13:6)
reconciled, to be **colqoq pievq huvq**
reconstruct, to **nieivq zao**
recount; relate; narrate **eilneiq neiq** (50:190)
recover, to **kaq**
recover from sickness, to **nal kaq**
recovered fully (from sickness) **kaq saq al; kaq sol**
recovering (from sickness) **kaq lal**
recreational activities **weiqyiq hoqdaof** (Chi); **yiqloq hoqdaof** (Chi)
rectify, to **zeidueif** (pf.); **zeiduaf** (Chi)
rectum **daoqbyu**
red **nil** (same word as "small")
red (to the extreme) **nilqul nei; nilqul qulssaq nei nil; nilceiq nei**
red, dark **nilqul pa qul nei**
Red army **Haoqjyul** (34:7) (Chi)
red-cheeked ground squirrel **hubaq baqnil**
Red Cross, International **siifgeif haoq siiqziif hyuf** (Chi) (50:154)
red deer **heiqceiv ceivnil**
red dirt **milnil**
reddish **nilpuq ceiq nei**
redeem; buy back former belonging **hhel huvq; pal huvq**
red eyes; envious **miavnil**
red flag **haoqqiq** (Chi) (34:7)
red flag carrier **haoqqiqse** (Chi) (26:100)
red flower **alyeiv yeivnil**
red face (as when embarrassed) **miavpyuq nilqul nei**
red face (as when healthy) **niltuvq nei**
red loach (type of fish) **deilnil**
Red River county **Haoqhoqxeif**
Red River delta **Haoqhoq lolqol**
red teeth (colored purposely) **seqnil nil**
reduce; decrease **hhe xu**
reduce amount (get less) **xu; suvq; naoq lal**
reed, a **tovqhaq**
refining pot **saol geelbaoq**
refine metal **gal lieif** (Chi) (26:34)
refinery **lieifgalluq** (Chi) (26:27)
reflect, to **fayif** (Chi)
reflect; react **nee puv**
reform, to **geigeiq** (Chi); **geicaof** (Chi) (34:10)
reform; adjust **zei'faol** (26:54)
refreshed, to be **hhaq bi bo huvq**
refute, to **eil duv; eil loq**
regain consciousness, to **deivq huvq lal**
region; place; country **milhaoq; qilyiuq** (Chi); **difqil** (Chi)

register **zufceiq** (Chi) (50:216)
register, to **buvq teiq**
regret, to **nyuq puv maq qaol**
regular **galkov**
regulate; adjust, to **zaol pal** (50:166); **ceil soq; tiaoqjiq** (Chi)
regulation **gyulliq** (Chi)
regulation; rule **tiaoqlif** (Chi) (50:166); **ziifduf** (Chi) (26:47); **sezeiq** (Chi) (50:156)
rehabilitate; rest and build up strength **hhaqma bi meil** (50:179)
rehabilitation of a person's reputation **haoqseil puv huvq** (50:75)
reins for horse **moqcav**
reject; scrap something **hhe zei**
relapse (in sickness) **nal puv**
relate; recount; narrate **eilneiq neiq** (50:190)
related by marriage, to be (man's side) **huljil pyu nei niq lal**
related by marriage, to be (woman's side) **miqssaq pyu nei niq lal**
relationship **gueilxif** (pf.); **gualxif** (Chi)
relative; friend (very close) **yoqcol**
  relatives **ciciq** (Chi); **laobiao** (Chi); **aqyivq aqnil**
  relatives on father's side **hyulzao**
  relatives on mother's side **nilzao**
  relatives, close **ciiqyeil**
relax, to **sov niv**
relax; loosen **pieiq juq**
relax restrictions **pieiq yeil** (50:49)
release, to **pieiq; pieiq duv** (50:155)
release; to untie **peel**
reliable, to be **neehaol sil; lavqdal** (46:179)
reliable; trustworthy **hoqhhyu aol**
relieve; succor **eq haol**
relieved; satisfied **naolhaol sil**
religion **zaoljaof** (Chi) (50:220)
religious ceremony **holmoq**
  religious ceremony, to hold **holmoq aol**
religious day **nee'lao lao**
reluctantly **maq hhyul meil**
rely on; lean on **dal; pieiq dal; haol dal**
remarry (a woman) **yil pal**
remember, to **nyuq teiq** (10:28)
remind, to **eil nyuq** (11:126)
remnants; survivors **yazeil** (50:19)
remnants; vestiges **jav gav e aqzeiq**
remold; transform something **geicaoq** (Chi)
remote, to be **galmol kaq; galmol mol**
remote places **lavqhhuvq lavqliv**
remotest corner of the earth; ends of the earth **aoqdaoq milseil** (50:166)
remove, to **geigeiq** (Chi) (34:10)
  remove someone from office **hhe sa**
rent out (and get half of the proceeds back) **aolpav**

pav

repair, to **zaol duvq; xelli** (Chi)

repair workshop **jilxel ceiljeil** (Chi) (26:33)

repeat (vb) **(vb) puv (i.e.; leiv puv); (vb) huvq** (i.e., **eil puv; eil huvq** = to say again)

repeat again, please (i.e., Could you please repeat that?) **haljivq loq**

repeatedly (vbA) (vbA) **meil** (vbB) (**yil yil meil ngyul** go repeatedly and cry)

repeat one's mistake **zyul puv**

repent; change mind **nyuq puv**

repentance, to show **zyulduq nyuq hev** (50:76)

replace, to **bavq taq huvq**

replow, to **ceiq puv** (11:18)

reply; answer **eil puv**

reply with a song **laq qoq**

report, a **baofgaof** (Chi)

report, written **baofgaof soqhhaq** (A=Chi)

reporter; newsman **naqgaq buvqssaq** (50:188)

representative; delegate **deifbiao** (Chi); **dafbiao** (not pf.) (Chi)

representative of the people **sseiqmiq deifbiao** (pf.); **sseiqmiq dafbiao** (26:101)

repress; suppress; put down **yaqpeiq** (50:193); **ssiivqpieiv; zeifyaq** (Chi)

reprisals, to make; make false charges **wuqcavq xa huvq**

reptile in tropical jungles (similar to crocodile) **ssolgov alpeel**

republic **gaofhoqgoq** (Chi)

reputation **pyuqduq** (34:15); **yoteil**

reputation; fame **yo'lal** (**yo'lal aoq zaq** - to ruin name, reputation); **colteil; teilsal**

request, to **sal; aol** (13:31)

request; beg **sal**

request a leave **qija** (Chi)

request from an official (demand) **yaolqeq** (Chi) (26:46)

require; need; want **guq** (50:190)

reread, to **zol puv**

research, to **piav puv**

reserve, to **toq leev**

reserve army **hefbifjyul** (Chi)

reservoir; dam **syukuf** (Chi) (50:158); **eelquvq laobao** (50:158)

resign; to leave one's work **hoqhhaq xeiv huvq** ('throw away one's rice bowl'); **safbal saf saq** (Chi) (26:29)

resolute; firm **jeiljyuq** (Chi)

resolve, to **jyuqdif** (Chi)

resources (as natural) **ziilyeiq** (Chi) (50:219)

resow, to **seiq dov pal**

respect, to **zyulzif** (Chi) (26:120); **zyulzaof** (Chi) (26:29); **zueilzof (zualzof)** (Chi) (34:15); **sol pyuq**

respect; praise; honor **saol pyuq**
respect; revere; esteem **zyuljif** (Chi) (50:221); **caofjif** (Chi)
respect one another **qaq qaq yaol maq hu nil**
responsibility; duty **zeiqsseif; fufzeif** (both Chi)
responsibility; each has a share **aqsol liq dal wuqbo**
responsibility system **fufzeiq ziif; zeiqsseif ziif** (both Chi)
responsibility, to take on **pi**
rest, to **hhaqnaq naq**
rest; stop **naq**
rest easy **qu yal** (11:162)
resting place, a **naqduq** (46:168)
restrain self, to **yoqhhaq jol teiq nia**
restrictions on **xeifziif** (Chi) (50:185), **hu ceiv** (50:185)
results **ceiqgo** (Chi)
resurgence; reversion **zaoq huvq**
retail; to sell retail **liqsef aoq** (A=Chi)
retain, to **bi jav; maq bi bial**
retaliate, to **diq puv huvq**
retire, to **tyufxel** (Chi) (50:172); **liqxul** (Chi)
retract, to (as arms and legs) **hhe kuv** (26:24)
retreat, to **di; naoldi di** (11:42, 26:98); **neema puv zaq** (26:44); **di naolhhuvq**
retrench; simplify; reduce **hhe xu** (50:89)
return **hhuvq; soq miq** (46:127)
  return; come back **huvq**
  return; go back **huvq li**
  return home from fields **yalsol hhuvq; xalsol hhuvq lal** (11:199)
  return something; give back **bivq huvq**
  return to suffering **saq puv**
reveal, to; to show **bilduv nei**
revenge, to get **zaol huvq; soq huvq; baofceq** (Chi) **hhaqjo soq** (the latter also means: 'to return labor')
  revenge for someone beating you **diqjo soq**
  revenge for someone lying to you **hheivqjo soq**
revere; esteem; respect **caoqjif** (Chi)
reverse; setback **cofzeiq** (Chi)
review; repeat **hu pal, zol puv**
review lessons **zol puv zoldaol daol** (50:177); **fuqxiq** (Chi)
review what studied **zolpuv hu**
revise; adjust; regulate **zaol pal** (50:166)
revisionism **xelzeil zuyif** (Chi) (50:190)
revoke, to; to withdraw **bavq hhuvq**
revolt, to **puv lal** (50:134); **geiqmif aol** (A=Chi)
revolt; rise in rebellion **lilpuv lav puv** (50:205)
revolution **geiqmif** (Chi)
Revolution of 1911 **Xilheif geiqmif** (34:4, 50:188)
revolutionary soldier **geiqmif zafsiif** (Chi) (26:44)
revolutionary spirit **geiqmif zilseiq** (Chi)
revolutionist **geiqmifjal** (Chi)

revolutionize to socialism **seifhyuf zuyif jeifseiq** (Chi); **geiqmifhuaf** (Chi)
revolve, to **gaolzua**
reward, material **miaoq nei qiq pyuq**

rhesus monkey (Macaca mulatta) **miuvqhav daoqnil**
rhinoceros **neivqniuq kyulteiq**
rhymed dialogue **dyufke ciiq** (Chi)

rib **bialnaol; bialhhal saqyyuq**
rib; side **jaqhhal**
ribbon **zaoqbuvq**
rice (general for cooked) **hoq**
rice (general for unhusked and uncooked) **ceil**
rice (glutinous) **hoqniaoq; haoqniaoq**
rice (glutinous, purple) **ceilnav; hoqniaoq niaoqnav; haoqniaoq niaoqnav; niaoqsol**
rice, broken **ceilgeeq**
rice, cold **hoqgav**
rice, cooked **hoq**
rice, early variety **ceilkol; ceil ceilkol** (46:205)
rice; food; meal (cooked) **hoq**
rice, fried (with egg) **alwuv hoqlul**
rice, grain of **ceilsiq**
rice, husked **ceilpiul**
rice, late variety **ceil le**
rice, mountain variety **daolceil**
rice, new (as in 'eat new rice') **hoqsiivq** (11:28); **ceilsiivq hoq**
rice, non-glutinous **haoqceiv**
rice, overcooked (burnt) **qavqkul**
rice, red **hoq nil**
rice, white **hhopiul**
rice ball **hoqcuv**
rice box (for carrying cooked rice) **hoqgav baoqtevq**
rice bran ('reddish') **haqpeeq peeqnil**
rice bran ('soft') **haqpeeq peeqnaoq**
rice bud **hho'quv**
rice budding **hhobaoq hhoduv duv**
rice cake **hoqniaoq niaoqbiav**
rice cake (sticky rice) **niaoqbiav; haoqniaoq niaoqbiav**
rice chewed up for baby **hoqhhyuq**
rice container made of bamboo **alniq hoqbav**
rice cooked done **hoqmiao**
rice crust (sticks to pan) (see: rice, overcooked - burned)
rice dumpling (to make) **za'lei lei**
rice field, irrigated **deiceil**
rice fistful (when eating) **hoqcuv**
rice grain **ceilneev; ceilsiq**
rice grain (cooked) **hoqneev**
rice grain (husked, not cooked) **ceilpiul**
rice granary **ceiljil**
rice gruel **hoqqavq eelcal** (10:10)

rice harvest **ceil yeiq**
rice head **ceilnaol; kalnaol**
rice head, new **ceilsiivq kalnaol**
rice husk (empty) **ceilhovq**
rice husk (outer, hard) **haqpeeq peeqhav; peeqhav**
rice in bloom **ceilbao beivq**
rice newly harvested **ceilsiivq hoq**
rice noodles **milseiv**
rice partially cooked **hoqceil**
rice pounder (all) **meicaol**
rice pounder mortar **meihovq**
rice seedlings **hhokeeq (hhocuv cuv** = to transplant rice seedlings)
rice seedlings, old **hhokeeq keeqssei**
rice seedlings, to transplant **hhocuv cuv**
rice seedlings bed **seiqpaoq**
rice seeds **hhossyuq**
rice seeds (to sow in seedbed plot) **seiqpaoq paoq**
rice stack **ceilbaol**
rice stalk **ceilbol**
rice steamer (wooden) **savqbaoq**
rice stem **hhobaoq**
rice stem flute (to blow) **hhobaoq meel**
rice stems to develop **hhobaoq baoq**
rice steamer cover **hoqpiq**
rice straw **hhoyyuq**
rice straw stacks **hhoyyuq ceilbaol**
rice stubble **ssaqbeiq**
(rice) table **lolbieil; jaziiq lolbieil**
rice-threshing machine **ceil diq jilqiq**
rice to be pounded **ceil taoq**
rice to be washed (before cooking) **ceilpiul ciq**
rice weevil **ceil byuqnav**
rice which is burned; rice which sticks to the pot **qavqkul**
rice worm/insect **ceilbyuq**
rice wrapped in leaf **hoq pavqtov**
rich **beq; loqbeq** (27:11); **sulhhaq loqbeq** (13:3)
rich, become **beq dav; loqbeq beq** (26:119)
riches, to be proud of **jaqbuq buq**
rich family **sulmeeq**
richly **biqsei nei**
rich man, a **sulhhaq aqda**
rich man, a cruel **zeiqbo havma**
rich man, not cruel **zeiqbo aqhhol**
rich people; other people **sulhhaq; sulmeeqssaq**
rickets **ssueiguqbif nalgol** (A=Chi) (pf.); **ssuaguqbif nalgol** (A=Chi) (10:1)
riddle **bavkaq** (pf); **bakaq** (11:178)
riddle, to guess a **bavkaq caq** (11:178)
ride **ziiq**
ride a horse **moq ziiq**
ridgepole, a **yaol huqbyu daoqma; xaol huqbyu daoqma**
riding horse, a **ziiqmoq**
riding saddle **ziiqhhav**

rifle; gun **miqbev**
right (correct) **hoq**
right (hand) **jaqmal; mallavq**
right and wrong **meeq dyul** (50:155)
right away; quickly **cal nei; laqcal** (11:112); **kolkol laqcal**
right deviation (pol) **yef** (Chi)
right deviation capitulation clique (pol) **yefqi teqxaq zuyif** (Chi) (34:6)
right deviationist (pol) **yefpeif** (Chi)
righteous cause **dafyif** (Chi)
right hand **mallavq; jaqmal**
right moment, at the **saqhaol; siqse za nei**
right now **niaoq'aol niaolhav**
right of accusation **eil duv qeiqlif** (C=Chi)
right of appeal **bu puv qeiqlif** (C=Chi)
right of exemption **hofmiei'qeiq** (Chi)
right side **mal pyu; jaqmal**
right then **yul taq luldu**
right to vote **biaojiqqeiq** (Chi)
right way; path **galma daol**
right wing; the right (pol) **yeqpeif** (Chi) (50:200)
rigorous; strictly **ssiqnei** (50:193)

ring (as worn on finger) **lavqnyul lavqgaol gaol**
ring (as worn on thumb) **lavqma lavqgaol gaol**
ring a bell, to **hhe gyuq**
ring for a finger **lavqgaol**
ring of a bell **gyuq**
ring finger **nyulzeil** (11:128)
rings to form around sun **naolma beeljoq joq**
ringworm **joqzyul**
rinse; bleach; clean **ceibu**
rinse mouth (or brush teeth) **meiqloq loq**
riot; rebellion **baoflueif** (pf.); **baofluaf** (Chi)
ripe (used for ripe fruits, crops, and cooked food) **ovq; miao**
ripe enough **ovqleel nei**
ripe enough to eat **ovq duvq; zaq deil**
rise (suddenly) **zei tul lal; beil tul lal**
ritual head of village **milguq (milguq lavqcavq** = his helpers)
river **lolbaq** (clf. **lol**) (11:34)
river, big **baqma; taoqtiv lolnavq**
river, lower section **eelmiq** (op. **eelmeil**)
river, upper section **eelmeil** (op. - **eelmiq**)
river bank **lolzeil**
river bend **lolhhuvq lolliv**
river outlet; mouth of river **lolmiq**
riverside **lolzeil** (13:30)
river source **lolheiq; lolmeil; eelmeil**
river valley **loldei**

road, flat **galbil**
road; path **galma**

road, side of **galdaoq galzeil**
road, very wide **galma dallul; dallul**
road, winding **galhhuvq gallavq**
road going down **galtyuq**
road going up **galdav**
roadside **galdaoq galzeil; galzeil**
road which is flat **galbil; galma galbil**
roam, to **del hha; gao hha** (**coldel del** = a person who roams)
roam around looking for food **hoqbiol leiq zaq**
roar; rumble **gyuq**
roar of tiger (or large cat) **gyuq**
roast, to 1. **ca**; 2. **peev**
roast duck **oq'a oqpeev**
robot, a **jilqif** (Chi) (50:79)
rock, a **haqluv**
rock cliff **hhaqpuq**
rocky area **haqluv luvdaol**
roll, to **leeq**
roll and tie **leel tovq**
rolling about **qao hha**
roll in muddy water **aqlao lao** (46:164)
roll of cotton prepared for spinning **saqlei**
roll of thread **kaollee**
roll on the ground, to **aqpuv puv** (26:10)
roll up, to **leev dav**
roll up onto something, to **puv dav**
roll up sleeves, to **leev**
roof **hoqbyu; xaolbyu**
roof beams **laqhyul hoqbyu**
roof of house **yaol hoqbyu**
roof tiles **meelhov** (A=Dai)
room, a **bavlov; lovkaq**
rooster; cock **hapyul; aqha hapyul**
rooster, very strong **deilluv**
rooster spur **hadavq**
root (as of plant) **alqil; daoqqil**
root; base **daoqpeiq**
root, side (not tap root) **qilseiq; alqil qilssaq**
root, small **daoqqil qilsal; daoqqil qilssaq**
root, tap (main) **daoqqil qiltaoq; alqil qiltaoq**
roots of broom grass **leiqgaoq alpul**
roots of plants **kalqil**
root up and break (as wild boars) **byuq qov**
root with snout, to **byuq puv; byuq zeiv**
rope **alcav; cavdu**
rope, to make **xu; alcav xu**
rope for a plow **miaqcav; ssaoqdaoq; bavqmieiq**
rope for tying cattle **niuqcav**
rope made of coconut husk (coir) **sseilcav**
rope to guide buffalo right and left when plowing or harrowing **kaolbev alcav**
rope to tie around village or village gate **galcav; sulpeel cavlei**
rope to tie buffalo **niuqcav**

rope to tie on loads **jalsoq**
rosin **taoqsuq ziq**
rot, to **buvq**
rotate, to **aqpuv lilpuv puv**
rotation **yoqpuv puv** (50:220)
rotten **yobuvq**
rotten (as meat) **buvq; buvqlavq qeilsuq nei** (50:52)
rotten (as wood) **peq; peqdaq**
rotten; corrupt **buvqlavq nei**
rough; coarse **sav**
rough, very **savyov nei**
roughly **savtuv pa tuv nei; savtuv nei**
round, in a circle **leecei nei**
rounded **hhao'lao nei**
round sum, a **qiq puq laq luq**
roundworm (intestinal, ascaris) **wuqdeiq buqdeil**
row a boat, to **he**
royal; kingly **hhellaoq**
royal family **hhellaoq qovq** (used of dragon in 11:201)

rub; stroke **sov**
rub, to **ssivq**
rubber **zaqgev; xafjaol** (Chi)
rubber shoes **jaolheiq** (26:72) (Chi)
rubber tree **zaqgev albol; xafjaol albol** (A=Chi)
rubbish **gaoqbeeq; gaoqbeeq dalssei**
rub eyes, to (as when wake up) **miav leiqleiq**
rub off, to **qiv**
rub one's feet **keeljyuq jyuq**
ruin; get bad **biav**
rule, a (as a grammatical rule) **gyulzeiq** (Chi)
rule, to **taoziif** (Chi) (34:16, 50:169)
rule; custom **yo'liq**
rule; regulation (as in the army) **ziifduf** (Chi)
ruler; lord (to be) **soqpaq gee; zyuqma gee**
rulers of the sky **aoqzyuq** (30:2)
ruler's wife **zyuqma aqpiq; zyuqma miqssaq**
rules (strict) **jiliq** (Chi)
rules and regulations **tiaoqlif** (Chi) (50:166); **sezeiq** (Chi) (50:156)
rules and regulations (detailed) **xifzeiq** (Chi) (50:183)
rumble; roar **gyuq**
ruminate, to **zalpuv puv**
rummage through; search **piav puv** (50:160)
run, to **xeiv; quq** (11:221)
run about; do exercises **xeiv hha**
run after, to **naolhao xeiv**
run and disappear **xeiv bial**
run and hide **xeiv hhovq; xeiv bial**
run apart, to **xeiv hhoq**
run around in circles **teiq sil teiq piav**
run away **xeiv leev; xeiv duv; xeiv yoq; xeiv bial** (27:11)
run down to **xeiv al yi**

run into (as fire) **quq peev**
running contest **xeiv'qeiv qeiv**
running sore, a **alnal nal**
run over here **xeiv al la**
run seeking something or someone **lolqo nei**
run up to **xeiv al la**
rush up **quq**
Russian language **Hhoqgoq** (34:5); **Sullieiq; Hhoqyi** (Chi)
Russians **Hhoqgoq; Sullieiq**
rust **sulnil**
rust to form **sulnil duv; sulnil tuvq**
ruthless; merciless **neegaq maq tavq** (50:180)

---

sacred grove of village **hhaqma; hhaqma hhaqcaoq**
sacred grove offering **hhaqma tul; hhaqma lol; hhaqma aol**
sacred tree (make yearly offerings to) **hhaqma albol; milsiil albol; milsaol albol**
sacrifice, religious **helhaoq**
sacrifice, religious (to make) **helhaoq aol**
sacrifice, to make a (food, eggs, chickens, pigs, etc.); **helhaoq daol dav; xilseil** (Chi) (34:116)
sacrifice for burial ceremony **yaqmoq**
sacrificial offering **zalhel**
sacrificial pork (in sacred grove ceremony) **saqhel**
sad, to be **nyuq saq; neesaq saq; neema geel**
sad (lit. 'cold in heart') **neema gav**
sad, very **neema hhoqcil geel; neema ceiv**
saddle and frame for packhorses **moqhhav qeivkeel** (the whole set)
saddle for packhorse **qeivkeel**
saddle frame (for packsaddles) **moqhhav** (B=Chi)
sadly **neema nalyov nei**
safeguard; defend **haollaol** (50:176); **weiqhuf** (Chi)
sake of (for the) **balnei**
salary **colhhaq hhaqpyuq** (45:3); **gaolziil** (Chi)
saliva **qalju; eelqal**
salt **caqdevq**
salt bowl **caqdevq caqhaoq**
salt container made of bamboo **caqdevq baoqcavq**
salt pounder **caqluv; caqdevq hoqbiav**
salty enough **caqdevq qul**
salty, too **caqdevq haq**
salute, to **wuqduq niei** (50:189); **ziifjif** (Chi)
sambar deer **heiqceiv**
same, the **za; qa; paoq; qiq qa; qiq qa paoq; qiq qa naldul dul; nallao dul; laqmeil**
same age (approximately) **qiq pieiv qiq dol**
same as; equal (amounts) **qiq kov miav nei**
same as; like **aqmeil ngeel** (10:11)
same generation **qiq pieiv qiq dol**
same village **qiq puv laolhaol**
sample, a **yafpi** (Chi)
sand **halceil**
sandals **seiqnaov; seivqnaov**
Sani language **Saniqdoq**
Sani people (a branch of the Yi) **Saniqssaq; Sanissaq** (A=Chi)
sanitation; hygiene **hhyufseil** (Chi) (50:177)
sap **alziq; ziq**
satellite **hhyufxil** (Chi) (50:177)
satellite, communication **naqgaq hhyufxil** (B=Chi) (50:168)

satellite, scientific **kilxoq hhyufxil** (Chi)
satiated (see: full)
satin; brocade **bu'lavq**
satirize; mock **eil kyuq; eil buvq**
satisfactory **leevdov nei** (50:174)
satisfied; eat one's fill **deiv**
satisfied; heart is easy **neema za; needeq lal; neema lal; neema salduq ssivq**
satisfied; relieved **naolhaol sil; neehaol sil**
Saturday **Xilqil kuvq nao** (A=Chi); **Xilqil liuq** (Chi)
sausage, to make **wulzoq zoq**
save; protect **haol leev**
save, to (as a burning building) **jiqyoq** (Chi) (26:75)
save, to (as a life) **boq (wuqhol boq** = to save a life - 26:13)
save, to (as money) **jiqyoq** (Chi) (26:75)
save up, to **taqssaoq; taoq ssaoq; taqssaoq laq; ssyuq taq**
saw, a (for cutting wood) **saolsul**
saw, to **yeiq**
sawdust **saolsul sulpovq**
say; speak **eil; eillul**
say directly, to **eil qiq kov**
say happily **eilheiq qeil**

scab **nalbyuq; nalhhov** (and see: **alnal nalbyuq byuq**)
scabies **geeq**
scabies of the neck **laolgeeq**
scald pig's bristles off, to **hhavqhao tal xa**
scale for weighing **savjil; savjil savmiav**
  scale for weighing, large **savjil jilma**
scales (of fish) **ngaqgeeq; hhov; ngaqhhov**
scalp (headskin) **wuqgeel**
scapula; shoulder blade **lavqbiav saqyyuq**
scar **nalbiol; nalheiq; alnal nalbioq**
scarce; sparse **kal** (11:55)
  scarcely **kul lul kal lal nei**
scare, to **guv; navqguv**
scarecrow **zalguv**
  scarecrow, to make **zalguv ceq**
scarlet **niltel nei**
scatter, to **leiq hoq leiq ceiv**
scattered out here and there **jolhhal maq ssaoq**
scattered thinly **kalseil nei**
scavenge for food **syuv zaq**
scenery painted on backdrop for drama or art troupe **bufji** (Chi)
scent, good **solxeiv**
scheme; plan; project **falhhaf** (Chi)
school **soqhhaq zolyaol; xoqxaof** (Chi) (50:191); **soqhhaq zolduq**
  school age **zolhuvq** (50:191)
  school bag **soqhhaq paltaol** (50:157)
  school, junior middle **culzaol** (Chi)
  school, primary **xaoxoq** (Chi) (11:176)

school, senior middle **gaolzaol** (Chi)
school mate; classmate **soqhhaq zolqoq; zolqoq**
school term **xoqqil** (Chi) (50:191)
school vacation; term break **fafjaf** (Chi)

science **kolxoq** (Chi)
science and technology **koljif** (Chi) (34:19); **kolxoq jifsuq** (34:19)
scientific method, according to **kolxoq galquv tav** (A=Chi)
scientific satellite **kolxoq hhyufxil** (Chi)

scissors **zyuqdal**

scold; push; sting; bite **deiq**

scoop out, to **beq**

score in a game (as in basketball) **bi'feil** (Chi)

scrape off, to **jeiv; piav xa**

scratch **piav**
scratch open, to **qiq piav piav pao**

screen (metal) **salcual** (Chi)
screened (as a room) **lovkaq to laq**

screw (as used in machinery) **loqsiil** (Chi)
screw and nut **loqsiilmaof** (Chi)
screwdriver **balzii** (Chi) (26:29)

scribble, to **leiq buvq**

script (as in linguistics) **soqmiav**
script, Hani **Haqniq soqmiav**

scrotum **davqwuv** (**davqwuv wuvsiq** = testicle)

scrutinize balloting **piaof luvq taq** (A=Chi)

sculpture, to make **molkol zaol**

sea; ocean; big lake **lao'laoma**

seafood odor; smell **salhe nei**

seal, to **miaoq kavq**

'sealed book' (something which cannot be known) **maq hev qivq e miqnieiq**

seal off; blockade; close **miaoq cyuq; laol quvq** (50:51); **diq cyuq; faolso** (Chi)

search; find **qo**

search for; visit each other **qo zaq**

search; rummage **piav puv** (50:160)

sea slug **heiseil** (pf.); **haseil** (26:118) (Chi)

season, the **zivq; ba'la**

season, to **dov**

seasonable; right time **yotovq**

season; moment; time **yotovq**

seat **jolhhal**

seat for driver (as car, etc.) **jafsiizof** (Chi) (26:98)

seat of trousers **laqheiq**

second cry of newborn **ceil niq puvlaol** (for the whole village)

second rice crop **ssaqbeiq beiqceil**

secondary occupation; sideline occupation **fufniq** (Chi)

second son; middle son **ssaqhhaol; aqhhaol**

secretary, general **zaosuljif** (Chi)

secretary, recording **miqsul; suljif** (Chi) (50:157)
secretly (vb) **hyuq (vb)** (**hyuq suv** = to smoke secretly)
section; chapter **zal** (Chi) (50:207)
section; joint **alciivq**
section (as of bamboo or wood) **lo**
section (as of flower or melon) **caoq**
security regulations **maq bi hev e meiqzaq**
see **mol; hu mol; mol lal**
see, to; to know **hu duv** (esp. in seeing through something)
see; read; look **hu**
seed **alssyuq**
seed; kernel; bean **neevsiq**
seedbed **hhoqpaoq**
seedling **kalssaq**
  seedling (rice) **seiqpaoq** (11:143); **hhokeeq keeqssaq** (46:159)
  seedling (to thin) **hhoqcaol hhe**
  seedling (vegetable) **hhoqzi**
seed of fruit **malneev; alneev**
seeds of vegetables **hhoqssyuq; hhoqyyuq**
seek; look for **qo; leiq** (13:4)
seek a lover **baqsal sal**
seek asylum; take refuge **xeiv hhovq**
seek for, to **leiq**
seek in every way, to **tyuqdil davdil dil; tyuqqeiq dav'qeiq qeiq**
seems to be; appears the same **naldul dul; aqmeil**
seen, to be **mol zaq**
seep, to **zeil duv**
seesaw (to play on) **daoqmeiv meiv; daoqmeiv dilmeiv meiv zaq**
see someone off, to **seqsa**
see through, to **hu duv**
select; choose **ceil**
select out, to **ceil duv; deiq duv** (46:131)
self **yoqhhaq bulduq**
self-confident **ziifxifxil** (Chi)
self-criticism **yoq ca yoq eil** (50:219); **jeitao** (Chi) (50:83)
self-esteem; self-respect **ziifzueilxil** (Chi)
selfish **neema neexeivq** (50:219)
selfish; miserly **neexeivq; neexeivq xeivq**
selfish departmentalism **beihhyuf zuyif** (Chi)
selfless; unselfish **gofsseiq zuyif** (Chi) (26:110); **dafgaol wuqsiil** (Chi) (50:30)
self-reliance **yoq aol yoq duv** (50:219); **ziifliq geilseil** (Chi)
self-respect; self-esteem **ziifzualxil** (Chi)
self-sufficiency **yoq aol yoq zaq** (50:219)
self-supporting (by one's own labor) **hoq hovq yoq dol**
sell, to **aoq**
  sell one's properties **aoq zaq** (50:13)
semicolon **feilhaof** (Chi)

semi-colonial; semi-feudal society **baf ziiqmiqdif baf faoljeif seifhyuf** (Chi) (50:5)
semi-conductor (electrical) **bafdaofti** (Chi)
seminal fluid **qoq'eel**
senate **calyifyeif** (Chi)
send (person) **heil; miaoqheil heil**
send off **seq sa; bavq sa**
send on an errand, to **miaoqheil heil**
send out, to **bavq sa**
send something **peif** (Chi) (**feiljil peif** = to send an airplane - 26:78)
senior middle school **gaolzaol** (Chi)
sensation (tingling) **he qivq**
sentence to corporal punishment **pafcu xiqfaq** (Chi)
sentence to death by firing squad **pavqcavq bev**
sentence; word **doq**
sentry post, a **luvq col jol duq**
separate; divide, to **bil heq**
separate; drive apart **leiq hhoq**
separate; take apart **bavq xa** (26:33)
separate, to **lav pav; taoq pil; hhoqloq nei hhoq; bil pav; feilliq** (Chi)
separate, to be (space between) **kaq**
separate; wean **hhei; hhoq; cev**
separate or leave **hhoq**
September **Hhyuqla siq**
sequence; order **lo'qo** (50:159)
sergeant **lieiqza** (Chi)
serious; grave **yeiqzaof nei** (Chi)
serious; important **teiq** (50:195)
serious and sudden disease **nalteiq nalcal**
serow; antelope **heiqceiv ceivnav**
servant, a **lavqmeevq** (35:51); **hhaqheil; ssaqhav**
servant girl **jeilma**
serve, to **haol** (Chi) (26:106)
service **fuqwuf** (Chi)
service, meritorious **gaolxil** (Chi)
sesame, black **naoqsiq**
sesame, white **naoqseil**
sesame seed oil **xalyeq (pf.); xalyiu** (Chi)
set, a (as of clothes) **zuvq**
setback; reverse **lav kyuq** (50:29); **cofzeiq** (Chi)
set fire to **keq (miqzaq keq); keq peev**
set fire to jungle **millaol keq peev**
set free, to **pieiq duv** (50:155)
setting; composition (as of a painting) **bufji** (Chi)
setting sun **naolma qeiq**
settle (as a dispute) **pil zaq; alkaq pil zaq**
settle down (live there) **yovq cuv**
set up (as a ladder) **bavqcuvq**
set up a stall for animals **zeiqssaq zeiqkuv cuv**
seven **siivq**
seventy **siivq ceil**
several **meenia** (10:pref.) (**meenia ceil huvq** = several tens of years; i.e., 30, 40, 50, 60)

several days later **meenia nao naolhao**
severe; stern; strict **yeiq; yeiqjif** (Chi)
sew, to **guvq**
sewing work **guvqduq**
sew up; sew back on (as button) **guvq cuvq**
sexual arousal (for female) **aqbeivq hav** (taboo)
sexual arousal (for male) **aqqoq hav** (taboo)
sexual intercourse, to have **lyuq zaq** (from male perspective, taboo); **zaol zaq** (more polite)

sh, sh! (to quiet someone) **xil** (13:6)
shabbily dressed (in rags) **ju lu ja la meil; peil jal laq jal**
shack; shed **xalqaol; yalqaol**
shackle for feet **keeljul**
shackle for hands **lavqjul**
shade; a cool place **aoqsiq siqdaol**
shade; shadow **aqbal; balhhaq**
shadow; shade **balhhaq; aqbal**
shake, to (from being weak) **biaoq**
shake; quiver **niv; niv niv niv nei; niv meil niv alnei**
shake hands, to **lavqcavq cavq**
shake head (in wonderment) **wuqduq yevq yevq**
shake head ('no') **wuqduq hhev hhev nei**
shake head ('yes') **wuqduq niei niei nei**
shake something down (as leaves, fruit) **ssuv xa**
shaky; not firm **yeivleiv leiv nei**
shaking **biaoqhhe nei**
shallow **teiv**
shallow, very **teivleiv leivssaq nei**
shaman **aqhhuv yiuvq ma; aqhhuv yiuvq nia e col** ('a person who can go into a trance') (**nilpaq** = not. pf.)
Shan; Dai (Tai) **Biqcaoq; Aqcaoq**
Shancha (a magazine sponsored by the Yunnan Academy of Social Sciences) **Salcaq** (46:120)
shape; form; appearance **yoyaovq** (50:189)
share; part **baol; saqbaol; qiq bil**
share, to **saqbaol bil**
share equally, to **qiq kov miav nei**
share someone's cares and burdens **saqbaol qiq haol**
shark fin **ngaqdaol; yiqciif** (Chi) (26:118)
sharp (as knife) **tav**
sharp, very **tavyol pa yol nei; tav pa tav nei** (11:57)
sharpen, to **siq**
sharpening stone **siqluv; sivqduv moqsiq** (latter is poetic term)
sharp eyes (able to see well) **miav gaol**
sharp iron **saol dalqei**
sharp mouth; talkative person **meiqzu tav**
sharp-pointed **qeiltav nei** (50:82)
sharpshooter; expert marksman **miqbev lavqzil**
sharp-witted; alert **neema bel**
shave (or have haircut) **sev (meiqmaoq sev** = to

shave)
shavings (wood, from planing) **sovpovq** (11:149)
she/he/it **aqyoq**
shear, to **niaov**
sheath **tobeiv**
shed; shack **xalqaol; yalqaol**
sheep **aqyol; yol**
sheep (female) **aqyol yolma**
sheep (male) **aqyol yolbu**
sheep day **yol nao**
sheep hour **yol zeq** (B=Chi)
sheep year **yol huvq**
sheet (for a bed) **hoqdaq; cuaqdal** (Chi)
she herself; he himself **aqyo bulduq**
shelf (for books) **suljaf** (Chi)
shell, a **salkyul**
shell case for bullet **ziihovq**
shelter, a **xeiv hhovq duq**
shepherd; cowherder **zeiqssaq luvqssaq**
shine, to (be bright) **bia**
shine, to (star to shine) **aqgeel sseivq**
shine (as the sun) **cuvq**
shine brightly **bia lil bia loq**
shining; bright **bia; laqju nei** (26:10); **geelsseivq nei** (26:100); **miavbeivq lovq beivq**
shirt (army) **ceiqsal** (Chi) (26:72)
shirt; jacket **peilhaoq; peilhaoq daodaq; daodaq**
shiver, to **saqzuq zuq**
shoe a horse **maqzavq diq** (A=Chi)
shoe made of bamboo strips **haqguq sseilnaovq**
shoe made of palm bark **sseilnaovq**
shoes, put on **ziiq** (11:20)
shoes; sandals **seiqnaov**
shoes, wooden **moqheiq** (clf. **zaol**) (11:76)
shoot, to (as gun) **bev**
shoot; to fluff (as cotton) **bev**
shoot and hit **bev sso**
shoot a basketball **teq** (Chi)
shoot a slingshot **xavpiq bev** (A= Chi)
shoot at (by firing squad) **pavqcavq bev**
shoot down, to **bev xa**
shooting stars **miqzaq miqseil; daqzaq miqseil**
shoot into, to (as an arrow) **bev cuv**
shoot to death **bev sil; bev tov**
shop, a **puqzii** (Chi) (26:2)
shop, a (or a company) **gaolsiil** (Chi)
shopkeeper; manager of a shop **zagyuf** (Chi) (50:207)
short **niaol; biov; niaoldyuv**
short (in height) **biov** (**biovlov lovssaq nei** = very short in height)
short (in length) **niaol** (**niaoldyuv pa dyuv nei** = very short in length)
short, very **biovlov lovssaq nei** (11:58); **niaoldyuv pa dyuv nei** (11:58)
shortcomings; weak points **dyulduq**

shorten (in height) **lav biov**
shorten (in length) **lav niaol**
short life **colssil ssilssaq** (26:100); **ssilcovq**
short stories **duapieil xaosoq** (Chi)
short time, in a **ciiv nei qiq heiq**
should (vb) **(vb) wulbo** (11:40); **(vb) wuqbo (hhaqnaq naq wuqbo** - should take a rest - 26:33)
shoulder **bavqtavq**
  shoulder bag **paltaol** (also other bags)
  shoulder blade; scapula **lavqbiav saqyyuq**
  shoulder joint in animal **lavqtov**
  shoulder to shoulder **bavqlavq bavqzaol zaol; bavqzaol zaol**
shout loudly **gul jiq gul jiq; guljiq jiqma** (46:139)
shout out; call out **gulcaq** (13:3)
shovel, a **caca** (Chi)
show, to **bi hu**
  show; reveal **bilduv nei**
  show; to appear **naldul dul**
  show; to display **tixeif** (Chi)
  show a movie, TV program **pieiq** (41:191
  show concern, to **hu meeq; hu leev**
  show forth, to **biaoxeil** (Chi) (26:100)
  show interest, to **laqhaq qeil**
  show off, to **jaqbuq seil; dalbuq buq**
shrew (small rodent) **paqpuv lavqsil**
shrike (bird) **zallaq**
shrimp **ngaqsaq albaol**
shrimp flake; sliced shrimp **xalpieif** (Chi) (50:183)
shrink, to **hhe kuv**
shrivelled, to be **hhyulzuq zuq**
shroud, a **moq li e peilhaoq yoja (moq li e** = a polite way of saying a person has died)
shrubs (flowering) **alyeiv yeivcaoq**
shudder; shiver **saqzuq zuq** (11:43)
shut; close **piq**
shut an umbrella **beelkaq piq**
shut in, to **saol; xovq laol**
shut mouth, to **muvqquvq**
shy **savqdol bo**
shyly **molsavqbo; savqdol**

siblings (born of one mother) **qiq ma bossaq**
siblings etc. **meilnaol** (50:168); **aqmol duma**
sick; hurt; ill **nal**
sick and weak **nalgol nalniei**
sickle **yeiqma**
  sickle with saw-like blade **yeiqhuvq** (11:137)
sick, to become **nalgol sso lal**
sickness; disease (to have) **alnal nal** (26:47)
sickness, incurable **aol gov laq e nal peiv**
sick of something; dislike it very much **aqyeil biul**
sick person **colnal**
side (to the) **bialzeil**
side; direction **pyu**

side; rib **jaqhhal**
side of road **galdaoq galzeil**
sideburns **baqseil**
side of path; road **galma galzeil** (11:36); **galma bialzeil**
side of torso **bialhhal**
sieve, a **jiqkal**
sift, to **jiq**
sigh, to **savqheiq heiq**
sight; vision **miavkeel** (50:154)
sign, to (or to make one's mark) **lavqnyul tyuq** (lit. 'make finger print')
significance; meaning **yifyif** (Chi)
sign name, to **colmiaol buvq**
sign; omen **dulmav mav** (50:201)
silk **guvqkaol; byuqkaol**
silk thread **byuqkaol; guvqkaol**
silkworm **guvqkaol aqma**
silt **halceil leildei** (1. a river bank of sand, 2. silt on a field or path)
silver; money; white **piul**
silver, pure **piulsol**
silver and gold **piulsiil** (11:82)
silver chain **piulcav; meiqkav alcav**
silver dangles on front of woman's headdress **seilbeiv**
silver leaf monkey (Presbytis cristatus) **almiuvq miuvqpeel**
silver lump **piuldev**
silver lump (looks like horse's hoof) **piuldev moqseiq**
Simao (town in Yunnan) **Siilmaoq** (10:pref.)
similar **dul; dul lal**
simple (as simple life) **puqsuf** (Chi) (26:74)
simply **neejav meil; jabu nei**
since; from that time **nei kavq; neikavq**
sing, to **cal**
sing about life, to **yodeivq ssil deivq** (46:170)
sing a folksong **lalbaq ssil**
single; only **aqteiq; laolngaoq**
singer, a **lalbaq ssilma** (11:122)
singing of birds **meel**
single (op. of double) **aqteiq**
sing songs (in home) **lalbaq ssil**
sing songs (in mountains) **aqzil gul**
sink in water, to **neevq**
Sipsongbanna **Xilsual banaq**
sister **dulma; naol** (shortened form of **milnaol**)
sister (older) **alba; alzeiq** (Chi)
sister, elder sibling **aqyivq; alba**
sister, eldest **alba bama**
sister, second eldest **alba miqhhaol**
sister, youngest elder sister **alba miqli**
sister-in-law (YB) **meiqma**
sister, lovely little (TE) **duma ssaqmiq**

sister's husband (older sister) **aqsaoq**
sister's husband (younger sister) **ssaqmavq**
sit, to **jol** (also means; to be at, to stay)
  aqhhuv jol
sit down, to **jol xa; aqhhuv jol**
site for house **zaolhhaol**
sit on heels **daoqzul zul**
situation, good (good times) **huvqlavq meeq**
situation; circumstance; affairs **qiqkuaf** (Chi)
situation (benefit for all) **dalja meeqduq** (50:30)
six **kuvq**
sixteen **ceil kuvq**

skeleton **saqyyuq loqkol**
sketch; outline **galyaof** (Chi)
skill; ability **besiil** (Chi); **jifsuq** (Chi) (26:33)
skilled person, a **lavqqivqssaq**
skilled farmer **xa zaq havma**
skillful **qivq; suv; lavqqivq**
skim and throw away **he zei**
skim off, to **he dav**
skin; leather **saqgeel**
  skin blemish **saqsiq**
  skin of animal **saqgeel**
  skin of snake (skinned by people) **ollol saqgeel; ollol lolhhov**
  skin rash **covqleivq; covqleivq kovq**
  skin ulcer **alnal nal**
skirt **laqlaol** (clf. = **xo**)
skull **wuqhov**
sky **aoq aoqdaoq** (11:133)
sky; far edge of **aoqzeil leil to**
sky; heaven **aoq; aoqtav** (50:165)
skyblue **niulhaq**
sky to be overcast **aoqcyuq cyuq**

slander, to **eil cavq** (50:49) **halnil; halnil nil; halnil nilcuvq; eil buvq**
slander (the crime of slander) **eil nal eil kyuq zyul** (50:215)
slant, to **bilqeiq qeiq**
slap, to **baqpov diq**
  slap (sound of) **teivq** (46:151)
slavishness; servility **aqqo daoqmiq** ('other's tail')
sleep, to **yiuvq** (**xavq** = to stay overnight)
  sleep; fast asleep **yiuvq sil**
  sleep, place to **yiuvqduq; xavqduq** (latter is also a place to stay overnight)
  sleep, time to **yiuvq deil** (26:46)
  sleepily **javqleel nei**
  sleep soundly, to **javqleel nei yiuvq**
  sleep, unable to **maq yiuvq sil**
  sleepwalk, to **yiuvqmu mu**
  sleep well, to **ssao nei yiuvq** (11:184)
  sleepy, to feel **yiuvqngyul ngyul**

sleeve **laqbaoq; laqbaoq baoqheiq**
slender (thin and long) **ja'la nei; ju nei** (for humans)
slender and tall person **col ju nei**
slice, to (cut) **yeiq**
slide away, to **jyu duv**
slide down, to **daoqteil teil xa; daoqsov sov xa**
slide show **huafdeil mu'luq** (A=Chi)
slingshot **xavpiq** (Chi)
slingshot, to shoot **xavpiq bev**
slip and fall (a person) **leeq; taoqsil**
slippery, to be **daoqteil teil** (26:99); **daoqjyu geiq nei** (45:62)
slippery and steep **baqdiq diq**
slit in the crotch (as in a baby's pants) **laqhaoq maq cuvq**
slobber (as an infant) **eelju**
  slobber, to **qalju zav nei**
  slobber bib for baby **qalju biqdaq**
slogans **kehaof** (Chi); **doqma**
slope **galtyuq**
slope (as a mountain) **haolteil**
slow, to be **piq** (Chi) (11:55); **le** (11:55)
slow action **piavsov nia (daov piavsov** = very slow)
slowly **loyei nei; loyei loyei nei**
  slowly; in no hurry **maq teiq maq cal; geiqleiq nei**
sluggish; dull; idle **eqleq deq**

small **nil; yonil**
small, very **nilkev nei; nilkev kevssaq nei**
small amount; little **naoq** (10:15)
small-group leader **miaoqbaol wuqduq duqssaq**
small intestines **wulssaq**
small letters **xiaoxi** (Chi)
small of back **juqzaoq pavq hhal**
small particle (or thing) **liqzii** (Chi)
small person **golbaq nil** (26:42)
smallpox **alzaq**
smallpox, to have **alzaq zaq**
smart, to be **hhaol**
smart person **colkyul**
smash and grab **diq zaq koq zaq**
smear, to **hao**
smell, to **naol hu** (try smelling)
smell bad; foul **beivqlavq**
smell essence of something **he**
smell good **sol; solxeiv nei**
smell good (as food) **xei**
smell of fire **miqhe**
smell of grass, weeds **jahhaq hhaqhe**
smell of meat **saqhe**
smell of seafood **salhe nei; sallavq nei**
smell out, to **naolhu hu**
smell sweet **qulsol**
smile, to **eel; eelseq niq; eelseq lev**

smile, to (show one's teeth) **seq lev**
smile in dream **eelmav mav**
smiling **eelseq lev nei; niq eel meil** (26:64)
smilingly **eelseq niq nei; eelseq lev nei**
smoke **aqhyuq**
smoke, to (as tobacco pipe) **suv**
smoke dry, to (as food) **teiv gee; ca gee**
smoke tobacco **hyuqniul suv**
smoke to billow up **aqhyuq hyuq**
smoky, to be **hyuqbovq bovq**
smooth; bald **julluq nei**
smooth, very **ju ju yaq yaq; ju ju geiq geiq**
smoothly **biulniq nei; biulniq pa niq nei**
smoothly; happily **yosuv nei**
smuggle goods **hyuq aoq hyuq hhel** (50:220)
snail, a **jajul loqniuv**
snake **ollol**
snake, black **ollol eelnav**
snake, green (poisonous) **ollol eelniul; eelniul**
snake, 'lazy' **ollol beivdev**
snake, spotted **ollol sovqeel** (steals chickens)
snake, water **eelcavq**
snake day **seil nao**
snake egg **ollol lolwuv**
snake hour **seil zeq** (B=Chi)
snake nest **ollol lolbeeq**
snake skin **ollol lolhhov**
snake year **seil huvq**
snare; trap (bamboo) **piavteiq; hhadaoq**
snare, using wood or stone **hhadaoq**
snare for birds **luljuv**
snatch, to **koq**
sneeze, to **heilceq ceq; halceq ceq**
snivel **aqbeil** (cf. **naqbeil**)
snore, to **kaoqhe he**
snout; mouth **meiq; meiqbaoq** (and see: 'snout of pig')
snout of pig **aqhhavq nalmeil; aqhhavq nalbaoq; aqhhavq meiqzu**
snow, to **haqju ju**

so; because of that **taoqngaoq**
so; such **laqmeil** (46:172)
soak, to **deev leivq; wuvq**
soaked thoroughly **nievq**
soap **yaqqiv; feiqcaovq** (Chi); **xalzaof** (Chi)
sob, to **ngyulsavq nei; ngyulngavq ngavq** (26:9)
sob; cry very hard **ngyul sil ngyul lo**
social ethics; social morality **byuldeivq liqhhaol**
socialism **seifhyuf zuyif** (pf.); **sefhyuf zuyif** (both Chi)
social relief **seifhyuf jefjif** (Chi)
society **huvqlavq** (50:154); **seifhyuf** (Chi) (34:33)
socks **seiqnaov naovbaoq** (note: **seiqnaov; naovbaoq** = shoes and socks)
sofa **salfaq** (Chi-Eng)

soft; fresh **naoq; naoqxu; naoqxo**
soft; tender **naoqxo nei; naoqxu nei**
soft and smooth **julluq pa luq**
softball **lyu'qeq** (Chi)
soft bone; cartilage **saqyyuq yyuqnaoq**
softeningly **povqsav nei**
soft feather; small body hair **saqhao haossaq**
softish **naoqzov nei** (11:56)
soft palate **lalssaq; ngaqngal laqliv**
soft sound (whispery) **doqteil teilsav** (26:86)
soft voice **yoteil teilnaoq**
solar energy **naolcalhhaq** (50:162)
solar energy stove **naolcal yuqduq** (50:162)
solar halo **naolma beeljoq**
solar period; solar term **jiqlif; jiqqif** (Chi) (24 in a year)
soldier **mavqssaq; daqjyul; daqjul** (Chi) (26:41); **geeldiq mavqssaq** (50:207); **miqbev bavqssaq**
  soldier, to become **mavqssaq gee; daqjyul gee** (A=Chi)
  soldier-engineer **gaolceiqbil** (Chi) (26:89)
solemn; grand **xav nei**
sole of foot **keelhhaq; aqkeel keelhhaq**
sole of shoe **naovdaoq**
solid; sturdy **zaqsiiq** (Chi)
solidarity; to make firm **zaol siivq** (34:10)
  solidarity; unity **neema qiq gao**
solidify, to **yodev dev**
solution; way **zalceiq** (Chi) (50:207)
solve, to **geijiq** (Chi) (32:3); **cu'li** (34:15)
  solve a dispute **alkaq kaq; alkaq pil; pil zaq; alkaq pil zaq; aol soq**
  solve a problem this way **weiftiq xilmol geijiq** (AC=Chi)
so many; many **hal dyul**
some **dyul**
some of **qiq mavq hhana** (10:pref.) (**qiq mavq hhana aqda aqma** = some parents) (26:68)
some of them **qiq mavq** (10:23)
someone else; others **aqqoq**
somersault, a **daoq lyul lyul puv**
  somersault, to turn a **daoqlyul lyulpuv puv**
sometimes **qiq taq hhana; qiq jol hhana**
son; child **ssaq**
  son, last **ssaqli**
  son, middle **ssaqhhaol; aqhhaol** (11:69)
  son, middle of several **ssaqhhaol hhaolma** (11:69)
  son, next to last **ssaqli lima** (11:69)
  son, oldest **ssaq yivq** (11:69)
  son, only (single) **ssaqyo yoteiq** (46:138)
  son, second **aqhhaol**
  son, younger (when several) **ssaqli lissaq** (11:69)
  son, youngest **ssaqli; aqli** (11:69)
song **caqgol** (Chi) (**caqgol cal** = to sing) (11:169), **golquq** (Chi)

song (ballad style, can sing in home) **lalbaq** (**lalbaq ssil** = to sing a ballad)
song (children sing) **aqnil dalya** (32:3)
song (courting) **aqzil** (**aqzil gul** = to sing a song outside home -- taboo to sing in home)
song, Hani **Haqniq lalbaq**
song competition **lalbaq ssilqeiv qeiv**
song of autumn **ceil diq aqzil**
song of praise **zafgol** (Chi) (50:204)
son-in-law **aqssaq**
son-in-law, new **aqssaq ssaqsiivq**
sons and daughters **ssaqmiq ssaqyo** ('daughters and sons')
sons and grandsons **yuq ssol ssaq**
son's wife **keeqma; ssaqmiq keeqma**
son who was bought **ssaqhhel**
soon, very **yoq yil joq lal**
soot **haqnav; miqsavq**
sore, a (ulcer type) **alnal**
sore to develop **alnal nal** (11:29)
sorghum **seillaoq**
so-so; not bad **maq bav**
so that ... **xilmeil ngaoq**
soul **sullal; yo'lal; yollal** (clf. = **mol; lal**)
soul-loss **sullal bal**
soul of the land **mil lal**
soul to be frightened away **sullal guv bial** (26:2)
sound, a **yoteil; doqteil; gulteil; gyuq teil**
sound; acoustics **yilxa** (Chi) (50:197)
sound, loud and pleasant **sseiv nei**
sound; voice **doqteil**
sound a cat makes **mil** (29:4); **mil'aol, mil'aol** (29:4)
sound good, to **nalhaq sal; salteil**
sound made when complaining of a bad odor **pul**

SOUNDS AS THE HANI HEAR THEM:

arrow leaving crossbow **teil** (may be said with unaspirated stop)
baby crying **wul wul al al nei gyuq** (AB=Chi)
bamboo instrument to scare birds **geldel geldel**
birds, insects, animals **civciv nei**
birds spreading wings **tuq, tuq, tuq**
bowl being broken **kovq tovq**
bubbling from a bamboo tobacco pipe **tuvq, tuvq, tuvq**
bulldozer **hhaoq, hhaoq** (pf.); **hhoq, hhoq** (26:30)
buzzing bees; engine; tiger; wind **hhuq hhuq hhuq**
calling to someone far off **kul** (27:11)
chirping sparrows **jil jil zal zal; jiv jiv zav zav**
cicada **cuq**
cracking **geivq, geivq, geivq**
crackling fire **luq, luq, luq; pilpil palpal** (11:21) (may be said with an unaspirated stop)
crying **ngyul teil** (26:4); **wulwul al'al nei gyuq**

dog barking **hhuq hhuq hhuq leil**
drinking water (gulp) **guvq**
drum, thunder etc. **duq**
ducklings **jyul, jyul**
engine; buzzing bees; tiger; wind **wuq wuq wuq**
high-spirited activity **yilhoq hoq**
insects **jyul jyul jyul leil**
jumping fish **koqcoq**
knocking **boq boq boq**
laughter **keivq keivq**
letters (as in the alphabet) **soqmiav zolteil**
liquid being drunk **ziilziil nei**
many birds flying **puq puq puq**
moving **biaoq, biaoq, biaoq**
pigs grunting **yuq eil yuq eil leil**
popping **pyuv** (11:10)
quarelling **ssav, ssav, ssav**
rain falling **teivq, teivq, teivq**
rattling **niv, niv, niv**
reading (aloud) **zolteil**
rice pounder going 'kathunk, kathunk' **gaoqdaoq laoq, gaoqdaoq laoq**
rubbing **kaqcaq kaqcaq** (Chi)
singing **calteil** (11:170)
sparrows chirping **jil jil zal zal nei**
spinning wheel **hhul hhul meil**
stream gurgling **hhaoq, hhaoq, hhaoq**
talking **lovq, lovq, lovq**
tiger; engine; buzzing bees; wind **wuq, wuq, wuq**
walking in rain, in mud **paljil** (26:95)
water **eelteil** (26:23); **covq covq nei**
wind blowing **huq, huq** (26:31); **suqsuq nei** (26:85); **hhuq hhuq hhuq**

sound pleasant, to **doqteil teilsal; teil sal ye nei**
soup, vegetable **hhoqcyuq eelcal**
soup, watery **eelcal; eelcal cal** (46:202);
sour **qeil; qeilgu nei**
sour, very **qeilgul pa gul nei** (11:62); **qeilgu pa gu nei** (11:132)
source (as of water) **eelmeil**
sour fish **ngaqsaq hhoqqeil**
sour food **zalqeil**
sour greens (esp. pickled Chinese cabbage) **hhoqqeil**
sourly **qeilgu nei; qeilbao nei**
south **naq** (Chi); **naqfal** (Chi) (26:34); **naqbuf** (Chi); **aqgee pyu** (lit. 'down stream')
south; down **naoqmil aqgee**
south pole **naqjiq** (Chi)

sow (female pig) **hhavqma; hhavqho**
sow, to **seiq**
sow seed, to **hhoseiq seiq**
soybean **neevsiq**
soybean condiment **aqciq; Haqniq aqciq**
soybean dregs **guqpovq**

soybean juice **neevguq eelcal**

space (room) for something **deil**
space between teeth **seqkaq**
spacious; broad **yeil**
spade, a metal **saolsyuv dalpav** (26:59)
spade, to **syuq** (note: this can also be speaking of a man having intercourse
spade hard, to **syuq kuv syuq luv**
spark from fire **miqseil**
sparrow **haqzal; haqzal naqboq**
sparrow-like bird **jaljul**
sparse **kal**
speak; say **eil; taol**
speak, to (talk) **gee (doqsii taq gee** = don't speak); **doqsii yeillul gee**
speak clearly **eil e loq** (11:163); **eil loq**
speak in polite way **doq gee zaq**
speak out, to **eil duv; gee duv**
spear **gaoq**
special; particular **maq paoq meil; aqzeiq meil** (50:164)
special agent; spy **teiqwuf** (Chi) (50:164)
spectacles; eyeglasses **miavkal**
spectacles, to wear **miavkal dovq**
speech, a **doqsii**
speech, to make **doqsii eil**
speedy; fast (as a spirit) **neivqkol kol**
spell, to **pilxi** (Chi)
spell out, to **pilduv** (32:3) (A=Chi)
spend; use **ssaoq**
spend money, to **ssaoq**
spend money freely, to **piul ssaoq duv; zeiq ssaoq duv** (**zeiq** = an old word for one's property, including animals)
spherical **hulle nei**
spice **zalsol**
spicy **cil**
spider **byuqzuq**
spill over **biq**
spin, to **hho**
spinal cord **ciivqnaovq**
spinal marrow **piultaoq**
spin a chestnut (put a stick in and twist it) **gaolleiq nieivq gaol**
spin cotton **saqlaq hho**
spindle **saqkaol paoq aol; paoq'aol; caol'aol**
spindle (bamboo or wood) on which thread is wound **qultuv**
spine; back **daolciivq saqyyuq** (pf); **daolciivq saqyoq**
spinning wheel **hhocal**
spinning wheel, to work at **hholcal hho**
spin tops, to **aolzei teiv**
spiral shell **loqniuv**
spirit (evil) **neivq; neivqhaq; yocavq**

spirit (of a person) **zilseiq** (Chi) (26:99)
spirit incantations, to repeat **neivqhaq tul; moqpil tul; moqpil galma meiq** (the last term is used for a 'spirit priest' 'showing way' to a dead person)
spirit of the clouds **joqhyuq aqpyuq**
spirit possession **neivqhaq guq zaq**
spirit priest **moqpil; byulmoq** (11:185)
spirit which lives in water, causes people to drown **eelhhuvq ssolnei galpeil**
spirit which protects the crops **hhoqzyuq aqpyuq** (46:182)
spirit takes person **neivqhaq guq zaq**
spiritual civilization **jilseiq weiqmiq** (Chi) (50:90)
spit, to **eelqal hal**
spit out, to **mieiv duv**
spittle **eelqal; eelqal qalma; zaoqpeiv**
splash a liquid, to **hal**
spleen **wuqpieil**
spleen of chicken **neenil**
spleen swollen **pieilheeq**
split, to **cevq** (as firewood)
split; divide; break up **bil hhoq**
split; open up **peivq**
split in two (as with knife or axe) **cevq pav; dev pav**
spongy **ovqdei nei; naoqzov nei; heimieiq nadul dul** (A=Chi)
spool of cotton **saqlaq saqlei**
spoon **kuqcavq; aqcavq; yuqcavq**
spoon (ladle) for dipping up rice **hoqkuq yuqcavq; hoqkuq aqcavq** (11:165)
sports **yifdaof** (Chi) (50:203); **tiyyuq** (Chi) (26:89); **tiyeq**
sports activities **tiyeq hoqdaof** (Chi) (50:165)
sports ground **caolca** (Chi) (26:45)
sports meets; games **yifdaofhyuf** (Chi) (50:203)
sports; physical culture **tiyeq** (Chi) (50:165)
spotted snake **ollol sovq'eel** (eats chicken eggs)
spray, to **pyuq duv**
spread (as a disease) **dovq xa heil**
spread (as sowing seeds etc.) **seiq**
spread; lay, to **deiq hoq**
spread on, to **leiq suq**
spread out (as a disease) **dovq xa heil** (15:62)
spread out (as a mat) **hoq**
spread out; open up **hhe piei** (50:206)
spread wings (as a bird) **daolpiei piei**
spread wings in flight (as birds) **daoldiq diq**
spring of water **eelbi** (11:166)
spring (of the year) **hhaol**
spring ancestor **hhaolduv aqpyuq** (46:156)
spring crops **kalssaq**
spring festival; June festival **Sseilkuq zaq; Zyuqzaq zaq; Joqzaq** (**Joqzaq zaq** = to observe); **aqpiq lol**

spring festival offering meat **zyuqzaq saqhel**
spring season **hhulduv ba'la; hhaolduv ba'la**
spring season god **aqpyuq Hhaolbei Leilseil**
spring up, to **pyuq**
sprinkle water, to **wulquvq seiq** (11:20)
sponge gourd **haoqkavq bilbiov**
sprout, a **alquv** (11:29)
sprout, to **alquv quv** (11:29)
sprouts, bean **neev'quv**
spruce (tree) **ssaolbol; salmuq albol** (A=Chi)
spur of rooster **hadavq; aqha hadavq**
spy, a **qu'qeiq hu e col; teiqwuf** (Chi) (50:164)
spy, to **qu'qeiq hu**

squander; spend freely **zeilnuv**
squat down, to **daoqzul zul**
squeeze **nieivq** (**cuvq** = if just fingers)
squeeze to death **nieivq sil** (also means: 'turn out the light')
squeeze to pieces **nuvqpieiv**
squirrel **hubaq**
squirrel, a kind of **bilqei aqma**
squirrel, chipmunk **piaqcoq**
squirrel, flying **hubiaol**
squirrel, red-cheeked ground **hubaq baqnil**

stab, to **cov**
stability and unity **hhaldif tueiqjiq** (Chi)
stable; firm **ssivqdao nei**
stable for animals **zeiqkuv**
stable for buffalo and cattle **niuqkuv**
stable for horse **moqkuv**
stable; steady **ssiivq** (50:179)
stack, a **(qiq) gaoq**
stack up, to **gaoq qu**
staff for supplying food in a messhall **hosiiqtuaq** (Chi)
stage, a (for concerts, dancing, music etc.) **haqhhal seilduq** (50:181)
stagger, to **biu lu biaoq laoq**
stair, a **davciivq**
staircase, a **davxov**
stake, a **dalhel**
stalk, a (for rice, buckwheat, corn and such) **albol**
stalk, a (for vegetables) **laqdul**
stamen (in a flower) **yeivniuv**
stammer, to **lalngavq ngavq; loqjiq**
stamp, a (postage) **yeqpiaof** (Chi) (50:199)
stamp into pieces **naoq nuv**
stamp on, to **naoqkoq**
stamp on ground with foot **caoqnaoq naoq** (26:5)
stamp with foot **teiv; aqkeel nei naoq**
stand, to **xovq**
standard; level **syupiq** (Chi) (50:158)
stand erect, to **taoqtul xovq**

standing, to be **xovq** (26:52)
standing committee **caqwuf hhyuyeiqhyuf** (Chi)
Standing committee of the People's Congress **sseiqmiq deifbiao dafhyuf caqwuf hhyuyeiqhyuf** (Chi) (50:142)
standpoint **liqcaq** (Chi)
stand up, to **tul; tul lal; cei; xovq tul lal** (26:37)
stand up, to (as ears of dog) **deiq tul** (29:4)
stand up, learning to **taoqtul tul zol zol** (45:46)
star **aqgeel alsiq; aqgeelsiq**
star, shooting **miqzaq miqseil**
stare, to **miav ssil nei; hu cuv** (26:51)
  stare angrily **miav deiq ssil**
  stare at something blankly, to **aqmavq deq nei; eqleq deq nei**
star to shine **aqgeel sseiv** (26:101)
stare, to **hu laovq**
start, to **bei; beibei; yobei; aol bei**
start a fire **taoqsuq; miqzaq keq**
start a project, to **lavqnieivq dovqbei**
start doing, to **aol koq** (26:89)
starter, a (as for a car, tractor, etc.) **qidaofqif** (Chi) (50:134)
start up (as start an engine) **xeiv tul la; caolzofga hhe niv** (A=Chi) (26:98)
start up (as start pushing a cart) **deiq tul** (26:64)
starvation **meivq kuv meivq luv meil**
  starvation for a long time **meivq hhohho meil**
starving with hunger **meivq sil meivq lo**
state, to; declare; announce **eil loq** (50:150)
state council **goqwufyeif** (Chi) (50:67)
state loan **jolqil** (Chi) (11:93)
station (as bus, railway) **ceilzaf** (Chi)
statistic **taojiq** (Chi) (15:28)
statue; picture **molkol**
stature **golbaq**
  stature of one's body **seduq**
stay, to **jol**
stay overnight, to **xavq; yavq** (clf. = **yavq**)
steadily; with steady steps **keeltuvq ssiivq** (50:179)
steal, to **hyuq; hyuq zaq**
steal a look, to **hyuq hu**
steal into and stay **hyuq xavq**
stealthily **hyuq zaq meil** (11:167)
steam; gas; breath **savq**
steam, to **savq**
steam (visible) **savqhyuq**
steam boiler **saolpao** (50:210)
steamed rice **hoqsavq; savq laq e hoq**
steam engine **zeilqifjil** (Chi) (50:210)
steamer for rice **savqbaoq**
steam up; warm up **laolsavq**
steam; vapor **savq'eel** (50:158)
steel and flint **miqdiq; dahojil** (Chi) (the latter is also a lighter)

steel materials **galceiq** (Chi)
steel rod **saol laqdul** (26:27)
stem (of fruit) **cavni** (note: this can also mean 'rattan vine')
stem (of plant) **daoqliq**
stem (of rice) **hhubaoq**
step, as in taking a step **keeltuvq**
step, in **keeltuvq qiq dov**
step; measure (as in politics) **bufceq** (Chi)
step-father **davceiq; danil; aqda danil**
step-mother **madavq; manil; aqma manil**
step over, to **ngaq; ngaq yoq**
steps **keeltuvq**
sterilization operation **jiqyeq sesuq** (Chi) (50:94)
sterilize (as bottle for nursing baby) **qavq sil** (10:19)
stern; severe **yeiqjif** (Chi)
sternum **nee'qil; neehha saqyyuq**
stick, a (to use for something) **daldul**
stick; dry branch **koqpial**
stick, forked **hupievq**
stick, sharp **dalqei**
stick; switch, a **dalciil**
stick in, to **cov; cov cuv** (46:153)
stick into, to **sil taol la; cyuq cuv; deiq tao**
stick on, to **deiq miaoq; miaoq; miaoq cavq**
stick out (as eyes) **lujeivq nei** (26:6)
stick out (as from a hole) **sil duv**
stick out; draw out **kovduv**
sticky, to be **niaoq; niaoqkavq nei**
sticky rice (glutinous) **haoqniaoq; hoqniaoq** (both)
  sticky rice (purple) **haoqniaoq niaoqnav; hoqniaoq niaoqnav**
  sticky rice (red) **haoqniaoq niaoqnil** (46:179); **hoqniaoq niaoqnil**
  sticky rice (yellow) **haoqniaoq niaoqsiil** (46:157); **hoqniaoq niaoqsiil**
  sticky rice cake, to pound **hoqniaoq niaoqbiav taoq; haoqniaoq niaoqbiav taoq**
stiff; hard **hhaol**
still; again **hhoqleiq siq**
still; quiet **quvqceiv nei**
stillness **jyuqlei nei** (26:6)
still to (vb) (as in: still to be sick) **(vb) siq** (46:214); **quvq**
stilts **seivmoq kovtov**
sting; bite; scold; push **deiq**
stingy, to be **laqpil cil; laqpil civ** (pf.)
  stingy person, a **neema xeivq; neexeivq**
stinkbug **aqqeil**
stipulate, to **gyuldif** (Chi)
stir, (as food) **he**
stir-fry, to **zabiav tal**
stir something up, to **lavhhul**
stir up, to **kov puv**

stir up (as trouble) **lav hhul**
stir up and down **zuv**
stir with a stick **lav**
stockings **naovbaoq**
stockings, to wear **naovbaoq baoq**
stock of gun **bevhov**
stomach **baoma**
stomach; abdomen **wuqdeiq**
stomach, pit of **needav**

stone **haqluv**
stone, flat **haqluv luvbiav** (46:130)
stone, huge **haqluv luvma**
stone, very small **haqluv luvjeivq**
stone mill **jivluv**
stone on which house posts are set **ssaoldaoq**
stone pile **haqluv luvgaoq**
stone roller **nieizii**
stones on which pot is set for cooking **hulcuv**
stone's throw, a **haqluv qiq teil e galma**

stool, a **naolmoq; naolzao; naolteil; baqdel** (Chi)
stool of bamboo or rattan **naolguq**
stop, to **naq; pieiq taq; leiq teev**
stop (vb), to **(vb) nieiq pieiq (ngyul nieiq pieiq** = to stop crying)
stop; prevent, to **laol cyuq; leiq cyuq**
stop; put down **pieiq taq**
stop; rest **naq**
stop breathing **savq ceiv lal**
stop something **teiv cyuq**
stop up; dam up **teev cyuq**
stop working **aqlavq pieiq** (26:71)
storage house (rice, vegs. etc.) **calkuf laqhyul** (A=Chi) (11:31)
store, a **saldieif** (Chi)
store (department); shop **gaolsiil** (Chi)
stored grain **toq taq laq e zalsiq**
storekeeper **toq leev aolssaq**
storm, a **aoqjiq aoqsseil**
storm (with wind etc.) **bozivq leilhhe**
storeroom **ceiljil**
story, a **dudaq; yeilgaq**
story, to tell a **dudaq gee; yeilgaq gee**
stove **yuqduq; miqzaq luqzii** (B=Chi)
stove, electric **dieifluq** (Chi)
stove, solar energy **naolcal yuqduq** (50:162)
straight **taoqtul meil; dol**
straight, very **dolssiq nei; gaol** (11:55); **gaolssiq nei; gaolssiq pa ssiq nei; taoqtul laltul meil**
straight and level **dolssiq nei ssol dei nei**
straight way **zoqleil nei**
strain something through sieve **jiq**
strain out; filter out **zeil**
strand of thread **cavleiq; cavdu**

strange, to be **gueif lao** (Chi)
strategist **zafnioqjal** (Chi)
strategy, long range **galmol neenyuq** (50:207); **zafnioq** (Chi)
straw (as rice) **hhoyyuq**
strawberry **caomeiq** (Chi)
straw mushrooms **haollul**
street **galzii**
street, on the **leivkaq deikaq**
strength **hhaq; hhaqhav; liqliaf** (Chi)
strength, to use all of it **hhaq tivq**
strength (to decrease) **hhaq daoq**
strength (to have) **hhaqhav; hhaqhav bo**
strength (to have unusual amount) **hhaqhav bo** (46:145)
strength (to increase) **hhaq dav**
strengthen; consolidate **gaoguf** (Chi)
strengthen; enhance **hhaq bi bo; lav ssivq; jalqaq** (Chi)
strenuous; heavy **faqzaof nei** (Chi)
stretch bent leg **keel kuv zoq** (11:218)
stretch of sandy shore **halceil leildei**
stretch one's neck to see **quq duv**
stretch out **zei** (**aqlavq zei** = to stretch out hand) (Note: also, throw away); **deiq gul**
stretch out; expand **ja**
stretch out a dogskin **keeqtuv galtuv tuv**
stretch out hand **lavq coq duv; aqlavq zei**
stretch out legs **hhe jyuq** (**aqkeel hhe jyuq**); **hhe joq**
stretch out to dry **lovq kuv**
strict; severe **yeiq; yeiqmiq; yeiqqeiq** (Chi)
strict rules **ji'liq** (Chi)
stride, to **keeltuvq tuvqma qiq**
strike; beat, to **diq**
strike and make a noise **diq ho**
strike and separate **diq hhoq**
strike down, to **taoq leeq** (26:25)
strike each other **diq kavq**
strike to death **diq seivq; diq tov**
string; thread **saqkaol**
stringed instrument **xeiqyoq** (Chi) (50:184)
stringed instrument (2 strings) **cil'aol**
stringed instrument (3 strings) **lavqhev** (to play the instrument = **bev**)
striped **galkov kov**
strive; fight; struggle **feifdef** (Chi) (34:2)
stroke; a (or some acute disease, as when the person cannot speak) **miqqusal**
stroke, to have a **miqqusal kovq**
stroke; rub **sov**
strong **hhaqhav; meil; daovq; daovqsiq nei daovq e** (**aqniuq**) (very strong buffalo - 11:150); **hhaqhav bo**
strong; healthy **hhaqhav havma**
strong, very **daovqsiq nei; jeilqaq** (Chi) (26:111)

strong and prosperous **fufqaq** (Chi)
stronghold; fort **bao'lyu** (Chi)
strong man, powerful man **miaoq aol havma**
strong, to be **hhaqhav bo**
structure **alciivq allo** (50:63)
struggle, to **beil; beil leiq beil sil; defzeil (Chi)**
(**beil movq** = wants to struggle)
struggle against **deiq kavq**
struggle all one's life **qiq ssil aqlo hhaq tivq**
struggle continuously **beil yil beil lal nei**
struggle to get **zafdef** (Chi); **defzeil** (Chi)
struggle up and down **tyuq beil dav beil beil** (26:111)
strutting **yevq yevq nei**
stubborn; obstinate **neetaoq taoq** (50:174)
stubborn; pigheaded ('thick ear') **naqtul** (50:213)
stubborn, to be **neema maq puv nia; maq nyuq puv nia**
stuck, to be **navq caoq; ya nevq**
student **soqhhaq zolssaq** (50:191); **xoqseil** (Chi);
taoqxoq mavq (A=Chi)
study; go to school **soqhhaq zol** (11:131)
study; learn **zol; nieiljef** (Chi)
study, a course of **zolnieiq**
study further **seilxoq** (Chi)
stuff in **deiq dov**
stuffy nose **nalbyu maq daol** (note: can also mean
'people who think only of themselves')
stumble, to **peiv lol**
stump (tree) **daoqliq; albol daoqliq**
stunned; frightened **eqleq deq**
stunned; stupefied **aqmavq mavq**
stupefied **laovq li**
stupid, to be **zoq**
stupid person **ssaqzoq; ssaqzoq zoq**
stupor **laovq**
sturdy; solid **zaqsiiq** (Chi)
sty, pig (can also sometimes mean 'prison') **hhavqkuv**
sty in an eye **miavqeil nal**
style **falsiif** (Chi); **weiqti** (Chi)
style and features **faolmaof** (Chi) (50:51)

subject **zuyi** (Chi)
subject; branch of learning **xoqkol** (Chi) (50:191)
subject; theme **zutiq** (Chi) (50:215)
subject; title; topic **doqmiaol** (50:164)
subordinate; lower level **aqhhuv qiq ciivq** (50:184)
subsidize; help out with funds **zeiqmiaoq bivq haol**
(50:219); **jiltieiqfeif** (Chi) (26:91)
subsidy; allowance **bivq laoq piul; ziltieiq** (Chi)
subsidy for loss of working time **colhhaq hhaqpyuq**
(50:182)
substitute regulation or system **qitif** (Chi)
substance **siiqti** (Chi) (50:153)
substance; essence **jilseiq siiqziiq** (Chi)
substance; matter **miaoqgaoq** (50:182)
substitute, to **deiftif** (Chi)

subvert; overturn **lilpuv zaol puv**
succeed, to **zaol pievq; ceiqgaol** (Chi)
success, to have **ceiqgaol jav** (A=Chi)
successor to **lavqcavq cavq** (26:101)
such; so **laqmeil**
suck, to **quvq**
suck brains out (what imperialistic landlords did before the revolution) **wuqnaovq cuv** (26:1)
suddenly **deiq niv nei; qiq heiq laltov nei; qiq haq laltov nei**
suddenly realize **kev nei nyuq loq**
suffer, to **saq** (**saq puv** = return to suffering)
 suffer hardship **saq al**
 suffering; miserable life **saq sil saq lo**
 suffering; poor **saq**
 suffering; tired of **saq qaq** (46:140)
suffer loss, to **zaolleiq; zaolsu** (B=Chi)
sufficient **hhyuq luvq ceil luvq meil**
sufficient food and drink **zaq luvq dol luvq**
sugar **poqbiav**
 sugar, brown (jaggery) **biavnav; poqbiav biavnav**
 sugar, malt **poqneiq**
 sugar, white (refined) **poqbiav biavpiul; biavpiul**
 sugar cane **poqqul**
 sugar lump **poqbiav biavnav**
suggest; propose; move **tiqyif** (Chi) (50:165)
suit (as to suit the occasion) **za**
suitable; applicable **aol e za** (50:155)
suitable; fit **za; hoq** (**maq hoq alnei** 10:17); **halza e** (15:3)
suitable; proper; appropriate **zahe nei** (50:155)
suitable way of doing things **lulsul**
sulk, to **deiq muv**
sulphur **zalsiil**
summarize, to **zaojiq** (Chi) (34:12, 50:220)
summary; conclusion **daoqdaoq ya** (50:184)
summer; hot season **aoqlaol ba'la** (10:7); **sseilzyuq ba'la**
summer vacation **cuja** (Chi) (50:157)
sum up, to **zaojiq** (Chi) (34:12)
sun **naolma**
 sun (poetic) **beel; beelma**
Sunday **Xilqil nao** (A=Chi); **Xilqiltieil** (Chi) (26:62)
sun-dried **lovq gee**
sun-dried bricks **caqbiav**
sunflower **naolma duhhoq**
sun is going down **naolma ya sil miv nei**
sunny; bright day **bia loq bia ceiv**
sunny side **aoqcal tei pyu**
sun rises **aoqbia bia**
 sun sets (and rests) **naolma xavq li qavq**
sunset glow **aoqnil**
sunshine **aoqcal cuvq; aoqcal cal** (10:6)
sun's ray **caoq aoqcal; naolkeel; naolma naolkeel; caoq naolma aoqcal**

sun shines brightly **aoqcal calhav** (10:6)
sun something, to **lovq**
sun's ray **naolma wuqcal; naolcal; wuqcal**
Sun Yatsen **Syul Zaolsal** (34:4)
super-conductor (electrical) **caoldaofli** (Chi)
superiority; advantage **sultavq meeq zeiq** (50:199)
superiority; preponderance **sultavq zeiq** (50:199)
superlative degree **hal**
supernatural being **Aqpyuq Miqyeil; Aqpyuq Molmil**
supersonic wave; ultrasonic wave (electrical) **caolseilbol** (Chi)
superstition **qeqqaq qeqga** (50:115)
superstitious idea **miqxif siilxa** (Chi)
supervise, to **huteiq** (50:40, 82); **jeilduq** (Chi)
  supervise each other **qaq qaq yaol huteiq zaq**
  supervising regulations **luvq leev faqgyul** (C=Chi)
  supervisory commission **jeilhhyuhyuf** (Chi)
supper, to eat **qivqhoq zaq**
supply, to **bivq neiq**
supply and market cooperative **gaolxaol hoqzoq seif** (Chi) (50:60)
supply falls short of demand **aoq naoq hhel miaq**
support, to (as a family) **qu (ssaqmiq ssaqyo qu)**
support; hold up **daltuv; daltuv tuv; ziilciiq** (Chi); **tuv teiq**
support someone in what they are doing **ziilyeiq yil** (A=Chi)
suppress, to; repress; put down **ssiiv teiq** (50:193); **ssiivq pieiv; zeifyaq** (Chi)
sure, to be **baozeif** (Chi) **lulsul**
surely; certainly **halmeil liq; yojil; doqjil; ngeeljil**
surgical department **wafkol** (Chi) (50:173)
surplus **aqzeiq**
  surplus food **zeiq e zalsiq** (50:200)
surname; clan **colqa**
surprised; amazed **naq pa naq nei**
surprisingly **naqhhaq nei** (13:12)
surrender, to (with hands up) **teqxaq** (Chi) (26:41)
  surrender; yield **wuqduq sal taoq** (50:139)
surround, to **luvq hhao; baol hhyuq** (Chi) (34:6)
surrounding **hhao nei**
survive, to **byuldeivq deivq**
survivor; remnant **yazeil**
suspect; doubt **hyuq nyuq**

swallow (bird) **jaljul lalhhaq; jaljyul lalhhaq** (26:60); **zilkuv lalssaq** (45:53)
swallow, to **mievq; mievq tao**
swallow, difficult to **kaoqnaoziivq nei**
swamp **laobao** (standing water)
swan (white bird) **zeilngyul** (clf. = **ssaq**) (11:151); **neivqhaq zeilngyul; aoqqaol**
sway, to **hhev**
swear, to (i.e., 'if I am lying may lightning strike

me') **laqnaq teil ceiv**
swear to follow a policy **xeilsiif** (Chi)
swear word **nuda**
sweat **kaoqpiul** (pf.); **koqpiul**
sweat, to **kaoqpiul duv**
sweat all over **saqcilleiq nei; koqpiul cal; koqpiul ju nei duv**
sweater **maoqxieif** (Chi) (11:155)
sweat of hands **lavqcil**
sweep, to **yav**
sweep clean, to **yav sol** (26:112); **yav leev**
sweep floor, to **hoqtavq yav**
sweet **qul**
sweet, a (as candy) **aqqul** (11:29)
sweet, very **qulju pa ju nei** (11:63); **qul qul nei** (11:57)
sweet and bitter (happy and unhappy) **qulhaq qulhaq nei**
sweet and mushy **qul qul bieiv bieiv; qulbieiv nei**
sweet fragrance **yyuqhe qulbaq nei**
sweetly **qulju nei** (11:56)
sweet potato **moqqul; moqnil; moqnil juma**
sweet words (esp. to loved one) **doqhhyul** (11:203); **doqqul**
swell, to **puq**
swelling to subside **suvq**
swift (bird that builds its nest in rocks and old buildings) **zeiljil**
swim, to **eeldiq diq; eelbeeq beeq** (11:110)
swindle; defraud; cheat **hheivq zaq**
swine fever **hhavqnal**
swing (ferris wheel type) **alhhe hhepuv** (to ride = ziiq)
swing (rotating long bar, one person on end) **aqjaol** (to ride = ziiq) (**aqjaol albol** = tree used for the long bar) (46:184)
swing (village swing, with 4 posts) **alhhe** (to swing = **ziiq**)
swing festival (June festival) **Sseilkuq zaq; Kuqzaq zaq**
swing on a swing **alhhe hhe; alhhe ziiq** (11:50)
swing one's hand **hhev**
swing-ring (to which swing rope is attached) **alhhe naqjul**
switch; stick, a **dalciil**
swollen to the extreme **puqcil pa cil nei puq** (11:59)
sword, a **toma** (clf. = **kaol**); **toma baqcevq**

syllable (gram) **yiljiq** (Chi)
symbol, a (as a letter is a symbol) **fuqhaof** (Chi)
sympathize with **hhosaq saq** (50:168)
sympathy for; allowance for **nyuq za** (50:165)
sympathy, to express; send regards **eil laol** (50:177)
symphony **jaolxayoq** (Chi)
synonym (gram) **doqlo lopaoq** (50:168)

syphilis; venereal diseases **niaoqnal** (sso) (note: this may sometimes be used for leprosy)
system **ziifduf** (Chi) (34:10); **ziifdufhuaf** (Chi); **tixif** (Chi) (**boqxoq ziifduf** = exploitative system - Chi)
system; a setup **tixif** (Chi) (50:165)
system of organization **tiziif** (Chi) (50:165)

---

table **lolbieil**
  table; desk **zoqzii** (Chi)
  table, round **lolbieil bieilhhao**
  table (as used in a book) **soqhhaq biaogeiq** (B=Chi)
  tablecloth **teiqbuf** (Chi) (50:162)
  table edge **lolbieil bieilzeil** (11:35)
  table made of bamboo **alniq lolbieil**
  table made of wood **jazii lolbieil**
tactics **ceiqnioq** (Chi)
tadpole **hoqbioq; hoqbioq aqma; aoqboq aqma** (45:41)
Tai; Dai; Shan **Biqcaoq; Aqcaoq**
Tai (Dai) water festival **Wulquvq hovqseiq zaq**
tail **daoqmiq**
tail, short **miqlil**
tail of a horse **moqmiq**
tail rope to hold saddle **daoqkee**
tail with long hair **miqbuq** (46:150)
take; carry **bavq; heil**
take; carry out **bavqduv**
take a bath **aqbul ciq**
take a chance **huzil** (13:6)
take along; guide; lead **seq**
take and (vb) **bavqssol nei**
take apart, to **piav; bavq xa**
take a step, to **keeltuvq qiq**
take away, to **heil**
take away (come and) **bavq lal**
take back, to **bavq huvq**
take by force **koq zaq**
take care of, to **zaolhul** (Chi); **nyuq hoq; hu leev; toq leev**
take care of each other; love each other **gaq zaq hhyul zaq** (10:pref.)
take off; undress **leiv**
take out, to **bavq duv**
take over there **bavq pyul** (see also: **bavq pyul yil; bavq pyul yi**, etc.)
take part in **kevq; caljal** (Chi)
take place, to **duv** (**miqnieiq qiq mol duv** = something took place; something happened)
take someone to a seat **ciil zul**
take something up **bavq li**
take turns, to **hev lal** (**nol sso al** = it's your turn)
take up; lift up **ciil tul**
talent **byulkyul** (50:165); **ceiqhuaq** (Chi) (34:68)
  talented person **byulkyul col**
talk; speak **gee**
talk and exchange ideas **bavq zil zaq**
talk animatedly **jaqbiei biei**
talkative person ('sharp mouth') **meiqzu tav; meiqzu**

deivq; doqdeiv deiv; doq miaq; aqpiq naqdeiv
talk back, to **eil puv**
talk freely, to **doqsii doqdeiv**
talk privately **doq gee'qoq**
talk properly **eilheiq za**
tall; high **goq**
tall and slender figure **gul nei; dalgul gul**
tall man, a **dafgofzii** (Chi) (26:82)
talon (bird) **seiqsaoq**
tame, to be **qu ya**
tamed; subdued (both of animals & children) **niuqgaq nei**
tank, army **taqkeq; takeiq** (Eng-Chi) (50:163)
tape measure **piqciq** (Chi)
tap root **daoqqil qiltaoq**
tar **beiqyeq** (Chi)
target, a **pavqcavq**
taro **byuqsiq** (9:26, 11:127)
  taro kinds **jivyov; byuqpeel**
  taro, wild **xoqbo laqdu**
tartar (on teeth) **seqxiq**
task, great **miqnieiq nieiqma** (26:104)
task, urgent **sseifwuf** (Chi) (26:81)
tassels of woman's turban **wuqhuv taoqbiq**
taste, to **zaq hu**
tasteless **bioq**
tasteless; unpalatable **yohe maq naol** (50:180)
tasting; to try tasting **cavqsiil siilhu**
tasty **keel; keelmil** (11:20); **zilhhel nei**
tax, grain **gaolliaq** (Chi)
tax money **ssase piul** (A=Chi); **syuf piul** (A=Chi) (50:158)
taxes **laoqliaq** (B=Chi)
  taxes, heavy **syuf** (Chi), **ceiqla zalpeil** (50:97)
  taxes, to pay **zeiq duv ceiqla soq; zeiq duv ceiqla bivq**
  taxes, various **zeiq duv ceiqla**
tax office **syuwuqjyuq** (Chi)
tax regulations **syufse faqgyul** (Chi) (50:158); **ssase faqgyul** (Chi) (50:158)
tax revenue **syufsel** (Chi)
Tazhai village (old name) **Oltol tavqzaoq** (and see: Dazhai)

tea **laqpeiv**
  tea, black **peivnil**
teach **meiq**
teach; care for **meiq miq qu miq** (26:106)
teacher **laosiil** (Chi) (9:92, 11:11); **seilse** (Chi)
teacher requirements **jaofxoq yaolqeq** (Chi)
teacher's training school **siilfaf** (Chi) (50:152)
teach; guide **meiq haol**
teach for a living **meiq zaq**
teaching and research staff **jaofyeilzu** (Chi)

team leader **dyufza** (Chi)
team member of unit (brigade, production) **dyufyeiq** (Chi)
tea plant **laqpeiv peivbol**
tear (in eye) **miavbil**
tear, to **hhe**
tear apart **hhe hhoq**
tear running (down cheeks) **miaveel laqja nei; miavbil duv**
tear stains **miavbil jukov**
tease, to **lav ceivq**
teat; nipple **aqqul qulsiq**
technology and science **koljif** (Chi) (34:19); **kolxoq jifsuq** (Chi)
teetering (not firm) **mu lu meiv leiv**
teeter-totter, to **gaoqmeiv meiv**
teeth **seq**
  teeth (upper) **wuqseq; tavqseq**
  teeth, bad **seqcavq**
  teeth, canine **seqziil**
  teeth, to grind **seqkovq kovq**
  teeth, two front upper **seqzaol**
telephone **dieifhuaf** (Chi)
  telephone conference **dieifhuafhyuf** (Chi)
telescope, astronomical **aoqtav hu e wafyeijif** (D=Chi) (50:166)
television **dieifsiif** (Chi)
  television set **dieifsiifjil** (Chi)
  television station **dieifsiifteiq** (Chi)
tell, to **eilgaq; eil sa lal**
tell a lie **moqlevq levq zavq; jaqmiaovq miaovq**
tell a story **dudaq gee zaq**
Temnick's cat; Asian golden cat (Felis temmincki) **haolnil buvqciv**
temper, a **piqqif** (Chi) (here used as: 'a buffalo's temper' - 26:58)
temper metal, to (by dipping in water, as a blacksmith) **ciq pieiq**
temper, to lose **civq peiv; sabaoq beil; civqbaoq beil**
temper; toughen oneself (as for a difficult task) **dueiflieif (duaflieif)** (Chi) (26:117)
temperature **quvqlaol** (50:177)
temple ('house of statues') **molkol kolyaol**
temple (of head) **naqpeiq**
temporary **zafsiiq nei** (Chi) (26:117)
temporary (or ahead) **gaoqwuq**
ten **ceil**
ten billion **yal milmil**
ten cents (figuring the Chinese way, only five cents in Hani figuring) **qiq haoq** (26:74); **niq haoq** (two times five cents)
tender (see: soft)
tenderly; softly **naoqxo nei; naoqxu nei**
tendon **saqguq**
tendril of a sweet potato **moqnil cavni**

Tengtiao river **Beqna lolma**
ten million **taol mil**
tennis **wa'qeq** (Chi) (50:175)
tense; nervous **calmil nei**
tent, cloth **beelpaoq**
ten thousand **mil; qiq mil**
terminology; technical terms **suqyi** (Chi) (50:157)
termite **aqyivq**
termite (in winged, flying stage) **hhocuv aqyivq**
term break; school vacation **fafjaf** (Chi)
term of imprisonment **xiqqil** (Chi); **hhaqkuv laol nao** (50:188)
term of office; tenure of office **gee nao** (50:143)
terms of endearment (see Appendix 7)
terraced fields (good) **loqsal** (46:178)
terraces in irrigated field **xaldei dalbaol; loqkol**
terrace wall **daobiao**
terrestrial heat **difsseiq** (Chi) (50:35)
terrified **naqseil ssuv; naqguv**
territory **zu'qeiq** (Chi) (35:15)
test; exam **kao** (Chi); **ceiqyeif ceiq** (Chi)
test, to **kaoyeif** (Chi)
test; examine; try someone **salhu; salhu hu** (8:26)
testicle **davqwuv wuvsiq**
testify; give evidence; bear witness **alkaq kaq** (50:222)
tetanus **poqsalfaol** (Chi)
tetanus, to come down with **poqsalfaol duv** (15:28)
text (as the text of an article) **kofweiq** (Chi)
text book, a **zolkaoq; soqhhaq zolpeiq** (26:18)
textile industry **faziiq gaolniq** (Chi)

Thailand **Teifgoq milcaq** (A=Chi)
thank; give thanks to **gaxif** (Chi) (**Noq yaol hha gaxif siq** = we must thank you. 13:14)
thank; to praise **biaoyaq** (Chi)
thank you **keellavq saq wul yaq** (note: this is somewhat artificial, and not always understood)
thank-you letter **gaxifsif** (Chi) (26:68)
that; there **yul**
that big **yul he nei**
that kind **yul qa**
that moment **tyultaq; yul taq**
that one **tyul; tyul mol**
that side; over there **yulzeil pyu**
that time; then **yul taq; tyul taq**
that way **yulmeil leil; tyulmeil**
thatch a house with grass, to **gyu**
thatch grass; cogon grass **eqjil**
thatch grass (other types) **sulpeel; pilsil**
thatch grass (to make shingles of it) **eqjil dalteiq teiq**
thatch house, a **eqjil laqhyul** (11:148)
thatch over, to **gyu kaq**
theater **jiqca; jifca** (Chi)

theater for dancing; singing; cinema **coqseil seilyaol**
theme; subject matter **doqheiq** (50:164); **zutiq** (Chi) (50:215)
then; after that **tyulmeil ngaoq**
then; at that time **galhhu** (long ago)
then; that time **yul taq; tyul taq**
then; therefore **taoqngaoq**
the next .. **naolhao qiq** (clf) (**naolhao qiq hhaq** = the next person)
theorist **li'lyufjal** (Chi)
theory; doctrine **xoqsoq** (Chi) (50:191)
theory of knowledge **sseifssiqlueif** (Chi)
there **tyulgei; yulgei; yuq'a**
there (as, 'at your place') **tyuq a**
therefore **tyulmeil nei**
therefore; then **taoqngaoq**
thermometer, a **quvqlaol ceilhuvq** (50:177)
thermos **sseiqsyupiq** (Chi)
these **xildyul; xiljivq**
these days; recently **xil qiq savq**
these people **col xildyul**
these things **miaoqgaoq xildyul; xilmiav nei**
they **aqyomavq; aqyo qiq mavq** (10:pref.); **aqya dyul** (31:3)
they; others **aqya** (27:12); **aqya mavq**
they themselves **aqya bulduq**

thick **tul; tulluq nei**
thick; dense **caolziv nei**
thick, very **tulxavq nei**
thick (of liquids) **peivnaovq nei** (11:150)
thick clouds; fog **joqtaoq taoq**
thicket of bamboo **haqbol haqcaoq; haqbol daol; haqbol dei**
thicket of jungle trees **albol bolcaoq**
thief **saolhyuq** (13:30)
thief, habitual **hyuq zaq zo**
thigh **saqpiaq** (human); **buldul** (chicken)
thigh bone (femur) **buldul dulma saqyyuq**
thimble **aqhhovq guvqdaq**
thin (of people) **gov; xeivq; colgov; colgov gov** (11:18) (may imply weak as well); **xeivqgov nei**
thin (of things) **baq**
thin, very **baqsov nei; baqka kassaq** (11:58); **baqka nei** (11:18)
thin and long **ja'la nei**
thin and pale **govniv nei; siilla nei**
thin and small **alssii ssii; alleiv leiv** (**Miqleiv** = Miss Shorty)
thing **qa**
thing; object **miaoqnieiq** (50:155)
things; goods **miaoqgaoq**
think, to **nyuq; nyuq hu; nee'li li; neenyuq**
think alike **halnyuq nyuq; haldul dul** (11:222)
think and understand **nyuq loq**

think clearly, to **nyuq gaol; nyuq za; nieiq nyuq**
think deeply and plan carefully **nyuq duvq nyuq cil**
think hard, to **neema jivqyal aol**
thinking; thought **neenyuq quv** (50:159)
think out; think through **nyuq duv**
think over, to **nyuq hu hu**
think over again, to **nyuq hu huvq**
think properly; clearly **nyuq za; neenyuq nyuq za**
think wrongly **nyuq bav**
thinly scattered **kalseil nei**
thin out seedlings **hhoqcaol hhe**
thin to an extreme **nilzav nei**
Third Plenary Meeting **Salzaol Qeiqhyuf** (Chi)
third world countries **dif sal siifjeif; dif sal siifgeif** (Chi)
thirsty; hungry **meivq**
thirty **saoq ceil**
this; here **xil; xilgei**
this big **xil he nei heeq**
this evening **niaoq'aolqivq**
this high **xil miav nei goq**
this kind **xil qa**
this long **xilmo nei mol**
this low **xilmiav nei biov**
this many **xilmiav nei miaq**
this morning **niaoq'aolsoq**
this much **xilmiav** (**xilmiav qiq bil** = all this much); **xilnav meil**
this much (a little) **xildyul dyulssaq**
this much (a lot) **xildyul**
this person **xil hhaq**
this side **xilzeil pyu**
this small **xilhe hessaq** (11:145)
this time **xil taq**
this way **xilmeil**
this year **yeiqnaohuvq**
thorn **algao**
thorn plant fruit **algao alluq luqnav; algao alluq**
thorough; everywhere; all affairs **wuqduq daoqmiq leev nei** ('from head to tail')
thoroughly **javq nei; leevdov nei**
thoroughly (from head to tail) **wuqduq daoqmiq li nei**
thought **siilxa** (Chi) (26:111)
thousand **taol**
thousand and one (a great many) **taol so aqyal; yogaoq gaoq meil**
thousands upon thousands **yotaol yomil**
thread **alkaol; saqkaol** (**kaol** = clf.)
thread (cotton) **saqkaol**
thread and cloth in loom **saqkaol naolnieil** (11:210)
thread on a spindle (for weaving) **kaollee**
thread spindle/spool **saqkaol kaollee**
three **saol; saoq** (Note: **saol** is used in combination with classifiers which are on the low tone; **saoq**

is used in combination with classifiers which are on the mid and high tones.)
threshing ground **zalsiq diqduq**
threshing machine (for rice) **ceil diq jilqif** (C=Chi); **toqliqjil** (Chi)
threshing mat **diqhhal**
threshing stick ` **diqdaq**
thresh rice and get into paddy bin **diq leev**
threshold (of door) **hhuteev; hhoteev**
thrifty **jiqyoq** (Chi)
thriving; prosperous **byuqssil byuqssav meil zeq** (50:46); **faqyaoq calsseif** (Chi)
throat **kaoqbaoq**
throw, to **teil** (27:12)
throw and hit **teil sso**
throw away, to **zei** (Chi) **zei duv** (A=Chi) (26:42); **baq zei; bavq zei; zei xa** (Chi); **suq zei**
throw back, to **naol zei meil zei**
throw into, to (as a basketball into a hoop) **zei tao**
throw oneself on **bialhhuvq**
throw towards **taoq pyul** (or) **toq pyul** (not pf.)
throw out, to **ngaoqhal**
thrush (laughing) **quqma**
thrush, black-throated laughing thrush **quqma baqnav**
thrush, greater necklaced laughing thrush **quqma quqsiil**
thrush, red-winged laughing thrush **quqseiv daolnil**
thrush, white-crested laughing thrush **quqma baqcal**
thrust in **taoq dov**
thumb **lavqma**
thunder **aoqjiq**
thunder, to **aoqjiq jiq**
thunder and lightning **aoqjiq jiqteiv teiv**
thunder god **aoqjiq aqbol**
thunder to roll **aoqjiq duq nei** (30:2)
thunder without rain **aoqjiq jiqhav**
Thursday **Xilqil yuvq nao** (A=Chi)
thus **yulmeil nei** (pf.); **yilmeil nei**

Tiananmen (Gate of Heavenly Peace) **Tieilhhalmeiq** (Chi) (50:165)
Tiananmen Square **Tieilhhalmeiq guaca** (Chi) (50:165)
Tibetan nationality **Zafcuq** (Chi)
ticket **piaof** (Chi) (26:90)
ticket for a train **hoceil piaof** (Chi)
ticket for food; meal ticket **fafpiaof** (Chi)
tickle, to **gevqdevq devq**
tidy, to be **soq do nei**
tidy up (cf. Eng. 'pick things up') **hhuv leev; zaol leev** ('make tidy'); **aol soq; aol suv**
tie, to **pavq tovq; kavq tovq; kavq leev**
tie a loose knot **taoqsuv suv**
tie down, to **leev teiq**
tie four legs of animals together **keelzaoq lavqzaoq kavqzaoq**

tie from the back **naoltovq tovq**
tie grass, to **kavq leev**
tie grass to stems of ripened rice **kaltov pavq**
tie hands and feet **keelzaoq lavqzaoq kavqzaoq**
tie high up **kavq ceq dav**
tie tightly **kavq siivq; kavq tovq**
tie together, to **kavq paoq** (46:190)
tie up; hang up **kavq ceq**
tie up (as person) **kavq tovq**
tie up (as things) **kavq leev**
tie with a rope **kavq puv; kavq cavq**
tiger **haqlaq** (clf. = **mol; laq**) (11:34)
tiger day **haqlaq nao** (11:32)
tiger hour **haqlaq zeq** (B=Chi)
tiger that eats pigs **saqzaq haqlaq**
tiger trap (made of wood and vines) **haqssiiq hhadaoq**
tiger year **haqlaq huvq**
tight **siivq (Nol hhoyyuq dyul zaza nei zaoq siivq.** You must tie these straws tightly. 11:108)
tight, fasten **kavq tovq; kavq siivq** (11:162)
tighten, to **to; to'liq nei**
tightly **siivqheiq nei** (10:26); **zilhevq nei**
tile, to (as a roof) **meelhov caoq** (A=Dai)
tiles, roof **meelhov** (50:173) (A=Dai)
time **siiqjeil** (Chi) (**siiqjeil taq bi yoq** = don't be late)
time, a (classifier for times) **lavq; taq**
time; hour **siqse** (Chi)
time, long **siiqjeil** (Chi)
timely; at the right moment **siqse za nei** (50:155)
time, period of **kaq**
time; season **yotovq**
time, to have **lov; jav** (**siiqjeil jav** (A=Chi)
times (math) **ceiqhaof** (Chi)
time to arise **tul tovq**
time to arrive **yotovq; siiqjeil hev** (A=Chi)
time to harvest crops **kalyei se leev tovq**
time to sleep **yiuvq deil**
time when **taq**
timid, to be **haniq niq; neenaoq neebaq**
tin **dyuq; cil**
tingling sensation **nal leil he qivq**
tiny **nilkev nei**
tip; top **wuqqei**
tire (as for car) **paoqleiq** (11:33, 26:99)
tired **qaq** (11:217) (**aol qaq** = tired of doing); **kyuq ya** (46:172)
tired, to be **daoqleil nei; hhaqkyuq kyuq**
tired and hot **qaq liq qaq, laol liq laol** (10:24)
tired and hurt **kyuq**
tired and sick **qaq lal nal lal**
tired and sleepy **daoqlei nei** (13:22)
'tired as a dead dog' **aqkeeq keeqsil** (27:12)
tired of walking **ssuq qaq**
tired of working hard **zeil kyuq** (A=Chi)

tired to death   **qaq sil laq e** (26:16)
tired to extreme   **kyuq leiq kyuq sil meil** (13:5); **kyuq sil kyuq leiq nei** (26:2); **qaq leel pa leel nei; qaq sil qaq lo; qaqtov nei**
tiresome   **kyuq sil kyuq lo meil** (26:6)
tiresome, very   **qaqleel nei**
tit (small brd)   **naoqcev aqma; kalyil aqma**
title; subject; topic   **doqmiaol** (50:164)
title of a book   **soqhhaq colmiaol; biaoltiq** (Chi)
title of a position (as engineer, professor, lecturer, etc.)   **ziiqceil** (Chi) (see also: 'academic title')

to you   **noq a**
toad   **paqbiav aqma**
tobacco   **hyuqniul; yahyuq hyuqyei**
tobacco; cigarette   **yahyuq**
tobacco leaf   **hyuqpavq**
tobacco pipe (men and women)   **balluvq; yalhhyul**
tobacco water pipe   **yahyuq boqlo** (9:163, 11:148); **yahyuq baoqdel; yahyuq balluvq; baoqdel**
today   **yeiqnao**
toe   **seiqnyul**
toe, big   **seiqma**
toenail   **seiqsaoq; keelsaoq**
together   **gao; qiq gao; civzaol nei qiq gao; zaoqgao**
together, to come   **jol zyul**
together with   **kevq meil**
toilet, a   **xiqduq**
token; symbol   **xafzeil** (Chi)
tomato   **haoqgo haolgo alsiq; falqiq** (Chi); **xilhaoqsiif** (Chi)
tomb   **luqbaol**
tomorrow   **neesoq; naosoq**
tomorrow evening   **nao'qivq**
tomorrow morning   **neesoq aoqsoq**
tomorrow or the day after   **neesoq salpeiq**
ton, a (wm)   **dyul** (Chi)
tone (as in language)   **seildiaof** (Chi)
  tone mark   **seildiaof fuqhaof** (Chi)
tone; mood; manner of speaking   **doq eil yoteil** (50:201)
tongs (as used by blacksmith)   **lavqniaov**
tongue   **lalma**
  tongue tip   **lalqei**
tonight; this evening   **niaoq'aolqivq**
to no avail   **aol duq maq jav; qiq daol maq cyuq** ('no value')
tonsils   **ngaqngal** (**ngaqngal hevq** = to treat sore tonsils)
too; again   **siq**
too; also   **liq**
tools for farming   **ceiqhhuvq miavhhuvq** (hoes, knives)
tooth   **seq**
  tooth, baby   **seqnaoq**

tooth, broken **seqhavq**
toothache **seq gol**
toothbrush **yaqsaoq** (pf); **yaqsuaq** (Chi)
tooth (canine) **seqziil**
tooth (incisor) **seqzaol**
tooth (molar) **bavqliseq** (like: 'wisdom tooth')
toothpaste **yaqgaol** (Chi) (26:73, 50:193)
tooth, poetic **seqbiaq**
top (wooden, for spinning) **aolzei**
top, on **wuqduq** (as in: **albol wuqduq** = top of the tree)
top; tip **wuqqei**
top, to spin **aolzei gaol**
top, very (as top of page) **wuqduq duqli**
topic (common) **- aq (xil mol aq** = this thing, animal etc., as the topic being spoken of); **a** (11:128, 129)
topple; fall over **lol**
tops, to play a game with **aolzei teiv**
torch, pine **taoqsuq aldovq**
torn **hhezeiv** (27:12)
totally correct **daov zeifqoq** (B=Chi)
touch, to **tyuq; taoq sso; lav sso** (50:26)
touch on, to **quq koq**
touch something, to **miaoq; taoq sso**
touch something (where cannot see it, as in a bag) **hhaq lal**
touch with finger; point **tyuq**
tour; sight-seeing **deihaoq hu** (50:200)
towards **pyu (yulzeil pyu pyul** = face toward that direction)
(vb) toward **(vb) pyul (hu pyul; xeiv pyul**, etc., 26:48)
towel (washcloth or face towel) **miavsiv**
town **ceiqzeif** (Chi); **ceiqsiif** (Chi); **laol** (walled city)
township **xal** (Chi)
township leader **xalza** (Chi)
toy, a **hhallul**

trachea; windpipe **kaoqhav**
track and field meet **tieiqjifseif** (Chi) (50:166)
tractor **tollaljil** (Chi) (26:26, 50:172);
tractor operator **tollaljil se** (Chi) (26:100)
trade, to (as occupation) **hhellavq aol maofyif** (Chi)
trade, to (with pack animals) **moqleiq yi; moqleiq zaq**
trade, to (buy and sell) **hhellavq**
trade for a living **hhellavq aol zaq**
trade for a living (selling) **aoq zaq**
trader; businessman **hhellavq aolssaq; hhellavq aol e col**
tradition **cuaqtao** (Chi)
traditions from Aqpyuq Miqyeil **Miqyeil yeilbei**
train **hoceil** (Chi) (**kol e hoceil** = express train)

train, to (and exercise)   **lieifxiq** (Chi) (26:46)
train, to (as for sports)   **syuflieif** (Chi) (26:89)
train, to (bring up)   **caofjef** (Chi)
train, to (develop)   **peiqya** (Chi)
train class (as first class, second class etc.)
    ceilxal (26:93) (Chi)
training (as in the army)   **xyuflieif** (Chi) (26:42)
train oneself   **dueiflieif (duaflieif)** (Chi) (26:102)
train ticket   **hoceil piaof; ceilpiaof** (Chi) (26:90)
train tracks   **hocei galma; hoceil galma** (A=Chi)
train workers (i.e., conductors, ticket takers, etc.)
    liqceilyeiq (Chi) (26:89)
trample on, to   **naoq pieiv; ssuvq pieiv**
trance, go into (as a shaman)   **aqhhuv yiuvq**
tranquil   **quvqceiv nei**
tranquilizer; sedative   **neesal naciq** (50:209)
transfer one's job   **diaofdaof** (Chi)
transferred from place to place   **bi jol pal; leiq tul**
transform, to   **bieifgeiq** (Chi) (34:10); **geicaof**
    (Chi) (34:11)
transform; change   **puv pal** (50:217)
transgress; violate; go against   **lilpuv** (50:176)
transition; interim   **gofduf** (Chi)
  transition period   **gofduf siiqqil** (Chi) (50:68)
translator   **falyiq** (Chi)
translucent   **biulniq nei biul**
transmitter-receiver   **selfa baofjil** (Chi) (50:155)
transparent   **bu loq nei mol qivq**
transplant rice seedlings   **hhocuv cuv; hhaoldaol duvq;**
    lima cuv
transport (as goods)   **hhe zaq** (50:203); **diaof** (Chi)
transport; carry   **miaoqgaoq hhe zaq** (26:49)
transportation company   **yifsul gaolsiil** (Chi) (50:203)
transportation unit (as in army)   **ssifsullieiq** (26:49)
transport for a living   **miaoqgaoq hhe zaq**
trap, dead-fall (dug)   **saqduq; saqduq duqbyul**
trap, metal   **saol piavteiq**
trap; snare (for catching birds or animals)   **piavteiq**
trapped, to be   **saqduq duqbyu ya dov; hhadaoq nei diq**
    teiq
travel expenses   **galhal**
treasure, a   **boq** (33:3)
treasure bowl   **baowuei (baowua)** (Chi) (26:118)
treasure box   **yopyuq miaoqgaoq baoqkev** (26:73)
treasurer; money collector   **piul se ssaoq zaq e col**
treasury bill   **goqkufjeif** (Chi) (50:67)
tree   **albol**
tree, good   **soq meeq**
tree, large   **soq heeq**
tree, old   **albol bolmoq; soqmoq** (this latter term
    sometimes indicates old people in Hani proverbs)
tree, young   **soqssaq**
tree of heaven   **ssiiqbol**
trees, expanse of   **albol boldei**
trees cut to make a field   **xal beiv**

tree stump **albol daoqliq**
  tree stump with roots included **albol daoqpul**
tree top **naqneil; wuqneil**
tremble, to **zuq**
trench; ditch **lolkaq**
trench (as for army men) **zafhaoq** (Chi) (26:48)
trend of thought; ideological trend **siilcaoq** (Chi)
trespass, to **hyuq xeiv dov al la**
tribunal; court **buduq**
Trickster (in stories) **Aljoqniq** (13:11); **Hheivqqivq Aqbiaq**
trip and fall **peiv leeq** (26:24)
tripod, iron (for cooking) **saolkeel**
trivial **qiq jivq maq cyuq**
trolls (live underground) **wulhyuq duvluv aqma ssaqnaol; wulhyul duvluv ssaqnaol**
troop; army **bufdyuf** (Chi)
tropical area **hyuqgyulxeif** (Chi)
trouble, to **aqzaq syuq**
troublemaker (to be) **lav beeq e col**
trouble someone, to **keellavq saq**
trough for horses **moqloq**
trough for pigs **hhavqzal hoqloq**
trouser leg **laqkeel**
trousers **laqcyuq; laqlil; yoja**
trouser seat **laqhaoq**
trouser waistband **laqheiq**
trucker; lorry driver **qifceilbil** (Chi) (26:49)
true; real **jil; yojil**
truly **yojil; yojil meil**
truly; honest **jilhev nei**
trumpet, a **lalbaq** (Chi)
trunk; box **baoqkev**
trust, to **pieiqdal**
trust; entrust **dal** (50:176)
trustworthy; reliable **hoqhhyu aol**
truth **yojil yoliq** (50:209); **zeilli** (Chi) (34:25)
try, to (vb) **hu**
try doing **zaol hu**
try to (vb) **(vb) hu hu (aol hu hu** = try doing)
try to do something **hhaoq zaq**

tube, a **boqlo**
Tuesday **Xilqil niq nao** (A=Chi); **Xilqil eif** (Chi)
tuition fee; tuition **zolpyuq** (50:191)
tumble, to **seiqtivq tivq**
tumble down **daoqteil teil**
tumpline (carrying rope) for women **wuqmieivq**
tumpline with wooden yoke **paoqkeeq laqcav**
tumor, a **puq; lu**
  tumor to be growing **puq lal lu lal**
tune of a song **golpu** (Chi)
turban (male) **wuqtov (wuqtov tov** = to wear a turban); **wuqduq wuqtov** (46:158) (**wuqtov lavqseiv** = black turban)

turban (woman) **wuqhuv** (**wuqhuv huv** = to wear a turban)
turbid; muddy **div**
turbulence; upheaval; unrest **milhaoq beeq**
turmoil; disturbance **lav beeq** (50:39); **daoflueif (daofluaf)** (Chi)
turn; twist **yevq**
turn around, to **puv; wuqduq zei puv**
turn back, to **xeiv puv yil; naolhhuvq puv; puv huvq**
turn back and forth **puv yil puv lal**
turned over **puv**
turn head, to **zeil pyul li** (11:162)
turn head around to look back **naolhhuvq zei puv**
turnip **hhoqpul** (11:78)
turnip, wild **alloq hhoqpul**
turn on (as a light) **hhe dovq** (29:4); **hhe sil**
turn out light, to **nieivq sil**
turn over (as paper, cake, etc.) **cev puv**
turn over (as rock; tree) **bavq pyul; deiq puv; diq hal**
turn over big object **ngaoq**
turn over quickly **puvlav teiv nei cev puv**
turn over repeatedly **puv lil puv la**
turn round and round (as car on slippery surface) **tyuq hhev lal hhev nei hhev** (26:99)
turn upside down **lilpuv puv** (somersault = **daoqlyul lyulpuv** 9:38); **puvlav nei; lav puv**
turn upside down to dry **piav gee**
turtle **byuqqul byuqbiol aqma**
turtledove **beilcaoq hoqhyuq**
tusk of elephant **ssama seq; ssama ssaziil**
tutor; guide of a great cause **moqmeiq laosiil** (B=Chi) (50:34)

tweezers **dalniaov niaovssaq**
twelve **ceil niq**
twelve o'clock **ceil niq se**
twenty **niq ceil**
twenty-one **niq ceil tivq**
twice **niq taq**
twigs **miqpial** (11:35)
twilight **aoqcal calziil**
twin **heiqmoq** (10:2); **ssaqzao** (little used)
twin sons **heiqmoq**
twine **cavpaoq**
twine, to make **cavpaoq paoq**
twinkle, to **aqgeel sseiv sseiv nei sseiv**
twist; turn; wrench **yevq; beil sil**
twist and break **heivq ceiv** (11:18)
twisted onto (as nuts and bolts) **yevq cavq** (26:119)
twist to death, to (as a chicken) **yevq tov**
two **niq**
two of them **aqyo niaq** (13:31)
two persons **niq hhaq; niaq**

type; model **diei'faf** (Chi); **moqfaf** (Chi)

type, to (on a typewriter)   **daziifjil diq** (A=Chi)
typesetting and printing   **peiqyif** (Chi)
typewriter   **daziifjil** (Chi)
typhoon   **jaqleil leilma mama** (50:162)
typical experience   **teil duv galquv**
typical news   **teil duv naqgaq**

U u soqmiav aqma hholqei niq ceil tivq mol e qiq mol

---

udder (as of cow, goat); breast **aqqul**

ugly **saoq sil laq** e (11:171)
ugly; dirty **cavqni**

ulcer **wulziil ziil**
ulcer of the skin; sore **nalnil**
ultrasonic wave; supersonic wave **caolseil bol** (A=Chi)
ultraviolet light **ziiwafxieif** (Chi)

umbilical cord **albeil**
umbilical cord, to cut **albeil niaov**
umbrella **beelkaq** (11:114)
umbrella, to close **beelkaq piq**
umbrella, to open **beelkaq tuv piei**
umbrella, to use **beelkaq huv**

unarmed; empty-handed **lavq pul lavq nieivq**
unbalanced (as load on a horse); lame **qeiq**
unboiled water **eelceivq** (10:16)
uncertain; incoherent **bil lil bav lav nei; bil lil biav lav nei**
uncle (father's older brother; father's older sister's husband) **dalda**
uncle (father's younger brother) **alsuq** (Chi) (Note: **alsuq** can also be fictive, or an expression of respect to an older man.) (26:101)
uncle (father's younger sister's husband) **aqsaoq**
uncle, maternal **aqhhyu**
uncle's wife **aqmee**
Uncle Tom's Cabin **Talmu Bassaq e Yaolssaq** (57:156)
unclean **maq sol maq cavq meil**
unclear; dim; vague **suqlu hhaqlaq meil**
unclear mind **laovq laovq bia bia**
uncomfortable **jolsaq** (11:28)
uncomfortable; unhappy **neema maq sal maq hev**
uncooked; raw **zaol**
under **aqhhuv**
under (in location) **hul'a (wulquvq hul'a** = under water)
under (in numbers) **hul'a (xeivq huvq hul'a ssaqguq** = the children who are under eight 10:pref.)
underarm hair **lavqhhuvhaoq haocavq**
underground (do in a deceptive way) **hyuq leivq hyuq hheiv meil aol**
underneath **hul'a**
underpants **laqlil**
understand; know **hev; hev nia; nyuq hev; loq; nyuq loq; siq**
undertake a responsibility **alyeil pi; ceiqdal** (Chi)

undress; take off **leiv**
unecessary; not needed **leiqdaq nei** (26:74)
unexpected **naqhhaq sav nei**
unexpected; dangerous **geelsal**
unexpectedly **moqzei nei**
unfasten, to **peelbieiq**
unfeeling; callous; grim **neepeel neehhuvq**
unfold, to **hhe pao**
unhappy **neema maq sal; neema kyuq; haoqsuvq suvq** (50:46)
unhurriedly **maq teiq maq cal meil** (13:32)
unified front **taoyiq zafxeif** (Chi) (50:169)
unified leadership **zaoqgao seq to** (50:169)
uniform; the same **paoq; qiq qa paoq**
unify, to **zaoqgao** (50:169); **lavqcavq cavq; tuaqjiq** (Chi)
unify the country **taoyiq zugoq** (Chi) (50:169)
unit; a collective unit **jiqti** (Chi) (26:107)
unit in the army **lieiqbuf** (Chi)
unite as one, to **qiq bao bao** (46:124)
united front **taoyiq zafxeif** (Chi) (34:17)
unity **taoyiq** (Chi) (34:17)
unity; solidarity **neema qiq gao**
unite, to **tueiqjiq (tuaqjiq)** (26:114)
United States of America **Mei; Meigoq** (Chi)
universe **aoqssol milcaq haoqbaoq hul'a** (26:112)
university; college **dafxoq** (Chi) (11:145, 31:3); **xoqxaof** (Chi) (50:191); **yeifxaof** (Chi) (50:201)
university student **dafxoqseil** (31:3)
unlock, to **zovq pao**
unlucky **siqhel maq meeq; gaoqlaoq maq bo**
unmarried person (woman, man) **miqmoq yomoq**
unnecessary **leiqdaq nei** (or) **eiqdaq nei** (14:175)
unprecedented; without precedent in history **yeilbei maq bei** (50:154)
unremitting **ziifqaq** (Chi)
unrest; turbulence; upheaval (in the land) **milhaoq beeq**
unsatisfactory **neema maq lal**
unselfish; selfless **dafgaol wuqsiil** (Chi)
unshakable; firm **naoldi maq tyul** (C=Chi)
untidy **beeq**
untidy, very **beeqga nei; beeqga pa ga nei**
untie, to **peel; peel bieiq**

up; upper **zoqnia** (11:219)
up above **hultav; aqtav; niagaoq** (33:3)
up and down (as something swinging up and down) **aqhhuv aqtav**
upheaval; unrest; turbulence **milhaoq beeq**
uphold; safeguard; defend **haol laol** (50:176)
upper arm **lavqbiav**
upper leg; thigh **saqpiaq**
upper lip (see: lip, upper)
upper part of village **zaolwuq**

upper place **donia** (11:32)
upper side **hultav pyu; aqtav pyu; aqnia pyu** (9:12 - this also means 'the east')
upper strata; upper levels **safceiq jeifzuq** (Chi)
upper teeth **tavqseq**
upper world **davqtav wuqdu** (11:221)
upright **dolssiq nei dol**
uprising; revolt; insurrection **puv lal**
uproot **daoqpul hhe puv**
upside down **lilpuv meil; daoqlyul lyulpuv**
upslope, slight **davtuv**
upstairs (as in the attic) **gaoqzaol** (27:11)
upstream; upper **aqnia; eelmeil**
upstream dwellers **zoqniassaq**
up there **aqnia**
upwards **taoqdav**

urge on; ask to hurry **leiq cal**
urgent matter **miqnieiq nieiqteiq**
urinate, to **aljeil jeil; alsyuq syuq**
urinate, trouble in urinating **luqbul kovq**
urine **aljeil; alsyuq**
urine, smell of **silhe nei; sillavq pa lavq nei**

USA **Meigoq; Mei** (34:8)
usage **aolduq**
use; spend **ssaoq**
useful **aolduq jav** (11:121)
useless **aolduq maq jav** (11:121)
usual thing **jol lal hha e miqnieiq**

uterus; womb **beivqziv; aqlul**

uvula **lalngavq**

V v soqmiav aqma hholqei niq ceil niq mol e qiq mol

vacant; empty **aqnieivq**
vacuum **zeilkaol** (Chi)
vagina **aqbeivq; beivq; aqbovq** (taboo)
vague; dim; unclear **suqlu hhaqlaq meil**
valley **hhaqhaoq; laoltaoq; lolgov** (11:20); **lolxaq; hhaqkaq; hhaqmeil** (46:170)
valley with water **lolgov**
vanguard **xeilfaoldyuf** (Chi) (50:184)
vanguard and model **xeilfaol moqfaf** (Chi) (50:184)
vanish, to make **zaol mei**
vapor; steam **savq'eel** (50:158)
variegated **buvq lav buvq civ nei**
vase (for flowers) **alyeiv hualpiq** (B=Chi)
vaulting horse, a **muqma** (Chi)

vegetable **hhoqpavq; hhoqcyuq; hhoqniul**
vegetable, bitter **hhoqhaq**
vegetable, bitter (wild) **hhoqtaoq**
vegetable, green **hhoqniul; hhoqniul zalniul**
vegetable, sour **qeilzaoq**
vegetable field **hhoqyal**
vegetable field (planted in the rainy season) **sseilhhoq hhoqyal**
vegetable garden **keilsaq; keilsavq** (both)
vegetable leaves **hhoqdaq; hhoqcyuq alpavq**
vegetable seed **hhoqssyuq**
vegetable seedbed **hhoqpaoq**
vein; artery **sivqguq**
velvet **maoqniq** (Chi) (11:31)
verb, a **daofciiq** (Chi) (50:39)
verify; check **sol za** (50:70); **caq loq** (50:20)
vermillion **niltel nei nil**
vertical, to be **bilceiv nei**
very... **daov (vb)** (11:105 has samples)
very bad **daov dyul** (8:1, 12)
very, very .... **tuvqqil** (**tuvqqil bia** = very, very bright) (11:107)
very long time **qiq savq hev nei**
vest, a **beifsil** (Chi) (26:61)
vest for Hani men **peillal; peilhaoq peillal**
veterinarian **seqyil** (Chi)

vice battalion commander **fuf yiqza** (Chi)
vice brigade commander **fuf liza** (Chi)
vice chairman; vice president **fuf zuxiq** (Chi)
vice commander **fuf siillif** (Chi); **fuf ziihyul** (Chi)
vice company commander **fuf lieiqza** (Chi)
vice platoon leader **fuf peiqza** (Chi)
vice political instructor **fuf jaofdaofyeiq** (Chi)
vice premier **fuf zao'li** (Chi)

vice president; vice chairman **fuf zuxiq** (Chi)
vice regimental commander **fuf tuaqza** (Chi)
victorious, to be **seiflif** (Chi)
victory **seiflif** (Chi) (26:44)
Vietnam **Yiqnaq** (Chi) (50:202)
viewpoint **gueildiei** (gualdiei) (Chi)
vigilent; alert **nyuq hev**
vigorous; lively **deivqhhuvq deivqla** (50:151); **seildaof hoqboq** (Chi)
vigorous and graceful **colzaq aqquv** (50:84)
villa **biqsuf laqhyul** (A=Chi)
village **puvkaq**
village, fortunate **puvsal sal**
village, lower side **zaoldaoq; zaolhhuvq**
village, new **puvkaq kaqsiivq; puvsiivq**
village, old and big **puvma; puvkaq puvma** (46:122)
village, side of **zaolzeil**
village, small **puvkaq kaqssaq**
village, small and new **puvsiivq puvssaq** (46:123)
village, to establish **puv cuv; puvcuv cuv**
village, unfortunate **puvsaq saq**
village, upper section **zaolwuq**
village, whole **qiq puv qiq laol**
village director **cyulza** (Chi)
village edge **puvkaq bialzeil**
village gate **galtuv; laolkaq** (46:122)
village gate; set it up **galtuv tuv cyuq** (46:132)
village head **milguq** (in most villages); see also: **zyuqma; puvlaol soqpaq; puvlaol aqhhol**
village leader **cyulza** (Chi) (**cyulza bi gee** = to have a person be the village leader - 11:181)
village ritual head **milguq** (he leads the villagers in various ceremonies and offerings)
village regulations **puvlaol doqtevq** (50:185)
villagers **puvlaol**
village sacred grove **hhaqma; hhaqma hhaqcaoq**
village sacred tree **hhaqma hhaqbol**
village site **puvhhal**
village which is active **puvlovq lovq**
village which is happy **puvsal sal**
vine, a **cavni** (27:11)
vine, pumpkin **maldei albiao**
vine fence, a **yuqjoq joq**
vine to grow **alcav ju dav**
violate; run counter to **lilpuv puv** (50:176)
violate law **hhyuqfaq luafji** (Chi) (50:176); **weiqfaq luafji** (Chi) (34:88)
violence; force hav diq
violently **deiq ssil alnei; hhaqhav tivq nei**
viper, black **ollol eelnav**
viper, green **ollol eelniul**
virtue; moral excellence **neemeeq neezaq** (50:114)
visibility **miav mol qiq qeiv** (50:121)
visit, to **qu hu; seilhha; doqdeiv hha; calgual** (Chi)
visiting delegation **calgual tuaq** (Chi) (50:19)

visit selectively (visit scattered friends and relatives without visiting everyone) **seiqkaq coq**
vitality (as full of vitality) **deivhhuvq nei deivq**
vitality; life-force **deivqhol hav** (50:151)
vitalize, to **zeifxil** (Chi)
vitamin **weiqseilsuf** (Chi) (10:1); **dafbeiqziiq** (Chi) (11:49)

voice; sound **doqteil**
voluntarily surrender **yoqzyul yoqssiil ssiil**
voluntary labor **hhaqpyuq maq bo miaoq aol** (50:197)
vomit, to **yuqpeivq peivq** (10:21)
vomit out; skim off **he dav**
vote; ballot **teqpiaof** (Chi) (50:169)
vote, to **xeiji** (Chi)
voter; elector **xeimiq** (Chi) (50:191)
vowel letter (i.e., a, e, i, o, u) **yeiqyil ziifmu** (Chi)
vowels (finals in ling. sense) **yifmu; ssifmu** (Chi); **yeiqyil** (Chi)

vulva; vagina **aqbeivq; beivqhov** (taboo) **aqbyu** (the latter can also mean: 'a hole')

W w soqmiav aqma hholqei nil ceil saoq mol e qiq mol

Wa **Wa**
wag (tail) **lav**
wages **gaolziil** (Chi)
wagtail bird **jalcil; jalcil aqma** (searches for insects in the mud, with its tail bobbing up and down without stopping. Hani compare women bobbing up and down transplanting rice with this bird)
wail for dead elder **miqsaq ngyul**
  wailing song for dead **miqsaq** (13:40)
waist **daolciivq; juqbaoq; juqdev**
  waistband of trousers **laqheiq**
wait, to **doq**
wait a moment **gaol taq teiq siq**
wait and meet **doq cavq**
wait for **doq joq; doq zaq**
wait for a long time **doq sil doq lo**
wait for game (in ambush) **saqluvq luvq** (11:220)
wait for on the way **galdoq doq**
waken from sleep **nyuq; yiuvqnyuq tal; yiuvqsul**
  waken from sleep (by being disturbing) **lav sul lal**
  wake up **bel** (this can also mean: 'to recover')
  wake up and get up **piav tul la**
  wake up someone, to **leiq nyuq; leiq tul**
  wake up someone by calling **kul nyuq**
walk, to **ssuq**
  walk along; move along **ssuq niv** (11:27)
  walk back and forth, to **ssuqgal aol**
  walking stick; cane **zaqngeeq**
  walk past **yoq li**
  walk wearily, to **ssuqqaq**
wall (of bamboo or wood) **kaolto**
  wall (of mud) **caqtaoq** (to build = **caqtaoq taoq**)
  wall (of steel) **galtiq caqceiq** (Chi)
  wall; fence **laolkaol**
  wall, to build up **ziivq**
  wall in; fence in **aol cyuq; diq hhao**
  wall of building (the outside wall) **laolkeel**
wallow in a wallow (as a water buffalo) **aqlao lao; niuqlao lao**
walnut (generic term) **aqmeil**
  walnut (hard variety) **meilhav**
  walnut (medium-hard variety) **meilkaq**
  walnut (soft variety) **meilnaoq**
wander, to **qao hha; del hha**
want to (vb).. **(vb) movq; aol** (**Aqyoq caqdevq aol nga laq**? Does he want salt? - 11:187); **(vb) ma** (11:130, may be made up of: **movq** and: **a**)
want; need; require **guq** (190)
Wa people **Wacuq**
war **geel; geel diq** (50:207)

war, to fight **geel diq**
wardrobe **keelsuv** (Chi)
warlord, a **jyulfaq** (Chi) (34:4)
warm **laol**
warm, very **laolnuv nuvma meil** (11:59)
warm by the fire, to **miqca ca**
warm-heartedly **neema laolcyu nei** (26:40)
warm in the sun, to **aoqcal calseil laol**
warmly **laoldu nei** (46:147)
warmly **laolcyunei; laolxavq** (26:14); **laolcyu pa cyu nei**
warmth; enthusiasm **sseiqqiq** (Chi)
warm up; steam up **laolsavq**
warm up (as at a fire) **laol; laol dav**
warm up (in the sun) **laolsavq**
warm water **eellaol laolnuv; laolnuv**
warm weather **aoqhhaq quqsiqnei**
warning **jibaof** (Chi)
warped (as wood) **bilhhuvq laqhhuvq meil**
warship; naval vessel **bilquq** (Chi)
wart **cevqsiq**
wash, to **ciq**
wash away, to **wulquvq nei leiq zei; wulquvq nei bul zaq; ciq xa** (46:179)
washbasin **miavciq hoqbiav**
washbowl **haoqmaq ciq** (13:33)
wash by rubbing; scrubbing **leiq ciq; leiq bu**
wash clean, to **ciq sol** (10:16, 11:21)
wash face, to **miav ciq**
wash up and relax **keellavq ciq deil**
wash-water **eelcavq**
wasp, ground **biaqdul**
wasp, tree **biaqgoq**
wasp, young (edi) **biaqbyuq**
waste, to **leiqdaq meil bi jav**
waste (as time) **laffeif** (Chi)
wasted; no benefit **leiqdaq meil; yoqdaq meil** (11:115)
wasted work (no value) **aolbu** (11:115)
watch, a **biao** (Chi)
watch; look **salhu**
watchman **hu taq zaq e col**
watch over; look after **hu taq**
watch (wrist) **siqse lavqduvq; sebiao** (Chi) (note: clock is: **siqse** (Chi)
water **wulquvq; eelquvq**
water, clean **wulquvq gaolciv nei**
water, clear **eelgaol gaol**
water, cold (unboiled) **eelceivq**
water, covered with **leiqhhuvq** (26:57)
water, dirty **laolsil**
water, distilled **zeilliefsyu eelquvq** (A=Chi) (50:210)
water, muddy **milxeiv**
water, to (as plants) **seiq; bavq seiq**
water, very clear **wulquvq gaolciv nei gaol**

water, warm **laolnuv**
water boils **eelbeel beel**
water bubbles **wulquvq haolpuq; wulquvq pavqmeevq**
water bucket **eeltaoq**
water buffalo **niuqpeel**
water closet; outhouse; toilet **ceiqso** (Chi) (10:16)
water container, bamboo **eelbaoq**
water container, large **wulquvq buqssaq** (11:37)
water container, wooden **hoqtuv** (33:3)
water course; ditch **lolgal**
water course of wood or bamboo **eelloq; wulquvq coqbiq**
water cress **halsol**
water ditch **wulquvq lolgal**
waterfall **wulquvq coqceiv**
Water festival of the Dai **Poqsyu jiq** (Chi)
water from boiled rice (rice-water) **hoqqavq eelcal**
water god **wulquvq aqma**
water hole **eelbyu**
water jar **wulquvq buqssaq**
water level (as high or low) **eelquvq goq biov** (50:158)
water pipe **syuguei (syugua)** (Chi)
water polo (sport) **syu'qeq** (Chi) (50:158)
waterproof cloth **faqbuf** (26:95)
water-protector spirit, the **Laoqsseil**
water pump **syubol** (Chi) (50:158)
water-run rice-pounder **wulquvq meicaol**
water snake **eelcavq**
watershed **eelbil; eelbieil**
water source (for village) **lolhovq** (46:134)
water source (headwaters) **eelmeil**
water spring **eelbi**
water tap **wulquvq laoqteq** (B=Chi)
water (in bowl on the table to cool certain types of food) **zal'eel**
water transport **eeltav miaoqgaoq hhe** (50:158)
water trough **eelloq**
water well; water source for the village **lolhovq**
wave, to (with hand) **aqlavq hhev**
wave of water **eeldaol; eeldaol bi; eeldaol hhev**
  wave of water to come **eeldaol yaoq nei** (30:2)
wax **aqbiaq biaqsaoq; biaqsaoq**
  wax candle **biaqsaoq aldovq**
way; channel **tuqjif** (Chi)
way; form **xiqsiif** (Chi)
way; method **baffaq** (Chi); **lulsul**

we (exclusive) **ngalya**
we (inclusive) **ngaldu**
weak **hhaqhav nil; hhaqhav maq heeq; jaoq; daoqlei nei**
weak (person; animal) **gov; yogov govssaq** (34:4)
weak, become **hhaq jaoq yil**
weak; feeble **nalgol nalniei; hhaqhav ca**
weak; shaky **biaoq**
weak and limp **keelqaoq lavqqaoq qaoq; aqbiaoq biaoq**

weak and sick **nalgol nalniei**
weak and soft (as bones) **naoqzov nei naoq**
weak points (as in one's personality) **qeituv**
we all **ngaldu**
wealthy **loqbeq; hhaq sil hhaq lo**
wean, to **aqqul ceiv**
wear (general) **dao**
wear (as clothes) **dao; hhyuq** (pf); **hhoq**
wear (as flowers, bandages) **dovq**
wear (as gloves, socks) **baoq**
wear (as hats) **wuqcaoq caoq**
wear, put on **huv**
wear, tied around **pavq**
wear ornaments on head **wuqpavq pavq** (silver stars); **seilbeiv pavq** (tiny silver 'trumpets')
wear shoes **ziiq**
wear turban (man) **wuqtov tov**
wear turban (woman) **wuqhuv huv**
weasel, yellow (Mustela altaica) **biaqyil naqboq**
weather forcast **sseil sal cavqgaq** (50:165)
weather is dry **aoq kuv mil kuv** (50:165)
weather nice **aoqsal sal**
weave, to **ziivq; hhavq**
weaver's shuttle **juqbaoq**

wedding **miqsiivq ssaqsiivq bivq zaq**
wedding party, to arrange **yulbee bee**
wedding party, to hold **yulbee bee; miqsiivq ssaqsiivq bivq zaq e**
wedding party wine, to drink **yulzil dol**
wedge, a **caqcaoq** (for putting in handles, splitting wood, etc.)
Wednesday **Xilqil saoq nao** (A=Chi)
weed, a **jabeeq; jahhaq; biabeeq**
weed, to **muvq**
weed a field, to **yalmuvq muvq; xalmuvq muvq;**
weeds; dust **gaoqbeeq; goqbeeq**
weeds; grass **jahhaq; buduv bucaoq**
weeds in clusters **jabeeq; jabeeq beeqcaoq**
weeds which can be used as animal feed **janiul** (33:3)
weed terrace wall with hoe, to **xaldei daobiao sev**
weed with hoe, to **quv**
week, a **xilqil** (Chi)
weep; cry **ngyul**
weigh, to **sav**
weight (as of child) **savjil savmiav** (10:2)
weight (five grams) **savmiav ngavq keiq** (C=Chi)
weight, heavy **xao**
weight, light **pial**
weights and measures **savmiav ssol dalqeiv**
welcome **hueilyiq (hualyiq)** (Chi)
weld, to **geel cavq**
well! (interjection) **weil** (Chi)
well; carefully **meeqzav nei (meeqzav nei aol** = do it

well, carefully); **ssao nei; ssaossao nei** (**ssao nei zol** = study well - 11:21)
well; good **meeq**
well (water) **lolhovq; syu ciiq** (Chi)
well-behaved (as children) **gaol; keellavq sol** ('pure feet and hands')
well-cooked **javq**
weretiger **buqluq**
weretiger ceremony (to drive out) **buqluq puv**
west **beelya pyu; naolma ya pyu** (26:69); **xilfal** (Chi)
west; down side **aqgee pyu**
western **xilbuf** (Chi) (26:87)
Western literature **xilfal weiqxoq** (Chi) (50:183)
wet **jeill ssiqnaol nei** (11:61); **yozaoq; jeilso nei**
wet; damp (as ground from rain) **ciq**
wet, something to be wet (as clothes) **jeil**
wet all over **jeilso pa so nei; jeilbiuvq pa biuvq nei**
wet with dew **ciqhaq puvtav nei**
we two **ngaldu niaq**

what? **haljivq** (**Xil mol haljivq nga laq?** What is this thing? 11:100)
what a pity! **maq neivq haoq wul naq; maq neivq haoq wul yaq**
What did you say? (a polite request for repetition) **Haljivq loq?**
what did you say? (as when someone calls you and you do not hear clearly) **Haq'al.**
what do you (vb)? **halmeil ya laq?** (8:1)
whatever **haljivq jivq; haljivq liq**
what happened? **halmeil ngeel** (13:14)
what is it? **halmeil leil**
what is (it) called? **halmeil leil kul**
what kind of...? **halmeil leil** (**Aqyoq halmeil leil e col nga laq?** What kind of person is he/she? **hal qa...?** what kind of thing?
what matter? **halsiil**
what time? (as what time to have a baby) **hal taq luldu** (15:5)
what want to (vb) **haljivq (vb) movq** (8:27) (**Nol haljivq aol movq ya leil aol.** Do what you want to do. 11:104)
What was that? (when not sure what was said) **Haljivq loq?**

wheat **meiqzii** (Chi); **dafmeiq** (Chi)
when? **hal taq** (**Nol hal taq hhuvq lal?** When will you come back?)
whenever; whatever time **hal taq** (26:23)
whenever (vb) at that time (vb) **hal taq (vb) hal taq (vb)** (**Nol hal taq meivq ngaoq hal taq zaq.** Eat whenever you are hungry. 11:104)
whenever meet up with **hal puq nei**
where? **halgei**

where exactly (just where (vb)?) **halgei gei** (**Aqyoq halgei gei li**? Just where exactly did he go? 11:103)
where -- there (Where the fire was strongest he went to put it out. 26:70) **halgei ... halgei**
whetstone **siqluv**

which (clf., clf.) **hal mol mol**? (**Hal mol mol**? which one? **Hal taq taq**. Which time? 11:85)
which are (have) **hal jav**
which direction? **hal pyu; hal pyu baq**
which kind? **hal qa**
which night? **hal yavq**
which person? **hal qiq hhaq** (11:99)
which side? **hal pyu baq**
which two people? **hal niq hhaq** (11:99)
while (vb) **(vb) taoqngaoq** (13:2)
while (vb) and while (vb) ... (on the one hand ..., and on the other hand...) **qiq pyu ..., qiq pyu...** (13:11) (**qiq pyu ssuq, qiq pyu doq gee** = on the one hand they walked, on the other hand talked; or, while walking they talked)
whip, a **dalpial**
whip, to (as a horse) **hhe ziivq; ziivq**
whirl, to **aqpuv lilpuv puv**
whirlpool **laqhhev; wulquvq taoqhhev hhev**
whirlpool, large **taoqdaol daolma** (30:2)
whirlwind **jaqleil leilhhev; jaqleil leilhha** (not pf.)
whiskers **baqseil**
whiskers, chin **meiqmoq**
whisper, a **doqsav; teilsav**
whisper, to **doqsav sav; teilsav sav**
whistle **jalxul xul; jalxyul xyul**
white **piul bia; bahhuq nei**
white, very **piulseiq pa seiq nei; baba nei** (11:57)
white; silver; money **piul**
white cloth **palpiul**
white cloud **joqhyuq hyuqpiul**
white feather; white fur **haopiul**
white flag **beiqqiq** (Chi)
white hair of pig **hhavqhao haopiul** (46:134)
white-headed **wuqduq ba nei** (46:140)
white horse **aqmoq moqpiul** (46:188)
white of egg **wuvpiul; alwuv wuvba**
white of eye **miavpiul**
whitish **piulseiq nei**
whitish; light (shade) **ba**
whittle to a point **dalqei sev**

who? **aqsol**
who all? **aqsol sol** (**Aqsol sol lal**? Just who all came? 11:103)
Who could know? **Aqsol hevnia ya**? (26:2)
whoever **aqsol sol** (3:7); **aqsol liq** (11:129); **aqsol mavq**

Who knows by whom? **Aqsol nei aqsol hev ya?** (13:4)
whole body **moljoq**
whole day; all day **aoqcil qivq nei; qiq nao aoqcil** (**aoqcil aol qivq** = to work a whole day)
whole group, the **baljoq nei** (26:114)
whole house, the **qiq yaol yaoljoq**
whole life, the **qiq ssil aqlo meil**
whole night, the **qiq yavq yavqjoq**
wholesale **pilfaq** (Chi)
whooping cough **beiqssiqkeq nalgol** (15:28) (A=Chi)

why? **haljivq** (10:1); **haljivq alnei** (**Haljivq alnei ngeel nil?** Why? What is the reason? 26:80), **haljivq nei**
why did (vb) **halmeil ssolnei** (**Nol halmeil ssolnei Dafjyul gee li ya?** Why did you join the army?)

wick; lamp **aldovq dexi** (B=Chi)
wide **yeil; bieil; bieillo nei; piei nei**
wide, very **yeillo nei; yeillo loma meil**
wide prospects **galquv yeil nei bia**
wide-range; extensive **gua'faf** (Chi)
wide road **galma dallul** (B=Chi)
widow **miqcyuq; miqcyuq aqma**
widow, to become **miqcyuq cyuq**
widower **byuldaoq aqpaq; byuldaoq**
widower, to become **byuldaoq daoq**
width the same **qiq kov miav nei yeil**
wife **miqssaq; miqma; miqsolssaq** (esp. when speaking of one's own wife); **ssaqnaoq aqma** (term of endearment, very polite)
wife and husband **miqssaq huljil**
wife of father's younger bro.; wife of mother's bro. **aqmee**
wife of husband's younger brother **nilma** (called by brothers and their wives); **aqyo aqmee** (called by nieces and nephews)
wife of ruler **zyuqma miqssaq; zyuqma aqpiq**
wife of younger brother **aqyo aqmee**
wife's brother **aqmol; aqyo aqhhyu; ssaqguq aqhhyu**
wild, to be **maq qu ya qao**
wild; uncultivated **beilcaoq** (**beilcaoq haqbol** = wild bamboo)
wild animals **nilzeiq**
wild banana **alzeiv**
wild boar **hhavqteiq**
wildcat **alhaol; ha'qiq** ('chicken snatcher')
wilderness (old fields that have grown over) **saqpeeq**
wilderness (virgin forest with few trees and bushes) **diqsiil**
wild fruit **beilcaoq alsiq**
wild ginger **meilquv**
wild goat **heiqceiv ceivnav**
wild person; ogre; chimpanzee (never seen, so actually a mythical type figure) **miaqlo miallo aqma**

wild rice stalk **ceil'aqma**
wild taro **alssi; alssi moqgaoq**
wild yam (large, yellow) **eilla**
wild yam (small, white, edi) **guqsav**
will; willpower **yifliq** (Chi) (50:197)
willing to (vb) **(vb) na (aqyoq aol na** - he is willing to do it) **xul**
willow tree **aolnaovq; aolnaovq albol** (26:117)
will-o'-the-wisp; phosphorescent light; ignus fatus **neivqdovq**
willpower; will **yifliq** (Chi) (50:197)
wilt, to **jaoq** (11:39)
win, to **diq hhaq; hhaol; hhaol zeiq; diq hhaol**
win; gain, to **zeilqi** (Chi)
win at gambling, to **duq hhaq**
wind **jaqleil; lil; leil; aqlil** (latter is old, poetic term)
wind, cool **jaqleil leilsev**
wind, strong **jaqleil leilma**
wind 'hole' (in mythology) **jaqleil duqbyu**
winding, to be **puv li puv lal**
winding path **galhhuvq gallavq**
wind instrument **bawul** (Chi); **gaoq bil** (Hani)
window **caqbyu** (10:7, 26:37) (this is more of a hole in the wall for the smoke to escape)
window (with glass) **bolliq caqbyu** (A=Chi)
window, to close **caqbyu diq cyuq** (10:7)
window, to open **caqbyu diq pao** (10:7)
windpipe; trachea **kaoqhav**
windstorm **bo ziivq leil hhev**
wind to blow up fiercly **jaqleil bo tul la** (30:2)
wind up (as wind up a top to spin it) **aolzei leel**
wind up (as wind up a toy) **nieivq puv**
wine; liquor **zilbaq; beiqje** (Chi)
wine, good tasting **zilbaq zilkeel**
wine, poisonous **zilbaq zilduvq**
wine cup **zilhaoq**
wine jar; liquor jar **zilbaq buqssaq**
wine made of sticky rice **zilbaq zilqul**
wing **aqdaol**
wing of chicken **hadaol**
wings, to beat (as bird) **daoldiq diq**
wink eye, to **miavmiv miv**
winnow, to **hhal**
winnowing tray **hhalma**
winter **caoq; caoqgav ba'la; aqgav ba'la** (10:7)
wipe, to **siv**
wipe out (in sense of killing all) **diq mei; zaol mei** (46:202)
wire **geeqkaol** (26:73)
wire; rope **alcav**
wisdom; intelligence **ziifhyuf** (Chi)
wisdom tooth **bavqlivseq**
with **naogo; kevq meil (aqyoq kevq meil yil** = go with him)

with (as 'with a hoe') **nei**
with; from **nei**
withdraw (as from battle) **naoldi di**
withdraw (as money from a bank) **bavq huvq**
wither, to **jaoq**
withering flowers **alyeiv yeivjoq**
without moving **qiq niv maq niv** (26:52)
without stopping **qiq taq maq leiq nei** (26:65)
with what? **haljivq nei**
witness (one who saw) **hu mol e col**
witness; go-between **colkaq**
wives of brothers **heeqssaq meiqma**

wolf **heiq'eil aqkeeq; haqyeil**
woman **ssaqmiq; ssaqmiqssaq; haqmiq ssaqnaol; ssaqmiq ssaqnaol; miqhhovq** (old word)
woman, old **aqpiq ssaqmoq**
woman gets married **sulmil yil**
Woman's Association **fuflieiq** (Chi)
women **ssaqmiqssaq mavq**
womb; uterus **aqlul**
wonder; contemplate **salnyuq**
wood **daoqtao; daoqma**
wood, a piece of **daoqtao qiq tao**
wood and bamboo borer **haqbyuq**
wooden bowl **albol haoqmaq**
wooden chopping block (meat, vegs.) **saqteil**
wooden container (used when threshing rice) **diqloq**
wooden hammer (decoration at village gate) **albol diqpuq**
wooden house **daoqma laqhyul** (26:69)
wooden stake; wooden stick **dalhel; miqkoq dalhel**
woodpecker **qyul'aqma**
woods; deep inside **laolqaol**
woods; jungle **albol bolcaoq**
wood shavings **sovpovq**
wool **aqyol yolhao**
word **doqsii** (13:3); **soqdoq** (46:62); **ciiq** (Chi)
word, language **doq**
word, new **doqlo losiivq** (50:151); **seilciiq** (Chi)
word, old **soqdoq** (46:183)
word order **doqlo lo'qo** (50:201)
word; sentence **doq**
word, single or multiple **dalciiq** (Chi)
word of wisdom (esp. words of the ancestors) **hhaoldoq**
work; job **miqnieiq; aolnieiq; gaolzoq** (Chi) (26:26)
work, to **aol; miq aol** (and see: **xalsol duv)**
work, to go to **xafbal** (Chi)
workable; practicable **loqsiiq** (Chi)
work at a job **miqnieiq aol** (11:154)
work cooperatively **aol paoq**
work diligently **keellavq belzav nei** (26:42)
work, enjoyable **aolheiq qeil**
work energetically for development **faqfeif tuqqaq** (Chi) (26:75)

work in fields **xalsol duv; xal aol**
work in office **gaolzoq aol zaq**
worker **miq aolssaq** (26:2); **gaolsseiq** (Chi); **qeiqgaol** (work with tools) (Chi) (26:33)
worker, ordinary **gaolsseiq ssaqnaol** (A=Chi) (26:26)
work is enjoyable **aolheiq qeil** (11:196)
work for living **aol zaq hovq dol**
work hard; be diligent **miaoq aol xul** (10:pref.); **lavqguq daov deivq; aol sil aol lo**
work hard; to knead **laqnuvq lavq xeiv**
work hard while living simply **jeilku feifdef** (Chi) (26:75)
working people; ordinary people **ssaqjeil ssaqlaol**
work; livelihood **miqnieiq**
work more, get more **aol miaq zaq miaq**
work points **gaolfeil; gaolpeil** (Chi)
work points to be divided up **gaolfeil pieiq** (or, **gaolpeil** ..) (Chi)
workshop **ximeiq ceiljeil** (26:27) (Chi)
work team, a **gaolzoqdyuf** (Chi)
work unit **aolduq dalweif** (B=Chi)
work well; properly **aol leev**
world, the **siifjeif** (Chi)
World Health Organization **Goqjif Weifseil Zuziq** (Chi)
world peace **siifgeif hoqpiq** (Chi) (34:15)
worm (earth or ascaris) **buqdeil**
worm; insect **byuqssaq; aqzuq**
wormwood **eilheiq**
worn down (vb) **liq** (**duq liq** = for a hoe to be worn down from digging)
worn out (as clothing) **dao zeiv** (**naov zeiv** = worn out shoes)
worn out (from working) **aol biav**
worried, to be **neema beeq; neema qilkuq nei** (26:80); **neema teiq** (26:43); **nyuq saq** (26:51); **haoqlaol**
worried to death **neema qil sil**
worry, to **qil; neema beeq; haoq laol; nyuq syuq**
worthless **qiq daol maq cyuq**
worthy, to be **pyuq**
would; want to **movq**
wounded (vb) **nal** (**diq nal** = wounded by a blow; **bev nal** = wounded by a bullet)

wrap, to **tov quvq**
wrap rice in a leaf **hoq pavqtov tov**
wrap up, to **tov; pavqtov tov** (in leaf); **tov quvq** (26:86); **tov teiq**
wrench; twist **yevq**
wrestle (in a wrestling match) **lavqbavq yevq; laqbavq ceivq; lavqbavq qiq pul taoq koq**
wrinkle (as forehead) **zuvq; baqzuvq; zuvqteiv nei**
wrinkled; folded **bilzuvq meil**
wrist **lavqpul lavqciivq**
wristwatch **siqse; sebiao** (Chi)

write, to **buvq**
write down, to **buvq teiq**
write from memory, to **nyuqbuvq buvq** (50:118)
write on, to **buvq dav** (11:47)
writer **zoqjal** (Chi) (50:222)
written agreement **gee taq soqkaoq**
written characters **soqmiav** (11:23)
wrong; make a mistake (vb) **bav** (**aol bav** = do something wrong; **eil bav** = say something wrong; **nyuq bav** = think something wrong, etc.)

Wuliangshan mountains (along Lancang River, where many Hani live) **Wuqliaqsal**

Xia Xiaozheng (an ancient Chinese book about the calendar) **Xaf Xaozeif** (46:83)
Xinhua Bulletin **Xilhuaqseif** (Chi) (50:188)
Xishuangbanna (in extreme south of Yunnan, on the border of Burma, where many Akha live) **Xilsual banaq** (Chi) (called 'Sipsongbanna' in Dai/Shan)

yam, Chinese **moqdev**
Yani (Akha branch of the Hani, esp. those living in the Xishuangbanna area) **Yaqniq; Ssaqniqssaq; Aqkaqssaq**
Yangjie Township in Yuanjiang County **Yeiqjalxeif e Yaqgeil xal**
Yao people **Yoqsseiq** (Chi)
yarn **maoqxeif** (Chi)
yawn, to **hal pov** (46:152)

year **huvq**
year; age **huvq; alhuvq**
year after next **salpeiq huvq; sallal huvq**
year before last **huqnao huvq**
year, leap **ssyufnieiq** (Chi)
year, normal (not a leap year) **piqnieiq** (Chi)
years and months; epoch **huvqlavq** (26:86)
years gone by **huvqlo milhhu**
year, whole **qiq huvq huvqjoq**
yeast **diqciq**
Yeche Hani (a subdivision of the Hani living in Honghe) **Yilce; Yilcessaq** (Chi) (**Yiqceilssaq** = closer to Chi)
yellow; gold **siil**
yellow, very **siilnieiv nei** (11:58)
yellow dog **aqkeeq keeqsiil** (11:36)
yellowish **siilbia nei; siilnieiv nei; siilniq nei; siilzev**
yellow liquor **siilzov zilbaq**
yes; to be so **ngeel ssa; eiqya; ngeel**
yesterday **milnao**
  yesterday evening **milqivq**
  yesterday morning **milsoq**
yet **siq**

Yi (large ethnic minority in China, also called Lolo) **Laqhholssaq; Haqhholssaq** (11:30)

yoke (wooden, for carrying loads) **paoqkeeq**
  yoke tumpline **paoqkeeq laqcav**
yolk of egg **wuvsiil**
you (plural) **nolya**
you (sing.) **nol**
young (not many years old) **alhuvq nil** (11:195)
young adult **colhav**
young age **alhuvq naoq** (26:45)
young; childish; naive **nee hyuq maq hav** (50:200)
younger brother of father **alsuq** (Chi)
younger brothers and sisters **naoqbo aqnil**
younger brother's wife **meiqma**

younger generation; descendents **naoqssaq** (46:161)
younger relation **aqnil**
younger sibling / brother **aqnil**
youngest daughter **miqli**
youngest son **ssaqli**
young fellow **coldavq** (taboo); **xaohoqzii** (Chi)
young hero **alhuvq naoq e ssilxoq** (26:45) (C=Chi)
young male; young boy **aqda dassaq**
young man (in youth) **coldavq davq** (taboo); **seiqhoqziiq** (Chi)
young person **ssaqnaol**
Young Pioneer **Maofxeil dyufyeiq** (Chi)
Young Pioneer ('Red Scarf') **haoqlizil** (Chi) (26:111)
youngster **ssaqguq**
young woman **miqdavq** (taboo)
your **noq e; no** (**no beewul peilhaoq** = your quilted jacket - 26:39)
your house **no qovq bee**
Youth League **Gaofqiltuaq** (Chi)
  Youth League branch **tuaq ziilbuf** (Chi) (50:171)
  Youth League charter **tuaqzal** (Chi) (26:32)
  Youth League committee **tuaqhhyu** (Chi) (50:171)
  Youth League member **Gaofqil tuaqyeiq** (Chi) (50:171)
  Youth League secretary **tuaq suljif** (Chi) (50:171)
you two **no niaq**
you yourself **nol bulduq**

yuan (Chinese money) **biav; biavma** (26:76); **yiq yuan** (Chi)
  yuan, half a (50 cents) **biavssaq**
Yuanfeng (ancient Chinese kingdom) **Yeiqfaol**
Yuanjiang county (in Yuxi Prefecture) **Lalsa; Lalsav**
Yuanjiang river **Lalsa baqma; Lalsav baqma; Yueiqjalxeif** (Chi)
Yuanjan animals (repeated often in their rituals) **Lalsav zeiqssaq**
Yuanyang (in the south of Yunnan Province) **Yeiqyaq** (**Yeiqyaqxeif** = Yuanyang county)
Yunnan **Yyuqnaq** (Chi) (50:202)

z Z z Z z Z z Z z Z

Z z soqmiav aqma hholqei niq ceil kuvq mol e qiq mol

---

zero **liq** (Chi)

Zhou Enlai **Zel Eilleiq** (Chi) (34:20)
Zhu De **Zul Deiq** (Chi) (34:20)

Zu Hao (an emperor who reigned many years ago)
Cuvhaoq; Cuvzal (Cuvzal miqnieiq aol) (Chi)

INDEX OF APPENDICES

1. Comparison of the Hani and Akha Orthographies 803

2. The Dragon and the Son-in-Law 805

3. Genealogy 823

4. The Names of 56 Ethnic Groups in China 825

5. The Names of Provinces, Municipalities and Autonomous Regions 826

6. Sounds of the Hani 827

7. Hani Terms of Endearment 828

8. Set Phrases with the Negative 830

9. Hani Proverbs 831

10. Hani Riddles 834

11. Hani Concept of Time 835

12. Four-syllable Elaborate Expressions 836

APPENDIX 1:

COMPARISON OF THE HANI AND AKHA ORTHOGRAPHIES

Below is a comparison of standard Hani orthography used in China, along with the newly developed 'Hani' (Akha) orthography now used in China (see book 58), abbreviated below as 'CHA', and the Akha orthography as used in Burma and Thailand, abbreviated as 'BTA'. 'IPA' gives the International Phonetic Alphabet symbols used in China on the far right of both colums:

VOWELS: (Basically the same in all three)

HANI	CHA	BTA	(IPA)	HANI	CHA	BTA	(IPA)
i (yi)	i	i	/i/	a	a	a	/a/
ei	ai	eh	/ɛ/	u (wu)	u	u	/u/
yu	yu	oe	/ø/	o	o	ọ	/o/
ee;ii	ee	ui	/ɯ/	ao	ao	aw	/ɔ/
e	e	eu	/ə/				

(For an explanation of the Hani -ee and -ii vowels represented by only a single Akha vowel, see the Introduction.)

These vowels occur only in the orthography of the Akha in China, Burma and Thailand, but not in the Hani orthography:

HANI	CHA	BTA	(IPA)	HANI	CHA	BTA	(IPA)
--	ei	e	/e/	--	-m	-m	/m̩/
--	an	ah	/ã/	--	oi	oi	/ü/

CONSONANTS

HANI	CHA	BTA	(IPA)	HANI	CHA	BTA	(IPA)
b	b	b	/b/	h	h	h/k'	/h;x/
p	p	p	/p/	hh	hh	g'	/ɣ/
m	m	m	/m/	j	j	j	/dʑ/
d	d	d	/d/	q	q	c	/tɕ/
t	t	t	/t/	x	x	sh	ɕ
n	n	n	/n/	y	y	y	/j/

HANI	CHA	BTA	(IPA)	HANI	CHA	BTA	(IPA)
g	g	g	/g/	c	c	ts	/ts/
k	k	k	/k/	ss	ss	z	/z/
ng	ng	ng	/ŋ/	s	s	s	/s/
l	l	l	/l/	z	z	dz	/dz/

Note: /h/ in CHA (China Akha) may correspond to both /k'/ and /h/ in BTA.

PALATALIZED CONSONANTS

pi	pi	py	/pj/	bi	bi	by	/bj/
mi	mi	my	/mj/	ni	ni	ny	/nj/

(Note: In Hani **'ni'** is evidently always palatalized. If written in BTA: **'nyi'**. When followed by another vowel in Hani it becomes palatalized: i.e., **'nia'** (nya); **'niu'** (nyu); **'niao'** (nyaw); etc. In both CHA and BTA there is a non-palatalized **'ni'** and a palatalized **'nyi'**. In CHA the latter is written **'nii'**.)

BORROWED CONSONANTS (not found in BTA)

f	f	--	/f/	w	w	--	/w/

Note: In those Hani and China Akha words which are not borrowed from Chinese, and are preceded by the vowel **-u**, the orthography writes a **w-** before the **-u**. (**'wuqduq'** = 'head' in Hani; **'u̬ du̬'** = 'head' in Akha)

TONES

	ORAL VOWELS		GLOTTALIZED VOWELS	
	HANI/CHA	BTA	HANI/CHA	BTA
HIGH	--l (**bal**)	--ˇ (baˇ)		
MID	-- (**ba**)	-- (ba)	--v (**bav**)	--^ (ba^)
LOW	--q (**baq**)	--̬ (ba̬)	--vq (**bavq**)	--̭ (ba̭)

(A rising tone, borrowed from Chinese: (**baf**) **--f**
(This is not used in BTAkha, and not often found in China Akha.)

APPENDIX 2:

BEIYAOQ SSOLNEI AQSSAQ

(THE DRAGON AND THE SON-IN-LAW)

(This Hani story is found beginning on page 198 in the Hani grammar by Prof. Li Yongsui. We have made a few changes in the Hani, to be more consistent with this dictionary. The page number of the text in the grammar is included in parentheses. There is an English translation at the end of the story.)

1) Galhhu aqbei, molcyuq cyuqssaq xilmeil qiq hhaq jol. Nil nei qiq nao neikavq e aqda aqma sil. Aqyivq aqnil liq maq bo. Niq yei niq ceil ngavq huvq biao liq, miqssaq qiq hhaq maq seq meil jol.

2) Xilmeil qiq nao, puvkaq hholqei nee'lao lao, haqjil aqda qiq mavq lolpav pieiq zaq yil jil. Molcyuq cyuqssaq yul hhaq qiq ba naogo liq maq bi ba zaq na taoqngaoq, aqyoq qiq hhaq sol meil qiq pav pieiq yil.

3) Aoq pav hev liq (199) ngaqdeil qiq mol maq mol. Yulmeil liq aqyoq lavq hhuvq maq pieiq xu meil, haqluv haoqbaoq halsal milnia qiq gal qiq gal meil ngaoq puv. Naolma ya sil miv nei yul taq yaol, loldaoq taoqhovq yulgei deilnil alciiv heeq laq meil qiq mol mol lal. Aqyoq deilnil mol nieivq alnei hhuvq li al.

4) Aqyoq laqhyul hhuvq li taoqngaoq, ngaqdeil mol yaol zaqqul ya zaqqul ya leil salhu zaq. Nieiq'eil salhu nieiq'eil zaqqul. Hal sal salhu taoqngaoq, aqyoq neema hholqei, "Ngaqdeil xil mol liq, ngal aqmeil molcyuq cyuqssaq ngeel maq hev siq" leil nyuq. Yulmeil taoqngaoq, aqyoq ngaqdeil mol maq zaq peq meil, hovqtuv hholqei pieiq tao alnei bi jol.

5) Naolhao qiq nao, aqyoq xalsul hhuvq lal e aq, aqsol nei ngeel maq hev, hoq laol zal laol xei nei susi miao taq alnei jav. Aqyoq, "Neema (200) meeq e col qiq hhaq nei ngaq yaol hhosaq saq taoqngaoq, zaol taq laq e ngeel aq zeiq ya" leil nyuq. Yulmeil nei aqyoq zaolpeil lolqoq dyul yaol naogo, "Ngaq e yulgei hoqzal aqsol nei susi laq e ngaq? Hoq zaq kal yoq" leil gul yil.

6) Yulmeil liq, zaolpeil lolqoq dyul saq nei nalhaq dyu e liq, ngeel nga leil qiq hhaq maq eil. Qiq mavq ngaoq, "No ballal nei hoqzal susi taq e neivqhaq wuqduq maq bo meil mol pa jol a" leil eil miq.

7) Xilmeil leil meenia nao biao haohaoq, hal nao liq hoq laol zal laol xei nei susi taq e alnei hha zaq. Xilmeil qiq nao aqyoq ceiqhhuv miavhhuv bavq alnei, xalsul duvhheivq hheivq alnei hhuvq huvq lal taoqngaoq,

hhoheiq nei hyuq hu. Za nei alciiv qiq savq jol taoqngaoq, ngaqdeil mol (201) hovqtuv hholqei hhahha nei xeiv hha duv al la. Naolhao "kocoq" leil, qiq coq ngeel taoqngaoq, naolzao hultav xeiv dav alnei, ssaqmiq miqssaq gaqzav nei qiq hhaq pievq al.

8) Aqyoq naolzao hultav aqtav tul a taoqngaoq, wuqduq kav zavq. Aqyoq wuqduq ceilkaol dyul haldyul mol ya siq laongaoq haldyul nav. Haqjil aqda dassaq yul hhaq laqnil pyu lulhhuv alkaq nei zuv nei salhu. Ssaqmiq miqssaq yul hhaq wuqduq kav duv alnei caolpievq pievq haqhaq e tyul taq, haqjil aqda dassaq hhaq xeiv tao li alnei, aqyoq e caolpievq a nil teiq alnei, "Nol halgei nei lal e aq wul al? Ngaq yaol hhosaq xilmeil saq jil aqnei?" leil nalhaq miq.

9) Ssaqmiq miqssaq yul hhaq, "Ngal Hhellaoq qovq e ssaqmiq aqlil. Noq yaol hhosaq saq ya (202) leil ngeel taoqngaoq, no naogo yolqoq aol lal wul" leil eil.

10) Molcyuq cyuqssaq yul hhaq, "Ngal yaol ssaqcyuq cyuqssaq. Ngal nil nei qiq nao neikavq e aqda aqma maq bo, aqyivq aqnil maq bo meil heeq lal laq e. Ngal xaldei qiq loq maq jav, kul'a qiq kol maq jav. Nol salhu naoq. Jol e laqhhyul liq kaoldaol laqhhyul jol e ngeel siq e. Xilmeil leil qiq hhaq naogo yovqhhovq cuvzavq alnei, aqkal nol maq saq qaol, maq gav qaol e pa ngeel a" leil eil miq.

11) Ssaqmiq miqssaq yul hhaq, "Hovqzyuq dama sal e huq sal hulcuv saol siq maq jav maq qil sso nga. Ngaldu naolhao naoq sal hulcuv saol siq, hovqzyuq dama huq sal hulcuv saol siq nal lao bi dul sso nga. Hovqzyuq dama sal e huq sal deimeeq loq biavq maq jav maq qil (203) sso. Ngaldu naolhao naoq sal deimeeq loq biavq liq, hovqzyuq dama sal e huq sal deimeeq loq biavq nal lao bi dul sso leil eil e, maq gaq ya aq?" leil eil miq.

12) Haqjil aqda yul hhaq aqyoq e doq dyul nalhaq, miav salhu ngaoq, ssaqmiq miqssaq yul hhaq eel seq lev nei, aqyoq yaol hu cuv alnei hhoq jol. Aqyoq, "Milmi ssaqheiq mol lal doq hhyul saol doq huq aq miqteil maq bei meil, miqbiaol dulma seqbiaq huq a miqteil yeiv lal" leil e doqsii yul doq nyuq duv la al. Yulmeil taoqngaoq, aqyoq ssaqmiq miqssaq yul hhaq eil e doqsii dyul yojil ngeel wul yaq leil nyuq al.

13) Tyul yavq ngeel taoqngaoq, aqyo niq hhaq aqpyuq helgeel a wuqduq qiq heiq taoq alnei, tyulmeil cuv zavq. Naolhao qiq nao, haqjil aqda (204) yul hhaq hhoqleivq miqteil naolhao aqmeil colhhaq aol zaq yil movq a leil zaol. Aqyo miqma aqyoq yaol, "Nol colhhaq taq aol zaq yil yoq. Nol milcaq haolteil maq aol zaq laq e aqzeiq yul mavq li alnei, halgei hev nei aol zaq

movq ya leil helliq diq li. Yulmeil ngaoq xaldei tyuq a duv lal qivq nga" leil eil miq.

14) Haqjil aqda yul hhaq aqyo miqma nei eil laq e aqmeil helliq diq li. Naolhao qiq nao salhu li aq, xaldei loqma pievq saq. Kul'a loqkol pievq saq al. Aqyoq hhyul leiq hhyul sil meil hhuvq yiv alnei, aqyo miqma naogo eil miq.

15) Aqyo miqma aqyoq naogo xilmeil eil miq, "Aqkal niaoq'aolqivq hoq zaq deiv naolhao taq, laqhyul zaolhhaol liq halmiav nei aol movq leil, dalqeiv qeiv hu alnei helliq diq yil."

16) Aqyoq (205) hhoqleivq aqyo miqma nei eil laq e aqmeil helliq diq yil. Naolhao qiq soq tul lal aq, meelhov yaolma yaolsiivq ba nei qiq caoq pievq al. Xil naolhao aqyo niq hhaq salzav nei yovqhhovq cuv zavq al.

17) Yulmeil liq, davqtav wuqduq yovqhhovq cuv zavq e aoqcyuq qiq taq maq cyuq, jaqleil qiq taq maq bo meil sal zavq nei e miqnieiq maq ngeel nga.

18) Naolhao halmiav nei maq biao meil, maq meeq e col qiq mavq haqjil aqda yul hhaq naogo cuq biav cuq lyul aol lal al. "No miqssaq tyul hhaq neivqzei hhalniul nei pievq laq e nga. Aqkal col yaol zaq lal nga. Puvlav cev nei leiq zei teiq teiq. Maq leiq zei teiq teiq e ngaoq, aqkal qiq puv qiq laol meil liq, aqyo nei zaq saq lal nga" (206) leil eil.

19) Haqjil aqda yul hhaq bialzeil pyu e maq meeq e doqsii yaol qeq alnei, ngeeljil meil, beiyaoq ssaqmiq yul hhaq yaol hhuvq yil leil leiq miq. Beiyaoq ssaqmiq yul hhaq, "Nol bialzeil pyu maq meeq doqsii qeq alnei pa ngeel a. Tyul qa doqsii maq qeq haoq nga. Nol ngaq yaol pa leiq huvq naohaoq yaol, hhovqleivq saq puv hha puv pal nga" leil eil miq.

20) Haqjil aqda yul hhaq, "Saq e naohaoq saq e ngeel al. Nol maq lal e taq liq, ngal byuldeivq deivq meil jol aq wul" leil eil miq.

21) Beiyaoq ssaqmiq yul hhaq, "Nol ngaq yaol maq hhuvq yil maq na leil ngeel naolhaoq, nol ngaq yaol miqteil lal e yulgei hha seq huvq heil nga" leil eil miq.

22) Haqjil aqda yul hhaq ciil jiq ciil jiq meil miqteil ngaqdeil (207) nieivq e yulgei ciil heil alnei, aqyoq yaol hhuvq yil joq leil eil miq.

23) Beiyaoq ssaqmiq, "Nol ngeeljil meil ngaq yaol hhuvq yil joq leil leiq e ngeel al laq?" leil eil miq.

24) Aqyoq, "Ngeeljil meil laolngaoq, noq yaol xaq a hev nei aqsol seq hev na nga aq?" leil eil miq.

25) Beiyaoq ssaqmiq aq, "Nol ssaonei nyuq hu. Ngaq yaol maq leiq huvq e meeq zeiq nga. Ngaldu niaq xa al nei lavqqoq hhoq e naohaoq yaol, nol hhuvq huvq li e noq e zaol ssol xal, laqhyul tyul mavq qiq jivq maq jav wul naq. Nol ssaonei nyuq hu. Aqkal naolhao nyuq duv al la taq, qiq gal bavq huvq yil lul maq hha nga" leil eil.

26) Yulmeil e liq, haqjil aqda yul hhaq hhovqleivq maq nalhaq na. Aqyoq yaol lolbaq deiq puvq miq. (208)

27) Haqjil aqda yul hhaq aqyoq qaq sol meil laqhhyul a hhuvq huvq li. Aoqqivq qiq yavq ngeel taoqngaoq, meelhov yaolma dyul miqteil e kaoldaol laqhyul pievq huvq al. Xaldei ssolnei kul'a liq, qiq jivq maq jav. Saqnei miqteil aqmeil algao saqcaoq pievq huvq saq al. Haljivq liq aqyoq miqteil hal jav e dyul laolngaoq, qiq jivq maq jav al.

28) Niaoq'aol xil taq, aqyoq zaol leiq wul yaq leil nyuq al. Qiq nao maq leiq lolbaq yulgei yil yil meil ngyul yil.

29) Xilmeil qiq nao aqyoq, "Milmi ssaqheiq cuq puv colkyul jol ssolnei, milmi cuq doq nal e hovq sal biav wul yaq. Tyul liq milmi ssaqheiq cuq puv colkyul jol e, cuq puv qiq hhaq halmiav maq zyul ya. Ssaqdov aqbiaol qiq pav zyul kevq ya. Deima loq sal (209) zaq biav eelssaq deivq e, zaq biav eelssaq halmiav maq zyul meil, deima loq sal qiq pav zyul kevq ya" leil ngyul.

30) Hal ngyul ngyul alnei ngyul nieiq pieiq taq e aq, wulquvq hul'a nei beiyaoq ssaqmiq doqteil loqleil sav nei gaq lal, "Nol haljivq leil ngyul wul aq?" Aqyoq, "Ngal no naogo yiv movq ya" leil eil miq.

31) Beiyaoq ssaqmiq aq, "Nol yiv movq naohaoq, kol yiv naoq" leil eil miq.

32) Aqyoq, "Ngal noq yaol maq mol qivq ya. Halmeil leil yiv ya?" leil eil miq.

33) Beiyaoq ssaqmiq aqyoq yaol, "Nol miav miv alnei xaq a coq xa yiv" leil eil miq. Aqyoq miav miv cuv alnei lolbaq taoq yulgei coq puvq heil.

34) Beiyaoq ssaqmiq yul hhaq cuv nei hhoheiq yulgei haqpal hhavq haqhaq. Haqjil aqda yul hhaq miav (210) miv alnei qiq coq ngeel taoqngaoq, saqkaol naolnieil hultav coq dav al. Aqyoq miav biei alnei qavq salhu aq, Ao, yuq a liq yuq a qiq aoq bia. Alyeiv hal dyul jav, alzil hal dyul jol.

35) Yulmeil liq, aqyoq maq hu zaq lov meil, beiyaoq ssaqmiq naogo beiyaoq aqhhol jol e yulgei li. Beiyaoq joq mol taoqngaoq, "Aqssaq yiv al lal. Meeq al" leil eil.

36) Aqssaq yul hhaq davqtav wuqduq jol e miqnieiq aol alnei heeq lal laq e ngeel taoqngaoq, yuq a niq nao saoq nao seilhha taoqngaoq maq jol teiq qaol al. Aqyo yoqpaq yoqma naogo hhuvq li movq al leil eil miq.

37) Beiyaoq aqhhol, "Taq teiq. Aqzeiq meenia nao seilhha. Nol meelheiq meil aqyeil biul alnei maq jol movq ya leil ngaoq, neesoq aq (211) hhaqlei hhaqyal saoq yeil lihhal beiv li" leil eil miq.

38) Aqssaq, "Aoq" leil qiq heiq eil taoqngaoq, duv huvq yiv al. Aqyoq yavqduq a hhuvq yil taoqngaoq, aqyo miqma aqyoq yaol, "Aqda haljivq leil eil nga aq?" leil nalhaq miq.

39) Aqyoq, "Aqda ngaq yaol neesoq qiq nao nei hhaqyal saoq yeil lihhal hha beiv saq nga leil eil ya. Qiq nao nei hhaqyal saoq yeil lihhal halmeil beiv saq ya?" leil eil miq.

40) Aqyo miqma, "Nol taq qil. Aqkal neesoq nol hhaqyal saqpeeq yulgei li alnei, xalhhaoq saol lavq beiv, xaldaoq saol lavq beiv, alkaqlaq saol lavq beiv alnei, "Dalda Hhellaoq hhaqheil heil movq a yil" leil eil alnei, nol alkaqlaq yiuvq. Yulmeil ngaoq, miqnieiq saq al" leil eil miq.

41) Naolhao qiq nao aqyoq aqyo miqma nei eil (212) laq aqmeil, aqhhuv aqtav alkaqlaq qiq gal saol lavq beiv a taoqngaoq, "Dalda Hhellaoq hhaqheil heil movq a yil" leil eil alnei, alkaqlaq a yiuvq.

42) Aqyoq yiuvq nyuq tal lal alnei salhu aq, hhaqyal saoq yeil lihhal saqnei beiv saq al. Aoqqivq, beiyaoq aqyoq yaol, "Aqli, hhaqyal beiv saq al laq?" leil nalhaq miq.

43) Aqssaq, "Aqda, beiv saq al" leil eil miq.

44) Beiyaoq, "Meeq al. Aqkal neesoq aq, nol miqzaq keq li" leil eil.

45) Aqssaq, "Aoq" leil qiq heiq eil taoqngaoq, duv yiv al.

46) Xavqduq hhuvq yil taoqngaoq, aqyo miqma naogo, "Aqda ngaq yaol neesoq miqzaq keq li leil eil ya. Yeiqnao naohav yaol beiv sil laq e jahhaq, neesoq miqzaq halmeil leil bi dovq li ya" leil eil miq.

47) Miqma aqyoq naogo, "Taq qil. Neesoq nol xalhhaoq, xaldaoq, alkaqlaq qiq (213) gal jeibaol qiq baol baol. Dalda Hhellaoq hhaqheil heil movq a yil leil eil alnei, alkaqlaq yiuvq. Yulmeil ngaoq miqnieiq saq wul al" leil eil miq.

48) Naolhao qiq nao, aqyoq hhoqleivq aqyo miqma eil aqmeil xalhhaoq, xaldaoq, alkaqlaq saoq gal jeibaol saoq baol baol alnei, "Dalda Hhellaoq hhaqheil heil movq a yil" leil eil alnei, alkaqlaq a yiuvq.

49) Aqyoq nyuq lal aq, javq nei peev saq al. Aoqqivq beiyaoq, "Hhaqyal miqzaq keq saq al laq" leil nalhaq miq.

50) Aqssaq, "Aqda, keq saq al" leil eil miq.

51) Beiyaoq, "Meeq al. Yulmeil ngaoq neesoq aq xa saq li" leil eil miq.

52) Aqssaq, "Aoq" leil qiq heiq eil alnei duv huvq yiv. Xavqduq a yil alnei aqyo miqma naogo, "Aqda ngaq yaol neesoq hhaqyal dyul xa saq li leil eil ya" leil eil miq.

53) Aqyo miqma, (214) "Neesoq nol hhaqssyuq seiq a taoqngaoq, xalhhaoq, xaldaoq, alkaqlaq qiq gal saol lavq duq alnei, 'Dalda Hhellaoq hhaqheil heil movq a yil' leil eil alnei, alkaqlaq yiuvq" leil eil miq.

54) Naolhao qiq nao, aqyoq hhoqleivq aqyo miqma nei meiq la aqmeil aol yil. Aqyoq hhaqyal hholqei qiq nyuq yiuvq alnei nyuq lal e ngaoq, hhaqyal hhoq duq saq al sil.

55) Aoqqivq beiyaoq, "Aqli, hhaqyal xa saq al laq" leil nalhaq miq.

56) Aqssaq, "Aqda, xa saq al" leil laq miq.

57) Beiyaoq, "Meeq al. Neesoq aq, nol hhaqssyuq dyul hhuv dav huvq li" leil eil miq.

58) Aqssaq, "Aoq" leil qiq heiq eil alnei duv yiv.

59) Xavqduq a yil alnei miqma naogo, "Aqda ngaq yaol neesoq hhaqssyuq dyul hhuv dav huvq li leil eil ya. Xa tao laq e hhaqssyuq yaol (215) liq hha hhuv dav huvq nga leil, tyulmeil wuqcavq meil ngaq yaol bi saq movq a leil nei laolngaoq" leil eil miq.

60) Aqyo miqma, "Maq beq sso. Aqkal neesoq nol xalhhaoq, xaldaoq, alkaqlaq, qiq gal saoq neev hhuv. "Dalda Hhellaoq hhaqheil heil movq a yil" leil eil alnei, alkaqlaq qiq gal piav ziil alnei yiuvq" leil

eil miq.

61) Naolhao qiq nao, aqyoq hhoqleivq aqyo miqma eil e aqmeil zaol yil. Aqyoq nyuq lal e aq, hhaqssyuq saoq yeil saq nei hhuv dav saq al.

62) Aoqqivq, beiyaoq naogo hhaqssyuq hhuv huvq yiv al leil eil miq. Naolhao gee hu aq, saoq neev maq luvq nga leil eil. Aqyoq yaol maq luv e yul saoq neev qo huvq li leil eil.

63) Aqyoq xavqduq a hhuvq yil alnei ngyul. Aqyo miqma aqyoq yaol, "Haljivq leil ngyul wul al?" leil (216) nalhaq miq.

64) Aqyoq, "Hhaqlei hhaqssyuq saoq neev ca nga yil. Halgei qo yil ya?" leil eil miq.

65) Aqyo miqma, "Taq qil. Nol niaoq'aolqivq kavmiaq meenia mol sev. Aqkal neesoq xalzeil a hoqhyuq saoq mol dovq nga. Nol alkaqlaq qiq mol bev li" leil eil miq.

66) Naolhao qiq nao, aqyoq xalzeil a salhu li e. Ngeeljil meil, albol hultav hoqhyuq zeil do nei saoq mol dovq e ngeel. Aqyoq alkaqlaq qiq mol yaol muvq zil alnei, "teil" leil qiq lavq ngeel taoqngaoq, alkaqlaq dovq e qiq mol zavlav nei ya xa heil qavq al.

67) Hoqhyuq mol peivq alnei salhu aq, hhaqssyuq yul saoq neev cuvnei aqyoq e beillivq hholqei kevq al. Aqyoq hhaqssyuq yul saoq neev beiyaoq naogo bavq huvq li miq.

68) Beiyaoq qiq jivq maq eil qivq al. Aqyoq yaol hhuvq (217) huvq yil alnei, ssao nei deissaol. "Neesoq kavtev ssolnei kavmiaq eq, zaqhal eq alnei, saqleiq zaq li movq ssa" leil eil miq.

69) Naolhao qiq nao, aqyo mavq kavtev ssolnei kavmiaq eq. Aqssaq aq ceilpiul liq qiq leil eq alnei, saqleiq zaq li al. Qiq nao aoqcil qivq nei halleiq leiq qaq taoqngaoq, naolma ya sil miv nei taq, haqluv hhaqzeil qiq gal lal hev.

70) Yoqpaq aq yulgei a xavq kal leil eil. Aqssaq yul hhaq qavq salhu aq, haqluv hhaqzeil zeilma yaol taoqtul laltul meil, tojeil nei dev xa laq e aqmeil. Haqluv hhaqzeil hul'a ngaoq, lolbaq taoq taoqma navqyol pa yol nei, wulquvq quvqma niulyev pa yev nei, miav qiq heiq salhu liq, saqzuq zuq lal jil aqnei.

71) Yulmeil liq yoqpaq aq yuq a maq xavq (218) maq na. "Haqlaq meiqbaoq maq tao li meil, haqlaq laqssaq maq hha nieivq qaol nga. Xa xavq alnei ceivnav bev zaq movq a" leil eil. Aoqqivq yiuvq e taq, yoqpaq aqssaq

yaol aqyo keelmiqdaoq a hha yiuvq nga leil eil.

72) Aqssaq yiuvq al naolhao laolngaoq, aqyoq maq yiuvq. Sulhhaol qiq pav hev lal taoqngaoq, beiyaoq mol nyuq lal al. Aqyoq nyuq alnei, keelkuv zoq wul leil zaol leivq a taoqngaoq, aqyoq keelmiqdaoq a yiuvq lavq e aqssaq yul hhaq yaol hhaqhav tivq nei qiq naoq ngeel taoqngaoq, aqssaq yul hhaq haqluv hhaqzeil a leeq xa heil qavq alnei "paoqtaoq" leil, lolbaq taoq a zei puvq al leil nyuq.

73) Beiyaoq mol col yul hhaq sil wul yaq leil hhyul sil al. Yulmeil liq, aqyoq neema kyuq wul leil zaol leivq a taoqngaoq, (219) "Aqyaoq, Moq'yul ssaqteiq ceiv al" leil eil.

74) Yulmeil liq, aqssaq yul hhaq qiq zeil pyu jol alnei maq teiq maq cal meil, "Moq'yul ssaqteiq ceiv e maq ngeel meil. Aqda Taoqpaoq zoqnia zaqhal jil aq" leil eil.

75) Eil! Aqssaq yul hhaq lolbaq taoq a leeq puvq heil qav al yaolliq, halmeil duv huvq lal nil? Miqnieiq aq xilmeil leil ngeel lal ssaq. Aqssaq yul hhaq miqteil hhuv duv e tyul taq kavq e aqyo miqma nei meiq kyul a taoqngaoq, beiyaoq mol aqyoq yaol keelmiqdaoq a yiuvq leil eil e tyul taq, aqyoq yuq a yiuvqhheivq hheivq alnei kaoqhe jiq nei yiuvq sil wulleil zaol.

76) Beiyaoq mol yiuvq sil taoqngaoq, aqyoq tul alnei ceilpiul dalleil mol beiyaoq e keelmiqdaoq yulgei a bilceiv meil bavq taq alnei, aqyoq aq qiq zeil pyu xeiv yoq alnei jol. (220)

77) Yulmeil taoqngaoq, eiqsi leeq xa heil e aq, ceilpiul dalleil mol. Beiyaoq mol qiq jivq maq zaol jivq. Wulma ziiv milnia lavq maq piav qivq meil saq al. Aoqqivq tyul yavq aoqzaq tyulmeil yiuvq bia al. Naolhao qiq nao laqhyul a hhuvq yiv al.

78) Aoqqivq, beiyaoq mol nei aqssaq yaol hhoq gul li alnei, "Neesoq saqleiq li movq al" leil eil. Aqyo aqssaq yaol milma hhaqdaoq qiq gal a saqluvq luvq leil eil miq.

79) Aqyoq hhuvq yil alnei aqyo miqma naogo eil miq. Miqma, "Neesoq nol toma qiq kaol bavq alnei, yuq a luvq li. Siqse hev lal e ngaoq, ollol eelniul saoq mol zeildo nei lal nga. Nol miqteil naolhao yul niq mol dev tov. Alkaqlaq e yul mol pieilse taq dev. Daqzii hha (221) bo. Halmeil liq yul niq mol hha dev tov. Pieilse taq bi xeiv. Aqyo niq mol yaol maq seivq nia ngaoq, nol maq leev wul naq" leil eil miq.

80) Naolhao qiq nao, aqyoq toma bavq alnei yuq a luvq li. Seil qiq zeq hev lal taoqngaoq, ngeeljil meil eelniul niulma saoq mol zeildo lo nei, lalma ja nei lal al. Miavneev neevma niulgeil nei aqyo naogo quq la al.

81) Aqyoq toma hhe cei, hhaqhav tivq nei dev xa heil. Miqteil pyu ssolnei naolhao pyu yul niq mol meil dev tov. Maq dev tov laq e mol daoqmiq hhe kuv alnei xeiv al.

82) Aqyoq laqhyul yil hev aq, yoqpaq yoqma maq jol al. Aqyo miqma qaq sol aqyoq yaol doq cavq lal. Aqyo niq hhaq, puv lav cevnei se leev teiq teiq alnei, davqtav wuqduq hhuvq huvq lal. (222)

83) Aqyoq niq hhaq aqsol movq aqsol sal. Halnyuq nyuq, haldul dul alnei, cuv zavq laq e ngeel taoqngaoq, aqzeiq meil gaqzaq nia. Aqyo niaq gaqzaq hhyul qaol nei yoqhhovq halmeil cuv zavq, ssaqmiq ssaqyo halmeil qu zaq leil tyul mavq aqnu liyal meil qiq mol e dudaq ngeel wulnaq.

ENGLISH TRANSLATION OF "DRAGON AND THE SON-IN-LAW"
(with notes at the end)

1) Long, long ago there lived a very poor orphan young man. While still very young his father and mother died. He had no relatives. When he reached the age of 25 he still had not taken a wife.

2) One day the village was having a religious holiday. A group of men all went to fish by damming up a stream. They were not willing to take the orphan with them, however. So he went alone to go fishing by damming another stream.

3) Although half a day went by, he did not see a single fish. Even so he was not discouraged, but turned over stones and looked in all of the holes. About the time the sun was going down he saw a fairly large colored fish at the bottom of the dammed up water. He caught the fish, and went back home.

4) When he got home he looked at the fish and saw it was very beautiful. The more he looked the more beautiful it became. Whenever he looked at it he thought in his heart, "I had not realized that this fish is an orphan, like I am". So he was not willing to eat that fish, but released it into a wooden container of water without killing it.

5) The next day he returned from working in his fields. He had no idea who did it, but someone had cooked a hot meal of rice and vegetables and left it

there. "Probably some good-hearted person has taken pity on me and done this" he thought. So he went all around asking the neighbors, "Who of you has come to my place and kindly prepared a hot meal for me? Come and eat with me".

6) But though he went around and asked all the neighbors, there was no one who said they had done it. As for one group they said, "It was no human. It must have been a headless evil spirit who prepared a meal for you."

7) Even though several days passed, not a day went by but what there was food prepared for him to eat. So one day he took his hoes and machetes and pretended he was going to his fields. But he came back to the door of his house and stole a look inside. In just a moment he saw the fish in the wooden container swimming around, up and down. Then there was a splash, and with a jump the fish jumped out of the water up onto a stool, and became a beautiful woman.

8) She stood on the stool and combed her hair, which was very long and very black. The young man carefully looked in through the door. When the young woman had combed her hair she started braiding it. The young man ran in, grabbed her braids and said, "Where did you come from? Was it because you pitied me that you came?" he asked.

9) The young woman replied, "I am of the royal family of 'Hhellaoq'. Out of pity for you I have come to be your friend."

10) The orphan said, "I am very poor. From the time I was young I have not had a father and mother. I grew up without any relatives. I have no field and no garden. Please look around. The place I have is just fenced in. If I were to marry you I am afraid you could not stand the poverty and cold", he said.

11) The young woman replied, "In the past our ancestors did not leave us a heritage or even three stones to make a fireplace. But do not worry. What we'll gain will be better than that. Our ancestors left us no fields. But do not worry. The fields we will make will be better than theirs. Have you never heard of these things?"

12) The young man listened to what she said, and looked at her. The woman smiled and just sat there looking at him. He remembered the saying, "When you meet your loved one, before you speak three sentences she will speak to you with a smile." He thought the words the girl spoke were sincere.

13) That night the two of them bowed their heads (worshipped) at the ancestral shrine, and in that way were married. The next day the young man looked like he was preparing to go out and work for others for a living again. His wife said to him, "Don't go out as a daily laborer. Go to a mountain slope that is not cultivated, and drive in poles there to mark a field. If you do that, an irrigated terraced field will appear."

14) The young man went and drove in the poles to mark the field like his wife told him to. The next day when he went to look it had already become a big terraced irrigated field with terraced gardens. He was thrilled and went back and told his wife.

15) His wife then said to him, "Tonight after you have eaten your fill, go find a house site. Measure how big you want the house to be, and drive in the field markers."

16) Again he did as his wife told him, and went to drive in the field markers. The next morning he got up and saw brightly shining roof tiles on a group of new houses that had come into being where he had driven in the markers. After this the two of them lived there as a happy couple.

17) However, there is not a family in the world that has not had a cloudy, overcast day, with a strong wind blowing. They did not always live in comfort without having to work.

18) Not too long after that, a group of bad people came to talk to that man, telling him terrible things. "Your wife" they said, "was originally a 'weretiger'. Later on she will eat people. Drive her away from the village at once. If you do not drive her away, in time she will eat up everyone in our village and it will disappear."

19) The man believed the terrible gossip brought by the outsiders, and thinking it was really true he drove away the dragon's daughter. The daughter of the dragon said, "It looks like you have believed that the bad words of the outsiders are true. It is not proper to believe words like that. After you have driven me away, you will return again to your old suffering."

20) The man said, "I'm sure there will be suffering again. But the time before you came to me, I was able to live."

21) The dragon's daughter said, "If you really must

send me home, first you must lead me back to where you found me."

22) The young man quickly pulled her back to where he had caught the fish, and told her to go back.

23) The dragon's daughter said to him, "Are you really sending me back like this?"

24) He went on, "Of course! If this were not the case, why would I have brought you here?"

25) The dragon's daughter said, "You must think clearly about this. It would be better not to drive me away. If the two of us separate you will go back and have no house and no fields. Think carefully. Later when you think about it, there will be no way to take everything back."

26) Even so, the husband still did not listen to her. He pushed her into the river.

27) The man returned to his house all alone. When night came, the house with the roof tiles turned back to being a mountain shack as it was before. There were no longer any terraced fields or gardens. Everything returned to thorn bushes. So all of the things he had before he no longer had.

28) Now he realized that this time he had made a mistake. Every day without fail he went weeping down to the river.

29) One day he said, "Because I listened to divisive words of clever people against the one I loved, my happy family has now been broken up. Even so, I myself have to take partial responsibility for it. A good rice field with terraces can be broken by a small stream of water. But the field itself must take some of the responsibility for the destruction" he cried sadly.

30) He cried and cried. One time when he stopped crying he clearly heard the voice of the dragon's daughter coming from below the water. "Why are you crying?" she asked. "I want to come down there with you" he answered.

31) Dragon's daughter said, "If you want to come in, come on down."

32) "I cannot see you. How can I possibly come down?" he replied.

33) The dragon's daughter said to him, "Just close your eyes and jump in here." He closed his eyes and

jumped into a deep part of the river.

34) Now the dragon's daughter was at that moment in the process of weaving cloth near the gate. When the man closed his eyes and jumped in, he landed on the loom and the cloth she was weaving. When he opened his eyes and looked around, he saw that it was another world, with a different sky. There were many kinds of flowers and many kinds of birds.

35) However, he was not interested in looking at those things. He went with the dragon's daughter to the palace of the dragon. As soon as the dragon saw him he said, "Oh, my son-in-law has come. Good!"

36) Since the son-in-law had lived in the upper world and had grown up making a living there, after he had visited the dragon's home for two or three days he felt he could not stay there any longer. He said to his father-in-law and mother-in-law that he wanted to go back up.

37) King dragon said, "Don't be in a hurry. Visit here for several more days. Now if you are really fed up with staying here, tomorrow go clear a field for planting buckwheat, a field large enough to plant three bags of seeds."

38) Having given his consent, the son-in-law left. After he had gone back to where he was staying, his wife asked him, "What did father say to you?"

39) "Father said that tomorrow, in just one day, I must finish clearing a field large enough to plant three bags of buckwheat seeds. How can I clear land for a field big enough to plant three bags of buckwheat seeds in just one day?" he asked.

40) His wife said, "Don't you worry. Tomorrow you go to an old buckwheat field. Go make three cuts in the upper section of the field, make three cuts in the lower section of the field, and three cuts in the middle section. Then say, 'This is uncle Hhellaoq. I want some help.' Following this, sleep in the middle section. If you do that, the work will be done."

41) The next day he did just what his wife told him, and made three cuts each in the upper, lower and middle sections of the field. Following that he said, "This is uncle Hhellaoq. I want some help". And then he went to sleep in the middle section.

42) When he woke from sleep and looked around, there was a clearing for a field big enough to plant three

bags of buckwheat seeds. In the evening the dragon asked him, "Son, did you clear the field for planting buckwheat?"

43) "I have finished clearing it," the son-in-law said.

44) The dragon said, "Good. Now go out and burn the field tomorow morning."

45) The son-in-law grunted an acknowledgement and left.

46) When he got back to where he was staying he told his wife, "Father has told me to go burn the field tomorrow. How can I burn the jungle growth tomorrow that was just cut today?"

47) His wife said, "Don't worry. Tomorrow you go and make bonfires in the upper, lower and middle sections of the field. Call out, 'This is uncle Hhellaoq. I want some help', and then sleep in the middle section. If you do that, the job will be done."

48) The next day he again did what his wife told him, and made bonfires in the upper, lower and middle sections of the field. He called out, "This is uncle Hhellaoq. I want some help", and then went to sleep in the middle section.

49) When he woke up, the field was thoroughly burned. In the evening the dragon asked him, "Have you finished burning the field for planting buckwheat?"

50) "Father, I have finished burning it," he said.

51) "Good. If that's the case, go plant it all tomorrow" the dragon said.

52) The son-in-law grunted consent and left. When he got back to where he was staying he told his wife, "Father told me to go plant the whole buckwheat field tomorrow."

53) His wife said, "Tomorrow when you sow the seeds, dig three hoefuls each in the upper, lower, and central sections of the field. After saying, 'This is uncle Hhellaoq. I want some help' sleep in the middle section."

54) The next day he again did as his wife instructed him. After he had a short sleep in the middle of the field he awakened to see the whole buckwheat field planted.

55) That night the dragon said, "Son, did you plant the whole buckwheat field?"

56) "Father, I planted it all" the son-in-law replied.

57) "Good. Tomorrow go back and pick up all of the seeds" the dragon said.

58) The son-in-law grunted consent and went out.

59) When he got to his sleeping place he told his wife, "Father has told me that tomorrow I must go to gather all of the seeds I planted. In doing this he is purposely trying to make it difficult for me. He wants me to suffer."

60) His wife said, "Never mind. Tomorrow go to the upper, lower and middle sections of the field and pick up three seeds in each place. Then say, 'This is uncle Hhellaoq. I want your help', after which clean out a flat place in the middle section and sleep."

61) The next day he again did as his wife said. He thought he had picked up all of the buckwheat seeds and put them in three bags.

62) In the evening the dragon said to bring the seeds. Later when the dragon counted the seeds, he found three seeds were missing. He told the son-in-law to go find and pick up the three missing seeds.

63) The son-in-law went to his sleeping place and cried. His wife asked him, "Why are you crying?"

64) "I am short three seeds. Where shall I go looking for them?" he asked.

65) "Don't worry. Tonight you prepare some crossbow arrows. Then tomorrow there will be three doves at the edge of the field. Shoot the middle one," his wife said.

66) The next day he went to look at the edge of the field. Sure enough, roosting on a tree in a straight line were three doves. He aimed at the middle one, and "zing" when he shot an arrow the middle bird immediately fell down.

67) He cut open the bird and looked inside. He found the three seeds right in the craw of the dove. He took the three seeds back to the dragon.

68) The dragon had nothing he could say to this. He told the son-in-law to return to his sleeping place to

get ready for the next day. He wanted to go hunting, and would thus need the son-in-law to carry crossbows, arrows and food for the trip.

69) The next day they set off, carrying the crossbows and arrows. The son-in-law also carried a bag of rice, and they went hunting. Having hunted the whole next day and being very tired, about the time the sun was going down they came to a rock cliff.

70) "Let's stay here overnight" the father-in-law said. When the son-in-law looked around he saw that the cliff was straight up and down. It was as if it had been cut off straight with a knife. There was also a huge and deep river at the bottom of the cliff with swirling green water. Just giving it a glance made one shudder.

71) Even so the father-in-law insisted that they had to camp there. "You're not going to catch any tiger cubs if you are not willing to go into the tiger's mouth. I want to camp here and shoot wild goats" he said. At night when they went to bed, the dragon said his son-in-law must sleep at his feet.

72) Even though the son-in-law lay down there, he did not sleep. When it was a little after midnight, the dragon awakened. He thought (up a plan), and pretended to stretch out his legs, which were doubled back. Then he exerted all of his strength in straightening his legs out, so as to kick the son-in-law down the cliff. The son-in-law rolled down the cliff and went "kerplop" into the deep river.

73) The dragon was thrilled that that man was dead. However, pretending he was very sad he said, "Oh, the last of Moq'yul's line is broken".

74) However, the son-in-law was over at one side, and without hurrying he said, "Moq'yul's line is not broken. Father's food, furnished by Taoqpaoq, is finished." (i.e., father-in-law is about to die)

75) Oh, in spite of rolling down into the river, how did the son-in-law get out? He could do it because his wife has taught him to be clever. So when the dragon told him to sleep at his feet, the son-in-law pretended to be asleep and even snored like thunder.

76) Then when the dragon was sound asleep, the son-in-law got up and put the bag of rice crossways at the dragon's feet, following which he ran over and waited at one side.

77) Therefore what had rolled down the cliff a

moment ago was the bag of rice. The dragon could do nothing. It was as hard for him as if his intestines itched and he could not scratch them. They slept then until daybreak, and the next day they went home.

78) That night the dragon called the son-in-law and said, "Tomorrow we want to go hunting." He said the son-in-law should wait for game in the mountain pass.

79) The son-in-law returned and told his wife. The wife said, "Tomorrow you take a sword and go wait for game there. At a certain hour three huge green snakes will appear in a line. You must chop to death the first and last snakes. Under no circumstances must you strike the middle one. You must be brave. No matter what, you must kill those two snakes. Under no circumstances must you let them run away. If you do not kill those two snakes, you will not be saved."

80) The next day, he took his sword and went to wait there (at the mountain pass). At the hour of 'seil' (3-4 pm) truly there were three big green snakes coming in a straight line, with their tongues darting in and out. They had huge green eyes, and came rushing toward him.

81) He raised his sword, and with all his strength he cut them up. He chopped to death the first and last, just those two. The one he did not kill pulled its tail up and ran away.

82) When he arrived back home, the father-in-law and mother-in-law were not there. Only his wife came to greet him. The two of them very quickly collected everything and returned to the upper world.

83) The two of them were thoughtful of each other (lit., 'they gave each other the choice of what they wanted'). They thought alike and developed a wonderful marriage, and loved each other very much. As to how much they loved each other, and what kind of marriage they had, and how they took care of their children, all of that will have to be told in another story.

NOTES ON THE STORY

(The section numbers are used.)

1) The orphan theme is important in Hani culture. See also section 4).

2) On such days the villagers cannot go to their fields to work, but they can go hunting.

9) '**Hhellaoq**' is another term for the 'lord dragon', stressing his royalty.

18) A 'weretiger' (**neivqzei hhalniul**) is a person who, though relatively normal in the daytime, at night becomes a man-eating ogre or 'weretiger'.

29) This refers to the proverb,
Eelcil xul e eelnaoq alju,
Eelnaoq xul e hhaqzeil biav.
(Slow flowing water appears 'soft',
But 'soft' flowing water can break
down a cliff.)
-- 'Soft' water here means that slow flowing water does not appear powerful, but as it continues to flow it can even break down rock cliffs. In the same way his wife's detractors had worn him down with their bad words, so they should bear part of the blame for his sending her away.

71) This refers to the proverb,
Haqlaq meiqbaoq maq tao li meil,
Haqlaq laqssaq maq nieivq qaol nga.
(If you do not enter into the tiger's den,
You cannot expect to catch tiger cubs.)
-- If you want to do something important, you sometimes have to do something dangerous.

73) and 74) The names of **Moq'yul** and **Taoqpaoq** appear fairly early in the Hani genealogy. The first is 11 names and the second is 13 names after **Sulmil'yul**, considered to be the first human being. The dragon was acting sad and saying that the genealogy of his son-in-law was 'broken' (i.e., that he was dead and would leave no sons.) But the son-in-law was saying he was not dead, and that the father-in-law's 'food was running out'. This meant that he would die soon. The Hani have a legend which states that one's food, and thus one's lifespan, is controlled by **Taoqpaoq**. So when the 'food is finished' (**zaqhal jil**) it means that that person will die.

77) This refers to the proverb,
Wulma ziiv e,
Lavq maq piav qivq.
(Even though one's intestines itch,
One cannot scratch them.)

79) We learn later in the story that this "certain hour" was "**seil**" hour, which would be roughly 3-4 in the afternoon.

APPENDIX 3:

GENEALOGY

The Hani memorize their genealogy much like the Akha (see Lewis 1989:700). Following are samples of genealogies from: a Hani living in Luchun, an Akha/Yani living in the Menghai area of Xishuangbanna, and an Akha living in Burma. The first section (eight names in the Hani, 11 names in the Akha) is made up of 'spirits'. The section of the genealogy that starts with **Sulmil'yul** (Smˇ miˇ oˇ), who is considered the first human being, is the 'human' genealogy.

The next 14 names are the same in all three. The Hani genealogy given here breaks off from the other two after **Zyuqtaoqpaoq** (Dzoeˬ tahˬ pahˬ), but the Akha/Yani and the Akha go on for another 13 generations.

Where the Akha/Yani of China and the Akha of Burma and Thailand divide, there are many Akha living in Burma and Thailand who have a very similar genealogy for many more generations. Actually, the **Jeqhhyuq** (Jeuˬ G'oeˬ) line is considered by the Akha themselves to be the 'major' line for many clans. They often refer to themselves and their language as 'Jeuˬ G'oeˬ', partly to identify who they are not, such as the Jeuˬ Jawˇ or Jeuˬ Byaˬ (other brothers of Jeuˬ G'oeˬ).

Hani in Luchun	Akha/Yani in Menghai	Akha in Burma, Thailand
Aoqmavq		(Mˬ maˬ)
Mavqhhaol		(Mˬ g'ahˇ)
Hhaolheeq		(G'ahˇ neˬ)
-----		(Neˬ zaw‸)
-----		(Zaw‸ zeu^)
Heeqtaol		(Zeu^ toˇ)
Taolmavq		(Toˇ ma)
Mavqyaol		(Ma yawˇ)
Yaolneivq		(Yawˇ neh‸)
Neivqbei		(Neh‸ beh)
-----		(Beh smˇ)
Sulmil'yul	Smlmil'ol	Smˇ miˇ oˇ
Yultyuqli	Oltyuqlyu	Oˇ toeˬ loe
Tyuqlizaol	Tyuqlyuzml	Toeˬ loe dzm
Zaolmiqyeil	Zmmaoqyeil	Dzm mawˬ yehˇ
Miqyeilqa	Maoqyeiljav	Mawˬ yehˇ ca
Qa'qiqsiq	Javtiqsiq	Ca tiˬ siˬ
Qiqsiqli	Tiqsiqlil	Tiˬ siˬ liˇ
Libaoqbei	Lilpaoqbei	Liˇ pawˬ beh^
Baoqbeiwu	Paoqbeiwuv	Pawˬ beh^ u^
Wuhaoqssaq	Wuvnioqssaq	U^ nyoˬ zaˬ

Haoqssaqcol	Nioqssaqcaol	Nyoˬ zaˬ tsawˇ
Colmoq'yul	Caolmaoq'yul	Tsawˇ mawˬ oeˇ
Moq'yulzyuq	Maoq'yulzyuq	Mawˬ oeˇ dzoeˬ
Zyuqtaoqpaoq	Zyuqtanqpanq	Dzoeˬ tahˬ pahˬ
Taoqpaoqsa	Tanqpanqmanl	Tahˬ pahˬ mahˇ
Sa'luvbeq	Manlhaoqtan	Mahˇ hawˬ tah
Beqhaqbyul	Haoqtanjeiq	Hawˬ tah jeˬ
Haqbyulngyul	Jeiqleilniaol	Jeˬ le nyawˇ
Ngyulmoqzovq	Niaolqillavq	Nyawˇ ciˇ la‸
Moqzoqlu	Lavqtanlbyuq	La‸ tahˇ boeˬ
Lubieilbol	Tanlbyuqsyuv	Tahˇ boeˬ soe^
Bieilbolngeeq	Byuqsyuvlei	Boeˬ soe^ leh^
Ngeeqlitaol	Lei'lmbol	Leh^ lm boˇ
Taolliqyiul	Bolmanqbov	Boˇ mahˬ po^
Liqyiulbieiv	Manqbovtil	Mahˬ po^ ciˇ
Bieivnaoq	Tilsalbiev	Ciˇ shaˇ byeu^
Naoqhhel	Bievmazanl	Byeu^ ma dzahˇ
Hhelbei	Zanljeq	Dzahˇ jeuˬ
Beidol	Jeqhhyuq	Jeuˬ byaˬ --g'oeˬ
Dolnia	Hhyuqmeil	Byaˬ zeuˇ
Niadao	Meilqanl	Zeuˇ zuiˬ
Daoceil	Qanldeel	Zuiˬ ci^
Ceilzyuq	Madyu	Ci^ bya^
Zyuqquq	Dyussanl	Bya^ dehˇ
Quqtaol	Ssanlbeiq	Oeˇ ciˬ
Boqzeq	Beiqnmq	Mahˇ yahˬ
Hhaolzeivq	Nmqbeq	Piˇ mahˇ
Zeivqzil	Beqnol	Zahˇ dmˇ
Zilhhov	Hhyumeq	K'ahˬ pyeuˇ
Hhovsseil	Mapel	Nyoˬ dzahˇ
Sseilseiv	Salbiaoq	Dzahˇ lo^
Seivlao	Laossol	Lo^ nawˇ
Caqmeeq	Hhyujeiq	Nawˇ ce
Hhyullyul	Jeiqbiev	Ce sahˇ
Seilsol	Bievho	Sahˇ huiˬ
Keelcyul	Hogal	Huiˬ gaˬ
Cyulbiao	Galco	Piˇ saˇ
Biaozyuq	Coxanq	Saˇ dui
Zyuqheeq	Xanqlo	G'oeˬ cmˬ
Heeqhhul	Lozei	Lehˬ shawˬ
Heeqssaol	Zeike	Shawˬ tsuiˬ
Ssaolju	Kecei	Tsui dzahˇ
Juceiq		
Ceiqdee		
Deejei		
Jeigaq		
Gaq'eq		

Gaqbia (after Gaqbia there are four generations)

Note on the spelling: In the spelling of the Akha/Yani: '-m' = a syllabic 'm', and 'an' = a nasalized 'a', corresponding to what is written as: '-m' and 'ah' in the Akha of Burma and Thailand.

APPENDIX 4:

The names of fifty-six ethnic groups in China:
(cf. 50:223)

Hani names	Standard spelling
Alcalcuq	Achang
Aqcaoqssaq (Deicuq)	Dai
Baollaoqcuq (Deqhhaqcuq)	Benglong
Baohhalcuq	Bonan
Beiqcuq	Bai
Buqyilcuq	Bonyei
Buflaqcuq	Blang
Caoqxeilcuq	Chaoxian
Daqhhol'eicuq	Daur
Daolxalcuq	Dongxiang
Daofcuq	Dong
Deicuq (Aqcaoqssaq)	Dai
Duqlaoqcuq	Drung
Ehheilkeqcuq	Ewenki
Gaolsalcuq	Gaoshan
Gellaocuq	Gelao
Halsalkeiqcuq	Kazak
Haqhholssaq (Yiqcuq)	Yi
Haqniqssaq (Halniqcuq)	Hani
Hafcuq (Pyulniul)	Han
Heiqzeiqcuq	Hezhen
Hyuqcuq	Hui
Jilcuq	Gin
Jilnoqcuq	Jino
Jilpolcuq	Jingpo
Kol'eikeiqziilcuq	Kirgiz
Lalhuqcuq	Lahu
Liqcuq	Li
Liqsulcuq	Lisu
Loqbalcuq	Loba
Macuq	Man
Maoqgucuq	Mongol
Maoqnaqcuq	Maonan
Meiqbalcuq	Monba
Miaoqcuq	Miao
Muqlaocuq	Mulam
Naqxilcuq	Naxi
Nufcuq	Nu
Oqloqsiilcuq	Russian
Oqlueiqcyulcuq	Orogen
Pumicuq	Pumi
Pyulniul (Hafcuq)	Han
Qalcuq	Qiang
Sallalcuq	Salar
Seilcuq	She
Syucuq	Sui
Taqjiqkeiqcuq	Tajik
Taqtaq'eicuq	Tatar
Tucuq	Tu
Tujalcuq	Tujia
Wacuq	Wa (Va)
Weiq'wuq'eicuq	Uygur
Wulziilbiqkeiqcuq	Uzbek
Xiqbeilcuq	Xibe
Yaoqcuq (Yoqsseissaq)	Yao
Yiqgul	Yugur
Zafcuq	Tibetan
Zuafcuq	Zhuang

APPENDIX 5:

Names of **PROVINCES, MUNICIPALITIES** and **AUTONOMOUS REGIONS** in Hani.

Hani spelling	**Standard spelling**
Beiqjil Siif	Beijing city
Fuqjeif	Fujian
Galsuq	Gansu
Guadaol	Guangdong
Guaxil Zuafcuq Ziifziifqil	Guangxi Autonomous Region
Gyufzel	Guizhou
Heinaq	Hainan
Heiqlaoqjal	Heilongjiang
Hoqbeiq	Hebei
Hoqnaq	Henan
Huqbeiq	Hubei
Huqnaq	Hunan
Hhalhyul	Anhui
Jalsul	Jiangsui
Jalxil	Jiangxi
Jiqliq	Jilin
Liaoqniq	Liaoning
Niqxaf	Ningxia
Nyufmaoqgu Ziifziifqil	Neimenggu Autonomous Region
Qilhei	Qinghai
Saldaol	Shandong
Salxil	Shanxi
Saxil	Shaanxi
Safhei Siif	Shanghai city
Siifcual	Sichuan
Teiqhhual	Taiwan
Tieiljil Siif	Tiangjin city
Xiljal Weiqwuq'e Ziifziifqil	Xinjiang Autonomous Region
Xilzaf Ziifziifqil	Xizang Autonomous Region
Yyuqnaq	Yunnan
Zeiqjal	Zhejiang

APPENDIX 6:

SOUNDS OF THE HANI

duq meil duq alnei (or) **duq duq duq leil** the sound of someone knocking at a door; striking a drum; thunder

geivq meil geivq alnei (or) **geivq geivq geivq nei** the sound of something cracking

goq goqdeil goq the sound of hens clucking

goqgyul lilhhul leil the sound of roosters crowing

gaoqdaoq laoq, gaoqdaoq laoq the sound of a rice pounder going "kathump, kathump"

gu lu gaoq laoq the sound of a boulder or log rolling down a mountain

hhaoq meil hhaoq alnei (or) **hhaoq hhaoq hhaoq leil** the sound of a stream gurgling along

hhuq hhuq hhuq leil the sound of dogs growling

jiv jiv zav zav the sound of chirping birds

jyul jyul jyul leil the sound of insects

lovq meil lovq alnei (or) **lovq lovq lovq leil** the sound of people talking

luq meil luq alnei (or) **luq luq luq leil** the sound of a crackling fire

puq meil puq alnei (or) **puq puq puq leil** the sound of many birds flying

ssav meil ssav alnei (or) **ssav ssav ssav nei** the sound of quarreling

taovq meil taovq alnei the sound of big guns firing

teivq meil teivq alnei (or) **teivq teivq teivq leil** the sound of rain falling

tov tov tov leil diq tov knocking, as on a table or at the door

tuq meil tuq alnei (or) **tuq tuq tuq leil** the sound of birds spreading their wings

yuq eil yuq eil leil the sound of pigs grunting

APPENDIX 7:

HANI TERMS OF ENDEARMENT

There are various patterns of speech used by the Hani to show great respect to the one who is present and being addressed directly. These can be referred to as '**terms of endearment**' (**TE**).

1. The following begin with 'no' which literally means 'your', but in these cases it is simply the introduction to the term of endearment.

no alba dear older sister (used by an elder to someone in the younger generation on behalf of his or her child, showing that the listener is older than his or her child)

no algo dear older brother (used by an elder to someone in the younger generation on behalf of his or her child, showing that the listener is older than her or his child)

no alnia dear aunty (used when speaking on behalf of one's child, when the woman is younger than the male speaker)

no alsuq dear uncle (used when speaking on behalf of one's child, when the man is younger than the speaker)

no alsuq laosiil dear uncle teacher (used by same generation where the listener is a male, the speaker is older than the listener, the speaker has a child and is showing great politeness.) (or) **no dalda laosiil**

no aqbol dear grandfather (used by members of the same generation)

no aqcu dear sister-in-law (patterns the same as: **no algo**)

no aqhhyu dear maternal uncle (used by members of the same generation)

no aqmee dear aunty (used by members of the same generation)

no aqmee laosiil dear aunty teacher (used by a person of the same generation where the speaker is older than the listener, the speaker has a child, the listener is female, showing great politeness)

no aqmee Pyulniul dear Han (Chinese) aunty (for the pattern, see: **no aqmee laosiil**)

no aqnil dear younger brother (used by a person of an older generation on behalf of his or her child, showing that the listener is younger than his or her child)

no aqpiq dear grandmother (used by members of the same generation)

no aqpyuq dear great-grandfather/great-grandmother (used by members of the same generation, but on behalf of a great-grandchild)

no aqsaoq dear uncle (used by the same generation)

no dalda laosiil (same as: **no alsuq laosiil**)
no damoq dear uncle (the speaker must be a father or mother, and the speaker and listener must be of the same generation)
no malma dear older aunty (used by members of the same generation)

2. The following become terms of endearment when the tone on the final syllable is changed from mid to low.

algoq dear elder brother

alniaq dear aunty

aqcuq dear elder sister-in-law

aqdaq, aqdaq nol dearest father (very polite)

aqmaq dearest mother (very polite)

3. The following are used in addressing one's spouse in a very polite way.

aqnil aqda dear child's father (or) **ssaqnaoq aqda** (used by a young baby's mother when addressing her husband, or on behalf of her child).
aqnil aqma dear child's mother (or) **ssaqnaoq aqma** (used by a young baby's father when addressing his wife).

4. The following are used in addressing one's child's parents in a very polite way.

no aqnil aqda your dear baby's father (used by the same or an older generation, much more polite than "**no huljil**" = 'your husband')
no aqnil aqma your dear baby's mother (used by same or older generation, much more polite than "**no miqssaq**" = 'your wife')

5. The following are used in situations where the one being addressed is greatly to be pitied.

ngaldu algo eil eiq dear elder brother
ngaldu aqbol eil eiq dear grandfather
ngaldu aqnil eil eiq dear younger sibling
ngaldu aqpiq eil eiq dear grandmother
ngaldu aqhuq eil eiq dear aunty
ngaldu aqhuq malma eil eiq dear aunty

APPENDIX 8:

SET PHRASES WITH THE NEGATIVE

Hani has certain set phrases using negative couplets.

1. Some of these describe '**middle ground**' -- not too much of this, not too much of that.

maq cul maq xeivq not too fat, not too thin
maq gaq maq cavq not too pretty, not too ugly
maq goq maq biov not too high, not too low
maq heeq maq nil not too big, not too small
maq meeq maq dyul not good, not bad
maq mol maq niaol not too long, not too short
maq teiq maq yeil not too narrow, not too wide
maq teiq maq yei not too busy, not too free
maq ya maq dav not upper, not lower ('middle class')

2. Some describe something in a **couplet**, thus giving more emphasis to it, or making it clearer.

maq beiv maq laol not smart; foolish
maq bo maq jav not possess, not have ('not rich')
maq dul maq mav not to give serious thought to it
maq gaq maq hhyul not loving, not warm-hearted
maq li maq loq not clear-minded; not wise
maq nyuq maq dul not to give serious thought to it
maq puv maq lav not move, not shake
maq qul maq bioq not sweet, not tasty
maq yil maq lal not go, not come
maq yiuvq maq mi no sleeping, no quiting (to work day and night)
maq zaq maq dol not eat, not drink
maq zol maq hev not learn, not understand

3. Some are **virtually shortened proverbs**, like in English when we say 'Spare the rod and spoil the child', we really mean 'If you spare the rod ...'.

maq aol maq zaq (if you do) not work, (you will) not eat
maq diq maq nal (if there is) no beating, (there will be) no hurting
maq duv maq tao (if) nothing is going out, nothing will come in
maq eil maq loq (if you do) not tell, (it will) not be clear
maq hovq maq dol (if you do) not fetch water, (you will) not drink
maq meiq maq gaol (if there is) no teaching, (there will be) no wisdom
maq meiq maq kyul (if there is) no teaching, (there will be) no cleverness

APPENDIX 9:

HANI PROVERBS

Most of the following samples of Hani proverbs are taken from **Haqniq Doq'aqma** (36).

Almil maq jol,
Hucavq zyuqma aol. (36:223)
(When the cat is away, the rats are kings.)

Almiuvq maq dav albol maq jav,
Haqjil maq ssuq galma maq jav. (36:155)
(There are no trees monkeys have not climbed.
There are no roads men have not walked.)

Alwuv qiq siq niq taq maq diq.
Colssaq qiq hhaq niq taq maq sil. (36:155)
(An egg cannot be opened twice.
A person will not die twice.)

Aqbol maq hel,
Gaoqlaoq maq meeq. (36:3)
(If offerings are not made to ancestors,
'Good luck' will not be present.)

Aqma wuqduq yonil,
Aqpyul wuqduq yoheeq. (36:157)
(A female chick has a small head.
A male chick has a big head.)

Aqniuq xal aol e hoqpiul maq zaq.
Moq ceil zaq e xal maq aol nia. (36:224)
(The buffalo plows the field, but eats no rice.
The horse eats some rice, but plows no field.)

Aol zaq ssaqyo jolqil taq xa.
Hovq dol ssaqyo yiuvqja taq taoq.
(Diligent farmers do not stay idle.
Hard working people do not oversleep.)

Col aq colyul yaol gaq,
Zeiq aq zeiqsiivq yaol hhyul. (36:112)
(Old friends are loved more,
New animals are cared for better.)

Coldeivq miqmeeq hhyul a wuqhol jil,
Colsil luqbaol beq e ssaqssyuq mievq.
(To take away a living man's wife can end
one's life.
To dig a dead man's tomb can end one's
generation.)

Colmoq maq jol, doq yul maq jav.
Zeiqmoq maq jol, galjo maq loq. (36:17)
(When elders are not present,
There are no old sayings.
When old animals are not present,
No one knows straight paths.)

Dama niq hhaq alkaq ssaqnaol sal,
Eelma niq lol alkaq ngaqssaq zaq. (36:167)
(Children with both parents are happy.
Fish where two rivers join are beautiful.)

Doq hal jav e taq eil.
Piul hal jav e taq ssaoq. (36:117)
(Don't say all the words there are.
Don't spend all the money you have.)

Doq qiq doq nei eil ceiv,
Heiqceiv qiq lavq nei bev sil. (36:121)
(Give the final decision with just one word.
Shoot the sambar deer with just one shot.)

Eil miaq maq sal, Zaq miaq maq keel. (36:172)
(Say too much, it is no longer pleasant.
Eat too much, it no longer tastes good.)

Galdav li e aqkeel taq sil,
Galtyuq yil e paoqciivq taq hhaoq. (36:22)
(Don't let the leg ache when climbing the path,
Don't let the knee feel 'bent' when decending the path.) -- A type of blessing for someone setting out on a journey.

Hapyul deil e aoq bia naolngaoq,
Hama deil e aoq maq bia nia. (36:175)
(The day breaks only after the cock crows.
The day does not break after the hen clucks.)

Hawuv hyuq e maq nil.
Niuqpeel hyuq e maq heeq. (36:175)
(Stealing an egg is not a small matter.
Stealing a buffalo is not a big matter.)
-- ALL stealing is bad!

Haqniq sil e Lalsav,
Oqha sil e yuqlaoq. (36:27)
(A Hani dies in Yuanjiang. A duck dies in a pot.)
-- Said when something is worthy of doing.

Jaqleil maq bo,
Alpavq maq niv. (36:183)
(If there is no wind,
the leaves will not flutter.)

Jav e saqcul maq keel,
Meivq e hhoqtaoq maq haq. (36:182)
(If you have plenty of food,
Even fatty meat is not tasty.
If you are hungry,
Even bitter greens taste good.)

Laqnil duv e aoq hu,
Laqhyul tao e col hu. (36:131)
(When leaving a house, look at the sky.
When entering a house, look at the people.)

Maq meeq doq nei ceil,
Maq sol eel nei ciq. (36:134)
(If something is wrong, make it right with words.
If something is dirty, wash it with water.)

Maq ziiq moqssaq dyul,
Maq aol zo ssaq saq. (36:135)
(A pony not ridden will be lazy.
A boy who does not learn a skill will be hard up.)

Miqlaol sil e miqjiv sil.
Aqkeeq sil e keeqseil sil. (36:224)
(When a flame dies, the coals go out.
When a dog dies, the fleas die out.)

Neema hal nyuq solzal maq lal qivq.
Miav lo hal mol galma maq ssuq qivq. (36:199)
(Not all the wishes of one's heart can be realized.
Not all paths one sees can be taken.)

Ngaq jol wulquvq yaol hu alnei jol,
Col jol milhaoq yaol hu alnei jol. (36:200)
(Fish depend on water to live.
People depend on land to live.)

Yuqma gaq e piul, Yuqpaq gaq e siil. (36:103)
(Granddaughters are loved as silver.
Grandsons are loved as gold.)

Zeiq teiq sil, Col teiq laol. (36:217)
(Crowded animals bring death.
Crowded humans bring warmth.)

Zyuq maq jol laol biav.
Pil maq jol neivq beeq.
Qivq maq jol xal bial. (36:250)
(If there is no ruler, the country falls apart.
If there is no spirit priest, the spirits create chaos.
If there is no blacksmith, the fields are abandoned.)

APPENDIX 10

HANI RIDDLES

1. **Albol hultav haoqmaq qiq haoq jav. Aoqsseil maq sseil biao nia.** (**zilbeeq**) (4:31)
   A bowl in the top of a tree that cannot be filled when it rains. (a bird's nest)

2. **Alpavq qiq pavq, alqil yuvq qil.** (**lolbieil**) (4:32)
   It has one leaf, and four roots. (a table)

3. **Alzil maq dovq e dalciil.** (**juldal**) (4:32)
   A kind of stick that birds cannot roost on. (chopsticks)

4. **Aqma aqqul maq bo ssaq qu. Heeq la aqma ssaq maq hev.** (**aqha**) (4:33)
   The mother has no milk, but raises her child. When the child has grown up the mother does not know the child. (a chicken)

5. **Colpiul qiq hhaq hhoheiq duv yil. Qiq ssil maq hhuvq lal nia.** (**eelqal**) (4:35)
   A white man goes out the door, and is never able to return again. (spit)

6. **Duv li lalbaq ssil. Hhuvq lal miavbil duv.** (**eeltaoq**) (4:35)
   Going out it sings a song, returning it weeps. (a pail for carrying water) (Note: When going to the water source the pail jingles and jangles as if singing. Returning home, water slops over the sides as if crying.)

7. **Gyuq teil gaq e maq mol qivq.** (**jaqleil**) (4:36)
   We hear the sound but never see it. (the wind)

8. **Hucavq daoqpei seq lev. Alzil daoqpei daol piei.** (**alku bialhhaq**) (4:37)
   Around rodents it shows its teeth. Around birds it spreads its wings. (a bat)

9. **Jahhaq maq zaq e aqniuq.** (**tollaljil**) (4:37)
   A buffalo that does not eat grass. (a tractor)

10. **Moqceil maq zaq e moqpaq, naciq dol e haqzeil.** (**qifceil; feiljil**) (4:39)
    A stallion that does not eat horse food, a hawk that drinks 'medicine'. (auto; airplane)

11. **Yuqcavq kuq e maq lal. Juldal niaov e maq hhaq.** (**jaqleil**) (4:44)
    A ladle can't scoop it up, chopsticks can't get hold of it. (the wind)

APPENDIX 11:

HANI CONCEPT OF TIME

(Huvq, la, nao)

English	Hani	Animal year and day	
MONTHS			
January	Joqzaq siq (Zyuqzaq siq)	Haqlaq	Tiger
February	Joqnil (Zyuqnil siq)	Toqla	Rabbit
March	Saoqla siq	Laoq	Dragon
April	Yuvqla siq	Seil	Snake
May	Ngavqla siq	Moq	Horse
June	Kuvqla siq	Yol	Sheep
July	Siivqla siq	Miuvq	Monkey
August	Xeivqla siq	Ha	Rooster
September	Hhyuqla siq	Keeq	Dog
October	Ceilla siq	Hhavq	Pig
November	Ceiltivqla siq	Hu	Rodent
December	Huvq'yul siq	Niuq	Buffalo

DAYS OF THE WEEK

English	Hani	Chinese
Sunday	Xilqil nao	Xingqiri
Monday	Xilqil qiq nao	Xingqi yi
Tuesday	Xilqil niq nao	Xingqi er
Wednesday	Xilqil saoq nao	Xingqi san
Thursday	Xilqil yuvq nao	Xingqi si
Friday	Xilqil ngavq nao	Xingqi wu
Saturday	Xilqil kuvq nao	Xingqi liu

APPENDIX 12:

FOUR-SYLLABLE ELABORATE EXPRESSIONS

1. **AABB pattern:**

heeq heeq nil nil big and small, young and old
hhuvq hhuvq daol daol to go and come
ju ju geiq geiq smooth and slick
laovq laovq bia bia have an unclear mind
qul qul bieiv bieiv sweet and soft
yil yil lal lal go and come often; repeatedly
zaq zaq yavq yavq eat and sleep in idle manner

2. **ABAC pattern** with **(vb) sil (vb) lo;**

aol sil aol lo work with great effort
cyuq sil cyuq lo to be very poor; to cough a lot
doq sil doq lo to wait and wait for a long time
gaq sil gaq lo to love greatly
hhaq sil hhaq lo to be very wealthy
meivq sil meivq lo to be starving for food
nyuq sil nyuq lo to miss someone very much
ngyul sil ngyul lo to sob and cry very hard
pyuq sil pyuq lo to be very proud
qaq sil qaq lo to be very tired (45:58)
qoq sil qoq lo to invite with great urgency
saq sil saq lo miserable; suffering

3. **ABAC pattern** with **(vb) sil** (vb) ---

kyuq sil kyuq leiq to be very tired
teiq sil teiq piav quickly; hurriedly; in a rush

4. **ABAC pattern** with **(vb) leiq (vb) sil**

beil leiq beil sil to struggle
hhyul leiq hhyul sil with exceeding joy
kyuq leiq kyuq sil very tired; exhausted

5. **ABAD pattern**

bia lil bia loq to be very bright
ju lu ja la shabby
puv lil puv la turn over again and again

6. **ABAC pattern**

bia loq bia ceiv for the day to be bright; sunny

byuq ssil byuq ssav flourishing; prosperous
col ya col del flee hither and thither; a roamer
cuq biav cuq lyul to gossip; stir up trouble
hyuq leivq hyuq hheivq do in secretive, lying way
hhyul lul hhyul sav very happily; pleasantly
jil li jil hevq honest
miav mul miav lav make one's head swim
nyuq duvq nyuq cil think deeply; plan carefully
ovq duvq ovq ciq over-ripe
qeq qaq qeq ga superstitious belief
teiq li teiq cal nei hurriedly
teiq yil teiq lal nei hurriedly
xal ceiq xal kav 1. to plow and harrow, 2. to engage in farming

7. **RHYMING AABB pattern:**

bil lil bav lav 1. confusion on confusion; 2. incoherently; uncertainly
bil lil biav lav brokenly
bil lil hhuvq luvq to be bent
bil lil yovq loq leaning to one side (person; pole; building)
biu lu biaoq laoq to stagger
cil lil cuvq luvq twittering; gabbling
du lu de le 1. strings of beads, 2. bearing fruit
gu lu gaoq laoq carelessly stacked or piled
jil jil zal zal the sound of sparrows chirping
muv luv meiv leiv piled up so as to easily fall
qul qul bieiv bieiv sweet and mushy

8. **RHYMING: ABAB pattern** (of reduplication)

kaq caq kaq caq the sound of rubbing
kul lul kal lal scarcely

9. **ABCB pattern**

bilhhuvq laqhhuvq to be warped (as wood)
col miaq doq miaq 'many people, many words'
diq zaq koq zaq to invade and take over
keelqeiq lavqqeiq arms and legs to be crippled
keel sil lavq sil arms and legs to be paralyzed
lilpuv lav puv to rise in rebellion; revolt
lilpuv ssuq puv to go the wrong direction
lilpuv zaol puv to overturn; subvert
peiljal laqjal old, shabby clothing
pyuq gaq hhyul gaq friendship